Millarville Fair, Albert Sandeman driving team in pulling contest. Horse show activities in background.

Photo courtesy Michael Burn

FOOTHILLS ECHOES

©1979
Serial Number 291603
Register Number 267

Standard Book No. 0-88925-015-4

Published by
Millarville Historical Society
R.R. 1
Millarville, Alberta
T0L 1K0

Printed and Bound by
Friesen Printers
5720 Macleod Trail S.W.
Calgary, Alberta
T2H 0J6
Head Office: Altona, Manitoba

FOOTHILLS ECHOES

J. MacKay

Dedication

To the Beauty of Our Area
The Wildflowers
The Towering Spruce Trees
The Rolling Foothills and
The Mountain Vista.
   To all who made this book possible by volunteering
to submit material.

Acknowledgments

The Millarville History Society would like to express their thanks and appreciation to all who helped make this book possible

To our sponsors, the Millarville Willing Workers Womens Institute, also the New Horizon's Program for their generous grant which assisted us in getting started.

All those who sent in family histories and spent much time searching facts and writing articles; the typists and proof readers for selecting and cataloging pictures and all who submitted photos for the colored section. Janet MacKay for designing the cover and for her sketches which appear throughout the book. Michael. Burn and the Glenbow - Alberta Institute for any material of theirs we have used.

We appreciated the use of buildings offered in which to hold our meetings, particularly the Millarville School Library; the newspapers for publicity, and all who gave donations and loans.

A special mention to the memory of Leonard Nelson, who was a member of our group. His death in August, 1975, left a large gap.

We regret any errors and omissions.

Nita Foster

Foreword

The aim of "Foothills' Echoes" is to continue on from where "Our Foothills" left off. The first book took in the country from the 1880's up to 1940. Many of these stories are of the descendants of the early pioneers and of others who lived in the district prior to 1940, whose stories were not told. It also tells of the oil workers who came to the district to find work in the oilfields, many who had been farmers in other areas, forced out by the hard times of the "Hungry Thirties."

Primarily a ranching country, it is now a blending of two industries, ranching and petroleum. In the late 1930's and early 1940's, several good producing wells were discovered in the Millarville and Kew areas. Many of the farmers and ranchers of the district, feeling the pinch of hard times, worked on these wells and later on the production end of it. They were fortunate to have homes in the immediate area. The workers who had come from further places needed a place to live, so five small settlements came into being. These people became as much a part of the community as the permanent residents, and added greatly to it. When the drilling slowed down, many moved to the neighboring towns of Black Diamond and Turner Valley, others followed the work to the central and northern part of the province. Others bought land, stayed on to become ranchers and farmers.

As the wells became producers, weird looking pumps were installed at the well head, pumping steadily, attesting to the fact that some of Alberta's great wealth is being pumped up from below the fields where cattle graze and ranchers cut their crops.

Other stories in this book are of the city folk who wished to live in these lovely foothills, some on acreages, others on larger pieces of land, but all have one thing in common, a love for the land. They, as the oil workers had done before them, joined community ventures and have helped "Foothills' Echoes" become a reality.

The boundaries for this book are approximately the areas of the schools which were amalgamated into one school, Millarville.

Table of Contents

Executive and some of the workers. Back Row, Left to right — Alex Lyall, Una Ball, Pat Ophiem, Albert Thorssen. Next Row — Kathleen Tosh, Freda Purmal, Cathy Lineham, Mildred Macmillan, Norma Lyall, Gwen Kelson, Joyce Thorssen. Third Row — Stella Pekse, Phyllis Cannon, Ida Jackson, Peggy Nyland, Joanna Hanson, Janet Mackay. Front Row — Nita Foster, Veryl Laycraft, Jean Blakely, Doreen Chalmers, Betty Nelson. Workers and members who were not in the picture: Ruby McNab, Elaine Taylor, Roy Latter, Joan Goyette, Elaine Allen, Ernie Sylvester, Barbara Reimer, Ruth Hoy, Sandra Bull, Shannon Seamon, Inez Schofield, Marj Parker, John and Betty Atkins, Wilma Chalmers, Howard and Eleanor Davidson, Jane Fisher, D. W. Foster, Esther Jackson, John Jackson, Val Nicholson, Judi Powell, Ann Standish, Faye Grose, Carolyn Kemp, Arlie Laycraft, Pearl Laycraft, George Nylund, Pearl Nylund, John and Marie Nylund, Bob and Mary Parkins, Ted Pekse, E. Rummel, Lloyd Standish, Don Sim, Margaret Sim, Irene and Elwyn Evans, Bill Dube, Sig Bradshaw, Evelyn Smith, Nola and Keith Giles.

Acknowledgement

The Millarville History Society gratefully acknowledges the Alberta Government Historical Publication Grant, which assisted us financially and was greatly appreciated.

Chapter 1
Schools

History of the Millarville School

by Marjorie Parker

The old one-roomed schools have a certain nostalgia for those of us who were fortunate enough to have attended them or taught in them. There was a definite camaraderie between pupils and teachers as well as between pupils regardless of age. Teachers taught all the grades and often it was difficult to attend to all the individual needs of the students, therefore it became necessary for the older children to help the younger ones. There was little or no commercial playground equipment or planned activities during recesses and noons, and pupils were forced to use their ingenuity to amuse themselves and all ages participated in these activities. Although the Millarville School is an amalgamation of several schools with many teachers and many more pupils, it has not lost this camaraderie or ingenuity.

Amalgamation meant a whole new way of life for both parents and pupils. The one-room school was a little world of its own and many parents were loathe to have their schools closed and lose control of their destinies. Administration was handled by the local board of trustees who were in close touch with all needs. The trustees hired and fired the teachers, paid the salaries, provided supplies and paid for the upkeep and were in close proximity to all activities. With amalgamation came a broader coverage with only one trustee elected to represent not only Sheep Creek but also several other larger amalgamated schools in a still larger school division. Now the children would no longer walk or ride to school but travel by bus. Children or teachers were relieved of janitor duties because one janitor was hired to keep the fires going and clean the school. Instead of one teacher being responsible for all the grades, she or he could become more individualized and each one could confine their instruction to one, two or maybe three grades. Now the school would be warm when the children arrived. Instead of being exposed to the blazing heat of a newly-lit stove or the freezing cold if someone neglected to stoke the heater, there was an even, thermostatically controlled central heating system provided by a coal stoked furnace in the basement. The school doubled as halls for local community dances, picnics, meetings and plain old get-togethers, but after amalgamation many of the schools were sold and moved away which precipitated the need for building larger halls. Pupils found they had to adjust to the needs of many pupils instead of a few. Their horizons broadened because instead of being a big pebble in a little pool they were now a little pebble in a big pool. More stringent rules had to be made by teachers such as running in the halls or on the stairs, and the playground had to be apportioned to individual grades to ensure the safety of all. Even the dramatic prowess of pupils had to be curtailed. Instead of being in several events in the Christmas program, each child had to be content with a small part. This new way of life had its advantages as well as disadvantages for each little community.

Prior to amalgamation in January, 1952, the Millarville District encompassed the one-room schools of Fordville, New Valley, Sheep Creek, Square Butte, Plainview, part of Ballyhamage and part of Fish Creek. The New Valley school closed about 1944, when

Sheep Creek School Christmas Concert in the old Rancher's Hall. 1939. Back row, L. to R.: Mamie Willford, Jean Chalmers, Irene Willford, Josephine Waugh, Murray Jackson, John Pegler, Jim Chalmers (curtain). Centre row, L. to R.: Charis Blakley, Audrey Rawlinson, Fern Jackson, Hugh Rawlinson, Ann Jackson, Fred Hodgkins (hidden), Bob Cloakey, Robert Chalmers. Five in front, Phyllis French, Florence Willford, Dennis Blakley, Wally Larratt, Yvonne Hodgkins. Mrs. Jackson at piano.

the pupils were sent first to Fordville School, then to Sheep Creek, about 1946, and eventually to Millarville in January, 1952. Plainview School closed temporarily in 1943 when the pupils were bussed to Sheep Creek. In 1947, it was reopened and pupils returned to their home school until amalgamation. Square Butte remained open until the amalgamation. Jake Reimer had bussed his own and neighbor's children to Square Butte in a Jeep but when the larger school in Millarville was opened, he bought a regular bus and took the pupils from Square Butte plus others along the way to Millarville. Some of the children from the southern part of Fish Creek School District came to Millarville after their school was closed but most of them went to Bragg Creek. Fordville School was the last to give in to the amalgamation. Although pupils from other School Districts attended Fordville and eventually went to Millarville when it was opened, Fordville remained open until June, 1952, seven months after the four-room school in Millarville started to hold classes. The pupils of Sheep Creek moved with their school. However, the original one-roomed school of Sheep Creek was transported to Ballyhamage where it continued to be used from 1952 to 1956. Children were then sent to Red Deer Lake and the southernmost pupils who were not already attending Millarville, were transferred to the school. This old Ballyhamage School is now the Leighton Centre.

While Sheep Creek was at its original location west of Millarville, a two-roomed school had been built in addition to the original one-roomed school to accommodate the influx of oil workers' children. This two-roomed school was moved to its present site in Millarville where two more rooms were added with a full basement underneath. The building was moved in the fall of 1951 and while the two rooms were being added, classes were held at the Home Camp in the old dance hall which had been partitioned. Here Mrs. Katherine Beazley (Nevra) taught Grades one, two and three, and Mr. Dan Clarke taught Grade seven and up. Mrs. Tillie Deines (Grudecki) remained in the original one-room school of Sheep Creek where she conducted classes for Grades four, five and six. The Christmas concert in December, 1951, was held at the Home Camp and in January, 1952, all the children were bussed to the new four-roomed school in Millarville. The new school retained the name of Sheep Creek No. 4258 until about 1973, when the Foothills School Division changed the name to Millarville to avoid confusion with another Sheep Creek School in the province.

Millarville was under the jurisdiction of Calgary Rural School Division No. 41 until 1954 when it became part of the Foothills School Division No. 31 in the Foothills Municipality.

The Millarville School has evolved over the years in construction, academics and extra-curricular activities.

Perhaps the most noticeable change occurred in construction. As the school population grew, expansion became necessary. From 1952 to 1955 the four classrooms were adequate but in 1955 a portable classroom was brought in to relieve the overload in Junior and Senior High. The basement of the larger school was still unfinished. Memories of Physical Training, as it was then called, are still very vivid. The advantage of physical activity was greatly outweighed by the breathing of clouds of dust from a crude cement floor, activated by many scurrying feet and there were large bumps on many heads from contact with a projecting sewer pipe.

Fall, 1951 — Sheep Creek School moved to new location in Millarville. Basement being built on right, trucks that moved the school on left.

Millarville School about 1953. Brian Matheson in foreground. Jake Reimer's bus in background.

Millarville School — 1955-56. Note two room addition on back and unboarded windows. Ranchers' Hall before it was stuccoed in foreground.

Millarville School 1978. Note the portable on left, porch addition on front, new addition on back and boarded up windows.

The necessity of a Science laboratory finally brought results. The School Division allocated money to finish the school basement. Two large rooms and one small room plus a large central hallway were partitioned and completed. The small room became the lab complete with pedestals, cupboards and a sink. The two larger rooms were used for music, physical education, playroom and audio-visual. About this time a larger entrance was added. Now there was room for boots and room for children to remove them without falling down the stairs. It was about this time, too, that natural gas was installed in the portable and main school.

Soon, however, new problems arose. The school population was increasing and the new lab had to be taken over for a classroom. In 1969, the school embarked on an individualized math program and the large room on the east had to be used for this purpose. We were back to one large room for music, physical education and extras. This was partially solved by the School Division who rented the Ranchers' Hall from the community. Now there was a place for physical education. The hall floor was sanded and varnished, and activity lines were painted on the floor. The windows were covered with grating and the beautiful animal trophy heads were moved to grace the hallway of the school. This solved the space problem but new headaches were created. In inclement weather, pupils had to be checked to make sure they wore boots and coats, plus carrying running shoes for their Phys. Ed. Children became heated up by exercise in the hall and then came out in the rain, snow or cold to return to the school. They just could not understand why they had to dress warmly for such a short trip. The ceiling of the hall was not the regulation height for games such as basketball or volleyball, subsequently large round holes began to appear in the ceiling and walls.

Now the main school came in for more renovations. The portable classroom was abandoned. It had served its purpose but was very inconvenient for smaller children who were constantly in need of a drink or the bathroom.

It was decided that the children would be better under one roof so a class was moved into the east room of the basement and the west room was converted into a library and principal's office. The old portable school was used for art and music. Later, it became a classroom for math classes and eventually for kindergarten.

In 1976-77, the final phase of expansion began. After many years of anticipation, an addition was put on the north side of the school. While under construction, another portable classroom was brought in. This was removed after the addition was completed. The new part housed a gymnasium, Junior High washrooms and showers, library, ancillary room, workroom, principal's office and last but not least, staff washrooms.

The new addition was timely, but the height of luxury had to be the staff washrooms. Up to this time, the staff had to use the pupils' washrooms. Whether the latches on the toilets had been ripped off, swallowed by errant pupils, or just never put on, the fact remained that the toilets could not be locked when occupied. The pupils were urged to go outside at noons and recesses unless they had notes from home permitting them to stay inside. The rule was made by the teachers, of course, for a very good reason — not for the benefit of the pupils but for the teachers. It was the only time they could occupy the premises in peace and quiet without having to hook one foot under the door to ensure privacy. The result of one hooked foot was often one large cramp. However, Mrs. Beazley (Nevra) informed me that the teachers of the 60's and 70's never had it so good. Previous to this time there were no doors under which a foot could be hooked. This resulted in all the teachers congregating in the bathroom at one time, each one taking a turn at guarding the door. It was due to the perseverence of Mrs. Beazley who practically camped on the superintendent's doorstep, that the much needed doors were finally installed.

Over the years, there have been academic and course of study changes as well. At first, teachers were responsible for their room only. They taught all the subjects including Music and Phys. Ed. Then departmentalization began in Junior High. About the end of 1959, the Senior High School students were bussed to Turner Valley and Mr. Dube taught only grade nine. I had no great love for Math and Science and Mr. Dube did not particularly care for Literature and Language so a trade was made. He took the grades seven and eight for his subjects and I taught the language arts to grade nine. This was the time of grade nine departmental exams. Every phase of the dreaded exams was covered including many hours of perusing old exam papers from years past. Pupils knew that a stranger would mark the exams and assess their ability. This was good because a teacher could become emotionally involved with the pupils, but the exams were also unfair to a degree because they stressed factual content rather than effort. Pupils really had to put forth their utmost but some were reduced to shadows of nervous exhaustion by the time the exams were finally over.

Departmentalization was attempted in the lower grades but did not prove too successful. Now it has been restricted mainly to Phys. Ed., Music and sometimes Art.

There is a constant striving in education, as in anything else, to attain perfection. Different methods are tried in an attempt to reach all children regardless of learning ability. It may appear to be a trial and error method but how else can it be done? In 1969, under the principalship of Mr. Russ Bateman, an experimental Math program was instigated, called Individually Prescribed Instruction (I.P.I.). This was set up by the Provincial Department of Education. Two city schools, one in Edmonton and one in Calgary, and one rural school were chosen to participate. Millarville was honored by being chosen as the rural school. Professor Oliva Cleveland from the University of Calgary and Russ Pacey from Edmonton, director of program, held some interesting meetings for the parents to acquaint them with the program. A week's seminar was held in Banff the previous summer for the benefit of the participating teachers. To we teachers this was perhaps the best part of the whole program. In spite of faithfully attending the whole seminar, we had time to make new friends and enjoy Banff to the fullest. There was much interest among fellow teachers in and out of the school division and many came to observe. This program allowed the children to advance at their own rate of speed. There was very little formal instruction other than in problem areas. Numerous educational games and devices, as well as tapes were used to spur the learning process. The pupil came to the teacher only if he encountered difficulties. If a pupil was good in Math he could progress rapidly but the slower students found there was not enough formal grounding. The program extended over a three year period, when it was abandoned because of its cost and insufficiency in many areas.

In 1970-71, Spelling was adapted to the I.P.I. program. This was not a departmental implementation but rather one of the Millarville School, but it worked only fairly well. At this time, too, Mr. Bateman attempted a new reading program. Students were assessed as to their reading ability and received instruction in reading on that level, contrary to the grade they were in. This, too, worked only fairly well because the advantage of a pupil understanding work of a grade three level was offset by the emotional awareness that he or she was in grade six.

With the growing school population, it was decided at this time to send the grade nine children to Turner Valley along with the Senior High School pupils.

At this time, too, a resource teacher was hired by the Division. Mrs. Jean Davies travelled from school to school testing for disabilities and prescribing help for the same. This was a step in the right direction but Mrs. Davies was overworked and could not possibly keep up with the demands. The job covered too big an area.

When Mr. Don Green became principal, the School Division decided to hire resource teachers for each school. Anne Green became the part time resource teacher for Millarville. Her mornings are spent as a regular classroom teacher but in the afternoons, she works with children who have problem areas and who benefit from a one-to-one association — one pupil to one teacher.

Millarville also participates in the Science Fair where individual pupils set up projects which are judged on the school level. Winners go on to a divisional level and finally to a Provincial level.

Field trips are another method of learning in which Millarville participates. Visits to Heritage Park, Glenbow Foundation, the zoo, commercial plants and the Jubilee Auditorium increase the scope from past to present. At the Auditorium, children had a chance to see and hear symphony orchestras, and in spite of the popularity of loud, blaring, modern music, these sessions were thoroughly enjoyed, especially by Bob Lochhead, our bus driver, who was properly attired in dark suit, white shirt and black bow tie.

One field trip involving the grades one and five, took place in the air. Children were given a taste of flying when these two grades chartered a plane and had the pleasure of flying a circle route from Calgary to Millarville School, the envy of the remaining children at the school. There were a few green faces when we were about to land at Calgary, and as one experienced boy who had recently returned from a trip to Disneyland expressed it, "this sure isn't like flying in a big plane."

Perhaps the most extensive field trip was taken in 1967, by Mr. Russ Bateman and his grade nine class. David Ball, Greta Buikema, Peggy Lochhead, Terry Lochhead, Jackie Chalmers, Jim Standish and Duane West accompanied by Mr. Bateman, had the unforgettable experience of going to Expo. Students from Red Deer Lake, Millarville, Longview and some from Turner Valley travelled by C.N.R. from Calgary to Montreal via Edmonton. They were billeted off the Expo site at student compounds and visited Expo each day for a week. Prior to the trip many fund raising activities, including a turkey supper, were instigated by the students with extensive support from the community.

In 1975, Mr. Don Green took the Junior High on a field trip to Adams Lake, B.C. to observe the salmon run. This trip extended over four days and stressed geology and outdoor education.

Millarville also participates in the Outdoor Education program implemented in 1974-75 by the Foothills School Division to give the grade six classes an opportunity to learn geology and camping skills. For three days the children enjoy and learn from Mother Nature.

Off to Expo at Montreal, 1967. L. to R. Greta Buikema, Elizabeth Gant, Jackie Chalmers, Peggy Lochhead, Margaret Lochhead, Russ Rowlandson.

Sheep Creek School Skating Rink, December, 1954. Extra rink made for free skating. Note the lack of snow and no coats on children, in December.

Off to Expo, 1967. Back row, L. to R.: Dan Hoy, David Ball, Jim Standish, Greta Buikema, Russel Bateman, Dwayne De Visser. Front row, L. to R.: Elizabeth Gant, Peggy Lochhead, Jackie Chalmers, Terry Lochhead.

This program has now been extended to include the Junior High and grade five classes.

Mr. Green has also started an awards program. Each month a certain area of the curriculum is chosen and two pupils from each grade are cited for effort and proficiency in this area. They had the honor of taking time out each week to go to a special class supervised by Mr. Green. In this special class they could work on their own individually chosen project. Now the chosen children have a special fun half day.

There is also a yearly awards program. Special awards in areas such as Physical Education, Math-Science, Language Arts and others are given to pupils who have shown effort and proficiency. These awards are in the form of miniature trophies which the pupils may keep. It is a very exciting evening and an event which is held in high anticipation.

A graduating banquet is also held each June. This was set up to honor the grade eight class who would be leaving Millarville to attend Black Diamond. However, in 1976-77 the grade nine class was again taught in Millarville and so now it is held for that class.

Millarville has always been interested in sports and extra-curricular activities. Bill Dube pushed skating and hockey. The usual schedule was: Grades nine, ten, eleven — hockey — 8:30 a.m.; Grades three, four, five — hockey — recess; Grades six, seven, eight — hockey — 12:00-12:30 p.m.; All Grades — skating — 12:30-1:00 p.m.

In 1958, the Home Oil Company, through the help of Bill McIntyre, provided the boards to replace the old rink at the school. In December, an old fashioned "bee" was organized to set it up. Most of the players on the hockey team known as the "Big Rock" which played in the Bush League at Okotoks, were from Millarville. The school teams also enjoyed playing the fathers on Friday afternoons.

As hockey became more popular, an extra rink for skating was made so that even the youngest pupil could participate.

The flooding and caring of the rink was done mainly by the pupils. Yards of black hose snaked up from the well in the basement and out to the rink north of the school. The older boys took turns going out to flood the rink. About 1969, the School Division co-operated with the community in the building of a rink shack to alleviate the congestion of skate donors in the school. At this time a new well was drilled to supplement the one already in existence. Now the long lengths of hose could be abandoned from the school.

About 1973, another building, complete with washroom facilities, was moved from the Home Camp. This building was set down on the west side of the rink to serve exclusively as a hockey shack and a septic tank was installed. One end of the shack was a dressing room for the home team and the other end was for the visiting team. The room in between was a refreshment stand where hot dogs, coffee and hot chocolate were sold. In 1976, when the addition to the school extended on the north side, the skating rink had to be moved. A new rink was built on the east side of Ranchers' Hall and the basement of the hall converted into washroom facilities.

Hockey has always been a major sport in Millarville. It has expanded from school hockey teams to teams participating in local leagues. Today nearly all boys can enroll in the Tiger Mites, Pee Wees or Bantams, according to their ages and these teams play in the Valley Minor League.

Up until recent times, the boys were responsible for the maintenance of the rink. Hours of cleaning and flooding were spent by the older boys. It was very discouraging for many, after countless hours of wielding a snow shovel following a heavy snowfall, to return to find capricious nature had dumped another four or five inches on the rink overnight. Now, community fathers coach the teams, and have set up a schedule for the repairing, cleaning and flooding of the rink. Even the modern invention of a snow blower has alleviated much of the manual labor.

In 1950, the Royalite Oil Company sponsored the Oilfields Cadet corps in Turner Valley. In February, 1955, many of the boys from Millarville School joined this corps. They were encouraged by Mr. Bill Dube who became an instructor and then the Commanding Officer of the corps. On Friday, February 16, 1979, Mr. Dube was named Citizen of the Year by the Foothills Lions Club, for his work with this corps. The first cadets from Millarville were Mike Rogers, Roy Stuart, Gordon Peel, Jim Scatterty, Robert Backs, Peter Norand, Larry Potter, Mervyn Gorveatt, David Evans, George Bull, Jim Potter, Ken Adams, Vernon Blanchard, and Curtis Wheaton. Many others joined later and many attended summer camps at Vernon, B.C.

Volleyball and basketball have also come into their own, now that there is a regulation gymnasium in which to play. The teams are formed from the Junior High boys and girls with a few grade six students filling in if there is a shortage of players. These teams play in an Interschool League. Very often there are trips to the city to watch nearly professional teams play.

At one time, the Turner Valley Legion sponsored a track and field meet for surrounding schools. Pits were dug and high jumps erected. Recesses and noons were spent by all the pupils practising their skills. Now, a track and field meet is held in the spring for the Junior High students. Contestants are chosen first on school level, winners going on to compete at a divisional level. Cross country runners compete in the fall, again chosen on the school level, the winners competing against other schools at the Strathcona-Tweedsmuir School.

Mr. Gordon Day was the Physical Training instructor when Mr. Russ Bateman was principal. Gordon

was very interested in gymnastics and formed a Gymnastics Club which won many awards.

Extra-curricular events included Hallowe'en and Valentine parties, ice carnivals, skate-a-thons, teen dances, as well as the ever popular year end picnics and Christmas concerts.

Christmas concerts have always been the highlight of the year. Here would-be actors have the opportunity to show their acting ability. Mrs. Esther Jackson supplied the music for twenty-two years, then as more teachers could play the piano, they took over and Mrs. Jackson was retired from the job.

Young and old always wait anxiously for the crowning event of the evening—Santa Claus. Bob Lochhead performed this duty for many years. A crisis arose at one concert. The jolly old gentleman's suit was missing. It had been brought over to the hall but when the time came for Santa to prepare himself, the apparel was nowhere to be found. A frantic search ensued. It was a little disconcerting for the enthralled audience to have wild-eyed teachers dashing amongst them trying to locate the missing costume. At the back of the hall was a box-like extension projecting into the room, on which people sat if there was a shortage of chairs. An engrossed member of the audience had been sitting on the suit, pressing it neatly and at the crucial moment Santa's reputation was saved.

The annual school picnic was always well attended. Long tables were placed on the east side of the hall and parents brought pot-luck dishes. The tables literally groaned under the culinary art of the community mothers. At the picnics, awards were often given out and retiring teachers honored. The day was filled with races, track events and finally baseball games in which the mothers played daughters and fathers played sons.

Even teaching aids and supplies have improved over the years. At one time, if more than one copy of an exercise or test had to be made, carbon paper was used. Then the duplicating liquid poured into a flat tray produced up to twenty copies if you hurried and did it before the master copy dissolved into the jelly. Now, an almost unlimited amount of copies can be run off on a duplicating machine and the original master copy can be used again and again.

The 16 mm. projector that was purchased when Mr. Dube was principal was a boon to all in the community and many worthwhile and educational films were shown to parents and children. Then radios were given to the school and school radio broadcasts added variety to the every day curriculum. Television brought a new concept and specially designed school programs could not only be heard but also seen. Today, through special equipment called the Video Tape Recorder, students put their own programs on tape and watch themselves by re-playing the tape on the television screen.

Typewriters, overhead projectors, paper cutters, tape recorders and even hole punchers relieve the load of harassed teachers.

The most mechanical and merciless invention has to be the automatic school bell. Teachers used to set their watches faithfully and spend their recesses and noons carefully monitoring their watches so that the old brass bell would be manipulated at the exact time. It would never do for a parent to come past the school at five minutes past one and find their child still out playing. The teacher wasn't earning her salary. You felt like a bellringer of Merrie Olde England as you walked through the school and out on to the playground so that late comers couldn't say "I didn't hear the bell". Then an electric bell was installed. The walking was eliminated by flicking a switch and the principal or a teacher had to keep close tab on the time and dash into the staff room at the opportune time. Too often no one knew who was responsible for flicking the switch because often that teacher was farthest from the bell. Now a cold, automatic monster with face and hands, looks down on the occupants of the staff room and rules relentlessly by not only telling the time but ringing the bells as well. No one can procrastinate now. The bells are rung exactly on time and there is no longer that pleasant extra minute for having one more sip of tea or giving the pupils another precious minute of sunshine, on a pleasant spring day. I am glad I once taught at the time of the old brass bell when time was not quite so regimented.

Teachers have always had a soft spot in their hearts for Millarville. They have left reluctantly and usually the only reason for leaving was to forward their careers. Five principals have steered the ship of learning. Mr. Dan Clarke taught until 1954 when Mr. Bill Dube took over. He stayed for eleven years until 1965, when he became principal of the Turner Valley Elementary School. Mr. Russ Bateman replaced Mr. Dube in 1965 and stayed until June, 1973, when he took over the principalship of Black Diamond Elementary. Mr. Elmer Harke came in September, 1973, but remained for only one year before leaving the profession of teaching for one of theology. The present principal, Mr. Don Green, came in September, 1974, and shows every indication of remaining for a long time.

Following is a list of the teachers who taught at the Millarville School. I am including the names of the ones who taught at the original Sheep Creek School because all of these were honored at the 50th anniversary and reunion held in July, 1978, at the Millarville Race Track. These names are not necessarily in the order in which they taught: Patricia Jameson (deceased), Eleanor Galbraith, Irene M. Evans (Rickett), Selina M. Mulder (Hambling), Helen M. Gould, Lucy A. McWilliams, Sheilagh S. Jameson, Katherine A. Van Amburgh, M. Vair Anderson, Mildred Sawkins, John William Grant (deceased), M. C. Deines (Grudecki), Gertrude Duffield, John A. Thorburn, Dan H. Clarke (principal), Eileen M. Clarke, Freda McArthur, Stella Raffa, Mrs. Blake, Mrs. Karpoff, Margaret Young, E. Katherine Nevra, Agnes M. Munroe, Erma Wheaton, E. Pearl Laycraft

Millarville School teachers, 1965. L. to R. Bill Dube (principal), Stella Pekse, Helen Lyall, Marjorie Parker, Shirley Goerlitz (Taylor), in front. Picture taken before front porch was added.

(Cowling), William Dube (principal), Helen M. Lyall, Stella Pekse, Marjorie Parker, Margaret H. Kendall, Marguerite Davies, Shirley Taylor, Angelique Emmelkamp, Elmer Zelmer (deceased), Hope Alana Babiuk, Meriel J. Burke, Linda M. Schaal (Watkins), Russell J. Bateman (principal), Agnes Ball, Mary Lou Werner, Irwin Wurkington, Judy Herr, Elaine Jacobson, Linda Axani, Elmer Harke (principal), Louise Parkins, William Bruce, Gordon Day, Iris Frank, Jean Davies, Barbara Johnston, Don Green (principal), Anne Green, Alice Avery, Larry Veilleux, Debbie

Mrs. Stella Pekse's Class at Sheep Creek School. 1957. Nadine Armstrong, Doug Dube, Marilee Chalmers, Terry Lochhead, Penny McIntyre, D'Arcy Foster, Christine Thiessen, Peggy Lochhead, Hazel Yates, Pat Lochhead. Second row: Pat Ball, Brian Boulton, Debbie Garies, Randy Garies, Agnes Lyall, Tim Hampton, Anne Kirkhope, Joe Jacobson, Gene Blakley. Third row: Virginia Ingeveld, Bucky Kendall, Diane Davidson, Wayne Hampton, Audrey Standish, Jimmie Noyes, Kathleen Noyes, Doug Pritchard, Donna Paul, Craig Ryckman.

Thompson, Jim Fuerstenberg, Carol Capley, Toni Hampshire, Bill Cunningham, Lynne Cunningham (Deglow), Loretta Nelner, Patti Thorne, Marjorie Fisher.

The Millarville School story would not be complete without mentioning the people behind the scenes: the bus drivers, janitors, school aides kindergarten teachers and the parents.

To me, the most nerve racking job must be that of the bus drivers. They have the lives of the children in their hands. Every day they are faced with inclement weather, bad roads, bus failures and a few thoughtless children. A heavy responsibility is theirs.

Among the first bus drivers was Jake Reimer who, I feel, is due special merit. I have already mentioned that he drove a Jeep to Square Butte and then after the amalgamation, he bought a regulation bus and bussed the children to Millarville. He drove for twenty four and a half years, right up to two days before his death. In all that time he only missed about two days. Jake could be firm or gentle with his charges according to the situation and he was well loved by them. It was a sad day for both teachers and children when Jake was not there to entertain us while waiting, sometimes many minutes, for the High School feeder bus from Black Diamond.

In addition to Jake, the first bus drivers included Bill Lee and Bill McGuiness for Home Oil. In 1956, Bert Haney took over from Bill Lee. Bert drove until 1975, when Mac Clarke took over and eventually Bob Lochhead picked up the Home Oil pupils on his route. Other drivers include Ron and Jeanette Arkes, David Evans, Linda Codd and Evaline Prestie who now drives Bert Haney's old route. The last five are the present bus drivers.

Bert Haney, Gordon Blanchard, Bob Lochhead and Jake Reimer were the real pioneers of bus drivers. Many of the people west of Millarville did not have telephones in the 1960s, and announcing school closures over the radio was not thought of, as yet. These men never thought of staying at home in inclement weather. If one child was waiting on the roadside to be picked up, these faithful drivers felt it was their duty to go. When the wintry wind blew, teachers knew that they would have to forego the luxury of staying in a warm, cozy bed because the Mighty Four would be at the school with their small, partial, or full load of children.

Janitors in a school have a never ending job. Ask Vera Haney. Her day did not begin and end with cleaning the school and tending the fires. There were numerous frantic calls from the school — someone had jammed an apple down one of the toilets and there was a miniature flood in the bathroom which seeped through the floor and dripped on the teacher's desk in the room below. Haul out pails to catch the drips while mops were manned in the bathroom. Or — no water — the water line had frozen up in the little hole in the basement. There were never thirstier children or more children who had to go to the bathroom so badly

as at a time like this. While Bert and Vera Haney thawed out the frozen line, the more desperate cases donned winter attire and hiked to the old toilets back of Ranchers' Hall. Sometimes, when parents were entertained at the school, too many electric kettles and coffee makers blew a fuse — utter chaos — no tea, no lights, no heat, no water, no even tempers. Call Vera. For over twenty-five years, Vera Haney kept things running on an even keel. She did the janitor work for many years in the old Sheep Creek School west of Millarville. Then she continued her work in the newly located Millarville School until ill health forced her to retire about 1974. Vera's duties were taken over by Clark and Pat Jacobson and now their daughter-in-law, Doreen Jacobson, undertakes the job.

School aides have relieved teachers of many jobs, whether it be correcting books, typing and duplicating extra school work or helping children with difficulties. The first aide was Barbara Parker, who was hired in 1969 to assist in the I.P.I. program. Doreen Jacobson took over this job in 1970, followed by Cathie Scatterty in 1971. Cathie has continued working at the school assuming more duties. She is now secretary and librarian and all teachers including the principal, Mr. Green, agree that the school would just not function to capacity without Cathie. When Cathie assumed her extra duties, another aide was needed. Judy Malchow was hired and when she moved away, Ruby Lepp took on the job. In 1975, Pat Fisher became the new aide and still continues her work at the school. Pat not only contributes invaluable services but her sense of humor and penchant for playing jokes add to the sometimes hum-drum life of the school.

Pre school children find it much easier to adjust to the school routine if they have a little beforehand preparation. Kindergarten teachers now supply that orientation. Pearl Laycraft was Millarville's first kindergarten teacher. In 1966, she undertook to hold classes in the mobile home in which she and Ron lived near the Millarville store. Elaine Jacobson took over from Pearl in 1967-68 and conducted classes in Russ Bateman's house. From 1968 to 1973, Pat Fisher assumed the duty of kindergarten teacher. When she quit in 1973, Judi Powell replaced her and continues to teach these little ones for a half day, twice a week. She holds her classes in the old portable school.

It is only fitting to pay tribute to the parents of the students. They have always supported the school whether it be with money, physical aid or general moral support. When Mr. Dube was principal, the parents formed an active P.T.A. group with representatives from each of the former one roomed schools. Supplies and equipment were not as freely allotted by the School Division as they are now. In 1954, money was raised for a new 16 mm. projector and screen. Over seven hundred dollars was raised by various groups in the community. National Film Board films were shown to pupils on Friday afternoons and again for interested parents in the evening. Over the years, parents have made donations for Christmas candy bags, picnics and various other undertakings. When the new gymnasium was completed, programs and Christmas concerts are now held in the gym but a new portable stage was needed. The parents have contributed approximately three thousand dollars in grants and donations in the last three years, making it possible to buy, not only a stage, but a trampoline as well. There is also a parent advisory committee who act as a liason between parents and teachers and are a sounding board for the community. This committee more or less replaces the original P.T.A. At first there was a representation from the four corners of the community but now there is one representative for each grade in the school.

Last but not least — the pupils. Millarville School pupils have always accepted children from other schools, other countries and other faiths. When a new pupil enters the school, the children have seldom shown discrimination. All they ask is to be met halfway. Many children have perhaps come from fancier schools but after being absorbed by Millarville, they have been very reluctant to leave. I have mentioned the camaraderie and ingenuity of the one roomed schools. They are both evident in this larger school. Older pupils used to help the younger ones. They still do. There are now peer tutors from Junior High who go to the lower grades to lend a helping hand. Ingenuity is still evident especially on the playground. Even the presence of expensive commercial playground equipment does not stop the making of snow forts, grass or scrap houses. Many an argument has to be settled because some house builders have stolen some jealously guarded grass or scraps from another would be contractor. These children still enjoy the simple activities and games of the one roomed school.

Many students have brought honor to the Millarville School in the form of awards and trophies. In 1965, Dan Ball won the Governor-General's Award for obtaining the highest grade nine marks in Departmental Examinations in the Foothills School Division. There were also many honor students amongst the ones who wrote the grade nine Departmentals. The trophy case in the hallway of the school contains numerous plaques and trophies for both sports and academics. These trophies and plaques pay tribute to the pupils and their teachers.

I have attempted to set down the history of the Millarville School. My association with all the people involved has been memorable and I am proud to have been a small part of it. If I have omitted anyone or anything pertaining to this school or given any false information, I humbly apologize. The omission is due to lack of knowledge or memory rather than lack of intent.

SHEEP CREEK REUNION: On July 29, 1978, the 50th anniversary of the Sheep Creek School and subsequent extension to the Millarville School was celebrated at the Millarville Race Track. About four hundred persons enjoyed renewing old acquaintances. After the barbecue a short program was held in front of the grandstand where Elwyn Evans acted as Master of Ceremonies. Recognition in the form of a plaque was given to Mrs. Esther Jackson for her many years of contributions at Christmas concerts. Helen Lyall received a plaque for her teaching seniority of twenty years. Other teachers recognized for years of service were: Marjorie Parker, sixteen years; Stella Pekse, fifteen years and Bill Dube, principal, eleven years. Seth Peat was introduced as the only surviving member of one of the original school boards.

Mrs. Elsie Douglass was introduced. Her son, Jappy, who was also present, was one of the first students and Millarville was named after Mrs. Douglass' father, Malcolm Millar.

Three of the first bus drivers, Bill Lee, Bob Lochhead and Gordon Blanchard were presented and tribute was paid to two others, the late Jake Reimer and the late Bert Haney.

Mrs. Vera Haney, as janitor of the school for twenty-five years was specially honored.

Two families, the D. W. (Chubby) Foster and Elwyn Evans were introduced. Three generations of each of these families have attended the school. Of the nine students who started school at Sheep Creek in 1928, five were present: Katherine (King) Jeffrey, Marion (Waugh) Lyall, Jappy Douglass, Elwyn Evans and Fritho Mulder.

Mr. Bill Dube gave a short address and introduced the teachers present. The teachers each gave a short comment on personal highlights of their teaching days in Millarville.

The late Mrs. Patricia (Jameson) Steeves who taught from 1928 to 1933 and was the first teacher of the original Sheep Creek School was remembered at this time. The second teacher, Eleanor (Galbraith) Coton, 1933 to 1935; Irene (Rickett) Evans, 1935 to 1937; and Sally (Hambling) Mulder, 1937 to 1940 were also present.

Other teachers in attendance were Sheilagh Jameson; Lucy Harrell (McWilliams); Marjorie Fisher; Angelique Emmelkamp; Mrs. Mildred Sawkins; Mrs. K. Beazley (Nevra); Mrs. Tillie Deines (Grudecki); Mrs. Shirley Goerlitz (Taylor); Mr. Russel Bateman and Mrs. Pearl Laycraft (Cowling).

Numerous pictures were taken by Rudy Mulder and Al Deines. The happy reunion ended with a dance in the Millarville Hall to the music of Cliff Moore's orchestra.

ANECDOTES OF MILLARVILLE SCHOOL: New principals and teachers are often tested by students to see just how much discipline the teacher will exert. When Mr. Dube first became principal, he noticed smoke issuing from behind several piles of hay on the schoolgrounds. No panic. Instead of hoisting a fire extinguisher, Mr. Dube hoisted binoculars. Sure enough, when the bell rang, human beings emerged from

Sheep Creek Reunion at Millarville Race Track, July 29, 1978. Barbecue line up near Race Track Hall.

Sheep Creek School Reunion — July 29, 1978. Some former teachers of the Sheep Creek, later Millarville School. Front row, L. to R.: Tillie Deines (Grudecki), Irene Evans (Rickett), Stella Pekse, Angelique Emmelkamp, Russel Bateman. Second row, L. to R.: Marjorie Parker, Pearl Laycraft (Cowling), Mildred Sawkins, William Dube. Third row: L. to R.: Sally Mulder (Hambling), Lucy Horrell (McWilliams), Marjorie Fisher, Sheilagh Jameson.

behind the hay and were promptly nabbed for smoking, by the new principal.

One day, several grade five students showed signs of the flu. During school they became violently sick to their stomachs, necessitating numerous, quick trips to the bathroom. The fear of a flu epidemic was soon dispersed when it was discovered that the boys had found a bottle of beer and some snuff and had sampled both.

Then there was the little boy in grade two who thought his teacher had magic glasses. Even when she was writing on the blackboard with her back to the class, she knew what was going on in the room.

Cathie Scatterty and Pat Fisher changed their professions for an hour one day. It had been rumored that a local business man had won a snowmobile race which had extended from Red Deer to Drumheller. A phone call was placed to the unsuspecting victim. A reporter and cameraman from the Calgary Herald would like to interview and do a feature story on the successful participant. A hilarious noon hour was spent by the teaching staff attiring the two pranksters, complete with Herald staff cards in their hats, and proper gentlemen's clothes (a trifle bit too large). Down they went to the local businessman who fully appreciated the joke and had his picture taken with the two impersonators.

The first big event of the year is the Hallowe'en party. Costumed children parade from room to room and teachers are hard pressed to pick winners. One year, it was decided to have the children parade in Ranchers' Hall where everyone would have more room than in the crowded classrooms. A new feature was added. Unbiased judges, Bob Backs, Bob Rock and Bud Codd were asked to pick the winners. The audience not only enjoyed looking at the extensive and sometimes expensive costumes, but also guessing or attempting to guess who was inside each costume. Everything progressed quite nicely, until it came time to judge the older children. Consternation reigned. Nearly everyone was identified but one prancing, hump backed, red devil complete with fork and tail. He was performing all sorts of weird antics and everyone, including the judges, knew that this Satan was a winner. All unmasked as soon as the winners were chosen and when the devil removed his red stocking mask, lo and behold, our aide, Pat Fisher emerged.

PUPIL'S COMMENTS: Overheard by a teacher while on playground supervision one frosty February day, "here comes the old bear, and it isn't even spring."

A grade one class was being tested early in September. A small voice, the owner of which had been indulging in daydreaming, interrupted the teacher, "don't you know I'm still up here? I've been jumping horses."

When a small lad was dictating a story he was to recopy for a composition, and being hesitant about offering much information, several questions were used by the teacher to cultivate his imagination. After the third short sentence, without even taking a breath, he announced in a finalized tone, "and that's all I'm going to write."

During an oral language lesson, the children were to comment on, "what would you do if a dog whispered in your ear?" A small child answered as calmly as you please, "I'd probably wet my pants."

The Night I Slept on the Picnic Table

by Don Green

It all began in October, 1975, when two bus drivers, three parent chaperones and myself took two busloads of Junior High students from Millarville School to Adams Lake, B.C. The purpose of the trip was to observe "The Salmon Run," on the Adams River. The students and adults set up tents along the way and practised their camping skills. The trip was very successful and on our return trip we arrived at Golden, B.C. looking for a camping spot late in the day. I finally made a deal with the K O A manager for our total group and the work began. Tents had to be set up, supper cooked and preparation for bed. Finally, about 11:00 p.m., the students were tucked in, the bus drivers and chaperones had spread out their bedrolls in the busses and the camp was quiet — oh the peace and quiet.

I was tired as I looked at my pile of gear beside the bus — tent not up, bedroll still rolled — "do I have the energy?" I asked myself.

Just then a cry came from one of the tents, "Mr. Green, Mr. Green." I hurried over to the tent and looked through the flap. "Do you need help with your tent?" asked a tired, concerned grade eight student. "No — I am fine. Thank you, anyway, good-night," I said as I turned and walked back to my pile of belongings.

Sitting on the edge of the picnic table, I looked up at the clear sky and watched the stars. Then an idea began to form in my weary head — "clear sky, stars, cold — it won't rain — of course, I will sleep under the stars."

Quickly, I picked up my bedroll, spread it out on the table, took off my boots, crawled into the sleeping bag, and as I thought about what a good group of kids we had, drifted off into a deep sleep. My first and last sleep on a picnic table.

Millarville teachers have always had a tremendous sense of humor. No major calamities have occurred at Millarville but when a crisis did occur, it was met head on and afterwards a bit of the funny side could be seen. Following is an excerpt from a school report composed by a Millarville principal. This was com-posed and presented after a particularly trying year when everything seemed to go wrong. The occasion was a year end staff party. MILLARVILLE SCHOOL ANNUAL REPORT: Assets — six capable teachers; two aides; one intern; one part time Phys. Ed; one janitor; one hundred and forty hard working, intelligent students; forty concerned, interested parents; seven patient, tolerant, understanding husbands; two patient, tolerant, understanding wives. Liabilities — one school; six tired, worn teachers; two overworked, underpaid aides; one unemployed intern; one hundred and forty non-working, horse playing inmates; ten disgruntled, disinterested parents; one male chauvinist; one women's lib. affiliate; one poor water well.

From this you can see there is little balance or profit dividends to be divided among the shareholders. A brief resume will help to explain.

Our term began with great enthusiasm; we had forecast an enrollment of one hundred and forty-eight but counted only one hundred and thirty-six. Hence all prior planning and preparation were scrapped and we had to re-organize the troops. You will remember Mr. Day being here full time but was later shifted to part time. Re-organization left us with a class of forty-two in a combined grade. Departmentalization left us each with a share of the load. The year then progressed quite favorably for awhile. We had a successful candy sale earning approximately two hundred dollars for the school. Then the well went dry. We had to switch from our clear, cold, good tasting water to murky, foul tasting, smelly water. On looking back, this combination of candy and bad water may have been the source of many of our problems. It was only shortly after this that several younger students had problems with control of their excretory systems. As one grade one student put it, "he didn't really mess his pants, just his underwear." The agonized, pale expression on Jude's face caused the principal to heroically volunteer to look after him. After peeling off many layers, we finally arrived at the source of the problem. These briefs were removed and placed in a plastic bag outside the classroom window to freeze, later to be taken home via his lunch pail. Helen missed all the excitement being in hospital for an operation, but she was informed as the proceedings went along.

Our janitor's aide became quite efficient even leaving notes when the going got heavy and sticky. But because he knew he should never pass notes in school, he was relieved of his duties and now things are very much back to normal. Mrs. Haney then forced Bill, who was already overworked, to carry on some moonlighting. After much negotiation of wages, it was finally agreed to, and the union accepted him and he was in. He earned so much money, he bought a car and got married, neither of which could ever be done on an ordinary teacher's salary. Teachers were called upon to install coat hangers in the basement, all volunteer labor, of course.

We had numerous school parties which taxed the school resources, both pupils, but mostly teachers. Remember the ice carnival, Hallowe'en, Valentine parties, ski-doo parties and hikes?

Two incidents occurred which nearly took the life of the principal. One might even suspect sabotage or conspiracy. The first incident occurred on a cold wintry day when a school bus tried to pass another in front of the school, where the principal stood in earnest conversation with the lady bus driver's husband. Conspiracy! I should think so! Later in the spring of the year, the principal was still alive and more active than usual, so he was invited to ride the Primary teacher's ten speed bike. Due to some faulty mechanism a violent spill resulted immediately in front of the school before one hundred and forty cheering, excited onlookers. A very subdued, bruised and aching principal then returned to his lair, never to show his face again, afraid that further assassination attempts might be made. Who fixed the bike and arranged for the anxiously awaiting crowd of vultures?

Pearl, who had seen enough by now, decided to clear the air and surrounding area. Launching a Pollution Campaign, she and her crew amassed great volumes of — shall I say, "garbage." Seeking the aid of unwilling workers among the community, the goods were recycled out of the community. Articles have been appearing in the press lately which indicate that some unwilling workers found the wading in garbage, just too much. As a final clean-up gesture, it was decided to send all students swimming during June. This certainly did do the trick and we hope that we will all be able to complete the term and begin next year with a clean slate. Even this noble effort was fraught with problems, for some students began drinking from the bottles collected. Pearl, I'm sure, lost a few more hairs over this.

We are all tired and worn. Why even yesterday one aide, Grandma Scat had to be assisted to her typewriter and propped up with pillows in order that she function at all. This is the type of courage and gumption we have on our staff. Poor Mrs. S. has nearly died on us many times. 'Tis a good thing we had some new, fresh blood arrive in May. Our intern has been a real life saver. I'm sure she kept a lot of us from going under. Thanks, Lorna.

I sincerely thank each one of you for your support and help during the term. We launched a shaky, wobbly ship in September, but I think, during the year, in spite of the rough seas, the winds that blew, and the rain that fell, we have managed to come out with a strong ship. We are a seasoned crew ready and prepared to begin again next term.

Millarville Gymnastics
by Gordon Day

In the summer of 1968, I accepted an invitation from Carsten Carlson of Edmonton to have some of my students attend a work out and clinic with the German Olympic Team at the University of Alberta at Edmonton. Kevin Lochhead, Stuart Lochhead, Mike Zell, and Gary Smith with Teren Allen of Millarville and Tim Johnston of Turner Valley, who had shown a keen interest in gymnastics the previous term, accompanied me. It was a successful weekend, and shortly after the group entered a float, with great success, in the Nanton parade. Thus Millarville Gymnastics was born.

That fall, Mrs. Charis Cooper, Mrs. Nita Foster, Mrs. Donna Evans, Mrs. Myrna Fisher and Mrs. Wilma Chalmers volunteered their services as leaders (and incidently made up most of the first executive) and the first Gymnastics Club got under way with an overwhelmingly enthusiastic group of boys and girls. They immediately purchased green leotards for the girls and white slacks and singlets for the boys. Great support from the community added greatly to the success. That May, the first annual display was held. Since it was the Saturday before Mother's Day, each child presented his/her mother with a waxed crepe paper rose and each leader received a waxed crepe paper corsage. The flowers were made by Mrs. Opal Day of Nanton, who had been involved with the Nanton Recreational Training Centres, Okotoks Tumbling Club and Blackie and Cayley Gymnastics Clubs for the previous twenty years. The display was an unqualified success.

Over the following years, Millarville Gymnastics grew and each year added a new idea to its programme and traditions.

A color party was organized with the members being selected from those boys and girls who demonstrated the greatest leadership and deportment from the previous term. Floats were annually entered in the Nanton and Black Diamond, Turner Valley and Longview Shindigs, always with success. These floats, being the first performing gymnastics floats recorded in Alberta, received widely acclaimed notoriety, and were made possible by the hard working parents and community members and Keith Giles, who unselfishly offered his vehicles.

In 1970, the Oilfields Gymnastics Competitions were organized with Black Diamond, Longview, Turner Valley and Millarville competing. Again Millarville gymnasts realized great success.

Mrs. Grace Langford encouraged the group to enter a float in the annual youth Kick-Off parade in Calgary. Millarville's first entry won the grand prize and trophy.

The group put on displays at the Priddis Breakfast, concerts and senior citizen lodges, as well as a number of functions and concerts. A number of eager boys and girls from Turner Valley became anxious to belong to an organized club and joined Millarville Gymnastics and eventually gave rise to the forming of Turner Valley Gymnastics. Both clubs worked together in harmony sharing each others facilities.

Millarville Gymnastics with Gordon Day and some of his pupils.

Millarville Gymnastics Club who had prize winning float at Calgary Stampede Parade. Three at back. Gerald Scatterty, Dallas Donaldson, Jim Fisher. Gymnasts, L. to R. Andy Jones, Chris Langford, Mary Jane Hudson, Tim Cooper, Patty Fisher, Ann McCurry, Gretchen Cross, Greg Hudson, Barb Scatterty, Noreen Cooper, Steve Verhulst. Front: Alex Verhulst, Phillip Langford. Gordon Day, coach.

The success of Millarville Gymnastics has to be credited to the eagerness of the boys and girls, the parents and certainly, the community. I only wish that it were possible to list some of these people who helped form Millarville Gymnastics and support it but the list would be endless. The salute has to go out to every boy, girl and parent and indeed every member of the community. Credit also has to be given to the Calgary Herald, the Nanton News and the High River Times who faithfully supported Millarville Gymnastics with excellent coverage.

Addenda

After the organizing of the Oilfields Gymnastics Competitions, Kevin Lochhead became the first male to earn the bronze medallion and Tim Cooper the first to receive the silver. Noreen Cooper became the first female to earn the Gold Medallion. (It takes three years to earn a gold medallion.)

In Track and Field, Kevin Lochhead, Earl Allen, Rick Godwin and Terry Orum are considered all round athletes, breaking up to 13 records. Gary Smith and Dennis Hanson the outstanding distance runners. The outstanding female athletes, Teren Allen, Lacey Cooper, Jane Standish, Jane Glaister, Laura Godwin, Chris Langford.

Millarville School Athletics

by Gordon Day

Unhesitating support from the Millarville Home and School made it possible for the organizing of the first basketball, volleyball and badminton teams in 1967-68. Miss Babiuk helped with the girls' teams. The boys' teams realized unparalled success winning every available trophy at the time. The teams continued to maintain their strength for several years. The first practices were held in the basement of the school. The following year, the enthusiastic parents converted the Ranchers' Hall into a gymnasium.

The four schools in which I taught formed the Oilfields Athletics. This gave rise to greater opportunity for the schools to work together and improve their skills.

The same year, the Royal Canadian Legion, Turner Valley Branch No. 78, asked me to form the Oilfields Track and Field Championships. The first meet lasted two days with keen competitions. Millarville edged ahead with 629 to Black Diamond's 609. Turner Valley and Longview placed 3rd and 4th respectively. Millarville continued to dominate the meet being the first school to earn the trophy for successfully winning the meet three years consecutively. Black Diamond won it the fourth year but Millarville regained the title the following year. Turner Valley won the meet in 1972, and has maintained the title since with Millarville the second place contender. In 1972, the meet was made an inter-community competition extending the age limits from 12 years to adults.

Millarville students have managed to hold the individual athletic titles. Earl and Teren Allen were the first to win the Legion awards for outstanding performance in track and field. Rick Godwin was the first Bantam boy to win the Legion Track and Field Medal. Many regional and provincial records were broken by Millarville Athletes.

Fordville School No. 1908

by Ida Jackson

Fordville School was built in 1908 on N.W.¼-Sec. 25-T.21-R.3-W.5. As there is a reasonably complete history of the school in the book "Our Foothills", I will list all the teachers and histories of some of the teachers, also a few humorous incidents. The first teacher was:

Miss Roxana Alexander	Miss Una Condy
Miss Alice Freeborn	Miss Muriel Law
Miss Hilda Bland	Mr. A. E. Sturgeon
Miss Phyllis Sharp	Mr. E. Williams
Miss Ellen Heathcote	Miss M. M. Saville
Miss Lucy Jones	Miss Jenny Ethridge
Miss Edna Frost	Miss F. Hunt
Miss Helen Armstrong	Miss Edith Potter
Miss Phoebe Johnson	Miss M. Watson
Miss M. A. MacIsaac	Miss Margaret King
Miss Kathleen MacDonald	Miss Mary Stanger

Mrs. E. E. Huntley (Miss Edna Frost), taken in 1916 on her own pony "Rory", in front of the Knights' home.

Mrs. Pratt	Miss Ruth Cleveland
Miss Jenny Finlayson	Miss Eddler
Miss Georgina Dunlop	Miss Thompson
Mr. Robert Standish	Miss Hewlitt
Miss Marina Dmitrieff	Miss Crossman
Miss Matilda Grudecki	Mrs. Louelle Standish
Miss Peppard	Miss Spillar
Miss Hayes	Miss A. Peirce

Joan Barker, Freda McArthur, Mrs. Bothamly (Phyllis Sharp).

Bill and Marjorie Winthrop's 25th wedding anniversary. Standing, L.-R.: Ida Jackson, Eunice Park, Ellen Patterson, May Whitney, Bill Patterson, Leonard Nelson, Bill Lee, Grant Standish, Bill and Marjorie. In front: all ex-Fordville pupils.

Fordville Humorous Happenings

The water well was hand dug and often in the spring and summer, you would drop the pail in to get water, and bring up a drowned gopher.

Some cold mornings when you were hoping for the school to be warm, the one who lit the fire would have grief, and the stove pipes would fall down and soot all over.

There was a flagpole but I don't remember ever having a flag; although some of the boys sat one of the teachers around the bottom of the pole with the feet in a particular position and was unable to get up. The girls came to the rescue.

The school lake was always a great attraction and a boat of sorts was built. Two of the boys went out in it and it capsized. They were wet and late getting into school. They took all their clothes off in the boys' outside toilet and put them on the fence to dry. The girls always wore overalls to ride horseback to school and they were taken off at school, as you always wore a dress in school. So the boys were supplied with these overalls, and had to come into school while their clothes dried.

Another prank was to bring a dead muskrat (if one could be found) from the lake and put it in the drawer of the teacher's desk.

The schools all had a hand school bell, so some of the boys had it stuffed with plasticine so it wouldn't ring.

Square Butte School

The following is a list of pupils, teachers and trustees of the Square Butte School from 1922 until its closure in 1950.

Students: Dick Lyall, Peggy Lyall, Annie Silvester, Albert Silvester, John Silvester, Olive Rawlinson, Arthur Silvester, Isabella Silvester, Daisy Silvester, May Silvester, Ernie Silvester, Alice Silvester, Charlie Silvester, Minnie Silvester, Jim Silvester, Tommy Silvester, Jean Fisher, Harry Fisher, Jean Malcolmson, Lizzie Malcolmson, Hilda Jones, Bethune Vanderburg, Vivian Connop, Dorothy Virtue, Jim Virtue, Gordon McLay, Joe Bannerman, Hilda Beck, Mary Beck, David Beck, Marthe Ingeveld, George Ingeveld, Nina Ingeveld, Agnes Petersen, Axel Petersen, Mabel Petersen, Olaf Petersen, Jimmie Petersen, Lilian Petersen, Amelia Petersen, Annie Ball, Arthur Ball, Gerald Ball, Bob Campbell, Tommy Campbell, Dorothy Campbell, Eunice Campbell, Hazel Campbell, Bill Kendall, John Kendall, Frank Kendall, Marie Kendall, Joan Kosling, Albert Gouy, Rene Gouy, John Gouy, Dolores Gouy, Elizabeth Fulton, Warren Fulton, Bobby Purdy, Florrie Hulme, Tony Craig, Stan Keeping, Arthur Reimer, Bernice Reimer, Edith Reimer, Bev Birney, Audrey Birney, Norma Anderson, Margaret Nylund, George Nylund, John Nylund, Eleanor Nylund, Eldon Lyall, David Wildman.

Teachers: Betty deMille, Helen Lee, Mrs. E. Jones, John Vanderburg, Mrs. C. Kosling, Ruth Carnat, Mrs. Grace Jennings, Mr. O. Joyce, Fred Watson, Mr. E. Foerster, Jessie Patterson, Marie Edlund, Dorothy Campbell, Mr. Harry Hamilton, Helen Greig, June Collins, Margaret Bowman, Margaret Cullen, Mrs. G. McLay, Margaret Hallburg, Helen Pocover, Joan Kosling, Nina Ingeveld, Mrs. Sutherland.

Sect.-Treas.: S. W. Virtue, J. T. Ward, A. Northover, Elizabeth Rummel.

Chairman and trustees: George Lyall, Mrs. George Lyall, E. Silvester, Albert Stagg, J. T. Ward, W. G. Trevenen, Dan Bannerman, Fred Kosling, A. Northover, M. Ingeveld, Joe Bell.

School Fairs
by Edna Jones

In the late twenties and early thirties, Fordville school was one of six in the area taking part in a school fair program, and the highlight was the local school fair held at Red Deer Lake Hall on Labour Day each year. This was a project of the provincial government and the seed was supplied, and in many instances grown, by the Agricultural Schools at Olds, Claresholm and Fairview. In the spring of each year a parcel arrived, containing enough seed for each participating pupil to take home and plant in the family garden where, with tender loving care, it would hopefully produce a sample of potatoes, peas, carrots or even a bunch of sweet peas worth showing at the fair. The Fordville district, being liable to summer frost, we often had to be satisfied with root vegetables, but in a good year these would be supplemented with a sample of Netted Gem potatoes and even some green beans.

Beside flowers and vegetables there were classes for what is now called domestic science, cooking, can-ning, needlework, as well as penmanship and art. The boys, and often the girls, could also show a calf, lamb or piglet, and even if your farm had neither garden nor stock, there was a class for a collection of pressed weeds and another for a collection of weed seeds.

If a pupil had been very dedicated and had received enough red, blue, and white cards, indicating first, second or third prize, together with a few special prizes, the top award was a week at Olds to further his education.

Ballyhamage 1948. Back row, L. to R.: Alex Macklin, Joyce Ritchie, Alan McNab, Miss Burton (teacher). 2nd row: Bill Holliday, Irene Brunt, Beverly Ritchie, Marilyn McNab, Johnny Field, Annie McNab, Dorothy Ritchie, Dorothy Wood. Front row sitting: Freddy Cane, Eddie Cane, Shirley Taylor, David Brunt, Kenny Ritchie, Joy Threlfall and friend.

Old Ballyhamage School, built partly on the road, replaced by Sheep Creek School about 1952.

Old Sheep Creek School moved to Ballyhamage, used for a few years before becoming Leighton Centre.

Last Ballyhamage class. L. to R., Back row: Shirley Taylor, Beverley Schaal, Linda McNab, Mr. McDougall (teacher), Freddy Cane, David Patterson, Danny McNab, Garry Schaal. 2nd row: Bobby Taylor, Lorne McNab, Violet McGillis, Bonnie McNab, Louise Cane, Arthur Taylor. Front row: Louise and Anne Patterson.

Ballyhamage School about 1935. L. to R., Back row: Florence Field, Geraldine Holdsworth, Edith Field, Miss McDougall (teacher), Mary Stewart, Marjorie Barlow. 2nd row: Stanley Wilkinson, Bobby Holdsworth, Ruby Field, Roy Cable, Evelyn Field, George Yule. Front row: Nevill Cannon, Ronnie Birkenes, Ben Martman, Stanley Stewart.

Plainview School Class of 1930. Back, L. to R.: Nita Adams, Lulu Robinson, Jack Adams No. 1, John Anderson. (with bat), Raymond Johnson. 2nd row: (3 girls) Marjorie Johnson, Peggy Calderwood, Emma Adams. Remainder from L. to R.: Evelyn Nash, Hazel Adams, Charlie Iceton, Mable Adams, Jack Adams No. 2, Louise Adams, Laurie Lochhead, Herb Adams, Henry Anderson, Dennis Foster, John Iceton. Tacher Miss O'Connor.

Last students to attend Plainview School. Art Peel, Jean Smith, Donna Evans, Raymond Smith, Gordon Peel, Verna Orum, Mike Rodgers, Earl Orum, Melvin Adams, Ken Adams, Joy Orum, Glen Sim, Phyllis Peel.

New Valley School term 1939-40. L. to R. Anne Kohler, Thera Hovis, Louis Kohler, unknown. Front row, L. to R.: Jim Kohler, Ronnie Scatterty, Bud Hovis, Lilibeth Kohler, May Kohler.

New Valley School, Sept. 1940. L. to R. Ronnie Scatterty, Louis Kohler, May Kohler, Lilibeth Kohler, Thera Hovis, Pat Stockton, David Glaister, Bud Hovis.

... ... first ... of ... ...
newspaper, ... the "Weekly News."
I hope everybody will like it, and please
do your best to keep it up. If you think
of any good new ideas, just tell the editor
of that subject about.
The names of the different editors and their
jobs are as follows:
Editor ----------------- Isa-May de Palézieux.
Editor-in-Chief ---- Margaret Deane Freeman.
Sports Editor -------- William Fisher.
News Editor -------- Joan Oliver.
Humorist ----------- Lillie Frayn.
Question Box ------ Frank Cowger.
Health ------------- Charlie King.
Liar Club ---------- Elliène Burns.
As yet we will only make our paper two pages long
and lengthen it if it gets any better, and if
we get more material to put in it. Editor.

News.
With the opening of a new year of school our
teacher, Mr. Scott is teaching on a new schedule set out
by the government. It includes grades 1 - 6 divided into
two divisions. So far Division one has been taking
arithmetic spelling, reading and the study and use of see
Division 2, in place of seas has been studying the cave
men, making books and implements concerning them.

Although Thursday is Thanksgiving - We have
decided to take our holiday on Friday, in order to ha
a longer week-end.

Chapter 2
Churches

Christ Church, Millarville

1940-1979

Our Foothills, the first history of Millarville, Kew, Priddis and Bragg Creek, recorded the early history of Christ Church, Millarville up to 1940. This will be a continuation of the church story covering the subsequent years.

During the period from 1940-1952 the usual pattern of ministers staying for short term periods was in practice. The Reverend George Lang came to Millarville in January 1940 and left in October 1943. He was followed by Reverend Edward J. I. Hoad in November 1943. The Reverend Charles P. Bishop succeeded Mr. Hoad in February 1946 and remained in the parish until January 1948. Through the next year as there was no resident minister, visiting ministers took services when possible. The Reverend Douglas A. Ford came to Millarville in March 1949, remaining until 1952 when Waverley D. Gant arrived. As this period (1940-1952) covered the war years and the transition period immediately following, money was scarce and the church had difficulty in carrying on financially. However, through the years, full support was given the church by many members. W. E. Deane-Freeman was Rector's Warden from 1928 until 1943. Tom Jameson was People's Warden continuously from 1928 until 1947. Francis Sinclair-Smith was Rector's Warden for many years and also served as Treasurer of the Cemetery Fund.

Hugh Macklin took over as People's Warden and Secretary Treasurer in 1950. He continued in this work until 1975. Through the years when financial help was badly needed, the Millarville Ladies Guild gave generously to the church in many ways. This help was much appreciated.

The Anglican Young People's Association was formed during Mr. Lang's ministry. Mr. Lang and succeeding ministers were interested in young people and worked with them, making this organization very worthwhile. The A.Y.P.A. was involved in the work of renovating the old vicarage which had been vacant for many years. With much volunteer help it was redesigned as a church hall or 'house' as it was always called, the forerunner of the present Church House. Through the years the A.Y.P.A. put on plays and skits and various forms of entertainment. These efforts were enjoyed by the community.

After Mr. Gant took over the charge in 1952 a change of organization was instituted. Until about 1956 Millarville and Priddis and the adjoining parishes were cared for by the minister in Okotoks. At that time a reorganization took place with Okotoks being linked with the Midnapore parish. Mr. Gant moved to the rectory provided in Black Diamond and acted as rector for Black Diamond, Hartell, Turner Valley, Priddis and Millarville. The combined parishes took the name, Meota, a Plains Cree name meaning 'good camping ground'.

Christ Church, the centre of a large community, has always served people of all denominations. Perhaps due to its location in a district of few churches, Millarville has enjoyed the whole-hearted loyalty and support of people of all faiths.

Through Mr. Gant's long ministry there have been many changes. The country in early years was settled by ranchers and farmers. In the course of time considerable subdivision has taken place; many new homes appeared, lit by electricity both indoors and out. The country has become prosperous and the way of life with improved roads and transportation has become vastly different. The church has been well maintained, with many improvements being made over the years. The largest renovation took place in 1959, when all the logs in one wall and a considerable portion of another were replaced. The unique beauty of the church has always been preserved. The beautification of the church grounds has been supported by the whole community. Credit for such a beautiful setting for the historic building of Christ Church is due to many dedicated people.

In the early seventies it was felt by those interested in the Church that a new organ was needed. The old one having served well from early times. A large outlay was necessary for this purchase. In response to a request for support, many interested people from near and far contributed generously. A new organ was installed and the church is fortunate in having D. Michael Stanfield as Organist. The old organ still stands in the church, a tribute to those old timers who drove many miles with teams in order to provide music for services.

One of the early flower festivals at Christ Church, Millarville.

On a visit to England in 1962, Mrs. J. R. King, a member of Christ Church and the Ladies Guild, attended a church flower festival. Flo King was very interested in this lovely idea. It was due to her enthusiastic report to the Guild members that the now well-known Flower Festival at Millarville came into being. For the Flower Festival, held the first week-end in August, the church is decorated with many flower arrangements done by enthusiastic local gardeners and others from the surrounding district. Tea is served in the Church House Saturday and Sunday from two to five. A special service on Sunday afternoon is a summer highlight of Christ Church. In the early years a bake sale in the Church House was an added attraction, especially to city visitors, but as the ambition and energy of all concerned dwindled, it was abandoned.

For the first few years much appreciated help was given by several Calgary Florists in the form of arrangements and boxes of beautiful cut flowers. Eventually, as it was felt the unique log structure of the church lent itself to the use of wild flowers, home grown flowers, grasses and driftwood, it became purely a community effort. Flower festival contributions go toward church upkeep.

In recent years the festival has changed in that a different theme is chosen each year thus creating interest and bringing in many different people. Through the years attendance has remained consistently high, many making a trip to the festival an annual outing. As

The 80th. anniversary celebrations began with Louise Bruns playing the old organ for its retirement, her grandmother Mrs. Frank Patterson had played it for years. The dedication of the new organ followed.

a result of Flo King's idea and with the continued support of many people, the Millarville Flower Festival has been enjoyed by all those who arrange their lovely flowers to beautify the church, the visitors, and even the ladies who put time and effort into preparing and serving an excellent tea.

In 1976 Christ Church celebrated its 80th Anniver-

20

Hugh Macklin who lit the 80th. anniversary candle presents the light to George Jackson, a fourth generation member, to light the dedication candle projecting to the future.

sary with a special service. Parishioners and friends of many years standing were in attendance. Thought and organization went into making this event one which shall always be remembered.

In January, 1978, to celebrate the Gant's 25th Anniversary in "Meota", a parish dinner was held at the Flare and Derrick in Turner Valley, attended by parishioners from all four points — as well as numerous friends from churches all around. The enthusiasm of all testified to the regard in which Dorothy and Waverley and their family are held.

Christ Church Millarville will continue to hold its special place in the life of Millarville and district.

Christ Church — Millarville

In its most recent quarter century, Christ Church has in one respect not changed at all. For it continues, as heretofore, to witness to the presence of God in the midst of the community, to the call of God to find new life in Him, and to the love of God for all his creatures, whether they reciprocate or not.

Peripheral things **have** changed. No longer does the congregation, as was the case up to twenty years ago, have to huddle around a wood burning heater at the back of the Church, on specially bitter Sundays, for a quick twenty minute service. Now it can luxuriate in the even warmth of an efficient forced-air furnace. No longer need the Church provide a wind proof shelter for the parishioners' horses. Now it ensures a snow free parking area for their comfortable automobiles. Today's worshippers doff their hats to the hardiness of their Church-going forebears who knew nothing of such latter day luxuries.

Some old-time hazards still remain, however, like the river crossing near-by. Perfectly safe in its frozen winter state, it becomes perilous in spring and late fall and even chancy in mid-summer, as it was on one occasion when the cars of an entire bridal party became stuck in mid-stream. The girls had to remove shoes and stockings and wade to shore in their finery. The wedding eventually got performed. It was agreed by everyone there that this adventure made it the most unique nuptial event in the history of the parish.

Christ Church Millarville
— 1957 —

J.M. MacKay /79

Celebration of the Gants' 25 years in "Meota" parish. L. to R. Mrs. Axon, Bishop Goodman, Dorothy and Waverley Gant, Mrs. Goodman and Archdeacon Axon.

Bread and butter issues are never far from the minds of Wardens and Vestry for if the Church cannot remain financially viable, it must close its doors. In the early fifties this viability was in some doubt, a not unfamiliar crisis, historically. It was then that the "Calf Program" was launched as an attempt to stabilize the parish budget. In subsequent years as many as two and a half dozen calves, bearing the Church's own brand, were put into the hands of willing ranchers for finishing and ultimate shipment. The Church realized the proceeds. The program was a success, albeit a source of disquiet to personnel in the Diocesan office when the Annual Statistical Report came in from the Millarville Church with the entry: "Anticipated revenue for the forthcoming year: Increment from thirty calves assuming they all live to see the abbatoir." This was not the sort of statistic accountants like to deal with, but it served to underline the fortuity the agricultural industry and the Churches in its midst must live with.

The decade of the fifties also saw the demise of the old Church House. It had been one time a Rectory, but had long since been refurbished as a Parish Hall. Now as the floor joists began to rot, the piano leaned drunkenly toward the middle of the room. The door on the ancient space heater would drift open to release clouds of acrid smoke, hardly to be described as "a sweet smelling savour". The building had become unsafe, but funds were scarce. A patch up job would still leave the monumental inefficiencies of the kitchen. At that point the Women's Guild asked to be given the task of dealing with the problem. The Vestry acceded to their request with alacrity and the women went at it with characteristic daring and verve. The present Church House is the result. A spate of gargantuan money-raising events paid for it. Its maintenance has remained in the Guild's capable hands since.

A Junior Women's Guild was established in the parish during the sixties. It coordinates its efforts with those of the Senior Guild, and matches the older group in enthusiasm and creativity. Its fabulous annual Art Mart is the most publicized of its imaginative projects.

Since it is a country parish, it has seemed sensible to make the most of the Church's agricultural setting. The traditional Harvest Festival Service has always given recognition to the hand of the Creator. To this has been added the observance of Rogation in the spring. The blessing of God, then, is called down on seed and soil and sower. This is a revival of an ancient practice fallen into disuse in this country. Appropriate symbols decorate the Church, even on occasion, chickens and lambs.

In similar vein, the Senior Guild introduced, in the early sixties, an established British Church custom, the mid-summer Flower Festival. Artistically composed arrangements inside and out complement the hallowed atmosphere of the old building. The many visitors are reminded that man does not live by bread alone, that the earth also produces some of those ineffable values that feed the soul. Christ Church parish was perhaps the first in Canada, certainly the first in Western Canada to introduce this custom.

The eightieth birthday celebrations of Christ Church in 1976 were marked by the dedication of a new electronic organ, and the launching of a full-blown, long term landscaping program. With the generous support in effort and money of many benefactors, a long step was begun toward providing this gem of a Church with a setting concomitant with its spiritual and historic worth.

In the late seventies, the congregation was successful in turning back an attempt by the Historic Sites Branch of the Government of Alberta to take the Church, hall, cemetery and grounds under its aegis. This would have made parishioners little better than custodians in their own house of worship. It was realized that a worshipping congregation is the best guarantor, not only of the historicity of the edifice but more vitally, of the maintenance of the building as a symbol of the living Presence of God.

Overflow 80th. anniversary participants hear the service via a public address system, in the shade of a colorful canopy, which was set up between the church and the church house.

22

Long may it continue so — a haven to administer solace and joy and inspiration and challenge and peace, in response to the varying needs of its people.

The Church House

In 1937 an unused rectory which was just east of Christ Church was renovated to serve as a parish hall. For a number of years it served the church and community well for many functions — showers, wedding receptions, turkey suppers, teas, card parties and as a home for a very active A.Y.P.A. As well it was used for teas after Harvest Thanksgiving and Confirmation services and for various meetings connected with the parish. But having been built in 1908 the building began to feel its age and by the mid-fifties the main room floor had quietly slipped into the dirt cellar. For several years following this sad state of affairs church meetings, confirmation teas and card parties were held in the homes of various Guild members.

In 1959 at an annual meeting of the Millarville Ladies Guild, with only seven members present and a bank account of a few hundred dollars, they voted to build a new parish hall. One of the members offered to loan the Guild, interest free, the money for the new building. The men of the parish tore down the old rectory and a local and community minded carpenter Bert Haney was hired to oversee the building. He hired Seth Peat and Jake Reimer to help and many local men gave their time as well. A calf sale was held to raise some of the money. Even Guild members were pressed into service during the building. In late September they painted the outside, fighting bluebottle flies with every brush stroke-some descendants of these same flies remain to this day. By late fall the ladies proudly presented to the vestry the keys for a serviceable building albeit without water or plumbing and with only plywood floors.

All this activity was commendable but it was not getting the building paid for and so the Guild members turned to their kitchens. Many schemes were devised to raise money, nearly all of them connected with food. They let it be known that they were available for any type of catering — nothing was too large or too small — farm sales, horse shows, weddings, concessions and barbecues were all taken on.

The first large undertaking was to provide food from early morning to late at night for the Kay Cee cattle sale. For three days the ladies worked at the sale only to go home and fry more chicken and make more beans for the next day. One and sometimes two people were kept busy bringing supplies from Calgary. Another large project that went on for several years was to provide food for the Pony Clubs that stayed at the Race Track. This meant arriving at the Hall at 6 a.m., stoking up the old coal stove and cooking three meals a day plus cocoa and cookies at night for 50 or so hungry young people. For several years during the summer months, two ladies would take turns baking

pies, cakes, bread etc. which Lee's would sell at their establishment. Various tours were also catered to — one was a bus load of Eastern tourists. They thought that we had very healthy water in the district because it contained so much iodine. Little did they know that by accident the water taken to the Church House for the supper had accidently been pumped through a rubber hose tainted by the flavor of weed spray. Many harvest suppers, teas and bake sales were arranged — anything that would bring in a few dollars. Also at this time the Guild began to cater to the Bar Pipe annual cattle sale which they have continued to the present time. All this was done with a membership of about twenty ladies.

With all these ventures by August of 1962 the Ladies were able to have a party and with a dozen red roses paid back the last of the money which had been loaned to them. Work did not stop here however as many things were still left to be done to the Church House. During the next few years they were able to add hot and cold water, indoor plumbing, linoleum to the floor and much other needed equipment. Fortunately about this time a Junior Guild was formed and much of the load was taken from the Senior Guild, and none too soon as many of the senior ladies could not face another brownie or stir another pot of stew.

Millarville Sunday School
by Nora (Andrew) Krake

In 1949, the Reverend Douglas Ford and family came to Okotoks to be our Anglican Minister. His territory was a large one, taking in Okotoks, Black Diamond, Turner Valley and East and West Millarville.

There has been mention of the beautiful little Church at East Millarville elsewhere in this history book so I will not relate on it, except to say that the services held there in the older days, when it was

Millarville Sunday School Choir 195. Front row, L. to R. Sandra Wheaton, Joyce Cowan, Marlene Peat, Joan Douglass, Elaine Matheson. Centre: Peggy Ann Haney, Linda Rishaug Dianne Shick, unknown. Back: Glen Wheaton, Curtis Wheaton, Jim Andrew, Lillian Haney, Bob Haney.

candlelit, seemed more beautiful and inspiring than in later years with electric lights, especially as it was in the log church and built in such beautiful country.

In West Millarville, our services were held in the Home Oil Recreation hall and although thanks are due to a great many people during those years, we must say a special thanks to Ole and Kay Nevra, who were always so very kind.

In the fall of 1950, under the guidance of Rev. Ford, a Sunday School was started with classes held at Millarville School. The first teachers were Mrs. Bert Chalmers and myself, helped at times by other mothers.

When the Sunday School was started there had to be lessons and supplies provided and we had no money. I do know that had we gone the rounds asking for donations, there would have been plenty, but we were very independent and decided to do it on our own. Now it is against Church laws to have a raffle but I bought a large grey plush elephant and although I knew it was truly against the rules we sold tickets on it. I am sure the Good Lord looked down and smiled at our attempt and He blessed our endeavors, as the raffle was a big success and so our Sunday School began.

The Sunday School flourished, the parents were most co-operative in all respects and children came from three years and up — no distinction was made as far as race, creed or color and we loved them all. Mrs. Chalmers taught the older children and I had the little ones. I have so many fond memories of those little ones who are now grown and married with families of their own.

The next on our list was a choir and with the very able help of Mrs. Dan Hume, who lived in the Millarville area our little choir was formed. Mrs. Hume was very gifted in voice and music and the children had good help. Practice sessions were held at Mrs. Dick King's as it was most central. Even the little three and four year old children soon learned the more simple hymns and took delight with being with the older ones. With the help of the mothers we were able to make choir robes for them all and we sang at our church services. The highlight was singing at church at East Millarville one Sunday evening at a candle-lit service.

Although I could relate many amusing incidents during those years, one seems to stand out in my memory more than others. One little girl, soon to be three years old and eager to start Sunday School, had been taught to sing "Jesus Loves Me", verse for verse, because, as her mother said "They always sing that at Sunday School." Now, I was not aware of this and so the first Sunday she came, I had chosen the hymn "God Sees the Little Sparrow Fall" and while the rest of us sang this little hymn our new little girl stood up and very proudly sang "Jesus Loves Me".

As in all cases, the children grow up, Church is replaced by Sunday School and each seem to go their own way but no matter where they are, I am sure they have fond recollections of their younger years at Church and Sunday School at Millarville and I am sure

the love and understanding, and the Spiritual Guidance has been a help to all.

Rev. and Mrs. Ford were very well thought of during his stay and we all missed them very much. Their kindness and love to us will always be remembered but what was our loss has been someone's gain and in 1952 Rev. Ford left Lethbridge, back to Calgary and then to Saskatoon, Sask., where he is now Bishop of Saskatoon. Their family of two boys and one girl are all grown. Michael is married with one child and is teaching school at Mississauga, near Toronto. Stephen is married with two children and is a computer programmer for the Bank of Commerce and Kathy is single and is a lawyer in Saskatoon.

Millarville Ladies' Junior Guild
by Elaine Allen and Faye Grose

The organizational meeting of the Millarville Ladies' Junior Guild was held on November 21, 1963. The purpose of this group was to complement the work of the Senior Guild of Christ Church, Millarville. These young mothers with small children had to structure their time differently than the Senior Guild members, and so formed this group.

In the early years, many fond memories were collected during their sewing sessions when layettes were made, quilts stitched for overseas missions, and choir gowns designed for the Church. They gave financial support to the Sunday School and enjoyed tours to Calgary to see the Vocational Rehabilitation and Research Institute, Christine Meikle School, and Providence Creche.

Money was raised by catering to weddings and sales. In 1965, the first Old Fashioned Tea was held in May, an idea conceived by Flo King. It has been an annual event, even surviving one blizzard. In 1976, tradition was broken in favour of catering to the 80th Anni-

Millarville Ladies' Junior Guild, 1975. L. to R., back row: Cathie Scatterty, Dorothy Jackson, Jo Ann Jackson, Julie Boulton, Cheryl Arthurs, Ruby Sinclair-Smith, Corinne Smith; 2nd. row: Linda Bull, Vivian Watson, Patty Webb, Carolyn Kemp, Marisa Zarillo; 3rd row: Susan McPherson, Faye Grose, Sandra Bull, Val Nicholson, Inez Schofield, Judi Powell, Elaine Allen.

versary Celebrations of the church. Thanks to Val Nicholson, the first Art Market was held in October, 1975, and has been a worthwhile venture ever since. Now, a large portion of our funds are used to maintain the Church House. Also, at times we have assisted the Senior Guild with expensive projects in the Church, and helped them with their Flower Festival in August.

Our social calendar has included pot luck suppers, pancake breakfasts, children's Christmas, and tours of interest such as the University Observatory at Priddis, to which all the family has been invited.

The monthly meetings are usually held the first Thursday of each month at members' homes. The abundance of pick-up trucks at a neighbour's house indicates the meeting is in progress, covering the business agenda and often including a speaker, perhaps the home economist or a lawyer.

Currently, we are actively supporting the community library, some school projects, and the Landscaping Committee for Christ Church. Each July, pies are made for the Meota Parishes booth at the Millarville Races and again in November, pies are sent to the Bar Pipe Cattle Sale. Each fall the church is decorated for Harvest Sunday.

In the past, charitable works have included; donations to Children's Hospital, Calgary, for a bed; obtaining a respirator for Turner Valley Hospital; making favour trays at Easter and Hallowe'en at Turner Valley Hospital; giving toys, clothes and money to the Salvation Army, Lacombe Home, and Eden Valley. Special events have been sponsored by the Guild. Many young people enjoyed the Good Grooming Programme and the Babysitting Course. A "Lady Beware" programme was attended by many ladies from the community.

The Junior Guild can attribute its success to the dedication and hard work of its many members throughout the years. Some charter members who are still involved are Linda Bull, Lucille Glaister, Dorothy Jackson, Cathie Scatterty, and Ruby Sinclair-Smith. Following, is a list of past executives:
Abbreviations:
P. = President
V.P. = Vice-President
S.T. = Secretary/Treasurer
T. = Treasurer
S. = Secretary
V.R. = Vestry Representative
1963/64
P. — Dorothy Jackson
V.P. — Lucille Glaister
S.T. — Joy Zell
       Cathie Scatterty
1965
P. — Shan Cross
V.P. — Lucille Glaister
S.T. — Marg Schonhofer
1966
P. — Linda Bull

V.P. — Ruby Sinclair-Smith
S. — Dorothy Jackson
T. — Chris Graham
1967
P. — Linda Bull
V.P. — Ruby Sinclair-Smith
S. — Cathie Scatterty
T. — Vivian Watson
1968
P. — Bev Macklin
V.P. — Elaine Allen
S. — Cathie Scatterty
T. — Vivian Watson
1969
P. — Sharon Green
V.P. — Linda Bull
S. — Marg Schonhofer
T. — Marg Wright
1970
P. — Sharon Green
V.P. — Dorothy Jackson
S. — Elaine Allen
T. — Marg Wright
1971
P. — Cathie Scatterty
V.P. — Val Nicholson
S. — Corinne Smith
T. — Lucille Glaister
1972
P. — Sandra Bull
V.P. — Sharon Green
S. — Val Nicholson
T. — Julie Boulton
1973
P. — Ruby Sinclair-Smith
V.P. — Susan McPherson
S. — JoAnne Jackson
T. — Julie Boulton
1974
P. — Susan McPherson
V.P. — Faye Grose
S. — JoAnne Jackson
       Judi Powell
T. — Jill Ross
1975
P. — Faye Grose
V.P. — Julie Boulton
S. — Judi Powell
T. — Jill Ross
1976
P. — Julie Boulton
V.P. — Patti Webb
S. — Val Nicholson
T. — Corinne Smith
V.R. — Elaine Allen
1977
P. — Faye Grose
V.P. — Patti Webb
S. — Marissa Zarillo

T. — Pat Sirois
V.R. — Elaine Allen
1978
    P. — JoAnne Jackson
    V.P. — Linda Bull
    S. — Judy Williams
    T. — Evelyn Smith
    V.R. — Sandra Bull
1979
    P. — Linda Bull
    V.P. — Patti Webb
    S. — Judi Powell
    T. — Evelyn Smith
    V.R. — Sandra Bull

Wedding Pranks

by Phyllis Cannon

Over the years the people of the Millarville district enjoyed the pranks that were played on newlyweds. Various modes of transportation were used to convey them from the church. The following pictures are a few of the examples.

This antique fire engine was waiting for Maudie Glaister and Ronnie Birkenes at their wedding in 1945.

David Cannon and Betty King as attendants at the Birkenes wedding, revelling in their part of it.

What a surprise Nevill and Phyllis Cannon received when they came out of the church on seventeenth avenue in Calgary, 1947!

Nevill Cannon running alongside to make sure that the "contraption" stayed together, at the Birkenes wedding.

Charlie King getting ready to throw confetti down Nevill's neck.

26

The dubious condition of the buggy and the harness added to the hilarity of the event. Nevill and Phyllis on board.

Jane Gourlay's wedding, 1950. The groom, Buz Hayes, came from the east so the sign read "Imported sire —".

At the back of the buggy the famous sign "Watch Millarville Grow"!

The team were known to run away on occasion, but behaved well for Jane and Buz. Jock Gourlay driving.

At Jim and Kathy Silvester's wedding, the party were stranded in the river crossing below the church. Here Art Silvester is going for help.

Chapter 3
Hamlets and Post Offices

Foothills' Echoes

by Joanne Hanson

The nights were clear and frosty
As the land lay waiting Spring
Mating coyotes hilltop howling
Echoed with weird and chilling ring.

The cows roused from their slumber
Stiffly rise their calves to feed
Ever watchful, gaunt and anxious
Waiting the hayrack to fill their need.

The sun came up in splendor
To color distant mountain peaks
The rattling chains and horses snorting
As the rancher fords the creeks.

The way of life is just so peaceful
Hard work, but here man is king
The wood smoke curls from chimneys
From log cabins near the spring.

With the find of oil comes changes
Life's tempos soon increase
Soon the drilling derricks rise
And the sounds of mud pumps never cease.

Trucks loaded with drill pipes and tubing
Driven by men both young and old
Came to our foothills to live and work
To share in the hunt for rich black gold.

Soon oil camps and towns spring up
Shacks clustered near gas line or spring
The ranchers too, reaps many profits
As new echoes round the foothills ring.

Excitement reigns as wells gush oil
And separator and tanks spring up
More work, more money, happy times
Would this prosperity never stop?

But again the changes came
Drilling ceased and wells drained low.
People moved away, a few were left
Again the rancher fields will sow.

But as we look back to busy times
And the many friends we knew
That way of life in search for oil
Echoes foothill memories too.

Hamlet of Millarville

by Jean Blakley

The Hamlet of Millarville is the only one of five small settlements which sprang up in the Millarville district, to accomodate the oil workers during the 1940s, to still be in existence today.

The land where it is situated was originally the homestead of Robert Turner, who came to the area in the 1880s, and who also gave his name to Turner Valley. Shortly after the Turners left the district to settle near Okotoks, the land was owned by three ladies, the Misses Watt. They rented the flat where the school, hall and other buildings now sit, to Monte Fraser, whose main interest was polo. The long flat made a fine polo field and the first building was a small log house where the polo players rested and had their refreshments.

When Mr. Rawlinson bought the property in 1922, he had other uses for the flat, so plowed it and in the process, uncovered many wooden polo balls.

In 1926, Norman Pegler bought a small acreage from Rawlinson and built a grocery store. The Forward and Walton Store was further east, where Jody Fisher lives now. They also had the post office in the building which W. H. King had built in 1910. The post office was not moved to its present location until 1941.

With the discovery of oil in the district, families started moving into Millarville, renting a piece of land from Rawlinson, and either built a house or moved one

Hans Backs in front of his garage at Millarville.

in. Ginger (Eric) Douglass had a garage for a time. McFarlands had a lumber yard, with Mr. Jorgenson in charge. The small hamlet even boasted a restaurant, first moved in by Cowling, and operated by him and his wife. It was later taken over by Grace Myer and her mother, Mrs. Cunningham and at one time Vi Schultz managed it. Red McCorkel managed a lumber yard. Gene Robertson had a bulk station and his father and mother, Mr. and Mrs. Jack Robertson also lived at Millarville.

Jones and Grace Myer, Barney Babb and Vi Schultz, and Frank and Marie Flewelling had their homes near each other, with the McLeod family nearby. Al and Mrs. Grainger, and family, and Chuck and Edith Cowan were also residents, as well as the Sewells, the Martins, Mr. and Mrs. Orville Cunningham and their daughter Pearl, who worked for Jappy Douglass when he took over the store in 1944.

Dick Lampman and his family moved into the Millarville district from B.C. Dick did a bit of shoe repairing in his spare time. Other residents were Mr. and Mrs. Ken Campbell, Mr. and Mrs. Levi LaFrance, Phil Buckingham and his family and the Judsons. All of the children attended Sheep Creek School before it was moved to Millarville.

Jappy Douglass had a small coffee shop in his store, and most of the young girls in the district worked in it or the store at one time or another.

Vern and Gladys Theissen lived where Veryl and Arlie Laycraft now make their home. Mrs. Ossie Lister lived in this house for some time.

In 1950, many had moved on, following the work. Mr. and Mrs. Bert Haney and their children came from Ontario, and eventually bought an acreage from Mr. Rawlinson and built a home. The Sheep Creek School was moved to its present location.

The building which had been the restaurant was moved to Turner Valley and has since been used as an office of the local insurance agency.

Several other families lived about a mile up the road on the Chalmers ranch, Mr. and Mrs. Art Bird and their daughter, Pete McNary with his wife and two daughters. A one time janitor of Sheep Creek School, Jenson and his wife and family, also lived on the Chalmers.

There were many others living in the community, some for only a short time, many who will be mentioned in some parts of this book either in connection with their work or with the school. Many former students may recognize themselves in some of the pictures.

Bullville

by Joanna Hanson

Bullville was a small community of oil workers who rented lots from Seth Peat, north and west of the old Sheep Creek School. They were close to their work and most of them had families so being close to a school was important.

Picking up the bull gang for Major Oil. Albert Hughes, driver. L. to R. Bill Gent, Norman Tollefson, Henry Burquist. Front row, L. to R. Glen Hazen, Elmer Lohner, Ardell Tollefson, Grant Burquist, Sid Adams, E. Hagen.

About 1940, people began moving in. Some were Evelyn and Norman Tollefson, Stearns, Ardell and Dorothy Tollefson, Hank ahnd Verona Beebe, Ellif and Maude Hagen, Glen and Annie Hazen, Hank and Rachel Burquist, Grant Burquist, Sid and Maxine Adams, Nick and Helen Dannyluck, Mr. and Mrs. Seth McNary, Les and Enid Peat, Fred and Gladys Diabert, Clare Francis, Elmer and Lily Lones, Steve and Myrtle Alexander, Dan and Eileen Clark, Jimmy and Helen McPeet, Nate and Eileen Beebe, Agnes and Ossie Lister, Everett and Tillie Potter.

There was a good spring up the hill and everyone packed water from it. Afterward they wondered why they never piped it down to their homes. Their lot rent was $2 a month and they burned wood for both heat and cooking, buying it from neighboring farmers. They bought some loads of coal from the Priddis mine which was so oily it gave a terrific heat but the soot that formed in the stoves and chimneys in long black, sticky masses soon choked stoves and chimneys, requiring cleaning every few days, a very filthy job. Finally, they hooked onto a nearby gas line and everyone had clean heat in houses, garages and even the outhouse. What comfort!

Many had gas fridges as they still had no electricity, just coal oil lamps and the pump-up variety of gas lamps and irons.

As the oil companies quit drilling in that area and the larger production companies took over the smaller ones, there was no more work so they all left for other parts.

Majorville

This was a small settlement a few miles north west of Millarville Hamlet. The Major Oil Company had drilled some successful oil wells in the area, hence the name, Majorville. Home Oil and Royalite moved in with drilling rigs and soon this was a very busy area. The second World War brought rationing so many workers brought their families and either moved a house in or built one.

The Peat family owned the land on the east side of the road, the W.½ of 8-21-3w5 and the W½ of 17-21-3w5.

Major 12 well being drilled in the Millarville area. L. to R. Nibs Baton, Mark McKain, Ossie Lister, Slim Rosen, Unknown.

Fred Hodgkins had the land on the west side, the E.¼ of 7-21-3w5. The quarter joining Hodgkins on the north was owned by Jim Kerr and his wife, Rose. At the end of the valley north lived Joe Waugh and his family. On her father's land, Jean Waugh had a store, "Foothills Grocery" and later a coffee shop was added, with Jean's sister Josephine helping in store and coffee shop.

During the Second World War, with gas rationed, Drilling Contractors and Royalite put on busses to take the workers to the drilling sites. In times of bad weather, when the roads were nearly impassable, the crews unloaded and loaded at the little coffee shop, and very happy to get a hot cup of coffee after a hard day on the rigs. The Waugh girls operated the store for about four years, then sold to Mr. Brown, who lived there with his wife and daughter.

"Little Red" Young with his wife and daughter were early residents. Young was a tool push for Drilling Contractors, and his close neighbor, Bert Young (no relation) also lived there with his wife and daughter. George Fox and his neighbor, Benny Mitchell with his family, lived nearby. John Thompson and his wife Ida built a good house and when they left, sold the house to John Kendall, and it was moved to the Kendall Ranch several miles west.

Inside drilling rig. L. to R. Ray Wickens, Harry McMillan, Ossie Lister, Unknown, Steve Alexander, Gus Gamage.

Dan Matheson, with his wife and two children, had earlier lived on Bill Jackson's place, then moved to Majorville. Dan had been a farmer in Manitoba, so besides working for Home Oil, also had a small herd of cattle, leasing land from Home Oil for summer pasture. His children, Brian and Elaine, like the other children at Majorville, walked the two and a half mile to Sheep Creek School.

Hans Backs and his family also lived here, and others were the Mowatts, Dan and Mrs. Hume, Joe Raymond, Ossie and Mrs. Lister, Jake Severin and his family, Jim and Grace Fraser and their two daughters, Doreen and Kay.

Tommy Gilchrist with his wife Violet and boys, were residents. Like Dan Matheson, Tommy was raising cattle and working for Home Oil. When his herd of cattle became too large, they bought a ranch at Youngstown and moved there. The Posgate family also lived at Majorville.

Across the road on Fred Hodgkins' land, Jesse Sloan with his three children, Murial, Bob and Marian. Harley Hanson with his wife and two daughters, and the Sebrasse family had their little houses there.

Ernie Ducommun and his family lived in Joe Waugh's home when he sold his place to the Home Oil, and later Harold and Minnie Marshall lived there. Others who lived on the Peat land were Donna and Len Metz, Clyde Henry, Mr. Hill, Joe Raymond. As with the other small settlements, it had a floating population, so many who lived here may be missed.

All these homes were heated by gas, which was plentiful, although a bit wild. Small flares lit up the valley, until the Conservation Board put a stop to it. Rent was very cheap, with the ranchers usually charging only a couple of dollars per month.

As the drilling ceased, the families left until all that remains of the little settlement is a warehouse, which had been used by Home Oil.

Evansville

by Joanna Hanson

The first settlers began moving their shacks on to the south side of the Elwyn Evans place near the road in 1939. Gas lines were run on top of the ground so they were able to tap them for free fuel. There were no regulators so the gas was wild and not refined, probably coming from the Model wells. Most of the stoves were for wood or coal, with homemade burners. A surge of gas or turning the valve on too much sent the stove lids flying. Water came from the water line that ran from the pump house on the river on Evans' which supplied water to Incomes one and two wells, and the Home Oil wells.

Gallups put in a store and later Mr. and Mrs. Barney Hogg operated it. The lot rent was $2 per month and many fixed their grounds with lawns and flowers.

Near the river the Bert Baters had their home as he ran the pump house, also a Mr. and Mrs. Homes, who, on going out for the day, leaving her clothes on the line, came home to find Evans' cow had chewed them all up. That cow had a taste for soap suds. The Homes place was built so far up with lumber, then the upper part was canvas. It was very attractive, new furniture throughout. They put a water proofing on the canvas and being highly inflammable went up like a torch. Again the family were away.

Some of the people who lived there were: Gene and Edna Robertson, Mr. and Mrs. Bill Snider, Mr. and Mrs. Penard, Tom Kelly (who later married Jean Waugh), Barney Babb, Mrs. Vi Schultz, Mr. and Mrs. Bonnerman.

Dan Bell lived there for years and I believe he was the last one to leave that site. About a half mile further south were another group of homes. Mr. and Mrs. Cal Andrew, Jack and Maude Robertson, Ed McCaffery, Mr. and Mrs. Leftwich, Norman and Agnes Chaput.

A half mile west lived Phil Deschene until Hjalmar Nylund moved on to the battery, living there for many years. A Mr. Mainwaring lived in Evans' bunk house where many antiques were kept which the older David Evans had brought from Wales. The young man used to hang his clothes on a line over the stove. While he was on afternoon shift the clothes caught fire and a strong north west wind was blowing and the bunk house was completely destroyed. Fortunately, the wind blew the flames away from the house and no damage was done to it.

Home Oil Camp

When the Home Oil Company started a drilling program in what was called the "North End" most of the workers were living in Black Diamond, Turner Valley and the "South End". When a few good producing wells were completed a small settlement started where Home No. 2 had been drilled on section 33-20-3-W5. Drilling Contractors were drilling wells nearby for Home Oil, so built a house for their tool push, Cody Spencer, and he and his wife Eileen were the first occupants, but it was later taken over by Red McLaren and his wife. On the day that the second World War was declared in September, 1939, Harry and Helen

Home Oil Recreation Hall the day of the grand opening. Ethel Foster on steps.

McMillan moved into the house they had built. These were the first two houses built on what would become Home Oil Camp.

In a very short time many more houses were built or moved in and the population of the settlement increased rapidly. The camp was situated on a slope looking westward to the mountains. Warehouses were built, also garages and boiler and eventually a recreation hall for the enjoyment of the employees, with a much used pool table. However, no store was ever built so the Millarville Store benefited greatly and the mail was picked up there also.

The students were bussed to Sheep Creek School, then in 1950-51 that school was moved to Millarville and while it was in the process of reconstruction, all the Sheep Creek students were taken to the Home Camp and School was held in the recreation hall. This delighted the pupils, as at the old school site there was only outdoor plumbing, so they enjoyed the running water and indoor plumbing.

Over the more than thirty years the camp was in existence, the population varied, with families moving in and others moving out. Following is a list of names who either worked for the Home Oil Co. or were residents of the Camp: "Bid" Lowery, Gordon Webster, Ole Nevra, Hugh McNain, Herb Kirkland, Harold Kelly, Bill Kelly, Mr. Wiggins, Len Bauer, Archie Dick, Charlie Nolan, George Bennett, Win Parker, Geoff Parker, Percy Bennett, Bill McIntyre, Dan Hume, Don Campbell, Ray Endicott, Tom Grisdale, Russel King, Tommy Lyall, Alex Lyall, Joe Clancy, Bob Pruden, Jim Stafford, Roy Sim, Jim Fraser, Sam Webster, Danny Dudenhoeffer, Fred Dudenhoeffer, Sid Peel, Bruce Whitford, Dan Fraser, Alex Todd, Roy Foster, Les Foster, Chub Foster, Don Odlum, Nelson Odlum, Neil McNeil, Rudy Mulder, Eric Mulder, Fretho Mulder, Bill Johnson, Dan Matheson, Bud Flood, Don Storey, Oliver Yates, Jimmy Green, Merle Wickstrand, Johnny Cox, Rod Richardson, Len Scott, Jack Jameson, Ben Dichau, Al Moody, Sid Smith, Jack Stuart, Pat Tourand, Ossie Lister, Ernie Ducommun, Monty Stewart, Bill Stewart, Blackie Raymond, Clare Johnson, Glen Brown, John Shaw, Frank Patterson, Nap Larosee, Walt Kinder, Fred Rishaug, Hank Rishaug, Tim Blakley, Tip Johnson, Harry Cowan, Tom Kelly, George McIvor, Phil Samson, Gus Slack, Henry Anderson, Mr. Kirkland, Orville Cunningham, Fred Longacre, Shorty Hudkins, Fred Willock, Wes Mitchell, Len Metz, Mack McLeaod, Eddy Hunter, Art Rest, Harry Garries, Ted Swiften, Tommy Gilchrist, Harold Marshall, Nate Beebe, Les Vetters, Charlie Nolan Jr., Aubrey Baxter, Bill Bateman, Bob Burton, Glen Hazen, Gordon Larratt, Dan Daniels, Don Saunders, Arnold Gorveatt, Leo Olhauser, Dave Leman, Lawrie Lochhead, Bill McInnis, Bob Cormack, Carl Neese, Bill Orr, Joe Raymond, Don Sim, Hjalmar Snelvet, Elmer Anderson, Joe Carr, Gladys Orr, Mrs. Dan Dudenhoeffer, Mrs. Marsh. Some names may have been left out, so apologies to them.

All the homes are gone from the site, either sold or moved to other locations, and even the flares which lit up the country are few, due to conservation regulations. There is very little left to show what a thriving community it had once been. The hall was sold and moved. However, there are still work crews and some of those are Bill McIntyre, Fred Rishaug, Walt Kinder, Tip Johnson, Ken Roberts, Greg Debore, Wade Ewing, Dave Genert, Ron Utter.

Some of the earlier employees are working for Home Oil in Swan Hills and other locations, many have retired, but the memory of that small settlement lingers. Many were the donations for community efforts, such as the new Ranchers Hall at Millarville, also donating trophies for junior hockey teams at the Millarville School, and other projects.

Kew Store and Post Office

by Jean Blakley

In 1907, Gornal and Taylor, partners in the Gate Ranch, built a store on the N.W.¼ of 30-20-3w5. At this time the closest store was at Millarville, which also was the nearest post office, although some of the residents did get their mail at the Lineham post office at Denning's ranch. Harry Ewing worked for Gornal and Taylor on their ranch, also hauled the store supplies from Calgary. When the partners grew tired of the store, Ewing bought the stock and took it to his homestead and had a store for a couple of years.

Up until 1911, there wasn't a post office in the district, but that year George Bell became the first Kew postmaster, with the post office in his ranch house on Section 6-21-3w5. He named the new post office by spelling John Quirk's cattle brand, Q. Mr. Bell sold his ranch to Bill Patterson, and moved to Vancouver. The post office was then moved to the homestead of Harry Nadin, where he also ran a store. This was on the N.W.¼ of 19-20-3w5. When Bell took over the post office, the mail carriers had been Joe Waite and George Davidson, but after 1914, Robert Gillespie returned as mail carrier, and about this time he bought a Model T Ford, to carry the mail from Calgary to Priddis-Millarville-Kew.

In 1917, the store and the post office was in the original building, with William Edgerton as postmaster. In the first book, "Our Foothills" a document is pictured, an application by Sam Virtue, and was signed, William Edgerton, Postmaster. Feb. 9th, 1917.

In 1918, the business once again changed hands, when Edgerton sold to Mark and Bert Hodgkins. On one of the porch supports, a knife carving read, "Marian Hodgkins, waiting for the mail, 1918."

1920 brought new owners, when Hodgkins sold to Forward and Walton, who owned the Millarville store. Enoch Walton was postmaster, holding this position for more than twenty years. During this time the mail carriers varied, Ford Lochhead, for a time, and for four years during the 1920's Joe Waugh, first with team and wagon, and weather permitting, a Model T Ford. By this time the mail was picked up at Midnapore, taken by the old route, Priddis, Millarville and Kew.

After Enoch Walton's death in the early 1940's, Ford Lochhead took over the store and post office, and following were a succession of owners, Iceton, Jack Stagg, Jack Grant, Howe and finally Lawrence and Nina Lochhead.

In 1952, Lawrence and Nina Lochhead moved about a mile east and operated the business out of their home. A rural route ended the Kew post office in 1955. At the present time the mail comes to the district via R.R.1 Millarville, with Veryl and Arlie Laycraft as the carriers.

All the old buildings are no more. Michael Rodgers built his house on the site of George Bell's original post office and when the old log house was torn down, the post office wicket was still intact. Harry Nadin's house is gone, and one would have a hard time finding the location of the old Gornal and Taylor building as the road goes over it.

Millarville Store and Post Office, 1892-1941

by Jean Blakley

In April, 1892, Malcolm Millar was sworn in as Postmaster of the newly-formed Millarville Post Office. He had previous experience in this capacity when he was serving with the N.W.M.P. at Fort Walsh in the Cypress Hills. The post office and store were located in his ranch house on his homestead, the S.W.¼ of 11-3-w5. The store was the only one for many miles and catered to the needs of the settlers in the area. It also served as a trading post for the Indians, who brought their furs and buckskin goods to sell or exchange for groceries.

The first mail carrier was J. Dickey, then in 1895 Robert Gillespie had the contract until 1911, when Joe Waite took over with George Davidson also hauling for some time. In 1914, Mr. Gillespie once again had the contract.

In 1910, W. H. King had a store built on the hillside above his ranch buildings on the N.W.¼ of 2-21-3w5. In 1911, the post office was moved from Millar's ranch to the new King building. Mr. R. W. Shaw ran the post office for a few years, then from 1916 to 1918, Humphrey Brewis took over. The business was then sold to A. J. Twist, who was also in charge of a store at Priddis. In 1919, Twist sold to Forward and Walton, with Mrs. Annie Walton as the Postmistress.

There was a succession of mail carriers, with Ford Lochhead for some time, then in the 1920's Joe Waugh did the hauling for four years. He used horses and wagon, or in the winter, sleigh. He later bought a Model T Ford, which could only be used in very dry weather. The roads were just dirt trails, no gravel at that time, also no bridges over the creeks. On mail days, which was twice a week, the hitching rail in front of the store would have several horses tied to it, the owners inside, and if the mail was late, no one minded.

1902. Millarville.

A ranching settlement devoted entirely to raising of stock, twenty-four miles south-west from Calgary.

Adames, E. D.
Adams, Thos., rancher.
Aird, Alex., rancher.
   James. rancher.
Anderson, Gilbert, Sr., rancher.
   Gilbert, Jr., rancher.
   Herbert, rancher.
Barnes, H. H., rancher.
Bell. George, rancher.
Billings, Chas., saw mill.
Brown, S. V.
Carey, Eugene. rancher.
de Matherby, R., rancher.
Dempsey, Jno., rancher.
Dutson, Arthur, rancher.
Evans, David, rancher.
   R., rancher.
Fitzgerald, R., rancher.
   W. D., rancher.

Freeman, J. Deane, rancher.
Jackson F. A., rancher.
Joseph, Harry, rancher.
Kettleson, A. C., rancher.
Kieran. J. R., rancher.
King, W. H., rancher.
Lee, Walter, rancher.
Macdonald Angus, rancher.
Macpherson, A., coal mine owner.
Marsack, Fred, rancher.
McKinnon Jno., rancher.
Millar, Malcolm T., rancher and postmaster.
Noton, G. H.
Paton, Sam, rancher.
Phillips Walter, rancher.
Quirk, Jno., rancher.
Ridley, I. H., rancher.
Rodman, Caleb, rancher.
Senior, Fred, rancher.
Sinnott, Harry, rancher.
Standish, Joseph, rancher.
Turner, Robt., rancher.
Waite, Joseph.
Warren, J. C., rancher.
Webb-Peploe Rev. R. M., Anglican.
Welsh, A. P., Justice of Peace.
Williams, Norman, rancher.
Wright, Frances., rancher.

MILLARVILLE 1911

A post office on Sec 12. Tp 21, Rg 3, west of the 5th Mer., in the electoral division of Macleod. Is 15 miles from De Winton the nearest railway. Reached by livery and by regular semi-weekly (Wednesdays and Saturdays) stage. Has telephone connection with outside points. This is a ranching settlement. Mails semi-weekly.
Postmaster—Malcolm T Millar
Church of England—Rev C W Peck

Anderson H rancher
Cudlip J rancher
DeMille W V saw mill
Fisher Creek Lumber Co
Fisher & Macdonell saw mill
Frazer M rancher
Freeman W Dean rancher
Kennedy C H rancher
Kierans S rancher
Knights C R rancher
Lee G F rancher
Macpherson A coal mine owner
Millar Malcolm T postmaster
Millarville Trading Co general store
Phillips Thos rancher
Shaw Morris mail carrier
Smith H A rancher
Welsh Alfred P J P
Winthrop E L rancher

MILLARVILLE 1914

A post office on Sec 2, Tp 21, Rg 3, west of the 5th Mer, in the electoral division of Macleod. Is 15 miles from Le Winton the nearest railway. Reached by livery and by regular semi-weekly (Wednesdays and Saturdays) stage. This is a ranching settlement. Mails semi-weekly.
Postmaster—W H King
Cudlip J rancher
Davidson George mail carrier
DeMille W V saw mill
Durard A rancher
Evans David rancher
Fisher Creek Lumber Co
Fisher & Macdonnell saw mill
Fraser M rancher
Freeman W Dean rancher
Hulme Clayton rancher
Kennedy C H rancher
Kierans S rancher
King W H postmaster & rancher
Knights R rancher
Lee G F rancher
Macpherson A coal mine owner
Millarville Trading Co general store
Phillips Thos rancher
Segar Oil Co
Smith H A rancher
Welsh Alfred P J P
Winthrop E L rancher

MILLARVILLE 1924

a P.O. and farming settlement in Okotoks Prov. Elec. Div., 12 miles north-west of Okotoks on C.P.R. Calgary-Macleod line the nearest C.P.R. telegraph and Dominion express office, and the business centre. Farming and stock-raising.

Adams Thos farmer
Aird Campbell farmer
Alta Govt Phones
Barnes Geo rancher
Chalmers Bretam rancher
Chalmers James rancher
De Mille Ora farmer
Evans David rancher
Fisher Elizabeth rancher
Fisher Robt farmer
Forward & Walton gen store
Freeman L C farmer
Freeman Ronald farmer
Greenwood Ernest farmer
Jackson Willie rancher
Jamison Thos farmer
King Carlton farmer
King W H farmer
MacKay Wm farmer
Millar Malcolm rancher
Mitchell Lineham farmer
Mortimer Frank farmer
Nelson Chas farmer
Peat James farmer
Phillip Thos farmer
Postmistress Mrs Anne Walton
Rawlinson Edw farmer
Stanhope J A farmer
Stanhope Stanley farmer
Waugh Joe farmer
Winthrop Edwin farmer

MILLARVILLE 1928-1929

a P.O. and farming settlement on S11 T21 R3 W5, in Macleod Prov. Elec. Div, 12 miles northwest of Okotoks, on C.P.R. Calgary-Macleod line the nearest C.P.R. telegraph and express office, and the business centre. Farming and stock-raising.
Aird Campbell farmer
Alta Govt Phones
Bannerman W boiler tender
Bartlam William farmer
Chalmers Bertram rancher
Chalmers James rancher
Christ Church Rev A J Wright pastor
Evans David rancher
Fisher Elizabeth rancher
Forward & Walton gen store
Freeman L C farmer
Fulton John rancher
Fulton J S rancher
Jackson Willie rancher
Jamison Thos farmer
King Carlton farmer
King W H sec treas M D 191
Lees Bros gen store
Lyall George farmer
MacKay Wm farmer
Millar Malcolm rancher
Mitchell Lineham farmer
Mortimer Frank farmer
Mulder A rancher
Municipal District of Stockland No 191

KEW 1914.

A post office on Sec 30, Tp 20, Rg 3, west of the 5th Mer., in the electoral division of Macleod. Is 35 miles from Calgary, the nearest telegraph and 25 miles from Okotoks the nearest railway station. This district is situated toward the head of the north fork of Sheep Creek, in the foot hills and is only adapted for ranching. Reached by stage and by livery. Mails weekly.
Postmaster—Harry Hadin
Church of England—(supplied)
Anderson John rancher
Bloss Chat farmer
Brawne M F farmer
Brotton E C rancher
Burns P & Co ranchers
Chubb Ernest rancher
Cornall Wilfred T gen store
Cuthbertson Herbert rancher
Cuthbertson Joseph rancher
Dempsey John rancher
de Roaldes George rancher
Dubern Henri rancher
Ewing Wm farmer
Felton Oscar farmer
Flynn Patrick farmer
Fulton John rancher
Hadin Harry gen store
Howie J H plasterer
Johnson John rancher
Lockhead Charles rancher
Lyall George rancher
Lyall Thomas rancher
Morrison Charles farmer
Morrison James rancher
Nichols H F rancher
Read Arthur rancher
Scott Samuel rancher
Stagg Albert rancher
Stagg Robert rancher
Sylvester George rancher
Taylor E Louis rancher
Yeoman Maurice farmer

KEW 1911.

A post office on Sec 6, Tp 21, Rg 3, west of the 5th Mer. in the electoral division of Macleod. Is 35 miles from Calgary the nearest telegraph and 25 miles from Okotoks the nearest railway station. This district is situated toward the head of the north fork of Sheep Creek, in the foot hills and is only adapted for ranching. Reached by stage and by livery. Mails weekly.
Postmaster—George Bell
Church of England—(supplied)

Anderson John rancher
Bell George postmaster
Bloss Chat farmer
Brawne M F farmer
Brotton E C rancher
Burns P & Co ranchers
Chubb Ernest rancher
Cuthbertson Herbert rancher
Cuthbertson Joseph rancher
Dempsey John rancher
de Roaldes George rancher
Dubern Henri rancher
Ewing Wm farmer
Felton Oscar farmer
Flynn Patrick farmer
Fulton John rancher
Gornall Wilfred T gen store
Howie J H plasterer
Johnson John rancher
Lockhead Charles rancher
Lyall George rancher
Lyall Thomas rancher
Morrison Charles farmer
Morrison James rancher
Nichols H F rancher
Read Arthur rancher
Scott Samuel rancher
Stagg Albert rancher
Stagg Robert rancher
Sylvester George rancher
Taylor E Louis rancher
Yeoman Maurice farmer

They could have a good visit with their neighbors, exchanging news and friendly gossip.

When Joe Waugh was mail carrier, the mail was picked up at Midnapore, then on to the old route, Priddis-Millarville-Kew. Mr. Waugh would stay at the old Midnapore Hotel at times, as it was quite a long trip by horse and wagon. Originally, the mail had been picked up in Calgary.

Luke Forward had a truck, hauling cream, etc., to Calgary, bringing out supplies for the store and did general trucking for the ranchers. He became very ill, then Jim Colley took over the trucking. When Mrs. Walton became ill and bedridden for a few years before her death, Angus MacKay served as Postmaster until 1941, when the post office was moved one-half mile west to Norman Pegler's store, which had been built in 1926.

The building which W. H. King had built and which had served as post office for so many years, was accidentally burned in about 1948.

Millarville General Store
1926-1979

It was in 1926 that Norman W. Pegler built the store on the present site. He hauled his freight over rough roads from Calgary with horses. At that time bread was 10¢ a loaf and twenty lbs. of sugar cost $1.65. In 1941 the Post Office was moved into the store and the mail came out from Calgary three times a week. After 18 years in Millarville, Mr. Pegler sold the store to Jappy Douglass in 1944. By this time the oil boom had brought many new residents to the district and the store reaped some of the benefits. Mr. Douglass built on a coffee shop and he moved the McFarland Lumber Yard Office from High River and attached it to the store. In 1956, Jappy was seriously injured in a shotgun accident and consequently sold the store and purchased some land at Gem, Alberta, where he took up ranching.

Mr. and Mrs. Carl Orthner were the next owners, staying for two years, when they then sold the Clark Jacobson. Clark was very busy building the store and stock back up as it had become very run down, however he only had it from September, 1958 to April 1959 as he decided store-keeping just wasn't his field and sold to the Arlie Laycraft family of High River.

Nora Andrews ran the Post Office for the Orthners and also for Clark part of the time. Veryl Laycraft became Post Master in March 1959 and kept this post for 15 years. Arlie and son Ron were partners in the store and they built up a good stock and spent much time and money on insulating, painting, improving, landscaping etc. During their time, daily mail came to Millarville, and from this a Rural Route out of this Post Office. Clark Jacobson was the first Mail Contractor to haul the mail on this Rural Route. He stayed on this job for several years, giving the best of service, rain, snow or shine. His wife Pat was always a very faithful helper. In 1968, Ron Laycraft decided to go to University so his Father bought his share of the store and Arlie and Veryl carried on alone with part time help until Arlie began to suffer from Arthritis. In 1974 the store was sold to Nick and Janet Cooke from Okotoks. Nick and Janet worked hard for the next four years, had a family of two girls and made many changes, like adding to the living quarters etc. Nick was Post Master for the four years. In the fall of 1978 he left for the coastal area around Vancouver after he had disposed of the store to Mr. and Mrs. John Clarke of Calgary. Karen Clarke is the new Post Master and Arlie and Veryl Laycraft are still hauling the Rural Route mail which they started to do when Nick Cooke took over and Clark Jacobson wished to retire. We hope the Clarkes will like this community and stay for a good many years.

Chapter 4
Halls

Race Track Community Hall

by Stan Jones

In a community where the spiritual, educational, recreational and commercial facilities are spread over an area roughly five miles long and seldom more than two hundred yards wide, it was inevitable that the location of a community hall should pose a problem, however at an organizing meeting held at Fordville school on Saturday, November 9, 1946, there was no doubt in the minds of those present. It was to be built at the Millarville Race Track and named "The Agricultural Hall". At this meeting, John Jackson was elected President, and I, Stan Jones, was elected Sec.-Treasurer. Rudy Mulder and Arthur Patterson were named Trustees, and after deciding that the hall was to be 30 by 60 with a full size basement, and that all funds were to be deposited in the Calgary Treasury Branch, we went home.

The following spring at a meeting held on April 10th, it was obvious that the Race Club did not want a hall at the race track, as the purpose of calling the meeting was "To discuss an alternative site for the proposed hall".

The first motion, to re-approach the Race Club was defeated 7 to 5, and then three other sites were considered. A group in west Millarville had been talking of replacing the old Rancher's Hall and there were some who felt we should amalgamate. The next motion had this in mind when a site on Sec. 12, 21, 3, W5th, across from Bill Lee's store was proposed. This was defeated 11 to 1, and two other sites were left; one acre in the SW corner of Sec. 1, 22, 3, W5th, offered by S. C. Prichard and Sons, and one acre in the S.W. corner of Sec. 25, 21, 3, W5th, offered by Jack Lee. The Lee site was chosen by an 8 to 4 vote, and the name changed to "The Fordville Community Hall".

A timber berth which John Jackson held on Sec. 36, 21, 3, W5th, was taken over and a quantity of logs cut, and sawed with Mr. Barraclough's mill, all by volunteer labour. We then cleaned out the rest of the logs and piled them up. There is no record of a meeting in 1948, but in the spring of that year we borrowed Royal Burrow's mill and with Murray Croston as sawyer, and volunteer labour again, we were really in business. All the sheeting needed for the hall was

hauled down to Royal's and planed with his planer, enough 2 inch stuff for studding and joists was held back and the balance was sold.

The next summer, a deal having been made with Jack Lee for the land, an excavation was made for the basement, and Gordon Blanchard, who was going to be boss carpenter, started on the forms for the footings. Up to this point there had been lots of enthusiasm and no difficulty obtaining help, but suddenly a change came over the whole project and although we had a site, enough lumber for a hall, and a pretty good wad in the bank, there was something wrong. It turned out to be the location. A lot of lobbying had been going on to get the Race Club to reconsider, so we decided to call a general meeting.

At this time there had been talk of a hall in the Westoe area, Priddis had been considering building a new hall, the west Millarville group were still interested, and all were represented at the old Fordville school which was still the local meeting spot. This was an excellent meeting and it really cleared the air. While everybody had their say, it was obvious that the younger members of the Race Club were still in sympathy with our original intention of building the hall at the Race Track, and when it was moved by Winston Parker, and seconded by Bob Winthrop "That we re-approach the Race Club for a site", it was passed unanimously. On July 18th, John Jackson and I were asked to attend a director's meeting at the Race Track to answer questions, and as far as I was concerned, to convince them that what we had in mind was a community hall, and not what one director insisted in calling a "dance hall". After stating our case, we were asked to leave the meeting, and were later called in, to be told we could go ahead, and at last our hall had a home.

A community sale was held at the Track that fall and just over $2000 added to the bank roll. A blueprint had been made by Manning and Egelston Lumber Co. in 1947, and on the basis of that, plan, tenders for the construction of the building were called for, with the provision that we receive credit for any volunteer labour. Brown Bros. Construction of Black Diamond were the successful bidders, and after the basement was installed by what was then willing and plentiful volunteer help, they went ahead with construction. This must have gone on during the winter, as minutes at a meeting on February 20, authorized the Sec. Treas. to pay Brown Bros. "the second third of the money as agreed, and the last third on completion of the building".

From then on most of our troubles were financial, and the last third of the money turned out to be quite a problem. $3000 may not seem a big sum at the present time, but in those days, it was more than most people made in a year. At a meeting, still at Fordville school, it was proposed to borrow the money from a bank, with as many local residents co-signing the note as possible. This was quite unacceptable to the manager; he wanted only one signature on the note and that had to belong to someone with at least enough money in his account to cover the note. It might be noted here, that this was standard procedure with banks at that time — they would not loan money unless you were able to prove to them that you had the money, and therefore did not need it. We then found a bank which would loan the money with several co-signers, but by that time the only people we could get to sign had no money anyway, so the deal fell through.

The next effort was more successful. We canvassed the district for personal loans repayable in twenty years at 5% interest, and soon had the money. I might add here, that one old-timer I touched for a loan told me that while we said we were going to pay the money back, and no doubt thought we would, he had seen many similar schemes and none of them had ever paid off. It was with a great deal of personal satisfaction that, as Sec. Treas., I made out a cheque in his behalf for the full amount two years later; he declined the interest. At the Annual Meeting for 1959, there is a motion recorded to repay Oswald Madson $100, the last of the loans.

The first dance was held in May, 1950 with May Lock's orchestra from Okotoks. It was a great success. The hall was still not stuccoed, but shortly after, Jim Brown from Turner Valley took care of that detail. Our main source of income was from dances which, with the exception of the one held after the Races, were not very profitable, and was supplemented by any other projects we could dream up. On at least one occasion we ran a chicken supper after the Races, and for several years operated the refreshment concession.

During the 1963 flood, there were several feet of water in the basement, but prompt action by the neighbours prevented any serious damage to the kitchen. In 1964 the Hall, Races and Agricultural Society were combined into one organization, an arrangement which continues today. Natural gas was laid on in 1968, and with the addition of indoor toilets, and the upstairs kitchen, which were built on in 1972, our hall is as comfortable and modern as any in the country.

The New Ranchers Hall
by Elwyn Evans

The first rumblings about a new hall at Millarville started about 1948. There were a few meetings, each one smaller than the one preceding with nothing decided. There were also joint discussions with residents east of Highway No. 22 who also were planning a community hall but as so often happens when two groups of citizens try to combine as one nothing comes of it.

The spark that finally started Ranchers Hall going must be credited to the Willing Workers Women's Institute. They hired Ossie Hogg to dig the basement on the E. H. Rawlingson flat. That hole in the ground finally shamed the men into action. A meeting was held and the following men were elected to office, Bert Chalmers, President, W. Jackson, vice-president, and Virgil Ohlson, Percy Bennett and Ole Nevra as directors. Somehow or other I, Elwyn Evans, got sucked into being secretary-treasurer, a position I had for sixteen years. Donations from individuals and ladies groups followed. Virgil Ohlson drew up the plans and Bob Campbell was hired as the carpenter. The directorate put up money and bought a new 1950 Ford car from Hans Backs at cost, had books of tickets printed and started a car raffle. Well, raffling that car, though it was a financial success, gave the directorate more headaches than building the hall. Ticket sales which at first went very well, but as time went on sales dropped so that the directorate hired a young man who (so he said) had handled car raffles before. Sales picked up and everyone was pleased, then nothing was heard for some time. Inquiries showed that the raffle ticket seller had got married and gone to Ontario in the car on his honeymoon. There was no legal recourse so all the directorate could do was gnaw their finger-nails. However about two weeks later he returned having only sold twenty tickets. He suddenly joined the unemployed.

It was now the early part of December, 1950 and the directorate was fortunate to obtain a permit from the Calgary police to park the car on eighth Ave. to sell tickets. Merle Backs, Vera Haney and Elmer Anderson sold tickets on the sidewalk and they did a fantastic job. The car was drawn for at a dance held in Kew Hall early in January, 1951 and the winner was a young man J. A. Hantho, now a medical doctor in Calgary. He has been reported to have said that winning that car changed his whole life. Well it might have, but it also added some grey hairs to the directorate.

Meanwhile the construction of the hall was coming on well due to the help from the community and from the oil companies especially the Home Oil Co. The opening date of the hall was set for the second Friday in December, 1951, so for the last month everyone worked on the hall. Two incidents that happened at the opening deserve mention. The night before opening, when we were at last finished, called for a small celebration. As often happens, too much firewater led to fisticuffs between two Millarvilleites. The rest of us considered that to be the official opening. Also on that last day before opening it was decided to paint the benches green with paint guaranteed to dry in twenty-four hours. Something went wrong with the result that there were many green bums opening night.

The New Ranchers Hall was built and opened but it took almost another twelve years to pay off the cost. This was done through dances, suppers, turkey shoots and bingos. It was the bingo games that finally put things in the clear and the credit for them goes to Robert Chalmers, Robert Backs and Fred Rishaug. They did a wonderful job.

For the last few years the Ranchers Hall has been rented to the Foothills School Division as a gymnasium so still serves the grandchildren of the original directorate of which there are only two still living. One may note that of all the brands displayed in the hall there isn't one belonging to a member of that group. Somehow they never got around to putting theirs up. This story may tell posterity who built the New Ranchers Hall.

Kew Hall

by Nita Foster

In the winters of 1929-30 and 1930-31 dances and card parties (admission 50¢) were held by the community to raise money to build a hall. These events were held in houses and Plainview School. At this time Plainview School was condemned for dances, but Charlie Minue, a teacher, took all responsibility for these dances and they continued. Ford Lochhead also sold subscriptions for the Turner Valley Flare and the hall received half of the proceeds.

The lumber was shipped to Okotoks where it was picked up by Harvey Johnston on his big trucks and hauled to North End Turner Valley School because of mud roads. E. L. Kendall, Harry Foster and Pat Rodgers hauled it to Kew with four horse teams and wagons with the help of many more neighbours. Sandy Russel was head carpenter and all the neighbours helped, a real community project. The brick chimney was built by Jim Howie with Chub Foster helping. This was Jim's last job as a brick layer. The Hall opened in 1932 with a free dance.

By this time Turner Valley oilfields were booming and the dances at Kew were large affairs and really wild and woolly. One 17th of March dance is really remembered. The oil workers said, "Let's clean these old ranchers out" and one Irish rancher hollered, "Let's clean the bloody Hall". In half an hour the hall was cleaned, people were in the rafters, out the closed windows and out the doors. One oil worker ended up in hospital for ten days. Everything calmed down and the dance went on. But the ranchers showed this was their hall.

This hall was used for years for a great many functions. At one time a big attraction was boxing with the

Hodgkin boys, Thompson boys and many good boxers coming from the relief camps stationed west of Kew. The school held many good Christmas concerts there. All picnics and baseball functions were centered around the hall usually ending with a party in the hall. A wedding dance, the first in the Kew district, was held in the hall for Chub and Nita Foster. Chub bought a 45 gallon keg of beer for this event. The keg cost $11.00 and $5.00 was refunded when the keg was taken back. That keg of beer made a good time and a lot of people happy.

For a few years the hall was not used so it was decided to donate it to Square Butte as their community was growing and needed a recreation place. Very few of the old timers that helped start the hall are here, but we still have Mrs. E. L. Kendall, Mrs. Jane Fisher, Lizzie Rummel and Mrs. Walter Phillips.

Rancher's Hall Moved to Heritage Park

by Jean Blakley

For eighty-one years the old Rancher's Hall sat on the same spot on the Fisher Ranch at Millarville. Joseph Fisher Sr. had donated the land and the building of the Hall was a real community effort. Logs were cut and hauled to the site and almost all the ranchers had a hand in the building of it. Up to that time, 1895, there had been no public building in the district. Until 1950, when a new hall was built four miles east of the old Hall, it was in constant use as a gathering place for dances, church, school and meetings of all kinds. After the Sheep Creek School was built in 1928, the annual Christmas concert was held in the Hall, so many former students of the school, some still living in the Millarville-Kew districts, and many others who had attended dances in earlier years, had a fondness for the old Hall. This was demonstrated by their attendance at the party given for the opening of the Hall in its new setting in Heritage Park on October 2nd, 1976.

Play at old Ranchers Hall, March 1938. On stage L. to R. Mrs. N. W. Pegler, Richard Lyall, Selina Hambling, Rudy Mulder, Mrs. W. Jackson, Tommy Lyall, Erick Mulder, Jean Waugh, Elwyn Evans, Irene Evans.

In the early spring of that year, Heritage Park showed an interest in moving the old building into Calgary, to renovate and preserve it. It was rapidly deteriorating, having been used as a storage place for several years. The Fisher family were pleased to know that the Hall could be saved, so gladly gave consent to its removal.

It was quite a job, jacking up the heavy log building, and it was surprising to find most of the logs in fairly good condition. When it was finally loaded on dollies, with the logs well braced and minus the floor, it was taken into Calgary, and set down in a section of the Park to be known as Old Town. Close by is the Sam Livingstone house. The Fisher and Livingstone families have been close friends since the two senior members of the families came to the country in pioneer days, so it was appropriate that the two buildings should be situated nearby.

By the end of summer, an amazing change had taken place in the old Hall. A few new logs, windows and doors, a new floor, and an addition built on where in the early years had been a "Ladies'" and a "Gentlemens'" rooms, plus a kitchen. The entire interior had been renewed.

On October 2nd, 1976, the building was ready for the grand opening. Invitations were sent out to all former and present residents of the Millarville and Kew districts. The guests were met at the Park entrance and taken to the Hall in an assortment of horse drawn vehicles. For many, it was the first time in many years they had been behind a team of horses and for many of the younger ones it was a first experience.

When all of the guests had gathered the ceremonies took place with Archdeacon Cecil Swanson making the dedication. Short speeches were given by members of some of the oldest families of the Millarville-Kew districts, including Joe Fisher now owner of the land on which the Hall had been built, Nettie Ware, daughter of John Ware, who had helped in the building of the Hall, and Elsie (Millar) Douglass, daughter of the first

Millarville people entering old Rancher's Hall at its new setting in Heritage Park. Oct. 2, 1976.

Millarville postmaster. The daughters of Joseph Waugh, and early pioneer of the area, presented a picture to be hung in the Hall. Eunice (Shaw) Park of Priddis, presented a dance program, which had been used many years before at a dance in the Hall. A large framed photograph of Joseph Fisher Sr. was presented and later hung in the Hall.

Tables were set up in the main part of the Hall and in the new addition a long table was centered by a suitably decorated cake and mounds of sandwiches, courtesy of the Administration of Heritage Park. A silver tea service, loaned by Mildred (Millar) MacMillan, graced the tea table, which was presided over by two granddaughters of Joseph Fisher, Olive (Piper) Schwarz and Mary (Blakley) White. The lunch was served by many young ladies wearing old fashioned costumes. Some of the guests were also wearing old fashioned clothing, and this gave an old time setting for the event.

Since the opening day, several more pictures have been hung in the Hall, each having to do with the early life of the Millarville-Kew districts. One small picture of the old Hall, drawn by a great-grandson of Joseph Fisher Sr., Stephen Fisher, has been framed and is also on the wall.

The Hall is now used as a tea room and light lunches are also served.

Home Oil Recreation Hall

by Nita Foster

As the Home Camp population grew there was a need for a place for recreation. There was a lovely place on the hillside amongst the trees for picnics, but a building was needed so the Home Oil Company provided a hall with a big kitchen and washrooms. This was something special as no other hall in the area for miles around had washrooms inside. This hall was a great asset to everyone as not only Home Oil people used it, communities all around used it. Sunday school was held for many years and it was used for a school when the Millarville school was reconstructed and

Millarville friends gather in the old Rancher's Hall at the opening day at Heritage Park, Oct. 2, 1976.

moved. The young people used it for teen dances and a wedding reception and dance were held in it for Roy Sims' daughter, Jean and husband Doug Godkin. Fred Rishaug's Mother and Father held their 50th Wedding Anniversary celebration here. Many Christmas concerts for the schools were there and the Home Camp itself always had Christmas parties, staff parties and other social events. The hall was well used for many years but as the work in the oilfields moved the people of the Home Camp left, leaving a big hall empty. Harold Marshall and Johnny Eden bought this building and moved a section each to their farms west of Millarville where they are still located. This is another landmark that is in the past and only a memory.

Chapter 5
The Changing Scenes

The Changing Scenes

In these beautiful foothills of Alberta, with its ever changing view of the mountains, which is south west of the growing city of Calgary, there have been varied changes.

The pioneers came in the late 1800's, some by covered wagon, some by ox cart and Red River cart, and later by railroad. They filed on homesteads and started raising cattle. They were a hardy breed of men and women.

Later, the people from the British Isles settled here, some to raise fine horses, and cattle, and also cultivated the land. They had their old country habits' and had a Polo Team and Races.

As more settlers came, more land was cultivated and more cattle raised. Everyone had a half section of land or more in order to make a living. Life progressed in this farming and ranching area. Schools and roads were built, and so life went on.

In the 1930's there came what were referred to as C.P.R. squatters. Times were very difficult and hundreds of people were on relief in Calgary. The Federal and Provincial Governments and the city of Calgary gave $600.00 to any who applied, to buy equipment and a C.P.R. quarter of land in this area. They paid $25.00 down on the land and no more payments for four years. The government kept $200.00 of the $600.00 and doled it out at $10.00 per month. They had to build living accommodation, clear the brush off the land, cultivate it, and try to make a livelihood. There were many who came out here, some were not able to make it, quite a few were successful, and have contributed greatly to the community. It was very difficult to say the least.

As Calgary grew, so did the urge of the people to leave the city and own a piece of land, raise their families in the country. The people bought 20 acres, some less, some more. They have built beautiful homes and commute to Calgary to work. They are also contributing greatly to the community in these beautiful foothills. Who knows what the future holds for all.

THE RANCH

Down at the end, of a winding road,
There is a log cabin, so it's been told,

With a creek and a barn, and outhouse too,
All sheltered in a valley, with a mountain view.

There's a sign on the gate, that all will know,
Of the horses near by, for racing and show,
Chewing the rails, on the bunkhouse door,
To the squeak of bedsprings, and the occasional snore.

While down at the barn, in the first morning light,
All wet and shiny, and shaking with fright,
A filly is foaled, with some help to attend,
And untangle the legs, that just wouldn't bend.

The cook sounds the gong, that breakfast is soon,
As the smell of fresh coffee, drifts into the room,
And the pump handle squeaks, as the water is drawn,
To freshen your face, in the mountain dawn.

We enter a kitchen, of an appetite's dream,
For a breakfast of eggs and ham, potatoes and beans,
And if we're in luck, as the cook's been about,
There could be a taste, of your favorite trout.

Long are the days spent on feeding, on fencing, or painting,
And all of the chores, it took in the making,
A trip to the mill, for the lumber to build,
Or carry the rocks, we brought from the hills.

The noon sun is high, as the children are fed,
To go reluctantly, off to their beds,
And soon the afternoon heat, shadows to shade,
As the final rounds of the upper hay field, are made.

There's a chill, to the early evening breeze,
Which carries the wood smoke, up over the trees,
As the horses drift down to the house, for the night,
To peer in the windows, by the fading light.

We come to the ranch house, its shelter and sound,
Each from their labors, wherever they're found,
Sore from the tractor, the saw, or the saddle,
To rest in the kitchen, amid a cookery rattle.

Soon dinner is served, from a barbeque rack,
With salad and steak, and corn cobs in a stack,
And plenty of sour cream, for those on a diet,
Who say it's low calorie, to those who won't try it.

Away from the kitchen, and out into the dusk,
We stay low and keep moving, for our belts gonna bust,

To work with the horses, the mares and the foals,
For the Thoroughbred horse sale, is one of our goals.

As the yard lights come on, and the stars are out,
And the still of the night, echoes the coyotes shout,
We seek a soft chair, by a crackling blaze,
To talk till late hours, of the coming days.

From an embered hearth, to a darkened stall,
Today fades to tomorrow, and lights up the wall,
With our wish that tomorrow, your dreams will unfold,
Down at the end, of your winding road.

Paul R. Whitman/78
(SW 33-20-4-5)

Old Ranch Buildings

Ranch House.

David Evans ranch home, built about 1900.

George Lyall's home at Kew. Hjalmar Nylund on horse.

The Kendall ranch at Kew. Originally the Quirk ranch but from 1922 to 1973 the home of the Kendall family.

House built by Lawrence (Pud) Lang on the S.E.¼ of 7-21-3W5, now owned by Frank and Maude Sharp.

"Monea" the home of the Deane-Freeman family of Millarville.

Log house built by "Doc" Lee on the S.E.¼ 34-21-4W4.

The home of Pat and Nina Rodgers at Kew. Homestead of Mrs. Mary Waite where she and her son Joe made their home, bought by Mrs. Basilici in 1911.

The Billy Cochrane house at Millarville, originally the home of the Rev. Webb-Peploe, bought by Cochrane about 1906. He had the vertical logs painted black and white, his racing colors.

Arthur Ball's original home at Kew, built in 1936.

Hjalmar Nylund standing in front of original George Davidson house built about 1905. Was home of the Nylund family for many years. Been owned by Jim Ward since 1922.

Old Lineham ranch house on South Sheep Creek. Picture taken in 1910.

House on the Cannon Ranch at Millarville. Built about 1900. .

The MacKay Ranch House. Previously owned by John Turner later Francis Wright.

George Bell's Homestead House. First Kew Post Office.

Log home of Jimmie Spooner built in 1905, later the home of the Wildman family. Large tree had just been pulled out.

House on the homestead of Jack Johnson, on the N.E.¼ of 1-21-4W5, built about 1909.

Haying and Harvest Methods

by Jack Ollive

Some of the homesteaders started cutting their hay with a scythe and before they had the brush cut and land cleared, used to cut the slough grass and in the wet years would cut in the water, then drag the grass out to the edge to dry. It is surprising what one will do when there is no choice.

The horse drawn mowers were noisy and prone to breakdown, and for some of the wild hay had to be well maintained, and have a good team that would keep a good pace up, or it would start to chatter and stall. One time-consuming chore was the mower knife sharpening. The large wet stone was the most popular method used. These were mounted on a four legged frame with a seat on one end so the operator could sit while his feet were busy pumping the pedals that powered the stone. Water had to be used to wash the granules of stone away, otherwise the wheel would become black and smooth, so would no longer cut. The water also kept the mower sections from losing their temper by dissipating the heat. Some wet stones were mounted so the bottom ran in a trough to hold the water; others had a pail above them that had a small hole so the water would dribble onto the stone.

If one hit a stump or hummock of earth with the mower, the tongue would break. Most of them had a five foot cut, and it wasn't until the odd oil bath mower with rubber tires started to be made, that mowing wasn't a trying time.

Haying methods over the years have changed with the new ideas that have come up from time to time, and as manpower became more expensive, and each man had to produce more to survive in the ever changing farming picture. More sophisticated machinery has made the farmer and rancher more dependent on goods and services provided by the machine companies, whereas in the old days, if one had a mower, hayrake and a wagon, one could and did, improvise to get the job done.

The basket hayrack was used to haul many a hay crop in, and the backbreaking work of pitching the

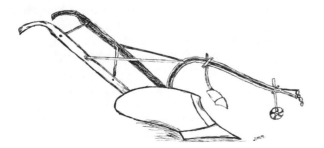

loads on and off, always in a hurry for fear of the weather changing.

Often the farm wife did the stacking, also the building and tramping the loads as the man threw the hay on the hayrack. But as always, there was progress, and if one could afford it, there was a pickup elevator that was towed behind the hayrack, and by driving down the windrow of hay, it would elevate it onto the back of the load and a man with a fork could build a load more easily. There were few of these in the district though.

Some people used slings to unload the hayrack either up into a loft or onto a stack. The slings were laid in the bottom of the hayrack and half of a load was placed on top of them; then another sling was laid on top and the remainder of the load built on that. These slings were made of rope or cable, with three lines parallel about three feet apart, having wooden slats across to act as spreaders. The slings were in pairs with a trip in the middle operated with a rope. When the load was elevated with a team and rope up to a track running just under the peak of the barn roof, the load was held in position with a catch arrangement; then it could be run along the track in the loft to wherever desired, the trip rope pulled and the load dumped. If one wanted to build a stack, the same arrangement could be mounted on poles so the track would run over the stack location, or a vertical log

Stacking greenfeed at W. Parkers about 1948. Stan Jones on stack.

Putting straw in loft with a sling.

held in place with cables, and a swinging gin pole suspended from the log would put the slings above the stack. Slide stackers were widely used. This was just a large ramp made out of poles and boards. The hay was brought in with a sweep which was a pole or timber frame, about fourteen feet wide by three feet high, with a swinging arm on each end. A team of horses were hitched to each arm — these arms helped contain the load of hay and also kept the sweep in an upright position. Usually the dump rake was taken down the windrow and the hay was bunched to make the sweep pick it up cleaner. The load was then hauled into the stacker and right onto the stack. One man could drive the two teams when gathering a load, but two men were needed to slide it up onto the stack. The horses were then backed up until the sweep had slipped down the ramp. Then the teams were turned around the sweep, being pulled the other way for the next load.

The hay had to be levelled out on the stack after each load. Otherwise, the stack would not settle evenly and would not shed the rain. Needless to say, there were clouds of blue smoke around when one team was too fast or slow, and the load would end up on the ground beside the stacker, or someone would let their team go too far, and the sweep would be on top of the stack.

There were many variations of this type of stacker. Some had a rope and pulley arrangement on each side so the teams could be unhooked from the sweep and hitched to the rope. This way, each man could drive his team outwards from the stack, and could see to keep the sweep even on its way up the stacker.

Then there was the pushpole stacker and the loads were brought in in the usual way and left at the bottom of the ramp and another team would push the load up with a long pole with a roller and baffle arrangement. This pole was thirty to thirty-five feet long with the team hitched to the heavy end, with it in front of them like an extended wagon tongue. When the load was pushed up onto the stack, the team would back up and the breast straps that were attached to the pole, made the whole assembly roll out of the way in readiness for the next load. Some of these would range from twelve feet high, to one model that was used on the Bradfield Ranch which must have been twenty feet. A crew of men with two sweeps, a man on the pole team, and a couple on the stack, and maybe three dump rakes could put up fantastic amounts of hay in a day. One of the rake teams would have nearly a full time job re-raking, that is, cleaning up the loose hay behind the sweeps. If one had to stack where it wasn't feasible to take the stacker, four poles could be laid up on a pile of hay and the next sweep load could be slipped up on top, after each load one would have to lift the poles up on top again, but it was still faster and easier than forking the hay up.

Another popular home-made haying outfit was the overshot stacker; this was used in conjunction with a buck rake. This rake was usually twelve feet wide

Gene and Pearl Ollive with a buck rake.

Stan Jones stacking hay with push-pole stacker.

mounted on two wheels with poles, or two by six planks for teeth. These teeth were a foot apart and usually eight feet long. A horse was hitched to each side and a seat for the man in the centre at the back. This seat was a sliding affair so the man could slide it back and counterbalance the teeth, and this way the chances of them catching on anything or sticking in the ground when going back for another load was lessened. When the load was on, there was no way of lifting the teeth, and they just slipped along the ground. When the load was delivered to the stacker, it was pushed onto a similar set of teeth with these attached to long poles or timbers with the ends anchored to the frame of the stacker. With a team hitched to a rope and a series of pulleys and levers, the entire load was thrown onto the stack just like a man with a pitchfork puts a forkfull into a rack. The advantage of this outfit was the stack was packed hard with each successive load and a skillful man with a fast team could toss the load to whatever end of the stack he chose. The wind, however, was a factor and if it wasn't a calm day there would be a lot of cleaning up around the stack, but these stacks would shed the rain as they were well packed. If it was a tall crop of hay, it would be all a man could do in the winter to pry a forkful loose, for it would seem to be all in one piece.

Sometimes a hayknife was used to cut a stack in half if only part was needed. There were two kinds of hayknives, one was like a square mouth shovel, having three mower sections on the bottom edge. There was a step on it, and by putting one's weight to work, would be able to cut about eighteen inches into dry hay. Any moisture or ice, and it wouldn't work.

The other kind was a steel blade about three feet long and four inches wide with serrations along one side. These were kept sharp and by two handles on the end, the stack was sawn the depth of the blade. One could also put a couple of strands of wire (barbed) over a stack attached to a weight or drag, and a team of horses on the other end a stack could be severed with a few passes of the wire.

There was a combination sweep and stacker called a Jayhawk that was pushed in front of a tractor or even a car or light truck. It had a standard sized sweep and a frame made of angle iron, in a pyramid shape and a wheel on each side about twelve feet apart. These wheels operated a winch when desired and as one approached the stack, the winch would lift the load of hay to the top of the stack. The only trouble if one didn't start to lift far enough away from the stack the sweep wouldn't be high enough to reach the top.

About this time tractors were being used more and more for haying and various homemade sweeps were used with them, then the farmhand came on the market. This was a hydraulic loader with a variety of attachments and was soon adopted by most farms. This machine could sweep the hay in, and put it on the stack and also could be used for moving the stooks of grain into the threshing machines, and soon the horses were finished both for the haying and the threshing in the country. Some who had the larger herds to feed in the winter and were lucky enough to have a tractor that could be started in the cold weather fed their cattle with the farmhand using the grapple fork or a forage fork and were able to take the hay directly from the stack to the cattle, and not touch any of it by hand. Some developed the art of stacking without leaving the tractor seat, so finally it was possible to do away with the manual labour.

Soon there were frames made to pile the hay into, so that anyone could make a good stack without handling it by hand. There were many catastrophies when these farmhands were being mastered with sweep teeth stuck in the ground and anything else that was in the way from tractors to the feeders on the threshing machines. Most of the tractors that were used in the forties and the fifties were too small and narrow, and many outfits were tipped and bent into pretzels. One man even had a load elevated and hit the clutch too hard. Tractor, load and all came over backward, but he survived.

They say one of the hardest things to do is to pull a steel farmhand tooth out of a tractor tire.

Soon most people started to think of the new baling systems that were on the market. For a while, there were a few machines that made a small round bale with a few wraps of binder twine around it, then the square pick up balers came, that had automatic twine or wire tie, which made them popular as compared to the ones that were used to bale hay out of the stacks, and had to have a couple of men to run the wire through the compressed hay and tie it. These were used mostly by farmers that were shipping hay on the railways or other means over long distance where space was a consideration.

The Country Guide and other farm papers used to have plans for hay balers and stackers of various kinds, and these were often winter projects for the farmer. One plan was for a baler with a long pole for leverage and a wooden chamber, the hay being forked in, and compressed with the lever arrangement man-power being the energy, and then the wire threaded through and tied by hand, but this was for someone with lots of time, small amounts of hay and an abundance of patience. There was a model available commercially which consisted of a bale chamber and a long arm to which a horse was hitched and driven around and around. Every revolution made one stroke of the plunger in the baler. Needless to say, this also was very slow.

With the automatic baler, there were lots of ways to handle the bales. Some were elevated directly from the baler onto a wagon which was towed behind, then when a large enough load was built by hand, the wagon was unhitched and hauled off to the stack or barn. Sometimes a bale elevator was used to unload the bales. Often, bales were dropped onto the ground behind the baler and a truck or wagon with a short elevator on the side would put the bales onto the load where they were built by hand.

One can buy a thrower that will shoot the bale from the baler to a wagon towed behind. There were high sides on the wagon, and no attempt is made to build the load.

Then there was the stooker, which was a sled towed behind and a man stood on a platform and placed each bale onto a frame, and when he had formed a stook of six or ten bales, he would release the load leaving a fairly weather proof stook, which could be picked up with a farmhand or other kind of loader. Soon there was an automatic stooker, and these were, and still are, very popular, for the other kind made a breed of men that had long, strong right arms from heaving bales all day long. The other arm was used to hang on in case there was a change in the speed of the baler, which if one happened to have turned with a bale would pitch him off of the stooker in a hurry. Now there is the bale wagon that picks the bales off of the ground, builds the load, and when backed into the stack the load is upended and becomes part of the stack.

Some machines operating in the district now chop the dry hay out of the windrow and blow it into a large wagon where it is compressed hydraulically, and when full, the load is dumped, leaving a neat and even stack. These stacks are usually arranged side by side, and a truck with a stack mover can pick up four of these

stacks at once and transport them to a feeding area or stackyard.

The round bale has come into its own again, but now it is the large one with weights around fifteen hundred pounds, with some a little lighter, and these have to be handled by large loaders or other hydraulic systems.

There are some farms that are turning to silage as a means of beating the weather. This can be carried on even when there are light showers, for the grass or grain is cut green, chopped and blown into a wagon or a truck, transported to either a pit silo or an upright model. Silage can be kept for several years if need be, with little spoilage.

With the adoption of the tractors on the farm, and power mowers, haying became easier and more work could be done by one man. Now, there is the mower conditioner that mows, crimps or crushes the hay and delivers it into a windrow so there is no need for the hayrake, except to turn the windrow to hurry drying. Swathers can also be fitted with crimpers and these are also used to cut and windrow the hay.

The old dump rakes were horse drawn — it was a job done mostly by the women or children and was one of the most dangerous jobs, going with many people badly hurt or killed on them.

Then came the side delivery rake, and some styles are nearly trouble free, many being used to turn the windrows of hay as well as the grain swathes.

A part of the early years of harvesting in this area was the grain crops and the trouble that was had with lodged fields. This is when the crop is heavy and usually green, and has been knocked down by the wind, rain or snow, and had to be cut one way with a binder pulled by four horses, although sometimes three were used on the small binders. These binders were made in six, seven and eight foot sizes and the later power binders were ten feet wide. Most of the grain crops grew very rank when the land was newly broken. Many times the fields would be wet, and there would be no traction for the bull wheel which powered the reel, canvases and the knotter, as well as the knife. Then all would be plugged up and would have to be cleaned out by hand so one could get going again. These were the worst conditions for a binder, and many days of trouble were en-

Joe Standish binding grain, 1930.

dured to get the grain cut, and then the stooking which meant standing the bundles up against one another to facilitate drying. Usually six or eight were in a stook, any more and a few days of rain or snow, and they would go mouldy, if the wet weather was warm enough, the grain would sprout.

Many hours of backbreaking work would be put in digging bundles out of the snow if the crop was caught out by an early winter and feed was needed for the cattle. After a chinook or a thaw, followed by a freeze, they would be frozen down, then a sharpened shovel would be used to cut them free.

There were threshing outfits that went around the district for those that wanted their bundles threshed. Most of the outfits had four or six teams of horses with a man for each, and two field pitchers whose job it was to speed up the loading in the field and one or two spike pitchers to help with the unloading into the thresher.

Now it is all done with the swathers and combines. The large crews are gone forever. It is surprising just how many old threshing machines there are sitting around the farms just one step away from the scrap yard. There were always the hair raising situations with loads of bundles upside down on hillsides and a lot of skill was developed by the men in how to build a load on their racks from the ground so that it wouldn't slip off on the way to the thresher. The horses soon caught onto following along the rows of stooks when spoken to, or an occasional touch of the reins with the bundle fork as the lines were usually tied to the top front of the rack when one was loading, and the team was quiet.

Feeding the threshing crews was a major job for the farm wives, and each would try to outdo the other. The day started off with a good breakfast before dawn, a midmorning lunch, then it would be dinner time. The afternoon lunch was about four o'clock, then supper after dark, with the last loads going through by the lights of the car or truck. Now, the combines roll all day and into the night until the dew makes the grain too damp or "tough".

The hydraulic farmhand was used to replace the bundle racks and men. Two of these and four men could do a lot of threshing in a day but it was an ex-

hausting time throwing the bundles into the thresher. Some of the more inventive farmers mounted their farmhands onto truck chassis with the differentials turned upside down so that it could be driven backwards at the same speed that was usual in the conventional direction. The seat was turned around as well as the brake pedal, clutch and steering wheel. To watch these machines go out across a smooth field at twenty to thirty miles an hour was a sight to see.

Land cultivation in the area started on the small farm with the walking plow and a team of horses. A disc was needed to work the furrows down and a set of harrows to smooth the earth and kill the newly sprouted weeds.

Some of the first seeding was done by broadcasting the seed by hand and dragging a willow bush over the land to cover the seed. Then the Cyclone seeder was used. This was just a canvas bag carried with a shoulder strap. This seeder had a spinning plate on the bottom turned with a crank to scatter the seed in a uniform manner. One step, one turn was the rule of thumb. Harrowing after covered the seed.

There were sulky plows with one bottom and a seat for the driver pulled by four horses and two bottom gang plows pulled by six horses. Hit a stump or a rock and they would be on their side in a hurry.

Progress has changed all this, now tractors pull plows having up to twelve bottoms, reminding one of the plows pulled by the huge steam tractors that were

John Jackson and 8 horse outfit.

Threshing grain, J. Jackson's.

Breaking plow built by Howard Hampton and Milley Raymond.

used to plow up the prairies except now they don't need men to ride the plow and manually adjust the depth of each bottom. Now a flick of the hydraulic lever and it is done.

Chisel plows tear the land up and come in widths to suit the tractor power, some to forty feet and more.

The discs are no longer six or eight feet wide pulled by four horses but hydraulically controlled units almost as wide as the chisel plows. The seeders put the seed in the soil at one level, the fertilizer at another, and the grass seed at still another.

To have hayland plowed costs as much as most of the land was worth in the late thirties and early forties.

What will happen in another hundred years? Perhaps covered with houses — a barren waste — or?

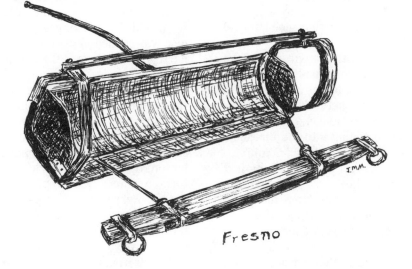

Fresno

Maintenance Grader

Grader (Road Building).

Road Gang, 1929 at Millarville. (l-r) Bill (?), J. Nelson, D. Barrable, J. Lee, D. Cameron, C. Williams, C. Nielsen, A. Wilderman, foreman, C. McEachran, S. Purdy, J. Jackson.

Road Building

In the early 1920's roads in the Priddis-Millarville area were adequate for the amount and type of traffic of the period.

Most people only planned on two or three trips to town during the year as it was a long drive with a horse and buggy, and meant an overnight stay. All discussions of these trips started "If it doesn't storm." By the late twenties, though, things were changing. More people owned cars, and now a trip to town only took an hour or so — if it didn't rain. If it did rain, the roads became a quagmire and the trip became a nightmare. In the winter there were snowdrifts and icy patches to contend with. Naturally there was a great deal of dissatisfaction and a demand for better roads, so the municipality got into the road building business with some help from the province.

Road Gang, 1929, at Millarville bridge on Sheep Creek.

On the first roads brush was cleared by hand, then plowed with a team of four horses, then built up and smoothed with a slip.

The slip, which was similar in shape to a wheelbarrow, but without the wheels, was approximately three feet wide. It was pulled by a two horse team, the driver steering it with the wooden handles, which also served to dump the load.

In time this was succeeded by the fresno. It was about twice the width but shallower in depth, and the wooden handles were replaced by a metal bar across its width with a central handle which served the same purpose as the wooden handles on the old slip. As it was capable of moving twice the load, it required a four horse team. Maintenance was done with a four horse team.

One of the first road bosses was Ed Winthrop, but by 1929 enough men were involved to hire a foreman, and Art Wilderman got the job.

This same year the bridge across the North Fork Sheep Creek (since renamed Three Point) was put in at the Millarville Ford, so there was a convenient road to Turner Valley.

The fill for the bridge was put in by fresnos, largely by local men among whom were Jim Nelson, Dennis Barrable, Jack Lee, Duncan Cameron, Conwil Williams, Art Wilderman, Charlie McEachern, Scotty Purdy, John Jackson, and the cook — Bill Smallwood.

The next advance was the purchase of a Caterpillar tractor. True, it was old and broke down often, but it was a tractor and it was now possible to cover a lot more territory in a shorter time.

Millarville crossing of Sheep Creek, 1928. Joe Jackson.

In 1932 Russel and Macleod completed the building of Highway 22, linking Calgary and Turner Valley, and providing the Millarville-Priddis area with a choice of shopping areas. All types of road-building equipment were used — horses, mules, tractors, fresnos, dump carts loaded with elevating graders.

The problem area was the Patterson slough, between sections 35-36, Township 21, Range 3 W5M. With Art Wilderman as roadboss it was corduroyed with poplar, then covered with a thick layer of dirt and gravel.

This was a learning period for roadbuilding everywhere, so while they were good in good weather, there were still problems, especially in the spring when there were many frost boils to make them almost impassable. It was many years later before they learned that a road should be graded one year, then left for the frost boils to happen so they could be fixed before the road was finished.

Today Highway No. 22, is a hard surfaced road, maintained by the province. The district roads are built and maintained by the Municipality with modern roadbuilding equipment, and no longer is it necessary to preface the trips to town with "If it doesn't storm."

Earliest Sawmills of Millarville-Kew District

In an area where timber was plentiful and the need for lumber great, it was inevitable that there would be many sawmills, some of these were large operations and others quite small. Apart from the need for lumber, there was also the need for employment. Most of the early homesteaders, trying to get started on a shoestring, were happy to be able to make a few dollars. Many rode from their homes, worked all day, and rode home in the evening to do chores.

One of the early mills was owned by Charles Edgar Billings and supplied lumber for many of the first buildings in the Millarville area. This mill was sold to V. N. deMille in 1907, who moved it to his ranch on section 25-21-4w5, and operated for several years until a disastrous fire put an end to the operation. A full account of this mill is told in the previous book "Our Foothills." This section was logged over several times in the ensuing years and is now the site of the Brown-Lowery Natural Area.

On the N.W.¼ of 6-21-3W5, Joseph Fisher had a steam operated mill on Fisher Creek. A Mr. McDonald was hired to run it and he and his family lived in a log house near the old Ranchers' Hall. Many of the local homesteaders were hired to do the logging and also to work in the mill.

On the N.W.¼ of 20-20-4w5, Mrs. Spooner and her sons Arthur and Hiram operated a mill on Ware Creek, also here giving employment to many of the Kew settlers.

After the devastating fire of 1919, which started in the month of May of that year, much valuable timber was burned, but there was much which could be salvaged. A company was formed the following year, with many local people buying in at $25 per share. Although there is not a complete list of all who bought

Buildings at Ware Creek Sawmill, about 1920.

shares, members of most families in the area were included, the Ohlsons, Bert Chalmers, Bill Bradford, John Broomfield, Jim and Seth Peat, Richard Knights, Will Letts, J. McGregor, Bill Adams. There are many other names of men who worked there and may also have been shareholders, such as Ford Lochhead, Burl Posgate, Herb Adams, Jerry Woodford. Bert Chalmers was secretary, Will Letts was in charge of the logging operations, and Dan Morrison, an Okotoks old timer, set up the mill, which was on the same quarter section and almost the same spot as the Spooner mill had been several years before. Bunk houses and a cook house were built with Bert Hodgkins doing the cooking.

When the sawing began, much of the lumber was bought by the Municipality to build culverts for new roads being built.

Shortly after the Ware Creek Sawmill was finished, the land was homesteaded by Gavin Calderwood, who sold to Joe and Jane Fisher and is presently owned by Elizabeth vonRummel.

Sawmills in the Square Butte Area
by Dick Lyall

I can't remember too much about the sawmills of the early days. There was one called Ware Creek mill and some others.

The mill I remember most was Larratt's Mill. They started on the Van Wyck place near Priddis in the 1930's moving to northwest of Millarville. Then in the late 1930's they moved to section 8-21-4w5. After that they moved back to Millarville.

In those days lumber could be bought for a song. I think about $10 per thousand was the top price.

Vic Jensen started a little mill on the Ingeveld place and Jim Colley had a small mill which he moved from place to place. Alex Lyall had a small mill on the Pierce place and at their own place for some time.

Ted and Dick Smith moved a mill on to our place around 1950 and were there for several years. They logged and sawed lumber on various sites for many years. Lester Letts had a mill for a while on the Chalmers ranch at Millarville and also on the South Fork.

Royal Burrows had a small mill on his place. I believe the Croston boys ran it for him. Also Jacksons had a mill north of their home for some time. Bill Kendall had a mill on Fisher Creek and has had it for several years. I apologize for any names I have missed.

The Kendall Sawmill

Bill Kendall's first logging venture was on the ranch in 1948, consisting of a winter's cut of a few thousand feet, which he did in his spare time; skidded the trees out on the river flat by horse and sawed them up in summer with Barraclough's mill, run by Jake Reimer.

Kendall's Mill.

In the winter of 1952-53 he logged on George Ingeveld's land, 100,000 board feet, and had it sawed with Murray Jackson's mill, the sawyer being Jim Colley. It was during this winter's work that Bill broke his arm, when a tree length load of logs, skidded behind a cat, caught on a stump and swung sideways.

The next step was a Timber Berth in the Forest Reserve on the "northeast slopes of Square Butte. The first winter 1953-54 the trees were pulled out to the Ranger Station flat on the North Fork of the Sheep River, now Three Point, by caterpiller tractor and sawed in the summer on Murray Jackson's mill. This was a slow procedure and in February 1955 a camp and mill were established on the Timber Berth off the north end of Square Butte. Lumber was hauled out on a road the truck drivers used to say was built on the day Bill was riding a crow — a bit steep on some grades.

When the camp was established here the whole family moved to the site. The two oldest children, Donna and David, were going to school so stayed with grandmothers during the week, and went to the bush camp on weekends. When Spring came the road was impassable except for horses and wagon so the children started out from the ranch on Friday after school on their father's reliable hunting horse, Pete. One Friday night they failed to appear on schedule so, after waiting an hour, a search was launched. Just around the corner from the camp they were coming on foot, leading Pete — a more bedraggled trio was never seen — mud from head to foot, horse included.

Even this trail-wise horse had failed to anticipate a bog hole masked by mud and water that had broken out in the middle of the road. In he plunged and was up to his belly before he could stop. Fortunately, he didn't panic, just stood still and the children stepped off his back to dry land and then wondered how they were going to get him out as the sides of the hole were straight up and down. Finally, encouraged by shouts and pulling on the reins, he managed to get his front feet on dry land and with great lunges succeeded in struggling to better footing. The children were so frightened and unnerved they walked the rest of the way leading the horse.

This site was soon logged out, and in 1956 more timber berths were purchased at the head of Fisher

Creek and the mill and camp were moved there to a scenic spot with a much better access road. However, there were a few trials on this road too, such as the time Bill spun out on the steep pitch of a hill and rolled backwards into two feet of snow and willow brush on the side of the road; coming abruptly to a halt, high-centred on a barrel full of diesel fuel, which had rolled out of the back of the truck as it lurched out of control. Then there was the time in the spring thaw, when most of the night was spent in a mud hole — but finally with the aid of planks and a sturdy jack, mobility was obtained.

In retrospect it seems that the years spent on Fisher Creek were one long camping spree; the meadows equally delightful in winter or summer. The sparkling stream, in its idyllic setting, contained many a leaping trout; a continuous source of sport and adventure for the children on weekends and summer holidays. It was there they all learned a great love of the outdoors and a lesson in initiative and self-reliance.

It was at the camp on Fisher Creek that we awoke one morning to find the tracks of a huge grizzly which had passed within 20 feet of the cabin door during the night. The track of the animal was such that Bill, who wears a size 12, could put his foot inside with room to spare. Needless to say, fishing and hunting activities were somewhat curtailed. Even the dogs had been notably silent that night, not wanting to call the prowler's attention to their presence.

Then there was the time that Earl Orum, who was skidding logs, dropped onto a beaver dam with the cat in the middle of winter. At once all work on hand was abandoned at the mill and an expedition was launched with the sawing crew and the old Allis Chalmers cat used on the mill to act as anchor. They worked to get

Sawmill on Fisher Creek. Bill Kendall and Don Foy.

him out before the outfit was frozen in. Supper stayed on the stove late that night.

In 1960, after several profitable years on Fisher Creek, Monte was six years old and would be starting to school. It seemed advisable to establish a base outside the Forest Reserve, so the mill and camp were moved to the property of father-in-law, Fred Kosling, where a small retail yard had been established.

Timber was now purchased from the Fish Creek watershed and a road was built into the area to haul out the logs in winter. During this time the mill was powered by diesel engines of various makes, G.M., Buda, and a generator supplied electricity. Unfortunately a fire destroyed the mill and when it was rebuilt it was powered by three-phase electric motors, electricity supplied by Calgary Power. At this time a refuse burner was added — a landmark to all who passed by.

When the timber was logged on Fish Creek a further supply was purchased west of Bragg Creek on Ranger Creek. However, the Department of Lands and Forests changed their policy to a quota system, which meant a clear-cut operation, all timber utilized and a production quota set for a 5 year period. This proved a disastrous decision south of the Bow River, as all operators in the area south to the Livingstone River eventually lost their quota areas because they couldn't meet the production required by regulations. This was when the sawmills began a post and pole operation to meet clear cut requirements.

At the end of 5 years this company was forced out of the Forest Reserve, so turned to the Morley Indian Reserve for timber. The agreement reached here was successful as the trees were felled by the Indians who laid claim to the timber and the balance of the work was done by Kendall Lumber crews and machinery. The trees were hauled full-length to the mill — a distance of 50 miles.

In the winter of 1975 the stress and strain of the business began to take its toll and Bill decided to end the mill and logging operations. It was not until January 1977 that the last of the log inventory was processed through the mill.

And so it was, with the help of many able and reliable men, that Kendall Lumber Limited was established and operated successfully for 25 years. The business continues to operate as a retail yard with the materials supplied by other operators.

Chalmers Sawmilling

by Jim Chalmers

Besides ranching Dad seemed to have a yen for sawmilling. He was Secretary Treasurer of the Ware Creek Lumber Co. for several years. Then in 1933-34 he cut timber on the S½ of 15-21-3-5 (C.P.R. land he'd purchased to the north of the original home place). I believe these logs were some of the first to be sawn in the Millarville district by W. B. Larrett and sons — Gordon and Herb. In 1938-39 we logged the rest of the home property and Lester Letts sawed these logs using

Sawing outfit in the Millarville area, 1950, used by Chalmers.

Jim Chalmers with horse used for pulling logs from the bush.

the old M.D. Cat. for power. This Cat had its own roof and also a big front wheel besides tracks. This was sure an awkward outfit to drive e.g. besides brakes and clutches you used a steering wheel for the front wheel. Lester also had his own planing mill and dressed a portion of this lumber.

In 1946-47 Dan and Fred Dudenhoeffer, my brother Robert and myself took logs out of the Evehorn Valley in the South Sheep Forest Reserve. Dad, Fred Dudenhoeffer and myself sawed these with John Barraclough's portable mill, we also sawed logs Buck George had taken off the old Joe Simpson homestead, (this mill was located on Bob Carry's land, about one half mile east of the Forest Reserve).

Lester had moved his mill down to the Highwood country in the early forties where I had helped him log and saw quite a bit of timber for Joe Bews on the north fork of Sullivan Creek. By this time he had acquired a steam engine which I think is the best type of power you can use on a mill. In 1949-50 we logged the W. H. King place across the river from Millarville. We hauled most of these logs home with teams and sleighs. Lester moved his mill and steam engine over to saw for us again. Some of this lumber was used to build the new Ranchers Hall. About the mid fifties Lester bought the timber off of Jim Wylies Rat Farm and hauled them over here to be sawn.

In 1960-61 we had Clarence and Ken Boggs log my other place (the old Harold Smith place E.½35-19-4-5) west of Turner Valley. The following winter Clarence and Ken Boggs and myself sawed these logs.

Besides selling lumber a fair amount of lumber was used for the Ranch from these mills. Lesters mill and steam engine ended up in Heritage Park.

Logging and Lumbering

by John Jackson

In 1933, Johnny Barraclough logged S.E. Sec. 21-3-W.5 on land owned by Otto Roedler. Owning no sawmill, he got Walter Larrett to saw the logs. The lumber was used to put up a house and barn on S.E. Sec. 32-21-2-W.5. In 1937, he got a sawmill from Bill Mitchell of Priddis and logged S.E.¼, Sec.5-22-3-W.5. His son, John learned to run the saw and this became lumber. This mill was sold and a portable mill was purchased. John and I logged and sawed lumber on S.W.¼, Sec. 30-21-2-W.5 intending to build a house for Ida and myself, but it ended up in a chicken house and sold the rest. I then did some logging with Bob Winthrop and Bill McAmmond. We logged N.W.¼-Sec. 36-22-4-W.5. Sim Van Wyk taught me how to set up the mill and saw. Irving Standish and I logged on the Jim Brown land — N.W.¼-Sec. 3-22-3-W.5 using Barraclough's portable mill. This lumber was used to build a house for Irving, which was later moved to Sandy Cross' land, S.W.¼-Sec. 7-22-2-W.5. Also, we built the house we presently live in.

Royal Burrows also did a great deal of logging and lumbering as he also had a mill. I bought a planer from him for $300.00. My boys and I logged N.E.¼-Sec. 31-21-3-W.5 and got lumber for the present barn.

In recent years I dismantled the mill and shipped it to Whitehorse, Yukon.

SONG OF THE SKI
by Joan Kendall

A whispering sound
  like a song in the night
Like a flick of a wing
  on a wild soaring flight.

A sweep thru' the woods
  in a soft singing rhyme
The silence of winter
  the beginning of time.

Behind lies the ferment
  the tight pressing mass
Ahead lies the wonder
  the ascent to the pass.

Up on the summit
  this urge to be free
The sweep of the mountains
  the song of the ski.

Sports and Rodeos

Millarville Ball Team. Back row: Nevill Cannon, Bruce Stanhope, Alex Scatterty, Bill Fisher, Ronnie Birkenes. Front row: David Cannon, Bryce Standish, Bob Winthrop, Dode Bull, unidentified.

Millarville Ball Club 1939. Back row: Bryce Standish, Lloyd Standish, Glen Batdorf, Roy Latter, Dode Bull, Alex Scatterty, Bill Fisher. Front row: Harry Fisher, Bob Winthrop, Ronnie Birkenes.

Frank Sharp on Cyclone.

57

Rhonda Lansdell, Little Britches Rodeo, Innisfail, July 14, 1974.

Noreen Cooper on Papoose barrel racing at Stampede Corral. 1973.

Cam Lansdell on Strawberry Lil at Calgary Stampede.

Donald Chalmers riding in the National High School Finals in Helena, Montana in 1977.

Joe Fisher on Midnight just before he lost his stirrup.

The Muskeg Kids from Kew in Calgary Stampede Parade, 1952. Frank Kendall, Mary Blakley, Dibby Kendall and Dennis Blakley, outriders, Ivor Lyster, driver, Mike Rodgers, driver assistant.

Frank Hodgkins.

SEDUCTION
by Joan Kendall

Midnight cowboys
Goggled and grim
Pause for breath
On the Canyon rim.

The thrill of the chase
Has stirred their blood
The pack moves off
Like a surging flood.

The snarling roar
Now fills the night
Across the mountain
Before dawns light.

The bucking lurch
The belching wail,
The riders hurtle
Along the trail.

Drenched with sweat
Desire complete;
Glorious glut
The soul replete.

Horse Racing Days at Millarville Race Track.

J. Nelson

The first good horse I had was named Red Skin. I won the boy's race with him and my Father won the saddle horse race on him. I sold Red Skin to the late Clem Gardner one day at Fordville School. Mr. Gardner decided he would ride him home. I could see that Red Skin didn't like Mr. Gardner when he got on him. He just stood there with a hump in his back so Mr. Gardner banged him in the ribs with his heels then Red Skin bucked him off in the middle of the school yard.

The next good pony I had was Home Maid. She was never beaten at the Millarville Races. The third good pony I had was Some Baby. He won the quarter mile race four years running and also won the saddle horse race.

The best day I had at Millarville was winning the first race on a horse named Hup Six and winning the next two on Home Baby. We used to go to the track on Sundays and Wednesday evening to gallop ponies and two old sports used to go and hide in the bush with stop watches to get a line on our ponies.

Millarville Fair

The true old style country fair is almost a thing of the past, but for the hundreds who each year, attend the Priddis and Millarville Fair, it is very much alive.

This big little fair is different from most country fairs in that it has remained strictly agricultural. In fact, it is one of the few truly agricultural shows that is left.

The directors of the fair have kept out commercial entertainment and side shows.

The Priddis and Millarville fair was started in 1907 and was held in Priddis until 1915. Then it was held in Millarville.

For many years it alternated between the two sites. Then it was held at Fordville about half way between the two places. After this friendly tug of war it was finally agreed in 1946 to make a permanent home for it at the Millarville Race Track. Since then it has blossomed in its beautiful foothills setting.

The beauty of this fair is that it is a family enterprise as well as a community effort.

Everyone from Junior to Grandad wants to get into the act.

There is art, handicraft, baking and needlework, grains and grasses, flowers and vegetables, poultry of all kinds, sheep and swine, cattle, horses, and even floppy eared rabbits.

The full day of horse show events includes everything from Western and English classes to cutting horse and jumping competitions. All breeds of cattle both beef and dairy are groomed to perfection.

This is the kind of fair where competition is keen but friendly.

You can sit on the grandstand and watch Junior show his pony while the loudspeaker tells you that Grandad got first with his peas.

However, as soon as the doors open to the various buildings housing the displays you must go and see for yourself.

The mouth watering lemon pies, and chocolate cakes, the homemade bread, the beautiful floral arrangements, and the vast array of garden vegetables all give you the feeling that we are indeed fortunate to live in this part of the world.

Yes, the Priddis and Millarville Country Fair is still very much alive.

Millarville Racing and Agricultural Society (Amalgamation)

For years three organizations used the facilities at the Millarville Race Track — the Millarville Race Track which owned the land and had built the track, grandstands, horse barns and pari-mutuel building — the Race Track Hall Association which had built the hall and the Priddis & Millarville Agricultural Society. The Agricultural Society had added several exhibit buildings to the site. All three organizations had their own meetings, each had president, secretary, treasurer and a number of directors. This of course meant that a very large number of persons were involved, each with their own interests paramount, in what was essentially one community project.

About 1964 the Millarville Administration Board was set up. This Board had the responsibility of deciding what were the most pressing needs of the entire establishment, regardless of the desires of any one of the three organizations. They decided what buildings or repairs were to be done, they amalgamated the insurance under one policy, paid for the utilities, and were responsible for preserving the grounds from further flood damage, caretaking and general maintenance. In order to obtain money for this work the Board assessed the three organizations for certain amounts of money, taking into account their ability to pay. However in the event of a disaster or several rained-out events they had no borrowing powers as the land and thus the building belonged to the Race Club.

This Board was an improvement over the past but now there was four presidents, four secretaries, four treasurers and numerous directors. For a number of years many local people had felt that an amalgamation of the three organizations was essential if the Race Track facilities were to serve an expanding rural population. Also about this time fairly large provincial government grants had become available to Agricultural Societies for capital expenditures, but in order to apply for these grants the Agricultural Society had to own the land.

After several very stormy meetings and with the help of community minded accountants and attorneys a new constitution was finally drawn up for an organization to be known as the Millarville Racing and Agricultural Society. The Millarville Race Club signed over the land and buildings and on February 20th, 1969 the new organization became effective. A board of directors was elected which included a chairman for each of the three original groups and a secretary and treasurer, was hired who also was to serve as caretaker and live on the grounds.

All this has proved most successful — grant money was obtained from the government, an equal amount was borrowed from a local bank and an addition which included indoor plumbing was built on the hall. This was only the first of many improvements to the grounds and buildings. The Society is on a firm financial footing — the facilities are used more than ever and individuals are still able to work for that part of the organization in which they are most interested.

Fashions over the century
by Phyllis Cannon

From the time that mankind started to clothe himself fashions have played a great part in changing life styles. The following pictures over the last century try to tell the story of the dress of the pioneers; the trend to a less restricted form of dress of the "Flapper" era; the "made over clothes of the difficult thirties; through the wartime, and the very daring styles of the sixties, and swinging back to a gentler form of dress in the seventies.

Mrs. Kidd, housekeeper for Frances Sinclair-Smith, 1920.

Grandmother Margaret Lyall, about 1850.

61

Tailored suit and hat of 1944. Irene Evans and son Milton.

Peggy and Dick Lyall, about 1917.

Leonard and Jim Nelson, about 1912. Sailor suits were fashionable.

Maggie Bell, Georgina Roberts, early 1900.

Another bride and groom, Ronald and Maud (Glaister) Birkenes, 1945.

A stylish Miss of the 1950's. Note the "bobby sox". Alice (Evans) Melvin.

Military garb of W.W.1.

Irene (Rickett) Evans at Normal school, 1931. Matching beige and brown suit and hat.

In 1941 it was the one piece bathing suit. Mrs. Frank Lee.

Breeks and Prairie Belle high boots were the choice of Freda McArthur to wear for fishing, 1915.

Mrs. Barraclough, 1916; note furs.

Peggy (Lyall) Nylund, about 1927.

Bathing Beauties, Banff 1915.

Skirts were shorter by 1939. L. to R. Betty King, Joan Oliver, Margaret Deane-Freeman, Isamay dePalezieux, Doreen Oliver, Maudie Glaister.

Betty (King) Nelson and friend, 1934. Dark skirt made from men's trousers.

Friend of Marj Parker's 1935. Note bias cut dress.

This is a typical bride and groom of the wartime 1940's. Gordon and Ruth (Chalmers) Maberley.

Ladies' Pant suit and Western jacket, worn by Ruby and Stuart Sinclair-Smith, 1978.

65

Marj (Van Der Velde) Parker and friends, 1937. The tunic dress was the rage!

Baby picture of Stastia Cross Carry.

Lorna Cannon in her Bikini, 1979. "You've come a long way, baby".

King Edward basketball team. Back row, L. to R. Winnie Clark, Anna Harley, Gladys Smith, Donna Orpe. Front row, Alice Thurston, Jean Fisher (holding ball), Margaret Derry. 1922-23 basketball season.

Oh! Those "mini skirts" 1972. Mary (Birkenes) South at her wedding shower.

Stastia Cross Carry,
9 years of age.

The long gowns of 1976, at 80th anniversary of Christ Church Millarville. L. to R. Edith Trotter, Irene Evans, Helen Preston, Edith (Knights) Pallister.

A swim party, 1920's. Friends of Irene Evans.

Fred Kosling and Jack Lynd. Cowboys Sunday best, about 1911.

Old Time ranchers, 1900. 2nd from left — Dave Evans, next W. H. King; others unknown.

Note the split skirt that Freda McArthur wore for riding, 1916.

Stastia (McNab) Risdahl in her "pedal-pushers",
1965.

Look at the well cut Western suit and natty coordinates worn by these two ranchers, 1976. L. to R.
Elwyn Evans and Winston Parker.

Chapter 6
Organizations

NORTH FORK COUNTRY
by Joan Kendall

Come to the North Fork country
  follow the canyon trail
Past the sleeping ranches
  up the beck'ning vale
Through the sunlit meadows
  in a golden glow.
Lazy cattle grazing
  the sparkling river flows,
Past an old log cabin
  past an old log barn
Past a hardy settler
Smiling tough and strong.

Come to the North Fork country
  look for the trails afar,
Find the ghosts of hardy men
  who trailed a blazing star.
Follow the grass grown pathways
  lost in the past and time.
Blazed by many a sturdy hand
  born in a sunnier clime.
Dark the spires of timber
  against the summer sky
Shadows on the pathway
  a shade of coolness lie.

Come to the North Fork country
  take the Hogsback trail,
Twist along the canyon rim
  tread the blackened shale
Beyond the stunted jackpine
  on the boundless height
Infinite yawns the canyon
  what an awesome sight!
Clover in the sable rock
  by a giant hand
Chasms, cliffs and shaley slopes
  thread a splintered land.

North Sheep Stock Association

by Ernest Silvester

The North Sheep Stock Association was formed in 1919. The first meeting was held in Carl Ohlson's house. 1978 is the sixtieth year the association has been in operation.

The first elected officers were:
President: J. F. Dole
Vice President Carl Ohlson
        Secretary-Treasurer: A. E. Hunter
Executive Committee:
George Silvester
R. Basilici
J. F. Dole
C. Ohlson
A. E. Hunter
    Other members in 1919-
J. C. Beck
Andy MacKay
Walter Phillips
John Anderson
H. Nichols
Pierce Brothers
George Lyall
Ernest Silvester Sr.
W. S. Bannerman
W. H. Bradford
D. J. Stewart
J. McGregor
O. Anderson
McBee

The area covered by the Association was Ware Creek, North Sheep, Mesa Butte, Fisher Creek, Muskeg and Three Point area. For many years the yearlings were taken into the Muskeg, but in the late 30s and 1940, the cougars and grizzly bears were doing so much damage they quit using the area. The Indians got seven cougars the next year and the ranchers got a bear hunter to thin the bears out. The muskeg area was not used for ten years. In 1951, myself and brother John Silvester needed pasture so badly, so asked the Forestry if we could try the area with cows and calves. We were told we could if we could hold them. On the 5th of June, 1951 we took about 80 head of cows in the muskeg. It was raining and snowing when we took them in. Two days later there was three feet of snow. It was two weeks before we could get to the muskeg. The cattle had lived on Spruce bark and willows, but there were no losses, thanks to the good shelter. Some

Cattle being driven to Forest Reserve pasture. L. to R. Nina Rodgers, Jane Fisher, Pat Rodgers, Mike Rodgers.

of the members who have used the area through the years were: R. H. Rodgers, J. Fisher, H. Foster, T. Macmillan, E. L. Kendall, McBee Brothers, Bell Brothers, J. Grant, Les Foster, John Silvester, I. Lyster, Fred Wildman, Tom Wildman, S. McRea, MacKay Brothers, G. Ingeveld, J. Andrews, W. Andrews, R. Vanderham, Ernest Silvester, M. Rodgers, Bill Lucas, Bill Stewart. The Wildman permits were

Gate at entrance to Bow Crow Forest Reserve at North Fork.

used by Mrs. Wildman and son David for a few years, being turned over to Ernst Geiger when he bought the place and the cows.

Present members are: Peter Fisher, Ron Mitchell, K. Macmillan, E. Evans, D. Glaister, Charlie Silvester, Ernst Geiger, D. W. Foster, H. Hampton, Joe Mercier, Ernest Silvester, H. McBee.

When the Association started the cattle went in May 15th to Nov. 15th. At this time many of the ranchers weaned the calves and took the cows to the straw piles in the Okotoks and Tongue Creek areas until the end of April, once again bringing the cows home to calve and back on the Reserve again. There were three times as many cattle run in the Reserve as there is today. Now we are allowed in the Reserve June 15th to October 15th., two months shorter seasons, but the bush has grown up so thick it has drastically reduced the grazing area. To this day there are only two original names left in the Association, that being Silvester and McBee, but Peter Fisher still carries on the Basilici permit being a grandson. The rangers count the cattle on and off the reserve. In the early days everything was done by horseback.

70

Millarville 4-H Beef Club

Many years back, a club was started in the district. This club was Government sponsored. As most farmers at that time stayed away from anything pertaining to the Government, it was not very successful and died a natural death. In the late 1940's another club started, sponsored by private individuals. They showed their calves at The Priddis and Millarville Fair — the prize money was very good. It was from this club that the Millarville 4-H Beef Club came into being. The first leader was Charlie King. The achievement day was held at High River in conjunction with several more clubs. The club grew under Charlie's good guidance and after about two years, it was decided most people preferred Calgary. The show and sale then went to Calgary in competition with about twelve other clubs. The next leader was Bill Massie of the Red Deer Lake district. The Millarville Club won many awards. Grand Champion Calf, Best Barn Display (Decorating and clean stalls), Best Showman — each year the club received some of the top awards. The Club continued and Bill Jackson became leader, having started as a member in the club and stayed until he was twenty-one. The next leader was Harry Hobbs. The club grew under his guidance to about 60 members, when it was decided to split into two clubs, East and West Millarville. Harry Hobbs led the East Millarville, and Ike Halferty became the West Millarville Club leader. Ike led the club for several years, until Bill Massie Jr. took over for one year. The two clubs have now amalgamated again, under the leadership of Wilf Waters.

RULES AND REGULATIONS GOVERNING THE MILLARVILLE 4-H BEEF CLUB

1. Club meetings shall be carried out according to parliamentary procedure.
2. A yearly membership fee of one dollar shall be charged to each member.
3. Any member missing one club meeting inexcusably will be asked to resign from the club year.
4. The validity of an excuse will be decided by the majority vote of the club members.
5. Club meetings shall start at two o'clock sharp.
6. Any member missing one feeding report shall be asked to resign from the club year.
7. All feeding reports must be sent to the secretary within the first ten days of the following month.
8. Two club members shall give talks each meeting unless otherwise stated by the club program for the year. Subjects of talks to be chosen by the President.
9. Speakers shall be chosen by the club president.
10. All subject material shall be in the form of notes.
11. There shall be a minimum of three minutes and a maximum of five minutes for each talk.
12. All meetings shall be held as stated in the club program for the year.
13. All club members should aim at from 425 to 500 points in club efficiency.
14. The secretary shall forward an official receipt to the donors of gifts, prizes, trophies, or money to the club.
15. Each member shall write a thank you note to the donor of any gifts, prizes or trophies that are won by the individual.
16. Each member shall be required duties during the Achievement Day Show and Sale in Calgary.
17. Each member shall be required to have on Achievement Day:
    A. A wine colored shirt bearing the Millarville and Alberta 4-H crests on the left sleeve.
    B. A pair of khaki pants.
    C. A grey tie (man's length).
    D. Well polished shoes.
18. Small exceptions to this constitution shall be made with a majority vote of the club members and advisory committee when necessary.
19. All club members shall abide by the rules of this Constitution.

Stockland 4-H Beef Club

by Jackie Chalmers

Since the inception of the Stockland 4-H Beef Club in 1963 it has grown and developed into a strong club with members from the Millarville, Kew, Square Butte, Red Deer Lake, Black Diamond, Turner Valley and Okotoks districts.

In the fall of 1963 several meetings were held with parents, prospective members and the District Agriculturist to discuss the formation of a beef club. A general format was decided upon and a name adopted. Stockland was chosen as a name not only because the members were from cattle country but also because it was the name of the Municipal District in the earlier days and the head office was at Millarville.

Strong leadership and much enthusiasm has been instrumental in making the club the success that it is. The first leader was Mr. Frank Hunter, a rancher from south of Black Diamond. Other leaders over the years have been George Abbis, Jim Hunter, Albert Sandeman, Stuart Robertson, Mrs. Henrietta Thorne and the present leader is Bill Weireter.

The main project of the club was to learn about beef. During the 4-H year talks and demonstrations were given on the various aspects of beef production. Some of the topics discussed were judging of beef animals, breeds of beef cattle, cuts of meat, feeding and care of the animal and showmanship.

Until recently all the emphasis was placed on a show steer but some innovative changes took place within the club. There is a heifer project which continues from year to year and a member also has the option of raising a carcass animal which is judged after slaughter — an interesting project with the introduction of the European breeds.

The Stockland Beef Club took all the prizes for showmanship at the 1977 Heifer Show. Margaret Ann King, Andrew Campbell, Edie Chalmers, Mark Opheim, Shelley Crooks, Neil Campbell, Fiona Lagarde.

The club isn't all work and no play. Social events such as toboggan and skating parties are held. Oftimes other clubs are invited to participate. Curling with other clubs has become very popular in the last few years. The Calgary Exhibition and Stampede Board have made tickets available at a reduced rate for Rodeo Royal and the Ice Capades. Stockland has taken advantage of this many times.

The club has participated in the Seed Fair or Roundup which is held in the spring at the Calgary Exhibition Grounds.

Through the years the club undertook many money-raising projects. They were involved with bottle drives, sprnsoring dances and raffles. Perhaps the most successful has been the cutting and selling of firewood. Each year they all gather at various members homes and cut and split fire wood. Each member is responsible for selling a cord of wood.

A special project that the club has been involved in is the cleaning of the ditches for the Alberta Dept. of Highways. This is a province wide project and the

Donald Chalmers with his Grand Champion calf. June, 1973.

government pay the club for their work. Everyone who has helped clean up the ditches on the highways would like to see disposable diapers outlawed by the government.

Stockland has been a strong supporter of the camping program at the Kinsman Camp Horizon at Bragg Creek.

For many years a float was entered in the High River Little Britches Parade which was always a fun time.

Four years ago the club took on a unique and challenging project. They are sponsoring a child in Taiwan. This sponsorship allows Hsu-Shin-Tung to attend school and he and his family to be properly clothed and fed. Each month a different member writes to him and tells of all the activities that are taking place here.

The club year ends in June with an Achievement Day and Sale. This has been held at either High River or Blackie over the years. Clubs from all over the Foothills District compete. Twice the overall Grand Champion has been won by a member of Stockland. Fiona Lagarde won in 1972 and Don Chalmers in 1973, both had Limousin cross bred steers.

An accomplishment that the club is very proud of took place at the Heifer Show in 1977 at Okotoks. The

TOP STEER AT HIGH RIVER. This 1,170-pound dark-red Limousin-Angus steer, shown by Fiona Legarde of the Stockland 4-H Beef Club was judged Grand Champion at the Foothills 4-H Show and Sale June 9. Fiona won the Canadian Imperial Bank of Commerce Trophy, Alberta Limousin Association Trophy, and $100 cash from the Canadian Limousin Association. Shown with Fiona, left to right: Jackie Chalmers, 1972 Alberta Limousin Queen; Stu Robertson, Stockland 4-H club leader; John Kendall, assistant Stockland leader; Eugene Guertin, manager of the Canadian Imperial Bank at High River and Bob Rowland, manager, Parrish and Heimbecker at High River, donators of the winning banner.

top six chosen for showmanship were all from the Stockland Club, Fiona Lagarde, Neil Campbell, Shelley Crooks, Mark Opheim, Andrew Campbell and Margaret Ann King. The Reserve Champion Heifer was won by Laura Jorgenson in 1974 and Fiona Lagarde in 1978.

Each year many members participate in public speaking. The club is especially proud of the Campbell boys. Gordon competed at the Southern Alberta Junior Public Speaking Championships in 1975 at Lethbridge. His brother Andrew went to the Championships several times placing second at one competition. Andrew did very well at the Provincial Selections in 1974 and 1975. He was a guest at the Western Stock Growers Convention in Edmonton where he addressed the assembly. The following year he journeyed to Quebec in a Provincial Exchange.

To wind up the year a banquet is held annually. Awards are presented and the parents and members have been entertained by such colorful after dinner speakers as Ed Noad, Tom Primrose, Mary Dover, Allan Baker, Ted Pritchett, George Crawford Q.C. and others.

A TRIBUTE TO A COWBOY
(TIP JOHNSON)
by Dave Glaister

An old cowhand has donned his spurs
and rode to the great divide.
He was the oldster's friend,
the young hand's lasting pride.

There will be many friends to greet him there,
a pow wow sure to be
Men he rode the range with, Sam Howe, Hardwick and
   a brother,
of these he'd long to see.

His friends behind will miss him,
for better hands were few
He could rope a horse or brand a cow,
of this so well he knew.

When the boys all saddle up
and there's work at the old corral,
the thought will sure pass 'round, I wish old
   Tip was here
he could do this job so well.

When in the fall the boys head west
for the round-up and a spree,
Sadness will be felt there, at the stall
that bears the mark of the old Bar Tee.

In the evening bunk house glow
At the game he loved the best
He won't be heard to say
"I'll call and bet the rest."

From Millarville to Bassano
The race horse was his pride.
At the track you'd always meet him
With a good one by his side.

And if you'd listened close boys
You might have heard him quote
"She's a good one fellers, the blood of Chub
runs strong beneath her glossy coat."

To the redman he spoke in native tongue
Bears Paw, Crowfoot, Lefthand, to name a few
These men of the plains, they knew him
of friends no finer hue.

So when you've ridden out boys
Remember well his kind.
These men are getting fewer boys,
So good and true defined.

Team Roping In Millarville
by Jackie Chalmers

The Chalmers Arena at Millarville is the setting for a weekly get together of team ropers.

The sport of team roping originated in the south western States. The art was perfected on the open

Brian Crowe and Edie Chalmers at Lorne Wells Roping School 1978.

73

range where it was necessary for one man to catch the head and his partner to rope the "heels" or hind legs. This method was used when a "Critter needed to be doctored." Team roping has now moved into the rodeo arena and has become a great spectator event and highly competitive.

Robert Chalmers and his family operate the arena at Millarville using several cross bred heifers and steers for roping. Throughout the summer ropers gather to practice and compete in Jack-pots. Points are accumulated with trophy buckles, breast collars and various other awards presented at the end of the season.

When it becomes too cold to rope outside in the fall the ropers all moved to Bob Winthrops Arena for the winter.

Team roping is a sport for young and old. There are some very good ropers from age eleven and up.

A "Century Club" has been formed in Millarville with Robert Chalmers as President and Lynn Chalmers as secretary treasurer. The directors are Cliff Vandergrift, Delbert DePaoli, Fred Gladstone, Bill Beattie, Inj Betts and Joe Wells. The ages of the team must add up to one hundred years or they cannot

rope together. Old fellows like Bill Renard can rope with young ones like George Bull. There are saddles and buckles up for the winners of the "Century Roping."

1974 Highest Selling Angus Bull
by Lucille Glaister

After looking over, under and all around for a red out crossbull in the annual 1974 Calgary Spring Bull Sale, Dave and Lucille Glaister of the Mesa Creek Ranch, West of Millarville, saw a bull they wanted. At that time they didn't know that particular bull was destined to be one of the highest selling Red Angus bulls in history.

Red Emulous 69D won his age group, Junior Champion and then Grand Champion and with his stall mate went on to win the best group of two bulls.

The Glaisters met with the Sibbalds (from Cochrane area) and found they also wanted to buy the Emulous bull. By pooling their resources they decided to go the limit. When the dust settled every one caught their breath and found they were the owners of Red Emulous 69D for $15,000.00, the highest selling Angus bull at the Calgary Spring Bull Sale of 1974.

L. to R. Frank Slezina, Mrs. Slezina, John Sibbald, Wayne Sibbald, David Glaister, Gary Slezina. Lucille Glaister, Kathy Glaister.

Founders of the Square Butte Testing Station, 1973

To the Red Angus breeder the backbone of the beef industry is the commercial cowman — with this in mind Dave Glaister, Mike Rodgers, Dave Wildman put their heads together with the Red Cattle Company and John Kendall and set up a testing station. The station was set up on the NW¼ of Section 9, being Dick and Helen Lyall's ranch West of Millarville in the Square Butte district. Dick Lyall acted as Manager and herdsman and Helen Lyall acted as secretary bookkeeper for the operation.

The station used the same program as the Ellerslie test station. The feed formula was the same except Square Butte used hand feeding to produce sound, range ready yearling bulls.

This project started on the banks of Mesa Creek in Square Butte. It has advanced and expanded to become one of the major recognized beef tests in Alberta. Although the centre is no longer here, it is pleasing to know that an enterprise started in the foothills of Millarville has gone on to aid in the betterment of Alberta cattle.

L. to R. Dick Lyall, Mike Rodgers, David Wildman, David Glaister. Helen Lyall in front.

Three Point Riding Club
by Charis Cooper

Even though we lived in horse country there was only pleasure riding and cattle chasing for our young people, so in the summer of 1967 a group of interested

Sleepy cowboy race at gymkhana at Jacobson's arena, 1969.

Barbara Reimer and Charis Cooper in stake race at Jacobson's arena. 1969.

Eddie Behm, 1916, at Monte Fraser's ranch.

people met at Square Butte Hall and formed the Three Point Riding Club.

Gymkhanas were the main form of entertainment and were held at the open arenas of Jacobsons, Lysters and Chalmers. Old and young tried their skill at these games with the most enthused being the younger children, who on their little, fat ponies very soon became adept at tackling any event no matter how formidable. It was fun to watch these youngsters try to balance an egg on a spoon and ride the course with such concentration, or watch them race at full speed around the barrels or stakes with such a great sense of competition.

Some of these young people went on to compete in horse shows and rodeos, and we like to think the riding club helped them with their horsemanship.

Near accidents occurred as people and horses usually bring about such results, but no one was ever seriously hurt in the years of holding the gymkhanas.

There were also trail rides in the Forest Reserve which were always well attended by the families with the smaller children riding with their Moms or Dads.

In the spring of each season we would hold a meeting to elect new officers and view any pictures that were taken the year before, these usually being movies taken by Jake Reimer or Alex Lyall, and these could be very amusing to say the least.

In the fall we would close the season with a dance to help everyone relax and let down their hair after a summer of competition.

ODE TO EDDIE BEHM
by C. Lineham

There came a lad from the Northwest States
Around Nineteen 'O' Four.
A lad made up of wild west dreams
In a frame not five foot four.

He searched each town
While working 'round
For land his name could claim.
Land called 'home' from which, he vowed
He'd never leave again.

He settled West
In a forest nest
In the shadow of a Rocky peak.
And for a time, to hear mankind
An echo he would seek.
He cut his home from the timber near
With a dog and horse for kin.
His dog, folks say, would shut the door
Once Eddie let him in.
His horse stood ready to ride for supplies
Or simply just to ride.
For the hills were home to Eddie Behm
'Twas in the hills he died.

He was one of the very first jockeys
To eat dirt off the Millarville track.
I was told of a time
When his gritty grin
Was the leader of a motley pack.
His flapping arms
Set the beat for his mount
As he thundered the last quarter mile.
And he rivalled the sun
Stretched full in the run
With his face dressed in a smile.

He was certain of a notion
That the only decent motion
Was the riding of a horse
From A to B.
For on a salty summer's day
He'd bought a Model 'T', to say
You'll have to prove to me
You're better than a beast.
That 'T' she tried her best
When Eddie put her to a test
Alas, he wouldn't read the book
On how to guide her.

He called her seat a saddle
And her rpm's a rattle
And she couldn't cross a creek
So what the heck.
"I'll put her up on blocks"
And there she sat among the trees
In the wind and rain
But never was she bridled.
Too soon old age's smoulder
Forced a shotgun to his shoulder
Should a stranger try to
Keep him from a nap.
So came a reputation
With the strictest implication
That his solitude
Was his alone to snap.
His faithful dog had passed away
His horse grew weak and thin.
The North wind blew much colder now
Through Eddie's tattered skin.
'Though an unseen twig while riding
Had stolen the sight of an eye.
He wouldn't leave his hand-hewn home
'Till fifty years passed by.

But sixty years had come and gone.
And a frost of Sixty-nine
Had slept in the cot where Eddie lie
And whispered, not much time.
He knew Old Death was waiting
As it does for all mankind.
It stalked him from the ridges
It stalked him from behind.
A wind as cool as icicles
Forever at his side
Filled his dreams with pale white steeds
Who teased him to a ride.
He knew that Death was waiting
Could feel its presence nigh.
So slipping on his silver spurs
And a hat tipped to the side
He grabbed the reins of a ghostly horse
And to the hills did ride.

Come winter
When the cold, cold snow
Lays frozen to the ground
And Jack Frost paints your windows
You may hear a mournful sound.
But startle not, nor shiver
Just pull the covers 'round.
For Eddie Behm is riding
From the foothills into town.

Boy Scouts of Millarville

by Art Patterson, John Jackson

A movement started by Lord Baden-Powell in England, 1908, took root for a few years in the Millarville district, when Captain A. J. Cawthorne came to this country in the early 1920's. He saw the merit of

Mounted Boy Scouts. Standing: Bob Standish, Larry Williams. Seated, L. to R.: unknown, Bill Hackett, two unknown, Ken Gush, unknown, Clifford Cane. 1922.

Boy Scout training, and with the aid of Rev. Alexander, (Christ Church rector at the time), and a few neighbors, mustered together a group of boys. There were about twenty of us in all, and we were proud to take part in the troop. Mr. Cawthorne was a good instructor, who knew how to give orders. He started his program by asking what we thought was the **main** factor that won the war. Of course we had many reasons, but then he said:

"Boys, those may be reasons, but the main factor was discipline, and discipline is what I intend to get from you boys!"

This remark was more than a little awe-inspiring, but later we found our leader not only to be firm, but just, and in the ensuing months we learned many things. First, we were taught the Boy Scout motto: Be prepared; and the slogan: Do a good turn daily. All this revolved around the Boy Scout oath:

"On my honour, I will do my best to do my duty to God and country, and to obey the Scout law; to help other people at all times; to keep myself physically strong, mentally awake, and morally straight."

Physical fitness and self-reliance were of prime importance, so we learned various fitness excercises,

Mounted Boy Scouts Camp in Forest Reserve near Ware Creek. L. to R. Bob Standish, unknown, Clifford Kane, standing unknown, Dick King. 1922.

first aid, morse code, semaphore, the art of knot tying, and club swinging. The first set of clubs was made by Mr. Knights out of a broken neck yoke, thus demonstrating how one could improvise. A bugle donated by Pat Burns was a prized possession. Dick King was the bugle boy who aroused us all at the crack of dawn with reveille.

For sport, the game of cricket was played on the sloping greens of the Fordville school yard, under the guidance of Mr. Knights.

One of our favorite activities was camping. We learned how best to live off the land, how to light a fire in the open with a limit of two matches, and various other little gems. The highlight of our first season was a camping trip conducted by one of our troop leaders, Mr. Howard de Mille. With all the necessary gear, pack ponies, and mounts for all, the troop headed for the hills; destination, the point of Ware and Lynx creeks. For ten days the camp was set, just inside the forest reserve. We spent our time fishing, hiking, and doing camp chores. Our spare time was spent picking those luscious wild strawberries, which were hanging by the handsful from the ledges.

Some of the points a good scout club must follow when on the trail are; be alert, leave the site as you found it, put out camp fires carefully, and leave some sign so others may follow on your trail. The reason we bring this last point into the story, is because Rev. Alexander, being a rugged outdoors man, riding a gaunt old sorrel, was going to rendezvous with the group at the campsite Sunday morning. He hoped to see how things were going, and preach a little sermon. Whatever went wrong we don't know, but he was unable to pick up our signs! He searched in vain for the troop, only catching up with us as we were coming back out. To say the least, he was not amused!

To help raise funds for the necessary equipment, such as badges and uniforms, Mr. Cawthorne wrote and produced a play. With the help of some local talent, the play was shown at Priddis, and was well received. Mr. Otto Roedler played the piano for dancing afterwards.

As the years go by, and the memory dims, there will be some who say it was not quite so; however, this is how we remember it.

Below are the names of the boys who took part: Jim and Len Nelson, Mike Knights, Jack, Frank, and Bill Lee, John and Bob Standish, Allan Greenwood, Dick King, Clifford Cane, Larry Williams, George and John Jackson, Bill and Art Patterson, Jess Hackett, Lester Letz, Arnold Bruning, Buster Jaquish, Hugh Peak, and others we don't remember.

Mounted Boy Scouts

Jim Nelson

The Millarville Mounted Boy Scouts, as far as we know, was the only Mounted Boy Scout troop in Canada. Mr. A. J. Cawthorne was our Scout Master and we were very lucky to have him as leader. Mr.

L. to R. Mike Knights, George Jackson, John Jackson, Leonard Nelson, Bill Patterson and Arnold Bruno. Members of Mounted Boy Scouts.

L. to R. Mike Knights, Bill Patterson, George Jackson, Arnold Bruno, Jim Nelson. With catch of trout taken from Lynx Creek.

Cawthorne organized the odd mounted Church parade. One parade I remember was when Mr. Cawthorne bawled me out for riding a bronk in it. What happened, we were all lined up in front of the church and the people. We had to make a fancy dismount and the bronk I was riding did not like it so she ducked her head and bucked me off and ran away. Three of the other scouts tore off down the road to catch her.

Mr. Howard deMille took the troop on a camping trip west of Kew, on Lynx Creek. We had one big tent to sleep in. We made a mistake when we put the tent up: we had the door facing west. One night a wind and rain storm came up and the wind came in through the door and lifted the tent up and dropped it down and broke the ridge pole. We had to go out in the rain and dark and cut another pole to put the tent up again.

Lynx Creek was full of trout so we had lots of fish to eat.

Willing Workers Women's Institute

by Esther Jackson

The history of Willing Workers and many of their activities is recorded in Our Foothills history.

However, a few things come to mind which were not included, one of which is Women's Institutes affiliation with Associated Country Women of the World (A.C.W.W.) organization. Their headquarters is in London, England and they do a tremendous amount of work helping women in foreign countries by teaching them homemaking, etc. They hold a convention every three years in member countries. In 1965 the convention was held in Ireland in Dublin. Two of our members, Mrs. Kathleen Tosh and Mrs. Esther Jackson went to that as contributing members. The 1968 A.C.W.W. convention was held in the United States in Lansing, Michigan, Kathleen Tosh and Esther Jackson attended that, accompanied by Mrs. K. Kendall. In 1977 South Africa was hostess country. The convention was held in Nairobi, and Mrs. Stella Pekse attended. It was a never-to-be-forgotten experience for those who had the good fortune to attend these conventions and to meet women of many races, colours and creeds from many parts of the world.

Federated Women's Institutes hold trienniel conferences in the different provinces throughout Canada. In June, 1976 three Willing Workers members; Mrs. Pekse, Mrs. Evans and Mrs. Jackson travelled to Charlottetown, Prince Edward Island to attend the conference held there that year. The program included an all-day tour of the Island, with a visit en route, to Cavandish to the birthplace of authoress L. M. Montgomery and the home of Anne of Green Gables. Another interesting place visited was Confederation Square in Charlottetown (the home of Confederation) built by the Canadian Government to commemorate Canada's 100th birthday.

A highlight of all the years was the 50th anniversary held at the Race Track Hall on November 28, 1976. More than one hundred persons were invited including four former charter members; Mrs. William MacKay (Jennie Chalmers) first secretary-treasurer, now of Calgary, Mrs. Marian Mitchell, Black Diamond, Mrs. William Pallister (Edith Knights) and Mrs. Richard Knights, (Netta Stanhope) both of Calgary, all past

members, now widely scattered. Neighbouring Institutes, Turner Valley and Westoe Wanderers and other special guests. Much preparation had been made, the hall nicely decorated by Nita Foster and Helen Preston. An anniversary cake was made by Jo Ann Jackson and tastefully decorated by Edna Jones (the daughter of a former member, Mrs. Joe Standish). A program of a skit and musical numbers prepared by social conveners Irene Evans and Kathleen Tosh, corsages made by Kathleen Tosh and a large bowl of punch made by Stella Pekse. All other members helped wherever they could. All that was needed was the co-operation of the weatherman, but he let us down, and it was a stormy day. Despite that, more than fifty persons braved the elements and came. Mr. and Mrs. Habberfield came from Strathmore and Mr. and Mrs. Christie from Cochrane. We were very gratified that they came. It must have been a rough trip for them.

We were very happy that one charter member was able to be there, Mrs. Marian Mitchell made the trip from Black Diamond and she cut the anniversary cake.

We now have twelve members and keep busy making quilts and afghans, hooking rugs among other things. We give special cash prizes to Millarville fair and 4-H Girls' Club, contribute to Institute Girls' Clubs and A.C.W.W. projects and District IV foster child, among others.

Socially we have card parties in the winter months, and a get-together at some nice place in summer. We are proud to have had two constituency conveners from our group. The late Mrs. N. W. Pegler served during the years 1935 to 1937 and the present convener Mrs. Nita Foster who is starting her third year.

Mrs. W. H. King, Mrs. Hackett, Mrs. Pegler, with hand quilted quilt.

Marian Mitchell, Charter member of Willing Workers W.I. cutting 50th Anniversary cake for W.I.

Before closing I wish to pay tribute to our husbands and families who, through the years, have helped in so many ways to make Willing Workers W.I. a good organization to belong to. Bless them.

Square Butte Community Club
by Peggy Nylund

Mr. and Mrs. Sam Virtue came to the district in 1919 and soon after they started house parties and surprise parties. They knew all the old time dances. The school was built and ready for use in 1922. There were Christmas concerts but just when they started all the community affairs I am not sure, but when they did everyone got together and had a good time. It was a place where families could all go together and enjoy themselves.

When the schools were all amalgamated to Millarville in 1950, the old Square Butte School was still used as a community center.

Margaret and John Kendall had the first bridal shower there. There were many others after that. The music was all local talent. There were picnics, ball games, bingo, card parties. Folks came from near and far to gather at the school. One picnic in particular had an egg hunt in the trees and much to the surprise of many, when they found the nests, instead of eggs they found peanut butter.

Last but not least of all activities were Sunday School and Church Services held in the school.

There were many pleasant memories of the old school. It burned down but I am not sure of the date. The teacherage had been moved away. A little shanty stands guard where the old school once stood. It is very hard to see where it once stood as the trees have grown up and the road has been changed.

The Kew Hall was moved to Square Butte in 1959 and ready for use about 1960. Eleanor and Howard Davidson had the first bridal shower in the new hall. Mary Ann Highmoor had the first wedding reception, but there have been many more showers and receptions since, much activity in the last seventeen or eighteen years. Also many improvements to the grounds and hall. Another room, kitchen and washroom built and many other improvements. Much entertainment goes on there — trail rides, snowmobile rides, with lunches and suppers served after the outings.

The Square Butte Ladies' Group still carry on their good work. Norma Lyall, Una Ball and Agnes Ball have been with the group and are still active members and many new members have joined the group. Many of the original members have moved away or passed on.

While on holidays with Norma and Alex Lyall, we went to see Mr. and Mrs. Paul Gardner at Costa Mesa, Calif. Mrs. Gardner was one of the first members of the group, back in 1941.

The Square Butte Community Association
by Joan Kendall

The Square Butte Community Association grew out of sporadic merry making that took place in the old Square Butte School house and neighborhood house parties. There was always the Christmas concert with a dance afterwards that everyone enjoyed.

In 1937 Miss Dorothy Campbell came to teach at Square Butte School and she initiated dances in the school. Musicians were gathered from the neighborhood: Mary Bell with her guitar, Cyrus McBee with his violin and guitar, Mr. and Mrs. Fred Kosling on the accordion and piano and sometimes Jim Howie with his violin.

There was always an enthusiastic attendance so under the leadership of Mrs. Fred Kosling a club was formed to carry on parties throughout the year. When the school was abandoned by the pupils when they were bussed to Sheep Creek School (Millarville), the old school house was taken over by the community; and a teacherage which was on the premises was joined to the building for a kitchen.

The Square Butte school house was originally a small log building but during the thirties when the school population blossomed due to oil well exploration and people moving to the hills to escape the prairie dust bowl, a frame addition was affixed, one wall removed and the old roof supported in the middle by a post. Anyone who attended the dances at the old school house will attest to the fact that this post in no way impeded the progress of the dancers — even in the wild convolutions of a square dance.

The school year wound up at the end of June with a community picnic, rain or shine, foot races for young

Working bee when Square Butte Hall was put on foundation. L. to R. Jack Robertson, John Kendall, Art Ball, Al Belanger, Pat Rodgers, Les Foster, Mike Rodgers. December, 1960.

and old and a ball game that became a tradition. If the roads were impassable for cars — the horses were hitched up and the revelry went on as usual. If the weather was fair everyone went home, did the chores and returned for a dance. It seems sad to think that the progress of modern living has doomed the community picnic; and we are all so satiated with entertainment that the thought of this old-time fun makes us weary.

After twenty years this old school house began to sag and was in need of repair. The community looked towards the Kew Hall which was standing unused. By mutual arrangement with Kew people — some of whom, the original builders, were also members of Square Butte, it was agreed to move the hall to its present location on land which was given by Tillie Hulme. An association was formed in order to get title to the land.

The hall was moved late in 1959 by Schumaker's outfit and local volunteers and was on the foundation by Dec. 8. However, it was not till the first Friday in February, 1961, after much community work, that the first dance was held. Mr. Fred Kosling played a few bars for the first opening waltz.

The next year, 1962, a beef supper was organized in February and became an annual event for twelve years till it fell under the wheels of progress. The Safety Round-up singers from Calgary under the leadership of Sgt. Don Hanson provided wonderful entertainment during these years. The night of the first supper the weather decided to have a fling, when one of the old time chinooks blew in — turning the road and yard to a sea of mud — a real mess — there being no gravel on the new site. This was not the only event where rubber boots or four-buckle overshoes were a "must" to get to the door, and cars were left on the road, but finally gravel did get hauled.

There have been continuous renovations to the hall to accommodate crowds and the variety of functions held; the majority of the work having been done by volunteer help from community members. The Square Butte Ladies' Group have contributed support in the form of money; the most notable example being the installation of plumbing raised by their seventeen mile Walkathon which they aptly named John-a-thon. In 1975 an addition was added to make more seating facilities and a larger kitchen. It is only by the unstinting work done by the hands of community members, and their unfailing support of events, that the hall continues to operate in its present capacity.

The Square Butte Ladies' Group

by Joan Kendal

The Square Butte Ladies' Group was initiated in April 1941, after a baby shower for Peggy Nylund (Lyall) proved to be an enjoyable occasion. It was decided to meet in individual homes once a month, and as it was wartime; to join the Red Cross for the purpose of knitting and sewing for soldiers and refugees.

Some original members of the group were Mrs. Paul Gardner (whose idea it was to form a club), Mrs. Bell, Mary Bell, Mrs. Gladys Grainger (McLay at the time), Miss Helen Greig (Mrs. Dick Lyall), Mrs. Maurice Ingeveld, Martha Ingeveld, Mrs. Godkin (Mrs. McLay's mother), Mrs. Katherine Kendall, Mrs. Carrie Kosling (she did not rest till the club was organized), Joan Kosling, Mrs. George Lyall, Mrs. S. A. Lyall, Mrs. Peggy Nylund and Mrs. Ella Quigley.

After the war, the group raised money to give to various charities which included the Cancer Fund, Heart Fund, Red Cross and Crippled Children's Hospital. Since that time the group has extended their donations to include the Women's Crisis Centre, Retarded Children, Christ Church and 4-H Clubs. They also send two children to the Kinsmen's Camp Horizon each summer. Several Greek children have also been sponsored through Save the Children Fund; a project which has continued for thirty years.

During the years before the roads were gravelled and transportation was more difficult; the Ladies' meeting was the event of the month and was held in the afternoon. No one allowed any circumstance to stand in her way and any means was employed to get there, — be it walking (which involved fording creeks in bare feet), riding horseback or grinding through muddy roads by truck or car. There was the time when Alex Lyall spent many hours traversing a stretch of muddy road on the way home from a meeting, even to the point of taking the wheels off his car when they became so clogged with the heavy gumbo, they no longer turned.

Over the years there have been many events put on by the Ladies to raise money for their various

Some of the Square Butte Ladies. Back row: Miss Mary Bell, Mrs. K. Kendall, Mrs. Jean Andrews and son, Ron, Mrs. Elsie Ingeveld, Mrs. Kosling, Mrs. Peggy Nylund. Front row: Mrs. Seth Peat, Marian Stewart, (her mother), Mrs. Marie Stewart (nee Kendall), Mrs. Norma Lyall, Mrs. S. A. Lyall, Mrs. Betty Lyall. Picture at Wildman home.

projects. At first bazaars and bake sales were organized, but as these were a terrific amount of work — a whole year's effort — they looked around for other means.

For quite some years, during the fifties a Strawberry Tea was held each spring in the Rancher's Hall, but the most noted event, which continued uninterrupted is the "Gingham Ball". Begun in 1953 in Rancher's Hall, it was held there each year on Farmer's Day till 1961 when Square Butte's new hall was put in use. Fred Kosling and Tom Wildman were the first doorkeepers at Rancher's Hall and Fred Kosling continued in this capacity till arthritis crippled his hands and he could no longer change the money. The Gingham Ball is still an annual event.

On June 8, 1974 the Ladies held their famous Walkathon, starting from Turner Valley to Square Butte Hall — a distance of seventeen miles. This event, which they called the John-a-thon, was to raise money to install plumbing in the Community Hall. They succeeded in raising $1,650.00 (One thousand six hundred and fifty dollars). Fourteen members took part and the first trio to reach the hall were Mary Ann Highmoor, Agnes Ball and Norma Wildman, who made the distance in an incredible five hours. The walkers were urged on and ably supported with drinks and snacks along the way by Alex Lyall and Dick Smith. Besides this tremendous effort the Ladies have continued to assist the Community Hall in its many renovations over the years.

In 1967 the Ladies' Group catered to the Barbecue at Millarville Races on July first and have continued to

This is to certify that _Norma Lyall_

completed _17_ miles while walking in the JOHN - A - THON on

Saturday, June 8, 1974.

The Square Butte Ladies Group wish to sincerely thank

you for your support.

Mary A. Highmoor, President

Bev Patterson, Secretary

do so till the present time. Besides these larger projects the Ladies have made quilts to raffle, catered to wedding receptions and put on bake-sales.

In 1965, the twenty-fifth anniversary, a supper and social evening were held for members and their families. Engraved silver spoons were given to original members who were still active in the group.

Square Butte Ladies' Group. First picture. L. to R. Kamma Henriksen, Agnes Ball, Norma Lyall, Mary Parkins, Una Ball, Ruth Page. Second picture, back row, Connie Brown, Agnes Ball, Doreen Marthaller, Jody Ball. Middle row: Karen Banjovich, Dorothy Weir, Norma Lyall, Jo Shelley. Front: Alleyne Wyler, Lucille Glaister, Joan Kendall, Liz Mitchell.

Down through the years many ladies of the district have belonged. The original enrollment in the group was about sixteen members and at present there are fifteen members.

The original concerns and interests of the group remain the same — to give a helping hand to others and at the same time keep a finger on the pulse of neighborhood life.

Kew Club

In the 1930's ladies living in the Kew area decided to form a club to get to know each other better and have some social activities. They went by horse and buggy or horseback looking forward eagerly to their once a month get togethers. Sometimes they had social gatherings and card parties in the evenings.

During the war years it was a Red Cross effort, knitting, sewing and quilt making.

One of the first showers was given at Hartell's Home when Nita Adam's became the bride of Chubby Foster.

Some of the first members were Mrs. Middleton, Mrs. Getteg, Mrs. McKeever, Mrs. Calderwood, Mrs. Robison, Mrs. Bill Johnson, Mrs. Frank Chambers, Mrs. Bill Iceton, Mrs. Walter Phillips, Mrs. Harry Foster, Mrs. Ford Lochhead, Mrs. Bud Dameron, Mrs. Dan Dudenhoeffer. Mrs. Paddy Rodgers.

Later new settlers moved in Mrs. Sid Peel, Mrs. Roy Sim, Mrs. Bob Lochhead, Mrs. Laurie Lochhead, Mrs. Cam Lansdell, Mrs. Harley Hanson, Mrs. Danny Dudenhoeffer, Mrs. David Evans, Mrs. Leo Olehauser, Mrs. Everett Danforth, Mrs. John Iceton, Mrs. Albert (Eva) Iceton, Mrs. Harry Orum, Mrs. Frank Adams, Mrs. Lynn, Mrs. Art Peel.

I remember Mrs. Bernie Vandergrift riding over to one of our meetings on her favorite saddle horse when she was well over seventy.

There were showers given for brides, new babies, in homes or the Kew Hall. Trophies to youth groups, skating and toboggan parties with wiener roasts, suppers, and farewell parties.

Kew Ladies' Club, 1943. Mrs. Robison, Nita Foster, Mrs. Harry Foster, Mrs. Pat Hartell, Mrs. McKeever, Mrs. Phillips, Mrs. Bob Calderwood, Mrs. Middleton. In front: Kenny Foster, Mrs. Hazel Adams, Loretta McKeever, Mrs. Hallie Lochhead.

Kew Ladies' Club. L. to R. Mrs. Kendall, Mrs. Rodgers, Mrs. Hanson, Mrs. McArthur, Mrs. Phillips, Mrs. Adams, Mrs. Foster, Jem Lochhead.

Kew Ladies' Club. Back row: Mrs. E. Patterson, (Joanna Hanson's mother), Harley Hanson, Hallie Lochhead, Leah Peel, holding Linda, Mrs. McArthur (teacher at Plainview School), Clara Adams, Joanna Hanson, Mrs. Elsie Sim. Front row: Rose Marie Lochhead, Maureen, Margaret, Trina, Jem and Nina Lochhead, Mrs. Orum, Donna Evans.

One of the Highlights of the year was the Kew picnic. This was held on the Lochhead flats one of the most beautiful spots along the Three Point Creek. The Lochheads always gave ready permission for people to use this area for recreation; we often gathered to play ball on Friday evenings or Sunday afternoons. There was a good swimming hole there too.

The men would help prepare the ground after cutting off the grass and setting up the tables and benches under the trees. They collected funds to pay for treats and prizes.

All the community attended and many from neighboring areas too. There were various foot races and contests for young and old, followed by a big ball game. Tables were ready and everyone had brought a pot luck dinner which was set out Smorgasbord style with plenty for all. Followed by ice cream, watermelon and treats. What a Happy time. The Annual Christmas concert was held in the hall, again the ladies and husbands helped cutting the tree and trimming tree and hall. One old timer remembers Mr. Lochhead bringing the old white mare, horns well placed with Santa and Pack aboard arriving just at the right time.

We had people teach us crafts too. One summer Mrs. Tip Armstrong taught us Leather craft. They lived on Shatlo place. After the Plainview school went to Millarville and the Hall to Square Butte, the club disbanded leaving many happy memories.

"500" Club

The "500" Club was started in 1965 by the late Tom Wildman and Ted Pekse. The first players were Norma, Tom and Fred Wildman, Stella and Ted Pekse, Cubby Tosh, Al and Alice Belanger and the children.

Through the years the players have been, Gram, Frank, Anita, Bill, Joan, John, Margaret Kendall, Tom and Irene Campbell, Robert and Jeannette Reimer, Frank, Liz and Freda Stewart, Jake and Barbara Reimer, Fred Kosling, Keith and Nola Giles, Art and Agnes Ball, Judy and Ken Foster, Sid and Eileen Barker, Edie and Duane Durieux, Dick Smith, Helen Preston, Happy and Cam Lansdell, Mary and Bob Parkins.

We play once a month. In June or July we have our annual barbeque. The yearly prizes are then presented. Some of the players no longer play, some have passed on and some have moved on, but the rest of us are still playing.

The Millarville Nursing and Ambulance Association No. 500

by Veryl Laycraft

This Auxiliary to Calgary St. Johns Ambulance was founded in 1969. Living in the district at the time was a very Qualified First Aide Instructor by the name of Opal Gamble. She taught many First Aide classes in Millarville and surrounding areas such as Priddis, Red Deer Lake, etc. It was she who fostered and encouraged a good many of us to keep working as First Aiders, also to strive for higher awards in St. John courses.

It was also due to her influence that a group with First Aide Certificates, around Millarville, decided to band to-gether into an Auxiliary Association of St. John. Members of this group were Frank and Bill Kendall, Bob and Margaret Lochhead, Jake Reimer, Joanna Hanson, Donna Evans, Elaine Lyster, Wilma Chalmers, Don and Jean Morrison, Gail Wildman as R.N., Eveline Prestie, Ron and Veryl Laycraft.

Monthly meetings were held at the homes of the members. Ron Laycraft was the first elected President, followed by Bob Lochhead and Frank Kendall. Elaine Lyster carried the position of Secretary Treasurer until she moved out of the district. Records

were kept of duties and duty hours, with reports going in regularly to St. John. First Aide was administered at the Millarville Races and Fairs, to other activities such as the Black Diamond Rodeo, Priddis Breakfast, Riding Academy work shops, school Track meets etc. We always went in to the Calgary Stampede to help man First Aide Stations on the grounds also taking duty hours at the Parade. From 1972 on some of the members began selling their land and moving out of the district. Elaine Lyster moved to Vilna, near St. Paul, Frank Kendall to Lacombe, Bob and Margaret to Innisfail, Joanna Hanson to Turner Valley, Gail Wildman to Sangudo. Jake Reimer and Opal Gamble were deceased. There was only five of us left to carry on the Association so it was decided to disband in 1975. Out of the original membership of this group there is only Wilma Chalmers and myself with First Aide Certificates left in this district.

Oilfield Army Cadet Corps

The Oilfield Army Cadet Corps was formed in Black Diamond in 1950 under the sponsorship of the Royalite Oil Co. Ltd. It was moved to the Turner Valley Militia Armouries. With the closure of the Armouries the Corps was moved to Sheep Creek School in 1958 where almost all the Jr. High School and High School boys joined and at one point brought the Corps strength up to 73 Cadets, the highest the Corps ever held. The Corps was affiliated with the Service Corps, later the Calgary Highlanders (Militia.)

Captain Bill Dube became commanding officer of the Corps in 1955 and continues to this day. Captain Dube was twice elected President of the C.S. and C. for Alberta and the North West Territories (Cadet Services of Canada.)

The Corps has won the top efficiency award for S. Alberta several times and individual cadets have won trophies, certificates, and awards in many areas both at local training and summer camps in British Columbia and Manitoba (first aid, wireless, swimming and field sports, shooting, hunter training, driver mechanic etc.)

Parades were held at Sheep Creek School for seven years with cadets being transported from Black Diamond and Turner Valley. Many training schemes and camp outs were held in the wilderness area to the west. Proper gun handling and shooting competitions were a top priority and most cadets won shooting badges. Several cadets achieved master cadet gold star status, the highest award after four years training.

Tom Owens, Stuart Sinclair-Smith and Bill Dube Jr. received commissions and became instructors with the Corps. Sgt. John Scheuerman (Militia) was also an instructor with the Corps.

OILFIELDS ARMY APR
CADET NEWS 62

Seven first-year cadets took the St. John Ambulance First Aid Tests at High River and all passed. Dr. C. W. Forsyth tested the group.

Those who received the St. John's badge were:

Cdt. Thomas Anderson, Turner Valley; Cdt. Allan Carr, Cdt. Robert Gratton, Black Diamond; Cdt. Linton Hardisty, Turner Valley; Cdt. Russel Prichard, Midnapore; Cdt. Melvin Scheuerman, Cdt. Barry Luchia, Turner Valley.

The Oilfields Annual Inspection is scheduled for Friday, May 18 at Millarville at 7 p.m.

————:o:————

Cadets Stand Inspection At Millarville

[Herald Correspondent]

MILLARVILLE—The A. Gardner trophy for most efficient army cadet corp in southern Alberta was presented to the Oilfields Army Cadet Corp No. 2383 at its annual inspection at Millarville recently.

The corp won the award at a previous inspection. Presentation was made by Major S. Ellis, commanding officer of RCASC (M) High River.

Following the march past the cadets presented demonstrations in precision drill, rifle, national survival, first aid, wireless and sports. Chief instructor of the corp is Capt. W. R. Dube.

Awards, based on yearly averages, were presented to Cpl. C. Jones, best turned out cadet in the senior group; Cadet M. Scheuerman, best turned out cadet in the junior group; Capt. W. Haney, best shot; Cpl. J. Yee, efficiency trophy, senior; Cadet T. Anderson, efficiency trophy, junior.

GORVEATT TROPHY was presented to Cadet Melvin Scheuerman by Major Scott Ellis at the Oilfields RCAC inspection. Trophy was for best first-year cadet. Times photo.

GARDNER TROPHY was presented to Cadet Captain Bob Haney by Major Scott Ellis at the Oilfields RCAC inspection last week. Trophy was won by cadets last year for being most efficient corps in southern Alberta.

OILFIELDS ARMY CADET inspection by RCASC Major Scott Ellis was held at Millarville last Friday evening to the music of the RCASC band. Cadet demonstrations and presentations were held later in the hall. — Times' photo.

1962

Cadets' March Past At Millarville

The Gardner trophy, emblematic of the most efficient Army Cadet Corps in rural southern Alberta, was presented to the 2383 Oilfields Corps by RCASC Major Scott Ellis at Millarville last Friday.

The Oilfields cadets won the trophy last year. It has been up for competition eight times.

The presentation was made following the cadets' march past and inspection by Major Ellis, Col. M. Finlay, Major R. Butterfield, Capt. W. Dube, Capt. D. MacDonald, Capt. C. Forsyth, RCMP Cpl. D. Simmons, Black Diamond Mayor T. Brown, Turner Valley Mayor J. McInnis and Turner Valley Legion president, J. Oakes.

The RCASC (M) band, led by Jack Pickersgill Jr. played for the march past.

Following the field inspection, demonstrations including first aid, wireless, rifle drill and national survival were given in the hall. Presentations followed.

Gorveatt trophy for the first year cadet was presented to Melvin Scheuerman by Major Ellis; Best all round cadet in the corps was awarded to Cpl. Chris Jones by Major Butterfield, CS of C representative from Calgary; perfect attendance trophy was presented to Cdt/Cpl. Jim Yee by the Turner Valley Legion president; Best Rifle Shot trophy went to Cdt./Capt. Bob Haney (who also received the Gardner trophy from Major Ellis) and was presented by Capt. MacDonald, cadet training officer for southern Alberta.

Good cadet work earned Cpl. Gord Cutting an award and Cdt. Tom Henderson won a cadet award. Cdt./WO 2 T. Owens was elevated in rank in another presentation.

Cadets taking part in the demostrations included (ranks omitted), besides those already mentioned, L. Rest, R. Jones, W. Heyland, M. Robinson, W. Prichard, W. P. Dube, D. Measor, D. Thompson, A. Tosh, W Weireter, D. Hardisty, R. Prichard, D. Stauffer, F. Klok, W. Stuard and cadets Luchia and Carr.

The Oilfields unit is sponsored by High River RCASC (M) 153 Company.

Oilfield Cadet Corps lined up for inspection with drill rifles on the Sheep Creek School grounds at Millarville. 1961.

Stitch-In-Time 4-H Club
by Agnes Ball

The club was organized in September 1971 as a Clothing Club with Elaine Lyster as leader and Nita Foster and Wilma Chalmers as assistant leaders. The meetings were held once a month at Ranchers Hall, Millarville. Wendy Foster was elected President and she was also junior leader. Debbie Lyster was vice president, Sheila Giles, secretary, Elaine Ball, Treasurer, Carolle Sutter, News Reporter and Marty Ransom, Librarian. There were 14 girls all involved in clothing projects. The Square Butte Ladies Group became sponsors of the club. Denise Lyster suggested the rather unique name and it was adopted. The club collected stamps to send to a Leprosy Colony in New Brunswick and also wintered a pony for Camp Horizon as two charity projects. Their fund raising event was a December Coffee Party which became an annual event.

At the Public Speaking held in March 1972, Wendy Foster and Debbie Lyster were the winners in the senior section with Vicki Chalmers runner-up. The winner in the Junior section was Sheila Giles with Carolle Sutter runner-up. The efficiency winner at the May Achievement day was Debbie Lyster.

The Club reorganized in August 1972 at the home of Keith and Nola Giles. Elaine Lyster and Nita Foster were leaders and a new project "Leathercraft" was added. Wilma Chalmers and Nola Giles were assistant leaders. There were twenty-three members and three pee wees. Debbie Lyster became president, Elaine Ball, Vice president, Joanne Ball secretary, Sheila Giles treasurer, Kathleen Ball, Club Reporter and Laura Kendall Librarian.

In the spring of 1973 the club had a display booth at the Calgary Seed Fair at the Kinsmen Centre.

The Public Speaking winners in March 1973 were Debbie Lyster and Vicki Chalmers in the senior section with Sheila Giles in the juniors and Patric Lyster in the pee wee section. The winner of the efficiency award in May was Sheila Giles.

The club took a trip to Banff in early June to end the 4-H year.

In the fall of 1973 when the club reorganized Nita Foster became leader and there were five assistant leaders, Wilma Chalmers, Nola Giles, Carol Ricks, Judy Foster and Agnes Ball. Sheila Giles became president, Joanne Ball vice president, Carla Giles Secretary, Marty Ransom, Treasurer and Beth Ricks news reporter. There were twenty-four members.

Winners at the Public Speaking in March of 1974 were; Sheila Giles and Marty Ransom in the seniors with Vicki Chalmers runner up and Joanne Ball in the junior level with Lance Chalmers runner up. Edie Chalmers won at the pee wee level. The winner of the

Stitch-in-Time 4-H Tour of Fort Whoop-Up, Lethbridge, June, 1974. Front row, L. to R.: Lance Chalmers, Deanna Chalmers, Lisa Godwin, Edie Chalmers, Kate Ball, Anna Tieman, Steve Verhulst, Sherry Reimer, Lisa Arkes, Ron Arkes. Back row: zig zag, Christine Verhulst, Beth Ricks, Carla Giles, Sam Kendall, Sheila Giles, Twyla Giles, Marty Ransom, Bev Bull, Joanna Ball, Bernie Arkes, Laurel Harke, Wayne Harke.

efficiency award at May Achievement was Joanne Ball.

The year end was highlighted with a trip to Fort Macleod and Lethbridge in June which all the 4-H members will remember.

Thirty-four members reorganized the club in September, 1974. The same leaders helped as did the previous year and the club was grateful in having Rilla Wills who was a tremendous help to the girls in sewing. Joanne Ball became president, Laura Kendall was vice president, Beth Ricks was secretary, Vicki Chalmers treasurer and Edie Chalmers, news reporter. Sherry Reimer was librarian and Tracy Shelley was stamp collector.

The group adopted Mrs. Jim (Stastia) Carry as official 4-H grandmother. The 4-H members enjoyed having Mrs. Carry join them in their meetings and 4-H activities over the next two years.

The club made stuffed animals for the Childrens Hospital and also donated money to buy a square foot in the Kinsmen Research Centre for handicapped children as two of their charity projects.

The Public Speaking winners were, Joanne Ball in the senior section with Greg Bruce runner up. The junior winners were George Jackson and Laura Kendall with Steve Verhulst runner up. Susan Ball was the pee wee winner. At Achievement in May, 1975 Twyla Giles was the efficiency winner. In June the club travelled to Banff for a day to end another successful 4-H year.

In September of 1975 when the Stitch in Time Clothing and Leathercraft Club reorganized, Agnes Ball became leader. Nita Foster, Nola Giles, Wilma Chalmers, Pat Opheim, Karen Stromstedt and Mary Warren were assistant leaders. Twyla Giles was president, Beverley Bull vice president, Brenda Warren secretary, Traci Shelley treasurer and Shelly Turner Club reporter. There were 22 members.

The winners of the public speaking were Shelly Turner at the senior level with Ritchie Trostem runner up. The junior level winners were Susan Ball and George Jackson with Jody Kemp runner up. The efficiency award was won by Deanna Chalmers. A trip to the Drumheller Badlands in June concluded another 4-H year.

The club was not reorganized again until September 1977. It became a multi-project club. Dorothy Jackson became club leader and head of the crafts project.

Agnes Ball led the foods project. Mary Warren led the clothing project. Bill Jackson led the small motors project and Wilma Chalmers headed the leathercraft project. There were 25 members. Debbie Codd was president, Lisa Godwin, vice-president, Roxanne Schofield, Secretary, Pam Lyken, treasurer, Sherry Reimer, Club Reporter and Susan Ball, Stamp Collector. The club held a slide presentation in Feb. 1978 and gave a donation from the profit to the Crippled Childrens Hospital as one of their charity projects. They participated in the Provincial 4-H Highway Clean-Up in May 1978. As well as completing their winter projects, five members, Tasha Allen, Laura and Lisa Godwin, Marie Laycraft and George Jackson participated in a summer pheasant project.

The public speaking winners were Heather Jackson and Susan Ball with Tasha Allen runner up. They were all junior speakers.

At Achievement in May 1978 prizes were awarded in each project and an over all efficiency winner was not chosen.

The 4-H program has seen many changes over the last few years and owes its' success to the help and encouragement of many community people.

A special thank-you to Mrs. Irene Evans and Mr. Ted Pekse for their support of Public Speaking in the Stitch-In-Time Club.

Continuing Education in Millarville

The Foothills Continuing Education Council was organized early in 1973. The first chairman, Jean Moore of the Foothills School Division, and Diane Osberg, secretary, of High River, were mainly responsible for the early success of the Council.

Each of the communities within the School Division soon had volunteer representatives on the Council. These people plan and administer the courses on a local basis, arrange for instructors, the use of facilities and evaluation of the program. The first representative in the Millarville area was Dorothy Jackson, who since the autumn of 1974 has been assisted by Faye Grose.

The first course offered was a powder puff carpentry class taught in 1973. The winter of 1974 saw a furniture re-upholstery course, followed by a landscaping course in the spring. Since then, there have been several courses in carpentry, furniture re-upholstery, furniture refinishing as well as many gardening courses.

Several courses that were later taught elsewhere in the Council had their beginnings at Millarville — taxidermy, tanning of skins and leather braiding. One of the first classes in ballroom dancing was held here in 1975.

Craft classes have always been popular. Some that have been taught are: decoupage, ceramics, pottery, flower arranging, quilting, leather tooling, crocheting, photography, sewing, basketry, drawing, Christmas crafts, and crafts using nature's materials.

Sometimes, courses require special facilities for instruction. The Millarville community has always been able to provide the necessary facilities for courses such as brick laying, plumbing, house wiring, meat cutting, curing meat and sausage making, welding, engine repair, cattle grooming and hoof care, western equitation, and nature interpretation.

For those interested in the culinary arts, there have been classes in Oriental cooking, yeast breads and pastry, microwave cooking, dried foods, barbequing, salads and summer dishes, and other cooking classes.

The interest in the dog obedience classes was such that no less than eight classes of dog obedience have been taught since that first class in September, 1975.

The representatives strive to offer a wide variety of courses. As a result, there have been classes in hair care, conversational French, Transactional Analysis, keep fit, yoga, cross country skiing, defensive driving, driver education and first aid.

Continuing Education has received assistance from Alberta Agriculture through the District Agriculturist and District Home Economist in programming several courses — income tax management and estate planning, horse management, parliamentary procedure, as well as courses related to foods and home management.

Courses associated with various types of gardening, from greenhouses to pruning of trees and shrubs were continually requested. The keen interest in these classes brought together a group of people who, as a result of these classes, decided to form a club, thus the Millarville Horticulture Club.

Another club that was formed and has grown rapidly as a result of specific classes, is the Sheep Creek Weavers. Many classes have been taught in primitive and off-loom weaving, 4-harness weaving, spinning, nature and commercial dyeing of wool, and color and design in weaving.

Since the inception of the continuing education program there have been over 100 courses offered within the Millarville community with approximately 1400 registrants. Many times the course enrollment was so large that the class was divided into two classes. There were a few times also that the required eight people did not register and the course was cancelled.

Many of the courses have been taught by local instructors. These classes have provided an opportunity for these people to share their knowledge and expertise with others in the community. When local instructors were not available, instructors were brought in from other areas, including S.A.I.T. and other institutions.

Classes have provided an opportunity for the people in the community to learn new skills, develop new hobbies, meet new people and take a night out for relaxation.

As long as there is sufficient interest within the community, and the Foothills Continuing Education

Council receives financial support from the Department of Advanced Education, the people of Millarville can look forward to more courses in the future.

Leighton Centre For Arts and Crafts

The idea of The Leighton Centre was originated by Mrs. Barbara Leighton, widow of the internationally renowned artist A. C. Leighton. Mr. and Mrs. Leighton had lived in many parts of the world during which time, Mr. Leighton painted constantly. After many years of traveling, the Leightons settled in the Millarville-Okotoks area. After Mr. Leighton's death in 1965, Mrs. Leighton attended the Alberta College of Art, where she received her degree in Fine Arts. Initially she began holding classes in the basement of her home for small groups of friends who were interested in learning such crafts as batik and silversmithing. However, she soon found that more space was needed for classes. She purchased the old Sheep Creek Schoolhouse and had it transported to its present location. The old school house was given a complete new personality by being remodeled to become the main studio of the Leighton Centre. The facelift which was given to the old building was carefully planned to blend with the rural atmosphere and to maintain its rustic appeal. Old barn wood was subtly combined with cedar shakes to form interior walls on which were hung paintings, batiks, woven hangings and dried weeds and flowers. The heat for the building was provided by an antique "his and hers" stove, which was converted to gas. The official opening of the Leighton Centre for Arts and Crafts was held in October, 1970.

Classes at the new Centre proved to be so popular that it was felt that another studio, specifically for weaving, must be added. Again Mrs. Leighton showed her ingenuity by re-modeling an old building which she had moved to the Leighton Centre. This building is also heated by an authentic old stove which has been converted to gas. There is a wide variety of looms ranging in size from small table models, on which beginning students can make table mats, wall hangings or purses, to large floor looms for making rugs, curtains, bedspreads, etc.

It was felt that even with the addition of the weaving studio that there was not enough room and once again, an old building was obtained, and remodeled to initially provide a separate building in which to hold childrens classes. At present however, it doubles as a children's classroom and a pottery studio. It is well equipped with a new modern kiln and three potter's wheels, as well as a wide variety of glazing materials, which encourage students to experiment with mixing their own glazes.

Over the last few years, the Leighton Centre classes have expanded to include an extremely wide variety of art and crafts. These activities include oil painting, watercolour, weaving, pottery, sculpture, leathercraft, whittling, silversmithing, copper enameling, batik, silkscreening, spinning, dyeing, caning, macrame, sandcasting, stain glass, quilting and sketching.

The Leighton Centre has attracted adult students from Calgary and surrounding areas, and in its short life has become a focal point for the pursuit of art and crafts. Further to the above it should be added that the Leighton Centre caters to young people as well. Particularly in the spring and fall months school children from Calgary and the Foothills School Division have attended classes at the Leighton Centre. It has given us great pleasure to see small children, some of them exposed for the first time to country scenery, work so enthusiastically and happily in what must be an unparalleled setting. Such has been the success of the programs offered that some schools make a visit to the Leighton Centre an addition to their regular art program. Classes are also held during the summer months where children learn such things as weaving, pit fired pottery, river crafts and sand casting.

Other groups have availed themselves of the attractions afforded by the Leighton Centre. Included here are Senior Citizens, Professional Organizations, and special childrens groups. Within reasonable limits, the Leighton Centre strives to structure its programs according to the special needs and interests of its patrons.

One of the leading attractions at the Leighton Centre is the magnificent art gallery located in Mrs.

Main Studio Leighton Centre.

Weaving Studio Leighton Centre.

Leighton's residence. Featured among the many paintings are the works of such noted Alberta artists as Illingworth Kerr, Maxwell Bates, John Snow, Rick Grandmaison, Jim Nicoll, Marion Nicoll, Janet Mitchell and Ken Esler, not to mention of course the large and impressive array of paintings by A. C. Leighton himself. These paintings may be seen through guided tours specially arranged in advance, although Mrs. Leighton has been known to conduct impromptu tours for unexpected visitors.

The Leighton Centre grew out of a desire by a single woman to perpetuate a tradition so dearly held by her late husband. The Leighton Centre stands today as a tribute to her success and as a contribution to the cultural heritage of Southern Alberta.

Millarville Horticultural Club
by Judy Williams

The Millarville Horticultural Club blossomed from the desire of many gardening enthusiasts in the District to become more knowledgeable as well as sharing their valuable experience with novice gardeners who were seeking help. On April 21, 1976 a public meeting was held at the Millarville Race Track. Dave Zukerman the District Agriculturist and Arlene Chesney a Horticulturist with the Alberta Department of Agriculture explained how to form a club. All in attendance agreed there was a need for such a group within the community due to an influx of new landowners.

On May 6, 1976 the first regular meeting was conducted by the newly-elected executive of Grace Bull — President, Linda Bull — Vice-President, Judy Williams — Secretary-Treasurer, Dorothy Jackson — Educational Director, Ann Vale — Chairman of Tours, Betty Nelson — Chairman of Plant Sale, and JoAnn Jackson — Director-at-large. There were 40 members during the first year.

Informal tours to our local home gardens have created an enjoyable atmosphere for discussing individual horticultural problems and viewing a wide variety of fruit, vegetables and flowers. The Agricultural Research Centre in Brooks broadened our gardening techniques through displays and talks with their specialists. We observed first hand the importance of selecting the best variety for our particular weather conditions and soil.

During those long winter months Guest speakers, as well as our own members have discussed tree pruning, weed control, starting seeds, forcing bulbs, growing vegetables, identifying wild flowers, using dried materials for decorating and colour-co-cordinating our flower beds. These programs have attracted men and women of all ages from numerous surrounding communities.

A grant from the Alberta Horticultural Association has enabled our Club to supply labels and plant material to beautify the Millarville Church grounds during the landscaping campaign.

The funds from our Annual Plant Sale are being used to build a reference library on all aspects of indoor and outdoor gardening. These books are available for all our members to borrow and read in order to improve their gardening skills.

Sheep Creek Weavers

The Sheep Creek Weavers was started by Mrs. Freda McArthur in her home in Black Diamond in 1973, with Eleanor Walpole, Margaret Fulger, Fern Davidson, and Doris Griffith. We moved to Griffith's Memorial Centre (also started by Freda McArthur), and added Rosemary and Jennifer Baxter.

In 1974, we moved to the Valley neighbors in Turner Valley, where we organized with Freda McArthur as president and Ruth Page as secretary. We were 2 years obtaining our charter. We then moved to the

Cushions by Freda McArthur, Sheep Creek Weavers.

91

Race Track Hall for Foothills Continuing Education Classes with Rosemary Baxter as instructor.

We undertook to demonstrate our craft at the various schools of the widespread district, including Red Deer Lake, Black Diamond, Turner Valley, Longview, Eden Valley, Strathcona-Tweedsmuir, Glenbow, Heritage Park, Banff, Millarville Fair, Calgary Exhibition. At present, Rosemary is working to obtain her degree in Fine Arts at the University of Calgary after taking several courses at Banff School of Fine Arts.

Classes and workshops have moved their locale around to the various homes and find the Christ Church Parish Hall at Millarville ideal for their purpose. Besides weaving, we are now proficient at spinning and nature dyeing. We offer prizes each year at the Millarville Fair in these arts.

Having obtained several grants from local Recreation Boards, the Society now owns several looms and other weaving equipment, and is working towards a home to keep them in.

Having discovered the Woollen Mills at Carstairs, we no longer wash and card our own wool, but all have done plenty of it. Many of our twenty-acre people are raising a few sheep for their fleeces, as we use locally grown material as much as possible.

An exciting event coming up sponsored by the Sheep Creek Weavers is a Sheep to Shawl Contest, one at the Calgary Round-Up in March, 1979, and one at the Millarville Fair in August.

The Millarville Community Library

In 1975 it was decided to start a Community Library at Millarville. At the first meeting Jill Ross was appointed Librarian and other Board Members were Mr. Green, the school principal, Kathy Scatterty, who is the School Librarian, Linda Bull, Doreen Chalmers, Coreen Smith, Elizabeth Campbell, Sharon Raduloff, Muriel McCreary, and Janet MacKay.

The school library was located in the basement with the Community library having one end of the shelves for their books. Then in 1977 an addition was built on the school and in the fall all the books were moved into the spacious new library upstairs. The community now has their own section in one end for their books.

It was a great day when several people went to Calgary to buy new books with the money from the Government grant and donations from several organizations in the district. The Alberta Government gives a grant each year and the same amount has to be

Library (Books on Shelf).

Putting books on shelves when library started in 1975. Linda Bull in front, Jill Ross at shelves.

raised by the community. This money is to be used for buying books.

All work has been on a volunteer basis and many new books have been bought and catalogued. At the present time, 1978, there are over a thousand books on the shelves.

The Happy Gang
by Joanna Hanson

The club was first started by oil workers' wives in 1942 when the oil field work was booming. It was an exciting time with everyone friendly and anxious to do something worthwhile for the community. Later, farm wives joined. They held suppers, strawberry teas, picnics, dances, card games, catered at weddings and sales, gave showers for new brides and new babies and

Millarville Happy Gang. Back row, L. to R.: Barb Godwin, Veryl Laycraft, Barb Birch, Pauline Lyken, Karen Clark. Centre, Inga Erhler, Joan Smouse, Mary Gordon, Linda Codd, Myrna Fisher. Front: Joyce Backs, Wilma Chalmers, Donna Evans.

flowers for the sick. They gave trophies for 4-H and other clubs, also giving donations to Unitarian services and the Red Cross. When any member moved they received a going-away gift.

Every birthday, members received a cup and saucer. I remember as long as Mrs. Peat lived some of the girls took lunch and a cup and saucer for her birthday.

Since oil workers were a moving population there was an ever changing membership, so I will try to give as many names of members as I can remember of those who lived in the Millarville area throughout the years as perhaps this will be the only place they will be mentioned in our book.

Flora Haley, Hazel Bird, Verona Beebe, Eunice McNarry, Maude Hagen, Anna Hazen, Rachel Burquist, Maude Robertson, Euella Dickau, Tillie Potter, Eileen Beebe, Grace Chalmers, Belle Lampman, Claire Halburt, Ethel Jorgenson, Rene Werner, Esther Jackson, Betty Nelson, Agnes Lister, Millie Matheson, Donna Metz, Mary Peat, Avis Rishaug, Jean Malcolm, Jessie Martin, Gladys Theisen, Merle Backs, Minnie Nelson, Phyllis Gunderson, Joy Rawlinson Lewis, Eileen Clark, Mabel Mullins, Vera Haney, Elizabeth McClean, Irene Evans, Clara Johnson, Elsie Ducommun, Mrs. Fortier, Margaret Lochhead, Leatha Dube, Doreen Chalmers, Wilma Chalmers, Eveline Prestie, Veryl Laycraft, Joyce Backs, Phyllis Godwin, Donna Evans, Alma Paul, Pat Jacobson, Shirley Taylor, Glenda Bateman, Trina Smith, Barb Godwin, Mary Edwards, Janet MacKay, Linda Codd, Grace Landford, Pearl Laycraft, Myrna Fisher, Greta Verhultz, Maya Kieboom, Inga Elhers, Pauline Lickin, Lori Rock, Judi Malchow, Mary Gordon, Jean Schmaus, Nola Giles, Marlene May, Karen Clark, and Barbara Birch.

So many wonderful friendships were formed at the gatherings.

Chapter 7
District Highlights

The Millarville Meteorite
by Chuck Hayward

The chances of finding a meteorite are one in a million. There have only been 44 known meteorites recovered in Canada.

In the Spring of 1977, I decided to break up some hayland that had been cleared and rototilled in 1973, when my plow turned up an unusual looking object. I immediately stopped and examined it, noting the burn marks on the exterior and the unusual weight (40 lbs.). Not knowing for sure what it was, I threw it up on the sod and went another round. By this time, I was firmly convinced I had recovered a meteorite.

I contacted the Department of Geology at the University of Calgary, explained to them what I had found and they immediately came out, examined it, and confirmed that it was, indeed, a meteorite. Dr. J. E. Klovan, head of the department, compared it to a "beautiful piece of sculpture".

Dr. J. T. Wasson, the moon rocks specialist, from U.C.L.A., was invited to the unveiling on November 16, 1977 at the University of Calgary. The information he had compiled was that the meteorite was formed 4½ billion years ago. Its density and high metal content indicate it was once part of the core of a larger body, perhaps a destroyed planet which broke up approximately 60 million years ago and the pieces travelled through outer space, orbiting the sun, until approximately 100 years ago one of the pieces streaked through the atmosphere and slammed into the earth.

This meteorite is recorded around the world as "THE MILLARVILLE METEORITE" and has been placed on permanent display in the University of Calgary's Gallagher Library of Geology. Small pieces were taken from one end and are on display at the Smithsonian, Institute The National Museum in Ottawa, The British Museum, and the University of Southern California.

Geodotic Survey

Geodotic Survey of Canada, Triangulation Station No. 27605, commonly named Priddis. From survey observations, it has a known position, Latitude 50°, 50', 16" north, Longitude 114°, 15', 30.6" West.

This station was one of many established in the national framework control system in 1927. The station is marked on the ground by a bronze tablet set in a foot square and a two foot high cement monument. This station is located in S.E.¼ section 6, Township 22, Range 2, W.5, M. This station and other stations in the area form a basic reference framework structure for various surveys required for engineering, mapping, property definition, and other purposes.

Chuck Hayward and the Millarville Meteorite.

In much the same way that the skeleton of the human body has the job of supporting the various physical organs in their correct relative positions, allowing them to function in harmony, Geodotic markers enable various types of surveys to be tied into each other properly.

^{0} — degrees
' — minute
" — second.

A Brief Summary of Home — Millarville Wells
Nos. 1 and 2 at Millarville
by Russell F. King

Early in the spring of 1937 I was working on Floyd Welker's rigging-up crew in "Little Chicago". After rigging up and spudding Granville No. 1, Three Point No. 1, Model-Spooner-Reward No. 1 and National No. 1 we were moved to Millarville in June to rig up Home-Millarville No. 1 in L.S.D. 8 Sec. 33-20-3-W5. It was a new "Oil Well" unit owned by Home Oil; H. R. "Bid" Lowery was their popular Field Superintendent, Dr. J. O. G. "Pete" Sanderson was geologist and Snyder & Head were the drilling contractors. This hole was eventually abandoned in Nov. or Dec. of 1937 after many mechanical difficulties due to a crooked hole. I believe this well is now known as Home-Millarville No. 1A.

In April 1938 the rig was moved a quarter mile west to L.S.D. 6 in the same section to drill H.M. No. 2. Newell and Chandler were the drilling contractors. This well eventually bottomed at 8495 feet with a bot-

tom hole pressure of 3030 lbs. per square inch and a casing head pressure of 1990 lbs. per square inch. I believe it eventually produced slightly over a million and half barrels of A.P.I. 41 gravity oil which, I believe, was a record for Turner Valley.

About Dec. 18, 1938 I started to work for Home Oil, welding some water lines that had been frozen. A few days later I worked a 25-hour shift for Newell & Chandler helping to remove and lay down drill pipe, then run in tubing and install the well head and hook up a line to the flare pit. The well was swabbed about Dec. 27 and shut in until the next day, when the well head pressure had reached 1000 pounds. Don Campbell and I blew the well to clear it of any remaining drilling fluid. Home Oil management were all there, as well as Pete Sanderson and many others. Everyone was very happy and excited, as well as the Newell & Chandler crew.

The well was shut in for a few days to give it a small acid wash, then blown clear and started steady producing about Jan. 3, 1939. "Don" Victor Odlum became our field manager and Al Jensen arrived about the same time to fill out our original crew of four.

As drilling increased more operators were needed, as well as lease crew, and new personnel were hired.

After war was declared in Sept. 1939 Don Odlum, who was a Captain in the reserve army, left soon to go in the army. His brother, Nelson Odlum, became our new field manager until he left to go in the army early in 1940. He was followed by Gordon Webster in Feb. 1940, as field manager.

As well as those already mentioned, others we enjoyed working with until I left in March 1943 included, and I hope I haven't missed anyone,

Home Millarville blowing in. 1943.

George McIvor
Winston Parker
Harold Kelly
Herb Wiggins
Bill Kelly
Erick Mulder
Dan Campbell
Ray Endicott
Bill Stewart
Bill Gallup
Jack Fulton
John Hallgren
Hugh McNain

Charlie Nolan
Rudy Mulder
Jimmy Stafford
Fred Hall
Tom Bleasedale
Bill McIntyre
Percy Bennett
Les Foster
Chubby Foster
Tom Lyall
Jim Fraser
Herb Kirkland
"Peace River Mac" McLeod

Jack Thompson
Bob Washington
Hugh Willford

Dude Willford
Dave Welsh

Men still working when Home Oil took over:

Grant Burquist
Harlin Hanson
Hjalmar Nylund

Everett Potter
John Schick
Vern Theissen

QUIRK CREEK GAS PLANT — by Art Duitman

Following the oil play of the middle to late thirties, when the Turner Valley field expanded north and west into the Millarville ranching country, rancher and oil man settled down to routine co-existence. The oil men extracted their oil, separated and shipped it in buried pipe lines to market. The only evidence of them being in the area was the occasional battery or pumper, and several gas flares visible at night dotted against the hills.

Time passed with the usual series of good and bad years, cattle prices fluctuating, late spring storms with resultant calf crop losses; wells dying off, and flow lines plugging up, until the years 1968, '69 and '70 when another type of oilmen came to the district: These were the gas men who were searching for gas pools known to exist along the foothills of the Rocky Mountains.

Major Oil

by H. Hanson

About 1940, Fred Shoultz, along with Mr. Bell and Mr. Harris formed a company, Major Gas, Oils and Waterlines. They had two rigs drilling at one time, but most of their work was done in production, laying pipe lines, putting in separators, and general bull gang work. Later they started Western Petroleum. Mel Fulton was field boss for many years. They employed over seventy men. Some of the batterys were Major 1, 2, 3, and 4. Some of the first men on production were Jack Robertson, Bob Washington, Mark Hovis and Everett Potter. These were good jobs at $4.20 per day.

After fifteen years on the bull gang then on production, Jack Schick was field superintendent until the field was unitized and Home Oil took over and the operators were dismissed.

Continental became another branch of the company and moved into the Leduc field.

The names of men who at some time worked for Major Oil are the following:

Sid Adams
Hans Backs
Nate Beebe
Lloyd Beatty
Gordon Barker
Grant Burquist
Hank Burquist
Ralph Campbell
Granville Ducheney
Phil Ducheney
Morris Edwards
George Fox
Mell Fulton
Big Gurb
Bill Gent
Glen Hanson
Harlin Hanson
Al Hagen
Glen Hazen
Albert Hughes
Dan Hume
Ivan (Slim) Haynes
Jim Kerr
Dick Lyall

Elmer Lohner
Vern Mowatt
Pete McNary
Rod McKenzie
Al Moody
Dan Matheson
Ben Mitchell
Frank Nelson
Lorne Mitchell
Hjalmar Nylund
Bill Nutt
Sid Peel
Edwin Peat
Seth Peat
Everett Potter
Jack Robertson
John Schick
Ed Swiffen
Len Smith
Fred Scott
Vern Theissen
Jake Severen
Ardell Tollefson
Norman Tollefson

Quirk Creek Gas Plant.

97

The survey crews had been in the country several years earlier. They crisscrossed the land, measuring elevations and distances, and fastening their little flags for each "Jug" and "Shot" location. Working along with the Surveyors were the Geophysical men with their long strings of cable.

The first well was drilled early in 1968 by Columbia Northland on a farm-out from Imperial Oil Ltd., on 6-5-21-4 W5 just inside the Forest Reserve, with the second on John Kendall's land north of his home. Six other wells were drilled in rapid succession, three farther west and three south. Two "dry" holes were also drilled. A total of 450 Billion cubic feet of gas estimated to be stored below the rolling hills.

The decision was made to build a gas plant on 2 and 3-4-21-4 W5, two miles west of Kendall's Mill. This was something new for the Millarville district, and posed a serious problem to residents and livestock, as the gas was sour, i.e. very poisonous, and ninety million cubic feet would be processed each day.

The residents naturally voiced their concern at several meetings with the Gas men and members of the Conservation Board. The Plant was to be built despite their objections, and Stearns-Rogers were hired to design and construct the Plant.

A constant stream of men and equipment passed through Millarville during 1970. Huge trucks became a familiar sight along the district roads; a few large towers even required two trucks, one driving forward and the other backing up. These very heavy loads were not allowed on Highway 22 and were transported on back roads and past Millarville Race Track.

The Plant slowly rose on the shoulder of the hill, with the three hundred and fifty foot stack towering above the surrounding area — even some of the lower hills.

The men required to operate the Plant arrived in the summer of 1970 for their training program. Six of these moved with their families to Turner Valley, one found his home in Millarville, three others at Priddis, and the balance decided to enjoy city life in Calgary. Mr. Murray Jackson of Millarville and his men were kept busy on road construction and grading.

Construction of the plant was completed, ready for production, by February, 1971. Gas was turned on first of all from the well on Kendall's land, to pressure up the Plant. The emergency shut-down system was tested, depressuring the Plant and creating the first huge flare from the lower one hundred foot stack. The Plant was again pressured up, pumps for the various fluids were started, and more gas was turned into the Plant through the well heaters at the wells. After about four hours of flaring gas, the gas was sweet and was turned into the sales gas pipe line.

The next few days were very busy, with more wells being started and Plant production increasing to the ninety million mark. There were the usual start-up problems to be solved, but the Plant continued to operate and a sulphur block started to grow — a bright yellow block beside the Plant. From then on sulphur trucks were to be seen on the road to Okotoks.

Years have passed with the usual ranch problems, and Plant problems and co-existence between rancher and oil man continues much as before.

Submitted by Art Duitman, who is an Instrument Technologist with Essor Resources Canada in Calgary.

Oksi Hill Garden — Portion-N.E.¼-Twp21-Rge.3-W.5
by Mary Julia Dover O.B.E., C.M., D.U.C.

1978 may well be the year of the trees. After a long winter of snow, and a fairly damp spring, there was a burgeoning of flowering by the crabapples, hawthorns, maydays, willows followed by lilacs and honeysuckles. More than ever, wild roses bloomed throughout the summer. These were the foundation of the garden.

Oksi Hill was purchased in 1958, a small panabode built in 1960, added to in 1961 and later in 1971. The origin of the name came from David Crowchild, chief of the Sarcee Indians, who with his sons fenced the property. Each day at noon, when there was a luncheon break, David would smilingly say "Oksi", "Oksi" — "This is good". On being questioned, he explained that the word meant good, happy, welcome, and came from the Blackfoot. After gaining the Chief's permission, the property was registered with the name Oksi Hill, and imprinted in hieroglyphics on the surround of the fireplace. The tiles were the handwork of Ceramic Arts, Calgary.

How is a garden founded, or conceived, or designed? The land of Oksi Hill acreage reaches from its northern fence at the south edge of Chance's Lake, up a great steep hill, its northern slope clothed in a forest of coniferous and deciduous trees, beneath which is deep, thick growth of shade-loving shrubs, and a dense carpet of flowers and mosses. It is no ordinary woodlot. Black birch are a good size, and two white birches were found amongst them. Up the steepest slope, Cornus or dogwood grow from the water to the crest, changing colour with each season from brilliant sealing wax over snow to summer green. There is a wild cranberry patch. In spring, buds show deep red. The following leaves a little like

Mary Julia Dover O.B.E., C.M., D.U.C.

98

maples — green in summer, red in fall, and clusters of white flowers turn to bright scarlet fruits, sharp to taste, but attractive to small flocks of grossbeaks and waxwings.

The southern slope of the great hill is bare of trees, but clothed in thick growth of bunch grass, the fodder of the buffalo, and natural drifts of sun and chinook-loving field flowers, bergamot, daisies. Early each year, life returns with the chinook and the first sight of the crocus followed quickly by shooting stars. Annora Brown gives them the delightful name of Indian Chief. The hill levels into a saucer where there are sloughs — willows, no springs, but deep fertile black soil.

Throughout the first few years, steps were faltering because of real waste through abysmal ignorance. Probably this was for the best, as soil values and plant preferences had to be discovered. Best examples are probably — if blueberries grow at Rocky Mountain House, surely here. If the flag of Canada must contain the maple leaf, "Acer Saccharum", it must prosper. The different acid and alkali, sun and shade tolerance, coupled with the diversity of zone, had to be learned.

On a day long before Canada's 100th birthday, a cheerful voice said on the telephone, "The Samaritan Club has reserved 10 centennial crabapples for you. Will you please pick them up. The bill is $2.50 each. Thus, the collection of flowering trees began.

An early pleasure of the garden was discovery of ancient paths. Animals, wild and later tame, had followed each other to grass, water and migration, their life span since time forgotten. Later, the Jackson and Standish children walked and rode to Fordville School over a still well-marked trail. There is never an ending, rather a crossroad turning toward another

separate direction. It is beside the paths that plantings have been made.

A long row of peonies bloom in early July. They are double and single, red, pink, and white. Nearby, pears, Preston lilacs and honeysuckles. Farther around the large slough, apples — Dolgo and Rescue — bloom and bear fruit. At the south end a Pinetum has its beginnings, with Ponderosa, Bristle Cone, Swiss Stone, Austrian, and Lodge Pole. Spruce — Norway, Green and Blue, also Koster. Many are of a great size. There are two firs, the Douglas or Abies Taxifolia and a Mountain Fir, a gift from Western British Columbia.

Junipers are well represented. The native upright Scopulorum and imported Blue Haven, as well as many of the prostrate varieties, blue, green, purple, gold.

Oksi Hill would be nothing without its wild flowers. Beside curves in the paths clumps of Anemone Canadensis turn in the wind — also Arnica, Clovers, Fleabane and tall Asters. After rain, violets are underfoot, the little Early Blue and Ramping White Wood Violet. A yellow amusement is Zizia Aptera or Heart-Leaved Alexander. In their rarity, Smilacina Racemosa and Stellata appear in hidden patches. There are many more.

Oksi Hill has become an absorbing interest and constant challenge. Perhaps in one hundred years it may have matured. It is a private garden, the venture solely of the owner. There have been no grants or assistance, and none applied for.

Visitors are welcome — Sunday for tea seems best. One of the greatest pleasures is to welcome busloads and carloads of old age pensioners. Their day is Thursday.

Chapter 8
Utilities

The Millarville Rural Electrification Association Limited

In the late 1940s some of the residents of Millarville and east, were getting tired of the constant trouble with the individual power plants, or worse yet, the lamps and the lanterns — they saw too, that actually the power wasn't too far away, if only they could get together and bring it into the area.

A great deal of time and effort by F. E. B. Gourlay, R. H. King and R. G. Spooner, together with the other 11 members, was put into the job of organizing a co-operative to bring electric power into the area. They realized that except for water, electricity was the greatest asset to farm living. The other 11 original members were: T. Jamison, N. E. Hoy, W. M. Johnson, T. Pekse, J. R. King, G. W. Bull, W. C. Parker, MacKay Brothers, B. T. Chalmers, E. J. Preston, G. C. Smale.

There was the odd lighter moment in the frustrating days of canvassing, planning, meeting, etc. They told later of calling at this one particular house, and when asked the question as to whether he would like power they got this answer, "What the hell do I want power for? My bank account is my power". He never did take the power. At another house the farmer said no, whereby the lady of the house spoke up and said — "you've never gotten anything for me in all these years — you're getting the power for me now." He was one of the original members.

Different meetings were held with various officers of Calgary Power, and various routes were discussed, until on June 12, 1950, the members met and it was unanimously agreed that the Millarville Rural Electrification Association Limited be formed as a co-operative for the purpose of securing power in the Millarville and surrounding area. For the first meeting all were in favor of R. G. Spooner as Chairman and R. H. King as secretary of the meeting.

Following the meeting all the Director's held a Director's meeting with Mr. Anderson, Calgary Power representative. At this meeting F. E. B. Gourlay was elected President, R. H. King as Vice-President and R. G. Spooner secretary. Their charter was granted on June 28th, 1950.

Soon the financing was all arranged, construction was begun, and in short while the electric lights came on in the area. There is the story being told about one household where the electricity was put in. A new refrigerator was bought — however there was complaints that it didn't keep the food very well, upon investigation by the salesman it was discovered that the plug was pulled out every night to save on the use of electricity.

Mr. Spooner resigned as secretary in 1952, and his place was taken by Mrs. Anne Standish, while in 1954, B. T. Chalmers took over from Mr. Gourlay as President, as Mr. Gourlay was leaving the area. In 1956, Mr. Chalmers resigned due to ill health, and F. Ball has been president from that time.

In 1952, extensions were added to the east, and to the north, and from that time on, it has continued to grow. From the small beginning of 14 members it has now over 400 members, and covers a large area. It stretches west along the Sarcee Reserve, with the reserve as its north boundary, almost to Bragg Creek, the forest reserve is the west boundary, to a point west and south of Turner Valley, angling again north and east to take in members south and east of the immediate Millarville area. The Eastern boundary is a line north and slightly east of the Millarville Church.

It is a far cry from the faint lamplight dotted sparsely through the area, which was the way it once was, to the myriads of lights dotted everywhere, as one drives into the area at night.

Memorandum of Association Meota Gas Co-operative Association Ltd.

Registered June 19th, 1962.
1. Robert Chalmers, Millarville, Rancher.
2. Stanley Jones, R.R. No. 1, Midnapore, Field Supervisor.
3. H. C. Bond, Priddis, Rancher.
4. Jas. Griffith, Priddis, Rancher.
5. Hugh Powell, Priddis, Shipping Clerk.
6. W. J. Rishaug, Millarville, Oil Worker.
7. D. E. Evans, R.R. No. 1, Midnapore, Rancher.
8. John Schaal, R.R. No. 1, Midnapore, Rancher.
9. C. R. Hopper, Priddis, Rancher.
10. Leo Ohlhauser, Turner Valley, Rancher.

Meota Gas

by Stan Jones

Meota Gas Cooperative Ass'n is Alberta's first consumer owned and operated gas utility. The idea was developed and the association formed in Millarville, but for the first ten years it operated mainly in the Priddis district.

When the Alberta Gas Trunk Line was put through the district in 1960, the first question everyone asked was if gas would be available to the farms and villages along the way. The answer was yes, but not until the system had been in operation for at least one year. In the meantime a Gas Services Advisory committee had been set up to work out the details of gas service for the farm hook-ups. This body, with J. G. McGregor as chairman, decided that the stretch within the Municipal District of Foothills would be turned over to Valley Gas Co.

A canvass of the area was made by officers of this company, and all potential consumers were interviewed. We felt that while the price to be charged per M.C.F. was quite reasonable, the monthly service charge of $6.00 was too high. Despite the fact that the first two M.C.F. were included in that figure, Meota charges $2.00 per month. The main objection was their insistance that the cost of regulation equipment, meter and the cost of installing it, had to be financed by the company and could not be paid for in cash. Their estimate of the cost involved was $400.00 and interest at 12% would be charged monthly. At the present time this does not seem an abnormally high rate of interest, but at that time it was considered exorbitant. We appealed to the Public Utilities Board, but were told they had no jurisdiction in the matter; a further appeal to the Advisory Committee resulted in a meeting with Mr. McGregor who assured us of his sympathy but stuck to his original decision. Only one man in the entire area had accepted the deal as outlined at that time, and while the rest of us stalled, we were told by a representative of the company that if the taps were not made before the line was pressured up, we would be out of luck. Fortunately, we found that provision had been made for taps anywhere they might be needed, when the line was installed.

About this time at the annual Credit Union banquet in Calgary, I was talking to Harold Webber of the Cooperative Activities Branch and mentioned our problem. He was very interested, as he was a member of the Gas Advisory group and said that he had been unaware of the details of the proposition which had been made to us. He asked if we had ever considered forming a cooperative utility as a charter had recently been issued to a group of the Lethbridge area and suggested that we investigate.

Bob Chalmers, the late Harry Denning Sr., and I drove down to Sunnyslope just outside Lethbridge, where a Mr. Chapman very kindly drove us around their small system which had been installed, and was to be operated by Canadian Western. He also gave us all the financial details which we found were the same as for rural electrification. We called a meeting to be held in Millarville school and as a result the decision was made to form a gas cooperative. Present at the meeting was Jack Fears representing Glaholt and Associates, a Calgary engineering firm. This began a long and fruitful association, as without Jack's drive and determination, it is doubtful if Meota would have lasted long. Ten men had the courage and foresight to put up a dollar each to become the charter members. It took courage to put up the dollar, and the foresight is reflected in the fact that there are now thousands of farms enjoying natural gas service provided by cooperatives.

The following summer can only be described as frustrating. While we had the wholehearted support of the Cooperative Activities Branch, the support of the Dept. of Mines and Minerals was less enthusiastic. In fact, we got the distinct impression that somewhere behind the scenes there were forces at work determined to see the demise of Meota before it got off the ground. This was where Jack Fears really shone. He had dealt with the Government before, and as soon as we were slapped down in one direction, Jack would go at it from another direction.

Application to install a line to the Chalmer's buildings went astray while a similar application from Valley Gas was approved and we had a line cutting our potential territory in two. Letters to Edmonton had accomplished nothing until Jack Fears suggested a personal letter to Premier Manning. Just two days later we had a call from a deputy minister's secretary requesting a meeting, which was no problem, and the following day a carload of minor officials arrived and were taken on a tour of the area. Later, while my wife fed them tea and cookies, they looked over our plans, checked our finances, thanked us for a pleasant afternoon and left. We were then asked to set up a meeting with Mr. Somerville, deputy minister of Mines and Minerals, in Calgary for the following week. We held the meeting at Glaholt's office and it was almost a case of standing room only. After an hour or so, Mr. Somerville appeared quite satisfied that we knew what we were doing, and told us to re-submit our applications for permits and he would approve them the same day. We felt that the battle was won but there was one fly in the ointment. It was then Oct. 22nd and normally very close to freeze up. It would be uncharitable to wonder if this had influenced Mr. Somerville, but we had an exceptional fall, and by Christmas C. R. Hopper, Herb Bond, John Schaal, Elwyn Evans and I were enjoying natural gas service.

These installations were made with iron pipe as plastic pipe had not yet been licensed for underground gas lines, and during the winter we read everything available on the possible use of plastic gas pipe, with the result that when it was approved the next summer we were ready to install several miles to service a further group of thirteen farms. Tom Adams had taken on the job of supervising construction and was prepared to learn about plastic pipe on the job. We were advised by the supplier to cement the thirty foot lengths of P.V.C. two inch pipe together with the couplings provided, lay it over the ditch on short boards or posts, leave it overnight to dry, and lower it into the ditch the next morning. The first stretch was a most imposing sight that night, but the next morning it was a different story as it all came apart. There were more long faces in Priddis that morning than there were when the result of the 1936? election was announced. Phone calls were made, telegrams sent, and soon the scene was swarming with experts. The explanation was fairly simple — while the pipe was P.V.C., the couplings were A.B.S. and the two will not stick. After the joints were all cleaned with solvent and the proper couplings used, there were no further problems.

In the following years, the system expanded slowly as even with the use of plastic pipe, the cost was quite high. We suggested to the provincial government that they consider a revolving credit plan similar to that used to finance rural electrification, but their feeling at the time was that until natural gas was available over most of the province this was not feasible. After the present government came up with their assistance plan, business really picked up, and at the end of 1978, there were 201 outlets in our franchise area.

Since the first year, Tom Adams has been in charge of all new construction and has acted as serviceman. Jack Fears has transferred his enthusiasm to other fields, and Jim Lineham is now resident engineer. I acted as Secretary Treasurer for three years, then Secretary Manager until retiring in 1974. John Patterson has been president for several years and when the position of Bookkeeper was created, Mrs. Geo. Park filled that office for sometime. Mrs. Jack Steen is now in charge of that end of the business.

Chapter 9
General Articles

Municipal Government

contributed by L. C. Van Tighem

Stockland No. 191 was gazetted as a small Improvement District January 15, 1913. It comprised all Township 22 Range 1 W5th, and all Townships 19, 20, 21 and 22 in Ranges 2 and 3 west of the fifth Meridian. The records have some gaps and it would appear from the information on file with Department of Municipal Affairs, Edmonton that the Councillors for the area were as follows:

Division 1 — J. A. Grant 1915-23; Norman F. Brown 1924-25; R. W. McKinnon; W. J. Lockhart; E. W. Gould.

Division 2 — H. Denning 1915-22 (grandfather of Harry Denning); and J. T. Broomfield 1924-28.

Division 3 — W. Edgerton 1915-16; Gerald Webster 1917; There is an interim period when J. A. MacKay was councillor in 1918; B. T. Chalmers 1918-21; Chas. Billings 1922-23; A. J. Cawthorne 1924-43. Mr. Cawthorne represented the area on the Executive of the Association of Municipal Districts and Counties for one term — 1942.

Division 4 — J. Standish 1915-20 and J. R. Kieran 1921-42.

Division 5 — J. Sheepy 1915; R. Sheepy 1916; J. R. Godlonton 1917; Walter G. Birney 1918-1955. Mr. Birney was a councillor when Stockland became part of the M. D. of Turner Valley in 1944 and he continued on when Turner Valley was amalgamated with the M.D. of Highwood in 1954 to form the M.D. of Foothills.

Division 6 — R. Stanton 1915-21; W. Bannerman 1922; C. J. Standish 1923-37; T. Van Wyk 1938; W. W. Stewart 1939-43.

Division 7 — In February 1922 there was a Ministerial Order which changed the divisional boundaries and a new division was added. Mr. George Silvester was the only councillor this division had, and he like Mr. Birney was a councillor in the M.D. of Turner Valley during its existence and a councillor in the M.D. of Foothills until 1955.

It is evident from the above that the Councillors were dedicated men who had the respect of their electorate judging by the length of the terms.

There are seven divisions in the M.D. of Foothills No. 31. Division 4 covers Range 3, 4 and part of 5, west to the Forest Reserve, north to the Sarcee Reserve, and south to Sheep Creek.

Following the history through after Mr. Silvester left municipal life he was followed by Bob Carry. Mr. R. L. Carry served M.D. of Stockland from 1941-43; M. D. of Turner Valley 1944-53; and M.D. of Foothills 1955-65. Mr. Tom Davenport, Priddis, served for five years 1966-70. The present representative of the area is Fred Ball who started council in 1971.

The first Secretary shown on the Department record was Mr. E. A. Hayes who was also Secretary of the M.D. of Sheep Creek 190. He was followed by Mr. Percy F. Peirson from 1916 to 1920. In 1921 George McKee became Secretary and he continued until 1925. W. H. King then became Secretary Treasurer. He held this position for 16 years until ill health forced his retirement. Angus MacKay filled out the term until Stockland became part of the M.D. of Turner Valley in 1944 when Mr. Percy Wray was appointed Secretary. After the amalgamation L. C. Van Tighem was secretary treasurer until December, 1976. Mr. T. J. Motil took over the position in 1977.

Place Names of Millarville-Kew

Ardmore Ranch. Original home of A. P. Welsh and named by him. Later known as Spooner Ranch, now Cross' Bar Pipe Ranch.

Big Horn Ranger Station. Named for the Big Horn Sheep which have always been in abundance there. Harry Holness had squatters rights here, sold to the Gov't in 1907, to be used as part of the Forest Reserve.

Brown-Lowery Natural Area. Section 25-21-4W5. Formerly deMille land. Bought by Home Oil and presented to Alberta Gov't.

Bucher's Mine. Well known place in Forest Reserve. Named for Warren Bucher, who had mine there.

Cache Ranger Station, on North Fork of Sheep Creek.

Coal Mine Hill. Here Joseph Fisher had a coal mine about 1910-12.

Death Valley. Fisher riders found skelton of a white man here, thought to be a trapper who had gone into the area and disappeared. The men brought the skull to Fisher's Meadow, where it was placed on a fence post and sometimes used as a football.

Death Valley Creek, sometimes called Sinnot Creek for nephew of John Quirk, who settled for a time on land on this creek.

Fisher Creek, named for Joseph Fisher, first settler in the area.

Forget-Me-Not Mountain. Was a look-out station.

Fordville School. Mr. Ford had the land on which the school was built.

Frenchmen Place. Name given to two places, the de Roaldes ranch at Kew and the deMalherbe ranch at Millarville.

Frenchmen Valley. A valley north of Fisher Ranch. Several Frenchmen homesteaded here.

Hoadley Hill. Once owned by Mr. Hoadley. S.E.¼ of 6-22-2W5.

Pratt Valley. Named for early settler, north of Jackson's ranch west of Millarville. Became the site of many oil producing wells and where the small settlement of Majorville was.

Rancher's Hall. First community hall in Millarville area. Built on Fisher's ranch, N.E.¼ of 6-21-3W5. Now in Heritage Park.

Sheep Creek Canyon. Well known attraction in Forest Reserve.

Smiley's Cabin. Trappers cabin on Ware Creek, in Forest Reserve. Named for Lee Smiley, who had a trapline in the area. He was found dead in his cabin. Lloyd Middleton has a cabin there now, also a trapline.

Square Butte. Largest hill in these foothills, 5552 feet above sea level. Named for its square shape when looked at from the east.

Turner Valley. This valley starts a mile south of Millarville. Named for the Turner family who ranched where the hamlet of Millarville is now, and ranged their horses in the valley.

Waite Valley. A valley running south from the North Fork of Sheep Creek. Named for Mrs. Mary Waite and her son Joe Waite, who homesteaded on the west half of section 25-20-4W5.

Ware Creek, Ware Mountain and Ware Ridge. All named for John Ware, early rancher of the Kew area.

Whiskey Creek. This was on the trail used by whiskey runners to bring in liquor illegally.

Windy Point. On the road to the Big Horn Ranger Station.

Yeskey Creek. Near South Sheep Creek. Named for a very early rancher.

Hunter Sheep camp. A Mr. Hunter pastured a large band of sheep here in the Forest Reserve.

Johnson Hill. Steep hill up from Fisher Creek bridge. Probably more accidents here than on any other.

Kew Post Office and District. Named by George Bell, first postmaster by spelling Quirk's Q brand.

Macabee Gap. At south end of Ware Ridge. Named for Macabee Brothers, early ranchers in the area.

Majorville. A small settlement of oil workers, named for Major Oil Co.

Merino Pass. Between Kew and Bragg Creek. Louis Merino had ranch by the small lake.

Mesa Creek. Small creek in Kew area.

Millarville. Named for Malcolm Millar, first postmaster.

Morley Trail. This trail started at Morley, through Bragg Creek and on south. Used by the Stoney Indians before the white men came, as a trail to hunting grounds further south, and used until recently fenced.

Muskeg. Area in the Forest Reserve for cattle grazing by members of North Fork Cattle Association.

Muskeg Creek. Tributary of North Sheep Creek (Three Point).

Nigger Quarter. Homestead of Chat Bloss, taken over by Tom Spencer, a well liked Negro who lived there for several years, died in old log shack there. Now owned by Tucker and Ross.

North Fork of Sheep Creek. In recent years named Three Point Creek, and in very early years, Quirk Creek.

Plummer's Corner. N.E.¼ 35-21-3W5, once part of the Bradfield Ranch then owned by Pat Burns, then by Jim Plummer, who came from England. His house was the first on this land.

Pothole Creek. Small creek in east Millarville, runs through Cawthorne ranch and through Bar Pipe Ranch.

Bits From The Past
by Billy Trevenan

Summer is coming and I have just had a letter from Mrs. Nylund about a further edition of "Our Foothills". I don't think it needs any improvement, but will try and think up a few things. There is mention in the book of the flu epidemic in 1918 and 1919. I was in that as I was not working, so I helped flu patients for three months, and it was chiefly owing to the fact that I had a couple of bottles of whiskey in my saddle pockets that I was able to help, as a hot drink at the right time saved several who would have gone, otherwise. One lady, who was a strict teetotaler, was very ill but her husband said we would have to do something, so we got a dose of whiskey with a couple of aspirins and we took turns all night keeping her covered. She got rather hot but woke up the next morning and her temperature was normal and she got all right. I don't think she ever knew what cut her sickness and her husband never told her, I know that.

I stopped in to see another man who was supposed to be sick (he was). He lived in a big house with a little stove burning briquets in the corner of a big room. It was 42 below outside and nearly that inside. I kept my chaps on all night as he had the only bed. The next one was not so lucky; he died while the Mountie who came along and I were trying to help. Incidentally, without the Mounties it would have been a very rough winter. They were good people.

I kept on going north to Calgary and stopped at Mr. Parkers west of Midnapore. They were all sick. Frank Blake arrived, coming from Calgary. The hired man had died in the night and small Jessie was the only one

Bridge party at N. W. Pegler's, Nov. 1938. L. to R. Irene Evans, Erick Mulder, Selina Hambling, Mrs. Pegler, Elwyn Evans, Charlie Nelson, (clowning with false moustache and monocle), Mrs. W. H. King, W. H. King, Mrs. Nelson, Mrs. W. Jackson.

who seemed to be on the mend. Frank went to the barn as the cow had not been milked or the horses fed for 2 days. Jessie and I went to work in the house, got some hot food into the rest of the family. Frank and I stayed a week and got the family back on the beam. It was a rough winter, that was.

Another trip a couple of years after that, I had a bunch of colts for Mr. E. J. Kieran on my place west of Kew. They were doing all right, but we had a Chinook for a day, then it switched right back to 30 below and froze the whole country into a sheet of ice. No chance for horses to feed so had to get them out in a hurry. I cut the heads off 4 sheaves of oats and took a few feeds of oats on the pony. I got them to MacKays the first day and got them on the road early the next morning. I was glad the last mile was down hill as the colts would get off the road in the deep snow and had to be pulled back onto the road by main strength and it was getting a bit short by the time we got home.

Trips with horses in the old days — Trucks were just starting. I went to Harold Bannister on the Bow to get a mare that Mr. Cochrane had bought. I led her off on an English saddle. She had crippled two horses when they had tried to lead her but she knew I was green and I led her 40 odd miles and had no trouble. As my old Scotch boss said "The Di'el looks after his ane," could be the explanation.

One trip I have never forgotten, I picked up a Clyde gelding for Mr. Adams. The horse weighed 1900 lbs. and was really mean. He had got away from a dray and got back to just west of Okotoks where he was raised. He led until we got around Midnapore, then he started running past me and kicking at my horse, so I got off and put a new rope on him, put a half-hitch round his nose, tied the end to a telephone pole and threw my hat at him. It took him a few minutes to get on his feet again and then he came the rest of the way like a gentleman.

I had a nice job another spring, I looked after the stallions for Mr. Adams and he got me to take them out to various places they were to stand that summer. The first one went to Kew; I walked him out to Kierans from Victoria Park where they had been all winter, and left at 6 in the morning on the 20 odd mile walk to Kew. We both enjoyed it. The next one was McNeill; he went to Springbank just across the river from Clem Gardner's. He was a gay big horse and was a handful at times. It was quite a thrill standing on a hill west of Calgary and seeing the city laid out below you. The big horse made quite a picture, standing, looking all over the country as if he owned it and was just waiting for his mares to come out and join him.

The next one was John Jacket; he went 50 miles northwest of Edmonton. We left Edmonton at 4 in the morning in a C.N.R. freight car and we stopped every time we came to a wide place in the road. All the crew got out and sat in the sun for awhile and talked to the natives. We got our 50 miles just after noon and I had four miles to walk him in and the mosquitos — they were the kind that bite a piece out then fly up in a tree to eat it. I put a blanket on the stud and he got there all right. Then Mr. Adams asked me to go to High River and get Rivetter out of there. He had wrecked two outfits that had tried to move him, so I got Pete Gerlitz and we went down. He would load all right then start to kick things to bits, so we loaded him and there were two sharp turns before we got on the road. He was just starting to act up so Pete hit the first turn on high. He had just started to go up in the air but he lost the truck and had no place to go. He just got back on his feet when we hit the next turn. He went down again. He travelled 200 miles like a baby.

Among the men who could do things I never could do were Eddie Bowlen and Jappy Rodgers; they could ride a rough horse and give a good one lessons. Then I rode for awhile with D. P. McDonald; he would ride a horse all morning in the Ghost River country, pull the saddle off him at noon and you would think he had just started. He was the easiest big man on a horse I ever saw and his horses were nearly clean thoroughbred.

Then there was Little Arthur who rode Lowes' high jumpers. He rode a horse for a bet at the 1912 Stampede. The Texans and Mexicans could not believe their eyes.

In the days before Women's Lib was with us, a lot of girls held up their end. The Sexsmith girls were from High River (they rode side saddle). I have seen the eldest girl tie her horse up to a corral and get on him alone and turn him loose and he would buck for at least a quarter of a mile, then he would settle down. I always thought Bun Dewdney (who died last month) was one of the tops. She could ride a turning pony or a five gaited horse and rode a good race. Also Nan Black was a good girl on a racehorse. They both rode horses for Old Joe at Chinook. Penny Ridge, who is still with us, was another good race rider. You can add May Atkins and Mildred to the list with Audrey and Joan Gardner and the Littlewoods. They could all ride anything. I've left out a lot of people, but I worked with all these. Cochrane has always had a lot of good riders. I judged a show up there once and had 16 girls, 18 and under, all on nearly Thoroughbred ponies. I looked at them and said, "I wonder if you could ride bare back." They were all off their ponies, the saddles in front of them, grinning at me. I worked them hard and you could not beat them. I tossed up for the prizes as they were all good. In the old days, the girls used to tie a dress on their saddles and change at the dance.

These are memories that one is proud of, a grand lot of people.

Kew Memories

by Leslie Foster

The old Kew store and post office has disappeared and with it many of the old characters who have gone the way of all men. So, in tribute to these old timers and also to refresh the memory of those that still remember, I will attempt to recall a little of the life as I saw it some fifty years ago.

Take old Joe Waugh, for instance. He hauled the mail from Midnapore to Kew Post office every Tuesday and Friday the year round through hell and high water and I don't use the phrase loosely. He kept a relay team at Priddis. One time I remember, Sheep Creek was running high and wild with days of heavy rain. Old Joe just lit up his stub of a pipe, pulled the harness off the horses, threw the mail bags on one and rode the other into the swollen creek and swam them across. He arrived at Kew a little late but as unconcerned as if it was a regular occurance. Now, that's what I call mail service.

There was a hitching rail in front of the Kew store and the characters that hung their reins over that pole would put western fiction to shame. Men as different as day and night but all with the same belief that this was the greatest country that God ever created. They gathered in the evening to get their mail and visit a little after their days work was over.

There was Walter Phillips, with his close clipped mustache and high pitched English accent. You could tell him away off in the evening dusk, as he sat one sided in the saddle, sort of off centre like and rode a high headed prancing sorrel mare. Walter was a joker and always had people laughing. He said that when he left the old country so many girls came to kiss him good-bye that they capsized the boat. At this stage, Mrs. Phillips "Georgie" would say "Walter" and the old boy would shift his feet a bit and look down at the ground and grin and you knew darn well he was already cooking up another story.

From the west another fast stepping horse would come into view and you could tell by the stately figure in the saddle it was Gene Kendall from the former Quirk Ranch, a slow speaking American. He wore well fitting buckskin jacket and chaps. Gene was a shrewd business man and a real friend to those who knew him well.

In from the south would come John Gettig riding a big Hamiltonian "Old Bones" they called him. He had been injured as a colt and healed with a crumpled muzzle but he was all horse. John came from the States, Pennsylvania, and a better hearted and hospitable man you will never find and his good wife, without a doubt, could grow the best garden, fry the best chicken and make the best beet wine of anyone from Pouce Coupe to the Ozarks.

As the shadows grew longer and old Joe was about due with the mail, you would hear the sharp clip clip of a big single-footer crossing the creek behind the store and my dad, Harry Foster, would literally shoot up to the hitching rail aboard that good road horse Paddy, known for miles around for his road eating gait.

These old boys all kept road horses for fast travel over long trips. Good horses around cattle but exceptional for stamina and speed. A fast horse was the only dependable means of transportation in a hurry. My dad had long bushy eyebrows that gave him a fierce look but he was gentle underneath. He could stand more cold than an Eskimo and was never seen with his coat buttoned up. In his early years he freighted for Hudson's Bay Co. from Prince Albert, Sask. to points north with oxen and dog teams.

Well, enough of Kew on mail days but I must tell a few stories about a few more friends of mine. Jim Howie lived just north of us, a very big man, 325 lbs. and he didn't wash too often and soap was a scarcity in his shack. I thought a lot of Jim and visited him often. He was a good fiddler and I loved to hear him play. My mom warned me I'd have to eat with Jim sometime or I would hurt his feelings. I couldn't always say "Thanks, Jim, I can't stay." Well that day came; he caught me in a weak moment and I stayed. Did you ever eat boiled pig with the hair on? Ha. But Jim meant well even if he didn't scald his pigs.

One night I was making my way from Turner Valley to Wolf Creek where Buck Stockwell and I had a fencing job for the South Fork Stock Association. I was riding horseback and dragging a pack horse loaded with groceries. I heard a man cussing at the top of his voice. Up the road ahead of me I found it to be Bob Carry, stuck in the mud with his Model T coupe and it was raining like heck and black as Toby's hide. There was Bob, with a lariat up under the radiator, up through the floorboards and tied to the low pedal (you oldtimers will know what I mean by low pedal) He was out on the end of the rope with his wooden leg jammed into the deep mud and when he pulled, the old Ford took a little groan, and moved up a little then Bob pulled out the wooden leg and moved back some and pulled again. It was common procedure for Bob, as the trail ran up the Lineham Ranch flats and many little creeks and wet places were encountered. For a tough guy, Bob was the champ.

Eddie Behm was a little fellow that lived away back up against the Forest Reserve. He and I were friends for fifty years. He had been a jockey for Johnny Kieran years back. About 1916 or 1918 he homesteaded up west here, went to town for a haircut a couple of times a year. Outside of that he didn't travel away from home much in his later years. He was a good cowboy and axe man, and worked a lot on local ranches; small as he was he excelled in pitching bundles and he was known a long way out on the prairie where he worked with the big steam outfits until the snow flew, then came home and holed up for the winter. He used to shoot coyotes by moonlight through a crack in the logs of his shack, with a ten gauge shot gun. He set a horse carcass out on the hillside within range to draw the coyotes.

Some said Eddie was a recluse and others said he was a hermit, but he was a good guy. He lived his life as he wanted it. He is gone now and we miss him. He was part of our Kew hills. May God rest his soul.

John Broomfield recently celebrated his 89th birthday and we all wish him luck in his next fifty, after that he is on his own. I worked for John for some years off and on during the depression and he was tops as an employer, a very generous man. I was only getting about fifteen a month and on Saturday nights when I went girling, John would hand me a five and say "You'll need some money." so you see his generosity got me in the red. I had to stay with him as my wages were always overdrawn. John was a kind of backwoods philosopher, had many wise sayings that I have remembered through life. One time, seeing a fellow make a bad job handling a colt, he said to me "To break a colt or train a dog you have to know a little more than they do." When asked his opinion of the weather, he would say "only a fool or a greenhorn prophecies the weather in this country." You ask John Lefthand and he would say "Plenty bad winter coming, white man got a big woodpile."

We were trailing some cattle from the Valley ranch to Stavely late in the fall when the weather turned bad on us and it was terribly cold. John walked behind the herd and led his horse to keep warm, while I (eighteen and all cowboy) thought it beneath my dignity to walk. Finally, after seeing a frozen patch on my cheek grow bigger, he looked up at me and said "Sooner sit up there and freeze like a man than run behind like a dog, eh?"

John had an old black team called Darky and Dude that I fed cattle with in the winter. Old Darky didn't pull much and worked with his rump nearly under the rack and left Dude do all the work. This used to bother me and when the boss wasn't looking I'd take a long line to Darky and make him step up. John saw this and said to me "Don't hit him, he's worked under there for twenty years and he is not going to come out now."

Well, John, I enjoyed working for you and I have enjoyed being your friend and neighbor for fifty years.

First Sheep Hunt

by David Glaister

I don't believe there is a conquest in a man's life that can compare with his first trophy in a hunting ex-

Nevill Cannon and Bill Kendall with grizzly they shot at head of Three Point Creek.

pedition. Speaking for myself, I know there never will be quite the same enthusiasm, excitement and grand memories in any other hunt as there was on my first sheep hunt in 1943.

The hunt was by no means a dashing success, trophywise, as only three sheep were sighted and these were females, but to a young lad of fourteen who had never sighted a Big Horn Sheep before this was conquest enough, and to make him vow that as long as he was fit and able he would keep returning to this magnificent mountain country and try for one of these elusive trophies.

I have noticed with youngsters through the years that they are not so hard to please. Every part of a hunt carries some thrill, preparation, setting camp, taking care of horses, packing and many other small jobs that to the older hand have become chores of necessity.

A real good mix-up with a pack string, with packs bucked off, horses hung up, can be a nightmare to the older group but through the eyes of the youngster on his first trip out it will stick longer than any staged rodeo.

To be taken in and accepted as a partner by the seasoned hands of the experienced can give a young sportsman one of his most cherished thrills. These youngsters, too, can be the very best company, always

Pack horses on Highwood Pass.

eager to help in any way, at any time. They are never greatly deflated by failure and always eager to try again.

On my first hunt, I will never forget the fireside sessions at night, as my uncle, Pat Rodgers and a friend, Frank Sharp, both of much experience, swapped tales of years gone by, of hunting elk on the Highwood with an old trapper friend and Pat telling of wounding a ram on the lower slope of Mount Rose, running out of shells and roping it with his saddle horse and finishing it off with a hunting knife. How my mane stood straight up as they told of shooting grizzly and black bear under difficult circumstances throughout the mountains.

To have the different mountains, creeks and trails pointed out and told their names, names you have heard so many times and always longed to see. They stuck in my memory a lot faster than the name of my school teacher or the paths thereto, for that matter.

Quite often when I'm making up a bed or rolling out a fine sleeping bag in a camp, I think of my first night spent on this trip. We stayed in an old trapper's cabin on the forks of Ware and Link Creeks. There was a rough plank bunk in one corner and this was to be my uncle's and my resting place for the night. What a night. Did you ever spend eight hours (mostly all awake from excitement) on a rough blanket stretched over planks and not daring to move for fear of waking your loudly snoring companion? A youngster can be in utter misery from cold or hunger and he won't let a peep out of him for fear you might turn back or give up the chase. Let this happen to the older set and he will never stop belly aching.

Tim Blakley and Les Peat, with loose hide of large black wolf shot by Tim. April, 1937.

On that first trip of mine my uncle was naturally always in the lead much to my horse's dismay, and he never quit jigging, this giving me at times such a severe stitch in my side, I could have shot him without shedding a tear, but I never uttered a word. It was a small price to pay for the honor of being along.

At the time of my first hunt, sheep were very scarce in our area and I believe they were suffering from lung worm thus they were closed for some years and I was not able to return until seven or eight years later. When I did return with a young friend, Jody Fisher, I had no trouble finding my way about as my first trip stood clear in my memory. Sheep were more plentiful and had made a good come back. We had no trouble getting a ram.

I have returned many times to this grand mountain country and each trip has its cherished memories but none can compare with that splendid and inspiring first trip.

It is hard to say when a boy is really old enough to take to the hunting field. I suppose it depends a lot on how he has been raised. I know there are boys of twelve that would make excellent company and boys of eighteen that I would not accompany on a bet, they would cause you nothing but trouble and anguish.

It was a great pleasure for me to be accompanied by the young son of a doctor on several trips on which he got his first deer and sheep. His enthusiasm and gratitude was most rewarding. He was a most willing companion. I am sure that now while he is studying medicine he must have moments of relaxation in his memories of his first trips hunting.

So if you ever have the companionship of a well behaved youngster along on a hunting trip and you tell, him not to ask so darn many questions because he is spooking all the game in the country, say it with a smile because ten to one he will be taking everything very seriously.

Reminiscing

by Peggy Nylund

I can remember my Mother, Mrs. George Lyall, telling about a cow we had. We called her Shorty. She got into the house we lived in, got herself turned around in a small space and when Mother went in to the house, the cow was looking in the glass doors of the cupboard. Mother was afraid that she would put her horns through the glass. Mr. Jack Stagg had built the cupboard for her.

Another time Mother had us dressed for Sunday. If I remember right, company was coming. I went outside with my white dress on and the rooster took after me and I was all covered with blood. The rooster came out second best; he lost his head.

Another incident I remember was when we were going to a birthday party for Bob Fisher. Mrs. Ward and Jimmie, Mother (Mrs. George Lyall) Dick and myself. That was in the horse and buggy days. Dick was doing the driving and something went wrong with the buggy. We left it on the road between Howie's and the Johnson place, and took the team and walked the rest of the way. It was a dark night. Bob Fisher took us home in his truck. We went back for the horses and buggy next day. Mr. Bill Nelson came along and helped fix the buggy. He was a very nice man, called by most "Wild Bill.)

Mrs. Ward and Jimmie stayed at Fisher's all night.

Chinook for Christmas

by Jean Blakley

About 1925, a raging snowstorm was followed by bitterly cold weather, just prior to Christmas. The main road to Calgary from Millarville was through the Sarcee Indian Reserve and up over the Weasel Head Hill, and these roads were completely blocked, not that many cars used the roads, especially in winter. My brother John, sister Kathleen and I had come into Calgary the previous week to do some Christmas shopping and visit friends. Our problem now was how to get out home to Millarville in time for Christmas, and it was Christmas Eve already. Luckily for us, our married sister, Maybelle and her husband had come into town by team and sleigh, to do their shopping, and were staying with friends in South Calgary. The children had been left on the farm in the care of their grandmother, Mrs. Stanhope, Sr.

We three took the street car to South Calgary to meet the Stanhopes. We were told it was 40 degrees below zero F. and it felt every bit that cold. The sleigh box was filled with hay, but as this was before the warm outdoor clothing of today, we had to get out and run behind the sleigh to get warm. The trip took several hours and it was nearly dark when the Stanhopes let us out at the Lower Meadow gate where Dr. Roenisch now lives. Their home was two miles south while ours was about six miles west.

The snowdrifts were unbelievable, and with John breaking trail, we took off through the Meadow, our lower ranch. I have often wondered since why we didn't go onto the Meadow house and light a fire and stay the night. At the time no one was living there but there was always wood and a stove, but we were determined to get home. The further west we went the deeper the snow seemed to be. We finally reached the road by the Millarville post office, but there had not been any traffic on it, not even a saddle horse. By the time we reached the MacKay ranch I was sure my end was near. I asked John if it was true that one became warm when they were freezing to death, and he thought it was true as he also was becoming very warm. I redoubled my efforts and trudged on in his footsteps, feeling very much like the page following in the footsteps of Good King Wenceslas. In fact, I was really getting very warm and when my brother and sister stated that they also were getting warm we realized what was happening. A Chinook was blowing, that lovely soft breeze from the Pacific that makes this foothill country so different from any other part of Alberta.

By the time we had arrived home we had loosened our coats and were very happy to see the lights of the house. This sounds like a "Johnny Chinook" story but it is very true.

Water Divining

by Jean Blakley

Water diviners, or witcher, as they are more commonly known, are often scoffed at, but all over the world water has been found in this way where none was thought to be. In these foothills, where there are creeks aplenty, good water wells are hard to find. Many have spent time, money and a great deal of effort in trying to locate a good well, then through "witching" have had success. One farmer in Millarville had thirteen wells drilled with no success, then as a last resource consulted two water witcher. Each pinpointed an area in almost the identical spot and when drilling was done water was found.

"Water Witching" 1950's; Leonard Nelson, Mrs. Hopkins, and Betty Nelson.

Tim Blakley witching for water.

111

The first step in witching is to procure a divining rod, usually a green willow, although many use a steel bar. The witcher then starts walking slowly over the chosen area, and if he feels a "pull" walks on then retraces his path to where the pull is the strongest. There is no guarantee at what depth water may be found. One home in Millarville was built high atop a hill, and a flowing well was discovered by a witcher at about fifty feet, and in some places at a much lower altitude water wells are deeper.

Not everyone has this mysterious power. Without it, one can stand at the exact spot where a witcher has had a great "pull", use the same rod and feel nothing. Among the more successful diviners in the Millarville and Kew districts: Bill Winthrop, Oswald Madsen, Bill Jackson, John Jackson, Leonard Nelson, Tim Blakley and one very good lady diviner, Maudie Sharp. All of these have had good water wells to their credit.

Milking a Cow in the Church Yard

by Chub Foster

Mr. and Mrs. Doc Robison and their sons Bud and Howard moved to Kew from Strathmore in the early thirties. Bud was given the job of trailing the milk cows to their new home which took him three or four days. He had food with him and when it came night he tried to find a small field to hold the cows and his horse. It was getting late as he came to the Millarville Church yard so he put the cows in it. These cows were all in full milk so Bud had to milk them every night and morning. This morning Paddy Rodgers and I were trailing a herd of cattle home, so were on the road early and as we came past the Millarville Church yard Bud was milking his cows. One cow was near a tombstone so Bud sat on it for convenience. This was the first time I saw Bud.

Accident on Kew-Millarville Road

by Nita Foster

An accident happens because precautions were not taken. The bridge on the Kew-Millarville road had a new plank floor put on it about the first part of July 1928, but no guard rails. The next week Billy Jackson was coming home with a four horse team from work, in a bad hail storm. As he came upon the bridge a big clap of thunder frightened the horses, and they plunged over the end of the bridge into the creek. What a mess with harness all tangled up, but the horses were not badly hurt.

The next week, July 23, Herb Adams was going to take his family for a ride in the new car he had bought from Mr. Peglar of the Millarville store. The whole family, seven children and Herb and Hazel were really excited about their first real car. They only lived about one hundred yards west of the bridge, so didn't have time to get up any speed as they came onto the bridge when Herb felt he had no steering, thus going over the end into the creek. No one was hurt, but Herb strained

When Herb Adams' first car went over the bridge with nine passengers, no one was hurt. July 23rd, 1928.

July 24th, 1928. Taking wrecked car out. Not much left on top or windshield.

his back getting the car up enough to get Hazel and the baby out, and Hazel had a very badly sprained thumb. There were many people in that evening to see who had been hurt. Next day the neighbours came and put up a gin pole to hoist the car out. Our poor car with no windshield and no top. But we still had many good times in it after all.

Names

by Norma Lyall

Some of us never like to grow up, throw away, or part company with anything that belongs to us. When your ancestry is Scottish then that is doubly true.

Who ever heard of a good Scotsman parting with anything, even a name, if it is possible to hang on to it.

My Father, Colin Campbell Stewart of Davisburg, really started something when he married my Mother, Ettie Stewart of Byemoor.

That should have ended it but not yet. My brothers, Vernon and Stanley complicated things even more when they married twin sisters, Mary and Rose Stuart of Rimbey. If you think that is coincidence, how about this? My Mother's sister Thelma (Stewart) McClean of Calgary, a widow for a few years, married her cousin, Lorne Stewart of Lion's Head, Ontario.

I am glad I broke the pattern by marrying Tom Wildman. How do my children and grandchildren figure it all out? They do not. Even I get confused at times; as for Tom, he had a terrible time trying to figure out my relatives. Alex, my second husband, says that he is not going to try.

Horse Auction Sale

by Jean Blakley

My father was first, last and always a horse man. On his ranch, the horse was king, cattle secondary. Many fine mares and stallions were imported from England and he had built up a fine herd of horses. When my father died in 1914, there were, by count, 1400 head of these horses running in the Millarville and Kew areas. Before the Forest Reserve boundaries were made, he had a large lease in what is now the Bow Crow Forest Reserve.

After my father's death, the family made their home in Calgary, returning to the ranch in the summer. In 1915 and in 1916 many of these horses were sold, and I have records of many being sold to Clem Gardner of Pirmez Creek, also to other ranchers. In 1917, nearly 500 head were taken to the Bassano country on shares. In 1923, as the boys were now older, the family returned to the ranch to live full time. There were still many horses running in the hills so about 1925 it was decided to round up some of these and sell them by auction in Okotoks.

After grazing out all winter, the saddle horses were "soft" so they were put in the barn and conditioned with oats and hay and much currying to get off the old winter hair. When they were in good shape the gathering began. By this time the hills were greening up. When over a hundred head of horses had been collected, they were driven to Okotoks and held in the stock yard corrals there. The leader of this particular bunch was a French Coach horse named Black Diamond. He and the other horses were becoming very restless with the many people sitting on the corral fence. One young Okotoks fellow bet he could ride any horse there. Bets were taken and a rope was thrown in the general direction of Black Diamond, but with one great leap he cleared the fence and took off down the railroad track, his long black tail waving goodbye. However, the other horses were whinnying for him to come back. He turned and running very fast, once again cleared the fence. This time he was roped, snubbed, blind folded and saddled and our hero got aboard. About two jumps and his feet lost the stirrups, his hands found the saddle horn and when the wildly bucking Black Diamond got close to the fence the would-be rider made a wild leap and landed on the

fence. He loudly declared that he couldn't ride that black brute.

The sale progressed and most of the horses were sold. Black Diamond eventually went to Peter Welsh and was taken on the rodeo circuit with Welsh bucking string.

The day of the big horse ranches was over. To-day one can scarcely find a trail for riding, so many acreages and land owned by newcomers, with gates wired or locked, and no trespassing signs. The Forest Reserve offers the only riding trails.

The Charge of the Longhorns, 1914-18

I. and E. Evans

In case this priceless true story that happened during the first world war should be lost, I shall try to relate the details as they were told to me.

In those days, there were no cattle liners or possum-bellies, so cattle were driven from the Millarville area to the Calgary stockyards to be sold. In the fall of the year ranchers would round up what they wanted to sell and get the various bunches together, and start for Calgary with a herd that may have 200 to 400 head. In those days horns were left on and steers would be at least four years old or more so their horns could be rather long.

The route was usually through Priddis and across the Sarcee Indian Reserve and over the Weasel Head Bridge and thus to the stockyards. This time the riders had a hard time getting the cattle to start over the bridge and when they did start the rattle of the bridge planking caused them to stampede. No rider could get on the bridge to head them until all had crossed. Up the hill went the cattle on to the flat plain where the soldiers in training at the Sarcee Military Camp were camped.

The tents were in the form of a box with an open end. Into this open end the cattle stampeded and when they came to the closed end they didn't stop. My father, David Evans, who was one of the riders said he had never seen such destruction. All tents were levelled; some carried away on the steers long horns. Stacked rifles were scattered like spilled matches, field guns were upset and some of the cavalry horses had broken loose and were running with the cattle. He said also that the soldiers were running as fast as the cattle only in a different direction.

It took over three weeks before all the cattle were found and rounded up again. Some were found in the Springbank district but the majority were found in the area now known as Broadcast Hill.

Fortunately, no soldiers were hurt seriously. My father never mentioned any damage claims. Maybe the men in charge thought it would have given the soldiers a vision of what they would meet when they got to the battlefield.

Happenings in the Square Butte Area
by Peggy Nylund

In July 1919 a fire went through the Hudson Bay, and Mr. Dole's lease land, later leased by Mr. Kendall, now by Zahava Hanen. There were many other fires but I do not recall the dates.

Dad was away helping to fight the fire, Mother was in a Calgary hospital with our twin brothers. Uncle Alf Pierce and his son Alf were staying with us. He sent Dick and I off to bed while the sun was still shining; we thought it was terrible to go to bed so early.

Dad and Mother came home with the twin boys so we were all together again, but sad to say, the twins passed away before they were a month old.

There were also many floods, one in 1922 when Mr. George Silvester lost his pig and pig house in the flood. Another flood in 1942, when my cousin Tommy Lyall came to our place to get Hjalmar to take him to Calgary to his Army base. They had a time to get the horses across Fisher Creek to pull the car up onto the road. Next morning Hjalmar had trouble crossing the creek to get home. He and the team went down the creek, but a Guiding Hand brought them out of the water. One horse went back to the other side. The late Gordon McLay got one horse and Hjalmar and the other one came out on the home side. He was shaken up and very wet and cold. Our foot bridge landed down at the Wildman place. Those were the days when we battled muddy roads, floods and snow drifts.

Many times we were stuck going down Johnson's Hill, never mind coming up the hill. It was a lot better when the hill was straightened and no bends. Some of us are still here to tell the story.

There have been many oil wells drilled in the Square Butte area; the Cotton Belt well, which was shut down, also one on the Joe Bell place. The Quirk Creek Gas Plant was built.

Some of the land in the Square Butte area has changed hands, and some sold into acreage lots. Homesteads still owned by relatives, or parts of some, are Minnie Marshall, Jim Silvester. Mr. Northover's place is owned by Fred Kosling. The Jim Ward place has been owned by him since 1922. The George Lyall place which had been bought by son Dick, is now owned by Mr. and Mrs. Don Green, teachers and principal of Millarville School. Part of R. McBee place has been sold.

Some of the folks that have lived in the area for a number of years and are still living there, are Alex and Norma Lyall, Barbara Reimer and some of her family. Dorothy and Jim Davis, Bill and Joan Kendall, Fred Kosling, Ernie Silvester and family, Jim and Kathy Silvester and family. Minnie Marshall, Fred and Una Ball. Art and Agnes Ball, and David and Jody Ball.

Bob MacKay's Letters From Morley

Bob MacKay and Johnny Bearspaw. 1971.

Morley, Alta.
Feb. 10th -1943

Dear Bob,
Brother I have received your letter and open it I fine Fifteen Dollars in it and was very glad and thankful as the whole world.

This $15 will sure help a lot and today is the first time have sat on a chair but I haven't try to walk outdoor yet and but you didn't tell me what would you want in buckskin wear so I may try and fixt up with you this coming spring if you and I keep well and may I say Happy New Year to all you MacKay boys so this is all for now.

from your friend
Job Stevens.

Morley, Alta.
Dec. 26-45

to
Bob MacKay
Millarville
Dear friend
I have received your letter which had accompany with Xmas & New Year present for me. I was very glad and appreciated for it. For this the mountain seemed to be more beautiful as I look at it.

I hope all your relatives and friens are getting along fine. I am getting along fine now. I hope to see you when spring comes along if it is ever going to be. We are having lots of snow down here much more what it should be.

I'll be very glad to be in the New Year on account of the present which you have sent. I would like you to write and tell me what you want such as Buckskin coat, jacket, gloves or moccasins.

I shake hands with you with Mary Xmas and best wishes for you all and Happy New Year.

yours truly
Red Cloud
Indian.

Morley, Alta.
Dec. 10 1946.

Dear Bob,

Well I am going to tell you how I am going its about one feet of snow in Morley we got quite a bit of snow since last fall and the people down here is all right & been out hunting myself this fall I don't kill anything myself the horse slip on me on the hillside and broke one of my rib I am still in my house well I will be seeing you next summer if I am all right that's all the news I can tell you my son. and David Bearspaw's wife got sore eye for two month and hardle see but she is getting better now that was all I can say

from
Red Cloud

shake hands to you all and best wishes.

Stony Indian Reserve
Morley Alta.
Dec. 30th 1946

to
Bob MacKay
Millarville
Desr Sir

I was very greatly full of satisfactery and cheer the way I got the letter from you.

The snow has been too deep for me to go out to shoot squirels beside that I think I am getting too old and weak to do it.

I received the sum of twenty-dollar bill O.K. I would say thanks a lot from way down deep in my heart so-long and best wishes for yourself & wife also your brother for the New Year

Yours very truly
Red Cloud.

Stony Indian Reserve
Morley Alta
April 26th 1947

to
Mr. MacKay
Millarville
Dear Mr. MacKay

Will drop a few lines to let you know that I have been getting along fine same as ever. I hope all of you brothers are the same way

I will tell you what we are getting for our ration is just a very lean meat from the elks. So if you have any fats or grease let me know about it I will go over and get it so I will be seeing you then this spring.

It was hard winter this year

yours truly
Red Cloud

Stony Indian Reserve
Morley Alta.
Dec. 22nd 1947.

to
Bob Mackay
Millarville
Dear friend

Will drop in just very few lines to you.

I will tell you that I didn't go around much last summer. It's for that reason I didn't come to visit you

I hope you all getting along fine as usual for this coming Christmas day.

I would say it's grand to be alive for another Christmas I got along fine up to this time so far also very much the same with the other people here.

I wish you a very Merry Christmas and good cheer for the coming year.

Yours truly as ever
Red Cloud.

Stony Reserve
Morley, Alta.

to
Bob Mackay
Kew, Alta.

Will write to you again Mr. MacKay.

When I came near Christmas I was kind of a bit hard up but when I went to the post office I got a letter and opened it and found some money in the envelope. I was very surprised but filled with joy at the same time. With that I had my Christmas and New Year celebration.

My wife and I are still getting along fine. I hope you are the same.

I guess that's all I can say to you. The main thing I want to say to you is this "THANKS" ever so much for that Xmas present I got from you.

I'd like to say Hello to you and wife Also your brothers with their wives sorry I don't know their names.

I remain yours truly
Red Cloud.

Morley, Alberta.
Dec. 1948

to Mr. Bob MacKay
Kew, Alta.
Dear Mr. & Mrs. MacKay

I am enclosing parcel containing present for both of you to say a very Merry Xmas to you with it.

I hope it will delight you. Also I would like to say best wishes for all the coming year.

I remain yours
respectfully
Red Cloud.

Morley, Alberta
May 25-50

to
Mr. Bob Mackay
Kew Alta.
Dear Sir,

I am enclosing a pair of gloves which you wanted.

We sure glad to meet each other, didn't we? I've been so proud to have a friend like you in every ways. I think from now on I'd get fat from that grease of suet I got from you. I still want to see you again for I didn't had enough to meet you at the time I've been up there, I guess you didn't expected me to visit you, didn't you.

Good bye to you all
thank you from
yours respectfully
Red Cloud.

Stoney Indian Reserve
Morely Alta.
August 14-50

to
Bob MacKay
Kew alta.
Dear Son Bob,

I have been an orphan now since for the last three(3) days. I would be having poor and mournful life for the rest of my time. The biggest hurricane had been attacked where my wife and I were. Also some people were with us. Enoch Rider, Noah Ear & family. My wife & Mrs. Peter Ear & two of Alex Ear's children were all killed suddenly. Some of us survivers also got hurt but I am still alive & not as healthy though. That's the news I want you to hear.

Shake hands with you all. I'll be at Longview from 16th to 23rd of this month and be coming back to Morley

yours respectfully
Red Cloud or Christian name
as Lazarus Dixon

Morley Alta.
January 6th -51

Bob MacKay
Kew Alta.
Dear Bob

I've been thinking about you again up to this time.

If you had joyable Xmas and New Year holidays it'll be splendid for me to hear that.

I've been wanting to say hello to you but nobody are willing to take me over there for this reason that the car is running by money. It's hard for me to get money that's why.

I've used up all that grease you gave it to me.

You know when the last time I met you I was coming home since then I never go away from my house.

May God bless you all. Happy New Year to you all and same.

yours truly
Red Cloud.

Morley Alta.
January 31st 1951

to
Bob MacKay
Kew Alta.
Dear Son,

I've been very much appreciated & thankful for your letter which found me around the Xmas holiday.

I never been away since I got home after I see you up there. I've been having the hardest time for the winter, although it has been a very good winter. I always want to see you every time I think of your mother. I can't be able to go up and see you right now for the road not very good. Anyway I want you to spare few suey grease, please, hope you are all well at present time, would like to say good bye to you all

Your father
Red Cloud
P.S. I got your $20 that you enclosed to me. Thanks a lot.

Morley Alberta
March 1951

Dear Bob

I have been sick for two month and I not feeling good yet. I am always thinking of you, I know you always gave me grease and I am hungry too and no money. I can hardly walk too very weak I hope you all feeling well. I always pray God for you that's all and wishing to see you this summer if God helps us all. That's all I can say shake hand

your father
me Red Cloud.

Stoney Reserve
Morley Alberta
March 1954.

Dear Bob,

Just a few lines to you. Well all our friends are gone except me I'm left alone. I'm writing this letter because I want fat grease. I sure would be glad if you can spare me some. We're really close friends that's why I'm asking you to do that. I'm really short of groceries these days cause I can't work now. That is why I am asking you to do this for me. I really hope you're feeling fine. Myself I'm fine. Long time ago I know that you were really my friend. It's hard to get money now-a-days so that's why I'm asking you that. This winter lots of people can't hardly get their grub cause they isn't any work.

This is all I can tell you now.

I shake hands with you.

Chief David Bearspaw.

116

Brown-Lowery Natural Area

In the Millarville-Kew district there is a section of land that has been set aside as a nature and wild life sanctuary. It is just one square mile in size, section 25-21-4W5. Originally the land had been owned by V. N. de Mille who had a large sawmill and his ranch buildings on the N.E. ¼ of the section.

Over the years since de Mille had quit logging, and lumbering, the land had been logged over several times. When the Home Oil Company bought the place in the 1940's, it was leased to neighboring ranchers for cattle pasture. It has always been a favorite home for wild animals, especially bear and there still are a quantity of these in the area.

When Home Oil presented this land to the Alberta Government about 1968, it was decided it would be an area for foot travellers only. A fence was built around all four sides, with a parking space provided near the gate on the west side. Paths were cleared and foot bridges put over the little creek that runs through. This is an ideal place for anyone wishing to take a nature study walk through the cool shady forest, and there are many flowers and fungi, that grow only in these places, to delight the photographer. As no cars

are allowed in the area, one is never disturbed by noise or crowds.

Nature
by Janet MacKay

Do you really know how interesting nature can be in these foothills? There is a great variety of flora and fauna, if we just take time to observe and really listen.

Identification of all the different species of birds and flowers can be almost a lifelong study. The animals aren't so difficult. We have the whitetail deer, mule deer and some moose. There are elk, mostly in the western part of the district.

Bears are seen occasionally, although most people do not appreciate them. Those wonderful mousers, the coyotes, are with us. Their song is one of the true wild songs of nature. There have been a few wolves in the district over the years.

Going to the smaller animals, the mice and gophers are the most plentiful. We do need the predators to keep them in check. The hawks, owls, coyotes and weasels all do their bit.

Most things in nature run in cycles, even the butterflies. In the thirties there were thousands of rabbits all over the country. Many a family earned much needed cash by hunting them for the fox farms. They have never been as plentiful since then, and there probably won't be now that there are so many people in the country. A great deal of brush has been cleared off the land since those days.

If you get out in the winter for a walk or on skis, you will see many interesting tracks in the snow. The weasels travel a considerable distance, working back and forth across a field in search of mice. Their tracks will disappear beneath the snow for a few feet, they probably hear a mouse under there.

Other animals are skunks, badgers, porcupines and sometimes a mink along the creek. The beavers also build their dams along the waterways. These are just a few of the animals, there are many more.

There are too many birds to name them all. We all know our robins, bluebirds and of course the happy little chickadees. The coldest day doesn't seem to faze them. Anyone who puts out feed for them is rewarded by many pleasant hours of watching. The downey and hairy woodpeckers also come to the fat in the winter.

The bluebirds seem to be making a nice comeback after being almost completely wiped out in June 1951. It started raining, turning to snow and giving us about a foot of heavy wet snow. The birds were wet and cold and they just perished. It took several years for them to recover. People seem to be more concerned now and they put up boxes that the starlings can't get into.

There are nest boxes along Highway 22 between the Priddis corner and Turner Valley. In the summer of 1978 quite a few of these houses had bluebirds and others had tree swallows nesting in them. Identification of all of the birds can be very frustrating at times

Bluebird Hovering

Mountain Bluebird

Goldfinch

Yellowthroat Warbler

Housewren

Vesper Sparrow

Robin

SUMMER BIRDS

118

Chickadee

Bohemian Waxwing

Hairy Woodpecker

Redpoll

Evening Grosbeak

Snowbird

J. MacKay
78

WINTER BIRDS

119

but a most rewarding hobby. Learning their songs and call notes is the next step.

Each bird of one species has his own rendition. Then one bird may have several slightly different songs. That is especially noticeable with the meadowlarks. He will sing one song, maybe half a dozen times, then change to another combination of notes, and almost sound like a different bird.

The flowers are easy to observe, but learning to identify them all isn't done in one season. Some of the most beautiful are very small. In the deep woods, there are several members of the orchid family, also the wintergreens, all very lovely. On a north slope of a hill, where there are spruce and all the mosses and lichens, you will find these. As well, the tiny twin-flowers grow in these locations.

If you take the time to photograph the flowers close up, you will realize how beautiful they really are.

The rare flowers should never be picked. In the case of the tiger lilies and orchids, the bulb of each flower that is picked dies, because the leaves that feed it for the following year are on the stem.

The rose is Alberta's floral emblem and many road-side ditches are pink with them in June. Later the red hips are food for many birds.

The many mushrooms and fungi are really quite fascinating. One season there may be a great number of one variety and then they may not show up again for several seasons. In 1969, the morels were growing all through the aspen woods. Then in 1976 the very poisonous amanitas, brilliant orange mushrooms with white spots, looked like jewels in the shade of the aspens.

Nature study is really a fascinating subject, with something more to learn each year. Do get out and really look and enjoy yourself.

Photo by J.M.M.

Photo by J.M.M.

Photo by J.M.M.

Photo by Winston Parker.

Photo by Les Boulton.

Cenotaph at Millarville church yard.

Photo by J.M.M.

Photo by B.N.

Photo by Winston Parker.

Photo by Winston Parker.

123

Photo by Keith Giles.

Photo by W.C.P.

Photo by Veryl Laycraft.

Scene at Millarville.

Photo by J.M.M.

Photo by Janet MacKay.

Photo by Winston Parker.

Looking west to John Ware Ridge at sunrise. Photo by Noreen Cooper.

Looking west from top of John Ware Ridge. Photo by Wayne Hampton.

Photo by Wayne Hampton.

Sheep Creek Canyon in Bow Crow Forest Reserve.

Photo by Wayne Hampton.

Forget-Me-Not Mountain from the Muskeg.

Photo by Keith Giles.

Photo by Winston Parker.

Photo by Winston Parker.

Photo by Janet MacKay.

129

Photo by Keith Giles.

Photo by Betty Nelson.

Major Tank Farm.

Photo by Janet MacKay.

Ruins of the barn on the John Ware ranch at Kew.

Photo by Keith Giles.

131

Photo by Stewart Sinclair-Smith.

Photo by Keith Giles.

Photo by Barb Godwin.

Photo by Janet MacKay.

Photo by Les Boulton.

Photo by Betty Nelson.

Millarville Races, 1954.

Millarville Fair, 1963.

Photo by J.M.M.

Photo by J.M.M.

Photo by Winston Parker.

136

Chapter 10
Veterans

Morris McLay   Maurice P. Shaw   Walter J. McArthur   Charles R. Knights   Walter Ball

Jim Carry

Jack Bell

Jack Lee

Jack Adams

Val Mack

138

Roy Foster

Ford Lochhead. Picture taken in Sweden after his escape from German prison camp.

L. to R. Dave, Hank and Vic Scheuerman.

Lois (Burrows) Warren

139

William James Ware

Isabella Silvester

Richard (Dick) Lyall

Arthur Silvester

Albert Iceton

William A. Fisher

Lawrie Lochhead

Wilfred George Purmal

141

Robert L. Carry

Bill de Mille

John Leonard
Nelson

Grant Burquist

Margaret Deane-
Freeman

Fred Ball

Francis Sinclair-
Smith

Jackie Cudlip

William Trevenen

Albert Stagg

142

George William
(Curly) Sand

D'Arcy Foster

Hugh Rawlinson

Frank Ball

George Ingeveld

Mollie (Hartell)
Duxbury

Frank A. Shaw

Nevill Cannon

David Kendall

Arthur Ball

Edward H. Raw-
linson

Jack Little

J. F. Pat Hartell

Leslie Douglass

J. G. Lineham

Jack Surtees

Fred Lewis

Arthur J. Stanhope

David Glaister

G. L. Parker

John Ballachey

Henri de Roaldes

William Bell

Frederick
Anthony Knights

Winston Parker

143

Wm. Dube

William S. Tosh

Harry Fisher

Jimmie Virtue

Maurice Ingeveld

George McNab

Harry Rawlinson

Sue Rawlinson

Tommy Lyall

Joe Bannerman

Fred Rishaug

Miles Adams

Ronald Birkenes

Thomas Adams

Jack Adams

Harold Marshall

Phyllis Piper

Helen Gould

Richard von Stralendorff

W. Geoffrey Hulme

Dorian W. (Jappy) Douglass

Merton Olson

Donald Bannerman

Irene (Adams) Waite

South African War Veterans. Gerald Webster, left with flag, was one of only seven Boer War Veterans still alive. 1971.

L. to R. Don, Ab, John and Doug Morrison. Lewis in front.

Chapter 11
Family Histories

Elizabeth Doreen Adamcik (Adams)
by Betty Adamcik

I was born to Herb and Hazel Adams, who at that time were living on a farm south west of Millarville. There were three brothers and six sisters in our family, as Phyllis, Ruth and I were the youngest, the rest of the family were mostly grown up and gone during our growing up years.

The Oil Well boom came into full swing in the years that we lived at Millarville, of course the face of the countryside as well as peoples ways of life were drastically changed. My Dad, besides farming, worked at the Tank Farms in that area for a good number of years. I can still remember vividly the Tank Farm across the road from us and the big gas flare that burned continuously, sometimes soaring great heights into the air when they blew it as they cleaned out the well.

Another event that sticks in my memory while we lived at Millarville was the out break of World War 2. All three brothers and sister Irene served in the Armed Forces during the war, thankfully they all came safely home.

The first school I attended was Plainview, three and one half miles to the west of our place, what a ride, especially on a cold day. Many a time we got to school to find the fires had just been started, so the teacher would make us run around and around the school house to warm up. How well I remember a white horse we rode to school who shied at anything and everything, leaving us on the ground, to walk the rest of the way either to school or home which ever way we happened to be heading at the time. However we survived these rigors of life and are probably better people for it. By the time I was in grade five my sisters and I started going to Sheep Creek School, attending that school for the next four or five years until my Dad and Mom sold the farm and moved to another one south of Priddis. While there I attended Fordville School for my grade nine. For our High School education my sister Phyllis and I went to North Turner Valley High School, having to board at someones place in the Valley during the week, going home for the weekends.

While attending High School I began going steady with my husband Frank Adamcik. After finishing High School we were married in 1950 and lived on Frank's farm in the Red Deer Lake district, where we farmed for 21 years. We had a family of four children, two boys and two girls. Our oldest boy Vernon worked in the Artic on the Oil Wells and was killed in a plane crash in 1974, that took the lives of thirty-two men, all on their way to work in the North. Our second boy Frank Jr. is a brick layer working in Calgary at this time. Our two girls Michelle and Maryanne are still going to school at the time of this write-up.

In 1971 we sold our farm at Red Deer Lake and moved to another farm in the Harmatten district, 14 miles north west of Didsbury. We have a cow-calf operation set up on our farm and this is our main occupation right now. We are happily settled on our farm and have many outside community activities besides belonging to a newly formed Toastmasters Club, which is a self improvement project.

Out of our large family that was raised in the Millarvlle district, all but two brothers have settled in Alberta to make their living and raise their families. My Dad and Mom as of now are residing in a Nursing Home in Calgary and come out to stay with us for 4 or 5 days once in a while. It is still a joy to visit and converse with them as their minds are as bright and alert as ever, even if they have slowed down physically.

The Millarville district where I was born and raised will always remain a beautiful spot to me, and hopefully the people who live there now appreciate it as much as we do who had their beginning in that special part of Alberta.

Clara and Francis (Frank) Adams
by Clara Adams JE

In April, 1900 Frank Adams, his mother and four brothers, Tom, Jim, Sid and Herb; two sisters Ida (later Mrs. Noah Haire) and Jenny (later Mrs. George Sylvester) came to Turner Valley to join their father Thomas and brother Bill who came out from Ontario one year earlier. They took up land in the Millarville-Turner Valley area. 30-20-3W5 was Frank's land.

Here they lived the hard life of the first pioneers. At times even packing in supplies on their backs when the

L. to R. Clara Holdsworth, Frank Adams, Clara Adams, Doreen Adams, wife of Frankie Adams.

L. to R. Frank Adams, Allan Carr, Hubert Rendell with a fine catch of fish from the Highwood River.

wet springs made travelling by teams impossible. Frank then worked for Dominion Land Survey for six years as chain man. They went east as far as Winnipeg doing correction work. Then west to Vancouver completing and correcting work done earlier by surveyors. Then when that work was completed he and friends went to work for the C.P.R. as a section hand up through the Rogers Pass.

He started working for Royalite Oil Company freighting supplies from Calgary and Okotoks. Working at various jobs in the plant yard. While there at the risk of losing his own life he realized two men who had been sent down to clean the yard sump were unconscious from gas. He gave the alarm, then dragged them to the edge where they were lifted out just as he slumped into unconsciousness. It was a year before he was able to resume work. As a tool dresser on a cable tool rig he had his hand badly crushed one year. In 1934 Frank married Clara Lawrence who had come from Taber with her parents in 1928. They lived at Whiskey Row north of Turner Valley, going to the North Turner Valley School and later Turner Valley where her two sisters and a brother attended high school. Later her folks moved to the Mercury Camp.

The first year Frank and Clara lived in Turner Valley, then moved to the homestead at Kew. Frank was a watchman at a Royalite plant working from 9 p.m. to 6 a.m. shift for six years. He then was pipe line walker, 7 miles north and back one day and the next 7 miles south and back but a welcome change from night shift, although he and other line walkers went if it was 30 degrees below or 90 degrees above through mud and snow.

After working for the Royalite eighteen years and because of poor health, he quit the company receiving no pension.

Going back to full time farming, his health was restored. They now had a family of three boys, Frank, Melvin and Kenneth born at La Rosees Nursing Home in Turner Valley. Close neighbors were Herb Adams and Bedford and Norma Boggs. Home Oil drilled wells No. 1, No. 2 and No. 3 on Frank's land. Home Oil Company bought the land and Frank bought three quarter sections. Section 30, NE ¼ and NW ¼ from Bill Patterson in 1940. His cattle brand was JE.

Then for a time they lived on his parents place as they were both in poor health. Mrs. Adams died in 1942 and the father Thomas in 1944.

By now Frankie was school age and had to walk to North Turner Valley School four miles. In his second year we won the right from the school board for Frankie to go on Dan Dudenhoffer's bus to Millarville. Then the Plainview School reopened and he and Melvin rode horseback as we moved back to Kew. They had good crops and gardens there. They loved country living and had good neighbors, so were sad to have to give up as Frank again was not too well, and sell to V. Hammel of Calgary. They retired to Turner Valley.

Frank married Doreen Robinson of Springbank and have two daughters Carol Lynne and Patricia Dianne. They own their own trucking business and live in Calgary. Melvin married Joan Patterson of Black Diamond, liked farming, but is now employed by Fording Coal Company living at Elkford B.C. They have two boys, David and Darcy and one girl Sharon. Kenneth married Sherron Iceton of Turner Valley and owns and operates a back hoe. They have two girls, Bonnylou and Serena and a son Murray and live in Turner Valley.

Frank passed away in June 1973 but Clara continues to live in Turner Valley.

Adams, Herb and Hazel
Z3

In 1900 Herb Adams came to Alberta from Port Hope, Ontario at seven years of age with his parents Tom and Maria, five brothers and two sisters. Herb, with his older brothers Tom, Bill and Frank came with their father to land north west of Turner Valley where they first lived in a makeshift cabin built around a tree. One day cabin, tree and all burned up so they built a dug out in the hillside and did they ever have a good time when they weren't helping build the house and barn. Mrs. Adams and the other children lived in Okotoks until the house was built. There was no school in the area and Mrs. Adams taught the children as much as she could. The boys worked for other settlers as soon as they weren't needed at home. At the age of ten and eleven years Herb worked for Mr. Malcolm Millar herding sheep in the summer time. One

146

Herb and Hazel Adams 50th wedding anniversary with Herb jr., and wife Rilla with first grandchild.

summer Herb and Frank worked for Mr. Joe Fisher herding horses. Each boy had a stallion and a band of mares in different valleys and they often thought they would let the stallions get together for some excitement, but they never did.

In 1910 the Plainview School was built and Herb went for three winters when Mrs. Carl Ohlson was the teacher. Herb then went to Calgary to take a plumbing course where he was very lonesome after being with a large family. He would come home over weekends whenever he could catch a ride with a rancher that was in for supplies. He even borrowed a bicycle once and rode the 35 miles to the ranch over the prairie trails on Friday night and had to go back Sunday afternoon. Then in 1914 war broke out and Herb had to forget his plumbing career. He did join up but was discharged to go farming. In August 1915 he married Hazel Paul who had come to the district with her parents from Montreal in 1903. The Paul's first lived around Calgary and Red Deer Lake. Herb and Hazel spent their first winter working for Andy Thompson south of Black Diamond.

Then for the next few years they moved around renting places finally buying the John Anderson place on the Kew Millarville road. In the winters Herb worked at the MacPherson mine at Black Diamond, the Denning mine west of Turner Valley and the Bucher mine west of Millarville. Herb worked out most of the time, leaving the farm work to Hazel and the kids. But these were good times growing up as a large family. Summertime included swimming in the cold creek, baseball and picnics. We spent winter time skating, tobogganing and at dances in the old Ranchers Hall. We all worked hard but there was always lots of fun.

Herb Adams in mine.

In 1927 Herb went to work for the Royalite Oil Co. of Turner Valley and worked there until he retired in 1960. By this time they had moved to a farm south of Priddis. In 1962 Herb and Hazel sold their farm and moved to Summerland B.C. They had thirteen good years of retirement in B.C. then came back to Calgary December of 1975 where they now reside. Herb and Hazel raised a family of seven girls and three boys. Nita born 1916, married Chub Foster. Jack born 1918 married Eunice Campbell. Hazel born 1920 married Stewart Cameron, Anna born 1921 married Bill Stickle. Herb born 1923 married Rilla Turcott. Tom born 1924 married Jessie Brown. Irene born 1926 married Joe Waite. Betty born 1930 married Frank Adamcik. Phyllis born 1932 married Jim Mangan and Ruth born 1935 married Gene Girioux.

In 1975 Herb and Hazel celebrated their 60th Anniversary with an open house at Millarville Race Track Hall. All their family was able to attend except Jack who now lives in Ontario.

Jack Adams
by Eunice Adams (Campbell)

This is of Jack Adams, eldest son of Herb and Hazel Adams who were residents of Millarville area for many years.

Jack grew up on the farm of his parents with seven sisters and two brothers, he remembers how the old house bulged with family and friends. He went to

Jack Adams with his mother and father, Hazel and Herb Adams and wife Eunice.

school at Plainview, Sheep Creek and Turner Valley High. Jack loves all sports and took part in them all, he remembers the ball games and what a time they had, also swimming after the chores were done. Then there were those great dances at Kew and Ranchers Hall, wild and wooley they were.

Jack began his working career with Royalite Oil Company and he lived with his aunt and uncle for awhile and also batched. He then married Eunice Campbell, who had as a young girl lived with her family in the Kew district for a couple of years and went to the Square Butte School, then they moved back to Calgary. Jack joined the army and served five years in different parts of Canada and most of it overseas and retired as a sergeant.

After the war he resumed working for Imperial Oil on the rigs and pipeline, then he was transferred to Ontario where he was active in pipeline inspection and laying of the lines for the company. After thirty years he took an early retirement and decided on a new career where he is a Supervisor of the Letter Carriers of a division of the Burlington Post Office in Ontario.

Jack and Eunice have three children, John and his family of Edmonton, Alberta; Dawn and her family in Burlington and Bob also in Burlington.

The ties of the West are still strong and the memories happy ones.

History of Ryan William Adams
by Ryan Adams

My father, William Adams, was born in Silverdale, Staffordshire, England. My mother, Alice Adams, was born in Edinburgh, Scotland. Both came to Calgary at an early age. My father's family started Adams Radio Parlors in Calgary. My mother had a dancing school called Murdoch School of Dancing.

I arrived August 20, 1935, after my mother walked to the Western Hospital at 14th Ave. and 3rd St. S.W.

because my father's car had a flat tire. This experience must not have daunted my mother, because two sisters were born after me. Sharon is a figure skating teacher. She lives with her husband, Arthur LaRiviere, and two daughters in Acme, Alberta.

Vicki and her husband, Garry Willis live in Calgary. She is a dancing teacher and choreographer. Vicki teaches at the University of Calgary.

I went to Calgary schools until I went to the University of Oklahoma. I came back to Canada with a degree in Petroleum Engineering and a wife. She was born Marilyn Katherine Brokaw on September 8, 1936 in Shawnee, Oklahoma. Her parents, Willard and Katherine Brokaw, were educators. Marilyn's mother taught elementary school. Her father was a teacher, principal, and finally superintendant in Shawnee Public Schools.

I brought my new bride to the oil "boom town" of Drayton Valley, Alberta, in 1957. We left our car and crossed the Saskatchewan River on a raft, carrying our few possessions. The streets were rivers of mud. We lived in a 10'x20' skid shack with no running water. We were soon moved into a company bungalow, however.

Our daughter, Sandra Lynn, was born in Edmonton, December 18th, 1958 while we were still living in Drayton Valley. Later we moved to Edmonton for a short while. Our son, David William, was born there on August 1st, 1960.

A month later we moved to Calgary. Our third child, Katherine Alice, was born in Calgary, December 9th, 1963.

Our oldest daughter Sandy was responsible for our move to the country. It started with a horse. Her interest in horses and riding soon led to looking for a place to keep them. One summer day I happened to find one of the most beautiful spots in the area, and I bought it "on the spot". Marilyn was angry until I brought her to see it. One look at the mountains, and wildflowers and she was happy. We bought the property N.E. ¼, Section 31, Twp. 21 Range 2 West of the 5th from John and Ida Jackson in 1969. We built a cedar cabin and spent our weekends and summers here. In 1972 we moved here permanently. We soon met our neighbors. They pulled us out of ditches, gave us advice and help on animal care, fencing, gardening and helped us make the transition from city to country living.

Our children enjoyed horse shows, 4-H clubs and entering the Millarville Fair.

Sandy was taught to ride by Joe Selinger at ST. George's Stables. David was more interested in rodeos. Alice became interested in the piano and was taught by two area residents, Linda Kundert and Bettijo Smith. All three children attended Red Deer Lake School until they went into Calgary for high school.

Our neighbors have made us welcome and we feel at home in this area.

Tom and Jessie Adams ⊥T – ε̇ – T⊥

Tom was born in 1924 at Kew where his parents, Herb and Hazel Adams farmed and he attended Plainview school. He joined the navy in 1942 and served in the Atlantic. In 1948 he married Jessie Brown who had grown up in the Turner Valley area. The first years of their married life they spent in and around the Edmonton area while Tom worked for Imperial Pipeline and Imperial Oil.

They came to the Bradfield Ranch on March first, 1953 and for six weeks it rained every day. Farmers need the rain but it isn't one of the finer things of life for a young mother with three small children and one on the way. In December number four joined the crew. Now there were Thomas Jr., Leslie, Gwenda and David. At this time Charlie Urquhart also took up residence with the family as a friend, household helper, field hand and an instigator of many an interesting pastime. Together Jessie and Charlie made cheese (which worked if they would have left it a little longer) made beer (which wasn't half bad) and tried to grow mushrooms (which was a total failure). So life was never dull.

Sometimes dull might have been more fun! One morning two "hobos" straggled into the yard and asked for a loaf of bread. As the house was so far off the road it gave Jessie food for thought. Add the fact that Tom was no where about, and it gave Jessie food for fear. At any rate they turned out to be two young boys who had hitch-hiked from Moose Jaw and they had not eaten in days but they were hoping to find Jim Brown who had fed and employed them before on the farm. So the Adams took them in and gave them room and board plus $1.00 a day and put them to work. Over the years Donny returned many times. Often when everyone was in Calgary he would move in and do the chores and wait for our return and just as often he would leave abruptly.

It is the coming and going of friends and the warmth our homes offers to us all that makes us thankful for the day we left the oil patch and took up farm life. The few years we lived at the Bradfield although uneventful are nice to remember.

Tom and Jessie's Wedding. July 6, 1948. Hazel Adams, Gordy Schultz, Jim Brown, Jessie and Tom, Kate Brown, Herb Adams.

Tommy started school at Millarville as did Leslie and although we moved to Priddis April 1, 1957 they completed that school term there. Gwen and Dave started school at Priddis and all six children (Including Dan and Tim who were born after we moved to Priddis) finished their junior high education at Red Deer Lake School. They then went on to Calgary High Schools.

Now that the family is almost grown Tom often remarks that he and Jessie will soon be on their own. However, for his new home he custom built a kitchen table four feet wide and seven feet long. His children have settled at such great distances from home too. Tom married Judy Jenkins from Duchess and they live in Calgary. Les married Mary Ann Stotz from Black Diamond and they also live in Calgary. Gwen married Wayne Blatz from Meadow Lake, Sask. and they live with their three children near Turner Valley. Dave lives in Black Diamond and Dan and Tim are still at home. Most Sundays we all live at Priddis.

The Story of William (Bill) J. Adams

by Louise Anderson

Bill Adams, second son of Thomas and Maria Adams was born in Port Hope, Ontario in 1887. He came to Alberta with his parents in 1900 and eventually filed on homestead S.E. ¼ 20-20-3W5. He married Vivian Willford in 1910, the third daughter of John and Frances Willford who trekked by covered wagon from Nebraska to Okotoks in the fall of 1899, after six months on the trail.

Around the time he and my Mother were married, Bill (my Dad) worked for the Calgary Petroleum Products Co., Well No. 1. Better known as the Dingman, this was the first producer in the Turner Valley Field. It blew in on May 14th, 1914. Dad drove freight wagons for Dingman, hauling supplies from Calgary and Okotoks and coal from the Burns Mine up the Highwood River. Mother cooked for the Dingman crew. They were with the Company until 1915 during which time their first three children (of eleven) were born. They were Robert (Bert), Olive, and Miles (Porky).

The family was living in the first small frame house they had built on the homestead and Emma was eight months old when the 1918 Flu Epidemic struck. Every member of the three Adams familys were stricken with the exception of Bert (eight years old) and Dad's youngest brother, Sid (in his teens). These two rode from place to place making firewood and soup and tending the needs of the sick ones and livestock. Dad took sick after returning from Okotoks where he and his elder brother Tom had made a trip for supplies. Tom took sick the following day and did not survive.

Dads next job was for the Lineham ranch. Mable was born there in 1919. Sometime in the early twenties Dad worked on a Government Survey crew, running lines and building roads. Their tools were horses and

149

L. to R. Kenny Foster, Keith Foster, Herb Adams, Vivian and Bill Adams. 1959.

scrapers and picks and shovels. Prior to 1922 the family moved into the big house on Ewings, S.W. ¼ 20-20-3W5, where I, Louise, the fourth daughter was born. The Dave Stewarts were living on Sam Scott's S.E. ¼ 19-20-3W5 across the road. Their sister-in-law, Mrs. Norman Stewart (R.N.) was visiting and assisted at my birth. The Ewing quarter later became the home of Granny, Bob and Gavin Calderwood for many years until it was sold to Sid Peel in the 1940s.

In 1923 we moved onto the Lusk quarter (better known as the Pocket Place). The folks started building the log house on the homestead. Jack was born in 1924 and the following year we moved into the unfinished log structure. There were just the rounds of logs, sub roof and dirt floor, the doors and windows empty openings in the unchinked logs. The family spent the cold winter of '25-'26 in a tent set up inside the log walls. Mable recalls George Lefthand of the Stoney Indian Band coming during the winter and noticing the cold feet on the dirt floor. He returned several days later with moccasins made of sheepskin, which were greatly appreciated.

Dad started working for the Royalite Oil Co. in 1929. He rode saddlehorse to work until one time his mount fell on him dislocating his shoulder. Then, he bought his first Model T Ford. Getting to work in the wintertime through the snowdrifts was sometimes quite a struggle, until he devised a way of mounting skis under the front axle of the car. He was able to keep the road open longer, altho on some of the corners the occupants of the vehicle got many a thrill. He was also very sports minded, enjoying baseball and played on the local team. He was a crack shot with a gun which greatly augmented the larder during the lean years prior and during the Dirty Thirties. In later years he and his brother Frank had many trophy heads mounted of deer, moose and goat and sheep. He was a superb dancer and on occasion called for square dances at the Kew and Rancher's Halls. Bert and Porky used to supply the music in these establishments with fiddle, banjo and guitar.

I, like the older members of my family, acquired my education at the Plainview School. The Christmas concerts were always the highlight of the year. I recall Mr. Enoch Walton, Proprietor of the Kew General Store and Post Office, visiting the school on the last day before Christmas with his annual gift of candy for each child. As youngsters, Jack and I were close companions, riding, playing and working together. We raised a coyote pup which we dug out of a den on the Strallendorff place. Shortly after it was fully grown it broke it's tether and raided the chicken pen one early morning. My older brother, Porky shot it, not knowing it was our pet coyote! Another incident I recall most vividly occurred while we were hauling gravel for Everett Headly who was the new owner of the Jim Short S.W. ¼ 21-20-3W5. We each had a four horse team on a haul one mile west of the homestead and were paid five dollars a trip. On one trip we were caught in the worst electrical storm of my existance. A bolt struck nearby, knocking both ourselves and one of the teams unconscious.

Two stories my folks used to tell of Jim Short comes to mind. In those early years Okotoks was the homesteaders nearest supply and R.R. Depot, ordinarily a two or three day trip depending on the load haul. Short had a pet moose which he used to drive on a light buggy or cutter and would make the trip in a day. Everyone marvelled at the distance covered so effortlessly with the moose. The second story concerns a rabbit hunt that Jim and two companions engaged in one winter. Short was wearing white rubbers which one of his companions mistook for a rabbit under the bushes, and blasted with his shotgun. Luckily the distance was such that only a few pellets penetrated.

Our log house was situated on the lip of a shallow draw. During run-off times in early spring a healthy stream of water rushed past the door. I remember as a very small child one such spring time when the folks were away for supplies, it was decided we should make a swimming hole. We damned up the creek and it wasn't long filling up. But the water was frigid so we spent several hours heating pots and kettles on the kitchen stove, which we dumped into the dreadfully cold, muddy pond. Of course, it didn't help a bit but we were having quite a time until two neighbor girls rode in to find about four very nude, very cold and dirty would be bathers who scurried into hiding in nothing flat.

Between 1926 and 1933 three more daughters were born. Joan arrived in 1926, Jean in 1930 and Lavone in 1933. It was during the summer of '33 that Dad and his good friend Harry Hunt took a holiday trip through B.C., in Harry's new Graham Page touring car. Equipped with a built in radio, it must have been the latest in luxury. When they got to Francois Lake west of Prince George, Dad was so impressed by the tall timber and tales of big game and fish that he filed on another homestead there. There was some mix-up regarding the location of the property, for when Brother Bert and Charlie Grant went out to prove up that fall, they found it twenty miles away and on a steep sidehill. They built a small log cabin and were joined shortly after Xmas by my Mother and the youngest members of the family with the exception of myself. Mable was the eldest at thirteen.

The family was unprepared for the severe winters with deep snows of Northern B.C. The nearest town and doctor was nine miles away mostly by ski or snowshoe travel since rarely the road could be travelled in winter by horse and sleigh. Luckily, the latter was the case when Lavone at fifteen months swallowed a handful of Dodd's Kidney Pills. Bert borrowed the neighbors horse and cutter to take Lavone and Mother to the Doctor. It was twenty-five below and the baby was in a coma. Miraculously, she survived. Another near tragedy was averted the time when Jack, aged 8 while whittling tripped and slashed Joan in the upper arm. Mother immersed the arm up to the shoulder into a 100 lb. sack of flour, which stopped the flow of blood and saved her life. Joan carries the scar to this day.

The family returned to Alberta in 1935. Bruce, the last member of our family, was born on the old homestead in 1936. They moved to Black Diamond in 1947 and Dad eventually sold the property to Sid Peel. In 1950, Mother and the three youngest moved to B.C. buying a small acreage near Lemon Creek in the Slocan Valley. Dad joined the family in 1952 after retiring from the Royalite Oil Co.

In 1968 Mother's health failed. They sold the acreage to Bruce and bought a home in Slocan, B.C. Mother spent most of her remaining two years hospitalized and passed away in January of 1970. Dad joined her in November of 1972. They rest in the Slocan Cemetery along with my Grandmother, Mrs. Frances Willford and her Mother, my Great-Grandmother Stimpson.

Bert: (better known as Bob) settled in the Wildwood, Alta. area after returning from Francois Lake, B.C. He worked at logging, construction and carpentry in the Wildwood, Edson and Hinton areas. He built and sold several houses in and around Edson and Hinton. He was a carpenter for the Hinton Pulp Mill when his health began to fail. In 1974 he moved back to Edson where he lived until his death in 1975. He married Florence Ernest and raised two sons, Bobby and Larry and two daughters Gwen and Judy.

Olive: Married Sam Webster, Blacksmith and employee of Home Oils now retired at Longview, Alberta. They raised three sons, Billy, Gordon and Ron.

Miles: (Better known as Porky) worked for Carl Ohlson and Bill Jackson before joining the Army in 1942. He went overseas with the Royal Canadian Engineers and served under the command of Gen Montgomery with the No. 1 Road Construction and mop-up division in France, Belgium and Holland. Upon returning in 1945 he got work on the oil rigs and in 1949 was with a test rig sent to the Queen Charlotte Islands. He was a driller for five years before moving to

Slocan, B.C. in 1961 where he still resides. He married Maryann Hodgkinson and they raised one daughter, Edna Marie.

Emma: Married Tom Maxwell, Postmaster at Wildwood, Alberta for many years. They raised three sons, John, Michael and Stewart. Tom passed away in 1976. Emma makes her home at Wildwood.

Mable: Married John Stuart. They left the oil fields in 1962 and moved to Perry Siding, B.C. where they bought a farm. They raised five sons, David, Gordon, Ed, Jim and Raymond; two daughters, Linda and Carol.

Louise: Married Irvin Anderson, Tugboat operator on Slocan, Arrow and Kootenay Lakes. They raised two sons, Gary and Jesse and one daughter, Aline.

Jack: Joined the Royal Can Infantry in 1943. Before going overseas in the fall of 1944 he took up heavyweight boxing in the Army and won several bouts in and around Calgary. He was killed in action during the Leopold Canal landing on Oct. 11, 1944. He is buried in Nymwegen, Holland.

Joan: Married Rusty Michiels, farmer and truck driver. Had three sons, Allan (killed in a lumber mill accident on Vancouver Island), Jerry and Randy.

Married Thor Hird, Farmer and Logger. Have two sons, Gene and Benny and one daughter, Freda.

Jean: Married Jack Cowley, Logger and Miner. They raised three sons, Ron, Bob and Bernie and two daughters, Pat and Debbie.

Lavone: Married Clarence Cowley (Brother of Jack) Logger. Killed in logging accident in 1966. Lavone raised one son, Lloyd, and four daughters, Darleen, Susan, Sandy and Charlotte. She lives in Golden, B.C.

Bruce: Has followed the sawmill circuit as worker, operator and foreman at Slocan, Golden, Enderby, Clinton and 100 Mile House, B.C. Married Joyce Collins and has four sons, Gordon, Don, Barry and Larry.

Married Sally McPherson and have one daughter, Brenda. They presently live at 103 Mile House, B.C.

Prelude to the Poem "Foothills Storm"

Jobs and money were hard to come by in the late Thirties prior to the war involvement in 1939, so it was every one's duty to share the load whenever we could. In the following poem, Everett Headley (school teacher) hired my brother Jack, who was then thirteen years of age and myself of fifteen, to haul gravel for his new house and retaining wall he was building on the edge of the coulee of the Jim Short place. We hauled the material from a gravel bank on the road allowance just south of the Ewing buildings, overlooking Waite Valley to the West.

FOOTHILLS STORM
by Louise Anderson

We laid our shovels on the loads, and swung the
    teams around;

Their sharpshod hooves then biting deep into the
  hard packed ground;
These last two loads of gravel would complete the
  concrete wall,
In the valley to the Eastward — it was a one mile
  haul.

The road wound south along a ridge, then east
  down the other side;
Off to the west between the hills, ran Waite
  Valley three miles wide.
Pausing often on the upgrade to let the horses rest;
Now their breathing came more quickly; their
  heaving sides now streaked with sweat.

When we gained the hilltop, far westward in the blue
A grey-black, rolling cloud took shape — how
  rapidly it grew!
We urged the horses onward, knowing well a storm
  was due;
A deadly calm hung on the air — the horses sensed
  it too.

Just a little further, just one more gentle rise;
Then we'd be on the topmost hill and start down
  the other side.
Then the wind set all a-tremble; there commenced
  a distant roar;
Gathering force and strong momentum — objects in
  its wrath was bore.

The sun went out behind the clouds that seemed to
  roll along the ground,
Interlaced with streaks of lightning; thunder
  made a deafening sound.
With brilliant flashes all about us and dancing
  along the wire fence,
The hair of the horses manes and tails standing
  up in weird suspense.

In my head a light exploded, without sense of
  shock or pain;
Just a dim yellow light bulb, when the gulf of
  blackness came.
There seemed to be no lapse of time — I was
  awakened by the rain;
My head upon the double trees amid the tugs and
  chains.

The big bay horse upon the left was stretched out
  on the ground;
The others, rising, shaking, trembling with
  bellies white with foam.
Acrid fumes of burning sulphur hanging heavy on
  the air;
All the posts along the roadway had dark burn
  rings to wear.

Half an inch of hail had fallen; all the world
  was ghostly white;
Thunder rumbled far to northward; thinning clouds
  let in the light.

With limbs so numb and shaky, I pulled myself
  upright
And quickly looked back to see if my brother was
  all right.

He lay outstretched upon his wagon, arms hung
  limply o'er the edge;
Not a single muscle moving — from appearance he
  seemed dead!
He stirred just as I reached him — eyes like fire
  in his head;
In a voice — 'twas but a whisper, "I'm o.k." was
  all he said.

I laid hailstones on his forehead to try to clear
  his brain;
Then I helped him up upon a horse — he clenched
  his hands around the hames;
All the horses on their feet now but much too
  weak to pull
The heavy loads of gravel. So we left them where
  they stood.

I chose the big sorrel Belgian, somehow crawled
  upon her back—
Where no other man had ridden excepting he — my
  brother Jack.
Home we went on legs so shaky, slipping sliding
  in the mud;
Every head so bent and weary — while the sun
  laughed from above!

James Sydney Aird

Born in 1896 in Millarville, the first white child.
Educated in Calgary and attended Mount Royal
College. Syd served in the Armed Forces during World
War I overseas with the University of Alberta bat-
talion. He was married in 1919 to Margaret Jackson.
To this union were born two sons; Jackson and David,
both educated in Calgary and graduates of the Univer-
sity of British Columbia. Both are prominent in their
fields of endeavour. Syd was a life member of Knox
United Church and was a Past President of the
Southern Alberta Old Timer's Association. He lived his
entire life in Calgary with the greatest interest in the
country and its lore. James Sydney Aird passed away
November 15, 1976.

Jackson Aird lives in B.C. and has two children,
Jacqueline and Brian.

David Aird lives in Toronto and has two children,
Jamie and Jeffrey.

William Alexander Aird (Bud)

Born July 4, 1895 at Calgary, NWT and resided at
Kew until the age of six. Educated in Calgary, atten-
ding A. E. Stark, Central Collegiate and Mount Royal
College.

He was a member of the Southern Alberta Old
Timers Assoc. and a Charter member of the
Associated Canadian Travellers formed in Calgary
and consequently became President of the Edmonton

The children of Alexander and Isobelle (Shortt) Aird, taken Sept. 1950; L. to R., J. S. (Syd) Aird, Winnie (Aird) Lehodey, Alice (Aird) Beckett, and W. A. (Bud) Aird.

charter. His business and residences encompassed all prairie provinces and Ontario.

William married Hazel Eilheck in 1920 and of this union twins were born in 1926; Russell William John, now residing in Scarborough, Ontario and Beverley Catherine Grace residing in Calgary.

W. A. Aird (Bud) passed away December 28, 1954.

Winnifred Grace Lehodey (Nee Aird)

Winnifred Grace Aird was the first baby born in the new maternity wing of the old General Hospital on 12th Avenue E. in 1900. She attended public and high school in Calgary and graduated from the Holy Cross Hospital in 1923. Winnifred nursed in Shaunavon, Saskatchewan where she married Maurice M. Lehodey. Two children, Isabella and Maurice were born to this union.

Isabella has two children, Kevin and Given. She and her husband, George L. Nelson farm in Wilcox, Saskatchewan.

Maurice Marcel and his wife Doris live in Calgary. They have three children, Robert, Brian (who attended the U. of Alberta) and Dianne who is a World Cup skiier.

Winnifred presently resides in Lethbridge, Alberta.

Alice Isabella Beckett (Nee Aird)

Alice Isabella Aird was born in Calgary in 1906. She attended public school at St. Hilda's College. After her mother's death she assisted her father in managing a general store in McAuley, Manitoba. After her father's death she moved back to Alberta where she married Ernest E. Beckett in Edmonton and was widowed three years later. Alice has always been in business and professional endeavours and is most interested in the Arts and Music and travel.

As a family we have enjoyed the heritage that has been passed on to us and it is our hope that our children and grandchildren will also enjoy it and always be proud to be Canadians.

Gordon Harold and Betty Akins   —A4

by B. Akins

On June 4, 1950, Gordie and I came to work for Mr. Cyrus McBee on his ranch, located on the SE¼ 30-21-4-W5th, right up against the Forest Reserve at Square Butte. A very quiet but beautiful place.

As Mr. McBee was getting on in years he needed someone to handle the ranching chores, and Gordon Akins was his choice. He took care of the feeding of cattle in winter, calving in the spring, and during the haying season the neighbors Tom and Joe Bell, also Dick Lyall, who lived 4½ miles east, came to help. Then Cyrus and Gordie returned their help to put up hay. This type of neighborliness also served when there was firewood to be cut, also at branding time. Many hands shortened the work and no one was "out of pocket" as Cyrus would say. This was very deeply appreciated by each rancher.

Gordie followed the rodeos before coming to work for Cyrus, his specialty being riding bulls and bareback broncs. He was one of the first to ride the Brahma bulls after they were imported to this country. So he was nicknamed "Brahma Akins" by the boys in the rodeo circuit. He was also known as "Slim" or "Red".

When school was out in 1950 I brought my daughter Barbara from B.C. to Cyrus's ranch. She really loved it out there, and had many adventures with her dog and an old horse called Shorty, that Cyrus allowed her to ride. It was during one of these adventures that

Betty Atkins standing by the old 1949 Ford.

L. to R. Mary Bell, Barbara Akins, Mrs. Bell.

The Jack Allan Family. Back row, L. to R.: Rory Allan and Matthew Jacobson. Middle row: Ellen, Jim, Dave, Danny Allen, Rod Allan and Jack Allan. Front row: Joe Jacobson, Doreen Jacobson, Sarah Jacobson, Gustina Allan.

resulted in Barb losing the sight of one eye. This was very sad, but outside of this, her memories are happy ones.

Barb received her education through correspondence the first two years we were at the ranch and then we made other arrangements so that Barb could receive her education. She boarded with Betty and Tom Lyall, who also lived in the Square Butte area, during the week and came home on weekends. This went on for one school year. She could ride the school bus with the other Square Butte children and Jake Reimer driving. The next year Mrs. Grace Chalmers boarded Barb during that school year, she lived quite close to the Millarville school, I'd say about a half mile.

It was in the Spring of 1954 that we parted company with Mr. McBee. We still remember him fondly. He was always kind and generous with us.

We also remember all the folks that lived around Square Butte at that time. I don't believe we have met their equal anywhere. They are a special brand of people. They never missed a chance to give a helping hand where needed. This friendliness and good will are unforgettable. They welcomed me into the Square Butte Ladies Group, and I strived to attend all their meetings which were held once a month. It was very pleasant meeting these women and working with them towards a good cause. I hesitate to mention their names as I am bound to forget someone.

Jack Allan Family

Jack was born in Okotoks June 1st, 1921. He was the first born son of Clark and Barbara (Mitchell) Allan. Barbara was a neice of John Lineham, pioneer of Okotoks. When Jack was eleven years old he moved

with his parents to Black Diamond, where he got his first taste of ranching. On Friday nights after school he would head out west of Turner Valley to the McGregor place where Bill Luscombe lived. Jack claims he had many close calls with unseen dangers in the long dark walks.

He worked on various jobs in the oilfields until the second World War. He joined the R.C.A.F. and was stationed in Vancouver where he met Miss Ellen Margaret Hicks, who was working for Dr. Dumont at that time at Vancouver. They were married and returned to Black Diamond for about a year, then moved to Edmonton, where Jack operated an oilfield trucking company for twelve years.

Once again, however, the urge to be a rancher brought Jack back to Millarville where he purchased a quarter section of land, the N.W. ¼ of 30-20-2W5, from Gene White, which had formerly been owned by Bert Mickle.

Jack and Ellen Allan.

Jack is presently employed by the Imperial Quirk Creek Gas plant.

Jack and Ellen's family of four include David, who attended Oilfields High School and is married to Gustia Tecklinburg from Okotoks. David got his ticket for Plumbing, Heating, Gas fitting, and steam fitting and now works in the Brooks Hospital. They have two sons, Danny and Roy.

Doreen married Joe Jacobsen, has a son Matthew and a daughter Sara. She has another month at the University and is planning on teaching school.

Jim is still single and has been employed by the Calgary Herald for the last eight years. Rod is attending Mount Royal, working at Dominion Oilfields in Calgary at present.

Garnet and Elaine Allen

Brand — E R.R.
Sec. 3, T. 22, R. 3, W. 5

We met in Calgary in 1950, where we were both employed. We were married at Dawson Creek in the spring of 1951, and took over Garnet's family farm at Hillmond, Saskatchewan.

We grain farmed there for seven years. Our two eldest children, Earl and Teren were born there. In 1957, we decided there had to be something better than grain, so Garnet came down to Calgary to look for land.

We bought our ranch from Jim Brown, who moved to Turner Valley. We moved November 11th weekend in 1957. We have never regretted our move and really love the area. I think the one thing we will never take for granted, is having all the water we can use, which was very scarce back in Saskatchewan.

Our last two children were born here. Tasha, who is in grade seven at Millarville, and Ward, who graduated last June and is helping his Dad on the ranch, Earl has his B.Sc. in Agriculture and works for Crestview Ranches. Teren is a Registered Nurse at Foothills Hospital in Calgary. She was married last fall to Bill Clarke of Calgary.

Alice Randmel — Nee Alice Muir Anderson

by Jean Perry

Born 1897 at Carnoustie, Scotland, eldest of five children born to Wm. M. and Jane Anderson. Emigrated to Canada with family in 1903 at age 6. Lived in Calgary for 2 years where she started school. The family then moved to Sheppard, 6 miles out of Calgary, where she attended school for one year. Another move was then made to Millarville where Alice's father homesteaded. She started classes at Fordville School as soon as it was built in 1908, walking 3½ miles each way. Alice later took a business course at the Garbutt Business College in Calgary, then joined the staff of the Bank of Montreal in Three Hills. While there, she met Reidar Randmel, newly out from Norway and also employed by the Bank of Montreal.

They were married in 1923. The first of their three daughters was born in Alberta in 1924. Reidar went to California to find work and Alice followed when the baby was 9 months old. They settled in Yuba City where Reidar was employed in a bank and then joined the Pacific Gas and Electric Co. as accountant. Two more daughters were born to them in California. Alice worked for many years in the office of the Del Pero Meat Packing Plant, and at a later date Reidar also joined this company as accountant. Alice died in 1956 and Reidar one year later. Two of the daughters still reside in Yuba City.

Children: **Gloria** — born 1924, Alberta. Married Don Hubbard (now a widow). Three children — Donald, Laurie and Victoria — 8 grandchildren.

Eunice — born 1926. Married Renzo Del Pero. Three children — Rickard, Lisa and Robert. Resides in Yuba City.

Betty Ann — born 1927. Married Ed Ingalls. Both work as Commercial Artists in San Francisco where they make their home. No children.

David Anderson Family   MH

I, along with my Mother, Mrs. Jane Anderson, brothers Kenneth and William, sisters Alice and Jean moved from the Millarville district to the Carbon district in 1916, here Mother bought a farm which I helped operate.

In 1939, I married Grace Guynn and we bought land of our own in the Webb school district and in 1945 we moved there, here we farmed and ranched. We grew mostly wheat, some barley and oats for feed. We had good pasture land with the Ghost Pine creek running through it, so kept a fair herd of cattle.

1929, Dave and Kenneth Anderson.

155

Spring was a busy time for we had to keep careful watch on the cows at calving time — many times we rescued a cold and shivering new-born calf and brought it in the house to warm and dry it. We also raised hogs, turkeys and chickens so had to have hired help the year around.

Farming and ranching was much more mechanized in the 1940s and 50s — tractors replaced horses, we had trucks, cars, bale loaders, hoists, lifts etc. which made work much easier. We also had telephones and electricity — hence stoves, fridges, deep-freezes etc. which made work much more pleasant.

We often think of our parents, grandparents and other pioneers who came here long ago, worked so hard, endured so many hardships and did without the conveniences which we enjoy today, they paved the way and we owe them much.

We enjoyed the busy life of farming and ranching, always found time to visit our neighbors, go to parties, picnics, rodeos, etc., went fishing at Pine Lake, the Red Deer river or local dams and each fall went big game hunting.

We have three daughters, Joyce Farthing, Myrna Jensen and Kay Hicks, seven grandchildren — Laurie and Jason Farthing, Monica, Drew and Nichole Jensen, Vicki and Angela Fredell — we see them often and now have more time to enjoy them.

We retired to Calgary in 1959, did some travelling and have many happy memories of friends in the Millarville, Webb and Carbon districts.

Jean Perry — Nee Jean Anderson

by Jean Perry

Born in 1900 in Barry, Scotland, second child of William M. and Jane Anderson. Arrived in Canada with family at the age of 3. Lived 2 years in Calgary, one year in Sheppard, then moved to Millarville at age 6. Started school at Fordville at age 8½. Later, took a business course in Calgary and went to work in Saskatchewan in the Bank of Toronto. Two years later, I returned to Alberta to join the staff of the Royal Bank in Hanna, Alta. In 1928 I went to California where I stayed with my sister Alice in Yuba City, and worked in the office of a fruit packing plant. Returned to Canada in 1931 and married George Perry, C.N.R. Conductor, and took up residence in Mirror, Alta. Our three children were born in Mirror. Moved to Edmonton in 1953 when my husband transferred to Passenger Service. He retired in 1956 and died in 1975. I still live in my own home in Edmonton.

Children:

Claire — born 1932; married David W. Smith who teaches at University of Guelph, where they make their home; Three children — Nancy 18, Sheila 17, Sandra 9.

Sheila — born 1934; married Wm. F. Howlett, Imperial Oil Ltd., Calgary office; Sheila is employed by Dome Petroleum; Three children — Patricia 19, Neil 18, and Jill 15.

Georgene — born 1942; married in 1968 to Wm. Munn (now separated), no children; School teacher-librarian; Lives in Edmonton.

Kenneth Anderson

Kenneth Anderson, second son and fourth in the family of the late William M. (Stoney) and Jane Anderson, pioneers of the Millarville district.

Attended school in my primary years at Fordville and finished in the Carbon district. One of my teachers was Mrs. Annie E. Wright who was THE Anne of Green Gables. She drove with horse and buggy 12 miles to our school and never missed a day, even at 60 degrees below zero.

Friend with Ken and Lottie Anderson.

In 1926 I met Wilf Carter, who had come out from Nova Scotia for a job harvesting and we worked together on the Threshing gang.

In 1928 I met my bride to be, Charlotte McKeown from Belfast, North Ireland and we were married in 1930. We farmed a section of land on the Ghost Pine Creek until 1945 when we moved to Powell River, B.C.

Our family consists of a daughter, Patricia, she and her husband Chuck Opheim live in the Millarville area. Chuck is salesmanager for Texas Refinery Corp., they have two children, Mark age 16 and Sanna age 14.

Our son Ian Anderson also lives in the Millarville area and is a salesman for Texas Refinery.

My wife and I are retired in Powell River, B.C. and hope to travel as much as possible in future.

William B. Anderson

Anderson, William B. (Bill), youngest of family of William Muir Anderson, late of Millarville, Alberta.

I was raised in the Carbon district, attending Gamble School, and Mount Vernon School, followed by High School at Three Hills and Carbon.

I joined the Bank of Montreal at Three Hills in 1927 and served in various branches throughout Alberta. In 1952 we settled in Edmonton, where we still reside.

In 1937 I was married to Orvilla McCue of High Prairie, Alberta, a teacher, who served in several Northern Alberta districts, and for a time with the Edmonton Public School Board. Latterly, she was employed on the faculty of the Alberta Vocational Centre.

Our family is as follows:

Son — Alistair (Al), educated in Edmonton, and at University of Alberta. Employed by Government of Alberta. With wife Barbara and two small daughters, Kimberly and Kathryn, resides in Sherwood Park, Alberta.

Son — Keith, educated in Edmonton, and at University of Alberta. Employed as instructor at the Alberta Vocational Centre. He and his wife, Carol reside in Edmonton.

Daughter — Elaine, educated in Edmonton, has several years service with Bank of Montreal. Her husband, Roger Bissonnette, is engaged in the operation' of Caltech Laboratories Ltd. With small daughter Jackie, they make their home in Sherwood Park, Alberta.

Vair Anderson

by M. Vair Anderson

In September, 1944, almost 34 years ago, I assumed the position of principal of the three-roomed Sheep Creek School. On December 27 of that year, I married Flora Massie, and we spent the first year and a half of our married life in a Sheep Creek School teacherage.

After two years we left and I became principal of the Glenmore school near Calgary. After four years there, I left teaching and worked in Calgary for twenty-one years.

For the last four years we have lived in Clearwater, B.C. We have two sons, Bruce and Byron. They are both married and working in Clearwater, Bruce as a

Vair Anderson with Sheep Creek pupils in 1945. L. to R. Benny Dichau, Bob Moody, Phyllis Adams, Betty Adams, Alfred Moody, Anne Jackson, Fern Jackson, Charis Blakley, Vair Anderson. Front: Wally Larratt, Harvey Potter, Billy Martin, Audrey Rawlinson, Mona Fisher, Yvonne Hodgkins, unknown, Lorraine Fisher, Marian Sloan.

doctor and Byron as an electrician in one of the sawmills.

Our memories of the Millarville district are very pleasant. Both Flora and I love the foothills and spent our early years in or around them, south west of Calgary. Very pleasant, also, are my memories of the Sheep Creek School, the pupils I taught there and of my associate teachers, Mrs. Mildred Sawkins, Mrs. Eric Mulder and Miss Grudecke, now Mrs. Allan Deines. We remember well the generosity and friendliness of the people of the district. We remember, with pleasure, climbing the big hill north of the school, ball games at the school, Christmas concerts and a general feeling of friendliness in the community.

We also remember the morning we slept in and awoke up with headaches and a smell of gas in the air, because of a leak in a gas line behind the teacherage. We remember the flares that lit up the whole valley and surrounding hills at night.

When we think of "our foothills" we don't wonder that so many of the early settlers in the west chose the Millarville and Kew districts for their permanent home.

Andrew Family

by Nora (Andrew) Krake

Calvin Lewis Andrew was born at Maymont, Saskatchewan, December 1909, oldest of a family of five and took part of his schooling at a little country school. Later the family moved to a farm in the Drummond Creek district, 25 miles S.W. of North Battleford. The rest of his schooling was taken at the little school in their district and Cal and his brother ran the farm after their father died.

In 1934, Cal married Nora Newhouse of the Wilkie district and they moved into a little house on their own farm.

Those were the dirty thirties when a complete crop yielded six bushels of wheat and not enough oats to fill a wheelbarrow. Cream sold for $1.50 for a five gallon can, eggs at 5 cents a dozen and a six hundred pound steer netted $2.79. But those were happy days — no one went hungry on the farm, with plenty of meat, vegetables, eggs and milk. Those who did not live in those days have missed a good deal of life — the Bennett buggy, covered cutters in the winter, friendly card parties and dances that cost 25 cents per man — "Ladies, please bring a cake." I am sure those were the happiest years, especially as we had added two sons to our family — Tommy and Jimmie.

However, far away fields look green and Cal came to the Turner Valley oilfields to seek work. I stayed with my sister-in-law for a week. Cal phoned to say he had a job with Bill Ross at Black Diamond and was getting $5 a day. We were all so excited and I can remember sitting down with pen and paper and listing all the things we would buy and all the money we would have in the bank. What a dream.

Cal and Nora Andrew in their store at Turner Valley.

The boys and I left a week later and arrived in Black Diamond, and we lived in a suite in the Welcome Inn. That was in November and in January Cal took pneumonia so we went back to Saskatchewan.

In March we headed back to Alberta, a trip never to be forgotten. We started out in our truck, red body and yellow fenders, packed with what little furniture we had, pickles, fruit and canned meat and thirty dollars in our pockets, all our worldly goods. From Wilkie to Hanna, a distance of over a hundred miles, we had seven flat tires. I drove while Cal patched the inner tubes and we finally arrived and stayed the night with friends. Arriving in Black Diamond we managed to rent a house over by the school and with the twenty dollars we had left, put the down payment on the gas and power and in a few days Cal went to work for Anglo-American Oil Co. who were drilling oil wells in the Millarville district.

The next year we bought a little three roomed house at Little Philadelphia and had it moved to one of the Butler lots in the west end of Black Diamond. In 1944 the Company moved the house to Income 1 Tank Farm and later moved us to the Miracle Tank Farm where we lived until 1960. Many happy years and good friends were made during those years. I worked in the post office at Millarville for a few years before we moved to Turner Valley.

While at the Miracle Tank Farm we kept a few cows and horses and had the brand, after our two boys, Tommy and Jimmie and this brand is still kept by Jimmie.

Both our boys took their schooling at Millarville Tommy took one year at Olds Agriculture School then went to work for Purity 99 Plant at Hartell, later moving to Fort St. John to work on oil rigs. In 1957 he came home and went to work on an oil rig on Plateau Mountain. In April of 1957 he was killed in a car accident near Lacombe, Alta. on his way to visit his grandparents in Saskatchewan. He was 21 years old at the time of his death.

Jimmie took his grade twelve at Mount Royal College in Calgary, then took a course in Electronics and went to work for Burrows Business Machines for three years and then worked for Co-op Fertilizer Plant when it opened in Calgary. In 1969 he married Susan Beamish of High Prairie and moved to a ranch in the High Prairie Area. He worked for Buchanans Sawmill for five years then went to work for the Dept. of Highways, where he is still employed. They have one son, Sean Crawford, who attends school in High Prairie.

In 1960, Cal and I bought the Turner Valley Drug Store and moved our home into the town. We turned the dispensary into a coffee shop and had a good business and made many friends. In 1965, Cal died of a heart attack, a wonderful man, well thought of by all who knew him and a wonderful husband and father.

I carried on the store until 1965 and then married Russell Krake of North Battleford, Sask. The store and house were sold to my brother-in-law, Bill and Elaine Andrew.

Russell and I are now living in Battleford, Sask., retired, but spending our time with hobbies, fishing, curling, bowling and handicrafts. We spent two years looking after a regional park and two years managing a fly-in fishing camp in Northern Saskatchewan, but now we are enjoying life with family and friends.

Wallace and Jean Andrew
by Jean Andrew

Wallace Andrew, son of Leona (McBee) and Jim Andrew, married Jean Robinson of Innisfail in June of 1954 and moved directly to the Square Butte district, settling with his uncle Cyrus McBee on his place.

We were welcomed to the community with a shower. Neighbors were friendly, although the nearest

Andrew Family Orchestra. L. to R. Wallace, Jean, Ron, Sherry.

was four miles away. We celebrated our first anniversary with a group of them in the unfinished new house (only place large enough). In December of 1955 Lora Leone was born. The following summer we moved into the new house. At times it seemed lonely, living at the end of the trail and a difficult trail to travel in times of bad weather or spring break-up. However when we did get out, it was to good times, and Square Butte dances where Wallace helped out with the music and lots of friendly visiting and exchange of work. There was an abundant supply of fish and wild game of which we enjoyed our fair share. Sunday visitors were a common occurence and it was nothing to have 10 extra for dinner and a different 10 for the evening meal.

In 1957, about Millarville Fair time, a son Ronald arrived on the scene.

Jean was a member of the Square Butte ladies club and started writing the district news to the North Hill News. Wallace started the boys' baseball club with practise at the Foster's. Later John Kendall took this over.

Our Uncle Cyrus died in June of 1960, and we continued to live on the place. The following year Square Butte and the area close by had a baby boom and Sherry Lynn Andrew was one of them. At this time we had the bad news that we could not get the school bus to come for our children and so Lora stayed with the John Kendalls and went to school at Sheep Creek from there. We felt this was too much and so sold out and returned to the Innisfail area in the spring of 1963, where we could get our children out to school and other activities. Many were the good times we had there and many are the wonderful friends we still have. Square Butte will always hold a special place in our hearts.

Wallace Andrew with a fine catch of fish caught in Fisher Creek.

Arkes Family. L. to R. Ron, Wendy, Ronnie, Lisa, Bernie and Jeanette.

Arkes Family

Jeannette and Ron Arkes were both born in Holland. Jeannette was born 24th. August 1940 in Borne, Overijsel. Ron came into the world 18th. September 1925 in De Bilt, Utrecht. Jeannette came to Calgary with her parents in January 1955. Ron was born on a dairyfarm, where he grew up. He then joined the Armed Forces and spent four years in the Dutch East Indies, (Indonesia) of his six years service.

He came to Canada and worked for the P.F.R.A. Then he was employed as herdsman at the Lazy F T ranch in Hussar for six years. After that he managed the Model Dairies Jersey Farm for two years. He rented three quarter sections and farmed for two years but life was too lonely so he became a truck driver and worked for Midland Superior and Melchin Transport. On the highway near Airdrie he met his wife to be, whose father had a flat tire.

In 1959 he rented the old Pearson place, South of the Red Deer Lake Store, where Jeannette and Ron got married and started a small dairy. Later they bought a big dairy farm by Conrich but after six years they moved back to the hills.

In the meanwhile they started their family and Wendy was born in 1960, Bernie in 1962, Ronnie in 1964 and Lisa in 1966. All four of the children attended Millarville School. Jeannette and Ron both became active School Bus Drivers in 1968. They built their home on N.W.¼, S26, T21, R4, W 5. In 1976 Lesley Bishton joined the Arkes family at their farm. 1978 saw Jeannette and Lesley starting an Animal Health Supply, Pet, Feed, Tack and Saddlery Store in Turner Valley. In conjunction with Ron they are all actively involved in School Bus Safety and training of Safety Oriented School Bus Drivers.

Wendy (Foster) Ashbacher
by Wendy Ashbacher

In November, 1953 I was born as the one and only daughter of Chub and Nita Foster of Kew. In the fall of

L. to R. Wendy and Darrel Ashbacher. Front, Zane.

1960 I started my schooling at the Sheep Creek School, now the Millarville School, and continued my high school education in the Turner Valley High, Black Diamond, Alta.

During my years at home I spent many hours outside with my Dad either helping or hindering him. School sports were a big interest in my younger years and I was always involved in community organizations. For three years I was secretary-treasurer of the Three Point Riding Club. My memberships into 4-H clubs consisted of two years in the Millarville Busy Beavers Food Club and four years in the Black Diamond Buttons and Bows Clothing Club. I helped organize the Millarville Stitch-In-Time 4-H Club and was a member for one year.

In October of 1972 after completing grade twelve I continued my education in Edmonton at the Alberta

Vocational Centre taking a Laboratory and X-ray Technician course. I got my certification in May of 1974 already having spent a year working in the Athabasca Municipal Hospital, Athabasca, Alberta. In June of '74 I returned to my parent's place and worked for my Dad for awhile. August of '74 found me getting a part-time job in the Turner Valley Municipal Hospital and I worked there until May of 1975 when I went back to work on the farm. September found me short of money and looking for a job again, this time taking me back north to the Breton General Hospital, Breton, Alberta where I am still employed.

On August 27, 1977 at the C. K. Giles Ranch, Darrel Ashbacher of Hoosier, Saskatchewan and I were married. January 20, 1979 found us with a son, Zane Darrel. We still live in Breton but hope to live on our land at Oyen, Alberta one day.

John Atkins

John is the elder son of the late Mr. and Mrs. Richard Atkins. Born at Lake Forrest, Illinois in 1905, he came with his parents and sisters to Springbank on the western outskirts of Calgary. He attended the old West Calgary School at 45th Street and 17th Avenue (where the 17th Ave. Drive-In Theatre is now located), and Sprucevale School.

During this period of time, the family was engaged in dairying and John acquired a great interest in breeding and showing Holstein cattle, taking part in many of the milking competitions held at the Exhibitions. After much saving, his ambition was realized when he purchased a registered Holstein of his own, and from there built his herd.

John has two sisters, Mrs. May Blake, Washington, Mrs. Irene Standish, Langley, B.C., and a brother, Kenneth in Black Diamond.

After his parents retired, John and Betty Watt, only daughter of Mr. and Mrs. Alex Watt also of Springbank, were married in 1943. Betty, born in Scotland immigrated to Canada with her parents and brothers in 1924. In 1925, they moved on to a dairy farm neighboring the Atkins. That farm is now part of "Strathcona Heights".

Wendy (Foster) Ashbacher.

John and Betty Atkins with sons Gordon and Norman.

160

John and Betty continued to dairy on the original home site for several years before moving further west in Springbank, near "Artists View Point", directly south of the CFAC T.V. transmitter.

In 1947, their first son Norman, was born who inherited a great love and admiration for Holstein cattle and now operates his own dairy at Leduc. A second son, Gordon was born in 1949. He too became keenly interested in livestock, primarily Holsteins. He studied Veterinary Medicine in the Saskatoon Veterinary College and is now a partner in a Calgary Veterinary Clinic. Gordon and his wife JoAnne make their home in Calgary.

In the spring of 1970 John, Betty and family moved to the Millarville district on part of the original Joe Standish farm, dairying there for a few years. Due to John's failing health and no room for expansion, Norman moved the herd to Leduc where he and his wife, Marjorie enjoy breeding, showing and exporting Holsteins. John and Betty remained in the Millarville district.

Ralph Ayling

by L. Ayling

Ralph was born in England, and came to the Alix district of Alberta in 1910. He farmed at Alix and other areas of Alberta, and was Manager of the Buffalo Hills Ranch at Arrowwood for fourteen years.

I came from the Fraser Valley area of British Columbia to Arrowwood in 1934. Our daughter Doreen was born in Calgary.

From Arrowwood we moved to Millarville. We bought the Calling Valley Ranch from Frank Standish in September, 1944. At that time it comprised the N.W.¼, Sec. 12, T.22, R.3, W.5 of deeded land and a half section of government lease.

Ralph brought some registered Herefords, dairy cattle and horses from Arrowwood. He kept grade beef cattle on the lease pasture. This wooded area was very pleasant and interesting in the summer. There were wild flowers and berries, and a small lake completely surrounded with trees whose branches met to form a

The Frank Standish house, a warm cozy little house, contributed by Laura Ayling.

shelter for the cattle. I believe Frank Standish called it the barn.

Ralph rode with Guy Pallister on the P. Burns Ranch, and Mr. Fortney on the Anchordown Ranch. There was the usual problem with strangers who open pasture gates and neglect to close them. When cattle wandered away in this wooded area they were difficult to find and round up. On one occasion they found the strays in some dense brush north of the Priddis corner.

Neither the phone nor power was available. The nearest phone was at the Hugh McNain home near the Priddis corner.

Jack Lee brought our supplies from Calgary during the winter when we were snowed in. The highway along our property was very slippery and treacherous. Our work horses were kept busy pulling cars out of the ditch. One car overturned. Fortunately the two couples and their small children escaped injury. Another time a Mounted Police car went off the road. Bill Prichard was helping Ralph. The footing was rough and slippery for the horses. Finally they made a sudden lunge. The car hit Ralph and he suffered several cracked ribs. The Mounties took him to the Col. Belcher Hospital in Calgary to have his ribs taped, and brought him home.

Mr. and Mrs. Charles Bull were the only people we knew when we moved to Millarville. Our neighbors made us welcome, and we enjoyed the years we spent on the Calling Valley Ranch.

We sold the property in 1947 to Mr. E. D. Arnold and Mr. and Mrs. Tom Day. Since then we have lived in British Columbia, Calgary and Turner Valley.

Ralph has been in the Twilight Nursing Home in High River since November, 1976.

Merle and Hans Backs

Hans and I moved to Millarville with our three children, Eveline, Bob, and Phyllis in the spring of 1943.

First, I will go back a few years and tell you a little about us before that time.

Myself, I was born in Minnesota and came to Canada (Enchant, Alberta) when I was 4 years old. I've done many things in my life that my children and grandchildren still like to hear about.

Times were hard when I was growing up. My dad was a camp cook and Mother and us children took care of the farm. When I was thirteen I wanted a piano but because Dad couldn't afford it he bought me a violin for 10 dollars; it's the one I still have today. This lead me to playing in an orchestra for dances in the Enchant area for a few years.

Some of my endeavours for making money at this time included trading my Dad a colt I had raised for a big sow that was due to have little ones — she had only one little pig and it was born dead. Next I tried farming — I bought the grain, paid my brothers to seed it and harvest it but due to grasshoppers, cutworms, and drought, I came up losing instead of gaining. Also, I

Hans Backs Family. Back, L. to R.: Bob, Phyllis, Eveline. Front: Merle, Gwen and Hans.

tried my hand at coyote hunting along with brother Archie. In the early fall we started training our young coyote hounds. Taking three of these in a crate on the democrat we set out after the coyotes. They were plentiful on the prairies then. When we found one we started to circle it, first in a large circle then drawing in closer as the coyote got used to us. When we got close enough we released the hounds and they would soon have Old Mr. Coyote. A prime hide was worth about $20.00 at this time. Mind you, not many of the hides were prime — many were small or mangy and not worth much money.

One of my more successful endeavors was cooking for a threshing crew. I made $6.00/day cooking for 12-17 men. My dad, who cooked for about the same size of crew, made $10.00/day because he was a man.

Next, I took up barbering and beauty culture, and became a travelling hair-dresser spending a day or two in each little town; Enchant, Traverse, Lomond, and Vulcan.

Deciding there was more money in cooking I moved to Calgary and cooked in a boarding house, then on to Didsbury where I cooked in the hotel.

Near Christmas time of 1934, I decided to quit my job and go home. (My family had now moved to James River Bridge.) It was during the Christmas season that I met Hans.

Now, to tell a bit about Hans' life. Hans was born in Hamburg, Germany, and came to Canada when he was 19 yrs. old. Hans was the only son of a band master. When he was a young lad, Hans had a tough exam coming up in school. On the fateful day he decided that he would play sick and miss his exam. He complained of severe stomach cramps so his mother and dad sent for the family physician. Upon examination, the doctor declared that Hans had acute appendicitis and that an immediate operation was necessary. Now Hans was in a dilemma — trying to decide which was the lesser of two evils — to tell his dad (who was a very stern gentleman) that he was not really sick, or to have the operation which he didn't really need. He decided on the latter; he not only had his appendix removed, but was rewarded with a gold watch from his father for being such a brave boy. I'm sure he had many guilt feelings over this, but it has afforded his children and grandchildren many laughs over the years.

When he was 19, Hans was reading in the newspapers "Go West Young Man", so he decided, along with two of his friends to come to Canada. He got a job on the Reed Ranch in Olds. It was a great new experience for him. He loved the life — especially the horses — and soon was riding with the best.

Hans and I met at Christmas, 1934 and were married in May, 1936. We lived in a little two room log cabin in James River Bridge which he built and where our first two children Eveline and Bob were born. Times were hard in these years. We left the farm in 1939 and moved eleven times in the following two years — including the towns of Olds, Carbon, Vulcan, and back to Olds when he joined the army in the fall of 1941.* In the spring of 1943, Hans got an honorable discharge because of difficulty in obtaining his Canadian citizenship papers due to loss of birth certificate during the war.

At this time we moved to Millarville where he was a roughneck on the oil rigs. We lived in three different houses in the district called Majorville, and moved to Millarville in the summer of 1945. Our house was immediately north of where Arlie Laycraft now lives. Hans started a service station and bulk station situated where Laycrafts house now is. (The original garage building was bought by Seth Peat and moved to his farm west of Millarville. This is the house that George Connop now lives in.)

Approximately three years later he bought out the garage started by Ginger Douglass located where it still stands and is now owned and operated by our son Bob.

Originally the garage was an Esso station but before long Hans changed to B/A which is now Gulf. At this time he worked about sixteen hours a day, working in the service station during the day, and hauling gas at night.

During these years, Hans fixed up a half-ton truck with a canvas covered frame and benches inside with which he drove the Millarville chidren to school, which was still located 2½ miles west of Millarville.

At this time too, I remember, there was a community pasture where everyone kept their milk cows. Then too, we all made use of the community well located south of where the municipal garage now is. We all carried water from this well.

*Our third child, Phyllis, who was later to become "Miss Rodeo of Canada" was born in Olds in 1940.

In 1946, our last child, Gwen, was born here in Millarville.

In 1951, we sold our house in Millarville to Ken Thompson for 10 head of cows and calves, and bought and moved to the property belonging to Karen King. These were happy years for Hans and I and our young

E A S T E R   B I R D

VICTORIA PARK, CALGARY, JULY 11, 1967, BILL NORRIS UP
BIG CHEESE(2nd)   7 FUR.   1:27:2   LINA PAGE(3rd)
H. L. BACKS, OWNER - TRAINER

Hans Backs' "Easter Bird" winning at Calgary. L. to R. Hans Backs, young fellow wanting to get in picture, John Heath (at horse's head) Merle Backs. Bill Norris the jockey.

163

family. The children were able to have saddle ponies, and I kept and milked 3 milk cows and shipped cream.

In 1964 Hans indulged in a dream of his and bought two thoroughbred mares. This was the start of a different life for us. He gradually relinquished the management of the garage to our son Bob and started spending more and more time with the horses, until in 1967 he did his own training at the track. He had a very successful year, with both fillies he raised from his original purchase being handicap mares, and a mare that he claimed winning 5 races for him that year. I was never far behind him — from race meet to race meet — never missing a day at the races — betting on every race. Win or lose, I had a ball! I remember once, Hans gave me some money to make a bet for him and I forgot to make the bet. His horse won the race so I had to get busy and get betting so that I could make enough money to pay Hans his winnings. I did it, but it was a long time before I told him about it.

It was a sad day for us when, on Dec. 8 of that same year, Hans suffered a fatal heart attack.

As a family, we tried to carry on with Hans' plans for the horses until in 1970 I was involved in a car accident in which I broke my neck. I spent many months in recuperation.

In Dec. of 1970 Eveline and her family bought the home place and took over the horses.

I bought a double-wide mobile home and have it on the home place where I still live.

The past few years I have been enjoying watching my ten grandchildren growing up, and doing some travelling which has included trips to Alaska, Hawaii, Italy, and the States, many of which I was accompanied by my very good friend, Cubby Tosh. We are planning on seeing more of the world in the future.

Backs, Robert and Joyce (Lee)

Robert Hans Backs born at James River Bridge, Alberta on March 11, 1939, only son of Hans and Merle Backs. He moved to the Millarville district in 1943 with his family, where his father was working in the oilfields. Robert attended Sheep Creek School and then Red Deer High majoring in mechanics.

Joyce Anna Lee born May 13, 1940 at Calgary, eldest daughter of Bill and Ethel Lee. She attended Sheep Creek School and graduated from Turner Valley High School. She was also employed at the Canadian Imperial Bank of Commerce in Calgary.

Robert and Joyce were married in the Millarville Christ Church on August 23, 1958. In 1960 Robert and his father formed a partnership in Millarville Motors, this partnership continued until his father passed away in 1967. Robert then purchased his mother's interest in the business and a Limited Company was formed.

In 1968 a friend, Lyall Ismond of Bragg Creek was working for a company that sold snowmobiles. Robert was soon selling snowmobiles as a side line, but this soon grew to be a big part of the business. It helped to fill in the slow time in the winter months. Robert and

Back: Robert and Joyce Backs. Front: Beverly, Terry, Brenda.

Joyce have had many pleasurable and memorable occasions connected with snowmobiles; from trail riding to getting involved in racing with old and new friends. They have been lucky enough to win three all expense paid trips to different parts of the world. This is something they would not have done on their own.

Robert and Joyce have three children, Beverly Ann, born on November 19, 1959; Terry Robert, born October 15, 1961; Brenda Lynn, born on June 24, 1964. Beverly is a Beautician having received her licence in 1978 and is employed in Calgary, Terry is now attending Oilfield High. Brenda is attending school at Millarville.

The George Bailey Family
by Arlene Dear

My father, George Bailey, was born in Elkhorn, Manitoba, 11 March 1899, the second son of Russell and Mary Bailey. In the year 1900 they moved to Alberta and settled on the Bailey Flats near Bassano. A few years later they moved to Blackfalds where my father

Branding time at Cannons'. L. to R. George Bailey, Stuart Cannon and Bill Bailey.

grew up. He often reminisced about the pleasant memories and experiences of his early years. My grandmother Bailey died in 1919, at which time the farm was sold and my father went to work for Clay Howard near Cayley and Parkland.

In 1923 he married Phyllis Mounkes, second daughter of Alfus and Rebecca Mounkes of the Big Rock district near Okotoks.

For a time Mom and Dad farmed the Gier Place and then moved to the "Homestead" in the Ballyhamage district. Here my brother Alvin was born in 1928 and my sister Betty in 1930. I started to school at Ballyhamage where Miss Eileen Jameson was the teacher at that time.

From here we moved to the Dutton Place north of Sheep Creek in the New Valley district. We had to cross Sheep Creek on a saddle horse to get to school, an experience I shared with Maudie Glaister and Margaret Freeman.

From Dutton's, we went to Black Diamond and the Lineham district.

In 1940 we moved to Calgary where my father worked in the bakery business until his retirement; he died of a heart attack in August 1969.

Alvin is married, lives in Calgary and has three sons — all married. Betty is married, lives in Calgary and has two daughters.

I married Herb Dear from Lockport, Manitoba, in October 1942, and we have four sons, Doug, Ron, Tim and Bob. Doug, Ron and Tim are married. We have three grandsons and one granddaughter.

Herb has worked for the "Gas Co." for more than thirty years and has had many opportunities to work in these districts at one time or another.

Some of my fondest memories come from the time my family spent in the foothills districts, such as the excitement and hospitality of Cannon's Branding Day, visiting our neighbours the Stewarts, Riches and Barlows. I heard my first radio broadcast over a

crystal set at Barlows. Attending the Millarville Races, Black Diamond, High River and Midnapore Stampedes, where my father often saddled bronks for the cowboy contestants and my uncle Bill Mounkes calf-roped. Christmas at my grandparents with all the families in attendance. Christmas concerts at the country schools.

Each fall we look forward to a weekend drive through these familiar foothill districts and once again enjoy the fall scenery and recall the happy memories of time spent here.

The William John Bailey Family
by Mildred May (Bailey) Unser

My father, William John (Bill) Bailey was born in Elkhorn, Manitoba in 1897.

In 1900 the family moved to Bailey Flats (so named after them) near Bassano. They later farmed at Black Falls.

After the death from diptheria of Grandmother Mary Georgina Bailey in 1919, my Grandfather Russell Rose Bailey sold the farm and the boys, my Uncle George and Dad, worked around Cayley. My Dad then went to the "T.L." Ranch to work for Mr. Riddell. That was where his brand, the ⅄ was originated. (Now registered to Edmund W. Mounkes).

While at the "T.L.", he met my mother Alice Mildred (Millie) Mounkes, the eldest daughter of Alfus Calvin and Rebecca Mounkes. They were married March 23, 1921.

The "T.L." was their first home and from there they moved around the Okotoks district, finally settling on the Stanhope farm. It was about three miles north and a little west of Black Diamond. Mabel and Stan Stanhope's buildings were a half mile east of ours. Our place had a huge red barn on it which could be seen for miles.

It was there I started school at New Valley. Mr. George Scott was the teacher — the best I ever had and I shall never forget him. I took grade 1 and started grade II when my Dad died of a heart attack. He died

Family reunion, July 1976. L. to R., Back row: Doug, Ron, Bob, Tim. Second row: Sharon, Candy, Phyllis Bailey, Arlene, Herb. Front row: Jana, Tyler, Todd and Jayson.

Bill Bailey on Jug with May on Mickie going to Black Diamond.

early one morning in the fields while threshing for Mr. Luscombe, September 25, 1931.

I have some very happy memories of our time there: — .... of calling on Elliene Burns on my way to school. She lived half-way between home and school and of stopping in on my way home for some of Mrs. Burns' dessert (I wouldn't eat supper, but I sure liked the dessert!).

... of going home with Isa-May and Jacqueline de Palezieux after school. Mr. and Mrs. de Palezieux were always so very nice to me, I loved to hear the girls tell of their trips to Switzerland. Isa-May could draw horses beautifully and try as I would, I never mastered the art of drawing a horse. Dad would wait so long after school and if I didn't appear, he would ride all the way over the big hill to the west of us (to de Palezieux's) and bring me home. How he kept his patience, I will never know.

... of riding with my Mother and Dad to Black Diamond. They had two beautiful riding horses, Jug and Kid, and I had my Shetland "Mickey" — my pride and joy.

After my Father's death, and because he left no will, our possessions had to be sold and the related death taxes paid. My Mother and I moved back to my Grandparents' farm — eleven miles south and west of Okotoks. I went to school there from grade II to VI at Sky Glen School.

My Mother married James (Jim) Grondahl in 1934 and we moved to Calgary, where my two sisters were born. Marjory lives in Calgary. Marleen married Wayne Cameron and they live with their two children in Edmonton.

In 1941 I took a hair styling/cosmetology course at Jacobson's Hair Styling Academy and after completion, married John Stupak in October, 1942. Our son, William Michael (Bill) was born October, 1944. In October of 1947, John died of cancer.

My dear friend, Dorothy Berenik, whom I met on course, worked with me at various beauty salons. We then opened our own, the "Dorothy-May Beauty Salon" which we operated until five years ago.

In 1966 I married Lawrence (Larry) Anton Unser. We live in Calgary and he is with A.G.T.

Bill is married and has two children, Shannon Lee and William Michael Jr. Bill works for the Calgary Fire Dept. My Mother is well and lives at Mount Royal House in Calgary. My stepfather passed away in 1963.

In summary, I am grateful to have been part of this pioneer heritage and proud to be an Albertan today.

Theresa (Ball) Reneau

Being uprooted from the city and transplanted on the South East ¼ of 33-21-4W5 wasn't about to turn me into a lover of nature over night, however I was started on the road to having a great respect for Mother Nature.

The arrival of the truck with all the worldly goods of Arthur and Annie Ball and their seven children, was

John and Theresa Reneau.

the reason I had found myself all alone with my baby brother Arthur and a flickering coal oil lantern which was casting all kinds of eerie moving shapes around us. The rest of the family had taken off through mounds of mud to assist the truck driver. Within minutes of being deserted I was sure my time had come. An owl had picked just that time to give out with his very unfamiliar and haunting hoots. I don't think my brother Arthur ever did or ever will travel as fast as we did, as I picked him up and took off down that road, we did pass a moving object in the darkness that seemed to be moving just as fast though. The flying object turned out to be my brother Walter as he had heard the same hoots down the road. We came in for a great deal of teasing from all the rest of the family, they said I couldn't have hit the road at all as my shoes were clean, but Walter was stuck in the mud when he heard the hoots and just took off leaving his shoes behind. Through the weeks to come the many strange sounds of the wilderness such as the cougars and coyotes were to keep all our eyes popping and our breath sucked in, as we had not even seen a squirrel before arriving on the homestead.

Dad only had the frame of the house up and the walls covered with shiplap, the warping of which left our house well air conditioned. Now this wasn't too bad on our arrival in September, but by late October and November we could have managed very well without it. I remember awakening one morning to find my breath had frozen my cheek to the dampness of my pillow.

Dad became very much of a hero in our eyes as he rose each morning to get the wood going in the stove. All of us children would then go through the wierd manouvers of putting our clothes on under pounds of home made blankets then dashing for a choice spot around the warm stove before having to take that dreaded hike to the little house out back, then dashing quickly to the house to crack the sheet of ice on the water bucket before we could wash. This ritual was closely supervised by Mom, as we all thought the job could be done well enough by dipping one finger into the water and then gingerly applying it to a very small portion of our faces. As the water had to be packed quite a distance from the neighbors we had a very good argument for Mom when it came to washing and wasting the water, but we always lost.

Dad used a willow branch to locate the water and it did the job well, but as it twisted and turned it never told him just how much water was down below. One day we heard great whoops of joy and when we went running we found Dad sitting partly under the house, holding a cup of water and waiting for more to seep into the hole he had dug. This first well did not produce much water but Dad did find one not too many feet away, which he dug and cribbed by hand and it was in use for many years.

We had to take turns making the trip to Kew for the mail and to greenhorns like us it was a great adventure. I always looked forward to my turn as it meant meeting people and a day out. However, one day I bit off more than I could chew. Chester Hodgkins had said I could borrow his horse, Brownie, if I would pick up all the mail for the neighbors. It was February and the weather had not been too good, but with lots of confidence and little know-how I started out. Everything went fine until I was heading back home with the mail tied in a sack on the saddle horn. I had just left Elijah Hargreaves when the Blizzard started and Brownie became very unhappy. I got off to open a gate and with that Brownie reared up and took off along the fence line and into the brush with me yelling and running behind. I finally located the horse, but somewhere along the way he had lost his saddle and with it the mail. While I was looking for the horse, I had visions of being found frozen to death, but when I found all the mail and Chester's good saddle missing I was afraid I wouldn't be. After following the tracks for what seemed like miles I located the mail and saddle. As I had never saddled a horse before I would rather have practiced on any horse but the one facing me. His games were over for that day though as he stood very calm and let me work up steam calling him some choice names Mom would never have approved of. When I finally had the saddle on, the cinch tied in some wierd invention of my own, I slipped falling directly under Brownie and, worn out, I told that fool horse to go ahead and walk on me.

My brother Fred and his wife, Una, resided on the homestead until May, 1978, and have eight children. My brother Arthur and his wife. Agnes, are residing on the homestead close to the original site and have three children. My brother Gerard and his wife Bea, live in Victoria and have five children. My sister Wyn, and husband, Jack Ollive, live in Priddis and have one son. My sister Annie and husband, Dale Elliott, live in Calgary and have four children. Our dear brother Walter passed away suddenly on December 2nd, 1977, in Edmonton, leaving his wife, Hilda, and four children. Hilda recently moved to Surrey, B.C. with two of her children, son Stephen and daughter Arleen.

Ball children alongside log section of original home. Front, L. to R.: Arthur Ball, jr., Charles Reneau, Annie Ball, jr., 2nd row: Gerard Ball, Ainsley Reneau, Wyn Ball holding Patricia Reneau, and a friend, Shirley Oxford.

I married John Reneau of Calgary in Our Lady of Perpetual Help Church, we have five children. Ainsley married Kay Harlos and resides in Calgary. Charles married Heather Keeler and resides in Calgary, with their four children, Michael, William, Susan and Teresa. Patricia married Ralph Blair and resides in Calgary. She has four children, Mitch, Rory, Johnny and Debbie. Judy married Stan Priebe and resides in Calgary with their two children, Ricky and Rhonda. Randall married Diane Gentry and resides in Calgary and has two children, Candace and Jesse. My grandson Mitch Blair has a son, Joshua, making us Great-Grandparents, but it still seems like yesterday, when we were spending our first night on the old farmstead.

Mother and Dad, Annie and Arthur Ball, (great-great-grandparents) celebrated their 60th wedding anniversary in Calgary, July, 1976, and are still living on the North Hill.

Fred and Una Ball   UXL LR
by Fred Ball

Just a little insight into our family history, grandfather Ball was a machinist and fitter in Lancashire, England, while grandfather Robinson was a cattle buyer and exporter in County Mayo, Ireland. Mom went to England to work in a Munitions Plant and it was there she met Dad. Dad was in the dry goods business in Rochdale, Lancashire, but due to being gassed in World War I, and ensuing lung problems, the family doctor advised him to move to a drier climate.

Fred and Una Ball.

I started school in Rochdale and when we moved to Ireland for two years I attended school in Ballina, County Mayo. Dad emigrated to Canada with the idea of going to Australia, and worked his way west finally settling in Calgary and working at the Holy Cross Hospital. He then sent for Mom, Theresa, Wyn, Walter and I. We stopped at Winnipeg and seeing a pile of snow on the station platform I jumped off to see what it was like as we had not seen snow before. The train took off without me but due to the quick action of a man at the station he managed to get me back on board.

Dad later worked for the City of Calgary and as the Depression was then on, Dad and Mom decided to eke out a living on the land. They bought the original quarter SE 33-21-4-W5th for $2.50 per acre from the C.P.R. and paid $25.00 down payment, this was 1934.

Dad and Mom sold our home in Calgary and bought a team of horses, a cow, and some equipment. We purchased our plow, disc, and wagon from Cozarts Ltd. which was located where the No. 1 Calgary Co-op is today. We children emptied our little banks and came up with a partial payment on a $75 — 1927 Chev. car. We had all thought a car was a necessity but it

proved to be one thing we could get along without, it was traded to Chester Hodgkins for horses.

Dad, Walter and I put up the first one roomed house and the family, which included Frank Gerard, Annie and Art, officially moved in on Sept. 4, 1934.

Dad's first trip to Turner Valley for groceries, was in Chester's small Chev. Coupe driven by Slim McKague. This proved to be the first of many adventurous episodes, travelling dirt roads and crossing creeks without bridges. While attempting to cross Sheep Creek at Paddy Rodgers. Slim told Dad, "Really nothing to crossing creeks providing you just took it easy". However, Dad said later "When I saw the radiator disappear under the water as we nosed down the bank, it was then I knew we wouldn't make it". After wading out and going to the nearby ranch Lizzie von Rummel pulled the car out with a team. Alex Lyall often took Dad and Mom to town for groceries before we bought a truck in 1938.

Over the years with the combined efforts of all our family the brush was gradually cleared, the land broken and sowed to hay for due to frost it was futile trying to grow grain.

While attending a dance at the Alazhar Temple in Calgary Una and I met — Una was from Pine Lake and graduated from Red Deer High School and Garbutts Business College, Calgary. She worked in the accounting department of the C. M. & S. Co. — Fertilizer Sales Office. We were married the day Calgary won the Grey Cup in 1948, and we have four sons and four daughters. Maureen Joan Sikorski, Daniel (Dan) Ernest, David Frederick, Colleen Marie Nelson, Glenn Charles, Keith William, Elaine Susan, and Kathleen (Kate) Mary. Maureen, David and Colleen have written their own stories.

Dan graduated from Turner Valley High School in 1968 and University of Calgary in 1972 with a B.Sc. in Chemical Engineering. He worked for Baroid of Canada for over a year, and is currently with Getty Oil (Canada) Ltd. as Production Foreman out of Drayton Valley.

Glenn graduated from Oilfields High School in 1974. He worked for Canadian Western Natural Gas for over a year as a backhoe operator, then with G.R.M.

Dan, Glen, Keith, Elaine and Kate Ball.

Contractors for two years. Glenn is presently ranching.

Keith graduated from Oilfields H.S. in 1975. He is presently in his fourth year of Mechanical Engineering at the University of Calgary.

Elaine graduated from Oilfields H.S. in 1976. She has worked for A.G.T. for two years in the Master Records Department, and has plans to go into the accounting field.

Kate will graduate from Oilfields H.S. in June, 1979. She hopes to enroll in a secretarial arts course in Calgary.

Our home (SE 22-21-4-W5th) faces the remains of an old coalmine opened by Joseph Fisher in 1912. Coalmine Ridge overlooks our ranch and the old Morley Trail which wound through the valley.

Lionald and Maureen (Ball) Sikorski

by Maureen Sikorski

I am the eldest of the eight children of Fred and Una Ball. Growing up was a combination of early rising, chores (mainly outdoors) long hours of riding and haying. One of the chores which we could never seem to please everyone with was the milking schedule — either we were bringing the cows in too early and waking someone up or we were visiting with the Davis' on the crocus hill who were supposedly getting in their cows and then making someone wait. All things considered though, growing up was thoroughly enjoyable.

I attended elementary school at Sheep Creek under the guidance of W. Dube, principal, and Jake Reimer, bus driver. Mom and Dad being primarily interested in our scholastic accomplishments often found our interests wandering to the card games which occupied our three-hour-per-day bus trip to and from school. In order to attend high school we were bussed to Turner Valley High School in Black Diamond. After graduation I moved to Calgary and enrolled in a secretarial course at Henderson's Business College.

My first job was as a secretary at Spalding Hardware. It was while working there that I met Lionald Sikorski. Lionald had moved here from Ituna,

Saskatchewan (about ninety miles north-east of Regina). Lionald is the eldest son of Adolphe and Anne Sikorski and has one sister — Christine.

We were married in 1972 and have been blessed with two children — Leana Catherine born August 21, 1973 and Michael Anthony born January 17, 1977. At present we are residing in Calgary with hopes of returning to the Foothills Country.

David and Jody (Ransom) Ball   UXL RR

by Jody Ball

David was the third child born in the family and since Danny and Maureen were already playmates, David and his cousin Pat became inseparable buddies, building treehouses and getting into lots of mischief.

Hunting became a big part of early teenage fun, providing extra pocket money and excitement. The boys received 30¢ for squirrel hides and $10-$40.00 for beaver pelts. David and Dan remember awaiting their chance at beaver in the early spring once returning at 2 a.m. with one weighing over 60 pounds.

David attended Millarville elementary and later Turner Valley high graduating in 1970. After which he tried several different occupations but preferred driving tractor-trailer units.

It was during David's last year of school that we met on the school bus. After graduating from high school in 1972 I commenced employment with A.G.T. as a Service Representative. We were married on September 14, 1974. David and Pat began building our house in June 1975 on the SE 22-21-4-W5th facing Coal Mine Hill. David and I moved in August with much excitement. He was still working on the house and although it was almost completed we had such modern

Jody and David Ball with their children, Deanne and Shanna.

Lionald and Maureen Sikorski with their children, Leana (L) and Michael.

conveniences as running water — a garden hose which ran upstairs from the pump, heat — several blankets on the bed, and a toilet — which was filled by the garden hose. The first few months were a lot of fun and quite a change from the hurried confusion of town.

Since then we have been gifted with two girls, Shanna Marie on May 29, 1976, and Deanne Michelle on April 13, 1978. We are presently continuing the family tradition of ranching.

Ron and Colleen (Ball) Nelson

by Colleen Nelson

I was born in the summer of 1954, the fourth child of eight and smack in between all of the boys. That to me was my childhood trial and tribulation. But being from a large family has more good points than bad. Along with our cousins the long evenings were always filled with football, baseball, soccer or hockey depending on the season. Consequently I turned out to be somewhat of a tomboy.

I took my first two years of high school at Lord Beaverbrook in Calgary, and the third year at T.V.H.S., Black Diamond. Shortly after graduating in 1972 I moved back to Calgary and joined the Royal Bank where I am still employed.

In 1976 I married Ron Nelson from Devon, Alberta. He has spent most of his life in connection with the oilfields. Ron's parents, Ernie and Vera Nelson, lived in Royalties and later Black Diamond moving to Devon with the outbreak of the Leduc Oilfield discovery.

At St. Patrick's Church, Midnapore. Colleen (Ball) Nelson, Ron Nelson, his mother, Vera, and brother Lloyd. June 26th, 1976.

Ollive, Winnie (Ball)   G ◇

When Mom and Dad, Arthur and Annie Ball, found a ¼ section of land to homestead on I, along with my brothers and sisters were happy with the thought of living in the country. I thought it would be like a long vacation away from the city. Dad bought a team of horses and a running gear from McLean's auction, he built a rack and loaded it with as many of our possessions as it would hold and set off with my brothers Fred and Walter to build a house. A couple of weeks later Mom hired a truck and as most of our furniture had to be sold for the money to buy lumber for the house, we did not have too much left. I think the truck driver was very doubtful of Mom's directions when she was telling him to follow an old wagon trail through the bush, he said "You know, a fellow could get lost in here".

Dad and the boys had the house partially built and as soon as the stove was unloaded we gathered wood and had our first meal outside. Mom had brought along a large pot of stew and we ate it off pan lids, pie plates and cake tins, as we could not find the dishes and were too hungry to look for very long. Coming from Calgary we were so surprised to find the evenings so dark, we had not spent an evening away from the city lights. However, we soon adjusted to kerosene lamps, wood-burning stove, outdoor plumbing and having to haul water — as we did not have any choice in the matter.

Mom and Dad sent to Edmonton for school correspondence courses, as there was not a school in the district and I was soon busy teaching my younger brothers and my sister. Mom and Dad started clearing brush and sawing logs and after my older sister Theresa left to work in Calgary, I also had to look after my younger brother Art. Our land had such dense bush on it, I was afraid to let him outside as he was just over two years old I thought he would never be found if he wandered away. Consequently, as I kept him with me while I was teaching the others, he learned to read and write when he was just over three years. About six years later around 1941, the children were bussed to school and their first real schooling was at Square Butte school — a small one room log building. The

L. to R. Winnie Ollive, Arthur Ball, sr., Gene Ollive, Mrs. Ollive, Mrs. A. Ball, sr., Pat Ball.

school teacher at that time was Mrs. Fred Kosling. She was a super teacher, she tried to keep a "No Nonsense" attitude, but her fondness for children was easy to see. I do not know how she managed to teach both my brother Frank, and Frank Kendall, as they were both so full of devilment. During the six months my brother Frank attended Square Butte, I think we had to pay one half the price of a piece of glass for the bookcase twice, the other half being paid by the Kendalls. At that time the grade nine pupils had to write departmental exams from Edmonton and both Franks passed with flying colors, much to my surprise, as I only had my brother half-way through grade seven when he started school. He still fondly remembers Mrs. Kosling and the special effort she put into teaching him.

We used to attend the Christmas concerts and some of the dances, Fred and I used to ride horseback as we did not have a car or truck. Most of the people came in wagons or sleighs, according to the season. There were only a few cars or trucks parked outside the little school house.

The first dance I recall — Otto Roedler and Mrs. Kosling played the piano, Jim Howie and Cyrus McBee the violin. Mr. Kosling had his accordian and Dick Lyall played the harmonica while his brother Alex called the square dances.

In the early 1940's Miss Margaret Halberg (Mrs. Koch now) called a meeting, as she was teaching at Square Butte at the time. She suggested we form a committee and hold dances and parties on a regular basis. Mrs. Kosling was elected president. I had the honor of being the secretary treasurer. Alex Lyall and my brother Fred were our entertainment committee. Our orchestra was local talent, Mrs. Kosling on the piano, Mr. Kosling accordian, Mary Bell guitar and Cyrus McBee with his violin. Later on Jake Reimer was our purchasing agent, he bought a piano from Jack Robbins and a second hand lighting plant. The lighting plant was installed in an old out-house. At every dance it started out working just fine, but somehow to the delight of the younger generation, we had several moonlight waltzs, while poor Jake was out fixing the plant. I never did find out if we had a faulty lighting plant or just some amorous pranksters, anyway we had some wonderful times. Instead of collecting at the door, we passed the hat at supper time. I remember once when we had a Halloween party, after buying a box of apples and a few candies we were left with thirty two cents in the funds.

One day as we were going to a dance, we passed an encampment of Indians who were fencing for Kendalls. Fred invited them to the dance, they happily accepted and quite a number of them showed up. They were very good dancers, so light on their feet and I just had a ball — until it was time for supper. As the Indians were our guests they were served first. There was one elderly lady, who thought when she was offered a sandwich or a piece of cake, it meant that we

were giving her the whole plateful. She had come equipped with a large flour sack and everything was emptied into it. It just about broke my heart to see a large dish of Mrs. George Lyall's lemon filled buns (the highlight of suppertime to me) heading for that sack. Paddy Rodgers could see just what was going to happen and he was up and had a couple of buns before they hit the sack. He said "darned if I am going to miss out on those buns."

Mrs. Tom Lyall — (Auntie to everyone) always made our coffee. She made it in a large copper boiler and Square Butte served the best coffee in the country. She also kept an eye on the babies; we had our nursery and kitchen combined. Even during World War 2, when sugar was rationed, we would go without at home just so we could arrive at Square Butte with a cake complete with icing. I still think of the dances at the old school house, as part of the "Good old Days." They added much pleasure to my life.

Later on I taught Jody & Peter Fisher and Michael Rodgers for a couple of years as they were not on the bus route. One day we were all skating on the creek nearby. It was a wonderful day, the creek had flooded the previous night and the ice was like a sheet of glass, we were all enjoying ourselves so much that our lunch hour had extended to three hours. We finally noticed a car parked outside the little school house, thinking it was the school inspector, we had our skates off immediately and were running up the path to the school. Peter said "Do you think we are all going to get fired?" On arrival we found it was just the "Rawleigh Man" peddling his liniments and salves etc.

While I was staying at the Fishers' ranch, Joe was breaking a lovely Palimino mare. I wanted a ride on her so badly but she was quite frisky and I was not a very good rider so he would not allow me on her. One day in spring, the creek flooded and washed away the bridge. The Fishers had to leave the car on one side of the creek and cross on a fallen log to the house. One day Joe was going to Calgary, he asked me to wait beside the creek while he rode across and sent his mare back to me. He made me promise not to ride her to the barn as she was still not well broken. I promised, but when she came across the creek, she looked so friendly, I thought, well here is my chance for a ride. As soon as I mounted she took off like a flash. It did not help having Joe jumping up and down on the other side of the creek shouting and threatening me. I was wearing a full flared skirt at the time and I could feel it flying out behind me like a sail. I could not hold the mare at all, and as we flew by the schoolhouse, the boys all ran out shouting "You are going to get killed." Both the corral gate and the barn door were open and I thought for sure she would gallop right into the barn and knock my head completely off. However she came to a stop at the door. My legs were shaking so much I could hardly unsaddle her. Another time the Fishers were driving me home for the weekend. I got out to open a large wooden gate. As Joe was driving through I let the gate go not knowing it would swing and catch on the car bumper. While he was putting the gate back together, he was mumbling his favorite phrase — "The darndest school mam yet."

Later on I worked in the Intravenous Lab. in the Holy Cross Hospital. One day I was taking a patient to his room in a wheel chair when the wheel fell off. I was on my hands and knees trying to get the wheel back on when the head nurse came along with some visiting doctors. I suppose, not wanting them to know we had some chairs which were not substantial, she passed by quickly saying "This is Miss Ball, we never know just what she is going to do next." When I left the hospital I went back home for a couple of years and then I went to work for Zellars Ltd. downtown in Calgary. I stayed there for over ten years, going back to the farm to visit and sometimes to help with the haying. I was going with Jack Ollive at the time, we had known each other since we were in our early teens.

One weekend I took Mom and Dad out to Happy Valley for a picnic and the place was swarming with bees. Somehow one got in my purse. When I was in Zellars washroom the next day combing my hair, out came this real mad bee, buzzing around. The girls tried to get out so fast they were jammed in the doorway screaming. They finally got into the lunch room and the bee was still going after them. The manager came running out of his office and when we finally got the bee out of the window, he said "I knew Miss Ball was behind this". I could never understand why someone as sensible and as reserved as I was could get into so much trouble. Of course I could not get anyone to believe that the bee had not come from Jack's hay field.

I later married Jack, and we farm about eight miles east of my parents homestead. I have a son Pat who is a geologist and is in the oil industry. His hobbies are fishing and skiing. My hobbies are gardening and collecting house plants and rocks.

We have a camper and as Jack is an avid photographer we re-live our holidays many times over. We both belong to a camera club, which we enjoy.

Our brand is G ◇ which the Ollives have had since around 1937.

Walter Joseph Ball

by Hilde B. Ball (nee Northmore)

Walter is the second son of Mr. and Mrs. Arthur Ball who homesteaded on land S.E. ¼ of 33-21-4-W5th twelve miles north west of Millarville in 1934.

In 1934 Walter was eleven years old and made the trip with his father and his older brother Fred from Calgary in a wagon with a milk cow tied behind, to the land that was to be their home. Both the boys helped build the house and haul timber from the nearest saw mill.

Walter spent a lot of his time shooting rabbits for which they sold for five cents each. He was a very good

Walter J. Ball.

shot and very rarely missed. He was using a single shot 22 which at that time cost $4.95 and was a great deal of money to spend. A box of fifty shells cost 25 cents.

When Walter was twelve years old he left home and went to work for a neighbour and later on he worked for another neighbour where he joined a threshing gang and went around the countryside threshing grain for all the neighbours.

Walter loved horses and during his teenage years owned several of his own. He loved to ride and was a very good rider.

At the start of the Second World War he was one of the first to join up and arrived overseas in England when he was barely seventeen. This is where I met him, getting married in September 1943 in Thornton Heath, Surrey, where I was born. He was with the 1st Medium Regiment R.C.A. and saw action in Sicily, Italy, N.W. Europe, Germany, Holland and France. It

Walter Ball Family. L. to R. Doreen, Steven, Hilda, Arlene, Theresa.

was while there that he was "Mentioned in Dispatches" and was awarded a bronze oak leaf cluster for brave conduct.

Walter (I called him Wally) and I lived in Calgary for six years where we had two daughters Theresa and Doreen born in 1946 and 1949. We moved to New Westminster, British Columbia in 1951 and lived there and in Vancouver until 1953 and then moved to Mission City when Wally started working for Trans Mountain Pipe Line Company. We enjoyed life there very much, but in 1957 we were transferred to Edmonton, Alberta when Wally was made the Station Operator there.

In 1958 our son Steven was born and in 1963 we had our fourth child and third daughter Arlene.

Theresa married Gilbert Lylick in 1967 and reside in Leduc, Alberta with their two children Robin and Sherri.

Doreen married Arthur Andrews in 1966 and reside in Surrey, British Columbia with their two children Glenn and Jim.

Steven and Arlene are still residing at home.

Walter was particularly happy the last seven years of his life while building his lake front cabin at Skelton Lake in the Athabasca district 100 miles north of Edmonton. He was always busy fixing the cabin and loved to take his children and the neighbors' children water skiing. He also got a lot of pleasure taming the squirrels and feeding them peanut butter crackers and watching the birds and wild life.

Walter passed away December 2nd, 1976. We had thirty-three years of happy married life together. We all miss him very much but remember him as a devoted father and grandfather, a loving husband and a very fine man.

I have now moved to Surrey, British Columbia.

Ball, Frank Gerard

While I could never refer to them as the good old days, my early years in the country were a mixture of good wholesome fun and hard work; the winter months were spent largely with a combination of both, hunting rabbits and squirrels — the rabbits were sold to a fox farm at a nickel a piece and the squirrel pelts sold from 18 to 30¢ each. The rifle I used was purchased from Eaton's mail order catalogue for $4.50, this was the same rifle with which I shot my first deer (at age twelve) which was an occasion for a family celebration.

Age was no barrier in those days, boys worked at the side of grown men at harvest time, and in the fall of 1943 I worked for Doug Beatty in Okotoks stooking for $5.00 a day and threshing for $6.00, and it was a proud day when I arrived home with a staggering pay cheque of $160.00. The early winter months were spent harvesting Christmas trees which were pedalled from door to door in Calgary. As we were seven miles from the nearest school our education was acquired from correspondence courses from Edmonton. In this manner I finished Grade 6 and then at 17 I attended

Beatrice and Frank Ball.

Square Butte School and completed Grades 7, 8 and 9 under the capable supervision of Mrs. Kosling.

I have fond memories of our early years in the country, swimming in Whiskey Creek, dances at Red Deer Lake, Priddis and Kew, skating parties on Whiskey and Sheep Creek and the much looked forward to school Christmas concert at Square Butte School.

In 1945 I left the country for the bright lights of Calgary where I worked for Burns Packing Plant and stayed there about a year, working ten hours a day at 52¢ an hour. Life in the packing plant held no promise for me so I followed my early dream and joined the Royal Canadian Navy, ironically on April Fool's Day, the first day of April, 1946 as a second class stoker. I was sent to Esquimalt, B.C. for basic training, six months later I was drafted to the light cruiser H.M.C.S. Uganda — a drastic change from a country boy to a member of the crew of which was then Canada's largest warship. During that time I met Beatrice Pithie, legal steno, who, two years later, became my wife. The next twenty years with the R.C.N. proved to be a cyclone of events, a variety of ships, cruises to various parts of the world, from the Arctic Circle to Cape Horn, with a trip to the Far East for good measure. During this period with the Navy we

Frank and Beatrice Ball on their honeymoon, getting stuck in the mud on their way to the farm.

Elliot Family. Back row, L. to R.: Dale, Anne, Wendy. Front row, L. to R.: Kenny, Brian, Tony. Scott in front.

managed to have five children, Gerald and Michael were born in Halifax, N.S. and Theresa, Rosanne and Patrick are still living at home. At the end of twenty years' service I decided to try my hand at being a civilian again, and was released from the Navy in April, 1966. After a brief stint as a security officer with the Attorney-General's office I took employment as Chief Engineer with the Dep't. of Recreation for the City of Victoria and remained in that position until July, 1975 at which time I took employment with the Corp. of Saanich as Municipal Building Maintenance Sup't. where I remain to this day.

Anne (Ball) Elliott

Being very young when we moved to the Square Butte district, I cannot recall much about the first few years on the farm. The school was about seven miles from our place and we had no way of getting there. We took correspondence courses from Edmonton the first few years. Later on we went to Square Butte School by bus which was Mr. Purdys family car.

Dad had huge gardens which seem to need hoeing all summer long. Also carrying water for plants, chickens and turkeys, which was a never ending job for all of us. A friend used to stay with us during the summer vacation and our job was to keep calves out of the oat field. Every day I would suggest playing dog and sick him on the calves every time they went near the field. The summer was half over before he realized he was doing all the work.

During the war Dad was laid up with a bad back, Fred and Walter were in the army which left Frank and I to run the farm. We thought we were doing very well till one little calf which was our pet became sick, it turned out we forgot to water him. Dad never did find out why that calf died.

As we grew up our entertainment was going to the dances at Square Butte, Kew, Millarville, Priddis and Red Deer Lake. We really had some good times.

I left the farm in 1946 to work in Calgary and go to night school taking a business course.

I married Dale Elliott from Winnipeg in 1950, and the ladies of Square Butte put on a lovely dance and shower for us. That was the last time I was in the old school house.

For years Dale and my brothers Walter and Art spent many a winter day tramping the hills around Square Butte, big game hunting. We just about lived on wild meat all winter.

We have four children, Wendy, married Wayne Hoffman, daughters Tonia and Brandi Anne; Kenny married Delore Heatherington, son Cory, daughter Deana; Tony, married Bev Engle, son Scott and Brian, at home, and a daughter Jessica.

Dale operated Ernie's Garage for a few years, then bought Gleichen Standard Transport which we operated from 1966 till selling to son Tony and Son-in-law Wayne in January of 1978. We are now semi-retired, he is still operating Dale's Pickup and Delivery, for which sons, Kenny and Brian, are operating their own trucks.

We are still living on the north hill in Calgary, just a few blocks from where I lived with Mom and Dad before moving to the farm.

Arthur and Agnes Ball   ◇B
by Agnes Ball

Art was only one year old when he came to live on the SE¼ of Section 33, Township 21, Range 4, West of 5th, where he resides today. He was born in Calgary April 8, 1933.

There wasn't any way to get to Square Butte school so his older sister Winnifred taught him correspondence until grade 5. Mr. R. Purdy drove the school bus to Square Butte that year, (quite an undertaking in those days as there weren't any gravel roads and the Fisher Creek had to be forded). The following year the

Art Ball Family. L. to R. Agnes, Joanne, Allan, Susan, Art.

Purdys started a school in their home and this continued for one term. After this Jake Reimer drove a school bus to Square Butte School. He drove one of the first four wheel drive Jeeps in the country.

Art worked at home after he finished school. In the winter of 1958, Mr. and Mrs. Ball (Senior) moved to Calgary. Art ranched in a partnership with his brother Fred until 1977 when the partnership was dissolved and Fred moved to his new home on SE¼ of Section 22, Township 21, Range 4, West of 5th.

Art and I were married July 4, 1959 at St. Joseph's Catholic Church in Calgary. I was born January 18, 1937 (Agnes Mary McHarg), at home on my parents' farm near Okotoks. Mother had scarlet fever and she couldn't be admitted to hospital so Dad had to bring the doctor and nurse to her from the main highway through 12 foot snow drifts with a sleigh and horses. I attended Big Rock School from grades 1-6 and attended Okotoks school until I finished high school.

I then attended the University of Alberta in Calgary and taught school at Priddis from 1957-1959 when Art and I were married.

Our eldest daughter Joanne Marie was born May 14/60. She attended public school at Millarville and high school at Oilfields High School Black Diamond. She graduated in June of this year (1978) and is enrolled at the University of Calgary this fall. Our son Allan Joseph was born October 27/61 and attended Millarville school and Oilfields High where he is now in grade 12. Our youngest daughter Susan Teresa was born December 13/65 and is in grade eight at Millarville school.

Home of Art Ball Family.

When Art and I were first married we had electricity in our home but a wood and coal stove and no plumbing. We were lucky to have a very good wood and coal cook stove that Art's mom and dad left. I soon learned to make all my bread. However I dreaded baking bread on windy days because of chimney fires.

In 1965, we had a full basement poured just west of the house and Bill Kendall engineered moving our house onto the basement that summer. By fall we had a propane furnace and Art had the plumbing installed when I brought our youngest daughter Susan home from the hospital in December.

Art enjoyed hunting and used to travel as far as the muskeg between the Elbow and the North Fork, seldom coming home empty handed. We lived entirely on elk and deer meat. As the game laws changed and it became less of a sport, he lost interest and hasn't hunted for the last few years.

One of his prize trophies is a large grizzly he shot in October 1968 about three miles northwest of our place. It had killed a young heifer belonging to one of the neighbours.

Art along with Dick Smith organized the Turkey Shoots at Square Butte Hall which were held quite regularly in the 1960's.

We have both been active members in the community association. I have been a member of the Square Butte Ladies since July 1959. Our girls have been members of the 4-H Stitch-In-Time Club at Millarville and I have helped as leader and assistant leader.

Lately all of our family have taken up cross-country skiing which seems to be the best way to enjoy our beautiful countryside in the long winter months.

The Larry Ball Family

The Larry Ball family lived in the Millarville district from May, 1974 to August, 1978. Larry Ball was born and took his schooling at Perdue, Saskatchewan. In 1943 he joined the Navy and served until the end of the war. After his discharge he moved to Calgary, where he has since been active in the construction industry. Thelma (Hautzinger) Ball was born in Big Valley, Alta. and moved to Calgary with her family in 1943. Larry and Thelma were married in 1951. In 1954 they were blessed with Laurie, in 1955, with Douglas and in 1959 with Janice. In 1968 they bought 25 acres of land from Mr. Salter, 28-21-3-W5. After much clearing and planning in the ensuing years, they started to build a home in 1973. In May of 1974 they moved in and spent four lovely years in the beautiful Millarville district. In August, 1978 they sold to Mr. and Mrs. G. Clark and moved back to Calgary and are residing at 31 Cedarwood Mews S.W.

Mr. and Mrs. J. M. Ballachey

by Isamay (dePalezieux) Ballachey

I was born in 1921 on the homestead of my parents, Mr. and Mrs. E. A. dePalezieux, in Millarville. Apart

Ballachey family, Feb. 19, 1972. L. to R. John Edmund Ballachey. Isamay Ballachey. John Ballachey sr. Front: Barbara and Brenda Ballachey.

from the four years from 1923 to 1927 during which my parents operated the Buffalo Head ranch west of High River, Millarville was my home until the time of my marriage. My sister Jacqueline and I rode horseback to New Valley School for our public school years, a distance of about three miles. For reasons of warmth, particularly in the winter, and convenience, we usually rode 'bareback' which caused some laundry problems during the horses' spring shedding season. We went on to High River for our high school years either boarding with friends or in a rented house.

It was a wonderful childhood with many happy memories of visits back and forth with friends, swimming and skating parties, the Millarville Fair and the Millarville Races, and Sunday services at the Millarville Church which often involved the use of a team and cutter in the winter. And lots and lots of riding. We used to go on horseback to the Millarville store for the mail and groceries at least once a week, in the early years to Forward and Waltons and then to Peglers.

Following graduation from high school I took a business course at the old Mount Royal College near Mewata Barracks in Calgary and after working briefly in a law office went on to Edmonton to attend university in the first year B.Sc. in Nursing. This was followed by three years training at the Calgary General Hospital — one of the most rewarding periods of my life. I graduated in 1945 and was married one week later on September 22nd, 1945, to John M. Ballachey of High River at St. Stephens Anglican Church in Calgary.

The next four years were spent in Edmonton where John, a veteran of the R.C.A.F. and a recipient of the D.F.C., studied law, and where our eldest daughter Barbara Julie was born on January 15, 1949. We

Ballachey family enjoying a ride. L. to R. Brenda on Haida. John on Dandy. Isamay on Miss Wine. Barbara on Willow.

Mike and Karen Banjavich.

returned to Calgary that year and have resided there since but in 1956 bought the ranch homesteaded by George Sylvester in Kew. Our second daughter, Brenda Elizabeth, was born on July 11, 1952, and our son John Edmond on December 12, 1956, both in Calgary.

Over the years we have spent many happy days at the ranch where the children learned to ride and developed a love of the outdoors — and where more recently we have taken up cross-country skiing and re-learned the joys and frustrations of growing a vegetable garden. John became involved in the cattle industry shortly after we purchased the ranch and was particularly interested in the Charolais breed. He played a major part in the formation of the Canadian Charolais Association and the subsequent importation of European cattle. The name Chinook Ranch is registered to us and also three cattle brands, JMB, ₿, V∃ , and one horse brand, ₿ .

Both our daughters were married at the beautiful Millarville Church, Barbara on February 19, 1972 to Gerald L. Forseth of Calgary where they now reside. Barbara is a professional artist having studied in Montreal and Calgary where she obtained her B.F.A. and Gerry is an architect, a partner of Donnell & Forseth. Brenda was married on August 25th, 1973 to Gary R. McKenney of Lamar, Colorado. They met in Ft. Collins, Colorado where both were in the faculty of Agriculture at C.S.U. Upon graduation they spent two years, from 1974 to 1976, operating Chinook Ranch and are now back in Ft. Collins where Brenda is continuing her studies. Our son John is living in Calgary and has held various jobs since completing high school at Brentwood School on Vancouver Island.

Banjavich

BANJAVICH, KAREN LAURAINE — The only child of Gordon and Eileen Gray, born in Tillsonburg, Ontario, six months later we moved to Woodstock, Ontario where I spent the rest of my childhood and teen years.

BANJAVICH, MARK JOSEPH — The eldest son of Mark and Catharine Banjavich, born in Welland, Ontario and moved to Woodstock Ontario in 1956 where I finished my highschool years as did my only brother George.

We were married in Woodstock May 26, 1962 and took up residence in Toronto for two and a half years. Mark was transferred to Calgary in the fall of 1965.

We became interested in the Millarville district when Connie and Rick Brown moved to the Square Butte area, since Karen and Connie are first cousins we spent a considerable amount of time visiting and getting to know some of the other people. After much searching we bought twenty acres two miles south east of Millarville on Highway 22, in 1975.

Mark now has his own distributing company in Calgary (Condoco Distributors Ltd.), where Karen helps out occasionally. Karen is a member of the Square Butte Ladies Group and we both love the Millarville area and plan on remaining here.

Joe Bannerman

Joe was born August 18th, 1922, on his father's ranch, the S.W.¼ of 29-21-4-W5, near Fisher Creek. He is the son of May and Dan Bannerman. Dan's father, Joseph M. Bannerman, was a very early pioneer of the Calgary area.

When Joe decided to put in an appearance, a doctor had been sent for from Calgary, but due to the poor condition of the roads, the baby came several hours before the doctor arrived, and when he got there, mother and baby were doing nicely, thanks to father.

The following year, 1923, Dan, May and their young son moved down to the Jimmie Spooner place, the East half of 2-21-4-W5, when he decided to sell his ranch and return to England. There was a section of lease so it was an ideal place to raise cattle. Dan also had several pens of silver fox, and as Joe became older it was his job to keep the fox in rabbits and gophers, and with this much practice, he became a very good shot.

L. to R. Joe Bannerman, with his mother and father, May and Dan.

He attended Square Butte School for several years, riding his pony for transportation. The family lived on the ranch until 1939, when they sold and moved into Calgary, where Joe attended Crescent Heights High School. After graduating from high school, he joined the R.C.A.F., remaining to the end of the war. During this time he met his future wife, Ada McLean of Powell River, B.C. After their marriage they lived in different parts of British Columbia. Joe started his own firm, Bannerman Construction, presently operating out of Sparwood, B.C.

Joe and Ada have a family of four, one son and three daughters. Their son Donald was born February 13th, 1947. He and his wife Fiona have a son and daughter. They make their home in Sparwood.

Janis Elaine was born July 7th, 1948. She and her husband, Walter Finn, have one son. Their home is in Nova Scotia.

Jo Ann Lorene was born March 18th, 1953. She is married to Kent Roger and they have one son and one daughter, live in Sparwood.

Tracy Lee, born January 25th, 1959, is married to Lloyd Krikke. They have one daughter, also live in Sparwood.

Leonard W. Bargus

by Kim Bargus

My family originated in Oxfordshire, England approximately 800 years ago. At that time the family name was Burge, and in subsequent years, the name changed five times, until the early 1800's, when it became Bargus. The earlier members of the family were predominately farmers and soldiers. It is thought most of the family died at Nazeby, supporting Charles 1st and the royalist cause. The family moved to Sussex in 1850 and twenty years later my great-grandfather Walter Bargus was born. He married and had four children, Walter, Ernest, Matilda and Leonard. Walter

married but had no children, Ernest and his wife had a daughter, and it was left to Leonard to carry on the family name. In 1929 Len married Hazel Wilson and one year later a daughter, Daphne was born on November 20th. Ten years later, on November 20th, 1940 a son Leonard was born. On December 9th, 1940, Leonard senior was killed by a delayed action bomb. At the age of thirteen, Leonard junior joined H.M.T.S. Mercury, a navel training ship and three years later enlisted in the Royal Navy. During the next few years he served in everything from the battleship H.M.S. Vanguard to submarines. He became a navy boxing champion, and took part in a variety of sports. He met and married Ann Norris and in 1960, a daughter, Kim, was born. In 1966, a son Paul joined the family and the same year, they left Sussex and came to Calgary. Although reasonably happy in the city, they yearned for country life again, and in the fall of 1975, they bought the old Eden place (NW¼ 3-21-4-W5M). My father is employed by Steeplejack Services Ltd. in Calgary as their purchasing agent. My mother is a supervisor at the Carriage House Motor Inn. I attend Oilfields Senior High School and hope for a career in accounting. My brother at present attends Millarville School and his future is a little uncertain, particularly if he misses doing his chores too many times.

Margaret Joan Barker

by M. J. Barker

Margaret Joan, seventh child of Richard and Mary Knights. I left Millarville in March, 1922 to go in training at the Holy Cross Hospital, Calgary, graduating in April, 1925. Being a Special Nurse for country cases took me far and wide, and as a relief Operating Room Supervisor at the Galt Hospital in Lethbridge I obtained a wealth of experience.

John and Joan Barker, 1933.

On June 29, 1926 at Christ Church, Millarville, I married John Barker and lived at 225-20th Ave. N.W., Calgary until 1933, when we went to Banff where Jack was employed as Branch Manager of the Union Milk Co.

In 1939 we moved to Chilliwack, B.C., first visiting George and Violet Barnes and family, former Millarville neighbours, and then settling on our own farm where we raised mink, later transferring our interests to dairying.

I worked as Supervisor at the Chilliwack General Hospital, and later as Assistant Matron of Valley Haven Rest Home.

John died June 19, 1964, after which selling the farm at 382 Gibson Rd., I retired to 550 Kipp Ave., Chilliwack, my present address.

John (Jack) Barlow & Family

Jack was the only son of Harvey Richard and Edith Olive Barlow, born June 7, 1916 on Jocelyn W. Littleton's place at Red Deer Lake. In 1921, along with his parents and sisters, Jean and Marjorie, they settled on the home quarter, NE¼ 15-21-2 W5th.

Jack attended eight grades of education at Ballyhamage School. Being a born farmer, he was unable to join the Armed Forces during the War years (1939-1945) as he was physically unfit. He stayed at home and helped his parents. He didn't work all the time, but attended the local concerts and dances in the district. Jack was a member of the Young People's Association at Christ Church (Anglican) in Millarville, and a member of the Sunny Social Society, commonly known as the Triple "S" Club.

On October 18, 1948 he was married at Christ Church, Calgary, to Betty Munn (Boys' and Girls' Supervisor) of Calgary. Jack and I resided with Jack's parents — the house was partitioned off so we lived separately. Both our oldest sons were born there; Richard in May, 1949 and David in August 1950. Our daughter Evelyn was born in March 1953, Calgary; prior to Dad and Mother's retiring from the farm in September 1953. Richard attended Grade one at Ballyhamage School. Brian, our third son, was born in May 1956 at Calgary. We had nothing but dirt roads off from the mail route roads, until the school buses commenced in 1957.

We sold the farm in June 1956 to Albert Banner. In July we moved to Alvin Federsen's farm at Red Deer Lake, which we had bought. The two older boys attended Red Deer Lake School. They would walk a half mile in good weather and one mile in bad weather to meet Ritchie Stanton's school bus. Dampness in the house brought sickness to the family. Jack sold out in May 1957 to Mr. Hobbs (race horses) of Calgary. Later that month he bought a quarter section a mile south and a mile and a half west of Cremona. However, it would not be vacated until the end of October 1957. In June, Bill Norrie of Red Deer Lake transported our household effects to our new farm home. The children and myself stayed with my sister and husband, Joan and Earl Nielsen in Cremona. Jack stayed with Mac Graham to do some root picking and haying. It was the latter part of July that Jack finally returned to his family in Cremona. Lots of jobs were available so he was kept busy. He eventually moved onto the farm on November 2, 1957, the temperature was at 10 degrees F. Kathleen was born in January 1959 at Didsbury and in December of the same year Jack had, for the first time in his life, electricity in his home. As the children grew up they all attended Cremona High School for grades 1 through 12.

Sadness came to our family on July 30, 1967. Our eldest son Richard, then 18 years old, drowned in the Little Red Deer River at Water Valley. He had rescued his sister Evelyn but got into difficulties. In January 1968 he was awarded (posthumously) the Silver Medal for his bravey, "Life of Alberta", which was presented to Jack and myself by Grant MacEwen in Edmonton.

David is a heavy duty mechanic living in Calgary and married to Candace Grey of Calgary (June 26, 1971). They have two children, Jeremy and Heather.

This house was built in 1921 on the Barlow place — N.E.¼-15-21-2-W of 5.

The Jack Barlow family taken at Jack's and Betty's thirtieth wedding anniversary October 18, 1978. Back row, L. to R.: Kathleen, Brian, David, Evelyn. Front row: Jack and Betty.

179

Evelyn married Allan Myram (a childhood sweetheart) on July 10, 1971. They live on 80 acres in the Cremona area with their two sons, Andrew and Tony.

Jack and I sold the farm in May 1972 to Tom Standish and bought the Cremona Corner Service Garage. We took up residence in a trailer in the Mountain View Trailer Park where we have been for just over 6½ years. We sold the business in September 1975 and are semi-retired during the winter months. Brian has been working on oil rigs for a few years, starting as a roughneck and, at present, is a driller. Kathleen is at home with us. She is working in Didsbury as a bookkeeper and in the evenings works as a bar-waitress in the Cremona Hotel. Jack keeps busy helping local farmers from spring to after harvest and sometimes works in a lumber mill during March. When the Pioneers Apartments were built just over a year ago, for Senior Citizens, Jack was asked and is now the maintenance man for the home.

John D. Barraclough

I was born on February 4, 1921, about where the Calgary Airport is, the only son of a family of seven. My oldest sister Annie passed away in 1929. I have a twin sister Hilda. My parents are Johnny and Emily Barraclough. We moved to the Millarville district in 1928. What education I got was at Ballyhamage School, riding horseback three miles; later, at Fordville School. As I grew up, I did some lumbering, and sawed lumber with Dad's sawmill. In 1945 I moved to Calgary, and in November, 1945 Lois Williamson and I were married. I then took up coal mining, and in March 1946 moved to a mine at Alexo Alberta, near Nordegg. I mined coal until 1954, when the lure of gold took us north to Yellowknife, N.W.T. With a lot of hard work and studies I held the position of Safety Supervisor for Giant Yellowknife Gold Mine until 1966. We then moved to Whitehorse, Yukon to take up the position of Mine Rescue Superintendent for the Yukon.

In 1973, had the Honour of becoming a Serving Brother in The Order of St. John. The investiture was held at Government House in Ottawa with the Prior of the Order in Canada, His Excellency the Governor General presenting the Honour.

We have four daughters — Vicki, married Richard Hancock in 1965; Cathy, works in Edmonton; Becky, married Jim Andrei in 1975; and Margaret, at home.

In the spring of 1978 Cathy married John Aldrich, and they live in Edmonton.

Daisy Battle

My parents, Alice and Ernest Silvester, came out from England in 1910. They took up a homestead at Kew and settled down. This is where I was born in 1920, almost in the middle of their thirteen children.

My education was obtained in a little log school house called Square Butte. In those days education

Henry Battle and son Lorne at Bow Falls.

didn't seem so important and the school only taught up to grade nine. From there I went out to do house work for eight dollars per month, at such places as Kendalls, Tom Phillips and Grandma McBee. I also helped milk cows for Royal Burrows.

I married Henry Battle in 1944 at the Millarville Church. We worked on ranches for a few years. Gwen arrived while we were working for Charles Bull. When Gwen was six years old we moved to Royalties where she started school and her dad got a job at the Commoil Plant. Lorne came along when Gwen was eight years old. When she was fifteen and Lorne seven their father had a heart attack which eventually took his life.

At this time I was janitor's helper in the Longview School, where I continued for three years. After this I went to work for Joan Boyd, looking after children, doing house work and a little of everything that goes on, on a ranch.

Gwen finished her education at Royalties and Black Diamond. She then decided on a Nursing Aide course in Calgary. When she finished that she worked in High River and Calgary. She decided to go to British Columbia where she and her friend obtained jobs at Williams

Back row: Daisy Battle, Gwen McFaul, Jim McFaul.
Front row: Lynn, Kevin and Averil McFaul.

Lake. While working there she met Jim McFaul and married him on September 6th, 1967, in the Millarville Church. They now have a home in Kelowna and have two daughters and a son.

Lorne obtained his education in Longview and Calgary. He now works in Wetaskiwin in the Shur Gain Feed Mill. He married Rhoda High on August 16, 1975. At the present they have one daughter.

I live in Longview in my little log house.

Mamie (Willford) Beattie
by M. Beattie

I was born in Turner Valley September 8th, 1928 and moved away from there when I was about two years old.

My Dad, Ed Willford, bought a farm in the Millarville district the S.E.¼ of 20-21-3-W5. He moved the family from Turner Valley to the farm with horses and wagons.

Included in the family was my mother, May Willford, my brother Hugh and sisters Florence and Irene. We lived on the farm approximately fifteen years. While there we attended Sheep Creek School. We had three miles to go to school. We rode horseback and walked. About a mile and a half from our farm was a family by the name of French. They had one girl going to school, her name was Phyllis. When we rode the horses to school we would give Phyllis a ride. Boost her up one side of the horse — she would fall off the other side, making us late for school. We would end up letting her walk.

There were the Chalmers, Jacksons, Rawlinsons, Blakleys, Cloakeys, Larratts, Hodgkins, Pegler,

Waughs and Ingerveld that started to school about the same time.

Every year Sheep Creek School had their annual Christmas Concert. This was held in the Rancher's Hall, west of Millarville. As the years went by there were more folks moving into the district, more children to go to school. Another school was built, children were bussed in from Kew and I don't recall the other places off hand.

We had a multitude of teachers at Sheep Creek, just to name a few, Miss Galbraith, my first, Miss Rickett, Helen Gould, Miss VanAmburg, Mr. Anderson, Miss Jameson, Miss McWilliams and Mrs. Fisher.

In July 1947, I went to work in the Horse Shoe Cafe in Black Diamond, I worked there several years and at the Valley Grill in Turner Valley. My folks sold the farm at Millarville and moved to Turner Valley.

In 1951 I married the only fellow left in Turner Valley, Don Beattie. He was walking the pipeline from Turner Valley to Calgary. We lived in Turner Valley about a year or two then moved to Leduc. Don worked in the oil fields until 1965. In 1955, we had a daughter, Yvonne. She is married and has two children. From 1965 we were in the Motel business. At the present time we reside in Fort McLeod, the only place the wind blows every day.

E. Katherine (Nevra) Beazley
by Kay Beazley

I was born in Stettler in 1915. After completing secondary school in Stettler I attended Normal School in Calgary 1933-34.

In 1943 I married Ole Nevra. Ole was born in Hoksund, Norway in 1904. He came to Alberta in 1926 and was married shortly afterwards. In 1934 Ole came to Royalties and worked for Brown, Moyer and Brown. In 1936 he was promoted to Field Superintendent. The same year Anker was born, and shortly afterwards his mother became sick and passed away.

The year following our marriage, we moved to the Home Oil Camp at Millarville where Ole continued employment in the same capacity.

Anker attended Sheep Creek School in 1944-51, from there he moved to Red Deer graduating from Red Deer Composite High School. He completed his first year of a Chartered Accountancy course in Edmonton. He passed away suddenly in 1957.

I taught grades one to three at Sheep Creek School from 1951-56, and after our move to Calgary I continued teaching until 1970. Ole held the position of Personnel Manager and Safety Supervisor until his death on July 8th, 1959.

In September 1967 I married R. G. (Bob) Beazley. Bob was brought up and received his schooling in England, coming to Canada in 1926. He is president of Miller & Beazley Ltd. and through his business over the years we both have many friends in the Millarville area.

N. G. Beebe and Family

Nate and Eileen Beebe were both raised on farms in the Hastings Coulee district near Forestburg, Alberta, Eileen being the former Eileen Evans.

Nate farmed in that area in the early years and was also a coal miner.

They have three children, Vernon, Mona and Marjorie. Vernon married Gwen Finley from Oxford, Nova Scotia and they live in Calgary.

Mona married Jeffrey Bulock, originally from England. They live in St. John's, Newfoundland and have two boys, Graham and Martin.

Marjorie married Bryan Carr from Midnapore, Alta. and they live in Aldergrove, B.C. They have three children, Darrel, Dale and Shannon.

The Beebes moved to the Millarville district in 1945 and lived there for eight years. Nate worked in the oil fields there. The children attended Sheep Creek School, both before and after it was moved. Eileen was at one time a member of the Happy Gang Club, which was really enjoyable.

They moved from Millarville to Midnapore in 1953, which has become a part of Calgary now. Nate became employed at the Holy Cross Hospital as a steam engineer and has worked there for the past 24 years.

Their fond memories will always be at Millarville, where many of their friends still live.

Mr. and Mrs. L. J. Belanger

(by Mrs. L. J. Belanger)

On a holiday in September, 1955, we visited Mr. and Mrs. Frank Sharp, with a real estate salesman showing their ranch FOR SALE. After climbing to the top of north end of Nigger John ridge, we felt we were almost in Heaven, and just had to have that property. We owned Rossdale Apartments, and West-end Tog Shop for Men, and I was part-time clerk in H.B.Co. Ladies Shoe Dept., in Edmonton. None of it had any attraction after the view from the ridge top. We sold our property, bought the ranch, moved in April, 1956.

The old picturesque log house on NW¼-22-20-4-W5 had been built about the turn of the century, and what a spacious place it was, with a good well and pump right out the door! We bought cows with calves, from Percy Bennett, registered a brand JA for both the cattle and horses, naming our holdings J-Ay BAR Ranch.

"Al" Belanger was always interested in Community concerns, travelled many miles and did a lot of talking to get Calgary Power Service into the area, helped with moving the old Kew Hall to it's present location at Square Butte, got the Rural Mail Route extended (for personal gain and for others) and was willing to lend-a-hand anytime. An unfortunate mower accident damaged his health, and coupled with having our car go through the ice late one night at 42F. below zero, by the Rodgers' place, forced our retirement from ranching, and hastened Al's death from emphasema. "Paddy" Rodgers was an angel in disguise when he

A hunting we did go. Uncle Deric Chartrand, Al Belanger, Alice Belanger. Dry bones was all that we found but we sure had fun on our first hunting trip in the hills. 1956.

rescued us from the ice that midnight, and Mrs. Rodgers gave us hot coffee.

We sold the ranch and lease to the Rodgers, and their son Michael and wife moved in. We moved to High River.

"Al" was born in St. Albert, Ont., came West with Sister, Mother, and Grandparents, to Edmonton, 1911. He homesteaded at Sarrail, Alta, 1917; a charter member of A.W.P., 1921; trucked from Meanook to Edmonton, 1936-42; farmed at Clyde, 1942-48; operated a Highway Store and Gas Service at Hercules, 1948-50; lived in Edmonton, 1950-56.

I was born in Sintaluta, Sask., coming to Calgary, 1913, when "Daddy" Bentley began barbering there. Bentleys moved to various places over the years, mostly at Pincher Creek, where I attended High School, then Normal in Calgary, 1927, teaching in Athabasca area, 1928 to Dec. 1931, when I married. I have been a member of A.W.I. since 1938; of U.F.A. since 1946, and was a "Squarette" with the Square Butte ladies. I love riding, and had the most beautiful horse (caught wild on the range by Tex Worobetz) which I rode to the meetings when the weather was unpleasant.

We have a foster-daughter, Mrs. Edith Moore, Quesnel, B.C., and a foster-son, Trevor Stoutenburg, 'Maitre de' of Vallhalla Inn, Kitchener, Ont.

Here is my "home-made" roll call verse for one meeting, with my apologies to Bryan Waller Procter:

SPRING

The mud! the mud! the sea of mud!
The wet, the black, the sticky mud!
With the clouds above, and the mud below,
And slush wheresoe'er I go;
If a storm should come, and make it deep,
What matter? I shall ride, or sleep.

I'm in the Hills! I'm in the Hills!
I'm where there are no ills.
With the blue above, and the green below,

And beauty wheresoe'er I go;
If a storm should come, and change the scene,
What matter! I shall ride and dream.

Miles and Mary Crichton Bell
by Mary C. Bell

This is a short, short story about the decendants of George Bell and his wife, Mary Elizabeth Crichton Bell, who were married in Christ Church, Millarville, April 24, 1905. George Bell was the first postmaster of the Kew district, naming the district by spelling the brand of John Quirk's, Q.

Miles, their only son, was born in June, 1907 and Mary Crichton, their only daughter, was born in July 1908. Miles was born in Holy Cross Hospital in Calgary and Mary arrived at the ranch on a hot summer day.

It was on September 1st 1914, that the Bell family arrived in Vancouver to make their future home. The children obtained all their schooling at the coast and continued to make their homes there after both their parents had passed away.

Miles began his business career with the Royal Bank of Canada. After leaving the bank, he was stationed with Pacific Command in Victoria and then in Vancouver during the war years. He then became a paymaster with Crown Zellerbach Canada Ltd., Paper Products Division, in Richmond, B.C. until his retirement some six years ago.

In July, 1949, Miles married Brenda Davey and in July 1950, one year later, their only son, Derek Norman, was born. A childhood interest and hobby lead Derek to his present vocation as a branch manager of a photographic supply house in North Vancouver. He makes his home in West Vancouver.

After her school years, Mary was a stenographer with B.C. Telephone Co. for fifteen years before leaving to serve with the Canadian Army Medical Corps for two years. On her return she joined Dominion Directory Co. Ltd., an affiliate of B.C. Telephone Co. until her retirement over five years ago. She now enjoys her leisure time doing volunteer work, playing golf and birdwatching.

Miles, with his family, has returned to visit in the Kew area, and Mary, too, has returned on several occasions to enjoy renewing the friendship of those long-time family friends and their decendants who still reside in the Millarville and Kew areas.

Percy Thomas Bennett — Pat Bennett

Percy was born August 4, 1904, in Herefordshire, England, the third son of an English Father and Welsh Mother, Elizabeth and William Bennett. There were three boys and two girls in the family, all born in England except the youngest girl. They are, Bill of Fort McLeod, Frank in Pincher Creek, May in Calgary and Mertle of Vancouver.

Mr. Bennett Sr. came to Canada in 1910 to find employment and look for land suitable to raise

Percy and Pat Bennett, taken at George Lane Park, in High River, 1966.

livestock. It was in the area around Lundbreck that he finally decided to settle, so in 1911 he sent for his family and met them in Winnipeg, then on to what was to be their home for many years.

In 1920 he got the job as Manager of the McEchin Ranch, or better known as The Rock Creek Hereford Ranch, and he held this position until the ranch was sold in 1936. So it was here the family grew up. Mrs. Bennett passed away in 1925.

Percy took his schooling at the Northfork and Diamond Schools, about six miles from the ranch, and at the young age of fourteen he went to work for different ranchers in the district, some of them being Fulton, Dennis Folley and the Waldron.

In 1926 when Peter Welsh went east with his rodeo string to put on shows in Toronto, Ottawa and Winnipeg, Percy and his brother, Frank, went along to look after the stock and compete a little. Percy drove the chuckwagon. Things went well, and the boys had a great time, until Percy had the misfortune to get a bad bite from one of the bucking horses, and ended up in the hospital with blood poison in his hand. This not being at all to his liking, he persuaded the doctor to let him out to travel with his friends, and by the time he got home his hand was a terrible mess and he was lucky not to lose it.

In the spring of 1927 he went to Banff to work for Jim Brewster, as a Packer. There was lots of this kind of work to be had, as most of the ski camps got started at that time. They hauled everything — all the lumber, stoves, beds and tables with horses — no roads, just pack trails. In the winter he got the job, along with another lad, of freighting, with four-horse teams, the material to build the camp for the dam at Kananaskis Lakes. When they made their first trip up the lake, Percy's team and sleigh went through the ice. It was a good thing there were two outfits, the horses had to be unhooked and pulled out one at a time. It was thirty below zero, and Percy's load consisted of all the men's bedrolls and grub. There was no sleep for anyone that night as they had to build bonfires to dry out the bedding, and this took three days. In the early thirties when work was hard to find, Percy took a job as one of three meat cooks at the Relief Kitchen at Stampede Park. On Christmas Day, 1931, they fed over three thousand men a full course meal, including turkey and Christmas pudding.

In 1934 he went to work for the Federal Government as a Park Warden, stationed on the Clearwater in summer and the Yaha Tinda on the Red Deer River in winter. It was while he was working at this job that Percy and I were married on September 6, 1935. I had met him three years previous to this time, while I was working for a well-known Bragg Creek couple, Mr. and Mrs. Chummy Cresswell for four years.

I am a native of the Priddis district. Born in Calgary, October 13, 1910. My Father came to Canada in the fall of 1897 from his home in Carmarthenshire, Wales, the third child in a family of fourteen. Mother was born in Lancaster, England, in 1881, the third child born to Mr. and Mrs. John Devereux. She had one sister and one brother. Dad's first job after coming to Canada was with the C.P.R. west of Fort McLeod, where they were laying the first line through the Crow's Nest Pass. In the spring he arrived at Priddis and worked for some of the early settlers, breaking sod with a team and walking plow. As time went on he got acquainted with many of the old timers, including John Ware, whom he spoke of with a great deal of admiration.

Mother came to Canada in 1903 where she met my Father at the Bradfield Ranch, and they were married on October 13, 1905 in Calgary. I have one brother born in 1906, L. C. Williams, Calgary. John, my younger brother, was killed in 1936 while building his house two miles west of Dad's place on the south fork of Fish Creek.

We children went to the Priddis school, then to Fordville for a couple of years.

After Percy and I were married he stayed on as a Warden for two years. In 1937 we lost our only son, born in Banff hospital July 21, 1937 — William John Bennett.

Percy Bennett with Quarter Horse Stallion bred by Tip Johnson, owned by Percy. 1963.

In the spring of 1938 Percy went in partnership with a well-known old timer of the Banff and Lake Louise areas, Jim Boyce, who had been in the tourist business for some time. We spent our summers on the trail taking out fishing and hunting parties. One of the best I can remember was when we had Carl Rungus as our guest. Mr. Rungus passed away many years ago, but will live on through his paintings of the mountains and animals.

Through one of the ski instructors at Banff, we were invited to start a western dude ranch in Quebec, ninety miles north of Montreal. So in June, 1940, we bought twenty-four broke saddle horses and all the equipment, and headed East to Mount Tremblant. It took six days for the horses to get there by box car, and then there was no accommodation for the horses, as this place had been opened as a ski resort two years earlier. Today it is the biggest in the East. It was a lot of work to get a barn built and trails made, all the feed had to be shipped in from Ontario and most of the horses sent out for the winter. Percy's Dad had gone down with us, but left for home in the spring. Percy and I stayed till the fall, then sold the horses and came back West. I don't think the men cared for the Frenchmen and black flies!

After our arrival back to Calgary, came the task of finding a place to get started ranching. The Home Oil Company had some land two and a half miles south and west of Millarville and they were kind enough to lease it to us for the time being. Percy went to work on one of their drilling rigs, working mostly night shifts, so he had time to work at other jobs on the place, getting very little sleep. He did this for three years, and by 1946 we were able to start buying a section of land one and one-half miles south of Millarville, from a couple that were about to retire, Mr. and Mrs. (Eugene and Jacqueline) de Palizieux, old timers of the Millarville district. We moved in November in some terrible weather. We had a few cattle and ten milk cows, and Percy had built me a fair size chickenhouse of cottonwoods, so we moved that too, and for twenty-three years I graded and sold my eggs to the Economy Store in Turner Valley. Returns from the eggs made it possible for me to go into Registered Suffolk sheep, which I had until I sold out. Percy had been buying and selling horses since we came back from the East. We had wanted to get into Quarter horses, so in 1952 went to Montana and bought a yearling stud colt from "Dong Dear", by the name of "Birdtail's Dandy", but before long he was known as "Turk". His service was much in demand, and at age five had served ninety mares in one season. His colts are all over Canada. Turk was part of our family for twenty-three years, and it was a sad day when we lost him in 1974 of a twisted bowel.

I lost my Mother in 1952, and Percy's Dad in 1956, and also my Dad in 1960.

We cleared quite a bit of brush during these years and sowed it to timothy hay, which Percy hauled to the race horse men at Stampede Park. In 1949 he took the job of calf-starter at the Stampede in Calgary and was there for eighteen years.

He helped to build Millarville Hall, and enjoyed curling at the Black Diamond Rink. He was also on the Rodeo Committee at High River. We quite often took in the Priddis and Millarville Fairs where I first showed at the age of ten years. Dad was one of the originators in 1907. He showed Clyde horses for many years.

Between 1967 and 1969 Percy sold three quarters of our place: To — Bob Young, Lawyer S.E. ¼ 35-20-3-5. To — Jim and Helen Thompson, Lawyer N.E. ¼ 26-20-3-5, N.W. ¼ 25-20-3-5.

Percy passed away in January 14, 1972, after three years of illness. I stayed on the ranch for two more years then sold the home quarter to Walter Semchuk, P. Eng. — N.W. ¼ 26-20-3-5.

Norm and Pat Benny

Norm, son of Phillip and Frances Benny, was born and raised in Calgary, attended Langevin and Crescent Heights School. After finishing school he apprenticed with the Electric Light Company and obtained his Journeyman Electrician certificate and has been working there for the past twenty years.

Pat, daughter of Kelly and Hilda Ozelle, was born and raised in Nelson, B.C. After finishing High School she moved to Calgary where she completed a Certified Nursing Aide Course and worked at Baker Memorial Sanatorium before marriage and the Calgary General Hospital for a year after her marriage in September of 1963.

We have three children, Jacquie b. February 28, 1965, Laurie b. March 23, 1967, and Kelly b. November 27, 1969, who were born in Calgary. We lived on the North Hill in the Brentwood area until June, 1978 when we decided to leave the hustle and bustle of city living and move to the country. Norm is building our home in Millarville and has found it a great challenge.

The children are enrolled in Millarville School and seem well adjusted and happy with the change from the city schools.

As a family we enjoy cross-country skiing, swimming and hiking and hope to resume these activities when our home is finished.

Bernhardt — Jack, Linda and family

Linda and I first explored the Square Butte-Millarville area in May 1975, seeking a new home for our family as my employment presented us with the opportunity of transferring from Oakbank, Manitoba, a small village on the outskirts of Winnipeg. We finally decided, and it was an easy decision, on a 53 acre parcel of land formerly owned by Mrs. M. Lyall. It was ideal, not only because of its proximity to the Imperial Oil Quirk Creek Gas Plant, but also because it represented the ultimate in country living — an active community combined with the luxury of the wilderness — and the Rockies thrown in free of charge. I moved onto the property June 1, 1975 and lived in our truck camper while beginning my new job as an engineer with Imperial Oil. Linda and children stayed behind in Manitoba until the sale of our house was completed, and came out on July 7, 1975. Our first summer and autumn was mainly spent building a new log home and getting settled. It was a trying experience in many ways and we moved in on Linda's birthday, Dec. 23. An unforgettable moment was that same evening, trudging through the forest in the moonlight with our children age 8 and 5 and cutting our first Christmas tree.

Our interests in the following 2 years were mainly in hiking and roaming the countryside, enjoying and finishing our house, gardening (potatoes as big as your head) and going to community functions at Millarville and Square Butte. Our children participated in skating, hockey and baseball at Millarville and also the Millarville Art Fair.

Our 2½ years in the foothills also more than amply exposed us to the combined blessings and fury of the chinooks — a legend to behold and partly responsible for our eventual selling.

We moved December 21, 1977 to Oakbank, Manitoba — a little sad but enlightened to the magic and moods of the mountains, and feeling a certain magnetism that will bring us back many times to the good friends and neighbours we came to know. Our home and property was purchased by Mr. and Mrs. R. Dixon of Calgary. We are presently residing in Oakbank, Manitoba and are developing and operating a family style restaurant.

Benny children, left to right. Jacquie, Laurie and Kelly.

Warren and Laura Bernhardt.

185

Nick and Shirley Berjian

by Ruby McNab

Nick and Shirley with their two lovely daughters Carla and Kim joined our happy community the fall of 1975. Nick Berjian sold his Willow Creek Ranch at Claresholm, which he owned for 10 years, and bought the ranch in our district, the S.W.¼ 25-21-R2-W5. It is one of the prettiest quarters in our area. Catching up on the lands history, Nick and Shirley discovered it had changed hands many times. Norman Anderson bought it from Long John Goerlitz in 1919. In 1925 Norman had the Natural Gas installed for allowing the gas line to go through his property. He spent his time farming and developing the grounds until it resembled a park. He sold out to Watts, in 1945 who sold to Bill McGuire in 1948. Who later sold to Ann Boon of Banff, in 1964. The ranch consisted of 400 acres then. It was managed by Ann Boon's brother Bill Sadler and family for four years. Ann Boon sold out to speculaters. During this time they subdivided the ranch into parcels leaving 167 acres. This was bought by Relco Management and managed by Rudy Enzman. Nick residing in Bayview S.W., Calgary was looking for a place within commuting distance to the city. When looking over the land of hills and valleys covered with trees, flowing springs and cultivated pastures, Nick decided this was the haven for his Full Blood Simmentals. He purchased it from Relco and built it into a going concern for his Simmentals. It wasn't long until Nick and family often could watch from their living room window deer mingling contentedly with his Simmental herd.

Nick, Shirley and daughters were pleased when attending the 1979 Simmental Spring shows they came home with the Grand Champion and Jr. Grand Champion.

Jack and Marie Putzie from Claresholm now retired in Claresholm helped Nick on the Ranch for three years.

Nick, after his many enterprises, decided that this is the life. His wife Shirley, an R.N., who divides her time between the city residence and the ranch, agrees. Although the ranch is always buzzing with activity, friends and visitors are always assured the same kind of old fashion hospitality that the pioneers of this district were so famous for.

Bill and Sharon Bieber

by Sharon Bieber

Bill and Sharon Bieber, along with their son Timothy, born in 1974, moved to the Millarville area in 1975 from Calgary, and settled on the farm of Gordon and Rila Blanchard. (N.W.¼-23-21-3-5) Tera-Lynn was welcomed to their family in July, 1976.

Both Bill and Sharon are from rural backgrounds; Sharon from a farm at Marwayne in east-central Alberta, and Bill from rural southern Alberta towns where his parents were in business. They met at University in Edmonton, where Bill was a medical student and Sharon in the Faculty of Education. After graduation, in 1969, they married and moved to Calgary where Bill interned at the Holy Cross Hospital, and Sharon taught junior high school physical education.

At this point the wide world and international travel was beckoning them to expand their narrow horizons, so in the fall of 1970 they set off. Working in places like the West Indies and Tanzania for 3 month stints, and travelling all around the world in between, certainly did broaden their perspective of the world community, and give them a new realization of the privileged lifestyle we in the western world lead in relation to the greatest percentage of the world population. They returned to Calgary resolved not to become caught up in the materialistic rat-race of many of their contemporaries, but found the pulls back into this way of life very subtle, yet very strong.

Moving out of the city to a small farm five years later was not only a step of returning to their "roots" to allow their children to be raised in the healthy country environment, but a step in the direction of a search for a simpler and more basic lifestyle that depends less on material possessions and more on relationships and the satisfaction of good hard work. They raise a few sheep, to produce the wool that Sharon spins for knitting and weaving, and a few percentage Simmental cattle. They have chosen the name Sunridge Simmentals as their herd name. Bill still practices family medicine in south Calgary, and thoroughly enjoys the change of pace and roles which the farm provides in the evenings and on weekends. Sharon loves the freedom to "do her own thing" in growing a healthy garden, raising the lambs, entertaining the children, attending one of the local ladies' Bible study groups, pursuing hobbies, and all of the tasks of a homemaker.

However, the opportunity in 1978 to relieve a missionary doctor in Papua, New Guinea for one year aroused their spirit of adventure again, and on March 28, they packed their bags and two children and set off!

Nick Berjian, Kim, Carla, and Shirley.

Their history must stop at this point, as it is being written en route to Papua, New Guinea. Bill and Sharon and their family look forward, after their return home, to many years in the community that they have come to enjoy so much, and to many new friendships in this community.

The Ronald Birkenes Family

by Maud Birkenes PIE

I was born in Okotoks September 10th 1921, eldest daughter of David and Margaret Glaister. Grew up on the farm, S ½-3-21-2W5. Those early years were quite uneventful but when I started school, that was a real adventure.

I was nearly eight years old when my parents decided I would have to start school. There was no school close by. Ballyhamage was about four miles north of our farm and that was the place where I would have to go. It was decided I would board at Jamesons. They lived quite close to the school and Eileen Jameson was teaching there at that time. I had a little black Shetland pony called "Jimmy" that went along with me as my means of transportation. "Jimmy" had only one pace and that was slow, so poor Eileen had quite a time getting me to school on time.

After a year I graduated to a much bigger horse. She was a grey, part Percheron called "Dolly" and I started off to school from home. I had a mile to ride by myself and and then I joined the Cannon children (Helen, David and Neville.) We rode the other three miles together. My Dad built stiles at all the gates as I had trouble climbing up on old "Dolly".

After about four years I started to go to New Valley School. This school was two and a half miles west of our place and was opened January 1928. There was the North Fork of Sheep creek by the Deane-Freeman place which had to be forded and some times in the spring it got very high. When exams had to be written in June and the river was high, my Mother would ride with me to the swinging bridge. This was a narrow foot bridge hung by cables and used by the pipe line walker who walked the oil line from Turner Valley to Calgary. This bridge was just up the river from the crossing. I

would walk across the bridge (it used to swing when you got out in the middle of it) then I had a mile to walk to school.

At night I would meet my Mother at the bridge and ride the rest of the way home. Some times I would ride to school, the river would be all right in the morning but if it was a very hot day it would be much higher at night. My Dad would come down to the river and wait for me on the other side while I made my way across. He would have a lariat with him and I used to wonder if he would be able to catch me if my horse lost his footing in the swift flowing stream and I had to swim for it. He used to tell me "Just slide back and hang on to your horse's tail, she will get you across all right."

The ice in the winter used to cause some problems too. My horse was shod but she hated to venture out on the glare ice if there had been some flooding and freezing.

There sure were some cold rides, sometimes you would have to get off and walk and lead your horse and swing your arms to try and get warm. When it was time for High School I decided I had enough of school. I had missed a lot of school with illness and my friends were all so far ahead of me. I had heard a lot about Olds Agriculture College so in the fall of 1939 I struck off for Olds. During the years 1939-1940-1941 I went to Olds Agriculture College and took a course in Home Economics. I really enjoyed my stay there. It was a wonderful experience and I met young people from all over Alberta.

In the summer of 1941 I received a letter from Elizabeth Rummel, who was helping Erling Strome run Mt. Assiniboine Lodge south of Banff. This lodge was a two day trip from Banff on horseback (there were no roads in there) or if you really felt energetic you could hike in. In winter the only means of travel was by ski or snow shoe as the snow gets very deep in there. I spent a wonderful summer looking after cabins and doing lots of riding and hiking in my spare time. That fall on my way out I got myself a job in Banff for the winter. I loved the mountains and that was a wonderful winter. I was close to the skating rink so I could do a lot of skating and I even tried a bit of skiing on Mt. Norquay.

When spring came I went home for the summer of 1942. The mountains were calling again so I went on a Youth Hostel trip with the Oliver girls. We joined the Youth Hostel and used their accommodations. We travelled across country by horseback from Priddis to Bragg Creek, Jumping Pound, Morley to Canmore. We were away for a week and it was quite an adventure. It was a very wet year and we had a great deal of trouble with muskeg.

That fall I thought I would try a bit of city life. I went to Calgary and started looking for a job. Jobs are not very easy to get when you haven't any experience in anything. I was bound I would get something so I finally ended up with a job in Burn's Meat Packing Plant. This was during the war and my job was pack-

Maud and Ronald Birkenes on their wedding day.

Birkenes family on Mary's wedding day. L. to R. Mary, Maud, Ronald and Margaret.

ing bacon for the soldiers overseas. I quite enjoyed my winter at Burns but when spring came I longed for the country again. I was not home very long when I received a visit from Elizabeth Rummel. She was going to run Skoki Lodge, near Lake Louise, for the summer and she needed some help. Skoki is twelve miles north of Lake Louise and the only way you could get in there then was to ride or hike in the summer or ski or snow shoe in the winter. The Lodge had not been used for a while and sure needed lots of cleaning and repair work done. We spent a very busy summer there and went back again for the skiing season after Christmas. I stayed with Elizabeth at Skoki until the spring of 1945. I was home only for short visits during the spring and fall.

In June 1945 I married Ronald Birkenes and my days in the mountains were over.

Ronnie was born in Champion May 13th 1921. He spent his boyhood on the farm in the Lomond district and went to Brunetta School. When he was about ten years old he came to stay with an aunt and uncle (Albert Cane of Millarville) and went to Ballyhamage School. From there he went back to Champion to take his high school. The W.E. Deane-Freemans of Millarville needed some one to help with chores so he moved back to Millarville, stayed with the Deane-Freemans and rode seven and a half miles to Turner Valley High School taking his Grade xii.

In March 1938 he went to work for the Valley Pipe Line in Turner Valley. He boarded at Watchorn's boarding house. When war broke out in 1939 he joined the Air Force, taking his training at Calgary, Dafoe, Sask. and Toronto. In 1941, he went overseas. He was stationed in England, Palestine, Egypt, Bengazi. He served in Halifax Bombers. In 1944 he was awarded the D.F.C. He was discharged in the spring of 1945 with the rank of Flying Officer. He then went back to work for the Valley Pipe Line. He bought a small house on "Poverty Flats" and we lived there until 1957.

There were two big events during those years on the "Flats". In 1946 Margaret Elizabeth was born and in 1948 Mary Dianne made her appearance.

In 1954 there were some houses for sale up on "Snob Hill". The houses were much bigger and had more conveniences and they were situated right in the middle of the golf course. Ronnie and his daughters took up golf. Brown's Bowling Alley was going full swing by this time so the whole family took up bowling. Life was really busy up on the "Hill". There was a big garden and a big lawn with lots of grass to cut.

There were two big events in 1969. In July there was a wedding. Margaret married Marc Dallas of Turner Valley. Now with Margaret married and Mary off at the University, we decided it was time to move out to our place at Millarville. We had bought a quarter section (N.W. ¼-14-21-3W5.) in 1959. A new house was built and in November we moved to the country. Ronnie's life long ambition of being a farmer was finally going to be realized. A milk cow was bought and right away life in the country had begun. Ronnie was still working in the oil fields and driving back and forth to Turner Valley was getting tiresome. Some more cows were bought and there was plenty of work to be done.

In 1972 he retired from the Oil Company and became a full fledged farmer. In June, 1972, there was another wedding. Mary married Jim South of Manning and moved to Calgary. Now we are alone again.

It is now 1978 and there are four grandaughters. Margaret and Marc live in Turner Valley. Marc is an electrician and is an area foreman with Alberta Gas Trunk Line. They have two daughters, Danielle Renee, born in 1971, and Dionne Michelle in 1975.

Mary and Jim live in Okotoks. Jim is a back hoe contractor. They have two daughters, Kimberley Dawn, born in 1975 and Jamie Dianne born in 1978.

Charlie and Frances Birney Family *FC ℛℒℐ*

Charlie was born April 28th, 1907 the eldest son of Mr. and Mrs. W. G. Birney of Red Deer Lake district. That is where he grew up and went to school. Charlie farmed and ranched most of his life. His horse brand was F C and cow brand was ℛℒℐ . Charlie moved to the DeMille place in 1930.

Frances was born February second, 1909 the eldest daughter of Mr. and Mrs. Withell of Calgary. That is where she grew up and went to school.

Charlie and Frances were married September 30th, 1936. Charlie worked as a derrick man for Major No. Five and No. Twelve oil wells. Their two girls were born while they lived on the DeMille place. They moved back to the farm at Red Deer Lake for a while. In 1945 they moved to the Sid Bannerman place at Square Butte which they bought. They owned the East half of 22-21-4-W5 and the North West quarter of 23-21-4-W5. The home site is now owned by Fred Ball. While at Square Butte Frances was a member and secretary for the ladies' group. Charlie took the children to

L. to R. Beverley, Charlie, Frances, Audrey Birney.

Back, L. to R.: Bob, Audrey (Birney), Larry. Front: Donna, Rod and Tammy.

Joe and Bev (Birney) Czipoth and girls, Debbie, Fran, Cindy.

school at Square Butte part-time in the Jeep from the North.

They were both active in community affairs, picnics, social gatherings community plays and many other functions that took place in the district also functions at the Ranchers' Hall, Millarville. They left Square Butte district in August 1954 to live in Calgary. They were a loss to the community when they moved

away. Charlie worked for Alberta Distillers Limited, Calgary. Frances was a member of the River View United Church, Calgary. Frances passed away at a young age of 49 years on January fourth, 1959 after a long illness. Charlie's sudden death came on July 10th, 1969.

Beverley, their eldest daughter, was born January 20th, 1938; she started school at Red Deer Lake, then went to the Purdy home, now Jim Davis place, to be taught by Mrs. Purdy. Then she went by Jeep to Square Butte school until 1950 when all the children were taken by bus to Sheep Creek School now Millarville School. She finished her schooling in Calgary. Beverley married Joe Czipoth they have three girls, Debbie born September 14th, 1956, Cindy born December 11th, 1957, Fran born August fifth, 1964, they all live in Calgary.

Audrey their youngest daughter born September 16th, 1941, started school at Square Butte, then in 1950 went by bus to Sheep Creek, now Millarville school. She finished her schooling in Calgary. Audrey married R. C. (Bob) Egan, they have four children; Donna born October 28th, 1960, Larry born January 31st, 1962, Rod born May 11th, 1967, Tammy born March second, 1970. They all live in Calgary.

Harold L. Biswanger
by H. L. Biswanger

I was born on Jan. 3, 1928 in Calgary, Alta., the second born of six children, two boys and four girls, to Lillian and Ernest Biswanger. Lillian is the oldest daughter of Lillian and Jessie Aldridge of Okotoks;

Harold Biswanger building home, 1956.

Ernest, the youngest son of nine children of Lidia and George Biswanger of Nova Scotia, descendents of one of the oldest families in Nova Scotia — dating back to 1590 for the Rodgers, and 1650 for the Biswangers.

I went to school in Calgary, taking grade school in Bankview, Mount Royal and Sunalta, and high school in Western Canada High.

I was working for my dad at an early age of 12 or 13 at painting and carpentry trades on weekends and holidays. I had a scaffold collapse under me at about 14 years of age, and I landed on the edge of a board. So after ten years, my back gave me trouble ever since. I dug the basement in grade nine for a house we were going to build in the spring. This basement I dug by hand with a shovel and steel wheeled wheelbarrow. This was done in winter, the ground frozen solid. I set fires at night with old street paving blocks, and covered them with sheets of tin to keep the heat down. The next day I dug out the thawed dirt and repeated the operation. This took three months. I received $100 for this, as it was the going price at this time for a machine to do it.

I spent any time I could get away in summer holidays at my grandfather Aldridge's farm at Okotoks. I always wanted to become a farmer. So three years after leaving school, I and school chum Albert Vanner started to deal on the Ed Blair farm — S.E.¼, Sec. 27, T.21, R.3, W.5 and N.W.¼, Sec.22, T.21, R.3, W.5, — but foot and mouth disease hit the west in cattle in 1951 and money was very tight, so we could not get a loan. So I bought the S.E.¼, Sec. 27, T.21, R.3, W.5 myself. I spent the summer cutting and peeling and treating poplar posts to fence the place. I borrowed a team from Gordon Blanchard or Jack Lee to move the post around the fence line through heavy bush, and then drove them in by hand. I pastured my cattle along with Aunt Olive Aldridge's and Harry Barker's cattle for one year.

I sold to my uncle Bill Aldridge who in turn sold to Cliff Green. I then bought N.W.¼, Sec.6, T.21, R.28, W.4 seven miles north east of Okotoks.

While I was at Millarville, I started doing some carpentry work for Bob Winthrop, and so 28 years later

I am still doing work for Bob, and many others in the Priddis, Millarville, Red Deer Lake, DeWinton and Okotoks areas, along with the odd job at Calgary, Cayley, Three Hills, and for the Macklin Bros. west of Olds.

In 1957 I pastured cattle and helped farm the land on the farm that Albert Vanner bought from Jack Barlow (S.E.¼, Sec.22 and N.E.¼, Sec.15, T.21, R.2, W.5) in the Ballyhamage School district. In 1962, together with my brother Merton we bought the S.E.¼, Sec.24, T.21, R.1, W.5, from Eric Goddard, south of DeWinton. Mert built a house, and I pastured my cattle here.

One harrowing experience I had here was in the spring of 1963. I was in the process of unloading a seed drill off a flat deck wagon. I unhooked from the wagon with my M.M. tractor which I had just got out of the garage in Okotoks with a new motor job. To have the work done on the tractor, I had to take the front end loader off. As I was used to the extra weight in front of the tractor, I had to climb out of a wide ditch to pull the drill off the wagon. I got square in the ditch and I was standing on the platform in low gear. I started to engage the hand clutch and the tractor reared up, fully engaging the clutch, and throwing me off balance and on to the ground behind the tractor. I turned over and looked up in horror, to see the tractor standing straight up and starting over right behind me. I scrambled away on all four, just as the tractor crashed to the ground behind me, missing me by a foot. As the motor was still running when it hit the ground, the first thing I thought of was, my new motor was still running upside down. As I reached under to turn it off, it quit — and only then did the realization hit me and I went into shock. I sat on the side of the ditch for about an hour. I then walked to Bill Heater working in a field about a mile away to get him to turn the tractor over for me. Nobody came by for five hours, till the school bus came.

I was married Dec. 1964 to Jean Standish, but the marriage did not work out, so I moved back to my own farm at DeWinton.

That December, the end of the first week, was about the coldest I could remember, and for many others, 30 degrees below with a wind from the north east equaling a chill factor of 90 degrees below Fahrenheit.

I joined the Millarville Racing and Agriculture Society in 1965, and I have been the concession director for 12 years, and main board director for 3 years, also director of the DeWinton Historical Society.

Blackie, William (Bill) — 1886-1963
by his daughter Jean Harper

Came from Scotland in 1926 with his wife Catherine and three of their four children — Walter, Hellen and William, leaving the eldest child Catherine to finish her nurses training. They first farmed in the Edmon-

W. Blackie.

ton area, then moved to Twin Butte in Southern Alberta in 1936 where he was manager on a ranch. In early 1940 he, his wife and young daughter Jean, the only Canadian born of the family, came to the Anchordown Ranch, as manager for Mrs. Dorothy Dewar of England. When they first arrived, there was no house on the West Anchordown (it having been destroyed by fire), so they took up residence on the White place (later owned by Ed Hehr), while a new log home was being constructed by the Crostons who owned a nearby saw mill. While they lived on the West Anchordown, Jean attended Fordville School. In late 1941 they moved to the East Anchordown where he continued to manage both ranches.

Mrs. Blackie passed away in July, 1942.

In 1943 Mrs. Dewar was killed in an accident with a horse in England, after which Mr. Blackie and his eldest son, Walter, rented both ranches for a year. During this time Jean attended Priddis School.

Harper and Blackie Family.

In the spring of 1944 both ranches were sold. Mr. Blackie and daughter continued to live in the Priddis area and Walter went to Arrowwood as manager to the Arrowwood Farming Co. In early 1945 Mr. Blackie and Jean went back to the Twin Butte country. From there, Jean joined the Canadian Women's Army Corps. and after a year's service, she and her Dad again returned to Priddis to the Percival place purchased by Mrs. Dorothy Weir and managed by Mr. Blackie.

In 1948 Jean married John Harper of Midnapore. They were married in St. James Church, their wedding being the fourth in 40 years to be held in this little church. In 1949 Mr. Blackie married Mrs. May Lowe and they resided on the Lowe farm until he passed away in 1963. He will be remembered for his willingness to help his neighbours and for his love and knowledge of horses and cattle. He was always very interested in community affairs and served on the Priddis Hall Board during the start of the hall renovations. He was also a member of St. James Church and helped out there too.

Jean and John Harper owned and farmed the Powell place — S.W.¼-34-22-3-W5 until they sold it in 1964 to Pat Burns and moved to Rocky Mountain House where they dairy farm. They have four children, all born while they lived at Priddis — Merridith, Keith, Kevin, and Shelagh.

Walter, who was with his father on the Anchordown, and his wife have been with Mannix Farms of Calgary for a number of years. Bill Jr. and his wife are with Peter Bawden Drilling World Wide and are at present in Jakarta, Indonesia. Hellen lives and farms with her husband and family at Grassland, Alberta. Kitty, the eldest, who remained in Scotland, immigrated to Australia in 1948 with her husband and family. She is now a widow and lives in Sidney, Australia. In December, 1962 she came to Canada to visit her father after a parting of 36 years, and also to meet her sister Jean for the first time. She was still here at the time of her father's death.

Dennis T. Blakley

Dennis was born June 7th, 1933, at Tees, Alberta, second child and eldest son of Tim and Jean (Fisher) Blakley. In 1935, his parents moved back to the Millarville district, living on Joseph Fisher Sr.s homestead, the north half of 6-21-3w5. He attended Sheep Creek School, mostly riding on behind his sister on her pony, Baldy. Often when they got down the road a bit and met up with the Hodgkins, Dennis got on behind Freddie and Yvonne on behind Charis, and usually a race was on to the school yard. Living on the south side of Fisher Creek, which could become a raging river in the early spring during the run-off, or after a heavy rain, the Blakley children had many unscheduled holidays. Other times the creek was frozen into a sheet of glare ice, so then walking was the order of the day. No school busses at that time.

Dennis Blakley and friend.

Dennis soon had his own pony, bought from a Morely Indian, Isaiah Powderface, and named by his previous owner, Chiniki Lake, an odd name for a horse, who was as odd as his name. He didn't have any intention of becoming a kid's pony, would run away at the drop of a hat and if that didn't work he would try to throw his rider. However, he was soon traded off for a much more reliable pony, this one from the Sarcee Reserve. Gypsy came with a bill-of-sale which read, "Guaranteed free from vice". Seldom do you see such a bill-of-sale, but Gypsy lived up to it and many small children learned to ride on her. She became a long time member of the Blakley family, living to the ripe old age of 27 years. When Dennis outgrew her she became his sister Mary's pony.

Dennis learned to handle a gun at an early age, and anxiously awaited the day when he would be able to go big game hunting in the mountains. There were no roads into the North Fork district of the Forest Reserve at this time so all hunters had to pack in all their supplies on pack horses. One September when sheep hunting opened, Dennis and his cousin Peter Fisher, equipped with all the camping necessities, set out on their first big game hunt. One week before, Pat Rogers had taken in a party of hunters, among them Jody Fisher and David Glaister. Dennis and Peter would have liked to have gone along but Pat thought that would be too many. However it rained, it was cold and they didn't get any game. On top of all that a precious bottle of rum slipped out of a pack and wasn't found, but Pat told Dennis and Peter just about where it had been lost. The weather changed, Indian summer set in so things looked promising for the young hunters. After a week and no news, the parents of the two began to worry a bit. There were a lot of grizzleys in the area where they were hunting, which often frightened the horses into leaving camp and their riders stranded on foot. However, about 10 days later, while Joe and Jane Fisher were at the Ranger Station talking to the Ranger, they could hear weird noises coming from a

distance in the evening dusk. It turned out to be the two young hunters, and each had got a Big Horn Sheep, but by the time they had packed their game out of the canyon, they were very tired and hungry. Their grub was all packed so they decided to start for home without eating. They had found Pat's bottle of rum, so on their way home they thought a few sips of rum would help the hunger pains, so they had a few sips then a few sips more. By the time they got to the Ranger Station, the noises that had been heard were coming from two quite tipsy boys. When Pat Rogers saw the sheep that evening he told the hunters "You may very well go hunting and you may also get a sheep again, but you won't ever find another bottle of my rum." Dennis had many hunting trips after that but none to compare with the first.

Like most young fellows of the area, he went to work in the oil fields on the drilling rigs, but by this time very little drilling was being done in the Millarville district. His first job was at Strathmore, then on to Saskatchewan, and to many areas in the north country.

When a chance came to go to Lake Louise as a guide for Timberline Tours, owned at that time by Ray Legace, Dennis went very eagerly. This was a great life and his friend Ivor Lyster was also there, so the two of them had some great times. Legace's horses wintered at the Ya-Ha-Tinda, the Government Horse Ranch and it was a real adventure in the spring, trailing the horses back to Lake Louise.

In 1962, Dennis married Dianne Scheilke of Black Diamond. At the time he was working in the oilfields, but shortly after worked on road construction, with the Municipality and also with J. C. Ohlson, then with the Forest Service, with the highway crews. After getting his own heavy equipment, he has been in this business ever since. While working in the Wandering River country, north of Lac la Biche, he bought land and here he and his family make their home. The closest place is Breynat. While farming, he also works with

Georgina (Jo), Dianne, Dennis and Nelson Blakley. 1978.

the Dept. of Highways, and maintaining roads for oil companies.

Dennis and Dianne have a family of two. The eldest, Georgina, (Jo) was born in Turner Valley and attends high school at Lac la Biche, a daily round trip of 100 miles by bus. Their son, Nelson, was born in High River. He attends school at Wandering River, a much closer bus trip. A small daughter, Theresa Lynn, passed away in 1963.

Dianne and the rest of the family all share Dennis' love of horses, each having their own saddle horse. There is a lot of room up there for riding.

Gene Blakley

I was born in Turner Valley, November 4, 1950, the youngest son of Tim and Jean Blakley. In 1956 I started school at the Sheep Creek School at Millarville. Here life progressed fairly normally under the guidance of Mrs. Pekse, Mrs. Lyall, Miss Davis, Mrs. Parker and the Principal Mr. Dube. The only reason I attended school fairly regularly was because of our bus driver Jake Reimer. This man was so punctual that Dad always said you could set your watch by his arrival to pick us up for school each morning. I suppose our Postal Service could learn a very valuable lesson from this man.

Sheep Creek School will always hold a dear spot in my heart. This was a place where you formed

Gene Blakley resting after climbing Loder Peak.

friendships and morals that you carry with you for the rest of your life. Mind you, we had our share of panties run up the flag pole and smoking behind the Ranchers' Hall, but this establishment has produced everything from fighter pilots to engineers.

From Millarville I went to Turner Valley High School located in Black Diamond. I always wondered why they didn't call it Black Diamond High School. Here Tim Hampton and myself found out Mr. Ford's 1949 automobile could be used for something other than the sedate Sunday drive. After achieving the nickname "Boomer" I graduated from this post of higher learning in 1968.

My next move was to Calgary where I worked for Crane Supply on their order desk and eventually accounts receivable. Being never one to stay in one place I went to work for S. E. Johnson Plbg. and Heating. That lasted for about eight months and then a move to Banff was in order. There I worked for The Banff School of Fine Arts as Assistant to the Building Superintendent. I enjoyed Banff very much because of the many fine people that work there only because of the care they feel for the mountains. Again the moving bug hit me and I relocated in Calgary again to work for Scott National Paper. I stayed here for two years working as a Sales Representative. I guess this was the place I realized that I disliked wearing a suit and tie. So, in 1971 I decided to return to school.

Mount Royal College had just moved to their new location in South West Calgary and were offering a course in Aviation. With a great deal of B.S. I gained entrance and tried to gain feathers. By the summer of 1972 I had received my Private Pilots License and about one-half of my Commercial license. But as all good students I required more money to attend the following fall so off to find a job of sorts. This job of sorts turned out to be a fire spotter position with the Alberta Forest Service. Here my job was to fly over designated patrol routes in the Bow-Crow Forest keeping an ever-watchful eye for smoke. By the end of that summer we (Paul Slager — an Alberta Forest Service pilot and close friend — now deceased) chocked up seven smokes, one fire and a drug inspection waged on our craft by the R.C.M.P. I couldn't believe they called this work.

Gene Blakley on top of the mountain.

193

I finished up with the course the next season but that first summer with the Forest Service seemed to stir something I couldn't explain in me so I returned to them the following summer to chase smokes again from a lofty perch. With the coming of fall, forest fires are a rarity so Joe Burritt offered me a job as his assistant in Recreation with the same outfit. This was a very enjoyable position until Edmonton decided that a degree in Forestry was required to do this job.

Well, there I was out of work and aviation looked very dim indeed for any "Sparrows". So, I went to the Motor Vehicle Branch and got my Class One license to drive Semis.

I drove for about five years, hauling everything from gravel to hydrochloric acid. I found these old rascals of the road had much in kin with their brothers in the sky and decided this wasn't such a bad life at all.

In 1978 I returned to the Forestry as an Equipment Operator for Joe Burritt and the Recreation gang. In this, my duties consist of working on snowmobile trails (grooming) and operating any and all equipment they send my way.

For the first time in many years I actually had a paid vacation coming. So, Cody Olhauser and myself packed our packs and headed for New Zealand and Fiji for about two months. That sure was nice to be away and still be receiving a pay check at home.

With all these benefits of steady work I may not be overcome by that bug again.

Jean (Fisher) Blakley

I was born one very hot day in August, 1909, in the old Calgary General Hospital on 12th. Ave, next door to my Grandfather Stagg's home. My Mother had all her children born in Calgary, probably due to the fact that her parents were living there. I was raised on my Father's ranch at Millarville, until it came time for my older brothers and sisters to go to school. There was no school near the ranch, so the family moved into Calgary, living at first in the Riverside district, then when a new house was built in South Calgary, we moved there, and I started my first year at King Edward School. During the coldest weather we took a lunch and one of my earliest memories is the smell of my lunch coming from the newspaper in which it was wrapped. At that time there were no wax or plastic paper, even the bread from the stores came unwrapped. However, the good smell of my lunch was so tantalizing I usually ate most of it by lunchtime.

A very poignant memory of that time was the long lines of soldiers marching into Calgary from the Sarcee Military Camp. We lived very near that road, and with most of the neighborhood children, followed along with many weeping women who were saying "Good-bye" to their loved ones, on their way to the battlefields of Europe, during the first World War. There were no radios to broadcast the news and how well I remember our Scottish neighbor, who received

Tim and Jean (Fisher) Blakley.

the morning paper, reading to us the latest war news and also the casualty lists.

While living in South Calgary, our summers were spent on the ranch at Millarville. Happy was the day when someone came in with the team and lumber wagon and our summer supplies of groceries were loaded in the wagon and often a few assorted cousins to spend the summer with us. One return trip to Calgary in the fall was unforgetable. We started out, with Mother driving a one horse buggy with a horse named Punch between the shafts, and Cubbie, Harry and me in the buggy with Mother. Our sister Maybelle was riding alongside on her saddle horse. This was usually an all day trip, and at noon we stopped near the Hunter ranch at Priddis to eat our lunch. Cubbie and Harry jumped out of the buggy, and Maybelle pulled the bridle of Punch, to feed him some oats. Punch was still hooked up to the buggy, with Mother holding the driving reins. This was a very stupid thing for ranch raised people to do, especially since Punch was a notorious runaway horse. As soon as his bridle was pulled off, away went Punch. Mother was thrown out first and I went sailing through the air with the buggy seat. Usually there was very little traffic on this road, which was the main one from Millarville, to Priddis, on through the Sarcee Indian Reserve to Calgary, but I remember Jack Johnson coming along with a team and wagon, hauling supplies to the store at Kew. He may have been the one to get Mr. Gillespie with his Model T Ford to take us in to Calgary. I suffered no ill effects but Mother was badly hurt and spent some time under a doctor's care. As for Punch, his wild flight ended up in a hay stack. I'm not sure if Mother ever drove him again, but I doubt it.

In 1919, we moved to British Columbia, living the first summer in Vancouver. Mother bought us each a wool bathing suit which itched very badly. We were very green about that large ocean and our swimming ability was nil. Cubbie, Harry and I played on the beach of English Bay nearly all summer, and we finally did learn to swim, but this was after Harry and I decided to go for a ride on a log we found floating in the bay. We were having a fine time until we realized we were on our way somewhere and it wasn't the beach, but was in the general direction of Japan. At that time there was a Negro life guard named Joe, who patrolled English Bay in a life boat. Luckily for us he spotted the two young urchins clinging to the log, and very frightened. He caught up to us, took the two of us in his boat and gave us a very good lecture, then on with him in his boat for a long ride. Harry and I also spent a great deal of time down at the piers, looking at the large ocean liners, such as the Empress of Russia. I think it was here that Harry fell in love with the sea, as in later years, after he had received his discharge from the Air Force, he moved to the West Coast, bought a boat and made his home there for the rest of his life.

From Vancouver we moved to Victoria. I didn't go over as soon as the others, as there was a diptheria epidemic there and I was the only one of the family to get it, so spent a month in an isolation hospital in New Westminster. We lived in Victoria, going to school there for about three years, then returned to Calgary, once again to King Edward school.

Then came the happy day in the spring of 1923, when Mother decided we would all move back to the ranch at Millarville. Sid and Louise Bannerman had been living on our Fisher Creek place, Dad's homestead. Sid then rented the Lang place across the road from us, where Frank Sharp now lives, and we moved back to our old home. We still had some saddle horses and the older brothers broke a few more to ride. North of our place had once been settled by homesteaders who had moved out, so there were very few fences, making this an ideal place to ride. One of my favorite rides was up on the high ridge where once a family named Toole had homesteaded. Here in May, the large blue forget-me-nots grew; they do not grow in the lower altitudes but up there, the hills are blue with them, and still are today. Mr. and Mrs. Joe Waugh and their girls lived nearby and I usually made my way there, where I was sure to get a nice snack.

About 1925, I met Tim Blakley at a party given at the Sturrock place for Bob Carry. Tim was working at Carry's at the time. However, we were not married until 1928, and shortly after we moved to the United States, living in Oregon, then in Hoquiam Washington, where our daughter Charis was born in 1930. When Charis was two years old we came back to Canada. While living at Tees, Alberta, our first son Dennis was born in 1933. Then in 1935, being homesick for the hills and Chinooks, we moved back to Millarville. At first we lived on my father's homestead, the north half of 6-21-3w5. This was during the hungry thirties, and jobs were very scarce, but Tim got work on the drilling rigs in the south end of Turner Valley. We rented a house in

Black Diamond and in June 1937, our second daughter, Mary, was born in Mrs. La Rosee's Nursing Home.

When drilling started in the north end near Millarville, we moved back. Charis started school at the old Sheep Creek School, then when Dennis became old enough, he also attended. In 1946, we moved a half mile west, very close to the road and on the good side of the creek. Much as I love that creek, it caused many problems, getting the children across for school and many dark nights taking Tim across on a horse to where his car was parked, when he was working night shifts on the rigs. The return trip through the flooding creek was always a little scary.

In 1950, we had a second son born, Eugene (Gene.) He, like his sisters and brothers before him, attended Sheep Creek School but in Jake Reimers school bus. Changes were being made every year. We had the power installed, where for so many years we had used coal oil and gas lamps. Then the luxury of natural gas after many years of wood, coal and oil heating.

There have been many other changes in these hills, some not so beneficial. Much of the land has been sold and broken into small parcels, fenced and in some cases, the gates are locked. All the old riding trails are blocked off, including the old Morley Trail, over which the Stoney Indians travelled to and from their hunting grounds further south, years before the white men came. There are few places left to ride, unless one goes to the Forest Reserve. The newcomers have yet to learn that these hills are imperishable. For hundreds of years they have withstood the onslaught of beast, man, fires, floods and other dangers, but still the grass grows green in the spring and the trees grow thicker every year. They would be amazed to learn how often in the very early years the country was blackened by forest and grass fires, but in a few years all traces were obliterated, so I am sure a rider on a horse can do little damage.

We have sold our cows and some of our land. We just enjoy life, visiting with family and friends. All of our children love this country, especially the creek where four generations of Fishers and Blakleys have swam, fished and played for over ninety years. No matter what happens, I am sure these hills will endure.

Timothy A. Blakley ↲B

Tim was born in Sand Dune (now McLeod), North Dakota, November 6th, 1904. He is the son of Adin and Clara Blakley, both born in Minnesota. In 1910, they moved to Brocket, Alberta, with their son Tim and his sister Ethel. Another daughter, Elsie, was born after their arrival in Alberta. Other members of the family had gone to the Cypress Hills and taken out homesteads up on the Bench, the high tableland which has an altitude of 4800 feet, about the same as Banff. After a few months at Brocket the family decided they would also go to the Cypress Hills. Tim's father settled at first in the Nine Mile Coulee, not far from the homestead of the grandfather, Albert Blakley. Walsh and Irvine were the closest towns and to get up to the homesteads meant a long haul up the Graburn Coulee from Walsh, or up the Bull Trail from Irvine. If the loads were too heavy, an extra team was required to get back up to the Bench. One of Tim's aunts, Mrs. Ida Rogers of Stettler, recalls when she and her husband arrived to take up their homestead, they were met at Irvine by Tim's father. All their stock and other belongings had come by freight car from North Dakota, so after getting reloaded started up the Bull Trail, but half way up the long hill, the soft prairie horses from North Dakota became too tired so they spent the night part way up, with Ida sleeping on a load of oats.

Grandpa Blakley's homestead was not too far from where the cairn is now to mark the spot where Corporal Graburn was killed by an Indian in 1879. He was one of the first Mounties killed in the west.

There was a school in the Cypress Hills, far enough from home for the children to ride horseback. There was also a hall used for dances and as all the Blakleys were very musical, playing various instruments, were often in demand to supply music for these affairs. Many years later, in the Millarville district, Henry Monroe, a very fine fiddler himself, told how he had learned to play the violin by watching Adin and Albert Blakley playing for dances in the Cypress Hills, where Henry had been raised. Tim's younger sister, Ethel, sometimes chorded on the organ while the men played and when she missed a note, Grandpa would reach over and tap her with his bow, without missing a beat.

This was real ranch country, with miles of unfenced grasslands, abounding in game of all kinds. Tim learned to handle a gun at an early age, hunting with the men of the family. There were few, if any,

hunting restrictions, so there was wild meat on every table.

There were short stays in Walsh and Medicine Hat, where the children attended school. Two more sisters were added to the family, Ruby and Maxine and a baby brother, who passed away and was buried at Walsh.

In 1918, the family left the Cypress Hills and moved to Stettler, where Tim's mother passed away, leaving five young children. The father took them to the United States, but they were soon back in Alberta. Another move, this time to Condor, Alberta. This was a sad time for the family. Ruby, a younger sister was stricken with diphtheria and passed away, and a year later, Albert Blakley, the grandfather, passed away.

Tim's father decided he had enough of the cold Canadian winters, so in the early spring of 1923, Tim and his father went to Oregon, and later the rest of the family joined him there. However, it wasn't long before Tim was back in Alberta. He was working for Bob Carry in the Kew district when he met his future wife, Jean Fisher. Jim and Stastia Carry spent a winter on Bob's ranch and when they left the following spring to join Conklin and Garrett Shows, where they had a Wild West concession, Tim went along as a trick rider, with a well known Black Diamond cowboy, Pat Nichols, as a bronk rider.

On October 29th, 1928, Tim and Jean were married at Vulcan, Alberta. After their marriage, they moved to Salem, Oregon, where Tim's father and sisters made their home, later moving to Hoquiam, Washington, where their first daughter, Charis was born January 27, 1930. They returned to Alberta in 1932, having lived in Idaho and back to Salem, before deciding to come home. They lived at Tees, Alberta, where their son Dennis was born, June 7th, 1933. However, being lonesome for the hills (and the Chinooks) brought the family back to the foothill country, to the homestead of Joseph Fisher, the north half of 6-21-3-W5.

These were the "Hungry Thirties" and jobs were very scarce, but Tim got a job in the oilfields at the

Tim and Jean Blakley.

The Blakley family. L. to R. Gene, Mary, Dennis and Charis. 1978.

south end and they rented a house in Black Diamond where their second daughter Mary, was born in June 1937. Drilling had now started in the north end in the Millarville area, so a move was made back to their home. Charis started school at Sheep Creek, as did the others as they became old enough.

Tim bought more land north of their home with some lease for summer pasture. This was the N.W.¼ 24-21-4-W5. Working on the rigs and farming the land kept him quite busy, but usually every fall when Sheep hunting opened in September, he would pack in to the mountains. There were no roads into the Forest Reserve at that time, so everything, tents, grub etc. were carried by pack horse. The Big Horn Sheep was the game most sought after by Tim and his friends.

In November, 1950, another son, Eugene David (Gene) was born, and he, as his sisters and brothers had done, attended Sheep Creek School.

In 1957, Tim quit the oilfields, giving all his time to raising cattle, until 1976, when acute arthritis caused the cattle to be sold, also some of the land, but the saddle horses were kept. As often as possible, Tim and Jean visit the Alberta Cypress Hills Provincial Park, where the Blakley homesteads taken up so many years ago are now a part of the Park.

Ed and Bertha Blair, 1948.

Ed and Bertha Blair
by Jack Robbins

Ed and Bertha Blair came to Millarville district around 1938. They purchased a raw ¼ from the Canadian Pacific Railway — S.E. ¼, 27-21-3.

Before the Blairs came to Millarville, they farmed at Carmangay, Alberta. Carmangay was very dry in the thirties, so they looked most of Alberta over before moving to Millarville. On their ¼ section, the Blairs built a log house and barn, and also broke some land. They then rented ½ section at Priddis and turned the ¼ over to Bertha's sisters, Mary and Elizabeth, and her brother Albert Bunchcuski.

In 1943 or 44, Ed and Bertha bought another ¼ at Millarville from Jack Lee (N.W. 22-21-3). They farmed this ¼ for about 10 years, until Bertha's health failed. In 1953 they sold the home quarter to Jack Brunt, and the adjoining quarter to Harold Biswanger. Ed and Bertha then moved to Calgary, where Bertha died within a year or two. Ed retired to Tempe, Arizona in about 1958. Despite his age, Ed drove from Tempe to the Priddis and Millarville area every year to visit relatives. Ed died in 1974, at the age of 82, while making arrangements for another trip to Alberta.

Blanchard, Gordon
J4 Brand

I was born in 1916, Sweet Grass, Montana. Rilla and I were married in 1937 at Shelby, Montana. We moved to Black Diamond in 1938. I worked in the Oil Fields for eight years.

Our family, Garry, Vern, and Irene were born in Black Diamond. As both of us were raised on the farm, we decided to buy a farm. We bought a quarter of land in the Plainview district. We did not like the location, and we sold to Harley and Joanne Hansen.

In 1945, I worked for Ginger and Jappy Douglas. We lived on the Millar farm near the Sheep Creek River, now known as Three Point. We bought Mrs. Peterson's farm in 1947 (N.W.¼-Sec.23-T.21-R.3-W.5). At that time there was only a wagon trail. It was so muddy we moved with horses and wagon. There were only ten acres cleared, and a log house on the farm.

The old Fordville school was closed in 1952. I got the job of driving the school bus to Millarville and Black Diamond. In those days there were very few gravel roads. Our road was high graded the fall of 1952. When it was wet we had to leave our vehicles at No. 22 highway and walk home. School bus driving was no fun with the poor road conditions and no phones. Now everyone has phones and good roads. I drove the school bus for seventeen years.

All the family worked hard to improve the land. We milked cows by hand and shipped cream, raised pigs and chickens. In 1960 we changed over to range cattle and laying hens. We enjoyed selling eggs to all the surrounding neighbours.

When we sold out in July 1975, we had approximately 110 acres of land cleared. Dr. Bill Beiber of Calgary bought our farm.

Our family are all married now. Garry married Elaine Foster, and they farm in the Hoadley district. They have two boys, Bradley and Trevor.

Vern married Donna Cunningham and live near Fort St. John, and have two children, Tammy and Michael.

Irene married Roger Jones and live in Turner Valley. They have three children, Andy, Peter and Kathleen.

Now we have retired and live in High River, Alta. — 129-3rd Ave. S.E.

Clarence and Ardell Boggs

Clarence was born January 26, 1906, in Moville, Iowa, coming to Canada with his parents and seven brothers and two sisters to the Daysland area in April, 1911. They lived there till 1929 when they moved to the Turner place west of Okotoks. Clarence attended the Agricultural College at Vermillion, graduating in 1929.

Gordon and Rilla Blanchard at Aden, Alberta, 1937.

Gary, Verne and Irene and horse Shorty, 1943.

Ardell and Clarence Boggs and son Elton.

They then moved to the Stewart place at Kew. With a family of this size they played baseball and hockey, having nearly enough to form a team of their own. In 1931, they moved to the place where Leo Ohlhauser lives now. One brother, Bedford and his wife Norma owned a quarter section at Kew for many years. They moved from the area and Clarence farmed it for many years till it was sold to Lionel Kane. Clarence worked for Carl Ohlson for a time and in March 1935 he married Ardell May Fisher. They moved to Bashaw for the next five years, where their first son Elton was born in 1937.

In 1940 they returned to the oilfields and he became a well operator for Renown and they lived on the lease for the next twenty years.

In 1942, another son, Kenneth was born. When the oilfields unitized they moved to a place near Sheep Creek which they had bought. The next eighteen summers he worked for the Sheep Creek Cattlemens' Association, riding in the reserve with Alex Murdock as his boss.

He worked for Chubby Foster for two years, then selling their land, they now make their home in Black Diamond. Clarence still feeds cattle for Don Thomson. He always loved stock, showing his first calf in 1922 in Edmonton in the boys and girls feeder calf show, winning grand champion and in 1929 winning grandchampion for a pen of three sheep.

He raised Hereford cattle and always had good saddle horses and Percherons, still having some registered Percherons. In 1939 he brought some Neutria Beavers from South America as the pelts were valuable. He raised them for a time and also had some Angoras. His love of animals led him to doing clay modeling, in which he was quite successful.

He did a good deal of taxidermy, a wolverine one of his best work.

Elton Boggs married Donna Patterson, they have three children, Glen, Shirley and Tammy and live at Elkford, B.C. Kenny married Alice Silvester and they have two children, Corine and Arland, also live at Sparwood, B.C.

Phyllis Sharp (Mrs. Bothamly)

Phyllis Sharp (Mrs. Bothamly) taught school at Fordville in 1911. These are some of her memories.

One very warm summer's day in 1911, several of us school friends were bathing in Chance's Slough. A lovely place to bathe, woods around the slough, but it had the reputation of harbouring leeches. So, we had to watch ourselves. While we were there, a thunder storm came on. One brave little girl, Joan Knights, made for the bank, collected all our clothes, and put them in a sheltered place under the trees. We all stayed in the water until the storm wore itself out. The leeches didn't seem to matter any more.

One day in the late fall, some of the children brought a beautiful wasps' nest on a long twig from a bush, as a contribution to our nature study. I put it up in a good place as I thought an old wasps' nest a fine ornament. One winter afternoon the stove gave more heat than usual and wasps began to crawl out of the nest. Great excitement prevailed, but we got the nest and the wasps outside without anyone getting stung.

One Sunday afternoon Mary Knights, Ruth and I went for a ride with Charlie Knights. I don't know where we went, but we were in a wood with a brook going through it. I saw some bushes that looked very familiar, and sure enough, they were black currant bushes laden with fruit. We gathered lots of them — probably into our hats. A heavy shower came on, and our only shelter was Charlie's coat. But, wet as we all were, we got our black currants safely home. Mrs. Knights made us a pie next day. Black currants are sour by their very nature, but there are ways of sweetening them. In this instance, Mrs. Knights smothered them with a thick layer of sweetened whipped cream, which had a marvellous effect on them. We all enjoyed them. Charlie Knights and Dick often provided partridge and prairie chicken, or large trout for supper. They were delicious. One day a flock of wild swans came down on the School Lake. Mr. Knights shot one of them. It was enormous. It was hung on a hook from the cellar roof and reached to the

Sheep Round-up, Robert Chalmers (left), Clarence Boggs (right).

Mrs. C. P. Bothamly, (Miss Phylis Sharp). Taken in front of the Knights' home on one of the Knights' horses in 1915.

floor. Except for our elders, we all spent an evening plucking it. It was cooked next day, but was tough beyond words and had a fishy taste. I don't know what was done with it.

One winter day at lunch time the children were romping in the school room. In their rather rough play Belle Jackson, who must have been about seven years old, received a push from Justin Dean Freeman, which sent her against the stove. She got a nasty burn on her hand. I did what I could for it, but had no proper remedy for burns at the school. On the Saturday of that week I went to Mr. Jackson's house to see how Belle was getting along. I still remember the warmth of the greeting I received. I felt a friend of the family right away. Soon afterwards I received a kind invitation to supper, and that was a happy occasion. The Jackson family were friends I was sorry to leave when I resigned from the school.

Occasionally I went to Calgary, travelling with the mail driver. I think the distance was about thirty miles, a large part of which was through the Sarcee Reserve. We had two mail deliveries a week. Most of the local mail boxes were outside the school. I loved the school, and often wished afterwards that I had stayed with it.

Mr. and Mrs. Les Boulton and Enid Knoepfli

Mr. and Mrs. Les Boulton and Enid Knoepfli moved to the Millarville area in the fall of 1950 by the purchase of the property that was owned by Art Hall. This property is more locally known as the Turner Place as it was owned for years by the Turners, who came from Scotland in 1886.

Lester, the youngest of three sons, was born of an old-time English ranching family at Blacktail P.O. on Willow Creek, sixteen miles west of Stavely. Education was received at Kohler Coulee School, a one-roomer, about one steep coulee and a mile west of Blacktail, and also at Stavely, Calgary and Banff.

Iva and Enid Knoepfli were born in Calgary. They were the daughters of Jacob A. Knoepfli, of Swiss descent. Mr. Knoepfli was a building contractor in Calgary, where he erected many homes and also the York Hotel. Iva and Enid were friends of the Streeters, who also live on Willow Creek. It was on one of the girls' visits to the Streeter Ranch where Lester and Iva met.

Lester and Iva were married in November of 1945 in Knox United Church in Calgary. They spent the summers in the town of Stavely and at the Blacktail Ranch, and the winters in Calgary. This happened for several years, until they moved to the "Old Stone House" on the Turner Place, in the spring of 1951. They brought with them their two-year-old son Bruce, born in 1948, and their new arrival, Brian, born in 1951.

Raising purebred Hereford cattle and trying to farm, a new venture for Lester, took up most of his time. The cattle were branded 2UH. This brand was issued to Tom Boulton in 1894 and is registered whole animal.

Attending to business interests in Calgary, cooking and raising a family took up most of Iva and her sister Enid's time. Enid was always ready to drive a grain truck, tractor or a baler if the help situation became a little thin.

In August of 1952 we moved into the new home located on the NW corner of 35-20-2-5. It was sure nice to have the modern facilities. It was in November of this year that the third son, David, arrived. It was also in 1952 that Mrs. Ida Little came to live with us.

On July 16, 1954, Michael Guy was born. He was not allowed to stay very long with us. At the age of three months he died of virus pneumonia. He is buried at Christ Church, Millarville.

In July of 1956 Neil was born. As Aunt Enid always said, he was the last of the Mohicans. It didn't look as if there was any use in trying to get a granddaughter for Grandma Boulton. Neil was her ninth grandson.

Like most of the ladies in the district, Enid and Iva were members of the Millarville Ladies Guild. During their tenure, many events were catered to, and it was during this time that the new Church House was built.

In the fall of 1959, Lester and Iva bought the Spooner place. This was operated as a feedlot and ranching operation until 1964, at which time it was sold to the J. B. Cross family.

It seems only fair to mention Jack Willis at this time. Jack was an Englishman who worked for Art Hall at the time the Turner Place was sold to Boultons. He was a most faithful and ardent worker. He stayed on the place from 1952 into the 1970's. Jack loved horses and gardening. He passed away on January 22, 1978 at the age of 99; his birthday was Valentine's Day.

Another member of the family was Mrs. Ida "Shorty" Little. Auntie Ida was born in Kitchener, Ontario. She and her husband, Art, ran the General Store in Hartell. She came to the Boultons in 1952 and stayed until she moved to the Mayfair Nursing Home in 1975, where she still resides. She is now 96 years old. Mrs. Little was a good cook, and a nana to the boys.

The three eldest boys rode the bus to Millarville School. Bruce played hockey; all the boys participated in 4-H, showing Hereford calves. After 1962, the four boys attended Okotoks School.

In 1969, Bruce married Julie Ann Fox of Okotoks. They have one son, Greg, who was born in 1974. They now reside in Red Deer, where Bruce is engaged in the construction industry with brother David.

Brian is running the farm at the present time. On November 4, 1978, he married Hughena "Joe" McInenly of Arrowwood.

Neil is presently working in Calgary.

Cecil B. "Jim" Boyer
by Geoff Parker

Born of a well-to-do family in England, well-educated, he came to Alberta in the 1920's as a remittance man. He acquired the NE¼-5-22-2-5, where he lived and kept a few horses. Jim had learned to box, in the "Old Country", and was exceptionally good at it, which he proved on more than one occasion.

Jim was fond of horses, and was a very good horseman, taking part in many of the Calgary horse shows. I remember one Spring Show, Jim and Tally Shoebothom, feeling no pain, dressed up as ladies and rode in the Ladies' Hack Class; which delighted the crowd, and gales of laughter rocked the old arena.

After several years Jim moved to an acreage north of the William Norrie Store at Red Deer Lake. It was here Jim married Peggy Carruthers. Jim kept a couple of milking goats. When it came time to spend a few days in Calgary (celebrating), Jim would put the goats in the back of his half-ton and park it in front of the Empire Hotel, where it was convenient to come out twice a day to feed, water, and milk the patient, forbearing goats.

From Red Deer Lake they moved to Deep Creek, B.C., where they had one son.

Jim travelled back and forth to Alberta on a motorcycle (having a little difficulty at times when it wouldn't neck-rein) to work for Johansen at the race track.

Jim died in 1976, his wife and son are still living at the Coast.

Lillian Marie (Haney) Bradley

I am the eldest daughter of four children. My parents, Bert and Vera Haney, moved from Seaforth, Ontario, to Millarville, when I was ten years old. I attended the Sheep Creek School, and I belonged to the 4-H sewing Club, and the Square Dance Club at that time. We were active in skating, dancing and bowling.

On March 8th. 1958, I married Howard Bradley of Turner Valley. We lived for a short time in High River, where Howard was employed in the oilfields. We moved to Black Diamond where we rented à house, later to Turner Valley, where we resided until 1965. We moved to Didsbury, where Howard was employed in a gas plant.

While we lived in Didsbury, I went to Calgary every day and took a Certified Nursing Aide course from

Lillian (Haney) Bradley.

which I graduated in 1970. I worked for a few months in the Calgary General Hospital, then worked in Didsbury to be closer to home.

In 1971, Howard got a transfer to Rimbey to operate a gas plant there. I then worked in the Rimbey Auxillary Hospital. During our time in Rimbey, we lived on a farm and had several head of cattle, which we really enjoyed. While I lived at Rimbey, Howard was employed at Coronation, but I would not move there, so in 1975 we moved to Two Hills, where Howard was employed by an oil company. We have purchased a new home in Two Hills.

I have been active in bowling, ladies baseball and curling. I attend several bonspiels every year. I belong to the certified Nursing Aide Association, past member of Oil Wives, belong to the Canadian Legion, and was secretary for minor hockey.

We have five children. Debby, married to Brian Laschowski, lives at Vegreville. Debby was a 4-H member and is very good at crafts and fancy work.

Stuart just graduated from Grade 12, plans on taking up plumbing. He is active in hockey, playing for Vegreville Jr. B. hockey team as a defenceman. He works as a carpenter now.

Cheryl is still going to school in Edmonton. Has belonged to the 4-H sewing Club and enjoys horseback riding.

Roddy goes to school, is active in hockey. After completing a course in Rodeo College, has competed in rodeos as a junior steer rider.

Daryl is our baby, 4 years old and looking forward to going to kindergarten, and is very interested in hockey and likes rodeo as well.

Ivor Braine

Ivor Braine came to this district from Staffordshire in the depression years, at the age of nineteen. He worked for Hugh Macklin for a season, under a government assistance scheme of $5.00/month plus $5.00 for the farmer. He soon became fed up with working for the other fellow, stooking tall, green, heavy, poorly tied oat bundles, which insisted on doing everything but stand up. Then and there he decided to get some land of his own, where he could be his own boss. He acquired the N.E.¼, Sec. 21, T.21, R.2, W.5, where he built a meagre log cabin from the poplar poles close at hand. To supplement his income, Ivor ventured into the chicken business. He purchased three or four hundred baby chicks, and a coal oil brooder that would hopefully brood the chicks and also help to heat his house. The thing was ill designed and all but burnt the place down. Things were not going well! What with the loneliness, the long, dark, eerie nights, and his deathly fear of ghosts, Ivor was most unhappy. Early one morning, a large brown bear in search of food or possibly a chicken dinner, came crashing through the rickety cabin door. That was the last straw! Ivor leaped out the window vowing never to return — "The bloomin' bear can have it!"

From here, Ivor went to live at Gilberts, on the Sparrow Ranch, where he started one of the most useful businesses that ever accommodated the neighbors through these hills. It was a trucking service that would take the farm produce to Calgary, and deliver your grocery order back to your door. Money was in short supply, so Ivor would often pick up your cream cheque when he was gathering the empty cream cans for return. When it came time for him to pay the bills at William Bros., he would take the cream or egg cheque and sign it on the spot. On one occasion, Ursula, the cashier at Williams Bros., said to Ivor, "If you are going to sign everyone's cheques, for God's sake go around the corner so I can't see you do it."

Those were the days of mutual trust, and we were grateful to Ivor for his service. He left this country in about 1936 or 37, and the last we heard, he was back in England.

Fred Brawne

Fred Brawne was born in Port Perry, Ontario, in 1862. He married Margaret Burton, who was born in Chatham, Ontario, in 1872. After they were married, they lived in various places in Southern Ontario, as Fred was a section foreman for the C.P.R.

The Brawnes had two daughters, both born at Ringold Station, seven miles west of Chatham, Georgennia in 1904 and Winnifred in 1906. The Brawnes decided to go to Alberta to homestead, Fred first going alone, then Margaret and the two daughters coming by train to Calgary in the spring of 1907. Fred had filed on land east of Cayley, but found the land too rocky, so when his family arrived they lived in the town of High River for a short time then that summer moved to a homestead in the Waite Valley, in the Kew district. The homestead was the S.E. ¼ of section 12-t.20-r.4 w5. They moved to their new home, bringing their belongings and furniture in wagons, with a cow or two led behind. They lived in a tent on Oscar Felton's place until a log house was built, with the help of the Feltons and other neighbors. A bank barn was also built, some land broken in which some grain was sown

L. to R. Fred Brawne, Mrs. Brawne, Georgennia and Winnifred.

and a garden patch worked up. They moved into their new log house in the late summer.

They had quite a few neighbors nearby, most of them, like the Feltons, had recently settled on their homesteads. The Brotten family lived on the quarter section joining them on the north, with the Malms and the Morrisons west on the same section. The Cuthbertsons were to the north.

At first, the Brawnes received their mail at the Lineham Post Office. Mr. Harry Bescoby carried mail and supplies there from Okotoks. The post office was on the south side of the South Sheep Creek and fording this could be very hazardous during the spring run-off and after heavy rains. They later got their mail at the Kew Post Office, which was at that time in George Bell's ranch house.

Fred worked at Spooner's saw mill on Ware Creek in the winter. The mill was located about six miles north west of the homestead.

The closest school was Fordville, several miles to the north-east, built in 1908, much too far away, so when Plainview School was built in 1910, Gorgennia attended school there, Jessie Felton taking her in a horse drawn buggy. Living on the homestead was very interesting for the two young girls. The Indians would visit and Mrs. Brawne would give them fresh baked bread, also butter and vegetables. They could watch cowboys from the Quirk ranch brand and handle cattle on land about a half-mile from their house. The Quirk ranch was located a few miles north west but many cattle were kept on several sections of land near Brawnes. This ranch was sold to Burns in 1910, but many of the same men stayed on, working for the new owners.

About 1912, Fred rented land east of Black Diamond so that the girls would be closer to school. They did not remain there very long. Later the homestead was traded for land at Westcott, Alberta, and cattle, furniture etc. was loaded on a box car at Okotoks and once again moved to a new home.

Fred Brawne passed away in Calgary in 1927 and Mrs. Brawne passed away at Chatham, Ontario, in 1950.

Georgennia married Bengamin Kershaw in 1928, and they lived in the Westerdale district for 32 years. They had one daughter, now Mrs. Robert Jackson, of Olds. They have two children, Karen and Darwin.

Winnifred married Tom Collinge and now makes her home in Surrey, B.C. She has two daughters and two sons.

Aileen married Henry Prohl of Three Hills and their children are: Doug, Norman, Bernice, Raymond, Edward, Darlene, Stan and Patricia.

Edith married William Peterson of Strathmore, and their children are Vance, Lynn and Kenneth.

Frank Collinge of Red Deer has six children: Tracy, Frank jr., Nancy, Noreen, Lyndia and Peter.

Jim Collinge lives in Vancouver, has a family of three, Gus, Laurie and Micheal.

Champion "HILARI" of Briggs Arabians

Picture taken in dining room of homestead in the Waite Valley. L. to R. Georgennia and Winnifred Brawne, 1910.

Briggs, Arthur Edward
by Arthur Edward Briggs

In the summer of 1978, my wife and I purchased the balance of the S.E. ¼ of 15, Township 21, Range 3, West of the 5th. The quarter section had been in the Chalmers' family for many years. I understand that Jim and Robert cleared the place which is now in tame hay and pasture. My wife picked a spot for our new home overlooking a beautiful valley with the mountains stretching for miles in the distance. We have three daughters, Lisa, Lonni, and Lana. All are presently attending Millarville School.

My wife's folks immigrated to Canada after the Second World War from Sweden. They worked in Shelly, B.C. for a few years, and finally settled in Calgary.

I had the good fortune of having three grandfathers, although I only knew two of them. My grandfather Clamp, an early pioneer who worked for Great West Saddlery, died young. Arthur Briggs of the old Calgary Tannery and eventually of Briggs Furriers

and Tannery Limited, adopted my father Roy, and so I was born a Briggs. I married in 1967, and Maija and I have worked together in business ever since.

Our family all love animals, and we have in our care a few very beautiful Arabian horses. We applied for brands, and received a M̂ E left hip for cattle, and a L̲ right hip for our horses.
3 We lived in the country west of Calgary before moving to your beautiful Millarville.

Jim and Kate Brown K J

In 1946 Jim and Kate Brown sold their farm at Okotoks and bought the Bradfield Ranch from Pat Burns. After they made their down payment they owed $2000.00. Over the next two years Jim made $2400.00 working as a mason and he paid off the debt. When someone recently remarked to Kate that it was unbelievable that they could have lived on $200.00 a year she laughed and said "Well, you know in those days $2.00 bought more groceries than you could carry."

On the Bradfield. Charles Urquhart, Kate Brown, Jim Brown, Nigger the dog.

203

James Brown's 82nd birthday. Front row: Chris Schultz, Andy Schultz, Matthew Schultz, Stacey Brown, Stephen Brown, Jeff Blatz, Kathy-Jo Brown, Ben Blatz, Mitchel Brown, Russel Brown, Jenny Parks. Kneeling: Phyllis Zuk, Jim (Buster) Brown, Charlie Brown holding Cameron Brown, Jessie Adams holding Jennifer Blatz, Gwen Blatz, Linda Brown. Middle row: Joe Brown, Patty Brown, Judy Adams, Gerry Brown, Jim and Kate Brown, Colleen Brown, Ruby Brown, Joan Schultz, Gord Schultz, Rita Brown, Jim Brown. The bunch in the back who wouldn't line up: Bruce Schultz (on truck), Wayne Blatz, Mike Zuk, Mike Brown, Les Adams, Bill Brown, Dan Adams, Jack Brown, Tom Adams Jr., John Brown, Dave Adams, Wendy Schultz, Tom Adams, Art Schultz, Tim Adams.

And carry groceries they did. Jim's dad and Charlie Urquhart moved on to the farm before Jim and Kate and they brought their groceries to them. The road being almost always impassible, it meant a long walk to their shack by the creek carrying bags of provisions. The Bradfield was a lovely farmstead, close to the creek, surrounded by flat hay meadows and tall spruce but it's least endearing feature was the road. Almost a mile long and an instant sea of mud when it rained and a mass of drifts when it snowed, it was the deciding factor that made Jim and Kate move on to Turner Valley. They kept the farm for a while and rented it to their daughter Jessie and her husband, Tom Adams, but eventually they sold to Garnet Allen.

Today they live on the property they bought when leaving Bradfield Ranch but they have recently sold this property as well. However, they retained a lifetime lease on their home and you'll find them there most days.

Brown, Richard E. & Constance D.
Y4H

Constance Dianne only daughter of Edwin and Elizavata Hunter born in Windsor Ontario, a sister to Edwin Thomas Wayne and later to Michael Joseph. Moved to Edmonton in 1952. After living in many dis-

tricts, we finally settled in Eastwood where unknown to me another family was also building. The family turned out to have five boys, one of which was to become my husband.

Richard Erle born 1945 in Edmonton, lived with a family of eight in N.E. Edmonton. Attended schools at Cromdale, Eastwood, Eastglen, and graduated from SAIT (Architectural Tech.) in 1966.

Moved to the Eastwood district in 1959, where I met the 'girl next door, Connie.

Married July 8, 1966 in Edmonton at St. Alphonsus Church. Geoffrey Erle born Feb.19, 1970, long and gangley. (21½ in. and 6 lbs.) Lived in Edmonton until 1970 when we were transferred to Calgary, with Imperial Oil.

Connie started teaching music at the Square Butte Hall in the spring of 1971. This introduction to the area, started us looking for land. After much searching, and many disappointments, we rented the Ivor Lyster place from Jack LaMarsh and Terry McMahon, who had just purchased it from Ivor. (NW¼, 13, 21, 4 w. of 5th). When the quarter was subdivided into 40 acre parcels, we purchased the North 40 with the house and buildings. We later determined the house had been built by Jim Colley in 1953.

The name we choose for our home is attributed to the following story: It was early spring of 1975, when we were burning some wind rows at the East end. I had just lit 3 piles and was about to step back and admire my work, when I caught a glimpse or something crawling out of one of the burning piles. It was a bear, slightly scorched. The bear headed South and I 'calmly' went down to the house for some help.

When we returned to commence the search, I was accompanied by a neighbor, Ron Shelley. I recall, the longer the hunt became, with us circling looking for tracks, the **bigger** that bear became. Finally with expert tracking abilities (4 Hrs. later) we located the bear some 400 yards from where I had last seen him. The two year old cub was badly burnt but still able to canter. With steady hands Ron raised his rifle and fired. A well placed shot found the poor animals foot. Another two hours saw the hunt to an end with the bear out of his misery.

Thus the name: 'Burnt Bear Ranch'. Registered Herefords, of course.

Mrs. Georgina W. Brucker/Miss Georgina W. Dunlop, Teacher 1930-32

I was born, raised and educated in Calgary and at 18, nearly 19, started teaching at Fordville School. I boarded with Mr. and Mrs. Arthur Wilderman and enjoyed the community with its rural, unique and social atmosphere so strange to my urban conception of life. I was followed by Mr. Standish, who was married to Dorothy Dudley-Smith, school and church acquaintance.

There was never a dull moment. My first experience was Murray Standish arriving with a broken arm professionally attended to, but the next year en route to school broke the other arm scaling the obstacles of a newly constructed agricultural complex.

After "round-up time" I arrived at school to find "Christophersons" etc. using the premises and grounds. A certain fear captivated me as this was new to me; steers, cows, etc. being the same sort of animals, viz. cows.

A near disaster took place when my inspector, from complaints, informed me I could no longer teach grade 10 during school hours. The tens were most helpful doing their work, marking and putting on the blackboard exercises etc. so I could start teaching them from 4 to 6 p.m. Fortunately it was then, and I was young, but as I remember they were a credit in writing the provincial examinations.

Mrs. Nellie McLung visited with us to speak about her literary accomplishments, in particular "Sowing Seeds in Danny". McLungs were personal friends and I went to school when Mark was there.

I spoke at some gatherings of my experiences travelling in the U.S., south and east to Ontario. I had a post card type of projector. How primitive! I was also interested in art and music, so many of the students became interested too. I had access to library books from Calgary so we had a fresh variety every month.

Christmas concerts and school dances were terrific. My first Santa Claus was my older brother arranged by Art Wilderman whom I had requested to act. Tap-dancing was really enjoyed.

Most interesting to me was Corrine's aptness and knowledge during lambing and calving activities, Mr. Wilderman's right hand, and usually at school on time. Rosie Jensen seldom walked to school. She raced, skipped, hopped onto a horse's back, using a pat on one side or the other to get her nearer her destination. She never went around the bush or through a gate; just a leap over the top. Her shoes were left at school and ready to step into.

The girls saddled one of the Wilderman's horses so beautifully, then came to get me from school so we could go swimming. Rosie was hoisting me onto its back, but not realizing her strength and my hundred and fourteen pounds, sent me flying over the top some distance from the horse. Also, they hadn't told me until later there were leeches in the lake. Such things in the water horrified me, but this was ordinary life to them. I soon harmonized with rural routines, also practised whistling and yodelling enroute home from school.

Art Junior always sat on his large Roger's Syrup lunch pail to read or learn "The Shooting of Dan McGrew", or some other Robert Service poem, then rise up and be on his way without it. He memorized easily and had a tremendous appreciation of literature he enjoyed.

Dad was from Belfast, Mother from near Bristol, and I married an R.C.M.P. officer, so I continued to live in many places from Toronto, Niagara Falls to Vancouver. After fourteen years, we were in Calgary long enough to qualify to adopt our son who is now a lawyer in Toronto. Almost any time now we plan, after twenty-two years in Vancouver, to return to our house in Calgary.

The Brunner Family

The Brunner Family — Mike, Lyn and daughters — came from south-western England and lived in Bragg Creek for some years, before moving in 1978 to the W½ — SE¼ Sec. 4-22-4-W5, on land originally settled by Jake and Barbara Reimer.

Mike Brunner lived in British Columbia from 1946 to 1956, where his family owned a dairy farm near Lake Windermere. After the death of his father, in 1960, the family moved to England, where Mike learned his trade as an electrician.

He met his wife Lyn, a hairdresser, in 1966. They have two girls, Heidi and Michelle, who attend the Millarville school.

Wilfred and Emily Brunt

by Sharon Brunt

In 1917, after the Halifax Explosion, Emily Day came with her family to Calgary. Wilfred, known to most as "Jack", arrived in the year 1921. They were married in 1928, living near the old Calgary Airport. In 1932 they purchased land from the C.P.R. for seventeen dollars per acre, much of which was bush that had to be cleared with an axe. Although their neighbors were very skeptical of the method, the land was cultivated by four horses.

At first, Em was not really impressed by the looks of the place and would have liked to return to their establishment near the airport instead of setting up house in a one room shack and having to haul water from a spring a quarter of a mile away. As time passed, more rooms were added to this shack and was their home for eighteen years.

The closest school was Ballyhamage and so it was here that their family began their education.

The family consisted of four children: Charlie married Pauline Haberer in 1958, they have two children, and presently live in Mulino, Oregon; Florence, who was married to Vic O'Brien in 1955 and had four children, is now living with her husband, Ken Walker, in Penticton, B.C.; Irene married Art Reimer in 1957, they have five children, and presently live in Blind Bay, B.C.; David married Sharon McEathron in 1973, they have one child, and presently live near Black Diamond, Alberta.

Things were tough, but they were not always so grim. One night, Jack worked particularly late and so after the children were asleep, Em went to look for him. Perched on his tractor seat, Jack could see a billowing white object heading straight towards him. To his great relief, he found that it was only Em in her white night dress, coming to see how much longer he planned to work that night.

W. Friley purchased their land when Jack and Em decided to move to Strathmore. In 1953, they returned to Millarville, buying Ed Blair's land. They are presently residing in Turner Valley.

Buitendyk

by P. Buitendyk

I came to Canada in 1924, worked on farms and ranches until 1927, when I bought some sheep and ran them in partnership with George D. MacMorris in the district south of Alderson, Alberta. I sold out in 1931 and returned to Holland. I was married there and came back to Alberta in 1932 with my wife and her eight-year-old son, Fred.

After looking around I bought the N½-2-21-2-5, which at one time had been part of the Sparrow Ranch and was locally known as the Dowker place. We built a house and barn with the help of one of our neighbors, Ben Maartman, and moved onto the farm in September.

Our main income was from cream, which we shipped twice a week to Calgary. The cream was picked up by Ivor Braine, and later by Andy Templeton, who brought our groceries back on the return trip.

In 1933 our daughter, Joy Astrid, was born in Calgary in the Holy Cross Hospital. I received word of the happy event via the barb-wire telephone through Stan Gilbert, where the only phone in the district was located.

Step-son Fred Vitringa took his schooling first at Alexandra School and later at Ballyhamage.

In the fall of 1939 I sold out to Chappy Clarkson of Turner Valley, and moved into Calgary, where Fred continued his education at Western Canada High School, and Joy went to Sunnyside Cottage School. I joined up with the Calgary Highlanders and went Overseas with them in 1940.

On return to Canada in 1945 I was employed as Settlement Officer with the Veteran's Land Act, with my headquarters in High River. In 1954 I purchased a Real Estate and Insurance business in partnership with T. R. Liddell.

In 1965 my wife died.

Joy is married to H. Westland; they have three children and reside in Calgary.

Fred Vitringa is married and lives in Holland, but he retains his Canadian citizenship.

I am remarried, retired from business, and live in High River.

Bull, Gerald and Sandra

by Sandra Bull

Gerald Bull was born January 21, 1944, the second son in the family of George and Grace Bull. He attended Sheep Creek School and Olds School of Agriculture. During his school years his thoughts for the future were to follow what his parents had begun, to raise Hereford cattle and farm.

I was Sandra Oldfield of the Vulcan district. I was raised on a farm in that area and trained to be an elementary school teacher. We were married on December 16, 1967 while I was teaching in Turner Valley. On our wedding day a fierce and blinding

Gerald Bull family Nov. 1973, Sandra, Gerald, Ryan (3 months), Duane (2 years).

prairie blizzard hit, forcing wedding guests to stay in Vulcan till the afternoon of December 17.

On June 9, 1971 Duane Gerald was born and two years later in September Ryan Charles joined our family.

In 1975 we moved from the home place to S.E.¼ of section 8-21-2 W. of 5. It was during that summer we also acquired section 28-20-2 W. of 5, probably better known as part of the MacKay Brothers Ranch to complete our farm.

Community work has been important in our lives with Gerald keenly involved in the Millarville Racing and Agriculture Society serving as President of the main board in 1968-69 and President of the Fair in 1976-77. I have enjoyed the work and fellowship of the Millarville Ladies' Jr. Guild.

Farming has its ups and downs, pleasures and pains, who could find it dull. We are interested and challenged by the cattle industry, and proudly use the "keyhole" brand ℧ brought from Washington by Gerald's Grandfather.

We have enjoyed our life in the Millarville area and look forward to many years in the future.

Bull, George and Grace

George Bull was born in Ellensburg, Washington, son of Charles and Kate Bull. He came to Alberta in 1923, settling in the Millarville area a few years later. The Bull Ranch dates back to 1924 when Charles Bull and sons bought into the Curtice Cattle Co. Charles

George, Brenda and Gerald Bull on "Sally" about 1947.

Bull retired in the late 1940's and still enjoys good health at the age of 100.

During the 1930's and 40's Dode travelled the cattle show circuit in Canada, and the United States with great success. It was not uncommon to have visitors looking at cattle at the ranch.

Bull Ranch stock was regularly exported to Russia, the United States and other parts of Canada. Dode is the past President of Alberta Hereford Breeders and the Alberta Cattle Breeders and is recognized as a Hereford enthusiast judging at many stock shows.

Baseball was the chief recreation. Anywhere, anytime there was a chance to play ball — Dode would be there. Still an avid sports fan today, Dode enjoys golf with his friends at the Turner Valley Golf and Country Club.

Grace Bull was born Grace Campbell of Stavely and trained as a nurse at the Holy Cross Hospital in Calgary. In 1937 she and Dode were married and began married life in the Millarville area on the ranch. She has always enjoyed the outdoors and during busy seasons of haying and harvest was often the extra hand needed. During those years 4 children were born, George, Gerald, Brenda and Larry.

Her varied responsibilities were that of a Mother, cattle breeder and a gardener. There was also time for considerable community work in areas such as leader of Millarville 4-H Food Club, past Secretary and President of Millarville Agricultural Society, and an active member of the Millarville Senior Guild. In more recent years Grace was the first President of the Millarville Horticultural Society and also manages to join activities at the Turner Valley Golf Club.

In 1973 a new home was built on the north end of the ranch (NE¼ of 8-21-2-W5). This was soon landscaped and most certainly admired by the passerby. Grace is active with community projects as well as taking grandchildren (of which there are 8) on jaunts in the motorhome. Dode helps farm in the busy seasons and is, according to his 5 year old grandson "the best combine man."

Grace and George (Dode) Bull about 1945.

Both Grace and Dode enjoy a good game of bridge with their friends and have been known to disagree over the finer points of the game.

by Sandra Bull
Brenda Galloway

Larry D. and Roxanna M. Bull

Larry was born December 3, 1946 in Calgary, the youngest son of Dode and Grace Bull. He grew up with his two older brothers, George and Gerald, and his sister Brenda at the Millarville ranch. He attended Sheep Creek School and later the Turner Valley High School, finishing his schooling at the Olds Agricultural College. Larry participated in community sports and activities, in particular played with the Millarville Men's ball team.

In 1973 Larry married Roxanna, daughter of Ron and Jan Edwards of Turner Valley. Roxanna was born November 29, 1952 in Calgary, and moved to the Stettler area in 1962, then to Turner Valley in 1965. She attended the Turner Valley Jr. High and then the Turner Valley High School where she finished school. As an avid horsewoman, she enjoyed participation in local horse clubs, rodeos and gymkhanas.

Their first year of marriage was spent on the ranch, and in 1974, they purchased a farm in the Herronton area, east of Blackie, where they currently live. Here they farm and have a small herd of cattle; some of the cattle being descendants of the original Herefords of Charles Bull.

Larry and Roxanna have two children, a son Dallas Leslie, born in 1976, on the same birthdate as his grandmother Grace Bull, February 29. A daughter, Laura Grace, born March 31, 1978.

Burn, Margaret (nee Wardle)

Margaret was born in Northumberland, England, March 1931. She was married in 1954 and came to Canada in 1957, with one son, Peter, aged two. The family lived near Penticton, B.C. until April 1963, when they moved to Calgary. They now had three sons.

Coming from a country background in England they were delighted to meet the Blakleys and the Fishers at Millarville and discover their mutual love of horses.

After spending many happy weekends and holidays at the Fisher cabin on Ware Creek, where their nearest neighbor was Eddie Behm, they bought the house on the N.W. ¼ 34-20-2W5 from Jack King when he decided to move back with Charlie on the home place in 1969.

Sons Peter, Marcus and Miles attended Millarville and Oilfields High School.

Margaret was a very active member of the Gymkhana Club and has also been very interested in the Priddis and Millarville Fair and Horse Show, helping with the different classes of the horse show. She has her own saddle horse and enjoys riding around the hills near her home in East Millarville.

Katherine and Harvey Burrows on their 25th wedding anniversary.

History of Harvey Burrows
by Lauren Hitchner

Harvey was born in Bassano hospital in 1932, the only son of Royal and Janette Burrows, and moved with his family to the Millarville area in 1937. He attended Fordville school and later went to Western Canada High and to Olds Agricultural College.

When 19 years old, he married Katherine, the only daughter of Gordon and Helen Larratt of Millarville, and went into partnership with his Dad, importing a large herd of registered Quarter Horses from Colorado. Harvey, who was an accomplished horseman, designed the indoor arena which was built on the ranch using home-sawn lumber and unskilled labor.

In the early Sixties Harvey and Kathie, with their three children, Laurie, Royal and Matthew, moved to the Two Rivers Ranch at Cochrane as general manager. While at the ranch, Harvey was responsible for importing and training the legendary Quarter Horse stallion, King Leo Bar. During this time at Cochrane another daughter, Heather was born.

Harvey was not destined to remain a horse trainer. so left the Ranch and moved first to Calgary and then to Colorado where they and their four children have settled in Greely. Here Harvey designed and manufactures tub grinders for farm use. The eldest daughter Laurie is married to Rick George of Greely and has three daughters, Carrie, Brandy and Tracy. Royal Jr. is married to Susan, a Colorado girl and they also live in Greely.

Jeannine Burrows
by Laurne Hitchner

Jeannine is the fifth child born to Royal and Janette Burrows on October 3, 1944, and was raised on their ranch at Millarville. Jeannine always had a love of horses and was her Dad's right hand; preferring to work with colts rather than do housework. One of Jeannine's favorites was her Quarter Horse mare "Slipperanna", which she trained herself and even though Jeannine was petite and the tall mare was high-spirited, she became one of the best racehorses on the Quarter Horse Tracks and Jeannine was very proud of her.

Jeannine attended Sheep Creek School and Turner Valley High, where she met Kenny Powell, youngest son of Lester and Mary Powell. Jeannine and Kenny were married in 1961 and went into the horse business at the ranch at Millarville. Jeannine travelled with Kenny during his rodeo career, packing kids and diapers along. They have four children, Randy, Dick, Tracy and Wayne. The Powells are a close family, enjoying their Quarter Horses and Brahma cattle on their ranch at Seba Beach, Alberta. The boys are active in rodeos and are kept busy breaking and training horses.

Lauren Burrows

by Lauren Burrows

Lauren is the sixth child born to Royal and Janette Burrows on April 6, 1946, and had the good fortune to be raised on their beautiful ranch north-west of Millarville. Some of her fondest memories are of riding with her sister Jeannine and their Dad, attending to ranch chores, or for fun in their indoor arena which became a meeting place for friends, neighbors and local cowboys. The Burrows ranch was a constant flurry of activity, preparing for the girls 4H meetings, helping Mom bake buns and do-nuts for rodeo Sundays and serving coffee and cake to the many horsemen who dropped in to visit.

Lauren (Burrows) Hitchner and family. L. to R. Tara, Kimberly, Sherri-Dale, Keith, Lauren.

Lauren attended Sheep Creek School and Turner Valley, spending hours on the school bus driven by the good natured Gordon Blanchard. She came to appreciate the ole bus though, when she attended Wm. Aberhart High School in Calgary for Grade XII and had to walk seven blocks to School.

Following graduation she attended U of C. majoring in oral French, followed by her first teaching job back at Turner Valley High School. In May 1966 she married Keith Hitchner, eldest son of Dan and Alberta Hitchner of Meadowbank.

Keith and Lauren moved to High River in 1967 where she taught in the High School for one year before retiring to raise a family consisting of two girls, Sherri-Dale in 1969 and Tara in 1970, little sisters for step-daughter Kimberly. Lauren and Keith and family continue to be very active with their cutting horses and manage to squeeze in training and showing between husband's Band, Highwood, at major Rodeos, Fairs and Nightclubs across the country, Lauren hasn't returned to teaching due to busy schedule of helping in Keith's office, caring for her growing girls, working with their horses and oil-painting and travelling some with Keith.

Lois Yvonne Burrows

Third daughter of Royal and Janette Burrows, attended Ballyhamage school for grades seven, eight and nine; Western Canada High, Calgary, and Henderson's Secretarial College. I spent three months working for Knights Bindery on Centre Street, Calgary, then decided it was time to do something more constructive so joined the Canadian Women's Army Corps. Basic Training was taken at Kitchner, Ontario. Being an inveterate walker anyway, the route marches in the surrounding country-side was a most enjoyable experience. Always "marker" of the Platoon, gave me the opportunity of "setting the pace" to suit myself and I was not always popular with the diminutive girls bringing up the rear.

Posting day saw me headed for Ottawa and National Defence Headquarters, Directorate of Staff Duties, attached to No. 12 Administration Unit and billeted in a lovely old mansion on Chapel Street; two doors down from the residence of Prime Minister MacKenzie King. I remained here till the war's end and the repatriation of the troops from England, taking my discharge in August, 1946 at Lonqueil, Que. I thoroughly enjoyed the whole experience, the discipline, parades and the notable dignitaries from other countries who came to Ottawa from time to time; among them, General DeGaulle, General Smuts, General Eisenhower, Eleanor Roosevelt, and of course the day of the "Victory Parade" when peace was declared and we paraded before Lord and Lady Athlone who took the reviewing stand at the entrance to the Peace Tower on Parliament Hill. It was unforgettable.

Lois, Wendy, Kevin and Bedford Warren.

After my discharge, I took up residence in Montreal, working first for a Cut Glass Firm, then the Prudential Insurance of America, and lastly with Trans Canada Air Lines. This suited me to a "T" and I availed myself of every opportunity to travel as much as possible.

I missed the foothills of the Rockies so after five years I returned. Not too long after I met and married a very nice gentleman, Bedford Warren of Bassano, who it turned out descended from people who had homesteaded in the Millarville area in 1886, a Mr. and Mrs. John Cook Warren. We were married in the log Christ Church on April 25, 1953, by Rev. Waverly Gant. This was significant for us as Bedford's grandfather had been one who had assisted in its construction and at least one of his Aunt's had been married there as well. Our wedding was the last candlelight service using "real" candles set in pine beams above the alter and down the center aisle; also the last reception held in the original Church House.

We resided at Bassano, in the Lathom district, for the first five years of our marriage; our children, Kevin and Wendy were both born at Bassano.

In 1958 we moved to the Big Rock area, Okotoks, where we still reside. Both our children attended school in Black Diamond and graduated from Turner Valley High School. Kevin went to Olds College, graduating in Agricultural Mechanics and is now a Journeyman Heavy Duty Mechanic, presently self-employed. Wendy attended Henderson's Secretarial, is working in Calgary and married Lawrence Frantz, Dec. 3, 1977. Bedford spent nine years with Farm Credit Corp., at the Calgary Office and then in High River, resigning to return to the farm where we are employed raising cross-bred Limousin cattle. I spent three years with the Oil and Gas Conservation Board in Black Diamond but resigned to look after the farm during the period Bedford spent with Farm Credit Corporation.

The Royal Burrows Family
by Janette Burrows

Royal came to Alberta in 1916, with his parents, a brother and his wife, and a sister and her husband, They had heard fabulous tales of land under irrigation, to be had from the C.P.R. Thinking that one must have irrigation as they had in California, to raise a crop; they each got a quarter section in Gem Colony, 17 miles N.E. of Bassano. It was rough going as life was pretty hard in war time and worst of all, his father got the Flu' in 1918 and died of it; one of only two deaths of Flu' in the whole community. Several were very ill but recovered. So Royal was then 17 years old and had to take his father's place, running their quarter for his mother, who was never very well. Thinking he was now a man, he asked me, Janette Royer to be his wife to help him and to help care for his mother. By that time we were only 18 and 20 years old and started our married life in 1920. Soon we had three little daughters who learned to ride almost as soon as they could walk and rode with their daddy all over the prairie when he rode for our cattle as there was free grass for everyone but no fences, so it took lots of riding to keep track of our cattle.

We moved to the Millarville country in 1937 to get away from the irrigation and to be nearer the Calgary market as we always had cattle and hogs and milked from 18 to 40 cows to keep off "relief". We moved in with horses and wagons and $10.00 in our pockets. We rented 5 quarters with 30 acres of crop land in 5 small pieces, but before long we teamed up with Jack Brunt and bought a breaking plow and 12 work horses and broke 60 acres for us and 60 for Jack. Very hard work as we had to clear the land of poplars first and pick roots after, but boy! did we have good land.

After 4 years we moved to the Wilkinson place, after Charlie Wilkinson was killed in a high-way acci-

Royal Burrows Family. L. to R. Lauren Hitchner, Jeannine Powell, Fae Winthrop, Janette Burrows, Royal Burrows, Theresa Patterson, Lois Warren, Harvey Burrows.

Royal Burrows on his cutting horse.

Edward and Bernadette Butrenchuk. Wedding picture. June, 1978.

dent; his three children found it hard to manage their 5 quarters and small herd of milk cows. We ran this for 4 years for $50.00 a month rent and were to leave the same number of stock as there was at first. Which we did.

With our three good girls and a little son Harvey, who was 5 years by then, we did pretty well, but could never find hired help as the Second World War took all the able bodied boys from the West, so we did with the girls. They stooked and hauled hay and did chores and we never had a happier or better lot of hired help.

After 4 years the Wilkinson girls wanted to sell tneir place as their young brother had grown up, so we bought the ranch called the West Anchor Down. The owner was killed in a jumping accident in England and it was up for sale by sealed tender, and we bought it for $10.50 an acre. We loved it there and finally built a new house, shop and 200 ft. by 50 ft. arena which we called the "play-pen". We used to put on small rodeos and broke lots of colts there, also trained our cutting horses as by this time we had a couple of good studs and a 40-60 mare herd. Never made much money but had lots of fun.

Our girls all moved to neighboring ranches as wives to younger ranchers. Theresa married Arthur Patterson in 1940. Fae married Bob Winthrop in 1942. We had added two more daughters to our family, Jeannine born in 1944 and Lauren in 1946. Lois married Bedford Warren in 1952 and Harvey married Katherine Larratt the same year. The youngest girls, Jeannine married Kenny Powell in 1961 and Lauren in 1966, to Keith Hitchner.

Royal sold the farm and tried to retire but couldn't be idle so rode two of his best Quarter Horses to Canadian Cutting Championships and now in his later years is in partnership with son Harvey as Canadian Distributor for a Hay Grinder, which he has designed and built in Colorado. They are doing quite well in this business. Royal is now 78 years and still going strong. No retirement for him.

Edward and Bernadette Butrenchuk

In the spring of 1973, Ed took up permanent residence in Millarville on 20 acres in NW 26-21-4 W5, formerly a part of a quarter section belonging to Ted Cloakey. Originally from Winnipeg, Ed moved to Calgary in 1968 to begin a profession in petroleum geology. In 1978 he brought his wife, Bernadette Thibodaux, also a geologist, from the swamps of Louisiana to the foothills of Alberta.

With weekdays primarily taken up with working in an office in downtown Calgary, the Butrenchuks look forward to quiet, relaxing weekends where they can devote their time to their animals and home (and a visit from the stork in August 1979).

Buxton, Ellen (Hackett)

Ellen Hackett Buxton recently attended the fiftieth anniversary of her Calgary Normal School class. After teaching a few years she married Clarence Buxton. They lived near Consort before moving to Hixon, near Prince George. Having retired from farming in 1972, they find life has few dull moments since their family includes nineteen grandchildren and one great-grandchild.

George, the eldest son lives with his wife, Doris Schoder, a son Andy and daughter Cathy at Port Coquitlam, B.C. where he is a land surveyor with the Federal Dept. of Mines and Resources, presently resurveying the Indian Reservations of B.C.

Robert is Wood Superintendent for Dunkly Saw Mills at Hixon. His wife, Joyce Walker, teaches kindergarten. Their older son, Robert, completed a course in electricity at Cariboo College, Kamloops. James and daughter Leslie are students at home.

Anna Clare is a teacher at Wildwood, Alberta where her husband, Ernest Vankosky, farms. Their oldest son Doug, and wife Cindy Becker, live at Dawson Creek, B.C., where he is employed by Northland Utilities, while Cindy works at the Toronto Dominion Bank. Todd is a student in carpentry at Dawson Creek College, while Gary is in high school.

Buxton Family. Back, L. to R.: Todd Vankosky, Clarence Buxton. Front: Ellen, Anna Clare and Ernie Vankosky.

Frances teaches Home Economics in Prince George Senior High School, and her husband, Ben Down, trucks gravel for the city. Their children are Susan and Christopher.

Betty and husband, William Gaal, live in Prince George where Betty works at the Regional Hospital, and Bill for B.C. Hydro. They have a son William. Their daughter Tammy is married to Dave Letchford, a social worker at Ft. St. James. They have a son Christopher.

Linda operates a Beauty Salon in Prince George. Her husband, Eugene Chartier runs a loader for a city contractor. Their family includes son Dean, and daughter Karen.

Mary's husband, James Lockyer, owns a logging truck and works for Swanson's Lumber Co. at Prince George. Their children are Lauralea and sons Brent and Trevor.

Marlene, who is Mrs. Randall Speed, is drafts woman for the Engineering Dept. of Public Works, Prince George. Lee and Tracy are her daughters.

Joseph (Joah) F. Canby and Family
by Roland F. Canby

History of Joseph (Joah) F. Canby and his wife Mary Jane Canby, also four of their children who lived on the homestead in Millarville. Two of the children were born while living there, map of 1894 shows No. 256208 S.W. ¼ of 28-21-3-W5. Joah F. Canby and his wife

Buxton Children. Top row, George, Betty, Anna Clare, Frances, Bob, L. inset, Linda and Mary. R. inset, Marlene.

Mary Jane Canby, wife of Joah Canby.

Mary Jane (Bleckley) Canby were both born in Bolton, England. Joah was a druggist in England. Evelyn May Canby, a daughter, and a son, Norman F. Canby, were also born in Bolton, England.

Roland F. Canby, a son, was born while on the homestead in 1906 as also was a son, Thomas, in 1909.

As my older brother and sister have both passed away, I will try and give you as much information as I can as I was very young when we lived on the homestead.

I was born in 1906 and I remember my father telling about the day I was born when my father took my mother to the hospital. On the way back home he saw a fire in the distance that looked exactly like it was his house, so he whipped up the horses to make them go as fast as they could to get home, as he had left my older brother, Norman, and my sister May at home alone. Well, the fire was over the hill in back of our place, so they were safe and sound.

I also remember going with my older brother, riding in a wagon up the hill to bring back spring water for the house for drinking water and domestic use. One time it was so cold riding in the wagon I stuck to it.

My older brother, Norman, worked some in Calgary for the C.P.R. Railroad yards. My sister Evelyn May, May as we called her, used to go by horseback to bring back supplies and would be gone a couple of days. I understand she had to go through some Indian territory going for supplies and some Indians would escort her on her way. (This was the Sarcee Indian reservation, which the road to Calgary from Millarville went through.)

My brother Tom (Thomas) was younger than I, born in 1909. I really don't know how long we lived on the homestead, but we did move in to Calgary and my father built some houses to sell.

In about 1912 or 1913, my parents, through a Calgary real estate agent, traded some property in Canada for some property in Tulare, California, sight unseen, in the San Joaquin Valley. This transaction proved to be very misrepresented, so he returned to Calgary and had a lawsuit over it, but after winning the lawsuit was unable to benefit by it, so he returned to California where he had traded the property and worked for a time as a butcher. In 1917 he bought a farm out in the country and farmed the land and raised his family. Both he and my Mother lived out their lives on the farm, both passing away in the 1950's. One more son was born to them after they came to California, Jack Canby. Myself, (Roland), Tom and Jack are still living in California.

My wife Lena and myself just celebrated our 50th Golden Wedding anniversary in May. We have two sons and one daughter, eight grandchildren and four great-grandchildren. We hope to go up soon to see if we can locate where the homestead was. (This land is now owned by Mr. A. E. Thorssen.)

The Cane Family
by Annie Cane

Clifford's father, Albert, came to Canada from England on a sailboat in 1886, the trip taking 30 days. He was 14 years of age. He recalled working in one of two Calgary barber shops for $2.00 a week, and Saturday change. In later years he cooked in lumber and mining camps near Trail, B.C.

In 1905 he returned to England and married the former Sarah Sadler. On their return to Canada they settled in Calgary, working for the Burns Ranch.

In 1910 Albert moved his wife and year-old son, Clifford, onto the SW¼ 22-21-2 W5th. It was the last

The Cane Family. L. to R. Clifford, Edward, Mrs. Sally Cane (Clifford's mother), Fred, Annie and Louise in front.

Joseph F. (Joah) Canby, early homesteader of the Millarville district.

213

homestead in the area northeast of Millarville, Alberta. Here Clifford was raised and later went to the newlybuilt Ballyhamage school in 1919 which was half a mile away — when teachers could be hired. During these years the Cane home had a spare room where the teacher could board. On completing school at Ballyhamage Cliff, nicknamed 'Slim', took up farming with his parents — fox farming, lumbering and selling hatching eggs.

In 1936 Clifford met and married the former Annie Field of Calgary. Annie took her early schooling at Calgary's Col. Walker and Elbow Park schools. On completing school she took work as a domestic until her marriage. Annie and Clifford settled on the home quarter and built a new house. During the War years they raised two sons, Edward and Fred, and a daughter, Louise.

On the passing of Clifford's mother in 1963, the home quarter was sold to Dr. Cruse of Calgary. Following a lengthy search for a new farm further from the expanding City of Calgary, Clifford settled on the E½ of 8-33-5 W5th in Eagle Valley, a district West of Olds, buying in March 1963 from Bob Phillips. A year later (March 11, 1964), Annie, Clifford, and Fred moved to their new farm in Eagle Valley.

To date, Annie is involved with the Eagle Valley W. I. and Sundre General Hospital Auxiliary. Clifford and Fred are raising purebred Herefords. Edward is married and living in Toronto, working as an Accountant. Louise is married to Gordon Cutting, formerly of Millarville, now working in Calgary as a welder-mechanic. They have a daughter, Lori, and a son, Mark.

David Stuart Cannon
by Florence Elizabeth Cannon
A-C

Born in Calgary in 1918, raised with his elder sister, Helen, and younger brother, Nevill, on the old homestead ranch, purchased by their father — Albert Stuart Cannon in 1900, and mother — Miriam How Cannon in 1913, of East Millarville, Alberta. The

David Cannon and son Lloyd (age 3), Jan. 17, 1960.

RED STAR LINE MAIL STEAMERS.
M. K. KENDALL, AGENT, LONDON.
North Buildings, Eldon Street, E.C.
Near Broad St. Railway Station
4, ADELAIDE STREET, W.C.
Charing Cross, W.C.

No. 2192   Received £1

To pay £13 — 3 — 7   March 21 188 9

Please supply bearer with one

Steerage Ticket to Calgary   (State) NWt

for Steamer WESTERN   and charge to my account

NAMES.	AGES.	REMARKS.
Albert Stew. Cannon	18	Balance due to be paid to L.K. before 9 o'clock p.m. day of departure.

This Ticket is issued subject to the Conditions of the Company, mentioned therein, and can only be used by the parties named thereon and upon the date mentioned.

NOT TRANSFERABLE.
Agent [signature]

Passengers leave London every Thursday. } Steamers from Antwerp every Saturday
Passengers leave Hull every Wednesday.

214

Mrs. Miriam Cannon, Florence Cannon, June 21, 1953.

FLORENCE ELIZABETH CANNON was born in 1921 in southern Alberta, in the Porcupine Hills, where mother and dad were working at the time. Grandma Remington was mother's doctor for me, Edith, Ruby and Evelyn. I finished my Grade 8 schooling at Ballyhamage School in 1937, with Mary McDougall from High River our teacher. We managed nicely through the pioneering and depression years, with the excitement of the community activities most of the time, people getting married, etc., right on through the years after the War to the '50s. I lived in Calgary on the North Hill, clerking for The Patricia Bakery and Coffee Shop — one day I was quite surprised to have David and Mother Cannon in for coffee. Neighbors from the community were very seldom in that Calgary area. I transferred over to the National System of Baking in 1951; life at that time in Calgary was very carefree and jolly, not too cumbersome with industry, etc. One could look around and see the moon and stars above the city lights. A couple of years passed, to 1953, when David and I were married in Christ Church, Elbow Park, in Calgary. We left everyone at five o'clock — a beautiful sunny evening — to motor westward through Banff to B.C., and across the border into Idaho and Montana. We came back to Waterton Lakes, and home through rain storms, which ended a beautiful trip the First of July, at the Millarville Race Track.

Lloyd David Cannon

Born in Calgary Feb. 17, 1957, at the Holy Cross Hospital. He was a very happy baby and grew up to school age much too fast. He kept himself interested outside with his dad, mostly around the tractors and cars. The snow disappeared early, the middle of February in '57, and the water was running all over, so the farmers started working the land early in March. In 1963 schooldays arrived for Lloyd, driving for a full ten years in to Millarville on Bert Haney's school bus, and from there in to Turner Valley High School in Black Diamond. Then with a car of his own Lloyd

Lloyd Cannon with pail of drinking water, Jan. 17, 1960.

homestead land was (NE¼-10-21-5) plus, a few years later (SE¼-10-21-2-5) and (NE¼-11-21-2-5); A-C, the original brand, is still being used.

The three children rode horseback to Ballyhamage School, 2 miles north of the home place. They walked on snowshoes in winter through the bush, catching bush rabbits with snares. They left home early, to pick up the rabbits for Clifford Cane, who took them to Calgary to the Colpitts Fox Farm. They also had to cross over the gas line being built at the time from Turner Valley to Calgary which was dug by men with shovels. One of the boys at school frightened the kids about crossing over the ditch, by saying the line would blow up. In 1966 it did blow up along that same gas line — David wondered at the time if the same school-boy would have heard of it. The Gas Company in Calgary was very pleased to have had help in finding the trouble as quickly as they did, when David phoned in from Francis Sinclair-Smith's early one morning, before daylight, May 17, 1966.

World War II started in 1939; Helen and Francis Sinclair-Smith were married; Nevill joined the Air Force, and David stayed at home on the farm with their mother. Mrs. Cannon passed away one week after her 80th birthday in June, 1959, at Nevill's family home in Okotoks, Alberta.

New Year's Day, 1971. L-R: Andrew Campbell, Lloyd Cannon, Marcus Burn, at Cannon's Farm.

drove himself, to finish his Grade Eleven; then on in to Calgary, where he lived and worked at Midnapore for the Redi-Cut Lumber Company. He still lives in Calgary, employed with The Highfield Corporation, looking forward to a career in carpentry.

Nevill G. Cannon 1921-1975

by Phyllis Cannon NC

On October 28, 1921, at Calgary, the third child of Stuart and Miriam Cannon was born. He was christened Nevill Gladstone Cannon — Nevill being a name handed down for generations on the Cannon side of the family, and Gladstone from his mother's side, dating back to the time of W. E. Gladstone.

He spent his early childhood in the usual way of farm children, and had a love of horses, as his father before him, so learned to ride at an early age. This came in handy when it came time to start school, as Ballyhamage was quite a distance from home.

One of his earliest recollections was the visits of the Indians when they came through his father's place. His father could converse with them in their own language. However, Cannons had a dog who had a hostility to these people, so he had to be controlled, forcibly, while they were there.

Nevill also remembered his father learning how to drive. Stuart had bought a new car and thought the corral would be a good place to practise, so he went round and round several times before he could get out through the gate again.

The children rode to school but when the snow became too deep they used snow-shoes. At that time, anyone who had a car couldn't use it in the winter because without heaters and anti-freeze it became too hard to start and too cold to ride in.

During the good weather the Cannons took a lot of trips, so on June 10, 1932 the children were very excited about a drive to Red Deer, which would take all day. However, it was not to be, because when his father was preparing the car for the trip, he died, leaving a bereft family.

1932 turned out to be a very dry year, and Nevill remembered a shortage of feed and the loss of several of their best cows. It was devastating for his mother, left with three children to raise and still new to the ways of a new country. However, the children helped all they could, and with the resilience and stamina his mother had, they continued to make a happy life for themselves. Nevill helped his Uncle Tom Philips with the fencing; at times the posts were bigger than he was!

He and his brother David had a natural ability with machinery, so it was understandable that they would try to rebuild an old car. What a laugh they had when they tried to get it going, only to find they had one speed forward and three reverse.

Times were hard so Nevill took an outfit of horses and Fresno and during the summer worked on the building of municipal roads to work off the taxes. With all the jobs to be done around the farm there were many days when school was missed. Miss Jameson was teaching at Ballyhamage at the time and was very aware of the situation.

Nevill and some other boys were on a Nature Study hunt one day when they found a number of small frogs.

Nevill Cannon 1949.

216

They found the teacher's lunch kit and deposited the frogs therein. Imagine the reaction when her mother opened the lunch kit, to be met by a barrage of little green frogs that leaped all over her kitchen.

Later on Nevill worked for Mr. Charles Bull. He enjoyed his stay there, even though he found it quite startling to be awakened, not by an alarm clock but by the raucous sound of someone hitting the lids of the cookstove with a poker. He felt he learned so much from this wise gentleman, and always thought of him as a good friend.

Like most families, they weathered the Depression, enjoying dances in the country schools, playing on ball teams, participating in Young Peoples, and having a home where the neighbors always enjoyed playing cards and visiting.

Towards the end of the '30's war clouds were gathering. At this time both Nevill and David were in the Calgary Highlanders Reserve unit in Okotoks. The Second World War broke out in September 1939; early in 1941 Nevill decided to join the Royal Canadian Air Force, so he took a course in mechanical engineering in Calgary, preparatory to enlisting June 6, 1941.

His greatest hope was that he would be posted to England, where he could see his relatives, but his mechanical abilities soon put him at the head of a

Phyllis Cannon 1949.

group of men who flew to various stations in Canada, servicing planes. It was a great experience and kept him off rudimentary things like route marches, but it denied him going overseas.

It was during this time that he and a number of other Air Force boys were invited to a party hosted by the Alberta Wheat Pool for its staff, at the Glencoe Club. That night he met a girl by the name of Phyllis Rowan; little did they know their paths would cross again, three years later. Meanwhile, it was 1943 and the war raged on.

By the end of 1944 it was obvious the Western World Allies were winning the war so Nevill asked for his discharge from the R.C.A.F., and to his surprise it was granted, because he was a farmer. That winter he worked in Okotoks trucking with Vic Rehn. While he was still in the Air Force, with the help of his mother he had bought the E½-12-21-2-W5, from Tom Roberts. In the spring of 1945 he went back to the farm.

At a dance at Red Deer Lake in November, 1945, there was that girl he had met at the Glencoe in 1943. They renewed acquaintance, and after a courtship of a year and a half they were married at Scarborough United Church in Calgary, on July 5, 1947. Phyllis came from Sylvan Lake, so it seemed natural since she had worked in Calgary, to choose that city for the wedding, as a central point between her home and his. Because Nevill had been the instigator of many a prank on young newly-weds in the Millarville district they thought they were safe from retaliation. Not so! Waiting for them outside the church was an old buggy and team, which toured them all over the city. The temperature was 80 F degrees — results — a very sunburned bride.

Nevill built a house on his place but there was not enough broken land to farm so the following spring he worked for Art Hall on the Turner place. That fall, 1948, they moved to the Bruce McLean place, where they farmed for three years.

They seemed destined to be plagued by bad luck. In the three years, the crops were hailed out, frozen out, and left out over the winter. In the fall of 1949 Nevill came down with polio.

Their first son was born in July, 1951. By January, 1952, they moved back to their own half-section — sadder, wiser, and very much in debt. In September of that year their second son arrived.

The next few years saw Nevill working in Black Diamond for Ken Atkins in the autobody business and doing his farming on weekends. During this time in May, 1956, their third son was born. Perhaps the pace may have been too much, because in January, 1958, he was slowed down by a heart attack at age thirty-seven. After three months' rest, they decided to sell the farm and move to Okotoks, which they did in August of that year.

They bought four acres from J. Patterson, and although they had been unaware of it, they were forced to become developers in order to sell any lots. From

Nevill and Phyllis Cannon's Silver Wedding anniversary.

1959 to 1968 Nevill worked for Elmer Piper, Phil Bice, and the Coca Cola Co. in Calgary, but he always wanted to run his own business. The opportunity was offered him in January 1968 when the business known formerly as Halpenny Motors became available. This was a coincidence because his father had owned this same business in 1930.

He enjoyed running the Automotive and Autobody business for seven years. During that time he relished the trips to the States and Eastern Canada with his family, and of course those pleasure-filled hunting trips in the fall with his good friend Bill Kendall.

Destiny intervened, and while he was at work on a sunny spring day, April 11, 1975, he succumbed to a second heart attack.

He enjoyed life and liked people and could truly be called "a gentleman of the Old West." He was laid to rest in the lovely little cemetery at Christ Church, Millarville. As a living monument he left three fine sons to carry on his name.

His wife, Phyllis, still lives in Okotoks.

Phyllis Cannon

Phyllis Margaret was the third child of Leonard and Elva Rowan, formerly from Thessalon, Ontario. An older brother and sister and a younger sister completed the family. She was born in Calgary July 17, 1921.

Her childhood to age six was spent on the family farm at Redlands, Alta. The dry years were beginning, so her father moved the family to Drumheller. That year he put in the first mine spur to East Coulee. The next year the family moved to Sylvan Lake where her father built many of the local roads using horse-drawn outfits.

They were on a farm there where Phyllis attended school to Grade VI. They then bought a farm south of Sylvan Lake and the school was Marianne — a one-room school where the teacher had Grades I to X.

After Grade X Phyllis and her sister rode four miles for Grade XI to Sylvan Lake again. That

January the temperature never rose above 30 F degrees below zero. Lots of memories of frozen face and fingers. The next two years she finished her education in Red Deer, resident in the Dormitory for country students. This was a grand experience of meeting new people and learning independence.

After this Phyllis and her older sister cooked for two winters and a summer in their father's lumber camp near Rocky Mountain House. This is a story in itself as the appetites of fifty hungry lumberjacks kept a couple of kids really busy. The hours were long but it was a great learning experience.

The two girls left in the spring of 1943 to take business courses in Calgary. Phyllis worked for the Alberta Wheat Pool until she married Nevill Cannon in 1947.

Graham Neville Cannon
written by P. M. Cannon

The first son of Nevill and Phyllis Cannon was born in Calgary, July 22, 1951. Graham spent the first seven years of his life on the farm. During this time he enjoyed riding the "Cat" tractor with his dad, and getting grubby around anything mechanical.

He rode the school bus to Okotoks during his first year of school, and remembers many frightening trips

Graham and Rhonda Cannon with children Joel and Jody.

on a muddy road that had no gravel on it. Sometimes, when the driver couldn't go any further, one of the high school girls would walk with him to see he got home safely.

His dad's illness in the winter of 1958 decided the move to Okotoks in August of that year.

Graham was in Cubs and Scouts and enjoyed these various activities. He also enjoyed ball and hockey games, but his real interests lay in the artistic field. He liked model building and did well in many contests.

When he was in Grade X at Okotoks his parents bought into a garage business and then his model building became a reality and he got his first car. From there on it was his hobby.

He went to Lord Beaverbrook High School in Calgary for Grade XI and Grade XII. He enjoyed Drafting especially, and appreciated the great people — namely, the principal and teachers who left such a lasting impact on his life.

The year after he finished school he lived in Calgary and worked in an upholstery shop. The next year he came back to work with his dad in the autobody business. Although he got his ticket and did a good job it affected his health, so he decided against it as a life's work.

In May of 1974 wedding bells rang and he married Rhonda Poffenroth of Red Deer Lake. She is the second daughter of Harvey and Vicki Poffenroth.

That summer he decided to run his own upholstery business which he started in a part of his dad's building. He was only in it a few months when his dad passed away. His mother ran the garage business for a year, then rented it for another year. When the building was sold in 1977 he carried on his business at home.

On April 1, 1976, their first child, a son, was born. They gave him the name, Joel Neville. The following year, on July 26, 1977, a wee daughter, Jody Lynn, was added to the family.

During the summer of 1978 Graham and Rhonda decided to go back into the garage business. They purchased the property known formerly as Hill Top Service and at this time of writing have a new building nearing completion, and are looking forward to a life in the business community of Okotoks.

Lorne Leroy Cannon

written by P. M. Cannon

On September 17, 1952, a second son joined the Nevill Cannon family. Quiet by nature he was much like his father, and at an early age showed the mechanical tendencies in his background. His first five years were spent on the farm in the Millarville area. He enjoyed playing in the wide open spaces and was happy to be around his dad, especially when he had anything to do with machinery. Lorne was six years old when the family moved to Okotoks; he had to start school within a month. It was quite a transition from the quiet country life he had known up to then.

Lorne and Sheila Cannon with children Lorna and Stuart.

As soon as he could he joined the Cubs organization and really enjoyed its activities. He continued on into Scouts and later to Venturers. Most of all he liked the camp experiences — back to nature.

During those years the family took a trip every summer, usually to the Coast or the States. The children were expected to save or earn some money to buy clothes for the next school year. Lorne had a paper route which he started when he was eleven years old. Cutting lawns also augmented his income. This made him quite an astute shopper.

Nearly every week-end the family enjoyed a fishing and camping trip, usually with friends like the Kendalls, and Lorne learned to fish at an early age.

His schooling was taken in Okotoks, with the last two years at Lord Beaverbrook in Calgary. It was natural that he would excel in the Automotive classes. By this time his dad was in the garage business so Lorne helped in the automotive part of it.

When he finished school he tried a bit of rodeoing — bull riding! He got a few minor injuries which probably slowed his ambitions to pursue this sport to any great extent. At this time he travelled with Dave Garstad, taking cattle to the States. What an opportunity this was to see the country!

In the late fall of 1972 he decided to spend some time in California. He was able to work for some friends who had horses, so between exercising horses and hauling hay he put in six months.

In April, 1973 he returned to Okotoks and went to work for his dad. Very shortly thereafter he met Sheila Booth at a dance at DeWinton. Sheila is the daughter of Jack and Joyce Booth of Irricana. She was teaching at Okotoks and boarding at Volds in DeWinton. She was very interested in horses and during her summers had worked for Bill Collins at his stables in Edmonton.

The romance bloomed and the following year on July 20, 1974, they were married in the lovely old

Christ Church at Millarville. They took up residence on the former Harris place, now owned by Harry Denning, south-west of Turner Valley. At High River on January 4, 1976 a daughter, Lorna Jean, was born.

During this time they kept a few cattle and of course some horses. After his father's death in 1975 Lorne started his own business, known as Foothills Waste Disposal, with business from Turner Valley to Claresholm.

On December 20, 1978, a son, Stuart John arrived. The family is now in the process of relocating, so time will tell where they will be.

Randy Douglas Cannon
written by P. M. Cannon

On a beautiful May 17th morning, 1956, a third son was, born to Nevill and Phyllis Cannon at Holy Cross Hospital, Calgary. His mother maintained she had one for her side, he was so much like her father, Leonard Rowan.

Randy spent only two years on the farm and probably of his few memories of it the most vivid was his encounter with a swarm of wasps; very aggressive after his brother Lorne jabbed a pitch fork through their nest.

The fall of 1957 was the time of the Asian 'Flu epidemic and Randy had quite a siege of it. By August of 1958 the family had moved to Okotoks. This was a new experience for a wee fellow who previously had had a lot of space to roam around in. It wasn't long before he had little friends to play with.

When he was five he went to Mrs. Johnson's kindergarten and looks back fondly on her kindness and teaching.

During his 'growing up' years he joined Cubs, Scouts, Young Peoples and enjoyed the many trips with his parents and brothers. His last journey with his parents was when they took a camper trip to Ontario in 1972. He was sixteen and had just received his licence, so was able to drive part time. He had quite a scare in Des Moines, Iowa, when he got into a traffic circle and couldn't get out.

Randy took his schooling at Okotoks and at Lord Beaverbrook High School. Later he worked with his dad and became very adept in 'Autobody', but after his father's death he didn't seem to want to pursue this. During the ensuing years he has worked at many things — running machinery, laying carpets, carpentry, etc., and as yet has not decided what he will settle into for a life's work.

Cavers, Joan
Eldest daughter of William J. and Marjorie Oliver of the Diamond L Ranch, Millarville

Our family lived at Millarville from the Spring of '33 to the Fall of '49. Mr. George Scott taught me Grades 8, 9 and 10 at New Valley School and I graduated from Grade 12 at Central High and a 1-year business course at Western High School in Calgary. I helped Dad and Mother at the ranch during the war years and then worked for Brewster Transport Co. Ltd. of Banff at their Columbia Icefield Chalet for two summers and at Sunshine Ski Lodge during the intervening winter. Thence, back to Calgary in secretarial work for a number of years, predominantly with Royalite Oil Company. When Bruce and I were married in 1960 I was working as International Travel Advisor with Canadian Pacific Airlines. We moved to our ranch at Water Valley early in 1961 when our daughter, Sandra, was three month's old. We still reside at Water Valley and Sandra has graduated from Grade 12 at Cremona High and is presently completing a two-year course in Forestry at NAIT in Edmonton.

Jim and Wilma Chalmers and Family
by Wilma Chalmers   J.H.C.

Jim Chalmers, eldest son of Bertram and Grace Chalmers, was born in High River on August 23, 1926. He grew up on the Ranch at Millarville and attended the Sheep Creek School.

One of Jims early recollections concerns the day the adults were away to town. He and his brother Robert decided that since they were always banned

Randy Cannon, 1979.

Jim Chalmers family. Back row, L. to R.: Jamie, Marilee, Linda. Front row, L. to R.: Lance, Sharon, Wilma, Jim, Vicky and Deanna.

A L E X A N D E R   M U I R

LIVE STOCK EXPORTER AND SALES AGENT

902 Burnside Place
MONTREAL, P.Q.

SHIPMENT TO: W. Eastwood & Sons, 29 Woodside Lairage, Birkenhead.

For Account Mr B.Chalmers, Millarville, Alta.

No. Cattle 21 Steamer Nidarholm Sailed Oct.14th/33

From Montreal Destination Birkenhead

Car Nos.	No. Hd.	Off. Cars	Avg. Wgt.	Marks
273158	21	21800 lbs.	1040 lbs.	One clip on right pin.

SENATOR P. BURNS, HON. PRESIDENT
SENATOR D. E. RILEY, PRESIDENT

L. McKINNON, CALGARY, 1st VICE-PRESIDENT
M. J. STAPLETON, JENNER, 2ND VICE-PRESIDENT
JAMES MITCHELL, MEDICINE HAT, 3RD VICE-PRESIDENT

JACK BYERS, MANAGER
E. W. BRUNSDEN, SECRETARY

DIRECTORS
W. H. McINTYRE, MAGRATH
GEO. G. ROSS, ST. KILDA
W. I. MONKMAN, NANTON
R. R. MACLEAY, HIGH RIVER
J. J. BOWLEN, CALGARY
R. GILCHRIST, WILD HORSE
E. D. ADAMS, CALGARY
J. B. CROSS, CALGARY
E. HUNTER, SPRING POINT
M. HIGDON, MANYBERRIES
H. G. MINOR, MEDICINE HAT
E. E. CAPERS, HIGH RIVER

The Western Stock Growers' Association

28 MICHAEL BUILDING

Calgary, Canada

PHONE M4787

November 29, 1933.

Mr. Bert Chalmers,
Millarville,
Alberta.

Dear Sir:-

We beg to enclose our cheque for $544.31 and all documents covering shipment of twenty-one head of cattle from Millarville on the S. S. "Nidarholm" sailing from Montreal on November 14.

Draft was received from Great Britain for all cattle on this boat and was cashed at the rate of $520 which gives you an average return on your twenty-one head of $25.92.

Yours very truly,

THE WESTERN STOCK GROWERS' ASSOCIATION

E. W. Brunsden

Record of 21 head of cattle shipped to England by a Millarville rancher, Bert Chalmers. After all expenses the average return was $25.92 per head.

Record of 21 head of cattle shipped to England by a Millarville rancher, Bert Chalmers. After all expenses the average return was $25.92 per head.

from the garden they would take this opportunity to stock up on carrots. They hid their loot under a hay rack. Unfortunately for them the bare patches in the rows of carrots gave them away. Their mother, being a strict disciplinarian, saw to it that the carrots were found and Jim and Robert had a steady diet of carrots until they were all eaten.

Jim spent his younger days helping his family on the ranch. At that time they had a herd of purebred Aberdeen Angus as well as grade cattle and were also in the business of raising and selling horses. Jim helped to break these horses so they were ready for sale.

In 1942 Jim took a course in Farm Construction and Tractor Mechanics at the Tech in Calgary. While taking this course he boarded in Calgary during the week and hitch-hiked home each week-end to help with the ranch work.

As so many farm boys do Jim decided to try the rodeo business and for several years he rode bulls in the stampedes. In 1947 he won first at Black Diamond and second day money in Calgary. He would help with ranch chores in the morning, go to the stampede and ride, then head home and help with the haying.

As a young man he not only helped at home with the ranch and saw mills which his father operated but also helped with various jobs in the area. He helped John Jackson saw for McHargs at the Big Rock, Jack Robbins and Tommy Campbell when they sawed at Priddis, and Lester Letts when he sawed logs for Joe Bews on the north fork of Sullivan Creek. One summer he was hired by Boyd Johnson to help build some of the Major oil wells on the MacKay land, using his team of horses to raise the derricks piece by piece.

By working for his Dad on the ranch, he purchased the E½ 35-19-4-5, a piece of land which his grandfather and father had previously owned. In 1978 geologists found that the muskeg on this land contains the longest record of vegetation and climate in southern Alta. — a record spanning over 19,000 years.

I, Wilma Lee, eldest daughter of Bill and Norley Lee, was born November 15, 1932 in Lloydminster, Sask. My family lived in Lloydminster until 1935 then we moved to Turner Valley. I grew up and was educated in Turner Valley.

Jim and I met in 1949 and were married in the Spring of 1950 in Christ Church Millarville. Our first home was a small house (dubbed 'The Honeymoon Cottage') located on the western edge of the Chalmers home quarters. Many old timers in the area will recall the charivari put on for us by the neighbors.

Mrs. Chalmers, always active in community affairs, enrolled me as a member of the W.I. and also the Happy Gang Club shortly after we were married. I am still a member of the Happy Gang.

At that time we were using mantle and gas lamps. Being a town girl I was scared silly of the gas lamp so would only light the Aladdin lamp in the evening and leave the gas lamp for Jim to light when he got home

from work. Jim hauled our water from a well which he had dug by hand. Our fridge was a wooden box set into the ground next to the well and operated the same as a dumb waiter. We had wood fires in the cook stove and in the air-tight heater.

The first fruit cake I ever made was mixed up in the afternoon by my sister Beatrice and me. Jim built up the fire, we popped the cakes into the oven, then went to the movies in Turner Valley. After the movies we went up to my parents place for coffee. Mom almost choked on her coffee when she heard what we had done. But such was Jim's expertise as a fireman the cakes were done to perfection and the fire was out by the time we got home that night.

On December 24, 1950 our first daughter, Marilee, was born. She always felt that Christmas Eve was a bad time to be born and arranged to have her birthday parties near the first of December.

In 1951 Mr. Chalmers took Jim and Robert into a partnership on the ranch.

In 1953 our second daughter, Linda, arrived on June 19th. In preparation for the new addition to the family Jim doubled the size of our house. By this time we had electricity and used stove oil instead of wood, we were really getting modern.

In 1954, on November 16th, our third daughter, Jamie, was born. On June 6th, 1956 daughter number four, Sharon, arrived, and on July 23rd, 1957 daughter number five, Vicky, was born.

The first phones in our area were on a Turner Valley line. However very few people were able to get on this line as it was one the oil companies had run in for their own use. Jim's brother, Robert, managed to get one of these phones in his home. When the AGT lines were finally put in we were all on a Calgary exchange, thus, we had to phone long distance from our home to the main ranch buildings, a distance of less than half a mile.

In the early 60's under the leadership of Edna Mae Dudenhoeffer we started a Sunday School for the children of the district. It was held in the Sheep Creek School and several of us served as Sunday School teachers.

In 1962 our only son, Lance, was born on November 12th. At this time we again doubled the size of our house and Valley Gas was installed that Fall; now we were completely modern.

In 1963 Opal Gamble taught classes in St. John's first aid and I became a first aider. After several years of first aid classes we formed a group known as St. John's Ambulance and Nursing Brigade No. 500. First aid duties included the Millarville Races, the Fair, walk-a-thons, horse shows, etc. The group disbanded eventually because so many members moved away.

In 1964 our sixth daughter, Deanna, was born on August 13th.

For several years during the late 60's Jim served as President of the Millarville P.T.A. In 1970 he became

Secretary for the Turner Valley Oilfields Curling Association and is still acting in that capacity.

From 1969-73 I helped Gordon Day with the girls' gymnastics at the Sheep Creek School. During this time I was also with the Stitch-In-Time 4-H club, acting as a leader for sewing and then for leathercraft for a period of six years.

The winter of 1974-75 Jim was assistant coach for the Pee-Wee team in hockey.

Mr. Chalmers passed away in 1969 and Mrs. Chalmers in 1972. In 1974 Jim and Robert decided to break up the partnership and Jim bought Robert's share of the home place. We moved to the house formerly lived in by Mr. and Mrs. Chalmers.

Marilee married Fred Hughes from Innisfail in 1968. They have three children, Nora, Stacy, and Clinton and are now residing in Bowden.

Linda married Wayne Mason from Turner Valley in 1970. They now have three children, Maria, Sherry, and Paul and reside in Turner Valley.

Jamie married Wade Smith from Hanna in 1971 and they have two children, Pam and Marty. Jamie and the children now live in High River.

Sharon married Clifford Smith (Wades brother) also from Hanna, in 1974, their two children are Kelli and Shawn and they reside in Black Diamond.

Vicky is engaged to Walter McCaghren and is presently living in Calgary. Lance and Deanna are still living at home.

Robert Chalmers

by Doreen Chalmers

Cattle Brand —7V on the Left Rib, and ⅄ on the right hip. Horse brand ⅄ left thigh. The old original Brands of Chalmers and sons were ⅄∩ cattle and B⊃ Horse Brand.

Robert was born on June 20, 1928 in High River. He lived on the home place S.W.¼ Sec. 10 T21, R3, W5 until 1974 when he and his family moved to the N.W.¼ Sec. 10, T21, R3, W5.

Robert is the second son of Bert and Grace Chalmers. He received his education at Sheep Creek School. The rest of his education was obtained through books on the care and training of animals as well as many night school courses.

Robert has always been an avid horseman and broke many horses for the ranch. He and his sisters Ruth and Jean helped their father at a very young age move cattle from summer to winter pasture and back again. He competed in rodeos whenever he could. He rode bulls and saddle bronc. In 1951 he won the Novice Saddle Bronc riding in High River and in 1952 the Novice Saddle Bronc riding in Calgary. Robert's father Bert did not like rodeo because he didn't think rodeo and ranching were compatable so in 1952 Robert quit his rodeo career to become a full time Rancher and family man.

In the 1940's Robert trailed the Chalmers cattle to Okotoks, Aldersyde, Mazeppa and Dewinton for

A new member is added to our family. July 24, 1976. Doug's Wedding. Back row: Robert, Doreen, Jackie, Don. Front row: Edie, Lynn and Doug. Photo credit: Janet MacKay.

several winters to strawpiles. He rode with Clem Gardner for some of these trips. As well as the Chalmers cattle he also trailed George Silvesters cattle to strawpiles at Longview and Okotoks in the fall and back in the spring. He also helped Clarence Ginrich trail Bucking Horses for the Calgary Stampede from Black Diamond to Calgary in 1947 and 48.

Robert and Alex Murdoch gathered wild horses on the reserve for three winters and trailed some of them to Calgary with Wilf Gerlitz in 1951 for the Horse Sale.

Robert has ridden on every Roundup in the Fall since 1941.

On September 22, 1951 Robert married Doreen Nichols, third daughter of Jim and Edith Nichols of Black Diamond. In August 1952 Jacqueline Louise was born, Douglas Wayne was born in June 1954, Donald Robert in March 1959 and Edith Mary in February 1964.

In 1953 Bert Chalmers suffered a stroke and never could work much after that. Robert began managing the ranch after this and he and Jim ran the ranch as partners, Robert looking after the cattle and he and Jim doing the farming and haying.

In 1969 Bert Haney built a new home for Robert, Doreen and family. Ours was the last of many good houses which Bert built in the Millarville district. Prior to this we lived in the original ranch home of Roberts folks with no plumbing etc.

In 1968 Robert built an arena where many of the local families participated in gymkanas etc. Doug, Jackie and Donald participated in all events and won many ribbons with Socks and Sandy.

In 1971 Robert started team roping. He did real well until in 1972 he lost the thumb on his right hand due to a freak accident. Everyone kidded Robert about his brother trying to chop his hand off because he had chopped his two middle fingers off with an axe when Robert was only five years old.

In spite of this handicap with only two fingers left on his right hand he went back to roping and won the Permit Buckle for Canada in 1973. He has won several trophies since for his roping.

After the death of Robert's Mom in 1972 Robert and Jim decided to split their partnership. This finally came about in 1974. In August of 1974 we moved our house to the present location. It was a very hard move to make due to sickness and other complications but we are all much happier now. When we came we only had a well with very good water. We now have a barn and shop, lots of good corrals, a roping arena and we have planted over 200 trees. Because of having a very good neighbor, Leonard Nelson, we were able to plant several large spruce trees with the help of another good neighbor, Jody Fisher, with his tree planting machine. Due to tender loving care we have only lost two trees. Mr. John Standish also gave us several fruit trees and perennial plants.

Robert has been Secretary-Treasurer for the South Sheep Creek Stock Association since 1953. He was chairman of the Ranchers Hall Board for several years and has served on the Turner Valley Municipal Hospital Board for many years. Robert is chairman of the Century Team Roping Club at the present time and also a director of the Millarville Races.

Doreen (Nichols) Chalmers

in 1932 in Black Diamond

I attended school at Black Diamond Public School, North Turner Valley High School and Garbutts Business College. I worked at Lake Louise, Calgary and Valley Pipe Line before getting married in 1951.

My mother always told me, "Never marry a farmer. All you do is work from morning to night." I wasn't married too long when I found this out. It was my job to cook for all the hired men, threshing crews and Branding crews. When you are young and healthy the work never seems that hard.

It wasn't all work and no play. We attended dances at the old Ranchers Hall and the Kew Hall, later moved to Square Butte. When Jackie was a baby we took her to all the dances and she would sleep on the space that was provided for the babies. When Doug came along Granny Chalmers or Granny Nichols would baby sit for us and Grandpa Chalmers always baby sat for Jim and Wilma.

I am afraid like most young brides I wasn't a very good cook. Lucille Dudenhoeffer (Glaister) came to visit one day when I was making pies and she was astounded at how I was treating my crust. Thanks to Lucille I can now make pies. The first time I made pumpkin pies Robert ate one whole pie and half of another one so I guess Lucilles lessons were a real help to me.

There were several young couples in the community at this time with one or two children. On Sunday afternoons we would take turns gathering at each others houses. The men would play poker while we tended babies and cooked supper. One Sunday we were all gathered at our house and we decided to have chocolate cake and angel food cake for desert. Jackie Mackay baked a chocolate cake and Lucille said she could make delicious Angel Food cakes, only we didn't have any eggs so I went to the hen house and gathered the nice fresh eggs. Lucille made the cake. It was perfect when it went into the oven. When it came out it was about one inch high. What a disappointment. Lucille was the only young bride that was a known good cook, her home made bread was delicious, but her angel food was a flop. We were all so dumb we didn't know that you couldn't use fresh eggs for angel food cake. What fun! We all ate it and enjoyed it. David always said my brown gravy was better than Lucilles even if her angel food cakes were better. I never did know if that was a compliment or not.

When the weather was warm on Sundays we would take picnic lunches and go for a drive, many times with Norm and Gwen Haynes and kids or Lou and Betty DePaoli and boys.

Over the years I have taught Sunday School at the Sheep Creek School, worked at the school as a volunteer to help with Math, held several offices in the Happy Gang Club and was Secretary for the Millarville and District Recreation Board for many years. I was Secretary-Treasurer for the Rancher Hall board for many years. At the present time I am Secretary for the Millarville History Society and Vice Chairman for the Priddis and Millarville Fair. I am also a director and volunteer worker for the Millarville Library Board. I canvas for Red Cross and Cancer in the spring. In the summer I am kept busy with my greenhouse, gardening and team roping.

Jackie Chalmers — Jackie received her education at Sheep Creek School, Oilfields High, Lord Beaverbrook, Mount Royal, Bozeman University in Montana and the University of Calgary. She has travelled a lot and done many interesting things. She went to England and Scotland after graduation from High School. She worked in Oklahoma in a School for Emotionally Disturbed Children for a time. She has worked and lived in Arizona and travelled to Mexico, California

Jackie Chalmers on Sandy.

224

and many other states. For several seasons Jackie worked at Spruce Meadows in Public Relations for their International Jumping Shows. Jackie has done some free lance stories about pioneer women which have been published. At the present time she is working for Transcon Livestock Ltd. in Calgary.

Jackie was a member of the Millarville 4-H Food Club and the Stockland Beef Club for many years where she won several awards for Public Speaking, as well as several Achievement Awards.

Jackies first love is riding on the reserve with her Dad helping to move cattle. When Ted Grant and Andy Russell had their book published "Men of the Saddle", Jackie was the only girl to have her picture in the book. She is an avid horsewoman. As well as Jackie, Robert, Doug and Donald have their picture in this book. Jackie was Limousin Queen in 1972, and took part in several stock shows.

Douglas Chalmers — Doug received his education at Sheep Creek School and Lord Beaverbrook High School. After graduation he travelled through the British Isles, Europe, United States and Mexico for about eight months. He finally decided Canada was the only place to live. Doug is now a Commercial Pilot and Flying Instructor. He took some of his training at Springbank but most of it in Saskatchewan. Floyd Glass who owns Athabasca Airways needed a ranch boy who was interested in cattle to work for him on his ranch in Prince Albert, in return Doug would get flying lessons. Doug got the job. Floyd soon found out that Doug was too good at looking after cattle and he had him spend too much time on the ranch and not enough time in the air. Doug met his wife to be, Lynn Crothers at Prince Albert. She was a flying instructor for Floyd Glass. Doug took several hours flying lessons from Lynn. From Prince Albert Doug and Lynn moved to Saskatoon where they were both flying instructors for Pultz Aviation. Doug and Lynn were married on July 24, 1976 in Christ Church, Mill. What started out to be a small family wedding turned into a large "Ukranian" wedding with friends and relations from Ontario, British Columbia, Saskatchewan, and Nova Scotia with campers, trailers and tents spending the weekend. Lynns' folks are from Ontario so we held a team roping and gymkana for them on Sun. They had never seen team roping before. Many neighbors and friends turned out on Sunday to participate or watch.

Doug and Lynn worked for a time with Pultz Aviation as instructors. From there they moved to La Ronge, Sask. to work for Athabasca Airways where Doug was the Base Manager and both he and Lynn were flying. They were flying Indians, hunters, fishermen and freight in and out of the bush and lake country in Northern Sask. Long hours, from daylight till dark even in the summer, isolation and the risky flying made them decide to come back to Alberta to live, in the fall of 1977. They both worked for a time in Calgary in their chosen profession. They finally got tired of the rat race in the city and they are now

Doug and Lynn Chalmers by one of the planes they flew in Sask.

managing a feed lot east of Calgary. They both have horses and do a lot of team roping now. All their spare time is spent swinging a rope. Lynn worked for a while for Bob Backs in the office before they took the feedlot job. Lynn is Secretary-Treasurer for the Century Team Roping Club this year.

Doug was a member of the Stockland Beef Club for several years and president for two years. He won rate of gain for his calf nearly every year.

Donald Chalmers — Brand ꓕↆↆ right rib.

Donald loves Long Horn cattle and he started his herd with a heifer he bought from Allie Streeter in 1973. He has had to sell some of them to help pay for his education. Donald received his education at Sheep Creek School, Oilfields High School and Bishop Grandin High School. He is now attending school in Casper. Wym.

Donald started riding horses at a very young age. He couldn't lift the saddle high enough to put it on Socks so he tied it up in the box stall and tied Socks underneath it and then let the saddle drop onto his back. He would then lead Socks up to the house so I could tighten the cinch for him.

Donald went to Steer Riding School when he was twelve. He would try riding the range bulls whenever we weren't home. Before he was old enough to drive himself to Rodeos he talked Doug into going to a Bull Riding School with the hope that big brother would drive him to all the Rodeos. Doug competed in a few Rodeos and broke his arm and decided he didn't like Bull Riding.

Donald competed in Bull Riding in the High School Circuit and won second for Alta. so he qualified to go to Montana to the National Finals. He split second, third and fourth for the World. As a result he is attending College in Casper, Wyoming on a Rodeo Scholarship. He is taking his teaching degree in Industrial Arts and riding the College Rodeo Circuit. After completing his first Semester he was placed on the Deans Honor Roll in Casper College with one of the highest averages in College.

Donald was in the Stockland Beef Club for many years and his calf won the Grand Champion for the Foothills Division in 1973. He also won rate of gain several years with his calves.

Edith Chalmers — Edie received her first nine years of Education at Sheep Creek School. At a very early age she and Joe Bateman became playmates. When the weather was fit they would take turns walking across the field to play together. Rip, Donald's old Newfoundland Dog was their constant companion, until Rip would see Donald come home from school and then he would run to meet him.

Edie is now in Grade 10 at Bishop Grandin High School in Calgary. She is taking her Senior Matriculation courses. She leaves for school at 6:30 a.m. and doesn't get home till 5:15 p.m. It is a very long day but she likes school and her marks are good.

Edie was in the Stitch in Time 4-H Club and now in her fourth year in Stockland Beef. She has always done well in her public speaking and has won rate of gain for her calf several times. Edie likes to ride horses and help her Dad with the cattle. She is learning to team rope and won a rope for the most improved student and placed second in the jackpot at Lorne Wells last Roping School held in our Arena.

I sometimes think we should have had four boys instead of two of each because our girls prefer to work outside with their Dad. Jackie is an excellent cook and has been cooking since she was old enough to stand on a stool and read a cook book. Jackie takes after her Aunt Jennie (Chalmers) Mackay. Robert always said she was the best cook in the country. Aunt Jennie told me before Robert and I were married that if I could make good doughnuts I would pass the test but Aunt Jennie still makes the best doughnuts.

Poems Written by Jackie Chalmers — Submitted by Doreen Chalmers

Who loves cows, horses and the wide open sky?
You do, Dad
Who loves furry kittens, new born calves and playful puppies?
You do, Dad
Who's always ready to lend a hand with 4-H calves, fixing cars or learning to rope.
You are, Dad
Who's a winner with his friends and his family?
You are, Dad
And who loves you for all these wonderful things?
I do, Dad!

Love, Jack 1977

Who spends hours in her garden so we can reap our harvest?
You do, Mom
Who has time for each of her kids and every one of their friends?

You do, Mom
Who finds time to drive to 4-H, sew a quilt and time a roping?
You do, Mom
Who holds the community and the family together thru the good and bad times?
You do, Mom
Who loves you for being such a special person?
I do, Mom!

Love, Jack 1977

D. Charles H. Clark Family

Charles Clark joined the Alberta Forest Service in June of 1954. His first posting as a Ranger was at the North Fork Ranger Station, just west of Millarville. His wife, Arlin, and three daughters, Elaine, Rae and Verlyn moved into the fine old log cabin for an enjoyable, but all too short, two years. The closest neighbor was George Silvester, about a half mile away.

Charley's work was associated primarily with cattle grazing under permit in the reserve. Each herd was assigned a definite area and usually settled down well enough, although some, especially younger cattle, would wander at times. In the spring, checks on areas containing poison weeds had to be made and during the danger period stock was moved to a safer location. Some losses to bears occurred and an attempt was made to eliminate the guilty predator. Salt grounds caused problems since numerous wild horses in this area would try to prevent the cattle from using them. Overgrazing in the creek valleys had to be checked constantly and corrected when necessary.

As time went on, a fair amount of logging, especially on Fisher Creek by Bill Kendall, began. This new industry made improved fire-spotting and radio contacts more important, so a new Lookout at Forget-Me-Not was built and Jim Killmeister installed as towerman. A new road was made from Sheep Ranger Station (Big Horn) to Forget-Me-Not via Northfork Ranger Station and the Lookout could then be serviced via truck. The work out of North Fork Ranger Station headquarters had all been done by the use of horses previously. In 1955, elk, moose, deer and mountain sheep were in abundance. The grazing potential was excellent and good quality cattle were brought in to graze and fatten on it. Timber supply was rather limited, unfortunately.

For recreation, the girls liked to ride horses, pick berries, fish and swim in the creek. Schooling was by Correspondence School and exams were written at Millarville. We all enjoyed the socials and old time dances at Square Butte and Millarville. The old Square Butte Hall had trouble keeping the roof in its rightful place when the Lyalls, Silvesters, Rodgers, Fishers, McBees, Lysters, Nylunds, Marshalls, Kendalls, Koslings, Fosters, Glaisters, Bells, Wildmans all got in time to the McBee, Lyall and Kosling music. Many good dances were enjoyed at Millarville also.

We must thank all the people around North Fork Ranger Station for the fine business associations and never to be forgotten sociability.

Charles and Arlin, now retired, live in Pincher Creek.

Elaine married Ivor Lyster and lived in the Millarville area long after we left. They had three children. They now live in the Vilna, Alberta area.

Rae is married to Oris Lyster and lives in the Stettler area with her two girls.

Verlyn has two boys and lives at Ardrossen, near Edmonton.

Allen, our oldest is married and lives in Edmonton. He was not with us at North Fork since he was already working out in 1954.

The Clark's

by Martha Clark

DeVone and Martha Clark were born and raised at Beechy, Saskatchewan. They were married in June, 1941 and became active in farming. In 1953 they, with their two children, Carole and Garney, moved to farm at Landis, Sask.

In 1964 Garney moved to Edmonton for training with N.C.R. and while in Edmonton, he met Katherine Kendall, from Edson, who was employed in secretarial work. They were married in July 1965, and settled at Landis to resume farming operations.

The Clarks sold their farm-holdings at Landis, in August 1978. Mr. and Mrs. Garney Clark, Cameron and Suzanne make their home on an acreage at Millarville, and Devone and Martha will retire in Calgary.

Clark Family. Back, L. to R.: Devone, Katherine, Martha, Garvey. Front, L. to R.: Suzanne and Cameron.

History of Louise Lee

by Louise Clark

I was born in 1936 — my parents were Jack and Corene Lee. As a small child I moved along with my parents from the quarter N.E.¼, Sec. 27, T21-R3-W5, to the S.W.¼, Sec. 25, T21-R3-W5, which my dad

Russell, Louise, Calvin, Darcy.

purchased from my grandfather, Art Wilderman. This land ran along Highway 22. I grew up on this land with my three sisters and one brother. I resided in the area during my school years, attending Fordville and Sheep Creek Schools. From there, I worked in the Royal Bank, located in Turner Valley. I then decided I would apply for a position in the telephone office, also in Turner Valley. For the next five years, I did this type of work, resigned for a short time, and this time applied for a position in the High River A.G.T. office until 1961. At this time I resigned, and married Russel Clark of Hoadley. We have two boys, Darcy, 15 years, and Calvin, 11 years. In 1970 we purchased the building used as the Anglican Church at the time of our wedding in 1961. We are remodeling the building. We also own the land adjoining the building. We are involved in the dairy industry. Our brand 4F on R.R. is the brand that belonged to Grandad Lee, also to my Dad. It now is registered in the name of Russell G. Clark, so is still in the family.

M. H. and Alice Clarke

by Alice Clarke

Malcolm (Mac) was born in Lloydminster, Saskatchewan, raised on a farm in Rex District. Losing his mother at a very early age, and being the youngest of nine on a small farm in hard times. The elder left as soon as they were old enough to work out. The younger ones, mostly boys, dragged themselves up until only Mac and his father were left. With little time for school in the early '40's, his dad sold the farm for a song, leaving nothing for any of the family. Mac then worked for different farmers, until the late '40's and was then making appearances at the dances, ball games, etc. in my community.

Born in Wainwright, Alberta (Alice Shadbolt), I was raised on a farm in the Hope Valley district. After a couple of years of sharing the same interests in life, we decided to get married. Mac sold his wood sawing outfit and the Model A car we had so many laughs and accidents with, and came to Calgary in January 1950. We worked at De Winton, where our only son Ken was born that summer. Later, we went to Olds for W. W. Hunter. In the fall of 1951, the crops were snowed under and by spring the mice were so plentiful the cats couldn't stand to eat another one. They all drank milk out of the same dish while we sat milking the cows and watched.

From there we went to the Warren dairy farm at Didsbury. The pay was good but so tied down. One day a foreman from the Butterfield Ranch north of Cochrane, came to see if we would like to go ranching and Mac was only too glad to accept the first ranch job. The place was formerly owned by Mrs. Little (across from the Weedon School — now in Heritage Park). I had four men to cook for and they called me "Ma". It was rather funny to go to a dance, not being known in the district, and have these fellows say "Let's dance, Ma." I had to make these fellows pancakes every morning and to save time would mix them the night before, put a cloth over them and set the bowl in the hallway to keep cool (no fridge). One morning as I lifted the cloth there were brown spots in the batter and thought, Oh, my God, those darn mice got into the batter. Upon dipping a spoon in, found raisins the boys put in after I went to bed.

On another occasion the middle-aged secretary for the ranch came out to spend the night. She always slept in her sleeping bag on the floor downstairs. We had an empty bed that night so convinced her that she should put the bag on the bed. The next morning two of the boys pulled her thumping down the stairs and outside onto the veranda and then left in a fit of laughter. I was called to unzip the bottom of the bag so she could get her feet out while she was muttering what a dirty trick and how lucky she had a bag with a bottom zip as she slept in the nude.

After three years, the men were gone — two married and Ken was going to Westbrook School. The ranch owner in Montana was in financial difficulties and finally came to say he had to sell but couldn't say when, so we couldn't look for another job. One day some people drove in and said they were buying the place. We weren't leaving as we hadn't received a lot of wages so a couple of weeks later they moved in with three small children and a hired man and we all lived together until the boss came back from the States and paid us off.

Jobs were hard to find so Clem Edge asked us to help him on his Ranch 50 at Beaupre until we found work at Crossfield, where we spent the next few years, mostly at a purebred Hereford farm for John Hehr — the most honest man in the business. John's bad heart grew worse and Stan, the youngest son, married and was ready to take over so there wasn't enough work to keep us. We went west of Cochrane to the Two Rivers Ranch (between the Bow and Ghost Rivers, now owned by the Stony Indians). Later made a two-month stop at Clem Edge's again before coming to Priddis in

June 1961 to manage the Crestview Ranch owned by D. S. Harvie and previously owned by Van Wykes. After ten and a half years there we then came to a different life style at W. Lee's — Bill's Corner Service in April '72, where we are at present. Mac did a lot of school bus driving when we first came.

Our son Ken is now living near Edmonton. We have moved around a lot but it has been worth it. We have met and worked with so many nice people. A lot of them look us up and we laugh at the good times we had together.

One evening (we had nieces and friends from Ontario visiting) when Roy Thomson came in and said he had bought a donkey. I wanted to look at it as I had never seen one before. Next thing we knew in came the donkey and stood in the kitchen, scared to blink an eye. We put a hat on him and admired him while my niece (Hazel Flanagan) held my dish pan in case of an accident — which fortunately didn't happen.

Joseph and Catherine Coates

Joseph Robin Coates was born in Tisdale, Saskatchewan on November 10, 1952 the son of Bruce and Verna Coates. The Coates later moved to Estevan, Saskatchewan and then in 1962 they moved to their present home in Regina, Saskatchewan. Joseph completed his high school education in Regina. He then later obtained his private pilot's licence with an aviation career in mind. In the fall of 1973 he moved to Banff, Alberta where he was employed at Mt. Norquay.

Catherine Mary was born in Regina, Saskatchewan on March 29, 1954 the younger daughter of Herb and Isobel Padwick. She was educated in Regina and during these years devoted most of her time to the equestrian world. Cathy trained under Robin Hahn of the Canadian Olympic Team and Hugh Wiley of the United States Equestrian Team. In 1973 she was a member of the Pony Club Team that represented Canada in Japan.

Catherine resided and worked in Regina until 1976 when she and Joseph Coates "high school sweethearts" were married. They then joined her Mother and Father in the purchase of Belmar Ranch. S.E. ¼-27-21-3-W/5.

Mrs. Margaret Coates
by Marilin (Coates) Henry

Mrs. Coates came to teach at Plainview School early in 1948, replacing the teacher who had started the term.

She had taught for many years in country schools — first when she was very young (when some of the pupils were older than she was,) and later in life, when a family illness brought her back teaching.

She was extremely happy in the Millarville-Plainview district. She felt very much at home with the wives and mothers in the district, where the

Mrs. Margaret Coates, teacher at Plainview School at Kew.

friendly community spirit was so similiar to the community in which we had farmed many years. Mr. and Mrs. Sim, who lived next to the school, were very kind to her, and their friendship lasted through the years until she passed away June 30th, 1973. Little Glen Sim, at four years of age, was her delivery and messenger boy, bringing mail, eggs and milk. She thought his sayings and expressions were delightful.

Families in the area at that time were the Sims, Dudenhoeffers and Karys.

She was so pleased upon arriving at the teacherage to have a warm fire and the kettle singing to welcome her. I remember once, when the spring thaw came, the vehicles were having difficulty getting through, she walked from the Plainview School to Millarville to take a bus to Calgary. She had visions of her daughter at fifteen, and alone for the first time, getting into dire difficulties.

She used to love to drive back to the area every summer, after teaching at Plainview. It is such a beautiful countryside, with the rolling foothills and those beautiful mountains almost at your finger tips. I had the privilege of spending the last week of the school term with her, and sharing some of the friendly spirit at a community picnic, going horseback riding with the Karys, Sims and Dudenhoeffers, and swimming in Sheep Creek. Good memories indeed.

Red and Sherry Cochrane

by Sherry Cochrane
Sec. 2, T. 22, R. 3, W. 5

We moved from Hamiota, Manitoba to Alberta in Nov. 1965. We worked at Stan Jones for 6 months, then moved to the Skyland Angus Ranch in May, 1966. We

worked for Mr. W. A. Friley for two years, until he had a dispersal sale.

We have two children, a boy, Murray, who was three years old when we moved to this district, and a girl, Loree, who was a year and a half.

Fred then worked for the Alberta Wheat Pool for a little over a year in Hussar, Alberta. We left there to work for Alberta Gas Trunkline in Cavendish, Alberta. We stayed in Cavendish for three years, then transferred with A.G.T. to Wainwright in September, 1969. We are still in Wainwright district and a year ago bought a quarter section of farm land with buildings.

Bud and Linda (Lee) Codd

Bud was born in Assiniboine, Sask. Later with his parents and five brothers and one sister, moved to Manitoba, where they farmed.

In Bud's late teens, along with his older brother, they moved back to Saskatchewan, around the Burstall area, where they rough-necked on oil rigs and farmed. After a few years with rancher, Clark Jacobson, Bud decided to move into Millarville district with Clark, where they set up a ranch. Still ranching with Clark, Bud went into the general trucking business. He then began driving a milk truck for R. Linden, after he met Linda Lee.

Bud and Linda (Lee) Codd on their wedding day.

L. to R. Darryl, Bud and Deb Codd, December, 1972.

229

Linda was born in Calgary and raised at Millarville, the youngest daughter of Bill and Ethel Lee. She received her schooling at Sheep Creek School. Linda enjoyed swimming and got her Royal Life Saving Awards at Turner Valley Pool and Y.W.C.A. in Calgary. She also worked at the Turner Valley Telephone Office.

Bud and Linda were married at the Christ Church in Millarville. They moved to Hartell and operated a service station. Bud also drove school bus to Turner Valley and Black Diamond, later getting into building tractor cabs.

Bud and Linda had a daughter Deborah (Deb) and four years later a son Darryl, both born in Calgary.

The Codd's sold their service station and moved to the Millarville area (N.W. part of the S.E. ¼ of 14-21-3w5.) Linda is now driving school bus at Millarville and Bud is working at Millarville Motors Service Station. Darryl attends Millarville School and Deb goes to Black Diamond Oilfields High School.

Gwen (Stockton) Cohoe

Mayme M.

Gwen Stockton Cohoe — daughter of Mayme Martin, Strathmore, went to school in New Valley and after her Mother's remarriage in 1939 attended Sunalta and Western Canada High. She took a correspondence course in Chemistry and was later employed in the lab at Canada Cement Co., Exshaw, Alta.

In 1944 she joined the C.W.A.C.'s, taking her training in Ont. Later posted to Winnipeg, then Chilliwack, back to Winnipeg where she was on loan to the Navy Lab. After demobilization she worked for a time in the Calgary CO-Operative Store.

On Jan. 24, 1948 she married Norman Edgar Cohoe of Cochrane. They had 5 children.

Charles — Castlegar, B.C. who has an Insurance business there.

Cathryn Cohoe Bennett, R.N. who is a hemogoblin specialist at the Jr. Red Cross Hospital, Calgary. Her husband is a buyer for the city of Calgary.

Robert — who is an automotive salesman in Edmonton.

Bonnie — who graduated with a Bach. of Finance degree in 1977 from U. of C. and is now taking 4th year Education at the U. of C.

Lynn Cohoe Williams is a co-ordinator of Activities at the Alberta Mental Hospital, Ponoka and lives in Wetaskiwin. Lynn's husband is asst. manager of the Treasury Branch in Leduc.

Gwen and Norman are still residents of Calgary and enjoy having their family around them.

Jim Colley

Born in Ontario, Jim came with his parents to Alberta, settling first in the Rosemary district, where they ranched. In 1927, with his parents and sister Annie, they came to the Millarville district, driving their

Jim Colley, left, "Peace River" Mack, right. Spring, 1940.

cattle and sheep. They first lived on the N.W.¼ of 16-21-3W5, and had adjoining land.

Jim was a very good mechanic, could probably do more with a motor than anyone in the country at that time. Forward and Walton had both the Kew and Millarville stores, with Mr. Forward doing the trucking to keep both stores in supplies. When he became ill and unable to continue with the trucking, Jim took over the job. Here his talent for mechanics proved its worth as Mr. Forward's old truck needed constant care to battle the roads it had to travel. The road to Calgary from Millarville at that time was through Priddis, the Sarcee Indian Reserve then up over the Weasel Head Hill, quite an accomplishment in dry weather and a real challenge in rain or snow. There was no gravel on any part of that road.

After the death of his mother, Jim and his father lived on the Stagg place for awhile. Mr. Colley bought the S.W.¼ of 13-21-4W5 and the two of them batched for some time. Jim had a sawing outfit and travelled around the country sawing lumber for many people, either large or small amounts.

About 1938, Jim spent a winter trapping at Harold Creek, where his friend Harry Fisher had a trap line in the winter and was a ranger during the summer. They were trapping lynx, as well as other fur bearing animals, and did quite well.

In 1943, Jim was married to Neva Croston. He joined the Armed Services and with his knowledge of trucks etc. he became a driver instructor. He was stationed at Red Deer for a while, but was transferred

L. to R., Back: Sharon and Linda. Front: Jim, children of Jim and Neva Colley.

to Eastern Canada, but was back in Alberta when his first daughter, Sharon, was born in 1944.

After the war was ended and Jim had received his discharge, they moved to the land his father had lived on and started dairying. The road in to the place was at most times impassable, and when Sharon started school, Jim would bring her by saddle horse nearly two miles to meet the bus. Two more children were born, Linda in 1947 and Jim jr. in 1951.

John Meim had bought the N.W.¼ of 13-21-4W5, joining Jim's land, and he and his family lived there for only a short time. Jim needed more land so bought Meim's land. Here Jim built a new house and moved to this location as it was much more accessible, a better road to get the children to school.

In the spring of 1958, Jim sold his land to Ivor and Elaine Lyster. In looking for a likely place to start a new life he chose New Zealand. Hearing that cars were at a premium there he changed his Volkswagen car to the right hand drive and had it shipped to New Zealand. Arriving in that country he had no difficulty finding a job. His mechanical knowledge was put to good use, driving machines for ditching, road building etc.

As a hobby Jim built small boats, and his son sailed these in the waters around Auckland, where they lived for several years.

Sharon is married to Ron Gordon and makes her home in New Plymouth, New Zealand, as does Linda. The only son Jim Jr. returned to Canada and makes his home in Calgary.

Jim's health failed and he is in a nursing home in New Plymouth.

Nick and Janet Cooke

After selling their house in Okotoks and a Coin Laundry business in Calgary, Nick and Janet Cooke bought the Millarville General Store from Arlie Laycraft and began to operate this business in June 1974.

The next year in May, a little dark-eyed daughter, Stacey was born and two years later another little daughter, Heather joined the family.

Janet, being an ardent horse lover and trainer, soon had a horse, and it wasn't too long until Nick became a horse-owner too. They enjoyed many rides around Millarville and were members of the Ridge Riders Club from Priddis. Several times they took part in long distant rides with other Horse Clubs. They both enjoyed and excelled at cross-country skiing, taking advantage of our excellent snow conditions at every opportunity.

Coming from the coastal regions of Ireland, they began to long for the salt water, so in 1978 they sold the business to Mr. and Mrs. John Clarke from Calgary and moved to Salt Spring Island, British Columbia.

Elsie and Bill Cooper

Elsie is the sixth girl of Bud and Lola Field. She graduated from Western Canada High School and went into nursing. She married William Cooper from Raymond, Alberta. He is a salesman in Medical Supplies. They have two girls, Colleen and Sandra and one son Clint. Bill's job took him across the border. They moved with their family to Albuquerque, New Mexico, to Denver, then to Salt Lake City. Now, after ten years, they have moved back to Calgary.

Elsie and Bill Cooper, son Clint, Friend and Colleen. Insert of daughter Sandra.

Elsie Cooper.

Charis (Blakley) Cooper and her school pony, Baldy. Summer 1938.

Cooper, Charis Jean (Blakley)

My parents were living in Hoquiam, Washington when I was born in 1930, January 27. Consequently out of the four children in our family I was the one who was the American citizen, a fact which has since been rectified.

Over the next two years my parents and I lived in Salem, Oregon and Bonner's Ferry, Idaho. In 1932 we moved to Tees, Alberta and stayed until 1935 when we moved to the Millarville area. There were four in our family now as my brother Dennis was born at Tees in 1933, June 7th.

We moved to the homestead of my Mother's father, Joseph Fisher, who had first arrived there in 1884 with a herd of cattle and had spent the first winter in a dugout which we kids used to poke around in, in the hopes of finding something very extraordinary, which we never did.

All of Mother's family lived in the area at that time and we had some rousing family gatherings especially at Christmas time when we would congregate at my Grandmother's house located in East Millarville and called the Meadow. The first couple of years we would go by team and sleigh with hot rocks at our feet and many blankets tucked around us so the seven or eight mile trip did not seem so bad.

There were many adventures living as we did and one I remember vividly was the winter morning a visit

was paid to us by a huge black wolf. We were awakened by a cow bawling and looking out the window we saw the wolf trying to grab one of the two heifers that were with the cow. Dad got one leg in his pants and grabbed his gun, then stepped outside and fired at the wolf, hitting him in the spine, rendering its hindquarters helpless. Dad then finished pulling on his pants, pulled on boots and jacket and went after the wolf, who was trying to pull itself away with its front-quarters. As Dad came near, the creature tried to leap at him and some horrible white vapor was coming out of the wolf's mouth. Dad shot again and the wolf went down but it still took a blow on the head with an iron bar to finish it off. This wolf turned out to be one of the biggest ever to be shot in the district.

In the spring of 1937 we moved to Black Diamond for a dual purpose, Dad started to roughneck on a rig in the Longview area and to await the birth of my sister, Mary, who arrived on June 26th.

I started to school in Black Diamond, then the following spring, in 1938, we moved back to the farm on Fisher Creek and I started to school at Sheep Creek. It was a two mile walk and the first mile I was alone and I was sure there was a terrible animal lurking behind every bush waiting to attack me as I possessed the usual active imagination of an eight year old. The next mile I had lots of company with three Jackson children and two Hodgkins.

In the fall of 1938 my parents presented me with a grey pony with a white face so he was named Baldy, and he carried me to school for many years. The first few months we had to get used to each other so I spent a good bit of the time being thrown to the ground but he never did run off and leave me, so I would crawl back

Cooper Family. L. to R. Lacey, Dick, Charis, Tim and Noreen.

on an ' we would continue the journey to school. These schoo... onies were smarter than the kids they carried. As we would ride by the Rancher's Hall, Baldy would look up the big hill on the north side of the road, then he would whinny and his school yard pal, Fritz, ridden by the two Hodgkin kids would appear, then off to school we would all ride, quite often having a race to see who had the fastest pony. In 1939 my brother joined me on Baldy's back and we continued this way for a few years then my sister started school and Baldy's load was increased to three.

The next year the little one-room school was joined by a bigger building with two more classrooms as more people were moving into the area due to oil wells being drilled all over the country. The school paddock fence was torn out and that was the end of school pony transportation.

My first job was at Millarville store, working for Martha and Jappy Douglass, where I was store clerk, coffee shop waitress and gas jockey. This was in 1948, then in 1949 I went to work in the Turner Valley telephone office as a telephone operator, until 1952 when I moved to Edmonton to work in the long distance exchange there. This brought about my meeting Richard (Dick) Cooper, who was born and raised in Edmonton and had just obtained his journeyman electrician certificate. We were married on January 30, 1954 and over the next nine years we lived in apartments in Edmonton and had three children.

Lacey Jean, born April 26, 1955.

Timothy Richard, born November 5, 1956.

Noreen Elizabeth, born December 2, 1960.

I kept thinking of our foothills and the Rocky Mountains so in 1963 Dick finally gave in and we moved to Calgary. In 1964 we bought some land at Millarville just south of the Home Oil company and moved out. Sheep Creek School was no more as there was now a big school at Millarville and this is where our children would go by school bus and not school pony. The first year we had to drive our children one mile to catch the bus as there was no road, only a trail to our place.

When this trail was snowed in or otherwise impassable the children either walked or we took them by horse to meet the bus so they had a small taste of school pony transportation. The next year the municipality put in a road so the school bus was able to come to our gate.

In 1971 Pat Hartell decided to sell his ranch, N.E. 8-20-3-W5. We were the lucky buyers and we live here now with a beautiful view of Waite Valley, the foothills and the Rocky Mountains. We have a small herd of cattle and a few horses as we love to ride in these hills. In the winter we all cross-country ski.

Lacey has just graduated from the University of Lethbridge and is teaching at Brooks, Alberta.

Timothy is in Edmonton working for Pacific Western Airlines as an Aircraft Maintenance Engineer.

Noreen will graduate from high school in June and plans to enroll at Southern Alberta Institute of Technology and take the Television, Stage and Radio Arts course.

At every opportunity they all come home to enjoy the great outdoors and partake of family gatherings we still have as my parents still live on the place on Fisher Creek.

Harriett (Crossman) Copithorne

My brief residence in the Millarville district was from September 1948 to June 1949. I was employed as teacher of Fordville School and lived in the home of Mr. and Mrs. James Cawthorne. It was pleasant being with them and I have warm memories of those fine people. Also Hughie, who always had an amusing story to tell.

School enrollment was quite low that year but the students were interesting and bright. I especially remember the three "big girls" — Ruthie Adams, Lila Croston and June Hehr, and their lively noon-hour chatter about their boy friends.

One of the nicest things about my year at Fordville was the thrill of being in the beautiful foothills country with the Rocky Mountains in full view. It was my first introduction to the mountains, and was so deeply impressed, I guess, that I chose to remain in an area where I can enjoy a view of the Rockies — always magnificent but never the same.

Another memorable event was the first dance I attended at Rancher's Hall. The place was packed and everyone seemed to be having a really wild time. I was not at all sure that I liked being there. However, I soon learned to appreciate the capacity of the people in that community to put aside their work and troubles on Saturday night and go out and have one helluva good time. A great philosophy! I hope it is still the same out there.

Glaister-Coulter, Joan

I was born in 1953 at the Turner Valley Hospital, eldest daughter of David and Lucille Glaister. My first home was a tiny, two-room house on my paternal grandparents place, East of Millarville, SW½ 3-21-2 W5th. Although I don't remember my first two and a half years spent on the Valley View Ranch, it was during this time that the beginnings of a very special relationship developed between my Grandmother Glaister and myself. My parents moved to the old Frenchman's place off highway 22 (NE½ 14-21-3 W5th) when I was about three but I returned to Valley View as often as possible and would cry when I had to return home. The hours I spent with my Grandmother listening to the stories of her childhood and the "olden" days, helped me to develop a strong feeling of family roots and an undying love of these foothills. My Grandmother was a fine horsewoman and with her coaching and the help of my father I, too, learned to love the feel of horseflesh. Many of the long, lazy summer afternoons of my childhood were spent rambling about on the back of one of my favorite horses, Sugar or Snooks. I have often heard my mother say that a gentle horse makes a fine babysitter.

I showed my first pony in the Millarville Fair at the age of four and didn't miss any of the children's classes for the next eight years. I started school at Sheep Creek, Millarville, when I was five, riding Bert Haney's school bus from the Ballyhamage ranch which my parents were then renting. I don't remember much about my early school days except a very strong dislike being cooped up and having to spend time away from my horses and the beautiful woods and fields of Ballyhamage. If I hadn't had kind but strong coaching from my first and most loved school teacher, Mrs. Pekse, I am sure I would not have completed as much school as I did. After Grade Nine I attended the Turner Valley Oilfields High School in Black Diamond for two years and finished Grade XII at Henry Wisewood in Calgary. Having developed an even stronger dislike of school, I could not face the thought of further institutionalized learning. I wanted God's open spaces. I found I learned best in my own way for my own reasons. I had no idea what I was going to do with my future.

In the Spring of 1970 I accompanied my Dad to Ten Mile Cabin on Brewster Creek where he was to help Al Johnson shoe the Mt. Assinniboine horses. I spent one short afternoon in the company of Al and the staff at Ten Mile but left knowing that somehow I would return, and return I did. I applied to Assinniboine Lodge to be a dishwasher and ended up head cook. This was my style of education, working in the tourist industry. I learned most of the things that school teachers had tried in vain to teach me over the last twelve years. For the first time in my life my mouth was shut and my eyes open. I met people of every nationality, including Tensing Norgay who, along with Sir Edmund Hilary, was one of the first men to stand on the top of Mount Everest. People like this showed me, a country girl, that I too was capable of achievement beyond my dreams. As a result of lessons learned that summer of 1971, I went on to cook in

places like the Banff School of Fine Arts, the Bugaboo Lodge, Emerald Lake Chalet, Mt. Stevens Chalet, and at Sunshine Village. I spent approximately five years in and around the Banff area. While at Mt. Assiniboine I climbed my first mountain. I accompanied Al Johnson to the Corners where I experienced my first horse round-up. I learned to tie the diamond hitch, cure saddle sores on my own rear and to deal with the constant threat of Grizzly bears. I cooked on wood stoves with the light of a Coleman lantern. One incident I clearly remember while cooking at Assiniboine was the night of the helicopter. I had prepared a lovely ham and sweet potato dinner which I had left in the warming oven when someone yelled "helicopter". I rushed to the window to look and turned back to find my dinner ruined. The helicopter had flown over the chimney and the soot from the stovepipes was blown over everything. With 28 hungry people waiting in the dining room, I had to improvise a meal from what could be salvaged. One question I was constantly asked was "what makes a good cook?" I learned from incidents like the one above that a good cook is a person who can read and interpret a recipe, who has a vivid imagination, and a large, appreciative group of people with a sense of humour. In the Bugaboos I cooked at Boulder Camp with cold running water, two Coleman stoves and no oven. This is where vivid imagination comes into play.

I went to England when I was 18 to stay with a girl I had met while working at Assiniboine. Arriving at Margaret's place, Low Woods Farm on Low Woods Lane, was like walking into the pages of Black Beauty. During Margaret's stay at Mt. Assiniboine I taught her the art of Western riding. She now taught me something of the English method of riding. Indeed, I learned the finer art of horsemanship through Margaret's patient coaching, a few scares, and a runaway. I visited the Quorn Hunt and travelled extensively over the rolling English Midlands. Continuing on to Wilshire, where I stayed on Manor Farm, I visited the Veil of the White Horse Hunt and experienced my first hunt ball. With some sadness I learned a bit about English etiquette as regards the 'hunt'. I had romantically fallen for one of the young men who worked as a whip with the hunt and was disappointed to learn he could not attend the ball as he was a hired servant of the hunt and was therefore not admitted. From England I travelled to Scotland and visited with a friend of the family's, Catherine McDowell, before returning home a month later.

Upon returning to Canada I felt an urgent need to head back into the mountains. I worked until meeting my husband-to-be, Michael Coulter. In keeping with my somewhat spontaneous character, we had no courtship. Within a week of meeting and following our first date I knew I would marry this Texas cowboy. On November 8, 1975 at Christ Church, Millarville, Michael Gordon Coulter, of Wichita Falls, Texas and myself were married. Three years later, on June 20,

1978, while Alberta's wild roses were in full bloom, our daughter Jennifer Joan was born.

Michael, Jennifer Joan and I now reside at Mesa Creek Ranch, where Michael and I work alongside my parents with the running of their ranch operation.

Cross, Donald J. A.

The Donald Cross family moved to the Millarville area in September, 1964. Their home is located on the N.W.¼ 20-21-2W5 and was purchased from previous owner, Mrs. Bill McLaws. This quarter was originally homesteaded by Tom Phillips in 1904.

In the spring of 1964, Donald and his father, J. B. Cross of Okotoks, bought the Ardmore Ranch from Les Boulton and established a commercial cattle operation for Bar Pipe Farms. Peter Welsh, first owner of the ranch, had given it the name 'Ardmore' in 1890 and it was well regarded in Hereford circles when used by a subsequent owner, A. G. Spooner. The name was restored to the ranch in 1978 when the commercial cows were sold and the place was once again stocked with registered Herefords.

Donald was born in Calgary, April 5, 1932 and received his schooling at Strathcona School for Boys and Appleby College, Oakville, Ontario. Summers and holidays were spent at the family cottage on Willow Creek at the a7 Ranche, homesteaded by grandfather, A. E. Cross. Donald obtained a Bachelor of Commerce from the University of Alberta in 1954 and a Masters in Business Administration from the University of Western Ontario in 1958. That same year he married Shirley Ann ('Shan') Holman, born May 24, 1936 in Regina, schooled in Calgary and the University of British Columbia. They have four children, Pamela Helen, b. April 10, 1959, Gretchen Kathleen, b. October 6, 1960, James Charles ('Jay') b. March 14, 1962 and Jill Marnie, b. October 10, 1967. The children have attended Millarville School and Strathcona-Tweedsmuir School. The two oldest girls presently attend the University of Western Ontario.

Donald is a past president of the Millarville Racing and Sports Association, Vestry member, Christ Church and Fair Director for the beef section. However, his greatest volunteer time commitment is to the Calgary Exhibition and Stampede and he is currently President-Elect. The family own and operate hotels and a fishing lodge in the N.W.T. Shan is active at Christ Church, Leighton Centre, Strathcona-Tweedsmuir School and is a Fair Director. For the past eight years the family has spent all possible leisure time skiing and hiking in the mountains.

The Ronald Cross Family

by Allene Cross

In February of 1973 Ron and I and three of our four children moved from Calgary on to what is known in the area as "the Spink place". Ron is from the Ponoka area, I from Gleichen. Our children were all born in Calgary.

The three who moved here with us are Cathy, Gary and Tracy. Our eldest girl, Terry, is married to Ken Winnick and lives in Calgary with their children, Craig and Serena. The brand we use is was first used by my grandfather and is registered in the North West Territory Brand Book.

Melvin Croston

I was born in Calgary, Alberta in June of 1925. This was the beginning of the depression years. My father, Bert Croston, worked at anything he could find to do. I was fifth in a family of eight children, but being a child, and not knowing the problems that go with providing for a large family, we were happy. My brothers and I used to roam the hills and explore Bride Creek near where we lived.

I attended King George School in North West Calgary. I also attended Mount Pleasant, where I completed junior high.

In 1940 our family moved from Calgary, out to a ranch that was known as Anchordown Ranch. At the age of fifteen, I got my first lesson in log cutting and sawing the logs into lumber. We, (my father, brother Murry, and future brother-in-law, Jim Colly) continued to work at this occupation for the next four years. It was all done as piece work, so it meant long hours, and much hard work.

In 1944 my father was bedridden with a stroke, and by this time I was no longer in the lumber business, so went to work on a ranch for Peter Massey at Red Deer Lake. I worked there for two years. This was my first introduction to farm life. There I learned to milk cows, feed pigs, clean barns, and good things like that. It was not all work though, as we were able to go on hunting trips with Royal Burrows. These hunting trips were the highlight of our time there.

In about 1948, our family purchased a farm about two miles from the little village of Caroline, Alberta. This is near Innisfail, Alberta. My brother Murry and I once again went to work in the lumber business, Murry managing a planing mill, and myself, a saw mill when the slack season came on the farm.

In about 1952 an opportunity in the oil field presented itself. I was going to be a roughneck! After many trials and tribulations, I was promoted to derrick man. I worked for several more years and was made a driller.

In 1959, I met the most wonderful gal who was to become my wife, though I didn't know it at the time. Eileen came out to cook for us. She continued to cook for us until 1961. By this time, I decided I couldn't live without her, so we were married. One of the greatest pleasures of my life, was her six year old daughter Debbie. Everyone loved her. She was such a happy child. Soon I adopted her and life was great!

In June of 1962, R & B Drilling Co. asked my wife and me to go to Alaska for them. Eileen was to cook for a crew of thirty five men and I was to drill for them. We talked it over, and accepted the job. We spent three very happy years out on the Aleutian Chain, around Anchorage, and the Keni Peninsula, as well as Dutch Harbour. After three years we were transferred back to Canada.

About a year later, a beautiful baby girl made her debut in our home. This one being Rebecca Dawn, our second chosen daughter.

In 1965 Murry and I decided to sell the farm, so we had an auction sale and sold the farm equipment. We moved into Calgary, where I bought a hardware store. It didn't take long to realize I was no business man, so we sold the store, and tried my hand at real estate for a short time, only to find out this wasn't my cup of tea either. So, because we like to eat, I went back to the oil rigs.

It was about this time our first chosen son came into our home. Stephen Douglas was a joy beyond compare! and as the days went by, life was truly beautiful!

By this time my job had taken me into northern B.C. (Dawson Creek), where work was to last for two years for sure and maybe three. As it looked as though we were going to be there awhile, we bought a farm just out of Dawson Creek.

In 1966, our second chosen son came to live at our house. Timothy Allen! We felt truly blessed, two girls, and two boys! We spent eight good years on the farm where the children learned to love farm life. We have so many good memories. We were all very happy.

Archie Moore, was recruiting men for overseas, and he phoned to ask me if I was interested in a contract overseas (Archie used to work derrick for me, but now he was in the office). Once again we talked it over, and decided to take it. This time there were three more of us to think about. Anyway, on April 6, 1974 I started my first contract overseas. We chose South East Asia, Singapore! This move was very hard on my wife. Cultural shock, along with a bad case of homesickness, was very hard to adjust to, however, after six months, things were much better.

We lived in Singapore for two years, and life had never been like this before! Strangely enough, we did miss it after we left there. While we lived there, I worked in various exotic places such as Bruni Sri-Lanka, Indonesia.

The company I work for decided to move all the families to Malta, in the middle of the Mediterranean. From here I work in the Persian Gulf, offshore from Abu-Dhubi. I work twenty eight days in, and twenty eight days out.

Life does have its ups and downs over here on this side of the world, but we like it, and plan to stay a few more years. When we get enough of this craziness, we plan to return to a sleepy little town somewhere in Canada.

Tom and Joy Crowe   I-J

by Joy Crowe

The ad appeared in the Calgary Herald. It read,

"Married man to work on ranch southwest of Calgary. Small bungalow house available".

At the time, we were living on a rented acreage at DeWinton and commuting each day to work in Calgary. This was getting to be a hectic grind and we were ready for a change, so we looked into the job advertised. Two weeks later, in October of 1975, we moved to Priddis to work for "Crestview Ranch".

Our first home was the cozy little cottage located on the Friley section across the highway from Gordon Prichard. We really enjoyed that house and many of our visitors were awed by the marvelous view of the mountains from the west balcony. In November, 1976 we moved to the new house built on the old "Tom Day" place which had been bought by Crestview. Although we lost our mountain view, it certainly was nice to move into a new house and we are enjoying it just as much.

I was born and raised at DeWinton. Tom was born in High River and raised in Stavely. My dad, Johnnie Hamilton, and an older brother presently live on the farm at DeWinton and the rest of the family is divided between Calgary and Weyburn, Sask. Tom's folks live in Stavely, although a lot of time is spent in Cardston running the auction market there, which the family purchased in the fall of 1975. Tom's dad, Jim, auctioneers and his mom, Marguerite, does the books. One brother works in the yards and another trucks cattle, so it's a real family business. Another brother and two sisters work and go to school in Stavely.

My schooling years were taken in Okotoks and Tom's in Stavely and Claresholm. We both attended Olds College in 1971-72 and were married the year after we graduated, in May of 1973. We resided in Calgary until November of that year, when we moved out to DeWinton.

Rodeoing is our greatest interest. We both compete in the calf roping; Tom in the Foothills Cowboys' Association, while I belong to the Canadian Girls' Rodeo Association, on which I also hold a position on the Board of Directors. In the summer, week nights are spent exercising horses or practicing, while weekends find us on the road to a rodeo, which take us to Saskatchewan and B.C., as well as many in Alberta. Between rodeoing and holding down a part-time bookkeeping job in the city, I still find time to do some leatherwork. I learned this hobby in 4-H a few years ago and get a great amount of enjoyment and satisfaction out of it. This winter I got Tom interested in it too, and many winter nights are spent working on belts or wallets.

This winter we have taken up cross-country skiing. It's great fun and also a good way to stay in shape for roping in the spring. With all these interests and hobbies to occupy our time, we haven't yet given thought to starting a family. This spring we will both be a quarter of a century old, so still have plenty of time ahead.

Although we do not presently own any cattle, we do

hope to someday have a piece of land and some critters grazing on it with our brand, ⊔ on their ribs. This may be years in the future but it is something to work for and look forward to.

But for now, we are most happy living and working where we are. We have met a lot of fine people and made some great friends; the Howards, McBees, Cooks, Allens, Chalmers and the Harvie family (just to name a few), and hope to make many more. Our two years of living in this district have been good to us, and we are looking forward to however many more we may be here.

Frances Ada Jackson Croy

Born in a log cabin on the Jackson ranch on April 4, 1911 and rumor has it that there was that day a severe blizzard and our father was unable to secure the services of a mid-wife (Mrs. Ada Bennett, who lived on the Tom Phillips farm), until after he and our oldest sister Mary had delivered me.

I have very happy early childhood memories, running wild on the ranch, along with my older brothers and sisters.

Attended Fordville School starting about age seven. As a rule, we walked the mile and a half, but in the winter months we either rode horseback or went in the sleigh, drawn by a team of horses. Later, after my brothers George and John graduated, the Joe Standish children and also Bill and Bob Winthrop and I went to school together, usually on horseback.

In that era there was considerable open range, and in the summer months one project I very much enjoyed was taking salt out to the range cattle. If memory serves me right, Dad or one of my brothers would tie the rock salt to the saddle horn and I'd cut the cord when the horse and I got to the salt lick, as I could not lift the salt.

One of my closest friends was Mrs. L. C. Freeman, who was a regular visitor, walking over the hills to have tea with us. She always had a fear of horses, but it was necessary for someone to bring home the Freeman groceries, so every Wednesday, Ronald would harness up the team, hitch them to the democrat and point them in the direction of the Tom Phillips' where Mrs. Freeman would pick up Mrs. Phillips, known to us as "Auntie May", and Mrs. Phillips would drive to the Walton-Forward Store at Millarville.

In 1930 I had some heart problems, and the decision was made to have me leave the "high" altitude of our ranch and go to Vancouver to stay with my sister Isobel (Gorman).

After I recovered, I attended Harradine Commercial College in Vancouver, B.C. for two years; then University of California at Berkely; also Traffic Management at Merritt College in Oakland, California.

Spent over twenty years in the railroad industry, then fourteen years with Tigu Leasing, North America Car Corp., San Francisco, California, returning April 30, 1978 as Customer Service Manager.

Married Robert Rich in Vancouver, B.C. in 1932, and moved to California where Robert was subsequently killed in an accident. No children. Married Walter Croy in 1946 and lived in the San Francisco Bay area until 1974 when we moved to an apple orchard at Sebastopol, California, about 55 miles north of San Francisco.

My sister Mary has now retired from the nursing profession, lives with us, and sister Isobel (now Poykko), lives next door to us.

We often reminisce about our happy and carefree days in our beautiful Alberta foothills.

Dalton, Gloria and Al

Gloria and Al Dalton with daughters Celina and Kimberley, established residence in the Millarville area in 1977. In tradition of their pioneering forebears, a love for the countryside and natural setting led them to build a home high in the foothills surrounded by the breathtaking beauty of the Rocky Mountains.

Originally from Edmonton, the family lived in Eastern Canada for fifteen years. During this time they made their home in Windsor, Brampton, Toronto, Montreal and Winnipeg. Both sides of the family have their roots in the land, coming from ancestors who homesteaded in Saskatchewan and the Peace River country at the turn of the century. Original family lines stem from England, Normandy and the United States.

The Daltons have established permanent roots here because of their love of Alberta and its wonderful people.

James Frederick and Dorothy Davis
by Dorothy Davis ⊔ ⊐
SE¼ 34-21-4-W5

I am the youngest son of the late Fred and Lilian Davis. Born in 1915 on the home farm eight miles east of De Winton in the Davisburg district. My sister Lil and husband Ernie Irving live there now.

As a small child I had trouble with my lungs and have been fighting it ever since. I got my schooling at Davisburg school (a one room school which was heated by a pot bellied heater). I rode horseback with my brother Martin and later on when Lil was going to school we went in the buggy.

Dad had cattle and pigs as well as grain on the farm so could handle horses or tractor in the field. We all had chores to do feeding pigs, cattle, and milking cows. I have done a fair amount of riding, rounding up cattle, trailing cattle from Gladys Ridge, Blackie and Davisburg, to Calgary Stockyards. I helped neighbours when they needed help, worked for Sheep Creek Municipality with horses and slip. While at home I learned to skate and play hockey on the Highwood River. I also went to lots of house parties and Country

Dorothy and Jim Davis. May, 1978.

Club dances. I had my own car in my twenties (which was something in those days) so I had a way to take my girl friends out.

In the spring of 1941 I went to work for Clyde Lester of Keoma (this is where I met my wife Dorothy). I stayed until work was finished in the fall, then went back to my parents and worked at De Winton airport.

I was the youngest daughter of Brenda and the late Don Dingwall of Summerland, B.C. I was born in 1921 at Chancellor, starting school while there. In 1928 Dad decided to change from a farm to a store in N.W. Calgary. He didn't like it, six months later we were back on the farm again south east of Irricana. I got my education at Craighdu school (a one room school heated also by a big heater). All farm kids have chores to do, my brother was very small for his age and I was the husky one, this meant I had to pack grain and water to pigs and shovel a lot of grain. Ken and I stooked the crop together.

Jim and I were married in April 1942 and we rented some land east of Okotoks from Jim's brother so the crop was divided in three. A year later this land was sold, and we moved to another rented place north of Okotoks. Just before we moved in, Don was born. We weren't too sorry as the house was air conditioned (could see daylight up beside the stove pipe). Again the land was sold a year later. In April 1944 we moved N.E. of Strathmore staying there six years. During that time the rest of our family were added. Leslie, Reta, Gene and Brenda. We grew grain, milked a bunch of cows and raised chickens. Don and Les learned how to milk cows while here, they also started school. We were hailed out three times in six years.

Jim couldn't stand the grain dust, after looking around for some time, decided to buy in the Millarville area where just greenfeed is grown. On the day we looked at the place it had rained and there was no gravel from the mail boxes on. We got just past Mrs. Gouy's drive (where Ray Gessler lives) and couldn't go any further so we walked the rest of the way. Our feet were enormous by the time we got back to the car. I always said this country had the best mud. At the mail boxes, we met a man with the biggest cowboy hat I'd ever seen; it was Jake Reimer (it made me wonder what kind of people lived here). It turned out fine, Jake and Barbara became good friends and neighbours. We met another stranger on the road moving cattle. We stopped and asked him about the country. he said the grass was as high as your knees, so we decided to buy, We bought the S½ 34-21-4-W5 from Bruce McLean (who had Harold Marshall taking care of it). The west quarter was all bush, while the valley on the other quarter was cleared and seeded to hay. The N½ of 34 and SE¼ 24-21-4-W5 was lease which was included.

It was the first week in November 1950 when we moved to our new home. The last day of moving Jim and two boys were in the big truck packed with stove, beds, etc. I had the car with the other three kids. When we arrived the kids got out and ran all over, they had never seen trees or hills like that before. Jim and I unloaded then the kids started worrying 'What if Santa Claus couldn't find them out in this place?' after all Christmas wasn't far away. After telling them Santa knew where to find them I put the three to bed while Jim and the boys went back for the chickens and the dog. I had just got the kids to bed when Harold Marshall came by for the rest of his things. He was on his way to a dance at Square Butte (the first Friday of the month) he said that was a good way to meet people, for us to come to one of the dances. They took place once a month on the first Friday. So in December the Reimers and Davis family went in the bus. Meeting so many people in one night and knowing me, I had them "paired up" wrong.

We came here with great enthusiasm with horse drawn machinery, a tractor, a hammermill, 6 milk cows, 3 heifers, 1 bull and 3 calves. It's a good thing we were young and had high hopes and a young family to help because things were sure tough. There was a work horse on the place called Freddy. Jim helped John Gouy cut logs the first winter and Freddy skidded them out. With the money Jim made along with cream money (which brought from $10.00 to $11.00 a can) we managed to save enough to buy another horse from John Schaal. Now we had a team.

The first years we hayed with the Reimers and Gouy's. They helped us and we helped them in return. Jake, Barbara and Marie taught me a lot. As our family got older, we were able to hay by ourselves, but were grateful to all who helped us.

When we were still raking with horses, I was raking, Jim was sweeping the hay in; he had a sweep in front of the tractor. He'd hook onto the stacker and throw hay onto the stack where the boys were stacking it. A black cloud had come over and it started to thunder and lightning. Jim told me to quit, but there were only a couple of rounds left. One bolt of lightning hit close to the rake, away went the team. My first thought was to hang on and guide them towards the stack, if I can only make it, I did. Jim helped me off and one of the boys grabbed the team. I looked like a

238

Jim and Dorothy Davis with their family. L. to R., Front: Brenda, Leslie, Gene, Reta, with Davis nephew in front. Don, holding horse Flicka, niece on horse. 1958.

wet rag as the others took me to the car. To this day I hate thunder and lightning.

We had many problems trying to pay for the place. We were trying to get more range cattle by saving our heifers. Milk cows helped provide food and paid several bills. The whole family helped cut posts and rails (which we sold) cutting, trimming, and skidding. I was from the prairies where there were no trees, I had never seen a Swede saw before. The only time I used an axe was for chopping wood, which we did a lot of now, as it was the only way to heat the big log house. (I learned the hard way.) We cut logs several winters with John Gouy and Garnet Allen sawing them for us for a share.

In 1952 Bruce McLean gave the family a saddle horse (named Flicka). Now the kids had a horse to get the cows with, that is when they could catch her. It was a real chore to look for cows in the bushy west quarter, even worse when it was raining.

We always milked a lot of cows, sometimes up to 16 by hand, it was only the last few years that we got the milking machine working. In February 1976 we sold the milk cows, after milking cows for 34 years, sure missed them at first. The only part I didn't like, was having to work in the field all day then finding the cows and milking them after that. It always took me a little longer to get them as I walked, I was no rider, especially in the bush. The whole family were taught how to milk, also mow, rake, drive truck and tractor and service them.

Jim had to go out to work during the summers to help pay for our place. When the Power came in 1955 Jim helped Jake and several others put poles in (which paid $1.00 an hr.). Other jobs were working on highway — $1.30 per hr., building Okotoks school, helping Jack and Joe Waite and doing odd jobs for ranchers. Jim helped Ted Cloakey build an addition on his house in return we got pasture for our heifers.

By 1960, we had more range cattle and managed to pay for our place. It could never have been done without the help of the whole family. At this time we

bought different machinery and were able to do custom haying. While the boys were still at home they and Jim worked for Bill Kendall who logged our SW¼ (that quarter was sold in Dec. 1977). During the last six or eight years we've had some brushing done and after working up the land, seeded it to hay. When our family left home Jim and I carried on as best we could.

There were some bad spring snow storms since we moved here. One on 4th or 6th June 1951, we got over two feet of snow, it was sure hard on the cattle. It had rained so Jake left the bus at Charlie Birneys. That was one time the boys didn't go to school. Jake rode a horse to Birneys driving the bus from there, there were no phones to let him know if there was school or not. We were without power during some of the spring storms but we always made out.

In the spring of 1969 we borrowed money to buy a house in Calgary. This is the first time we ever had a bank account. Now we had to get ready so we could move the house out. Bill Kendall sent Johnny Eden to dig the basement, Ken Foster dug the water and sewer line, Fred Ball took care of backfilling after cement was poured. Brenda and Jim helped Jake with the plumbing and heating. Brenda wasn't well that summer, so she painted some of the rooms while Jim and I baled and hauled straw. In November we moved to the new house with all the luxuries of running water, propane furnace and stove. Imagine no more hauling water up that hill or wood to pack in. No more sawing and splitting wood for heat. To many people today it may not seem like much, but to those of us who have never had it, sure helped with the chores.

After moving from the old log house, I sat and thought about the tales it could tell if it could talk. I've been told at one time the upstairs had been used for school for some of the kids from the east end of the community. We ourselves had many a party there and who knows what else that house experienced before we moved in. One cold winter night, when we had a good fire going in the heater (the pipe went into same chimney as fireplace) Les was washing his feet beside the heater, when the chimney caught fire. Everyone got busy to get it out, some on the roof putting snow down the chimney, some packed water, and I put wet clothes on the wood on top of fireplace especially around the chimney. We finally got it out, but Les never finishing washing his feet (too scared I guess). One thing about the old log house it was always cool, no matter if it was winter or summer.

Today the family and some of their friends manage to come out on weekends to help with branding, haying etc. Branding is a great time for the whole family. Our brand is ⌐D RR (which was Jim's Dad's). I make sure I have enough food (wieners, beans, potato salad, pies, cakes). The kids have a great time catching calves and throwing them to the ground in victory. My job is vaccinating, although sometimes I get too handy with the syringe.

We've experienced all the problems of a growing

family such as dolls, toys, horses, boyfriends, girl friends, cars, trucks, speeding tickets and accidents, all a part of growing up. No matter what, the kids were always there when we needed them.

Fun times were at picnics and dances at the old hall where the whole family (no one thought of babysitters in those days) came to enjoy the food and music. Mr. and Mrs. Kosling, Mary Bell, and Cyrus McBee supplied the volunteer music, sometimes Elsie Ingeveld would play her piano accordion. Alex Lyall and Harold Marshall were floor managers. All the ladies in the community brought food and shared the job of preparing and serving the lunch and doing dishes. Aunty Lyall always made the coffee until she was no longer able. The younger ones had as much fun as the adults and when they got tired, they were put on a shelf to sleep. Some never did go to sleep (might miss something).

Another place we often visited was Priddis hall, where they also had a place for the younger ones to sleep. The Whitneys supplied the music and Jack Ollive was usually the floor manager. The Priddis and Old Square Butte hall echoed with music and laughter those nights.

Later on Jim and Jake spent a lot of time fixing up a new hall, when it was brought in. The whole community got together to run cement for the foundation. Barbara and I worked alongside the men, shovelling sand and gravel while our girls put water into the mixer. The young fellows helped on the wheel barrows. With the whole community helping, trying to provide a new place for social functions, it certainly didn't take long to get things done.

Due to Jim's poor health we are unable to attend as many of the get togethers as we would like, but do manage a few from time to time.

Donald and Margaret Davis

by Margaret Davis DJD

The eldest of five children, Don was born April 6, 1941, at the Holy Cross hospital in Calgary. His parents, Jim and Dorothy Davis, lived near Okotoks at the time. Brother Les was born a year later shortly after they moved to the Strathmore area. Later on Reta, Gene and Brenda came into the picture. Don was a very quiet child and reminiscences are made how he was the only grandchild allowed to sit beside his grandfather's sickbed. Although only two years old he would sit quietly for hours and occasionally they would shake hands. Even so, he could still get into a little mischief. Brother Les was afflicted with severe eczema and had to be cleansed with mineral oil rather than water. After one such "bath" Don decided Les needed some ashes in his hair. The adornment was not particularly appreciated by mother.

Don started his school years at Strathmore in 1949; in November, 1950, the Davis family moved to SW¼ 34-21-4-W5th, known as the Doc Lee place. Don rode

Don Davis Family. Dianna, Don, (holding Donna) and Margaret. Debbie in front.

Jake Reimer's bus all the years he attended Sheep Creek School.

There were several summers that Jim had to go out to work to support his family. Often he was gone for weeks at a time which meant the rest of the family had to pitch in and help with all the work. They all had to work hard; milking, haying, cleaning barns, etc. Even so, they were able to entertain themselves with the simplest of occurrences. One afternoon when milking should have been done, Dorothy found Les and Gene fighting with Don as a spectator. When she asked Don why he hadn't stopped the fight he said that they weren't hurting anything and that he was enjoying the spectacle.

At 16 Don quit school and went out to work. His employment started with Calgary Power, continued with the Department of Highways and then to farm labour. Some of the farmers he worked for were Earl Morrow, Rudy Mulder and George Park. For awhile he worked at Kendall's Sawmill. In June of 1964 he started work at Swift Canadian in Calgary and moved to Midnapore.

On October 10, 1964 we were married at Red Deer Lake United Church. My parents, Don and Dorothy McKay, moved to Midnapore from Turner Valley in 1955. I attended school in Midnapore until 1962, when I had to finish high school at Henry Wise Wood in Calgary.

After our marriage, we lived in Midnapore where our first daughter came into the world. Dianna was born May 30, 1965. In April, 1967 we moved to the Bert Ollive place at Priddis; and in September of the same year Don went to work at Calgary Feed Service. September 10, 1968 brought the arrival of our second daughter, Debbie. For several summers Don did custom haying in the Priddis area.

240

On April 1, 1973 we moved to Leslieville area just two miles from brother Les. On July 31, 1973 our third daughter Donna was born. Since our move to the Leslieville area Don has combined truck driving with farming with the hopes of sinking our roots permanently in the Leslieville area.

Leslie and Louise Davis
by Les Davis
LKD — SE¼ 34-21-4-W5

I was born in 1944 second son of Dorothy and Jim Davis. Mum and Dad lived north east of Strathmore then, I don't remember too much about Strathmore. Mum and Dad milked a lot of cows and Don and I learned how to milk before we were 5 years old and we also fetched the cows.

We both started school while we lived there. I do remember it was a flat country, seemed like the only trees were the ones that were planted around the buildings. I know they had some terrible blizzards while we were there.

We moved to Millarville SE¼ 34-21-4-W5 in Nov. 1950, there were lots of hills and trees to climb. There was always chores to do, as Dad always milked lots of cows. We all helped in the bush, cutting, trimming posts, rails, and logs. I couldn't help with the haying as much as I would have liked due to bronchial asthma, which I have had since a small child. I missed a lot of school because of this.

The road just went to Reimers at first and no gravel from the mailboxes in. Jake left the bus at Charlie Birneys lots of times, and we rode in his jeep the rest of the way, which was a rough ride and crowded as the Reimers were in there too. Jake only missed one day

Les and Louise Davis with their children Kenny and Treena.

that I remember, sometimes his was the only bus that showed up. One time Jake couldn't make the Birney hill so the kids with the biggest feet, my brother Don was one, made tracks ahead of the bus to the top of the hill. Jake was a good bus driver and riding the bus was a good experience. I was fond of all sports and took part in most of them.

We kids fought a lot when we were at home, but if anything happened to one, the other four were right there.

My first job was helping Mr. McCallister of Priddis during haying. I found it hard as the hay bothered my asthma, anyway I earned enough money to pay for my correspondence course in typing. I hunted squirrels in winter for extra money.

The following summer I worked part time on the old Van Wyk ranch. Mac Clarke was manager. I rode across country on horse back. I worked every summer to help put myself through school. We had to buy all our own books then. I worked for Calgary Power and A.G.T. I was determined to get my education and I took my grade 12 in Okotoks staying with my grandmother. When I still lived at home I worked for Walley Andrews and Bill Kendall. George Park of Priddis was the last one I worked out for that way.

Don and I stayed at one of the cabins at Midnapore. I worked for a few construction companies, also Swift Canadian. At one place I worked a pressurized tank blew up and hit me in the eye. Thanks to Diane (Winthrop) who was employed at the same place, and Mrs. Gamble for relaying the message about the accident to the folks, as at that time the telephone line ended at Gambles. I still have trouble with that eye.

I met Louise when Don was going with Margaret. Louise is the third daughter of Don and Dorothy McKay of Airdrie.

Louise said the first time I took her out to the farm, she thought it was a real hillbilly place. Dark old log house, no running water — just cans with water in the corner, no telephone, no fridge, and just a woodstove. Gene was sitting beside the stove with his cap on, the peak was pinned to the top with a safety pin. Reta and Brenda were at the table playing cards and arguing, their jeans had patches on the knees. Mum was at the cupboard in her patched jeans and shirt that was too big for her. I guess she didn't think too badly of us, as she married one of the hillbillies. Louise learned how to milk cows while going out there. She learned a lot about farm people with my help. Farm people don't always have money for lots of things and they do without, so they can pay their debts.

Louise and I got married in August, 1966. We lived on an acreage west of Midnapore. I rented some land and bought some second hand machinery. I had a few head of cattle, some I bought and some Dad gave me for money I lent him. We both worked while at Midnapore. Louise at Lacombe Home and the last place was at Currie Barracks where she met Major Spence the first time. I drove a truck for different firms the last was for Crone. I worked up north the first winter leaving Gene and Brenda to help Louise with the cattle. We decided that someday we were going to have a farm. I got a farm loan and bought land in the Leslieville district. While working at Crones I bought my first truck. The winter of 1970 we moved to Leslieville. I worked out quite a bit while there to help make payments. I soon had 2 trucks and was building a business up. Our daughter Treena was born in July, 1971. As the farm work bothers me, the doctor advised me to leave the farm because of my health. I got Don to come up and do the farming and I was trucking, but this didn't work out. Our son Kenny was born in 1974, and while on the farm Mum said Kenny rattled like I did when breathing.

I got the Imperial Oil Agency in December 1974 and moved to Vulcan, sold my farm later. I still have 4 trucks and Louise helps all the time with books etc. My health has improved since I left the farm.

I have had good times and bad times, one of my trucks called Country Bumpkin burnt up in Calgary. I have tried many things in my life, farming, working in Service Station, hauling cement, cattle trips all over the country, hauling mail from Calgary to Nelson, B.C.

I still like to go back to Millarville, walk through the trees and hills and look at the cattle.

Bill and Reta (Davis) Dubie

Our family lived at Strathmore, Alberta when I was born in 1946, (in Calgary at the Holy Cross Hospital). We moved to Millarville on November 1, 1950.

Winters were cold and we'd all huddle around the heater to keep warm while listening to radio. Our residence was a two-storey log house where five of "us" kids played, fought and grew up together. Mom must have had her hands full with three boys and two girls; especially when it came time for my sister, Brenda, and I to do the dishes. There was always a disagreement as to whose turn it was to wash. Oh, I hated those dishes, but most of all it was the roaster that presented problems. In one particular instance, the dishes were finally done and I decided to sit down for a rest after the long, tiring ordeal. Brenda was up to her usual tricks, and just as I was to plunk myself down, she pulled the chair out from under me. Consequently, I landed with a thud on the floor while Brenda said with a laugh, "Geez, you almost put a hole in the floor!" I don't know if it was the embarassment or what, but I was mad to the point of tears.

During haying time, we all had to put in our share of work as well as other chores. One particular day when I was out haying with Dad (on Michael Rodgers' old place), I was half way up the hill when the tractor stopped. Dad came over to see why I had stopped and found out that it had run out of gas. We couldn't finish the work without gas (tractors don't run too good without it), so off Dad went while I stood on the brake and held the clutch, hoping to stay in that exact spot until he got back. Shortly, he brought back some gas

Bill and Reta Dubie and family, Terry, Sandy and Eddy.

and we completed the job. During another haying job, Dad had the misfortune of running over our dog, Laddy, with the mower, cutting the dog's legs off, as he ran out in front. I took the dog to Mrs. Gamble's, but unfortunately he couldn't be saved. After leaving home, I'd often go out to the farm on weekends and on holidays to lend a hand with the haying.

We all did our share of the farm work including milking cows, feeding chickens and gathering the eggs. Late in the evenings, once a week, one would go out to check the lease cows, either by walking or by horse, while the others shared the rest of the duties. First thing in the morning, the boys would milk the cows while the girls made breakfast before heading off to school. After school the job of hauling wood and coal had to be done, so all was ready for the next day. When Don and Leslie left home, Brenda and I took turns milking.

Education facilities were at Sheep Creek School (now Millarville School) up to Grade 9. One instance that stands out in my mind was in Grade 6 or 7 when Larry Bull set up a boxing match (he was the champion), but found out that nobody wanted to tackle with him. So, rather than let the match go to waste, I decided to take on the job of his challenger. However, I ended up with a black eye and a bleeding nose. I guess you could say that he won? Besides taking part in boxing, my favourite sport was baseball where I played catcher and field and thoroughly enjoyed it. One time when we played ball at school, I was on first base. Brenda had just hit a beautiful home run. I had never played that position before and so had problems figuring out which side of the base to stand on. I tried hard to stay out of the way, but didn't do so well and Brenda went flying. One base on a home run hit. Hooray for our side! During the winter we would go skating out on the slough until we got cold and one day Mr. Dube let "us" girls play hockey. What a game! One thing I did learn was to duck hockey sticks after a few bruises.

One of the special people in all the kids' lives was Jake Reimer, the school bus driver. He was always nice to everyone and on holidays or special occasions, he would treat each kid to a pop and a chocolate bar. Many times he would stop and let us pick up his and our mail. I was the bus monitor with the responsibility of keeping everyone in line (or at least try to). The older boys were usually no big problem as they always played cards at the back of the bus while my sister, Brenda held all the books and sometimes the cards.

During the time that we were cutting posts and rails, we were going through the bush and I used to ride in the bucket of the tractor. The lever got caught in the trees and flipped the bucket, giving me a wild ride right into the bushes. Obviously, I didn't have any future plans of riding in the bucket again. In the lumber mill business, there were two people at the mill . . . one to unhook the horse and one to roll the log into the pile. In one particular instance when my brother, Gene, was riding "Twilight", the horse ran half way down the hill, hit a stump and broke the harness. Gene didn't even notice the log gone and kept right on going. Sure wasn't too profitable a haul!

The boys were always coming up with bright ideas and one day they decided to play pretend branding. And guess who was the animal to get branded??! They took the poker from the stove and planted it right on my rearend. I let out a yelp, but they couldn't figure out why, as they were sure that it wasn't **that** hot. As a result, I ended up with blisters and believe me . . . they weren't pretend either! The branding of cattle takes place once a year. My brother, Gene, gets the calves out and we all take turns at holding them. One year, when the branding was finished on the calves, we were going to try out a brand on my husband, Bill, but somehow he really wasn't too interested. Wonder why?!

On completion of Grade 9, I went to Okotoks for 2 years where I helped take care of a farm for some people on holidays, and cared for Jenkins' mother, for five to six months. In 1966, I went to Calgary where I worked at the Father Lacombe Nursing Home for 3 to 4 months and then moved on to Parkdale Heating for three years. At that time I lived at the Wheel Inn Motel in Midnapore. It was also then that I borrowed Gene's car which was full of gas when I left, but somehow arrived back without any gas. The guage read 'E' anyway.

For ten years I worked for various Mohawk Oil places and that is where I met my husband Bill Dubie, who at the time was a trucker. After we got married, we moved to Langley, B.C. (in NOVEMBER 1977) and started our own business called "Cherokee Transport". Two months later, we moved to Camrose, Alberta . . . where we are presently residing with our three children: Terrence James, Sandy Marie and Edward William.

At the present time (1978) I am taking a veterinarian course and will carry on with it. Upon completion I will be a vet's helper. To help me along, I have two horses to look after for practice.

Gene and Shirley Davis
by Gene Davis
SE¼ 34-21-4-W5

I was born at the Holy Cross Hospital in Calgary. I lived on a farm at Strathmore for three years then moved to Millarville, November, 1950. We lived in a two storey log house (that still stands today). I slept upstairs with my brothers. In the winter the house was so cold that when you woke up in the morning to wash you would have to break through the ice in the pails. We had to haul our water from the spring house in milk cans either by tractor or in the truck.

Everyone had chores; I started when I was five. I had to chop fire wood, milk cows and help with the haying. When doing the haying I used an old horse rake, and we fenced the stacks in the hayfield. Wood splitting was done for half an hour every night after school. I would usually have enough wood split and stacked to go half way up the house. I had to get up every morning at five thirty, milk cows, have breakfast and be ready to board the school bus at seven thirty.

At age eleven I had my first job with John Gouy helping cut and skin posts. I worked so hard one day I fell asleep on the post pile, John didn't seem to mind, he came by and asked if I had a good sleep.

Dad worked on the highway and it was our job to find the milk cows on the hill. If we couldn't find them we had to stay out till we did because the cows had to be milked. Once while looking for range cattle in the lease we got caught in a real downpour of rain. Mom and I had gone east and the others went west. We got lost and kept going in circles until the rain stopped. We were a little scared and wet but found our way home later.

Gene and Shirley Davis with their children, Jamie and Tammy.

243

In grade nine the principal would send me down to flood the skating rink while he took notes for me. That sure was nice getting out of some school work. Grade 10 was started in Black Diamond. I played football and tried to participate in most other sports.

During the days there wasn't much to do on the farm we would make our own toys. They were made from wood, tin cans, nails and old spark plugs. After they were put together we would have tractors, balers and rakes. We also built our own log cabin in the trees; we had a wooden floor in it and lined all the walls with cardboard. The little wooden house is still there but a tree has fallen over it. On one of my lazy days I took Les's bow and arrow and was pretending to be fishing on top of the hammermill. The bow fell in the hammermill and I went in after it and couldn't get back out. After much yelling my brothers and sisters helped me out. Mom still doesn't know how I got in or out of there today. I would also go squirrel hunting (during my teens) and sell the skins for extra money. Top price for a skin was fifty cents.

At age eighteen I left home to work for Swift Canadian for four and a half years. I then worked for Burnco for two years. In the spring of 1973 I started work for Atomic Interprovincial Transport Ltd. driving a truck. In 1976 I was made warehouse foreman which is my present position.

While still working at Swift Canadian I met my wife Shirley (Racz) and were married on October 17, 1969. On December 7th, 1971, we had our first child, a boy, James Paul and on December 23, 1975 he had a sister Tammy Kay. We are presently living in Calgary in Mayland Heights. Some of our spare time is spent at the farm in Millarville where the rest of the family gets together quite regularly. We enjoy the farm very much.

Brenda (Davis) Smyth
SE ¼-34-21-4-W5

In 1950, when I was a year and a half, our family moved from Strathmore to our home place at Millarville, Alberta . . . described as S½-34-21-4-W5. We lived in an old, log house where winters were so cold that water would freeze in water pails and cans . . . and that was in the house!

A farm always has lots of chores and we all had our share to do, with time to play after the work was done. I learned to milk cows at the ripe old age of four by practicing on an old cow named Beauty. After the milking, we'd separate the cream and milk, feeding the calves with the skim milk. Our next job was putting up the hay, and we had to work extra hard when Dad got a job working on the highway. The work eased some in 1959 when we got our first baler, with me riding the rack; the youngest of the "clan". The days were busy, but Dad always found the time to play with "us" kids when all the work was done.

School days started at Millarville and continued to Grade 9. From there, we were bussed to Black Dia-

Brenda (Davis) Smyth, July, 1978.

mond for the remaining years. During this time we did all our studying by lamp-light. In Grade 8, a fight developed between Randy McLaws and me, which the principal took advantage of . . . he made us clean the library out and we were told to fight out behind the skating rink where he couldn't see us. From then until Grade 10, I was "Miss Goodie Two-Shoes", at which time I took Bookkeeping and learned the art of signing into class and then skipping out to go downtown for a half an hour or so and then come back to complete ten minutes of work. By some miracle, I passed!

As with any school, there's lots of activities and I took part in all kinds of sports. Playing football with the boys was a riot, but the principal soon put a halt to that. Darn it! Never could figure out why. At school picnics, I managed to strike-out two ladies who had never seen such a "mean" left-handed pitcher. Later on, in 1970-71, I played ball for an Okotoks team and for A-1 Auto Body in Calgary.

In 1957, John Gouy, who lived in the community, discussed going into the lumber business. He and Dad undertook the job of a lumber mill business for a year and a half. We did all our logging by horse. John had a horse that my brother, Gene, would always ride, but it went through more harnesses than all the other horses put together, because it would never walk. Some days, Dad would have to make up two sets in one day. All was done by horse . . . we cut all our own posts and rails, too.

Our methods of playing were a lot different than kids nowadays. We built our little stackers and sweeps, and during our spare time, our imaginations helped us to build fantastic works of art. Take for instance our tractor . . . made out of a block of wood. It had everyting you would expect a tractor to have . . . like wheels on the outside, a spark plug and six-inch spikes for a gear shift. What a prize! Then, there was our baler made out of a sleigh with a piece of tin down the center. It was a real time saver! We'd tie the hay manually and shove it through the attached pipe and out came the bales. Our fence posts were another thing . . . treated in rusty water, with string to hold them together. Along with these mentioned forms of construction, we were also able to put together a log cabin in the trees.

An independent me left home at the age of sixteen, leaving the farm life behind (and my first boyfriend, Alan Orum, whom I met at fourteen). In order to earn some sort of living, I took a job babysitting, cooking and housecleaning for Bill and Bernice Dinter. I saved every cent I earned and was able to put myself through hairdressing school. My brother, Leslie, provided me with a place to stay, while my other two brothers, Gene and Donald, provided the transportation to and from school. Working hard, I soon was "labelled" a hairdresser.

Hairdressing kept me busy, but in 1973, a change took place in my life when I married Robert A. Smyth. Like all newlyweds, we needed a place of residence and took up one in the Amy Lorne Trailer Court. Three years later, in 1976, we formed "Double 'B' Transport", a trucking business. My jobs were now two . . . my hairdressing and bookkeeper of our business. All was going well until Bob got very sick. He passed away on January 25, 1977 of cancer.

It's a funny thing how a person keeps on when losing a loved one, but they do. I picked myself up and took over the business with my brother, Don, doing the driving. Faithfully, he took care of the truck for five months while I recovered from back surgery. As soon as I could get around, I went back to hairdressing, but sold the truck in January 1978.

My life is full and although I was always taught to be seen but not heard, things are sure different now. Everybody who knows me from back home say I have a new image, talking a mile a minute. They ask me if I like the new me and here's my reply "Why Shore!" During the summer I enjoy riding my horse and in the winter my free time is taken up on my ski-doo, to which I was introduced by Duane Durieux. He gave me my first ride. This past winter (1978), the story of the "Runaway Ski-doo" took place. I had been out ski-dooing and decided to go in the house for a quick coffee. After that, I figured that I should go out and put my machine and father's away, so I started up Dad's and warmed it up by tearing around the house a couple of times. I left his running and started mine, but the throttle got stuck, and from the house to the bridge, which is about 100 yards, I was doing 50 m.p.h. By that time, I realized that I couldn't handle it at that speed, and turned the key off. While checking it over, I could see my father at the door yelling that the choke was stuck. I yelled back, "No, eh!" I played around with the throttle and being left handed, I had to stand on the ground when I went to start it. All of a sudden, it took

off and I jumped on as it was going by. A short distance later, it tipped over and threw me off, but I wasn't going to let that "critter" get away, so I hung on, dragging behind for six or eight feet . . . all the while trying to shut the key off. It did get away, and I watched as it went through the neighbor's fence after crossing the ditch. Half way up the hill, it turned and came down, back through the fence, tearing the hood apart and the ignition switch as it hit the barb-wire. Dad was concerned and ran out to see what had happened. It was just like the western days . . . with the horse waiting and watching at the rails for the hero to come and save a lady in distress. You could see that I wasn't going to be defeated as I rode the "tamed bronco", with Dad towing it home with the tractor.

My hairdressing continues at Salon Jamal and I welcome all my fiends to "try us out".

Davidson, Eleanor M. (Nylund)

On the 15th day of July in the year of 1941 in the city of Calgary, Alberta a daughter was born to Hjalmar and Peggy (Agnes M.) Nylund. The new arrival being a sister for Margaret, George and John. Given the name Eleanor May by her grandfather George Lyall and her uncle, R. J. Lyall. Raised and schooled in the Square Butte and Millarville areas.

I went to work in The Royal Bank of Canada, Turner Valley, Alberta branch in September 1958. I married Howard M. Davidson of Black Diamond, Alberta in May 1961. We lived in Turner Valley and Black Diamond until May 1964 when we moved to Calgary, where we still reside. We have two daughters, Shelley Lynn and Shirley Ann. Shelley is sixteen and in grade eleven at Bowness High School. Shirley is seven and in grade two at Montgomery Elementary School.

While working for Canadair Flextrac Howard went on several field trips between 1969 and 1976 fixing tracked vehicles. He travelled to points in Alberta, British Columbia, Newfoundland, The Northwest Territories and the Yukon, to several states in the United States of America and also to the jungles of Peru, South America. He is presently employed by Conmac.

L. to R. Back row, Shelley Lynn, Eleanor (Nylund) Davidson, Howard Davidson. Front, Shirley Ann.

The Dawson Family

by Norma Dawson

The Dawson family moved to Millarville, from Ottawa, in the Summer of 1976. There were four of us then, Rick, Norma (Ping), Angela and Jeff. Krista happened along in December of that year — the only one of us to be born in the West. We settled on twenty acres (NW 20-20-3-W5M) and began our new life in the Foothills.

In August of 1975 we came to Calgary for our summer vacation. Naturally we fell in love with the area, especially the majestic Rockies, and when we returned to the East, Rick began talking about opening an office out here. The following Spring our wish came true and in June, Rick was named Branch Manager for Calgary for A.E.S. Data Limited.

Our moving-in day wasn't until July so we stayed with Rick's brother in Red Deer Lake for a few weeks. At that time I thought Red Deer Lake was country — until Rick brought us out to Millarville to see the acreage he had bought for us. As we travelled along Highway 22 I thought, "When are we ever going to get to this place called Millarville"? Finally we saw a sign which read Millarville — 1 mile, but we bypassed that and had to travel six miles along a dirt road before we eventually reached our new home. Needless to say I was a little discouraged — it seemed as though we had travelled a hundred miles! After living here though, and having visited communities around Calgary, I know we have settled in the best area.

In 1977 we tried our hand at being the small-time Farmer. We acquired a very old horse named 'Plug' who was given to us, and we all went out and bought cowboy boots. We also bought some baby ducks, chickens, turkeys and two pigs. They were all so cute and we thought it was great because we could finally say that we had "chores to do". Then the summer was over and it was time to take the pigs to market and kill the fowl to fill up the freezer. The latter took a little getting used-to, but we always celebrated with a party after, which helped to get through the dirty work.

You would think after moving from a 60' x 100' lot in Ottawa to our twenty acres in the Foothills we would be happy — but we got greedy and decided we needed more land. We didn't want to leave the Millarville area and after looking for a few months we bought forty-seven acres in the Square Butte area (SW 13-21-4-W5M).

This is where we built and are still in the process of finishing our log home. Although Byron Palmer and Bruce Wright did the actual log building, Rick (and anyone he could con into it) peeled all the logs by hand.

This year we plan to keep busy finishing the house and finally getting Dawson Tree Farms started.

Debnam, Bruce and Loraine

I was born May 1947 and raised in Calgary the eldest of seven children. My wife Loraine (nee Hayward, b. Feb., 1948) was brought up in the Red Deer Lake area. I met her while she was attending University at the Calgary campus. We were married in June 1969 at Red Deer Lake and moved to the quarter section owned by her parents just north of Millarville. Although welding is my livelihood I have always been interested in horses. Loraine and I have belonged to the Ridge Riders club for many years and I have team roped for the last three years. Our

Rick, Ping, Angela, Krista, Jeff Dawson.

Holly Debnam.

246

daughter now rides a mare that was given to me when I was seven years old. I took great interest in this side of the outfitting business in the Northwest Territories owned by my father-in-law, Chuck Hayward. Coaching Minor League Hockey has been another activity I have been involved in for many years.

In September 1971 our mobile home was totally destroyed by fire, but with the help of our generous families and friends we were soon able to begin again with another mobile home in the same spot.

Our daughter, Holly, was born on August 13, 1974 and two years later we sold our home to Loraine's brother Ed and his wife Pam. In partnership with Ken and Judy Foster we purchased 100 acres (NW 31-20-3-W5) formerly owned by F. Sharp. The construction of our home on this property was truly a community affair with time, labour and interest given by many and we are very proud of it.

Allan and Tillie Deines

Allan Deines was born in Calgary. He spent some of his early years on a ranch near Millarville starting school at Fordville and then finishing his education in Calgary. In 1945 he went to work in the oil fields at Turner Valley being employed by Commonwealth Drilling and later by Drilling Contractors. In 1951 he left the oil fields and went into construction with his brother in Calgary.

Matilda (Tillie) Deines (nee Grudecki) was born in Empress, Alberta, and spent her childhood on her parent's farm near Acadia Valley, Alberta. She received her elementary and secondary education at Acadia Valley and graduated from high school at St. Theresa College in Medicine Hat.

After attending Normal School in Calgary she taught for two years in a rural school near Three Hills from 1942 to 1944. From there she went to the Calgary School Division and taught at Fordville for one year. In 1945 she was offered a position at Sheep Creek School teaching Grades 4, 5, and 6, which at that time was situated two miles west of Millarville. It was while she was here that she met her future husband, Allan Deines. They were married in Calgary in 1948. She continued teaching at Millarville until 1954.

In 1955 they moved to their farm five miles north of High River (NE¼ 36 19 29 W4) which they had purchased in 1950 where they still reside. In 1961 Tillie went back to teach at Blackie and in 1962 to High River where she still teaches at Spitzee Elementary. Allan and Tillie have three children, Marilyn who is working with Amoco Petroleum in Calgary, Gerald working with Deines Arctic Services, and Barry who plans to take an engineering course.

Matilda Deines (nee Grudecki), Teacher — Fordville

I was born in Empress, Alberta and spent my childhood on my parents' farm near Acadia Valley. I received my elementary and secondary education at Acadia Valley and graduated from high school at St. Theresa College in Medicine Hat.

After attending Normal School in Calgary, I taught for two years in a rural school near Three Hills. From there, I went to Fordville for one year, 1944. In 1945, I went to Millarville School until 1954.

Conrad and Mollie Deines
written by Allan Deines

Conrad and Mollie Deines emigrated from Germany to Calgary in the early nineteen hundreds. They made their home in Calgary where he worked for the Calgary Brewery. They had a family of ten children, Emil, Ronald, William, Alma, Alfred, Lea, Dorothy, Allan, Walter, and Mollie.

In 1932 they purchased the former Knights property (NE ¼ 24 21 3 W5) about five miles north-east of Millarville. After selling the Knights place they bought a farm three miles north-west of Lee's Store (NE ¼ 15 21 3 W5) disposing of it in 1949. He continued working for the Calgary Brewery until his retirement.

Henri A. de Roaldes
by Joan de Roaldes

Henri de Roaldes was born in the South of France, on March 9th 1900. A few years later his parents separated and he lived with his paternal grandmother at the Chateau d'Arifat at La Salvatat, until the age of

Henri de Roaldes, bugle boy, 1st W.W. 1915.

Joan and Henri de Roaldes at their Calgary home, 1976.

nine, when he joined his father, Count Georges de Roaldes at Millarville, Alberta, where he was homesteading on the N.E. ¼ of 22-21-4W5.

At the age of fifteen he went overseas with his father as a Trumpeter in World War 1. He and his father served throughout the war and on return to Canada took up land at Bowden, Alberta.

He married Agnes Ransom of Nanton, on September 3rd, 1924, and there were five children. His first wife passed away on January 25th, 1934, and when the 2nd World War broke out, he placed his children in the Wood's Christian Home at Bowness, and went overseas with the Canadian Army Service Corps, serving in England and on the Continent.

At wars end he returned to Canada to reside in Calgary, where he worked for the Soldiers' Settlement Board, later going into Real Estate. He also served in the Canadian Militia for 12 years. In 1954, he married Joan Tregillus of Calgary.

On September 26th, 1968, his father passed away in Santa Barbara, California at the age of 94.

In 1973, Henri and his wife took a trip to England and France, where Henri had a brother and sister residing in Paris. They took a motor trip through Southern France, where they visited his old home and met other relatives. He also visited the Beaches of Normandy, where he landed during the war.

In 1976, he suffered a stroke and passed away on October 10th, 1977.

Robert Jordon Dick
by Billie Russell

Born in Edinburgh, in the late 1880's one of a family of five children. With his brother George he immigrated to Canada. In 1906, having established themselves at Pincher Station, they sent for their parents George and Mary Dick and sisters Jean and Mary.

In 1914, when war was declared, he joined the army and served overseas. After the Armistice, he and his English war bride Hettie, settled on a half section on Ware Creek, the home quarter N.W. ¼ 22-20-4W5. They milked cows, cream fetching a good price in those days.

Mr. George Dick, Bob's father, purchased the Taylor place on Quirk Creek in 1920 (his neighbor was J. F. Dole (Kendall Ranch). He made his home with the Bob Dick's until 1923 and later with his daughter Jean Russell. During this time Bob Dick served as Bailiff of Calgary and in 1923 they moved there.

In 1924 Bob Dick entered into partnership with his brother-in-law Alexander (Sandy) Russell. Lee and Jenny Constable purchased the ranch in 1941, selling out to Maud and Frank Sharp in 1945. Mr. Lorenzo Belanger and wife Alice took over in 1956. Mike Rodgers and his bride Ella May made their first home on the home quarter in 1963 later selling to the Imperial Oil Company in the late 1960's. The Imperial Oil Company maintain the home place as a company picnic and barbecue site.

Bob Dick died in Vancouver in 1948, he and his wife Hettie had no children.

Kay and Bob Dixon and Family
by Kay Dixon

The Dixon family (Kay, Bob, Suzanne, Sydney and Bradley) purchased the house and property from Jack Bernhardt located on the NW 14-21-4-W5M in November 1977.

R. K. (Bob) Dixon, son of Wm. J. and Ethel Dixon (nee Fisher), was born in Calgary where he attended public and high school after which he attended the University of Oklahoma and graduated as a petroleum engineer.

Kathleen (Kay) Dixon, daughter of Wm. W. and Winnifred Myers (nee Symonds), was born in Lethbridge where she attended public and high school and subsequently graduated as a registered nurse from the Royal Alexander Hospital in Edmonton.

Kay and Bob Dixon.

The Dixons were married on September 20, 1952 and began their world travels in the oil and gas business. Their Canadian residences included New Sarepta, Drumheller, Calgary, Wetaskiwin, Gordondale and Spirit River in Alberta, and Regina, Swift Current, Weyburn and Forget in Saskatchewan. The Dixons also lived for a number of years in Angola on the west coast of Africa where the Dixon children attended school in Luanda and Johannesburg.

The Dixons returned to Canada and Calgary in 1970 and have lived there ever since.

Suzanne, the Dixon's eldest daughter graduated from the University of Calgary in 1978, majoring in languages. Sue was married to Mr. Michal Rassmussen, very recently and is now living in Fort Macleod.

Sydney Kathleen, the Dixon's number two daughter is presently attending university in Windsor, Ontario, where she is majoring in Interior Design.

Bradley, the youngest of the Dixon children, was born in Wetaskiwin, Alberta. Brad must have established a record for the number of schools that he has attended during our travels and he has recently graduated from Henry Wisewood High School in Calgary. He is now working in Calgary.

Bob is employed as the President of Merland Explorations Limited in Calgary and still is obliged to do a great deal of travelling.

Kay is employed full time in trying to keep the Dixon household together as well as being the manager of a few small family businesses.

The Dixons hope that their long-term moving and travelling is now over and they can spend more time at their home in the Millarville area.

Fern (Jackson) Dorsch

Fern Elizabeth Dorsch daughter of William and Esther Jackson Jr. Born in Calgary and spent childhood and teen years on the ranch at Millarville. Attended Sheep Creek School and Olds Agricultural College. After graduating from Olds moved to Calgary to work for Crown Trust Company and obtain business course by night at the Calgary Business College.

Married Walter Dorsch in 1953, moved to Edmonton in 1955. Worked for Canadian Fire Insurance Company, Western Propeller, and Snap-On Tools until daughter Terrill Lee came along in 1959. Two years later Lane Walter appeared on the scene. Moved to Denver Colorado in 1962 and from there back to Calgary in 1964.

Appointed social convener for Southern Alberta Pioneers as well as secretary for the Calgary Co-op Guild. Served four years on the Public Relations Committee for the Calgary Co-op.

Started back to work full time in 1970 with the Alberta-National Drug Co. where I am still employed in the Store Modernization department.

I am still very involved with the Southern Alberta Pioneers Association as well as been active in the

Fern (Jackson) Dorsch with her horse Sally.

Calgary Singles Club and the Parents without Partners Club. My interests are golf, dancing and all forms of art.

I still have a soft spot in my heart for Millarville and the many good times had at the old Ranchers Hall. Also the times my brother Murray would gather all the

Fern (Jackson) Dorsch with her children, Lane, (left) and Terrill. 1964.

kids around in our old chev truck and head for a Friday night dance not caring how far we had to go or what the weather was like.

One incident I'm sure my mother still remembers is the time the four Jackson kids went up to the Ranchers hall after a dance and gathered up all the chewing gum from under the benches and proudly came home chewing a wad as large as our mouths could hold.

Douglass, Dorian Wingfield (Jappy)

B2P CD ―∧⋝

Born at Bassano, Alberta, November 20th, 1915, son of the late Leslie Douglass and Elsie Douglass, who now lives in Calgary. I married Martha McQuillin on February 18, 1944, in Calgary.

I started school at Millarville because there was no school at Gem. I lived with my grandparents, Mr. and Mrs. Malcolm Millar. Dick King would come and pick up Gordon and I when we started at Fordville. Rode horseback when old enough, to Sheep Creek and New Valley schools. I was in the first class at Sheep Creek School fifty years ago in 1928.

One outstanding event was when my horse ran out of control. Peggy Waugh was coming in the opposite direction on her horse and I ran into her and knocked both of us and our horses down.

I would come home during the holidays in summer and help with the haying.

Jappy and Martha Douglass and family, June — 1978.

I joined the Air Force in 1942, stationed in Calgary and Eastern Ontario, as an Airplane Mechanic. I received my discharge in 1945.

I bought the store at Millarville from N.W. Pegler in 1944, and was there about ten years. On leaving there I bought the ranch at Finnigan, on the Red Deer River, from my father. I am still enjoying this good life. I have since bought a ranch across the river north of Dorothy, about twelve sections. My son Ken lives there. The other two older boys, John and Neil, have their own places south of me. They look after the home place. as well. I bought a house in Bassano so the children could go to school as it is much too far from the ranch.

My oldest girl, Joan, married Ronn Christianson and lives ten miles from us. My youngest two boys and two girls are still living at home. I am very proud of my children. My only regret is that I should of had another eight. They are so comforting to have. I don't imagine my wife would have appreciated that.

Eight children, (1) Joan Margaret, married Ronn Christianson of Gem. (2) Kenneth Leslie, married Donna Milne of Gem. (3) John Gordon. married Sharleen Lund of Duchess, (4) Neil Malcolm (5) Barbara Helen (6) Sheila Dorothy. (7) Russel Dorian. (8) Stuart Eric.

Downey, Bill and Sheila

Sheila came to the Millarville district from Longview and originally Rosland with her parents, Everett and Tillie Potter and 3 brothers Harvey, Jim, and Larry. They rented land about 2 miles west of Millarville from Seth Peat, along with numerous other families who mostly worked in the oil fields. She took her schooling at the Sheep Creek School until grade 11, and then went to the Turner Valley High School.

Bill came from the North Turner Valley district, where he moved with his parents from Hartell and originally Killam. They were married in 1956 and lived in several different places until 1962 when they moved on Bill's folks place. In 1974 they bought a farm at Bluffton where they now live.

They had 5 children, 3 boys and 2 girls. The boys were all in Cubs, Scouts and Cadets. Daniel, who took all his schooling at Turner Valley and the Oil Fields High School, was fatally injured in 1976 in an industrial accident. Bill Jr. who took his schooling in Turner Valley, Oil Fields High and also Rimbey High. He now lives in Black Diamond where he drives truck and also works the rigs. Monty went to school at Turner Valley, Bluffton, and Rimbey High. He lives at Bluffton and also works on the rigs and drives truck. The girls are both at home, Randina went to school in Turner Valley and is now at Bluffton, Lorraine went to kindergarden at Turner Valley and is taking her schooling at Bluffton.

R. Lloyd and Elaine Drake

by Elaine Drake

We were both born in Alberta and grew up in the Crowsnest Pass, except for three years when Lloyd's family moved to Calgary and he attended High School there.

We were married in 1949 and lived in Blairmore where our three sons Randy, Loren and Daren were born in 1950, 1955 and 1960 respectively. In 1965 we moved to Calgary and in 1968 we had another son — Michael the only one still at home.

By 1974 we had decided to leave the city and bought 40 acres in the Davisburg area and built our home. We enjoyed life in the country, especially gardening. When we sold the property in 1976 it was with the intention of building another home on another acreage. Unable to find a piece of land that appealed to us we rented an acreage on Gladys Ridge for four months and then bought a home in Okotoks.

It took us eight months, but we found what we wanted in the Millarville area — 40 acres (E ptn. SW ¼ 23-21-4-W5M) with trees and a creek near the mountains.

We started to build in September of 1978 and moved into our new home in March 1979. We enjoy the peace and quiet and beauty of the countryside and appreciate the friendliness of the neighbors.

Bill Dube (Sr.) and Family

Bill Dube and his family arrived in Millarville district in Sept. 1954 where Bill took over principalship of Sheep Creek School and taught grades 9, 10, and 11 in one room. He was born in Glaslyn, Saskatchewan, and his wife, the former Leatha Phillips, came from Kansas City, Missouri.

Bill, along with his two brothers, served in the Canadian Active Services. He received University degrees at the University of Saskatchewan. After teaching a few years in Saskatchewan he came to Alberta. His son Bill jr. was born in Saskatoon and Doug was born in High River, Alberta.

Challenges at Sheep Creek included getting an extra classroom and teacher, building a strong sports program and getting young people involved in extra activities (cadets) and also having students show good progress in school.

With the excellent co-operation and backing of local people and local organizations the school raised about $800 to purchase the school's own film projector and sound system.

Many young people became interested in Cadets and in February, 1961, there was a high of 71 cadets enrolled at Sheep Creek. Bill went to several cadet training camps including two at Banff as Company Commander. Twice he was elected Pres. of the Alberta and N.W. Territories branch of the Cadet Services of Canada.

In 1965, Bill taught at Black Diamond and in 1972 he took over the principalship of Turner Valley Public School. He has held a variety of positions in the Foothills Teachers' Association, including President and has been President of the Foothills Principals' Association.

In 1965, the Dubes purchased a quarter section of land west of Millarville, formerly owned by Norman Thomson, and built a home there. Here Leatha has turned a bare hill top into a beautiful spot. Wherever the Dubes have lived her "green thumb" has left a bit of beauty. The trees around the teacherage at the Millarville school were planted and cared for by her.

Bill Dube jr. is presently teaching at High River and Doug is at the University of Calgary.

In 1978, the Foothills Lions Club presented Bill sr. with the "Citizen of the Year" award.

A challenging chore at Sheep Creek School was to keep the ice rink going in spite of the Chinooks. Many nights Bill flooded the ice until 2 and 3 A.M. One cold night he became so engrossed in his work and the beauty of the cold clear night, discovered when he was leaving the rink his boots were frozen in the ice.

Skating and hockey were greatly stressed. Senior boys played hockey prior to school time, middle grades played hockey at recess (with extended time) and the lower grades for the first half hour at noon and then there was skating to music for all for the next half hour.

Bill recalls one incident at Sheep Creek School when a couple of lower grade boys sneaked snuff and a bottle of beer and tried them both at the same time. Punishment was delayed to give their teacher time to think it over. Their suffering from the anxiety of waiting was punishment enough.

Carl Ducommun

I was born in High River in June, 1940. Lived in Longview for a year then the folks moved to the Rat Farm, near Olhauser's farm, living there until 1944, when we moved into a log cabin owned by the Home Oil Company and at one time was the home of the Waugh family.

I started school at Millarville, the Sheep Creek School, after Mother and Dad moved to the Home Camp in 1946 and I went to this school for eight years, until 1954. The folks moved to Calgary and I took my grade nine at King Edward Junior High. From there the folks moved to their home at 67 Meadow View Rd. and I graduated from Western Canada High in 1958.

I then went to work for the Forestry, as look-out man on Blue Hill for two months, then was promoted to assistant Forest Officer. I was at the Red Deer Station for three years, then transferred to the Elbow Station. After four years there, was transferred to Kinuso, Alberta.

There I met Donna Sloan and we were married in July of 1968. I left the Forestry in October of that year and moved to Calgary to work for the Calgary Fire Dept.

Carl and Donna Ducommun with Michelle and Shane.

Our daughter Michelle was born in January, 1971. That fall we moved to High River, where our son Shane was born in May, 1973. We are living in High River and I commute to Calgary.

Ernest H. Ducommun Family

Ernie was born in Cleghorn, Iowa, U.S.A. in 1914. He moved with his parents to High River at the age of 12 years. He received his education in High River. Later worked for Guy Weadick on the Eden Valley Ranch.

Elsie was born in Calgary in 1917. She moved with her parents to a farm, one mile west and a half-mile north of Aldersyde. She received her education at the Maple Leaf School there.

Ernie and Elsie met in High River when Elsie was working for Mr. and Mrs. Heseltine.

They were married in 1935 and lived in the town of High River for two and a half years, then moved to Longview. Ernie started working for the Anglo- Canadian Oil Company.

The summer of 1938 a daughter was born, Marjorie Ann. In 1940 a son, Carl, came along.

They moved to the Rat Farm, west of Turner Valley, where Ernie was a separator Man. In 1942 he went to work for the Home Oil Company and they moved to the Waugh place west and north of Millarville.

In 1944, Marjorie started school at the Sheep Creek School then in 1945 they moved to the Home Townsite, and Carl started school in 1946.

They moved to Calgary in 1954, where Ernie was caretaker at the Home Oil Office on 6th Ave. W. About 1958 or 1959, he went to the Home Oil terminal east of Calgary, later known as the Cremona Pipe Line. He worked there until he retired in the spring of 1976.

Marjorie married John Janzen from Glenwood, Alberta. They are living on a farm near Olds. John is a heavy duty mechanic for Mobile Oil Company.

Carl married Donna Sloan from Kinuso, Alberta. He is a fireman for the City of Calgary and lives in High River.

The Ducommuns have six grandchildren and live at 67 Meadow View Road, Calgary.

Ernie Ducommun family. L. to R. Ernie, Margy, Carl. Seated, Elsie.

Art and Pat Duitman
by Pat Duitman

The Duitman household in Devon was thrown into a state of confusion in the spring of 1970 when Art announced that we were being transferred to the Imperial Oil Quirk Creek Gas Plant, west of Millarville.

It was with mixed feelings that we turned onto Highway 22 to visit the site of the plant. We hadn't gone very far when we were sold on the idea of living in that beautiful country with its wide open spaces, the Rockies in the background, and such a sense of freedom. The excitement of the children — Jack, then fifteen and Mary-Lou thirteen — increased the farther west and south we drove. By the time we reached Quirk Creek we had pretty well decided to try to find a suitable place to live in the district.

We stopped at Millarville Store, where we found that the log house on the hill, the old Jameson Place, might be for rent. We were lucky enough to rent the house. Our belongings, cats, dogs and sundry were transported, and we soon settled in. The children went wild exploring, and I was amazed to find that after all I could face mice, bats, shrews, etc., and did not go into hysterics when I spotted a moose peering through my kitchen window.

The children found the school bus quite an experience. Mary-Lou attended Millarville School, and Jack went to Black Diamond. I must have driven hundreds of miles to various sports events. The track and field program at Millarville was the best we encountered anywhere.

Our city friends found Ballyhamage a perfect setting for good old-fashioned Sunday gatherings, and our Christmases were most enjoyable in such quiet and cosy surroundings.

Although a Catholic, I found myself belonging to the Anglican Ladies' Guild, and the first thing I volunteered for was cooking stew for a cattle sale. I nearly fainted when the rancher came to the door and handed me twenty-five pounds!!! of beef and mountains of vegetables. The sale was on Monday, so after mass on Sunday the Duitmans formed a production line in our kitchen and prepared the stew. After that I was more careful about volunteering! My association with those Guild ladies is one I will always treasure.

We have the warmest feeling for the Millarville people: They took us "as we were" and made us feel a part of the community.

We were at Millarville a little over two years, moving to Red Deer where we spent three years, and back to Calgary in 1975.

Art is in the office of Esso Resources Design Engineering now, and is finding his work challenging and enjoyable.

Mary-Lou has found her niche in the business world, and Jack is trying out different lines of work, all of which seem to be truck-related.

As for me, I have found adjusting to big city life much harder than I thought I would. Maybe after all I should "Thank God I'm a Country Gal: at heart. Submitted by Mrs. Pat Duitman, (J. A.) now living in Calgary.

Peggy (Haney) Durand

Peggy was born in Seaforth, Ontario, in 1945 and moved to the Millarville area in 1950 with her parents. She attended Sheep Creek School for grades one to nine, also Turner Valley High School for Grade Ten. She attended Calgary School for Nursing Aides in 1963.

Moving to Rimbey in January, 1964, she was employed at the Rimbey General Hospital. In 1965 she married Charles (Shorty) R. Durand of the Leedale district. In the spring of 1969, moved to Rocky Mountain House and had part time employment with the

Peggy (Haney) Durand.

R.C.M.P. then in 1970, moved to Red Deer. Started working for the Red Deer Regional Hospital in 1974, and has remained at that job.

The Durands have two children, Melody, born in Rimbey in 1966, and Wendelyn, born in Rimbey in 1968.

Edith (Reimer) Durieux

I was born on November 18th, 1939, on the Anchor Down Ranch, to Jake and Barbara Reimer. At the age of two, we moved to the south half of section 4-22-4W5, where Mother is still living. The first school I attended was Purdy's, where the Jim Davis family now live. Later on my Dad bought a Jeep and bussed us to Square Butte School. Later on Square Butte School was closed and then Dad bussed us to the Millarville School.

During those years we spent all our spare time on our horses. We had a lot of fun riding with the Birney girls. Part of our summer was spent helping with the haying at home and at Bells.

In 1956, I met Duane Durieux. On finishing school at Millarville I went to Calgary and worked for the C.P.R. Telegraph Office. On December 21st, 1957, I married Duane Durieux and we started our married life at Red Deer, Alta. Duane was then stationed at the Penhold Air Force Base. On July 19th, 1958, our son Marty was born in the Red Deer Hospital. Then Lana, our daughter, came along on December 15th, 1959.

In April, 1962, a message came saying we were transferred to One Fighter Wing, France. Duane thought this was great, but with two small children and a dog, I wasn't very happy. However, Mom kept my little dog and we flew to France. We lived in Belgium for thirteen months, then were transferred again to Two Fighter Wing, further south in France. While living there, in 1963 Mom and Dad came over to visit us. We toured nine countries and had the best time of our lives camping. Mom and Dad flew back to Canada and we still had almost three years to spend in Europe. In 1964 we were transferred back to One Fighter Wing where Marty started Grade one. At this time Duane was working on 104 Starfighters. Lana started Grade one in 1965 and in 1966 the happy day came when we flew home to Canada.

We were now stationed at Cold Lake, Alta. For the next ten years Duane spent most of his time on 104 Starfighters and I went to work as a meat wrapper and cashier. In 1975 we were again transferred, to Moose Jaw, Sask. Here our son graduated from Grade 12, and our daughter finished grade eleven. After 21 years of service, Duane decided to end his career with the Armed Services. On June 27th 1976, we left Moose Jaw and came back to where I was raised, west and north of Millarville. Lana graduated from the Oilfields Jr-Sr. High School.

Both kids are still living at home and out working. Duane is working at Millarville Motors and I'm still wrapping meat, but for Safeways now. My free time is spent riding with Mom.

Mrs. A. Durrant — Formerly Miss Peirce

I taught one year at Fordville School (1951-52). It was my first year of teaching, and the last year Fordville School was located in the Millarville area. The community was very much divided on the question of consolidation. However, the school was later moved into Midnapore, and the children bussed to Sheep Creek School. I understand Fordville School was used as a school for two or three more years, then it was used as a Scout and Cub Hall. The building was eventually demolished about 6 years ago.

I have been teaching continuously in Calgary since 1954, and presently have a Grade 1 and 2 class at Eugene Coste Elementary School.

Fordville School, 1951-1952.

Fordville School; back row: Walter Jackson, Bill Jackson, Bill Winthrop, Dennis Hehr. Front row: Gordon Prichard, unidentified, Bob Jones, Tom Owens, Jim Cawthrone.

Mollie (Hartell) Duxbury

We moved to the Kew district from Pekisko in the early spring of 1935. I can remember Dad hauling a few loads up there with a team of horses and a hay rack, which was quite a trip in those days.

My sister Dot and myself were allowed to ride along and help move the cattle, which was a two day trip. One of my earliest memories was meeting Wilf Middleton, and Buddy Simpson, who was a bachelor.

One night, when we four girls were having our Saturday baths, in the old wash tub beside the kitchen stove, Buddy came calling and with a few squeals and a lot of scrambling, we soon cleared out of the kitchen.

We had a lot of good neighbors and a lot of good times when we were growing up in that district.

We girls went to Plainview School and Miss Pat Jameson was the teacher when we first went there and the following year Mr. Hedley took over.

One night I can still remember; we had been over at Doc Robisons for supper and we were returning home after dark by horses and sleigh. There was lots of snow on the ground and they had a winding road out of their place through the trees. We girls were all singing "Jingle Bells" at the top of our voices. All of a sudden we hit a bump and the next thing we knew we were all rolling in the snow.

In the spring of 1943 I joined the Airforce. It was in the Forces that I met Frank Duxbury, my husband. We were married in August 1946 after we were both discharged. We have lived in Medicine Hat ever since and raised a family of five, Darlene, Glen, David, Kenneth and Mary Lynn.

John and Erna Dyck Family History

John Dyck and his wife Erna (nee Penner) grew up in the Grassy Lake district of Southern Alberta. They were married in 1946 and purchased the family farm from John's parents. They developed this into a registered seed operation and farmed until 1965.

As early as 1960 John had become interested in continuing his education. In 1962 he enrolled in the Lethbridge Junior College and the following year the family moved to Calgary to continue attendance at the University. It was also an opportunity for the family to see how they liked living in a big city. At this time the family was comprised of the original couple plus five children: Dennis was born in 1948; Wayne 1950; Robert 1953; Carol 1955; and Patricia on Christmas day 1960.

The experiment seemed to please the whole family and after teaching in Lethbridge for one year, the family moved to Calgary in July, 1965. By 1968 the

Mr. and Mrs. John Dyck with daughter Pat.

family had tired of the city and purchased twenty acres west of Calgary. In January 1970 a house had been built and the family with two horses and a German Shepherd puppy moved in. In 1972 the second house on acreage was sold and LSD 11 and 12 in N.W. 36-20-4-W5 were purchased from Mr. and Mrs. L. H. Foster at Millarville.

Dennis and Wayne had been married by this time but Bob's mother was sure that Bob would never get married. So Bob looked after the ranching operation in his spare time while working for Michael Rodgers during the latter's illness in the hospital.

In 1974 the present residence was built and the family came to live in Millarville. John continued teaching in Calgary, commuting on a daily basis; Carol was in attendance at the University of Calgary while Pat took Grade nine in Oilfields High School in Black Diamond.

The following spring the family was forcefully reminded of the wisdom of Shakespeare's observation, "In the Spring a young man's fancy turns to thoughts of love." Bob had been smitten by a fair young lady who had somehow become lost in the woods. A year later Bob and Shelley were married. Another year later they purchased a farm east of Edmonton.

Without Bob's help it has become difficult to carry on the ranching operation. The sojourn at Millarville has been pleasant and will always be treasured by this family.

The Ted Eden Family — Brand ED

by Annie Eden

I was the first daughter of Mr. and Mrs. Ernest Silvester, early ranchers of the Kew district. I was born on the homestead December, 1910. I went to the Square Butte School the first year it opened, in 1922. There were only nine pupils going to school while I was a pupil there. After I finished, I stayed around home most of the time until 1938 and in May of that year I went to work for Mrs. S. J. McBee of Longview, until January 1942, when I married Ted Eden. Ted was born in England in August 1898. He was in the Army from

L. to R. Bill and John Eden, taken at Kew.

1916 to 1918, then he came to Canada, to the Longview and High River areas.

When we left McBees we went to Walter Hanson's to work. Then we came to Turner Valley to my brother Arthur's place, which now belongs to my brother Charley. We lived there four and a half years. While there we got a few cows and the brand ED on the right rib. We have two boys, both born in Turner Valley, John, May 1943 and Bill in August 1945. We used to move every six months or so. In 1948 we moved down to the Highwood River, just over the hill from Longview, in the Jim Maloff house. We had goats to milk there.

In July 1960, we moved to a quarter section belonging to my dad, the N.W.¼ of 3-21-4W5. The boys helped with the work so they each got half the land as Ted and I were not able to do all the work.

While on the place at Kew we belonged to the Square Butte Community Club and I belonged to the Ladies' group most of the time I was in the district. I also belonged to the Millarville Willing Workers W. I. for a few years and enjoyed it very much.

On December 25th, Christmas day, 1968, Ted passed away very suddenly. I continued to live on the farm at Kew until we sold the place in September, 1973. I moved to the town of Sundre to make my home. My son Bill, had bought a farm here, where he and his wife Maureen and son Joe live. My son John bought a farm near Sangudo, where he lives with his wife Allison and their two children, Heidi and Buckley.

I belong to the Sunshine Seniors Club and the Hospital Auxiliary. I keep busy knitting and making hand stitched quilts.

Lester Harold and Helen Einboden

by H. Einboden

My Husband was born and raised on a farm in Downsview, Ontario, on the northerly outskirts of Toronto, Ontario. I was born in Toronto and raised in Downsview, Ontario.

We came to Calgary in 1960 and lived there for one year, then returned to Toronto, with the thoughts of coming back some day to Calgary.

Annie and Ted Eden, 1942.

Many holiday trips were taken in Calgary and then in 1977 we came west once more, with the intentions of looking for retirement property in B.C. But we never got any farther than the acreage we bought in the foothills. Our acreage is located on the Cawthorne Estates where we built our home.

We raised three children. Dianne (Mrs. Murray Byrne) is a public school teacher in Malton, Ontario. She has three girls — Dawn, Cathy and Robyn.

John teaches trades in a Hamilton, Ontario high school. He has a girl and a boy — Maureen and Edward.

Our youngest son is Edward. He is a machinist in Toronto. He has a girl and a boy — Rebecca and Jeffery. Edward and his wife, Pam, and the children are planning to move out to Calgary this coming summer.

Lester has one sister, Ruth, living in Calgary and a brother, Howard, who also lives on the Cawthorne Estates. The rest of his brothers and one sister live in the east.

It has been a beautiful experience living here in the west, and being permanent residents of the foothills.

Einboden, Pat (Jones)
Submitted by Pat Einboden

I was born in Calgary on March 19th. 1938 the second child of Edna and Stan Jones. I started to school at Fordville travelling back and forth in the district's first school bus driven by Mr. Barraclough. When

Howard and Pat Einboden and children, Gordon, Theresa and Timothy.

Fordville School Students. Back row, L. to R.: Melvin Venus, Ronnie Scatterty, Reggie Pallister, Noreen Croston, Daisy Pallister, Nora Pallister, Lilibeth Kohler, Harvey Burrows. Second row: Brent McLean, Roger Jones, Allen Pallister, Lila Croston, June Hehr, Anne Scatterty, Marilyn Sharpe. Front row: Pat Jones, George Bull.

Fordville closed in 1952 I completed my education at Millarville. During this time I was active in the Millarville 4H Beef Club and was the club's first Secretary. Mr. Fred Bell, who recently wrote a book on his 4H experiences, was the District Agriculturist at the time.

After leaving school and until my marriage I worked as a nursing aid at Turner Valley Hospital. One of my favourite patients was Mrs. L. C. Freeman who insisted on being decked out in all her jewellery every morning.

On March 2nd. 1956, Howard Einboden, who had recently come from Ontario, and I were married in Christ's Church, in Millarville by Rev. Waverly Gant, a cousin of Howard's. Our first twenty-one years were spent at Red Deer Lake, beside the community curling rink. We built a house on the site of the Watkin's Machine shop which burnt shortly after it went into operation.

In 1977 we moved back into the Millarville district when we bought a site; located on the Cawthorne Estates. NE. 35-21-3-W5th.

We have three children; Gordon, born May 24 1959, Theresa, Jan. 17th. 1961 and Timothy, July 8th. 1967.

Peggy Elhorn (nee Latter)
Written by Peggy Elhorn

Eldest daughter of Roy and Grace Latter; born Sunday, July 24, 1949. Attended Westoe, Red Deer Lake and Henry Wise Wood High School (1955 to 1967). Attended University of Calgary and University of Alberta and recieved B.P.E. and teacher's certificate.

Memories: school bus rides (just missed having to ride horseback to school) — Alex Macklin, Walt Thiesen, Mom and Dad, my bus drivers; baseball games; 4-H Club Millarville Beef meetings; public speaking; school track meets and picnics at Millarville racetrack; horseback riding to the lake and down

The pony, saddle, bridle and a complete Western outfit was won by Peggy Latter, eldest daughter of Roy and Grace Latter in 1958. Grace won a horse, saddle and bridle at the last Midnapore Stampede in 1934.

township lines with friends; toboggan parties at Stan Genert's and MacKay's place; going to square dances with Dad and Mom at Millarville Hall; swimming hole on Sheep River; the river crossing near Charlie King's farm, where he towed me and truck out from; Millarville Fairs; going to Calgary for High School football games; chinooks in the winter; walks on our farm to. the spring and far side; little springs of water spouting from the hillsides at our farm; wild flowers; the ᵇˡᵛline of lights of Calgary; the gas smell from Turner Valley; Dad driving a road grader; milking a lot of cows; our dogs; the windmill near our house; the playhouse; good friends and good times; my family and neighbors being there.

Family: I have been married to Herb Elhorn since 1971 and we have two boys (to date), Colin M. born October 14, 1976 and Wesley B. born April 8, 1978. We are living in Edmonton, where Herb is a sergeant with the Canadian Armed Forces in the Airborne School. We have travelled to Germany, Cyprus, and across Canada to Alaska. We love camping, fishing, bowling, hockey, football and dancing. Herb is from Wanham, Alberta (Peace River-Lassiter Project) and the third of five children of Al and Ruth Elhorn. Al Elhorn is a step-brother of the late Jim Carey.

People and History; Dad, Mom, Judy, Kath, Colleen and Dean; Uncle Cal and Nora of Black Diamond; Mrs. Evelyn Spink, Cathy and Aunty Pam; Grama Wylie; Joannie Lariviere; Mrs. Stasia Carey; Mom and Dad's friends, Uncle Harvey Goerlitz; Auntie Mary; Aunty Ellen and Uncle Bill McGuire and kids; Uncle Bill Ireland and Aunt Eleanor; McBees; Schaals; Grama Barkley; Grampa Barkley.

Mom and Dad shared their room with me when I was born, now the upstairs bedroom of our house. Grama Latter used to push me in the buggy, down to

get the cows. Then one winter night we had our mattresses downstairs around the furnace to sleep and keep warm; the huge snowdrifts that were left after the roads were cleared by the snowplow; the homework we did by kerosene lantern (with mantles); the climbing of the windmill where you could see for miles; love of all we know about grandparents. Our old International ½-ton truck is still on our farm and so is our home.

Walter and Alice Erickson

by Mayme Martin

Having no desire for induction into compulsory army draft, young Walter Erickson emigrated from Sweden to United States in 1911-12.

In summer he worked on farms and during winter in logging operations, gradually working his way west to Tacoma, Wash. where he was a laborer.

Alice and her family also emigrated from Sweden and settled in the Chicago area before travelling west to Washington State. She worked as a domestic and soon became known as an exceptionally good cook. She was employed for several years by Senator and Mrs. Harrigan in Tacoma.

Walter and Alice met in 1916 and were married in early 1917. They both continued working at their respective jobs.

In 1920 they decided to come to Canada and homesteaded at Lathom, near Bassano. During the winter months they both worked in Calgary, earning sufficient funds to build a comfortable house on the homestead. They farmed at Lathom until 1938 when they sold and moved to Millarville, purchasing the McGrath place, W½ and S.E. ¼ 30-20-2-W/5.

Much of this property was rough bushland, but the Ericksons being industrious by nature began improvements. Walter cleared and broke many acres of land, a back-breaking job, while Mrs. Erickson grew a large vegetable garden, beautiful flowers and raised a large flock of chickens.

In 1947 they sold their farm and moved to Calgary for the winter. The following spring they moved to the Vancouver area, settled on Lulu Island.

Following a series of building houses and moving, they finally settled at Cloverdale. Walter worked for the Surrey School Division until he retired on pension.

Mrs. Erickson passed away about 1965 and Walter a few years later.

Friends and neighbors remember the Ericksons as popular and hospitable people. They also remember that Walter always referred to his wife as "the woman," so they assumed that Mrs. Erickson had a Nordic name too difficult to pronounce. It was somewhat of a surprise when they learned that her name was "Alice."

Mrs. Erickson told friends that with the first money she earned in America, she purchased a hat and forever discarded the habit of wearing a headscarf as she did not want to be identified as an immigrant. She is remembered as a statuesque woman of almost 6 feet tall and of regal posture.

The Ericksons left their former friends and neighbors a legacy of fond and unforgettable memories.

The N.W. ¼ is now owned by Jack Allan and the south ½ by Hugh McPherson.

David Maxwell Evans

I am the eldest son of Irene and Elwyn Evans. I am of the third generation of Evans to live on our ranch at Millarville. My Grandfather and Grandmother Evans came over from Wales in 1897, when what is now Alberta was the North West Territories. Our brand was first recorded then and we are still using it today.

I was born in Calgary and raised on the ranch here at Millarville. I attended Sheep Creek School, then later to Technical School in Calgary and took an Agricultural Mechanics course. When I was finished, I came home to the ranch and went into partnership with my father.

I married Donna Hanson and we have three sons, Donald David Evans, Daryl Elwyn Evans, and Cameron Scott Evans. We are still living on the home place.

David Evans Family. L. to R., Back: Donna, David. Front: Donald, Daryl and Cameron.

David Evans with "Spotted Prince" who brought top price at Calgary horse sale, Appaloosa section, $1520.

Donna Mae (Hanson) Evans

I am the second daughter of Joanna and Harley Hanson. I moved to Millarville with my parents in 1944. We lived on the Freddy Hodgkins place, then moved to Jackson's where we spent a very happy time swimming in the river and playing with dolls amongst the big old spruce trees.

My dad was a derrick man on the oil wells, later working as an operator on the pumping stations. Later, until his retirement, he worked for Silver Wood Dairies.

I started grade one at Millarville School, at the time it was called Sheep Creek School, but after a year and a half we moved to Kew district where I attended Plainview School. We bought the Gavin Calderwood place. We had a dairy herd so always saw the sun come up. I lived there all my growing up years and very enjoyable years they were. We had so many really nice neighbors; we used to sleigh ride up and down the big hills making it so slippery when our dads came home for work they couldn't make the big hill. In the summer we had picnics. The Kew picnic was the big one of the year, the neighbors all got together, and it was really fun. All the kids would go swimming in the creek.

My Mum usually stayed home and did the chores and it was sure nice to always have a good supper waiting on the table and to know she was there when I came from school.

In grade six, Plainview School closed down and we were all bussed to Millarville School at its present location. Laurie Lochhead was our first bus driver, later Bob Lochhead took over and was a driver for sixteen years. At Millarville I finished my grade eleven, as that was as high as we could go there. Mr. Dube taught grade nine, ten and eleven and at that time we took departmentals. I always wondered how he did it; just about 100% passed. I then went to Mount Royal, where I took a Medical Dental Secretary course. Later I worked for Dr. S. Goodfellow, a dentist, until I married David Maxwell Evans, the eldest son of Irene and Elwyn Evans, who was born and raised at Millarville. We still live on part of home place, where we built a house.

David still farms with his dad and we both drive school busses. We have three sons, Donald David, Daryl Elwyn, and Cameron Scott. The three boys have all attended Millarville School. Elwyn also attended Millarville School so the boys are the third generation to attend the same school; we will wait and see about

Donald, Daryl and Cameron Evans, sons of Donna and David Evans.

the fourth generation. After high school at Oilfields High School, Donald went on to S.A.I.T. where he took Power Engineering. After Daryl finished grade twelve he decided to stay home and help his Dad. Cam is attending Elboya School in Calgary. Hope to spend many more years here in the foothills.

The E. Evans Family   N2U 3/-

submitted by Irene (Rickett) Evans

I have often said (in fun) Oh I'm imported, in a way this is true. I arrived in Millarville Sept. 2, 1935, to become the third teacher at the original one-room Sheep Creek School. Previous to that I had taught for several years at the Grassy Slope School north east of Hanna.

The two years I taught at Sheep Creek proved to be a very interesting experience for me. The school was comparatively new, the heating of course was a bit of a problem — two pot bellied wood burning stoves to keep one on the hop. Your reward — the wonderful aroma of burning wood. More than half the pupils were in the lower grades. All in all they were a good bunch.

This last year 1978 when we celebrated the 50th anniversary of that dear little school what a thrill it was for me to have ten of my former pupils present.

The school board consisted of Margarite Pegler, Bert Chalmers and W. Jackson Jr. Mr. Ted Rawlinson was the sec.-treas. My salary was not a large one $75.00 a month but it went a long way in those days.

During the two years I taught at Sheep Creek I made my home with the Peglers who then operated the present Millarville Store. Margarite and Norman were both very friendly and out going people. They treated me like one of the family, and always made my friends welcome.

June 30, 1937 Elwyn Evans and I were married in Calgary, in the presence of a few close friends. Upon the advice of Grandfather's close friend Mr. W. H. King we left immediately for the west coast. When we returned home some six weeks later, we really settled down to the serious business of making a living ranching in the foot hills.

During the years between Nov. 14, 1938 and Aug. 22, 1942 our three children; David, Milton and Alice-Ann were born at the General Hospital in Calgary. They all took their public schooling and some junior high at Sheep Creek and from there went their different ways.

Winter time at the Elwyn Evans ranch.

Our old house was a bit of a challenge wondering what could be done to add to our comfort. The kitchen after raising the ceiling, putting in new cupboards, digging out the old cellar and adding a small utility room, and a cement cistern became the most used and versatile room in the house. Believe it or not it served as a kitchen, dining room, bath room and laundry room. Friends and neighbours sat on the bench under the south window never dreaming that a bath tub was in that box. When you lifted the lid there it was taps, cold, hot and drains — what an improvement over the old wash tub.

We solved this problem along with others by having Mr. Bert Haney build us a new home in 1962.

When your family have reached maturity and have completed their High School, then you begin to wonder where they will find their niche in life. David took a course in Agricultural Mechanics at Tech, and has been in partnership with his father since 1964. David and his wife, the former Donna Hanson live in a new by-level house on the home quarter (SW3 21-3-W5). Donald, Darryl and Cameron the three Evans boys are all still at home.

Milton after completing Grade XII took a two year course at the Technical School in Industrial Electricity. He is now employed by Alberta Gas Trunk Line having been with the company for over 15 years. He has done well with the company and now has a very good office position.

Elwyn Evans Family. Back, L. to R.: Elwyn, David and Milton. Front, L. to R.: Irene and Alice.

Shirley Rae Hutchenson and Milton Evans were married at Christ Church Millarville Oct. of 1962. They have lived in Calgary now for 12 or 14 years, have two children, a daughter Kelly, 11 years and a son Stuart, 7 years.

Alice graduated from Mt. Royal College with a diploma in Social Welfare work. She worked for some time for the Government in Edmonton in the department of adoptions. While in Edmonton she met and married Dr. Robert R. Melvin. They have two children, Michelle 12 years and James, 8 years.

Before closing I think, since Elwyn is not writing a personal history for this edition that he deserves a small paragraph. He has given time, talent and effort to the community, to mention a few; The Millarville Fair, Sec.-Treas. Meota Gas Co-op, Sec. of Ranchers Hall board for 16 years, Director of Social Credit Group, North Fork Stockmens Association. Personally I have confined my outside interest to one organization, the Willing Workers Institute. It has been my privilege to attend three Federated conferences; one in Winnipeg, one in Banff and one in Charlottetown.

It is gratifying, especially to Elwyn to know that the third and fourth generation have taken over Cambrian Ranch, established by Dave Evans in 1897.

We now live in semi-retirement on the home quarter.

As my friend, Dr. David Lander, would say we are "Over the Hill" so it is our privilege, we hope to do some travelling reminisce over our pioneer heritage and dote on our grandchildren.

Evans, M. H. (Bud) and Colleen

by Colleen Evans

From early childhood I longed to see the Rockies. My Father would return to Toronto after a trip west each year with pictures and stories about Calgary and the mountains. I remember my embarrassment as he walked into Union Station with a ten gallon hat on his head. Very few people travelled in those days and they knew very little about the different regions of Canada. I spent summers on my United Empire Loyalists ancestor's farm on the St. Lawrence River where I enjoyed the farm animals, haying and most of all the solitude.

Bud was born in 1928 and raised in Port Credit, a little town west of Toronto on Lake Ontario. He enjoyed books about cowboys and listening to western music on the radio. When the teacher asked for a composition based on what he saw from his bedroom window, he wrote about a cowboy riding a horse towards the mountains!

He graduated from Port Credit High School. Bud attended M.I.T. and graduated from Ryerson College in Electronics in Toronto. Bud worked for C.B.C. radio and was on the first camera crew when television first started. We were married in 1951 after I graduated at the Toronto East General Hospital and then I worked as Afternoon Supervisor at the hospital.

M. H. (Bud) and Colleen Evans with their sons Malcolm and Campbell.

Front row: Ron and Elizabeth Carlyon, with son Rod and dog "Cinnabar". Second row: Rod's grandparents. L. to R. Stan and Elizabeth Eveleigh, Violet and Edward Carlyon. Top row: Rod's great-grandmothers, Mrs. Louise Gill and Mrs. Mary Eveleigh.

In 1955 our first son, Malcolm, was born in London, Ont. where Bud was working in a steel mill. He then went in steel sales in Toronto and commuted to Acton when we had our second son, Campbell in 1957. I took lessons in oil painting and sketched the countryside and showed in art shows.

Bud was transferred as manager of a metal service centre to Winnipeg in 1960. I was a member of the Winnipeg Sketch Club and the St. James Art Club and the Antique Arts Club. The boys attended Queenston Public School and I took my turn as President of the Home and School for a year. The boys were active participants in the cub group and joined the Winnipeg Ski club winning prizes the first year.

In 1968 Bud transferred to Calgary to open a branch. I joined Calgary Newcomers Club and the boys attended the John Ware Junior High School the year it opened and continued to E. P. Scarlett. Malcolm graduated Strathcona Tweedsmuir and Campbell from E. P. Scarlett. Cam then left university to open a business, Rocky Mountain Messenger, with his brother. Our desire to move from wall to wall houses became a reality in 1977 when we bought eighty acres Ptn NW 36-20-4-5 from Nita and Chub Foster with one of the most beautiful views of the mountains we had ever seen.

We were just getting settled in the house when Bud went on his first cattle drive to the mountains with the Fosters. Although it rained all weekend he returned with a smile on his face and looks forward to returning each year. The men take part in calving and branding with Chub, our brand being ℰℂ. Bud took a sausage making course in Millarville in the evenings. When I'm not working at Rocky Mountain Messenger I'm busy identifying mushrooms, wildflowers and birds, also taking up my painting again.

Family of Stanley and Elizabeth Eveleigh
written by Elizabeth Eveleigh

My husband, Stan, was born in London, England, and emigrated to Canada when a boy of fourteen. He

lived in Manitoba for six years, working on farms most of that time. Later, when work became less plentiful, he moved to New Toronto, Ontario, where he obtained a job in Goodyear Tire & Rubber Co.

I was born in Port Credit, Ontario, a village between Hamilton and Toronto, on the shores of Lake Ontario. I met Stan in 1926 and we were married in 1929.

We have two children, a boy William, and a girl Elizabeth Anne; both received their Public School and High School education in Port Credit. Bill followed the electrical trade and married an American girl, LaVerne Gebhart. They have their own electrical business and live in New Jersey, U.S.A.

Elizabeth graduated from teachers' college and met Ron Carlyon while he was attending Queen's University. He graduated as a geologist in 1959 and they were married in May of the same year. They moved to Regina, Sask., and from there the firm Ron was working for transferred them to Calgary. They have one son, Rod, who was born in October, 1960.

During our visits each year with the family in Calgary we made plans for the four of us to buy a farm or ranch. We had all lived on farms so knew the work involved, yet preferred this life to that of the city.

In 1967, Stan obtained early retirement and we sold our home in Ontario and moved west. My mother, who had made her home with us since the death of my father, also came with us. We stayed with Elizabeth and Ron for three months, during which time we directed our attention to farms and ranches for sale. In August we found a farm, the home of Dessa and Hugh Macklin, situated on SE¼ of S3-T22-R2-W5. After due consideration we decided to buy the land and form a partnership, and raise Appaloosa horses and Black Angus cattle. Our brand is 4-E (4-E halfdiamond). Originally this land was owned by F. H. Wolley-Dod, who built the beautiful home, with barn and out-buildings. Stan and I have renovated the old house and live there quite comfortably. Ron, Elizabeth and Rod lived in the cottage while building their home on the south of the farm, where they now live.

Rod received his education at Red Deer Lake School and Bishop Grandin High School in Calgary, and in the fall of 1978 entered university in Edmonton. Rod and Ron train their own horses and are well-known in the Show Circuit, winning many trophies and ribbons.

My mother, Mrs. Louisa Gill, has for the past year been a resident in the Father Lacombe Nursing Home. She is now in her 92nd year. She too has enjoyed the life here, and always remarked about Alberta's sunshine.

It has not been all work, we have enjoyed many leisure hours on the farm. There is still time for each of us to follow our own particular hobbies. We are all interested in the community and help out when and where we can.

Delaine and Rudy Evenson

by Delaine Evenson

I was born in Jan/48 along with a twin sister, Diane, the second and third daughters of Robert and Fae Winthrop. We grew up on the home place (SW 26-21-3-W5), and attended school at Millarville and Turner Valley High. Growing up with a twin sister had its trials and tribulations and was often frustrating to our parents. Mother always remembers one time we had her thoroughly confused. She had baked us a cake to have when we got home from a date and heard us come home around midnight and thought, "Gee, they're home early!", and then went back to sleep but several hours later heard us come home again! We had come home just long enough to get the cake and leave again.

I attended one year of high school at William Aberhart in Calgary and then went to Business College. In 1965 I married Gordon Stauffer (of Turner Valley) but after two years the marriage failed. We

had one son Chad born in Sept/67. I began working at Western Supplies Ltd. (plumbing wholesale), where I worked for the next six years. During the summer of '68 Chad and I moved home and we commuted daily to Calgary, me to work and Chad to the Providence Crech's Day Care Centre. In 1971 I bought a mobile home and moved it to the farm so Chad and I could have a home of our own. That same year Dad built an indoor riding arena to practise team roping, which was becoming very popular in Canada. There were lots of ropers coming to practise twice a week and one of them was Rudy Evenson.

Rudy was born at Beechy, Sask., in Sept/1928. He left school when he was thirteen years old to go harvesting for his Dad. (Driving a team of horses hauling bundles for the threshing outfit.) He never did get back to school and continued working on farms and ranches in the district. Then in the fall of 1947 he came to Alberta with some friends in an old Model "A" Ford truck. He worked at several ranches around High River, including the Bar U, Mount Sentinel, 7U Brown Ranch; the Riverbend and Koch Ranches at Longview and the 44 and SN Ranches at Claresholm. He was rodeoing during this time and spent two summers ('53 and '54) at Cody, Wyoming riding bareback broncs at their evening rodeos each evening all summer. In 1958 Rudy went to work for J. B. Cross at Okotoks and spent the next three winters in California looking after his polo horses. 1962 found Rudy at the Riverbend with Morris Erickson breaking and training horses. Then in Sept of 1965 he started to work for the Department of Agriculture as a Brand Inspector at the Calgary Stockyards, where he works today.

Rudy always liked roping, both calf roping and team roping and spent most of his weekends off to a roping or at Winthrop's practising. During the practise sessions I often put in cattle and ran the chute but before long I got the roping "bug" too. Since Rudy was Dad's partner and such a good roper I'd get him to head some for me so I could practise heeling. The first thing he knew he was the one that got heeled! We were married in April, 1973. We had two children, Dean

Delaine, Dana, Chad, Dean and Rudy Evenson.

Bob Winthrop and Rudy Evenson, 1974 Canadian Champion Team Ropers.

George born Apr/75 and Dana Jeannine born Aug/76. We built a new house on the home place and still do lots of roping and Chad now 10, has started roping too. I am a member and a Director of the Canadian Girls' Rodeo Association and compete in the team roping at the All Girl Rodeos.

The Faltus Family

The Faltus family came to the Millarville area in January, 1965. We settled and built on the original Ernest Chubb homestead, which faces the John Ware Ridge. In the fifteen years we have been in the area we have seen many changes in the land and its inhabitants.

John Ware Ridge as seen from the Faltus acreage.

When we first came out it was a novelty to see people driving by, now cars and campers come by in a steady stream on their way to the campsites on Ware Creek.

The Faltus family consists of Morris and Helen, father and mother. Brian, the oldest and his wife Betty and son Douglas. Rick and his wife Eileen and children, Kathy and Ricky Jr. and Jerry, the youngest son of Morris and Helen.

We started out building our place as a summer retreat, but are now living out there all year round. The family is originally from Calgary, where Morris's occupation is a Building Superintendent, Helen is a housewife and Jerry is completing his grade twelve. Brian works as an electrician, his wife Betty works as a payroll clerk, Rick is Plant Operator for Gulf Oil in Calgary and Eileen works for the City of Calgary in the office.

Our goal is to someday retire in the area and to establish a trend for the rest of the family to grow into.

The people of Millarville owe it to the land and to themselves to keep the land and area of Millarville beautiful for future generations to enjoy.

John A. and Wilma J. Farkas

Brand ⌢F. R.R.

In the year 1928, my father George Farkas, immigrated to Canada from Kosicka-Bela, Czechos-

lovakia. At this time, I was two years old. By the spring of 1935, Father had saved enough money so that my mother, Mary Farkas and I could join him on a farm in the Red Deer Lake area.

I started school at Red Deer Lake, then in 1936, my father bought a raw half-section in the Ballyhamage District — Sec. 22, T.w1, R.2, W.5 (presently the John Given place).

The Ballyhamage School (then taught by Sheilagh Jameson) was located on the S.W. corner of our land, and the horse barn and pasture were across the road on the west side.

My childhood memories are happy and exciting ones while living in the Ballyhamage District. I remember sleigh-riding on the hill, the school picnics, and the Christmas concerts, which were gala events for everyone. I recall one year the school picnic was held at the Millarville Race Track Grounds. I had won a money prize in a foot race, while a fellow student won a book. As I loved reading, and could never get enough books to read, we soon exchanged our prizes.

Although we lived only a half mile from the school, I occasionally rode a speedy swayback mare to school. Often as I approached our gate, an older student, Ben Martman, would come along on what looked like a thoroughbred. Knowing that I could not hold the horse back, he would start to gallop and then the race was on. I would hang on for dear life, and I believe those experiences taught me how to really stay on a horse.

I remember racing on foot one day with Roy Cabel and Bob Holdsworth. Bob was barefooted, but he could still outrun us through the brush, brambles, thorns and all!

One of the highlights of my life then, was going to Calgary in a Model A Ford truck, which had no heater but was naturally air-conditioned. Roads, at that time, were something else again. Other memorable times were when my father bought me my first .22 rifle and when we got a new battery operated radio.

Farkas daughter's wedding picture. L. to R. Lori, Wilma, Cathy, Lawrence, John, Don, and Allan in front.

263

Our land was cleared with an axe, by my father and a couple of hired hands. The trees were cut three feet up, leaving stumps which were pulled out by a four-horse team. My job was to drive the team while Dad cut some of the roots and hooked the chain around the stumps. Teddy Cuffling did some of the breaking for us with a steel wheeled 15-30 McCormick Deering tractor. The barn was built from poplar logs, which were skidded home from the east quarter.

One of my jobs was to fetch the milk cows every day. Although some had bells on, there were many times when I would come home without them, as they would bed down in the heavy brush and I would walk right past them.

In the fall of 1939, my parents sold out and bought a farm in the Red Deer Lake-Midnapore District where I finished my schooling.

In 1955, I met and married Wilma Jean Rost of Innisfail, Alberta. We have two sons, Don George and Allan John, and two daughters, Cathy Ann and Lori Jean. Our eldest daughter is now married and we have a granddaughter, Candy Lynn. I also have a younger brother, Fred, a geologist, married and living in the area.

All of our children have actively participated in the Millarville East 4-H Beef Club. My wife, Wilma Jean, myself, and our eldest son, Don, still carry on with our farming and ranching operation.

My mother passed away in 1977 and my father now resides in Calgary.

Down through the years I have seen many changes in the District and the city of Calgary. Calgary has grown so much bigger now, but not necessarily better.

Constance Mabel Felton

Born in Calgary, Alberta, in 1898, daughter of Elfie Mabel Idalie (Shaw) and Walter Fitzray Phillips (1874-1949) Mother died in 1901 and Father remarried in 1903 to Georgina Scott. We lived in Millarville until 1910, then moved to Kew (N.E.¼ of 24-20-4w5.) where I attended Plainview School (demolished in 1967). The school was several miles away and most of the children went by horseback. During the winter months I packed oats in a saddle bag or a sheaf of hay in a gunny sack for my horse while I attended classes. The school was one-room: grades 1-8 for 10-12 children. Chores took up the major part of the days, with milking, feeding the animals, water and wood carried in before leaving for school, and similar chores waiting to be done after school.

We milked cows to sell the cream, which we kept cold by placing the large cream cans in the spring, which also provided an adequate supply of water for the whole ranch. Hay was completed entirely by horses and manpower, and kept for our own use. Our main diet during the summer months was potatoes, carrots and pickled beef which was stored in crocks or barrels. Eggs were preserved in crocks of water-glass or greased with butter and placed pointed-end down in

Connie Phillips Felton riding Frank at Kew, 1915.

Lizzie von Rummel, Isobel Fulton, Constance (Tuck) Phillips, Nina von Rummel. Picture taken by Jane von Rummel while camping at Ware Creek.

oats (to keep the air from the eggs.) These were used during the winter months when the chickens were no longer laying.

I have fond memories of my childhood playmates: Lizzie, Jane and Nina (von Rummel) Basilici; Molly, Isobel and Douglas Fulton and Dolly Read, our many

Constance Felton and family. L. to R. Bruce Chapman, Vera Felton, Constance Felton, Wade Felton and sister (Grandchildren) and Dolly (Felton) Chapman.

264

horseback riding expeditions, home rodeos, summer fairs, camping trips and gay sing-songs at the Basilici home.

In 1919, I married Irkeland Felton (born in 1885 — Harvard, Nebraska, died in 1964.) and we moved to Penticton, B.C. We had four children: Ethelyn Irene (Tily) living in Penticton. Victor Vernon, living in Okanagan Falls, B.C. Dorothy Hazel (Chapman) living in Okanagan Falls, B.C. Ralph Frank, living in Penticton, B.C.

For many years I worked as a housekeeper in Penticton, then moved to Rock Creek, B.C. where I worked in the Rock Creek Hotel. Some time later I moved to Midway, B.C. where I worked in the Midway Hotel for Mr. Carl Thomet, a well known pioneer of the Midway district. The hotel was sold in 1960, and I took a job as the school custodian in Midway until retiring in 1967. I am still living in Midway, President of the Senior Citizen's Group, active in the welfare of the community and receive great enjoyment from helping and competing in the local Fall Fairs.

Through my life I have seen many changes . . . from a pioneer type of life to great scienic wonders . . . television, extensive air travel, to landing a man on the moon.

The old homestead was sold soon after my father's death, but the original log cabin, which I called home, in Kew, is still standing.

John Stanley Field

by Ruby McNab

John is the youngest of Bud and Lola Field's children. Was born April 18, 1940. He left home when

John Field. This was always the little kids job on the farm, feeding the pail bunters.

John Field family. L. to R., Bev, Janice, Jennifer, Jacky, John.

he was 17 and joined the Airforce. Stationed in Trenton, Ontario. Serving in the Airforce for five years during which time he furthered his education, receiving a degree in engineering. After his service in the Airforce he took a job with General Motors in London, Ontario. Starting at the bottom of the ladder and working up to District Service Representative Terex Sales. He was transferred back to Edmonton in 1975, the first time he was back in his home province to stay for any length of time for 19 years. For the next three years his job took him flying all over the U.S.A. and Canada. Receiving another promotion he was transferred back to London with his family in the spring of 1978.

John has a son Jay and daughter Debbie from his previous marriage. He and his present wife Bev have three girls Janice, Jennifer and Jacqueline.

John and his wife Bev. belong to the Curling Club and are just as active on the Golf Course.

John is gifted in singing and loves it. Many an evening either around his fireplace in the winter or a barbeque and swimming pool in the summer you'll find him surrounded by friends and neighbours joining in along with his wife and girls as he plays his guitar and sings.

Robert Henry Field, Jr.

Robert was born January 2, 1933. He took his education at Ballyhamage School and remained in the district helping his folks on the family farm. After his father's death in the spring of 1968 he continued with the farming and taking care of his mother. He has always been active in Community affairs, and always had time to lend a helping hand to relatives and friends and neighbours when needed. His great ambition is to take time out from so much hard work and take a real holiday. He has seven sisters older than himself and one young brother John, who works for General Motors in London, Ontario.

Ready for a country dance, Robert Field, 1965.

Harry and Nellie Fisher on their wedding day, August — 1977.

Robert Field and friends, branding calves.

Harry Edwin Fisher

by Jean Blakley

Harry was born in Calgary May 10, 1912, son of Joseph and Elizabeth Fisher. The family at this time were living in the Riverside district, having moved in to Calgary from Millarville so that the older children could attend school. When Harry was two years of age, a new house had been built in South Calgary, and the family moved there.

South Calgary was an interesting place for a boy to grow up in. In 1914, the houses were built a distance apart, and it was much like living in the country. There were many sloughs where a boy could swim in the summer and skate in the winter. There was plenty of room to roam around and still be near enough to take a street car to downtown Calgary, which boasted

of a couple of moving picture Theatres. There was an abundance of prairie grass and quite often a prairie fire. One particularly bad one brought out the Calgary fire department. A small group of boys admitted starting it to see if the fire could jump Brackman's Slough, one of the largest in South Calgary.

The road to the Sarcee Indian Reserve passed very near the Fisher house, and here the Indians would tether their ponies, and take the street-car from 34th Ave. into the city, asking Harry and his two sisters to keep an eye on them, which they did, also riding them. Often the Indians would not return until the last street car, late at night.

During World War I, this same road was used by the Army to go to the Sarcee Military Camp. Needless to say, these were but prairie trails, used mostly by saddle horses and wagons with teams. Not far from Fisher's house was a steep dip in the road, and cars, being what they were at that time, were usually stuck in the mud. Cars were a great novelty to the young fry, and they enjoyed watching the officers (who rode in the cars) trying to get their vehicles unstuck.

The foot soldiers usually had a break from their long marches near 34th Ave. and the Fisher children and their young friends would carry pails of water to where the soldiers were resting, very happy to get a cup of water and the water carriers were also happy when the pail was passed around among the men and a few nickles and dimes put in.

Harry started at King Edward School in 1918, and the following year the family moved to Victoria, B.C., remaining there for three years, then returned to Calgary. In 1923, in the spring, they moved back to the ranch at Millarville. Harry rode several years to Square Butte School, which had opened the previous year. At this time school was held from late spring until cold weather set in. He later stayed with the Jim Ward family and had a shorter distance to ride.

In 1929, the house on the Fisher ranch burned while Mrs. Fisher was spending the winter in Calgary. Bob Fisher was at the lower ranch, the Meadow, so the old log house became home. Harry worked with ranch work and worked on other jobs. He worked in the oil fields, spending some time on a drilling rig at Fort Norman, in the Northwest Territories. In the 1930s he was a forest ranger, at the Aura and Harold Creek Stations. At this time, rangers were required to supply their own horses, no 4 wheel drive trucks at this time.

When World War 2 started, he joined the R.C.A.F., stationed in the Queen Charlotte Islands, then later in England. After his discharge, he moved to the west coast, bought a boat and did commercial fishing, later becoming a fish buyer.

Harry remained a bachelor until he married Nellie Burns in 1976. They lived very happily in New Westminster until his sudden death in February, 1977. His wife still lives in New Westminster.

Jane Fisher

by Jackie Chalmers
October 1978

Our member of the month is Johanna Von Rummel, but better known to her friends and neighbours at Millarville as Jane Fisher. Jane was born 80 years ago to Baron and Baroness Von Rummel of Munich, Germany.

She remembers her mother as somewhat of an adventuress, as a result much of her childhood was spent travelling throughout Europe. Jane and her two sisters, Lizzie and Nina received their schooling from a governess while living in Italy, Austria and Germany.

It was quite a surprise to the girls when their mother came home with the news that she had bought

Jane Fisher at ranch on Ware Creek returning from a ride in the Forest Reserve with niece Charis Blakley and son Jody on "Tom Thumb" and Peter on behind Jane. 1941.

some land in Canada and they would be going over soon to see it. She had purchased a section of land for approximately $11.00/acre.

Jane's first introduction to the cowboy life and his skill with horses was in 1908 at Shepperton, England. Her family was living in London for the summer and the girls were enrolled for riding lessons. It was here that the three girls befriended George Welsh, a trick roper; a friendship that lasted for many years. George came over to the first Calgary Stampede in 1912 and placed 2nd in the trick roping, a thrilling feat for three impressionable young girls at their first rodeo.

Jane first saw the foothills country west of Millarville in 1911 — during this first visit the family only stayed a short time. The girls were so insistent upon returning to the wilds of Canada that their mother consented to coming back the following year.

The first few years in Canada were carefree for the girls, with many hours spent riding in the foothills. For three girls "crazy about horses" it was like one long vacation.

With the advent of World War I many changes took place. The family money lost all its value as the German mark became very inflated — it was also impossible to get money out of Germany.

Jane, her two sisters and her mother had to come up with some way to make a living. Their decision was to raise Clydesdales and break them for work horses. The girls embarked on a breeding and horse breaking program with a Clyde stallion named "Northern Star" and a bunch of mares. No small feat for three petite frauleins.

The girls did everything with the horses including breaking them to drive and doing their own farrier work. The ingenuity of the fairer sex showed through when they rigged a trap to front foot the horses for trimming. One girl chased the horse along the side of the corral where they had a loop rigged up on a hook on the corral rail. When the horse stepped in it the other two girls jerked the loop tight — the Clyde would struggle 'til it went down. Once down Jane held the head while Lizzie tied the three feet together.

It was at this time that the first tractors were introduced and there wasn't a ready market for work horses. Teams that should have sold for $300.00 a team had to be sold for $40.00 a piece — a big disappointment after all their hard work.

Luckily, their main source of income was milk cows. From their ten cows, the girls sold cream for many years at $1.00 a gallon.

In 1933 Jane married young Joe Fisher, the son of one of the first settlers in the Millarville area. Mr. Fisher Sr. took up his homestead in 1883. Joe and Jane gradually started to build up a cattle herd comprised of Herefords. To help meet family expenses Joe worked in the oil patch. Jane stayed at home raising two sons, Jody and Peter, and also looking after all the outside work — from putting in the crops to raking hay. She never wanted a hired man saying, "I'd rather

Jane Fisher, Christmas time at the ranch.

work outside than cook for an extra guy''. She claims a dislike for cooking but one would never go to the Fisher home without being greeted by warm hospitality and good food.

Jane's career in the hayfield started in 1913 when she learned to drive a single black horse with shafts to rake the neighbours hay. She never missed a summer raking hay taking progress in her stride as she graduated from a single driving horse to a tractor. Jane retired from the hayfield in 1976 after developing some problems with her legs. She speaks fondly of those 67 years in the hayfield.

One of the highlights of Jane's life was her champion home-grown Palomino stallion — Kew Gold Dust. With "Dusty" she travelled to many of the local horse shows; winning Grand Champion Palomino in the 1949 Calgary Horse Show. Because of his many wins Dusty was chosen to go to the CNE in Toronto, even at a fair of this calibre he placed 5th. "He was the colour of a gold coin and had a thousand pictures taken of him,'' Jane recalls. She was honoured when she and Dusty were invited to lead the V.I.P.'s in carriages from the Palliser Hotel down through 8th Avenue for Stampede breakfast during the early '50's. They also led the Grand Entry of livestock at the Stampede.

Jane portrayed her love of the foothills in note cards she has drawn in the last few years using the

hills, mountains and trees as subject matter. She tells of drawing and writing stories with her sisters when she was just a youngster in Europe.

Joe and Jane were members of the Stock Growers for many years, gradually acquiring more land and expanding their operation at Millarville, 30 miles S. W. of Calgary. Their son Peter and his family have taken over the ranch now.

Jane truly epitomizes the breed of woman that helped develop the many early ranches of the area; hard-working, ambitious and far-seeing.

John E. Fisher
by Jean Blakley

Son of Joseph and Elizabeth Fisher, John was born in Calgary May 5th, 1905, the same year Alberta became a province. He was raised on the Fisher ranch at Millarville. There was no school in the Millarville area so the Fishers had to keep a home in Calgary, so the children could go to school. John first attended the old Riverside School then later when a new house was built in South Calgary, then King Edward School. Summer holidays were spent on the ranch at Millarville and John and his brother Joe would delay their return to Calgary in the fall as long as they possibly could. When the family moved to Victoria, B.C. he went to school there for a few years.

In 1923, the family moved back to the ranch. This was during the roaring twenties, the big band era, and John, like so many of the youths at that time, loved the music of the saxophone and he had a yen to own and play one. Saving his money, he bought a fine looking one, which he kept very polished, shining like a silver dollar. Learning to play the saxophone without a good teacher didn't produce very good music and there were no teachers in the area. He didn't get much encouragement from his brothers and sisters, who com-

John and Hazel Fisher on their 25th wedding anniversary, Jan. 20, 1959.

pared his music with the howling of the coyotes, so the saxophone was soon given up.

About this time he had a chance to go with an outfitter to take a party from Hollywood into Kananaskis Lakes. This was a big game hunting party. Going into that area at that time was done all by horseback and pack outfits, and John had a great time, with one sad note; his brother Joe had loaned him one of his top saddle horses, which got away from camp and was lost. In spite of several trips back into the mountains, the horse was never found.

John was a player for the Kew hockey team, who were in a league with Millarville, Priddis and Turner Valley. The Kew team had some excellent players and won the trophy cup three years in a row, thus retaining possession of it. The cup is still in the district, on display at the Millarville School.

About 1927, the Turner Valley oilfields were booming and John went to work for the Royalite Oil Company as a roughneck on the drilling rigs. The towns of Black Diamond and Turner Valley were having growing pains, with mostly shacks and roads that were knee deep in mud. Most of the roughnecks lived in the Royalite bunk houses. Here John was given the name of Pee Wee, which stuck with him long after he had outgrown it.

In 1934, John was married to Hazel Stagg of Black Diamond, and the next few years were spent working on rigs in the north and south ends of Turner Valley, then when drilling was at a low ebb in these fields, he went on wild cat rigs, at Strathmore, Pine Lake and in Saskatchewan. Hazel and the family lived in their home in Black Diamond during these jobs, but in 1952, when John went to Fort St. John as drilling superintendent for Pacific Petroleums, they bought a home there so Hazel and the boys moved up.

John and Hazel have a family of four. Carolyn, their only daughter, was the eldest. She was married first to Jim Harrison, having two children by this marriage, Patty and Michael. By her second marriage to Jerome Laboucane, she has two sons, Joe and Stacy. They live at Mile 55 on the Alaska Highway.

Garry married Florence Eklund and they have four daughters, Debbie, Pamela, Jacqueline and Joni. They make their home in Eckville, Alberta, where Garry is in the cement business for himself.

Brett married Esther Netterfield and they have two sons, John and Tommy. They also make their home in rural Ft. St. John, where Brett is in the construction business.

The youngest son, Bob, married Arlene Alexander and they have two children, Michelle and Douglas. Bob works for the B.C. Railway out of Ft. St. John.

John passed away in 1966. Hazel makes her home in Ft. St. John.

Joseph Fisher ⅂

Joe was born September 28th, 1902 in Calgary. He is the second son and third child of Joseph and Elizabeth (Stagg) Fisher, early pioneers of the Millarville district. He was raised on the ranch on Fisher Creek, and learned to ride at a very early age. Many of the old time cowboys worked for his father, breaking horses to be sold to the R.C.M.P. and many other outlets, so Joe had an early education in horse breaking. Although his father, Joseph Sr., knew horses from A to Z and was reputed to be one of the best judges of light horses in the west, he was no rider of the wild ones, but he enjoyed watching the cowboys ride the bronks. Tom Livingstone once remarked, watching Joe ride a bronk, "How his daddy would have loved to see him ride."

Joe's father loved the foothills so well that it was given to his son as a middle name, but his son didn't think too highly of this and the younger members of the family were threatened if they dared tell what the initial F. stood. It wasn't until many years later, on applying for his birth certificate, that he discovered that he had been registered as just "Joseph Fisher" Foothills had not been included in the registration.

There were no schools for the Fisher children to attend near the ranch, but for a short time school had been held in the old Rancher's Hall, which was situated on the ranch. Some of the Toole boys, whose father had a homestead north of Fisher's, also attended. About 1912, a home was bought in Calgary, in the Riverside district, and the older children attended Riverside School, and here the Fisher boys learned, among other things, to defend themselves. They usually had a saddle horse or two in town, and a barn and corral was built to accommodate these and horses brought in from the ranch to be held for selling. A team of horses were kept for the use of Joseph Sr., to pull the democrat, which was as essential for travel as the family car is today. Joe's older sister, Maybelle, was the terror of the Riverside district, galloping around on her pony.

Joe and his brother John would postpone going back to Calgary in the fall for school, often staying alone,

Joe Fisher judging at a rodeo at Black Diamond.

and on one of these occasions they saw such a sight come out of the timber that they ran into the house and remained there for days. What this thing was they were never able to explain, but whatever it was they were never to see anything to compare with it. No one could ever convince them that what they saw was not real.

When Joe was about 14 years old he had a good horse, Polo, who had been pre-empted by his younger sister. On her 7th birthday he was told that if he gave Polo to his sister he could have his pick of a large bunch of horses. Many horses were gathered and Joe picked a beautiful mare, who became his top horse. Not many 14 year old boys have the privelege of having their pick of so many horses.

It was inevitable that Joe would try his hand at rodeo riding. He rode in many local shows, Calgary, and rodeos put on in Eastern Canada and the United States by Peter Welsh. A clipping from the Calgary Herald about 1926 reads "A young rider came out of the chutes and put up such an exhibition of bronk riding that even the oldest cowhands described as salty. Hooking his mount, the noted old outlaw 'Wildfire', high in the shoulders, the young cowboy, Joe Fisher of Kew, turned in a ride that was thrilling in the extreme and one that will undoubtably land him in the money. His father used to raise the famous JN outlaws in pioneers days." This last remark made his mother furious. Outlaws, indeed not!

He was the first rider to have a qualified ride on Five Minutes to Midnight, and at one rodeo drew the famous old horse, Midnight, but lost his stirrup and was disqualified. At some rodeos where he competed he also served as pick-up man and says he knows of only one other rider to do this — Wayne Vold.

Somewhere along the line he took time out to take a welding course, and he worked at this and also in the Turner Valley oilfields.

He was married to Jane (Johanna Louise von Rummel) in 1933 and they ranched on the homestead of Jack Dempsey, an early and well known Alberta cattleman. They built a large log house and a smaller one which was used as a schoolhouse for his two boys, Jody, born in 1934, and Peter, born in 1936. It was the old problem of no school close enough for the boys to attend, so for a few years teachers were hired and the little schoolhouse used. The time came when the boys needed to go to a larger school, so it was decided to move to the Fisher homestead about seven miles east. The log house they had built on Ware Creek would have to be moved. This was done by James and Reimer Trucking and was quite an undertaking. There were three creeks to be crossed, Ware, North Sheep and Fisher Creeks before the house could be set down, no bridges on which to cross and in many places trees had to be cut down to allow the large load to proceed. That same evening the chimneys were put back in place and Jane cooked supper. The little log schoolhouse was

also moved down to the new location and has been used as a guest house for many years.

Joe and Jane were members of the North Sheep Stock Association for many years, running their cattle on the Forest Reserve. They raised some fine horses and one of these, Dusty, a Golden Palomino, Jane showed at many horse shows, winning awards, and Joe took Dusty to the Toronto Royal Fair one year.

Joe last competed in rodeos in 1936. He won first at Sundre, on to Innisfail, where he split first and second with Slim Watrin of High River, each receiving as his share $12.50. Prize money was much smaller at that time. At Crossfield he again won first money, but with hungry cowboy friends and travelling expenses he arrived home with less money than he started with. For several years he judged at the Calgary Stampede.

A few years after moving to Fisher Creek, Joe bought a section of land, 6-20-3-w5. Jody and his family lived on this place until it was sold. When Joe retired from actual ranching he worked as a real estate agent. He enjoyed this very much as he liked being with people.

His son Peter and his family have taken over the ranch, as well as land Jane owned, the old John Ware holdings. He is using his grandfather's brand. His family is the fourth generation of Fishers living on the homestead.

Joe presently makes his home at the Big Hill Lodge at Cochrane.

Patricia Helen Fisher
born in Drumheller, Alberta, October 17, 1942
written by herself

I was raised a true blue city girl, but as a child I used to spend all my summer holidays on a farm. At about the age of 14 I decided that I would **never, never** marry a farmer as there was far too much work to do on a farm. So what did I do at the ripe old age of 19, I turned around and married a rancher, which is just about as bad.

Peter and I were married on September 8, 1962. Our wedding day was the day following one of the heaviest snow storms this district had had in years. We were married in Calgary with a reception to follow. Due to the fact that there were so many people from this district that we couldn't invite to the supper, Peter's folks, Jane and Joe Fisher had decided they would have a party at their house the same night. What a party! On account of the storm the power lines were still down, so candles were used for light. Of course they didn't have running water, as few people did at that time in this district, and only the wood stove for heat. They didn't need this as every room in the house was packed with people, with standing room only. It was a great party, certainly not your everyday, run of the mill, wedding parties.

Peter and I then lived for the first month of our marriage working on John Cross's ranch west of Nanton. Peter was roto-tilling at the time and we lived in a

Peter and Pat Fisher on their wedding day, September 8th, 1962.

L. to R. Stephen, Peter, Russel and Lisa Fisher.

trailer there. After that we moved back onto his mom and dad's place (N.E. 6-21-3-w5) and lived for the next 5 months in the little log cabin that they called "the schoolhouse". This cabin was like a little doll's house. It was one room about 12' x 14'. No water again, but it had power and a little gas burning stove for heat. The Fisher place was the furthest west on the Turner Valley gas line at that time.

Everything would have been rosy at this time except for one minor detail, I was pregnant, and terribly sick on top of it. Everyday started with me stepping out of bed and making a dash for the "slop bucket" — sick to my stomach again. After many mornings of this Peter informed me he couldn't take this anymore and was going "home to Mother's" (who lived next door) to have his breakfast in peace. This suited me fine until a few nights later in bed a mouse ran across my face and I informed him that I was going to live with his mother until he killed all the mice in the cabin. Consequently we **both** ended up living at his mother's place for a short time.

Another amusing thing about me being pregnant was that the community had never had a wedding shower for us before we were married (that was the custom then, they had the shower after the wedding). For some reason they never got around to having the shower until January of 1963. I was very sick at this time and the Doctor had put me in the hospital and kept telling me he would try and let me out on Friday so I could attend the shower. Wouldn't you know it, come Friday, Dr. Landers said, "I couldn't go home." At this time there were no phones west of Bill and Esther Jackson's place, so it was almost impossible to cancel the shower. Peter had to go to the wedding shower by himself and explain to everyone that I was pregnant and sick in the hospital. He had to stand there and give the thank you speech all by himself. This has always amused me. Maybe because I was so sick myself, that old saying, "misery loves company", is true.

Russell was born on June 29, 1963 at Turner Valley

Hospital. It was a terrible stormy night again and I can remember Peter's Uncle Harry Fisher was visiting from B.C. and he said to me, "you will have the baby to-night, as all the Fisher women have their babies in a storm", and I laughed and said, "sorry Harry, not this time, its not due yet." Well Harry was right, and what a trip and what a storm! It washed the bridge out at the race track and the one at Millarville was impassable. Lucky for me we got through before the water got that high.

By this time we had moved into the house we are presently living in, still on Jane and Joe's place.

Our second son, Stephen Peter was born on August 19, 1965. He had long red hair at birth and was a delight to all the nurses at the General Hospital in Calgary.

Our daughter Lisa Jane was born on June 5, 1968. At this time Peter was away working on an oil rig at Canmore. Peter's father had to take me to the hospital in Calgary that night. He was so nervous that I was quite sure we would never make it to the hospital alive, never mind in time!

In 1968 Russell was 5 years old and I felt that he needed something to keep him busy so I offered to take over the kindergarten at Millarville as Mrs. Pearl Laycraft (who was teaching it at the time) was going back to full time teaching. She was a big help to me and I had classes 2 mornings every week from October to May. The mothers of the children I was teaching would take turns looking after Steve and Lisa for me as they were too young to attend. These mothers were a great help to me also. Those 5 years have some of my best memories and many of those children still live in this district and some are now in high school. They will always have a special place in my heart.

I now work full time at Millarville School as a Teacher's Aide. I have been here for the past 3 years. I find my work very rewarding, working with children and a great staff.

Of course, Peter and the kids are my pride and joy and I feel very fortunate to have on top of all this a great community like Millarville to live in.

271

Fisher, Peter Eugene
born in Calgary, June 13, 1936

As a youngster, I lived with my family (Jane and Joe Fisher and my brother Jody) one mile east of the forestry boundary on Ware Creek.

Our only close neighbors were two bachelors, Eddie Behm and Gavin Calderwood. We did not have a very good road to our place, but if the driving conditions were just right we could drive Dad's 1936 Plymouth down the Ware Creek flats and get out that way.

My brother Jody and myself took correspondence lessons for our early schooling with the help from a Miss McDonald, who lived beside us in a little one room log cabin, which we called the school house. Later on Miss Winnie Ball took her place. My cousin Mike Rodgers, who lived 4 miles east, joined us for his grade one in 1945.

Mom and Dad had a few head of cattle and Dad worked part time on the oil rigs, having to sometimes ride horseback to work in bad weather. My Mom liked living back in the hills working the livestock and doing a lot of the farmwork herself.

It was somewhat of a lonely life for children to grow up in compared to the lifestyle of youngsters nowadays. Our annual outing was to go to the Calgary Stampede for one or two days. My Dad worked at the Stampede for 17 years.

Our main visitor was my Grandmother (Elsa Basilici), whom we all called Omi. She lived part time with us and part time with one of her other daughters, Mrs. Nina Rodgers. She was a wonderful person and taught us many things, including how to play poker when I was six years old. Another frequent visitor was my Aunt Elizabeth Rummel, whom we all called Aunt Lizzie. She is well known in the Banff area having operated various lodges in that vicinity and later on owning her own summer resort near Mt. Assiniboine.

Home of Joe and Jane Fisher on their Ware Creek Ranch. Picture taken in 1933 just when house was finished. This large log house was moved down to Fisher Creek in 1946.

During the summer our main pastime was the wonderful fishing along Ware Creek. It isn't nearly as good nowadays.

In 1946 due to the poor school conditions we moved our log house to my Grandfather's homestead (N.E. 6-21-3-W5) 3½ miles west of Millarville, where the house still sits today.

I attended Sheep Creek School, 2 miles west of Millarville, until I completed grade 11. I finished grade 12 by attending Mount Royal College in Calgary one year and Turner Valley High School the next.

In the spring of 1955 I went to work driving a tourist bus for Rocky Mountain Tours in Banff. I returned to the same job for the summer of 1956 and part of the summer of 1957 for Brewster Grayline.

In the fall of 1957 I went to Tech in Calgary taking a Survey course, which I completed in the spring of 1959. At this time I went to work for Calgary Power in Canmore and later to the Calgary office in 1961. It was there that I met my wife Pat (Gray). We were married on September 8, 1962. For the first six months that we were married we lived in the same little, one room cabin that I had gone to school in as a child.

In the spring of 1962 I quit Calgary Power and went into Partnership with my brother Jody, doing custom rototilling and cattle ranching. In 1967 we dissolved the partnership and I have been ranching on my own ever since.

Pat and I still live on my Grandfather's homestead, 3½ miles west of Millarville. We have three children, Russell born 1963, Steve born 1965 and Lisa born 1968.

Peter and Pat Fisher with their family, Russel, Steven and Lisa, helping Dad build a porch.

Robert Wilfrid Fisher
by Jean Blakley

Bob was born in Calgary November 8th, 1900, second child of Joseph and Elizabeth Fisher of Millarville. His father was a great admirer of Sir Wilfrid Laurier, the Liberal Prime Minister at that time, so Bob was given Wilfred as a second name. Bob was raised on the family ranch at Millarville until the family was forced to go to Calgary for schooling. The first Calgary home was in the Riverside district, with barn and corrals to accommodate the many horses brought in from the ranch for selling. This was of great interest to the many children of the area, who spent much time watching the activity in Fisher's back yard. The children attended Riverside School until a new house was built in South Calgary, and the children attended King Edward School. William Aberhart, the Social Credit leader was principal of the school at that time.

About 1922, Bob with his sister Maybelle and her husband, Stanley Stanhope, moved out and took over the lower Fisher ranch, the Meadow, selling hay and raising sheep. They lived here until the Stanhopes bought land nearby from Mr. Williams.

Bob loved engines of all kinds, and at one time took a mechanics course at the Hempel School, which was

Bob Fisher and two friends at Banff.

situated near the Langevin Bridge, in Calgary. He had one of the early tractors in the Millarville district and went from ranch to ranch, sawing large piles of wood, which at the time was the usual source of heating.

For a few years he worked at many and varied jobs, living at times on the ranch on Fisher Creek, later moving to the Meadow, where his mother came to live with him in 1929. The house on the Upper Place had been burned to the ground, so from then on the Meadow became home. Mrs. Fisher had been living in Calgary and the place on Fisher Creek had been rented when the fire occurred.

Bob was usually a peaceful man, unless he thought

his rights were being tampered with. On one such occasion, he got into a fight with a neighbor and soundly trounced the older man. He was taken to court in Okotoks, fined for assault and then to add insult to injury, when he went out to his car to drive home, he found his car had been ticketed for improper licensing, another fine.

He bought the John Anderson land in the Kew district, the S.W. ¼ of 28-20-3w5 and an adjoining 80 acres. By this time he had a good herd of cattle, pasturing them on this land in the summer. The Meadow was well known as a great hay producer, and as it was one of the few frost-free places in the area, he raised a large garden. The potato patch was usually green after the first snow.

Bob was a strong supporter of the Social Credit Party, and during the thirties at political meetings in the old Rancher's Hall, many heated arguments arose, with Bob right in the middle of them.

After his mother's death in 1947, Bob batched, had never married. In 1963, after driving his cattle to the summer pasture, he passed away very suddenly. The Meadow was sold to Harold Roenisch, and he and his family make their home there.

William Allan Fisher

I was born in Victoria, B.C. but spent most of my young years in the Millarville district. In 1928, I started school at the newly opened Sheep Creek School, being transported there on behind my sister's horse. Later that fall, Mother and I moved into Calgary, where I attended Haultain School, until spring, when we returned to Millarville, living at the Meadow. I then went to New Valley School.

I left New Valley School in 1937, after which I worked for W. J. Oliver on the McKinnon place (now Graham Ranches). The following year I worked for Bert Chalmers, Tim Blakley and Herb Adams. In 1953 I worked for Francis Sinclair-Smith and joined the Army Reserve in Okotoks and in June 1940 I took two weeks training at Sarcee Camp in Calgary. I moved to Turner Valley in 1941 and began working in the oilfields, but joined the Royal Canadian Navy Reserve in August. I took basic training at Calgary and Esquimalt, B.C., from there to Halifax in July 1942. I then went to Saint John, N.B. to pick up H.M.C.S. St. Croix, and served in the North Atlantic convoy until December, when I came home on leave and was married to Marie Nesbit of Black Diamond. I returned to the St. Croix and the North Atlantic until March and then the Mediterranean for a month.

We went back to Halifax in April, then back on North Atlantic Convoy until September 19, 1943, when the St. Croix was torpedoed and sunk. I was picked up by H.M.S. Itchen, which was torpedoed September 21, two days later. I was rescued by a Polish merchant ship, which landed in New Jersey. I went to the hospital, where I found I was the lone survivor of H.M.C.S. St. Croix. After a week in hospital, I went to Ottawa and then on leave. I spent three weeks helping

Bill and Marie Fisher.

Bill Fisher Family. L. to R., Back: Steven, Anna, Bill jr., Betty, Keith. Front: Bill and Marie.

the fifth Victory Loan Drive, travelling around the country speaking.

I returned to Ottawa, where I was stationed until April 1944, then to the West Coast. Our daughter Betty was born in August 1944. She and Marie joined me at Victoria in May 1945. We stayed there until the end of the war then returned to Black Diamond.

I worked for Royalite Oil Company until they sold to Gulf Oil in 1968. I worked in Turner Valley until Gulf Oil transferred me to Westerose in 1972, where I am working now.

Our family are all on their own now so Marie and I enjoy fishing, camping, golfing and snowmobiling.

Our eldest daughter, Elizabeth Joyce (Betty) was born in Calgary in August, 1944, and is working and makes her home in Calgary. Anna Louise was born in Calgary, also works and makes her home there. William Thomas, born in Turner Valley in 1950, served in the Armed Services from 1969-1976, married Louise Williams. They have one daughter and make their home in Drayton Valley. Steven Mark was born in Turner Valley in 1952, has one son and one daughter. Steven is now serving with the Canadian Armed Services in Germany. His family are also in Germany. The youngest member of the family, Keith Allan, was

born in Turner Valley in 1956. He is married to Gloria Nadeau, has one daughter. They make their home in Calgary.

Marie and I are long time members of the Canadian Legion and at one time had the distinction of each being president at the same time, Marie of the Ladies' Auxiliary and I was president of the Turner Valley Branch of the Legion.

Ellen Louise (Jackson) Flood

by Esther Jackson

Ellen is the second oldest daughter of William and Mary (Minnie) Jackson. She was born near Priddis in 1899 NW¼ 24-22-3W5. Received her education at Fordville School and later took up dress-making. She was married in Calgary to Orval Dowling of Priddis. They had six children; Robert, Lloyd, Helen, Myrtle, Beulah and an infant who passed away at an early age.

They farmed for some years around Cayley and Vulcan and in the 1930's bought a farm at Goodwin near Grande Prairie.

Their little girl, Myrtle died at the age of three before they moved north and both of their boys died at

Ellen (Jackson) Flood.

the age of 20 from a rare muscular disease. This was a sad blow to them.

In the 1940's they moved to a farm at Leslieville, it was soon after that when their marriage ended in divorce. Orval died in 1967.

Ellen worked at cooking for construction crews for some years then married James Flood, a fireman. They worked for oil companies for some time, then, went to live in Taber. Ellen's two daughters were married while they lived there. Helen married, Glen Stanley and Beulah married Nick Lazaruk.

Ellen and Jim later moved to Lethbridge where Jim died in 1974. Ellen and her two daughters now live in Lethbridge.

Erlwin Foerster — Teacher at Square Butte School

by Margaret Blaine, daughter

ERLWIN FOERSTER was born in Ontario May 5, 1871. He taught school in Ontario for a number of years, beginning at age 17. In 1910 he came west with his wife and family and then taught for many years in various places throughout Saskatchewan and Alberta. He taught in the Square Butte school No. 4008, at Kew, Alberta, in the year 1932-33.

This school was constructed of logs and was obviously built by the early pioneers of the district. My father bought a cabin in Turner Valley and had it moved on to the school grounds as a teacherage where he and my mother lived.

I think all the children came to school on horseback. Some of the pupils were Joe Bannerman, Billy Kendall, Joan Kosling, Elizabeth Fulton, to mention only a few names I remember. Elizabeth Rummel was secretary-treasurer and Dan Bannerman and Mr. Northover were on the school board at that time.

It was my father's custom in all his schools to go out at noon and have a baseball game going. He was the pitcher and umpire for both sides. Everyone, large and small, got into the game. This was an enjoyable part of school life. My mother taught the children singing as she was gifted in that way.

My father enjoyed the remoteness of the area, the foothills, the trees, the animals and the birds. He was a lover of nature as shown in the poem he wrote:

To A Chickadee

Kind chickadee, you stay with me
    When all around is dreary;
No other bird has stayed with word
    To make my winter cheery.

No words can tell my thanks so well
    As this big bone for dinner,
That hangs before my cabin door,
    Lest hunger make you thinner.

And may it bring on joyous wing,
    Around my forest shanty,

More velvet caps that search for scraps
    When frost-proof meals are scanty.

— Erlwin Foerster —

Foster, D. W. (Chub) and Nita

by Nita Foster

Chub was born at Empress, Saskatchewan in 1919 in a sod shack. In 1920 his parents Harry and Mabel Foster and two boys moved to Stoney Plain, Alberta. After swamp fever killed their cattle and some horses, in 1922 they moved to Kamloops, B.C. and from there in 1928 they moved to Kew. Now Chub was happy because he was on a farm and had a horse. He rode to school at Plainview for all his schooling. Chub liked to ride so much he always went with his Dad to take the cattle out to the straw piles at Okotoks no matter what kind of weather. Then he spent weekends riding for neighbours, also trailing cattle to Calgary stock yards. When Chub left school he worked for Mr. Kendall, Mr. Phillips and Paddy Rodgers. He bought some milk cows and started a dairy in 1937.

In 1938 Chub and I were married. I am Herb and Hazel Adams eldest daughter and grew up in the Kew district. I attended public school at Plainview then two years at Sheep Creek School and two years at Turner Valley High. When I left school I went to work at Okotoks, Longview, Turner Valley and a year in Calgary. Chub and I lived in a little log house we had built on Mr. Foster's place with a log barn and increased our dairy herd, going into purebred Ayrshires. As we needed more land we rented different places and moved six times, dairy and all. Finally we bought part of Chub's Dad's home place. This was a big step without much money so Chub went to work for the Home Oil Co. I kept the dairy going and helped as much as I could with the other outside work. Chub worked for eleven years at the Home Oil Co. By this time we were getting some range cattle so after 26 years we sold our dairy herd and went to straight

Nita and Chub Foster with their family. L. to R. Nita, Chub, Wendy (Foster) Ashbacher, Darrel Ashbacher, Judy Foster, Ken Foster with son Clayton, Nona Foster, Keith Foster.

Taking cattle to summer pasture behind Forget Me Not Mountain. Nita Foster, Buck Stockwell, Chub Foster.

Keith Foster

range cattle. About this time I registered Harry Foster's brand ∨⅂ that he had taken out in early 1900's. Then in 1963 I went to work in a cafe as cook in Black Diamond, often going to work at six o'clock in the morning or working the late shift at night. After three years this was too much, so I just worked three or four days a week cleaning houses in this area.

In the last ten years with our family on their own Chub and I have had more time to do things we like. Chub likes to go to sales, also cattle and horse shows. I was involved with 4-H until two years ago and I have taught Leathercraft and Quilting for Adult Education. Now my big interest is in the Women's Institute. We are still active in our ranching operation but take time each winter to go for a holiday and have been to Hawaii, Mexico and Arizona.

We have two boys and a girl, Ken born April, 1942, married Judy Young and they have three children; Shannon 1968, Tami 1969 and Clayton 1976; Keith born 1944, married Nona Vinson, two children; Lenore 1974 and Brandi 1976; Wendy born November 1953, married Darrel Ashbacher, one son Zane 1979.

Keith Foster

by Keith Foster

I came into this world January, 1944 at the Turner Valley Hospital as the second son of Chub and Nita Foster, of Millarville. I took my schooling at the Sheep Creek School and Turner Valley High. During my school days I belonged to the Cadets under instructor Bill Dube. I left school before I finished my grade eleven and went to work for Ray Legace at Lake Louise as a guide and packer. I did this work for three summers and worked on the oil drilling rigs in the winters. The third winter I went into selling real estate in Calgary, but when spring came the outdoor call was strong so I went to work for the Provincial Parks. I spent that summer on a lookout north of Fort McMurray. I had a long lonesome four months with only radio contact with the outside world, but it made me think about the future, so I spent my time studying forestry. By September I was moved into Fort

McMurray for awhile, then assigned to be an assistant ranger at Anzac. I had many hair-raising experiences there amongst the Indian people, also with the weather. It was great experience, and I worked to be Fire Chief with seventy men under me fighting the big

Nona, Lenore and Brandi Foster. March 1978.

276

Athabasca fire in 1967. I was often taken by aircraft to other big fires, one being the fire west of Banff. After three years at Anzac I was transferred to Federal Parks and was posted at Willow Creek in Jasper Park. I lived out there with my horses and dog for three years, only coming into Jasper periodically for supplies.

Then I met Nona Vinson who worked for her father Tom Vinson at the pony barn at the Jasper Lodge. Nona was barn boss and could guide out a party on a trail ride trip or a hunting trip with the best of them. We were married on November 27, 1971 at Hinton, Alta. Two weeks later we were transferred to Dauphin, Manitoba to the Riding Mountain National Park as area manager. What an experience that first Christmas, in a big house with no furniture as the shipping van had been delayed, also it was the first time either of us had been away from our homes at Christmas time.

Now we have two girls, Lenore born May 1974, and Brandi born February 1976. We have been active in horse sports events and I have a great interest in team roping, getting into the Manitoba Provincial final three years. Nona is a high point winner in the Gymkhana events of the area. The girls love their horses so hope they will be cowgirls too.

Ken and Judy Foster.

Foster, Kenneth Leigh   ⌐⌐ R.R.

I was born April 1942 in Turner Valley, eldest son of Chub and Nita Foster. All my schooling was taken at Sheep Creek School. I was in the Royal Canadian Army Cadets for several years. The summer of 1957 I spent in the Vernon Cadet training camp.

From the time I quit school, I have been involved in the farm operation with Dad and registered my brand ⌐⌐ right ribs. I also worked for several contractors at various jobs. For ten years I worked on seismograph crews, travelling all over Alberta and B.C. In 1968 I started a construction business.

I consider these Foothills home, as my great-great-grandfather, J. Ennings, great-grandfather of my mother Nita (Adams) came to the Okotoks area at the turn of the century and is buried in the Okotoks cemetery. My grandfather J. H. Foster moved onto this section (36-20-4-5) in 1928.

I married Judy Young from Bowness. Judy was born July 1946 in High River, Alberta. The family moved shortly after that to Calgary and then in 1950 to Bowness where she took all her schooling, graduating in 1964 from Bowness Composite High School. She worked as a stenographer in Calgary until moving to Millarville. We have two daughters, Shannon, March 1968, Tami, July 1969 and one son, Clayton, April 1976.

In 1965 I bought the SE¼ 34-20-4-5, but we live on the home ¼ NE 36-20-4-5. I was involved in the first executive of the Millarville and District Recreation Board which began in 1972.

Tami, Shannon and Clayton Foster, children of Ken and Judy Foster.

Leslie Foster

I was born on the bald prairie in a sod shack, at Josephine, Saskatchewan, between Alsask and Empress, in 1913. My Mother and Dad were early homesteaders, arriving before the railroad. It seems most of the people in the west originally came from Saskatchewan.

When I was about six years old, my Dad sold out, that was in 1919, the last of the good years. My Dad used to say he was the last one to sell out — the rest walked out. Certainly some hard years followed. However, he bought a new Model T Ford and we drove across country to a ranch he had bought between Lac St. Ann and Wabamun. It was pretty rough country then. It took us about ten days to make the trip, can be made easy in a day now. We had only prairie trails to follow. From Stony Plain west we cut poplar to make corduroy to cross the wet places, but we finally got the Ford to the new place. I don't really remember that Ford coming out again.

Silvia, Matthew and D'Arcy Foster.

Well, we hit the cattle slump in 1922 and lost everything. Dad signed a quit claim deed and we literally walked out. He got a ticket for Mom and the baby (Chub) and Dad and I rode the freight to Kamloops. Imagine a nine year old with his first pair of bib overalls taking the Yellow Head route on a freight and seeing the Rockies for the first time. Boy, it was an experience I will never forget. We lived in

Ann and Leslie Foster with Gloria (Toots) and Gordie. 1948.

Bruce and Gloria Ockey and family. L. to R. Bruce, Gloria, Holly, Shawna, Michelle.

Gordie and Jeannie Foster with their family. L. to R. Jeannie, Darrelle, Dana, and Derek.

278

Kamloops for six years and liked it very much; it was a nice place to grow up in.

When I was fifteen, we moved to a ranch at Kew. Dad was manager for L. M. Hanan, a San Francisco shoe manufacturer. I went to school a couple more years at Plainview and Sheep Creek, rode horseback summer and winter. In fact, we did everything on horseback. When I got old enough to talk back I went out to work on ranches clear down to the border. Learned about cows (Heaven forbid) and how to break horses, which I followed until I got my first oil well job. I stayed in the oil patch from then on, came home and helped on the ranch when jobs were scarce.

In 1945, I married Ann Miller from Lethbridge. Yes, you guessed it, she originally came from Saskatchewan, too. We bought out the ranch in 1947 and still operate it.

We raised two boys and one girl. They are all married and live within 40 miles, Gordon, Gloria and D'Arcy. Gordon married Jeannie Gibb from Hillspring. Gloria married Bruce Ockey from Calgary. D'Arcy married Sylvia Smith from De Winton. We have seven grandchildren. Gordon and Jeannie have two girls and one boy, Darrelle, Dana and Derek. Gloria and Bruce have three girls, Holly, Shawna and Shelley. D'Arcy and Sylvia have one little boy, Matthew. So life goes on and is enjoyed by all.

Roy and Ethel Foster. April, 1979.

Roy Foster

by Roy A. Foster

Likely some of the earliest events that I remember in my childhood days, took place during the wet spring of 1928. That was the year my father and mother with their family of three boys, moved from Kamloops, B.C. (where I was born). Father took the job of running a ranch for Mr. L. M. Hannon. During those years, the main road from Calgary to Millarville, and Kew, took a route over the "Weaslehead Bridge", which skirted the Sarcee Army Range, and the old Currie Army Camp in southwest Calgary. The road wound through the Sarcee Indian Reserve to the Hamlet of Priddis, and then wound up and around the hills to Millarville, Turner Valley and Kew areas. That spring, the Foster home as we know it today, was in the early stages of being built.

During the years that followed, prior to 1939 and during the "Dirty Thirties," my childhood days were full of joy with few responsibilities. I'm sure that the responsibilities associated with my father and mother during those years were far from joyful, with untold hardships, and some heartache. However, they faced the daily tasks with vigor, aggressiveness, and smiles. As a young boy during those years, I used to play a lot of hockey on various sloughs, and creeks during the winter months, and did lots of good creek fishing, and exploring during the summer. Those were the years when the North Sheep, Fisher Creek and Ware Creek

supported and supplied any number of good sized Trout and Grayling.

The Snow-Shoe and Cottontail rabbits were in abundance. Every kid in the country had a trap, or rabbit snareline. We all grew up with a .22 rifle which supplied many good meals of Prairie Chicken and Ruffed Grouse.

Summer was a busy time collecting Magpie and Crow's eggs; which represented one point each, and gopher tails also!! Magpie and Crow legs were also point getters, which when all were turned into the school teacher for counting an equal amount of money (one cent per point), would be paid by the Provincial Government.

We also shot rabbits and gophers which represented money when delivered to Dan Bannerman's Fox farm!!

The money earned would quite often be used to have a real exciting party by riding horseback to Turner Valley to see a movie of "Buck Rogers" or "Hop-a-Long Cassidy".

Usually once during the winter hockey season, Ford Lochhead, or Dan Dudenhoeffer would load up the back of their half ton trucks with all the neighborhood kids and take us to the old Victoria arena in Calgary, to watch the Turner Valley Oilers take on the Calgary Stampeders, (excitement at its best).

I also recall setting gopher traps on top of the straw

piles, where hundreds of Prairie Chickens would feed during the long winter months.

Other good times involved walking several miles to play hockey on the ice at Olhausers "Rat Farm", if the ice was in good shape!!

As we lived on the north side of the North Sheep (now called Three Point), and Plainview School was on the south side, we had to ford the creek in the morning and at night. It was also my job to deliver one quart of fresh milk to Mr. Walton who owned the Kew Store and post office. The delivery was made on my way to school. The delivered milk (fresh with cream on top) brought a credit of ten cents per day, which was deducted off our family grocery bill at the end of each month. Occasionally I would take two chocolate bars in lieu of the ten cent credit!!

The crossing of the creek each day, I am sure, must have been an untold worry to my family. During the spring break-up and heavy spring run-off, the normally calm little creek would turn into a rampage. Many times during the maximum depth of the water, during the evening return from school, I would stay at the Lochhead or Rod Richardson home. The communication would be a "Wave" to my father who would be waiting on the north side, knowing the creek was too wild to cross, even with a good horse.

Ethel and Roy Foster's family. L. to R. Gerald Roy, Brenda Leigh, Ferol Lorraine, Eldon Vernon.

Gordy Maberley tells of a day when five or six of us kids were walking on the dusty road between Lochheads and the old Kew Store — likely in the vicinity of the Kew Community Hall (now Square Butte Hall). It was a hot mid-summer day during the mid thirties. We all had our fishing poles, on our way to go fishing. Gordy says it was I, who said, "O.K. everybody lets all whistle", and likely that was an ideal place, time, and atmosphere for anyone to be able to "whistle".

Many happy times were spent with my school pals,

and it seemed the Lochheads, Richardsons, Dudenhoeffers and Icetons became second homes.

It seemed there were always lots of hired "Cowhands" for my Mom to feed, or lone cowboys passing through who would be welcome to a cowboy's free meal, regardless of their appearance, even if they wore a six gun!!

Untold stories filled the bunkhouse where my older brothers Les and Chubb would be, until the early hours of the morning. Stories were told, and songs were sung, that were not for children's ears to hear!! Mouth Organs, Jews' Harp's, Guitars, Banjos and "Spoons" were common musical instruments at the bunkhouse after a hard days work. Cowboy songs and yodelling would shake the rafters of the old bunkhouse, which could be heard clear over to the Boss's House, and likely some whiskey still "Brew" found its way to the bunkhouse concealed in the saddle bags of some cowboys saddle!!

Several oil company rigs would be drilling from time to time in the Kew area. I recall the old wooden derricks with cable tools drilling at a location approximately 1½ miles directly west of our house. This was the "Brock", and Mr. and Mrs. Bert Campbell and their family lived there for several years after the camp and "hole" was abandoned. The old Richfield wooden derrick and cable tools drilled in the northwest corner of the Bill Senior place, and in later years another Richfield well was drilled very near the original hole; this time with a bigger steel rig and rotary tools. The steam boilers were fired with oil which was trucked in. We, as kids, used to ride horseback or walk to the boiler house for a shower quite often. The crews always had a good laugh when some "Roughneck" would turn the high pressure cold water hose on us while in the shower.

During the mid thirties it was always a happy occasion to go to a far away, good neighbor, to an invited Sunday dinner.

I recall Father polishing the harness and grooming a "snappy" little team, and during the summer months we would all ride in a plush two seated buckboard to such homes as Gettigs, Kendalls, Joe and Jane Fishers, Paddy and Nina Rodgers or Mr. and Mrs. Sandy Russell and of course, others!! In the winter months it was a similar situation, with a good team, polished harness complete with sleigh bells, and a double deck box (partially, filled with hay; and rocks which had been heated in the oven the previous night, for Mom's feet) on a well painted and maintained set of bob sleighs.

My dad was likely the greatest wild berry picker in the country, and many summer Sundays were spent at the south-end of "Nigger-John" ridge west of the old Iceton farm, picking wild raspberries and saskatoons. (Mom made the best saskatoon pies.)

My parents, and family were also great friends of the Sarcee and Stony Indian tribes. The long trail of Indians, (using every mode of horse travel imaginable) would be heading south to the big ranches for fencing, cutting brush, and other jobs, and would always spend one or two nights camping at or near our house. Many tents of all shapes; sizes and colors would sometimes be pitched in our holding field; and some of the older Indians would even sleep in our barn, or hayloft.

Mother would give them tea and flour, and Dad would give them tobacco, and feed their animals. (There were always lots of dogs.) I'm sure such friendship between Indian and white man is gone forever!! and the good neighbour attitude was respected by the whole tribe, and appreciation was always evident by the laughter of the small children, and the smiles of the shy squaws.

On the return trip back to the Reserves in late fall, the Indians would again camp at our ranch. For Mother and Dad, (and sometimes us kids) there were always presents of beautiful beaded guantlet gloves, chaps or buckskin coats. These genuine handcrafted presents were yearly tokens of appreciation by the Indians, for the friendship shown by my family. (Friendship amongst brown and white that likely is gone forever.) Visits by my Mom and Dad were also made to those neighbors who were living alone. People like Jim Howey, Eddie Behm — George Fleming, Dunc Grant, Arthur Reid and others. These visits were always happy occasions also!!

It seems evident in my mind today that my parents were great friends of great and genuine neighbors.

Childhood and school days soon passed, and my first job was working on a threshing crew for Joe Standish. I then worked for Paddy Rodgers, feeding cattle, chores, fencing and sharpening fence posts (with a good sharp axe).

Part of the time I would be up at Joe and Jane Fishers, when they lived up on Ware Creek. I would haul feed in the winter time from the Bill Patterson place up to the original Joe and Jane Fisher ranch. I would help Jane do chores, and fix fences when Joe was away at some of the big rodeos during the summer months. The ranch and farm life didn't seem to attract me, as it had for so many kids. The war was now raging in 1940-41, and I was becoming anxious to reach 16, so I might stand a chance of enlisting in the Airforce or Navy. At this time I thought there must be something different in the world, other than living on the north bank of Sheep Creek.

I enlisted in the RCAF in the spring of 1942, (under age) and served in the youth training program of the B.C.A.T.P. (British Commonwealth Air Training Program) at the old badminton building at Medicine Hat. Originally during this period I trained as an airframe mechanic. After boot-camp in Edmonton, and technical training in St. Thomas, Ontario, I was transferred to No. 1.S.F.T.S. at Camp Borden, Ontario. I went overseas in October 1943; served in Bomber Command, and later with a Beaufighter Squadron.

After the war I used my war gratuities to take a 2 year Diesel Engine course, and attended the same old badminton building in Medicine Hat which had been converted from a war training school to a Veterans Vocational Training School. (This old building no longer stands at the west end of Allowance Ave.) The advancement Diesel Engine training was located at the Wartime Army Facilities in Red Deer where the training was completed. This is where I met Ethel Longacre who was training for a nurse in Red Deer. Ethel was one of 12 children, who had been raised by her late father on a dried out farm northwest of Taber at Retlaw, Alberta.

We were married in Okotoks on April 24/48. The reception was held at the Foster home at Kew. Those attending the reception were transported into the Ranch in relays by two jeeps (which my brother Les and myself owned). The roads commonly known as trails were something to remember!!

Prior to wedding I had started to work for Home Oil Company at Millarville as their Field Mechanic.

Ethel and I bought a little two room house from Mr. and Mrs. Ozzie Lister at the location where Bobby and Jo Ann Jackson now live. We later moved to the Home Oil camp where we lived in a company house until 1950.

We now had our first son; and the R.C.A.F. took my interest away from Home Oil and the oil industry. I rejoined the R.C.A.F. in 1950.

For four years I was attached to the Salvage and Aeronautical Inspection Board at No. 6 Repair Depot in Trenton, Ontario.

Our responsibility was to pick up all RCAF crashes from a line running from the high Arctic to the Gulf of Mexico and from a point east of the Ontario — Manitoba border. This operation took me to many isolated areas of Canada. From remote crashes in Northern New Brusnwick, isolated lakes in Newfoundland and into the high Eastern Arctic. These years were busy flying years in the RCAF — Canada had recently started flying jet aircraft. The Korean war was on — the first F'86 Sabre jets and the old twin boom Vampires were piling up, in, and around the big airbases at Bagotville, Quebec — Chatham, N.B. — North Bay, Ontario — Trenton, Ontario — St. Hubert, Quebec and others, as well as crashes in many swamp, bush, and tundra isolated locations.

In 1954, I changed from ground duties to flying duties. Ethel and I were moved from Trenton, Ontario to the old Currie field (now known as Atco Industries and Mount Royal College) at Lincoln Park in Calgary where we were to stay for almost nine years. We lived in married quarters, and I was attached to Canadian Pacific Airlines as a resident Flight Engineer with 129 Acceptance and Ferry Flight. These following years were likely exciting for me, but very lonely for Ethel and our children.

Our duties at 129 A & FF at Lincoln Park were varied, but primarily we tested new aircraft out of the factories in the U.S.A. and Canada and delivered aircraft to user Canadian bases throughout the world. During the N.A.T.O. Mutual Aid Program we delivered Jet aircraft to Turkey and Greece. These 150 aircraft were accumulated at Trenton, Ontario where we would fly approximately a 10 day shake down, and then ferry them across to Greenland and Iceland — Scotland — England, France, Sardinia, Italy and over the Persian Gulf region into Greece and Turkey. I accumulated over 6000 hours of flying time in 27 different types of piston and jet engine military aircraft.

It is interesting to think back and remember I flew in the last Norseman aircraft in the RCAF — John Bissett (an ex Spitfire pilot and prisoner of war in the Burma Campaign) and myself ferried the old single engine Norseman from Whitehorse in the Yukon to the Airforce Museum storage site at Mountain View, Ontario — I also flew in the first dual seater F104 Starfighters that were delivered to RCAF Stn. Cold Lake, from North American Aviation in California. Other types of new aircraft delivered were the first C119 Boxcars from Henreitta, Georgia and the little L-19 army spotter aircraft from the Cessna plant in Wichita, Kansas. Deliveries to the U.S. plants included B-25 bombers to Hayes Aircraft in Birmingham, Alabama and deliveries of Dakota Aircraft (United Nations) from Elarisch, Egypt to Lincoln Park, Calgary.

Due to loss of hearing caused by aircraft engine noise, I was returned to a non-flying job, and transferred to the F104-Starfighter Squadron at Cold Lake. Due to a series of events, I requested release from the Airforce and received my official release in the Spring of 1963. By this time Ethel and I had four children. Two boys Eldon and Gerald, and two girls, Ferol and Brenda, who are now all healthy and grown-up.

For a short time after my release from the Airforce I worked as a heavy duty Mechanic for the Government at Lincoln Park. All Western Airbases were slowly being closed, and Lincoln Park finally was officially closed down and we were terminated.

I began working for Brake Drome Ltd. and stayed with the company in various capacities until 1976.

Since that time I have worked for Hutton's Ltd. in Calgary and I am responsible for Technical Service and Sales in the Heavy Truck and Industrial Division.

Ethel and I sold our house in Mapleridge, Calgary and bought a double wide Mobile Home where we now live back in the country, where I was raised as a boy — "It is still the best country in the World."

Ruth Gallagher, (Cleveland) Former Fordville Teacher

Since Fordville, I taught seven more years, spending three years in Airdrie. My last teaching position was with the Department of National Defence at Camp Wainwright. There I met Bob Gallagher who was with the Queen's Own Rifles. We were married in 1958 and have since lived in Camp Borden, Calgary, West Pakistan, Winnipeg, Montreal, England and Ottawa. Then Bob commanded the United Nations Forces in the Middle East. He was posted from Damascus, Syria to a diplomatic posting as Military Attache to the United Nations in New York City. We have been living in Manhattan — in the heart of New York City for the past three years.

Living in New York is much faster paced than any other place we've been, and being diplomats leads us on a merry chase as well. We are out socially almost every night of the week — to functions dealing with the United Nations. Bob is Canada's Military Attache to the U.N. and one of Canada's delegates dealing with Peacekeeping, Disarmament and the Special Political Committee — so we have to keep up with all entertainments involving those. Many ideas and much information is exchanged at social functions.

We have three teenagers who keep us busy, too. Sean had a job as a waiter, but is trying to get into Columbia University. Neil is studying for his baccalaureate at the United Nations International School. Moira is also a student at the United Nations School, doing an equivalent to Grade 8.

Galloway, Ronald D. and Brenda L. (Bull)
NE¼-8-21-2-W5

Ron was born in Victoria, B.C. and is the oldest son of Mr. and Mrs. Douglas L. Galloway. His parents moved to Calgary where he attended St. Mary's High School and Mt. Royal College. After his schooling he worked for the Royal Bank for a number of years including the bank in Turner Valley. Ron is now employed as the general manager for an oilfield service company in Calgary.

Ron married Brenda Louise Bull in 1964. Brenda is the daughter of Grace and George Bull, and grew up with her brothers on the Millarville ranch beside Christ Church. She attended Sheep Creek School and Oilfields High School. After a year at a Calgary business college, Brenda worked for an orthodontist in Calgary. During her school years 4-H played an important part in her life with many years in clubs such as sheep, food, and clothing. Brenda now enjoys weaving and teaches 4-H'er's and adults.

Ron and Brenda have two children; Douglas Michael born in 1965 in Ft. St. John, B.C. and Graham Ronald born in 1967 in Edmonton, Alberta. Because of Ron's work in the "oilpatch" they have lived in such places as Fort St. John, B.C., Saskatoon, Sask., Houston, Texas, Edmonton, and Calgary. In 1977 the Galloways built a home at Millarville on land originally owned by "Grandad" Charles Bull.

Paul Gardner
by Peggy Nylund

Mr. and Mrs. Gardner came to the Square Butte district the year 1939 or 1940. They lived on the S.E. ¼

Paul and Bernice Gardner.

22-21-4-W5 later owned by Charlie Birney then Fred Ball. Mrs. Gardner was a member of the Square Butte Ladies group.

It was Mrs. Gardner who helped start the ladies group. That was April 1941. It was a loss to the community when they moved away. They moved to the Mowatt place between East Millarville and Black Diamond in the early 1940's. They have two children, their son Glenn was born in March 1943. They were still at East Millarville and Black Diamond. Then they moved to Innisfail. Their daughter Leslie was born March 1946.

In 1953 they moved from Alberta to Costa Mesa, California, where Mrs. Gardner taught School.

Their family is married and have families of their own. Glenn lives in Calgary and Leslie lives near home.

Early in 1978 Alex and Norma Lyall and myself, Peggy Nylund, had the pleasure of visiting the Paul Gardner's at their home in Costa Mesa California. We had a real nice afternoon going over old times when they lived in Square Butte district.

Mrs. Gardner's parents Mr. and Mrs. George Cunningham also lived in the Millarville district, North of Millarville on the 22 Highway.

A personal note of my own I missed the Gardners when they left Square Butte as Bernice and I had become very good friends.

Ernie Geiger   9C

I was born July 23rd, 1945, in Rheineck, Switzerland, the youngest child of Ernst and Louise Geiger. Under compulsion, I made it through grade and high school in this little town at the shore of the Rhein River, though helping at the neighbors farm was always more interesting than doing homework. This of

Ernie Geiger.

course reflected itself in my marks. Nevertheless, I made it through school somehow and started my apprenticeship as a carpenter in a nearby village.

Since I was to take over my father's contracting business, I also had to attend foreman school — more schooling! At this age it wasn't the neighbor's farm so much that occupied my time, but the town's gymnastics team, and the beautiful mountains of the Alps, and Dolomites. Just as any young Swiss, I had to spend some time in the army, where I served with the Engineers.

After this, I felt it was time to see some other parts of the globe. Canada was the first country I wanted to visit and spend one or two years to see the country. Well, it's been eleven years now and I still haven't seen very much of this big beautiful country. Looking back at that May 10th, 1968, as I stepped off the train in Calgary with hardly a word of English in my vocabulary, gives me mixed feelings. The first few months were pretty tough going, due to this language barrier.

In 1970, I met my friends and now neighbors, Ron and Liz Mitchell, which improved my language problem considerably. My interests changed from mountain climbing and skiing to horses and hunting in which Ron was, and still is, my teacher. 1972 saw me fortunate enough to purchase the first little piece of land from Gert and Ron Sullivan; this being 20 acres of the S.W.¼ of 26-20-4w5. A little old house was moved onto the place which was to be my home until I had the time and cash to build something better.

In the summer of 1973 the company I worked for in Calgary asked me to go to Hay River, N.W.T. where we were to build a high rise apartment. This was a welcome chance to improve my cash situation. When I came back south after this job, I obtained my Canadian citizenship, of which I am very proud. Working back in Calgary didn't satisfy me at all, so I decided to be my own boss, which worked out very well. At this time I started to build my new home. When there was time to spare I would help Dave and Lucille Glaister on their ranch, since I had become more and more interested in cattle. Yes, right back to my first hobby.

As it turned out, I never did live in my new home. Just as it was completed, in early summer 1976, I had a chance to buy the N.E.¼ of 2-21-4w5 from Mrs. Norma Lyall, so I sold my acreage, and turned to something bigger and better. With the new place, I got the cattle, brand 9C left or right rib, three quarters of lease of section 11-21-4w5, plus the Forest Reserve grazing permit. Just over a sleepless night, ranching had changed from a dream to a reality. It is a way of life to me far more enjoyable and satisfying than pounding nails.

Before I finish, I would like to express my thanks to my friends and neighbors for their help and advice to make this dream come true.

Gierens

My wife Christel and I bought a 20-acre parcel of land in the S.W. part of section 27-20-4w5 in the Kew district, very near the John Ware Ridge. This land has changed hands many times over the years. The original homesteader was Ernest Chubb, who settled there before 1910. We had bought from Mr. David J. Morse of Calgary.

We have a family of two daughters, Marianne and Annette. We all love this lovely foothill country. We are presently using the land for recreation and keep a few hives of bees in the summer.

The only permanent residents, year round, is a family of skunks under our woodshed.

Gessler, Ray and Ruth

In the spring of 1975, Ray and Ruth Gessler, daughter, Sandy and son, Mike, moved out from Calgary into their new home, which they had built themselves over the proceeding ten months.

The house is a large chalet style located on twenty acres in a subdivision which was previously the Ted Cloakey farm and before that was known as the "Gouy Place" (4 miles north of Kendall's Mill). The Cloakey barn is situated on this acreage, an unusual result of the subdividing.

Ray, a supervisor for an oil company, and Ruth, a school secretary, commuted to Calgary daily to work.

Gessler house at Kew.

Sandy attended Black Diamond High where she was a cheerleader for the basketball teams. Mike went to Millarville school and participated on the basketball, volleyball and bantam hockey teams.

The family owned some livestock (horses, cattle, dogs). Ray and Mike participated in local cattle drives and brandings which produced several incidents, amusing and otherwise, but always interesting. Mike's horse, a maverick pinto named Rusty, more than once took the bit in his teeth and ran away with the frantic lad, his dad in hot pursuit. This same horse also had an apparent dislike for water and tried to fly over rather than ford a stream as a normal horse would. Several times Mike was all but unseated and somewhat shaken.

On one occasion when their Angus cow, Candy, came into season, hurried arrangements were made to have her serviced by Jackson, a bull owned by neighbor Ernie Silvester. Ray, by now a "seasoned cowboy", put Candy's two calves in the barn and saddled a horse, intending to simply herd the cow down the road. Not wanting to be separated from her calves, the cow had other ideas and proceeded to run him in circles. Undaunted, Ray next put a halter on her and by means of a stout rope wrapped around the saddle horn attempted to lead her. The cow dug in, the horse began to buck and almost threw him and Ray, dismounting entangled in the rope, decided leading her on foot was the only solution.

All this produced fits of laughter from Ruth who, retrieving the camera from the house, hopped in the car and raced around by road to meet Ray coming across country, in an attempt to shorten the ordeal, dragging and cajoling the ornery beast. However, Ruth's attempt to record the event for posterity was failed when she was informed, as she was about to trip the shutter, that there was no film in the camera. All ended well as Candy finally met Jackson and afterward returned home much more peaceably.

Putting up hay in the fall was very enjoyable to Ray who considered it part of the romance of "ranching". It received much less enthusiastic response from Mike.

In the winter of 1976-77 the Gesslers sold out to Pat and Susan McMahon and moved back into Calgary, at the same time acquiring a quarter section in the Bergen area, to which they moved their stock. While now residing in Calgary they cherish fond memories of their country home, the new friends they made in the area, and the many experiences that occurred during their time there.

The Giles Family

by Keith and Nola
The Malawahna Ranch $\frac{S}{T}$RH

We were born in Calgary and raised on mixed farms on the east boundary of Calgary. Today, all our farm land is a part of Calgary.

My wife, Nola Maybin, was an only child. Her parents were both from Northern Ireland. Mr. Maybin came to Canada in 1908, worked on farms for a small wage, as many did, then turned his hand to road building in southern Alberta. One job was the rebuilding of the highway through the Frank Slide at the base of Turtle Mt. In later years he took up farming east of Calgary, one mile east of the Imperial Oil Plant Refinery. Nola's mother came to Canada in 1922 from Belfast. She was a private secretary in Calgary; she passed away in 1947.

I am one of six children of Irish and Norwegian descent. Tom, my father, had his ticket to sail for Canada on the Titanic, which went down April 15, 1912. As fate would have it, he broke his leg one day before he was to sail and wound up in the hospital. He came out one year later, west from Halifax, and joined his brother Jack, in Calgary. At a later date Jack was in the construction business. Among many contracts, they cut down the Centre Street hill to the bridge as it is today. As well, they did concrete work on the city streets near the old RCMP Barracks, 9 Avenue East, and the Elbow and Bow Rivers. They also did work on Government Grain Elevators southeast of Calgary, and on the Glenmore Dam and Reservoir. In 1922, Dad married Clara F. Anderson from the Shepard area. They went farming later near Hubalta, and raised their family of six: two girls and four boys. I was a twin, but my twin sister, Audrey, was deceased in December 1928. My other sister resides on a farm northeast of Calgary, one brother on a farm near Airdrie, one brother in Didsbury, and one brother on a ranch in B.C. Our father died in July, 1948.

Nola and I were married in June, 1953. In 1960 we sold our farm and spent six months in Calgary, during which time I worked for the Health of Animals, blood testing cattle from Calgary to Banff. In the spring of 1961 we purchased a ranch near Kew and Millarville, and moved out to the ranch with Nola's dad. We continued ranching by choice. We acquired ¾ sec. as part of 32-20-3-5 at Kew Corner from V. Hammel, which was previously owned by Frank Adams (re: Our Foothills, page 109). We built a new ranch home in 1961 and out buildings later replaced all the old ones.

Keith and Nola Giles. January, 1976.

In the spring of 1962, Nola lost her dad, and in the spring of 1963, I lost my mother. We later purchased more property on the south side of the Sheep River, five miles west of Turner Valley PT 29-20-3-5 and PT 19-20-3-5, known as the Seeman Ranch. I was now in a cow-calf operation with Herefords wearing the $\frac{s}{T}$ brand and running up to 175 cows.

In 1965 we named and registered the ranch "The Malawahna Ranch", a west coastal Indian word meaning "sweet wind of the west", a most appropriate name for this area.

We have three daughters. The eldest is Sheila, born in January, 1959. She spent her school days at Millarville and Oilfields Jr. & Sr. High School in Black Diamond. She is now in her second year in a Secretarial Arts course at Mount Royal College in Calgary. Carla, our second girl, was born May, 1961. She is now in her last year at Oilfield High School. Twyla, our youngest, born in July, 1963, is in her first year at Oilfields High School.

Among the hobbies of our family are traveling, photography, rock-hounding, fishing, hunting, handicrafts, sewing, (man-hunting for three — with money!), skiing, and other sports. At this time we, and other friends, are involved in organizing the first motorhome club in Canada. It is registered as the Canadian Rocky Motorhome Club.

On October 29, 1977, due to my health, we had an auction sale. As I have had two open heart surgeries (November 1975 and June 1977) I had little choice but to retire and release the pressures and work load. We will continue to live on The Malawahna Ranch. Once again, we wish to thank all those kind folks that offered their help and kind words during the time I was ill.

You have never seen Alberta until you have seen Millarville!

Ruth (Adams) Giroux

Ruth P. Adams (Giroux) born in Turner Valley, Alberta, the youngest of Herb and Hazel Adams of Kew or Millarville. Rode horseback with sisters Betty and Phyllis to Plainview School for grade one and part of grade two, then was bussed to Sheep Creek School, Millarville, for grades two to six. In 1946, we moved to the Priddis area, and then completed grade six to grade nine, riding horseback, school bus and walking to Fordville School. High School was taken at Mount Royal College in Calgary, and a business course completed at Calgary Business College. Worked as a secretary at Osler, Hammond & Nanton Ltd., and G.M.A.C. of Canada Ltd., in Calgary. Married to Eugene Giroux in 1955, oldest son of Charlie Giroux, late of Millarville. We have a son Paul, born 1958, daughter Tobi, born 1961, and son Bradley born 1966. We moved to Edmonton in 1964, as Gene started teaching at the Northern Alberta Institute of Technology, where we still reside at the present time.

Giroux Family in Hawaii. L. to R., Back: Toby, Paul. Front: Gene, Bradley, Ruth.

John K. Given

by John K. Given

I came to Ballyhamage District in the spring of 1947. My wife came a little later and we were married June 7, 1947. Gordon was born in 1949, and now has a farm at Nanton, Alberta. Bett passed away after a long illness, in 1973.

Ray and Ella Quigley and family lived here for several years.

Norman and Lucie Given

by Daughter Roselyne

August 6, 1923, was a special day for Emily and John Barraclough of the Penman Ranch, at Springbank, west of Calgary. That day marked the birth of their daugher, Lucie Emily.

Five years after her birth, Lucie, her parents, sisters and brother left the Calgary area to move to Millarville, where they resided at the Cochrane place. After spending two years there, the family moved again, this time to the Billings place in the Priddis district. Later, in 1934 Lucie and her family moved for the last time to their own farm seven miles west of the Billings place.

During this time Lucie was attending school, first at Ballyhamage, then the Fordville School.

Growing up on Deer Play Farm, Lucie was able to indulge her love of drawing and painting by capturing the scenes of her daily life.

As a young woman, Lucie did not go unnoticed by members of the opposite sex. There was of course, one special admirer. Lucie and Norman were married 3 days after her 21st birthday in 1944, and settled in Priddis.

Two years later, in 1946, Lucie and Norm had their first and only son, Russ. Russ now lives in Calgary and is an Instructor at the U. of C.

Nineteen Forty Seven saw another member of the Given family on the scene, this time a daughter, Roselyne.

After six happy years in Priddis, Lucie and Norm moved to Turner Valley in 1950.

One year later, 1951, the third and final of their children was born, another daughter, Penny.

Leaving many friends and family behind, Norm and Lucie moved to Red Deer, where Norm established a successful business. The move was in 1959.

After living in Red Deer for over a decade and all three children grown and gone from home, the couple decided to look again for a new area in which to live. After many possibilities were looked into, they decided on Edmonton. That was three years ago, and the decision was a good one, for they are happily settled just outside of Edmonton at Winterburn, where they can enjoy the quietness of semi-country life.

Glaister, David and Lucille

as told by David B. Glaister

The first recollected remarks of my presence, by neighbours, was that I looked rather like a prune, red-faced and wrinkled. This event took place July 9, 1929 in a log house on the SE¼ of 3-21-2 W5th; Dr. A. E. Ardiel doing the honors. Father must have made a fast trip to Okotoks to acquire the doctor as we had no telephone until 1936. I neglected to ask in later years if this trip was made by horse power or motor power. Father was milking a bunch of cows and he always remarked about what a hot spell we had at the time of my birth. I can well picture the sweat dripping off the end of his nose as he did the evening milking. Some of the things I would always associate my father with (as I screamed and hollered my progress in the world) were milk cows, pigs, work horses and the sport of fishing and hunting, birds preferably. One of Mother's remarks about my advancement was that I did a considerable amount of squawking and making everyone's life miserable. This problem was solved by Tom Livingstone, who was helping Father at the time, "Give the damn kid a bone, he's starving to death". Mother said he hit the nail on the head, more food, less squawk. However, they seemed to pull me through the years of non-recollection of thought without too many mishaps; just a smashed nose on a two-by-four trying to see what was under the new bedroom addition and, later, at three or four years of age, a loose top log on

Glaisters. L. to R. Kathy, Jane, Joan, Lucille, Dave.

Joe Fisher's new garage fell, whacking me on the head and knocking me colder than a cucumber. Mother thought I really had it this time but after being held under the yard pump for a spell I set the anxious group at ease by coming back from oblivion. As I began to form my own lines of thought and memory, the Millarville Foothills District became a remembered paradise for a boy to grow up in. There was always lots of animals, wild or tame, the wild ones always an attraction. Snaring, trapping and finally the achievement of shooting gophers and trying to dig out coyote pups in the Spring, for the $5 bounty. For all the digging I did I sure didn't get many pups, maybe a dozen at most. I found an orphan fawn in the early Forties and what a time my sister Anne and I had with Falene, the name we gave her. Even the Game Warden came from High River to see our Falene. We shook until he said we could keep her, for she was not confined.

I feel that in recording some of our earlier history there should be a word about some of the hired help that worked throughout the district. They were residents in the area, some for quite a considerable length of time. I know, to the younger members of the families, these fellows were held in great esteem. They were a continuous source of humor, knowledge, tricks of their trade and, to this day, they hold my admiration. Not that there weren't a few duds in the bunch, but for most their contribution to the early history and shaping of the community was significant. I'll mention a few that worked for Father, as well as working for neighbours throughout the community. There was Jack Mackenzie, a Scotsman in his 60's when I knew him. He was an excellent heavy horseman who would go on periodic benders, overstay his leave and return quite broke and cranky, which did nothing for his relationship with his employer. But I, at 5 or 6 years old, loved him. He had a heart of gold and was a constant source of pocket knives, construction of slingshots, etc., much to Mother's dismay. I believe his latter years were spent at the Coast. Another was Fred Singer, whom I believe had some French background. He was a fascinating man that worked for Father, Cannon, Sinclair-Smith and Malcolm Millar, and was a resident for quite a number of years. Rod Redfern, worked for my Uncles, Joe and Harry Rodgers, breaking to drive a bunch of real rank old seven and eight year horses. A book could be written on this man's abilities with horse and gun. The Grant boys, Percy and Doug, who helped us hay, lived on the NE¼ of 34-20-2 W5th. And Leonard Nelson, a local man in his 20's who helped us hay through the mid-Thirties. I often wonder how he stood us, but marked it to his extreme good nature. With my consistent pestering and sister Maude and her girl friends' pranks after a full day's work in the fields, we must have been quite a strain.

As I was gradually broken in to milking the cows, feeding hogs and chickens, range riding, etc., it became clear my task was to eventually replace the hired men. The chores may have taken some persuasion but the riding was a different matter. We lived on our horses and, 50 years later, still enjoy riding. My eldest sister Maude, then later myself, had our first introduction to horseflesh in the shape of a shaggy, longhaired Shetland pony, handed down from our Uncle Tommy McMillan. Our escapades and adventures were burnt so deep into my memory that I swore no child of mine should ever have to ride a Shetland pony, and they never did. If there ever was a horse that knew all the angles, Jimmy was an expert. He could unload or outsmart me in an exultant manner then immediately go to grazing. He'd give me a quizzical gaze as I dug dirt out of my mouth or nursed a sprained arm and planned my revenge. However, we did have some fine ponies. Some of the best originated from the Stony Indians. I will never forget a Sunday afternoon visiting my Uncle Pat Rodgers at Kew, who announced I was to follow him to the barn, as he had something for me which, if I could climb on, would be mine. This was my introduction to Pocahontus and, needless to say, it didn't take me long to mount up. From that day forward, rain, shine, blizzard or whatever, she faithfully packed me to school for seven years. She never wore a shoe and I don't recollect her falling or limping a step at any time. The fun and relationship, as well as the responsibility to care for a pony, is something I am happy to have experienced — certainly it was a much more memorable experience than the modern child's ride on a school bus.

My schooling was quite limited. Grade 1 to 4 at New Valley School, Grade 5 at Balmoral in Calgary, 6 and 7 back at New Valley then Ballyhamage for 8 and 9. Then, as my Uncle Pat expressed it, I threw off my coat and went to work. I would like to mention a few high points of my school days, for one, the first day, because it is so foreign to the first grader of the 1970's. Mother took me in the Model T Ford, introduced me to the teacher, Eileen Cunningham, and marched out of the room. I had always been a loner as we had no near neighbours with small children. My sister Maude was nine years older than I, and younger sister, Anne, not yet born. Every face in the room was a total stranger. I am certain that if I had not been paralyzed with fright I would have bolted for the nearby willow brush. However, to my surprise I lived and many of those faces are good friends to this day. In 1941, going into Grade 5 I had somewhat the same experience as Grade One. My Aunt, Mrs. Roly Glaister, persuaded me to live with them in Calgary and go to school at Balmoral. She and my Mother agreed this would be superior schooling (I will question that to this day). I was extremely bushy to City standards. Up to this point my time spent in the City could be counted on one hand — perhaps one day at the Stampede and one day at Christmas. I hated each "city" day with a passion and only now feel it did a great deal to aid in the process of growing up and facing the world. I never found reason to quarrel or dispute with my teachers. They were all female and generally a great lot. One of our neighbours, Joan Kendall, taught me in Grade 8 and 9, and we still have many lively discussions of school days at Ballyhamage. Towards the end of my schooling I ran a trapline catching coyotes and weasels, this being a source of pocket money. I also rode a few green broke horses for friends and neighbours, thus adding a little extra cash to the kitty. I realize now that Father got the short end of the stick, for he provided, without cost, the hay and oats. I guess he felt I learned something, the horse learned something, and everybody was happy.

My first after-school job was for Willie Deane-Freeman on Section 4-21-2 W5th. This consisted of splitting wood, large cottonwood blocks split with a wedge, hauling hay on weekends and helping to start his Titon tractor, which I got a great bang out of, literally, for when it got going everything around banged and sputtered, including me. They were great, hospitable people. Mrs. Deane-Freeman was a wonderful cook and a connoisseur of fine tea. My first employment away from home, age 13, was for the Bull ranch, raking hay. Mr. Bull told Father "I'll pay him a dollar for the first day, increase it a dollar a day to four dollars, then hire or fire him". He gave me a pair of Clydes, one a young snorty bugger he borrowed from Percy Bennett and the other a real quiet old pelter called "Peanuts". The first time I unhooked them I had them facing home. With the other teams going by they just about got away on me and caused a serious wreck. The old fellow came up to me, "Don't you know", he says, "always face your team away from home when unhitching, they stand better". I never forgot that lesson, I also stayed on to finish the job. When I was through school, 1945 or '46, I tried to get into Olds College but the War Vets had priority and the school was full up. Also, Father's health was failing and I was needed at home. When work slacked in winter I worked in the bush with Murray Jackson. Murray and I got the idea to buy a power saw, a new gadget still in its technical infancy. The thing was called a Hornet, weighed 60 pounds, took two men to

handle it and taught us all about the 2-cycle engine. We had it apart so many times in adverse weather conditions. Mostly he worked with a cross-cut saw in order to make enough money to pay for the parts to fix the Hornet, in order that we might be able to pack it through two feet of snow, start it up and have it break down again. The bush work kept us in rip roaring condition with appetites to match. We cut logs for Les Foster, Elwyn Evans, and firewood for Fred Rishaug. The winters of 1947-'49 Murray and I worked on Jackson's timber, just east of what we now call the Whiskey Hill subdivision. I can't remember what we got paid but we had a boisterous good time anyway. Things were opening up after the War and our families had pretty good cars. We would beg, borrow or steal the wheels for the weekends, dances at Kew, the old Ranchers' Hall, Red Deer Lake, or picture shows at Turner Valley on Saturday with, of course, girls, girls, girls. Come Monday we'd be back in the bush without a penny to our names. One winter Murray and I worked for Murray's father. We drove a team apiece four miles into the bush, logged all day and brought the loads back at night, along with helping to milk fourteen cows before and after. Billy Jackson was a wonderful man to work for.

In 1946 brother-in-law Ron Birkenes, just out of the Air Force, came up with the suggestion we buy the Roy Dutton place (E½ 34-20-2 W5th) as Roy was trying to sell out. This place joined our farm on the South. I was seventeen and had either $1,200 or $1,500 in the bank. Using my savings for land purchase wasn't the most prominent thought in my mind at the time — a car or a few wild weekends were more in my line. But land it was, with a loan from Mother and my savings, Ron and I were proud owners of 253 acres at $23 an acre. Now, some thirty years later, I realize what good fortune this was for I couldn't have spent my money in a better venture. For ten years Ron and I worked the land along with my father's place, raising cattle, cereal grains and hay.

In 1951 Hughie Chalmers and I had a contract to cut and skid timber for Carl Ohlson on the old Lineham Ranch and it was about this time that I ran into a snag. This came in the form of a little dark-haired, dark-eyed girl that worked at the Turner Valley Hospital. Lucille Dudenhoeffer was a local girl that lived by the Plainview School and I knew her family quite well. Hughie and I rented a grey Percheron, from Lucille's father, to skid logs for our contract, so we had plenty of excuses to go calling. On week-end time off Lucille, usually with a girl friend, would ride down to the ranch to make sure we were really logging. This led to an engagement at Christmas, 1951, and a marriage on September 9, 1952 in the United Church at Turner Valley. We set up housekeeping on the home farm in a little two-room house, 14' by 28', which I acquired from the Home Oil Company for $600. We lived here for three years and added two more ladies to the family, Joan Lucille born October 9, 1953 and Jane Lynn born

August 16, 1955. I realized the property I had with my two partners could not support our growing family and a move had to be made. With an offer from Les Boulton, Ron and I dispersed the Dutton place for double our money. Then came land hunting with very limited funds, no easy task at any time. Two particular pieces of property I remember looking at were the Hicklin place west of Turner Valley and the Frank Adams place Southwest of Millarville. I loved the West and wasn't about to go looking East. On one of our stops at Bill's corner store Bill Lee told me the old Frenchman's place off Highway 22 was up for bid and that an old friend of Father's, Josh Littleton, was looking after the Estate. I presented a bid of $8 an acre on the SW¼ of 14-3-2 W5th and $35 an acre on the NE¼ of 14-21-3 W5th and the SE¼ of 23-21-3 W5th, which was the portion of the Estate lying west of Hwy. 22. This bid was sent to France, to the Estate of de Bernis and Durand and then followed an anxious waiting period. At last, with great joy, we learned our bid had been accepted. A few people had tried to snap up the two quarters along the highway but not one bid on the SE¼ 23 at any price. As the Estate desired to sell all parcels or nothing, our bid did the trick. Now we had a barn that was in better repair than the house, which had been built of logs by Walter Phillips prior to 1900. Nevertheless, in May 1956 we moved in — no power, no running water, and two baby girls. I know the hardest item to do without was refrigeration. We had a good spring and Lucille would run back and forth with every solitary thing that had to be kept cool. I rented a cat, brushed and broke 60 acres on the SE¼ of 23 and cut and sawed timber on the SW¼ of 14 to build some corrals and sheds. Calgary Power services were installed in 1957. Our third daughter, Kathryn Ann was born June 15, 1957 at the Turner Valley Hospital. I had realized from the start that the house was impossible. The bottom logs were rotten and the floor sills were gone. The kitchen had sunk close to a foot below the living room and the girls took great delight coasting downhill on their tricycles. In the winter months Lucille and I slept with the babies to keep them warm. The floor mop would freeze to the floor leaning on the kitchen stove. We were in a bit of a tough spot with trying to clear the land and make the payments. We had absolutely no means to improve the house accommodations. About this time we received an offer on the SW¼ of 14-3-2 W5th, from a Dr. Cody, which we found impossible to turn down. Lady Luck held fast, now Gourlay's sold out and no longer rented the Jameson place, where a very lovely home sat, now empty. Eileen and Sheilagh Jameson (close, good friends) were more than willing to rent their home on Sec. 16, 21-2 W5th, to us. And so it was, we moved September 1st, 1958 to Ballyhamage into the grand old log house built by the Tom Jameson family with its spectacular mountain view and gracious setting of trees, gardens and creek. I think it was Lucille that gained the most from this move — now we had power, hot and cold run-

ning water and lots of room. We made good use of it, having many lively parties and entertaining friends. This was an exceptionally lovely place for our girls to spend some of their younger years and, in looking back, I know it was some of our happiest as the girls were at such an interesting age. They had many pets, geese, lambs, calves, horses. The girls learned to milk, look after chickens, ride horseback and especially loved to accompany me hauling feed with the team and sleigh in wintertime. It was July, 1959 that 16 year old Eddie Stuart from Black Diamond came to help us hay, and stayed living with us for four years. He became something of a big brother to our girls. We still have a close association with Eddie, his wife Florence and family of three. They live in Houston, B.C., where Eddie is head saw filer for a large sawmill.

We were now farming Father's place, the Frenchman's place and the half section at Ballyhamage. This kept us busy but we always found time to take the girls out on Saturday or Sunday exploits into the hills, riding, hiking or fishing or just plain enjoying the scenery. Progress and change are to be expected — and so it was with us. Father and Mother wanted to retire. With some swapping, borrowed money and prayers, we were off on another venture. I bought a quarter and traded Father one home quarter for the NE¼ of 14-21-3 W5th, the quarter where he and Mother had built a comfortable new home and lived until their passing, (Mother February 22, 1973, Father February 19, 1974). We said farewell to Ballyhamage and moved back to the old home farm in April 1961. How we hated to leave Ballyhamage. I know this entire foothills country and if I had a choice of a building site there is none which could compare with that area. However, we were the new owners of the old home place and reality had to be faced; there was much to be done. We cleared and ploughed all feasible acres with Jody Fisher doing some work with one of the first rototillers in the area. We farmed here for eight years, milking, raising hogs and running

Back row, L. to R.: David Flundra, Lloyd Wilder, Dave Glaister, Michael Coulter. Front: L. to R. Kathy Flundra, Jane Wilder, Lucille Glaister, Joan Coulter.

about 50 beef cows. It was still a family enterprise, Lucille helping outside and in and the girls not missing a trick. The girls went to Sheep Creek School, catching the bus at the front gate. They were baptized, attended Sunday School and sang in the choir at Christ Church, Millarville. Their great-Grandfather had helped build this Church many years ago. Jane was more the domestic of the three. When Millarville Fair time came along, Joan and Kathy would be showing their ponies and Jane would enter sunflowers and cooking. Lucille was active in the Junior Guild, Sunday School and, as the girls came of age, she took an active part in Millarville's Busy Beavers 4H Food Club, being a leader for many years.

It always seemed we were in some sort of dilemma. Number one, I liked cattle, not farming, for which you need more land. Number two, the old house needed fixing and for that it would have to be put on a proper foundation taking considerable funds, of which there were none. Again neighbours and friendship played a part in our lives. At an auction sale on Lucille's home farm Ernie Silvester said, "Glaister, you always wanted to live in the hills, why don't you buy Tom Bell's place, he wants to sell." That little speech sent me into a heart-wrenching tailspin for about six months. I wanted that place so bad I could taste it. Not only was it a picturesque place, as far West as you can own deeded land in this district, but it was a big enough, economical unit to raise cattle on. It also came with a comfortable, modern home. Tom was approached at Easter and price was negotiated, which was reasonable — but, being 1,280 acres, the amount to me, with a mortgaged three quarters, was astronomical — and had to be cash. I always found if you wanted something bad enough you could do a lot of scratching. First, sell the farm for $200 an acre cash; the neighbours thought I was nuts, too much money. But, with the help of my cousin Perry Glaister, who said he would purchase one quarter, my friendly banker and Farm Credit Corporation, the deal was swung. The property consisted of the home quarter, NE¼ 9-21-4 W5th, homesteaded originally by Tom Bell's father; the NW¼ 17-21-4 W5th, homesteaded by Joe Bell; the SW¼ 9-21-4 W5th bought from W. J. Malcolmson; SW¼ 15-21-4 W5th bought from the CPR; the SE¼ 20-21-4 W5th and the NE¼ 17-21-4 W5th bought from Sam Virtue and the W½ of 20-21-4 W5th bought from Billy Trevenen. Again it was hard to move, leaving the home place my Father had founded and lived with Mother for 45 years, the very house in which I had been born. But, one cannot live on nostalgia and we moved on October 31st, Hallowe'en, 1968. Lucille said next time it would have to be a fire or an auction sale — no more moving, which sounded fine to me. There is nothing I hate worse than moving furniture. Our first visitors, upon arising the next morning, were a family of five coyotes teasing our dogs in the yard, which was highly amusing to the girls. The No. 1 project on our new ranch was an official name. Thought and family

discussion came up with the name Mesa Creek Ranch, named after the little creek that runs through the home quarter. It was registered and recorded in Ottawa and is used as a prefex for our Registered Red Angus cattle. The Bell's had run the place on a cow/yearling basis but we decided, to keep pace with changing times, to run a cow/calf operation. This entailed more corrals and sheds for early calving. We built the herd up to 170 cows running over half of these on the forest reserve as we had acquired Bell's permit along with the land. The first winter, 1968/69 John Howell stayed with us and as the place was new, we were not too organized. The weather was cold and the snow deep. We bought our first snowmobile, an old Twintrack and had a great time chasing Elk out of haystacks and exploring the ranch. The winter of 1969/70 we contracted the timber on the Trevenen place to Bill Kendall which gave us access to a good supply of lumber for our building projects. In the Spring of 1969 we purchased our first Red Angus bull from Jim Wright of Okotoks to breed our Hereford heifers. We were pleased with the result and as the "exotic" kick was in full swing, we sort of got the itch. However, we were a little cautious about going the exotic cattle route. At a roadside conflab with cousin Mike Rodgers and David Wildman, it was decided to take in some purebred Red Angus sales in the States. We have never totally convinced our wives that it was cattle we were after and not just a wild weekend. What a time we had meeting some grand ranch people in Washington and Oregon. We all purchased our first seed stock Red Angus females, launching us into the purebred business of which I have never been sorry. The cattle have been excellent for our particular needs and environment and the socializing aspect has led us far afield with many new and dear friends. In 1973 the opportunity to add to the ranch holdings was presented to us by Dick Lyall, our neighbor, who was retiring. Cousin R. P. Glaister purchased the SW¼ of 16-21-4 W5th and I acquired the lease rights to the NE¼ 16-21-4 W5th. This purchase fit in perfectly with our ranch holdings. In June 1977 Lucille and I accompanied Canadian breeders to the World Angus Forum in Scotland, visited relatives and spent some time in London.

My Uncle Pat Rodgers gave me my first heifer when I was born and I have been in the cattle business ever since. I guess I always will be, so long as the Lord allows. We have struggled through the rough spots and dug in with the good ones and it has been a very satisfying family way of life; I wouldn't change a thing had I the chance to do it over. Our girls are all married now, Joan to Michael Coulter, of Wichita Falls, Texas in 1975. They have presented us with our first grandchild, Jennifer Joan, born June 20, 1978. Michael and Joan have joined us in the ranch operation, making the workload much easier as Lucille and I start to slow down. Jane married Lloyd Wilder of Invermere, B.C. on June 3, 1978. They reside in Invermere where Lloyd enjoys logging and speculating in heavy equipment.

Kathy married David Flundra of Cochrane, Alta. on October 7, 1978. They reside at Cochrane where David is in the carpentry/construction business.

As I sit in our log living room that I built over the last few years, writing our history, I look out over the same mountains that shaded Grandfather James Rodgers and his brother Joseph as they walked with the I G Baker bull teams from Fort Benton in the Spring of 1883 to settle in the beautiful foothills country. I can only wish that some of their blood will pulse through the veins of many more generations here in the foothills.

Glaister, Elizabeth Anne

by Anne L'Hirondelle (Glaister)

Born in Calgary, April 12, 1938, youngest daughter of David Glaister and Margaret (Rodgers) Glaister. I grew up on the family homestead, the S. ½ 3-21-2W5.

For five years I rode three and one quarter miles to Ballyhamage School, a typical one room, nine grade establishment with a stove that looked like a drum on its side. Mild punishment was to stand in the corner behind the stove and suffer from the heat. Our gymnasium was the bit of land reserved to pasture our ponies during classes. As my trail to school took me along the crest of a large ridge of hills, the snow got so deep and crusty that I usually had a welcome holiday through out the month of March. In grade three I boarded a few weeks with my teacher, Mrs. Wonnacott, as the weather was so miserable.

Ballyhamage School closed down in 1949 and I then rode Bill Lee's bus to West Millarville to Sheep Creek School from September 1949 to June 1952. One year in residence at Mount Royal College in Calgary, then finished the last two years of high school boarding with my sister (Maud Birkenes) in Turner Valley. After a summer job in Lake Louise, a few months in Reeds China and Gift Shop in Edmonton, I settled down to working at the Royal Bank of Canada in Turner Valley. On September 1st. 1958 at Christ Church Millarville, I

L. to R. David, Patrice, Anne and Don L'Hirondelle. In front, Denise.

married Donald L'Hirondelle, (grandson of another Millarville oldtimer.) We lived five years in Lodgepole, a year in Drayton Valley, ten years in Edson and the last four years back in Drayton Valley. Don has been employed by the Pembina Pipe Line. Ltd. for the last twenty years. We have three children, David John, born Jan. 10, 1961. Patrice Anne, born Nov. 7, 1962. Denise Alice, born Jan. 10, 1966.

With my parents resting in peace at Christ Church, Millarville and the rest of my family living in Millarville I still "come home" as often as possible.

Glaister, Dr. R. Perry

Born in 1929 in Calgary, only child of Rowland Lindsay Glaister (brother of David Oliver Glaister, a long time resident of Millarville). As I grew up I spent many enjoyable weekends and summer vacations at my uncle's farm which was located a short distance east of the Millarville church (S½-3-21-2-W5). I can remember my Dad having to put chains on our Model A Ford to drive from Calgary to the farm as Highway 22 in the thirties was unpaved and nearly impassible during spring thaws or after heavy rains. In 1968 my cousin, David Glaister (Jr.), purchased Tom and Mary Bell's ranch near Square Butte, and shortly afterwards we acquired one of the quarter sections from him (SE¼-20-21-4-W5). In 1973 we purchased a quarter section from Dick and Helen Lyall which was contiguous to my cousin's and provided convenient access between our grazing parcels. My wife, Ann Elizabeth, and I have three children — Lawrence, Bill and Janice. At the present time we reside in Calgary where I am a Geological Research Advisor with Imperial Oil, but we enjoy most of our weekends in the beautiful Millarville Foothills.

Godwin, Phyllis (Backs)

Olds, Alberta, June 27, 1914 — a red headed daughter born to Hans and Merle Backs. Both parents being brunettes, Mom took a lot of teasing about this fact.

Our family moved to the Millarville area in the spring of 1943 and I started school at Sheep Creek school in 1947 under the strict teaching of Miss Duffield who punished Elizabeth (Sis) Sewell and myself the very first day of school for giggling — we had to stand in the corner for half of it. On up through the grades, various teachers and many great school chums to an amusing incident in about Grade 9 when Milton Evans brought a container full of sheep ticks to school and unbeknown to me, proceeded to dump them in my long red hair!

My last teacher was Mr. Bill Dube, a great principal who saw me through grades 9, 10 and 11 — and that was the last grade taught at Sheep Creek in 1958.

Always having a great love and interest in horses, I recall fondly our first family horse "Ol' Baldy", 28 years old. I was about 6 years old then and because of older brother Bob, and sister Eveline, I remember

Phyllis Backs.

always being upset because they wouldn't let me ride him as much as I wanted to. Finally, my parents purchased "Midge" — my very own horse — when I was 10 and just shortly after moving to "the ranch" — the quarter section previously owned by Kay King just north of Millarville.

Horse involvement took me on many memorable plateaus from training and riding Midge's foal "Tipperary" — to competing in barrel racing and other local horse show events — to being one of the first members of the association known today as the Canadian Girls' Rodeo Association — to the greatest year of all, 1959.

I was then 18 years old and a very naive country kid, when some of the merchants from High River asked me to compete for the title Miss Frontier of High River. I agreed, having no idea that the decision would lead me to the most memorable year of my life. Soon after winning that competition the town of High River sponsored me in the Miss Rodeo Canada pageant held in conjunction with the first fall indoor rodeo held at the Calgary Stampede grounds. What a thrill when I was announced the winner and remember the tears of joy when the announcer asked all the people from High River and Millarville to "please stand up" and half of the crowd stood.

A couple of days later, Mr. Fred Kennedy from the Calgary Exhibition and Stampede Board phoned to tell me they would like to sponsor me in the Miss Rodeo America pageant in Las Vegas, Nevada the following

month. Having never been on an airplane nor ever travelled more than 150 miles from home in my life and not much time to prepare, I was one scared kid. Anyway, I finally went by car, accompanied by Mom and Dad and my good friend, Linda Lee. We had a wonderful trip, many eye-opening experiences and the exciting outcome of the contest — I was named runner-up to Miss Rodeo America.

When I arrived home, the Millarville community put on a big "do" at the Ranchers Hall and presented me with a silver serving tray which I cherish.

The numerous rodeos and functions I attended throughout my year as "Miss Rodeo Canada" will long be remembered.

In 1961, I married Lyle Dahl. We had two children, son Cody and daughter Kelly. We were divorced in 1970.

My mother's words of wisdom at that time were "Honey, it's a poor 'ol hen that can't scratch for a couple of chicks" and those words gave me strength many times over the next couple of years when the going was rough. Then I went on to enjoy a very fascinating and rewarding career in Real Estate for 6 years.

I married Frank Godwin in 1977 and we are now living on our acreage at DeWinton. Cody and Kelly, who are now 17 and 15 years old are attending high school at Okotoks.

The Godwin Family
B-T Brand Location Left Rib
N½ 9-21-W5 Home Land Location

Ted and Barb both born in Montreal, Quebec, married in 1956 and Ted graduated from McGill university the same year. Moved to Cartagena, South America for 3 years. Moved out west to Calgary in 1959. Ted worked in the oil patch with various companies as projects Engineer and company president. Past director of Limousin Association, Advisory Import Committee for Dept. of Agriculture. We bought some land from Bob and Janet McKay in 1969, moved here in 1970, building barn house corrals, fencing, and

Godwin Family. L. to R. Barb, Rick, Lisa, Ted, Laura.

started to raise cattle (limousin). Ted retired from the Oil patch in 1976; he built a 12 acre pond which we enjoy swimming, canoeing and sharing the water with the wildlife.

Rick born 1958, Lisa born 1963, Laura born 1966. All are very keen sports persons and outdoor oriented. Rick played hockey for Okotoks for many seasons. Rick and Lisa enjoyed Stockland Beef 4H club. Laura belongs to the Millarville Multi-4H Club. The girls interested in raising sheep and rabbits. Both keen on riding their horses. Family participation at the Millarville Fair.

The Gourlays

by Shelagh Gourlay, November 28, 1978

The Gourlays, Jock and Alasdair, searched the Commonwealth countries for two years before discovering the Diamond L Ranch at Millarville in 1949. They had graduated in agriculture from Marischal College in Aberdeen, Scotland, and had been challenged by their father, Ernest Gourlay, to find a place to settle. Having already lived in Ceylon where Mr. Ernest Gourlay was a tea planter (now Sri Lanka), eastern Canada and Scotland, they knew they had found what they wanted most on the grassy flatlands along the north fork of Sheep Creek. The Diamond L Ranch was purchased from Bill Oliver, a well-known Calgary photographer, and Ernest, Joan, the two boys, and a daughter, Jane, arrived.

Jane did not stay in the west very long. She had met a handsome young easterner named Buz Hayes, and was married in the summer of 1950 at a festive western celebration. Jock and Al decided their sister and new brother-in-law should be treated in the bucolic tradition and they were returned home after the wedding at the pretty little Millarville log church on a hay wagon carrying a sign "Imported Sire".

The idea of the sign had come about because the Gourlays had ventured into the purebred Shorthorn cattle business. They had bought some of their herd from a Dalroy rancher named Walter McCollister and also imported a herd sire called "Millhills Jubilee" and some heifers from Scotland. They showed cattle at Calgary, Saskatoon, and Millarville. Using the excellent pastureland of the area, they also kept feeder cattle and sheep. The sheep were not very successful because of coyotes and poor market conditions and

The Gourlays, Sept. 1959. Picnic at the river ♀ Ranch.

they ate the last of the flock, getting rather tired of mutton by the time the ninth one went into the stew pot.

Jock was the next one to get married. He married Shelagh Wilson from Cobourg, Ontario, and set up house in what was known as "the bothy" a Scotish term for bunkhouse. The first winter they lived there, it lacked a foundation, so Jock piled manure around it to keep the frost out. In the spring, the house became rather aromatic with nice farm smells. John or "Gopher", was born while they were living at the Bothy and, Sheena, three years later, when they had moved to Ballyhamage, which they had rented from the Jamesons.

Meanwhile, Alasdair married Mary James from Port Hope, Ontario, and redecorated the bunkhouse to live in. The Diamond L Ranch was now beginning to look well inhabited. Mary and Al had two boys, Kim and Robin, and the Gourlays were fast approaching what might well be termed a "clan."

One of the exciting episodes of the ranch days was known as the "Flood." The boys had decided to cut a channel for the river so that it would not keep eroding the hay flats. In the spring as the river rose, it roared down the new channel and cut into the bank where the barns were. They thought they would lose all the buildings. Only with the help of the neighbours, using their trucks and caterpillar tractors to dump cement and iron down the bank, did they manage to stabilize it. Later, they drove piles in further up the river and directed the river away from the barns.

Another of the highlights was a Shorthorn Field Day at the Diamond L. Lord Lovat was visiting Calgary from Scotland and came out to judge cattle at the ranch and talk to the breeders and 4H clubs. He was a very tall, handsome man, and particularly striking in his Fraser kilt. Mrs. Gourlay had known the family as a girl around Nairn in Scotland. She was introduced to the imposing Lord Lovat and smilingly said, "How do you do? The last time I met you, you were a snotty nosed little boy." This statement broke all the formality of the occasion.

As the Gourlay family enlarged, they began to realize that the Ranch could not support their growing needs. It was decided to sell the family business in 1958. The whole family will always enjoy their happy memories of life and friends at Millarville.

Mr. and Mrs. Ernest Gourlay retired to Scotland where they resided for ten years before returning to Canada. On their return, they settled in Kelowna, B.C., where Ernest started a new career as an Orchardist.

Jock and Shelagh moved to Lethbridge where Jock joined a feed company for a few years before entering a financial career as a Stockbroker.

Alasdair joined Shell Oil in Calgary for the next 17 years before moving to Kelowna to carry on the orchard business started by Ernest. He and Mary still live there with Ernest's widow, Joan.

Jane and Buz now live at Port Hope, Ontario, where

they are enjoying life in a 100 year old stone farmhouse.

Bob and Joan Goyette
by Joan Goyette

I was born in October, 1948 in Calgary, the second daughter of Effie and Alex Scatterty. Mom and Dad had three older children, Ronald, Margaret, and James, before I came along. My first home was on the old Spooner Ranch where Dad was manager. I attended Millarville School until 1957 and then we moved to Calgary because of Dad's health. I attended Cliff Bungalow and Rideau Park Schools in Calgary. In March, 1959 my Dad passed away and in June, 1960 my mother married Oswald Madsen, an old friend and longtime resident of Millarville. In 1961 they built a house on the N.E. ¼, Sec. 23, T. 21, R. 3, W. 5, and we moved back to Millarville. I attended Millarville School and Turner Valley High School until 1966, and then I moved into Calgary with a friend, Mary South (nee Birkenes). I started working for Premier Dry Cleaners, but it wasn't long before I discovered that pressing clothes in the summer was a little too hot (110 degrees). From there I went to Greyhound Bus Lines, but sorting bus tickets soon proved to be just a bit boring, so I joined the Air Force for some adventure.

In January, 1967 I headed for Cornwallis, Nova Scotia for basic training and from there I was posted to Clinton, Ontario for communication training. Eventually I ended up being posted to Namao, Edmonton working as a teletype operator. This work I found to be quite interesting but it wasn't long before I met up with a military policeman named Robert Goyette, and that was that.

Bob was born in Carleton County, Ottawa in March, 1947, but as a baby, his family moved to Sudbury, On-

Joan and Bob Goyette and family.

tario to enable his father to work in the mines. After leaving school, he too worked in the mines for about a year, but then decided it wasn't the life for him, so he left Sudbury for other parts of Ontario working at a number of different jobs. In 1966 he joined the Army and became a soldier in Princess Patricia's Light Infantry. Later, he transferred to become a military policeman and was posted to Edmonton where he eventually became a paratrooper in the Airborne Regiment.

Shortly after joining the Airborne, Bob was transferred to Calgary, so thinking this wasn't such a good idea, I left the service and we were married in Millarville's Christ Church in December, 1968. One month later, we were posted back to Edmonton and I started working for the Alberta Wheat Pool. After Bob left the service in April, 1969 he worked at a variety of jobs and then in September, 1969 we once again moved back to Calgary and he took up the trade of plumber and gasfitter. I began working for the Alberta Wheat Pool in Calgary, and did so until the birth of our first child, Michael James in May, 1971. Michael was soon followed by David Jason in September, 1972 and in November, 1972 we moved back to Millarville into a house we had built on Block 1, N.E. ¼, Sec. 23, T. 21, R. 3, W. 5 (a 20 acre parcel we had acquired from my parents). Bob became a journeyman plumber and gasfitter in 1973, and in August, 1976 our third child, Douglas Oswald was born. Bob died in a tragic car accident in August, 1977 and the children and I left Millarville in July, 1978. We now reside in Okotoks, Alberta.

Drew and Chris Graham
by Drew Graham

In 1953, I arrived at the old F. E. B. Gourlay place in Millarville, part of S.W. ¼ 7-21-2-W5. Sheep Creek was in full flood and almost all the ranch buildings

Joan and Bob Goyette.

were washed away. The creek was later diverted from the barns.

In the fall of 1955, I attended the Olds School of Agriculture where I received my diploma and in the spring of 1956, Mr. Gourlay recommended me for the management job of Dr. Doyle's farm at Black Diamond.

Later, Dr. Doyle sold the farm to Johnny Langenhoff of Saskatchewan and I helped him move there and put the crops in before coming back to the "Diamond L" as it was then known, to run the place for my cousin, Ewen Graham. I think Ewen bought the place in August, 1957.

I cared for approximately seventy head of feeder cattle and sixty cows plus wintering calves and selling hay to Messers Hoy & Co.

In 1958, I met Chris Brown and returned to Scotland to be married in November, 1959, and we then moved into the other Graham house. In 1962, I was offered the chance of renting from Ewen and Nicky, with the exception of land at the front of the ranch house and some of the buildings. They backed me to a loan at the bank, enabling us in this venture.

While living on the Graham Ranches, I had various lads work for me; one in particular was Johnny Cowan from the race track, a very likeable fellow. Another year, Sid Sorrie from Scotland, who later brought his wife out and is now somewhere in B.C. Also while living there, I had my first of many meetings with Alec and Effie Scatterty who were on the Spooner Ranch.

In April, 1967, we moved to the Johnny Wells place, just north of the Rodeo Grounds at High River, which we rented until our return to the United Kingdom in 1971. Had we the necessary funds we would have purchased the Wells place.

Since returning to the U.K., the first two years were spent looking for a farm but prices were soaring by the month and also my mother died six weeks after our return which put "paid" to the idea of buying land in her name to save estate duty and it seemed hopeless to go and borrow huge sums ($140,000 for 150 acres) just for land before equipping. This of course is nothing now as land around here sells for approximately $4,000 per acre.

I am now an agricultural contractor at Edinburgh, Scotland, beginning in 1972 and do a great deal of oilseed rape swathing and have a couple of big 120 h.p. John Deere tractors, two swathers, two big balers and various other equipment including two forage harvesters, ammonia injection tackle ploughs and cultivators. I only wish I had some land to go with the contracting business.

We have had a grand selection of Albertans here in Edinburgh as the Royal Highland Showpound is only ten minutes from here. In 1971, we met Joe and Helen Preston and next was Louis Kohler. Had a good crack with him and his future wife. Also the Braids from John Campbell's, the Wells of High River, Margaret and Orrin Hart of Claresholm, with Dave and Lucille

Glaister among others, so you can see it is a small world.

We have three children; our son James, born September 5, 1964 and daughter Heather, born May 4, 1967. Both born in Calgary. Neil was born May 30, 1968.

Some day when the kids have left school, we hope to return for a trip to the Millarville area.

Graves, Margaret (Deane-Freeman)

by Cynthia Anne Beyer
The Deane-Freeman brand ⅊

Margaret Deane-Freeman was born and raised at Monea (on the north fork of Sheep Creek) from 1922 to 1941.

Monea was the home ranch of Joseph Deane-Freeman, which was first settled in 1886. After growing up at Monea, William Deane-Freeman, the son of Joseph, ranched at Lineham, returning to Monea in 1921 with his second wife, Mabel Rigg (nee Strong).

Margaret was the only daughter of William and Mabel Deane-Freeman. After attending New Valley School she went on to high school in High River, and then graduating, held a position in a bank in Calgary. After war broke out she joined the C.W.A.C. and later attained the rank of Captain.

Monea was sold to Winston C. Parker, a close friend of the family, in 1947, and William and Mabel moved to High River. William died in 1954 and Mabel in 1976.

Margaret's marriage to R. C. Graves of London, Ontario, in 1946, was the beginning of many moves for

Margaret Deane-Freeman and friend.

295

her. With her three children, Susan, born in 1947, Cynthia in 1949 and Pamela in 1950, she moved to Nova Scotia and Manitoba. While her husband was overseas she moved back to High River for one year; that was the start of memories of Alberta for her children. She moved to Germany, Quebec, England and Ontario in subsequent years. In 1963 they moved to Ontario to stay, first Camp Borden, then Exeter, Ottawa, and finally Thunder Bay on the retirement of her husband. My mother said one time she had moved twenty-seven times in twenty-one years of marriage. She completed and graduated from a course in Hotel-Motel Management, and on May 6, 1973, she died.

Margaret is survived by her three daughters and four grandchildren: Susan Doucette of Owen Sound, Ontario, and her daughter, Catherine Margaret; Cynthia Beyer of Mount Forest, Ontario, and her son, Christopher Burke and daughter Shannon Deane; Pamela Screve of Marseille, France, and her daughter Nathalie Anne.

Although Margaret and her family spent little time in Alberta she never lost her love of Monea. She requested that her ashes be scattered over the foothills of Millarville at Monea. Our mother retold many stories of growing up at Monea, skiing to school in the winter and riding horseback when the weather permitted. She talked of polo games, and parties

where babies slept in the bedding chest of drawers. She instilled in us a feeling of security, of belonging, a sense of heritage and love for this part of Alberta. This heritage is being passed on to a new generation — our children.

Burke and Shannon Beyer have both been guests of Winston and Marj Parker, who are still living at Monea today.

Don Green Family

I was born in High River and grew up in the Mossleigh area. I met Anne Pettit from Gleichen and we were married on August 2, 1958.

We taught in the County of Vulcan for nine years. Then we moved to Fort Vermillion in 1969, where we both worked in the field of education and enjoyed the north for five years. In July 1974 we arrived in Millarville. We lived in the teacherage until October, 1975. In August 1975 we bought the Dick Lyall place and moved there in October.

We have two sons, Barry, who was born on October 23, 1964, and Brian, who was born on September 1, 1967. Both sons enjoy working and living in the Millarville area with their interests being school sports and team roping.

We are looking forward to many more exciting and memorable years in the Millarville District.

Don Green, principal of Millarville School and family. L. to R.: Don, Anne, Barry and Brian.

Dorothy Gregg

Daughter of Edith and Harold Thomas married Roderic Gregg in 1938, lived in Edson, Alberta from 1938 to 1969 now retired and living in Victoria, B.C. four children — all married — eleven grandchildren.

Lloyd and Doreen Greig
by Lloyd Greig

I was born in Didsbury December 19th, 1929. My parents were James Stuart Greig and Greta Lily Isabelle Greig. I was raised in Didsbury and Olds district from 1929 to 1940, then moved to Trochu where I spent the remaining years growing up and going to public and High School.

I worked around Trochu and area until 1954 and then moved to Square Butte Area and stayed with Brother-in-law Richard J. Lyall and sister Helen while working for Millarville Motors, owned by Hans Backs.

I recall the good times I had with the Lyall

L. to R. Desmond Deane-Freeman, Margaret Deane-Freeman, Clive Deane-Freeman.

Lloyd and Doreen Greig.

families, Nylund family, and Wildman family and all the good entertainments at the Square Butte Hall and Ranchman Hall.

After leaving Square Butte area I moved to Calgary. Most of my working time has been spent with Simpson and Sears and Calgary Coop in Automotive field.

When Hjalmar and Peggy Nylund were in Calgary I had the opportunity to live in the basement suite of their home. When this home was sold Nylund's then moved into my home.

I sure enjoyed the Nylunds company because they were full of fun and pranks.

I will give you an example, Peggy says to me ''Lloyd you have a mouse in the house'', and of course brave Lloyd is going to catch that mouse. Here I am looking under the bathroom tub, by the way this tub had legs; with my pantlegs half way up to my knees when Peggy decides she was going to have some fun. She takes a straw from the broom and tickles my legs and Lloyd is not looking under the tub, but is half way under with fright.

I met my wife Doreen in Calgary and we were married in November first 1977. We are now residing in Calgary as we both have work here.

James Edward and Almena Faye Grose   Jᴣ

What a day that was! — the day we moved to the land we were fortunate to buy from Irving Standish. In one trailer load we moved our belongings slowly out to what was one day to become the home of Jim, Faye, Darren and Cory Grose. As the two young fellows who helped us move, unloaded and placed our furniture on the green cement floor of our basement, they asked where we would be staying until the house was finished. "Here!" we replied, to their amazement, as they looked around at the window holes covered with plywood, at the building supplies stacked here and

there, and at makeshift power and water resources. So began our life in the country with Cory, age one and Darren, age three, in August, 1972.

In the next six months, the house progressed to having rooms in the basement and an empty shell above it. Severe winds that first January were a forewarning to build everything securely for Johnny Chinook was always just around the next hill.

Adjusting to country life was different for each one of us. Jim, having grown up on a farm at Clive, Alberta, was soon interested in cattle and crops. Although he taught electronics at Lord Beaverbrook High School in Calgary, he also worked on the Meota gas line expansion, and installed septic systems. Then he did some custom haying, which, in September, 1978, led to him giving up teaching to enter custom farming on a full time basis.

Faye was born and educated in Kingston, Ontario. The city life and higher education had not equipped her for calving problems and driving machinery. However, she, in time, was able to do the baling, while Jim ran the balewagon. Periodically she took part-time social work jobs at the Children's Hospital or School for Unmarried Mothers in Calgary.

From the time they were five and three years old, Darren and Cory have been entertaining themselves in fields from Red Deer Lake to Black Diamond while their parents put up hay. Starting school at Red Deer Lake was a welcome relief. The time is soon to come when they will displace their mom in doing the field work.

The friendliness of the Millarville community soon leads one to involvement in activities and groups. Jim accepted the vice-chairmanship of the hall of the Agricultural Society which led, eventually, to taking the presidency after Jim McCreary. Plowing the road in winter, working the track in summer, and slinging hamburgers in the concession were all part of the job. He was also on the Meota Gas Co-op Board for a short time. Faye started in the Junior Guild in 1973 at the invitation of Dorothy Jackson who was great about welcoming new neighbours, and took her turn at executive positions. Faye has helped with Continuing Education classes.

Memories of good times with neighbours like the Powells, Kemps, Jacksons and Allens were collected while involved in community work, and — in terms of history — those memories are what have made our seven years in the Millarville Community pleasant ones.

Don and Nancy Gullett

by Nancy Gullett

Donald Robert Gullett was born July 1, 1930 in Picton, Ontario. Nancy Aileen Gullett was born April 17, 1935 in Sherbrooke, P. Quebec.

Don moved to Calgary in 1952 where he went to work in the oil supply business. He is still connected with the oil industry. Nancy came west via the Canadian Pacific Railway, and went to work at the Chateau Lake Louise. She and Don met while skiing at Lake Louise although they had lived most of their formative years within fifteen miles of each other "back East"!

Nancy is the daughter of Howard and Mary Church who for many years farmed near Napanee, Ontario and who have just recently moved to Cranbrook in order to be near all four of their children who are now confirmed "Westerners".

Don's parents, the late Dr. and Mrs. Don Gullett moved to Toronto from Picton in 1941, when he was appointed Secretary of the Canadian Dental Association, a position he held for many years. In 1971 he was commissioned by the Canadian Dental Association to write the "History of Dentistry in Canada". During his lifetime he was the recipient of many honourary degrees and awards, including the Governor General's Award. Mrs. Gullett now lives in Vancouver.

Don and Nancy were married at Central United Church in Calgary in 1962 and spent the first few years of their married life living in Calgary.

We have three children all born in Calgary, Jennifer Mary — February 26, 1964, Cynthia Margaret — October 15, 1965, and Heather Aileen Joan — April 6, 1970.

We took up residence on "Whiskey Hill", near Millarville, on August 28, 1976.

Mary Ellen Gush (nee Knights)

by Mary Ellen

I, Mary Ellen, was born in London, England, April 15th, 1896, being the eldest daughter of Mr. and Mrs. Richard Knights, who resided at Massingham Ranch, Millarville, Alberta from 1909- . I emigrated with my parents, brothers and sisters in March 1909 and lived with them at Massingham Ranch, until I was married at Millarville Church to Ernest Walter Gush on March 31, 1920. Ernest was also born in London and emigrated to Canada in 1910. He lived in Calgary before enlisting in the 31st Battalion in Calgary in December, 1914 going overseas and staying in the Battalion, until its return to Calgary and demobilization in June 1919. On our marriage, we returned "Home" to England and lived in my husband's home county of Huntingdonshire, where our daughter Joyce Mary, and our son Richard Humphry were born. Joyce trained as a nurse at Adderbrooke's Hospital in Cambridge, and later visited Canada, nursing for a short time at Turner Valley Hospital, also Chilliwack Hospital, returning to England owing to her father's ill health. After his death, Joy took further training, gaining her Midwifery and Health Visitors Certificates. After further practice, she married Ted, a chemist. They now have 4 teenagers, two boys and twin girls, a happy family, living in Cambridgeshire. Dick trained as an electrical engineer, worked at an electric power station, both in the north and south of England. He married and had one boy John, and a girl Margaret, both now of age. Dick died in 1975.

I often look back, in memory of the happy days we spent at Massingham Ranch, first our school days at Fordville School, the busy holiday days haying and riding, and the lovely Alberta sunshine, which I still miss here, where we have so many dull and wet days. Our skating and hockey games on the rink at Millars Store and at Priddis, the dances and surprise parties, not forgetting Millarville Church, which we attended, also cleaned and decorated many a time. Here's to my happy childhood and many old friends.

Hackett, Jesse

Jesse left the MacKay Ranch to work for Imperial Oil in the Black Diamond, Turner Valley and Longview areas. Starting as a pipe line worker, he gained experience in all the aspects of oil and gas production, and took part in the activities of an expanding industry, and in athletics.

In 1938, he married Nancy Clarke of Turner Valley. They have three children, — Angela, Wendy and James. Angela and husband David La Plante, with two children, — Ray and Rachel, live in Barrie, Ontario. Wendy and husband Robert Barron, operate a modern farm near Chatham. Lynley and Roberta are their at-

Standing, James Hackett. Sitting, Marie and baby Jeff.

298

L. to R. Nancy and Jesse Hackett and brother Bill Hackett. Taken at Chatham, Ontario.

tractive daughters. James, a pharmacist in Windsor, married Maria Fasano from Cochrane, Ontario. They have a son, Jeffrey. Jim, an experienced golfer, won an Ontario Junior Championship.

Jesse was transferred from the West to Imperial Oil's Eastern Production in Chatham, as Superintendent of Production, a post he filled until his retirement. He and Nancy are still Active in Golf and curling.

Hackett, William James

Bill left Millarville to attend high school in Claresholm. After attending Normal School in Calgary, he commenced his forty-seven years of teaching school. A Bachelor of Arts Degree, and a Bachelor of Education Degree from the University of Alberta, several special courses in guidance, and the experience of twelve years in rural schools, prepared

him for High School instruction. Also his association with the Dominion Provincial Youth Training Program, and his own athletic experience, were useful at Central High where he became Department Head of Physical Education. In the Guidance Department at Central, and at Aberhart High, he was priviliged to interview and advise many students. Later he watched with interest and pride the scholarly performance of many of them at University and in the professional world.

His wife, Eva Beattie from Nova Scotia, acquired a Bachelor of Arts Degree at the University of Alberta. After two years in a rural school, she taught high school at Dalemead, Red Deer, and Calgary. They have two children, — Barbara Jean and Barrie who died at the age of twenty-six.

Bill and Eva Hackett.

Intermediate Relay Race Record. L. to R. Peter Lochhead, Bill Egbert, Bob Rutter, Ted Allen, Bill Fayter. Standing — Bill Hackett, coach Central High School.

Thorpe family. L. to R. Phillip, Barbara, Sharon, Allan.

Barbara Jean completed an honors biochemistry degree at McGill University on scholarship. After graduation, she married Phillip Thorpe who had received a B.Sc. degree in Math and Physics from Acadia University, and a degree in Electrical Engineering from McGill. They live in Calgary where Phil is a systems analyst in the computer program for Shell Canada, Ltd. He and Barbara are active lay workers for the United Church. Barbara is a docent (teacher) at the Glenbow Museum, and works part time at the Calgary Conference Office of the United Church of Canada. They have two children.

Sharon is in her first year at university working towards a degree in archeology. Allan is completing Junior High and continuing his interest in the piano and the bassoon.

Hall, Faye Audrey (Nee Mickle)

Born — 1945 — raised at Jumping Pound until five years old, lived at Royalties for one year where I completed Grade One, then moved to Black Diamond area on Walter Erickson's West Half and S.E. Quarter of Section 30, Twp. 20, Range 2, West of 5th Meridian. I went to school at Millarville. In 1959, we moved west of Millarville to the South-half of Section 17, Twp. 21, Range 4, West of 5th Meridian.

In Grade Eleven (11), we had to go to Turner Valley to school. After Grade Eleven, I took a Secretarial course for one year in Calgary.

My favorite hobbies were helping Dad with the trapline and chasing wild horses near Square Butte. As our land bordered the Forest Reserve, I spent a great deal of time riding on the Reserve and staying at our Trapline cabin.

When I was seventeen, we moved to Lake Louise where we ran a trail riding business (Timberline Tours Ltd.) in the summer, took hunting trips in the fall, and ran a ski business at Skoki Lodge in the winter.

I was married in 1966 and continued to work at Lake Louise, where I raised my daughter — Deborah Lynn and son — Marty William until 1976, when I moved to

Fay (Mickle) Hall with son Marty William (back) and daughter Deborah Lynn.

Spruce View area after being divorced. I am residing at Spruce View on my parent's farm and my children are going to school at Spruce View.

I am working as a cook in a cafe at Spruce View at present.

The Hamilton Family

S.E.¼ 16-21-4 W5
by Harry Hamilton

After Mollie (nee Pierce) died in 1961, Harry later married Eileen Campbell and they and the girls continued to visit the homestead every summer for the next ten years. Harry had open heart surgery in 1968 and in 1973 which necessitated an early retirement and his selling the homestead and their Calgary home. Harry and Eileen moved to an apartment in south west Calgary and are still making this their home.

In the meantime the four girls left home and settled in several parts of Alberta. Patsy married Arnold Brogden of Priddis and they are still farming in that community. They have three children — Ken, Dawn and Teresa. Mary married Ralph Roy who at one time worked in the Square Butte district. They subsequently moved to Didsbury where Ralph worked as a welder and Mary nursed in the Hospital. They have two girls — Shirley and Kathleen. They later moved to Fort Ver-

Fay (Mickle) Hall at Deception Pass, near Lake Louise, July 1960.

The Hamilton family. L. to R. Gwen, Harry, Mary, Pat, Molly. Sharon in front.

Square Butte School. Class of 1939-1940. Back row, L. to R. Nina Ingeveld, Joan Kosling, Mr. Hamilton, (teacher) Rene Gouy, Frank Kendall, Alice Silvester. Centre row, L. to R. Bill Kendall, Charlie Silvester, Dolores Gouy, Gordon McLay (kneeling). Front row, L. to R. Minnie Silvester, Jimmie Silvester, Dibby Kendall. Absent, John Kendall.

milion where they set up farming. Although presently living in Grande Prairie they continue to run the farm at the Fort and plan to move back there when the girls are through High School.

Gwen married a New Brunswick boy Leon Carmichael who had travelled west, and they too are farming in Fort Vermilion. They have four children — David, Michelle, Paul and Chad. Presently they are living in the Fort but plan to build a home on the farm when it becomes self supporting.

Sharon the youngest girl did a little travelling and working in the States and then returned to settle in Claresholm. She is single and is presently a secretary for an accountant in the town of Claresholm.

Although we have left the Square Butte District we have many fond memories of times spent there. Friends and relatives still live there and we visit them periodically. Our wish is that Square Butte may continue to prosper and give pleasure to others for many years to come.

My Association With Square Butte

by Harry Hamilton

I married Mollie Pierce in February 1939, and that was my introduction to some wonderfully happy years in the Square Butte District, just west of Millarville.

We had a piece of land just north of George Lyall's farm, on the S.E. quarter of Section 16-21-4W5. All that we had on it was a log cabin, 20' by 20', but it was to become our home for the next year as I was appointed to teach in the Square Butte School for the year 1939-40.

What a happy year that was. I had about twelve students in grades 1 to 9 in the little log school. They all rode their ponies to school and stabled them in the shed on the school grounds. Sometimes the Kendalls would bring an extra pony for me and we would go on trail rides up the Butte and around the countryside. We called these our field trips and they proved most interesting and happy times.

We had several musical evenings in the school and at the old Ranchman's Hall, where the children performed, supplemented by talent brought out from Calgary.

All the while, we lived in our cabin during the week and spent weekends back in Calgary where Mollie conducted a Church choir and I sang. Some weeks the roads were too muddy for Mollie to attempt the trip, and then I would stay with Mr. and Mrs. George Lyall where they welcomed me with utmost kindness.

We terminated our residence out there in June 1940, but kept in touch with the district by adding to our cabin and spending our holidays and special occasions at Square Butte. We used the brand ↓T, which was initiated in the early 1900's by Mr. Tom Pierce who homesteaded when he came from England.

Square Butte School reunion 1972. Back row, L. to R. Charlie Silvester, Jimmie Silvester, John Kendall, Frank Kendall. Front row, L. to R. Dibby (Kendall) Stewart, Minnie (Silvester) Marshall, Alice (Silvester) Hampton, Mr. H. Hamilton.

In 1972, Square Butte School celebrated its 50th. anniversary and I was invited to be M.C. for the occasion. There were seven of the original twelve students present, and I include a picture of them taken at that time, accompanied by one taken in 1939.

Mollie died in 1961 and our four daughters have scattered. I sold the land in 1973 but I still visit and keep in touch with old friends in the Square Butte district.

From 1940 I continued to teach in the Calgary School System until my retirement in 1972. The little log schoolhouse at Square Butte, though now gone, was a happy beginning to a very satisfying teaching career.

The Howard Hampton Family
by W. J. Hampton

My father, Howard Hampton, was born on March 9th, 1920 at Vulcan, Alberta to James and Gertrude Hampton. Father has one elder sister, Beulah, who presently resides in San Jose California. James and Gertrude owned and rented various parcels of land in the Milo, Lake McGregor and Vulcan areas where they made a living by raising grain crops. During their residence in these areas Father attended Sunny Glen, Snake Creek, Sandpit, and Lake McGregor schools where he obtained his basic formal education. He also helped his Dad with the many tasks around the farm after school hours.

In 1937 James and Gertrude packed up lock-stock-and-barrel and moved to Longview, Alberta where they rented Tom Merriam's ranch (sec 17, S½ of sec 20, S½ of sec 19, NW¼ of sec 18 all in twp 18-R2-W5) and went into the cattle business. Father continued to work with his parents on the Merriam ranch until 1947.

In 1944 Father met his wife-to-be, Alice Silvester, who was employed at the Joe Bews Ranch west of Longview. Mother, born on June 19th, 1925, was the ninth child in a family of thirteen children born to Alice and Ernest Silvester Sr. who ranched in the Square Butte district. Mother received her basic formal education at Square Butte School and in 1941 at the age of sixteen she went to work as "choregirl" at the Joe Bews Ranch for $15 per month. She continued working at the Bews Ranch until 1945 with the exception of a three month interlude in January, February, and March of 1942 during which time she worked for Charlie Grenek in the Gladys Ridge area. By the time Mother left the Bews Ranch in 1945 her salary had escalated to $45 per month.

On March 12th, 1945 Mother and Father exchanged marital vows at Christ Church Millarville with Reverend Edward Hoad officiating. Mother and Father bought a little house and located it on the Merriam ranch where they resided until 1954.

Being very mechanically inclined, Father decided to start his own contracting business and in 1947 he purchased a TD-40 International Harvester crawler tractor. Soon realizing that when one is in the heavy equipment business breakdowns are much less costly if repaired through the use of your own skills rather than having someone else do it, so Father decided to purchase a welder. The welder which he purchased in 1948 cost $333 and is the same one he is using to this very day. Even though Father did receive some help from a friend he is basically self-taught at welding and can probably cast a bead which is as smooth and strong as that done by a fully licensed welder. Also in 1948 Milley Raymond and Father designed and built a heavy duty breaking plow (see photo page 51) which was one of the first such pieces of equipment to be used in this area.

In 1949 several major events occurred: Father purchased the NW¼ of sec 14-twp 20-R4-W5 from

Howard and Alice Hampton picnicking at Holden Creek on their way to the Muskeg with salt.

Howard and Alice Hampton. 1965.

Tim and Ronnie Hampton with son Kim.

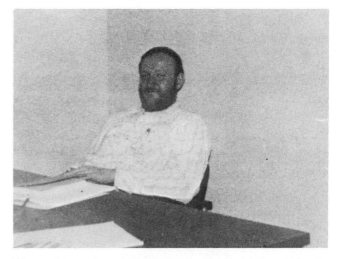

Wayne Hampton at his desk, Fox Lake Indian School.

William Iceton; the first of two children, Timothy Howard, was born in the Turner Valley Hospital July 16th; and Father opted for a larger TD-14 Crawler Tractor. It was with this cat that Father helped construct the road up to the look-out on Raspberry Ridge in the Highwood country. Father often tells of the time when he was on this job that the road slid out from under his cat and he managed to get the cat wiggled around so it was pointing down the mountain and he went a distance of 200 yards at a ninety degree angle before he came to the switchback below him. Father also helped build the "truck trail" which joins the North Fork and South Fork forest reserve areas.

Two years later in 1951 I was born in Turner Valley Hospital on July 5th. In 1953 Father made another addition to his line of heavy equipment by purchasing a new Towner Disc which cost $1650. This heavy duty disc was designed in the United States in an attempt to develop equipment that would be successful in cutting through the very hard and parched soil in the Kansas area. It proved to be a worthwhile piece of equipment which Father still uses on his own property to this day.

1954 saw the purchase of another quarter of land namely, the SE¼ of sec 14-twp 20-R4-W5 from George Wambeke. In October of this year the Hampton family moved house and all to this location where we have been residing ever since.

In this the beginning of Mother and Father's own ranching career they had a herd of 11 head of Hereford cattle marked with their brand AP on the Right Ribs. Also during this year Mother and Father obtained a forest reserve permit to run 25 cows and calves in the Muskeg during the summer months. This permit has since been increased to 40 cows and calves and 10 yearlings.

Up until 1962 Father continued to do contract work with his equipment to support the family and help pay for the land. This involved many many long hours of hard work on the part of both Mother and Father however it has not been without its rewards.

In 1959 Father purchased the NE¼ of sec 14-twp 20-R4-W5 and the NW¼ of sec 13-twp 20-R4-W5 from

Albert Iceton. It was also in this year that we made our first step into the modern 20th century by getting the welcomed convenience of electricity. In 1964 we put in a basement and built onto our home; in 1965 we put in running water; in 1971 we received telephone service and in 1976 we received natural gas. Up until this time our home had been heated by fuel oil and wood and then later propane. However in 1977 we moved back into the wood burning days with the installation of a Franklin Fire Place to help abate the escalating costs of the natural gas bill.

Tim received his basic formal education at Millarville School and Turner Valley High School (now Oilfields High School) and has chosen a career in the heavy equipment contracting business. He is married to Veronica (Ronnie) Richardson and they have one son, Kim Howard, who is presently in Grade One at Millarville School. They reside on the NW¼ of sec 13-twp 20-R4-W5. Tim and Ronnie run a few head of cattle with Mother and Father's herd and their brand is IT and Kim's brand is IS both on the Right Ribs.

I similarly received my basic formal education at Millarville School and Turner Valley High as well as receiving my baccalaureate degree in education from the University of Calgary. I commenced employment with Northland S.D. No. 61 in 1973 and since 1974 have been the principal of a twelve teacher school on the Cree Indian Reserve of Fox Lake located near Wood Buffalo National Park. At the time of this writing I am on sabbatical leave from Northland and am doing graduate work at the University of Calgary in Educational Administration. At the same time I am constructing a log home on the same quarter as Mother and Father's buildings. My home is nearing its final stages of completion and at the end of my sabbatical I will be returning to the north country to continue working with the Cree Indians, a people I deeply love and respect. During the summer vacation I usually help my parents with the task of haying. I too run a few head of cattle with my parent's herd and my brand is 7H- on the Right Ribs.

Bert Haney

by Lillian Bradley

Born in Johnson Township in Algoma near Sault Ste. Marie, Ontario.

Took his education at a small country school near Seaforth, Ontario, near his father's farm.

He worked at various jobs through the thirties, working on farms, driving cattle liners which one time tipped over killing most of the cattle. He also worked at Sproats Brickyard in the Seaforth area.

He married Vera Leonhardt who was from Phillip's Township, near Bornholm, Ontario. They moved to Seaforth where they raised chickens for a while.

Bert bought a house in Egmondville and he worked in Bells Foundry where they made threshing machines.

Dad loved the water and he liked to fish. I remember one time when some of them went on a fishing trip when the smelts were running. You catch them with nets, they came home with wash tubs full of them, and wondering what the heck to do with all of them. They spent the whole day trying to give them away.

Dad built several motor boats in his spare time, one of which was a twenty foot cruiser. Every Sunday we would pack up and go to Lake Huron for a picnic and a day on the water. One of the things Dad said he really missed in the west was the lakes.

In 1950 he came west to find work, settling in Edmonton with his uncle, Tom Townsend, working as a carpenter.

Coming to Millarville to visit his sister Esther Jackson, he found a job in Calgary working for Precision Machinery.

In June of 1950 Vera drove west with four small children. We stayed with the Jacksons until we moved into a small house rented from Hans Backs at Millarville.

Dad started to build a garage, but soon the garage door was boarded up and a picture window was put in its place and became a three roomed house.

He purchased five acres of land from Ted Rawlinson and moved the house across from where the school is now situated. Later years the house was sold to Sylvesters and moved. A new house was built in the same place along with a few other buildings.

In 1952 Vera started to clean the school, which she did until 1977.

The following year, 1953, Bert got a small school bus which he purchased from Bill Lee. He bused the kids from East Millarville area to the school. One day a week they had store day when all the kids were allowed to go into Bill Lees store and buy a treat before going home. All of them looked forward to this.

After school hours Dad's old red Dodge truck could be seen going to one construction job or another. Dad built many lovely homes in the area, the first being his sister's, the Billy Jacksons and Murrays' home. Later many more followed. He also built the church house at East Millarville and Bills Corner Service Station.

Bert and Vera took part in most of the community activities especially Ranchers' Hall. They bowled in a league in Turner Valley and Vera at one time belonged to the W.I. and the Happy Gang.

Dad loved hockey and went to many of the Okotoks Oilers and Centennial games in Calgary. Bert enjoyed hunting for big game and birds and every chance he had would be seen with his friends packing off into the mountains to hunt big game or to the prairie country to hunt for birds.

One time in Calgary after a few quick ones at the Royal Hotel, Hugh Cawthorne and Dad pinched a large watermelon from the back of a fruit truck, which was standing on the street corner. They then took their prize to Bert's nieces, Fern and Anne Jacksons to eat it. For dessert Bert ate the pansies in a bowl in the middle of the table.

In 1966 he bought a backhoe from a fellow in Black Diamond. That was the start of Bert Haney Construction. He started working around the country digging in water lines and septic tanks. At this time he bought a small Cat to back fill the ditches. Jim Scatterty started working for him around this time. He had a gravel truck which mostly worked for Burnco in Calgary. He bought a small gravel crusher with which he crushed gravel at the pit on the Jackson farm.

Bert passed away suddenly in February, 1976.

The Haney family at Millarville. L. to R., Back: Vera, Bert. Centre: Lillian, Joan, Bob, Peggy Ann in front.

Bert Haney, 1976.

Vera still resides at their home in Millarville.

Four children — three girls, Lillian, Joan, Peggy Anne and one son Bob. All attended school at Sheep Creek School in Millarville. Lillian and Peggy Anne both Nursing Aides from school in Calgary and both working. Joan works in a Dry Cleaning store in Los Angeles as a leather cleaner. Bob is at Jasper National Park as a park warden. Bert and Vera have twelve grandchildren and one great-grandson.

R. W. Handfield

This brief history is about the Handfield family consisting of Rod and Lise happily married now for the past 22 years, as well as sons Robert age 14 and Carlo age 12. Lise is French Canadian by origin and her family has lived in the Quebec City area for the past 300 years. Rod's family ties date back some 250 years to the time of the English conquest in Canada. Both our boys are born out west.

We bought our quarter the S.W. ¼-1-21-4w5 off Bob Oldrich, a well known artist who is remembered in High River for the Windmill he created in the Town Centre. Our common family interest is horses and the big controversy is whether we should ride Western or English. The issue has been settled by the horses, one of which refuses to accept anything but an English saddle. Our second interest is trying to find our husky dog which is always running away for extended periods of time. An amusing incident occured last year. I was trying to catch our dog "Kila" who in turn was attempting to round up a dozen head of neighbours' cattle. When the neighbour arrived on scene I expected the worst and apologized accordingly. His comments were as follows: "I am not worried about the dog or cattle, they know what they are doing, but if you continue, you will certainly have a heart attack". So much for dog chasing in Millarville.

Our involement in local district affairs has been negligible to date because of Lise's career (travelling school teacher in Calgary) and Rod's work load (self-employed consulting geologist). We do look forward to the days in the near future when we will spend more than weekends and Holidays in our Millarville home and get to know our district and neighbours better than we currently do.

Dennis and Patricia Hanson

Dennis and Patricia Hanson. Dennis was born in 1953, only son of Harley and Joanna Hanson. He went by bus to Sheep Creek School at Millarville for his grade school, then to Lord Beaverbrook for his high school. He was always very active in sports. He, with the neighborhood boys, always made a skating rink to play hockey in the winter and then when he was going to school in Calgary, played hockey there. Then he bought a Skidoo and travelled to many points in Alberta to compete in races, winning five cups. Now he and Pat have two Artic Cats.

Christmas Day. 1978. Dennis and Pat Hanson, with their children, Scott and Charlisa.

Scott and Charlisa Hanson, Dennis and Pat Hanson's children.

One winter Dennis and five of his friends went back through on their snowmobiles from Turner Valley to Fortress. One of the boys machines broke down and he went back to Fortress and caught a ride to Calgary. The other boys didn't miss him at first, then hunted for hours but running short of gas had to return home. It was with great relief they found Don was safe. The next summer Monte Kendall and Dennis covered the same area in dune buggies and had a marvellous trip.

He worked first at the Gas Plant at Millarville then to Ram River and now has his papers as a steam fitter.

He married Patricia Cole, only daughter of Ken and Winnie Cole of Calgary in 1973. They have two children, Scott Harlan and Charlisa Joanne. They now make their home in Medicine Hat.

Harley and Joanna Hanson
Brand U̲U̲

Harley was born in Park River, North Dakota, the fourth child of Martin and Gunilda Hanson. They came

Hanson Family. Back, L. to R.: Marlene, Donna
Front: Harley, Dennis, Joanna.

Harley and Johanna Hanson. 1978.

to Vulcan and made their home on a homestead close
to Lake McGregor in 1912.

In 1933 during the depression, he married Joanna
Scott who was born in Creston, B.C. She came with her
parents, David and Elizabeth Scott, one sister and four
brothers to the Champion district in 1918 in the Sanderson School district.

In 1934 Marlene Joan was born at Vulcan. In April
of that year, Harley and his brothers, Leonard, Glen,
and Marlin drove two six-horse outfits and one four-
horse outfit, loaded with machinery and household
effects to the Dovercourt district of Rocky Mountain
House. Marlin rode on horseback and herded cattle going the back roads. It was sometimes hard to find
enough feed and water for overnight camps. Prairie
horses knew nothing of muskegs and would walk right
out into them. They lost three horses one night that
way. I joined Harley on our homestead. It was a grim
winter. We lost most of the horses with sleeping
sickness and many of the cattle as the feed had little
food value and the prairie cattle weren't climatized.
Yet we had many good times; dances, picnics, ball
games etc.

In 1938 we returned to Vulcan where Donna Mae
was born. From there we came to West Naptha, south
of Black Diamond. Harley delivered milk for Jim
McGregor and Jim McDonald. We really liked the excitement of the oilfields. Marlene started school at
Glenmeade.

Harley started roughnecking for Newell and
Chandler and we moved to a shack on Freddie
Hodgkins at Millarville. There were so many wells
drilling in the area, the shack shook from the vibration
of the mud pumps. It was a cold winter, but the boys,
Harley as well as Glen and Marlin who stayed with us,
helped Freddie saw wood and the little airtight heater
was red hot many a night. In the spring, the river
flooded and we were cut off from the south end for
months, but Jean Waugh's store supplied the
groceries.

Harley worked derrick for years and we bought a
three room house from Ace Van de Work. They had
lost their baby Twyla while Ace worked at Priddis for
some time while he and Bill Bowie operated a
separator. After a nose operation Ace died. Pearl, his
wife, worked on the separator, one of the only lady
operators I know for a time, before she moved back to
Calgary to nurse in the Holy Cross Hospital. They had
one son Brian, who is a policeman in Calgary. While
living on William Jackson's place, Harley worked
separator for the Royalite. There were so many oil
workers in that area during those years.

In 1945 we bought the Gavin Calderwood place.
N.W. ¼ 29; 20, 3W,5 at Kew. There was no water so we
dug a spring out south of the place and Orums and we
used it for house and stock. It was so soft around it,
animals would mire down. The next year we had a 52
foot well drilled and always had a good supply of
water.

Donna and Marlene went to Plainview School
where Rita (Billo) Robison was teacher. Close
neighbors Orums, Sims, Peels, Lochheads and Adams
made an interesting neighborhood. Harley still worked
for oil companies, drilling contractors, Royalite,
Western Petroleum and Miracle.

We built up a herd of milk cows and I recall one
winter it was so cold a young visitor wanted to know if
we couldn't milk those cows with our mitts on.

Tommy Thompson of Black Diamond started a
milk plant and came for our milk if roads were
passable, otherwise we slung the 8 gallon cans over our
quiet mare's back and took them out to Adam's corner. In the spring the clay mud on that hill was so deep
we often left the cars at Frank Adams and walked
home. We gradually changed over to beef cattle.

We had very happy times there. In summer we had
a Kew picnic and ball games on Ford Lochhead's flat,
and we also had a Kew Club. We attend the Gospel
Chapel in Black Diamond.

Harley Hanson with his team of ponies.

In 1953 Dennis Harlan was born and Marlene married Donald Pearse of Calgary.

The Plainview School closed and every farmer paid $75.00 a quarter to have the road graveled so the children were bused to Sheep Creek School.

Up until this time, the phone at Kew store was the only one in the district, but now a few neighbors worked to get enough signers to join the mutual telephone company and have it extended as far as Peels. Even if we had a party line of 10, it was a real step forward.

Then the hydro was extended to our district and then next the mail route.

Donna married a neighbor boy David Evans (see Evans). Harley worked for ten years for Silverwood Dairies in Calgary. In 1965 we sold 20 acres to David Langford. In 1972, 40 acres to Ron Raricks and 40 acres to Sid Mueller leaving 60 acres for Dennis. He married Patricia Cole of Calgary in 1973. They have two children Scott Harlan and Charlisa Joanne.

We retired to Turner Valley where so many of our former friends and neighbors are living. We still enjoy going back up to the farm where Harley has ponies.

Percy Harbut

Percy "Herb" Harbut was an Englishman who was apparently in this country when the first World War started, as he went overseas with the Canadian Army. He returned with his bride and worked in Calgary until moving to Okotoks in the late twenties where he was in charge of the Imperial Oil warehouse. This building was on the C.P.R. tracks at the west end of town and served as the railhead for Imperial's Turner Valley operations. When it was closed during the depression, the Harbuts bought the N.E. 33-21-3-W5th where they farmed in a small way. Herb died in the Belcher Hospital and his widow still lives in Calgary.

Joseph Haracz

Joseph Haracz came to Canada in November 1946 from Italy after the war. He was in the Army and could not go back to Poland as it was a Communist Country.

He worked on a farming contract for two and one half years in Hussar, then went to Blackie and worked for Cecil Mitten on another farm. In 1950 he purchased the Everett Hedley farm located on S.W. ¼ of Section 21, Twp. 20, Range 3, west of the 5th Meridian.

In 1951 Joe's brother Stanley and his wife came from England. Both Joe and Stanley obtained jobs in Calgary, coming to the farm on week-ends. Joe worked for the city of Calgary Water Works and Stan worked for York Shaw Building Movers. They farmed this way until 1960 when Stan left his job and came to live in the small cabin on the farm. Joe and Stan raised yearlings until 1960, then purchased a number of cows and calves, selling them in 1971 when Stan became ill and could no longer look after them. In the fall of 1973 Stan had to leave the farm and move back to their home in Calgary because of poor health.

Joe retired from the City of Calgary in 1973. Stanley, Stella and Joe now live in Calgary and rent the farm out for pasture, coming out to visit as often as possible.

J. F. (Pat) Hartell
by Mollie Duxbury

I was born in Lemburg, Saskatchewan, on June 25th, 1895 and came to Alberta with my Dad, Mother and three brothers in 1899. We settled four miles west of Strathmore where two more brothers and two sisters were born.

As for school, it was 1905 before our parents got one. W. Miller, J. Lyons and my Dad worked for two years, writing letters to Regina, Saskatchewan. There was no Alberta then. Finally in 1905 a school was built about one and a half miles south east of Cheadle on the open prairie over a mile to the nearest fence.

We spent a short time around Trochu and in 1918 moved south of Black Diamond where Dad had bought the 8 Ranch. S. 8-19-2w5, and my brother Alex still lives on the land.

Wedding Group at 40th. Anniversary, 1959. Back row: Best man, Charlie Hartell, Brides Maid, Annie Minue, Flower girl, Elsie Snider. Front row: Groom, Pat Hartell, Bride, Molly (Brechin) Hartell.

In 1919 I married Mollie Breckin, from Dundee, Scotland. We lived on the ranch until 1924. Our first two children, Dorothy and Mollie were born there. Jean and Vi were born in High River. Moving south west of High River to the Spring Dale District, we farmed there until 1935. Then the big move — into the Plainview District.

I rented three quarters owned by Mr. Brown at Parkland. While living on same I bought the S.W. and N.W. quarters of section 8-20-4w5 from the Hudson Bay Co. for $7 per acre. At the end of three years I was supposed to have an equity of $1 per acre and have 30 acres plowed and some buildings. I managed and that was all.

For buildings — there were four oil well cabins about two miles away and with the help of my good neighbors and ten horses we moved them off the hill and across the valley and up another hill. They are still there, where Dick and Charis Cooper live. For the barn I cut the logs on Canyon Creek. The snow all went and I had to haul thirty foot logs on a wagon. Bob Calderwood showed me how to start a log barn.

For water there was a spring a quarter of a mile up the hill. I had to hitch up a team of horses to the home made sleigh and haul water every day for the house, pigs and chickens. This went on for about seven years. In the early 40's I got someone to start drilling. Over the next ten or twelve years we drilled five wells. One, 200 feet, no water, a little water in one at 100 feet; then my neighbor, Charlie Silvester, said he could witch one but it would be a little ways from the house. O.K. 700 feet from the house we got water at less than 30 feet. We had lots of water until I sold out in 1970.

The three girls, Mollie, Jean and Vi, went to Plainview School on horseback, while Dot took one year of correspondence courses. Then Dot and Mollie boarded in Turner Valley and later Vi went.

Jean was my right hand cowboy and farm helper. Walter Birney bought a lot of cattle in the late '30s and '40s. All the way from the North Sheep Creek south to the Highwood River and Jean, with some help, would drive these cattle, some of them pretty spooky, into Calgary. There were no trucks in those days.

Dot married Roy Davis and they live near the Pekisko Store. They have five children, Margarite, Barbara, Buster, Billy and Hazel, and to date, eight grandchildren.

Dot was in the Airforce, stationed at Gander, Newfoundland, where she met and later, home again on the ranch, married Frank Duxbury of Medicine Hat.

Jean married Vern Fedderson and they live on a farm just west of Turner Valley.

Vi married Tom Gilchrist. They live on a ranch at Youngstown and have a family of five, John, Stanley, Heather, Diane and Nita and to date two grandchildren.

We had a lot of good neighbors while we lived in the Kew district, the Middletons, Robisons, Dudenhoeffers and Adams, just to mention a few. In

40th. Wedding Anniversary of Pat and Molly Hartell. Back row: Elsie Snider, Fay Hartell, Walter Hartell, Charlie Hartell, Annie Minue, Rena Hartell, Nan Brechin, Joe Hartell, Molly Duxbury, Margarite Davis, Barbara Davis, Violet Gilchrist holding Heather, Bill Davis, Jean Fedderson, Roy Davis, Hazel, Buster Davis, Tom Gilchrist. Second row: Darlene Duxbury, J. F. (Pat) Hartell, Dot Davis, Molly Hartell, Ken Duxbury, David Duxbury, Frank Duxbury. Front row: John Gilchrist, Glen Duxbury, Stan Gilchrist. 1959.

the winter, house parties, from house to house, young and old, everyone welcome and you didn't need a bottle of hootch to start things going. There were also concerts and dances in the Kew Hall. I had the honour of calling the square dances.

In the summer the Kew Ladies Club did a lot of visiting and during the war years the "Willing Workers" did a lot of good. They sent a lot of parcels overseas. My wife, Mollie, was president of the group for quite some time.

We men, W. Middleton, B. Iceton, Dan Dudenhoeffer and myself, collected a few dollars and put on a picnic at the Kew Hall. Ford Lochhead would go to Calgary in the morning of the picnic for ice cream, watermelon, candy and peanuts. The young and old would have a great time with races of various kinds, ball games, horse shoes etc.

I enjoyed hunting, fishing, curling, base ball, in fact most any sport. I still enjoy a good card game.

I was president of the Turner Valley Curling Club for a short time, also president of the Turner Valley Telephone for about two years. On the committee of the South Sheep Stock Association, and fire warden for some years.

My wife Mollie passed away in 1970. We had fifty-one years together. I married a second time in 1972, to Mrs. Isabella Murray. We live in Turner Valley at 307 Windsor Avenue.

Charles Edward Hayward — 1924
Cow Brand 5H Rt. Shldr., Horse Brand H Rt. Shldr.

Born at Newlands, B.C., the seventh in a family of fourteen. In 1939 our parents died within a year of each other and the nine youngest were taken to Vancouver by the Children's Aid Society and placed in adoptive and foster homes. We lost track of each other until, in 1971, my oldest sister Ruth tracked us all down, and we had a family reunion in Quesnel, B.C. It was quite a reunion, some of us hadn't seen each other for 32 years.

I joined the R.C.A.F. in 1942 and while stationed in Dawson Creek, B.C., I met and married Laura Murray from Lymburn, Alberta. We were transferred to Whitehorse where Loraine and Gloria were born. Then transferred to Ontario where our son Ed was born. When Eddy was two, we were transferred to Calgary and we liked it so much we decided this was where we wanted to stay. I took my discharge from the Airforce, went to work for the City of Calgary, and we moved to the Red Deer Lake district in 1958. We lived on S.E.¼, Sec.21, T.22, R.2, W.5, previously owned by Albert and Connie Eckersley. We lived there until 1968, when we bought S.E.¼, Sec.23, T.21, R.3, W.5 from Dave Glaister.

I have always been an outdoorsman, and an avid hunter, so in 1968 we bought an outfitting business in the North West Territories. We trucked our horses 1,-500 miles north to the end of the road, then trailed them 240 miles into the Mackenzie Mountains, swimming the legendary South Nahanni and Broken Skull rivers. There had never been horses in this area before, and in some of this beautiful country the only human signs were stone axe cuttings between 200 and 400 years old. Though we travelled this vast country for eight summers, there are endless valleys and mountain passes that still remain unmarked by man or horse track. Prospecting has always intrigued me, and my dream is to return to the Yukon to resume my search for gold.

Our three children:

Loraine — married Bruce Debnam; have one daughter — Holly; live at West Millarville.

Gloria — married Barry Black; have three children — Dean, Becky, Shannon; live in Okotoks.

Ed — married Pam Jones; have one daughter, Amber; live at Millarville.

Everett Hedley

My family came from Durhamshire, England and settled near Cayuga, the County seat of Haldimand County, Ontario. My parents moved to Calgary in 1912 and I attended Hillhurst Public School with my two sisters. I graduated from Crescent Heights High School while William Aberhart was principal. He later became premier of Alberta.

After graduating from Calgary Normal School, I taught at Uphill School near Longview, Alberta.

I homesteaded at Enilda, Alberta, and taught school there for several years and played baseball and hockey for High Prairie, eight miles west.

I met Sheila Bowen who is a Welsh girl from Pembrokeshire. She was born in 1912 and came to Trochu in

1927 and to Kinuso later. We were married in 1932 at High Prairie.

We moved to a farm northwest of Turner Valley in 1934 and I taught at Plainview School in the Kew district for several years before becoming an operator for the Royalite Oil Company.

Shirley, our oldest daughter, attended Plainview school, Western Canada High School and Turner Valley High School. She was a good athlete and won the senior girls medal at the Foothills Sports Day at High River. She married Wray Lucas and they live on a farm north west of Rimbey.

Merlyn also attended Plainview School and graduated from Turner Valley High. She is married to Dave Basaraba and they live in Calgary.

Keith, our son, attended school in Turner Valley. He went to work for Semon and Lucas Construction and later had his own construction company, Hedley Construction of Carstairs.

While living in Turner Valley, Sheila was very active in community affairs. She was soloist at the United Church for 19 years. She also golfed, bowled and curled, winning many trophies.

I started to golf and curl, but was about average though I won two prizes with the Boles Hole-In-One Club as I made the hole-in-one in 1957. I was on the Turner Valley Golf Club Executive for many years as Handicapper and Membership.

History of the Sebastian Heemskerk Family
Block 3, Plan 1130, LK Pt. N.E. ¼ S-28, T-21, R-3, W5M Millarville.

Sebastian and Ave Maria Heemskerk came from Calgary, Alberta and settled in Millarville with their son Robert and daughter Deanna in November 1976.

Sebastian, son of Antonius and Sebastian Heemskerk, was born in Amsterdam, Holland. In 1953, along with his mother, father and eleven brothers and sisters, Sebastian arrived in Raymond, Alberta, where they worked in the sugar beet fields. They all moved to Calgary in 1955, and bought a farm in Maryland a few years later.

Residence of Heemskerks.

Ave Maria, daughter of Anna and Gordon Henderson, was born in Gorizia, Italy and later moved to Winchburgh, Scotland. In 1957, Ave Maria with her mother, father and brother came to Calgary, Alberta.

Sebastian and Ave Maria met in Holy Trinity High School and were later married in Holy Trinity Catholic Church in 1963.

A son Robert Gordon was born on March 12, 1965 and a daughter Deanna Marie on April 20, 1969. Both were born in Calgary and were baptized in Holy Trinity Catholic Church.

Sebastian owns and manages Key Concrete Ltd. in Calgary and Ave Maria works with Sebastian as Office Manager and Accountant for Key Concrete.

Besides enjoying their work at Key Concrete Ltd., Sebastian is an enthusiastic Curler. Ave Maria enjoys all kinds of music, dancing and loves to read.

Ed and Ella Hehr

by Ella

We came to the Millarville district in July, 1940 and settled on The West Anchordown Ranch (S.E.¼, Sec.32, T.21, R.3, W.5) — now known as the Bob Seaman Ranch. We came from Crossfield where our daughter June was born. I taught her the first two grades of school through the Department of Education, Edmonton. Then Mr. Barraclough started a school bus route and took the few children from here — Roger and Pat Jones etc. — to Fordville School. The teacher was Mr. Bob Standish.

We bought our own place where John Schaal now lives. We have been in Purebred Hereford cattle most of the time, and June won several champion ribbons in Calgary, showing in the Junior Beef Club.

Our son Dennis also went to Fordville School for several years until we moved to the Priddis district in 1952, and then to Red Deer Lake School. Our son, Neil also started school at Priddis, but the Priddis School was closed and all the children were bused to Red Deer Lake. He finished his high school in Calgary, as did all our children. Margaret was also a Priddis student, then Red Deer Lake, and completed her high school at Beaverbrook in Calgary. Neil completed high school at Henry Wise Wood, Dennis at Viscount Bennet and June at Mount Royal College, staying in the girls dormitory.

Margaret is now a nurse at the Foothills Hospital, June lives in Sacramento, California, Dennis is on the ranch here with us, and Neil works for A.G.T. in Edmonton.

Ed and I are still on the Ranch at Priddis raising cattle and have Dennis and his wife Anne here to help us. They have two children, Dean and Caroli, going to Red Deer Lake School.

Borge and Kamma Henriksen

by Kamma Henriksen

Borge was born in Denmark in 1922, in Hans Christian Andersen's hometown, Odense. I was born in

Henriksen Family. Back row, L. to R.: Jetta, Borge, Kamma, Ole. Front: Lene, Irene, Susan.

Svendborg. We were married July 1st, 1944 and lived in Svendborg for twelve years. We then decided to pull up our roots and immigrate to Canada. In March, 1957, we arrived in Calgary with our four children, Ole, Lene, Jette and Irene. Susan was born in 1962 and Steen joined us from Denmark with his family in 1974.

It was always our big dream to move to the country. In August 1976, we went looking and found just what we always wanted, a bountiful supply of nature. We bought 20 acres from Doug Kinnear in the S.W. ¼ of 21-21-4w5. And on April 28th, 1977, we moved in to our new home. It was a beautiful spring day and our dream had come true.

After driving to town working as a carpenter for the government, Borge has now decided to retire and work out here in our beautiful surroundings.

One of our enjoyable hobbies is raising and training Rottwiler dogs and showing them in shows in Western Canada.

Mary Ann (Wildman) Highmoor

by Mary Ann Highmoor

Born at Rimbey, Alberta in 1944 the youngest child of Tom and Norma Wildman. Our family moved to Square Butte in 1947 where I spent my youth.

In 1950 with the advent of centralized schools and school buses I began grade one at Sheep Creek School.School was always a pleasure and I enjoyed all the sports especially the many hours of softball we

David Wildman, 15, Mary Ann (Wildman) Highmoor, 12.

played. I can remember being in trouble numerous times through my school years for talking and giggling.

Many times during the fifties on Sundays, neighbors would get together and go for picnics in the South Fork Forest Reserve. Often Jake Reimer would take his school bus and load us all up and go for a picnic or to Turner Valley to a show.

I can always be thankful for my good fortune of growing up in the beautiful foothills of Square Butte. We had many advantages, living just a few miles ride or drive from the forest reserve which offered serenity and beauty which knew no limits. Beyond the beauty of the land were the good neighbors and friendly community.

I was involved in the various 4-H Clubs at Millarville, being a member of the first clothing club, then the cooking club as well as the beef club for a combined total of thirteen 4-H club years. The 4-H clubs were such a benefit to the young people of the district, but the leaders and assistants must be given credit for putting it all together to make it the success it was.

Mary Ann and Holly Highmoor. Christmas, 1975.

In 1961-62 I completed a commercial cooking course at SAIT which led to a two and a half year employment at the Palliser Hotel, Calgary.

In the fall of 1964 Earl Billington and I were married. Earl was born and raised at Lockport, Manitoba. As a young man he ventured west and met up with Phil Austin, Cochrane, who he worked for and struck a lasting friendship with the family. After this he worked at the Choco Ranch, Hanceville, B.C. as a ranch hand. While working here he had one eye taken out by a hondu when the rope broke after tying on to an old cow. Earl then went to Lake Louise and worked at Boyle's Garage for a few years and it was here that I moved after our marriage. On July 21st of 1965 Earl and three other young men were involved in a fatal highway accident on Highway 1 near the Great Divide.

I moved to Calgary and on October 8th, 1966 married Stan Highmoor from Flin Flon, Manitoba. In 1968 we moved to Medicine Hat for about ten months returning to Calgary following this.

In Calgary I worked at the Calgary Golf and Country Club, Phil's Pancake House, then at the Calgary Tower when it opened and until I quit in 1974.

Stan and I were ardent golfers and spent all of our spare time at this sport for many years.

On August 26, 1970 twin boys, Trevor and Travis were born but died shortly after birth.

In September 1971 Stan left, so I returned to live with mother and stepfather Alex Lyall, and commuted to Calgary to work for three years.

On March 6, 1972 Holly was born.

In December 1974 Holly and I moved to Sangudo to live with Earl Watson. I purchased a quarter of land and we are presently living here.

Chester and Kitty Hodgkins
by Jean Blakley

Chester was born in Okotoks, where his father was editor of the Okotoks Review, which was later sold to Charles Clark. Chester started riding for ranchers at a very early age. One of the first of these ranches was the Burn's ranch at Kew, previously owned by John Quirk, and later the Kendall Ranch. While working here, he became friends with Bob and Jim Carry, a friendship that lasted many years. His cowboying took him out to the prairie, where he met and married Kitty Brown.

Chester bought land in the Kew district, near Whiskey Creek, and after their marriage moved here. Anyone visiting their home could see the homesickness for the prairie in drawings done by Kitty, decorating the walls of their home. Kitty was an excellent artist and her drawings of prairie life were very true to life.

The Brown family had come to the Queenstown area from Scotland in the 1880's, maintaining a large cattle and horse ranch. Kitty and her sister Susan had the job of looking after the horses and the two were very good riders, spending many hours riding the wide open fenceless prairie. The one drawback to this was severe sunburn on their faces, so they devised a face mask to be worn, but quickly removed whenever another rider came in sight. However, this mask prevented very red noses.

The Hodgkins home was on the N.E.¼ of section 28-21-4w5 and here Kitty had made a lovely spot, with her flower garden, trees which she had transplanted and a vegetable garden in which she grew such fine vegetables that the area became known as the "banana belt". Inside the house, many beautiful plants bloomed. Kitty certainly had a "green thumb."

Chester had a string of bucking horses which were driven to rodeos near and far. No trucking horses in the twenties, but there were many young people ready and willing to go along to chase the herd. The Morley trail between Chester's ranch and Bragg Creek was muskeg all the way, and the riders in the rear were in grave danger, following the horses, and by the time the herd was through, the muskeg was so churned up the saddle horses would sink so deep, scarcely able to pull themselves out of the soft muskeg.

In 1923, Chester and Sid Bannerman put together a chuck wagon, horses and riders and were in the first Calgary Stampede chuck wagon races.

Kitty's homesickness for the prairie passed, and she came to look on the hills as home. They had one son, Guy, and when only seven years of age, he was very tragically killed by a horse falling on him.

Chester passed away at a very early age in 1944, then Kitty sold the land to Fred Hodgkins, who later sold one parcel to Jake Reimer and the rest to the Ball Brothers. Kitty moved to Calgary, where for many years she and Susan made their home with their two brothers, Dave and Austin Brown, and after the deaths of her brothers and sister, was in a nursing home where she passed away in 1977.

Hodgkins-Waters

by Bonnie Cofield

Stanley and Bunky Waters moved to the Louis Moreno place in 1957. Bunky was born and raised in the Millarville district, daughter of Frank Hodgkin.

Frank was born in Okotoks in 1898, the son of Okotoks first newspaper publisher. He liked competing in rodeos — saddle bronc and the wild horse race which he won several times at the Calgary Stampede. He also did a lot of boxing and became fairly well known as Cowboy Frank Hodgkin.

In 1923 he married Lakie Anna Rawlings who had come to Alberta from West Virginia in a covered wagon as a child. Frank worked on ranches in the foothills before settling on Whiskey Creek in 1932, (3-22-4-W5th). There they raised cattle and sheep. His brand was ⅄⸍ . They had five children; Jessie May (Babe), Lakie Fay (Betty), Frank Frederick (Pete), Columbine Kay (Bunky), and Peter Frank.

Babe married Victor Jensen and lived at Priddis

Frank, Peter and Lakie Hodgkins.

Frank Hodgkins on his saddle horse "Snake".

for a number of years. They have five children and now Babe is living in Ontario.

Betty married Harry Thomson and they ranch at Black Diamond and have six children.

Pete died in 1943 from rheumatic fever.

Peter Frank is married and living in British Columbia with their two children.

Frank and Lakie left their place on Whiskey Creek in 1959 and moved to Vanderhoof, B.C. Lakie died in 1963 from pneumonia and Frank passed away in 1974.

Columbine Kay (Bunky) was married to Stan Waters from Bragg Creek in 1949. Stan was born and raised in Calgary and later moved to Bragg Creek where he met Bunky. They were both very fond of horses and attended numerous horse shows and gymkhanas. They won the jumping at Calgary and smaller shows a number of times.

Stan worked for the Warden Service until his leg was badly broken in a logging accident. He spent

312

Bonnie and Bucky Waters on the Merino place.

Bunky (Hodgkins) Waters and her horse Cloudy on Whiskey Creek.

several months in the Banff Hospital and two years in a cast.

They moved to the Moreno place with their two children Bonnie Kay and Stanley Buck in 1957. Wilfred Cody was born in 1959. They raised cattle and horses and their brand is W-W. Bunky hunted squirrels in the winter as the prices were pretty good then.

In April 1961 they moved to a ranch they bought west of Stavely. Stan died in 1969 and Bunky still ranches at Stavely. Buck and Cody live in the Stavely area. Buck is engaged to be married in April. Bonnie is married to Randi Cofield from Stavely and has two children, Jory Tyler and Misty Fawn. Cody is attending Olds College at present time.

Colin Hogg
by Colin Hogg

My parents Alex and Mildred Hogg came from Scotland and England respectively. They were married in 1912 and homesteaded at Sundre, later moving to Elkton. I was born at Didsbury on December 13, 1920 and attended school at Elkton and Calgary.

I served with the R.C.A.F. for five years during the war.

In 1946 I married Ann Dick in Edinburgh, Scotland. We had four children all born in Calgary, Norman, Brenda, Richard and Ronald.

Colin Hogg, August, 1977.

I worked for the Alberta Government as a carpenter for twenty-nine years in the Calgary area. At present I am attending to the upkeep of the Medallion Ranch and enjoying my own two horses.

J. L. Holman

I, along with Ed and Kay Roberts and George and Dorothy Morrison, purchased ¼ section, actually 140 acres, from Bill and Marge Winthrop on July 1, 1971. Later that year, we moved a small residence onto the property, brought in the power and enjoyed it for week-end use primarily, until we built our permanent house. The property was sub-divided in 1975 and a permanent road was constructed giving us year round access. That same year we built a permanent house, drilled a well and brought in natural gas. We spend about half our time living in this house, the other half at a residence in Calgary. We have saddle horses on the property for use by our daughters Sally, aged 16, and Jane, aged 23, her husband Neil Stevenson and our grandson John.

History of Jane Louise Holmlund (nee Kendall)

I was born on May 30, 1949, the second daughter of John and Margaret Kendall. I attended Millarville School from grades one to nine. Following this I attended the Turner Valley High School, graduating in 1967. The fall of 1967, I commenced nursing school at the Calgary General Hospital, graduating in 1970. I worked at the Calgary General Hospital and the Holy Cross Hospital. In April 1971, I married John Holmlund. On June 16, 1973, our son Erik Scott was born and on December 17, 1975, our daughter Erin Marie was born. In 1974 we moved to Leduc, Alberta and have continued to live and enjoy this community, while John commutes daily to his office in Edmonton.

Edith Mary (Rodgers) Hood
by Mrs. D. L. Brown

Edith Mary was born on Aug. 21, 1894 in Calgary, Alberta, daughter of James Dublin Rodgers of Ireland and Maud Hull Pinkerton.

Her childhood and teen years were spent at Hillside Ranch, with brothers Jim, Jappy, and Pat and sister Marjorie. She spent some of her school years at St. Hildas in Calgary.

She has happy memories of life at Hillside Ranch, with Social outings of skating parties on the creek and dances and parties in the district.

She later worked at the Royal Bank in Okotoks until she met and married Benjamin Hood of Magrath, Alta. on June 21, 1921.

They had three children, Robin who died in early childhood, Marion, born in 1927 and Betty born in 1929. Marion now Mrs. R. W. Eastwood resides in Palma, Majorca and has two children, Penny and Peter. Betty, now Mrs. D. L. Brown lives in Toronto and has four children, Geoffrey, Michael, Sue and Sally.

Edith Mary Rodgers Hood and Ben Hood, Calgary 194?

Mrs. Hood lived an active social life in Okotoks as she liked to entertain and was a member of the St. Peters Anglican W.A., the I.O.D.E. and Book Clubs.

Mr. Hood died in 1962 and Edith moved to High River and lived there until 1972 when she fell and broke her leg. Since then she was confined to a wheel chair so she moved to the Beverly Nursing Home in Calgary where she now resides.

Otto Horman
by Otto Horman

Having an interest in agriculture I moved to the Square Butte area in October '63, when a position for ranch operator became available with C. A. Nabors of Calgary. Mr. Nabors owns Section 3-22-4-W5M. Our cattle brand is M̂ on the left hip.

I grew up at Viking, Alberta, where I attended school. I have two sisters and one brother older and a brother younger than me. Hazel, Gertrude and my parents live in Edmonton, Karl and Donald in Camrose, all are married except for myself.

After completing high school I went to Radio College of Canada in Toronto graduating in 1960, thereafter working at electronic service in Valleyview and Grande Prairie. Having had enough of the north country I moved to Calgary, again working in electronics until the move to Square Butte. I am still active in electronics and the pursuit of high quality sound and associated equipment which form a part time hobby.

Mr. Claire Nabors and his wife Lillian live in Calgary. They have three children, two girls and a boy. Susan and Charles live in Calgary and Barbara in California.

Otto Horman.

Josephine (Bird) Hounslow

by J. Hounslow

My parents, John C. and Nora L. Bird, my brother Ken and I, all born in England, came to Canada in 1909. We moved to the Kew-Millarville district in 1919 and were resident there for about fifteen years. Our land was purchased from a Mr. Brand through the Soldiers Settlement Board.

Neighbors to the west were Bob and Gavin Calderwood, their mother and sister, and to the east, the Jim McGregor family. Our stock brand was "bar C lazy B. ⌐∞

My brother and I attended Plainview School through Grade 9 and 8 respectively: enjoyed many good times and have reason to be thankful for the excellent teachers who presided there. I attended high school in Lethbridge and Calgary and graduated from Calgary Normal School in 1928 — fifty years ago this year. I taught at Plainview School for a time (1928-1930) and also on the prairie in Eastern Alberta and Saskatchewan.

I left the teaching profession but later returned to it and taught for 20 years in Calgary during which time I qualified for a Bachelor of Education degree from the University of Calgary in 1964. I retired in 1974 and became busier than I'd ever been as a teacher. Retirement is great, with time for dancing (Scottish Country Dancing) singing (I'm a member of the Calgary Music Makers Senior Citizens' Choir'') travelling, pursuing various hobbies and watching my grandchildren grow up. There's never a dull moment.

I have a son and a daughter. Michael is married, has four children and is in the insurance business. Nora Jo is married to Fraser Head. They have two children and both teach school in Calgary.

Re parents. My father and mother both lived to be a good age — 89 years. My father gave up his land at Kew and was Forest Ranger stationed at the North Sheep Creek post for several years. Always interested in race horses, he was active in this area until his death in 1966. My mother was a faithful worker for the Red Cross until crippled by arthritis. She died in 1969.

I have very happy memories of the years spent in the Kew district and loved riding horseback through the woods and valleys and climbing the foothills to view the beautiful scenery. I can vividly recall a forest fire which devasted, for a time, the wooded slopes of the "Gap" in 1919 and crept to within a short distance of the Calderwood place where we were living while our house was being built. All of the men in the district worked frantically, ploughing fire guards between the buildings and the fire, and that done, they drenched the roofs of the house, barn and other buildings with water to prevent fire starting from bits of burning debris carried by the wind. It was an anxious time for a while, but the fire was eventually controlled and burned itself out.

When I taught at Plainview School I boarded first with the Dave Stewart family and then with the Calderwoods, and walked the half mile to school. Later, I lived at home which was along the Kew Millarville road and then I travelled by horseback. It is interesting to note that many of my pupils were boys and girls who had formerly been my schoolmates.

Raymond Hugh Houston

by Hugh Houston ⊔⊣

I was born April 27, 1942, the second oldest in a family of three brothers at Lucknow, Ontario. I was raised on a mixed farm north of the village of Lucknow, where I received my education.

1960 was a year that moved me across the western provinces, working on various farms and ranches. The summer of 1961 was spent working at the Sedco Ranches, north west of Millarville. This country, I found, had a climate that appealed to me.

Moving on found Saskatchewan my home for a number of years. September of 1967, Millarville was home again, this time with my family, my wife Helen,

Hugh Houston

Josephine (Bird) Hounslow, teacher at Plainview School, Kew, with some of her pupils. About 1928-29.

315

Hugh Houston and sons Duane and Heath, at Sinclair Pass, B.C.

and sons Duane, born February 1964 and Heath, born March 1967. I worked as a mechanic at Millarville.

The next spring, the south 80 acres of the N.E. ¼ of 7-21-3-w5 was purchased from Mrs. Fred Hodgkins, and we moved here and still reside. This is a home for us and our Appaloosa horses. Horses have been used for many entertaining hours here, raising and training them. In 1971 I registered my brand ⊔H left hip for both cattle and horses.

Howell, R. John and Dianne

John was born in Calgary, where he received his education. He worked with his father Harold C. Howell, a local horse trainer and blacksmith.

John and Dianne Howell.

Jill and Penny Howell

In 1960, John began training race horses on his own. He first came to the Millarville area as a trainer for W. L. Falconer. During the winter months, John worked for some of the local ranchers where he met Dianne Langenhoff of Black Diamond.

Dianne was born in Humboldt, Saskatchewan and moved with her family to a farm east of Black Diamond in 1956.

John and Dianne were married in 1971 while John was living in California. In 1972, they moved to the Bob Stevenson farm where they now reside. They have two daughters, Penny, born in 1973, and Jill, 1975.

Both John and Dianne are active in the community, helping with the Millarville Races and Fair and various other activities. John is a director on the Agricultural Board and past President of the Millarville Race Club.

Nelson Hoy

Born in Montain, Ontario, April 15, 1913.

I grew up on a farm in Ontario, the oldest son of nine children and learned early in life how to straddle a milk stool and put froth on the pail. After leaving school, I worked for Sam Reed who had a purebred Holstein herd. Here I discovered a pleasurable side to the business; that of fitting and showing the cattle at local fairs in and around Ottawa.

A friend of mine came back for a visit from the west and after hearing his glowing account of this country, I wrote to Russ Broomfield and was offered a job. I got off the train at Stavely on April 3, 1937. Russ was such a congenial employer that I spent the next seven years working for him from spring until fall. There was no need for help after harvest so I spent the winters skidding tie logs for Swanson Lumber Co. at Hinton, Alberta.

On June 6, 1944, I married Ruth Kirk from Gull Lake, Saskatchewan. By the fall of 1945, we had acquired a few milk cows and sold milk to the Thompson Dairy at Turner Valley. I bought 240 acres at Millarville, (NW¼-8-21-2-W5th) and moved there in the spring of 1949. With purebred Hereford ranches on four sides, I had some trepidition about moving in with my Holstein bull, especially with no barn on the place and the fences in disrepair. I had the barn built by fall, but have found fencing to be a never ending job; and over the years have had a few red and white offspring as a result. Gradually I built up a purebred Holstein herd under the purfex "Tiny-Springs Holsteins" and was able to get back to the enjoyment of showing them at various fairs. It's good to know their bloodlines are scattered throughout Europe, Asia, Cuba, U.S.A. and Canada.

As a result of some good sales, I am semi-retired now and raise water-fowl and numerous other birds as a hobby.

Our only daughter Patty (Webb) lives near-by with her family.

Ray Garry and Doris Huebschwerlen

by Ray Huebschwerlen

Born January 13, 1942 in Edmonton, the only son of Darrell (d. 1977) and Grace Huebschwerlen. I attended school in Bowness.

Doris Louise was born April 23, 1942 in Calgary, daughter of John and Hilda Campbell. Doris attended school in Montgomery.

We were married in 1960 and have five children, Cindy Louise b. June 2, 1961, Donald Ray b. May 19, 1962, David Paul b. June 23, 1963, Tina Marie b. Jan. 1, 1965, and Dwayne Darrell b. Oct. 22, 1969.

We moved to the Square Butte area in December 1968 and lived there until December 1973. During this time the older children attended school at Millarville, and now the family attend schools in the Forest Lawn area. Cindy graduates from Forest Lawn High School in June, 1979.

I have been an auto body mechanic for the past twenty-four years and recently opened Ray's Auto Body Contracting.

During my adolescent years I looked forward to going trapping and hunting with my Dad, Curly Sand and Levie Smiley. The family still enjoys visiting and hunting with friends from the Millarville district.

Doreen E. Huffman (nee Oliver)

Born in Calgary, daughter of W. J. "Bill" and Marjorie Oliver, and in 1933 moved to the Diamond L Ⓠ Ranch on the North Fork of Sheep Creek directly east of the race track. In the 1930's and 1940's our family took an active part in community activities. In 1949 the ranch was sold to the Gourlays and later purchased by the Grahams.

We attended New Valley School until 1936 with George Scott and Eileen Cunningham my teachers. Our schooling was finished in Calgary and I attended business college. After working in Toronto for a year, returned to Calgary and worked for "Purity 99" oil company. On Oct. 2, 1948 Jack Huffman of Calgary, and I were married in the first candlelit wedding service held at Christ Church, Millarville.

We lived in Calgary until 1949 when moved to Redwater with Imperial Oil Ltd. Subsequent moves took us to Calgary, Toronto, Edmonton and back to Toronto where we now reside. Our two sons have graduated from university; Ken is travelling and Bob working in Cranbrook, B.C. Our daughter Jane is working and living at home.

Penny (Kendall) Hunter JMH ᴸᴿ

I was born July 8th, 1947, in Calgary, Alberta. My parents are Margaret (Cullen) and John Kendall. My grandparents are Martha and William Cullen and Katherine and Eugene Kendall.

My sister, Jane Holmlund, and brothers Buck, Ricky and Paul and I were raised west of Millarville, where my parents, Uncle Frank and Gram Kendall farmed.

I rode Jake Reimer's bus to Sheep Creek School at Millarville and later Turner Valley High. I took a secretarial course and worked in Calgary until I married Jim Hunter in 1968. We farmed Jim's parents old farm until 1974. We then moved to Athabasca where we now farm and raise cattle. Our land location is S.E.¼ of 30-65-20-w4. Jim's brand is J M H on the left rib.

We have three children, Wade, who is in grade one and Joey and Ronalee who are in kindergarten this year.

We enjoy living here with many varieties of trees, wildlife and birds.

Jim and Penny Hunter's children. Back: Ronalee. Left: Wade. Right: Joey.

Mrs. Joseph (Jean) Waugh, pioneer of the Millarville district.

Josephine Hyland (Waugh)

Perhaps what I remember most about my early years was the love that we shared in our home within our family and the willingness of mother and dad to share whatever they had with neighbors and friends.

The welcome mat seemed to be always out for friends and neighbors; dad loved to visit and share favorite experiences, view on politics or news items of the times. My favorite of all of his stories was the one he used to tell about a time when he was night herding cattle for Pat Burns out in the Nose Creek area. Dad had finished his shift and was riding into town since it was a Saturday night. The night was cool and crisp and there was a big full moon in the sky when suddenly a figure stepped from behind a rock and dad found himself looking down the barrel of a gun. As it turned out it was an RCMP officer and after deciding that dad was not "his man" he explained that there was a man-hunt on for Ernest Cashel and they had reason to believe that he was hiding out in the area. Cashel had escaped from the Calgary jail where he was waiting to be hanged for a murder he had committed. Dad said "that the barrel of that gun looked at least twelve inches across", and he was pretty uneasy for the rest of that ride into town. I'm sure that many of you who will be reading this will remember dad telling this story.

I left the Millarville district in 1945 and moved out to Vancouver and in 1947 I married Tom Hyland and moved to Seattle where I still live. Tom passed away in 1962. We had no family of our own but I have been blessed with six nieces and nephews and their families.

After Tom's death I became involved in real estate sales — I began selling homes and later became a broker and specialized in commercial property. I currently am working for a company who trains sales people. Perhaps I inherited my liking for people from my parents as working with people has been a very important factor in my life.

My life is very busy and full — I especially enjoy entertaining friends, cooking and the theatre and I can

Josephine (Waugh) Hyland.

always find the time to continue adult education. I am also active in a Toastmistress Club as well as in some volunteer work in church.

I have enjoyed a bit of travelling — in 1965 mother and I had a trip to England and Scotland. We visited the place where mother grew up which was a real thrill for me — even slept in the same hotel that mother's parents used to own and visited her best friend whom mother had not seen for fifty some years and a sister that she had not seen since she left her to come to Canada. Mother has never lost her enthusiasm and wit and I love to go to Vancouver and spend time with her.

Albert Iceton

Albert is the fourth child of William (Bill) and Georgina Iceton. When the Icetons arrived in Canada in 1924, the children numbered six. The adventures of young people growing up in pioneer conditions were typical of those days in the Kew area. After arriving in the district, two more brothers joined the family.

Albert worked wherever work was to be found in the farming and ranching places. He volunteered to enlist in the Canadian Armed Services, serving from 1942 to the war's end. He returned to Canada, married to Eva Holden of Dunmow, Essex, England. His

Albert and Bonita Iceton and Eddie.

Angela Iceton, daughter of Bonita and Albert Iceton.

English bride soon settled in to farm life. Two sons were born before Eva passed away in March, 1957.

Albert was employed by Home Oil for a few years, also worked temporarily at the Refinery in Turner Valley. He owned land in the Kew country through the V.L.A. He sold this land to Howard Hampton in 1961. He remarried in 1961, adding one son and one daughter to the family. Much more could be written of the farming and ranching days and even more of hunting and trapping. It is most difficult to put it all in a few words.

Melvin Iceton (1950-   )

Born Sept. 3, 1950 in Turner Valley, son of Albert and Eva Iceton of Kew. Attended Turner Valley and surrounding schools until graduating at Turner Valley in 1968. Worked at various jobs but ended up taking an apprenticeship in autobody. Married Barbara Sandeman July 21, 1973, daughter of Albert and Louise Sandeman of Turner Valley. Presently living in Turner Valley and employed at Sax Autobody Shop in Turner Valley.

Stanley and Maureen (Lochhead) Iceton

Stanley was born October 28th, 1947. His parents were Albert and Eva Iceton. He attended Turner Valley Elementary School and in 1967 completed High School at Turner Valley. He served an apprenticeship to be an Auto Body Mechanic in 1967, which was completed in 1971. He married Maureen Lochhead, daughter of Bob and Margaret Lochhead, born November 21st, 1947.

Stanley and Maureen have two daughters, Lisa, eight years old and Janine, five years old. They make their home in Turner Valley, where their children attend Elementary School.

Lisa and Janine Iceton, daughters of Stan and Maureen Iceton.

George and Elsie Ingeveld

Continuing the Ingeveld story from the book "Our Foothills" it mentioned that Maurice and Alodie Ingeveld had three children, Marthe, who was killed in an accident in the North Sheep Forest Reserve, June 1960, Marie-Louise (Nina) whose story is elsewhere in this book as Nina Lochhead, and George, whose story is told here.

At the close of World War 1, George's father remained in Europe employed by the Immigration Department until 1927. The whole family then returned to Canada, to the land that Maurice had homesteaded twenty years previously. George was then seven years old. This was his home for the next 42 years. He attended school at Square Butte and West Calgary.

George, like his father, Maurice, had a great love

319

30th wedding anniversary of George and Elsie Ingeveld.

and understanding of horses. At the age of 14 he began breaking horses for neighbors; soon his reputation spread, which meant that any horse that a rancher didn't care to tackle was sent to the Double N Ranch for George to break. Many of these horses were spoiled or had run out until they were six or seven years old. Although George never competed as a bronc rider at rodeos, some of the rank broncs he rode might have scored quite high on a rodeo judge's score card.

During World War 2, he served most of his time in Italy. He was serving in Holland at the close of the war, where he met his wife, Elsie de Vos. They were married in Calgary in 1947, then went to reside on the home ranch, where George had purchased some adjoining land, and was ranching in partnership with his father. They have three children, Roger and Virginia residing in Calgary, and Gerald, attending Olds Agriculture College.

"Buck Leo Jack" Quarter horse stallion owned by George Ingeveld.

George ranched with his father until 1955, when the latter passed away. In 1969, George sold the original ranch at Millarville and purchased a smaller 800 acre ranch south of Sundre, where he and his wife Elsie and their youngest son Gerald are raising Registered Quarter Horses and Polled Hereford cattle.

Roger Ingeveld

I was born in 1948 and lived with my parents on the original homestead until 1966 when I enrolled in the University of Calgary.

Attended Sheep Creek School for nine years completing grade nine with honors.

Attended Turner Valley Sr. High and was valedictorian for my graduation ceremonies.

Active in sports, 4-H and horsemanship throughout my youth and continue to be involved with horses and hockey today.

Graduated in 1970 from the University of Calgary with a Bachelor of Science degree. Later I completed courses for my Professional T Certificate but began a career in Chemical Research instead.

Presently residing in Calgary and working in the Petroleum Industry in chemical sales and consulting.

I often drive through the Square Butte area to reexperience the peaceful serenity of the countryside.

Roger Ingeveld.

Donald and Marion Irvine

We had been looking for a piece of property in the Millarville area for close to ten years that we felt would have some practical use as well as a view of the Rockies. During the late spring of 1969 we contacted Mr. Joe Fisher of Millarville who was in the real estate business and discussed the possibility of purchasing some property in the Millarville area. After a fairly short discussion, Mr. Fisher told us he had a few properties for sale but not to bother coming to see him unless we were ready to buy. A few visits to the area and we bought our property — which did not have a

320

road into it but I was assured that a road could be built for a very few dollars and no red tape.

The property we bought was the N.W. ¼ of 12-21-4w5, and was previously owned by George Ingeveld. Soon after we bought the land we became involved in the livestock business — we bought two horses from some friends and three black White Face cows from my real estate friend, Joe Fisher. The horses are still with us, together with a few more. However, the black white faced cows have gone. In 1971, Ivor Lyster and I started raising registered pure bred polled Herefords. We currently have close to 40 head of Registered pure bred polled Herefords and have built related facilities to handle our herd.

Our valley has changed quite a bit since Bob Parkins and I arranged construction of the road down to our place. We have four children, twin daughters, Joanne and Judy, and two boys, Jim and Jeff. The children were all born in Calgary, as was their mother. I was born in Ottawa and when still a young boy, my father, who was with the civil service, was transferred to Charlottetown, P.E.I.

Marion and I and the family continue to work toward the improvement of our place and the herd facilities, and plan for the day when we can build our home in the foothills of Millarville.

Harry Irving

by H. Irving

It was approximately 10 years ago that I bought the half section (east half of section 34, T.21, R.3, W.5) from the Adam's family, one of the pioneer settlers in the Millarville area. The place has beautiful evergreen trees on the back quarter section and a nice creek also runs through the back quarter.

The real estate agent who handled the sale was Lou Chambers, a fine horseman, gentleman and well known to many in the area.

I am a native Calgarian and am president of Irving Wire Products in the Manchester district of South Calgary. I played polo for 20 years but retired two years ago.

The brand for the ranch is the Z 3 on the left rib and has been in effect for many years.

My wife's name is Sheila; she is from Ottawa, and we have six children, Jill, Sandy (who is presently living on the ranch with his wife Pam), Fred, Sally, Polly and a new arrival Julie. All of the children have been active in equestrian activities and enjoy the country. We all like the Millarville area as it is in the foothills of the Rockies, the trees are beautiful, the land is hilly and rolling and there are many fine view points, particularly of the mountains to the west.

Present plans call for a permanent home on the property in the future but these plans have not been implemented yet.

Esther Olive (Haney) Jackson

by Esther Jackson

I was born in Northern Ontario in Algoma District near Sault Ste Marie. My parents were Matthew and Elizabeth (Townsend) Haney and I am of Irish, English and Scottish descent, I was the oldest of a family of one girl and six boys. Two brothers, Russell and Bert, and I were of my fathers first family. Russell was killed at the age of six from falling off a ladder in our tall barn. My mother died during the awful flu epidemic in 1918, Dad married again in 1920. They had four boys, the two youngest were twins, one of them died from an accident at the age of three.

My grandparents on both sides were pioneers in Algoma District, having moved there from Huron and Bruce counties when Algoma was opened up to homesteaders in the 1890s.

I received my public school education in a one-room school in our small village of Desbarats. More than seventy pupils were registered with one teacher. In this day and age it is hard to imagine a school like that, but we learned the three R's just the same. Discipline was surprisingly good probably due to the fact that a sturdy strap was kept handy, and teachers didn't hesitate to use it, especially on mischievous boys who delighted in putting small garter snakes (they are harmless) or toads or mice in the top drawer in the teachers desk where the school register was kept.

My main interests then were music and dramatics, and I got a lot of enjoyment out of practising for our school Christmas concerts. At the age of nine I started piano lessons and when I was eleven was chosen to play for the concert that year. After that I was called on sometimes to play the organ for church services, weddings and funerals and, years later, played for

Esther and Bill Jackson cutting the cake at their 40th anniversary party May, 1947.

321

Sheep Creek school concerts for some thirty years. I felt more than rewarded for this when I was presented with a plaque of appreciation at the school reunion held in 1978.

When I was thirteen we moved to Amherstburg, near Windsor. I went to high school there for a year, then my father bought a farm near Seaforth. My mother passed away a few months after we moved there. I went back to the Soo to stay with my aunt and to complete my second year of high school. After that I took a business course.

I worked in Kincardine and London, Ontario for a few years, and in September 1925 came to Manitoba to visit relatives there and in Saskatchewan. A cousin met me at the train in McAuley, Manitoba, and the first thing he asked me was could I cook. I told him I could boil water without burning it, then he told me that his mother, my aunt, had a poisoned right hand from being bitten by an insect while she was working in her garden, and that she had to keep her arm in a sling. She had had a girl to help her but she had just left to get married, so I arrived just in time to cook for the harvesters. I wasn't much of a cook but I soon learned to bake stacks of bread, biscuits and pies.

My visit turned out to be a long one for I liked the west and its friendly people so much that I stayed around there that winter and the next summer before coming to Alberta in November 1926 to visit my school pal, Marguerite Pegler. The Peglers had opened a store in Millarville the previous summer.

I came to Calgary by train and between Moose Jaw and Calgary came through the worst blizzard I have ever seen, and arrived five hours late. It snowed and it "blowed" across those prairies and we, the passengers, nearly froze as the heat had to be turned off to keep up enough steam to run the train (those were the days when coal was burned) and at that, it seemed to travel at a snail's pace. Marguerite was in Calgary to meet me and we had to stay there, at her sister's for a week, as the country roads were drifted and impassable. Finally we got word that Harry Trimmer, storekeeper at Priddis, was going to try to get to Calgary with his truck and that we could get to Priddis with him. He got through alright and after staying over-night with the Trimmers we came the rest of the way with Mr. Joe Waugh in his mail sleigh. That was my introduction to Millarville.

I have always been fond of reading Western books and magazines were my favorites when I was young and foolish, so I had a green easterners idea that in the west there were cowboys with chaps and spurs and six-guns, all over the place, but to my disappointment I didn't see even one in Manitoba or Saskatchewan, nor any in Alberta that looked like I had pictured them. I mentioned this to Norman Pegler and he told me with a twinkle in his eye that there were some real hand-some ones around Millarville so, sure enough, one day a tall lanky cowboy came into the store, complete with big hat, beautiful beaded buckskin jacket, white woolly chaps, boots and spurs (I think this was a put-up job). Little did I know when I met him, that I was meeting my future husband. I was satisfied then that there were real-life cowboys and not just fictional ones.

I stayed at Peglers that winter, helping in the store, and in May 1927, was married to Billy Jackson at St. Barnabas Anglican Church in Calgary and came to live in the "little log cabin" built for a blacksmith shop. It had been partitioned into two rooms and with the help of some gaily colored chintz curtains it looked quite cosy. We lived in it until the winter of 1928 when, with the help of Charlie Stockford and Carlton King, Billy built a log addition to it.

Our family arrived while we lived there, with the exception of Fern, who came along when we lived in Turner Valley. We lost our youngest little girl, Linda Marie in 1944, when she was just three weeks old. In 1951 my brother Bert, with the help of Billy and our boys, built a new house on the site of the one that was burned.

The depression years kept us busy making a living, but we had good times and nobody complained. For awhile there were few dances at the old hall, as money was too scarce to hire an orchestra, then Carlton King got a local orchestra together. At first there were three pieces, Gavin Calderwood on the violin, Bert Adams on guitar and yours truly on piano. Bert's brother Miles (Porkey) took Bert's place later, so, with our home-made music, regular dances were held at the hall again. Admission was 25¢ or ladies bring a cake. No one was turned away if he didn't have the "two bits". If there was any money left-over after expenses (sandwiches, coffee, etc.) were paid, the musicians divided it up. Sometimes we got a dollar or two each and sometimes a few cents except for New Years and July 1st dances which drew bigger crowds. Then we got $5.00 and thought we were rich. We really didn't care whether we were paid or not so long as everyone had a good time.

Like Billy, I enjoyed helping in the community. I joined Willing Workers W. I. in 1928 and was secretary treasurer from 1935 to 1953, also held all of its offices at different times through the years and I am still a member. I helped to organize a Girl Guide company, a 4H clothing club, was secretary of Millarville-Kew, Priddis and Bragg Creek Historical Society for several years while they were working on "Our Foothills." Was a member of Millarville Community Association and helped with fund raising when New Ranchers Hall was built in 1950, and have been an associate member of Southern Alberta Pioneers and their Descendants and High River Old Timers for quite a number of years.

On an evening in May 1967 Billy and I were given a very pleasant surprise when we were given a dinner party at Ranchers Hall for our fortieth wedding anniversary, sponsored by the Womens Institute and Millarville Community. We were presented with a clock, a coffee table a picture and three-tiered Anniversary cake. We considered this to be one of the highlights of those forty years.

During the past few years I have enjoyed doing some gadding around and hope to do some more.

I still live on the place that I came to, fifty-two years ago, as a bride. The years have been good to me and I have never regretted coming to Alberta. After spending the greater part of my life in the west, I think I can safely call myself a Westerner, Don't you?

George Jackson

George had planned to stay on the farm with his father and John, but like many other young men of the district, he found the lure of the oilfield irresistable, so he went to Turner Valley just before the Depression. When jobs became too scarce for him to make a living he returned to the farm. In 1935 he married Myrtle Meehan, the daughter of a pioneer Cluny farmer, who quickly became a favourite with the whole family. Oil was discovered in 1934, and within a short time jobs were more plentiful, so they tried the oilpatch again, eventually building a home in Black Diamond, where they lived until 1948, and where their two daughters, Georgina and Ruth, were born.

In 1948 he made the big decision to move his family to Calgary, as by now he was pushing tools on the northern wildcats, and could spend very little time with his family, so life would be easier for them.

George worked for Imperial Oil all his working life away from home, until he took an early retirement in 1964, for health reasons.

He spent his retirement on his hobby — gardening, and his home became the showplace of the neighbourhood.

On June 30th, 1971 Myrtle died, following a brief illness, although she had been in failing health for several years. The following year George and his brother Bill went on the Farmers and Ranchers trip to Australia, New Zealand and the Orient.

The same year he journeyed to San Francisco to marry Mae Johnson, a San Francisco widow and long time friend of his sister Frances.

George and Myrtle Jackson, 25th anniversary.

They had three trips, to Australia and Fiji, one to the Mediterranean area and Britain, and the other to Central America. Their other jaunts were closer to home, and on the return trip from a visit to the Spokane area, George died very suddenly in Fernie, on September 14th, 1975.

Georgina and her husband, Bob Bellman, live in St. Bruno, P.Q. with their three children, Scott, David and Jennifer. Ruth and Ron Evans, together with Michael and Joanne, have just returned to Calgary from Winnipeg, and will be moving into their own home shortly.

Mae has stayed in Alberta, and is a very dedicated parish worker in Acadia Valley.

Jack and Elsie Jackson

In the late nineteen twenties, a young fellow by the name of Jackie Jackson came from Cumberland, England to Canada. He hoped to make his livelihood on the N.E.¼, Sec. 25, T.21, R.4, W.5 near Millarville, working for V. N. DeMille.

In a few years he was joined by his sweetheart from England. They were married in Calgary, in December of 1930. They lived in a small house and had a few cattle. There was a house on the N.W.¼, Sec.32, T.21, R.3, W.5, so he got some of the neighbors, Art Wilderman, Bill Lee, John Jackson, and a fellow who worked for Syd Bannerman to move this house on Easter Sunday — so each came with his good pulling horses. All went well for a short distance until they came to the boggy land with plenty of nigger heads. The sills caught on the nigger heads and soon pulled apart — it was abandoned right there.

George Jackson family, L. to R. Georgina, George, Myrtle and Ruth.

Jack and Elsie Jackson.

Walter, Ida, Bill, John Jackson, July 1961.

They continued to live there and later moved across the road into a log house. It must have been a great shock to come from a town in England to the foothills of Alberta, where towering spruce trees swayed right beside the house. They later had a baby and returned to England, to what I am sure they felt was civilization.

John and Ida Jackson ∀R.H.

by John and Ida

I (John) was born on January 29, 1909 on the N.W.¼, Sec. 30, T21-R2-W5, in a log shack, the second youngest of a family of 9 of William and Mary Jackson.

I attended Fordville School and finished grade 8 — then worked at home on the farm. Ed Winthrop was road foreman and I worked on the road to pay our taxes. You were paid 40¢ per hour for yourself and 25¢ per hour for your team of horses. You supplied your own feed and boarded yourself. In the fall we worked for the neighbors threshing, with a separator that had no straw blower. I hauled the straw away with a team of horses on the straw buck. I finally graduated to riding the straw buck — a job I did not care for.

A great highlight in those years was when Jim Cawthorne organized a Boy Scout Troup. I was a

member for about 3 years. Each summer Howard deMille took the Boy Scouts into the hills around Lynx and Ware Creeks for about a week. We made pancakes with lumps in them, caught rainbow trout about 14 inches long, ate fish every day, and explored the country.

The summer of 1929, Art Wilderman was the road foreman. I got a job with him after harvest, and we put the approaches in to the first bridge across the north fork of Sheep Creek at Millarville, now called Three Point Creek.

Dances held in the schools were our chief form of entertainment; also, dances at the old Ranchers Hall. The men paid 50¢ and the ladies brought a cake for admission. Stan Stanhope played the piano, and Campbell Aird the violin. At the Priddis Hall the music was supplied by Otto Rhoedler on the piano and Slim McKeage on the violin. The great social event at the Priddis Hall was the Veterans Ball. All these dances would last until 3 or 4 o'clock in the morning. The children would be put to sleep wherever there was a spot to lay them, and everyone had a great time. There was also a great interest in hockey, which was played on the various large sloughs in the area.

In the late 1920's and 1930's there were a lot of partridge, sharp-tailed grouse, ruffled grouse, and thousands of bush rabbits.

Money was scarce in the thirties — you could buy 22 shells for 25¢ for 50 shells — so we shot rabbits, also snared them, and sold them to Colpitts Fox Farm for 2¢ per pound.

In 1934, on April 9, I married Ida Barraclough, daughter of Johnny and Emily Barraclough. We had but $5.00 in the bank and a few head of cattle. It did not cost too much to live. We grew a good garden and one could buy a large basket of tomatoes for 25¢.

In 1936 it was very dry and there was very little grass and hay. We sold cows for $11.00 per head, and 2 year old steers for $17.50 per head. However, all of us coped with the hard times and were happy.

John did some logging farther west and sawed it into lumber with my father's small mill. The lumber was hauled home and grew to a high pile. I was visualizing a new house, but my house ended up becoming a barn on the Joe Standish place, and a Service Station at Millarville for Ginger Douglas. The next lumbering became the house we now live in, which we built with the help of my father. Also, the barn was built later from our own lumber. We milked cows and shipped table cream, and also had beef cattle. Later, we disposed of the dairy cows and went into sheep.

We have two sons — Walter was born in 1937, and married Beverley Marsh, and lives in Calgary. Bill was born in 1939, and married Dorothy Hebson, and lives on the home quarter.

Life has been good to us — we have enjoyed it all, and hope to continue to do so.

Joe Jackson

by Catherine Jackson

After Joe left home, he tried several casual jobs during the winters, mostly in lumbering and construction, and finally settled down on a ranch at Millarville, with his brother Bill. By 1926 he had decided there was not a good living on it for the two of them, and besides, he was not that enthusiastic about farming.

Turner Valley was beginning to become more active, so he went there as a carpenter and handyman, working for Dalhousie and the old North-West Company, which were later integrated with Royalite. Within a short period, he had an opportunity to work on the rigs, and started as tooldresser with Howard Benfield, and later with Alf Patrick. When the more modern and efficient rotaries came to the Valley, he changed to them, working in all jobs until he finally became a driller in 1935, one of the first Canadians to do so.

In 1935, when the depression made work very intermittant, he changed to Snyder and Head, and worked for them for the next five years, after which he returned to Royalite which was then a subsidiary of Imperial. When Imperial sold to Royalite, Joe stayed with Imperial, becoming a toolpush in 1943. For the rest of his active career he pushed tools on the wildcats, eventually earning the nickname of "King of the Dryholes". He drilled in locations all over Alberta, southern Saskatchewan and north-eastern B.C. He did have one oilwell, though, when he was sent to Devon, because, as Tip Moroney told him, "We wouldn't want you to never have an oilwell. This one is between two producers, so you can't miss". He was philosophical about it, saying — "Well, the dryholes pay the same as the producers".

On July 16, 1927, he married Catherine Morton, the daughter of a Calgary businessman, built a house in the north end of Turner Valley, later named Whiskey Row, and lived there until 1934 when they picked up the house and moved to Black Diamond. This was their home for the remainder of the time that Joe worked in the Valley, and for the first few years he was wildcatting.

Joe, Marie and Catherine Jackson, 1946.

Catherine and Marie followed him, living in any accommodation which was available, including a caboose in Nordegg which they christened "Nordegg Castle". Marie's education was suffering from the constant moves, locations were becoming more remote, so we bought a home in Calgary. This was the end of our transient living, although when Joe could get a place for us, we still could spend the summers together. I now found myself with time on my hands, and joined the Girl Guides as District Commissioner, advancing to Division Commissioner, and eventually Area Commissioner for Calgary. It was arduous, but rewarding and kept me out of trouble while Joe was away. I have the Medal of Merit, presented to me by Lady Baden-Powell on her last visit to Calgary. In 1961, Joe drilled his last well before retirement, on the Forest Reserve northwest of Calgary. Then we took three months to see Canada, travelling to every province except Newfoundland, looking at every place we had ever heard about. We also visited some of the eastern states.

At this time the Guides were building their new Mockingbird Camp on Waiparous Creek with volunteer labour, and Joe supervised it. We both spent many long hours out there, among the chores we did peeling the poles for the fence. For someone who had never heard of, or seen a drawknife, I became very proficient. During the following winter he built (at home) all the bunks and cupboards for the Brownie House and lodge, which were installed by him and Dr. Noakes the following spring.

The North Hill Kiwanis Club had helped on the camp project, and Joe became interested enough to join them. He headed two committees — the youth group, and at the time of his death was working on a church register to be posted in hotels and motels.

He died suddenly in his sleep on September 3rd., 1963. In his memory, the Girl Guides and Brownies collected enough money to build a beautiful fieldstone fireplace in the lodge at Mockingbird. Beside it hangs his picture, and a bronze plaque donated by the Kiwanis Club.

Following Joe's death, I completed my term as Area Commissioner in 1965, then was free to travel. I have seen most of the Pacific Rim countries, including South Viet Nam, South America, Africa, Malaysia, and this year Jamaica. Hopefully, I will see many more before I am unable to travel.

Marie completed her high school and business courses, married in 1956, worked for several years while her husband completed his university courses, and now lives in Calgary with her children — Alexandra, 14 and Jeremy, 12. It is too early to say what their future ambitions are.

Mary A. Jackson

Mary A. Jackson was born near Millarville on a cattle ranch in a log house, the third child in a family of nine, of William and Mary La Penotiere Jackson.

Schools were not established in our district, so we lived at Priddis for a year to attend school. The first day, five of us found ourselves in the first grade as beginners. The next day, the teacher had our educational background established, and placed us in the appropriate grades. The next year we attended Fordville School. I later graduated from High School in Claresholm. I went to Normal School in Calgary for a year, obtaining a teacher's certificate. I taught school near Claresholm for 2 years. The winds were very bad and the school was staked down with iron rods. Storms came up very quickly in winter, and once I became lost in a blizzard. The dog who belonged to the people where I boarded, found me.

I had a desire for better education, and decided to go to the United States. I attended North West College in Nampa, Idaho, and after one year entered the Samaritan Hospital School of Nursing, which had a cooperative program with the college from which I graduated with a Bachelor of Science Degree. After graduating, the hospital and several doctors offered me an opportunity to study X-ray and Clinical Laboratory Technology, taking the courses in Seattle. I practised in these two fields for several years, and taught in the School of Nursing.

I decided that nursing education was my field, so I attended the University of Minnesota and furthered my interest. I graduated with a Bachelor of Nursing Education. My nursing career extended over 40 years,

Mary Jackson

and I worked in several different States in both large and small hospitals, and Schools of Nursing. I have held positions as Director of Nursing, Director of Schools of Nursing, and Instructor in Nursing. At the University of Oregon School of Nursing, I was Assistant Professor of Nursing Education. I found my career very interesting and challenging, and since retiring I miss the contact with the young people very much. I now live in Northern California at Sebastapol, which is north west of San Francisco — where there are beautiful apple orchards and flowering shrubs.

Murray and Iona Jackson

Born in Calgary in the year 1928. Attended Sheep Creek school until 1944, then went to the Olds School of Agriculture, graduating in 1946. I worked with my father on our ranch and dairy farm. My cattle brand right hip which I acquired in 1944.

Hunting and fishing were my main form of recreation, those were the days when it was worthwhile to hunt and fish and also a good way to get out of school and work for a couple of weeks a year.

In 1947 I went to work for Drilling Contractors, roughnecking on the old steam rigs, a lot better than the new modern rigs. Later that year Dave Glaister and I bought the first power saw in the neighborhood, it was a two man saw. We spent most of the money we made trying to keep the saw running, usually ended up cutting most of the logs with a cross cut and Swede saw.

In 1949 I bought a saw mill from Royal Burrows and went custom sawing until 1956, between busy seasons on the ranch.

I met Iona Altwater in 1950 while she was in training at the Calgary General Hospital. After she graduated we were married in June, 1952. We have three children, Linda Marie born in 1953 and presently working for Execucare Services in Calgary. Randy William born in 1956, working with me in the construction business and Clifford Murray born in 1959 and employed as a Power Engineer for Alberta Processors in Calgary. All three received their education at Sheep

Ione and Murray Jackson on their wedding day, June 4th, 1952.

L. to R. Randy, Clifford, Linda, Ione and Murray Jackson.

Creek School and Oilfields Jr.-Sr. High school in Black Diamond.

In 1957 I went back to the oil rigs on Flat Top Mountain and west of Sundre.

In 1958 we bought a caterpillar tractor to clear brush on our ranch and ended up in the construction business with cats and graders, building roads, clearing brush and doing oil field work.

In the fall of 1973 we moved our house from the home quarter to our own property on Kew road (S.W.5, twp21, Rge3, Wof5).

What a memorable day that was, to see a huge structure gently lifted and transported to its new location overlooking the foothills and the beautiful rocky mountains.

Robert and Jo Ann Jackson

by Jo Ann Jackson

I am the only daughter of Dr. and Mrs. C. G. Curdt of Calgary. Born in Calgary at the Holy Cross Hospital in 1942. Our family lived in Calgary for the first six years of my life, we were then transferred to Moose Jaw, Saskatchewan, spending almost three years there and then we were transferred to Ottawa. All that I can remember of Ottawa is the top of the Peace Tower and some of the rides on boats that travelled up and down the Rideau Canal. We lived for a time above a pharmacy in Ottawa, aha, my parents thought, as the proprietors were French, at last Jo Ann would finally learn some French, but all I did was teach them more English. We arrived back in Calgary in 1952 where I attended Parkdale, Queen Elizabeth and Crescent Heights schools. After high school I enrolled at the Southern Alberta Institute of Technology, taking the last one year course in Food Service.

I was employed by Canadian Utilities in Edmonton assisting the Home Economist in various demonstrations, cooking schools and appliance operations. We travelled throughout central and northern Alberta with these programmes.

I returned to Calgary and enrolled at the Hollingshead Business College where I learned to type and take shorthand with some bookkeeping and math skills thrown in for good measure. I scoured Calgary for a place that would employ me and finally found one with the RCMP. This job proved to be very interesting as well as challenging. It kept one alert, as happened one night after work. I went to my car, opened the door got in and turned on the ignition only to find a terrible bang and blue smoke come pouring out from under the hood. Some kind soul had attached firecrackers to the car's spark plugs.

It was while I was working there that a friend and her husband invited me to come out to a dance at the Rancher's Hall where I met Bob Jackson.

Robert Haney Jackson — is the younger son of Mr. and Mrs. W. Jackson, Jr., born in the Holy Cross

Back: Jo Ann and Bob Jackson with Jo Ann's parents, Alice and Dr. Clarence Curdt, on the occasion of their 50th wedding anniversary. October 10, 1976.

Shannon and Peter Jackson.

Hospital in 1933. I grew up on the ranch and went to the one room Sheep Creek School, located one mile east of the ranch until the school was moved to its present location in 1952. I went to the Southern Alberta Institute of Technology and took Farm Mechanics, returning to Millarville and the ranch to work with dad. Hunting, fishing and curling occupied most of my spare time.

Robert and Jo Ann Jackson — were married in December of 1967 at Parkdale United Church in Calgary. After a reception in Calgary and a wedding dance held in the Rancher's Hall we travelled to San Francisco for our honeymoon. We were just in time to hit a New Year's Eve storm near Great Falls on our way home and being too bushed from our long drive home we missed the last New Year's Eve frolic to be held in Rancher's Hall. Our first home was a 12 x 42 foot mobile home. Two children were born while we lived in that home. Shannon Claire arrived in January 1970 and Peter Joseph arrived in March 1972.

Things had gone quite smoothly until January of 1973 when we lost Pop, and then in May of that same year when Bob was thrown by a bull while selling our registered Hereford bulls at a sale in Brooks, Alberta. I will never forget the kindness shown by our neighbours that year when they seeded our crop. Bob was in the hospital for only two weeks and thanks to our Lord has recovered from that terrible accident.

The year 1973 was our year for change as we bought a new home and moved into our present home just about 10 feet further south from our old home. Shannon and Peter have since started school.

Bob has carried on his father's cattle brand, WJ right hip, keeping it active.

Bob was a director with the Red Deer Lake Savings and Credit Union for 10 years and is presently a director with the Southern Alberta Pioneers and Their Descendents.

Walter John Jackson

by Beverley Jackson

Walter John Jackson was born in Calgary, November 1937, the elder son of John and Ida Jackson

The pet Coyote, with Walter (l) and Bill (r).

of Millarville. He attended Fordville School for grades one through eight, riding on horseback to and from school everyday. The horse was named "Betty". She was black with a white star on her forehead and she transported Walter and his brother Bill faithfully during those years and lived to be quite an age.

When Fordville School closed in 1952, being one of the last one room schools in the area to do so, it was by bus to Sheep Creek, Millarville, for grades nine, ten and eleven. A year spent at the Southern Alberta Institute of Technology studying Drafting, concluded his formal education.

During his later school years, he was active in the Millarville 4-H Beef Club, from its inception in 1952, until 1957. He held most of the executive positions, and won two trips to the Olds Agricultural College. In 1953 and 1954 he won the J. Barraclough Challenge Trophy for General Efficiency and in 1956 a Judging Award.

As with other adolescents, he took music lessons for several years, featuring the trumpet. In later years it sounded like a "cracked coronet". One unusual feature of his boyhood was The Pet! An orphaned coyote was found in the field one day by his father. Bingo, as he was called, was about a month old. He was brought home, fed, and cared for. But alas! Bingo was not to be domesticated. After a few weeks, he was donated to the Calgary Zoo.

During the spring of 1951, an unusually heavy snow fell, resulting in an accumulation of two to three feet of snow on the level, and drifts five feet deep around

Betty, the school transportation. Walter (I) and Bill, and friend.

buildings and along fences. The storm started on the first of June with rain continuing for two days before turning to snow, which continued for three more days. The approach road to the farm was completely clogged with snow and fallen trees. Riding out to check on the cattle proved too much for the dog, and she had to be taken up on the horse also.

In October, 1965, Walter and I were married. We have one son Peter, and we reside in Calgary. Our main interests are photography and gardening, with hiking, camping and travelling when time permits.

During Walter's employment in Calgary, he travelled a good deal in Alberta and visited many out-of-the-tourist places. Together, we have seen a large amount of British Columbia, the Prairie provinces and southern Ontario. Also, we have had a trip to Hawaii, and two extensive holidays in the British Isles.

Travelling has provided us with ample subject material for our photography. Other rewards include meeting new people, visiting historical castles and cathedrals and appreciating some of the effort and manual labour that created these magnificent structures. Some of these buildings are 700 years old and still being used today — a remarkable feat!

A fairly recent interest is searching for information about the Jackson geneaology. We spent several days touring the Lake District in England visiting graveyards and talking to people who might be able to help us. Our success was limited.

We have property in the Millarville area which we use primarily on weekends. It gives us a change of scenery. Gardening, hiking and photography take up most of our time.

William Jackson Jr.

by Esther Jackson   WJ

William (Billy) was the oldest of the William Jackson family. He was born near Priddis on NW¼ 24-22-3 W5. He went to Priddis school for a short time until the family moved further south to NW¼ 30-21-2 W5 where his brother John lives now. There was no school in that area until 1908 when Fordville was built and he went there for awhile. Although he hadn't had much formal education he did a lot of reading. His interests were in agriculture, history, politics and that sort of thing.

Although rodeo probably hadn't been heard of in Canada at that time (the early 1900s) Billy and neighbor boys spent Sunday afternoons roping calves, riding steers and bucking horses. In 1913 he took part in infield events at the Calgary Stampede which he continued to do until 1925 when, riding in the wild horse competition, the horse fell with him breaking his leg. This ended his career with that part of the Stampede. He took part in the chuckwagon races as an outrider with Kew wagon. In the mornings during Stampede when the chuckwagons would stand on 8th Avenue handing out flap-jacks and bacon to Stampede visitors, he helped with the cooking.

Among the sports, hockey was his favorite. He played with Kew hockey team in the 1920s. They won three years in succession and were awarded the silver cup to keep.

Bill and Esther Jackson with their family in 1946. L. to R. Bill, Esther, Fern, Murray, Anne. Bob in front.

329

In 1918 Billy and his brother Joe struck out on their own. They bought NW and SW 5-21-3 W5 from the C.P.R. where they farmed until 1926 when Joe went to work in the oilfields. Billy stayed with mixed farming and for some years, dairying, and finally turned to ranching. Raising pure-bred Herefords.

Being of a friendly nature his home was open to everyone and it wasn't very often that he didn't have some of his bachelor friends staying with him. He had good friends among the Indians, both Sarcee and Stoney, and they often stopped in when passing through. He didn't believe in locking his door, ever, and as a result his house burned down one day while he was working away from home. His neighbors to the east (the MacKays) had noticed a fellow riding by before noon and Fishers, his neighbors to the west, had seen the same man riding by some two hours later so it was taken for granted that in the interval he had stopped in, cooked dinner for himself, and regardless of the fact that it was a very windy day had left a fire in the cook-stove. Billy came home that night to find nothing but a pile of ashes. While it was bad enough to lose his house, his biggest regret was losing his Stampede trophies, pictures etc. which could never be replaced. Luckily he had just finished building a small log place intending to use it for a blacksmith shop, but instead, he used it to live in.

For recreation Billy was very fond of dancing, and would ride to Bragg Creek and even further to a dance. He was secretary of Rancher's hall board for some years, also caretaker, so it was his job to light the wood fires and the coal-oil lamps and put a boiler-full of water on for the coffee, on dance nights. The dances usually kept going well into the small hours and it was a common occurance for some of the young guys, who had ridden a long distance, to bed down on the floor of his house for what was left of the night. Sometime before noon they would head for home after a hearty breakfast of flap-jacks and coffee.

Billy was one of those with a talent for witching water wells and was often called on to find wells by people in the district. He used a crow-bar but some "witchers" prefer a willow wand for "witching". The late Bill Hussey, a Black Diamond water well driller, often had Billy "witch" before he would drill a well. On one occasion Home Oil Company flew him to Northern Alberta to find water on a new oil-well site. He would never accept payment as he considered his ability to find water to be a "gift".

In May 1927 Billy gave up batching and got married. After two years of poor crops, being drowned-out in 1927 and dried-out in 1928, he decided to go to work in the oil-fields, so he rented the farm to Warren Fulton for two years and in April 1929, moved to Turner Valley where he worked for Calmont Oils. This wasn't a good move. The depression hit in 1930 and Calmont, like many other smaller oil companies shut down, so after a winter with little or nothing to do it was good to have the farm to come back to in April 1931. Money

was mighty scarce but there was always food for the table. Wild game was plentiful and Billy was a good shot.

Billy was always interested in the community and always willing to help with its projects. He was an active member of Millarville Racing and Agricultural Association and an honorary director, also a director of Millarville Community Association. He had been a trustee of Sheep Creek school and was a member of numerous other organizations such as Western Stock Growers, Hereford Breeders, U.F.A. and the Agricultural Bureau of Calgary Chamber of Commerce and was an active member of Southern Alberta Pioneers and Descendants and of High River Old-Timers and had served as president of both.

He and Esther enjoyed travelling in later years in parts of Canada and the United States. One of their most interesting trips was to Expo in 1967 with a party of Stampede members who chartered a plane to Montreal to take part in Alberta and Calgary Days at Expo. In 1972 Billy, and his brother George went with a Farmers and Ranchers tour to Australia, New Zealand and the Orient. His last trip was to Mexico when on January 19, 1973, at the age of 78, he passed away very suddenly while he and Esther waited to board their flight for home.

He was laid to rest in Millarville Christ Church cemetery among the hills he loved so well.

William R. and Dorothy Jackson
by Dorothy Jackson

At first, we didn't think we had much history, or there had been much change during our short lifetimes, but upon reflecting, we realized that our way of living and our community have changed.

Bill grew up and we reside on the land that his grandfather, William Jackson homesteaded in the 1880's. (refer to "OUR FOOTHILLS")

We both experienced sawing and carrying piles of wood to feed the forever hungry cook stove and pot-bellied heaters, then carefully carrying out the ashes, trying not to spill because you let the ash box get too full! Likewise, the water was pumped by hand, carried into the house and later carried out again.

Bill remembers cutting ice on Chance's Lake during the winter, and packing it in the ice house for use in the ice box during the summer.

We both rode horseback to country schools, Bill to Fordville and I to Stormount. The snowdrifts at the brow of Sandstone Coulee would get so deep that once my horse, after much lunging and struggling, could not get through. I had visions of spending the day there, and who knows, even freezing! However, my horse had his own ideas and managed to turn around and headed downhill and home. He had had enough for one day. Today those same size drifts are just great for our kids to glide over with a snowmobile — no challenge at all!

After high school at Millarville, Bill attended S.A.I.T. in Calgary, taking Agricultural Mechanics,

Dorothy, Heather (age 12), George (age 14), Bill Jackson. 1977.

Time out for consultation while showing sheep at the Millarville Fair 1977. Bill Jackson with George and Heather.

then returned to farm with his parents John and Ida Jackson. Bill has one brother, Walter who lives in Calgary.

I attended Okotoks High School and then Olds College. I was enrolled in the last general Home Economics course offered. It included cooking, sewing, horticulture, home nursing, bookkeeping, interior decorating, home management, and more. Everything one should know to be a good farm wife! However, I next attended the University of Calgary, taking teacher training, and taught at the Priddis School, grades 1 to 4, until it was closed in 1962. Living conditions were again slightly on the primitive level. I lived in a one-room teacherage — back to chopping wood and pumping water. The classroom had a water crock, wash basin, a hand bell, and the only means of making copies was one hectograph pad. However, there was electrical power.

During our growing up years, we were both active in 4-H. Bill was a member, and then leader, of the Millarville Beef Club. I was the first president of the Foothills Sheep Club and a member of the Okotoks Beef Club. Many times we met in the show ring, each striving for the champion honors. At that time, the winner of the interclub champion calf received a Bulova wrist watch. I still wear this much cherished watch. I was also fortunate and won an award trip to National 4-H Club Week in Toronto and Ottawa.

We are still active in 4-H as leaders in the Millarville Multi 4-H Club. Our son, George is keen on his small engine project, and Heather is taking the crafts project and is an enthusiastic 4-H public speaker. As 4-H members, they have far more projects and programs available to them than we had during our years as members.

When Bill and I were married, we farmed with his parents, raising beef and dairy cows. However, with regulations changing in regards to dairying, it was decided to change to sheep raising — a surprise to some people until they realized there was a resident shepherdess. I came from the sheep raising Hebson family. I have two brothers, William and Robert, and a sister, Linda. The new Okotoks Agriculture Arena was named after my father in 1978. I had exhibited sheep at the major livestock shows, from the P.N.E. in Vancouver to the Royal Winter Fair in Toronto, so was soon back in the show ring. My Southdown sheep appeared in the Calgary Exhibition and Stampede show ring for more than twenty years.

Although the farming operation and most of the land was sold in 1969 and 1970, we still have a few sheep that our kids enjoy showing at the Millarville Fair.

For a few years Bill worked at a veterinary clinic in Calgary, but is at present the Agriculture Fieldman with Foothills M.D. No. 31.

We moved from the farm site in 1971, into a new home on our own property. When building, we were fortunate to locate for our fireplace, bricks that were manufactured in the Sandstone Brickyard during the time my grandfather, Percy Pegler worked there. (The Percy Pegler Elementary School in Okotoks was named after him in 1976.) I can still see Grandad's face beaming with pleasure as he lit the first fire in the fireplace. At this same time, the branding irons W.J. - L.H., that Bill had inherited from his grandfather Jackson, were heated, and a cedar shake in the family room wall was branded WJ. Hopefully, occasions like this will help our children become more aware of their family heritage.

Both our families have been faithful community workers, and it often seems this family spends more time doing community work than we do at home. However, I'm convinced it has been the volunteer efforts of many community-minded people that have contributed to making Millarville such a great community in which to live.

With the progression of years, many of Bill's boyhood friends and neighbors have moved to farm and live elsewhere. The land once so vast to the homesteaders, is now rapidly being divided into smaller holdings or sold to non farmers.

Our children will be fourth generation on this land, but only time will tell if they will be able to choose to live here.

Margaret and Garman Jacobson

by Peggy (Waugh) Jacobson

I am the second daughter of Jean and Joseph Waugh, and was born in 1913 on the homestead at Millarville — N.E. ¼ 18-21-3 W5. I have been told that a lady by the name of Mrs. Iles attended my birth.

I grew up with my sisters on the homestead, and took part in all of the community activities along with the rest of my family.

In 1927 we moved to Midnapore for a year, and attended school there. Dad was carrying the mail from Midnapore to Kew at that time.

The Sheep Creek School was finally built in 1928, and we moved back to Millarville. I went to Sheep Creek School until 1931. Then I came to Calgary to finish my education at Western Canada High School, and after that my nurse's training at the Scottish Private Hospital. After graduating, I stayed on at the hospital and nursed for two years.

Garman and Peggy Jacobson, about 1968.

It was during this time that I met and married Fritchif Englund, a young farmer from Strathmore. We lived on the farm at Strathmore for three years until Fritz's death in 1942. I returned to Calgary later that year and began nursing once again.

In 1949 Garman and I were married, and we have lived in Calgary since that time.

Garman is the son of Garman Sr. and Anna Jacobson, who farmed in the Camrose district for a number of years. After his discharge from the army in 1945, Garman went back to work for Dench Cartage, where he had been employed prior to his enlistment in 1942. Later he was employed by several garages and motor dealers throughout the City, including Stampede Pontiac Ltd., where he worked until retirement in 1975.

The Jameson Family

The children of Thomas and Grace Jameson were: Hadassah Lowry (Dessa), later Mrs. H. G. Macklin; Eileen Elizabeth; Margaret Patricia, later Mrs. K. L. Steeves; William Thomas Lawrence (Larry); Sheilagh Somerville.

They were happy days for the Jameson children on beautiful old Ballyhamage Ranch. Playing along the creek in the lovely summer afternoons, learning to identify the wild flowers which grew there in such profusion, and enjoying bird song in the woods, sliding down the haystacks on winter moonlit nights, making angels in the snow, playing hide-and-seek on saddle ponies among the willow groves, were some of our childhood pleasures.

There were responsibilities too. Some of these included bringing in and milking the cows, rounding up the ponies for school, chopping and carrying in wood, picking berries, and as years passed helping with housework, raking and stacking hay, and stooking. There were some exciting occurrences, at times fraught with danger. One hot July day a sudden thunderstorm with golf-ball sized hailstones cut short a berry-picking expedition. Lush strawberries had to be hastily dumped and the pails and bowls used as head protectors. Our driving horses were spirited and at times there were run-a-ways. One of the most damaging occurred when we were visiting the Kennedys. The team hitched to our Californian cart was tied to a fence post, when a bunch of range horses, heading for the corral, swooped around the corner. The team, with the cart in tow and dragging a piece of the fence, joined the chase with dire consequences to harness and cart. Following days of school, homework and active play, there were evenings of quiet pleasure when our parents read aloud from Ernest Thompson Seton, James Fenimore Cooper, Charles Dickens, and many other favorite authors, a fine introduction to the world of literature. Sometimes before the flickering light of the fire, a neighbor told stories of the ghosts of Ireland. On other occasions evenings might be spent playing games, ending perhaps with a spirited game of Whist. It was a childhood long to be remembered.

Eileen Elizabeth Jameson

My earliest memory is about putting my new baby sister, Sheilagh, to sleep. I held her on my knee as we rocked and my song was a name, which oft repeated had a resonant ring to me. Ultimately we both fell asleep and tumbled onto the floor. Fortunately no harm was done — it was a child's rocker. I must have been six years old at the time. Another episode recalled from the early years was of school in the dining room with Mother as teacher, who had planned an appropriate schedule for each of us, and Dad preparing a very hot curried dish in the kitchen. Later Ballyhamage School was built and opened in the fall of 1919. The first morning at the new school was exciting — new desks, new books, and a big school bell. The family all attended this school and it was here that I took grades six to nine inclusive.

After completing high school in Okotoks and at Crescent Heights in Calgary, I graduated from the Calgary Normal School. My teaching experience spanned a period of fourteen years. During this time I taught in rural schools at Monitor, Irricana, the home school, Ballyhamage, Big Rock School, near Okotoks, Black Diamond, and Panima School, Okotoks. Teachers who taught during this period will recall the many vicissitudes of each experience: The two-mile

Eileen Jameson as Director of Nursing Education about 1963, in her office, School of Nursing, Calgary General Hospital.

walk in the morning at all seasons of the year or at some schools the joy in having your own saddle horse; sometimes starting the big old Waterbury stove, which baked our faces and froze our feet; dressing the little ones for their ride home — putting on scarves, mufflers, toques, overshoes, buttoning up, etc., helping them on to the barebacks of horses, and sometimes, too, it was necessary to bridle the ponies. They were great little children, resourceful and courageous. The Christmas Concert was a major event of the year; everyone helped — the Chairman of the Board volunteered to put up the stage for the one-night performance; some of the Mothers helped make costumes, others played the piano for drills, songs, and marches, then all helped the children to learn their parts — it was a cooperative enterprise which brought the whole district together and helped to cement relationships. The few minor crises were soon forgotten.

At one of my schools where I remained for six years, there were thirty or more children and grades from one to ten inclusive. On one occasion grade three was the only one missing. Teaching in a country school was a challenge but a very rewarding one.

Nursing had always beckoned, and in 1942 I entered the School of Nursing, Calgary General Hospital, graduating in 1945. A scholarship enabled me to take a post-graduate course in Obstetrics at the Royal Victoria Hospital in Montreal, following which I was placed in the Charge Nurse position of the Maternity Nursery at the General Hospital for four years. My involvement in Nursing Education began in 1953, when I obtained a diploma in Teaching and Supervision in Schools of Nursing at the University of Alberta. Over the next ten year period I taught Surgical and Medical Nursing Obstetrical Nursing and Nursing Arts.

From 1960 to 1973 I was Director of Nursing Education of the Calgary General's School of Nursing. By this time I had furthered my own education, obtaining a Bachelor of Science in Nursing from the University of Minnesota in 1956, and a Master's Degree in Nursing from the University of Washington, in 1964.

As poetry and all forms of Literature had always been of major interest to me, I appreciated the opportunity to choose some very good courses during the time at university. Some of these included Shakespeare, Greek Heritage, English Literature including Elizabethan drama, Poetry of the Renaissance, Romantic, and Victorian periods.

For many years I was actively involved in professional organizations, maintaining a special interest in Nursing Education. During Centennial Year, I was co-author of a book entitled "The Science, the Art and the Spirit", the story of Nursing and Medicine, spanning the period from 1883 until 1975. It has been a rewarding experience to participate in the gradual but continuing progress toward an enlightened form of education for nursing.

Pat and Leslie Steeves 1956.

Margaret Patricia Jameson (Steeves)

Pat inherited much of our father's gentleness and kindness and tended to be a peacemaker among the five children. She also had artistic skills which she put to good use in homemaking, needlework, gardening, etc. In later years she attended art classes and enjoyed oil painting.

With other members of the family Pat attended school at Ballyhamage where she took grades four to nine inclusive. She completed high school in Okotoks and then obtained a teacher's certificate from the Calgary Normal School.

As a young girl of seventeen, Pat commenced teaching in a rural school near Cayley. When Sheep Creek School, Millarville, was opened in 1928, she became the first teacher and continued in this position for the next six years. Later Pat taught at Red Deer Lake School and at Plainview. At one time Pat relieved for a teacher at Priddis for some weeks during a very severe winter. Here she lived in a small teacherage and during one night when the wood fire went out, water in a pail on the back of the kitchen stove was frozen by morning. The temperature that night was a recorded 60 degrees below zero (F.).

After spending some years at home on the Ranch, Pat went to Calgary where she attended Garbutt's Business College, completing a course in Business and Accounting. She had a 'head for figures', and was very successful in positions held in several firms in Calgary.

In 1956 Pat married Kenneth Leslie Steeves of Olds, Alberta. They lived on the farm for several years before moving into Olds. In 1960 they adopted an infant daughter, Norah Patricia. Pat died in 1965. Since that time her husband and daughter have lived near Parksville, Vancouver Island. In the fall of 1978, Norah was married to Allan Kent of Parksville.

William Thomas Lawrence Jameson (Larry)

Larry received his education at Ballyhamage and Okotoks. Although he obtained his admission to the Calgary Normal School, his main interest was always in the Ranch and he decided to take over its operation.

Larry on Sonny at Ballyhamage middle 1930's.

During the years he was at Ballyhamage he accomplished a great deal. Many improvements included clearing land for additional crop and pasture and building up a herd of herefords.

At this time tractors were in common use and although Larry bought and used a tractor, he continued to use horses also. His big Clyde teams remained a source of pride and pleasure to him.

At the outbreak of World War II, Larry was anxious to join the Forces, but farming was an essential service, and as his father was unable to manage alone, he felt that the operation of the Ranch was his first responsibility. He joined the Home Guard in Okotoks.

Larry died in 1953, following a brief illness.

Sheilagh Somerville Jameson

As the youngest child in a family of five I grew up with certain advantages and disadvantages. The others claimed I was spoiled — untrue of course. In our family, picking up chips from the wood-pile and gathering little sticks to serve as kindling to light the fire was considered a menial task from which each child in turn graduated as the next in line was able to take over. In the course of time this chore came to me. After some years I rebelled. There was no one younger to inherit the job and I feared that this would be my duty for the rest of my life. One evening at chip time I hid in an oat field and didn't appear until Dad had brought in kindling himself. When asked if I hadn't heard him call I confessed that I had and had answered, but not loudly enough for him to hear. This

Sheilagh Jameson, in her office, Glenbow Archives, in old library building in Memorial Park, Calgary; examining a Chinese letter book which had been donated to the Archives. 1970.

subterfuge didn't work and it became clear that there was no avoiding the chip duty. However, perspectives change; then before many years I went away to school.

After taking high school in Okotoks and Calgary, I attended Normal School and started my teaching career. There followed a number of years of teaching at Ballyhamage, Red Deer Lake, Sheep Creek and then at Midnapore, where I taught Grades VII to XI. Next I joined the Calgary school system, teaching elementary schools, chiefly Grades II and III.

In 1957, when on leave-of-absence from the Calgary School Board, I took a step which opened up a new career. I obtained a position with the newly formed Glenbow Foundation in Calgary. The concept of this organization devoted to the collection and preservation of the history of Western Canada, intrigued me, as from the stories my parents and their contemporaries had told of pioneer days in this country I had caught something of the flavour of history.

My first work at Glenbow was that of an historical researcher, then in 1960 I was asked to work directly in the Archives and became assistant to the Archivist, Hugh Dempsey. After a change in the organization in 1967, by which it became the Glenbow-Alberta Institute, Mr. Dempsey took a higher administrative position and I became Chief Archivist. At the time of writing (Spring 1979), I still hold this position.

In 1964, under Glenbow's sponsorship, I went to Ottawa to take a summer course in Archives Techniques and Administration, offered by Carleton University and the Public Archives of Canada. During my earlier years at Glenbow and while teaching I furthered my education by taking a number of courses at the Universities of Alberta and Calgary, Mount Royal College, S.A.I.T. and the Banff School of Fine Arts. Among these were courses in history, English, anthropology, journalism, creative writing and public speaking. In addition, I attended writers' workshop sessions for several years.

Writing has always been a part of my life. Indeed, when still in elementary school, I had a little article about a chic-a-dee published in the **Calgary Herald.** I thought then that I had arrived as a writer! Shortly I discovered that this was far from being the case; however, I continued trying. Among my more successful efforts have been a series of plays, produced by Alberta School Broadcasts; articles published in magazines such as **Canadian Cattlemen** and the **Alberta Historical Review;** chapters in the books, **Frontier Calgary,** 1975, and **The Canadian West,** 1977, published by the University of Calgary. At last, in April, 1979, my first book, **Chautauqua in Canada,** appeared in print.

I have found work with Glenbow and in the field of history most satisfying and rewarding. I am pleased and proud to have had a part in guiding the development of the Archives and to be involved in preserving and recording for future generations evidence of Western Canada's unique and significant history.

Marjorie Ann (Ducommun) Janzen

Hi, I'm Marjorie Ann Janzen, nee Ducommun. My parents are Elsie and Ernie Ducommun and I have one brother, Carl. Dad worked for Home Oil and I was born in High River, Alberta, on August 3rd, 1938.

My first home in the Millarville district that I remember was a log cabin about a ½ mile north of Waugh's store. One fall the cabin was being winterized and cement was being used to fill the cracks between the logs. Following this task we found cement all over Mom's dresser so I guess we had good air conditioning that past summer.

My 5th Christmas was spent with my family in the Black Diamond Hotel as we all had "gassed eyes" and had to leave our home until the leak had been found and fixed. Those were the days we used sour gas in the cook stoves.

Going to school in 1944 meant a five mile walk to and from school. Neighbors were kind and often picked us up but I can remember grade one, around 7:30 a.m. when Kathy Larratt would whistle when she reached the end of our lane and I would run down the hill and walk with her.

Around 1946, we moved to the Home Camp and lived 1 mile S.E. of the offices. There we had a bus to take my brother and me to school. Sheep Creek School was eventually moved to the Millarville town site and it was my school for grades 1 to 9. I have many pleasant memories of friends and I deeply regret missing the reunion — wish I could have seen many of you. Remember having to write an essay in grade 9 on

John and Marj (Ducommun) Janzen.

"Why I Like to Play Keep-Away with the Boys." Mr. Clarke was our teacher then. Recesses were spent talking, playing ball, football and marbles for the younger grades.

Since high school was not available at Millarville I went to Mount Royal with Anne Glaister and Eveline Backs. In 1954, my parents moved to Calgary so I attended Western Canada High School for grades eleven and twelve. Our home was sold and moved to Millarville town site as a home for the teachers.

In 1959 I graduated from the Calgary General Hospital School of Nursing as a registered nurse. During training, I met a young man from Glenwood, Alberta, on a blind date. My mom warned me about those kind of dates. In 1961, after attending Berean Bible College for one year, John and I were married and moved to Manning, Alberta, where John worked as a heavy duty mechanic for I.H.C. and I as a nurse. The north was good to us.

Today we have a ½ section of land west of Bowden. John works for Mobil Oil and I for the Olds Municipal Hospital. We have four children: Dan was born in 1962, LeeAnn in 1964, Tim in 1968 and Christine in 1971. Since farming is new to me John is busy teaching me many things — one not to ride the motorcycle over the barley

swathes when I call him to come in for dinner. He told me that meal was very expensive but I bet he's glad it wasn't through the rape swathes.

I am learning to play the saxophone. My two boys play the trumpet and LeeAnn the flute. They are in the County of Mountain View Band but I am still in the beginner's section.

So thanks, Millarville, for giving me a good start. Life is really great!

Betty (de Mille) Jenkins.

The class of 1922 at the Calgary Normal School under the direction of Dr. Coffin was a particularly enthusiastic group eager to start teaching. One of these was Wilfred Eggleston who later became Dean of Journalism at Carleton University, Ottawa. We all applied for schools in rural areas. One advertisement wanted someone able to ride horseback and talk French. After applying and being accepted, my brothers persuaded me not to venture into the wilds of Northern Alberta. The next ad was for Square Butte School. Mr. George Lyall hired me and also offered to let me board at their home. This proved a very happy home, good food and kind treatment. The salary was about five dollars a day.

Mr. and Mrs. Billy Hulme, who was our nearest neighbor to the mill, gave a house party to launch me and brother Howard drove me to Kew. There was still ice in the creek bottoms and patches of snow in shady

L. to R. Carolyn (deMille) Lancefield, Betty (de Mille) Jenkins.

336

Betty (deMille) Jenkins, first teacher at Square Butte (in 1922) and her husband and family. L. to R. Bill (father) Michael, Peter, Bob, Fred, William, Carolyn and Betty (mother).

places. The little school at Square Butte was really attractive, made of peeled logs with small panel windows. The desks were still in their crates when we arrived and had to be fitted together by Jack Bell and Lawrence Malcolmson. They were not screwed to the floor so they could be piled up and make room for dances. My sister had given me an old Victrola and a pile of old records.

The first pupils were Dick Lyall and his sister Peggy. Later two Malcolmson girls and Olive Rawlinson attended. After some persuasion Mr. and Mrs. Silvester sent three children, Annie, John and Albert on a horse named Felix. To make a shorter trip someone cut a path for them. Poor Felix used to be molested by cattle and other horses.

The cattle pushed their horns through the windows of the school, so Jack Bell made a pole fence around it. This provided a great gymnastic apparatus for the youngsters who "skinned the cat" and hung from their knees and did balancing acts on the poles. They also skimmed up trees like chipmunks.

It was a happy school life with pupils like Annie Silvester and Peggy Lyall so eager to learn that they fairly ate up the readers. It was an unnatural environment however for the boys but they bore with my ideas and struggled with spelling and literature. They made good progress, especially in arithmetic and natural science. When the end of the term came there were few dry eyes. The affection one feels for the first class is like one's delight in a first grandchild. As I was saving for University I could not afford to wait from Christmas until spring, as the new school held classes from early spring until Christmas, with their school vacation during the winter months, so I took another contract.

Jack and Grace Jennings

Mrs. Jennings came from Lomond to teach School at Square Butte. She stayed with Mr. and Mrs. George

Lyall. Dick Lyall was still going to school. That was the year 1928 or somewhere around that time. Mrs. Jennings went back to Lomond. Later Mr. and Mrs. Jennings came back and Jack was looking for work but no luck. That was in the hungry thirties. They went back to Lomond and their son was born. They came back to Square Butte again looking for work. Jack got a job cutting cord wood for Cotton Belt well. While they were living here their second son was born. Then back to Lomond to the farm.

Two more children were born a girl and a boy. Two of their children have passed away. Jack joined the army and they lived in Calgary.

Mrs. Jennings went back teaching after the children grew up. She also taught at Black Diamond for awhile, then went up North and taught the Indian children. Then she came back to Calgary. Mr. and Mrs. Jennings had parted and both remarried. Their daughter lives in Calgary and a son in Fort St. John. Grace passed away in March 1978. Jack still lives in Calgary.

Jensen, Marie (Edlund)

I began teaching at Square Butte School in September, 1935 and left at the end of June 1937.

I was born in Denmark in 1903 and came to Claresholm in 1904 at the age of six months. Here I attended the local schools and after graduating from grade twelve attended Normal School to receive my teachers' training. After receiving my first class certificate I taught in several rural schools before coming to Square Butte. I usually stayed in each school about two years as I was restless and wanted to move on.

While teaching at Square Butte I boarded with the Bannermans. My salary was $840 a year and out of this I paid $35 a month for board and room. $5 of this was for the horse I rode to school.

I remember Mr. Northover, a kindly old gentleman who lived close by a stream that we crossed every day. When the water was frozen it was often like a sheet of glass. Mr. Northover would chip the ice so we could cross safely. He loved to walk and as he did so he wrote beautiful little mottos in the snow with the stick he always carried. I used to look for these mottos as I rode to school and admired his beautiful writing with their messages.

I loved the setting of this school so close to the trees. From my pupils I learned much of the ways of the animals of this area and about the plants and flowers.

I remember one winter as being extremely cold. Many mornings the temperature was about —30 below F. as we left for school. In fact on two mornings it was —53 below F. I felt it was necessary to go to school as there were no telephones to call off school. One family sent their eldest children to school even on the coldest days.

After leaving Square Butte I came back to Claresholm district. I taught in the Willow Creek School Divi-

Marie (Edlund) Jensen. Teacher at Square Butte School.

New Valley School. Back row, L. to R.: Willie Kohler, Margaret Deane-Freeman, Bill Fisher, Bruce Stanhope, Annie Kohler, Gwen Stockton, Eileen Cunningham (teacher). 2nd row: Patsy Stockton, Bernice Freeman, Dorothy Frayn, Louie Kohler. Front row: Jimmie Kohler, David Glaister, May Kohler.

sion until I retired for the first time in 1946. I had married Einer Jensen in 1942, and we farmed until we moved into town in 1957.

However, in 1953, I was prevailed upon to teach in the Junior High School in Claresholm as one of their teachers had left. I taught Math and science in Jr. High until I retired permanently in 1967, after teaching about 36 years.

Einer and I have a daughter Gwen who is a secretary in Calgary and a son David who is a paramedic with the Calgary Ambulance. We have three grandchildren.

It may be of interest to some to know that my father, John Edlund, managed a theatre in Turner Valley in its early days and that my brother Edmer Edlund was a projectionist there. Edmer married Stella Klink of Turner Valley.

Eileen (Cunningham) Johnson

Eileen daughter of Mr. and Mrs. George Cunningham of High River taught at New Valley school for two years beginning Sept. 1937 until terms end June 1939. The following was contributed by her.

I also taught school in Sunshine district west of Crossfield and in the town of Parkland south of High River. I married my Scout, Ralph Johnson and taught

school in Edmonton for a couple of years till Bruce arrived. With the coming of three boys into our family I did not teach again in Edmonton. We adopted a baby girl and moved to Sherwood Park where in time I returned to teaching part time in Remedial Reading. I have taught this work here for 17 years and am still at it, though not for too much longer. It is hard to stop when you enjoy your work. Our oldest son Bruce is in process of setting up his own electrical business — finishes his Masters next month. Kim our second son is a pilot with C.P. Air and flies 747's to Hawaii, Hong Kong, Tokyo, Amsterdam etc. He took Computing Science at U. of A. but preferred flying. Darik, our 3rd son took Commerce and Business Admin. at University and is a buyer for Sherritt Gordon of Fort Sask. Lois; our daughter is in Vancouver picking up her University at night school, worked in Woodwards personel office but recently changed jobs to a fashion house.

Ralph is retired from Mutual Life but still works at a side line of District Manager for Edmonton Journal, is a lay-reader in our Anglican Church. I have played organ off and on for 22 years here.

Our boys are all married to lovely girls and we have two granddaughters who live on an acreage near us, so we see them often.

Wyman Harvey Johnson

Harvey was born in Dansville, New York, U.S.A. in 1890. His wife, Gladys, was born in Herefordshire, England, in 1891. Harvey had served in the armed services during World War 1.

In 1926, the Johnsons and their three children, Marjorie, Raymond and Patricia, moved to the Kew district, to a log cabin on the Dawes place, where Bob and Gavin Calderwood had previously lived. Harvey had the truck hauling for the Royalite Oil Co. and also hauled stock for the local ranchers.

Marjorie and Raymond attended Plainview School, and Mr. and Mrs. Johnson were actively interested in the Social Credit Party, that was just beginning. They also helped build the Kew Community Hall, which was later moved to the Square Butte district and is still used for community affairs. After five years in the Kew district, the family moved to North Turner Valley.

Marjorie (Johnson) Larmour was born in Edmonton in 1915. She and her husband have retired, and are travelling, but have their home in Edmonton. They have three children and three grandchildren.

Raymond was born in Edmonton in 1916. After serving in the Army during World War 2, he has worked in the oilfields, mostly in the north. Resides in Edmonton most of the time.

Patricia (Johnson) Mumby was born in Calgary in 1925. Her husband is in the oil business and they make their home in Pincher Creek. They have four children and four grandchildren.

Harvey passed away in 1954. Gladys resides in the Hardisty Nursing home in the city of Edmonton.

Chris Jones

I was born in Calgary on March 27th, 1946. My first years were spent on the farm where I spent a sheltered life attending school at Sheep Creek, until grade 9, and then went to Turner Valley High School. During the summers and after leaving school, I worked on several farms and one winter at the curling rink at Red Deer Lake.

In the spring of 1964, I started a sheet metal apprenticeship. After completing my trade, I met and subsequently married Brenda Leak on August 30th, 1969.

After living in Calgary for four years, we packed up our belongings and with our two children, Pamela and Shelly, left for Prince George, B.C. where we now live.

Jones, Elliene (Burns)

Daughter of Frank and Mabel Burns, born September 25th, 1921 in Sequim, Washington, U.S.A. My mother and dad lived at Hussar, Alberta at the time, but for reasons unknown to me, my mother went home to her mother's for me to be born. At six weeks of age, I was brought home to Hussar, where we lived until 1931. In July of 1931, we moved to the farm, four miles North of Black Diamond, formerly owned by the L'Hirondell's. This was great excitement for me, because for the first time I was able to attend school. At Hussar, we lived four miles from three different schools, which made it impossible for me to go. However with the aid of correspondence courses, I was ready to start grade five at New Valley. Those were very happy years for me, from the standpoint of companionship, which I had known little of previously. Under the excellent guidance of George Scott, the only teacher I had, I can look back to so many fond memories of Christmas concerts, school dances and

picnics on May 24th, that he so ably arranged out of his own time. I finished grade nine at New Valley which was the end of the line there. Times being what they were in those years, there wasn't the money available for tuition fees and board, to be sent where further schooling was available. I tried studying grades ten and eleven on my own, but found it was pointless. In 1939, my parents sold their farm to my Uncle Charlie Burns. We moved to Calgary where I took a hairdressing course. On completion of the course, my dad bought a beauty parlor for me, which I operated until 1949. In 1948, I married Ross Jones, he was working for James and Reimer, the oilfield heavy hauling contractors, and in 1949 was transferred to Edmonton, where we lived for three years. We returned to Calgary in 1952. Since that time I have changed occupations to being a bookseller. At present, I'm in my twelfth year in the Book Department at Hudson's Bay downtown. Up until just recently, my manager being Al Pallister, a familiar name of readers of this book.

J. Robert Jones
Feb. 4th, 1978

I started to school at Fordville the fall of 1948 and went for three years travelling back and forth with Mr. Barraclough, by car when the roads were fit and by team the rest of the time. At the end of this time Fordville was closed and we all went to Millarville, still with Mr. Barraclough. Mr. Dube had the cadets going strong at that time and I joined, eventually making sergeant. In 1961 I had one year at Turner Valley High school followed by a year at Western Canada in Calgary.

I started my apprenticeship in the sheet metal trade on July 1st, 1963 and have worked at it since, presently with Reggin Industries.

On June 9th, 1968, Christine Thiessen and I were married at St. Peter's, Elbow Drive and live in Calgary.

We have two children, Barry born May 27th, 1971 and Jason born April 16th, 1974.

Christine was the eldest daughter of Vern and Gladys Thiessen who lived in Millarville from 1948 to 1962.

Roger Jones
by Roger Jones

It was on Jan. 9, 1936 at the old Grace Hospital in Calgary that I was born, the first son of Edna and Stan Jones, who lived on the N.W., Sec. 33, T.21, R.3, W5th, and that was where I spent my childhood. I went to Fordville school for ten years — the same school my Mother attended, and the school that my Grandfather, Joe Standish, played a big part in originating in 1908. When Fordville closed, I took my high school at Millarville, and in 1953, went to work for Glen Champion and Art Cobb of Black Diamond on their gravel crusher.

Watching a dragline operate in the gravel pit close to the Fordville school had fascinated me, and for the next eight years I did little else. It must have fascinated the late Jack Sutherland, then Reeve of the M.D. of Foothills, who, when we were operating in his division, would sit for hours when the weather was good, watching the bucket swing back and forth.

In 1962, when Champion Construction sold out, I went into a venture of my own — "South Fork Transporation" — hauling sulphur from the plant at Turner Valley and loading it on cars at the old Imperial Oil warehouse in Okotoks. When this ended in 1969, I switched to a backhoe operation which I still conduct in Turner Valley.

Among my childhood memories, the most exciting was probably the day we had the runaway coming home from school. Most of the time we went in Mr. Barraclough's car, but when the roads were bad we went with a team. We went cross country with the team, and at one point there were two gates quite close together, and when we stopped at the first gate, Mr. Barraclough led the horses through, but they were a young team and knocked him down. They had barely got started to run when they came to the next gate, in which they got tangled up. At this point we bailed out in some disorder, but before Mr. Barraclough caught up, they got going again, rolling the democrat and smashing it up at the bottom of the hill. This democrat, which I believe had been bought from Malcolm Millar, was a cross between a democrat and a light wagon, and was the one that Herbert Welch used when he hauled the mail, and operated the stage between Calgary and Millarville in 1906. The remains were not worth fixing and were rolled into the creek, where the beavers later incorporated them into one of their dams.

The Priddis and Millarville Fair was always a big event, as both my parents entered many exhibits. I always had to gather a good supply of dry willow wood for the stove as this gave the desired heat for Mother's cooking. Other highlights were the odd dance and the Christmas concert, and the pre-Christmas trip to town was always a big event. Each summer I would spend a week or so with my grandparents and this meant a trip to town in the car and lunch at the Zoo. The rest of the time, when we were not at school, we made our own entertainment; hunting rabbits and grouse, fishing in the creeks, skating on the sloughs in winter, and having an inexpensive good time. In the spring of 1946, and again in 1947, I showed a calf at the Bull Sale in Calgary; June Hehr and Harvey Burrows also exhibited.

In 1959 I married Irene Blanchard, also from the Millarville district. Our first abode was a trailer which I pulled around to the gravel pits, but when winter came we bought a lot in Turner Valley and settled there. It was here that our first son, Andy, was born on July 11, 1960 at Turner Valley Hospital. Then on Feb. 3, 1966, our second son Peter was born in Calgary. The final member of the family, a daughter Kathleen, made her appearance on Oct. 25, 1975.

The R. D. (Doug) Jones Family

In 1968, the Jones family bought twenty acres of SE 35-21-2-W5 from Roy Latter. In subsequent years the land was cleared, fenced and seeded to pasture. Roy Latter "witched" a well and the water flowed abundantly, as predicted. In 1972 the Jones family built their home, also a small corral, and began cross-breeding domestic cattle to Maine-Anjou — an enterprise they still carry on, be it in a small way on twenty acres.

They have four children: David in Dental College, Saskatoon, Margaret and Mary both married and living in Calgary, and Dauna at home, attending school at Red Deer Lake. Doug is employed by Sun Oil Company Ltd. in Calgary.

O. Joyce

I was hired to teach at the Square Butte School in the Spring of 1930. The roads were in a very muddy condition at the time and I had a very difficult time reaching the Kendall ranch. I was told in a letter that I could get a ride out with the ranch truck from the Calgary Stockyards. Through some error I missed the truck although I waited at the Stockyards nearly all day. The next try was with the mail carrier from Midnapore. The mail carrier was new at the job. I believe it was his first trip. At each mail box along the way he had to examine and check to see if it was the right one for the letter or paper to be placed. Although we started at nine o'clock in the morning it was quite late and dark when we reached the Kew Post Office. The horses were almost exhausted wading through the deep mud. The driver was just as tired. Mr. Kendall had sent a man to get the mail and an extra horse for me. There were still a few miles to go although it was now ten o'clock.

At the Kendall ranch I had a log cabin for my use and I ate with the ranch hands. It wasn't long before I discovered that I could board with the Lyall family. This suited me much better so I made the move. I was soon to find that the Lyalls were a wonderful family. I was very lucky indeed. Mrs. Lyall was a hard worker and a wonderful Scotch cook. And I don't mean stintingly with food. There was always lots of it. I had been treated to this type of food where I boarded, going to Normal in Calgary and I liked it.

Mr. Lyall was quite skilful at the game of cribbage and I enjoyed making the effort to win once in awhile.

Another source of entertainment each evening at five o'clock was the Fibber McGee and Molly radio programme. During this half hour even the cows had to wait as all the milking ceased until McGee opened his famous closet door.

Mrs. Kosling's Father, Mr. Northover would drop

Ready to go home. Spring 1930, Silvester children, Peterson children, Billy Kendall, Joe Bannerman, Joan Kosling. Square Butte School.

1927 Ford and its owner, along with the Silvester children ready to go to Calgary one Saturday morning. 1930. Square Butte School.

in occasionally as he passed the school and provide a bit of philosophy, which I enjoyed.

I shall not soon forget a trip Dick Lyall and I made to Calgary in the OLD FORD. There was about one foot of snow on the ground when we left for Calgary. When we were ready to leave the City for home there was about one foot of mud. Poor Dick had to push the car nearly all the way. We arrived back at the Lyall home in time for me to have breakfast and go to school.

Oh! yes the school. There were the Silvester children, Joey Bannerman, Joan Kosling and Billy Kendall. For a time a family by the name of Petersen lived near by and so there were three Petersen children.

In later years I often had nearly thirty pupils in a class and ten or more different classes per week. It was then that I learned how to teach.

Mabel Kamphaus and Petersen Family

My parents' farm location at the time we lived at Millarville was N.W.¼, Sec. 23, T.21, R.3, W.5. My Mom, Johanna Caroline Christine Petersen, and my Dad, Jens Christian Petersen left Fynn, Denmark, the year of 1909, landed in New York and settled there 2 years on a homestead. Then they moved up to Biggar, Saskatchewan in 1911. At this time they already acquired 2 children. I do not know how long my parents

Amelia, Chris, Aksel and Gordon digging a well on Millarville farm.

homesteaded in Biggar, as they moved from there up around Airdrie, Alberta, and from there to Okotoks. At this time they had 5 children, and here at Okotoks is where the twins, Mabel and Oluf were born. This gave them 10 children. (Whoa; hold on; don't chuckle yet! There are 3 more after that!) They didn't know about birth control in those days. They knew about love. Love your neighbour. Love one another. Yes! I remember the great love people had for each other in those days. What happened? Where did it go? Nowadays they call it sex, along with all the four letter words.

I do not remember how old I was when Mom and Dad moved from Okotoks to Kew. I just barely remember starting school there. I remember the long narrow road cut out through all those tall, tall, lanky poplars — a mile and a half to walk. As I was walking to school with my older brothers and sisters, away up ahead, suddenly to my surprise, this big bobcat or lynx or whatever, jumped out of the ditch and crossed over the road in front of me. Well, I, as a very young girl, was so startled, I wheeled myself around on one leg and made a bee line for home. Man, was I scared!

Here, we also had missionaries come and teach us Sunday School. I remember they held it under the trees in summer.

Also, we had to haul our drinking water. We got it from a river near by. There at the river lived a real elderly man. To my young eyes at that time he seemed to be ancient. Long white hair, long white beard — I was very shy of him. But, we used to wait for him to come out and break a hole in the ice to get his water. Then we'd move in, and get ours too. His name was Mr. Northover. At Kew is where my brothers Gordon and Alfred were born.

Then Mom and Dad moved to Millarville where we went to Fordville School. Our teacher's name was Mr. Bob Standish. This was approximately 1934. This farm (N.W.¼, Sec. 23, T.21, R.3, W.5) is where my brother Carl was born. Now there were 13 children (baker's dozen). My dad was a strong man, a hard worker, and loved his children dearly. He worked for all the neighbours at one time or the other. He cleared the quarter section by hand. There wasn't much money around in the 30's. I remember Dad haying for Kennedy's — they paid $3.00 a week. That bought our sugar, coffee, flour, yeast, coal oil for the lamps, oats and wheat for seeding, and garden seeds. Mother didn't buy our clothes — she made them all from 100 pound sugar and flour sacks. Our house was made of rough lumber, no curtains on the windows. We had straw mattresses made from potatoe sacks, and goose and duck down comforters to sleep in, four children to one bed. Thank goodness for that, as we kept warmer in winters. Our heater was made from a big 45 gallon gas drum. We had a big oak table, and chairs, the only pieces of furniture we owned, besides the big black wood cook stove. I remember we bathed in a big round galvinized tub, which Mom used to wash clothes in, with a scrub board. This was a big one-roomed house, so Dad added a room on for him and Mother to have to themselves for privacy. I remember my baby brother Carl being born in there. Us kids were all curious, and were trying to see through the cracks in the walls where the slabs joined, so Dad hung a blanket up to stop that invasion.

Us kids had to do a lot of work too, help with the haying, milking, feeding hogs etc. I remember the Fordville School District paid all children for taking care of reducing the gopher, crow and magpie reproduction, by catching gophers, doing away with them, and saving the tails for a nickel; crow and magpie eggs as well. We raided all the nests we could find. With 13 kids in the family, we sure gathered in the eggs, and tails of gophers while our family multiplied. There are 38 nephews and nieces from those 13 children, as of today.

We also had to take turns to get to school one hour before the rest of the kids to light the stove to get the school warm for class to start. For this we got 10¢ a morning. At the end of class, one child would stay behind and sweep the floors and clean the blackboards off for the next day. This was also 10¢. We helped Daddy get a little money in the house for the bare essentials.

I know my Dad made this cutter (it's like a sleigh), pulled by a team or one horse. He put a canvas over it

Jim Petersen at Kew.

to close it in. Inside, he had pot-bellied black stove in the middle, so we could keep warm going to school. We had very little cloth, just running shoes for foot wear.

The families I remember the best were the Fishers, Toshes, Spooners, Scattertys, Halls, Lee's store, Dieneses, Jensons, Winthrops, Williamsons, Wilkinsons, Kennedys, Wildermans, Standishes, Barracloughs, and last was Hughie Cawthorn, as he was the boy that rode horse back 3 miles to our place, to tell Mother that our Dad passed away in Calgary hospital. My Dad was 62 then. That left Mom with still 10 kids to raise. I remember a few donations of new clothes from neighbours, I think.

I remember Bob Standishes home he built on the hill by the Fordville School. He had a half acre fenced in, a nice house, garage, and a beautiful sunken garden, sitting there in the middle of nowhere, just farmers all around, and poor ones at that. Yes! He worked hard on his home. It was just gorgeous. I used to work for his wife on weekends. He also had a lovely root house, where he kept his vegetables, and wines. One night some of the bigger boys broke into it and took his wine. The Petersen family was accused of that. But luckily when the police came to our house, we were all home. Yes, my dad was sure upset — I had never seen him so upset in all my life! But later we learned who the culprits were.

One evening Dad sent me for the cows. They were grazing on the old Hudson Place across the road from us. As I was chasing them home, I had a long green willow that I tore off a bush to switch them with. Well, all were walking home calmly, so I had nothing better to do, but push the stick in the ground in front of me as I walked, and it flung up, hit me in the eye, and left a sliver right in the centre of my pupil. Mom tried for 4 days to get it out. No luck, so she and I started to walk to Kennedys where Dad worked, picked up $3.00 in advance, and walked 18 miles before we got a lift to Calgary, where we saw Dr. Robertson to take it out. I wore one eye patch for one month after that, with drops every day. I was called the one-eyed bandit for a year.

I can remember hauling water from up near Bob Standishes place with the lumber wagon and three 45 gallon barrels. One night, about dusk, on our way back, my brothers Jim and Askel, and I were held up by three boys on horse back, handkerchiefs over their faces and they drew play guns. When we told Daddy he said, "Too bad you didn't think to throw a bucket of water over them". Isn't that just like boys.

There was a big lake just behind the school where we swam in summer and skated in winter. I remember we would all gather there after chores were all done, for a skate out in the moonlight. It was very lovely, especially when Billy Williams was along to skate with — my childhood crush.

We had a big corral for the horses, and a big red barn with a boys' outhouse at one end of the barn and a girls' at the other end. We took the corral gate off and used it for a teeter-totter over the corral fence, with 4 on each end. Whoopee! What fun!

I don't remember who mother sold our farm to. When we left Millarville in 1946, March 16, we arrived at New Westminster, B.C. This is where Mother, Mabel, Alfred, and Carl lived for about eight years. Actually it was 35 miles out of town at Sunnyside Road, on a chicken farm.

I married on September 23, 1948, am a mother of 2 girls and a son. My career is Practical Nursing. I now lived in Terrace, B.C. — 4706 Olson Ave., V8G 2A3. I would like to hear from anyone mentioned in here. Hello old friends, neighbours!

Ronimus (Rusty) and Helen Kary

Rusty was born in Odessa, Russia, in 1904, the son of George and Kathy Kary. The family first came to the United States, settling at Goodrich, North Dakota. In 1910, they moved to Hemaruka, Alberta, where his father took a homestead. This is the area where Dr. Harry and Dr. Dave Lander, well-known doctors in the Black Diamond district, first hung out their shingle. Rusty grew up in that area until about 1928. His brother Henry had the Corner Service Station on Highway 9, near Carbon so Rusty moved there to work for him.

It was here he met his future wife, Helen. She is the daughter of Gottlieg and Mary Ohlhauser, who came to Carbon from North Dakota to homestead. Helen was born in Minot, North Dakota, in 1906. She was the only daughter with six brothers, four of whom came with their parents from the United States, Ed, Emil, Teddy (Helen's twin) and Fred. Two more boys were born in Alberta, Art and Leo.

Helen and Rusty were married in September, 1930, and moved to the land Mr. Olhauser Sr. had bought west of Turner Valley. It was the homestead of Mr. Ridley, who had come to the district in 1895. The original log house was in quite good condition, and was Rusty and Helen's first home. Economic conditions were not very good at this time, the "Dirty Thirties" were just starting. The Karys were to receive

Rusty and Helen Kary before their marriage. About 1930.

Kary Family. L. to R. Patsy, Rusty, Helen, Buddy and Richard.

groceries in exchange for keeping the place in repair. However, sometimes the groceries were late in arriving and the pantry would become quite empty, but they were a very resourceful pair. Once, running out of coffee, they toasted dry bread in the oven until it was crisp and brown, rolled it with a rolling pin, put it in cans and used it as a substitute for coffee.

Rusty decided to hunt partridge for a change of diet. He counted his .22 shells, and finding he only had five, care was taken not to waste any. Luck was with him and he got three fine birds. What a feed they had for a couple of days! Those were hard but happy times.

The first child, Richard, was born in the log house, also daughter Lorna. Mrs. John Anderson and Dr. Hall officiated at both births. Their third and fourth children, Harold (Buddy) and Patsy, were both born in Turner Valley in Mrs. Larosee's Nursing Home.

The Karys lived in the log house until Mr. and Mrs. Ohlhauser came from Carbon to live. They bought a house, had it moved to the farm, and Rusty and Helen and their family lived with them until their own house was built. Later, they moved it to their own property, the N.E. ¼ of 16-20-3w5.

Rusty worked for oil companies, the Model, Phillips Petroleum, Anglo-Canadian and for Home Oil, where he was on the drilling crew when Home No. 3 was drilled.

As the children became of school age, they first attended North Turner Valley School, later Plainview School and when it was closed, they were bussed to Sheep Creek School by Dan Dudenhoeffer.

The Karys bought more land, the N.W. ¼ of 21-20-3-W5 and started a herd of Black Aberdeen-Angus cattle, buying their first heifers from Archie Hitchell.

In 1949, while working in the bush, Rusty had a very serious accident. A large tree fell on him, pinning him to the ground. Among other injuries, his hip was badly broken and he was in the hospital for several weeks. A pin had been put in the broken hip but caused such pain it had to be removed and skin was taken from his shin and grafted on the hip. It was a long time before he

L. to R. Lorna, Harold (Buddy) and Patsy, Rusty and Helen Kary's family.

New Valley School May Day celebration 1941. L. to R. David Stanhope, Jim Kohler, Lilibeth Kohler, unknown, May Kohler, Pat Stockton, Bud Hovis, Thera Hovis. Teacher's car and teacherage in background.

was able to resume his work, but he persevered and in time got along very well.

The following year, 1950, was a sad one for the family when they lost their eldest son Richard.

Lorna married Don Blair of High River and they had a daughter, Tracy. Lorna passed away in 1976.

Buddy married Marilyn Hill from Turner Valley. They have lived in Carstairs, Alberta, for several years, where Buddy works for Home Oil. They have three children, a daughter, Linda, and two sons, Wayne and Murray. They also have one grandchild.

Patsy married Garth Whitford, and they make their home in High River, where Garth has Navajo Trucking. They have a family of five, four girls, Tami, Cindy, Sherry and Shelley and one son D'Arcy.

Rusty passed away in 1965 and Helen makes her home on her farm, enjoying visits from her family and their children.

Ruth (Coffin) Keiver

I feel pleased the Committee asked me to contribute to your book. My time in your district was only for two years, term of 1939-40; 1940-41 as teacher at New Valley School. I left in June 1941 to be married to Alvin Keiver and moved to a farm near Three Hills, where I still reside.

I have many pleasant memories of those two years, such as the young people's group at Christ Church; Christmas concerts at school, visits to neighboring farms.

The first term (1939-40) I boarded with Mr. and Mrs. L. Mitchell. The next year the School Board built a teacherage on the school grounds, and living alone was not to my liking. I bought a Model T and went home to Calgary as many week ends as possible.

Both terms, the school only numbered 9 or 10 and so the pupils and I were more intimate than the class

rooms of today. Besides teaching, I was also janitor and fireman.

I taught at our local school the first year I came to Three Hills (1941-42). Then I quit, had three children and went back teaching at Torrington in 1957, I taught there seven years and then went to Linden School for four years. In 1968 I retired (so I thought) and did a bit of substituting until the next spring, I fell into a librarian's job, again at Torrington School and for the seven years I did that and last year I really retired.

Our oldest boy died in 1953 of polio and our other boy, Glen and daughter Judy are both married. Glen farms with Alvin, but has his own home on his land. Judy married a farmer and they live four miles west of Torrington. I have eight grandchildren.

As to my retirement, I really enjoy it. I have many hobbies. We are avid square dancers and also do quite a bit of travelling.

Jean T. (Waugh) Kelly

Third daughter, born in Millarville, to Mr. and Mrs. Joseph Waugh. Joe Waugh and his wife Jean were old timers and homesteaders in the Millarville district as you have read in "Our Foothills" Book One.

When Sheep Creek School first opened in 1928 I, along with eight other students, was the first to begin. Miss Pat Jameson was my teacher during the years I attended.

My growing up years in Millarville were happy years. I enjoyed horseback riding, dancing in the Rancher's and Kew Halls, playing Badminton, taking part in the plays that our Dramatic Club put on from time to time.

After leaving school my greatest ambition was to operate a business of my own, and become a career woman and be rich. However I tried a few different occupations in Calgary and also in Banff. These positions didn't particularly interest me — neither did the life

Foothills Grocery. Proprietor, Jean Waugh.

My Dad passed away twenty-one years ago, leaving an emptiness in all our hearts. Mother, who will be ninety years of age in March, is now residing in a private local hospital and is in fairly good health.

We have a family of three daughters. They were educated in Vancouver and all went to U.B.C. and all three graduated as teachers and still teaching.

Our oldest daughter, Barbara Jean, married Bill Johnson and they are making their home here in Vancouver with their two year old son, Paul, and another little one to arrive in April of this year.

Our second daughter, Janet McTavish, is married to Garry Linn and they are residing in Surrey, B.C.

Our youngest, Lorna Jo, is living in Vancouver and teaching in Delta, B.C.

After our daughters got married or went out on their own, Tom retired and he and I sold our home and moved into a self owned apartment, changing our name to "Riley" as we are now "Living the life of Riley" travelling when we feel like it and enjoying our friends and family, especially our little grandson.

Tom still enjoys singing and belongs to a local choir and I just keep busy. We have had a very good life here in Vancouver for the last thirty-two years but I will always have happy memories of the good old days in the foothills and of our many friends and neighbors.

in the city. When the Turner Valley Oilfield started to move northward I thought "This is my chance to go into business on my own" — so I opened "Foothills Grocery" on the north-east corner of my Father and Mother's quarter section of land. A year later I opened a coffee shop which my sister Jo operated. We were known throughout the oilfields as the "Chinaman" and "The Yew".

It wasn't exactly a glamorous career and neither did I become rich but we had a flourishing business and many good times. Best of all, I met my future husband, Tom Kelly, who worked in the oilfields and lived in Black Diamond. After four years I sold my store and coffee shop. Just as the drilling began to peter out in the north end, Jo and I went to Vancouver where I worked for the winter, returning to Banff for the summer season to work in a curio shop where I had previously worked. That summer Tom and I became engaged and were married in December of the same year, 1946.

We started our married life in Tom's little bachelor house in Black Diamond, but only for a very short time. Work was scarce in the Turner Valley oilfields at that time and it was so cold and the snow so deep, we decided to sell out and move to Vancouver where we have been ever since. Tom got work in steel construction and we bought our home with a suite upstairs, which my Mother and Dad occupied. There was a method in our madness, having "Built-in-Baby Sitters."

Tom and Jean (Waugh) Kelly and grandson, Paul Johnson, 6 months.

Pat Kelly

Pat Kelly was an Irishman and was reported to have a drinking problem. He was also said to be a licensed chemist (druggist). He worked for Cross at the A7 for many years, and was married while there. There was a daughter, but his wife must have passed out of the picture by the time he came to this country. He worked for Hugh Macklin and Bill Oliver and was working for Kieran's one fall when we threshed there. He ignored us completely and spoke only to Johnny or ''The Boss''. In later years he stayed with George Sylvester and George said he was extremely clean in his habits, and a good Catholic. I believe he qualified for assistance under the 7U Brown fund for worn out cowboys and died in High River.

George L. Kelson, 1895-1976. Gwynydd M. Kelson, 1908-

written by Gwynydd Kelson
Brand: $\overline{UE}$

George L. Kelson was born at Old Sudbury, Gloucester, England. He grew up on a farm and was educated at the local school. Apart from farming he took a tremendous interest in fox-hunting and all equestrian sports, and cricket. He came to Canada in 1927 and worked for the late Duncan McIntyre, who farmed north of Okotoks; later he was with Morgan Holden at Midnapore, where he broke and schooled horses. Mr. Holden always claimed that they set a record, seeding twenty acres of oats, non-stop. All the work horses were away working on road construction, so they had only two colts that had never been hooked up, and two saddle mares. They pushed the seeder out

into the field, hooked up the four horses. George drove them and Mr. Holden ran with buckets of grain to keep the seeder filled. Surprisingly it turned out a good crop of oats, without many misses.

On October 7, 1939, George married Gwynydd M. Thomas who was born in Okotoks, the second daughter of Mr. and Mrs. E. H. Thomas. She received her education at Panima School, Okotoks and Crescent Heights High School in Calgary, where Mr. Aberhart of Social Credit fame was principal; then went on to Normal School in Calgary. After graduation she taught one year at Laughlin Rural School, Chinook, then a year in Okotoks. She went to England with her mother for three months; on returning she taught at Pine Creek School near DeWinton until 1939. Holidays were spent on the farm. Horses were always her greatest interest. With her father's and George's help she schooled, rode and showed many horses in Calgary, Edmonton and any local shows and Gymkhanas in the district.

In 1939 George and Gwynydd farmed Cottonwoods Ranch, W½-S30 an N½-S31-T20-R1-W5, in partnership with Mr. E. H. Thomas, and later purchased it in 1949. They farmed with horses until 1947, when they pur-

Gwynydd Kelson on Chatter Box sold at Calgary Horse Sale 1946.

George and Gwynydd Kelson's wedding October 7, 1939.

George and Gwynydd Kelson with their team of Belgiums.

chased a John Deere "D" Tractor. They raised, bought, broke and sold a good many horses while they farmed with them. They still kept a few show horses and jumpers. Their horses got scattered as far west as Victoria, B.C. and east to Nova Scotia, and one even went to Bermuda.

They also raised cattle, pigs and poultry and had success in showing market steers in the Calgary Spring Show.

In the winter of 1972 they took part in the film "The Country Doctor" in which Dr. W. M. Gibson played the part of the doctor. It was done under the direction of Tom Radford of Edmonton, with Bob Reece and Reevan Dalsey assisting. Part of it was staged in this house. Their neighbor, T. Macmillan, also took part in it. It was quite a success, and has also been shown in New Zealand and Australia.

In 1976 George died as a result of an accident and his wife, Gwynydd carries on at the farm.

Alexander and Carolyn Kemp

Al is the son of Walter and Francis Kemp, and was born and raised in Calgary. Carolyn is the daughter of Walter Stewart and Adeline Pearson, and was born and raised in Crossfield.

After working in Calgary for 3 years, Al returned to school, at Orange Coast College in Costa Mesa, California, to study Fish and Game. He studied there for two years, then transferred to Humboldt State College in Arcata, California, where he continued in Fish and Game for another semester. Then in 1962 he came back to Calgary to work at the University until May, when he and Carolyn were married, and he started a new job as a draftsman in Edmonton.

At the same time Carolyn went to school in Crossfield, Calgary and Beiseker. In 1960 she entered the University of Alberta to study Medical Laboratory Science. She was ready to write the examination to qualify as a Registered Technologist when she was married in May, 1962.

Darrel was born in Edmonton in 1963 and Jody in 1964. When Jody was five months old the family moved to Moscow, Idaho, where Al entered the Faculty of Engineering at the University of Idaho and Carolyn was one of the medical technologists at Gritman Memorial Hospital. Al received his degree in Mechanical Engineering in 1967 and accepted a job in Toronto, Ontario. The family lived in Ontario for two years, returning to Calgary August 1, 1969, where Karen was born 12 days later. In 1970 the Kemps and three other families purchased the S.W. ¼ 31-21-2-W5 from Jean Standish. When subdivision approval was received in 1972, the family moved on to their parcel. The temporary house was a school bus "camper". Jody and Darrel were the only Millarville school students who lived in a bus. The weather during the summer of 1972 was less than ideal for building a new home and Al and Carolyn did a lot of the work themselves so progress was very slow. The family moved in to the unfinished new house on Christmas Eve, 1972, and the pool was first used in 1974.

The whole family took an active part in sports activities and community affairs. Darrel played hockey every year and both Darrel and Jody played baseball. Al coached baseball, with Carolyn as a stand-in, and Karen was a great spectator. Carolyn is vice-president of the main board at the Race Track for 1978-'79.

In the summer of 1979, the Kemps sold their home and purchased the N ½ 16-20-1-W5 from Wilbur McHarg. They moved August 30, and are in the process of planning another new home. The move was made with mixed feelings, as everyone was sad to leave dear neighbors and friends but looked forward to having more land.

Frank C. Kendall

I was born in Calgary in 1928, the third son of Eugene and Katherine Kendall. We lived at Kew on 33-20-4-w5. I attended school at Square Butte School through Grade 9. I then attended Mount Royal College for 4 years, graduating in 1948, I then attended 2 years at S.A.I.T. taking Industrial Electricity. I was in the Reserve Army while at M.R.C. and having learned marksmanship at M.R.C. won many shooting awards at Sarcee Range.

I went back to the Ranch, later becoming Vice-President and part owner of Kendall Stock Company. My brand is KU LR.

I was very active in the Square Butte Community, holding various offices. I was one of those who helped move the former Kew Hall to its present location as Square Butte Hall. I was also an officer in the Square Butte Gun Club.

I made three trips to Alaska, two were photography and one was hunting and photography and have shown my pictures in various halls around Millarville area.

On February 10, 1968, I married Anita L. Hill of Regina, Sask., and Calgary. We have two daughters, Dinah Maria and Meagan Colene.

In the fall of 1973, we sold the ranch to Z. Hanen. John moved to Amisk, Mother moved to Calgary and later to Lacombe and I moved to Lacombe. Our farm is located 1-42-28-w4 in the county of Ponoka. We have a mixed farm.

Our children attend Crestomere School and in 1978 are in Grades 2 and 4. We belong to the Lincoln Community Association, and the Crestomere Recreation Association and Anita has held offices in the Lincoln Community Circle.

Elizabeth Joan (Kosling) Kendall
b. September 19, 1924

I grew up on the homestead, SE¼ Sec. 17, T. 21, of my Father, John Fred Kosling; a wilderness home carved out of the bush; but it meant freedom for my father whose previous life had been working for others. Born in 1889 near Billings, Montana, he left

Fred Kosling at Coal Creek, near Burn's mine, with dog Zippy. March 1911-12.

home at 14 after an altercation with his father. His only communication with his family was a chance meeting with his brother in Boise, Idaho a while later.

He followed the cowboy life for some years, riding for ranches, trapping wild horses on the Idaho desert, following the rodeos. There was also a stint of packing for the U.S. Army, which included an ocean voyage to the Philippines to deliver a load of army mules. Starting at Fort Benton, Montana he went on board the freighter at New York, then to Brussels, Belgium, for part of the cargo of mules, the remainder loaded at Cherbourg, France. The voyage was through the Mediterranean, the Suez Canal and into the Indian Ocean. It was here a fierce storm was encountered that kept the crew battened below the decks with the mules for five long days and nights. Many of the mules died from terror and the crew thought they might follow them. On the morning of the fifth day they looked out a porthole and saw another large freighter tossing like a cork on the huge waves.

The storm did abate and when they reached the Philippines the mules were unloaded by slings into the ocean from where they swam ashore. A cargo was loaded and the ship returned home.

Then, in 1906, the great cattle ranges of the last frontier in Alberta beckoned and my father and two companions started by train from Boise to the Peace River country. This was the disastrous winter of 1906-07 and upon reaching Athabaska in April they were greeted by blizzard conditions and -40 degrees. Upon asking an old fellow they met how long the winters

Fred Kosling on his Sunday horse at Lineham Ranch. 1911.

lasted, he said he didn't know as he had only been there a year; they at once decided the country was not for them. My father stopped off in Edmonton but the other two decided they would return to sunnier climes.

After working there on construction, where the frozen ground had to be blasted, he moved on to Calgary and to jobs near Okotoks, first with Dave Thorburn at the Gladys Ridge, looking after Clydesdales, then to the Lineham ranch. This was in the days of the logging operations up the Sheep and Highwood rivers and many trips were made to the logging camps with supplies. These trips usually took three days.

After the death of Bill Lineham, my father left the Lineham ranch in 1915 and had various jobs. He did some packing for the Government surveyor Peterson. He also spent some time with Sam Brown the only Ranger from the Highwood to the Bow in those days. Sam Brown had been a timber cruiser for Lineham. On one occasion my father decided to go out on a patrol with Sam Brown to look over the country. They went up the South Sheep River and decided to spend the night in the old logging camp near Burn's Mine. They chose the shelter of a shack whose roof was partially gone but was dry inside; whereas the others were cold and damp from leaking roofs. It was a fine moonlight night and they awoke in the middle of it to see a Grizzly looking at them through the open door. No doubt these were his sleeping quarters too. Sam Brown grabbed his .30-.30 and fired a wild shot which wounded the bear. With a bellow of rage he made for them, but with the shot they were up and over the wall and into the blacksmith shop which had a stout door and a good roof of logs and sod. The bear raged and tore at the logs trying to get at them, while they inside, as helpless as rats in a trap, without gun or axe, prayed through the endless night that the building was stout enough to hold. Morning came and the bear left with a trail of blood behind him and the logs on the roof moved four feet.

From these adventures my father went to work for Carl Ohlson near Turner Valley, where he met my mother Caroline Hannah Northover, the teacher at Plainview School. They were married January 3, 1922 and went into partnership with Dave Stewart for a while. They decided that the homestead in the hills which had been filed in 1917 would be a better home and so in the Spring of 1925, when I was six months old, the move was made.

The early years were the homestead life — gathering wild berries in Summer and helping with the haying; my job driving the team as the hay was forked on the rack and then tramping down the stack. This was during the 1930's when the summers were hot and dry and the winters were cold. I always had a good horse to ride to school and go for the milk cows — a daily summer chore. In winter there was wood and water to get.

A time I vaguely remember, when I was about two years old, was the winter my father cut his foot with an adze while building the log blacksmith shop. Infection developed in the bone and he was forced to go to the hospital in Calgary and have the bone scraped. This resulted in six weeks in bed until the bone healed. My mother and her father, Alfred Northover, were left in the middle of winter to do the homestead chores. There were five cows to milk and my mother, who had never milked in her life was suddenly confronted with these animals, some of which were none too quiet. One cow in particular had to have her legs tied at every

Joan Kosling Kendall with her Grandfather, Alfred W. Northover. 1926.

milking. My Grandfather had never lived this life either and he wanted no part of the cows, but he did lasso their legs and hold them while my mother milked. I can remember being tucked safely away in a manger of hay while this struggle went on, always accompanied by loud shouts from my Grandfather, who believed that lots of noise around animals kept them under control. Great was the rejoicing when my father arrived home one dark night during a snowstorm, having walked ten miles from Millarville after getting a ride from Calgary with the mailman.

Fred Kosling brush plowing at homestead at Kew with eight horse team. 1921-22.

Another time, my father was clearing brush, again with an adze. He had the adze poised for chopping when, sensing something behind him, he turned to see a bear standing looking him over. He was so startled the adze dropped and chopped his foot at the instep. It was a nasty cut and by the time he got home his boot was full of blood. Infection was the big fear so iodine was poured in the wound. He was all winter with a sore foot, as every time it was safely on the mend something happened; first he kicked an ornery calf to get it moving and broke the wound open; then a few weeks later a horse stepped on the same foot — but, finally it did heal.

There were other problems with bears. We ran our cattle on timbered land and for a few years lost calves to grizzlies. Once my father found a big yearling beside the creek, dead from a massive wound clawed in its side either cougar or bear. Later he was walking through this timber at dusk to check on the cattle when around a turn in the path he came upon two bear cubs playing. He recognized them as grizzly cubs — one was dark brown; the other was white, an albino. He didn't wait to see where the mother was; just made a quick change in plan and turned as fast as possible towards home — having to go about a mile and a half in the dark. He decided that his calves were going to feed those growing cubs.

Part of his land, an open hillside, could be seen from our house, and one evening a few weeks later when we were at the barn, we saw a big bear and two cubs, one dark and one white, come over the hill half a mile away. About five minutes later a commotion of bawling and bellowing broke out from the range cattle in the vicinity and above the din rose the agonized bawling of a calf. A grizzly was teaching her cubs how to kill.

I ran to tell my father, who was in the barn. He only had a small calibre gun, .25-.35, but decided to go and see if he could get a shot at the bear. The area where the cattle were milling was densely forested so he climbed a large Poplar. Although he could see nothing but an occasional glimpse of the cows, he fired a volley into the air. The neighbors were contacted and the next morning a well-armed party of hunters went out — all they found of the calf was a hip bone, but they tramped over the whole area, firing off occasional volleys of shots. No doubt this alerted the bear to danger or she did not like her solitude disturbed because no more calves vanished after that. This particular land is where Hardee Lineham now lives. As a sequel to the story, about two years later Bob McKay shot a yellowish white grizzly on land to the North.

It was on this same open hillside where we saw the bear, that we had a garden for potatoes, high out of the frost. It was my job to go for potatoes on horseback and one hot day in August I was digging potatoes when my attention was drawn to a ridge to the West. A big pall of smoke and flame was pouring over the hill, billowing on the rising wind — a forest fire! Less than

half a mile from home. My galloping horse carried me homeward and on the road I met another galloping horseman, Dick Lyall, already going to alert the countryside. By dark a big party of firefighters was out to work through the night with axes, saws and shovels. Luckily the wind changed direction at dark and the fire turned back down the hill, burning in a huge horseshoe and its force died in the valley where it had started in a huge cottonwood struck by lightning. Rain a week later relieved the mop-up crew and the danger was over.

Before I went to school my mother taught at Square Butte School, two miles distant, so there was always the problem of what was to be done with me. Sometimes my Grandfather looked after me and many were the enjoyable hours we spent. He was always busy with a garden or walking in the woods and he taught me a love of both. When I was too young to walk far he carried me on his back in a little bag he made for the purpose. I also spent many hours with Mrs. George Lyall in her home and flower garden. When I was older my mother took me to school with her on horseback, where I was forced to keep school hours and be quiet. On the way home, to let off energy, I'd beat my heels against the flanks of the reluctant horse, trying to make it run, much to my mother's displeasure.

The big highlights for entertainment in my school days were the community dances; Rancher's Hall, Kew Hall, Red Deer Lake Hall and Square Butte schoolhouse and many were the good times as the rafters rang with the lilt of fiddlers and the mellow beat of the piano. My mother and dad played for the Square Butte dances — she on the piano and he on the accordion, accompanied usually by Cyrus McBee's fiddle and Mary Bell's guitar. Christmas concerts are a never to be forgotten memory of the old country schoolhouse. School days came to an end and I took teacher's training at Normal School in Calgary. It was war time and after one month, volunteers were called for, to go to remote districts. Early in October I embarked on the train for Edmonton and on to Mayerthorpe where I was to teach in a little school called Lily Lake — 10 miles West and North. It was a

Joan Kendall on her honeymoon at Elbow-Three Point Pass.

350

bitter winter, the snow knee deep by the end of October, but by April I was back in Calgary to finish Normal School. My next school was Balleyhamage just across the road from where the Leighton Centre now stands, and then on to a school at Madden west of Crossfield.

In 1947 I married Bill Kendall and from there my story is that of the sawmill days. From that time on I have held many positions including chief cook and bottle washer, bookkeeper, secretary and supply manager.

Since the closing of the mill and absence of crew there has been a return of quieter times and plans to take up the artistic pursuits I love so much.

John Scott Kendall
told by J.S.K.

I was born in Calgary, Alberta on September 28, 1926, second son of Eugene L. and Katherine Bryant Kendall.

I grew up on my parent's ranch (Sec. 33-20-4-W5, near Kew, Alta.), attending Square Butte School and later Olds Agricultural College, graduating in 1944. I was married Oct. 5, 1946 to Margaret Hazel Cullen of the Springbank district. We had five children:

Margaret Penny, born July 5, 1947, married James Hunter of Black Diamond, now living near Athabasca, Alta.

Jane Louise, born May 30, 1949, married John Holmlund of Canal Flats, B.C., now living at Leduc, Alta.

Eugene William Scott (Buck), born January 24, 1951, married Edith Lanman of Black Diamond, now living near Amisk, Alta.

John Roderick (Rick), born Feb. 2, 1956, married Ann Brookwell of Calgary, and lives here on the ranch property.

Paul Cullen, born May 9, 1962, still at home, attending High School.

I lived on the home ranch, working with my father and brothers following my schooling. After Father's death, I continued at the ranch until it was sold to Miss Zahava Hanan of Calgary in November, 1973, at which time, my wife and I purchased land (SE 34-40-9-W4) from Louis Delange near Amisk, Alberta, where we are presently residing.

My sons work the ranch with me, although Buck owns his own place near by. We grow grain, and raise cattle. This all keeps us pretty busy, but in the winter, we still have time to curl and ski.

Paul is interested in his school, his 4-H beef club, and finds time to ski also.

Katherine B. Kendall

I was born November 23, 1894, the second daughter of William L. and Martha A. (Dodge) Bryant, of Buffalo, Wyoming, U.S.A., where I grew up.

Katherine Kendall.

Although I am an American by birth, I am now a Canadian by naturalization, but I am very proud of my grandfather, Moses Dodge, who was the owner of, and also a participant, in the famous "Wagon Box Corral Fight", which took place near Fort Phil Kearny, Wyoming, U.S.A., in the summer of 1867.

Grandpa had a contract with the Government to furnish wood for the Fort, and on one of these trips the wood train and a small company of soldiers accompanying them were attacked by a horde of Red Cloud's warriors. The handful of soldiers and civilians were successful in fighting off the warriors by themselves and the use of the breech-loading Springfields, which were new at that time.

I attended Rock Creek rural school and the Buffalo grade and high schools. Two years after my father's death in 1911, I moved with the family to Los Angeles, California. I finished school there, attended normal school and business college. I then worked for six years and in 1923 came to Canada and was married July 26, to Eugene L. Kendall in Calgary. After a short honeymoon we went out to the ranch (Section 33-20-4w5) near Kew, which was to be my home for the next fifty years. The ranch was owned originally by John Quirk, who sold it to Pat Burns. Mr. Dole, then Ted Rawlinson, owned it. Mr. Kendall bought it from Ted Rawlinson.

We had four children: William Bryant, born June 16, 1924, married Joan Kosling. John Scott, born Sept.

28, 1926, married Margaret Cullen. Frank Cole, born Oct. 18, 1928, married Anita Hill. Marie Anne, born Nov. 21, 1931, married William Stewart. Sixteen grandchildren and six great-grandchildren have been added to the fold.

Mr. Kendall passed away August, 1948, but I continued living there until October 1973, when the property was sold to Zahava Hanan, of Calgary. I moved to Calgary, living there for three years and in September 1976 moved to Lacombe, Alberta.

Although I had stepped right from an office job in Los Angeles I was able to carry on the work due to my previous ranch experience. Although I must say I found it difficult without the direction of my mother.

I worked in the community and enjoyed my association with the Square Butte Community Club and Square Butte Ladies Club and also the Willing Workers W.I. of Millarville, which I first joined in 1927. I was also instrumental in getting a cairn erected in the Kew district honoring the late of John Ware.

The country where I went in 1923 has changed greatly and like all else, has responded to progress. The Kew Post Office was closed; dirt roads and open streams have been replaced by gravel roads and bridges. Tractors have taken over from the horses and the beautiful hills and valleys are dotted with gas well derricks. A large gas refinery plant sits on the top of a hill which once was grazed by cattle and horses. Great piles of suphur can be seen near the plant and heavy trucks haul daily from the plant. A sawmill came into being, on Fisher Creek, which has served the community well.

Square Butte School (1944-45)

by Margaret Kendall

When I first came to Square Butte (my first teaching school) in December 1944, there were only six students: Margaret, George and Johnnie Nylund, Jim and Tommy Silvester, and Marie (Dibbie) Kendall. They had been taking correspondence courses with Mrs. G. Granger as supervisor.

The school was very poorly equipped with books and such, as well as any sports equipment. I boarded with Mr. and Mrs. George Lyall, and did the janitor work at the school as well.

As I look back it was a very inadequate style of education as compared to that of today's, however, I think we were closer to the students and parents than what we are today. We had many good times, and the children were happy and co-operative, as we played games, went on hikes, etc. with younger and older ones together.

Kendall Stock Co. Ltd.

Incorporated Sept. 9th, 1922

Mr. Eugene L. (Gene) Kendall of Los Angeles, California, decided he wanted to fulfill a life ambition to start farming, so in the summer of 1921 he came to

Eugene Lamont Kendall, 1922.

Alberta and in due time purchased the Quirk Ranch at Kew, Alberta.

This was one of the oldest ranches in Alberta, first located in the High River country in 1882, and moved to the Sheep Creek district, which later became Kew. Two very well known cowboys moved the herd of cattle to the new location in 1887. They were Sam Howe and John Ware.

The ranch originally contained 3461 acres in all. There were 701½ acres deeded, comprising all or parts of Sections 27-28-33-34-T. 20 R. 4W5.

The lease land comprised all or parts of Sections 4-5-9 and 10, T. 21 R. 4W5 and sections 28 and 36 T. 20 R. 4W5, making 2117½ acres. Also S. 8-T. 21-R. 4W5 was leased from the Hudson's Bay Co. at $100 per annum but several years later the section was dropped.
Section 28, N.W. ¼ T. 20, R. 4W5, known as the Crow quarter was added some years later.

A license to irrigate was issued to John Quirk March 18, 1901. A water license for irrigation purposes was issued by the Dept. of Railway and Telephones at Calgary, the 16th day of December, 1930, to the Kendall Stock Co. Ltd., License No. 15 in the Bow River drainage and License No. 3 on Quirk Creek (formerly the North Fork of Sheep River). The license was renewed at Edmonton to water from Quirk Creek (North Fork of Sheep River) on the 15th day of March 1967. "The full right and liberty to construct, maintain and operate certain works, under the Irrigation Act,

Katherine Bryant Kendall, 1922.

Kendall family out for a ride. L. to R. Gene Kendall, Katherine Kendall, Bill, John, Frank and Dibby (Marie) Kendall.

through, over and upon part of the N. ½ of 23-20-4w5 was issued to the Kendall Stock Co. Ltd. Feb. 16th, 1928, at 10.20 A.M. Also the same rights were issued for S. 5-21-R. 4w5 at 10.18 A.M. of the same date.''

Mr. Quirk sold the ranch to Pat Burns of Calgary who in turn sold to John F. Dole of Calgary. Mr. Kendall purchased the ranch from Edward H. C. Rawlinson, who had a "Contract of Purchase" from John F. Dole.

Gene moved on to the ranch in January 1923 and by the summer he had brought in about 300 head of cattle. He maintained a herd of purebred Polled Hereford cows and bulls and many good purebred but unregistered cows in his grade herd. He later turned to the horned Herefords.

He bought from the Bar U Ranch at Pekisko a purebred Percheron stallion, "Templar" and two purebred females, "Ina" and "Pidgeon". He maintained a large herd of horses as all his work was done by horses at first.

The cattle were ranged on the lease land and in the summer on the Bow River Forest Reserve, although in later years they were all grazed at home.

Gene sold bulls at the Calgary Bull Sale for years and in 1933 he had the Grand Champion fat steer at the Calgary Bull Sale. He also showed cattle at the summer show during Stampede week and had the Grand Champion Bull there one year.

At one time he had several hundred sheep but the inability to get good shepherds forced him to sell all but they had done well for him.

One of the first things Gene did upon moving to the ranch was to clear brush, which was done mostly by the Stoney Indians and he also made and/or repaired 20 miles of fence.

Mr. Kendall lived here for 25 years but passed away after a lingering illness August 25, 1948. His family carried on until November 1st, 1973 when it was sold to Miss Zahava Hanan of Calgary and the families went their various ways.

Three Point Creek (formerly North Fork of Sheep River) bisects the crop land and Fisher Creek cuts through Section 10, so there was always water for man and beast. The spring at the home building was exceptionally good.

Before selling the ranch, the Imperial Oil built a gas plant in Section 4-21-R. 4w5 and its beam can be seen for miles. Many gas wells were drilled. Calgary Power reached every home; better and more roads were built and streams were bridged all which made the land more accessible and life easier than in 1923. It was a good ranch and home. The Kew post office was abandoned and Millarville serves the country now.

William Bryant Kendall

Born June 16, 1924 eldest son of Eugene L. Kendall, grew up on his father's ranch, the former Quirk ranch on the North Fork of Sheep Creek, (now Three Point Creek).

His early years were spent learning the ranching business, which involved a knowledge as broad as the work was hard.

Bill attended Square Butte School for Grades 1 to 9, riding horseback the distance of two miles there and back again. His energy was spent at recesses and noon hours on the sports he always loved — pitching for the baseball team, pole-vaulting over the schoolyard fence, and running endless miles in various games.

Sometimes the boundaries of the schoolyard were too confining. So on hot days he joined the other boys on a run to the creek for a plunge in the beaver dams.

Bill Kendall with his first coyote.

Bill Kendall with trophy mule deer. 1948.

This was the best of sports till the teacher wondered one day why the yard was so quiet; the girls not being able to make enough noise to cover the truants' departure and a stop was put to these ventures.

It was also great sport to hide in the ditches just outside the schoolyard fence and spook the cattle herds as they were driven by; till the enraged riders ran at them with their horses, or went to the school for further aid from the teacher.

When time palled there was the game of putting someone's horse out through a weak spot in the fence; with the owner's permission of course; so that an expedition could be launched outside the schoolyard to catch it. This resulted in several successful outings till one time the horse went further than expected and joined a herd of twenty or so others running in the two sections of lease adjoining the school. It required a day and a half of hard riding before it was captured and that put an end to that sport. It was too much like work.

After Grade 9, Bill attended Turner Valley High School for one year, took correspondence for one year and continued to work on the ranch. In 1947 he married Joan Kosling, his former classmate at Square Butte School. Their children are in various occupations around the country; Donna Lynn a Social Worker with the Federal Government in Saskatoon, Saskatchewan; David William a jet pilot with the Canadian Forces at

Cold Lake, Alberta; Philip Lamont with an accounting firm in Calgary, just writing his Chartered Accountant exams; Frederick Mark, a bartender in Vancouver and Katherine Laura still at home going to High School.

Bill's interest was always machinery, the animals taking second place, and in 1952 he began a small logging venture. This led to bigger undertakings and so it was that this business grew into Kendall Lumber Limited with the mill a landmark in the Square Butte area. (Its story told in another section). The Company is still operating on a limited basis.

Bill has always been an avid hunter, getting his first gun, a .22 at 12 years of age. At that time he had a small trapline where he caught coyotes, weasels and even a fox; and also trapped beaver which were flooding the lease land where his father ran cattle. His hunting ability continued through the years and many were the meals he provided for the table and many are the tophies that hang on his walls.

Primarily a big game hunter he has always been keen to hunt those most rare and wily species, the Mountain Sheep and the Grizzly Bear. He made two expeditions to Alaska with other hunting companions; once to Kodiak Island for a Kodiak brown bear and once to Fairbanks Alaska to Hayes Mountain for the rare white Dall sheep. Both were successful hunts.

In 1977 Bill shut down the logging and sawmill

Kendall Family. L. to R., Back: Joan, Donna, Monte, Laura, Bill. Front, L. to R.: Mark, David.

operations due to ill health, and is presently operating a retail lumber yard and still contemplating more hunting expeditions.

E. P. (Ed) Kenny

In February, 1969, Ed Kenny acquired an interest in the S.½ 33-21-2w5, in the Red Deer Lake area from Bob Winthrop and still farms the S.E.¼ of Section 33.

In November, 1969, he acquired the N.E.¼ of Section 14-21-4w5 in the Square Butte district, which was George Ingeveld's home quarter for many years. The original log barn and many of the log corrals built by George's father are still in use.

Ed's maternal grandfather, H. E. Price arrived from Philadelphia at Pile of Bones, N.W.T. (now Regina) in 1883 as a young boy and was the first naturalized citizen in the territory. Mr. Price later farmed in the Medicine Hat, Nanton and Redland areas during his long life. Ed's other grandfather (also Ed Kenny) arrived in Southern Alberta from Utah in 1895 and was the first ranch manager for the McIntyre Ranching Company. He subsequently was in partnership with Walter Ross in the Milk River area and later had ranches in the Gleichen and Redlands districts. He was also an early pioneer in oil exploration, primarily in the Okotoks area.

Despite this pioneer heritage, the present generation Kenneys are pretty much tenderfoot greenhorns (as their neighbors will agree) and the complexities of cow herding and barbed wire remain a mystery.

Ed has been engaged in the oil business in Calgary for many years and he and his wife, Nadine, and their five children (Susan, Beverley, Ross, Michael and Roger) spend very available minute at their second home at Square Butte where they run a small herd of Simmental Charolais cattle.

King, Charlie and Daisy (Pallister)

Charlie didn't go to school until he was eight years old as there was no school close by at that time. His mother taught his sister, Betty and himself until the New Valley School opened in January of 1928. He attended school there until the end of June 1936.

Charlie and Betty were some of the lucky ones that only had a mile to go to school and they always seemed to have a pony to ride. A lot of the children in those days had to travel 3 or 4 miles to school and had to walk either part of the time or all of the time.

In the fall of 1936 he attended the Olds School of Agriculture supposedly for 2 years. However, the first year Charlie was there measles and mumps broke out shortly after the Christmas holidays. As most of the people attending the college were from the country and had never been in contact with mumps or measles they spread like wild fire. He missed a month of school in quarantine. At one time almost ¼ of the school was quarantined with either the mumps or the measles.

Charlie graduated in the spring of 1938 which gave him the equivalent of 1 year of university in

Christmas 1971; Charlene, Margaret Ann, Daisy and Charlie King.

Family gathering 1976. L. to R., Back row: Evelyn and Ed McBee, Daisy and Charlie King. Middle row: Robert and Barbara Bruce holding daughters Valerie and Roberta, Margaret Ann and Charlene King, Dwayne and Charles McBee. In front: Tammy McBee.

agriculture, but liking outdoor life, he decided to let his schooling go at that and came home to help his father.

Shortly after returning from Olds he purchased 300 acres from Cecil Peacock. This being that portion of Section 33-20-2-W5 lying south and west of the north fork of Sheep Creek (now known as Three Point Creek). This land was in between the west half of section 34 and the north half of section 32, which Charlie's father owned. This joined their combined land together, as the home ¼, SE 5-21-2-W5 was now joined to the north half of section 32.

His father, Jack King, his sister, Betty and himself worked together for many years, raising purebred Herefords.

In 1953, Betty married Leonard Nelson, and that left Charlie and his dad working together on a share basis. In February 1957 the purebred Herefords were transferred to Charlie and he was on his own.

On December 27, 1960 he married Daisy Evelyn Bruce (Pallister). She had two children, Mary Evelyn, age 12, and Robert Elvin, age 10.

Evelyn married Ed McBee in February 1967. They live in a trailer on the farm. Ed drives a school bus, and helps with the farm work and the cattle.

Robert married Barbara Leaming in March 1972. They live in Calgary. Robert is a welder by trade.

Daisy and Charlie have two girls, Margaret Ann who was born in November 1962, and Charlene Wanda who was born in November 1966. Charlene is in Junior High at Millarville School and Margaret Ann is now attending Oilfields Junior Senior High in Black Diamond.

They are both interested in the cattle, and have been in the Stockland 4-H Beef Club ever since they were old enough to join.

Margaret Ann and Charlene King bring the registered Herefords home from the winter pasture. The herd was started by their grandfather, J. R. King in 1916 and is being passed down from generation to generation as both girls have cattle of their own from 4-H.

Richard Henry Cornwallis (Dick) King
by Jeanie (King) Slemko

Dick was born in 1910, son of W.H. and Lucy (Wilkin) King, spent his early years in the Millarville district. After his schooling in Alberta he went on to the University of British Columbia, graduating in 1936. He married Margaret Moffat of Victoria, British Columbia. They lived at the Big Missouri Gold Mine near Stewart, B.C. until 1941. There Dick was a geological engineer for Consolidated Mining and Smelting and Marg was the camp nurse.

In 1941, Dick and Marg and their two small daughters, Jeanie and Betty, moved back to Millarville to live on the W. H. King ranch. Dick worked for the Oil and Gas Conservation Board in Black Diamond as well as "ran" the ranch. Bill and Mary were born during the period that Dick and Marg lived at Millarville.

Marg, a girl from the city, quickly learned about the ranch life in Alberta. She learned to ride the "quiet" horses around the ranch, but was more enthusiastic about swimming. She found a good swimming hole in the North Fork of Sheep Creek (now called Three Point) where her four children learned to swim, not to mention all the cousins and friends.

R. H. (Dick) King and his wife Margaret.

Margaret King with children after baby's christening at Christ Church Millarville. L. to R. Jeanie, Margaret holding baby Mary. Front: Billy and Betty. Picture taken at ranch.

Dick was transferred to Calgary in 1951, and the ranch was sold except the bunk house and about 60 acres along the creek. The bunk house was moved onto the 60 acres and is now Dick's cabin where many gatherings have been held.

Marg died of cancer in 1963.

Dick retired from the Conservation Board in 1968 and worked in the Oil and Gas Department of Indian Minerals until 1977. Dick resides in Calgary but enjoys his cabin at Millarville.

When the first history book of the Millarville-Kew districts was in the process of being published, he served as president of the Historical Society for about ten years and was very interested in gathering the history of the area.

Jean Margaret married William Slemco and lives in Calgary. They have three children Margaret (Margy), Kathleen (Kathy) and Gordon (Gord).

Elizabeth (Betty) married Gordon Patterson. They have two girls, Dianne and Karen. Their permanent home is Calgary but at present they are touring Australia.

William Cornwallis (Bill) lives in Calgary but has lived in Waterloo, Ontario, Grand Cache, Alberta and Vancouver, British Columbia.

Mary Edith married Geoffry Goldie. They made their home at Prince Rupert and Ladysmith, B.C. aboard their sail boat. Mary died in a tragic accident at sea in 1978. They had no children.

As children, we remember "getting ready" for the Millarville Fair. During the winter we did all kinds of art and handicrafts etc. with the fair in mind. As soon as school was out we began working with our horses — standing still for mounting and dismounting, figure eights and circles at a walk trot and canter and lots of grooming. I even remember vacuuming the horses each day for the last week before the show. All the tack was well saddle soaped and polished. Plans were made for the Trotters and Cowells and their horses, the Kaylers and their rabbits, all to get to the ranch and then to the fair at the Millarville Race Track. Excitement ran high. In those days it was all local competition and a great deal of fun for everyone.

William Alfred (Bill) King

by Jeanie Slemko

Bill was born in 1902, son of W.H. and Lucy (Wilkin) King. He was raised on the family ranch at Millarville. He worked for several years for the Royalite Oil Company in Turner Valley. He married Muriel Price. In 1934, they moved to Duncan, B.C. where Muriel had been raised.

When World War two broke out, Bill signed up as an electrician and was posted to Terrace, British Columbia. After the war he returned to their home at Quamichan Lake, near Duncan, to work as an electrician and raise horses. There were two daughters, Sylvia and Pamela, both keenly interested in the

W. A. (Bill) King holding Mary Margaret Kayler.

horses also. In recent years Pamela has brought her horse to Millarville to ride in the show at the Graham Ranch.

Sylvia married William Creighton and lives in Victoria. They have two children, Eleanor and Sean.

Pamela married Michael Lenko and resides on the farm at Quamichan Lake. Their two children are Christopher and Rosilind.

Muriel has done a good deal of travelling in recent years but makes her permanent home on the farm at Quamichan Lake.

John and Doreen Kirby

We purchased land from Garnet Allen in 1965 (part of N.W.¼, Sec. 3, T.22, R.3, W.5), and finally moved out to Priddis in 1968, complete with two children, Richard and Jo-Anne, and Alf, a German Shepard who just loved his new back yard. The Kirbys are commuters. John and Doreen at that time ran Kirby Drug, Glendale Drug, and the Mardi Gras Card Shop. Richard and Jo-Anne attended Red Deer Lake School, and High School in Calgary. Richard graduated with a B. Comm., University of Calgary, and is now with Price Waterhouse, a C.A. firm. Jo-Anne attended college in Edinburgh, Scotland, and now resides in Lethbridge where she is a Speech Pathologist.

Michael Arthur Knights

I was born in the district of Hillington, Little Massingham, King's Lynn, Norfolk, England on February 8th 1905 the son of Richard and Annie Knights. My father was a Civil Engineer who spent a lot of time

Mike Knights.

away from his family while he built bridges and railroads on the Gold Coast of South Africa and other countries. He decided he would like to settle down and so he and my eldest brother Charles set sail for Canada. He bought a ranch at Millarville and then sent for the rest of the family.

I came to Canada with my mother, five sisters and two brothers in April 1909. The oldest boy Tony, sixteen to help mother and the youngest little girl, Edith two years old. We had a very rough crossing on the ocean and were plagued with icebergs, the ship striking one and making so much damage that we had to put ashore at St. John's instead of going up the St. Lawrence River.

We had a small log house to live in, so that a couple of the children went to stay at Ford's, later on known as the Bradfield Ranch. My father had started building a large two-storey house and when it was finished we were all together again. Later on he built a large barn and I remember well that any spare time that was available usually ended in the boys working on this structure. I went to school at Fordville, which was built on our land and just a mile and a half away from home. I worked on the farm for my father and also for neighbors until I was twenty-two years old.

I then took off for the Turner Valley oilfields where I worked for several years. Soon the depression came and this was a very hard time for everyone. I took some of my money and bought a gravel truck. I hauled gravel around Sylvan Lake and Eckville. However soon the pay for that was impossible and I had to sell my truck. After going from one place to another and staying with my folks and relatives through these trying times, we heard that men were being taken on and getting jobs in the Oilfields again. Married men were given preference and so Gladys Smith and I, who had been going together for quite a while decided we would not wait any longer and would get married "with nothing" and take the chance. I soon had a job and I

worked for the Royalite Oil Co. We had two children Marilyn and Arthur.

There were rumors circulating of how the Oilfields were closing down and so I decided I would like to try foreign fields, the same as my father before me. I left Canada in January 1947 for Venezuela, South America as a drilling supervisor for Shell Oil. Gladys and the children came down nine months later and it didn't seem to be so far away from everyone. Unfortunately, although the pay was very good and the camps were well taken care of, we decided this wasn't the place for us, so we came home, back to Sunny Alberta, which was having one of the worst snow storms they had had for several years. Roads were blocked and traffic was at a standstill. We were able to get into our house, which we had rented, in Black Diamond and I then started looking for a farm, which I had always wanted.

After looking at many, I finally decided I liked the looks of the Harmattan area, so I purchased the MacArthur place, as it was called, from Lem Beach. I came up and lived in a tent to cut and put up the hay. Also had had someone put in a crop of barley. We couldn't get into the house until August and then I moved my family up here. We started out by having to saw wood, we got a horse called "Ginger" for the kids to ride to school. This quiet horse promptly bucked them off the first time they rode it to school. We had one pup, which my wife couldn't resist when Mr. Goddard offered it to us. She was a female and presented us with 60 pups before we got tired and stopped counting. Had a team Mr. Noakes let me use until I got a small Case tractor. Gladys and I cut that first crop and we both would like to forget it as it almost ended in divorce, she not knowing anything of farming and my not knowing how to give "orders" to a woman.

We weathered disappointments, cattle prices dropping on account of foot and mouth disease, all the things that plague farmers. We went from coal oil lamps, coal and wood for heat, horses and rakes to electricity, natural gas for heating, larger tractors, balers and four wheel drive trucks. We became members of the St. George's Anglican Church and I have been the Minister's Warden for several years.

My love has been horses and I have had several which I think of with affection and pleasant memories. Matinee, who my father gave me, a four-year old by Ben Ara. Roughneck, who I had raised from a colt. A grey Arabian which I brought up here. He was a one man horse, very high lifed, too much for a farm horse. I found a really good cutting horse in "Sleepy Sam" as we called him — not so sleepy though as I won several trophies etc. with him.

Our entertainment consisted of going to card parties, dances, hockey games, baseball and rodeos in the summer. Square dances at the community hall later on and when we first came up here we and our neighbors had house parties so that we could teach our children how to dance. We really looked forward to these evenings. We had pictures and Talent shows to make a little money and we had Xmas Concerts to look forward to when we still had school in the Harmattan district. Progress finally catching up and the children bussed to other schools. Ours were taken to the Sundre School. We then used the school as a Community Center. I joined the Sundre Light Horse Association and had fun competing in gymkhanas and helping with the same. Also did some hunting and fishing when there was time to get away for a couple of days.

The men around here started a "Cutting Horse" Club and I joined that. We went around to neighbors places and to other districts to compete and also took our horses around to the Rodeos to be in these competitions. This form of entertainment phased out as do a lot of things when moneyed men with very expensive horses started coming to local Stampedes and we knew the competition was too great.

We built an arena at George and Bill Beatty's place and then went there for calf roping and team roping later on. We formed a Team Roping Club and we have had many very enjoyable days and evenings down there over the past years. Rope twice a week and have barbecues and a final party of the Harmattan Community Center at the end of November.

I am still feeding cattle and keeping busy haying, etc. Our daughter Marilyn married Leonard Turnbull and they farm six miles west of Olds. They have four children, Beverly Lynn, Roberta Joyce, David Arthur and Gary Michael. Our son Arthur joined the R.C.A.F. in 1958 and he travelled all over the country to different bases. At Comox, B.C. he met the former Edna Unger and they were married in Winnipeg and were finally living at Greenwood, Nova Scotia. In 1965 several Argus planes were sent down to Puerto Rico on Exercise Maple Springs, one involving submarines and the Canadian and United States Forces. Tragedy struck our little family when No. 2 crew of 404 Squadron, of which Art was a navigator, were lost, when their plane plunged into the sea. His wife Edna lives at Cumberland, B.C. where she is a teacher. Their three children, Cindy Lynn, Brett Arthur, and Shanna Denine live with their mother.

We have lived here for thirty-one years, talked of retiring but find it very hard to think of ever leaving here. We have had very good neighbors and friends around us wherever we have lived and have enjoyed living in this community.

Richard T. (Dick) Knights

by Richard T. (Dick) Knights

I am the eldest surviving son of the "Richard Knights" family written up in "Our Foothills" the forerunner of this book. My two older brothers having sacrificed their lives in World War One.

We all arrived in Calgary in early May, 1909, and soon learned to adjust to life on a Ranch near Millarville.

Dick Knights Family. L. to R. Kay Frew, Dick, Margaret McIver, Netta, Bob.

I was 15 years old at that time, and so was able to adjust more easily than my parents, and as the years rolled by, learned to do just about anything a Rancher has to do, like riding, roping, branding, shoeing horses, shearing sheep, milking cows, butchering beef, hogs and sheep, and farming in a small way, walking behind a single furrow plow, discing, harrowing and seeding, but haying was the main job every fall.

As our valley, where we lived was very susceptible to frost, we didn't grow much grain, however, in 1918 Father purchased a small threshing machine which we used to thresh what grain we did grow, and did a lot of threshing for our neighbours. I spent a lot of hours feeding sheaves into that machine by hand.

We all worked long hard hours in those days, but we also found time to ride, hunt and fish, play hockey and go to dances and visit neighbours.

I attended "Fordville School" the winter of 1909-1910. Roxy Alexander was our teacher, the first of many who taught at Fordville and a number of the early ones boarded at our house.

As the years rolled by, we had a good living, always plenty to eat, but didn't make much money, and then came Turner Valley and the urge to go where there were good paying jobs. And so I went to see a friend of our family, Sam Coultis, asking for a job with Royalite Oil Company and he said I could go to work with a pick and shovel. Being used to hard work, I left the Ranch after 20 years and started a career in the oil-fields.

In the fall of 1929 I married Netta Stanhope whose parents were farming north of Black Diamond, and we lived in Black Diamond. By this time I had graduated from pick and shovel to roughneck and worked on a well being drilled southwest of Hartell, "Foothills No. 3" and was able to have a house built in Black Diamond where we lived for 18 years and raised three children, Kathleen, Robert and Margaret.

Kathleen married Gordon Frew, who has had a long career with Inter-Provincial Pipe Line and is now District Superintendent of the line between Toronto and Montreal. They have five children and two grandchildren.

Margaret married Don McIver, now a Sergeant in the Mounties and stationed in Vancouver. They have two boys.

Robert also a Sergeant in the Mounties, married Mary Cowles of Edmonton, and is stationed in Edmonton and living in Sherwood Park. Bob joined the Mounties in 1954 and has served extensively in the north, places like Aklavik, Inuvik, Sacks Harbor, Arctic Red River, Eskimo Point, Rankin Inlet and Whitehorse. They have three children, two boys and a girl.

After roughnecking a number of years, I got promoted to driller until 1949 when I was transferred to Imperial Oil as Drilling Supervisor in the Leduc field. We lived in Devon, Alta., until I retired in 1959 and we moved to Calgary, where we still live and have a view of "Our Foothills" and the mountains.

Caroline Hannah (Northover) Kosling

1899-1961

Caroline Hannah Northover was born in Punknowle Dorset, England and came to Calgary with her parents in 1906. It was a move made when her father, Alfred Northover, then 40 years of age, decided that his lifelong desire to live in the colonies should be acted upon. The stone-mason, carpenter business in which he was engaged was disrupted when his father died and his brother fell ill. So the move across the ocean was made.

Carrie Northover attended Public School in Central Public School, a sandstone structure on 5th Avenue. She was always an exceptional student, excelling in English. In 1910 she won the Imperial Order Daughters

Carrie and Fred Kosling. Plainview School in background.

Mrs. Carrie (Northover) Kosling.

of the Empire Essay contest for which she received a set of Dickens classics. She won the R. B. Bennett Scholarship in Grade 8 for General Proficiency. In Grade XI, 1917 she was awarded a University Scholarship for 2nd highest marks in Alberta. She attended many schools during her High School years as the City was just developing; Alexandra, Stanley Jones, Balmoral and finished Grade XII in Crescent Heights graduating in June 1918. The Principal at Crescent Heights at the time was William Aberhart.

Her first school was ten miles East of Coronation, but she found the prairie life so bleak in winter that she looked for something different.

In January 1920 she came to teach at Plainview School, south east of the old Kew Post Office. She boarded with the Dave Stewarts and taught their children Bessie, Evelyn, Lilian and Cam. Among some of the other students were the Bill Adams, Lochheads, Ohlsons and Elwyn Evans.

It was here she met Fred Kosling. He and Mont Ohlson were riding by the school and as was the wont of young fellows decided they would like to meet the new teacher. The plot hatched in their heads that as an excuse they would ask her the way to Ohlsons. They tossed a coin as to who got the honor and the lot fell to Fred. He always declared she told him to go straight up an impossible hill in the opposite direction. But, in the end, he won out and they were married January 3, 1922.

She continued to teach for a time at Plainview and when they moved to the homestead further West she took a few terms from time to time at Square Butte

Going raspberry picking. In buggy, Mrs. D. Stewart, Mrs. Carrie Kosling. Evie and Bessie Stewart on horses.

Carrie Kosling off to school on Dexter.

School teaching the Sylvesters, Lyalls and Virtues. In the 1950's she returned to teaching full time for a few years at Midnapore, Spring Bank, Priddis and Red Deer Lake.

She was an enthusiastic community worker, supporting the formation of the Square Butte Ladies Group during the war time — a group that is still active. She also worked diligently for the Square Butte Community Association in its early days when events were held in the old Square Butte Schoolhouse.

Florence Krebs
by Florence Krebs

I was born in February, 1902 on the N.W. ¼ - Sec. 30, T21, R2, W5, the daughter of William and Mary Jackson, one in a family of nine. I went to Fordville School for the beginning of my education. In 1915, I left home and went to the Claresholm High School. After graduation, I attended the Calgary Normal School, graduated from there and then taught school at Richdale, a hamlet east of Hanna, for two years. In 1921, I married Glen Krebs, and in 1923 we migrated to the United States. We lived in Washington, and Nampa, Idaho. We have two children — Cloyd, a Doctor in Provo, Utah, and a daughter Madeline, who is a nurse. We have four grandchildren, and two great-grandchildren. We are now residing in Battleground, Washington.

John D. Lamarsh Family

The John D. Lamarsh family acquired its small farm (S½ of NW¼ 23-21-4-W5th) at Square Butte in the fall of 1969. The property was previously owned by Ross Marshall, Calgary businessman and long time resident of the Priddis district. The land is part of the original holding of the fabled Count Georges de Roaldes, who acquired it in 1905.

"Jack" Lamarsh, a Calgary lawyer, is descended from Samuel LaMarshe, a French Huguenot who arrived in Lower Canada in 1791 and shortly after established the family in Essex County, Ontario, where it flourished until the early 20th Century. Many members of the family then migrated westward, taking up homesteads in Saskatchewan and Alberta. Jack was born in Saskatoon, Saskatchewan, in 1937, son of Archie and Lucille Lamarsh. His father is a Saskatoon lawyer.

Jack's wife, Christine, is a native of Fife County, Scotland. She emigrated to Calgary with her family in 1961.

Jack and Christine have two sons; John, born 1966 and Craig, born 1968.

Jack and Christine acquired a small herd of beef cattle upon their arrival and sold calves for a number

John and Christine Lamarsh and sons John and Craig.

361

of years. They also spent the rainy spring of 1970 establishing a small tree nursery on their place. The garage and tack house were built in 1970 and the residence in 1975. These activities, together with hiking and gardening in summer and cross-country skiing in winter, have kept the family busy and happy at their country home at Square Butte.

Langford, Audrey Jean (A. J.)
Youngest daughter of William J. and Marjorie Oliver of the Diamond L. Ranch, Millarville

My early schooling was at New Valley School while I attended Junior and Senior High School in Calgary.

Following high school I trained at the Calgary General Hospital, graduating as a Registered Nurse in April 1949. I worked at the General for two and a half years in the Operating Room and Pediatrics Department.

In September 1950 I enrolled in a six month post graduate Pediatric Course at the Children's Hospital, Washington, D.C. On completion of this course I travelled to Miami Beach, Florida where I worked for several months. Subsequent travels and work included the Continent and the British Isles.

I was married in November 1953 to James A. Langford, architect and former player with the Calgary Stampeder Football Club (1949-50-51).

We moved to Kindersley, Saskatchewan in March 1954 and to Regina, Saskatchewan in October 1956. Since March 1, 1963 we have resided in Ottawa with our son and four daughters.

Cam Lansdell and family. L. to R. Cam, Happy (Gladys), Rhonda, Gordon and Doug.

was not exactly the "lap of luxury". Especially when the wind blew from the west and the snow sifted through the house making a nice drift on the east wall of the bedroom. In 1949, Cam bought the West ½ S12 T20 R4 W5th and the brand 7 Half Diamond from Bill Iceton. In the same year he acquired a section of lease 11-20-4 W5th and then in 1958 he bought the SW¼-14-20-4w5th, from Mr. Wes Way.

The Langford family 1977. L. to R. Bill, Leslie, A.J., Mary, Jim, Janet and Lorie in front.

Cam Lansdell and Family

Cam Lansdell was born in Medicine Hat, Alberta, and moved to Lacombe at the age of 2. He attended school at Lakeside and Lacombe and then in 1940 moved with his parents to Bentley, Alberta. He moved from Bentley to the Kew District in April 1945, where he purchased the East ½ S12 T20 R4 W5th from Mr. McCaffery, a Calgary lawyer. The only buildings on the place at this time were made of logs and the house

Gordon, Rhonda and Doug Lansdell.

While Cam was growing up on his father's farm near Lacombe, he learned to ride "cattle" as well as horses and therein got his start in rodeo. In 1938, he entered his first competition at the Ponoka Stampede and after this rodeoed for some 15 years. During this time he won many bronc and bareback events including the Canadian Saddle Bronc Championship in 1950. He was at Hanna in 1944, when the Cowboy's Protective Association had their organizational meeting and was the Bronc Riding Director from 1947 to 1952. Due to knee injuries, Cam decided to hang up his spurs in 1955 and get down to some serious ranching.

In 1944, Cam married Gladys "Happy" Parsons from Tees, Alberta. Happy came with Cam when he moved to the Kew District and set up housekeeping there. There was not much to set up though except a bed, table, and a few chairs. (Rodeo was not a well paying sport at this time.) They had 3 children; Douglas, born in 1945, Gordon born in 1947, and Rhonda (the straggler), was born in 1958.

While growing up Rhonda developed a deep love for animals and spent many happy hours with her kittens. One day a little brown and white pony named Tonka, became a part of her life and she joined the Gymkhana Club. She was a member for 7 years in 4H. At school she played basketball on the girls' team and also enjoys curling. At the present time she is living and working in Calgary.

Douglas Lansdell

Doug was born at Turner Valley, and attended school at Millarville and Black Diamond, then on to S.A.I.T. where he received his diploma in Mechanical Technology.

He enjoys sports, and played ball for the Square Butte and Millarville teams, also hockey which he still plays for the Hi Country Rustlers in the Commercial League.

In 1966, he married Phyllis Cameron and they have one son, Brent, born in 1969, who also enjoys sports and plays hockey in the minor league.

They purchased land south of Turner Valley, where they are presently engaged in farming.

Gordon Lansdell

Gordon was raised on the family ranch and attended school at Millarville and Black Diamond. After he finished school he spent two winters in Northern Alberta, doing seismic work and during the summers he worked in road construction.

He enjoys sports and played ball for Square Butte, Millarville, and Turner Valley. He still plays hockey for the Hi Country Rustlers in the Commercial League.

Gordon married Ann Borton in 1971, and they have a daughter Deana, who was born in 1975.

They are ranching in partnership with his father and reside on the home place.

Gordon and Ann Lansdell with daughter Deana.

Phyllis and Doug Lansdell with son Brent.

Deana Lansdell and friend.

Bal and Nancy Laskin and sons: Baruch, Lee and David

Bal (Balfour) and Nancy moved to the Millarville area during the Spring of 1975, having purchased the N.W. portion of 4-21-2W5 and N.E.¼ of 5-21-2W5 from Bull Ranches. They arrived with an infant, Lee, and their eldest son, Baruch, who was then two and a half. They have since had a third son, David, born in September, 1977. Because they each had a rural background, they sought a similar setting in which to raise their children. During their first year as beginner farmers, they bought fifty head of commercial heifers through which they met all of their neighbours while retrieving them.

Bal's Jewish Grandparents emigrated from Russia at the turn of the century and resided in Yorkton, Saskatchewan. Bal was born in Yorkton, preceded by a sister, Malca. His Mother, Florence, and Father, Bures, settled in Humboldt. Bures was an active farmer, businessman and served as Mayor of Humboldt for ten years. Bal fully enjoyed hockey and baseball, excelled at such track events as sprints and pole-vaulting, and is an ex-Dominion Highschool Curling champion. Always active in sales and promotion, he chaired many fund-raising drives and was an executive member of the Board of Trade, the Lions, the Fish and Game League, the Humboldt Curling Club. Parade Marshall of the Humboldt Fair as well as Manager of Junior "A" and Senior Hockey clubs. Bal attended the University of Saskatchewan and the University of Toronto in pre-law. At the time of moving to Millarville, Bal's companies, Norbal Sales and Developments Ltd., and The Ice-Man, dealt primarily in ice processing, storing and vending equipment throughout Western Canada.

Nancy's Grandparents provided another typical Canadian mix; Norwegian on her Mother, Clare's side and Scottish-American on her Father, Lee Lowry's side. Lee, after retiring from the oil well supply business, farmed both in Springbank and the Red Deer Lake areas. With the exception of her first few years, Nancy grew up in Springbank with her younger brother, Jon. She attended school there for ten years, transferring to Mount Royal College for Grade 12. Nancy graduated with a degree in Archaeology/Anthropology from Simon Fraser University in B.C. The University of Calgary offered a tempting bursary which she accepted, bringing her back home where she completed one year of postgraduate studies in Archaeology/Physical Anthropology. Throughout her lifetime she has enjoyed most sports, working for the city of Calgary Recreation Board during the Summers while in gradeschool and attending Pony Club on weekends. Snow and water-skiing seem to have been replaced by diaper-changing at present, however; since Nancy has an aptitude towards the arts: painting, sculpting and crafts — a balance is there because of the many Continuing Education Courses offered in the Millarville

District. Nancy joined the Millarville Ladies Junior Guild within her first year here and has since taken on the role of Director of the Art Section for the Millarville Fair.

Bal's and Nancy's sincere hope is that when another edition of Foothill's Echoes will be published, that the Laskin name will still remain.

Bernice (O'Conner) Latondresse

I taught at Plainview School from 1930 to 1933. It was my second school, the first being at Crossfield for two years, 1928 to 1930.

While teaching at Plainview I first boarded at Lochheads for two years then went closer to school and boarded with the Calderwoods for one year. There was just Mrs. Calderwood and her two sons. She was quite old, a very lovely lady, and could cook and tend her house very well. I stayed there one year.

The men on the school board then were, Mr. Foster, Mr. Gettig and Mr. Walton, who had the Kew Store. I had about twenty pupils from grade one to nine. They were a lovely group of children and I really enjoyed my three years teaching them. The grade nine pupils were very good students and easy to manage. One real treat was a gas stove. The gas line went right by the school so we had it instead of coal and wood. I rode to school part of the time from Lochheads and walked often in summer. I bought a car in the second year so went in to Calgary on the weekends. The road were not good at that time so I had many difficult times in the snow and mud. I could write a book on that alone.

Miss B. O'Connor and Peggy Calderwood out for a ride.

364

Each Xmas we had a big concert and I believe they were often held at the hall which was near the Kew store. I remember very well the one year, as after the concert was over then the presents and candy bags given out, we danced then I left for Calgary about three in the morning.

Jennie Richardson lived across from the store and is now in Delia, Alberta. She was one of my grade nine pupils.

I was married in Toronto and lived down there for one and a half years and came out to Carstairs but Bill (my husband) couldn't take the dust on the farm. We bought a grocery and butcher shop in Royalties. My two children, Billy and Bernice went to school and to the Black Diamond Church. Bill sold the shop and started with Home Oil. We must have been about ten years in Royalties and then moved to Drayton Valley Oil Fields. From Drayton we came back to Royalties as Bill was transferred to the gas plant there. While there, Bill had a heart attack and died in the Didsbury Hospital. We had been in Carstairs this time about five years. I went back teaching when Bill had his first heart attack and taught on after making it two years teaching there. I sold the house and moved to Calgary and got a teaching job with the Separate School Board. I taught nine years. I really moved a lot and never dreamed I would go back teaching after stopping for twenty years. It was difficult going back but I ended up enjoying my school years. It occupied my time after Bill was gone and I couldn't believe I taught nine years in Calgary.

I retired in 1972. I had a house but sold that and am now in an apartment. My daughter is in Drayton Valley and my son is in Spokane, married a year now. So, with thirteen years teaching before marriage and eleven years after I come close to twenty-five years of teaching. It seems unbelievable, but I guess time just flies. I am now trying to take some courses and do volunteer work. I find it hard not to be busy as that surely is a cure for ailments.

Jessie (Nesbitt) Latour

Having been born in Calgary in October 1917, I was the eldest daughter of Tom and Joyce Nesbitt, nee (Joyce Lochhead), I went often to visit my grandparents, Charles Lochhead, who homesteaded just south of Plainview School. In 1924-25, or thereabouts, my parents and five girls moved out to the Pocket Place, just south of Bill Adams homestead. My Dad worked in the Oil Fields and we went to Plainview School, our teacher being Josaphine Bird.

Then we lived in Black Diamond and Saskatoon coming back to the Short Place, just east of Bill Adams and south-west of Andersons. We went to school at Plainview around 1928, Charles Minue our teacher for a couple of years.

Then we moved to Turner Valley where I finished my schooling. Married, I have four children and living in Calgary since 1945.

Latter, Al-Dean Roy Donald
Written by Dean Latter

On October 3, 1959, the Latter family received the surprise of their lives. Not only was there a baby born in their farmhouse that night but the newborn was a bouncing baby boy! That baby was me. Most guys I'm sure would find it extremely good fortune to live with odds of four females to one male but believe me it does have its disadvantages. For example you have to reserve a few minutes during the day when you can grab a quick glance in the mirror or a few words on the telephone. And you have no choice but to be the guinea pig for any new dish they've cooked up. The part that came in handy was having four sisters who could catch, throw and shoot as well as most guys could.

I learned to skate in front of our house on the spring run-off. It was easy going downhill but a little more tricky getting back to the top. When the girls started school I was left to entertain myself and of course I found myself drawn towards all the mischief I could find to get into, much to my folks' dismay. I took to riding a bike like a duck to water and in my younger days when Mom would stop off for coffee at Lois Norrie's, Marilyn and I would race up and down the hill behind the gas pumps on our tricycles. She was different. At five years old we understood what it was like living with a whole household of the opposite sex.

One day, after inspecting what my Dad said was a flat tire, I am reported to have told him that "if I was a flat tire I'd be flat on all sides, not just at the bottom!" With logic like that Dad could see I was going to be a big help to him. I found myself often in the position of bargaining the girls into picking up a ball glove, a hockey stick or a football. I'd 'help' them do the chores if they'd come practise with me. The trouble with this scheme, I found out too late, was that they had already thought of it, and I ended up doing their chores instead of helping. It occurs to me now that those girls were always planning something. When I was five years old, one day wearing Mom's bright red coat, Kathy and Colleen coaxed me into the middle of the barnyard. They were safe inside the barn while I was left standing in the direct path of our bull, who had

Dean Latter, on Peggy's pony, 1963.

an immense hatred for the color red. Now they thought that to be extremely humorous. I can't understand why they no longer found it funny when I talked them into jumping out of the barn loft. Could I help it if they happened to land in the patch of stinging nettle beside the haystack we were jumping onto? We had an unwritten law among us that the youngest kid had to ride the smallest horse, which happened to be 'Stampede', the Shetland pony. Speedy, as we affectionately referred to him, was definitely the smallest. He was also the slowest and the most stubborn animal on the farm. However, he was also the smartest, as I unfortunately found out when, with my feet literally crossed under his belly, I was planning on making it clear to him who was boss. Speedy won, and I am still unable to live down that episode.

I finally reached that age where a boy drives a truck instead of a bicycle and the very first time I "borrowed" Dad's truck I'm sure he felt like chaining a bicycle to my leg forever. In a nutshell, when all was over, I had blown the transmission lines and almost dropped the vehicle out of sight in a snowbank, having taken a short cut through the coulee which no one had attempted to drive through in years.

While attending Red Deer Lake Elementary/Junior High School and later Bishop Grandin Senior High School in Calgary, all of my spare time was filled with some sort of sports activity. Fastball seasons were spent with the Midnapore Royals, Red Deer Lake Bantams, Kingsland Lions, Calgary Hillhurst and Calgary Parkdale, Calgary. While with Kingsland I was voted to the Calgary All-Star team, and with Hillhurst we won the 1975 Alberta Summer Games Fastball Section. Football seasons were spent firstly quarterbacking the Red Deer Lake Junior High team, then playing quarterback for Bishop Grandin High's Junior team. During hockey seasons I played goalie for the Priddis Pee-Wees, Okotoks Pee-Wees, Okotoks Bantams and Okotoks Midgets. We had all gone in to Calgary to cheer on the Okotoks Oiler men's game one night. Their goalie, Jerry Lomenda, who was also our coach, was hurt and they had no back-up. Jerry asked them to put me in. To this day I wonder if allowing only one goal to be scored was due to skill, a miracle, or the fear and knowledge that those 30-year-old gorillas we were playing were out to clobber that 13-year-old goalie which was me!

I joined the Foothills 4-H Sheep Club and even now I can feel the anguish of being dragged around the barnyard by an animal that weighed less than I did. At times it was a toss-up figuring out if I was trying to ride them or catch them, or distinguishing which end or whose end was up. The girls still find that funny, too! I won Public Speaking awards during my 4-H years. I can honestly attribute some of that ability to having grown up with four women. When you're the only guy you learn very quickly to speak up for yourself.

At this writing I am living on the farm with Dad and Mom. I make the drive to Calgary and back each day, as I am employed as a Sales Representative in the tire and rubber industry. I've added a new sport to my spare time — for the last two years I've been curling in the Red Deer Lake-Midnapore League with Colleen, Doug Allen and Joyce Winder.

As for growing up on the farm and living with four women? Let me say that I could never complain about being the only kid around. I could never complain at the lack of humor, though the quality of that humor sometimes remains doubtful. What I can say is that there are memories of my home that I'll always treasure. As it should be, I guess.

Latter, Colleen Eleanor
Written by Colleen Latter

I was born on September 25, 1955, the youngest daughter in the Roy Latter family. During my pre-school years I assisted my mother in handling her daily bus route as my other sisters were already in school and for the most part my brother hadn't arrived. When I wasn't riding the bus I was giving Aunty Ellen McGuire a hand with everything I could get my hands into, and of course offering the best advice a five-year-old could give.

Memories of my childhood are of family picnics and gatherings, my friends and our many relatives and the Red Deer Lake dances where Dad spent half the night calling square dances.

I remember the time we decided to brave the cold night air and camp out — in our front yard. That adventure led us to the surrounding and capture of a fawn that had wandered into Mom's garden. The five of us surrounded and were attempting to capture when Dad and Mom, who'd been awakened by our screaming, finally came to the rescue of the deer. Great White Hunters we were not. We named him "Patches" and nursed him through the winter and a goiter. He'd wait for us to get off the bus after school then wrestle with us for our left-over lunches.

One fall day our barn caught fire and the smoke could be seen for miles. Within minutes neighbors from every direction were pulling in to help us put out the fire before it swept through all our buildings. Some of those people were able to tell that the fire was on the Latter hill, others knew only that there was a fire and began to drive towards the smoke. Still others were city folk out for a drive in the country who came in, taking their blankets to help flail at the flames. Few words were ever spoken that afternoon until the fire was under control. All through that night and well into the next day our family kept watch over the smouldering piles of burnt wood and ashes, praying the wind would not change its direction. I clearly recall how painfully close we came that day to losing everything, including our home. It seemed that we never fully realize how close and how valuable our neighbors are until a tragedy like fire brings everyone together. We were fortunate to have so many friends who cared so much.

I attended Red Deer Lake School from 1961 to 1970 and Lord Beaverbrook Senior High School from 1970 to 1973. Throughout my school years I was involved in every sport that people would let me play. Besides sport activities there were other extra-curricular acitivities, which included Highland Dancing, Tap Dancing, Piano lessons, the Millarville 4-H Beef Club and the Foothills 4-H Sheep Club. I taught swimming classes at the Y.M.C.A. in Calgary and have been curling with the Red Deer Lake — Midnapore Curling Club. I played fastball with Red Deer Lake, the Okotoks Orphans and the Calgary Ace Rentals. I received one injury in all these activities, which was a broken collar-bone, acquired while engaged in a family football game.

I remember the great fun we had at the community Christmas concerts and the school picnics. There was a time when our family never missed the Millarville Races. Every winter we used to have skating parties down at the beaver dam just north of our farm and when summer came we would be partying on the Lake Road or camping over at the Millarville Race Track, where we had dammed up the river to make ourselves a swimming hole.

When Hallowe'en came around Mom would have costumes for all five of us and we'd head out to make calls on our neighbors. Mom would park the car as far away from their houses as possible so they wouldn't be able to identify us by the vehicle. They'd get one of us laughing and once that happened we were a dead give-away. They would hear the laugh, count heads, and announce proudly that we just had to be the Latter kids. We started to catch on to their head-counting method so we began taking one or two extra kids with us. That set them to thinking a little harder. I'm not sure if Mom didn't have just as much fun as we did, trying to fool everyone.

Upon completion of high school I was employed by Union Oil in Calgary in accounting until 1977. From there I enrolled at Mount Royal College, majoring in Therapeutic Recreation. I am presently employed with Sun Oil in Calgary, in their accounting department.

As for my plans for the future? I still enjoy the many hours we spend at the farm. There is just nothing like taking a break from the city and having the chance to breathe some good clean air. There are so many changes that have taken place in our area since I was born but the farm is still the same. I have no immediate plans but I can guess that whatever I decide to do it will be a very busy time for me.

Latter, Kathryn Winnifred

written by Kathryn Latter

Family and friends call me Kathy or Kate. My niece and nephew know me as Taffy. My folks lovingly referred to me with the entire name when I had some explaining to do. I was born July 16, 1954, third child of Roy and Grace Latter.

For as far back as I can remember I've been a sports fanatic, a pushover for stray cats, a lover of music and people, and a lot on the nutty side. In school I found my way onto every team I could be on: volleyball, basketball, badminton, soccer, curling, track and field and powderpuff football. Many times I was convinced that schools should have at least five gymnasiums and that at least half the day should be spent in sports activity. I have the feeling that all of us must have felt this way but Mum never gave up her attempts to make ladies of her girls. She had us in Tap and Highland Dancing and there were music lessons. We still chuckle over the occasions we danced on stage at the community concerts. Somehow I managed to find a reason to always be outside and conveniently I could seldom be found when there was housework to be done, or chores. When I was twelve I joined the Millarville 4-H Beef Club and three years later joined the Foothills 4-H Sheep Club. I brought home awards for Public Speaking, Showmanship and Achievement. The hardest thing about 4-H was giving up your animal after becoming attached to him for a year. As if I hadn't enough to keep myself occupied I played fastball for three years with the Red Deer Lake Midgets and the following two years with the Okotoks Orphans Senior B Ladies. I was a member of the community Hi-C Youth Organization and I taught Sunday School in the Red Deer Lake United Church. I was enrolled at Red Deer Lake Elementary/Junior High School from September 1960 to June 1969. In September, 1969, I began school at Lord Beaverbrook Senior High School in Calgary, and graduated in June, 1972. So many things spring to mind when I think of my school-days. One of the first memories was of the

Kathy Latter's class, 1961. Kathy is in centre back.

Ladies Sewing Circle Club which Mum belonged to, making blue crepe-paper skirts and bonnets for my Grade One girls' singing debut of "Alice Blue Gown" at a school concert. Grade Four, instructed by Miss Lillian Kelly, found us all trying to be musicians in the famed "Rhythm Band". By Grade Seven we had retreated back into our singing efforts with a Hillbilly presentation for the Home and School. Finally Grade Nine rolled around and the trip we had been looking forward to was a reality. Mr. and Mrs. Norman Floen packed thirty boisterous kids into a bus and headed for the Calgary C. N. Station, because we were on our way to Vancouver Island. What a graduation present that was! During my high school days I joined every club I could find to join. I sang with the school choir and still found time for a dozen sport activities. In 1971 the school opened the "men's only" Letterman's Club for Athletic Achievement to allow women into it. Approximately ten girls from our districts were immediately given memberships and we all received our school letters.

The bus rides to and from school were something to be remembered. I rode on Mum's bus to the Lake for nine years. I swear she knew what we were planning to do before we did it. When you misbehaved on Dad and Mum's buses you were given the front seat for a couple of weeks and if you were really bad you got the front step. I spent more than enough time in both of those positions. We rode with Dad once High School started. Dad even began an extra route on Friday nights so the kids from the farms could go in to the night football games held by the schools. One stormy night on our way home from school I remember Dad, Colleen, Elaine Taylor and I outside, trying to put chains on the bus so we could get home.

To fill in the spare time I had not already allocated, I worked at the Father Lacombe Nursing Home in Midnapore as a nurses' aide. With my schooling completed I moved in to Calgary and was employed as a secretary until September, 1974. During the year following graduation I drove to Okotoks at least two nights a week for fastball with the orphans. The next year Judi and I coached the Kingsland Girls Bantam A Fastball Team to the city championships in Calgary. My biggest thrill that year was being selected as an All-Star Coach for Calgary.

I moved to Edmonton in October 1974. I enrolled in Northern Alberta Institute of Technology in 1975. In 1976 I joined the Boys and Girls Club of Edmonton and worked in their Partners Program befriending a twelve-year-old boy. I am presently employed as Administrator of a large electronics firm.

It would be impossible to count the number of times our family has reminisced about our younger days. We often laugh so hard we cry. I have several favorite memories of growing up the way I did. One of the earliest was of Mum packing a lunch, Colleen and I taking it down to the field Dad was working and we'd have ourselves a picnic under the trees. The Millarville Fair was always a hectic time at our house — there was always something to do; it was a 5:00-in-the-morning start on Fair Day. The seven of us would be out tramping through fields, sloughs and trees, collecting wild flowers and grasses. Thank goodness that Dad could tell the difference between the wild flowers and the weeds that we had gathered. Though we only used them in power blackouts, Mum always had the kerosene lamps filled up and of course always handy, so we could never use that as an excuse for not doing homework or chores.

People would drop kittens off at the school and I'd agree to take them home because "I was sure Dad and Mum wouldn't mind". The best way to convince them that they wouldn't mind was to have the cat already at the house. I'd ride home on Howard Einboden's bus so they wouldn't see the animal until it was too late. I always knew that once they'd seen the kitten, being as much of a pushover for strays as I was, they'd never make me take it back. Mum said she could always tell when we were adopting a new cat at our farm.

Holidays were always a big event in our family. Easter Friday we'd color hard-boiled eggs and Easter Sunday we'd be up at 5:00 in the morning to find the eggs our Easter Bunny had hidden the night before. Once all the eggs were found we'd sit down to a brunch of devilled eggs. Even now all of us go through that same ritual which as become a family tradition. Christmas was the other really special day for us. Again, at 5:00 in the morning we'd be up, confirming that Santa really had stopped the night before.

We never seemed to be at a loss to find the humorous side of anything. I think our family photographs show that clearly. It is doubtful that there is one picture where there isn't one or all of us goofing around. It's no wonder our folks have a few greying hairs! Another of my fond memories is of Dad and Mum's 25th Wedding Anniversary. We kids arranged a dance and get-together at the Red Deer Lake Hall. It was to be a surprise but two days before we had to break down and let Dad in on our secret so he could keep Mum from asking so many questions. Many folks we had heard tales of but had never met, made it out that night; and long-time friends and neighbors had a reunion that to me seemed long overdue. There were hundreds of "I remember when . . ." stories exchanged that night.

There are some very special people who meant a lot to me when I was growing up, and they come to mind and make my memories even fonder: Bill and Ellen McGuire, Jimmy McGuire, Aunty Mary and Harvey Gerlitz, Robbie Fields, Peter Macklin, Billy and Edith Barkley. I seldom thought if I'd had a good life or a bad life but I hope my family will be lucky enough to have half of what I had. I hope one day to be back on a farm and enjoying the taste of country.

Whoever said "You can take the kid from the country but you can't take the country from the kid", was a very wise person.

Latter, Roy—Grace

written by Grace Latter

In 1948, Roy and I started our life together. Our home was on the land Roy and his dad had farmed since 1933. Roy's brother, Cliff, lives out at Shawnigan Lake, B.C.

Spring thaw was my first experience in living here. We would walk down the road and with hoes and shovels drain off spots that were flooding, so we could get out to town on Thursday. Thursday was **always** town day: delivering eggs and cream, then shopping for a whole week's groceries. It seems to me that we had more snow then, perhaps on the narrow roads the snow appeared to be piles higher. Roy and I made several trips home by toboggan, or walked. We had neither electricity or telephone when I came to the farm. It was an exciting time when our power was turned on in 1957. Many hours of homework and housework were done by the coal oil and gas lights. At one time we candled eggs by the gas light; this had to be done after dark so we could be sure to see the eggs.

Wallace McBee, John Given, Bill McGuire, Robert Field, Jimmy McNab, Bill Taylor, Jack Genert and Roy cleared a path through fields and bushland for the telephone lines. Our phone was the first to be turned on in our area and over the Christmas we had a private line — thanks to Walter Mosier and crew. When the other phones were connected we shared the line with four other families.

In the early fifties Roy played baseball in the area. Most of the players were farmers so when haying or fall work came along, baseball took second place. We worked with Red Deer Lake Hall Board until they moved into the school gymnasium. Roy and I were on the Hall Board from 1950 until 1969 along with a dozen other couples. Election of Officers Night saw the same couples trading positions from year to year. It was trying at times but we had many great times and dances and ALWAYS plenty of fun, which made all the work done most rewarding.

L to R. Mother-in-law Mrs. Barclay, Roy Latter, and daughter Judy.

Roy and I handled the Christmas Concerts for eight years or so. They were held in the community hall and each had the flavor and spirit of an old-fashioned Christmas. Jack Hervey and Ray Goodwin always found just the right tree . . . some so big we had a hard time finding a door in the hall big enough to bring it through! With the tree decorated with popcorn balls and such, enough oranges and candy for all and Keith Ingram poised at his trusty organ, kids from eight months to eighty years settled in for an evening of entertainment, all supplied by folks, both young and old, from our district. There is only one word which could describe this evening: WONDERFUL. The evening always ended with a rousing carol sing-song, lunch, which was brought by the ladies, treats for the children and a local Santa who seemed to add that special touch to a perfect night for each youngster. We knew most everyone and those we didn't know, we had met before the night was over. Many felt this was the one event that seemed to hold the community together. Roy emceed the dances at Red Deer Lake and Millarville for many years. He called square dances with Walter Birney until Walter retired and at that point calling became Roy's job. If he couldn't tire you out through regular dances a fast set of square dancing would exhaust or confuse the few remaining on the floor.

Our first daughter, Peggy Margaret Grace, arrived on July 24, 1949. Roy named her Peg and with a slip-up on the registration forms she came up with a double first name. This has caused some confusion through school — but she will always be Peggy. Of course she was our pride and joy being the first grandchild for my parents, Ray and Lawna Barkley, and living with and pampered by Roy's parents, Fred and Winnifred Latter. Grandma Latter loved having her there and every afternoon she would push the baby buggy down the field to get the cows for milking. Our daughter, Judith Lawna, arrived in our family August 19, 1950. She was also fortunate to receive the special attention of her grandparents, but only for a short time as Mom Latter passed away in September, 1950, and Dad Latter in April, 1951.

Norman Given was unfortunately almost run off the road in my rush to locate Roy to make that familiar trip to Grace Hospital and later that day, July 16, 1954, Kathryn Winnifred joined our family. Her two sisters thought this was just great — a real live doll to play with. Roy and I went square dancing on a Saturday night at the Stampede Corral and had a great time. It really became apparent what a good time we had when the following day, Sept. 25, 1955 Colleen Eleanor became part of our crew. Eileen Brown called the hospital three times, to get the same information: YES — another girl! This excited the older girls and ended countless arguments, as now each had her own live doll to play with. The way we were going we could almost plan for our own ball team. October 3, 1959 was a memorable day, or rather night, for all of us; our son, Al-Dean Roy Donald, had arrived. A BOY AT

LAST!!! He was born at home at 10:29 p.m. Let me just say that there was a lot of people doing some very fast moving around this house on the hill.

The December of 1956 we began driving school bus for Foothills School Division. We first took children only to Red Deer Lake School. Lo and behold!!! I am still at it 22 years later. We have taken pupils to Calgary high schools for quite some time, which was an experience in itself: writing letters for being absent, helping complete those late English assignments, and generally becoming a friend to a lot of young adults. This is the only run we have now as we gave up one of the bus routes four years ago. We have seen many changes in the district roads. We have driven over roads which were not much more than a well-beaten wagon trail, then high-graded and gravelled, and now some of these same roads today are of pavement and have acquired a government number status. I have had to put chains on many times just to plow through a lot of mud and snow. Once on the road running south of Red Deer Lake Store, now Highway No. 773, on Carnine's Hill (Beatty's Hill at that time) Eddie McBee, who now drives his own route from Turner Valley, got out and shovelled dirt from the side of the ditches under the wheels, just so we could get over the top of the hill. Robert Poffenroth would wait with his tractor on hand where the road had flooded over, to see that the bus got through; if not successful he would just hitch onto the bus and pull us through. Many parents came to meet the bus on bad days. If we weren't within fifteen to twenty minutes of our scheduled time, someone would come looking for us. The co-operation and concern of people made bus-driving most enjoyable. Not too many birthdays were passed by: half a dozen kids would always seem to

manage to be off the bus first, then stood outside, ready and waiting, to give the bumps to the 'lucky' Birthday Kid. Bussing has changed a great deal today, but so has everything else so why shouldn't school-bussing see the effects of progress. We used to drive to three schools in Calgary and now there are six busses from the area south of the city limits servicing seventeen schools in Calgary.

Roy and I have enjoyed a combined twenty-one years in 4-H clubs of varied natures, with five children. During this time we saw the kids through a total of twenty-two years of fastball. Each went through most of the athletic teams in Junior and Senior High School. Four of our kids taught Sunday School at Red Deer Lake United Church and were members of the Hi-C Youth Group there which Roy and I helped with. Roy and I sat through many hockey games and football games (powder-puff football included) in due course, and even took part in the usual family scrimmage. For variety, one season I coached the Midnapore Midget Girls' Fastball team. We cheered them all in their wins, stood by them in their defeats and comforted them in their injuries, of which we had our share. After three broken collar-bones, one broken nose, two broken toes, numerous broken teeth, sprained ankles, wrists and fingers — not to mention several pairs of shattered glasses, we all managed to come through the years in some semblance of order. Roy still claims we could have had one heck of a ball team!!! (we were just a few short in number). Though the family has gone its own ways and we have increased in number over the last several years, we get together as often as possible. We all feel very fortunate that our family's home and roots are found in a community that is proud of their past and looking forward with pride to the future.

Don and Margaret Anne Law
by Joan Goyette

Anne was born in November, 1936 the second child of Alex and Effie Scatterty. She spent all of her childhood in Millarville and attended Fordville and

The Roy Latter family. L. to R.: Kathy, Colleen, Dean, Judy, and Peggy. Colleen's first day at school, 1961.

Don and Anne Law and children.

370

Sheep Creek Schools. In January, 1953 she married Donald Coleman Law who worked on the Spooner Ranch for her Dad who was manager.

Don was from Sawyerville, Quebec but came out west in 1948. The first year of their marriage was spent on the Ranch and then they moved to Calgary where Don started working for Shaw Construction, followed by Consolidated Concrete and finally going to Barber Machinery in the fall of 1956. They moved to Black Diamond for about three years and then back to Calgary until 1966 when they left for Chilliwack, B.C. There they stayed for about six months and then moved back to Black Diamond and Don returned to Barber Machinery where he still works. They have five children: 1.) 1953 — Gloria Jean — married Thomas Walter Bayrack — two children, Robert James and Kathleen Marie Sparling; 2.) 1956 — Donald James — married Doreen Henry; 3.) 1957 — Donna Jane; 4.) 1961 — William Alexander; 5.) 1962 — Catherine Darlene.

Dorothy and Douglas Lawrence

In the spring of 1962, we moved to Dorothy's farm S.H. of 13-20-3, W of 5th from the Red Deer Lake area where I lived for twenty-seven years. We moved a house in, put in a basement and another two rooms were required. Dorothy's mother spent most of her remaining years with us. My brother-in-law John Iceton was living on the place so I used him to advantage. We had a lot of brush cut and most of it broken. I did considerable fencing.

I had disposed of most of my original herd so bought some cattle. They weren't used to us on foot so they gave us a bad time when we moved them.

The first winter was reasonably mild. We had a furnace installed and I built a round corral. We continued to milk cows and raise extra calves rounded out with a few hogs and poultry. There was always a need for extra income. Dorothy and son Garry were faithful choremen.

Doug and Dorothy Lawrence at Durham, England.

It was some years before we were able to install a modern water system.

As the years went on, methods and equipment changed and we required more feed. We were able to put feed up on shares and become established. Help was available.

We didn't seem to be able to take many holidays, but Dorothy and her mother did go overseas to visit relatives. It seemed the only reason I got off was because I bumped my nose or something serious.

Conditions got better, but boys grow up and so Garry got a job in local industry. We were feeling our years and decided to sell out. Inflation was in fashion. We sold the farm and had a farm sale in the spring of 1974. We realized a tidy sum. We bought a nice house in Turner Valley and moved following a wet snow storm that left people all around without power.

Like the rest of our generation, we've seen unbelievable changes in this part of the country since the late twenties.

Since we retired, we have taken a few trips. I work sometimes and otherwise enjoy life.

The Arlie Laycraft Family

by Veryl Laycraft

In the spring of 1959, the Arlie Laycraft family had an auction sale of farm equipment and livestock, and having purchased the store at Millarville from Clark Jacobson, they moved to this business in April of that year.

With them came their son, Ron, who was a full partner in this business and a daughter, Judy, a student at Mount Royal College, Calgary. Also a very loved member of the family, a white cocker spaniel, named Mickey, who almost lived to the ripe old age of nineteen.

L. to R. Charlie Iceton, John Iceton, Wilbur (Smitty) Smith, Mr. and Mrs. Wm. Iceton. Friends in behind, Robert Iceton, Evelyn Smith, Albert Iceton, Mr. Middleton, Lloyd, Mrs. Middleton, Joyce. On the 30th anniversary of Mr. and Mrs. W. Iceton at a picnic on section 1.

Veryl and Arlie Laycraft dispensing punch at Rancher's Hall, Millarville.

Laycraft family on the occasion of Ron and Pearl's wedding. L. to R. Judy (Laycraft) Sutter, Ron Laycraft, Robert Sutter (Judy's husband, Pearl (Cowling) Laycraft, Arlie Laycraft, Carrolle Anne Sutter, (2 years) Veryl Laycraft.

There was very little stock in the store as Clark had only owned the business from September to April, and was just beginning to get some stock on the shelves. All buildings were badly in need of paint and repair. Of course, there was no in-door plumbing and the floor sloped and sagged so much in the kitchen that when the pail under the sink ran over (which it invariably did), the water ran so fast to the far corner of the room that it was impossible to stop the flood. (I finally used this to my advantage to get a drain pipe, by threatening to drill a hole in the floor in that corner and let the water run into the so called basement.)

After all this, the first job was to level the floors. For years we repaired, painted, drilled wells, built fences and landscaped.

Ron married Pearl Cowling in 1962 and a trailer was moved into the back yard as their residence. From this trailer Pearl taught kindergarten for two years, also attended night school at the University of Calgary to get her degree in Education. They had at this time one daughter, Catherine.

Ron decided, after attending night school at Mount Royal College, to go to U of C also. So his father bought out his share of the business and he went on to get his degree in Economics, after which he went to work for Hudson Bay Oils, where he still is at the present time. (See Ron Laycraft story.)

Judy married Robert Sutter in the spring of 1960 and they went to live in Brooks, Alberta, where Bob had employment with Alberta Gas Trunk Lines. They had two children, Carolle-Anne and Roger, now seventeen and fourteen respectively. In 1969, while Bob was Station Chief at the Hussar Station, he died of inhalation of gas while on the job. A year after Bob's death, Judy and family moved to Calgary so that she could attend University. She received her B. of Ed., passing with distinction. She then took her family to Pullman, Washington, where she was able to get her Master's

Degree in Speech Therapy. She is, presently, living in Calgary and employed by the Separate School Board.

Arlie and Veryl continued through the years to operate the business and Veryl was Postmaster from 1959 to 1974; watching and helping the Post Office to grow from a small general delivery office to one with a Rural Route for Square Butte and Kew districts being sent out from Millarville, instead of Midnapore and Calgary. Pat and Clark Jacobson were the first Rural Route couriers from the Millarville Post Office, serving these communities faithfully, rain, snow or shine for seven years.

When Arlie developed arthritis, we decided it was time to step out, so consequently sold the business to Nick and Janet Cook, in 1974. On looking back over those fifteen years of long hours and hard work, it was with mixed feelings. While it was a good life, it was also frustrating as it seemed like you could only get to a certain point regardless of considerations or accommodations shown.

We have watched Millarville and district change from a farmer and rancher country to almost a commuter community. Many new homes have been built in many new sub-divisions.

"Who wouldn't want to live in our Foothills".

Increased enrollment of students has necessitated added rooms and a gym to Sheep Creek School.

After selling the store, we bought the little house up the road a ways and owned by my mother, Agnes Lister. She had decided to move into a Senior Citizens Home in Calgary.

We also took over the Rural Route from Clark Jacobson as he wished to retire. We were finally able to buy from Fernwood Construction, the acreage the house sits on; after two years of ifs, ands and buts from the Planning Boards.

We are still on our Rural Route Mail job.

Ronald A. Laycraft Family R L
by E. Pearl Laycraft

Even as a child the hills held a certain magnetism for me. I loved the picnics and drives we took in the hills. In September of 1958, I was very pleased to accept a position on the staff of Sheep Creek School. I taught here for two years, before returning to university; living in the teacherage and commuting to my home east of Hartell on the weekends. Everyone in the community was so kind to me, especially the Dubes. I tracked across Leatha's kitchen for water, and cheered my favorite hockey team in front of their T.V.

A teenage romance was rekindled when Ron moved to Millarville with his parents in March 1959, as the owners of Laycraft's General Store. Ron's parents, Arlie and Veryl (Lister) Laycraft, farmed for several years west of High River on the Round T Ranch. (See A. E. Laycraft story — **Tales and Trails p. 160.**)

My parents, George and Barbara (Connell) Cowling, farmed in the Tongue Creek district west of High River. — **Tales and Trails p. 70.**

Born in 1936, both Ron and I grew up as farm kids, attending country schools and high school in High River. Ron and I were married in 1962, and we moved into a trailer beside the store. Our eldest daughter Catherine May was born December 22, 1962, a beautiful Christmas present.

Ron was kept busy hauling groceries, stocking shelves and serving customers in the store. He helped with many of the Bingos held at Rancher's Hall, and usually found time to golf on Thursday afternoons.

I did some substitute teaching, finished my degree at the University of Calgary, and started an illegal kindergarten. I was never jailed for this daring escapade and indeed there has been a kindergarten in Millarville ever since.

Marie Elizabeth, our second daughter, was born November 1, 1967, a fun loving sister for Catherine.

Ron left the store to go to the University of Calgary in 1968. I returned to teaching the following year while Ron's Grandmother Lister cared for Marie. Ron graduated in 1971 with a BA in Economics and has been commuting to Calgary as a Production Analyst with Hudson's Bay Oil and Gas ever since.

In 1971 we purchased the N.E. ¼-16-21-3 W5M from the MacKay brothers, part of the former Wm. Moodie

L. to R. Marie, Catherine and Veryl Laycraft, summer, 1978.

homestead (**Our Foothills** p. 179). We moved the trailer to this land in 1972 and the following summer our new home was built.

One incident of our homesteading occurred the day we started fencing. I was driving the truck and Ron was standing in the back stringing wire by holding the spool on the crowbar. I thought I was traveling slowly enough, however when I looked in the rear-view mirror I saw Ron bombarding around. I slammed on the brakes and he scraped himself from the back of the cab in sort of a blue haze.

I think he got even with me the day it was some 90 degrees F. and I had to pack creosote posts through the willow bush. Between the sun and the creosote I was one exhausted, red blister by suppertime.

We've been trying our hand at farming again in the last few years. Ron's been breaking up some of the land and this year we cut the greenfeed with the binder. Our venture in grass feeding steers has had its rodeos and laughs too.

Our leisure time is also spent as a family. Ron enjoys golfing, snowmobiling, and building. The girls like riding, golfing, and skiing. I guess I'm happiest gardening.

We have been most fortunate to have had good health, kind neighbours and helpful parents. It's no wonder that we enjoy the hills of Millarville as our home.

Jack and Corene Lee

Born in Blackie, Alberta, 1916; Father and Mother — Ruth and Arthur Wilderman; one brother — Arthur; one sister — Betty.

Our family moved from Blackie to west of Priddis where my father looked after grandfather's (Wilderman) cattle on his ranch. When I became old enough to attend school, we moved to Calgary and resided on the North Hill.

Ron Laycraft Family. L. to R. Catherine, Pearl, Ron and Marie.

During the winter my father worked in the stock-yards in Calgary. When school was out for summer holidays, we moved back out to the ranch. In later years my father purchased the half section known as the Dickson place and sold it and bought land on highway 22, so we could be near the Fordville School.

In 1935 I married John L. Lee. He owned what was known as the Monk Place (N.W. 22-21-3-W.5), but we lived on the Miss Lee's quarter (N.E. 27-21-3-W.5) for a few years. We sold our place to Ed Blair, bought my father's place, which enabled our daughters Louise, born in 1936, and Marian, born in 1938, to be closer to school. Jacqueline was born in 1944 and the twins, Bonnie and Barry, were born in 1953.

Jack did commercial trucking for thirteen years and farmed in Millarville. We later sold out and moved north to Hoadley in the spring of 1959. We farmed there for thirteen years and then retired and moved to Vancouver Island.

Jack passed away in the summer of 1977 in Nanaimo, B.C. Our children are as follows:

Louise is married to Russell Clark. They have two boys and reside on a farm in Hoadley.

Marian married John DeWeese. They have one boy and one girl and reside on Vancouver Island.

Jacqueline married Gordon Hunt. They have two girls and one boy and reside on Vancouver Island.

Barry married Marilyn Wyness. They live in Leduc, Alberta.

Bonnie moved from Edmonton, Alberta to Vancouver Island.

William and Ethel (Moon) Lee   VY

Bill was born in Lindsay, Ontario, the fifth child of Henry and Jane Lee (see Our Foothills). He came to Millarville as an infant and has lived there since.

Bill went to Fordville School, worked in the Turner Valley oil field, then was in the general trucking business until 1943 when he sold the truck and went back to work in Turner Valley as a roughneck for Royalite Oil Company.

Ethel was born at her parents home in Midnapore, the fifth child of Willard and Nora (O'Brien) Moon, (see Sodbusting To Subdivision.)

Bill and Ethel were married in Calgary. In 1939 they bought the north half of the N.E. ¼ of 12-21-2W5. In 1946 they bought the S.E.¼ of 14-21-3W5 from Bill's brother Frank and started the service station, naming it "Bill's Corner Service." He continued to work for the Royalite Oil Company until 1949 when he quit and started driving a school bus and looking after the service station.

In 1972 the acreage on 12-21-3W5 was sold to Century Development Ltd. and later the service station was rented to Mac and Alice Clarke.

Bill and Ethel have two daughters, Joyce and Linda. Joyce married Bob Backs and they have three children, Bev., Terry and Brenda. Linda married Bud Codd and they have two children, Deb and Darryl.

Bill and Ethel (Moon) Lee on their wedding day.

Linda and Joyce Lee.

Bill and Ethel are living in their home just south of Bill's Corner Service, doing as little as possible and enjoying every minute.

Mrs. Ben Robert Leeds — Nee Marina Dmitrieff

Marina taught at Fordville School in 1941-1942, where she and her mother lived at Bob Standish's. The following year, she got on the Calgary School staff and taught for 2 more years at Rideau Park Jr. High, when she married Ben Leeds with the R.A.F. Marina and her husband spent the last 2 years of the war in England and then returned to Canada the summer of 1946. They both taught school in Cochrane for one year. Shortly after, Ben Leeds left the teaching profession and joined the Oil & Gas Industry, and their travelling days began all over again. They have a son, John Leeds (M.B.A.), and a daughter, Judy (B.A.) who both reside in Alberta.

The Leeds family lived in many places, including Edmonton, Lloydminster, Texas, Kansas, Calgary, Tulsa, and now spend 5 months of the year in their home at Lake Windermere, B.C., and the winters in Naples, Florida.

Marina's mother died in 1963 at the age of 86 years. They often recalled the happy year they spent at Fordville. The school children were delightful and the folks, pleasant and friendly. It was a great riding country and the beautiful scenery and wild flowers were something to behold.

When an acute shortage of teachers developed, Marina went back to teaching and taught for the next 13 years in Parkdale, Elboya and Elbow Park Schools in Calgary. In 1965 she retired, and in 1973 her husband took an early retirement, and since then they have been free to travel and enjoy the best of two worlds.

Leftwich, Lynch and Bess
by Avis Rishaug

My parents came to the Millarville area with the oil boom in 1942. They lived in a skid house which had been their home in Longview, (this building is still used as a home in Black Diamond).

They came to the Calmont camp at the foot of Home Hill. There were a number of families there. Among the ones I remember were, Walter and Mary Clarke and family, Bill and Naoma Crawe, John and

Lynch and Bess Leftwich at their Golden Wedding Anniversary.

Dixie Stewart and family, Finlay Judson and family and John Rose, and many others that I cannot remember. This group of people had a continuing penny anti game. Everyone had a tobacco can or jar of pennies, and they spent their evenings at one house or another playing. Sometimes there were quite a few playing and other times not so many depending on what shifts the men were working.

The Leftwich's left Millarville and followed the oilfields to Leduc, Redwater, Beaverlodge, Manyberries, and then into Saskatchewan and back. When Dad retired they returned to Millarville to live and stayed about five years before buying a piece of property in Newgate, B.C., that included a country store. Dad had a truck that he hauled lumber with, and Mother ran the store. They continued this way for a number of years until ill health forced them to retire. However they remained in Newgate until Dad's death, and then Mother returned to Millarville to live, eventually going to High River to the Medicine Tree Manor, where she resided until her death in 1977.

Mother had been a teacher, and at various times was called back to teach. She was also an excellent seamstress, and spent many hours sewing. My parents were a couple who were deeply involved with their family, and dearly loved all the grandchildren and great-grandchildren.

L. to R. Mrs. Leftwich, Avis and Fred Rishaug

Gordon and Ruby Lepp

Born in Hepburn, Saskatchewan in June 1935, I lived on a farm with my parents, Mr. and Mrs. Ben Lepp, who are now retired and living in Calgary.

Circumstances did not allow us to stay on the farm for very many years so we moved to Saskatoon where my father worked for Canadian Oil for many years. It was in Saskatoon that I met and married the girl of my dreams. Ruby Derdall, the only daughter of Mrs. Alice Derdall and the late Goodman Derdall who farmed near Outlook, Saskatchewan.

After we were married in 1956, Ruby and I only lived in Saskatoon until 1959 at which time it was decided that Calgary would be our new home. Since leaving school I spent most of the following years as a highway transport driver with various companies. It was in 1967 that I quit the road and started working on sales, which I am still busy at.

After having four sons born to us, we felt the city was no place to raise boys. Ruby's strong farm background prevailed and we purchased an acreage near Chestermere Lake where we lived happily for five years; our boys became involved in 4H clubs and were introduced to their own Welsh ponies, which we still have and raise.

In the spring of 1972 we sold our place and relocated on the original homestead of Alex Gouy in the Kew district.

Three of our sons, Ron, Rick and Rennie completed their schooling at Millarville and graduated from Oilfields High School in Black Diamond and are currently working in Calgary. The youngest son, Greg, is still attending Millarville School.

The three oldest boys have all taken an interest in hunting and done well, however Ron never did like to shoot anything he could not pack in his pocket so stayed with grouse and squirrel.

Our family is still enjoying the quiet life in Kew, and about the only complaint we have is that the gardening season is not long enough for Ruby. We enjoy

Lepp Family. L. to R. Back row: Ricky, Ron, Ren. Front row, L. to R.: Greg, Ruby, Gordon.

sleigh riding in the winter and have been involved with the Oldtimers in the Stampede for many years.

There have been some trying times and the most vivid one was hauling drinking water by horse and stone boat from the Davis ranch during a spring snow storm in 1974 when the power was off for five days.

A. George Lewis SL L.H. X̄ LTH.
by G. Lewis

I was born in Illinois, U.S.A. in 1898. After completing my high school I came to Vidora, Sask. in 1915. My father was a medical doctor. My brother Julius was killed in action in 1918.

I was married to Sophie Hansen from Valley City, N.D. in December, 1919. In 1927 we had our daughter Geraldine (Gerry). In 1929 we moved to my Uncle Lewis's farm at Blackie, which I inherited in 1957. In 1938 Francis (Frankie) joined the family. In 1950 we moved to High River so the children could attend school. Sophie passed away in April, 1951.

Shortly after returning to the farm I bought Section 5-22-4-W5M on Whiskey Creek from Joe Caldwell and Bill Howie and I believe they bought it from either Mr. Barraclough or Mr. Gilchrist. This land was used for summer pasture. The cattle were trucked in from the farm at Blackie. One incident that I do remember and I'll never forget when I was in a hurry to get back to the shack before dark and I d— near ran over Fred Ball who was chasing an old cow off the road at the bottom of the hill south of Reimers. I did enjoy the few years I spent in the hills until 1968 when I sold the section to Mr. Mawdsley and I do miss the good and kind people.

In 1952 Gerry was married to Ray Switzer of High River. They had four children, Gary, Deanne, Larry and Debbie. (Ray and Debbie dec.)

In 1955 I married Frances Kline from Phoenix, Ariz. We went on our wedding trip to Seattle and Vancouver taking up residence upon our return on the farm.

Frank was married to Gail Maisy from Herronton in 1959 and they have three children, Derrick, Bonna and Allen Gregory. They took over active operation of the farm in 1970.

Frances passed away on the 17th March, 1973. Last summer I revisited the Cypress Hills area. I was quite anxious to see the Jack McKinnon ranch where I played with an orchestra (trumpet) for a couple of dances in 1918-19. I was really disappointed to see all the buildings torn down, the government is rebuilding "Old Fort Walsh" on this site.

I am living in High River, and enjoying the companionship of my children, my grandchildren and my great grandchildren.

Lewis, Richard, Ellen, Lori and Richie
by Ellen Lewis

May 1966 brought the Lewis family to Calgary from Victoria, B.C. We lived in an apartment in N.W.

Calgary and spent Sunday afternoons driving in the country, dreaming about someday having a piece of land in the surrounding countryside. August 1973, that dream came true. We stumbled upon a very different looking home nestled in the trees with a meadow out front and a gurgling creek wandering through the 25 acres. The past five years have been very busy ones, fencing, painting, landscaping and clearing.

Mr. Lewis is a daily commuter to Calgary working for Sperry Anivac selling computers to keep his family happily settled in the country. Lori and Richie attend Millarville School and I keep the home fires burning. We breed Hungarian Vizsla Hunting dogs as a hobby so I am never at a loss for company even if it is the four legged variety. We are slowly acquiring pleasure horses and dream one day to raise Arabian horses. Who knows, dreams often do come true.

Hardee and Catherine Lineham

NW¼ 16-21-4 W5th
as told by Catherine Lineham
Hardee Lineham, b. May 17, 1951
Catherine Lineham (nee Elcombe) b. Nov. 20, 1949

September 30, 1930, Alfred William Northover of Millarville filed for Homestead Rights on the NW¼ 16-21-4 W5th. He realized Title, broke ten acres, fenced for a mile and sold it to his son, by the same name, for a dollar in 1932. Alfred the Younger held an Accountant post in Calgary but managed, over a 17 year tenure, to fence another one and a half miles and break a further twelve acres. He sold the quarter in 1949 to George Douglas and Ralph Donaldson Kinnear, of High River. The price was $1,000.00. Mr. Northover figured the land worth at $640, breaking at $18 per acre was $210 and fencing $150.00. James Graham Lineham, then residing in Calgary, purchased the property in May 1969, twenty years later, for $16,800.00.

The quarter is three miles West of Kendall's Sawmill. Heading SW is a good hour's walk to the top of

L. to R. Catherine, Hardee and Jim Lineham pondering procedure for second story floor joists. Fisher Creek in background.

Square Butte (Mesa Butte on the map). Running through from the West is Fisher Creek, reputed never to have run dry, compliments of the Mountains. From the top of the foothills, which surround the quarter, is an unobstructed view of the Rockies — in summer sun white-tipped oracles of peace; in mist and wind, great hulking masses of gloom. Neighbours are of diverse professions; teachers, ranchers, carpenters, cowboys, painters, potters, weavers and some of the most fantastic homemakers a countryside could boast.

Hardee, Jim Lineham's oldest son, was raised in Calgary, graduated, and attended the National Theatre School in Montreal, a course of theatrical study which took three years. One of his first professional acting jobs was at the Manitoba Theatre Centre, in Winnipeg, where we met. Two years later, August 25, 1974, we married in Stratford, Ontario between a matinee and evening performance of a play Hardee was in. That night we had our first taste of ". . . in sickness or in health . . .", as Hardee landed in the local hospital for treatment of a particularly sudden and violent case of bronchitis. Eastern dampness does much to perpetrate this condition. By this time it seemed to Hardee's Dad that the NW¼ of 16-21-4 W5th would sit idle forever. When he was contemplating its sale we were given the opportunity to make use of it and promptly decided to build a log house. Nothing huge, one that would not require any financial outlay in terms of labor as we, with Mr. and Mrs. Lineham's help, would do all the work. After buying a book on the subject we stomped around the bush on the property eyeballing suitable trees, felled them, limbed them and peeveed them into position for hauling out to the site. Jim and Cathy Sylvester loaned us horses, "Lady" and "June", their harness, and enough information to harness them and start to work. Lady was around 28 years old, had a bit of asthma and hated to work in mud. She could still haul a long wet log by herself, but not the 40-60 footers we had felled — these she refused to budge. June was added but she really hadn't done this sort of work before, however, she was young and strong. She would stand quite still (once you caught her) while the harness was put in place. When this was accomplished she would attempt to run backwards, forwards or sideways, getting herself and the stalwart Lady completely tangled in a mass of dangling, broken harness. She didn't like working in mud either. On a particularly dreary day, when we too were fed up with the mud, June chose to pull her trick. Hardee saw red, understandably, as we too were thigh high in muck, hauled back a fist and slugged June smack in the snout. Although neither Jim, Cathy or the ASPCA would approve, a point had been made. At summers' end the horses rested up before going back home. There were some pretty close calls, with both the horses and ourselves, the four of us physically and emotionally altered by the Fall.

We couldn't finish the house in one year — living in tents was not appealing past November and additional

L. to R. Jane Lineham, Hardee Lineham, Catherine Lineham.

finances had to be found. Tent pegs were pulled up and pounded back three summers in a row. Once, when we came out to camp a little too early, we lit the tent stove in our haste to get warm and practically burned it down. We've had black bears in camp four times — one through the side of the cook tent which took half a day to repair; one up on all fours, head buried in the refuse barrel, one on the porch (when the house was finished), and one at a distance. Deer, Moose, and Coyote are seen almost all year around, along with a great variety of birds. Rabbits are finally returning and the area, no matter what the season, is alive with activity.

On November 7, 1976 we moved our sleeping bags and tent paraphernalia into the house, turned on the furnace and celebrated. The house is warm in winter, cool in summer and, being approximately 1,100 square feet, has lots of room left over for spiders and flies. Certainly there is no use trying to deny them access.

At the present time, New Year's Eve, 1978, Hardee and I are permanent residents of "Square Butte", leaving only to pursue careers.

ROBERT F. LINEHAM, younger brother to Hardee, was born on Sept. 11, 1952. He graduated from Henry Wisewood in Calgary and went on to University taking courses to do with Science and Mathematics. He chose not to pursue the education, although his marks were good, and became a Cook. At one time he had a restaurant called Konnie's Kitchen, in Calgary, which he ran in partnership with a Glen Simpson. Konnie's had a regular clientele and line-ups for the downtown noon break. Unfortunately the location is now an empty hole scheduled for some new office or retail structure deemed necessary by the City planners. Bob has just completed constructing and finishing the outside structure of an indoor pool which his father has added to his own house. Bob shares an apartment in Calgary with two other fellows but spends a lot of time at his parents place helping with whatever needs doing.

JANE LINEHAM, born March 13, 1961, is currently completing her first semester of Grade XII at Henry Wisewood in Calgary. She lives at home (which is a few miles North of Millarville) and commutes to school. She is concerned right now with the question of a career, which means further study, or working for a year and then deciding what to do. After school Jane works with the Housekeeping Department of a major Calgary hospital.

Hardee, Bob and Jane are fourth generation Albertans.

J. G. (Jim) Lineham and Family
as told by Jim Lineham

I was born on December 16, 1912, in a farm house a few miles west of Youngstown, Alberta. Two of mother's brothers were present for the occasion, Dr. Jim Creighton and Dr. Bill Creighton. When Fin was born they thought it was all over and Bill said to Net (mother), "Good Lord Net, I think there's another one in there". I was born twenty minutes later and thus began the life of two twin brothers. Nothing very eventful has happened to either of them in the past 65 years; except that over those years they have been very close and tried to visit with and communicate with each other on all possible occasions.

I had an older brother, Bill, who passed away in February of 1973; and a sister, Janet, who has lived in Seattle for many years.

In 1919, following the first World War, Dad and Mother moved to Cochrane for a year or two and later to Okotoks where Fin and I spent several happy years growing into our early teens. One of the highlights of this time was camping up the Sheep River with brother Fin and a mutual friend named Norman Horning. Mr. Horning (Norman's father) ran one of the pool rooms in Okotoks and Norman got a set of numbered pool balls and snooker balls from his dad. We built a regulation-sized pool table behind Fisher's garage, made our pool cues from the Cedar posts along the CPR Railway tracks and gave them the proper weight by putting a few ball bearings in the handle. Used truck tire tubes served as cushions and, after covering the table with a flannelette sheet, we were in business. Competitions of both pool and snooker were held with the East end of town against the West. In later years, when we moved to Turner Valley, this prior "pool hall" experience stood Fin and I in good stead at "Buck's" pool hall.

To get on with the camping trips, these would last from five to six weeks during the summer. We would take such staple foods as salt, pepper, sugar, flour, smoked bacon, a few potatoes, matches and enough .22 bullets to last the trip, maybe 100 for each of us. We would build a shelter in the bush west of Hoadley's Point, (now the Golden West Horse Farm), make a fire pit, spread our blankets in the hut and start living. We ate such small game as partridge, prairie chicken, rabbits and fish from Sheep Creek. We kept our meat in a spring a few feet from the hut. It would keep for

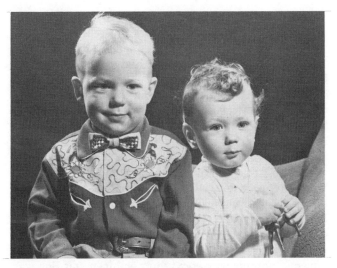

Hardee and Robert Lineham, at Redwater, Alta. 1953, ages 3 and 1½ years.

Jim and Jennie Lineham, about 1959.

several days if kept submerged in the very cold, clear water. Dandelions, pig weed, cattail reed roots and other herbs, in season, were devoured. We learned a lot about self-sufficiency and survival during these summers. Experience which has stood us in good stead over the years. In winter we would trap muskrat, weasel and the odd beaver from the dams which used to be east of the present Lions Club Park. We would stretch and flesh the hides in preparation to sell them at Simpson and Lee's trading post in Calgary. We earned enough this way to pay for our camping supplies for the following summer. It was a great way to grow up. However, life moves along and so did our family. We moved to Turner Valley on July 1, 1927 where we lived for a number of years.

I went to high school in Turner Valley and was taught by such teachers as Mr. Spence (Spence's shoe store in Calgary); Mr. James R. Shearer, a cousin of the movie actress Norma Shearer who was later a Justice of the Peace in Turner Valley. I mustn't leave out Roy W. Gould — I suppose he was a good enough teacher but he certainly didn't bring out the best in me.

On May 8, 1934 I went to work for the Royalite Oil Company as a Geological Assistant, an important sounding title but only important enough to pay $4.40 a day. This was hardly enough to buy clothes, tobacco and a few beers at the Black Diamond Hotel. It looked pretty good though following the first years of the

Depression. Things began to pick up by 1936 and by August 1940, when I joined the Royal Canadian Air Force, the economy was on the rise and hasn't looked back. Trudeau's French power block may put a stop to that during the latter years of the 1970's.

I enlisted (RCAF) with two people many readers may remember, Glen Lineham and George Scott, both now living in Calgary. I ended up as a Flight Lieutenant pilot on heavy bombers flying out of England. Along with thousands of other young men I did nothing spectacular — it was a job and some of us managed to survive. On the way overseas I met my wife-to-be on a train going to Montreal. Jennie Hayes Lawrence was a nurse on her way to St. Anne de Bellview, a military hospital in Montreal. My group spent about a week in a holding station before taking a train on to Halifax and then to England. During this week I was able to leave the station once or twice to visit with Jennie. We corresponded fairly regularly during the next two years and upon returning to Calgary we were married in the Chapel of the Church of the Redeemer on September 1, 1945. The next four years were a bit of a trial for both of us. I decided to go back to school and try for a degree in Petroleum Engineering. This was accomplished in June 1949 when I graduated from the State University of Oklahoma (Norman, Oklahoma). During this time Jennie worked as a nurse in various places both in Canada and the United States. With school finished we began to make our way back home and took a month to get back to Alberta. We visited an old Turner Valley friend in Midland, West Texas, named Walker Dabbs and his fine family. He was a drilling and production superintendent for the Humble Oil and Refining Company. After four years as penny-pinching students we were getting a taste of what life could be like and spent time in Los Angeles with Aunt Minnie and Archie Dutton, then with sister Janet in Seattle. Once settled home again I accepted a job with Imperial Oil Limited in Calgary. This seemed like the thing to do since I had been with Royalite for several years and for pension purposes had unbroken service since May 8, 1934. I went to work in Redwater, Alberta, first as a Reservoir Engineer and later District and Division Engineer in Devon, Redwater, Edmonton, Regina and Calgary.

During this time we had our first child, Hardee Thomas, who was born on May 17, 1951 in the Royal Alexandra Hospital in Edmonton. This was a great event in our lives as we had been married for seven years and had not been blessed with any additions. When we brought him home in a wicker basket we were overcome with pleasure and new responsibilities. Sixteen months later Robert arrived, September 11, 1952. He was also born in the Alexandra Hospital and in a few months developed into one of the most beautiful babies I have ever seen. I guess most parents feel this way about their children, but Bob was a beautiful child. He developed into a pretty good-sized man, being 6'2" and 220 lbs. at 20 years of age. The four of us moved around the country following the dictates of my job with Imperial Oil. The boys made many friends as did Jennie and myself. We moved to Calgary during the summer of 1958 when I was appointed Assistant Drilling Superintendent for Imperial Oil. The next several years were spent in this position with a man named George (Bud) Kelley. He is a cousin of Jennie's and we enjoyed working together.

On March 13, 1961 our family was rounded out with the arrival of Mary-Jane who was born in the General Hospital in Calgary. What an added blessing, now we were a family of five, all children normal and healthy.

We bought a house in Calgary, 94 Hallbrook Drive S.W., where we lived for the better part of the next 17 years. I had purchased the SW¼ 14-21-3 W5th from Dr. Cody's wife, Barbara Irene Cody, in February 1961. Joe Fisher was instrumental in our purchase of this land. He was a Real Estate agent for Meston Bros. of Okotoks at the time and when we went to look at the land the snow was butt high to a tall Indian and I was of two minds whether to buy or not. Fisher almost "shamed" me into it and we have been thankful to him ever since. We built an "A" frame house on it in 1963 and when we moved out from Calgary in July 1974 we constructed some additions. The history of this quarter is similar to that of many in the area. It was first surveyed by Dominion Land Surveyer, Edward Deville, in 1908 and although Armond de Bernis used it for a number of years he did not take out Homestead Rights on it until June 1, 1918. When he left Canada and returned to France during World War 1 he must have left this land "in trust" to the Montreal Trust Company who disposed of it to David Glaister through a public bid. They paid $9,280 for the NE 14-21-3 W5th, the SE 23-21-3 W5th and the SW 14-21-3 W5th and obtained Title on April 24, 1956. They sold the SW 14-21-3 W5th to Barbara Irene Cody for $4,300, who obtained Title on August 8, 1956. As mentioned previously I bought it from Barbara Cody in 1961, for $10,500.00.

We bought the NW¼ 16-21-4 W5th from Doug

Jane Lineham, grade 12 graduation.

Kinnear of the Tongue Creek country West of High River in May of 1969. I bought a few head of cattle from Dick Lyall who tried to teach me a little about the cattle business. Dick must have had many secret laughs with Helen and the girls over my attempts at becoming a "gentleman" rancher. We had a lot of fun though and enjoyed each others company. The history of this quarter is told by Catherine Lineham, Hardee's wife in another area of this book.

I retired from Imperial Oil on January 1, 1975 and incorporated myself into a small engineering company called Triple J Engineering Consulting Services Ltd. At the time of writing, this little one-man company is quite active providing me with a challenging occupation as well as some extra income for the three J's of the company — Jim, Jennie and Jane.

Ossie and Agnes Lister
by Agnes Lister

In October, 1941, we moved a small house from Longview to an oil well called Major 12, which was ten miles north of Millarville. Ossie was employed by Anglo-Canadian Co. as a steam engineer. While we were living here, he borrowed a team from a rancher friend, Charlie Birney, and hauled lumber from a mill

L. to R. Ossie and Agnes Lister, Mrs. Swift, Tom Swift. Some of Ossie's taxidermy work on wildlife heads.

to build an addition to our little house. I remember the terrible muddy roads, no gravel and 1942 was a very wet year. A happening comes to my mind while we were still at Major 12. Our friend, Charlie Birney, had let us have two hens that were setting, so over those awful muddy roads we went to Calgary for baby chicks to put under these hens. When we finally got home after being stuck in the mud several times, one miserable hen did not want those chicks and would try to pick them to death. In desperation, Ossie started choking the hen and was heard to say, "I am not driving all over that bad road to let you kill these chicks." After a couple of chokings she settled down and took the chicks and we raised a nice flock of fryers. Ossie's driller, Slim Rossen and family lived at the well site too.

After living a year at Major 12, we had to move to a deep test well, seven miles south of Turner Valley,

where we stayed for eight months. Tom Swift and wife lived next to us.

Once again we moved to a Majorville well site, north-west of Millarville. While here our lives were saddened by our son Mervin being killed while at work on Home Oil well 15, on August 21, 1943. Shortly after this we moved our house again to Bill Jackson's land, on the Kew road and later down to Jackson's farm, where it remained for years and we eventually sold it to Roy Foster. It had been moved six times.

In 1947, we bought a quarter section from Ed. Hehr, which is where John Schaal lives to-day. We ranched there, milking cows, feeding pigs, picking roots, etc., as Ossie had decided he had had enough of shift work on the oil wells. After five months of hard labour and

Four generations of the Lister family. L. to R. Veryl Laycraft (grandmother), Ron Laycraft (father), Agnes Lister (great-grandmother), baby Catherine Laycraft, Ossie Lister (great-grandfather).

Agnes Lister, Charlie Birney, Ossie Lister.

The Lister family at the 50th wedding anniversary of Ossie and Agnes Lister. L. to R. Veryl Laycraft (daughter), Agnes Lister, Harold Lister (son), Ossie Lister, Eileen Perry (daughter).

381

no profit we resold to Ed. Hehr and moved back to where Sheep Creek School used to be located. While there our close neighbors were the school principal, Dan Clarke, also the Everett Potters and the Berquists.

When Ossie accepted a job on a wild-cat well, near Devon, we rented our house to the Clarkes and stayed in the north for a year. On moving back to Millarville, Ossie went to work for Home Oil on No. 6 tank farm. We lived in a house supplied by the Co. and our good neighbors were the Dan Mathesons and the Burl Posgates. Ossie worked for Home Oil for five years, until his retirement. Then as the Clarkes had built their own house, we moved our Hagen house to Midnapore, where we lived until retiring to Fernie, B.C. Ossie died in 1965.

Note.

Since this was written by Agnes Lister, she has died at Turner Valley, at the age of 84. After she became a widow in 1965, she resided with family in Edmonton for three years but came back to Calgary and in a short time bought the Vern Thiessen house from Eveline Bruce and became a Millarville dweller again. She always looked on this as home and loved it here.

Veryl Laycraft (Daughter)

Roy and Gloria (Toombs) Litzenberger

by Gloria Litzenberger

Roy was born in Yorkton, and raised and educated in Regina and Saskatoon, Saskatchewan. Gloria was born and raised in Regina, Saskatchewan.

We met in 1959 and were married on July 7, 1962. We moved from Regina to Winnipeg where Tana-Lynn was born in 1965. From Winnipeg we moved to Calgary where our other two daughters were born, Peri-Ann in 1970 and Tiffany-Lee in 1974. In the fall of the same year we moved to the Millarville area, and have resided there ever since.

Tana and Peri both attend Millarville school and Tiffany, our youngest, attends Okotoks Day Care.

Roy is presently in his own business a data processing service to the oil industry.

L. to R. Peri Ann Litzenberger, Tiffany Lee Litzenberger, Tana Lynn Litzenberger.

We also operate a floral establishment in the Town of Okotoks.

Hopefully this will be our last permanent residence.

Jem Irene Lochhead

by Jean Blakley

Jem is the only daughter of Ford and Hallie (Earl) Lochhead. She was born September 6th, 1924, on her father's ranch at Kew. Mrs. Mary Peat capabley assisted at her birth. Jem's grandmother, Mrs. Charles Lochhead, who had assisted at the birth of so many Kew babies, had been injured in an accident the night before. While riding in a horse drawn buggy, the horse had run away, and Mrs. Lochhead had been thrown out, her leg broken when caught in a wheel.

Growing up in the Kew district, Jem attended Plainview school with her three brothers. The family was saddened by the death of the youngest brother, Lewis Edward in 1939.

L. to R. Jem, Bob, Ford and Hallie Lochhead, and the family dog.

One annual event which was looked forward to very eagerly was the Kew picnic. Here the many bachelors of the district enjoyed a day away from their own cooking. One particular picnic stands out in Jem's mind. Each year the single ladies versus the married ladies had a tug-of-war, and the teams put all they had into the pulling, making the rope very taut. On this particular day, each side was giving their best, when out of the crowd came a prankster, Walter Phillips, and with his very sharp knife, cut the rope. Ladies fell in both directions, mostly on top of each other, but when they got their bearings and their feet, they took off after the culprit, who headed in the general direction of Sheep Creek. For a man of his age he was very fleet footed, and eluded the ladies by hiding in the brush along the creek until they called off the chase.

After her Mother's death in 1966, Jem kept house for her Father. When he passed away in 1968, she lived alone at the ranch until she bought a home in Turner Valley where she still resides.

Lawrie H. Lochhead

by Nina Lochhead

In 1942 Lawrie joined the Royal Canadian Air Force and was stationed in many parts of Canada from Halifax to the Queen Charlotte Islands. He was on embarkation leave for the South Pacific when the war ended.

For a couple of years after the war Lawrie drove truck for different companies besides working on the farm with his father.

In 1947 he married Nina Ingeveld of the Square Butte area. At the time Nina was in her first year of teaching at the Plainview School. In 1948 their first child Rosemarie was born and in 1949 Nina went to teach at the Square Butte School.

In the spring of 1951 the twins, Patricia and Theresa were born. That summer construction of the new Millarville School took place and Lawrie worked on the crew. Later that fall Lawrie and Nina took over the

L. H. Lochhead family. Back row, L. to R. Laurie, Nina, Stuart, Pat, Terry, Russel, Rosemarie. Front, Randy, Laura Lynn.

Kew Store from Frank Howe. In January Lawrie bought a school bus and began the route from Kew to Millarville. The springtime brought their first son to join the family. That summer the Kew Store was moved east and a new building constructed. The post-office was also relocated at this time, and the site was on the corner of the Lochhead property in the fork where the southbound road joins the west one. While they ran the store and post-office Lawrie also trucked. In 1955 shortly after Randy was born they closed the store and post-office. A rural mail route later came into effect. Laura Lynn was born in 1956 and that year Lawrie went to work in Calgary for a construction company, remaining there six years.

In 1962, two years after their seventh child Russell was born, Lawrie suffered an accident while operating for a construction company near Red Deer. The doctors feared he might have to be hospitalized for a long time, and perhaps never walk again. At this time Nina was attending summer sessions at the University of

Alberta in Edmonton. Deciding that since it was to the advantage of the family that they could all be together she decided to take a position teaching in Wetaskiwin, where there was a newly built modern hospital. Fortunately the doctors hadn't reckoned with the stamina of the Scots, and Lawrie with much determination took daily exercises and in five weeks walked out of the hospital. The family, however, did move to Wetaskiwin where they remained for three years, Nina teaching school and Lawrie worked for a machine company.

The returned to their home in Kew in 1965 and Lawrie went to work for Canadian Well Services of Turner Valley and Nina went to teach in Longview. It was during this time that the three older daughters Rosemarie, Patricia and Theresa were married. Rosemarie has two boys, Gerald and Billy; Pat has two girls, Janet and Judy and also a boy Danny. Terry has three girls, Barbara, Shari and Carey Dawn. Rosemarie and Terry live in Calgary and Pat lives at St. Paul, Alberta.

1970 saw the family move again. They sold the ranch at Kew, and moved to Sundre. Here they purchased a half section farm and settled down to raising purebred herefords branded KEW. During their stay in Sundre Nina went back to the University of Calgary and obtained her B. Ed majoring in French. Stuart, their fourth child moved to Edmonton where he took up the electronic trade. He married there and has two children, a son Brent and a daughter Kristie. At the present time he is a foreman of a crew for Syncrude at Fort McMurray. While in Sundre the three younger children, Randy, Laura Lynn and Russell were very active in 4-H. Laura Lynn became the only 4-H member of the Olds District to win the Southern Alberta speaking championship in Public Speaking for 4-H held in Calgary.

After living at Sundre for three years the family moved again, this time to High Prairie where they bought a five-quarter farm and started farming it. Nina taught French at the high school in the town. Randy, the fifth child, left after obtaining his welding certificate at the Alberta Vocational College at Grouard. He is now working at his trade in Lethbridge. That same summer Laura Lynn left to take up a position of librarian in the elementary school at Ashmont. At the present time she is enrolled in a B. Ed degree program at the University of Calgary.

Russell is enrolled in the Alberta Vocational College at Grouard, but is quite undecided as to what he intends to become.

A family reunion of all the descendants of Charlie Lochhead, Lawrie's grandfather is to be held the summer of 1978, south of Turner Valley. It is expected there will be children, grandchildren, great-grandchildren and great-great-grandchildren of his there.

Plainview School

My First Year of Teaching — Nina Lochhead (Ingeveld)

In the fall of 1947 after only one year of university training I went to teach my first year at Plainview School in the Kew area. How little we had learned I found out when I arrived the first morning and wondered what on earth to do. The pupils were wonderful and helped me in every way. With the aid of the community they organized a dance to raise money for the Christmas Concert. Their concert by the way was composed by the students themselves. They wrote the script and carried out everything. Dan Dudenhoeffer was kind enough to take us in his sleigh to the Kew Hall to practice, Elsie Ingeveld helped with the music and Lawrie Lochhead got our tree.

True to form — the school teacher marries an eligible bachelor in the neighborhood. I married Lawrie Lockhead during the Christmas holidays. Now I didn't have to con the school boys into splitting the wood for my teacherage anymore, nor did my kind neighbor Roy Sim have to struggle with my sputtering gas lamp that I could never get to work properly. I also had help now to total up the register at the end of each month. Math wasn't my strongest subject.

Yes, those were the good old days and I think anyone contemplating teaching these days should have a chance to teach in a one room school for a time. Now that I have my B. Ed. and teaching my native language (French) in a modern high school, I sometimes wish I could turn back the pages of time and be back with those first students of mine. The nostalgia is strong, but progress is the word of the future.

Square Butte School

by Nina (Ingeveld) Lochhead

Square Butte was the school I attended for nine years. Therefore it was with much anticipation I went back there to teach in 1949. There were six families attending that year — Birney, Lyall, Nylund, Reimer, Silvester and Wildman, with twelve pupils in all. Today a class of that size would be considered paradise — but seven grades. That was a different story.

We had a good time that year. Being a small group we had time to do everything together — Junior Red Cross, ball games, hiking up the Coal Mine Hill, swimming in Fisher Creek and many more.

With help from Dick Lyall, Charlie Birney and Jake Reimer preparing a stage and Elsie Ingeveld with the music we put on a nice Christmas concert. That year the school saw many practices of the Drama Club besides many dances with music provided by the local talent of Mary Bell, Elsie Ingeveld, Fred and Carrie Kosling along with Cyrus McBee.

The following spring, Chas. Wilson, then Superintendent of schools for Calgary Rural Division 41, came to the school to make his inspector's report. He came three times before he actually found the school occupied. The first time we were away hiking on Coal Mine Hill, the second time we were fishing in Fisher Creek. The third time we were there all right but one student promptly climbed a tree and refused to come down until the brass had left.

Time marches on and with sadness I recall that that was the last year Square Butte School operated as a school. The following year it was consolidated into Millarville School.

Lochhead, Robert and Margaret

Robert C. (Bob) and Margaret Lochhead. Living here in the Caroline area for six years, it seems a long time ago that I was a kid at Kew.

Having arrived into the world on July 21, 1927, duly assisted by my mother, Hallie Lochhead and Mrs. Mary Peate.

I recall little of pre-school days, with the exception of one occasion when I ran down to the river where Dad was working and told him that my little brother Lewis had fallen from his high chair and all his teeth came out. Dad ran home and found everything was fine, including Lewis. He had not fallen at all. That was the first one I owed Mom. She said I was lonely and needed attention. Dad nearly gave me some said "attention" that day.

The nine years spent in Plainview School are pleasant memories. Mr. Hedley was my teacher from grade three to seven. He was also the only one to give me the strap. Granted, it was deserved.

George Iceton and I were killing flies with a pencil box instead of spelling. We used sugar as bait, and with means of an elastic band snapped the lid shut on the unsuspecting fly.

Much credit should be given to Mr. Hedley, he walked four miles every day to teach us, and received two hundred and fifty dollars a year if he did the janitor work too. Were not those the good ole' days? I wonder.

Lochhead Family. L. to R. Jem, Bob, Ford, Hallie, Margaret, Maureen (in white) Peg with cat, uncle Vern Lochhead. Kevin in front.

Summer seemed warmer then, and we spent most of our time in the creek, being called home by Dad's bugle at suppertime.

Rainy days found us at the Kew General Store. I must be getting old, I can remember buying a bottle of ginger beer for five cents, and not being able to finish it. I recall Mr. Walton, the storekeeper and Arthur Reed, and the way they used to argue about anything and everything.

Then there was Walter Phillips with his fiery temper and daring ways. Dad told of a time when Walter and some other fellows went to Calgary. They dared Mr. Phillips to make a U-turn around the cop directing traffic on eighth avenue. Walter merrily accepted the challenge.

The cop stopped him and asked where he was from. Walter cupped his hand over his ear and yelled "Aye"? The cop repeated the question with more volume, and Walter leaning forward asked "Eh"? So the cop shouted "Where are you from"? Walter said "Kew". The cop instructed him to get back to Kew, which Mr. Phillips did, — after collecting the bet.

My brother Lawrie, sister Jem and I, all rode to school on a horse named Roxy. Lawrie held the reins, and coming home from school one night, he took a turn too fast and all four feet went out from under Roxy, and there were the three of us sitting in order on the ground, Lawrie, Bob and Jem on the rear.

Grampa Charlie lived with us until his death in 1941. He always helped with the garden and farm work. I will never forget how mad he was when Dad wouldn't let him stack hay anymore. He was 80 years old, but it didn't stop him from shouting orders from the ground.

He was our "sitter" when Mom and Dad went away. We could count on potato soup and pancakes. Luckily, he was a better carpenter than a cook. One night after telling us to shut up about four times, he carried out a threat to go sleep in the barn away from the racket. We figured he would be back in as soon as we settled down, so we placed all the milk pails across the doorway. You can imagine the noise when he stumbled over them. It's a wonder I lived long enough to write this.

I will always remember how hard Mom worked and never complained. When I wanted some extra money for a bike, out came her egg money. She was the greatest. It was a trying time for Mom when Lewis died in 1939. But good friends and neighbors helped a lot.

When Lawrie went into the services in 1942, and Dad was trucking, the farm work fell to me. About that time consolidation of schools started and we were bused to Sheep Creek School at Millarville. One would have to say that Dan Dudenhoffer pioneered the bus industry with a sort of dog house built on an old Ford truck. We had lots of laughs trying to encourage that truck to school and back. One never knew but what they would share their space with Turkey Tom or a wiener pig.

The kids from the "Home Hill" had a bus to take them to school. It also served as a workman's bus. I recall one morning we were all jammed into this rig when it stopped to pick up two more girls. There were no seats left so I offered my knee to a pretty Miss. She accepted, and sat on it all the way to school and my heart was doing flip flops. Well, Margaret Robertson, that was her name, and I were married in the spring of 1946 — Good Friday it was — and ministers are hard to come by that day, they are all so busy. But Reverend Rex Brown took the time out of his busy day to perform the ceremony.

We lived in a granary while we cut and peeled logs for a house.

Allen Brooks, a cousin on Dad's side spent much of his early years with us, and was there to help us raise the logs. Allen was always good for a laugh.

Our first daughter Maureen was born in November of 1947 and followed shortly by Trina in December of 1948.

The thing I remember about Trina's birth was my mother-in-law saying that when the Lord said to replenish the earth, He didn't mean for me to do it all by myself!

Peggy was born in 1950 and Kevin in 1953.

I drove a school bus from the late fifties until 1972 when we moved. I enjoyed it very much and especially the extra curriculum trips with Bill Dube.

In the late 1960's, the country began to change, we were feeling the pull of city life. Acreages and small holdings were springing up all over.

Mom passed away in 1966 after a long bout with cancer, and Dad followed in 1968 with a heart attack while attending an historical meeting at the school.

Our centennial project arrived October 31, 1967. We named her Heather Gail. Our chosen daughter, Lori-Ann came to be with us in 1971 at the age of six years.

Raymond Trosten, Margaret Lochhead, Bob Lochhead. Front: Richard Trosten, Heather and Laurie Lochhead.

Our daughter Trina, who married John Smith from Turner Valley, lives on the farm with us. They have three children, Cindy, Christie and Sean.

Kevin married Vera Foster from Walter Valley and they have two children, Brian and Jannette. He worked for the Lamb Processors Co-op in Innisfail.

Peggy married Russell Rowlandson. They have lived in Ottawa, Toronto, Fort Smith, N.W.T. and are now in Jasper. They have two children Travis and Leigh-Ann. Maureen married Stan Iceton and they live in Turner Valley with their two little girls, Lisa and Janine.

This is a great country and wonderful community We are involved in the Nazarene Church, in school activities, first aid and Lions Club.

We are right back in the district where Margaret started school years ago.

Stuart and Christine Lochhead

Stuart was born in Calgary April, 2, 1952 oldest son of Lawrie and Nina Lochhead. He started school at Millarville going by bus. He enjoyed swimming and fishing in the river on Grandpa Lochhead's farm at Kew in the summer and hockey in the winter.

In 1971 he moved to Edmonton to finish his training as an electrician. While there he married Christine Kapp who was born in Loon Lake, Saskatchewan on April 10, 1952.

Christine and Stuart Lochhead and children, Brent and Kristie.

They now have two children, Brent A born July 23 in Edmonton and Kristie A born March 4, 1975 in Edmonton.

Stuart is now a journey man electrician and they make their home in Fort McMurray.

Lucas, Shirley (Hedley)

My father, Everett Hedley, moved to a farm northwest of Turner Valley in 1934. I attended Plainview School where my dad was teacher. During the first school years, I also attended Sheep Creek School for one year. I attended Sunalta Jr. High School in Calgary for grade nine and Western Canada High School for grade ten. My family then sold the farm and moved to Black Diamond in 1948 and Dad worked for the Royalite Oil Company and I went to North Turner Valley High School. I went to work for the Royalite Oil Co. in the office in Turner Valley, and later on worked for the Land Titles Office in Calgary. I married Wray Lucas of Semon and Lucas Construction in Calgary in 1962. We later sold out our interest in construction and bought a farm north-west of Rimbey, Alberta, in 1965. We still do a bit of part-time construction (building), involved with the 4H Beef Club for a number of years, and at present Wray is a Councillor with the County of Ponoka. We have a daughter Linda married to Dennis Tucker of Drayton Valley and they have a son, Nathan. Our son Guy is going to school in Rimbey for his grade nine.

My sister Merlyn attended Planview School, Black Diamond and Turner Valley schools and North Turner Valley High School, from which she graduated. Merlyn also worked for Royalite Oil Co. in Calgary. She married Dave Basaraba in 1965, who is an electrician at the University of Calgary. They have two sons, John and James attending public school. Merlyn and Dave have been involved in the anitque car club and in their boys hockey.

My brother Keith attended school in Turner Valley elementary and junior and High School at North Turner Valley High. He was in the Air Force for a short while, then worked for Semon-Lucas Construction then went to S.A.I.T. for carpentry. Upon completion he married Eileen Anderson in 1969 at Whitewood, Sask. He worked for Nu-West Homes and Springer Const. and gained enough experience that he has now formed his own company and lives in Carstairs, Alta. They have two sons, Kevin and Darren, Kevin is in grade two and Darren goes to Kindergarten.

My parents, Everett and Sheila Hedley sold their house in Turner Valley in 1977 and now live in Carstairs, Alta.

Joe and Helen Lukacs
by Zoli Lukacs

When the Hungarian Revolution broke out in 1950, Joe Lukacs was a university student on a tour near the Austrian border. At the outbreak of the revolution he slipped over the border, waiting a month in Austria before deciding where to go from there. Upon deciding to come to Canada, he returned to Hungary, to bring out his wife to be, Helen. After a series of misadventures, including being caught by borderguards and talking his way out of jail, they eventually left the country with a few friends, headed for Canada. After a "memorable" boat trip across the Atlantic, they arrived in Halifax January, 1957, and were married February 16, 1957.

Dad finished his university in Edmonton, graduating with a Masters Degree in Petroleum Engineering in 1962. After working in the oil industry for a period of time, which included living in Redwater and Cochrane, the family moved to Calgary in 1965, where he started a consulting company with some other businessmen, of which he became president.

There are three boys in the family, Zoli and Rick, born 1957 and 1962 respectively. While Dad was finishing his degree in Edmonton Joe Jr. was born in 1963 while the family lived in Cochrane.

Dad was introduced to the Millarville area while hunting in the area with Dale White, son-in-law of Tim and Jean Blakley.

He bought the piece of land, W½ 20-21-4-W5M from Dave Glaister in 1970. After a slow start and much clearing Dad (with Dave Glaisters help) got a small Red Angus operation going, joining with the Glaisters, the Rogers' and the Sibbalds of Cochrane, to form the Dynamite Breeders.

At present there is still much work to be done on the land, and living accomodations leave a little to be desired (trailers are a little inconvenient), but the family is looking forward to a long association with the land, and the people in the area.

Alex Lyall
by Alex Lyall

I was born in Calgary December 26th, 1911. My parents, Thomas Lyall and Sarah Ann (Pierce) Lyall came from England in 1906. They worked in and around Calgary then filed on a homestead in the Millarville and Kew area in 1910, the N.W. ¼ 14-21-4W5.

As a young boy I can remember my Dad and

Alex, Mother (Sarah), Richard and Tommy seated on big rock on Sec. 14-21-4W5.

Mother building the new log house in 1914. Most of that house is still standing today, in 1978. I remember when my folks, brothers and I wintered at the Dole Ranch, which had originally been the Quirk Ranch, then after Dole it was the Kendall Ranch for 50 years.

In the terrible flu epidemic of 1918, I and all the rest of the family were all down with flu.

In 1920 with my folks, we moved to Vulcan by team and wagon, where Dad had rented a grain farm. There I and my brothers went to Thigh Hill School.

We farmed eight years in the Vulcan district, then Dad and Mother bought a farm at Balzac twelve miles north of Calgary, in 1929. I farmed with my Dad and brothers until 1932 when Dad passed away from a heart attack. Then the depression of the 1930's came and the bottom went out of everything. The rest of the family and I carried on for three years, but with prices so low we could not make payments on the farm. So Mother, my brothers and I quit the farm and moved back to the homestead here at Millarville in 1935.

I have been living here ever since but the following years were slim pickings. Milking some cows, feeding a few pigs, and shooting some rabbits we all survived the dirty thirties. I also had a saw mill and sold lumber for five to ten dollars per thousand.

There were no gravel roads here then and in the spring time of the year when the frost was coming out of the ground, it was very difficult to get to Calgary with the cream, eggs etc. I had to travel early in the morning while the roads were still frozen and sometimes would have to wait until it froze again at night to get back home, and if it did not freeze I left the truck on the side of the road and walked home carrying groceries on my back. Then I had to ford Fisher Creek, taking my shoes off and wade through then get back into my shoes and keep on walking. Next morning it would be frozen so I could get the truck home.

Well, now along with all the hard going, I had some good times at the old Rancher's Hall, getting to the dances and badminton games by team and sleigh in winter and sometimes by car in good weather.

I played badminton with the local boys and girls, Leonard and Jim Nelson, Carlton King, Waugh girls, Bill Jackson, Bert Hodgkins, Val Mack, Eric Mulder, my brothers Richard and Tom, Joe Waite, Herb Larratt, Esther Jackson, Sally Hambling, Lyle and Merle Heine, Elwyn and Irene Evans, Bill and Ethel Lee, Jim Colley and some others. We also had a great softball team. We had good times in the Kew Hall at its first site before it was moved to its present site at Square Butte, on the N.W. corner of the Tilly and Harry Hulme quarter, the S.W. ¼ of 14-21-4W5. The land is now owned by Mr. and Mrs. Willson.

The old Rancher's Hall in later years was moved to Heritage Park in Calgary, where it is now, in 1978.

After the second World War, things began to get better. I went to the Home Oil Company in 1948, doing lease work and Tank Farm Operator, Compressor Operator, shift work day and night in all kinds of

L. to R. Marion Lyall, Tommy Lyall, Norma Lyall, Alex Lyall. Seated, in front, Betty Lyall.

weather. After a year or so later I bought a used half ton truck. The roads were gravelled and travel was much better. I used the truck to go to work and from there on I was able to buy a new car.

In 1957, I built a new house as Mother was still living. She passed away October 1970, aged 87 years.

I worked for Home Oil Co. for 23 years then took an early retirement in 1971. I continued ranching on the N.W.¼ 14-21-4W5, the S.W.¼ of 24-21-4W5 and the S.E.¼ of 23-21-4W5.

In May 1971 I married Norma Wildman, a widow and we both are living on the land I have here.

Norma has a son and daughter, David and Mary Ann, both living at Sanguda, Alberta.

I have two brothers, Richard, who passed away in 1972, age 62 years, and Thomas Henry living in the De Winton district.

I have seen a tremendous change in roads, ways of living, facilities and other things that are used today. Some difference to what we had in 1935.

DAD'S OLD BREECHES author unknown

When dad has worn his trousers out
They pass to brother John;
Then mother trims them round about,
And William puts them on.

When William's legs too long have grown,
The trousers fail to hide 'em.

Next Sam's fat legs they close invest,
And when they won't stretch tighter,
They're turned and shortened, washed and pressed
And fixed on me — the writer.

Ma works them into rugs and caps
When I have burst the stitches.
At doomsday we shall see (perhaps)
The last of dad's old breeches.

This poem was found pasted in an old family album, yellowed with considerable age.

Eldon and Barbara Lyall and Family YƎʀʀ.

I was born on March 18th 1942, first of four children of Dick and Helen Lyall of Square Butte. I lived in the Square Butte district until Mom and I moved to Trochu from 1942 to 1945 while Dad was overseas. Upon Dad's return in 1945 we moved back to Square Butte where Dad and Mom bought Grandad's (George Lyall) homestead and continued ranching operations.

I attended school at the original Square Butte School through grade three when the school was closed and we were bussed to Sheep Creek School west of Millarville, until that school was consolidated with other surrounding districts to the present site of Millarville School. As there was no grade twelve taught at Millarville I drove to Turner Valley for my last year.

Leaving school I went to work for Bill Kendall at the saw mill, then helped Wallace Andrews clean siesmic lines.

In 1960, I went to work for Allen Baker at the Bar U Ranch. Leaving the Bar U, I got a job with Alberta Gas Trunk Line Co. at Fort McLeod. Transferred to Brooks later on the same year and in September 1961 was transferred to Calgary as equipment operator.

On December 1st. 1962, I married Barbara Davis of the Meadowbank district west of High River. Barb is a daughter of Roy and Dot Davis and a granddaughter of Pat Hartell, who is well known in the Turner Valley district.

In 1965 our daughter Cheryl Ann was born and three years later Douglas Wayne was born.

I continued working for A.G.T.L. until August of

Eldon Lyall and family. L. to R. Douglas, Cheryl, Barbara, Eldon, Nancy Lee standing in front of Eldon.

1969 when we left Calgary to live in Delburne and Erskine and drove for G. & M. Transport to Stettler. The fall of 1970 saw us move to High River and go to work for Navajo Trucking Ltd., then for Bob Butcher at High River Co-op Oils.

Back to ranching and farming in 1971 when we went to work for Roy and Lenore McLean at Pekisko for almost four years. In 1975, Frank McInenly, my brother-in-law, bought into the Stavely Auction Market and we moved to Stavely to help him run the market. We spent two very busy and educational years there and then left to work on a farm east of Stavely.

In 1978 we resolved to find a business of our own. We bought a family business, Keely's Hardward and Furniture and moved to the town of Nanton.

Through the years since Grandad retired from ranching, and turned his brand over to us we have kept it, Y꜀ which was first registered in 1916.

Looking back we have no regrets about all our moves and experiences, as we have gathered a lot of warm and lasting friendships along the way.

Helen Lyall

Helen Lyall

On June 29, 1920, I arrived on the scene in St. Mary's Hospital Trochu, Alberta. My parents were Mr. and Mrs. Stuart Greig of Trochu. I lived with my parents until the fall of 1921 when my mother died. After her death, my grandparents Mr. and Mrs. McIntyre took me and raised and educated me. We lived for a short time with my aunt and uncle on the farm, then moved in to Trochu. In 1928 we moved to Calgary. I attended several elementary schools in Calgary and then took my High School at Central High School (C.C.I.) From there I went to the Calgary Normal School where I received my Permanent Teacher's Certificate. In 1940 I accepted my first teaching position at Square Butte. And in 1941 Dick and I were married.

Square Butte School

by Helen Lyall

Following my graduation from the Calgary Normal School in June of 1940 the next step was to find a job.

At that time there seemed to be more teachers than job opportunities. After answering several ads and travelling many miles I was getting rather discouraged. Then I heard through Harry Hamilton (who had been teaching at Square Butte) that the school would be available come September. At that time the Square Butte School was in the Calgary Rural District. I immediately went to see Mr. McVeigh who was secretary-treasurer at that time. Much to my delight, I was hired.

Labor Day afternoon found me on my way to my first school. What a long way it seemed from Calgary! After making a few wrong turns, we finally arrived at the school, took a look around it, then went on to George Lyall's where I was to board (and whose son I later married). That night was indeed a long one and I will admit I was really homesick.

However, next day the school term began in earnest. There were eleven pupils from grade one to nine and I also had two girls taking their High School by correspondence. It was an enjoyable year and we had many good times together. The highlights of the year were of course the Christmas concert in December and the school picnic in June.

I taught the next fall from September to December when I decided to work at becoming a full-time housewife.

The Square Butte School saw many pupils and many more teachers until it was closed in 1950 and the students were bussed to Millarville. Many community affairs were held in the old school after it was no longer a hall of learning. However, it was eventually burned down.

Norma Edith (Stewart) Lyall

by Norma Lyall

Born on May 7, 1920, the third child of Colin and Etta Stewart. Dad (b. Nov. 14, 1893, d. May 29, 1973) was a son of Morris and Agnes Stewart of Davisburg. Mother (b. Dec. 13, 1896, d. July 20, 1962) was the oldest daughter of William and Ada Stewart of Byemoor. I have two brothers, Stanley born Aug. 22, 1913, Vernon born March 3, 1924, and a sister Verna born March 29, 1916, died Nov. 1920.

My father was a roamer and we had lived at countless places by the time I was ten years old. In 1927 while living at the Forman place (home of the late Mrs. Flo King), Endiang, my father contacted polio.

My school days began in September at Endiang and continued in April at Halkirk as by then our family had moved. I only went to school in the fall and spring when the weather was warm as I had to walk 3½ miles.

Dad came home from Edmonton in June, 1928, but still could not walk without help. In the fall and winter of 1928-29, to keep food on the table, my Mother went to work as cook at the Ben Hronek Coal Mines north of Halkirk for $25.00 per month. Stanley was out working and helped with food too. The two years we lived at

Tom, David, Norma, Mary Ann. July 10, 1944.

Five generations. Back Norma (Wildman) Lyall, daughter of Etta Stewart. Etta Stewart, daughter of Ada Stewart. Front row: Ada Stewart, daughter of Susan Waters, (pictured) Baby, Mary Ann Wildman, daughter of Norma Lyall.

Halkirk we had no rain so that meant no garden or crops.

Conditions were bad when we moved to Rimbey in May 1930 and during our fourteen mile wagon trip to the farm we lost our only sack of flour. Next day we retraced our tracks to find that a herd of range horses had trampled it into the ground. We attended Crystal Springs school which was only a mile away.

My mother was well-known for her lovely patchwork quilts, marvelous cooking and neighborliness.

As kids, I can remember trapping gophers, collecting magpie and crow eggs for which we received 1¢ each, paid by the municipality. As a point of interest, you could only get 5¢ per dozen for hen eggs at the creamery. When I was twelve I became the janitor at the school, taking care of the firewood and packing the drinking water the one mile from home. After quitting school I had many jobs, basically outside work, at different neighbors, doing chores and looking after sheep. Later in 1939 I received top wages of $1.00 per day for this type of work.

In 1940 I married Tom Wildman a neighbor of ours. Our children David and Mary Ann were born and as there was no school close to our farm we decided to move to Square Butte in 1947.

The first outing we went to at Square Butte was a Halloween Party where we met all the neighbors. There Mrs. K. Kendall invited me to the ladies meeting the next week to which I attended and became a member of the Square Butte Ladies Group and have been active in it ever since.

In 1948 David started school at Square Butte which were the last years the school operated. He rode his horse most of the time in good weather, but the only problem he had was getting back on his horse if he ever got off or fell off.

David and Mary Ann amused themselves building tree houses then as David's talents increased, log houses. Mary Ann and the favorite old dog, Pal, did a lot of the log hauling.

After Tom's death in 1960 the farm business became my responsibility. I had never written a cheque or driven a car in my life, but I soon learnt. Fred, David, myself and at times Mary Ann ran the ranch until 1970 when David took over.

From 1960-70 I took in boarders who worked on oil rigs. At times there were up to five men working three different shifts which kept me hopping.

On May 1, 1971 I married Alexander Lyall and moved to his home on the hill.

In 1974 David moved to Sangudo and we hired Vern Blanchard to run the ranch for a couple of years.

In 1976 Ernie Geiger bought the Wildman Ranch and cattle.

Now Alex and I are retired on 53 acres enjoying ourselves traveling and gardening.

"HOW DO YOU FEEL"
Author Unknown

There's nothing the matter with me
I'm as healthy as can be (except)
I've Arthritis in both my knees
When I talk, I talk with a wheeze
My pulse is weak and my blood is thin
But I'm awfully well for the shape I'm in.

Arch supports I have for my feet
Or I'd be unable to be on the street.
Sleep is denied me night after night
But every morning I find I'm all right,
My memory is failing my head's in a spin
But I'm awfully well for the shape I'm in.

The moral is this as this tale unfolds
That for you and me who are growing old
It's better to say I'm fine with a grin
Than let folks know the shape we are in.

How do I know that my youth is all spent?
Well my get up and go has got up and went
But I really don't mind when I think with a grin
Of all the grand places my get up has been.

Old age is golden I've heard it said
But sometimes I wonder as I get into bed,
With my ears in a drawer, my teeth in a cup
My eyes on the table until I wake up,
Ere sleep comes o'er me I say to myself
Is there anything else I should put on the shelf?

When I was young my slippers were red
I could put both my heels over my head.
When I grew older my slippers were blue
But still I could dance the whole night thru
Now older still my slippers are black.
I walk to the store and puff my way back.
Finally,
   I get up each morning and dust off me wits
   Pick up the paper and read the o'bits.
   If my name is still missing
   I know I'm not dead
   So I get a good breakfast and go back to bed.

Richard James (Dick) Lyall

by Dick Lyall

I was born west of Nanton in July of 1913. My parents were Mr. and Mrs. George Lyall who homesteaded in the Kew district in the early years. With my parents I moved from Nanton to Kew when I was just a baby. As there was no school in the Square Butte district, my parents took my sister, Peggy, and I back to my birthplace in Nanton in 1919 so we could go to school. We attended the Sunset School west of Nanton until 1922. At that time we moved back to the homestead as that was the year the Square Butte School was started.

I finished my schooling at Square Butte at the age of fifteen years. After that I worked with my dad, also for the neighbors as well as the oil well companies for many years.

One of my greatest privileges in life was growing up among some of the real old time cowboys and Ranchers of the Kew district. It would take a whole book to write down all their names and experiences. Just to mention a few there were the Bell brother, Paddy Rodgers, Tip Johnson, Bill Livingstone, Joe Fisher. I could go on for pages. My greatest friend for

Dick Lyall Family. Eldon, Helen, and Dick Lyall. Front: Margaret Anne, Agnes and Carol.

years until his passing was Paddy Rodgers. My most earnest hope as I was growing up was that a little bit of me would turn out to be like them. Their schooling about ranching did not come from books. It came from hard work and experience.

In the late 1930's I rented the Bannerman place on shares and batched there. In 1940 Helen Greig came to teach at the Square Butte School. She boarded with my dad and mother. Being a curious nature I rode up to Dad's to see what the new teacher was like. I found her pretty and attractive and not too hard to get along with. A year later we were married and lived on the Bannerman place. Our son, Eldon was born there in 1942. We remained there until June 1942 when I joined the army. Our stock and machinery had to be sold and we moved our household belongings to Dad and Mother's.

Helen and Eldon moved to Calgary and lived with her grandmother for a time. Then after I went overseas they lived at Torchu with Helen's aunt and uncle Mr. and Mrs. T. J. Smyth.

After some basic training in Calgary and Camp Borden, Ontario, I went overseas as reinforcement with the Calgary Tank Regiment. Went through the Italian theatre of war before going on to France, Belguim, and Holland. Finally the war was over and we were sent to England. There we waited and waited, and waited from May until December. We finally arrived back in Calgary December 2nd, 1945.

In 1946 we purchased the ranch from Dad and Mother. We continued to live with them until the summer of 1948. In August of 1947 our oldest daughter, Margaret Anne was born. In 1947 we started building our own house. By the summer of 1948 we had the framework, roof and all outside walls done so decided to move in and live in it while we finished it. This was some undertaking but we finally made the grade. August 1951 saw the birth of our second daughter Agnes.

In 1955 Helen took a teaching job at the Millarville School She took a year's leave of absence during the 1956-57 school term and then went back in September

Dick Lyall Family. Standing Margaret Schmitke, Dan and Carol Scott, Barb and Eldon Lyall, Dick Lyall, Frank and Agnes McInenly. Sitting: Jay Schmitke, Cheryl holding Stacey McInenly, Helen Lyall holding Evan Schmitke, and Douglas Lyall.

Marion, Richard, Lynda Jean, Gordon and Don Lyall. 1954.

of 1957. Our third daughter Carol was born in October, 1956. Helen stayed with her teaching job until she retired in 1973.

Our life on the Millarville ranch was varied — some good years and some not so good — but all in all well worth remembering. We staying there until October of 1975 when we moved to Bowden where we bought a small acreage.

Eldon married Barbara Davis in December, 1962. They have two children Cheryl and Douglas. They now live in Nanton where they own a hardware store. Margaret Anne married Ken Schmitke in June 1968 and they have two children Jay and Evan. They live in Calgary. In January of 1974, Agnes married Frank McInenly. They have one daughter Stacey and live in Vulcan. Carol married Dan Scott in April 1977. They now live in Longview.

The Richard Lyall Family

by Donald (Don) Lyall

"Dash it all" and "Flippin" were two of Dad's favourite sayings. A real family man, he rarely swore, but could use one of his "sayings" to fit almost any occasion.

Dad was born in Calgary in 1909, the oldest son of Thomas and Sarah Lyall. He lived with his parents on the homestead, the N.W.¼ 14-21-4-W5, in the Millarville/Kew district until 1921, when the family moved to Vulcan. Here, Tom Lyall farmed for eight years.

Dad's schooling must have been something. The old school pictures have all the tousle-headed boys in bib overalls standing solemnly beside braided-haired girls. The one-room Thigh-Hill School is long gone, but I am sure the room was warm and friendly. From Vulcan the family moved to Balzac, where Tom bought a farm. Unfortunately, the depression years followed this move and like most things, farming was reduced to mere subsistance.

In 1932, Tom was stricken by a heart attack. The three boys, Richard, our father, and his brothers, Alex

and Tommy and their mother stayed with the Balzac farm for about three years.

Finally they were forced to move back to the homestead in 1935. Dad left the farm to persue a course in mechanics at the Southern Alberta Institute of Technology. During the late 1930's and early forties he worked for his uncle, E. O. Parry's Garage in Morrin, Alberta.

Dad and Mother were married in Calgary, in 1942, and made their home in this City. Mother still lives in her northwest Calgary home.

Mother was another one of those Millarville area people. The daughter of Joseph and Jean Waugh. She was born in Calgary in 1911, but grew up on the Millarville homestead, N.E.¼ 18-21-3-W5. The Waugh girls, Marion (our mother), Margaret (Peggy), Jean and Josephine, all attended school in Midnapore in 1927. During that year the Sheep Creek School was built, and the family moved back to the Millarville district. After completing her schooling in Millarville, Mother went to business college in Calgary, and then worked in the office of the Western Printing & Lithographing Co., for about two years. After that she went to Carstairs to work in the Beckner Dry Goods Store, as bookkeeper and clerk for three years, before she and Dad were married.

When we were all in school, Mother worked as a sales clerk in Eaton's for nearly five years, and then was employed by The Permanent, and worked in the mortgage department for twelve years. Dad worked as a mechanic for five years after he and Mother were married. Then Dad went into the building trade; working for several different companies. His last job was with Atco Industries, where he worked for many years before his death in 1972.

My sister, Lynda Jean was born in 1944. She is a graduate of the University of Calgary, and taught school for six years. While she was teaching, Lynda met James Nielsen, son of Virginia and Tony Nielsen, and Lynda and Jim were married in 1969. Jim is an assistant principal with the Calgary Public School Board. They have two children. Heather Jill born in 1972 and David James in 1977.

The Richard Lyall Family. Back row: Lillian (Gordon's wife), Gordon, Jim Nielsen, Donald and wife Noreen. Front: Lynda Jean, Marion, Heather and David Nielsen.

My brother Gordon, born in 1947, might be remembered in the Millarville area because of his red hair. After a couple of years at the Southern Alberta Institute of Technology, where he took electronics, Gord worked in the Millarville district for Alberta Government Telephones. He is still with the Telephone Company as a technical assistant.

Both Gord and I spent many summers with Uncle Alex and Granny on the farm, when we were kids.

In 1974, like many other Alberta boys, Gordon married a Saskatchewan girl. Lillian Dauvin, is the daughter of Emile and Helene Dauvin, who are long time farmers in the Peterson District, east of Saskatoon.

My name is Don (Donald for those formal types), and I followed my sister to the University of Calgary, where I took education. After teaching school for two years, I went to Mount Royal College, and took a course in public relations. I am presently employed by the Federal Government.

I am married to Noreen, who is the daughter of Howard and Norma Moore. The Moores are a true "Calgarian" family, having lived in Calgary all of their lives.

Being a native Calgarian, I am proud of the Lyall and Waugh families' connections to the Millarville and Calgary past.

Written by Marion (Waugh) Lyall in 1936

As we grow older day by day
And sun and shadows cross our way
We thank God for the little things
The things we had not counted much
Our dear Mother's gentle touch
Which does not flee away on wings.

It lingers in your thoughts a while
Her gentle touch and loving smile
Our Father too who understands
His always sympathetic ways,

His presence brighter than the rays
Of noon day sun and desert sands.

There by the fire the rocking chair
Where we have knelt to say our prayer
Each night, against our Mother's knee
And on the shelf near by there stands
The kitchen clock with crooked hands
Just placed where it will always be.

The table with its white scrubbed boards
Is set for supper fit for lords,
With bread and butter, milk and cheese
And through the open window comes
The song of birds and bees that hum
All carried on the summer breeze.

For the little garden gate that creaks
And the old shed with the roof that leaks
Where we at hide and seek have played.
There's the garden with its rows of corn
In which we weeded every morn
And then through wooded pastures strayed.

For all the hopes and joys of life
And all the pleasure, all the strife
And all the things that can and will
Make for us a happy home
Memories that last where e're we roam
And make our life worth living still.

Thomas H. Lyall
third son of Sarah and Tom Lyall

I was born in Calgary in October 1918. Our family lived on the homestead west of Millarville in the Square Butte district, from there we moved to Vulcan in 1921 and to Balzac in 1928. During the Dirty Thirties our father passed away. After his death we were unable to continue farming this large farm, and so we returned to the homestead at Square Butte in 1936.

The following years were very hard ones for Mother and brothers Richard, Alex and myself. We set about clearing and breaking the land for some grain and hay. Then it was the start of the war. In 1942, I joined the Armed Forces, and after training in Red Deer, Calgary and Vancouver, I was sent overseas. I was stationed in Jamaica in the West Indies for eighteen months. While stationed in Jamaica, I met my wife Betty, daughter of Mr. and Mrs. E. L. Christie of Ocho Rios, Ja. We were married on August 1, 1944. I returned home for 5 months, Betty arrived in December of 44 and I was on the move again, this time to England and Holland, returning home in January of 1946.

We built our first home on the homestead, and there our first daughter, Elizabeth was born in 1947. Our second daughter, Susan, was born in November of 1952. In 1946, I returned to Home Oil Company, for whom I had worked prior to joining the Army and I'm still employed with them, now in Head office in Calgary. In 1958 we moved to Home Camp and were later

Tommy and Betty Lyall on their wedding day. August 1, 1944.

Lyon, Sue (Rawlinson)

I came to Canada in, approximately, 1921, with my parents, "Ted" and Gertrude "Joy" Rawlinson and spent a brief time in Toronto and Montreal before moving to Kapuskasing, where Dad was superintendent of an experimental farm (see page 197 of the first edition of "Our Foothills".) He hated the snow and cold and nicknamed the place "Keep Us Cursing." At this time I was a prim and proper well behaved English girl and have vivid memories of my first school in the Canadian wilderness. The kids were holy terrors and I was as alien to them as they were to me. They did everything from putting me down a well to stringing me up. It made me very unhappy being the only outcast there. Twin boys who were reasonably human became my friends, and I soon learned that in order to be popular you had to be bad.

When we came west (again page 197) I went to a private school in Banff run by Mr. and Mrs. Greenham. The Margaret Greenham Theatre in Banff is named for this beloved woman in her memory.

I attended Square Butte and Fordville schools and finished my education in Calgary. Shortly after this I moved to Vancouver; in those years one could buy a ticket for one cent a mile. The great depression was moving up and jobs were nil. I worked at anything I could get, baby sitting, housework, hotel work and waitress jobs, (which were the most plentiful.) Being out of work for some time during one period I rented a room for $7 a month and couldn't even pay the rent. My patient and kind landlord (a Calgary man) carried me for two months, plus breakfast. A dear, funny old

L. to R. Elizabeth and Susan Lyall. 1965.

Sue (Rawlinson) Lyon and her cat, Snoopy. 1977.

transferred to Swan Hills, Sundre and to the Carstairs Gas Plant, returning to Calgary in 1963.

Elizabeth is married to Wayne D. Miller of Calgary and has three children. Randy, Jamie and Christie, all living in Calgary. Susan is married to E. Greg Strother of Calgary, they have two daughters; Leah and Laura. They reside in Calgary. Betty and myself are now living on an acreage east of De Winton in the Davisburg area.

man finally hired me and I got a job in the White Lunch at $7.50 per week, plus meals. I felt truly rich.

I eventually returned to Calgary and married Ted Fisher in 1937. After a short marriage I moved to Victoria, and put in an application to join the Navy. At this time they only wanted women cooks and as this did not appeal to me, my application was held in abeyance. I then took a welder's course and worked in the shipyards until hundreds of girls were laid off, including me. Jobs were now easy to get and I became a machinist, but in the meantime went to Vancouver to enlist in the C.W.A.C. but flunked the medical. Not liking the boss in the machine shop I returned to Calgary and again put in an application to enlist, this time at Currie Barracks. I then got a job as a fitter with an outfit under contract with Boeing Aircraft. The contract was quickly completed and I got a call from Currie. This time I made it and was suddenly in the Army. I was rushed into an ill fitting uniform and shipped off to Kitchener for basic training.

At the end of the war I returned to Victoria and my Navy brother Hugh and my Airforce brother Harry and I had a beautiful reunion and many nights together doing the town.

During this period I went to work at Royal Roads, for the Naval Officers Training Academy. Later had various jobs in laundries, bakeries, B.C. fish packers, creameries, post office, nurses' aide, electrician and service 'man' for Singer Sewing Machine Co.

Getting on in years my doctor advised me I had better slow up and find easier work, so I took a business course and upon completion got an interesting job with a hearing aid company. I married Bob Lyon in 1949 and later joined the Public Service as a secretary, then back with the Navy again at Dept. of National Defence for nearly ten years. Bob was also with D.N.D. before his death in 1968.

After a short time with D.N.D. I was talked into reporting for the Dockyard news, a side line that I came to love. Besides having a weekly column "The Lyon Roars" I worked up to human interest stories and everything pertaining to the Navy. This may have had some bearing on the fact that I received many official invitations to go out on one day cruises and exercises in the various Navy destroyers, frigates and the submarine H.M.C.S. Grilse. When my brother Hugh was alive he served on the H.M.C.S. Charlottetown and H.M.C.S. Ontario.

Toward the end of my Public Serivce career I transferred to N.S.D. in Edmonton at Namao, the largest Naval Supply Depot in Canada. I missed Victoria and the job was entirely different to my previous work and after a while the job held no challenge for me so I returned to Victoria. I had a few boring jobs and then worked for Health and Welfare.

I returned to Calgary in late 1970 and was hired by the Hudson's Bay Co. and am presently employed by the Carlton's Drycleaners and am a caretaker where I live.

I taught Sunday School for ten years at the Victoria Truth Centre and now belong to the Church of the Truth (Centre for Positive Living.) When time permits, my present interests are dancing, cooking, my church and constructive reading. Have recently learned different arts and crafts, including crocheting and macrame and am learning to skate again and am taking a course in the fascinating but strenous art of belly dancing. I have taken instruction in Transenden-

tal Meditation and many doctors agree that the benefits of the last two mentioned interests are too great to be ignored.

My mother lives with my sister Audrey in Calgary. Audrey is married to an Airforce man and they have two children. The family had many experiences during their Airforce days both in Canada and Europe.

My brother Harry was living with Ted Fisher and I in Turner Valley at the outbreak of war and could hardly wait until his 18th birthday to enlist in the Airforce. His Airforce history was extensive and he started at the bottom but like his father before him was later promoted to Captain.

Ivor Lyster Family $\overline{KO}$ ^{O}K
by Ivor Le Roy Lyster

I first saw the Square Butte country in July, 1949. Coming from a farm at Red Willow those hills looked pretty big. I worked for the Kendalls and Rodgers from 1949 to 1955.

While working at Kendalls in 1952, Dennis Blakley, Mary Blakley, Frank and Marie Kendall and myself had a parade outfit of eight pinto horses that we took to the Calgary Stampede. We called this outfit "The Muskeg Kids." Had a lot of fun that summer. In 1956, I wrangled dudes at Lake Louise for Ray Legace.

On December 27, 1956, I married Elaine Arlin Clark, a former Ranger's daughter. A bonus for packing salt for the North Fork Stock Association, I guess. Back to wrangling dudes in 1957 and fed cattle at Donalda the winter of 1957-58.

In the spring of 1958 we bought the West half of 13-20-4W5 from James Colley, who later went to New Zealand. We ran a few cows branded $\overline{KO}$ R.H. and horse branded ^{O}K L. H. Broke saddle horses and chased wild horses whenever I could. As one of my friends said, the best things of my life came off the Forest Reserve (my wife and wild horses.)

Ivor and Elaine Lyster with their family. Back: Ivor and Elaine. Front: Debbie, Patric, Denise.

Riders, Debbie Lyster, Wendy Foster, Elaine and Denise Lyster. Ivor and Patric in front. Horses, Buttons, Molly, Spook and Dixie.

We had three children, Debbie Elaine, born November 27, 1957. She married Peter Zapisocky and had one son, Christopher Micheal. Debbie passed away 1978.

Denise Rae, born March 23, 1959, is attending college at Vermillion, assistant veterinarian work.

Our son Patric Dale was born March 16, 1963, is at home, a sheep herder.

We sold our land at Millarville in 1971. Dr. A. Chopra bought acreage along the creek. Dr. Attarawala bought the rest of the south quarter in 1973. J. Lamarsh and T. McMahon bought the north quarter.

We then purchased three quarters of land at Vilna, where we now reside. Raising Purebred Polled Herefords and horses.

We miss the hills but not the deep snows of spring. The family are involved in riding clubs and Gymkhamas which was the love of their dad.

Ruth Maberley

It was fun growing up "one of the Chalmers kids", living on the hill at Millarville. There was always, as Mom used to say, "something in the wind" and many happy, exciting times, while the Chinook winds whistled around the big old log house. Being, very early, an inveterate tomboy, I must have been a real nuisance to Dad and the hired men around. However, this proved useful during the war years, when we helped in the grain and hay fields. Went on cattle drives and round-ups and helped chase horses out of the hills.

When Gordon Maberley came to work at Lester Letts sawmill, Dad said Gordon was the best hired hand we'd ever had. Well, I figured that even that was an understatement. After getting his radio ticket in Toronto, Gordy was in the U.S. Merchant Navy out of New York on Russian and African convoys, through the early war years. We were married in 1944 on Vancouver Island, after a year's engagement time, which he spent at sea in the Canadian Merchant Navy out of Vancouver. Dad had to sign for me to get a marriage license to take to Vancouver. I can still see the look on the license clerk's face as we walked up to her wicket. As plain as day it read "Why, he's old enough to be her father". When I met Gordy in Vancouver, my fat purse flew open as I threw my arms around him, and we spent the first five minutes of his leave retrieving all the things with which a purse is stuffed, that had scattered amazingly over the hall floor of the Marine Building.

While Gordy was at sea, I worked in Vancouver or Victoria, and took short holidays to meet his ship when it arrived at Tacoma, Vancouver or Port Alberni. We appreciated having Gordy's Mother, step father and family, the Calderwoods, as home base those years.

After the war, we spent a short time at Millarville and at Fort McLeod, a year on Lake Eire living in a light house, and then moved to Edmonton, where Colin was born. When Colin was a year old, we rented our Edmonton house which Gordy had built, and moved to a northern B.C. emergency airstrip where we lived for three years. Beatton River was about sixty miles of dirt road off the Alaska Highway. We had a thick old log cabin and had to really stoke our stoves all winter. The owls hooted, the wolves howled, and also, when the trapper was away, ate one of his dogs right out of his collar, not two hundred yards from our little cabin. We enjoyed the game and wild berries there, but it was mostly ten months of winter and two of black flies and mosquitoes.

We travelled with a Siesmic crew for two years from Pincher Creek to Sundre and Didsbury. When we settled in Calgary, we chose a little brother for Colin. Gordy has been with Calgary Power for the last twenty two years and we have watched our sons, and trees, and Calgary, grow up, in what seems now, a very short time. Colin was married in 1974, and Wendy fits into the family as the daughter we want. They live in Calgary, Wendy is a "landman-lady" for an oil company and Colin is a Journeyman carpenter. Davy is a second-year welding apprentice in Calgary.

We plan to move shortly to a spot west of High River to enjoy country living again, close to family and friends and "our foothills."

OUR HERITAGE
by Ruth Maberley

Have you found in idyllic setting a beautiful
   summer camp ground
And stepped from your car to discover pink
   tissue bits lying around.
Have you ever walked by a mountain stream
   close to the moose and the bear,
Where you felt so clean and close to God till
   you found a bottle there.
Now the tissue disintegrates quickly, and tin
   cans a bit more slow
But the glass will be there for ages, and
   generations will know

Of our years of selfish indulgence, and
  pollution of ocean and land
So all creation has suffered at the awful
  hand of man.
Will our great-grandchildren ever know the
  natural beauty here?
Will we guard our treasures in Canada, or
  will they disappear?
As we tear out the trees on marginal farms,
  and level the land, and take
The cream of the top of resources, and leave
  bits for our children's sake
Will we think of the children to follow, and
  plan, and be honest and fair?
We have loam, and wild game, and resources,
  and beauty, more than our share.
100 years have taken their toll of the land
  as we prospered and grew.
We must work and plan, so the hand of man can
  help the earth renew.
It's ours to use, but not abuse, then to pass
  on to future men
In better shape than it came to us, then it's
  up to them again.

Val Mack

Val was born in MacNutt, Saskatchewan, on the
10th of March, 1912. He left MacNutt in 1930 and
worked on road construction at Lanigan, Sask. for a
year. From there he rode the rods to Vancouver and
then back again for the harvest. There was very little
employment in the "Hungry Thirties". After the
harvest was over he went to Hartell, Alberta, and
there he met Fred Hodgkins. Fred had a small ranch
in the Millarville district and Val was hired to work on
the ranch. He also worked on Larratt's saw mill, and
also working in the bush logging for the mill.

Although times were very hard in the hills, there
were a lot of sports enjoyed, ball games in the summer
and badminton, hockey and boxing in the winter. Val
was a very active member of the Millarville Badminton Club, which had its headquarters in the old
Rancher's Hall. Other districts had Badminton teams
so there were many tournaments, with friendly
rivalry. The Rancher's Hall had a boxing club, and
many of the local small fry were taught the manly art
of self defence by the more experienced boxers, such
as Fred and Frank Hodgkins. When the Hall was
moved into Heritage Park, the heavy rings which held
the ropes for the boxing ring were still intact.

When war broke out in 1939, Val was one of the first
from the Millarville district to enlist. He joined the
Royal Canadian Engineers on September 6th, 1939.
After training in Canada he was sent to England, and
from there went on to serve in Sicily, Italy, France,
Belguim, Holland and Germany. When he received his
discharge in September, 1945, he found life very dull,
so rejoined the Army. He spent a year in Korea and

Val and Catherine Mack at wedding reception, Aug.
30, 1957.

three years in the Yukon. He put in a total of 22 years,
retiring from the service and making his home in Vancouver ever since.

On August 30th. 1957, Val was married to Catherine
Roberts of Port Arthur, Ontario. Apart from short
visits to Millarville and a few other Alberta points,
much of his time is spent in Vancouver.

Andrew MacKay
by Valerie Graf

Andy was born September 3rd, 1890, at Cape
Breton, Nova Scotia, to Murdoch MacKay and Annie
Ross MacKay. Andy and his eight brothers and sisters
moved to Gibbonsville, Idaho, with their parents
before the turn of the century. In 1904 the family came
by covered wagon to the Claresholm district, where
they settled on land west of the town.

MacKay brothers came to the Millarville district in
1915. They bought the John Turner homestead, the
S.E.¼ of section 9-21-3w5. Francis Wright had bought
from the Turners and lived on the place before selling
to the MacKays. MacKays also owned a section and a
half adjoining to the north and west and later acquired
the north half of 20-21-3w5. They were also members of
the North Fork Cattle Association and ran their cattle
in the Forest Reserve.

Andy married Annie Colley in 1927. Annie was born

Mrs. Andy MacKay (Annie Colley) with baby son Johnnie.

William and Andy MacKay. 1941.

April 27, 1907 in Commillie, Ontario. She came with her parents to Millarville.

Andy and Annie lived in Black Diamond with their four sons, John, Bob, Don and Ross. Andy worked for the Royalite Oil Co. before moving to their farm, on the former Butler and Quorn property. Andy had lots of cows so there was plenty of chores for the boys.

Annie was a great sports lady. She rode every day and attended any sports the boys were in. She was a life member of the U.C.W. and one of the ones responsible for building the Black Diamond United Church. She was also a member of the W.I. and War Workers and Red Cross. Her life was spent giving to others.

The boys were all sports minded, playing hockey, running, boxing and rodeo.

John is married to Hazel Bray and they have two sons. Bob married Jackie Renard in 1951, and they have six children, five girls and one boy. Don was married to Arleen Eastwood and they had three children, one died as an infant. They were divorced and Don married Deanna McLaren. Ross married Thelma Mifren in 1960 and have two boys and a girl.

Andy and Annie moved into the Beverly Nursing Home in Calgary in 1971. The home place was sold to Don, and Bob bought another quarter, built a house and moved to the farm.

Don was killed in a car accident Jan. 2, 1976. In July, 1976, Annie took sick and passed away July 31. Andy is still in the nursing home and doing well. He visits his brother Willie and his wife Jennie every Friday. Andy has thirteen grandchildren and five great-granddaughters.

Bob MacKay and Janet Bucher

Cattle brands — MacKay Bros. 5 U̅ Left Ribs
R. G. MacKay ⌐ Left Ribs

Bob MacKay and Janet Bucher were married on Dec. 18, 1941. They have spent all of their married life on the ranch at Millarville.

They have their own house a short distance west of the old ranch house. It originally belonged to an oil worker, "Peanut" Adams, and was on MacKay land, located a short distance from Sheep Creek School. That was before the latter building was moved to its present location. Bob had the house moved in the summer of 1942 and an addition was added in 1962.

Bob planted the first spruce in the spring of 1943. Since that time they have grown into beautiful big trees. There is also a lovely pine tree in the front yard that he brought home wrapped in his handkerchief. He found it growing out in the open field while he was ploughing. That would be about 1950.

Bob was born at Gibbonsville, Idaho in 1902. When he was two years old the family moved to the Claresholm district. There were seven boys and two girls in the MacKay family, Bob being the youngest.

He and his brother Murdoch took their schooling at Trout Creek, a country school west of town and in Claresholm.

Bob MacKay and friends, 1973.

Janet MacKay and friends.

In 1916 the MacKay's moved to the Millarville district, buying the Francis Wright place, the buildings being on the S.E. ¼ 9-21-3-W5.

Bob worked on several ranches in the district, also he would go out threshing in the fall. Several Millarville men would take their teams and bundle racks and work on the outfits around Aldersyde. At one time he worked for the Cheadle Cattle Company east of Calgary. He was a guide for a number of summers in the National parks including Banff, Jasper, Yo Ho and Waterton. That would be in the twenties and early thirties. He enjoyed those years on the pack trails in the mountains, and often speaks of them.

At one time Bob worked at John Hassa's Polo Pony Ranch in the Springbank district. That was also work with horses, breaking and training them, something he always enjoyed doing. He was a good horseman.

Since 1933 he has been at the ranch at Millarville. The MacKay brothers ran about two hundred head of Hereford cattle. William MacKay still lived on the ranch then and Murdoch was there as well. Some of these cattle were put on the forest reserve in the summer and Bob did a lot of riding up there looking after them.

He bought a quarter section from Dan Bannerman, the S.W.¼-29-21-4-W5. It joined the forest reserve and he used that place as his headquarters while riding. He later sold it to Cyrus McBee.

In the winter the cattle were driven down to the straw piles, generally S.W. of Okotoks. They had them at Tuckers different times, and at Herb Carr's. One winter when there was no feed in the South country the cattle were taken up to Olds. They went by rail from Okotoks.

MacKay brothers sold the cattle in 1941. After that Bob and his brother Murdoch gradually built up a small herd of around sixty cows. These cattle were always kept at home.

After Murdoch passed away in 1963 Bob kept the cattle for about two years. He sold them when he was no longer able to look after them because of his health. He is unable to do any work now but he stays cheerful and is good company.

Janet Bucher was born in High River. Her parents Warren and Margaret Bucher were homesteading in the Mossleigh district at the time.

The family moved to the Kew district in 1918, S.E.¼ of 36-20-4-W5. At that time there were three girls, Ruth, Janet and Hazel. Two more girls were born, Margaret at Kew, she passed away age one and a half years. Jean, the youngest was born in Okotoks.

Janet and her sister Ruth rode horseback to the Plainview School, Janet occupying the rumble seat, which wasn't always that comfortable, especially during a race. Ruth was never one to let another kid beat her. However, Janet survived.

She was lost one time while they lived at Kew. She and Ruth were walking home from the north field. She wouldn't stay with big sister, probably a stubborn little character. Instead of going south she turned east, and wandered around through the bush in the quarter where Batchelors house is now. It was in the spring and the searchers were able to see her tracks occasionally in the patches of snow. The hired man, Milo Brower found her asleep on the river bank. The water was quite high at the time. All she can remember about the whole incident was coming into the yard perched on Milo's shoulder.

The Bucher family moved again in 1923, to Okotoks. The girls took all the rest of their schooling in that town, which was quite small in those years.

Janet came back to the Millarville district in the spring of 1935 to the Malcolm Millars. She was there until the fall of 1937. During those years she did a great deal of riding around the beautiful Millarville countryside, quite often with Bob MacKay.

From Millarville she went to High River to work. Then in 1941 she and Bob were married.

She has always been interested in Nature, especially bird watching. That was long before it became as popular as it is today.

Photography and art have been very rewarding hobbies. There is gardening in the summer and the last few years Cross Country skiing has made the winters seem so much shorter.

Janet is the Librarian at the Millarville Community Library at the present time.

Several years ago she adopted a stray Shetland Sheep dog and after nursing her back to health she found the owners. They gave Janet a puppy in appreciation for caring for their dog that had been lost for two years. Janet is now an ardent Sheltie dog breeder and trainer and she has shown several of her dogs at shows and won many prizes and ribbons.

The MacKay Family

In 1904, the MacKay family came to Alberta at the time that it became a province, travelling overland from Idaho to Claresholm. Chief Joseph of the Montana Indians had recently been subdued. Although the MacKays were confronted by a band of Blood Indians at St. Mary's River, they continued on unmolested.

At Claresholm, Murdoch Angus MacKay and sons homesteaded and set up farming and ranching operations five miles west of the townsite, and in the Porcupine Hills. They supplied teams and equipment for the annual harvest that featured steam engines and wagons with pitch-fork loading, and when the railway to the Peace River was started, they provided horses and manpower for the grading operations.

In the spring of 1915, they moved to Millarville after purchasing the John Turner homestead and land associated with it. The trip from Okotoks was a day long affair. John, William and Robert drove two wagons and a democrat. The wagons were loaded with furniture and machinery, while the buckboard carried Mrs. MacKay, Mrs. Hackett and her three children.

Murdoch MacKay.

Andrew and Murdoch were involved with driving the livestock from Claresholm.

The story of the MacKays is well recorded in "Our Foothills". On page 102, it refers to William MacKay marrying Jennie Chalmers, and that they lived in Blackie, Banff, and in 1944 bought a home in Mount Royal where they live today. Since coming to Calgary, Jennie continued her interest in church and community work. Over the years, the Red Cross recognized her efforts by presenting her with a Life Membership pin, and more recently with a badge and a citation for her voluntary service.

They were honored in May, 1977, by a birthday party convened by Jackie MacKay and Ruth Maberley. Since Jennie and Willie had reached and passed their four score years, fifty nieces and nephews assembled at their home to congratulate them and wish them happy returns of the day. Hugh Chalmers and wife, Janie and Stephen, drove all the way from Denver for the occasion. Jackie Chalmers made the birthday cake enjoyed by all but especially by the many children present. Their home with its beautiful flowers and vegetable garden, is proof that Jennie and Willie still enjoy puttering in the soil.

Andy is a weekly visitor to Willie's home. For many years they have jointly supervised the MacKay family business. Andy's wife, Annie, passed away in Calgary in 1976.

Jessie, a sister of the MacKay brothers, married

Murdoch MacKay driving hay sweep.

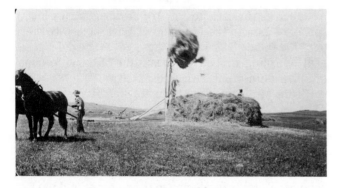

Lift dumping sweepload of hay. Bob MacKay with team, Will MacKay on stack.

William MacKay.

Jennie and Bill MacKay home in Mount Royal, Calgary.

Jennie MacKay receiving Red Cross awards.

Harry Shaver, a construction contractor who built many homes in Mount Royal and Elbow Park. They moved to Grande Prairie, but their two daughters were frequent summer holiday visitors to the MacKay home in Millarville. Clare and husband, Allan Tough, moved to Vancouver where Al died after years of suffering from a back injury. Clare continued work at the Bank until her recent retirement. Joan's husband was an instructor with the Royal Canadian Navy in Victoria. A recent trip to Australia is their first venture since his retirement. Their daughters, Leslie and Tracey, are students at the University. Their grandmother, Jessie Shaver, passed away at Victoria in April, 1977, at the age of 91 years.

Macklin, Alexander William Glyn (Alec)

I was born in 1935, second son of Hugh and Dessa Macklin. From 1941 to 1950 I attended Ballyhamage School where I took Grades 1 to 9. During the first two or three years I would spend the week with my grandparents and aunt and uncle, Pat and Larry Jameson, as it wasn't so far to ride to school. I'm glad to have lived in the era of reaching school by horseback. In spite of rainstorms and occasionally having to ride home sick, it was a pleasant means of transportation. There were always the side benefits such as the spring that a new-born fawn lay so close to my path I could have touched it. During my nine years at Ballyhamage we had several teachers: Mr. Lott, Beatrice McCray, Joan Kosling (Mrs. Bill Kendall), Margaret Cullen (Mrs. John Kendall), Bertha Wonacott and Edna Burton. Margaret Cullen boarded with us for a while and my brother, Jack, and I used to try to get a head start on her as we didn't want the other kids to see us riding to school with the teacher.

Feeling like a lost sheep and a country bumpkin, in Grade 10 I entered 1500-student-strong Western Canada High School in Calgary. During my high school years I boarded with my aunts (Eileen, Pat and Sheilagh Jameson) where, with four of us to get away in the morning, I enjoyed my share of the mad scramble and took my turn burning the toast. Following

Ballyhamage School spring of 1947, picture taken by the teacher Bertha Wonnacott. L. to R., Back row: Florence Brunt, Gladys Field, Robert Field, Annette Patterson, Yvonne Patterson, Alex Macklin (edge of picture). 2nd row: Anne Glaister, Irene Brunt, Marilyn McNab, Donna Patterson, Dorothy Wood. Front row: Gail Patterson, Len Brown, Ed Cane, Johnny Field.

graduation I took one year in agricultural mechanics at S.A.I.T. and then went home to work with Dad and Jack. By this time Uncle Larry had died so we were renting the Jameson place too.

I drove the school bus to Red Deer Lake School in the early years of bussing in our area, '57-'58-'59. Then I spent three winters working with seismic crews. In 1959, Peter Macklin came from England to live with us, and stayed until he built his own home on an acreage he bought from Vic Hanson. In 1961 Jack married Beverley Schaal. They lived in a small house in the yard (a former youth hostel building) until the spring of '64, when they moved to Ballyhamage, my uncle's farm at Millarville.

In the fall of '67 what had been home to me all my life was sold, when Stan Eveleigh bought the home quarter. The next spring Joe Mercier and his family bought the rest, apart from twenty-two acres Dad kept back to build a new home on. I stayed a few months with Mom and Dad after their first move, to the old Griffiths Place over the hill. The last few months before moving to her new home, Mother spent in the home of her childhood, moving to Ballyhamage after Jack sold it to Don Cross in the spring of 1968. Jack, Beverley and I bought a larger place west of Olds. Mother and Dad had a new house built that summer and moved into it in October. The following two or three summers they worked tremendously hard turning a bare hillside into a garden park, which offered great pleasure to their many visitors as well as to themselves.

In 1971 I married Anne Gant, daughter of Archdeacon Gant of Black Diamond. We built a small house on my land at Olds. In 1975 we sold this and moved a few miles west to Eagle Hill (near Sundre). Our last year on the Eagle Hill farm was one of sadness as Dad died in November 1977. His was a long, happy and productive life marred only by poor health in his last year, when for six months he was confined almost entirely to bed. Even then, though, he didn't lose his wit and sparkle.

The spring of 1978 saw us sell again and move to a new farm west of Eckville, my first time to farm away from Jack. Here we hope to stay put with our two children, Patricia Anne (born October 15, 1974) and Benjamin Hugh (born February 22, 1978).

Jack Macklin and Family
written by Jack Macklin

I was born on February 26, 1931 at the Holy Cross Hospital in Calgary, the son of Hugh and Dessa Macklin. My brother Alec was born February 7, 1935. We lived 4 miles S.W. of Red Deer Lake. The depression was tough, especially on the adults, but as a child I really didn't notice any real hardships. One of the clearest things I remember about the hungry thirties was one cold day in January, 1937, Bob and Bill Winthrop came along with a team and towed away our old Model A. Dad had traded it in on a work horse.

Another thing I remember of those years was Bert Griffith and Stan Gilbert's barb wire telephone which worked fairly well. The Second World War brought many new hardships, the loss of dear ones, and rationing of food and fuel. But it also brought a boom in our economy. By 1947 we were able to buy new vehicles, and Dad got a new Chevrolet ½-ton for approximately $1,365.00.

My schooling started at Ballyhamage School and I went there for nine years. We rode horseback for most of those years. In the earlier years I stayed with Tom Jameson, my grandfather, who was an oldtimer in the area. My first horse was a small Shetland pony, Sweet Pea by name. He abandoned me regularly. Aunt Sheilagh, who taught at Ballyhamage at that time, rode off and recaptured him and we carried on again. I spent many happy hours and days at my grandparents'. On many occasions Aunt Eileen would let me drive the old Plymouth.

From 1946 to 1949 I attended High School and then Technical School in Calgary. I worked for Whitburns Florists after school and on week ends, which I liked very much, and have been good friends of theirs ever since. In the early fifties I worked for Ray Goodwin in the Swan Hills. Austin Thompson worked with me, we had a great winter.

In 1954 we started dairying and shipped fluid milk to Union Milk Co. till 1961. Since I can remember I've been involved in community affairs. The Millarville Racing and Sports Association and the Priddis and Millarville Agricultural Society gave me many years of challenge and enjoyment. I was also on the Board for the Stockland Mutual Telephone Co.

On June 1, 1960 Beverley Schaal and I were married in South Minster United Church in Calgary. Beverley is the daughter of Walter and Lillian Schaal. On June 8, 1961 we had our first child, Barbara Anne. On January 11, 1964 Trevor John was born. Our first house was a small two-room cottage which we fixed up with running water and power; it was a castle to us. We had many good times there. In 1964 we purchased our first piece of land, the West half of S16-T21-R2-W5, from Sheilagh and Eileen Jameson. We lived at Ballyhamage till 1968. This was part of my grandfather Jameson's homestead. We still own 40 acres of the old homestead. Alec and I bought land up west of Olds in 1968, known as the Riverside Stock Farm. We farmed there till 1975; we moved to Eagle Valley then, and are there now. We built our first new house here and have enjoyed the experience.

I have been involved in the community up here too, with the Olds Co-op Association, the Eagle 4H Beef Club, and helped to organize the Foothills Natural Gas Co-op, which is a Rural Natural Gas Company.

Barbara started school at Millarville and Trevor in Olds. They both attend school in Sundre now, Barbara graduates in June, 1979. They both have been in the 4H Beef and Pony Clubs, and enjoy sports.

We have been in livestock for many years and our

brand is 000, known as the three links and is located on the right ribs. I got this brand from Joe Bowman. We went into exotics in 1974, breeding some of our commercial cows to Maine Anjou. We now have quite a number of percentage Maine Anjou cattle.

Jacqueline Helene MacLean (Nee dePalezieux)

by Jacqueline Helene MacLean

Born in Calgary; lived at Millarville until age 5. Then lived near High River until age 7. Returned to Millarville and attended New Valley School up to Grade X. Attended High School in High River.

Then in 1939 I was admitted into the University of Alberta in the Faculty of Nursing, graduating from the hospital in 1943. I worked in the Turner Valley Hospital for 6 months.

In February of 1944 I married Lawrence William Hannon, who was a Pilot Officer in the R.C.A.F. After the war he received his Law Degree at the University of Alberta.

Our 3 children are:

Judith Lynn Henning who is a Doctor and practising Medicine in Edmonton. Her husband, C. Roy Henning, is a Lawyer. They have a 4 year old son, Christopher.

Delia Lynn Hannon who has her Arts Degree, B.Sc. Degree, and is a Lawyer. She is living in Calgary at present.

John Robert Lawrence Hannon who is attending Medical School in Toronto.

In December of 1970 my husband passed away suddenly.

In April of 1972 I married Laurence Brent MacLean, who is a Bank Manager.

I now have two new sons:

Robert Brent MacLean and wife, Joyce. Both are teaching at Brentwood College on Vancouver Island.

Brian William MacLean who is teaching school in Hong Kong and is starting his 6th year there.

Larry and I are residing in Edmonton and expect to retire here.

Evelyn Mildred Macmillan

I was born in Calgary October 29, 1902 my parents Helen and Malcolm Millar lived at Millarville which was named after my father who had the first Post Office and Trading Post.

I had one sister Elsie who was eight years older than I who married Leslie Douglass.

I had a wonderful childhood being very fond of animals especially horses and dogs.

My mother taught me to ride early and I showed my pony "Jackie" in Calgary at four years of age and won my cup in Vancouver in 1912 for the best pony in all classes.

My mother, who rode side saddle, and I used to ride to church and as she was a hard rider I just had to keep up or be left behind.

My father being an old country man was a very good shot and kept us in game during the hunting season, unfortunately I hated the gun but had to follow him with the horses.

I used to harness the dogs to a sleigh in the winter time and a miniature "Haynes" wagon in summer and occasionally they would take after a coyote.

I started school at St. Hildas Girls' School with my cousin Elfie Thomas, later went to Mount Royal College while living with my Aunt and Uncle, finishing my education as a boarder at the convent.

Elfie Thomas, my constant companion, spent most of her holidays with us at Millarville. She also loved animals and we enjoyed swimming, riding and playing tennis. Having a tennis court we played at least five times a week at neighbors or the Tennis Club.

Millarville had a polo team, a visiting team from Pekisko stayed at the ranch and I had the privilege of cooling out their good ponies.

When I was sent to the Convent I found it very confining at first. The nuns being French and Irish were very strict but very good to us.

I hated the daily walks we all had to take in a group. At home they always said I walked half a mile to catch a horse to ride a mile.

We had wonderful neighbors by the name of Kings and their four children so we had many picnics.

Jacqueline MacLean (dePalezieux) and children, from left, Judy Hannon Henning, Lynn Hannon, John Hannon.

Mildred (Millar) Macmillan with her dog team at Millarville.

The highlight of the year was the Millarville Races. I wasn't allowed to ride in them; little did our parents know we had raced every horse we could put a leg across around that track.

During the war I was taken out of school to feed one hundred and ten head of cattle at Midnapore, one could not get a man for love nor money. I stayed with my Grandmother Shaw while my father was up at our place east of Athabasca having the hay shipped down. I borrowed a team to unload the carloads of hay down to a corral on Fish Creek and snake it out by a saddle horse.

I was asked why I didn't have a hay hook never having handled baled hay before.

On January 15, 1923 I went in training in the Holy Cross Hospital and finished three years to the day. My chum Eileen Thom and I went down to Portland, Oregon the winter of 1928-29. Canadian nurses were well liked and we enjoyed nursing there.

Several Calgary boys played on the Portland hockey team whom we got to know and enjoyed running around with that winter.

In 1932 I married Tommy Macmillan and we lived in Calgary for six months. Tommy bought the Nichols place at Kew and we built a bungalow and lived there for eight years and then moved to Riverdale Avenue in Calgary, later buying the Dr. Hackney home in Elbow Park where we lived while our two children Marilyn Sue and Thomas Kenneth were being educated.

We joined the Glencoe Club where Tommy curled, I bowled, Marilyn skated and Ken played badminton and was runner up to the Canadian Championship.

In 1960 we moved a bungalow from Calgary to the farm six miles west of Okotoks where Tommy continued to farm and raise Hereford cattle, Clydesdale and light horses.

I used to do a lot of riding, such as gathering the cattle in the fall of the year from the Forest Reserve. We put in many hours in the saddle.

In April 1976 I had the honour of being made "The Horsewoman of the Year", having helped with the

Alberta Light Horse Association with their shows for thirty-three years.

My husband died over three years ago and my son has taken over the farming and raising of the Hereford cattle which I still have an interest in.

My daughter-in-law, Alberta, and I bowl twice a week at the Glencoe Club and enjoy it.

Thomas Macmillan

Born December 4, 1909 only son of Mr. and Mrs. Thomas Macmillan of "Hillside Ranch" west of Okotoks.

He had five step-brothers and sisters, James, Edith, Jasper, Marjorie and Robert (Pat) Rodgers.

He rode to "Panima" school on a shetland pony.

Later he was with the Bank of Montreal. While he was with the Ford Motor Co. at Okotoks, he lived with his sister and brother-in-law, the Hoods.

Tommy married Mildred Millar in 1932 and he bought the H. F. Nicholls Ranch between the forks of Sheep and Ware Creeks at Kew and raised light horses and Galloway cattle.

There were two children, Marilyn Sue and Thomas Kenneth. When Marilyn was old enough to go to school they moved to Riverdale Avenue in Calgary and Marilyn went to Elbow Park School.

Two years later they bought the Dr. Hackney home in Elbow Park. Marilyn finished her schooling at St.

Tommy and Mildred Macmillan on boat leaving San Francisco. 1932.

Mildred (Millar) Macmillan on "Jackie" Champion saddle pony at Calgary.

Hildas girls' school and Kenneth at Elbow Park, Rideau, Western Canada High and Fort Collins, Colorado.

In 1939 his father died and he took over the home place "Hillside Ranch" leaving Jack McKenzie, who had worked for his father, in charge until it was divided up among the family.

There were between 80 and 90 purebred Clydesdale mares and eight stallions most of which he sold keeping about 20 mares and 3 stallions, also the hereford cattle.

They settled on the SW¼ Sec. 29 T20 R1 W-5 and as Tommy was becoming quite interested in farming he bought himself a tractor and tiller and began to break up and farm part of the place.

He bought a ½ section of land just west of the home place from Harry Rodgers and sold a ½ section "The Moore Place" to Helge Jensen who still lives there.

He continued to show the Clydesdales on the line and in harness and took many prizes, thanks to Duncan McMillan (no relation) who took a great interest in them and worked for us for over 25 years.

The family showed saddle horses in Calgary and Edmonton and Tommy enjoyed riding a good horse.

Tommy was a former Associate director of the Calgary Exhibition and Stampede, a past President of the Alberta Horse Breeders Association and for many years associated with the Clydesdale Association of Canada.

He was a member of the Southern Alberta Old Timers Association and a member of the Glencoe Club where he curled.

He was Secretary of the North Sheep Stock Association for many years and ran his hereford cattle branded ⊃ϵ RR during the summer and kept the little place at Kew which Andy Thom looked after for many years.

Tommy passed away on November 24, 1974.

Thomas Kenneth Macmillan
by TKM

I was born July 8, 1938 in Calgary, second child of Thomas and Mildred Macmillan, having one older sister Marilyn Sue, also being grandchildren of Thomas Macmillan of Okotoks and of Malcolm T. Millar of Millarville.

I was educated in Calgary attending Elbow Park, Strathcona Boys' School, Rideau Park, Western Canada High and university at Colorado State in Fort Collins, Colorado.

During my summers, while still in high school, I was a guide for Brewster Pack Trains out of Banff, which on many occasions led me to Mt. Assiniboine and the camp of Elizabeth Rummel. I participated in many athletic sports through junior and senior high school. I played junior football and baseball in summer and hockey and badminton in winter, culminating in the winning of the Alberta-Saskatchewan junior men's singles and the Saskatchewan senior men's singles championship in 1954 and was also Canadian Singles Finalist in 1954.

When through school I worked for Good Year Tire & Rubber Co. as an adjustor for a short time then was employed by Shaw Construction for several years working throughout the province of Alberta and on construction of the Rogers Pass section of the Trans-Canada Highway in B.C.

In 1962 I relocated and moved to the "Rabbit Hutch" in Midnapore, where the banker and I started a trucking business. After two years of batching and a shrinking waist line, I married Alberta McKevitt on December 12, 1964.

Tommy Macmillan on his horse, Jake.

Alberta and Ken Macmillan on their wedding day.

Ken Macmillan's truck, moving a cone crusher.

In July of 1968 we moved to the farm west of Okotoks to help out with the "Family Feuding and Farming" operation.

In September 1971 after much feuding and not much farming I went into heavy hauling and construction, starting a company called Southline Contractors Ltd. We moved many large gas plant compressor units and large vessels throughout Alberta and machinery to the far north.

After my father's death in 1974 we returned to farm at Okotoks where we live today. In the fall of 1977 we started a gravel crushing operation.

Oswald Madsen

by Joan Goyette

Oswald was born October 23, 1902 in Rind-Jutland, Denmark, one of six sons. He immigrated to Canada in July, 1923, landing in Quebec. From there, he took a train to Lloydminster and spent the fall there, harvesting. After leaving Lloydminster he lost his wallet containing the money he had made, so he ended up in a lumber camp in Rocky Mountain House. The men all ended up getting sick in the camp, including Oswald, so he headed for Calgary. After arriving there, he got a job on a farm which lasted a couple of years and then from 1926 to 1931 he worked for Voss Brothers, building grain elevators in just about every town in Alberta. In the early spring of 1933, he came to Millarville and went to work on the Spooner Ranch and stayed for about seven years. Following this, he worked as a carpenter for a couple of years at different airports and then in 1942 he headed for Fort McMurray and then on to Canol, N.W.T. to work on the pipeline between there and Whitehorse. In 1945 he came back to Millarville and bought the S.W. ¼, Sec. 22, T. 21, R. 3, W. 5, and rented a half section consisting of the S.E. ¼, Sec. 22, T. 21, R. 3, W. 5, and the N.W. ¼, Sec. 14, T. 21, R. 3, W. 5, from Alex Scatterty. In 1949, Oswald and Alex bought the N.E. ¼, Sec. 23, T. 21, R. 3, W. 5, and eventually in 1957 Oswald bought Alex's part and he now lives on this piece of land.

Oswald married Effie Scatterty, widow of Alex, in June, 1960. Effie came to Canada in 1930 from Fife, Scotland. She landed in Calgary and from there went to Nanton to work for the Brazil's. She thought she was going to the end of the earth when she made the trip from Calgary to Nanton and was quite frightened by the stories she had heard as a child about the Indians and the bears out west. She met Alex Scatterty when he was working for Ward Dick, and they were married in January, 1931. Their first child, Ronald Henry, was born in October, 1931 and they spent a couple of years in Calgary before coming to Millarville to the Spooner Ranch in 1933. Margaret Anne was born in November, 1936 and James Alexander in September, 1939. Following this, they bought some land (now owned by Ron Birkenes and Dr. Hanley), and left Spooner's for a time, but returned in 1946. In October, 1948 their last child, Joan Darlene was born and in 1957 they moved to Calgary because of Alex's health and he passed away in March, 1959.

Following Effie's marriage to Oswald, they returned to Millarville where they still live. They have twelve grandchildren and two great-grandchildren.

Oswald Madsen at the Spooner Ranch 1934.

Oswald and Effie Madsen.

The Mangat Family

by Binda Mangat

The Mangat household comprises of my wife Jasvinder, two sons, Navit and Sanjeev, my mother Sham, my father Basant Singh and myself, Binda Mangat. My father is enjoying his retired life after having worked for the East African Railways in Kenya for over thirty years.

Both my wife and I were born in Nairobi, Kenya.

I went to London, England in 1962 and worked for B.P.O. Telecommunications until 1974 when we moved to Calgary. My wife Jasvinder, worked for the Royal Free Hospital in London. We were married in 1968.

Our elder son Navit was born in 1969 in London, while the younger, Sanjeev was born in Rainham, Kent, England.

I have worked for A.G.T. since our arrival in Canada and Jasvinder has been employed by the Calgary Cancer Clinic.

Having purchased Blk. 1, Plan 1467 L.K., N.E.¼ 23-21-3-W5, from Joan Goyette in February, 1979, we hope to enjoy the good Millarville air and country living although the wilderness is somewhat different from that of Kenya.

Gwen (Backs) Manning

I'm the youngest daughter of Merle and Hans Backs. I was born in 1946 at Millarville and attended Sheep Creek School. I attended my first year of high school where the Turner Valley Golf and Country Club is now situated, later going to the new high school in Black Diamond.

From there, I went to the University of Calgary, returning to Black Diamond to teach math at the junior high school.

My fondest memories of my younger years were those when I became an active member of the Canadian Girls Rodeo Association. When I was 15 years old, I won the "Rookie of the Year Award" for the C.G.R.A. These years were very happy ones, with Mom, Dad, and I attending rodeos and race meets all over the province.

After University I continued to live at home, enjoying my teaching profession, and continuing with my riding, and helping Dad with his race horses. It was a good life.

In 1967 I married my high-school sweetheart, Stan Manning. We have two wonderful children Rob (9) and Buddy (7). Both of our sons are hearing handicapped which has lead us to making many changes in our lives. The first of these was moving to Calgary where the children could take advantage of the special education offered for them here. I have become very involved in the Society for Hearing Handicapped. I am education chairman for this society working to better the education for the deaf and hard-of-hearing in Calgary; a volunteer speaker on deafness; a volunteer at Children's Hospital working with parents of newly diagnosed deaf children; as well as a committee

Gwen (Backs) Manning.

Gwen (Backs) Manning with her family. Stan (back) Buddy, Gwen and Rob.

member working on setting up a standard curriculum for the deaf in the province of Alberta.

For the past 5 years I have been learning the deaf sign language, and would like to take an interpreters course sometime in the future.

Stan and I have the children actively involved in community baseball and football, as well as taking part in riding and swimming lessons. It's a busy life, but a very fullfilling and rewarding one as we watch our children learn to take their place in a "hearing world".

Harold and Minnie Marshall

Harold's parents, David and Alvina, came to Alberta in 1905, from Big Timber, Montana, with Harold's elder sister, Martha and two brothers, Fred and David. Harold's triplet brothers Roosevelt, James and Raymond were born near the Big Rock west of Okotoks and at the time of this writing, are the oldest living triplets in the Dominion of Canada. Shortly after the birth of the triplets, the Marshall family packed up, lock, stock and barrel and migrated to Erskine, Alberta, where Harold was born shortly thereafter, in 1910.

Harold spent a good part of his younger years in the Erskine area, working as a hired hand for local farmers, as well as participating in baseball and hockey leagues. In 1933, feeling the urge to move on, Harold decided to come to Turner Valley as he had heard so much about the oil fields and decided he had better see for himself. He says it was one of the biggest disappointments of his life.

He then went to the Cayley district where he worked as a hired hand for surrounding farmers for two or three years. Then, feeling a home-calling, Harold returned to Erskine where he rented farm land for three years. However, the yearning to return to the rugged foothills, the mountains and bush overpowered his desire to farm and he went to work for the British Columbia Forestry as foreman of the fire suppression crew in the summer and for winter employment, he

Minnie and Harold Marshall with baby cougar Harold captured with his shoelace.

acquired a trapline in 1939, on the South Fork of the Sheep River. This trapline became home for Harold, where he actively worked it until his death in 1978.

Harold entered the Canadian Army in 1944 for a year and following this, he rented the Ches Hodgkins ranch for three years. He then commenced employment for the Home Oil Company and stayed with them for twenty-three and one-half years. During this time he continued to work his trapline as well as work as Government cougar hunter for several years. While on the job, he got thirty-two cougars. Harold lived on the Doc Lee place during the time McLean owned it.

In 1952, Harold exchanged vows of connubial bliss with Minnie Silvester. It took a while for the wife to start hunting and fishing; however, after a few trips out, the wilderness became as much home to Minnie as it was to Harold. In fact, it became an unwritten law of the family that the wife was not to be left at home, especially when cougar hunting.

Harold and Minnie bought the S.W.¼ of section 2-21-4w5 from Minnie's dad, Ernest Silvester Sr. in 1962, where Minnie continues to live following Harold's passing. They raised purebred Charolais cattle, starting in 1967. Their cattle brand is PK right ribs which is the old Patrick Kerr brand which Harold got from Bert Young.

Willard and Doreen Marthaller

by Doreen Marthaller

Brand — DW left shoulder

Willard George Marthaller was born in Lethbridge, Alberta December 13, 1943. Willard went to school in Cayley and later worked in the southern Alberta area on ranches and feed lots and is now working for the United Farmers of Alberta.

Willard's father, Joseph L. Marthaller was born in Faith, Alberta and married (in 1941) Elizabeth Magdelena Rarick who was born in Burdett, Alberta. The Marthaller Family of six boys and two girls moved to Calgary in 1956.

Willard's grandparents on his father's side are Laborius Marthaller born in Speier, Russia and married Phillipina Krug who was born in Rosental,

Harold and Minnie Marshall, wedding picture, Feb. 14, 1952.

Doreen and Willard Marthaller with their sons Wayne and Dwight.

Crimea. Willard's grandparents on his mother's side are John Rarick born in Russia and married Helna Keller who was born in Dakota and are both retired and living in Foremost, Alberta.

Willard married Doreen Ruby Laing on January 30, 1971. Doreen was born in Calgary, Alberta June 14, 1947 and took all of her schooling there. Doreen also has training as a Medical Assistant.

Doreen's father, James Laing was born in Keith, Scotland (passed away February 11, 1979) and married Ruby Millar who was born in Minneapolis, U.S.A. Doreen's father came to Canada in 1928 at the age of 21 and settled in Calgary in 1928.

Doreen's grandparents on her father's side are James Laing who married Helen McIntyre, both born in Scotland. Doreen's grandparents on her mother's side are Frank Millar born in Iowa, U.S.A. and married (in 1907) Annie Newman who was born in England. They came to Canada in 1910 with their two daughters, Thelma and Ruby.

Willard and Doreen have two sons, Wayne Willard born August 31, 1972 and Dwight Ray born July 12, 1974 both in Calgary. The Willard Marthaller Family moved to Millarville in October 1976 and now live on Mike Rodger's father's place (Paddy Rodgers) on Three Point Creek.

Willard and Doreen love the area and both take an active part in the communities various functions. Wayne started attending school at Millarville in August, 1978 and Dwight started kindergarten there in August, 1979.

Linda Mason (Chalmers)

Linda Mason (Chalmers), second daughter of Jim and Wilma Chalmers, was born in Turner Valley, June 19, 1953. She attended the Sheep Creek School until the finish of grade nine then received her high schooling at Oilfields High School in Black Diamond. She took an active part in basketball, badminton, and volleyball during her school years. Linda was a member of the Busy Beavers 4-H Food Club for 4 years. She attended Sunday School at Sheep Creek School and then joined the Choir at Christ Church, Millarville.

In 1970 Linda married Wayne S. Mason from Turner Valley. They were married in Christ Church, Millarville. Their first daughter, Maria Louise, was born in Turner Valley on November 13, 1970. On October 3, 1973 their second daughter, Sherry Linn was born in the Holy Cross Hospital, Calgary, Alta. Their son, Paul Sydney James was born January 20, 1978, in the Holy Cross Hospital.

Linda has judged Gymnastics for 3 years now at the Turner Valley Elementary School. She has been a first aider with St. John's for 4 years. For a year and a half she worked at the Chuckwagon Steakhouse in Turner Valley as a cook-waitress and is presently working at the Valley Food Mart grocery store located in Turner Valley. Wayne, Linda, Maria, Sherry and Paul reside on Bailey Hill in Turner Valley.

Donald and Mavis Mawdsley and Family
by Don Mawdsley

Both my wife and I grew up on farms in Alberta — my wife near Barrhead, while my father's farm was near Chinook. We moved to Hamilton in 1956, the San Francisco area in 1959, and then to Calgary in the fall of 1968. Our family at that time consisted of Karen (9), Mark (7), and Susan (2).

The "lure of the land" resulted in the purchase of Sec. 5-22-4-W5M in March of 1969 from George Lewis of Blackie. The price, was the unheard of figure of $105/acre. (During the early 1950's, land was selling at Chinook for $10/acre.) In February 1970 the S½ and NW¼ of Sec. 6-22-4-W5M was purchased from Dr. Roenisch of Sheep Creek Ranch Limited.

We lived in Calgary but spent a good deal of time on the farm. During the summer of 1969 we ran a herd of steers on section 5. After they were duly branded the corral gate was opened and they quickly vanished into the bush. For a person from the prairie, where one can see for a mile or two in every direction, it seemed a sure bet that the beasts would never be heard from again. During the summer and fall of 1970 we built a house for a hired man, a machine shed, a cattle shed, 4 steel bins, corrals and installed a watering system for the livestock and the house.

Larry Fleury and family moved in to operate the farm in May of 1970. They left in the fall of 1971. Malcolm Kopas and family operated the farm from the fall of '71 until spring of 1973. Otto and Elsie Liske came in April of 1973. Wes and Joan Rabey purchased the home quarter and arranged with the Liskes to manage their operation until the spring of 1975. Prior to the farm sale Earl Orum built a marvelous road (somewhat like the San Diego Freeway) across section 5 to provide access to Section 6. Earl also cleared a lot of land and fence lines.

The Reimer and Ball families were fantastic neighbors in all respects. Their assistance and advice during busy times such as branding, round-up, fencing and numerous other occasions was invaluable. We will always have many great memories of the country and people we met and worked with in the Millarville-Bragg Creek area.

William and Marlene May

William and Marlene May of Calgary, in the summer of 1969, made arrangements to purchase the SE¼, Section 29, TWP 20, Range 3, West of the 5th Meridian from Mr. P. Lawson of Calgary. A home was built and the family moved to the area in late November 1969.

While Bill and Marlene May resided in the community, their children Suszanne, Billy, Janet, and Deanne attended school and kindergarten in Millarville, and later in February 1972 another daughter, Catherine, was a happy family addition. The three oldest May children were involved in the Millarville gymnastics club under the supervision of Mr. Gordon Day, then a teacher at Millarville and Suszanne was a member of the Millarville 4-H Club.

Due to a prospect of a Toronto transfer with the company Bill was with at that time, the Mays sold their property in March 1973 to another couple with five children, Mr. and Mrs. McKenzie of Calgary who still own and maintain the property, and Mays moved back to Calgary.

In the spring of 1978 the Mays sold their home in Calgary and have moved to Campbell River, B.C.

Freda (Knights) McArthur

I came with my Mother and seven other children to Massingham Ranch at Millarville in 1909. My Father, Richard Knights and oldest brother Charles had come to Canada from Little Massingham, Norfolk, England the year before.

I had a happy and well remembered childhood going to school at Fordville School and roaming the woods and fields on the ranch in my spare time. Of this there wasn't much as we had to mind sheep, help thin turnips, take tea out to the fields where the boys were working and generally make ourselves useful, but we loved these jobs, anything rather than housework. Winters were lovely, skating on the sloughs and creeks, tobogganing down the steepest buttes, and riding to school when the horses were not wanted for work "You'll be warmer walking." Maybe, but what fun to race the horses at noon hour and take them down to the School Lake for a drink.

Then came Grade eight exams in the city and three years working for my board to get through High School. I worked for Mrs. Monte Fraser and also for Mrs. Robert Turner during summer holidays to earn money for books. Willie Deane-Freeman came to town to fetch me home when the news of the second of my brothers being killed reached the ranch.

Freda (Knights) McArthur on "Dizzy". About 1916, wearing divided skirt.

There was such a shortage of teachers following the war that I was called to a school on the prairie south of Loyalist, Alberta, right out of Grade Eleven and here I met Walter the day he came home from the war. My teaching experiences will fill another book, I hope.

In 1920 I came back to Calgary to Normal School and in 1921 I was married in Youngstown, Alberta, to the kindest man on earth and tried for fifteen years to help grow wheat during the period now known as the "Dirty Thirties". We had four daughters, Effie Mae married Hector Marlow. Edith Mary married Wm. Wiltzen. Elizabeth Margaret who died in the Consort Hospital at the age of four and a half years. Muriel Joan, who married Robert Lewis. Nine years later, on Christmas Day, after we came home to the Oilfields Noel Christine was born. She married Hugh Goss.

When the drought and the grasshoppers finally drove us out in 1936, we gave up and came to Turner Valley where Walter got a job on the wells and we built a house near Hartell, which we moved to Black Diamond when we retired from Home Oil. Ardent fishermen and hunters, we enjoyed the oil field life as well as the bowling, curling and all spectator sports we had missed on the prairie.

After Walter retired in 1960 we plunged into community doings and were instrumental in getting the Griffiths Memorial Centre Association going and also the units and Lodge for the Senior Citizens and the Sheep Creek Weavers. I returned to my old association with Christ Church, Millarville, where Mother and Father are buried, and have been in charge of the Cemetery there since the inception of the Flower Festival.

During my life I have been lucky in that I have been able, not without a struggle, to be able to do most of the things I longed to do. Can you imagine a young girl kneeling on a splintery wood floor, putting her head down on a swivel chair behind a teacher's desk and thanking God she was a teacher (and had a school) at last. In 1945 I at last got to University, if only to Summer School to renew my certificate and was able

Freda McArthur (left) and Mrs. Hugh Downey with a fine catch of fish at Lineham Creek, 1937.

to resist the temptation to kneel down and kiss the stone steps as I went in.

In 1955 I went to Banff to the School of Fine Arts. I earned their certificate for Ceramics and for Creative Writing. In going from one building to another I used to see my Baby sitting in the shade peeling potatoes for the students noon meal and I still tease her about putting her Mother through college.

After Plainview School was permanently closed and became the last of the little white school houses, I went to Calgary to substitute in their schools, became interested in teaching the Special Classes, took some courses and settled in at Ogden until I retired in 1966.

Another happy interlude in my life was after Walter retired from Home Oil Co., we bought a holiday trailer but never trailed it further than the Junction on the Kananaskis Road. We went to work for Dobe Snyder there and I lived out back in my trailer and roamed all over the hills and fished in all the creeks with my "bear dog", a little black Cocker Spaniel named Philo. I'll tell you why later.

Now the hospitable doors of the High Country Lodge are yawning wide for us. It's lovely to have a place to go when you have to, that is, it's lovely for other people but not for us, please God, not yet.

Rolland McBee Family

(by Joan DePass)

In 1967 Rolland and Hilda McBee sold their farm in East Longview district and bought a half section of

At High River. Rolland and Hilda McBee.

land N.W. and N.E.¼ 20-21-3-W5. belonging to the MacKay brothers at Millarville.

They built a new home and cleared some land for pasture and continued ranching on a small scale. Still using the grazing permit on Fisher Creek that they had used since 1919. Rolland's health had been failing for a number of years and he spent very little time in their new home. He spent nine months in Turner Valley Hospital, before his death on November 25th, 1970. Hilda still lives on the farm and feeds cattle. She belongs to the Women's Institute at Millarville, also belongs to Sheep Creek Weavers, and belongs to the Unifarm at East Longview.

Their daughter Joan married Sydney Clive DePass of Jamaica, West Indies in 1958. They lived for six years on the Jack Cartwright place, originally the Larratt place, before moving to Turner Valley and Black Diamond. Clive is now an area Foreman for Canadian Pacific Rail, also a flying instructor. Joan is a registered Nurse at Turner Valley Hospital. They have three children, who attended school at Millarville for six years. Susan Jane born in 1959. Now studying for her Bachelor of Nursing at the University of

De Pass family. Susan, Joan, Clive, Kevin. Front: Cecille De Pass (Clive's sister-in-law), Stewart, Clive and Joan's son.

411

Smith Family. L. to R. Joy Lynn, Murray Wayne, James Roland, Laurel Maureen. Parents, Wayne and Virginia, Heather Lorraine on mother's lap.

Calgary. Stewart Clive born in 1960 graduated from Oilfields High School in 1978. Presently working for Canadian Pacific Rail apprenticing, while waiting an opening for an electrician. Kevin Bruce born February 29th, 1964, at present attending Oilfields High School.

Their youngest daughter Virginia who married Wayne Smith of Nanton in 1958, now lives at Prince George, British Columbia, where Wayne is manager for Beaver Lumber. They have five children. Murray Wayne born January 9th, 1959, graduated from High School now working in the lumber industry. Joy Lynn born January 3rd, 1960, married, and has a boy Sheldon. James Roland born July 2nd, 1963 attending High School in Prince George. Laurel Maureen born March 19th, 1965 and Heather Lorraine born December 14th, 1970, both attending school in Prince George, British Columbia.

Wallace and Joan (Smith) McBee
Brand M-F, R.R.

Wallace moved from the De Winton area to the Ballyhamage district to S½, Sec. 24, T.21, R.2, W.5, in August 1928, at the age of 12 years with his folks. He finished his schooling at Ballyhamage School.

Joan and Wallace McBee.

The nearest graded road at that time was two miles away, and it was ten years later that a road was graded for our use. The land was covered with brush and poplars and was without buildings.

Joan was born in Somerset, England and came to the Carstairs district with her parents at the age of 3. She grew up on the farm and attended Grand Center School. She walked 3 miles to school, summer and winter. While going to school she worked on Saturdays and after school, receiving 25¢ for all day Saturday, and 10¢ for after school.

Wallace and Joan met while on a threshing outfit in the De Winton district, the wages those days being $2.50 for a 12-hour day. They were married the next year at Crossfield, December 24, 1941. They lived in a log cabin in the Priddis district for the next nine months, and worked at a sawmill. During this time Wallace lost his mother. In the fall they moved back to the home place, and have resided there ever since.

In the fall of 1942, while we were trying to harvest, our first daughter, Helen — a twin and premature, was born. That year we got very little harvesting done due to wet weather, the threshing was finished the next spring. Edward was born in 1943, Florence was born in 1945, Carolyn in 1947, and Linda in 1951. The four oldest started school at Alexander School, and later went to Red Deer Lake School. Helen and Ed graduated from grade 12 at Midnapore and Western High School in Calgary. Florence and Carolyn graduated from Henry Wisewood. Linda started at Red Deer Lake School and graduated from Lord Beaver Brook School.

As the family was growing up, Wallace and Joan were kept busy with the farm, music lessons, and 4-H and school. Soon wedding bells were ringing. Helen married Ross Agnew in July of 1965 and lives at Chestermere Lake. They have 3 boys — Kevin, Brian and James. Florence married Donald Vander Velde, October, 1965. They live at Dalemead and have 3 boys — Shawn, Michael and Scott. Edward married Evelyn Bruce in February, 1967. They live in Millarville district and have 5 children — Dwayne, Charles, Tammy,

Carolyn, Florence, Helen, Eddie McBee in Millarville 4-H Beef Club.

Linda McBee, Millarville 4-H Beef Club.

Bill and Verona McGregor.

Kimberly and Karl. Carolyn married in February, 1969 to Richard Polowaniuk. They have 2 children — Darryl and Debra and live in Edmonton. Linda married Otto Wichert in November, 1971 and are now residing at Cache Creek, B.C.

McGregor, William Stewart (Bill)

Bill, the eldest son of James and Maud McGregor, was born in Saskatoon, Saskatchewan in 1916. Bill's mother having gone there from Youngstown, Alberta to be with her mother, Margaret McKay.

The family moved from Youngstown to the Kew area and Bill commenced school at Plainview, until the family moved to Black Diamond in 1928. He also attended Upper Turner Valley and completed his high school at Glenmede.

Verona's parents, Travis and Verna Rowles, were married in High River in 1916, and she was born in Frankburg, at the home of her grandparents, Otto and Annie Anderson. Verona's parents moved to Turner Valley in 1926, where she started school — in one

room, the grades being one to twelve, where Miss Garrison taught all grades. Completing her education at Black Diamond and Turner Valley.

Bill went to work for Anglo Canadian Oil Company in 1936.

On May 15, 1940, Verona and Bill were married from Christ Church, Millarville and settled on a farm he had purchased two miles south of Black Diamond.

Bill resigned from Anglo Canadian in 1945 to farm, ranch, and manage his newly-formed construction company, McGregor Johanson Ltd. The company grew quickly and still does oilfield construction work in Alberta and the North West Territories, including the MacKenzie Delta area.

Bill, Verona and family moved to Edmonton in 1949, and Bill, in addition to managing the construction firm, drilled several wells on a private basis with friends in 1951 and 1952. He formed a public company in 1952 called Mic Mac Oils, which was sold to Hudson's Bay Oil and Gas Company Limited in 1963.

In 1963 Bill incorporated a new company called Numac Oil & Gas Ltd., also headquartered in Edmonton, which company is listed on the Toronto and American Stock Exchanges. This company is active in the exploration of oil, gas and uranium in Western Canada.

Bill and Verona have two children. Their daughter, Donna, born in 1943, married Gilbert Gibb in 1965.

Gilbert is manager for the brokerage firm Walwyn Stodgell Cochran Murray Ltd. They have two daughters, Kerry and Heidi, the family resides in Edmonton.

Their son, Stewart, born in 1945, married Barbara Upstone in 1967. Stewart is a lawyer and partner in the firm of Cormie Kennedy. They have a son Scott and a daughter Marla, who also reside in Edmonton.

Agnes (Lyall) McInenly

Agnes is the daughter of Dick and Helen Lyall. She was raised in the Square Butte district, attending school at Millarville and Turner Valley High School. She is married to Frank McInenly, an auctioneer of Arrowwood. They reside in Vulcan, Alta. They have one daughter, Stacey, born November 26th, 1977.

Frank, Stacey and Agnes McInenly.

Karen (King) McInnis

by Jeanie Slemko

Born Karen Plathen in Finland, she was the second wife of W. H. King. She was a nurse and came to Millarville to attend Mrs. Walton. It was at this time she met W. H. King, and they were married in 1935. They had two children, John Rowley, born in 1936, and

John R. King

Olga (Biddy) King.

Olga born in 1937. After the death of Mr. King in 1941. Karen and her two children lived on at Millarville, where Olga and John attended Sheep Creek School. In 1949 Olga (Biddie) passed away.

In 1952, Karen married William (Bill) McInnis and they moved to northern Alberta, taking out land and farmed up there for many years. In 1974, they returned to Southern Alberta and have purchased a home in Longview, Alberta, where they are presently residing.

John Rowley King moved north with his mother, attending school at Spirit River, later went to Mount Royal College in Calgary. He married Rita Dandurand. They have four children and presently make their home in Vancouver, British Columbia. Their children are Wendy, David, Wade and Cathy.

McKeever Family

by Burneice McKeever

William H. (Bill), Burneice and Loretta McKeever moved from Gleichen to a foothills ranch south of Kew on the north half Section 7-20-3w5, owned by Johnnie McGregor, in May 1942.

We had farmed all our married life in the Gleichen district, but decided to take up ranching with our small herd of cows, and had a chance to rent the McGregor place. We moved into a small two roomed shack. How it rained that first summer and how cold it was that first winter. One morning it was 52 degrees below F and the wind blowing. We just couldn't get the house warm. The cream can froze almost solid in the middle of the kitchen floor and so did our feet.

The second year Mr. McGregor moved us into a larger house and my husband built on another room for a kitchen, making us four rooms, which was more comfortable. This house is still on the ranch. Our family consisted of one little girl 5 years old. The next year she started school at Millarville after the Plainview School closed. Our closest neighbors were Doc and Gertie Robison (my husband's sister), Pat and Mollie Hartell, Wilford and Maude Middleton. We gradually got acquainted with a few of our neighbors and went to dances at Kew. I joined the Ladies Community Club and was president of it at the time I left

Burneice, Bill and Loretta McKeever.

there and I got to know some nice people, who gave me a baby shower after I left, which was greatly appreciated.

As I sit here and write, I fail to recall any amusing incidents worth mentioning. Our time was taken up with farming, making hay, tending stock and getting in firewood for the winter. Pioneer days all over again for the third time in Alberta.

One day while churning in the old barrel churn, the lid came off and cream went all over the place. I was so disgusted I took off for town and left the mess. While we were gone, Mr. McGregor came to call, but I never did know how much he saw but the mess was still there when we got back.

The horses ran away with the hay-rack, one horse got bogged down in a soap hole and nearly died before we found her; one of our best horses ran away and we never did find him. The house caught fire just as my husband was about to go to the field for feed, and I screamed for help. Another ten minutes and he would have been gone and the house too, no doubt. Then, worst of all, my husband fell over dead with a heart attack while plowing the garden. He was buried in Calgary. This left me without a home as I had to give up the ranch, with no money and seven months pregnant with a new baby. I left there and went to Gleichen to live with my parents. My baby boy was born on July 17, 1944 and was named William Ross. I lived with my parents for four years, then my father died. I took my family and went to work for a farmer, Mr. Frank Corbiel and stayed there 22 years. Then I retired and bought the first home I ever owned and moved to Gleichen. I have a comfortable home with electricity, water and gas. Although I live alone I am doing very well and keep busy with sewing, gardening and social activities.

Loretta finished her High School at Cluny, worked a couple of years then married Frank's son, Gabriel Corbiel and now lives in Brooks. They have two children, Wade, 16 years old in Grade eleven, and an enthusiastic hockey player. Fay Ann is 14 years old in grade nine and now taking organ lessons.

My son, William Ross (Bill) received his High School education in Cluny then went to University for five years and got his teacher's certificate and B.A.

degree. He is now living in Calgary in Varsity Acres, teaching school there for nine years. He married Jean Yokoyama, and they have a little boy, Robin Stuart, four years old last April.

This is my two years on a cattle ranch west of Turner Valley. Denton Sammons (my brother) rented Mr. McGregor's ranch before we moved there and Buck George took it over after I left.

Brenda (Ballachey) McKenny
by I. Ballachey

Brenda and her husband Gary, who is from Colorado, spent the two years from June 1974 to June 1976 at Chinook Ranch in Kew. They are graduates of the College of Agriculture, majoring in Animal Science from Colorado State University in Ft. Collins, Colorado and came to Alberta shortly after graduating. While on the ranch they took over complete management including an A.I. program involving cross-bred heifers. Due to a very demanding schedule they were not able to become involved in many outside interests. Gary obtained his A.I. certificate after coming to Canada and studied for and received his private pilot's license.

Upon the sale of all the cattle on the ranch in the spring of 1976, Brenda and Gary moved back to Colorado where she is at present doing graduate work towards a Masters degree in Animal Science at C.S.U.

Ranald W. and Ann McKerchar (Ran and Ann)
by Ann McKerchar

Ran was born in Winnipeg, Manitoba. Ever since he was a wee lad, he always had a craze for horses. He got his first horse when he was a young teenager. He was well known in the city where there were horses, be it a Butcher Delivery Service, Riding Stable, Livery barn or his Aunt's farm. I am positive his continued presence was not always appreciated. By the time he achieved his position as an accountant, and his financial independence, he acquired better horses till finally he owned his first Registered American Saddlebred Stallion: Red Squirrel. He was the envy of more than just a few horse enthusiasts. In no time with his fervent ambition, he rated with the top Horse Show Contestants. From there he acquired a small stable of his own; taking in a few boarders. He was active in the breeding, training and some judging.

By the time "Red Squirrel" was due to retire; he took a trip to the U.S.A. and after meeting some of the, then, American Saddle Horse people and looking over their stock, he made the purchase of a beautiful black saddle bred Stallion with a white star and socks, "Connawings Dark Secret." He was a beautiful animal to behold.

I was born in Winnipeg and lived there most of my life till 1959. I also had a great love for horses, being raised by a father that was an avid horse enthusiast. I had the privilege of caring for horses and riding, although my riding was strictly for pleasure.

In 1956 after Ran's first wife and my first husband had both been deceased for some time, our paths met; our mutual interests were not long developing into a permanent relationship. We were married a year later. In 1959 Ran made his first venture to Calgary, to try and establish the basis for a future in the west, the real horse and Ranch country. As a result after a few short ventures we ended up in the Millarville district at the Graham Ranches.

Ran could not have found a more ideal place for his ambitions. His ambitions were not restricted to only the one; his favorite breed. He was keenly interested also in the Thoroughbreds: racing and showing Hunters and Jumpers. To add to the attraction were the beautiful Foothills and the mountain views. It seemed that this was all of both our dreams come true. Ran was in this Seventh heaven. At that time the Grahams were active in breeding of Thoroughbreds as well as very enthusiastic and active in the showing of these horses. Breeding, foaling, breaking and training were all part of the yearly program at that time, besides the care of the Show Stock. There was never a dull moment. The trophies and ribbons displayed in different areas of the Ranch are all the proof needed to verify the success of the horses and horsemanship on the place. Their ambitions never ceased. Their interest turned to the Three Phase Equestrian Competitions with more extensive and never ending training, consisting of Dressage Cross Country and Stadium jumping. The Western Canada Team training, then the Canadian Team training. It was a continual routine of Three Phase Events including competitors of the three western provinces, British Columbia, Alberta and Saskatchewan. Eventually leading to the Canadian Three Phase Equestrian Team training base at the Graham Ranches including the Millarville Race Track. Elimination led to the final, choice of the Canadian Three Phase Equestrian Team to represent Canada. It was very gratifying for Ran to be a small part of Canada's beginning participation in the Olympics. It was much more than his greatest expectations and hopes of most of his life time.

It gave me great pleasure to stand by him and share his enthusiasm and interest. In spite of fully sharing Ran's ambitions and interests I found my hopes and expectations came second to the equines. I found myself having no choice; instead having to cook for the extra single ranch hands plus all that goes with it, which certainly hasn't the prestige of a professional horseman. My spirits were not dampened for long.

I found the friendliness of the people in the community overwhelming and derived much pleasure and satisfaction in the community as much as I was able to. My lack of operating a motor vehicle in this modern age was one drawback of my own making.

The Millarville Races were one of my annual

highlights, and always found myself leaving the races with more than I spent on bets.

The Millarville Fair was an exciting and nostalgic event for me. Not only for the days the Fair was on but all the time it took to prepare the exhibits. The worst problem was not knowing how and by whom I would get my car load of exhibits across the road as that was always during the busiest time at the ranch, but I always found in the end everyone was behind me. If Ran wasn't available, whoever else was, would get my load over for me in time. It was always a very gratifying day and I always returned to the ranch with my fair share of ribbons and prize money, with everyone rooting for me when I returned.

Most of any spare time we had, was spent exploring the surrounding countryside. The points of interest in the Millarville area were ever so numerous. All the deserted old ranch buildings, the old N.W.M.P. Barracks, the remains of one of John Wares' buildings (presumably the barn) across from the Cairn erected in memory of this fantastic pioneer to mention just a few.

All good things have to come to an end, ours with Ran's health giving out on him. Our pleasant and happy memories shall remain with us as long as we live and feel a great privilege to have lived in Millarville and to have known so many wonderful people.

A. Bruce McLean Family   VI

by A. Brent McLean

My parents, Bruce and Belle McLean, with their two children, Brent and Beverley, moved to the Stan Stanhope farm (S.E.¼ of 31-21-2w5 and the N.E.¼ of 30-21-2w5) from Tilston, in Southwestern Manitoba in 1944. Both parents had been born on farms in this area of Manitoba. The N.W.¼ and the S.½ of 29-21-2w5 was added to the farm and later Dad bought the Doc Lee place (S.½ of 34-21-4w5) in the Kew district for pasture and hay.

Beverley and I attended Fordville School until it closed, then went to Sheep Creek School in 1947. My

L. to R. A. Bruce McLean, Beverley, Bruce jr., Brent, Bonnie and Belle. 1957.

416

sister Bonnie was born in Turner Valley while we were still on the Millarville farm, and Bruce Jr. was born in 1949, the year we moved to the Bill McGregor land south of Black Diamond.

Dad had a very bad experience while we were still on the Millarville farm. A big truck tire rim cut his nose off. He held his nose in his hand while a neighbor drove him to Black Diamond, where Dr. David Lander had his office in the Black Diamond Hotel. Dr. Lander called help in from the beer parlor, and with a man on each arm and leg, the nose was sewn back on.

In 1949, Dad went into the construction business in Edmonton and in 1950 the family moved to that city. The Millarville farm was sold to John Campbell in the early fifties, and the Doc Lee place was sold about the same time to Jim and Dorothy Davis.

I went to school in the United States in 1954, and after selling the construction company, Dad and the rest of the family moved to a farm at Langley, B.C., where he imported and raised Highland cattle.

Dad lives at White Rock, B.C. as do Beverley (Mrs. Ed Ackerman, Denise, Scott, Brent) and Bonnie (Mrs. Bill Buston, David, Romey, Neil). Our mother, Belle, lives on Curlew Island in the Gulf Islands. Bruce Jr. (wife Rebecca, Amos) after several years in Australia and New Zealand, lives and teaches school in Langley, B.C. I, my wife Maybert, Cody and Chelsea, have lived in Calgary for the past twelve years, where I am involved in the oil business.

Several years ago, while driving in the district, I saw a crew pulling a casing and abandoning an oil well. It was the same well I had seen being drilled from my Grade 5 window at the Sheep Creek School (old location) over thirty years earlier. The school, of course, had also been relocated.

The McLeod Family

Donna Metz

Donald J. McLeod with his wife Dorothy and five children, Jim, Gerald, Donna, George and Esther first moved to Black Diamond in 1936 from Fort St. John, B.C. Dad worked for the Royalite Oil Co. as a steam engineer. We moved to our new home in Riverbend, near Longview the following year. Jim, Gerald and I attended the Longview school until 1940. Joyce was born that year and the family broke up and Mother went back to Fort St. John with George, Esther and Joyce. Jim and Gerald worked out on farms and I went to Calgary and worked for my room and board and got my Grade Six at Colonel Walker School.

Dad built a small house at Millarville in 1941 and Mother returned in the spring of 1942, with George, Esther and Joyce. We were all together that summer but Mother packed us all up north again that fall and I took my Grade Seven in Ft. St. John. Wesley was born in January 1943 and that summer we all moved back to Millarville. Dad had gone to work for the C.P.R. and was running the pusher engines out of Field, B.C.

Donna (McLeod) Metz and friends. L. to R. Ann Jackson, Donna, Mamie Willford, Fern Jackson, Florence Willford. 1944.

George, Esther and I attended Sheep Creek School the 1943-44 term. Marvin was born in January 1945 and I quit school in May and went to work in Calgary until February of 1946, then returned to Millarville and went to work for Jappy and Martha Douglass at the Millarville Store. I met and married Leonard Metz that year. Len had just gotten his discharge from the Army and had taken a job in the oil patch. He lived with the Bert Chalmers family until our wedding in September, 1946. We bought a 3 room house just across the Creek from Bill Jackson's. In Sept. 1949, our first son, Donald Robert was born, and in 1950 we moved our house up the hill just north of the old Major warehouse. In Sept. 1953, our second son was born, and we named him Leonard Charles. "Rusty" became his nickname and he is still called that.

Later that year Len transferred to the Stettler oil field and we spent the next seventeen years living in Erskine. Our third son, Wesley John, was born November 1955.

We were all active in Church, Community, Boy Scouts and sports. Baseball filled most of the summer and they did well in it. Wesley played in three provincial play-offs and Rusty's team won the provincials three years and in 1970 Rusty's team won the Western Canada play-offs in Glenboro, Manitoba.

When Don finished his grade 12 at Stettler he went on to S.A.I.T. for three years and got his surveyors course and now works for Hudson Bay Gas and Oil out of the Calgary office.

In 1970, Len transferred to Sundre where we lived until Feb. 1978. Rusty and Wesley got their grade 12 and Rusty went into gas fitting and Wesley works for Calgary Power at Innisfail.

Rusty married Darlene Warhurst of Sundre, formerly of Red Deer Lake in 1976 and they are living in Sundre with their son, Christoffer. Don married Patricia Whalen of Calgary in Oct. 1974.

Len took a transfer to Fort St. John with Home Oil in February 1978. We had bought my grandfather's old homestead on Charlie Lake, just five miles north of

Fort St. John. We are building a log cabin there to live in, so it would seem that I have travelled full circle and am back to the place of my birth.

My father, Don McLeod passed away June 1972 and my mother, Dorothy passed away November 1977 at Fort St. John.

Jim McLeod lives in Whitecourt, Alberta. Gerald McLeod lives in Fort St. John. George McLeod has his home in Fort St. John but has spent the last four years in Iran with Haliburton Oil Well Service Co. Esther McLeod Beattie, Joyce McLeod McKearney, Wesley McLeod and Marvin McLeod all live in Fort St. John.

Jean (Smith) McLeod
by D. Lawrence

Jean was born in Turner Valley in 1943, daughter of Wilbur and Dorothy Smith. They lived on the South half of 13-20-4w5. Wilbur did trucking in the oil fields.

Jean started to school at Plainview and later went by bus to Millarville for some years. History doesn't relate how she did in school but they were probably happy days, as she is independent by nature.

Her father passed away during this period. Her mother stayed with the farm for a couple of years, then married Doug Lawrence, and the family moved to Red Deer Lake to his place. Jean finished her schooling and then served an apprenticeship as a hair-dresser in Calgary. She followed that line in later years.

In 1962, she married Jim McLeod, son of an old Okotoks family. They have lived in Okotoks most of the time since. Jim worked locally then for Firestone Tires for years until it went out of business. He is now engaged as an independent trucker.

They have three sons, Wade, Glen and Craig, who take an interest in seasonal sports. Jim and Jean curl and Jean has played on the ladies' ball team for years. For most of the past year, she has been employed at a retail outlet, so she hasn't let the world pass her by.

Jim, Jean, Glen McLeod. Front: Craig.

Pat and Susan McMahon with daughter Erin.

Patrick and Susan McMahon

Patrick and Susan McMahon and their daughter Erin were all born in Calgary. They bought the Ray Gessler house in the fall of 1975. Susan's parents reside in Calgary and her father John Cameron McCullough was born there. Her mother May Angela nee Lewis grew up in Turner Valley.

Pat's parents, the late George L. McMahon and Katharine McMahon, nee Staples, were both from the interior of British Columbia but came to Calgary in the early 1940's.

The McMahon Family
~J.M N.W. 13

Terry and Marie McMahon acquired 40 acres from Ivor Lyster in December 1973. They are permanent residents of Calgary. Marie originally came to Calgary in 1962 from Eganville, Ontario, in the Ottawa Valley, to work as a Public Health Nurse for the City of Calgary. It wasn't long before she found a handsome Calgarian, and she and Terry were married in 1964. They now have three girls; Nancy, 12 years; Jennifer, 11 years; and Megan, 8 years.

Terry grew up in Calgary and surrounding area. He graduated from the University of Alberta, and now has a busy law practise. In his spare time, he enjoys the work at the farm, first as a modest cattle rancher and now as a tree farmer. Marie spends her spare time spinning, weaving and dyeing, as well as helping at the farm.

Their cabin was started in the fall of 1974, and completed in July, 1975. It is used primarily as a weekend retreat. The cattle operation continued for the first few years. Now the land is used for tree farming, gardening, and recreation. All the family cross-country ski, hike and watch the grass grow.

The G. H. McNab Family

by Edith I. McNab

George Hunter McNab, second eldest son of Daniel and Margaret McNab, was born in Airdrie, Scotland in the year 1908 and came to Canada with his mother and two brothers in 1910 to join his dad at the Beggs' Ranch on the Dunbow.

He lost his mother at an early age, and shortly after, he and four brothers spent a short period of time at the Salvation Army Home and then numerous places after.

He attended many schools with moving around a lot; Mewata Park in Calgary, Panima, Melrose, Stormont and Okotoks. After finishing school, he went to work at the Sandstone Brickyard and from there to Hanna; then Royalite Oil Pipeline from Turner Valley to Calgary and several places from there on, ending up at Norman Anderson's, SW¼, Sec. 25-21-2-W5 for ten years, working hard, clearing land with a double bitted axe and breaking it up, general mixed farming, milking cows, etc. He earned poor wages, but gained much knowledge.

He planted many trees in the spring of 1923 and the spruce must be about sixty feet in height now. He also played the Hawaiian guitar quite well (a gift from Mrs. Anderson). In 1934 he met, Edith Irene (Field) born August 30, 1918, at Roundup, Alberta (near Granum), second eldest daughter of Robert Henry (Bud) and Lola Field. We married in 1936 and George rented his dad's place for a year and along with others hauled logs from back west to build a log house on the SE¼, Sec 23-21-2-W5, which he purchased from the CPR in the fall of 1937. In so doing, he had to relinquish the west quarter of the same section.

We named the quarter "Lone Pine" and in the early spring of 1938, we built the log house together and had scads of fun while doing it. Besides mixed farming, George worked out at different places, as it was during the depression and things were hard to come by.

George and Edith McNab at "Lone Pine" 1941.

Our daughter Annie Lila was born July 11, 1937 and son Alan Hunter April 28, 1939.

The Second World War broke out in September 1939, so George enlisted in February of 1941 with the RCAF and left for Brandon Manning depot on April 28 of the same year. He spent four and a half years in the Airforce, stationed at various stations in Western Command.

I stayed on the farm with the children. Sister Evelyn came to stay with us for a few months and then Sister Florence came to stay. We had horses and pigs, milked a few cows and raised chickens and turkeys.

There was always plenty to do so we were kept busy, which helped make the war years go by fairly fast. In those years there was no electricity, just coal and wood stoves, coal oil lamps, etc., and everyone seemed to manage quite well.

Daughter Linda Rose was born July 4, 1944, and son Lorne Eric November 5, 1945. The years to follow were very busy, the war was over and George was back home again, getting back into the routine of farming. Son James Lance (Jim) was born July 20, 1949 and daughter Stastia Laverne April 10, 1951. That fall, our crops were snowed under so George had to go out to work again in Calgary for 15 Works R.C.E. Currie Barracks.

We lived on this quarter, Lone Pine, until 1957 then moved across to the NW¼, Sec. 24-21-2-W5 (the old homestead). We named it Lonestead. George purchased Lonestead, on which we still have a residence, in 1948 through the V.L.A. from Willie Willis (George's step-brother). We sold the other quarter, Lone Pine, in 1967 to Jerry Sinclair and since it has been subdivided into two eighties. Jerry and family live on the south eighty and Lorne Marshall and Charlotte on the north. Both parties are in the oil business.

Our children took their schooling at Ballyhamage and Red Deer Lake, then high school in Calgary and are now all married with homes and families of their own.

Annie worked at home, doing chores, etc., on the farm while George worked in town. She also worked for some of the neighbors in the district, was married to Jim Smith from Scotland (a saddle maker) in 1963. They have a nice home in Medicine Hat, where Jim works for Hutchings & Sharpe "Western Store." They have no family.

Alan finished school and spent some time home, helping on the farm, was very good with machinery, worked the land and put the crop in, while his dad was working in Calgary and up in Banff, then he helped with haying and threshing, etc. After that, he left to work in Calgary for Triad Oil Company. He worked in various places in the north while with this company and then decided to go trucking. He met Rose Leoptke (a hairdresser) in Okotoks. They were married in 1960 and have a daughter, Lori, now going to Mount Royal College in Calgary. He and Rose were divorced a few

419

The George McNab family: L. to R. Statia, Annie, Alan, Linda, Lorne, Jim and dog "Rover".

years later, and have both remarried. He has worked many places with heavy equipment on road construction, etc., and is now working and living at White Court, Alberta with his new family.

Linda graduated from school with Senior Matric and went in training for a nurse at the General Hospital for three years, graduated in 1966 and went to Taber, Alberta to work in the hospital there. While working there she met Ron Fritz. He was born in Bow Island and raised there and in the Taber district. He worked for Carnation Foods at that time. They were married in 1967 and lived in Taber for seven years. Linda went on working at the hospital there. The Carnation Foods closed their Taber plant in 1972, so Ron got a job working for Canadian Western Natural Gas Co., which meant he and his family would have to move to Calgary. Linda works part time at the Rockyview Hospital. They have two children, Ronald Alan and Stastia Lynn.

Lorne (or Joe as he is known to many in the community) finished grade ten at Earnest Manning in Calgary then spent 1 year at the Devry Electronic School in Toronto. Following this he went to Sundre, Alberta to work for Kallas Gas & Electric and from there to Northern Geophysical, then came back to Calgary to work for Kohn Electric. He married Janet Marfleet from Sundre in 1968, completed his apprenticeship as a journeyman electrician in 1971 and left Kohn Electric to work for Alberta Gas Trunk Line, working himself into supervisor of electrical construction department and obtaining his "Master" electrical papers.

In March of 1977, he took a partnership in D. A. Electric and moved his family to Brooks, Alberta where he organized and now manages the Brooks division of the company. They have two boys, Donovan Hunter and Colin Lee.

James, known to all as "Jim," graduated with a Senior Matric then went to work for Kohn Electric and apprenticed as a journeyman electrician. He has now moved several times to where jobs took him, lastly Redcliff, Alberta where he and his family still have a residence. He is working at Burstall, Alberta at the present time. He married Marion (Ridley) of Orangeville, Ontario and they have a family of three, Paul James, Richard William and Heather Evelyn.

Stastia finished school and worked as a secretary with Pacific Petroleum 66 for seven years then was married to Randy George Risdahl of Calgary, a paramedic working in Calgary. They have two children Todd Russel and Linay Ann and are now living in Okotoks, Alberta.

James McNab (Jimmie and Ruby)

Jimmie was born on May 28, 1913 with a rough beginning. His mother died when he was two years old and his father then joined the Canadian Expeditionary Force serving overseas in the 1st World War. The five sons were placed in the Salvation Army Home during this period. From here the boys were split up at a young age and placed in different family homes.

Jimmie, being lucky, was taken in by Mr. Charlie Steiner of Vulcan who had seen him in the McBride home and thought he needed more tender loving care. Here he was raised as one of the family. Jimmie had various experiences working at different places while growing up. During his stay at the Steiner home he would take visits to the hills of the Red Deer Lake area where his father homesteaded. One time, when he stopped to visit the Johnny Barraclough family for a few weeks, it ended up a three year stay.

Jimmie was always one of those challenging, progressive individuals who would do almost anything for a dare. At the young age of 15 years while working for Mrs. Dave Wylie in the Red Deer Lake area he bet Mrs. Wylie's daughter, Cecilia, that he could beat her making an apple pie for the Priddis Fair. He made the pie at the Wylie's home and won First Prize. It never

L. to R. Jimmie McNab, with daughter Debbie and Wife Ruby (Field) (Nicknamed the Globe Trotter).

failed to bring tears of laughter when people heard just how the pie was made.

Another one of Jimmies stop overs was Bill and Ruth Hamilton's, as it was impossible to have the McNab brothers corralled in the same spot it was with great pleasure that Jimmie shared the company of his brother Johnnie who also often stopped at the Hamiltons. For years Johnnie threw stove for Dick Crosgrove of Rosebud, also for the Sheep Creek wagon outfit owned by Gene Goettler, driven by Sam Johnson. Hamiltons was the place Jimmie could relax, let his hair down and enjoy the company of friends and neighbors. Many hours were passed talking over the good times.

Another stopping place was his brother George's, who was married to Edith, the second of the seven Field girls. Consequently, it was on one of these visits that he met his wife Ruby, the fourth of the Field girls.

In 1942 Jimmie left Vulcan to take over his brother Johnny's farm, purchasing it from the Hudson's Bay Co. Jimmie married Ruby on June 7, 1944 and took up farming, naming their place the J. J. Ranch because this property was purchased and owned only by the two J. McNab's.

Our home wasn't much to look at but it was warm and always had lots of grub. Our friends and neighbors didn't care about us not having a big fancy home as they came to visit and it wasn't long before the old walls were ringing with laughter and good talks.

Sports was a number one topic in the McNab home, from boxing to hockey. Jimmie enjoyed a game of cribbage any time. He just loved to get his neighbors together for a game trying to prove who was Master of the game. Some of the champs being Harvey Gerlitz, Bill Sadler, Robert Field, Jack Genert and Albert Kromm. When Jimmie was getting beat he would say "Let's have another cup of coffee Ruby and we'll have just one more game as I'm sure I'll beat them this time". This was often at 11 o'clock at night. After years of playing Jimmie finally got the 29 hand while playing at Harvey's one night.

We were blessed with three children. Bonnie was born November 25, 1946 and Debbie April 22, 1952. Johnnie was born November 19th, 1956.

It was a great shock to us when we lost Jimmie suddenly with a heart attack on March 11, 1972.

Life isn't easy flying on one wing after sharing so much with one who enjoyed living for his family, and counting his blessings because he was part of our good neighborhood. Managing the farm keeps me busy along with working on tours. Tours have taken me all over the British Isles, Western Europe, Peru and across Canada. All over the United States, down through Mexico from Nagabis to Acapulco, Guadamala, through the Panama Canal, the Hawaiian Islands, Bermuda, Bahamas, Yukon and Alaska. Of all the places I've been I would not trade my little place in the Ballyhamage district for any or all of it. I love the

Bonnie (McNab) Taylor, husband Barry, children — Huff and Kari.

Debbie (McNab) Kobelka, with husband Ed and son Richard.

Johnny McNab with cousin Lloyd Cannon.

421

four seasons and it is always great to get home to rest where my roots are.

Bonnie graduated from Henry Wise Wood at seventeen. She was sponsored to run for Stampede Queen but married Lee Ellison instead. They were blessed by one daughter, Karie. After her divorce she enrolled in the first University course given at Mount Royal College for Nursing, graduating from the two-year program and receiving her R.N. She met and married Barry Taylor and moved to Victoria, B.C. They were blessed with a son "Huff". Bonnie specializes in the O.R. working on open heart surgery.

Debbie graduated from Lord Beaverbrook and went to Edmonton to finish her education. Here she met her husband, Ed Kobelka, who is a Toyota car salesman. Their son, Richard James, is their pride and joy.

Johnnie James took his schooling at Red Deer Lake, then attended E. P. Scarlett. He is now one of Cana Construction's crane operators going into his fourth year.

Dr. Thomas Melling

by Jean E. Melling

Dr. Melling was born in England and came to Canada at an early age, residing west of Edmonton. He received his medical degree at the University of Alberta. His first practice was at Tomahawk, Alberta. From 1936 to 1939 he was Medical Officer with the Department of Northern Affairs, posted at Chesterfield Inlet, Northwest Territories.

From there he went to Calgary and was associated with the firm of Drs. Bouck and Brodie until 1957, when he was appointed director of the Calgary Cancer Clinic. He held that position until his death in 1967.

His wife Carthena passed away in 1954. In 1956 he married Jean Pettis (nee Oro). They had a son Thomas Bryant, who at present is attending the University of Alberta in the faculty of Commerce.

Dr. Melling purchased his land at Millarville in the early 1950's. It was located at Sec. 15, S.E.¼ and N.E.¼ and N.W.¼ T.W.P. 21-4-5. Although the Mellings resided in Calgary, they spent as much time at their Millarville "home" as a busy medical practice would allow. In 1956 the land was sold to Jack Hunter of Calgary.

Don Mickle Memories of the Foothills

by Don Mickle

My memories of the East Millarville and Square Butte areas go back from early childhood, through the growing up years. We moved to the Walter Ericson place (the west half and the s.e. quarter of section 30-20-2w5) from the Cochrane area in the early 1950s. After a few years of farming on this land we moved west of Millarville to the old Fred Kosling place (south half of 17-21-4w5).

Don Mickle, Park Warden at Yoho National Park.

Don Mickle Family. Grace, Don, Flora and Johanna.

Dad had a trapline on the Forest Reserve and we spent a lot of time there. My most fond memories are of the area centered around the rolling hills of the Forest Reserve at our back door, dominated by Square Butte and the mountains towering behind. Wildlife was plentiful, even in the 1950s. It was thrilling to see the wild horse bands and watch them run over the face of the Butte.

We spent a few years in the Square Butte area, then our family moved to Lake Louise and the mountains in the early 1960s and we went into the guiding and outfitting business there.

I still live in the mountains and am a Park Warden in Yoho National Park. I met Grace MacKinnon in Lake Louise and we were married in 1971. We have two girls, Flora born in 1972, and Johanna born in 1974.

Bert and June Mickle T X

by June Mickle

My mother was a pioneer daughter of Bob Hamilton. She was born near Okotoks in 1896 and died

June and Bert Mickle at their home, Oct. 1978.

at Banff in 1968. Her first husband, Basil Roughton, was killed in a hunting accident in 1919. I was born a few months later. My mother and I lived in the Midnapore district and in Calgary, where she worked until 1936, when she married Tip Johnson. He was the pioneer son of old timer Ed (Wild Horse) Johnson of Priddis district. Tip died at Black Diamond in 1964.

When Tip and Claire were married, we moved to the old Ward place 10 miles west of Turner Valley, about one mile from the Big Horn Reserve. Our neighbors were Bob Carry and John and Annie Gettig. Also Sturrocks lived across from us.

Some of my happier memories are of that district where I attended many dances in the old Kew Hall, by horseback, sleigh and even skis. Sometimes I stayed overnight in the warm hospitality of Paddy and Nina Rodgers old log house.

In 1941 I met Bert Mickle from the old time family of Charlie Mickle from Jumping Pound. We were married in 1942 and had a real old western dance at • Kew Hall. People still remember that dance with a smile.

We lived on Bert's ranch near Jumping Pound where our two children, Don and Faye were born. When they were school age we sold the ranch to Sam Copithorne and bought a place four miles north of Black Diamond. Don and Faye attended Sheep Creek School from 1950 until they finished.

We moved west of Millarville to the old Kosling place near Square Butte. We built a new log house there and spent a few happy years. Bert coached the Square Butte baseball team for a while. He also worked on his trap line west of Square Butte. We got a wild horse permit and caught a few wild horses which we broke and used.

In 1963, we had a chance to buy Timberline Tours, a guiding, fishing and hunting business at Lake Louise. We managed Skoki and Temple Lodges also.

Many of the local boys came and worked for us in the summer, Keith Foster, Bob Haney, David Wildman, John Nylund and John Eden. Most of these boys have joined the Warden Service as the call of the mountains held them.

We sold Timberline Tours to Paul Peyto in 1976. When we sold the land west of Millarville we bought three quarters of land 26 miles west of Innisfail near Spruce View and the Raven River where we spend our winters.

In summer we run a novelty shop at Bow Lakes in Jim Simpson's Num-Ti-Jah Lodge on the Banff-Jasper Highway. In this business I have a chance to sell some of my paintings and leather goods which I make in the winter. Our son, Don Mickle, is a Warden. He is married and they live at the Park boundary west of Field. They have two little girls, Flora and Johanna.

Faye married Ron Hall of Cochrane. After ten years they got divorced so she and her two children, Debbie and Marty, live in a mobile home on our place. She works at the Co-op at Spruce View.

We kept Tip's brand $\overline{T}$ and also have our old Mickle horse brand $\times$. This is our story to date.

Lloyd and Betty Middleton $\stackrel{2}{\llcorner}$L.T. $\overline{AM}$R.R.
by Betty Middleton

Lloyd Wilfred Middleton was born in Fruitland, Ontario. He came west with his father Wilfred in 1935, when he returned to these parts, having homesteaded west of Turner Valley in 1906. His mother followed with his sister Joyce. He attended Plainview School, travelling by horseback.

When the war came he served in the army but was not overseas. Following the war, he returned to help his father on the farm. Later he took over the family farm, also buying the W. A. Simpson place, the N.W.¼ of 36-19-4w5. He pastures cattle in the Forest Reserve, gathering them at the annual South Sheep Creek Stock Association round-up held at the Cow Camp each fall.

Lloyd also did a considerable amount of trapping,

Lloyd Middleton and family. L. to R. Lloyd, Barbara, Karen, Betty. Wilfred in front.

Lloyd Middleton's cabin "The Retreat" on Ware Creek. L. to R. Joyce (Middleton) Bateman, Bruce Sturrock, Lloyd Middleton.

having a registered trapline in the Bow Crow Forest Reserve. Many will remember the little log cabin on Ware Creek which he built with the help of his fishing friends. It served many a passer-by with a place to stay overnight as well as a warming spot. Vandals finally destroyed the interior and windows of the cabin. This line at one time belonged to an old trapper named Smiley who was found dead in the original cabin. Ben Jarvis, who at the time, was working for the Forestry, packed out the body on horseback as there were no roads in those days.

In 1957, Lloyd married Edith Elizabeth Griffith, a registered nurse who was working in High River. She is the daughter of Charles and Amy Griffith of Priddis, where she grew up, later attending Western Canada High School and graduated from the Holy Cross School of Nursing. Her brother, Jim, still runs the family farm.

Lloyd and Betty have three children, Karen Christine, presently attending Mount Royal College taking a Secretarial Arts course; Barbara Ann, Grade IX; Wilfred Charles, Grade VI, attending Turner Valley School.

Wayne and Elizabeth (Lyall) Miller
by Elizabeth Miller

I am the eldest daughter of Tom and Betty Lyall and granddaughter of "Auntie Sally" Lyall. I have fond memories of growing up in the Square Butte District and attending Sheep Creek School. Now that I am involved in community life of my own I can reflect back to the Halloween, Christmas parties, picnics and Friday night dances, belonging to Explorers and many more enjoyable events and trying to bring some of these memories to my children and community.

After moving from Square Butte, I attended school at Olds, Carstairs and Calgary. I met my husband Wayne Miller in Calgary and we were married in 1967. Wayne was born in Olds, Alberta and attended school in Olds, Calgary, and Chilliwack, B.C. He returned to

L. to R. Randy, Christie and Jamie Miller.

Calgary in 1965 to work for Bow Valley Machinery where he is still employed. Wayne is an ardent curler and golfer, and as a family we also enjoy camping and boating, spending the last five summers at Sylvan Lake.

We have three children, Randy, Jamie and Christie.

Randy is a grade five student at Wildwood Elementary school. He enjoys reading, swimming and belongs to the 86 cub pack at Woodcliff Church. He also collects Super Hero Comic Books.

Jamie also attends Wildwood School and enjoys playing T. Ball and soccer. He also enjoys fishing with Grandpa Lyall and swimming.

Christie is currently attending day care part-time while I work. She also enjoys going shopping and curling and all the other busy activities of our family.

We have resided in the Wildwood District of Calgary for the past eleven years.

Charles W. Minue
one of the early school teachers.

I followed Miss Bird — April to June 1930, and boarded at Mr. and Mrs. Ford Lochhead.

I enjoyed the older children, but was not very good with the younger ones. The Kew Hall was built during my stay.

I enjoyed spending an odd evening with Enoch Walton at the Kew Store.

In July I went with the Gettigs, Nashes and Carry on a packtrain trip to the Kananaskis Lakes.

In the fall of 1930 I moved to Edmonton.

The Ron Mitchell Family ⬇
by Liz Mitchell

My dad's family, the John Keeler Cummings, came from Minnesota in 1909, and began the Independent Grain Co., in Calgary. My mom's family, the George Lamonts, came from Toronto, Ontario in 1905. They live in the Red Deer Lake District now, and celebrated their 50th wedding anniversary in 1976.

Ron and I knew each other for many years as both our fathers were active in Fish & Game work. Ron was born in Edmonton, but moved shortly to Calgary, where his dad started Mitchell Insurance Services, which he ran until his death in 1974. Ron's mom, Peggy grew up in Calgary, and was a championship swimmer, and fine athlete.

The Ron Mitchell Family. L. to R., Back: Ron, Liz, with their daughters Lisa and Pam.

Ron began his RCMP training in Regina, in 1961, and after 4 years, came home to work with his dad. I graduated from the General Hospital School of Nursing in 1964, and we were married the following June.

We bought 2 acres from Jack Waite, just north of the Halfway Store on Highway 22, and built a house there. The next summer we bought part of the Roy Cutting place, about halfway between Priddis and Bragg Creek. For the first winter, we lived in the original log house, and then built a new one the following summer. Lisa, our first daughter was born in June 1968, just in time to move into our new house.

The next summer Ron went to Little Dall Lake in the NWT, to guide hunters for Chuck Hayward. He liked it so well, that the summer Lisa was two, we all went north for the hunting season. Ron to guide, and me to help Ruby Sinclair-Smith with kitchen chores. It was a memorable time, and something we wouldn't have missed.

In 1971, we sold the Priddis place to Jack Herzog, and moved to our present place, SE¼ S1, T21, R4, W5, which we bought from Frank Sharp. Our cattle, leaseland, and Forestry Grazing Permit we bought from Mike Rodgers. Our second daughter, Pam, was born in June 1973.

I was secretary for the Square Butte Community for several years, and am in my third year as President of the Square Butte Ladies' Group. Ron has been secretary-treasurer of the North Sheep Stock Assn. for some years. Our cattle brand is —71 l.r. and 7 l.h. horses.

Mitchell, Wes and Edith
by Dolores Duchesnay

Wes is the son of Ben and Ivy Mitchell of Turner Valley. Edith is the daughter of Len and Grace Meister of Turner Valley. Wes and Edith were married in 1934 and had six children, Dolores, Carol, Shirley, Linda, a son Robert, and Darlene.

Wes and Edith moved to Millarville from Turner Valley in 1944, settling on what is now the Fred Rishaug place. Wes had his own welding outfit and did contract welding for Home Oil, Major Oil and other companies.

A couple of years later they moved to the old (Carlton) King place across from the Sheep Creek School. Wes looked after cattle for Bob Mowatt and started working for Home Oil. One Christmas Dolores and Carol went to find a Christmas tree. They found a beautiful one, cut it down and managed to drag it home. It turned out to be 20 feet long.

They moved to the Home Oil Camp in 1948 and in the summer of 1950 moved to Redwater. A son Robert and a daughter Darlene were born while in Redwater.

Wes is now medically retired and living in Redwater. Edith is working in Edmonton for Alberta Government Telephones.

Dolores is Mrs. Ed Duchesnay of Bashaw and has four children. Ed is employed by Home Oil in Bashaw. Carol is Mrs. Buddy Mills of Morrinville and has three children. Shirley is Mrs. Walter Marciniphyn of Edmonton and has four children. Linda is Mrs. Don Wheele of Wetaskiwin and has three children. Robert recently married and Darlene is single.

Mitchell girls ready for another day at Sheep Creek School. L. to R. Linda, Shirley, Carol, Dolores. Picture taken at the old King Place.

The Frank Mortimer Family

by Karel Whynot

There are three daughters and two sons in our family. Four of us, Karel (Margaret), Bill, Don and Barbara were all born on the farm in Millarville. Joyce was just a year old when our parents moved to the farm from Calgary in 1921. It was quite an experience for our Mother who had arrived in Calgary just two years previous from an English town in Wiltshire as a war bride. She had never experienced baking bread or making butter or raising poultry, but soon became proficient at all three.

My sister Joyce and I were among the first pupils to register at New Valley School the day it opened early in 1928. We were driven to school by our father in a horse-drawn sleigh when the weather was cold, and in fine weather we rode horses.

There were numerous gophers in the school yard in the spring and some of our recesses were spent drawing water from the well and pouring it down the gopher holes to drown them out.

In early December 1928, we moved to Calgary, where we attended King Edward School. There were two classes of each grade with at least thirty pupils in each which took a while in which to adjust.

In 1971, my husband John and I purchased property in Okotoks from Ed McLeod who told us he had bought a cow at the auction sale held when we moved from the farm, and had walked home to Okotoks with the cow in tow.

In 1975, Bill received a kidney transplant in Seattle, Washington; the donor was our sister Barbara. Up to the point of this writing it has been a success, for which we are all very grateful.

Joyce lives in Calgary and is an accountant at Conforce Products Ltd. Karel is married to John Whynot, a building contractor in Calgary. They have a daughter, Sharel Waddell, at Langley, B.C. A son, Shane of Calgary and one grand-daughter, Marin Waddell.

Bill is a sheetmetal and air condition contractor in Yakima, Washington. He and Betty have a son, Bruce; a daughter, Ann Field; one grand-son, Brian.

Don is a salesman for Taylor, Pearson and Carson, in Calgary. Barbara works with the Dominion of Canada Department of Agriculture, in Vancouver, B.C.

When I took driving lessons at the A.M.A. a number of years ago, I became acquainted with one member of the class in particular. During one of our conversations we discovered we were both from Millarville. She was Gwen Cohoe whose Grandmother and Grandfather's farm adjoined ours.

Don Morrison

The senior generation of Morrison's came to the west in 1903 from Kineer's Mill's, Quebec and took up land in the Big Rock district southwest of Okotoks.

Evelyn and Don Morrison.

My father John Warcup Morrison grew up and acquired his education there. He went into the teaching profession and taught school in many districts in Alberta. He joined the Royal Flying Corps in the first World War and returned to teaching after his return from service. He went to teach in the Hay Lakes district near Camrose and it was there he met my mother.

She was a native of Norway and came to Alberta at the age of four with her parents, who homesteaded land in the Hay Lake district.

Our generation of Morrison's were all born in that district, five in all. The eldest my only sister Karen (Mrs. John Minue), Absalom (known in your area as Ab) was the second. Then I and a twin brother were next (Doug and Don) and the youngest was a brother Lewis.

We too moved to the Okotoks area in 1931 and grew up and were educated there. By the time we finished our education World War II was underway and three of us joined up. Ab joined the R.C.A.F. and Doug and I joined the army going to the Calgary Highlanders. We returned from overseas in the summer of 1946 and it was not until the spring of 1947 that we moved to the Millarville district.

We rented the McFaul place with the intention of buying it through the V.L.A. The next four years were spent in a seesaw battle with the V.L.A. and in the end we lost the bitter battle. In all we stayed seven years in your district, then my brothers and father decided to go north to homestead in the Spirit River area.

I remained behind and worked for Bill Kendall at the sawmill and eventually moved to Okotoks where I live today.

While in your district my twin brother and I married two of the local girls. Doug married Verna the eldest daughter of Harry and Pauline Orum. She went north when Doug moved to Spirit River. I married Evelyn, the eldest daughter of Wilbur and Dorothy Smith.

At present my sister lives in Edmonton, Ab owns and operates a sporting good store in Dawson Creek, B.C. Doug and Lewis ranch in Spirit River. I live in Okotoks where I am employed by the town.

Upon reflecting back I believe the seven years I spent in your district were the best years of my life. I, being an avid fisherman and hunter, found the Millarville country unsurpassed for these pursuits. The fine people I met and became friends with left me with a wealth of memories I will always cherish.

I still hunt and fish and visit with the fine folks in your district and look forward to many more years enjoying your beautiful country.

Logan Campbell Mounkes
by Madeline J. Facette

It is with great pride that I write this article about my father, Logan Campbell Mounkes, born September 23, 1898, eleven miles west of Okotoks. He was the oldest son of Alphus and Rebecca Mounkes, better known as Al and Becky. They were true pioneers of that area in the late 1880s.

As my grandfather's herds of cattle and horses grew, he had to start scouting on horseback for pasture. He finally decided on land in the Millarville area part of which had been purchased from Jack Little, about 1919. This is where true pioneers came into focus. My grandfather, my father and his brother Calvin started the process of putting up fences and building corrals. There was a small shack on the place, and as my Uncle Calvin said "It was more com-

Naomi and Logan Mounkes.

fortable to sleep under the trees with saddle blankets and their saddle for a pillow than it was in the shack."

Getting supplies and materials into this land was extremely difficult as there was no road into the property. The terrain was rough and rugged with numerous hazards to overcome, such as muskegs, bog holes, bears and other wild animals, coyotes, wolves and here and there a few skunks.

Corduroy bridges had to be built over the bogs and muskegs. This consisted of cutting logs to cover them so they could get the pack horses and wagon in. It took many weeks and months to complete the fences and corrals under some extreme weather conditions. All of this was done in the latter part of winter and early spring.

As soon as the corrals and fences were ready it was time to start the drive, herding the cattle and horses to their new home of lush green grass, valleys with beautiful clear running creeks, with lots of poplar, fir trees and shrubs for shade. The peace and serenity one found in this part of the country in the spring and summer was overwhelming. It was no wonder that my father loved it so much.

He wasn't very old at this time, and being the oldest of the boys it was his job to stay on the land and look after the cattle and to break the saddle horses. He had his old dog named Towser, who was his audience when he played his mouth organ at night until it was time to turn in.

My father was a very warm and caring man and there were very few people who knew him that did not like him. Anyone could sit and partake at his table. trappers, neighbor Indians, everybody was welcome. There was one trapper friend of Dad's that he used to talk about. I couldn't find out what his name was, but from what I could gather he was one of the meanest men around at the time and he had a dog that fitted his temperament very well. Dad was the only man who could walk up to this man's cabin and the dog wouldn't move. This kind of love for nature, people and animals stood Dad in good stead all down through the years.

There were many good stories about his rodeo days. Cowboys then entered into every event, bucking, wild cow milking, calf roping, chuck wagon drivers and outriders. It was long hard days, sometimes winning, sometimes losing, but it really didn't matter, they loved it. There was only one person that Dad had a grudge against, but what the grudge was about I don't know. It was with a certain person at the Calgary Stampede. They were both driving in the chuck wagon races when this fellow's wagon went into Dad's and took off the rear wheel, bringing Dad in third. As he pulled into the infield he jumped from the wagon before it stopped and there were a few fisticuffs, which Guy Weadick, then president of the Stampede, broke up. That was the highlight of the evening, They got a standing ovation from the crowd and returned back to Millarville to remain friends all down through the years.

Logan Mounkes Family. Standing, Rebecca and Gail. Seated, Madeline, Barbara and Logan.

Bernice and Bill Mounkes with their daughters: Leona, Gertrude and Sandra, and son Edwin.

In 1919 when Dad was twenty one he took homestead Rights to one quarter in this section, and built a log cabin. Homestead rights meant you had to build a cabin and clear so much land. So Dad, along with a friend, Ed Allison, built the cabin using the same procedure as they had done with the fences and corrals. But this was right in the middle of winter. Dad continued doing what he had been doing all through the years, when he met Mother at the Kew rodeo. My Mother was Naomi Jelffs, born May 4th, 1904, in Niagara Falls, New York.

She came west in 1923 and married Dad March 25, 1925. They lived on the homestead until moving in to Calgary in 1935. He had attended Agriculture School in Claresholm and as a result did free lance landscaping. He did some of the first landscaping at R.C.A.F. Base at Lincoln Park, and R.C.A.F. Base Grand Centre, Alberta, including the golf course.

My Mother passed away Sept. 3, 1963, at 59 years of age. My father retired at age 65 and lived on Richmond Rd. from 1938 to 1974. He then moved to Jacques Lodge for one year. He passed away while in Thurso, Que. of a stroke, on August 18, 1976. He was interred in Burnsland Cemetery, Calgary, with my Mother.

Surviving are four daughters, Barbara Helen MacKenzie, Madelaine Jeannine Facette, Rebecca Ann Naomi Campbell and Gail Carol Hunter, also eleven grandchildren and seven great-grandchildren.

William Mounkes

In 1919 Alphus Calvin Mounkes, an early settler in the Okotoks district, searched the foothills for ad-

ditional pasture to supplement the grassland that fed his growing herd. After a week of riding, he located and purchased the square section that is known as Section 6, Township 22, Range 4, West of the Fifth Meridian. The south half of the section was purchased from Mr. Jack Little. The N.W. quarter was homesteaded by the eldest Mounkes son. The N.E. quarter was long-term Government Lease.

In 1935, an oil company decided to drill for oil or gas on the S.W. quarter of Section 6. The "Cotton Belt Rig" as it was known then, was hauled through the rough timberland by sleigh and horses, guided by good horsemen who understood the problems presented by the terrain. Cliff Vandergrift and Clarence Hart, and a few other such experienced men undertook the task of guiding the wooden well sections up the steep hills of the site by pulleys and cables. The wooden rig was constructed by rig-builder Johnson. In spite of the time and efforts put into the lengthy well-construction, the well was never tested for production but remained intact on the site for a few years.

During the years that the land was homesteaded, living quarters consisted of a long, low-lying log shack, which sat on a small hillside overlooking the spring that provided the drinking water. Though the original home has long since fallen down, its foundations and some framework remain in the same location.

In 1942, after the death of Alphus Mounkes, the south half was willed to the youngest Mounkes son, William, who in turn bought out Logan's interest in the N.W. quarter in December of 1946. The cattle were trailed to the summer pasture in a two-to-three day trail ride; and back again to the home place near the Big Rock in the fall for wintering. The summer pasture operation continued for several years. Even-

Bill Mounkes roping at Calgary Stampede.

tually as roads improved and cattle liners came into being, the trailing of the cattle to and from the home place to Section 6 became obsolete. During this time, William's only son, Edwin, played a major part in this successful operation.

In the early years, William (Bill) took an active interest in the rodeo life and at that time became a top-notch calf-roper participating in not only the Calgary Stampede (as early as age 17) but many surrounding rodeos as well. During his active farming-ranching years, his interest thrived, many times winning the dallied roping events, and ultimately winning the Canadian Calf Roping Championship at the Calgary Stampede in 1941. Like father, son Edwin also became active in the calf roping events and often, as in the High River Rodeo of 1950, father and son came away with top honors. On October 18, 1951, Bill was one of a group of championship cowboys who presented a mini-stampede in Calgary for Princess Elizabeth and the Duke of Edinburgh. As the events progressed, each cowboy explained his event to the royal party. Bill remained active for many years to become a well-known name in rodeo circles of that time.

Then in April of 1966, Bill sold the land that had become known as "the Hills" to Harold Roenisch of Calgary. Bill is now retired from the active farming and ranching life, as well as rodeo, but still lives on the original homestead at Okotoks with his wife of fifty years, Bernice. There were four children in the Mounkes marriage. Edwin lives on the home place at Okotoks along with his wife, Amy and four children. Leona, oldest daughter, married Cleo Dease who recently retired from the oil fields and have been living at Longview. They have three grown sons. Gertrude, middle daughter, married Bob Lore, a farmer, and they live at Brooks. They have three daughters and one son, also grown. The youngest member of the family, Sandra lives in Calgary with her young daughter.

F. R. Erick Mulder

I was born on a Sunday morning, on Jan. 13th, 1918 at Djombang, Isle of Java, in Indonesia; the youngest of 4 sons of A. Mulder, who for 30 years was a ranking

The F. R. Erick Mulder family, Sept. 16, 1978. L. to R. (seated) Fritho and Lilly. (standing) Valerie, David, Leroy, Silvia and Kathaleen.

officer of the Dutch Government, in what was then the Dutch East Indies. In 1920, my father retired and with his family moved to Holland, via Japan, across the Pacific, the U.S.A. and the Atlantic, to an estate near Assen in northern Holland.

In Nagasaki, in my mother's lap, while travelling in a rickshaw, I had convulsions and was in a coma for three days after returning aboard ship. In the fall of 1924 I went to school at Assen for six months until my father emigrated to Canada in the spring of 1925, and settled on the old Polkinghorne ranch (21-21-3-W5th) north of Millarville.

From 1925-1928 I rode 4½ miles to Fordville School where Miss Mary Stanger and Miss Margaret King were my teachers. In 1928 the Sheep Creek school was built and I was one of the first pupils under the tutorship of Miss Pat Jamieson, until 1933. I can remember coming to school early to light the fires (two wood stoves) for which I received the sum of 10¢ per day from the school board. During the "hungry thirties", the school board was without funds for some time, and when finally paid $34.90, I was the richest boy in the district.

During this time in the summer vacations from school, we cut and stacked 150 tons of wild hay, all with horses. I was the chief raker, while my two brothers, Erick and Rudy mowed and stacked. These were long hard days of labour, besides having the routine chores of milking 12 head of cows, shipping cream and tending over 100 head of beef cattle and as many sheep. I will always cherish the memory of those days and the evening rides on horseback to check the cattle for water and salt and to count them, as rustlers were rampant in those days.

I'll always remember the autumns with their early September snowfalls; the hundreds of huge flocks of geese winging their way south using the Turner Valley flares as a guide marker. Our 20 acre slough, one of the very few in the district that never went dry, with its flocks of mallard ducks, and nesting grounds for a myriad of Arctic terns and blackbirds, who when you approached their home, would dive-bomb just feet above your head and by their screams and chatter advise that you were not welcome. We had one of the last remaining flocks of sharp-tailed grouse (prairie chicken) in the district, and the treed areas were full of brush partridge with their eerie booming mating calls in the fall.

Visions and glimpses remain with me of herds of up to forty deer on the open hillside, the occasional cry of a cougar in the distance, tracks in the snow of lynx and in the spring a black bear and her cubs, who raised havoc with òur sheep and the neighbors pigs. These were pleasant, happy days with a uniquely happy family.

Our front porch looked S.S.E. down the length of the Turner Valley. After sundown we would be able to count 57 flares, up to 200 feet high. On some nights you could read by their light even though the nearest one was over four miles away. The single cylinder (one lunger) gas engines of the Royalite plant in Turner Valley could be heard from our house over 12 miles direct distant. We often predicted the weather from the way they sounded.

In 1933 Dad, Mother and I moved to Calgary and I went to Crescent Heights Collegiate Institute under the direction of Mr. William Aberhart, later to become the first Social Credit Premier of Alberta. In 1936 we moved to Vancouver where I attended the University of B.C. until 1938, when Dad passed away. I then started apprenticing with G. S. Eldridge and Co. and in 1940, wrote the examinations in Victoria and became an Assayer and Analyst for B.C. For a short time I was inspector of sulphite pulp (cellulose) for munitions, at Powell River, and then the assayer for Spud Valley Gold Mines at Zeballas on the N.W. of Vancouver Island.

On Nov. 18th, 1940, I joined the staff of Royalite Oil Co. in Turner Valley in the Gas and Gasoline Dept., (later to become the Madison Natural Gas Co. Ltd.) in their laboratory. In 1942, I was instrumental in discovering the great potash deposits in Saskatchewan from a wireline core of the Imperial Oil Radville No. 1, well (16-36-05-19 W2M) and in 1976 presented to the people of that Province, in Regina, one of the two known pieces of that core. This sample is now in the Museum of Natural History in that city.

During the 1940s, in conjunction with J. Webb of

Turner Valley, I was very active in the Fish and Game Association, we were instrumental in raising and releasing 75,000 young pheasants in the Millarville, Calgary and Brooks areas, the replanting of the first beaver in the Turner Valley and Millarville areas and several truckloads of elk in the Foothills mountain area to the west.

Between June 18th, 1943 and July, 1945 I was with the Canol Project in Norman Wells, N.W.T. as Petroleum Engineer with I.O.L. Here we did the first reservoir sampling under pressure and a complete reservoir oil analysis and those factors so important in the engineering of oil production. Of necessity we had to do all our own work as there were no service companies available, from logging, to acidizing, cementing and gun perforating. I installed 4 gas compressors to re-inject the produced gas for which there was no use or market. In two short years we developed 56 wells and had 4000 Bbls/day flowing to the Whitehorse, Y. T. refinery.

I came back to Turner Valley in 1945 as the Sr. Engineer for Madison Natural Gas Co. and in early 1947 was transferred to the Royalite Reservoir Engineering Dept. to initiate the first Canadian secondary recovery waterflood. This was started at Royalite No. 75 (6-2-20-3W5) on Aug. 6th, 1948.

On June 14th, 1946, I married Lillias Grace Halbert, the Chief Telephone Operator for AGT at Turner Valley. We have been blessed with 5 children:

David Erick, (47-03-15) B. Sc. (U of A) Computer Analyst with Computer Sciences of Canada Ltd. Calgary.

Valerie Anne MacDonald, (49-11-09) Secretary, Solar Turbines of Canada Ltd.

LeRoy Erick, (51-10-08) Computer Technologist (S.A.I.T.) with Computer Sciences of Canada Ltd. Calgary.

Sylvia Jean, (57-05-03) Fourth year, Forestry — U. of A.

Kathleen Janet, (59-02-12) Keypunch Operator, Cronkite Supply Ltd. Calgary.

On March 1st, 1950, I accepted the position of District Field Engineer with Home Oil Company, and moved to the Home Oil Camp at Millarville until 1957 when we moved to our quarter section ranch, S E ¼-18-20-2W5.

During this time my evenings were devoted to working on a thesis "An Engineering Study of the Turner Valley Oil and Gas Field", which gained my admission to the Professional Engineers of Alberta. A copy of this thesis is now in the Rare Book Dept. of the U. of A. and in the Glenbow Museum.

In late 1955, the world renowned firm of Petroleum Engineers Degolier and McNaughton spent two years attempting a study to Unitize the Turner Valley Field. They came to the conclusion that no agreement could be reached. In November 1959, an Engineering Committee of Gordon McGuffin of Royalite; Bill Batten of Western Decalta and myself of Home Oil Co., using computer programs, were able to put together a unitization package which was acceptable to all participants including the Energy Conservation Board of Alta. On June 1st, 1960 the unitization came into effect and waterflooding of this Field went into full operation. As a consequence during the last 18 years, there has been no decline in oil production, which had been dropping at a rate of over 10% per year and was nearing the economic life of this field.

On April 2nd, 1964, we moved into Calgary as I was transferred to the Head Office staff of Home Oil, in the Reservoir Eng. Dept. We still live at 749-80 Ave. S.W. Calgary.

On May 4th, 1943, I was received into the Order of Freemasonry at Corinthian Lodge No. 22, in Okotoks, and have been an active member since that time. For the 1975-78, Triennium, I hold the Office of Deputy General Grand First Principal of Royal Arch Masons International for the N. W. Region, extending from Alaska to South of Colorado, the first Canadian to have been so honored in the 200 years of the General Grand Chapter International.

My early years at Millarville, and this historic area, not to say the wonderfully kind and gentle people who have and now inhabit it, will always have a warm and tender spot in my heart.

Mrs. Erick Mulder (nee Jessie Thomson)

A teaching position at Fordville School was my reason for settling in the Millarville area. In October 1943, I arrived from Saskatchewan where I had spent most of my formative years and begun my teaching career. Comfortable lodging was found with Mr. and Mrs. Jim Cawthorne who lived close to the school.

After my marriage to Addy Erick Mulder, we lived on the Home Oil Lease where Erick was employed. At the same time, Erick also worked his half of the original Mulder farm, 4 miles N.W. of Millarville.

The routine of life on the Home Oil Lease was shattered one frightful night as our neighbourhood inventor, Jimmy Green, came to our door shouting,

This picture was taken the day Erick and Jessie Mulder and their daughter Sharon left Millarville to reside at the coast. L. to R. Jessie, Sharon and Erick.

"Run, the place is going to explode!" I grabbed our sleeping daughter and joined Mrs. Neese in a quick flight across field and fence to the safety of the Bower residence some distance away. Fortunately, a major catastrophe did not occur but Jimmy did have his living quarters slightly damaged from the resulting fire. However, this experience didn't deter him from continued experimentation.

I returned to teaching after our daughter, Sharon, was born. This time at Sheep Creek School with Mrs. Allan Deines and Mr. Thorburn as colleagues.

Christmas concerts were always the social highlight of the school year. They entailed many hours of practice and work on the part of parents, teachers and pupils. The Fordville concerts were held at the school on a make-shift stage and behind sheet curtains. Because Sheep Creek was a larger school, the concerts were sometimes held in the Rancher's Hall or in the Lease Community Hall. On those occasions, we enlisted the aid of helpful and willing parents such as Mrs. Billy Jackson.

In the early 1950's, we sold the farm, left Millarville and moved to British Columbia. The first few years were spent at the coast. After I lost my husband in 1955, I taught at various schools throughout the province. My daughter and I finally settled in Kamloops where I retired and we now live.

Rudy and Selina Mulder   F 7 K

Well, here we are again, a new history book in the offing and a whole new story to bring up-to-date. The last two stories we wrote of our family are in the book **Our Foothills** and the one not published yet, of the DeWinton-Red Deer Lake district. Both these stories were mainly concerned with the parentage of both our families; so this story is about us becoming parents ourselves and the role we played on the "Stage" which is described by Shakespeare as being "the whole world is but a stage" and where every person has a part to make a play "that will reflect itself in our unity and society as it is today". Yesterday we made today and today we hope for tomorrow.

When my parents left to live in Vancouver, B.C. in 1933, we, my brother Erick, and myself, were left here in Millarville on the old Polkinghorne Ranch which my parents bought in 1925 from the estate and described as Section 21-21-3-W5. The price at that time was $17.50 per acre including a beautiful house, and farm buildings from which to operate this section of land. Also included in this price were two ¼ sections of oil leases in fee simple being the S.W.¼ and the N.E.¼ which we still have in the family name today.

The years that followed were written in **Our Foothills** and it is actually with a small blank space of time in between that I want to begin. In 1937 when we were bachelors, Erick and I had to make a living by our own practical experience, and after many futile and frustrating attempts we seemed to have managed

Back row, L. to R.: Mrs. A. Mulder sr., Jessie, Selina and Rudy. Middle row: Erick, his daughter Sharon, with Connie and Joan, daughters of Selina and Rudy.

well by our own standards. Disappointments were overshadowed by the enthusiasm of "Being Interested"; we did not know the word "Failure" because as soon as it surfaced, we eliminated it by "Interest".

I remember in the hungry 30's that in order to make pocket money we would shoot and snare bush rabbits, load the model T Ford up full and take them to Thompson's fox farm in Midnapore where we got 1 cent each, cash on the spot. It didn't take long for our "computer" brains to figure out that our snares were covering expenses for the shells we missed and which cost money.

We would haul coal with four horses strung out on the sleigh from the mine of Swan's which was located

Rudy Mulder Family. L. to R. Back row, Douglas, Bonnie, Joan, Connie. Front, Rudy and Sally.

just a bit west of where Whiskey and North Fork Fish Creek meet. No roads in those days so we had to go across Roedler's place. One of us would leave at dawn and take two tons of lump coal, priced at $2.50 per ton to W. H. King in Millarville. (The post office at Millarville was owned by Walton and Forward, and was run by Angus MacKay, one of the four brothers who lived a mile west of Millarville). We would come home by evening after having had dinner there and having shoveled the coal into the basement; and for the whole day's work we would get $4.00 — for those days it was a bonanza. This procedure was also alternated with Norman Pegler's store in Millarville and Erick and I would alternate "union style".

In 1937, a new teacher came to Sheep Creek School. Her name was Selina Hambling, whose parents farmed around the Red Deer Lake area. In those days it was unheard of to think of romance before you had the means to support the consequences, so it took a year or two before we realized that we should get more involved in our planning. We had always a wonderful time together without involvement. I remember we were both in a play put on by Mrs. Esther Jackson which was held in the Rancher's Hall (the one now in Heritage Park in Calgary). Selina had the role of a country girl and I one of a disguised girl friend. Well, anyway, the rehearsal gang had a ball watching us kiss, which after all, was part and parcel of the play, "George in a Jam" and performed in the winter of 1938.

The year 1939 brought tension in our lives as the Second World War broke out. For a time we decided, with a few neighbours including Leonard Nelson and Doug Wilson, to join the forces. We would go once a week to Calgary in the Armories for many months and go through some drill performance; but this would get quite monotonous and it seemed that we actually were a nuisance to them — no equipment was available and we had wooden rifles and no uniforms. As we were very busy with cutting logs in the bush with Dude Willford, our neighbor, we decided to give that priority to the military activities. (We cut logs for three winters, cutting 100,000 B.F. in the winter months, with cross cut saw, wedge, and axe; no chain saws in those days. We piled them up for Jim Collie to saw up into lumber in the spring which we would sell and so accummulated a bit of cash.) Some of the other boys went on with the military and eventually made it overseas and came home after hostilities ceased with a lot more experiences than we had had with our work here.

In 1939 I went to work for the summer months for W. H. King, then Sect.-Treasurer of the Municipality of Stockland No. 191 (which was later, in 1941, amalgamated into Turner Valley Municipality and yet later, 1954, amalgamated into its present existence of Foothills No. 31 of High River). I had a wonderful time working for Mr. King in the role of "Jack-of-all-Trades" making $35 a month which was more than

Rudy and Fritho Mulder families. L. to R. Lillian, David, Roy, Valerie, Fritho, Rudy, Bonnie, Connie with Douglas on lap, Joan, Sally. 1950.

many a cowboy got working around. This coincided with the incident that our teacher of Sheep Creek School, Selina Hambling, was at that time boarding at Pegler's store, a very short distance from the Kings. Our association became so attached, especially through the help and interest of the two families, Peglers and Kings, and all the neighbors in general, that we decided to get married on July 10, 1940. Selina taught school until June 30th and after a unique honeymoon by packhorse trip of three weeks into the mountains to Kananaskis, Spray, Mount Assinaboine, back over Kananaskis to Burn's Mine, Gorge Creek, to North Sheep Creek (now Three Point), we arrived back to our home which was designed for two bachelors. It was in no time flat that Selina made her mark on the atmosphere and we started in earnest to look into the future, but never did the future interfere with present. We lived from day to day as we have since, each day being a new experience.

Our pack trip into the mountains was perhaps one of the last times one could enjoy the natural unspoiled beauty and convenience of the silent majestic togetherness one feels and can only be appreciated if one is actually involved.

To bring things to a more businesslike basis, we decided to split the section 21 into two halves; the south half going to Erick and the north half with the buildings to us. We had nothing to start with and so I went to work for the Home Oil south-west of Millarville in the fall and winter of 1940. I got $4 per day which seemed an awful lot then. I was on "pick and shovel" duty and here again my experiences in the seven months I worked there, were worth in later years, many fold the remuneration received.

Selina helped not only in the housework, but she was the moral background and stamina of all the detail that cropped up as we tried to make a "go" of this wonderful place we called "home". Our first daughter, Connie, was born in 1943; she is now happily married to J. D. Prentice with three children and lives on a farm near Calmar, west of Leduc. Then in 1946 came Joan, who is in the Adult Education section of the Alberta Department of Advanced Education and lives in Calgary. In 1949 Bonnie was born; she is happily

married and lives in Toronto with her husband, Bob Brown and two children. In 1953 we were blessed with a son, Douglas; he is now trying to find a place to settle down and is at present working on a cattle station 120 miles south of Darwin, on the northern tip of West Australia. Whether he will settle there is debatable; one never knows.

As years went by we accumulated more cattle, more machinery, always on a small scale, but slowly we became more and more self sufficient.

For years we hayed together with the MacKay brothers, Bob and Janet and Murdoch, and in 1948 we had an opportunity to work our way into half of Selina's parents farm in Red Deer Lake. After painful consideration of many different circumstances, we decided to move; and not withstanding it was only 15 miles away, it was very hard to make a decision, even though it was actually in the same district.

We had an auction sale in April, 1948, and that was the year that the roads were more blocked than open; our sale had to be postponed twice.

Now, after 30 years here in the Red Deer Lake area and in our own way of evaluating our accomplishments, we are very satisfied, to the point that since our children have gone their own way, we sold most of our land and retired in 1969. Little did we realize that even in our retirement, our interest in and zest for life had 110 meanings for the word "retirement." Instead we went on several long trips: overseas south to New Zealand, Australia and Indonesia; to Europe, over the Rhine to Switzerland, Venice, Rome and the Mediterranean lands and France's Alps and Paris and England. Also numerous winter months we spent travelling in the southern part of the United States.

And so in closing, it seems evident that as long as our bodies will cooperate with our spirits that the stepping stones laid in Millarville were the motivation of a life for both of us which is hard to equal if one can judge by the satisfaction it has given us.

Selina (Sally Hambling) Mulder

In June 1937, I graduated from the Calgary Normal School, this being the place where would-be teachers went to receive their one year's training for teaching. At that time it was located on the top floor of the Calgary Institute of Technology. Next came the job of looking for a position and those being the depression years, jobs were hard to find. You didn't usually look in the "want" ads of the Herald to find jobs — you heard of them by word of mouth and so it was that I heard from the weed inspector, Colonel Hervey, that the school of Sheep Creek was in need of a teacher. I donned my best and set off with my father to apply for the job, which meant I had to go in person to each of the trustees and school secretary for a personal interview. First I went to Norman Pegler, at that time owner and operator of the Millarville Store. He gave me the names of three trustees I would have to see:

Sheep Creek School, 1937. Teacher, Sally Hambling. L. to R., Front: John Pegler, Murray Jackson, Ann Jackson, Florence Willford, Yvonne Hodgkins, Fred Hodgkins, Audrey Rawlinson, Jim Chalmers, Hugh Rawlinson, Fern Jackson (hiding behind Fern is Mamie Willford), Robert Chalmers. Back: Harry Rawlinson, Hugh Willford, Jean Chalmers, Josephine Waugh, Ruth Chalmers, Irene Willford, in behind Ruth is Joyce Thompson.

Bert Chalmers, Billy Jackson, Sr. and Joseph Waugh. I guess the interviews were satisfactory as I got the job due mostly to the fact (so I heard afterwards) that Billy Jackson said "Give her a chance even though she has had no experience; I'd be glad if someone gave my girls a job without experience." I always appreciated that chance, for so began three of the most interesting and enjoyable years of my life. I loved teaching and during those years the children were enthusiastic and keen to learn all they could.

I had all the grades from one to nine to teach and one year I supervised a grade ten student, Josephine Waugh, who took correspondence. There were usually about 20 to 23 pupils in attendance. In those years the children did all the janitor work including getting to the school early to light the "pot-bellied" stove and haul water for washing and drinking from a spring about a quarter of a mile away in the bush behind the school.

We had many enjoyable times in those days doing our "three R's" and I especially remember the Christmas concerts in the old Rancher's Hall, which is now in Heritage Park. We teachers could always depend on Esther Jackson to help us with the music as she was an accomplished piano player.

Like many of my students, I walked 2½ miles from Pegler's Store, where I boarded, to the school, located on a hill beside the road on MacKay Brothers' property. Those lucky ones rode horseback; some came as far as five miles either by walking or riding. At recess we played many games, such as run-sheep-run, prisoners base, hide and seek, and baseball in summer. Sometimes in the winter the children brought their sleds or toboggans to school; however, we didn't get much snow in those days so the children went back to their old favorite games. They didn't have any fancy playground equipment like tires or monkey bars but made their own fun and were always busy and happy.

Of course, they had their mischievous times. I remember once when a .22 bullet, which had been put into the stove, broke the silence of our studies with a loud BANG! Needless to say, the culprit was thoroughly strapped. Once, when a student had to be punished by strapping, his sister said "Strap me also." Those were the only times I used the strap in my three years of teaching.

My career as a teacher came to a happy ending in July, 1940, when I married Rudy Mulder. In those days you hardly ever, if ever, worked at your old profession — you started a new one of housewife and mother.

Mr. and Mrs. Frank O. Nelson
by Mrs. Lillian McGonegal

Mother and Dad were both born and raised in Nova Scotia. Dad became a steam engineer and Mother a milliner.

Dad came west in 1906 and homesteaded at Millerdale, Sask. He drove an ox team, lived in a sod house and made porridge from slough water, polly-wogs and all. Six years later Mother came out as a bride and also lived in a sod house. They were blessed with five daughters, no boys, much to Dad's disappointment. They experienced all the hardships of the dry years and depression on the prairies.

In 1929 they moved to Sundre, Alberta, and later to the James River district. Farming on a quarter section of land became increasingly difficult and in the early 40's their house burned down. The girls were through school by this time and on their own so it was then Dad decided to move to Millarville. It was with mixed feelings they left but it was the best thing that ever happened to them.

Mother loved the beauty of the country side and especially the mountains. Dad enjoyed the excitement of working in the oil fields and the association with his fellow workers and last but not least the MONEY. People were very friendly. They enjoyed the community club, the Happy Gang and Mother had always been a staunch worker in the Women's Institute and she was delighted to find they had one in Millarville. Mother took great pride in her knitting, crocheting and all types of hand work and would exhibit them at the local fairs, being greatly rewarded with many prizes.

They returned to Sundre for a couple of years because Dad wanted to log his place, but they returned in May 1948 and the next year in April they bought a house from Mr. Hume and Dad worked as a battery operator.

Jack and Belle McCuaig, Dad's sister, had moved to Turner Valley from Sundre in 1942 and started work in the Valley. This was really great as they had always been close. Both families now owned cars and were able to drive back and forth for visits. Those were hap-

Mr. and Mrs. Frank Nelson, 1955.

py years and they enjoyed several trips during this period.

Allan, son of Jack and Belle, married Dorothy Welch in 1951 and lived in the Valley till 1959 where they moved to Stettler and later to Alix where he now resides, working for Chevron Standard.

Helen, daughter of Jack and Belle, married rancher Bill Massie of Midnapore, in 1941, where they still reside.

Probably Dad's main interest or hobby would have been hunting. He loved to hunt big game and he was a good hunter. As I recall, it was practically the only meat we had on our table during those difficult years. He was a great story teller too, nothing we would like better than to be privileged to sit up at nights and listen to Dad and his neighbor swapping yarns.

Mother's health had never been good and she had several major operations. Dad was reaching retirement age, so in 1956 they purchased a small house in Sundre and in October 1957 they moved back to be near their family. It was with a heavy heart they said farewell to Millarville and what the people there meant to them.

Mother passed away in August 1961, Dad in June 1969. Their daughters are still living. Ailsa-Peggy Elliott, R.R.4, Calgary, Winnifred Beaton, West Bank, B.C., Lillian McGonegal, Sundre, Alberta, Bertha Burk, Langley, B.C., Jean Bardal, Fort Nelson, B.C.

Jim Nelson

I was born at High River in 1906 and lived four miles west of High River for six years, then moved to a farm twelve miles west on the Highwood River. We lived there for four years then moved to Meadowbank

L. to R. John Standish, Jim Nelson, Bob Standish, Leonard Nelson.

district for two years. We then moved to the Millarville district in 1919. I worked at different jobs, farming, riding horses for Kierans, training for the Millarville Races. I worked on farms in the High River district and learned to play Polo there. I worked in the mud pits in Turner Valley with Art Wilderman. Went to work for the Royalite Oil Company in 1938. I took sick and lost the use of my arm. I worked on a battery of wells for Royalite west of Millarville until 1948, then I was sent to the Leduc oil field and worked for Imperial oil until I retired in 1967. Since I retired I put in my time gardening, fishing, curling and tying flies for fishing. I invented a small jig fly for catching lake whitefish and got a country wide reputation for it. It took most of my spare time to keep up tying these flies so I taught other people to do it.

I make my home at Devon, Alberta.

Nelson, Leonard and Betty (King) LN R.H.

Leonard Nelson and Betty King were married Oct. 1953 at Millarville Church. They lived the next fourteen years in Calgary, the first year in a suite in Sunnyside before getting a house in Windsor Park. But Millarville was always home, they spent nearly every week end at the shack Leonard batched in before going to Calgary. So when he was sixty they were happy to return to Millarville to build a home on the SW ¼ of 23-21-3W5. They enjoy being among their old friends and having time for their hobby, gardening.

John Leonard was born 1907 at his parents farm in the Old Brant district; being 22 miles east of High River; the second son of Charles and Lena Nelson. When he was two years old they moved west of High River. He started school at Big Hill school which was four miles east of the present Longview. He and his brother Jim attended Meadowbank school for two years before coming to the Millarville district in 1919. The moving took three days, their Dad hauled the furniture etc. on two hay racks and the boys age 12 and 13 drove the cattle; the June weather being mild, they enjoyed camping out at night.

Leonard and Betty Nelson, 1969.

Wyandotte Pullets on the range.

After finishing his schooling at Fordville school Leonard worked out for various neighbors as well as helping out at home. They milked about a dozen Holstein cows by hand but always had time to enjoy raising and training half-bred horses for Millarville Races. The Sundays before the races were more fun than race day, as they would meet with Kierans, Tom Phillips and Mr. Cannon to try out their horses. Leonard still reminisces about those days.

Before the war Leonard had a flock of Hampshire sheep, he had fun exhibiting at Millarville and Calgary, but the coyotes found them very tasty.

He joined the army in 1941, going overseas in 1942 and to the 14th Calgary Tank of the first Canadian Armored Brigade for action in Sicily and Italy. He was invalided home in 1945 with jaundice and malaria.

After his discharge he farmed in partnership with his father, at this time he started a small herd of registered Angus. In 1950 his Dad turned the home quarter over to him and Leonard bought a house in Black Diamond for his parents to retire to. He got a civil service job in 1953 with the department of National Defence in Calgary and let his cattle out on shares with the neighbors. Leonard bought the NW ¼ of 15-21-3W5 from his brother in 1954, trading the house in Black Diamond as part payment. Feed was grown on this quarter and the home quarter used for pasture. When they returned to Millarville Leonard continued to raise a few registered Angus cattle. He is proudest of raising Harrogate Revolution 2nd which he sold to Gordon Prichard and under Gordon's guidance this bull won fame in the Angus circles. Late in 1976 Leonard sold the quarter of 15 to Peter Reimer; so he now has to buy feed for his cattle and will be gradually reducing the herd.

Elizabeth Margaret, always known as Betty was born 1915 on the farm four miles west of the present village of Turner Valley, daughter of Jack and Margaret King. She was registered as being born at Lineham as that was the postal address of that area at that time. In 1918 her parents moved to a farm on the north fork of Sheep Creek, being about one mile south west of Millarville Church. Her Dad, brother Charlie

and family still live there. When she was five she had chicken pox which she passed on to Leonard her first gift to him. As there was no school in the district she started school age twelve when New Valley School opened January 1928; from there she went to high school in Okotoks in 1933 finishing in 1935. She had planned on going to normal school, but it being the hungry thirties and teachers not being able to get jobs, she decided to stay home and help out on the farm. Betty drove horses and later tractors during haying and harvest, helping with the cattle and kept a flock of chickens for spending money. She raised Rosed Combed White Wyandottes for years, selling hatching eggs in the spring, candling and grading the eggs the rest of the season to sell to the local stores. After her Mother passed on she had the house work to do so had less time to enjoy the outdoor life she liked so much until she and Leonard were married.

Leonard and Betty missed the farm animals when they were living in Calgary so Leonard started again on his childhood hobby of modeling farm animals. He had the natural gift of being able to make a small replica of a dog, horse, cow, duck, etc. out of a piece of clay or plasticine. Betty encouraged him to model and she took up ceramics so that she could make molds of his models and reproduce them in a more durable fired clay. As there were no ceramic supply shops in Calgary in 1955 they went to Spokane for supplies and a kiln. For a few years they made 4H trophies for the Alberta Hereford Association. Two well known horses Leonard modeled were Pagan Star and King Leo-Bar. When they came back to the farm, and had live animals to take care of Leonard lost the urge to model; perhaps he will start again when his cattle feeding days are over.

What amazes them most are the changes that have taken place in their lifetimes. Both born in wood and coal heated houses, with kerosene lamps, no plumbing or electricity to run deep freezes, refrigerators, washers, dryers, etc. The main mode of travel by horses, now cars and aeroplanes. No roads, just trails from one farm to the next. Both remember the first crystal radios, now colored television. The advances are wonderful, life is so much easier, but are people any happier for all these conveniences and luxuries. The Nelsons both enjoy it all and count their blessings. P.S. Leonard died suddenly from a heart attack August 3rd, 1978. Betty is planning on staying on the farm as long as she is able. It is home and she is where she wants to be, among very good and kind friends and neighbors.

Noel Noyes

The brief time that the Noel Noyes family spent in the foothills were among the happiest years of our life. We moved from Lloydminster in 1952 during the cold, wet month of February to the Roedler Ranch, then we also bought the Charlie Birney and Mrs. Gouy's home places.

Noel's parents were early settlers of the Lloydminster area, coming out with the Barr Colonists at the turn of the century. My people came out about the same time and settled in the Qu'Appelle Valley in Saskatchewan. My grandfather was Henry Jackman. His first job in Canada was as an horticulturist for the Qu'Appelle Nurseries. My mother, Mrs. Louise Ivie, also lived with the family in the foothills. Our family consisted of Noel and I and our three children, Jim, Kathleen and Meridith. Meri was born there.

Our closest neighbors were the Royal Burrows. Jeannine helped Jim break his first colt. Strange things happen in the foothills. Royal Burrows once granted a transient the right to live on the ranch, adjoining ours for free rent. A dispute came up over some minor event, and Ernie (his name was Ernest Running) came storming down to us with a story that he had put a hex on Royal. That same day, Royal was entered in the finals of a Quarterhorse competition in Calgary. He was standing in the top three. Going into town his car was involved in a traffic accident. Then he got to the competition late, rushed into the ring, his hat fell forwards over his head, the judge disqualified him and Ernie gleefully rubbed his hands. However, Royal gave Ernie his walking papers but he lost out that year in the Quarterhorse finals. The only time I

heard of Ernie again was when he hit the National news with the story of being lost and miraculously surviving in a storm, somewhere in the north.

One incident that stands out in my mind is the time Noel and George Ingeveld were haying on the home place. They had me raking hay on the hillside with a little Ferguson tractor. I'm not the best driver and as I was trying to turn upwards on the hill, I shifted into high instead of low. The unit took off like a bucking horse and I looked behind at the rake. I prayed, sprang, leaped and cleared the whole rig. It went rolling down the hill through the fences, across the road, the ditch, breaking trees and finally coming to halt at the creek bed.

Marthe Pallister was among my good friends and she would tell me stories of the early days and of the people. We spent many hours reminiscing of her father and how he came to train polo ponies, and how he brought a little culture with him. For years he had canvas paintings rolled up in the barn because there was no place to hang them. Marthe was witty, intelligent and ahead of her time. Once we went into an abandoned farm house. There was an old washboard there. She said "Let's take it before some other thief gets it." A day with her was a day of laughs.

We have wonderful memories of the Square Butte picnics and Christmas parties. It was a precious time and I often wish our Creator would label "The best years of our life" so we could appreciate them more.

Now we are retired to White Rock, B.C. and our home overlooks the ocean, but on a warm sunny afternoon, I miss the cattle, the hum of the fly, the smell of home-baked bread, watching the children disembark from the bus, and that wonderful feeling that alls right with my world.

Our son Jim works for the Parks Board in Yoho Park, close to the skiing and hiking he loves. Kathleen,

L. to R. Kathleen Noyes, Bucky Kendall, Meredith Noyes, Jim Noyes.

Noel Noyes at the ranch at Millarville.

after four years of art school in Calgary, is married to Douglas McKenzie, has a daughter and teaches at Michener Centre in Red Deer. Meridith married Richard Van Maarion of Seven Persons (from a ranching family) and is finishing her last year at the University of Lethbridge.

My mother is now eighty-three and still does her own thing. Noel took up Lapidary as a hobby and after he retired from farming, he began to do Lapidary and Gem shows across Canada. This is a most interesting and informative avocation.

I've always been sorry that our children didn't have the opportunity of spending more of their years in the wholesome, happy atmosphere of "Our Foothills."

George Edward Nylund   JN RR
by George Nylund

Born in Calgary April 22 1936, raised in the Square Butte district. I rode a horse to the Square Butte School until 1950 when Square Butte School was closed and we were bused to Millarville School.

Later I worked at various jobs. I married Pearl McGillvary December 1955 and lived in Turner Valley. Went to work for Home Oil Co. February 1956 in the Millarville Area. September 1956 we moved to Sundre for Home Oil Co. Then on to Swan Hills September

1958. Still working for Home Oil Co. Then we moved back to Sundre in July 1962. We bought a farm October 1968.

I left Home Oil Co. May 1976 to Ranch. We have three sons Hjalmar John born in High River 1956. Richard Allen born in Olds 1957. Dale George born in Barrhead 1959. John married Peggy Morton September 1976. They have one son Glen Lee born November 24, 1977.

I required my Dad's cattle brand JN Right Rib. December 1969.

Nyland, Hjalmar and Peggy
by Peggy Nylund

I went to Square Butte with my parents, Mr. and Mrs. George Lyall, in 1912. It was known as the Kew district; that is where we got our mail and supplies. When they put the bridge over Fisher Creek we received our mail at Millarville, and our supplies at Forward and Walton's Store, later at Pegler's store. In later years we had a rural mail route.

I went to Square Butte School. I took part in plays and Christmas concerts and also taught Sunday School at the Square Butte School. I was a member and president of the Ladies Group.

Hjalmar came to the Millarville and Square Butte district in 1928 and made his home with my folks. He worked for Calmont Oil and cut cord wood for the Cotton Belt Oil well west of Millarville. He also worked for McBee brothers moving cattle to and from the hills to the Longview district. In December 1933 we were married and lived in the Pierce cabin then moved to Auntie's (Mrs. T. Lyall) the spring of 1934, now Alex and Norma Lyall's place. The fall of 1934 Hjalmar went to High River to thresh for McBees, and I went to stay with my folks. In October, Margaret was born. We both worked at High River for a time. In April 1936, George was born. The fall of 1936 we moved to Mr. Jim Ward's place, N.W.¼ of 2-21-4W5. Mr. and Mrs. Warren Fulton had been living there but moved to Wardlow, Alta.

Our brand was JN, our son George has it now. March 1938, Johnny was born, then in July

George Nyland and his horses on the farm.

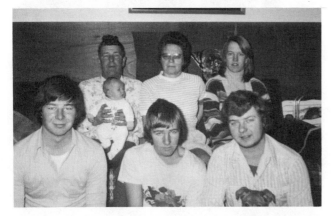

George Nylund family. L. to R. Back row, George, Pearl, Peggy Nylund, Baby Glen Nylund. Front, Dale, Richard, John Nylund and family dog.

George Lyall Family 1930. L. to R. Peggy, Dick, Mrs. Lyall, George Lyall.

Hjalmar Nylund Family. Back row, L. to R. Eleanor Davidson, 4th child, John Nylund, 3rd. child, George Nylund, 2nd child, Margaret Sim, oldest child, in front with father and mother, Hjalmar and Peggy.

1941. Eleanor was born. All our children were born at Grace Hospital in Calgary. We lived on the farm during the "Hungry Thirties" but never went without food. We appreciated the things we got when times got better. Those were the days when families and friends and neighbors got together, went on picnics and made our own fun. One sometime wishes they could roll back the years. We have a lot to be thankful for in this beautiful world.

Hjalmar went to work in the oil fields at Millarville in the fall of 1941 for Western Petroleum and Major Oils. In May 1942 he had the misfortune to go down Fisher Creek with his horses in a flood. He was riding one and leading the other. The one he was riding turned and went back to the other side but Hjalmar managed to jump and get hold of a bush and pull himself out of the water. The other horse went lower down the creek and got out.

Our children all went to Square Butte School until 1950, when the schools were amalgamated into Millarville and the children were bussed to school.

In the fall of 1953 we left the farm and moved to Major Tank Farm 9. It was nice to have electric lights and hot water for washing and other uses. Dick Lyall

Hjalmar and Peggy Nylund, Nov. 20, 1976.

took over the Ward place when we left. I became a member of the Millarville W.I.

We stayed at the tank farm until 1960 when Home oil took over. Hjalmar went to work for Alberta Gas Trunk Line in September 1960, at Brooks. December 1960 we moved to Calgary where he worked in the warehouse on the North Hill. April 1967 he went to down town Calgary to work in the mail office for Alberta Gas Trunk Line. He was there until he retired in May 1971 on account of ill health. In September 1971, we bought Mrs. Wilderman's house in Turner Valley.

We spent our retirement years visiting our families and friends when my husband was able to travel. We were able to go to three grandchildren's weddings, two in September and one in November of 1976, also a wedding of a friend. Hjalmar spent most of his remaining months in and out of the hospital. He passed away in Turner Valley Hospital after a long illness April 10th, 1977. I make my home in Turner Valley. I would like to end with a verse.

My times are in His hand,
A hand so safe and strong,
A hand which holds the sea
And guides the stars along.

GRANDMA SAYS

When the folks next to you act like those in a zoo,
A grumblin, growlin, and spittin,
It's a pretty good plan
To be calm as you can,
And do something useful — like knittin.

When a gossipin Suasan, with poison-barbed tongue,
Comes into the room where your sittin,
And starts to defame
Some neighbor's good name,
Count stitches out loud — and keep knittin.

When there's been a slight misunderstanding at church,
And others hint broadly of quittin,
Why, the very best thing
You can do is to sing
And stay at your post — and keep knittin.

When Satan moves in with his cohorts of sin,
Say, "You'll never find me submittin,
You irk me, I find;
So, get thee behind
And please don't disturb me — I'm knittin.

In the middle of problems, the big ones and small,
It's always most proper and fittin,
To trust and pray
Till the Lord shows the way —
And go right ahead with your knittin.

R. John Nylund
by Marie Nylund

I was raised in the Square Butte district, west of Millarville. I lived with my parents, Hjalmar and

John and Marie Nylund. Sheep Creek Canyon in Background.

Peggy Nylund, on the Ward Place at Square Butte until 1952. Along with my brother George and my two sisters Margaret and Eleanor, I attended Square Butte School and later we were bussed to Sheep Creek School at Millarville. Many a happy day was spent riding to Square Butte School on horseback and I recall the good times we all had. One humerous incident I plainly recall was one day when Cyrus McBee was moving his cattle west along the road towards Square Butte School. Being somewhat mischievous, a few of us school kids spotted him coming up the road towards the school and so we hid in the tall grass along the ditch. When Cyrus was oppsite us, we all leaped up and his horse went out from under him, and the cows scattered. We, of course, all thought it was the laugh of the day; however, Cyrus did not see the humour in it at all at the time.

In March of 1957, I went to work for John Ballachey at the Chinook Ranch, formerly owned by George Sylvester. At this time the road to the Chinook Ranch from the Kendall Ranch corner west was impossible to travel during the spring when the frost came out of the ground. It was on more than one occasion that I found myself on foot the remainder of the way to the ranch, leaving my truck stuck up to it's axles in the mud. I worked at the Chinook Ranch until 1963 and during my free time, spent many enjoyable hours hunting in the fall as game was very plentiful and only a short distance away to the Forest Reserve. My favorite time of the year was always haying season and I would always look forward to this time of the year. It was during this time of the year, however, that the barn caught fire after being filled with hay and was totally destroyed before the fire could be brought under control.

In 1963 I went to work for Alberta Gas Trunk Line and moved to Fort MacLeod until July of 1964. I then returned and again worked at the Chinook Ranch for one year. In 1965 I became employed as a Guide for

Bert Mickle, who owned and operated Timberline Tours at Lake Louise. I very much loved the mountains and after leaving Lake Louise, I felt that I would like to return someday.

In 1967 I became employed at Elkana Ranch at Bragg Creek. This job was on a Dude Ranch and involved a lot of patience with both horses and the riders. It was while employed at Elkana Ranch that I met my wife, Marie Merryfield. In May of 1969 we were married in Calgary and took up residence 2½ miles south of the Red Deer Lake Store. For a very short time we both worked in Calgary. At that time I was employed with Geo Space Canada, a Geophysical company, and Marie was employed with Alberta Government Telephones. Having both been raised in the country and having a great love for ranch life and the outdoors, working in Calgary did not appeal to either of us so we quit our jobs in Calgary and once again I moved back to the Chinook Ranch at Millarville on July 1st, 1969, only this time I did not have to do the cooking. We lived and worked on the Chinook Ranch for a period of 4 years to the date. On July 1st, 1973 we moved from the Chinook Ranch to Lake Louise where we have been living ever since.

Until April of 1977 I was employed "seasonally" with Parks Canada Warden Service as "Trail Crew Foreman". This job involved the maintenance of backcountry trails by saddle horse and pack horse. As a result of this job, I have been fortunate in having seen the entire park's back-country and variety of game. I purchased a good camera and took many pictures of my travels in the Park. As this job was "seasonal" (summer only), I became employed for 3 winters with the Lake Louise Ski Area on the slopes "grooming" by use of such packing machines as the Tucker Snow Cat, Thiokol and Nodwell. During this time both my wife and I tried our hand at skiing and enjoyed it very much. During the winter of 1975-76, I drove a speed plow for Parks Canada Maintenance Department and worked primarily on the Banff-Jasper Highway near Bow Summitt.

In April of 1977, I became "Senior Horseman" for Banff National Park. This job involves a lot of work with the Park horses, packing, care and transportation

John, Marie, Leo, Nancy and Guy Nylund.

440

of the horses and training the inexperienced Wardens to ride and pack. This job requires the majority of my time to be spent in Banff and therefore we plan on a move to either Banff or Canmore in the future.

My wife, Marie, has been employed with the Royal Canadian Mounted Police as a Secretary in the Lake Louise Detachment since June of 1974. We have two wonderful children; Leo James, aged 8 years, and Nancy-Lee Ellen, aged 2 years. Leo attends school in Banff and is in Grade two. He seems to have inherited a love for horses and is very interested in riding. He also enjoys skiing and drawing.

On the 7th of January, 1978, we sold our house in Lake Louise and with the help of the Lake Louise Wardens, we moved to Banff, to a small house on Squirrel Street near the Elementary School.

On the 27th of August, 1978, our third child, Donald Richard "Guy" was born.

The Oliver Girls,

Joan, Doreen and Audrey-Jean (A. J.)

In 1933 when Dad and Mother bought the Judge Ford place lying east of the Millarville Race Track we were city gals from the word go — didn't know the hind end of a horse from the front — so to speak. We moved to the Diamond L to live in the spring of '33. Dad's first cattle brand was LIV but it took up half the side of a calf so within a year or so he was able to acquire a two character brand ⟨⟩. In order for Dad to be able to cope with the roads to commute to business in Calgary, he bought 10 acres from Mrs. Joseph Fisher Sr. on the South side of the North Fork of Sheep Creek for $20.00, a truly exorbitant price! The access gate to the ranch was then opposite the Millarville Race Track entrance and it was on this piece of land that our home was built. Dad had bought some old bunkhouses from Royalite Oil used in early Turner Valley oil exploration days — Sam Rozell moved them in — and it was from these bunkhouses that our home and outbuildings were constructed. Old Blackie (William Arkinstall, a World War I prisoner-of-war and ship's carpenter) lived with us for some seven or eight years and did all the building by himself. What a great old Mr. Fix-it he was — could even make doll's eyes open and close again! What fun we three girls had when Blackie started tearing out partitions in the old bunkhouses — a real treasure hunt and piggy banks grew as we found all the loose coins that had gone astray in oilfield gambling days.

The Fred Andrews family came to work the ranch for Dad and lived in the old ranch buildings situated on the banks of the Sheep at the SE end of the ranch close to the Jack King homestead. They had four children and when September '33 came along there were six of us to start at New Valley School — Ernie, Florence and Bobby Andrews and Joan, Doreen and A.J. Poor Mr. Scott (George A. Scott)! — the Oliver girls were 3 real greenhorns to break in to a one room country

A.J., Joan and Doreen Oliver.

school. Joan was in Grade 8, Doreen in Grade 6 and A. J. in Grade 2. AND girls wore skirts to school — what an art it was to become to fold up the skirt, and whatevers beneath it, to tuck inside the "blanket cloth" slacks. The first year we walked to school — we didn't know how to ride — 1½ miles through the ranch fields. When spring breakup came the little creek running through the school quarter would flood by the time school was out and we would have to walk 3 miles around by the road past the New Valley Oilwell and down the Fisher Hill to get home. In winter when the snow got too deep or crusted or temperatures got down past 20 below someone would come to meet us in the fencing wagon on sleigh runners pulled by our first old team, Cappy and Lady. Replacing the Andrews family came Wes and Belle Frayn and their two daughters, Lil and Dorothy (Dot) attended New Valley School too. The second year we made sure we could ride — there was no barn and little shelter for the horses and what a time we all had catching our frisky horses on cold days. And speaking of cold days — if not enough students arrived to hold classes Mr. Scott would allow us to hold snowball fights (Doreen was pretty hard on windows it seems) and on warm spring days Mr. Scott would come out for afternoon recess to play baseball or football and somehow the school bell would get hidden and all of a sudden it would be time to go home; on other nostalgic spring days he would tell us to catch our horses (those who didn't ride horses would ride in his Ford Coupe with him), gather up our lunch boxes and head for the ford at the river. And speaking of school lunches — remember the old jacketed stove where our jars of 'somethin hot for lunch' were put to heat in a pan of water about 11 o'clock sending off agonizing whiffs of everything from hot chocolate to Boston baked beans! And detention was running X number of times around the school yard and Charlie King after some 14 rounds collapsed. And Joan's desk was next the coal bucket and opposite was Bill Fisher's desk and Bill was forever tipping her over — she still has blue Waterman's real ink in her hand from

441

one such occasion when she fell into the coal bucket and pen-with-nib stabbed her. And the desks — sidearm, side drawer, ink wells and pens with nibs — and no school buses!

Whenever we meet we three still agree that George Scott (Mr. George A. Scott — we used to call him GAS behind his back) was the very best teacher we ever had, and the best times of our lives were experienced at New Valley School in Millarville Country, and what we learned and lived there has enriched our lives forever.

P. E. Ollive

by J. F. "Jack" Ollive
Brand G ◇

Born in Upton Wirral, England, came to Calgary in 1911 and worked for Harry Chapman who had a dairy farm just north of Calgary, and after a bout in the hospital with typhoid fever contracted from swimming in Nose Creek, he came to Millarville to work on a horse ranch owned by Monty Fraser. Often their riding chores would be interrupted when a coyote would cross their path, and then the chase would be on. Monty carried a .22 revolver, so the larder was kept well stocked with ruffed grouse. I think a good time was had by all.

Dad moved on the next year to work for "Doc" Hays, the father of Senator Harry Hays at Carstairs. There, he was one of four men who did the milking — they each had a string of 29 cows to milk by hand, as there were no milking machines in those days. The forearms were to be held steady, no "pumping", as "Doc" thought this was too hard on the udders. Dad was happy there, as he liked cows.

Some time later, he and his brother H. V. "Bert" Ollive started a dairy farm in the Springbank area west of Calgary, but after a year or so, they called an auction sale, then joined the Lord Strathcona Horse. After a stint overseas, he returned to Calgary and worked at different jobs from Food Comptroller to

Winnie and Jack Ollive.

Store Keeper in the Palliser Hotel, and then for the Wood Vallance Warehouse which was taken over by Marshall Wells Hardware.

In 1923, he married Christina Whitmore who came to Calgary as a child in 1902 from London, England.

The depression came along, and in 1932 the staff was cut down at Marshall Wells, so for four years he worked at odd jobs. In 1936 he bought N.W.34, T.21, R.3, W.5 from Mrs. Allison and we have lived here ever since. In 1946, another quarter was added to the farm, S.W.34, T.21, R.3, W.5, being purchased from Mrs. De Mille.

Years were spent milking cows, sometimes as many as thirty, and finally we switched to range cattle but the pressure of renting land, putting up hay on shares, custom work, and a growing herd was too much, so half of the farm was sold and all of the cattle. Now feed is grown to sell, and life is not so hectic.

In 1967, I married Winnifred Ball and my stepson Pat is a geologist in the oil industry, being stationed in Medicine Hat.

Clara and Oscar Olson

by Pearl Olson

Clara and Oscar Olson came from Minnesota in 1910 and homesteaded in the Lomond district. They moved to the Carseland district in 1926 and to the Okotoks district in the spring of 1932, to the old Gier Ranch which is now the Bud Widney Ranch. They were only partly moved in when the district got that big blizzard of 1932. Many people will remember — lives and livestock were lost, power lines were down. They were marooned for at least ten days. The only way to get in or out for tobacco and mail was by saddle horse. This was Don's (their elder son's) chore. He had to get off the horse and lead it through the drifts.

They finally got settled, and as I sit writing, I remember with great amusement (though it wasn't really funny), Clara was so clean, she was washing down the upstairs and stepped over a trunk right into a stove-pipe hole. Well, her leg went through the floor as far as it could go, even splintering the ceiling of the room below. She ended up in hospital.

Pearl and Gene Ollive. 50th Wedding Anniversary, 1973.

Clara and Oscar Olson

They lived in this house for about three years, getting settled and becoming acquainted with the other people in the district, some of whom in later years were to become very dear friends.

It was during this period that Don came back to Carseland and married Pearl Melendy. Their younger son, Merton, grew up in the district and became great friends with David and Nevill Cannon.

After three years they moved to the old Templeton Place where they lived until they retired into Calgary in about 1953. Clara and Oscar always had time for a friend to drop in and have coffee and doughnuts and a

visit. If Oscar had to go in to town for repairs or anything, he always came in and got cleaned up first. You never saw him anywhere in his work clothes other than at work.

Don and his wife still live in Calgary and have more or less retired. They have one son, Garry, who manages "Don's Auto Body" and he is married to Bernice Paisley. They have a son, Terry, and a daughter, Laurie.

Merton joined the Air Force in 1942 and was sent down East. He was discharged in 1945; while in the Air Force he met Jane Watson, a doctor's daughter from Detroit. He married her in 1947 and they went down to Michigan to live. They have a son, Robert, and a daughter, Barbara.

Maybe the farmers of that era didn't have all the electrical appliances like they have now but they surely ate well. They had all the cream, butter, fresh eggs, fresh chickens, etc., that they could use. Clara was no exception, and could she cook! She will be well remembered for her fried chicken and home-made ice cream, also fresh baked buns. I wonder how many people will remember the Leftsa and Flatbread that she made for the Christmas Holiday Season, to eat with turkey. Very few people had ever tasted it before, but nearly everyone enjoyed it. I didn't have the patience to learn but the tradition is still being carried on in the Olson family because Clara laboriously taught Bernice to make it and she does a marvellous job.

Oscar passed away in 1957 and Clara in 1972.

We hope they found their life rewarding and we remember them with love and respect.

Merton Olson
by Jane Olson

Oscar and Clara Olson and sons Donald A., and Merton O., first came to the Millarville area in 1932; first living on the Gier Ranch. In 1937 they purchased the Templeton Ranch, and remained there until retire-

Clara and Oscar Olson, 1956.

Jane and Merton Olson, and son Robert, 1962.

443

ment, about 1953. They spent their retirement years in Calgary.

Oscar passed away in November, 1958, and Clara in January, 1972. Donald married Pearl Melendy in 1933. They have one son, Garry, and now have two grandchildren.

Donald founded "Don's Auto Body", and all of the family live in Calgary. Merton enlisted in the R.C.A.F. in 1942, and was discharged in 1945. He married Jane Watson in 1947. They have a son, Robert, and a daughter, Barbara. They all reside in St. Charles, Michigan, U.S.A.

Ole Olson
by Brian Berger

Ole Olson was born October 19, 1890, in Haugesund, Norway. At an early age he set out on his own, and for several years plied the North Sea as a sailor in the merchant marine. But his desire for change soon steered him toward America, in particular, the Dakotas. After roaming this territory for a short time, he and two friends set out for Canada. October 20th, 1909, the three wanderers arrived in Maple Creek, Saskatchewan. Immediately, Ole took up a homestead, on the east half of section twelve, township five, range twenty-five, west of the third. Robsart, Saskatchewan has since grown on this township. His need for work found him in the employ of a man named Keas, as a team driver, for five dollars a day. One cold day in December, while his friends were away after lumber, Ole had a visit by his neighbor, Mr. Carlie. He had just dropped by to pass the word that someone had stolen a quarter of beef the day before, and that he was now searching for the culprit. Being more than a little concerned by the suggestion Mr. Carlie had made, Ole spent that night in his shack, the door nailed shut, with rifle, revolver and knife nearby. Two days later Ole's companions arrived home and told of passing Carlie down the road a ways, with the beef over his horse. No doubt this made his next night's sleep more restful.

Ole was naturalized as a Canadian through the district court in Moose Jaw, Sask., on the tenth of December, 1912.

From September, 1916, through March, 1919, he served with the Royal Canadian Naval Volunteer Reserve. The years 1941 through 1947 saw him in uniform again, this time in the RCAF.

Ole married an eastern girl, Elizabeth Rose, and raised a family of two. Ole Adrian Olson, their only son, was lost during naval service during the Second War. Margaret Lorraine married Peter Berger, and had two boys of her own. She passed away in August of 1976. Peter now resides in Calgary.

The post war years found Ole in many parts of Alberta, as a carpenter. Some time was spent with the National Parks, in this position.

Ole Olson first came to the Millarville district in the mid-fifties. He purchased the northeast quarter of section nineteen, township twenty-one, range two,

west of the fifth. Soon he knew most of the people living around him, and enjoyed many years of friendship in the area. Ole passed away in December, 1970.

The land he once lived on is now the home of his grandson, Brian Berger, and his wife Laurlie. His only other grandchild, Bruce Berger, is now living in Edmonton.

Opheim, Charles K. and Patricia J. O4
NW 20-20-3-W5

We were married in Vancouver, B.C. May 1953, Chuck worked at mining and construction for several years. We then moved to Powell River, built and operated a motel. Chuck went into sales with Texas Refinery in 1957 and in 1960 we were transferred to Calgary.

After 10 years of city living the country called us back so we rented the Teskey place, south of the Race track, for two years. February 1972 saw our own home completed and ready to move into. However, Chuck conveniently broke his leg at moving time. So with the help of our wonderful neighbours (and a foot of new snow) we settled in. The spirit of the west was once again portrayed.

We have two children, Mark Jae, born 1962 and Sanna Jo born 1964. Both attended Millarville School.

Now after 9 years living in this area we know there is no other place to really live, but in these foothills.

25th Wedding Anniversary of Pat and Chuck Opheim. L. to R. Sanna, Chuck, Pat and Mark. May, 1978.

Mr. and Mrs. Robert (Bob) Oro
by Jean E. Melling

Bob and Elsie Oro resided on the property of Dr. Thomas Melling in 1955 and 1956. From there they moved to Clive, Alberta where they now reside, on the farm, formerly owned by his parents.

They have two sons, Gregory and Michael. Although their residency in the Millarville area was a short one, they made many friends, and enjoyed their association with their neighbors.

Alan and Karen Orum

Alan was born in the Turner Valley hospital on November 9, 1946. He started school at Millarville as

Alan and Karen Orum, 1976.

Harry and Pauline Orum.

the Plainview students were bused to Millarville that year with Lawrie Lochhead as their first driver.

He enjoyed the free and easy life of a farm boy helping with the farming with his father. He seemed to have his father's ability as a mechanic and overhauled trucks, tractors and cars. He soon had bikes, motor bikes and snowmobiles.

He soon was working after school and holidays for Jack Lawson. Then he worked on cats clearing and breaking land.

Alan married Karen Lynn November 19, 1967. He worked on the cat for his brother Earl and also worked for Bill Kendall for 13 years, working up to a sawyer. He also worked sawing at Cochrane. He now works for the municipality as a grader operator and Karen works in Calgary at Safeways as a meat wrapper. They make their home on the old home place.

Harry and Pauline (Krom) Orum

Harry was born in 1906 in Woodstock, Ontario, coming west with his parents at three years of age to the Crossfield area. They came west with team and wagons.

Pauline was born in 1915 in Coeur d'Alene, Idaho coming to Calgary with her parents then to DeWinton, later settling in the Red Deer Lake area.

Harry and Pauline were married in Calgary April 22, 1936 living for a time in Calgary then moved out to the Red Deer Lake area on the Underwood farm. Mr. Underwood was manager of John Deere Plow Co.

Then they bought the Sam Cultus place in 1942. NE ¼, Sec 30-20-3-W5 and moved in the fall to the Kew area. Here their three oldest children, Verna Joyce, Clifford Earl and Caroline Joy attended the Plainview School. On November 9, 1946 Harry Alan was born.

Harry was always in demand as a mechanic and every fall ran a threshing outfit for some neighbor. For a time they had milk cows, then after clearing

Orum Family. Earl, Verna, Joy and Alan.

more land he raised hay and grain. Pauline was an excellent homemaker and seamstress.

Harry worked at different sawmills; many years for Bill Kendall until he retired. Pauline died on October 18, 1976 and Harry on December 28, 1977.

Marion and Geoff Ovans

Geoff Ovans was born in Glasgow, Scotland. His family settled in Nova Scotia, and in the years of the threshers in the West, Geoff and his brother David worked their way across the prairies and settled northwest of Edmonton. There, Geoff met and in 1937 married Marion Gaskell, who had also come from England originally. They went immediately to Anchordown Ranch in the Priddis area, where Geoff worked on the dairy farm. A daughter Maureen was born in

1939. Later that year, with war in Europe threatening, the Ovans moved to Calgary just in time for Geoff to join up on the first day of Canada's declaration of war in the Royal Army Service Corps. New Year's Day in 1940 saw Geoff landing in England and he did not return until June, 1945. Geoff took up farming for a period of five years, and then went into the trade he had learned in the army — mechanics. Several garages later — via Mayerthorpe, Edmonton, and Mill Bay (on Vancouver Island), the Ovans' children grew up and settled in their various localities. Maureen, her husband and two boys live on Vancouver Island, as do Bruce and Jan Ovans and their young daughter. Two unmarried girls are away from home — one, Cicely, working in Edmonton, while the youngest, Lynn, works in Surrey, B.C.

Marion and Geoff are semi-retired. That is, apart from having a rural mail route, raising a garden, and a yard full of chickens. However, many are the times the conversation goes back to those years at Anchordown Ranch, Millarville (S.E.¼, Sec.32, T.21, R.3, W.5).

Herbert W. Padwick and Margret Isobel Padwick △Ḃ ᴸ·ᴴ·

Herb Padwick was born the eldest son of Frank and Mabel Padwick in 1912, in Winnipeg, Manitoba. He resided and worked there until 1939 when he joined the RCAF.

Isobel was born in St. Boniface, Manitoba; the youngest child of William and Susanna McKeand who had emigrated from Britain.

Herb and Isobel met in Winnipeg and were married in 1939, prior to Herb shipping overseas. After serving for six years, Herb retired with the rank of Wing Commander. After leaving the service, they moved to Regina where they had three children: Herbert William Jr., Frances Anne and Catherine Mary.

After 20 successful years with a local Caterpillar dealership, Herb and Isobel joined their two daughters and their husbands in Calgary in 1975. Soon after they purchased and established Belmar Ranch, a quarter section three miles north of Millarville. The legal description is SE ¼ 27-21-3 W5.

Along with their daughters and sons-in-law they established a registered Aberdeen Black Angus herd. Herb and his daughters also became actively involved with the local horse show scene, particularly with the Ron Southern's famed Spruce Meadows Stables. Isobel, who spent many active years on the national board of the YWCA, retired to run ramrod over her large brood.

Ruth and Gordon Page

told by Ruth Page

This is the saga of a pair of "rolling stones".

I was born in Windsor, Ontario, and moved, with my parents, Edith and Frederick Westcott, to

Back row: Matthew and Gordon Page. Front: Belinda and Ruth Page.

Kingsville, Warkerville, Kingston, Arden and finally London, Ontario. I joined the Canadian Navy as a Captain's Writer and was stationed at Cornwallis, Nova Scotia for almost a year. From there I was posted to Greenoch, Scotland on the Firth of Clyde, where I was on loan to the Royal Navy and it was there I met Gordon Page, a Deck Officer in the Merchant Navy.

Gordon was born in Edinburgh, then lived in Pittenween, on the East Coast of Fife, where his father Dr. Douglas Page was the local doctor. Gordon finished his schooling in Edinburgh, then as a naval cadet on the training ship H.M.S. Conway at Bangor, North Wales.

He served in the Merchant Navy in the North Atlantic, South Atlantic and South Pacific during the European war, then on ammunition and troop ships sailing around the coasts of India, Burma and Malaya, during the latter part of the war.

We were married in London, Ontario in 1947, and immediately moved to New Zealand. Gordon joined the Union Steamship Co. whose ships serviced the New Zealand coast, over to Australia and up through the Pacific Islands to the West coast of Canada and the United States.

We lived in New Zealand for six years — first in Wellington and then at Paraparaumu Beach, a small community overlooking the Tasman Sea. Our two eldest children, Belinda and Brian, were born in New Zealand. With a young family and no car, we didn't see as much of the country as we would have liked, but marvelled at what we did see, and met a most hospitable people.

When we came back to Canada, Gordon joined a Water and Waste Engineering Company, and we lived in Ajax, Ontario, then moved on to Thunder Bay, Winnipeg, (where Matthew was born), Edmonton, back to Winnipeg and finally in 1964, to Calgary.

In 1973 we bought an acreage above Pot Hole Creek and the following year the house was built and we forsook the bright lights of the big City and moved — our last move.

The children are grown and away. Belinda lives in

Kaslo, B.C., Brian graduated in Medicine from the University of Alberta and has just finished his second year interning in New Zealand, and Matthew is a Cadet Officer in the Canadian Air Force. So there is just Gordon and I, plus dogs, sheep and cat holding the fort.

It has been an interesting experience getting to know something of the various parts of Canada, Scotland and New Zealand. But after a total of twenty-one moves since we were married, we think it is time to stay put and where better than here on the hill above Pot Hole Creek?

Marthe (Ingeveld) Pallister
by Nina Lochhead

Marthe was born in January, 1914, in Brussels, Belgium. Her mother, Alodie Ingeveld, had returned from Canada in order to be with her own doctors in Belgium. Later that winter, her father, Maurice Ingeveld, sailed from Canada to get his wife and child and return with them to Canada.

When the first World War broke out in August, 1914, Maurice, Alodie and Marthe set sail again for Belgium where Maurice went to rejoin his regiment. The Germans had set up a blockade so there was no possibility of civilians landing on the mainland of Europe, therefore Alodie and Marthe spent the four war years with friends in England. This was where Marthe learned to speak English with a distinct accent.

After the war, when Marthe was five years old, the family moved back to Belgium. Marthe's education was now in both French and Dutch.

Marthe (Ingeveld) Pallister.

In 1919 Marthe was joined by a brother, George and in 1926 a sister, Marie-Louise (Nina). The family returned to Canada, to the Square Butte district in 1927. Here Marthe attended the Square Butte School. The following year the family moved to Calgary where Marthe resumed her schooling.

1932 saw the family return again to the Square Butte district, to Maurice's homestead. Marthe helped on the farm, especially after her brother went into the army at the onset of World War two. She was always ready to give a helping hand and a smile to anyone in need. During the war she was an active member of the Square Butte Red Cross.

In 1947 Marthe married Bernard (Bud) Pallister. Eleven years later, in 1960, she was killed in a jeep accident in the Forest Reserve west of Millarville and Kew.

Mrs. William Pallister (Edith Knights)
by E. Pallister

I, Edith Pallister, am the youngest of nine children born to the late Annie and Richard Knights, at Little Massingham, Kings Lynn, Norfolk, England, in July 1907; came to Canada with my mother, brothers and sisters in May, 1909. Father and my eldest brother, Charlie had come the year before and bought land at Millarville, Alberta. Of course I don't remember the trip to Canada, but was told it was quite an experience, as the "Lake Champlain" hit an iceberg near St. Johns, Newfoundland.

My childhood was spent on the farm at Millarville, and I attended Fordville School. After writing my grade 8 departmental examination and receiving my diploma, I had to stay home and help on the farm.

I was one of the original members of the Willing Workers Women's Institute. I have been showing at the Millarville and Priddis Fair since I was old enough to enter exhibits, and still enter my needlework, vegetables and flowers.

In 1927 my parents and I moved to Calgary, where I was able to get a job. In 1934 I married William Pallister. We lived in the Turner Valley district (where Bill worked in the Oilfields), and had two sons, Peter and William Jr. We had our ups and downs! In 1943 my husband had a heart attack and spent many long weeks in the Turner Valley Hospital under the care of Dr.'s Harry and David Landers. After a full recovery, he went to Egypt to work in the Oilfields for eighteen months. The boys and I stayed in Turner Valley. Upon his return, he still had "itchy feet" so accepted another tour of foreign work in Borneo — our sons and I going with him this time, in the fall of 1947. After two years, I came home with the boys, as the schooling was not up to par in the far east, and lived in Calgary. Bill returned to join us in January, 1951. We then bought a home in Calgary, where we have resided ever since, except for two years in Estevan, Saskatchewan.

After graduating from high school in Calgary, Peter joined the R.C.M.P. Force. He is married and has two sons and a daughter. He is now S/Sgt. in Hamilton, Ontario.

After graduating from high school, our second son, William Jr. went to Mount Royal College, and then became a salesman. He is also married and has two sons and a daughter. He now resides in Calgary.

I am so glad my Dad chose Alberta and the Millarville district to bring us to. I love the country and the scenery; when my time comes I will be laid to rest in the Millarville Cemetery. Christ Church, Millarville is so beautiful and the church that I attended during my childhood. My two eldest brothers, Charlie and Tony's names are on the cenotaph; both of them killed in action during World War I.

D. Byron and Laura (Brinkerhoff) Palmer
by Laura Palmer

Byron was born in 1942, at Oklahoma City, Okla. and moved to Regina, Saskatchewan with his family in 1952 and to Calgary in 1955. I was born in 1943, in Dallas, Texas, and moved to Calgary with my family in 1949. Byron and I were married in 1964.

The magnetism of the Millarville countryside is a very real phenomenon and not some tired cliche from a travel brochure like it may seem at first.

I was first introduced to this area as a child when a great many of our Pony Club competitions were staged at Graham Ranches and the Millarville Race Track. I was thoroughly entranced at the time and the magnetism was reinforced when my father, Bob Brinkerhoff, purchased the Dan Dudenhoeffer place in 1965, committing it in conjunction with the adjacent Shatto Ranches property to an exotic cattle breeding undertaking in 1969. We were less than two years out of university at the time, and eager to reacquaint ourselves with the foothill country, so became involved in this enterprise.

A stroke of luck found Byron commuting one day from our location at De Winton over to the Dudenhoeffer place, via Hwy. 22, when he noticed Joe Fisher tacking a "For Sale" sign on Bob Adam's property, just south of Bill Lee's Husky Station. Byron stopped to make a few inquiries, one thing led to another, and before long we had closed a deal to purchase the E. ½ of 11-21-3W5. That was late in 1969 when we were also involved in a thousand other projects, so it was early in 1971 before our Cee-Der-Log home was completed, Palmerra Beef Cattle Centre became a reality, and we were finally living near Millarville, whose magnetism had been drawing us closer all that time. (Jack Pierce, Ranger Oils, bought the Dudenhoeffer-Shatto Ranches property the end of December, 1973.)

Our eldest son, Davy (born 1965 in Denver, Colorado) was six years old when we moved and was

able to start Grade One at Millarville School that fall. Robbie was two and a half at the time (born 1968, Calgary) so all his memories are of this locale. John Cory, No. 3 son, came along in February, 1974, and spent only three years in our first house before we moved into our present location, high atop a hill on the south-central end of the half section.

After having built a fairly efficient, but small purebred cattle operation surrounding our original site, we decided to temporarily abandon cattle-breeding in favor of log-house building, and consequently sold the north 80 acres with buildings to Createplan Developments in June of 1977. However I don't believe we will ever abandon the Millarville area — it's home!

We may feel it is our duty and privilege to do our share of complaining about the weather, but the people here can't be beat and we are proud to be a part of the community.

Parker, Audrey (Rawlinson)
by Audrey Parker

I was born in Calgary June 15th, 1930, but raised in the Millarville district, where I attended Sheep Creek School from 1936-1947, then one year at Central High School in Calgary (now Dr. Carl Safran School).

In Calgary, I worked for the Kean family and attended Henderson College of Business. After completing the business course, I worked for S.S. Kresge Co. then went to work for D.N.D. (215 Workshop R.C.E.M.E.) at Currie Barracks. On July 4th, 1951, I married Ray Parker, who was stationed at No. 10 Repair Depot, R.C.A.F. (now Atco Industrial Park).

Ray was transferred to Montreal in 1952, and our daughter Joanne was born there May 20th, 1952. From Montreal to Sydney, Nova Scotia in 1955, where we went in by ferry and came out by the causeway that was built. Our son Ted was born there September 28, 1955. From Sydney we were transferred to Cold Lake, Alberta, where we were from 1958 to 1960. In 1960, we were transferred once again, this time to No. 4 Fighter Wing, in Germany.

While in Europe, on week-end and annual leave we visited many places, Switzerland, Holland, Spain, Belgium, France and Luxembourg, also England and many places in Germany. The highlight of a visit to England was to be able to see my father's home "Ballindune."

We came back to Canada in 1964 and lived in Edmonton. Ray was stationed at Puntzi Mountain, B.C. and I went there in July, 1965 and spent two months camping. Ray transferred back to Edmonton in 1965. In 1966 we were on the move again, this time to Sioux Lookout, Ontario. In 1967, we attended the World's Fair in Montreal. While we were at Sioux Lookout we had to be evacuated because of a forest fire. (I'll never forget it.)

Another move, this time to Beaverlodge, Alberta, but made our home in Grande Prairie, where Joanne

L. to R. Ray Parker, Ted Parker. Front: Audrey (Rawlinson) Parker and Joanne.

graduated from St. Joseph High School. Then from Grande Prairie to Calgary, where Ray retired with 30 years service. Ted graduated from Central Memorial High School in Calgary, where we now make our home.

Geoffrey L. Parker

Cattle Brand   TL R.R.

I am the youngest son of Mr. and Mrs. H. G. Parker, born in 1921 while my parents were living in the Red Deer Lake district. I attended a school at Red Deer Lake, Westoe, and the Olds Agricultural College.

Geoffrey Parker on Bee's Wax, Calgary Stampede, July 1945. Judge was Frank Sharp.

In 1938 while working for Jack Beatty in Red Deer Lake I became involved in Polo — to me one of the greatest sports there is, I played it for a considerable number of years.

In 1937 I ventured into rodeo, taking up saddle bronc riding and of course had a lot of fun wild horse racing. Those were the days before rodeo became professionalized.

I broke a lot of horses over the years. In the Thirties I'd get $10 to $15 per head.

I joined the Air Force in the early stages of the War, took wireless training and became a WAG. I was one of the many Canadians attached to the R.A.F. on coastal command and I am proud to have been on the famous Dawn Patrol Squadron. During my term on operations I was on the 58 and 59 Squadrons, R.A.F. and for a short time on the 423rd Squadron R.C.A.F. It was March 12, 1944 that we were shot down into the Atlantic, but very fortunately we were picked up before succumbing to exposure. I returned to Canada in 1945 and managed to ride in the Calgary Stampede while on leave — was discharged from the Air Force in the fall of 1945.

I worked for Home Oil, Millarville, for several months before renting the old W. H. King place in Millarville. Always interested in Thoroughbreds, I stood the Thoroughbred 'Sun Tryst', who left a lot of good quality colts and had several good stallions later on.

I worked for Clem Gardner in the Jumping Pound district then moved back to Red Deer Lake and farmed for a year. I became a livestock buyer for Burns and Company then worked for the Department of Health of Animals at the Calgary stock yards. I

Winston and Geoffrey Parker, Joan Gardner in background.

helped on a lot of the TB testing in the Millarville district.

In August 1955 Pearl Clifford and I were married. We purchased our present ranch north of Cochrane in 1956 where we still reside. We have two daughters, Patsy and Clem.

Parker, Winston and Marjorie

by Elaine Taylor
Cattle brand VL left ribs.

Winston Churchill Parker was born in Calgary in July, 1918. With his elder sister Jessie, he moved to the Red Deer Lake district the following year where his parents, well-known oldtimers Mr. and Mrs. H. G. Parker, began farming. His brother, Geoffrey, was born two years later. Prior to this time, Winston's father owned land west of Priddis and was employed by the Pacific Cartage Co.

Winston attended both Red Deer Lake and Midnapore schools before taking training at the Alberta Provincial Technical Institute (now called SAIT) in Calgary. Later, he returned to that location for Air Force wireless training, and again many years later for a photography course.

Son of a man who was a great horseman, Winston has always maintained a fondness for horses since childhood. He took part in many horse shows, particularly enjoying the polo pony and jumping classes. For several years he played polo at the Chinook Polo Grounds as a member of the High River team. In 1937, this team won the Western Canada Polo Championship.

He was fourteen years when his lifelong friend, Clem Gardner, first asked Winston to ride for him, gathering and moving the Stampede cattle and bucking horses in to the Calgary Stampede. He never missed a year riding for Clem, helping with the Stampede stock, also the yearly roundup and branding, except when he was overseas. He has always been proud to call Clem Gardner one of his closest friends.

Early in World War II Winston joined the R.C.A.F., in which he served over five years as a Wireless Air Gunner. He spent five months attached to No. 101 Squadron, Royal Air Force, and then when R.C.A.F. operational bomber squadrons were being formed he was transferred back to a Canadian squadron. Shot down on a bombing raid to Hamburg, Germany, he spent over three years as a prisoner of war, near the border of Poland. He was discharged with the rank of Flying Officer.

Following the war, he bought Monea Ranch from the Deane-Freemans and went to work for Home Oil, Millarville. He left the oil company to go ranching full time in 1951, and still makes his home with his wife, Marjorie, on the ranch located on the north fork of Sheep Creek, south of Christ Church, Millarville.

Marjorie and Winston Parker.

Parker cattle nearly home from summer pasture, riders, Winston Parker and Art Taylor.

Marjorie is the daughter of oldtimers Mr. and Mrs. Martin Van Der Velde, of the Dalemead district. She attended Normal School at the old Tech in Calgary and later taught school at Jumping Pound, Brushy Ridge, Ceepeear School in Calgary, Shepard and Strathmore. After her marriage she taught one year in Okotoks, two years in Black Diamond, and then from 1960 to 1976 she taught at Millarville. She retired in 1976 and now substitutes in the Foothills School Division.

In the tradition set by his parents, Winston has served his district in various capacities, having been an active member of the Millarville Race Club, Millarville Hall, and Priddis and Millarville Agricultural Society. For the Race Club, as a child, he sold programs; after World War II, for several years, he was either Clerk of the Course or Judge of the flat races; in recent years he has been the announcer at the races. He was one of the founding members of Millarville R.E.A., and at the present time is Vice-President.

An avid nature photographer, Winston still enjoys raising quality cattle and riding a good horse.

Robert and Mary Parkins   TE TE

Trails End Ranch (the E½ of 13-21-4W5) really is a suitable name for this piece of land, situated on the top of a hill. It was found at the end of a trail through Ivor Lyster's pasture and greenfeed, where we almost always got stuck, every time I came out at any rate. Bob bought the land from Graham ranches in 1960 and before Grahams it was owned by E. V. Keith. The original owner was Jack Johnson, who bought from the C.P.R. As far as we have been able to find out nobody had ever built on it before us. Indians may have camped on it as it was a well worn trail they used to Morley, so we have been told.

In 1961, Bob built a barn and a cabin so we could spend holidays and week-ends, with the hope that we

Bob Parkins, Standing, with grandson Skip. Daughter Vicki with her daughter and Si Romanowski, right, with twin calves.

could live here permanently. At times it seemed like a hopeless dream as the M.D. flatly refused to put a road through. In the summer of 1970, along with Don Irvine, Ivor Lyster, Tucker and Ross, they put the road through on their own. Bob added on to the cabin in the fall and we moved out to the foothills the 30th of November, 1970.

Country living, to me, was a far cry from Calgary where I was born March 2nd, 1921 and lived all my life. I've never quite figured out whether Ivor Lyster tried to discourage me or not; I do know he is happiest when he can tell stories on me. Unfortunately they are usually true. The country to me was a place where other people lived, never me. He still kids about my calving party, as he calls it. Bob went to an auction sale and left me with a heifer that decided to give birth. No heifer, before or since, has ever had so much attention, thanks to Ernie Silvester, Alex Lyall and of course, "Doc" Lyster. I almost needed a doctor myself. I guess I'll never live that one down. Incidentally, I never have seen a calf born and hope I never do. According to Ivor, I also rained out the Millarville Races and the ladies' Bar-B-Que on July 1st. He should have remembered to tell me to stay in Calgary that week end as he usually did, as I didn't enjoy it either. That was one of Bob's passing showers that lasted a week. I only wish the propane had lasted with it. We couldn't get up the hill, let alone down. Ivor had a Brahma cow up here that hated me as much as I hated her. I'm sure he kept her here just to torment me. I couldn't even go out on the front porch. He finally got rid of her when I threatened to shoot her. There is an old song called "You'll Get Used To It" and I guess that is what is happening to me, I'm getting used to it, I think.

My parents came from Moncton, N.B. to Calgary in March of 1912, where my father and his brother opened a shop next to City Hall and became Iddiols Bros. Locksmiths, the first in Calgary.

Country living has always been a part of Bob's life. He was born October 30th, 1916 in Scollard, Alberta, a little town south of Big Valley. I have to add that nobody seems to have heard of it except the people that came from there. His Grandmother came west in 1905 and opened a boarding house in Stettler, Alberta. His Father came to Alberta on a harvest excursion in 1908 and two years later moved his family out and went homesteading 30 miles S.W. of Stettler on the banks of the Red Deer River, which later became known as the Scollard District. In later years, when they were digging up dinosaur bones, the greater part of them were found on his Grandmother's old homestead. After his Grandmother's death, the family moved back to London, Ont. for a few years but the call of the west was too strong to resist. They returned to Scollard, where they bought a home just outside the town to raise their family of eight boys.

Before the war, Bob decided to go into business for himself and opened a grocery store. That wasn't a

Sign at entry to Parkins Ranch.

The Patterson family home.

very profitable business during the depression, so, when war broke out he closed up the store and came to Calgary and joined the Calgary Highlanders in 1940. That is where we met and were married on November 19, 1940. In January of 1941 he went overseas and became an instructor at pre-O.C.T.U. School (Officer Cadet Training Unit) in England. He returned to Brockville, Ont. in 1944, to receive his own commission and was stationed in Calgary a few months before returning to England, just before the war ended. It is fortunate he didn't choose the navy as every trip to and from England was proof that prairie farmers don't make the best sailors.

After the war he was employed by Imperial Oil, but left to work for Muttart Lumber, which later became Engineered Homes. He was with E.B.L. for 19 years.

In 1967 he went into partnership with some friends to form Chateau Home, a pre-fab business in Kelowna, B.C.

We have two daughters. Barbara married Ross Davidson, they live in Kamloops, B.C. and have five sons and one daughter.

Vicki married Ray Romanowski, and they have one son and one daughter and live in Calgary.

The Art Patterson Family
by Arthur L. Patterson — Brand N33 R.R.

The area of which I write holds fond memories for me, because I know no other land. My father, F. D. Patterson came to this country in 1889, and in 1902 he filed on the S.W.¼, Sec. 4, T.22 R.2 W.5 as homestead. He was also allotted the adjacent N.E.¼, Sec. 33, T.21, R.2, W.5 as South African script, for his service in the Boer War. From this quarter a good spring flows, making part of the head waters of the Pine Creek watershed. Running water in those days was a prime asset, so in 1902 he built a cottage close by that spring. That cottage is still intact and part of the home we live in yet. Dad's family consisted of four children: my half sister, Fanny now deceased, brother Bill of Ft. St. John, sister Jessy Riis of Kelowna, B.C. Of course my Dad, an old timer even then, was my hero, and as the years roll by, I find that he could accomplish more in

his travels with a team of horses, do more errands for the neighbours etc., than I was ever able to do even with the help of good roads, exceptional services, and a faster, more efficient mode of travel.

School, in those days, was of course the one-roomed type, ours being "Ballyhamage", now the Leighton Centre for fine arts. As we rode our ponies three and a half miles to school along that bush trail, little did we know or realize, that **this** lovely back woods country, scoffed at and belittled by our city friends would become a prize that many today strive to acquire.

The land is fast changing hands, but I like to remember the old crooks and the crannies where the upland game, like ruffed grouse, prairie chicken, and Hungarian partridge once flourished. It seems, the deer have been able to adjust, and withstand the inroads of subdivision and are quite plentiful, but the bush rabbit which used to nestle in the willows is almost a thing of the past. As a boy I remember what a thrill it was to see a rabbit sitting at the foot of every other willow bush. With the old single shot Winchester 22 we would endeavour to shoot a few rabbits; most every day there would be four or five bunnies to bring home. Some were fed to the laying hens, others were sold to the fox farm to make a few pennies to buy another box of 22 shells.

Ballyhamage School, built in 1919, was a spanking new building. A room of such magnitude, not equalled in this area was also used for social functions. Music for dancing was hard to find at the time, but we were lucky — Danny McNab had come into the district, and brought with him his button accordion. I was just a kid then, but to me he made the sweetest music of all. I was determined to learn to play that squeak box, so, with the able assistance of my mother, I learned to play a little. In the early thirties, the Priddis and Millarville Agricultural Society was hard up, so they decided to make a little money by holding dances at the Fordville School, admission 50¢ a couple. Again, there was no available music, so the Society purchased an accordion from Eatons mail order ($14.95), and we agreed if I would play for the functions at the rate of $1.50 per evening, the instrument would be mine. It was "high finance", but eventually the thing was paid for, and I have it to this day. P.S. — I do believe if you look in the records of the Priddis and Millarville Agr. Soc., you will find A. Patterson still owes $1.95 for final payment, on that squeak box. You see, I was out maneuvered by Gerry Berry and his Bush-Whackers.

School Fairs in the late 20's and 30's were popular events. The object of the exercise was to give the school kids, from a group of six or seven one-roomed schools, an opportunity to compete with exhibits of flowers, vegetables, grain and grasses etc. The student with the most points in the fair could win a short course at the Claresholm School of Agriculture. I was lucky to win most points one year. It was not because I worked very hard to achieve points, it was because the other guys did less. I spent one week at C.S.A. along with about thirty other kids who had gone the same route, and was again lucky to win the scholarship for southern Alberta. This was a six month, all expense paid course at the Agriculture School. So to make a long story short, the winter of 1930-31 was spent at the College. The instructors were all good guys and we learned a little and had a lot of fun, but they had quite a time showing us how to make a profit in the farming business; with wheat at 30¢/bushel, oats at 10¢/bushel, and cream at $1.80 for a 5-gallon can. Being 17 years old, having spent six months learning the art of farming, somehow I thought there wasn't much I didn't know. So, in the spring I started with great enthusiasm to put in the crop. The one thing, among many others that I didn't learn that winter, was never! never! put your finger in the drive gears of a Massey Harris seed drill and shout "Get Up" to your team. So, May 12, 1931, no middle finger on my left hand. With that sore hand, I remember hauling 3" by 10" fir plank from Midnapore to build subways on the mail route, the trips being up to 25 miles. On the first trip I had loaded about 1500 bd. ft. on the running gear, and was just pulling out from the station, when to my dismay a train pulled in from behind. Of course, the engineer had no way of knowing that my team had never seen a train, or that my hand was too sore to hold them, so naturally he blew the whistle long and loud! What with the rumble of the train, the snort and whistle, my lead team decided to beat that train to Wardens. Well, we finally came to rest when the train overtook us, causing the team to jack-knife into the ditch, breaking both the wagon tongue and the reach; also one wagon tire was missing. My lunch, which was bundled up in my rain coat, had bounced off a mile back. My cherished handwrought logging chain, "Made at Claresholm", fashioned and welded link by link, was lost. My hand was sore, and as I unhitched the team from the wreck, it started to rain, and continued to do so while we walked the twelve miles back home. That kind of day a fellow should forget, but never does.

In the early thirties, working your taxes out for the municipality was, for many, the only way you could meet your obligation, and the minute your obligation was met, you unhitched from the fresno and another rate-payer hooked on. Mill rate in Ballyhamage District was about 3½ mills on the assessed value. Road work for me was hard and tiresome. It entailed finding your four horse team in the bush pasture with the aid of a horse bell at 5 a.m., milk the cows, drive several miles on that uncomfortable steel wheeled wagon reach, to be on the job at 7 a.m. Then, wandering up hill and down dale filling and dumping the fresno with one hand while endeavouring to drive the team with the other. At 6 p.m., trundle on home at sunset, "in the cool, cool, cool of the evening to tell her I'll be there, to milk the cows". We were lucky though, because we did have a real good road boss, Ed Winthrop, the only man on the crew who had harness strong enough to hold that team of big Clydes when the plough hit a willow stump. Ed saw to it that we did a good honest day's work. The only time I remember we would get a little break was when Jack Brunt would mention the Social Credit Policy and $25.00 a month for all and sundry. At the mention of Aberhart, Ed would shout "whoa" to his team, the whole crew would grind to a halt, and there we would sit while those two argued and discussed the matter. Sometimes when the argument became real heated we would get up to an hour's rest. How sweet it was!

The council as a whole, and the municipality in general, was so hard up that on one occasion, after the road gang had risen early to drive five miles across country to be on the job at 7 a.m., the council ran out of funds at noon and we were asked to go home, leaving that chunk of road north of Bill Winthrop unfinished! In the name of progress, it takes awhile.

1938 was for me a most memorable year. I was down at the water hole getting the daily supply of water, when through the bush the rattle of wagon wheels was heard. On looking up, I saw a man with a team and wagon, with several cream cans sitting in the back. Close behind him were three young ladies riding horse back. The man introduced himself as Royal Burrows and said, "We have just rented the old Martman place, and we find it sure is dry up there. May we fill our cans from your spring?" I replied, "Yes, for sure, you sure can." But I wasn't looking at the man, or the horses, or the spring. I was fascinated by the pretty young ladies. My wife, Theresa, was one of those young ladies, the other two, her sisters. Some say I baited my girlfriend at the spring, others say twas love at first sight! We were married at Millarville Church, June 18, 1941.

We have raised a family of four. David Llewellyn, born in June, 1943, received his education locally, attended S.A.I.T. where he got his grounding as a surveyor. He worked for Mid West Survey Co. for several years. Tired of surveying well sites for oil companies who always wanted the job done "yesterday", he and a friend travelled through England and Europe, where they could more easily survey the sights and the girls. On his return in 1967, he decided to come home and

Arthur and Theresa with family, David, Louise, Anne and Don.

help us on the farm for which we were very thankful. In 1972 he married one of the Red Deer Lake School teachers, a nice young English girl, Felicity Coates. They have two children, Ian Hugh, born February, 1975 and Cathy, born December, 1976. They have lived in the house trailer on the hill for 6 years, but will be moving to the farm 4 miles south of Cayley next spring.

Laura Louise was born in September, 1946. She attended U. of C., became a teacher, and an accomplished pianist. She married Eldon Bruns from Pincher Creek in 1966. She taught school while Eldon finished his Masters in Wild Life Biology. They went globe-trotting for 2 years to places like Fiji, New Zealand, Australia, Asia and Europe, working and teaching as they went. On their return, they proceeded to raise a family; Matthew Clinton, born in 1972, and Christa Sharon Ann, born in 1974. They acquired an acreage north and east of Sylvan Lake in the Blind Man Valley, but have recently sold it and now make their home in Bentley, where Eldon is the Regional Biologist for the Red Deer District.

Margaret Anne, born in 1948, took part in 4-H and Pony Club at St. Georges Stables. She attended U. of C. where she attained her Bachelor of Physical Education degree. After teaching in Calgary for awhile, she decided to travel and join her sister in New Zealand. While she was in Australia, she met an English fellow, Chris Thompson who was teaching out there. They were married in Australia in 1972, and returned home via Asia and Europe. They have two children; Erin

Louise, born in 1976, and Claire Theresa, born in 1978. In 1973, they purchased an acreage five miles east of the weigh scales where they lived for 4½ years. Recently, they sold it and have made their home on forty acres S.W. of Okotoks. Chris has now received his Masters in Education and teaches at Strathcona-Tweedsmuir.

Douglas Arthur (Don) born in 1952, was active in 4-H and Pony Club at St. Georges Stables. He attended Red Deer Lake School and Lord Beaverbrook High School. He learned to play the trumpet and makes a little music on the piano, too. He worked for the Valid Construction Co. in B.C. for several years. He bought a home in Kamloops. His desire has always been to be in agriculture, so he has come home to throw his lot in with us on the farm. While in B.C., he met and married Sandra Greene, a pretty little trained nurse from Telkwa, B.C. They have one child, Kelly Arthur, born in 1975. At present they are living at the new location, four miles south of Cayley.

Last, but not least, and surely the better half, is my wife Theresa. She was a farm girl from the prairies but never tires of the beauty of our foothills and mountain scenes. She has spent untold energy improving our garden, also cares for house plants galore. She was keenly interested in farm activity and has helped in the field on many occasions. I think the pay-off was in 1958. She had spent many hours ploughing that sixty acre side hill with the old 99 with no wheel brakes. The going was tough, but eventually the job was done. Next year that land was seeded, everything going fine when alas! a hailstorm wiped it out. My wife is not one to swear, but on this occasion she said, "Oh heck, there must be a better way to make a living". So we bought a new 1960 Volkswagon and Theresa went off to University in Calgary to become a teacher. She took with her David, her nephew Jack Riis, Shirley Taylor, a neighbor, and a couple more all crammed in that little car. The net result was, she attained her Bachelor of Education degree, and has taught at Red Deer Lake for the last sixteen years. I guess it takes either a teacher or an oil well to make farming pay.

As I ramble on, there is one more thing I would like to mention that took my fancy years ago. It is the unique merits of the force of the Hydraulic Ram. This ingenious machine was invented by an unsung genius many, many years ago, to pump water from a moving stream. My Dad had purchased one of these in 1912 from an outfit in Illinois for $12.50. He set it to work, but it froze up that winter and broke the pipe. So there it sat, rusting away down by the creek for 20 odd years. In 1940, I harnessed the old machine again and for 22 years it served us well. Pumping 50 gallons an hour, 24 hours a day pushing the water 100 yards, and lifting it over 60 feet. In 22 years, that pump had lifted one and a half million gallons of spring water, yet our modern science will say that the hydraulic ram is both noisy and inefficient. But show me a modern pump which will do that work at no cost. What a thrill it was to see water running up that steep hill, when for so many years we had hauled it on a stone boat. In 1962 this outfit again froze up so we went modern and are now paying Calgary Power plenty to run a pump to do the identical work we once had done for free! This is progress.

Having reached the point in time when one is eligible to receive "treaty money", it is odd and a little disturbing when we look back and find "us kids" are now the old timers. Some say those were the good old days, but I don't see anyone suffering too much right now.

Now to my friends and neighbours, I would like to say:

"The world has been a better place, because you have passed this way

And o'er the hill the sun is slowly sinking
While day by day our time does shorter grow
We stop aghast and start a thinking
When trees and fields are buried deep with snow
All too soon we will be leaving
With our work but partly done
Missing you we will be grieving
But OH! we had a lot of fun."

Bill and Ellen Patterson

by Ellen

I was born on Christmas night in 1913, with my grandmother as mid-wife, the first child of Frank and Minerva Standish on Dad's homestead (N.W.¼ 12-22-3). When my dad went overseas in World War I, Mother, and by now three children, went to live in Victoria near Dad's folks. On my dad's return, he bought out his brother Clarke, and we then lived on S.W. 12-22-3. This was my home until in 1933, I married Bill Patterson, eldest son of Frank and Edith Patterson of the Red Deer Lake District.

It was a four-mile ride to school. We attended regularly, as we grew older, through good and bad weather, and on several occasions Dad met us with more clothing though we were already well bundled

L-R, Back row: May Standish, Corene Wilderman, Ellen Standish, Miss Finlayson (Teacher), Edna Standish, Rosie Jensen, Betty Wilderman in front. 1930.

up, chatting along with our cousins. Little did we realize we were out in blizzard conditions. I completed grade ten at Fordville, going during these years a few weeks to Priddis and Westoe Schools. I then completed a secretarial course at Calgary Commercial School.

Raised on a farm, I was no stranger to milking cows, driving a threshing team, haying, and all the other things farm life meant. Ice in the tea kettle on the stove in the mornings, wood stoves and ashes, coal oil lamps to clean and trim and fill, and ours being a hospitable home, lots of baking and meals to help with. Our parents were strict, but fair, and our home was full of children from Calgary all summer, and was a haven for the many bachelors and others. So we had house parties, went to dances bundled up in blankets, and hot bricks were in the sleigh. No car, for Dad's one experience with one lasted only a few months. Christmas concerts were highlights, and in the summer, ball games. Fordville had a strong school ball team, and with sometimes only sixteen pupils, big and little played ball, but few times were beaten by other schools. Sunday, three of us played for the Priddis Girls' Team, playing many teams from Calgary.

Christmas was always a very special time at our home, but Easter was too, with many guests, eggs cooked in every way imaginable and a rule was that you had to eat as many as you were years old — quite a feat for some of the older guests.

Bill was born in Calgary and attended Ballyhamage School, among the first students of that school. Growing up, he was quite a rodeo fan, and once won the Boys' Calf Riding at Calgary. He was an outrider for Harry Brogden's Chuckwagon for many years. Wilf Carter often rode and sang from this wagon in Stampede parades and street breakfasts in the 1930's.

After completing grade 8, Bill then worked out for farmers, mostly Mr. Gilbert of the Sparrow Ranch. When we were married, he put up hay, then traded the hay for logs to build our home. He worked one winter at Larratts Sawmill to get lumber to complete it, then worked for money to buy a few shingles and windows. We moved into our own home in February, 1935 on S.W. 4-22-W5, until then having lived with his folks. Our six children were born while we lived at this farm. Annette, Yvonne, Donna, Gail, Frank and Lorna (she passed away, age 3 months, and is buried at Millarville). During those depression years, Bill sawed wood and ground grain (a converted Reo motor being used for power), for neighbours — lucky indeed if he cleared $5.00 a month, but we had our own eggs, milk and vegetables. If luck held, we could get bread for 5¢ a loaf and beef sausages at Eaton's for 5¢ a pound; also, make believe coffee at 17¢ a pound, that is, if one could get to Calgary to get them. So, we got by, and most all around us were in a similar position. We had house parties, dances at the schools, and didn't gripe about our poor luck. It did hurt selling cows at a cent a pound, paying freight out of that. Our cattle brand was

SW4 — right hip. Bill next got a breaking plow and did custom ploughing. In 1940 he started working with Joe Houck for MD of Stockland, office at Millarville. In 1941 Mr. Houck quit and Bill was road foreman till he quit in 1957, while the districts changed to MD of Turner Valley, office in Turner Valley, and finally MD of Foothills, office in High River, where it is today.

In 1947, there being no school buses, and children having ridden over four miles to school, and some now needing higher grades than Ballyhamage offered, we left the farm, moving to Black Diamond. In 1957, Bill left the MD and started driving a school bus in Black Diamond, and had his own taxi business — "Bill's Taxi". In 1964, we moved to Taylor, B.C. to farm, and in June, 1976 sold the farm, retiring to Fort St. John, B.C., where we are active in Church and Senior Citizens' affairs, have many friends and lead a busy life.

In Centennial Year 1967, Ellen was the Southern Alberta Pioneers and Their Descendents, Pioneer Daughter. She was also a director of the Priddis and Millarville Agricultural Society from 1935 till she left the district in 1964.

Annette completed grade eleven at Turner Valley High School, then took two years dressmaking at S.A.I.T. She now teaches twice a week at N.A.I.T. in her chosen line. She married Mike Kusal of Edmonton, an electrician. They have two children — Deborah, an operator for Alberta Telephones, and Ivan, attending high school.

Bill and Ellen Patterson.

Yvonne completed grade ten at Turner Valley High School. She married Bob Nichols of Black Diamond. He was in the Air Force for ten years so travelled from Sept Isles, Montreal, awhile in Resolute Bay, Calgary and Whitehorse. They later both drove school buses in Black Diamond, but moved to Taylor, B.C. in 1968 where Bob drives a school bus, and runs an Auction Service. They have three children; Lorna, a hairdresser in Saskatchewan — married with two children; Andy works for Peace Woods at Taylor; Lisa goes to school there.

Donna completed grade twelve in Turner Valley High School. She worked as a Nurses Aid in Turner Valley Hospital. She is now married to Dan Goodison of Black Diamond. He has heavy equipment and works for Home Oil. Their three children, Shayne, Janet and Kim attend school in Black Diamond.

Gail completed grade eleven at Turner Valley High School, was a telephone operator in Calgary, married Charles Fairbairn of Calgary. He was in the trailer business in Calgary, Fort St. John, Edmonton, and now, manager of Vanguard Trailers at Richmond, B.C. Gail is an assistant manager of a department of Sears there. Their two children, Wesley and Karen are attending high school.

Frank completed grade twelve at Turner Valley High School, attended Mount Royal for a term, one year at University of Calgary, then two years drafting course at S.A.I.T., winning several scholarships. He then worked for various machine and oil companies in his trade. Now, in December, 1977, he has moved to Taylor, B.C., to take over Maintenance Supervisor at the oil refinery there. He married Karen Sillers, secretary to the Royal Bank in Calgary. They have two pre-school age children, Shannon and Gerrard.

Peake

by Hugh Peake

In November of 1921 I left home in the Dorothy district to help Miles Clark trail a bunch of horses to Morley where his brother, Alf had a small ranch. I had my own pony, a little bay mare. I stayed at the Clarks for about a week as the weather was very cold. I left there early one morning to ride to my Grandfather's and Uncle's ranch, Sam and Johnny Kierans, which was located about 8 or 10 miles south west of Midnapore. It was about 40 miles and it began to get late, and I wasn't too sure how much further it was to the ranch. I saw a ranch nearby, so I rode in for directions. It was Billy Jackson Sr.'s place. They put me up for the night and treated me so good. Mr. Jackson and my father, Arthur Peake had been good neighbors when Dad lived in that part of the country. The next morning the Jackson boys rode with me to Kierans — I believe George and John. I stayed with my Uncle and Grandfather until the end of June, 1922, at which time I returned home.

I attended Ballyhamage school and never missed a school day. I had plenty of chores to do at the ranch as they were race horse people. I believe they had about 20 head in the barns, including the work horses, milk cows etc. Some of the families attending the school were Jamesons, Pattersons, Cufflings, Canes and Fendells. I may have forgotten some.

I joined the Boy Scouts at Fordville and belonged to the Chickadee patrol. I used to ride to Midnapore for the mail occasionally. Neighbors who used to come to visit were the Elliots, Parkers, Jim Boyer, Charlie Keen and I guess many others whose names I don't remember. I used to climb a high butte north of the buildings at night to view the lights of the city of Calgary. I also attended the Millarville Races and I think won some stilt races. I married Claudia Galarneau of Gem in 1934, and we sometimes went up to the Millarville Races in later years.

Marie Peake

I was born in Calgary, July 26, 1911, daughter of Thomas and Ann Rimmer. I had four sisters and one brother, all younger. We lived at the "Big Rock", 6½ miles west of Okotoks. I started my education at Big Rock School, and finished at Sacred Heart Convent and St. Mary's in Calgary. The city didn't appeal to me so I returned home to help on the farm. I liked the outdoors and animals, especially horses. Always had a good saddle pony and loved to ride, so often made a few dollars trailing horses or cattle for neighbors.

In 1930, I took a mare up to Mr. J. R. Kieran's place at Millarville. That was the first time I had ever been there and thought it was the most beautiful spot I had ever seen. It was well after lunch when I arrived, but Mrs. Kieran (Mikie) gave me something to eat, while

Tom Peake Ranch, Dorothy, Alberta.

457

Mr. Kieran looked after the horses, both making me feel very welcome. We lived about 15 miles as the crow flies from there, but I visited them as often as I could, so they became Uncle Johnny and Aunt Mikie to me. I used to enjoy listening to Mr. E. J. Kieran, or "Boss" as he was known to friends and neighbors. He told some interesting stories of Ireland, thoroughbred horses and their pedigrees. I remember a neighbor coming to see the Boss one time and after being welcomed, was asked several questions, to which this chap replied, "I don't know, Boss". Finally the Boss became annoyed and said, "G.D. it man, don't you know anything?", to which he replied, "I don't really know, Boss".

About this time I had a bay, part thoroughbred, mare that I broke and later raced at Millarville. Sorrels have always been my favorite color in horses. So, when I saw Stratford Rock, a sorrel thoroughbred standing at Uncle Johnny's, thought, now I might get a sorrel colt from my mare. But as luck would have it, I got another bay filly. For the first time, I attended the Millarville Races in 1930. After that, I seldom missed, and believe I would have quit a job if I couldn't have that day off. I usually rode in the Ladies Race at Millarville, and in 1936 I rode for T. Stewart of Nanton, on a mare named Miss Claxton, winning my first cup. Didn't win again till long after I had married. In 1947, I won on a mare called Dewy, owned by Ed Stead of High River, and received a very nice trophy.

The year 1939, I married D. L. Patterson of Nova Scotia. A daughter, Mary Lynne, and a son, Gordon were born of this marriage. My husband joined the armed forces in 1940, and went overseas in 1943. War changes the lives of many and it did mine. We separated, each going our own way. I raised the children on my own, with help from my family when needed. Mr. Tom Farrel gave me a job in 1947, cooking at one of the Burns ranches, the O.H. I was there for 3 years, then in 1950 went to work for Claude Gallinger, who owned the 2 Dot ranch at Nanton, and managed by George Cumming. I have happy memories of the 2 Dot, as my children grew up there. After living there for nearly 10 years, the ranch was sold. The family was well grown up, and pretty well on their own by then. I took a trip out to the Coast to see Uncle Johnny and Aunt Mikie. I had a nice visit but thought Victoria was too damp, not enough sunshine for me. So, I returned to Alberta, took some short time jobs, and when out of work made my home with my sister, Mildred and brother-in-law, Gerald Gough (both now deceased).

In 1961, Mary Lynne married Ted Gobert and have a daughter Shannon, and son Robert. Gordon married Jackie Wien in 1965, and they have 2 daughters, Holly and Jodi.

1962, and back to ranch life again. In June of that year, I went to cook at the Bar C, north west of Cochrane. A very pretty spot, but only a summer job, from June till December, so I tried to get a year round

Marie Peake on Skeeter 1974.

job. In the spring of '63, I went to cook at the famous McIntyre ranch which is quite a spread. I stayed two or three months and soon decided I preferred my summer job at the Bar C, where I could still have my own horse, and was close to my family. So, I returned to my summer job which I had till August, 1966 when the ranch was sold.

In 1967, I went to help Mabel, Mrs. Lawrence while she was taking care of her mother, Mrs. Peake. I had met them several times, when I had been staying at Uncle Johnny's, Mrs. Peake's brother. While here at Mabel's, I met Tom again. Then, in 1971 we were married and live in the old home where Tom was born. We have around 100 head of cattle and a few horses. I still ride and thoroughly enjoy it, also help Tom outdoors when I can. If the cattle prices hold, or maybe even rise, we should be able to smile when we gather to ship in the fall.

We usually have a good garden, can really grow tomatoes in this dry climate. I do love growing flowers, and get a real pleasure out of my glads, sweet peas and stocks. All in all, we are quite happy on the sage brush flats.

Tom Peake

Cattle Brand — ⋁ R.R.
Horse Brand — ⥉ L.H.

To start my story, I was born in February, 1912 on the ranch where I am today. I have worked out, frozen out and burnt out, but am still here, and never got too far away from the Red Deer River.

My father passed away in 1947, and Mother in 1970. I married Marie Patterson in 1971 whom I met at Kierans in 1935, and we are as happy as two hound pups. I was seven before I started school, and the

Tom Peake's Dad's carvings on wall at Flying U Ranch 1976.

Tom Peake on Little Buck 1971.

school was 2½ miles from home. It was a small school, 14 x 20, and only ran in summer months. So, it was decided for me to go to the Millarville district and stay with my Uncle Johnny Kierans and boss E. J. Kierans (Grandfather), and attend Ballyhamage School. I didn't know my Uncle or Grandad at that time, but I knew the teacher, Lucy Morton which was quite a help. I landed there in the fall of 1927, and stayed till some time after July 1, 1928. They were batching then, but the grub was good and they treated me good, so no complaints. I broke four horses for them during my stay.

I must mention coming home for Christmas. They put me on the CNR train at Calgary, destination Rosedale, 25 miles from home. At that time they were building a new railway from Rosedale to Rosemary, which ran down the Red Deer River right by our place. I arrived in Rosedale Christmas Eve and was to ask at the hotel if Foley Bros. Construction had any men there going down the river, as they were hauling supplies regularly from that town, but that day there wasn't anyone. I met an old friend of father and mother's, George Bremner, an uncle of Eben Bremner, who ran chuckwagons at Calgary. He had a black percheron team and sleigh in town, and asked me to come and stay the night with him and he would take me home Christmas day. That meant a drive of 12 miles on the river ice with a shod team, as he lived on the river flat near East Coulee. They were sure glad to see us. They were making arrangements to send out a search party to look for me. There was no town of East Coulee at that time, not till the fall of 1928.

The spring of '29, I went to work for Billy Whitney and rep for him on one of the last government horse roundups. Anybody who had horses on the open range

and didn't have a man on the roundup, these horses were considered strays. They had to pay $3.00 per head to redeem them. The roundup lasted about 6 weeks, and we had 130 strays. They were advertised for 30 days and very few were claimed. Jim Tanton, better known as Fishie (or Fish), and I had the job of looking after the stray herd. We rode herd on them every day and corraled them in a small field at night. They were sold by auction at Brooks for the government. I bought one of the horses, branded 32 on the hip, for $4.50 (an Indian pony), broke him and sold him to Sam Johnson for $45.00 at Calgary when he was driving Gene Geottler's chuckwagon.

The fall of '29, I went to work for Jack Ogilvie, who ran about 300 cattle and some horses. His son, John Ogilvie now lives near Priddis.

In 1931, I broke horses for Billy Campbell. His ranch was on the Red Deer River, near Buffalo. After that job, I broke horses for T. L. Owens. He lived on the river near Jenner. He ran about 500 cattle and horses, also had three separate leases. The one near Buffalo was about 40 miles from the home ranch. I have made quite a few trips riding from home to Calgary, trailing in bucking horses to the Calgary Stampede, and several trips to Kierans after horses. I still do some riding, and when it comes June, I will limber up my roping arm, heeling calves at brandings.

My team has gone to greener pastures — several years ago — so I feed with a 4 x 4 truck. Horses are my weakness. I still have a dozen, but find it easier to look at them, than to break them.

Marlene (Hanson) Pearse

Marlene Hanson, eldest daughter of Harley and Joanna Hanson moved to the Millarville area in 1944.

Don and Marlene Pearse with sons Byron and Barry.

Georgie, Marlene and Seth Peat.

We lived on the Freddy Hodgkins farm and then on Bill Jacksons farm while I attended the Sheep Creek School (old location) for approximately 4 years. We then bought the old Calderwood farm at Kew and I attended Plainview School for 3 years. For my high school I went away to Three Hills to a boarding school and then 3 years for College in Calgary. After my second year of college, I married Don Pearse of Calgary. We have two sons Byron and Barry.

I have worked as a secretary most of my life and Don is a social worker. During our early married life we lived in Calgary, in the Lac La Biche area, Peace River area and then back to Calgary.

For our family the farm has alwa' been a real source of pleasure and especially fc our sons who loved to be on the farm as much as possible in the summers.

Byron now lives in Calgary and is a carpenter and Barry is a plumber, recently married Juanita Forsyth of Calgary and are planning on making their home in Turner Valley.

Seth Peat

by Marnie Berridge

Seth was born August 17, 1900, at Sheffield, England. His wife Georgie, was born August 19, 1904, at Westhope, North Dakota.

I never saw my Grandfather Peat, he died before I was born. His widow survived him by 27 years (died August 26, 1966) and even though she moved from the district in 1956, she was well remembered for her strength of character and sense of humor.

Mary Peat was confined to a wheel chair for more than three decades — if such a term can be used to describe the plight of this enigmatic woman. She was fascinating to me as a child, scuttling around in the course of a day's work and I marvel now that she was

able to completely manage her household from such an awkward position. Even the prospect of navigating the narrow ramp built onto the veranda did not daunt her, although I can well recall the unladylike sounds that rent the air when occasionally she misjudged her descent.

As the eldest surviving son, my father took over responsibility for the management of the farm when James Peat died. It was worked by the three brothers until after the second World War, and shortly after his return from service duty, Les sold out to Edwin and moved his family to the Okotoks area. By this time, Dad, a well-known bachelor in the community, had married Georgetta (Georgie) Millar, from Blackie, on June 9th, 1943. The following year, Nov. 10th, 1944, I was born.

The farm was more or less divided between the two remaining brothers, but, unfortunately, they did not always see eye to eye. It was finally agreed that the best solution was for one person to run the place and in 1956, my father bought out Ed and took over on his own. Dad later decided to sell out completely and in 1958, the property went to Keith Enterprises of Calgary. We moved "down the hill" onto a small bit of

Jack Schick and Seth Peat in Nora's Coffee Shop in Turner Valley.

land owned by Billy Jackson and it was here that my parents lived for the next twenty-one years.

My early school days were spent in the two room Sheep Creek School under the supervision of Mr. and Mrs. David Clark. In 1950, the larger facilities at Millarville were opened and in later years, high school students were bused to Turner Valley. Mr. Clark was succeeded by William Dube and his good-natured elder son was often the butt of our silly pranks. It was not unusual to find Billy hanging from the coat hooks by his belt or all trussed up in the bag used for softball equipment. Sports were an integral part of the school term and whether it was organized games such as hockey or volleyball or the spur of the moments snowball fights, nearly everyone participated. Lunch time also meant a short walk to the store for extra treats and if you were lucky, you were able to eat them throughout the film that often was shown before classes resumed.

Mr. Dube was an excellent teacher and it was largely due to his coaching that I achieved an Honors Diploma in the grade nine exams and shared the Governor-General's Award with Maureen Forster of Black Diamond. He was also Commanding Officer of the Oilfields Cadet Corps and as he supported females in the ranks, Elaine Matheson, Peggy Haney and myself had the benefit of many of their activities.

I started working in July 1962 for the Toronto-Dominion Bank and stayed with them for some thirteen years, both in Calgary and Vancouver. Wanderlust eventually became a reality and in February, 1975, I sailed for New Zealand. I worked for the N.Z. Post Office in Auckland and while on a week end holiday to Rotorua, a thermal resort, I met my husband, Tony. We were married on March 19, 1976 and continued living in New Zealand for eighteen months before travelling extensively throughout the Pacific area on our way to Canada. We operated a trucking business in Calgary for about a year and have now opened a service and machine shop in Ogema, a small town in southern Saskatchewan.

In the spring of 1979, my father was persuaded to leave his beloved foothills and he and Mother live in a mobile home on the station property. Their house at Millarville was purchased by family friends, Bert and Mary Normandeau of Calgary.

Sid and Leah Peel
Brand: S-P L.R.

Sid was born in 1903 at Norwich, Norfolk, England. He came to Strasbourg, Saskatchewan in 1922 and worked on a farm west of town, later he rented the same farm. Leah Delves was born in Saskatchewan in 1919. After Sid and Leah were married they continued to live on that farm for awhile. Then in the spring of 1942, due to the drought they decided to move to the coast, where Sid worked for Burrard Shipyards. With the weather being so wet, Sid suffered with asthma and returned east. He stopped at Millarville, where he knew George Fox to be. George was a former neighbor in Saskatchewan and had come out here a few years before to work in the oilfields. Sid got a job in the oilfields too and purchased the Bob Calderwood place, the N ½ of the SW ¼ 20-20-3-5. They moved there November 1st, 1943. Later they bought the south ½ of the same quarter and bought the Bill Adams quarter (SE ¼), also the NE ¼ of the same section.

When they moved to the place in 1943, the road was just a prairie trail. Later the municipality graded the road but did not gravel it. Many times they had to walk home after a rain as the Model A would become stuck. Off would come shoes and socks and they would walk home barefoot. The house they moved into was a big two storey affair. The upstairs was never finished, but they fixed one room and boarded the school teacher for a year or two. Downstairs you could see through the cracks between the boards on the walls. Manys the time Leah had to climb up on the roof in a strong chinook wind to throw salt or water down the chimney to put out the fire. In the winter they never knew who would be sleeping on the couch when they got up. If the

Marlene (Peat) and Tony Berridge on their wedding day in Auckland, New Zealand. –

Peel Family 1944. L. to R. Sid, Art, Leah holding Phyllis. Gordon in front.

Gordon and Art Peel on Flash. 1944.

wind blew the road in, the motorists would just come in and make themselves comfortable until daylight when they could get their vehicle mobile again. At times Sid would have to walk or ride the horse to Home Oil where he worked as the road was blown in. They got the power in August 1955 — a big event! Between 1957 and 1959 a new house was built, a family project. Sid worked with Home Oil from 1947 and 1962 and lived on the farm until his death in 1963.

Their eldest son, Gordon was born in 1938. He joined the airforce in 1955 and was stationed in Ottawa, where he met and married Anne Shone of Windsor, Ontario. They now live in Windsor and have five children, Syd, Nancy, Janet, David and Susan.

L. to R., Back: Janet and Art Peel. Front: Lorna, Jim Cathy.

Art was born in 1942 and took over the farm on his father's death. He married Janet Cameron of Turner Valley and they have three children, Lorna, Cathleen and James. Art was very active in the community, coaching the young boys hockey and baseball teams. He also played on the men's teams until they moved to Bezanson in 1973.

Phyllis was born in 1944 and moved to Calgary in 1962 where she lived and worked until 1967 when she went to work in Lake Louise for a short time. She married Bill Johnston and lived in Black Diamond until they moved to the home place at Millarville in 1973 when Art moved. Phyllis has three children, Edward, Christine and Robert.

Linda was born in 1949 and married Ken Stuart. She now lives in Cranbrook, B.C. and has three children, Trina, Leah and Randy.

Leah owned and operated the Turner Valley Bowling Alley from the spring of 1974 until she remarried in the fall of 1975 to Hank Rishaug of Black Diamond. They are now living in Swan Hills, Alberta, where Hank is employed by Home Oil.

Pekse, Ted, Stella and Elaine

We came to the Millarville district in March, 1949, after buying the Venus farm (formerly the Bartlam place.)

Ted was born and raised in the Lobley district north of Sundre. He farmed in that district before moving to Millarville.

Stella (Boyko) was born in Calgary and got her education in Calgary Practice School, Crescent Heights High and Calgary Normal School. She taught in Loyalist (west of Consort), Lobley, Reed Ranch, (east of Olds) and almost fifteen years in Millarville (Sheep Creek.)

Family gathering at Ted and Stella Pekse's 25th wedding anniversary. Ted and Stella in centre front.

Christopher and Tammy Brewer, children of Elaine (Pekse) and Bob Brewer, grandchildren of Ted and Stella Pekse.

Stella and Ted were married in Calgary in 1940 and continued to farm at Lobley until they moved to Millarville. They have one daughter, Elaine. She was born in Calgary in 1946. She took her schooling at Sheep Creek, Turner Valley, one year at the University of Calgary and two years in Edmonton. She got her degree as Batchelor of Science in Home Economics and has been teaching in Calgary.

In 1967, Elaine married Bob Brewer of the Red Deer Lake district. They have two children, Christopher and Tammy. They are living on an acreage in the Red Deer Lake district.

Stella taught for many years at Sheep Creek School as the primary teacher until illness made her resign. She was secretary-treasurer for the Priddis and Millarville Fair for seven years and is an active member of the Millarville Willing Workers W.I.

Penner, Harper

by Arlene Penner

Alex and Arlene Penner and Wallace and Glenna Harper own the east 40 acres of Section 20-20-3 W5. The land was bought from Art and Janet Peel in the fall of 1973.

Wallace Harper was born in London, England, but moved to Alberta while still a young boy. He taught school in the Medicine Hat-Drumheller area before moving to Calgary in the early 1940's. In Calgary he continued to teach and was appointed principal of two elementary schools — Kingsland and Acadia. In 1973 he retired and has since enjoyed working around his home in Calgary and around the acreage.

Glenna Gagstetter was born in Lacombe, Alberta, and after moving to different locations in the province, settled in the Drumheller Valley. She taught in the Drumheller area, where she met Wallace and was married to him in 1940. After moving to Calgary she continued to teach until the birth of her first daughter, Arlene. Another daughter, Maureen, was born two and a half years later. Glenna resumed teaching part time in 1954 and enjoyed her kindergarten students until her retirement in 1972. Since that time she has enjoyed travelling with Wallace and working around both home and acreage.

Alex Penner was born in Port Arthur, Ontario, but moved to Alberta when less than a year of age. He has spent most of his life in Calgary, attended school and university here and is presently teaching for the Calgary School Board.

Arlene Harper was born in Calgary where she has spent most of her life. She also attended school and university here, taught one year in both Calgary and Strathmore before her marriage to Alex Penner. The couple left for Australia for approximately a year of work and travel. Andrew was born in 1970 in South Australia, but travelled back to Calgary when only 2½ months old. The family has lived in Calgary since their return. A daughter Andrea, was born in 1972 and Arlene has been teaching part time for the Calgary Public School Board since the fall of that year.

Alex Penner first travelled to the Millarville-Kew district when only two years of age. It was then that he first met Curly Sand, and over the years a close friendship grew between the Penners and Curly. It was through Curly that Alex met many people living in the district, including Art and Janet Peel. Alex hunted and visited in the area for many years before he had an opportunity to purchase the acreage from Peels when they sold most of their land to move to Bezanson, Alberta.

The Penners and Harpers have been building a small house in the treed section of their acreage, to be used as a cabin at present and possibly as a permanent home for the Penners in the future. This has been a time consuming venture, since the house plans were drawn up by Arlene and Glenna, and Alex and Wallace, plus many great friends, have been doing all the building on their own.

Much time has been spent on the acreage and in the area by the Penners and Harpers and many new friends have been made.

Richard Perrott

The S.E.¼ of section 20-20-4W5 was purchased from Elizabeth von Rummel by Richard Perrott, fourth son of Elsie and Wilfred Perrott of Stavely, Alberta. There were five children in the Perrott family, one daughter and four sons.

Richard lived on his parents farm west of Stavely until completing high school then attended college in

463

Calgary. He worked for the City of Calgary Electric Light Department for seven years before accepting employment with the Alberta Motor Association.

Although he chose a business career he still kept an interest in the agricultural life and enjoys the outdoors. He returned to living in the country in 1972, taking up residence on his property west of Millarville.

Mr. and Mrs. Jim Plummer

Mr. and Mrs. Jim Plummer came from England in 1946, and bought the N.E. ¼, Sec. 35, T. 21, R. 3, W. 5. He worked for the C.P.R. at Ogden Shops, Calgary until his retirement in 1972. They built the first house that was on that land, and it became known as Plummer's Corner. They went back to England after he sold the land.

Everett and Tillie Potter

by Tillie Potter

I was born in the U.S.A. and Everett was born at Ohaton, Alberta. We were married in Camrose, Alberta, in 1930. We lived in that district for eleven years. Our children were all born there, Harvey, Sheila, James and Larry.

In 1941, we moved to Longview where Everett got a job with Major Oil Company, later called Western Petroleum. Most of the work was at the north end of the field, so in the spring of 1942 we moved our house two miles west of Millarville and rented a lot from Seth Peat. We lived there for nineteen years. Everett

Sheila and Bill Downey's Wedding reception. L. to R. Standing: Everett Potter, Jim Potter, Tillie Potter, Harvey Potter, Glenis Downey, Larry Potter, Hugh Downey. Seated, L. to R.: Nellie Downey (bridesmaid), Sheila and Bill, Bob Downey (best man).

was a battery operator. The Oil Company unitized the field in 1960, the Home Oil Company took over and the Western Petroleum men were laid off.

We then bought a house in Black Diamond where we still live. After moving here we worked for the School Division at the High School for twelve years.

Harvey married Peggy Demarce, they live in Pincher Creek where Harvey works for Shell Oil Co.

Sheila married Bill Downey. They live near Bluffton on their ranch. Bill has a trucking business.

Jim lives at home, drives truck for O R Contractors.

Larry married Arline Carter. They live in Drumheller, where Larry is a guard at the Correctional Institute. We have thirteen grandchildren. Our grandson, Danny Downey, lost his life while operating a grader for Foothills M.D. in 1976, at the young age of twenty years.

William Barry and Judi Marilyn Powell

Block 4, S.W.¼, Sec. 31, T.21, R.2, W.5

Originally from Saskatchewan, we moved to the Millarville District in August, 1972. We have 4 children — Kevin, Michael, Wendy and Christopher. Bill is an engineer, now owning his own company with a partner, and Judi a graduate nurse. We are immensely enjoying the beautiful countryside and friendly people of the district. Bill is active in school and sports activities — coaching hockey and baseball. Judi is active in community affairs and has also taught kindergarten since 1973. Most kids will remember Judi as the school chauffeur!

Isobel Poykko (Jackson)

Born 1904 on the homestead N.W.¼, Sec. 30, T. 21, R. 2, W.5, the daughter of William and Mary Jackson.

I went to school at Fordville, and later went to Business School in Calgary.

Everyone helped on the farm, and needless to say, I had many experiences. While milking, the cow kicked me over and I landed in a cow pad (manure) — that ended my milking. While stacking hay, not being too experienced, the stack was built on a slope. When we went out the next day, it had fallen over.

Mother sent my sister and me to borrow some Cayenne Pepper from a neighbor. Being curious, we ate some to see what it tasted like, and we drank water for hours after.

I later went to the United States, and after a few years resided in Vancouver, B.C. We are now living in California, where the apple orchards are very beautiful in the spring, and there are many more flowering shrubs and trees.

Eveline (Backs) Prestie

I was born in Olds, Jan. 12, 1938. We moved to the Millarville area in 1943.

Eveline Backs 6th birthday party. L. to R. Bob Backs, Darlene Mowatt, Phyllis Backs, Myrna Mowatt, Lorraine Severens, Loretta Young. Eveline in front holding her birthday cake.

We first lived in Majorville. One of my earliest memories of the area is walking from there 2½ miles to Sheep Creek School sometimes arriving there about recess time because I'd spent too much time picking wild flowers along the way. In 1945 we moved to Millarville where I had to walk 2½ miles in the opposite direction to school. Shortly after this bussing became prominent.

It was here when I was 9 that Dad bought us our first horse; however, I was 11 when my dreams really came true and Dad bought me a horse of my own. Nearly all of my activities in those years revolved around horses and riding. Due to the generosity of the R. H. King family many of the neighbourhood boys and girls were able to enjoy riding.

Most of the mothers didn't drive and there weren't

Eveline (Backs) and Vic Prestie with Gregg, Darryl and Tracy.

second cars in those days so if we wanted to go anywhere we either rode bikes, horses or walked. A special treat in school was going for a hike. A favorite being to the old swinging bridge and to the Carlton King place which we called the haunted house.

I took my grade 10 at Mount Royal College where my friend Anne Glaister and I were roommates in the dormitory. For Grade 10 and 11 I went to Innisfail and stayed with my Aunt and Uncle.

My first job was in the main branch of the Royal Bank in Calgary, at which time I lived for a while with the R. H. King Family and then moved to an apartment with 3 other girls.

In 1959 I married Clayton Bruce and lived in the DeWinton area for about 3 years where my two sons Greg and Darryl were born in 1960 and 1962 respectively. We then moved to Millarville where Tracey was born in 1964.

My second marriage took place in 1974 to Vic Prestie. As horses had been a major interest in both our lives it has been very fulfilling to both of us to establish a thoroughbred breeding farm. This has been a family venture with Greg, Darryl and Tracey taking an active part.

At present we are standing 3 stallions as well as boarding outside horses. Also it is interesting to note that the 3 mares Dad ran are still in our brood mare band. This year we have two fillies at the track which Vic is training himself. This takes a lot of effort and cooperation from each of us but it's a life we all enjoy.

Preston, Edger and Isabel
by Joe Preston

Edger Preston, known to everyone as Ed, was born in Spalding, Lincolnshire, the son of a watch maker. One of six sons and two daughters, he spent his boyhood there. At age sixteen he wanted very much to go to sea as an uncle, a sea captain, had done. His parents insisted that he go as an officer trainee but he stuck out for going as an ordinary seaman. They wouldn't hear of it so he shipped out to Canada in 1904.

He stayed in Quebec for a year working as a cook in a lumber camp. Then in 1905 with the few dollars that he had in his pockets, he came to Edmonton, Alberta. He worked for his brother, Percy, cutting logs and building school houses.

In 1907, he came to the Shepard district and worked for Pat Burns as a cow-puncher and later going to work for Mr. Bannister, who was known to his friends and associates as Foggy. He tells the story about when Mr. Bannister bought his first automobile, he drove it up to the back door, pulled hard on the steering wheel and yelled "Whoa" so loud he could probably be heard down at the Recardo Ranch, which was 2 miles up the Bow River. Needless to say he climbed the back steps before stopping. After this he had his garage built with doors on both ends so he could go right on through if he failed to stop.

Dad then moved to the town of Shepard and worked

Ed Preston Family. Back, L. to R.: John Edgar (Joe) and George Preston. Front, L. to R.: Edgar Preston, Helena (Preston) Sorenson, Mrs. Isabel Preston.

for several farmers in the district, one was Mr. Jacob Busslinger.

In 1909, Isabel Bone, his future wife, came from the smallest county in England, namely Rutland. Her father was a farmer but she never expected to come to such a rough and ready place as Alberta was in those days. She worked at different jobs until she came to Shepard in 1915 and they were married that year. They returned to Mr. Bannister to work for him, where they had their first child, George Alfred, in 1916.

He then rented the Hawks place, but after trying to farm on a shoestring, became fed up and moved to Shepard. There he went into the horse ranch business with Mr. Mooney, the store keeper, looking after a band of horses on shares. This deal went sour, so they moved to Calgary where another son, John Edgar, was born.

Ed then took a job with City Coal Co., unloading coal from railroad cars. At times he drove their truck, hauling coal. This truck had hard rubber tires and

50th Wedding Anniversary of Mr. and Mrs. Ed. Preston.

chain driven axels and was called Cole. After a time he decided he had swallowed enough coal dust to last him for the rest of his life.

In about 1920, he got a job at A. B. Cushing Mills and bought his first house at 1812-9th St. N.W. At this house, a daughter, Helena Marion, was born to Isabel and Ed. He stayed at Cushings and worked in a number of capacities from truck driver, to fireman, to yard foreman until 1939, when he was supposed to have retired, only to buy a farm at Millarville and work very hard for fifteen years or so. They moved into a shack on the Don Mortimer place until they could build a house.

In 1942, after rejection by the armed services for poor hearing, son John (Joe) came to work for him on the farm, the N.½ section of 31-20-2W5.

Ed farmed at Millarville until his death in 1970, at the age of 81. Isabel, who had stuck with him through good years and bad, died in 1972, at the age of 85.

Their daughter, Helen, married Walter Sorenson and is living in Edmonton. They have a son, Preston and a daughter, Susanne, both married. Preston lives in Calgary and Susanne in Lethbridge as Mrs. Bill Martin.

Their son George, a retired S.A.I.T. instructor, has two boys, Ted and George, both married and teaching school in Calgary.

In 1968, their son John (Joe) married Helen (nee Cannon) the widow of the late Francis Sinclair-Smith, and they live on Ed's farm at Millarville.

In tribute to my parents, I say no one ever had better ones. They never made it big or made a big show but when the chips were down, always came through smiling. If everyone had as fine a folk, the world could look to a bright future ahead.

Gordon Prichard and Family 7↓ L.H.

Gordon Allaison Prichard, the youngest of four children of Samuel and Harriet Prichard was born in October, 1923, at Camrose, Alberta. He lived his early years at the farm his father purchased in 1905. He attended Willowhill and Camrose schools and completed his education at Camrose Lutheran College.

During the three years he attended college, he worked after school and Saturdays at Mr. Brimsmead's Jewelry Store.

There were dry years at Camrose, so the family looked at land near Calgary. They finally settled on buying the old Chris Standish farm in 1941. There were springs with lots of water for their cattle. They sold their farm at Camrose in 1946, at which time Gordon had finished his schooling and moved with his family to their land near Priddis.

Sam, Bill and Gordon worked very hard breaking and clearing the land together. They kept adding land to their holdings, buying the Knowles quarter and one section of the old Burns' land, where Gordon's buildings are now situated, N.W. 1-22-3-W/5. Their holdings eventually became 1100 acres.

The Prichard family and friends at Doug and Kate's wedding.

Gordon and Rachelle Prichard with youngest son Greg, 1974.

By now, Sam Prichard had changed over to Herefords as they seemed to be more popular at this time, although he had a great love for the Angus breed and had top show cattle from 1917 to 1932. Gordon and Bill also had a small herd of Herefords of their own.

Mr. and Mrs. Sam Prichard had a home in the city of Calgary, where Mrs. Prichard spent most of her time in her last years. Sam had such a love for the country life that he wanted to spend most of the meaningful working time on the farm working with Bill and Gordon.

Gordon married Rachelle (Rae) Stanton, born in 1924 at Duchess, Alberta. She was the fourth child of Mervin and Blanche Stanton. Mervin had migrated with his family from Oregon in 1917.

Blanche Johnson had emigrated with her family from North Dakota in 1903. She was a true pioneer of the Carbon area. Blanche and Mervin settled in the Duchess area and later moved west of Didsbury. Their daughter Rachelle, spent her early childhood in the Duchess area and later moved west of Didsbury. She attended school at Duchess and Olds. She trained and served with the C.W.A.C. and also worked with General Engineering in Toronto. Rachelle studied at the Academy of Arts in Toronto.

Gordon built a small house close to his father's home but moved it later to his land on Highway 22, three miles south of the Priddis turn-off. Gordon built the original part of the big barn which at that time housed around 35 top Holstein milkers. Later the herd increased and addition was built on the barn, and after that there were around fifty cows milked every day. We are sure people always saw the Prichard barn lights burning. We started out with a lighting plant but always had milking machines. We got the Calgary Power in 1951. The Prichards, the Standishes and Winthrops were among the first to get Calgary Power at the north end.

When we first started out, it was coal oil lamps and wood and coal ranges. Over a period of thirty-one years we have changed from wood and coal, to oil, then to propane and finally to Natural Gas.

The highway has changed too. It used to be gravel

467

CALGARY BULL SALE '78

Left to right: Frank Slezina (judge), Greg Prichard, Mary Brown, Cheryl Prichard (Aberdeen Angus Queen), two purchasers from the United States, showman Gordon Prichard.

and very dusty. In the spring one would get bogged down in the mud holes on Highway 22.

Our children were bused to Millarville, Red Deer Lake and Calgary schools. Our children are:

William Wayne (Jerry), born 1946, works for a trucking business operating between Vancouver and Calgary. He married Lynn Rutledge, a secretary, in 1971. They have two sons, Gordon born February 1972 and Daniel born July 1973.

Russ Calvin, born in 1948, works as a Commercial Interior Contractor in Calgary. Married in 1975 to Virginia Dawson, a nurse from Toronto.

Douglas Allan, born in 1951, operates his own manufacturing company called Idea Factory, in Toronto. Married at his parents' farm in July, 1978, to Kate Houston Lambert, a model. They live in Toronto.

Bonnie Lynn, born in 1956. Married Wayne Robberstad in 1974. He has worked for the Salmon Arm newspaper since taking his Advertising Sales Course at Tech in Calgary, in 1974. One son, Tyler Jesse, born March 1977. They now live in the Calgary area.

Cheryl Susan, born in 1962. Had grades 1 and 2 at Millarville, continued to grade 9 at Red Deer Lake School and continuing grade 10 at Kelowna in 1978.

Greg, born 1967, has always attended Red Deer Lake School until moving to Kelowna in 1978.

In 1962 when the older boys became high school age, we moved into Calgary and built a home in the Chinook Park district. The boys attended Henry Wise Wood and Woodman and Bonnie was at Chinook Park Elementary. Later, Doug attended Lord Beaverbrook.

While we were in the city, Gordon worked one year with Gale and Company Real Estate and then with National Trust. After we returned to our farm at Priddis in 1964, Gordon continued in real estate for several years at the same time as having the dairy business with the help of the boys. The boys were able to drive their own cars by then, so they travelled into Calgary to finish their schooling. They were also very active in football, hockey, wrestling and girling. Bonnie went to Okanagan College to finish her schooling and she also took a business course.

In 1969 we sold our dairy herd and had been building up a herd of Angus cattle. Gordon still had his love for Angus since childhood and from watching his father raise Angus show cattle.

The Angus business has been exciting, prolific and a lot of fun. We have had many guests from around the world who came to view our magnificent bull, "Revolution" and his progeny. His progeny were very popular and marketed throughout Canada, United States, Russia and South America.

A very interesting group of people from New Zealand who toured our ranch, bestowed us with a lifetime membership to the New Zealand Angus Association. We hope some day to travel there and visit with them again.

A crowning achievement was the Grand Champion Bull at the 1978 Calgary Spring Show. Cheryl, our daughter being the Southern Alberta Angus Queen, presented her father with the Banner and ribbons for his achievements.

The bulk of our land is now owned by Crest View Ranches, but we still retain our homestead. We have taken up a second residence in Kelowna, B.C. as of August, 1978.

Cheryl now attends K.S.S. High School and Greg attends Bankhead Elementary. They are both active in sports, such as skiing at Big White and Greg plays hockey as well as playing in the school band. Cheryl sings in the school choir. They both attend church and Sunday school.

The climate is milder in Kelowna but we still love our Alberta home. The beauty of Millarville and Priddis areas, and the rolling foothills could never be surpassed.

Samuel Prichard

by Muriel Bevington, Doris Forester

Samuel Charles Allinson Prichard was born on his father's estate called Noyadd, Llangorse, Breconshire, Wales on April 18, 1883. As a young boy he had a very interesting life. In 1888 he sailed from Liverpool with his family to Chile, South America, where he remained five and one half years during a revolution. In 1893, it was sailing again, around the Straits of Magellan, and after many months arriving in Hereford, England. In 1894, his father was lured by the noted Restigouche River because of the salmon fishing. So it was sailing again. This time it was Halifax, Canada in 1894. Twelve hundred acres of land were purchased near Campbellton, N.B. There was a lake and to this day it is known as Prichard's Lake. The town of Campbellton bought the property recently for a water supply. A large park is being constructed there. Between 1894 and 1905, Dad was busy cutting cordwood and acting as a guide for sportsmen who came from the Eastern States. He was an excellent fisherman and hunter. He won trophies for marksmanship.

Another pioneer area beckoned. This time it was western Canada. He worked helping to survey the Wetaskiwin-Hardisty main line. He had a homestead on Iron Creek near Sedgewick, but gave it up in favor of land four miles from Ohaton, and at that time about eight or nine miles from the present city of Camrose. He was joined by his brother William. The two

Samuel Prichard and wife Harriet (Van Petten) taken in 1946.

brothers lived in a small shack and started clearing land. Water was a problem, and when a well was drilled many years later it was 275 feet deep. Power was supplied by the wind or a gas engine which worked spasmodically.

Many tales can be told of those early days. There was the terrible winter of 1907 when the snow was so deep. There were the prairie fires, a constant threat. There was the triple gang plow pulled by seven horses, all of which had to be fed and harnessed.

In 1909, Dad built a frame house and in April of that year he married Harriet Marie Van Petten, a true pioneer of the district. Her family came from Kansas in September, 1900. They had a post office and small store, called Skafse. Supplies were freighted in from Wetaskiwin by horse and wagon. The first year was

Will Van Petten and sister Harriet riding side saddle 1904.

rather frightening with fear of an Indian uprising. The water supply consisted of melted snow and slough water. After some schooling in a little log school called New Salem, Mother went to Edmonton. She was able to get a bookkeeping course at McTavish. Before marriage she worked in Wetaskiwin and at Johnsons Job Press in Camrose. Daughters Muriel and Doris were born at the farm in 1910 and 1912. Two sons followed, William, born in 1914 and Gordon, born in 1923.

In 1913, Dad decided to go into the dairy business, so he went to P.E.I. and hand picked twenty-seven milk cows. The cows arrived in December, and for several years it was hard work milking by hand and separating the milk to get the cream which was taken to Camrose by horse and buggy once a week. In 1917, Dad's first car was purchased. It was a Willys Overland with two seats and two little fold out seats.

About 1916 Dad became interested in Purebred Aberdeen Angus cattle. He began showing at the exhibitions, and Muriel won the Boys and Girls Class at the Spring and Fall Shows in Edmonton and Calgary in 1921.

Every summer, Dad showed Angus at exhibitions and fairs in Alberta and Saskatchewan.

Drought and hail were common in the Camrose area. There was a heavy snowfall in 1919-20. Feed was hard to get, and very expensive. Herefords seemed to sell better in Calgary, so for awhile Dad had both Angus and Herefords.

Depression struck, and in 1930 Dad and Mother tried to find land around Calgary. Finally in 1941, they found a place near Calgary and there was a spring with a good supply of water for the cattle. They moved to the Chris Standish place in 1942 — E½, Sec. 12, T. 22, R. 3, W.5.

In 1949, Dad cut and hauled logs which were trimmed to 6 x 9 inches. These were constructed into a house by building the same as a log house. The outside was stuccoed and the inside had wallboard. Unfortunately, the original log house built by the Standish's had to be moved, and later was demolished. Dad and Mother continued to spend their time in Calgary and at the farm.

During his lifetime, Dad was a member of the Aberdeen Angus and Hereford Cattle Breeders Association, a school trustee, a charter member of the Alberta Wheat Pool, director and president of the Camrose Fair Board. Mother was always interested in gardening. She was a member of the Calgary Horticultural Society. She was a member of the Red Cross and Women's Institute. She loved to travel and was able to visit her sister back in Kansas.

Mother died in 1957 and Dad in 1960. They were truly pioneers of western Canada.

William Stewart Prichard Family
by Ruth Prichard

William, known as Bill, was the oldest son of Sam and Harriet Prichard. Having purchased the Chris Standish land, S.E. ¼ 12-22-3-W5, in 1941, Bill moved from Camrose, Alberta, in December 1941 and attended the cattle until spring when the family arrived. Finding not much to do his first winter, he spent many hours getting to know his neighbours and having only a horse for transportation, he found many of his neighbours very friendly.

Bill farmed with his father and brother, improving the land by brushing and breaking, and also looking after their herd of purebred Herefords.

When his mother became ill and moved to Calgary, Bill found batching was not for him. He met the sister of one of his neighbours, Tom Day. Ruth lived with her parents and son, Gordon, North of Calgary, near the airport. After many months of driving to see Ruth, he asked her to marry him. They were married in July, 1951. Bill always said the car knew how to get to Ruth's place, after he headed north of Calgary.

Bill and Ruth took up residence on the farm. In the fall, Gordon at the age of eight, had to ride to Fordville School. Gordon's pony was very stubborn, and many a morning Gordon would have to dismount and lead her over a length of road where he could mount and continue to school.

When Fordville was amalgamated into the Millarville School District, his first bus driver was Mr. Barraclough and then, Gordon Blanchard.

Gordon continued schooling at Millarville and finished High School at Turner Valley. He was also a member of the Millarville 4-H Club.

In February 1963, Gordon joined the Air Forces, which he made his career. He was stationed at Winnipeg, Man., Summerside, P.E.I., Greenwood, N.S., Ottawa, Ont., and Comox, B.C. While stationed in Winnipeg, he met Augusta Pica, whom he married. They have one son, Robert. They reside at Comox, B.C.

Bill and Ruth left the district to take over his uncle's farm at Camrose in 1963. They sold their farm to Mr. Arnold of Calgary.

They have seven children. The older three girls, Doris, Kathleen (Kathy) and Wilma, took from grade 1 to 6 at Millarville.

Doris finished her high school in Camrose, going on to 2 years of University at Camrose Luthern College, then 2 years at University of Alberta where she got her Bachelor of Art Degree. She married Bruce Lockhart of Cold Lake, Alberta, in 1975. They reside at Fort McMurray, Alberta.

Kathleen (Kathy), their second daughter finished her schooling in Camrose. She married Bernard Markwart of Lougheed, Alberta. They have two daughters, Angela and Rosemary. They reside at Provost, Alberta.

Wilma finished her schooling at Camrose. She married Richard Davison of Sedgewick. They have two children, Shaune and Yolanda. They reside at Grande Cache, Alberta.

Jim wasn't quite old enough to go to Millarville, as he was to start the year we moved, but had an accident which hospitalized him for many months. He received all his schooling in Camrose and is now attending the University of Saskatchewan.

Barbara, Kenneth and Laura are still at home. Ken and Laura are in high school. Barbara has been working.

All children were in Camrose 4-H Beef Club, except Laura. Bill still raises Purebred Polled Herefords.

Purmal Place

S.E.¼ 26-21-3-W/5
by Freda Purmal

C. $\overline{WP}_{LR.}$
H. $\overline{WP}_{L.s.}$

Originally Hudson's Bay land. Probably leased to Charlie Hartell for cattle pasture, then purchased by Edwin Winthrop and later owned by his son, Robert Winthrop. S. I. Freda Purmal purchased the property in the early spring of 1971.

I was born in Calgary, December 1908, the eldest of six daughters of E. R. (Jake) and Annie Wilson Fullerton. The family moved to ranch at Bragg Creek in 1912. I attended grade school there and to St. Mary's High School and the old Commercial High School in Calgary.

For several years I worked for Jenkins' Groceteria and was in the grocery business in Vancouver, ladies' ready-to-wear in Victoria, service station attendant in Toronto and worked many years as an A.G.T. telephone operator and PBX operator.

While in Vancouver, in 1933 I married Wilfred G. (Bunny) Purmal, son of a pioneer Medicine Hat family. We had no children.

My family had long time associations with several Millarville families, the Staggs, Fishers and Wards, to name a few. In the 1920s we again became in close contact with numerous families of this community

Freda Purmal and "Prince". Ready for the parade in pioneers' section. July, 1971.

through local stampedes, boxing tournaments and dances.

During the mid 1940s my husband was discharged from the army and obtained employment with the Calmont Oil Co. While drilling in the Millarville area the employees were permitted to live on the Calmont lease; the land owned by Elwyn Evans. The camp was at the base of the east side of what was known as the Home Oil Hill. We lived there for several years until the company ceased operations.

Following several years of oilfield work throughout the country, we eventually settled in the Red Deer Lake area where we farmed for 15 years. Shortly after my husband's death in 1968 I had no desire to remain there and longed for a home in this district for which I had such great affection since childhood.

In the early summer of 1971, I had a water well drilled, proceeded with the house construction and had some old garages moved in for storage sheds. I hired the McFarland Dixon family from Eden Valley to build some fences before moving my Angus cattle here.

Rain, snow and cold weather set in early that fall and it was miserable weather when I moved into the wet cement basement on October 31st. I camped in the basement for four weeks before the upstairs was finished.

It was during this frustrating period of moving that I was asked to write the Bragg Creek history for the book "Our Foothills." I found this an impossible task to do alone so Joan (Burby) Merryfield joined me in sharing this project.

There has been little time for me to be involved in local activities owing to my farm work and previous commitments as an active member of the Southern Alberta Pioneers Association.

My principal interests are nature and wildlife, music and art. Books on local histories, ancient civilizations, astrology and archeology are my favourite reading material.

I count my blessings for the privilege of having wonderful neighbors and helpful friends. My only regret is that this location is devoid of evergreen trees and a mountain view. I can plant the trees but like Mohammed, the mountains will not come to me either.

To quote Lord Byron — "I love not man the less, but nature more."

*   *   *

The Purmal-Fullerton histories are recorded in the books "Our Foothills" and "Chaps and Chinooks."

On the Lighter Side of Life
by F.P.

LIQUOR AND LONGEVITY
The horse and mule live 30 years
And nothing know of wines and beers.
The goat and sheep at 20 die
And never taste of Scotch and rye.

The cow drinks water by the ton
And at 18 is mostly done.
The dog at 15 cashes in
Without the aid of rum and gin.
The cat in milk and water soaks
And then in 12 short years it croaks.
The modest, sober, bone-dry hen
Lays eggs for nogs, then dies at ten.
All animals are strictly dry:
They sinless live and swiftly die;
But sinful, ginful rum-soaked men
Survive for three score years and ten.
And some of them, a very few,
Stay pickled till they're 92.

—Author unknown

Raymond M. Quigley

Ray was born and raised at Carstairs, Alberta. He came to Priddis in 1940 and settled on the Doc Lee place (34-21-4w5). The next year he married Ella Given, youngest daughter of Kirk and Matilda Given. Shortly after their son Brian was born in 1943, they moved to the Ballyhamage district (S½ 22-21-2W5.) Their herd of cattle carried the N7-LR brand.

Ray played second base on the Millarville softball team. He worked at the Oil Ventures Ltd. oil well near the old Sheep Creek School. Their daughter Reta was born in 1946.

They later moved to what is now known as the Kingsland district of Calgary and hayed what is now Bel-Aire.

Quigley Family. Back, Ray and Ella. Front, Reta and Brian.

After living in Okotoks for a short time, they settled in the Forest Lawn district. Ray started working for the C.P.R. at Ogden Shops as a sheet metal worker in 1951 and retired in 1978 after 27 years of service.

Brian is the owner of Quigley Electric in Okotoks. He married Jean Gillard and they have two sons, Hugh and Scott.

Reta is a R.N. at Lethbridge Municipal Hospital. She married Bruce Berte. They have a son Randy and a daughter Taralyn.

Ella passed away in 1968. Ray married Winnifred Goss in 1970 and they are now living in the Palliser district of Calgary.

Westley and Joan Rabey

by Joan Rabey
RSW

Our families originally came from England, while both of us were born in Saskatchewan. Wes's family moved back to Ontario when he was very young and settled in Manilla, where his father owned a garage and service station.

Wes attended school in Manilla and the University of Toronto. After graduation he joined a seismic crew and has been in the oil exploration business ever since. He claims the shortest time he spent in any city was in Saskatoon, where Joan captivated him.

I was born and raised in Saskatoon and worked at the public library while completing university. We were married in 1946, coming to Calgary where we lived for twelve years before moving to England. After five years we returned to Calgary and have been there ever since.

We have three children, Noel, Karen and Warren. Noel and his wife Kay have a six month old son Owen. Karen makes her home at the ranch. Warren attends the University of Calgary.

We had often thought of owning land and in 1973 Karen made this her summer project. We bought the SE¼ 5-22-4-W5M in the Square Butte area and named it Medallion Ranch. Karen moved here in 1975 and settled in comfortably with a great deal of help from our neighbors, such as pulling cars out of ditches and tracking down errant horses.

We all enjoy our time spent out here but as I write this May 6, 1979, we have 4" of snow on the ground.

W. V. Ransom and Family

by Jody Ball

Bill Ransom moved to Millarville from Calgary in 1967 with his four children, Debi age 17, Jody age 15, Marty age 9, and Greg age 6. We lived on an acreage (ptn SE 17-21-4-W5th) in a log house built by the Mickle family in 1960.

Since we had previously been city dwellers and had absolutely no knowledge of the country way of life, we experienced a few memorable events. For example — awakening in —40 degrees F weather to find ourselves

Bill Ransom and daughter Jody, on her wedding day.

out of propane and freezing, learning that the five pound rug couldn't go through the wringer washer like it did in the automatic washer in town, and that when a faulty oven knob on a gas stove breaks — not only do the sparks fly but the whole thing bursts into flames (and singed my eyebrows and lashes in the process). Despite these minor difficulties our family grew to love the country and found it to be a valuable part of our lives.

L. to R. Marty, Debbie and Greg Ransom.

Later, we were joined by Rilla and John Wills who helped to run the household, as our father (a consulting engineer) travelled extensively and was away for several weeks at a time.

Debi married Jim Crowell in 1974 and is now residing in Edmonton, where she is employed as a registered nurse.

I married David Ball in 1974. We were gifted with two girls, Shanna Marie on May 29, 1976, and Deanne Michelle on April 13, 1978. We are presently ranching in the Square Butte area on SE 22-21-4-W5th.

Marty and Greg are living with our father in Calgary. Marty is enjoying her work in a veterinary clinic and Greg will be graduating from high school in 1980.

The Ron Rarick Family

The Rarick family consist of Ron, Margaret and their children, Ron Jr. Lesa, Susan and Billy.

Ron and Margaret moved to Millarville in 1972. They bought their place from Harley Hanson.

The Raricks raised a great variety of animals, Shetlands, Arabian horses, Charolais cows, sheep and chickens and ducks.

Ron has coached hockey for the past seven years.

Ron works in Calgary for Johnston Testers. Margaret teaches grade four at Black Diamond Elementary.

Harry Rawlinson

Harry Rawlinson, son of Mr. and Mrs. E. H. C. (Ted) Rawlinson was born in Millarville, November 13, 1923 and attended Sheep Creek School up until 1939. Also attended North Turner Valley High School in 1939 to 1941.

He joined the R.C.A.F. in 1941 to 1946 and trained for the air crew in Edmonton, Calgary and Lethbridge. His service theatres included first the West Coast (Bella Bella) then on to England, North Africa, Tunisia and many areas of the far east. In 1946 he was honorably discharged with the rank of Captain. In 1947 he joined the R.C.A.F. '418' reserve until 1958.

He worked for General Petroleum Co. from 1946 to 1948. In 1947 he married Betty Radke, a pretty nurse from Bashaw. They make their home in Edmonton and have three children, Chris, 19, Hugh, 17, and Elizabeth 15.

Harry worked for the Provincial Government from 1948 to 1956, then started his own business and had a service station up until 1975. He is presently employed with Alberta Government Telephones.

Edward Hugh Rawlinson
by Audrey Parker

Hugh was born at Millarville July 12, 1928. He attended Sheep Creek School, and after leaving school, worked on the bull gang for an oil company, digging ditches.

He joined R.C.N. at Naden, Victoria, then served on H.M.C.S. Ontario, and Charlottetown. After his discharge he returned to Millarville and started working for Haliburton Oil Well Service Company of Black Diamond. Later he went to Leduc and was a toolpusher for Pennant drilling Company.

He married the former Doreen Dinon of Calmar in June 1948. They had two children, Lynda and Brent.

Hugh was killed in an oil field accident in November, 1953, just outside Drumheller. They were closing in a well for Hudson's Bay Gas and Oil Co.

His daughter Lynda is married to Robert Assaly, a lawyer from Edmonton. They have two girls and a boy.

Son Brent has a sound equipment business in Calgary.

George Reid

The George Reid family moved to the old Roedler place in 1959 when it was purchased by Sedco Drilling Company and known as Sedco Ranch.

Our eldest daughter Isobel was already working and was only able to come home weekends. Elizabeth attended Sheep Creek School 1959-60. Our youngest daughter, Georgette was born while we lived there and because father wasn't home mother was driven to the General Hospital in Calgary by kind neighbors.

In 1961 we moved to the old Walter Birney place in the Red Deer Lake District. Both Isobel and Elizabeth were married from there. Elizabeth married Gordon Purcell on July 25, 1964 in the United Church at Red Deer Lake and Isobel married Jack Seewalt August 21 of the following year.

Betty and George Reid. April 22, 1979.

In 1966 George, Georgette and I moved to Midnapore where we still live. George is looking forward to retirement from his job as Cardiovascular Technician at the General Hospital in the next couple of years.

Isobel and Jack have a daughter Lisa and are in the hotel business. If you are ever passing through Vermilion, Alberta stop at the Brunswick Hotel and say hello.

Elizabeth has been working for the Department of Indian & Northern Affairs, Indian Minerals Division since 1969. In October of 1977 Elizabeth lost her husband in a car accident. She is presently residing in Calgary.

Georgette is in her last year of school and will graduate from Lord Beaverbrook High School this June.

Michael Lee Reid and Frances Anne (Padwick) Reid

4R Left Hip

Michael was born Feb. 13, 1942, in Baltimore, Maryland. The only son of Mrs. and Mr. Paul D. Reid, he was raised in a horse racing family, in a horse racing community called My Lady's Manor. He attended high school at Valley Forge Military Academy, served four years in the U.S. Marine Corps and later attended the University of Baltimore. After holding several jobs as a professional horseman, he joined the News American Newspaper where he covered crime, politics, government and court stories. In 1973 he was assigned as war correspondent to the Israel October War.

Anne, who prefers to use her middle name, was born in March, 1949, in Regina, Sask. The eldest daughter of Mr. and Mrs. Herbert W. Padwick, she attended Marion High School and excelled in ice skating and horsemanship. Her desire to skate was soon surpassed by her love for riding; and she went on to train under Robin Hahn of the Canadian Olympic Equestrian Team. In 1969 she moved to My Lady's Manor in Maryland where she continued her training under Hugh Wiley, a former member of the U.S. Olympic Equestrian Team.

It was in 1970, while Anne was riding with Wiley, that she and Michael met. They were married in August, 1970 and continued to live in Maryland. After a two week vacation to Calgary in 1973, Mike and Anne decided this was where they wanted to live. But, it was not an easy decision. Mike's career as a journalist was growing and Anne had completely involved herself in the Maryland horse world.

The arrival of two children, Jonathan Stuart and Samantha Fox added to their doubts of leaving a secure way of life and pioneering into a totally unknown country and careers.

Yet, the massive population of the East coast, the spread of surburban developments and the busy-body lifestyle of their community soon helped them make the decision to move in 1975.

On Dec. 14, 1975, Mike and Anne crossed the border in an old IH Loadstar truck after four days of rain, sleet and snowstorms. The border guards were very amused at the sight. Behind the truck was attached their Pinto, completely covered with ice and snow. The back doors could not be opened without much of their jammed packed belongings falling onto the only "unguarded border in the world". The cab was littered with old sandwiches, coffee cups and coke cans suspiciously smelling of rye.

After spending six months in Calgary with Anne's parents, who had moved to Alberta two years before, they purchased a quarter section from Glen Green of Millarville. The property, located three miles north of Millarville, is legally described as SE ¼, 27-21-3 W5.

Since moving onto the ranch, which was dubbed Belmar Ranch the Reids and Padwicks have concentrated on developing a registered Aberdeen Black Angus herd.

Arthur Reimer

Born in Calgary October 15th, 1936, Art lived his early life near Millarville, then in 1942 moving with his parents and sisters to the S.½-4-22-4W5, near Whiskey Creek.

He started school by going to Fordville while he lived with his grandparents, Mr. and Mrs. J. Barraclough, taking grade one there. Then he went to Purdy's, where Mrs. Purdy taught school. The Jim Davis family live there now.

Arthur and Irene (Brunt) Reimer. June 1976.

After his dad bought a Jeep to bus the children of the area to school, he attended Square Butte School. Mrs. Kosling was his teacher for several years and he learned to play the piano from her. Art admits adding several grey hairs to Mrs. Kosling's head.

From Square Butte, Art went to Sheep Creek School, where he met his future wife, Irene Brunt. After completing grade eleven, he went to work for Bert Haney, helping build houses for a short time, then to the Municipal District of Foothills, where he worked as a cat operator for six years.

On May 4th, 1957, Art and I were married and lived in a small house in Turner Valley until he was offered the foreman's job for the South End, of the Municipal District in 1960. He was foreman for the M.D. for eleven years, in which time he bought a house for his family in Okotoks near the water tower. In the summer the family lived in a trailer on the job sites and during the winter returned to their home.

In 1971, Art left the M.D. to built a resort at Blind Bay, B.C. on the Shuswap Lake with his partner, W. Edwards, which they sold early in 1973.

Our five children were born in Alberta. Darlene (1958) in Calgary, now lives in Salmon Arm, B.C. Howard (1959) in Calgary. Susan (1963) born in High River, Sandra (1964) born in High River, Sherri (1967) born in High River, live at home with their parents at Blind Bay.

Art now has his own industrial equipment, for digging basements, building roads, and general dirt work. He employs two men and says he just can't get away from dirt.

Barbara Reimer

I was born in Upper Hillhurst North West Calgary, on November 28th, 1912, to Johnny and Emily Barraclough. When I was three, my parents moved to a farm southeast of the Calgary Airport. At that time it was not an airport. I started school at seven years old in the Rocky View School. I went to school here for two years, until we moved again, to Springbank. We rented the John Penman Ranch, which is now Happy Valley, for five years. I went to Upper Hillhurst School in Calgary for four and a half years. All these years we had dairy cows and lots of work to do.

In 1928 we moved once more, to the W. H. Cochrane Ranch at Millarville. I quit school and worked for Dad, milking cows and doing field work of every kind. I also helped break horses to harness. After the first day I had to work them alone. I did a lot of riding, some of it getting the cows home to milk. I had a few horses buck me off.

There was lots of work to keep me busy; I have cut and skidded logs and piled lumber. I have done just about every job there is to do on a ranch. My older sister was killed at this ranch. My family moved again, to the Mrs. Elsie Billings Ranch, which is four miles south of Priddis. I was there three years and the family moved again, a little further west to the

Barbara Reimer getting snow for water at Bill Jackson's shack. 1941.

Kenneth Ball Ranch. I was still milking cows and getting soaked bringing them in with the rain coming out of my boot tops. Life had its ups and downs, but a lot of fun along the way.

In 1935 I met Jake Reimer and we were married on April 20th, 1936. We lived in any old shack we could get. One was the John Schaal place, then on to Vivian Shaws, about a mile south of there. We had a son, Arthur, on October 15th 1936. We then moved to the Anchor Down Ranch and worked for Mr. Ovans. Here, we had a girl, Bernice, on May 11th, 1938. Bernice was born in the back seat of the car that was taking me to Calgary. In 1939, Edith was born on November 18th, at home on the Anchor Down Ranch. Mrs. Dewer owned it at that time, but lived in England. Now the ranch is owned by Sedco Ranches. We took our little family into Billy Jackson's old homestead cabin a short way west. The oil wells were around here then and we had some work with them for a short time.

Barbara and Jake Reimer out for a ride on Dick and Joe.

Then we got land further west, the south half of section 4-22-4W5. Here we had a son, Robert, on July 4th 1946. We made this our home. We raised the kids in a lot of hard times, spuds and bread and for a change bread and spuds.

As times got better, we got a Jeep and used it for a school bus. Later we got a thirty-six passenger bus. I drove this bus when Jake would go hunting. With the bus and ranch we had a nice living for a lot of years. My husband passed away on November 27, 1970. We had a quarter section across the road from the home place. This I sold to Art and Fred Ball after I was left alone. Art Ball is now the owner. My four children now have the land. I live on it and it will be my home for as long as I live. My roots are down about two feet and no one can pull them up. I have a few cows and my horses that I just love. I love to ride and take the team and sleigh or the wagon in the summer, and anyone that wishes to come for a ride any time. I love this kind of pleasure, and sometimes Agnes Ball goes for a ride on horseback with me.

Robert and Jeannette Reimer
by Barbara Reimer

I was born July 4th, 1946 and named Gordon Robert Reimer. My parents were Jake and Barbara Reimer. I went to Millarville school in my Dad's school bus. I played a little hockey and had my high school at Black Diamond. I got my Grade 12 diploma. I worked for the M.D. of Foothills for two summer holidays and after finishing school, I worked for two years for the M.D. and in the winter months when there was no work, I trained on a fixed-wing for a short time; and then on to helicopters. I lived at home all these years, on the Southwest half of section four, township twenty-two, range four, west of the fifth. My work took me into the far north country.

I met Jeannette Howard and her three children: Brian, Sherry, and John, and we were married on October 2nd, 1971. I adopted the children and we lived in Calgary for one year. We then moved out to the eighty acres we got from Mother — W½ 4-22-4-W5th. In May 1973 a baby girl was born, Nancy Lynn.

In August that year I went for a plane ride with a fellow that was going from Eureka Island to a place about one hundred and fifty miles away. We crashed on a mountain side. We were not hurt, but the plane was a mess. I have seen a lot of the far north and it is nice in the summer, but in winter it is a bad place to be. In June, 1978, we bought a piece of land at Shuswap Lake and had a house built there. We sold twenty acres of land with the house on it and moved out to the place in B.C. The new owners of the twenty acres are Mike and Lynnette Brunner and their two girls, Heidi and Michelle. I am still flying helicopters, but for a Vancouver company, and I work mostly in B.C.

Mr. J. Austin Richards and Mrs. Gladys Richards

Pt. S.E. 27-20-4-W5th (68 acres)

In 1958, after a long search for suitable property, Mr. W. Roy Graves and I purchased 68 acres of the N.E. 27-20-4-W5th. from Mr. and Mrs. Joe Fisher, well known and long time residents in the Millarville area. In the fall of that year I had Mr. Albert Wentz of Turner Valley build an 800 square feet cottage and in 1959 Mr. Graves had a cottage moved in from one of the oil well leases in the area. Some years later I purchased Mr. Graves' interest in the property.

My wife is Gladys, only child of James and Lily Whalley of Calgary who came to Canada from Lancashire, England. I am the only child of John and Ethel Richards who lived in Edmonton and came from Cornwall, England. We are native Albertans. I was born in Edmonton and Gladys in Calgary.

We have three sons, Stephen James, John Austin and Donald Whalley, born in 1942, 1944 and 1949.

While the boys were young we spent many happy holidays and weekends in the country. Donald bought a horse and Gladys a palomino mare in foal, which we raised. When the boys were older and left home we gave the horses to neighbours.

The property is a rough triangle fronting on the road leading to the forest reserve and across from property owned by Thomas MacMillan. Three Point Creek is the eastern boundary and the monument to John Ware is on the other side of the creek. We attended the dedication by Grant McEwan, then Lieutenant Governor of the Province and an outstanding historian of Alberta.

Our lowest altitude is 4200 feet along the creek. The altitude, with late and early frosts, even in July, has restricted gardening although we find some root crops, if they escape the gophers, and lettuce and spinach, if they escape the deer, do quite well.

Other than for the garden and a lawn around our cottage the property has been left in its natural state, with three meadows, hills, and the spruce and poplar trees. We do have electricity and natural gas.

Directly south is John Ware Ridge rising to 4700 feet and giving a climber a wonderful view of the foothills and mountains to the west and the farms and ranches to the East.

My lifetime career has been banking. I joined the Bank of Montreal, Main Branch, Edmonton, in 1929 when Mr. Frank Pike was Manager. I retired in May, 1976, as Manager of the Fifth Street West Branch in Calgary. In the interim I served at Westlock, Hythe, Lacombe, Alliance, Forestburg, Calgary, New York, and spent three years on the Inspection Staff travelling over the four Western Provinces and four years as Special Representative when my duties entailed travelling in Texas, Louisiana, Oklahoma, Colorado and Montana to call on our correspondent banks and customers in those States.

Gladys was a secretary in the Main Branch, Calgary. We met in 1939 and were married in April, 1940.

Our activities in the district have been mainly with the Turner Valley Golf and Country Club where we have been members since 1973. I have served as Vice-President and President of the Club.

We have kept our Calgary home at 1047 Kerfoot Cr. S.W. using the country property for weekends, holidays, a retreat, golfing, cross country skiing and as an alternative residence for entertaining friends who welcome a visit to the foothills. Our son Donald is in Calgary now and has the use of the second cottage for summer weekends with his family. Our son Jim is in Edmonton where he has his business, Edmonton Paper Salvage Co. Ltd. and he and his family have used the property for holidays and look forward to a visit there when they come to Calgary. Our son John is an artist at Powell River, B.C. and has used the location for his paintings of southern Alberta.

We all enjoy the solitude, the peace and the beauty of the foothills. Deer and moose are frequent visitors to our salt blocks and occasionally we have a coyote, a bob-cat and porcupines. When we first went there we never saw Canada Jays or Ravens but now they are established in the area. As a bird watcher I have spent many happy hours and still have hopes of sighting an eagle.

My future plans are that the property will continue in the family with the hope that my sons and their sons for generations will enjoy the hours in the Foothills as I have.

John and Margaret Richardson

S.E.¼ S-23 T-21 R4 W5

Seven children:

    Veronica born on January 15/54
    Katherine born on April 7/55
    Shane born on June 23/56
    Christine born on Sept. 19/59
    Michael born on June 8/61
    Howard born on March 31/63
    Charlotte born on Sept. 9/68
    Mother, Margaret born Vancouver, March 12/36
    Father, John born Peace River, June 19/33

Our family has enjoyed this country since the late 1950's when we moved to Calgary from our wanderings in the oil patch with Sun Oil. We made week-end picnics on Three Point Creek and Sheep Creek a weekly habit. In the mid 60's, we were fortunate to meet and become good friends with Ivor and Elaine Lyster, located on the NW¼ S13 T21 R4 W5. which is now Rick and Connie Brown's abode. During our early acquaintance with the Lysters, we made frequent trips to the Forget-Me-Not and Mount Rose area via horse back. We camped under the beauty of a western sky and had many unforgettable good times. As most everyone in this country knows, Ivor had an irresistible urge to chase and rope wild horses, which he was the best at.

On several occasions I had the pleasure of accompanying him on such trips in the late winter when the snow was deep. The wild horses suffering from slow metabolism due to lack of bread, were not quite so frisky and were easier to catch. (Not that easy, Ivor named me "Fragile John" when on occasion I had bones repaired by the doctor.)

The turning point in our lives came one day in 1970 when Ivor mentioned a move he was making to help Michael Rodgers run his spread. Ivor subsequently moved four miles south to Paddy Rodgers' home place. He in turn, offered us his place to rent. In June of that year, we rented out our home in Calgary and moved to Ivor's.

After living at Ivor and Elaine's for two years, Elaine introduced us to the Millarville Racing and Agricultural Society. We subsequently accepted the post of Secretary Treasurer of that Historical Society. This new venture entailed a move to the Agricultural complex. Fortunately, just prior to our move, we purchased our present land location from our good friend and neighbor, Alex Lyall. After a rather hectic but informative four years at the track and many good times with horsemen, cattlemen, sheepmen, and chicken men, bless their hearts, we embarked on the task of building our present home in 1975.

We moved in on December 22 of that year. During construction, fond memories prevail of our Truss raising party at which 20 of our trusted carpenter neighbors attended (Peter Fisher and family included).

At this writing our family is growing rapidly and leaving home seeking new horizons for themselves. Our eldest, Veronica, is happily married with a son, Kim, to Tim Hampton and lives six miles south of our home. Kathy is in Calgary with her own Drafting and Design Business. Christine is in Jasper enjoying a guiding job at the Jasper Park Lodge. Shane is on the move as an operator on a seismic crew (taking lots of pictures), leaving Michael, Howard and Charlotte at home.

Our family enjoys the outdoors with its many rewards. We are very fortunate to have children who enjoy coming home to partake of these rewards, and who also derive much pleasure from each others' company. Our place is called Forget-Me-Not, after Forget-Me-Not Mt. which played such an enjoyable part in our early years in the high country.

The sweetest thing a man can hear
When water runs and spring is near
Must surely be two happy birds
Giving thanks with song instead of words
Through long dark nights, they've survived the cold
To cheer up your day with greetings untold
So give thanks to our friends who make morning a
 treat
And insure their good health with a morsel to eat.
                                              J. R.

Don. M. Ricks

The Don M. Ricks family moved into the district in 1971. They bought the old DePalizeux homestead (NE-25-20-3W5) and worked for several years (unsuccessfully) at restoring the original house before building a log home on the site. Like the previous residents of the place, they had a lot of privacy; only four-wheel drives and snowmobiles could negotiate their road for much of the year. Caryl was a weaver whose raw wool horse blankets and wall hangings became popular items. Because of her interest in fibers, the Ricks built up a small herd of llamas. As Don said, "If we're going to lose money raising livestock, we might as well do it with something more interesting than cows." Shortly after coming to the district, Don resigned his position at the University of Calgary to found a consulting business that conducted letter and report writing courses for business and government. All the Ricks were kept busy by events at the Race Track and other community activities, and their main winter pastime seemed to be driving kids to hockey games. Their four children — Beth, Jim, Cody, and Kate — all attended Millarville School.

Memories of "The Foothills"
by Jessy E. Riis (nee Patterson)

Stories in "Our Foothills" relate many things. My story will refer to a few nostalgic memories. For those younger ones, now living in the district, I hope they may be interested and somewhat amused. It may be a little difficult for some to realize that Grandmother's tales are really true.

I lived with my parents, Mr. and Mrs. Frank Patterson, on the farmstead where my brother, Arthur, and family live today. Things were vastly different

Ballyhamage School about 1926; Back row, L. to R.: Arthur Patterson, Larry Jameson, Sandy McNab. Sitting: Joan Wilkinson, Jack Barlow, Marjorie Barlow, George de Mille, Jessy Patterson, Cecelia Fendall, Sheilagh Jameson, Agnes Cuffling and Jean Barlow.

478

then. Our farm was very secluded in the hills and it literally was at the end of the long winding road that led to it.

Along with my two brothers, Bill and Arthur, we made our own fun. We seldom had other children to play with. What I missed most of all was a sister to share my secrets with.

We spent our days helping our parents with the numerous chores and sometimes having time to explore the woods and the small fields, maybe picking wild flowers, catching gophers, climbing trees or paddling in the creek. One time I remember we were told that if we sprinkled salt on the tails of birds, we could catch them. So we set out with a package of salt. Gullible as we were, we brought home a nest of baby robins. Bill had climbed the tree and carefully removed the nest; I sprinkled the salt on the poor babies. When we proudly displayed our accomplishment to our parents they immediately sent us back to replace the nest in the tree. Feeling very dejected we did so — our parents' wish must be obeyed.

In summer we would ride over the hills with two milk buckets slung over the saddle, to return home with the pails full of saskatoons. Mother would sort them and prepare them, to be exchanged for groceries at Jenkins Groceteria in Calgary.

Dad would make a weekly trip by team and democrat to Calgary, where he did the family shopping, picked up the weekly mail at Midnapore, and performed many similar errands for the neighbors. It was a rare occasion when we "kids" got a chance to go to Calgary with Dad, but it was with great excitement that we would wait in the evening for Dad's return. He always brought a treat — one pound of chocolates, which cost twenty-five cents, and maybe a surprise such as a can of honey or some strawberries, or the newest beverage known as "Iron Brew" — something like Coca-Cola.

The two most outstanding outings we had were the Millarville Races and the Calgary Stampede. The

"Skating Party" on the Cuffling Slough spring of 1922. From l. to r. Jessy Patterson, Arthur Patterson, Agnes Cuffling, Fanny Cuffling, Teddy Cuffling, and Bill Patterson.

whole family went to the Millarville Races on July 1st, and I always remember that was the day we feasted on watermelon. We three children would always go to the Calgary Stampede escorted by our step-sister, Fanny, (who was ten years my senior). We would drive with Dad to Miss Wilkins' place and from there Fanny would take us with team and buggy on to Calgary. We always considered ourselves very privileged, as few other children in the district were able to enjoy this momentous occasion.

One chore I'll never forget is fetching the cows in the evening. My turn to get them usually came about every third day. The cows roamed over two quarters of brushland; mounted on your horse, and faithful dog following, you would search sometimes for an hour or more. The mean old "critters" would deliberately stand very still so their cowbells would not ring, and you could not locate them. Then when you found them, they would purposely dodge in and out of the thick brush trying to evade you.

School days started for Bill and me in a small dwelling on the Mitchell place. (Mitchell's is what is known as the old Macklin place.) Mitchells had several children and as Bill and I were old enough for school and there was no school anywhere near us, Dad and Mr. Mitchell hired a governess to teach us.

A blackboard and a few necessities were acquired and we started our schooling. This lasted but a few months, when it was considered wiser to send us to Alexander School.

I'll never forget the first day we attended this school. After much preparation we were ready to leave early one Monday morning. I remember well, I wore a white calico dress with a bright pink silk sash around my waist, and a wide-brimmed hat my mother had carefully trimmed the night before. Bill had been well instructed by Dad on how to drive, and care for the horse when we arrived at school. Arthur was still considered too young to venture out on this long journey, but I was 6½ and Bill 7½ years old.

Along with our lunch in a lard pail was a small bag of oats for the horse, a slate and pencil — we very proudly set out on a new adventure. We had many gates to open. It was usually my task to open and shut them. We travelled about a mile to Mitchells where we were joined by four of the Mitchell children. Buster Mitchell, the older one, rode horseback along with us. We set out on our merry way, another four miles and no less than ten gates.

Arriving at school the horse would be unhitched and put in the barn and we were ready to start our school day.

At first we had our step-sister Fanny to protect us and settle our little squabbles, but when she left to attend school in Calgary Bill and I adopted a big brother, one by the name of Henry, to protect us. However, there was one little hitch. Henry demanded a bribe in the form of an apple, a bag of oats, or even a pocket knife. Things went well as long as suitable bribes could

"Walking Water" on the Patterson farm about 1928. The teamster is Douglas Haney a little boy visiting from Calgary.

be supplied but when Bill asked Dad for a nickel one morning Dad questioned why the need of a nickel. Bill confessed it was to pay for "protection" and Dad decided enough was enough. He called a meeting with other interested neighbors and soon they made arrangements to establish a new school, Bally-hamage. We rode horseback a distance of three and a half miles to Ballyhamage. With the exception of a short period, we continued here until I graduated from Grade IX in 1926. Then I went to Calgary to finish High School. As many interesting stories will be told of school days at Ballyhamage, I will not dwell on my experiences in this hall of learning.

Finishing Grade XII in 1929 I went to Normal School and graduated in 1930. It seemed that that was the thing to do in those days so I became a teacher. But times got hard about then and teachers were flooding the market so I did not teach the first year, but worked clerking in the Hudson's Bay store in Calgary. I taught school for six years after that. I taught a school near Three Hills, at Square Butte, and at Red Deer Lake. I spent very little time at home on the farm after leaving to attend High School in Calgary. Transportation was not as it is these days.

In 1939 I was married to Chris Riis of Blackfalds. We lived on the farm here until 1947. We had two children, Marilyn and Jack. In 1947 we moved to Leduc where we lived for a year, and in 1948 to the new town of Devon. We were pioneers in this town as we were one of the first six families to move there. Here another son, Roger, was born in 1950. Chris worked in the oil fields. We moved to Edmonton in 1966 — but Chris continued his work at Devon. In 1974 we retired in Lacombe and in August 1977 we moved here to Kelowna, B.C.

Marilyn, our daughter, was married to Grant Fletcher of Taber in 1960. They have three children, Janine 16, Judy 15, and David 12.

Jack is married to Roberta Robson of Vancouver and they have one son, Aaron, 1½ years. They live at Ladner, B.C.

Roger resides in Edmonton.

Square Butte School
by Jessey (Patterson) Riis

I trained as a teacher at Calgary Normal School, graduating in June, 1930. That was the era of the "Dirty Thirties". The year of 1930-1931 found me without a teaching position. There were many more teachers than schools to go around.

In 1931-32 and 1932-33, I taught at a school in the Pine Creek area, some thirty miles north west of Drumheller. This, my first experience, I found satisfying and rewarding.

However, it was not until I taught at Square Butte School in 1933-34 and 1934-35 that I realized the true meaning of friendship and the warmth of rural life.

A teacher never knows how her lessons have been taught or where those lessons have left their mark. It wasn't until I attended the Reunion of Square Butte pupils and teachers that something was awakened in me. Although you may find no trace of the old schoolhouse or the winding road that led you to it, and but a few of the seniors you once knew, you will find something else very inspiring.

Having long since dropped out of the public eye, this occasion gave me a "new old" feeling. As I met my pupils of thirty years past, now mothers, fathers and grandparents, I questioned silently, how I played a part in their lives? The answer was given in a hearty handshake or in the glint in their eye as I talked with them. I now realized I had not toiled in vain. I came away from that Reunion with a good feeling "deep inside me".

I could mention the Bannermans, the Fultons, the Gouys, the Ingevelds, the Koslings and the Silvesters and many, many more. I was always welcome in their homes, to be invited for an evening meal or to stay the night. Those were the days truly hospitable.

It seems strange now to drive to Quirk Creek and see the transformation. No more signs of poverty — a flourishing community rich in oil, with modern homes, good roads and school busses to take the youngsters to up-to-date classrooms.

When one witnesses the very modern, one has cause to reminisce. I think of the Christmas concerts held in the old half-log half-frame schoolhouse. I think of the oil lamps for lighting, and all the inconveniences but despite it all the joyful delight of children and parents alike. I remember the dust, and the drafty cracks and the completely inadequate wood burning stove that was continually much too hot or much too cold.

I think of the three supposedly "bad boys", George, Albert and Bob, and how in my "shaking shoes" I strapped one of them (who was, incidentally taller than I) thus nipping any further trouble "in the bud". From that time on they were "good boys" who always caught my horse and saddled it ready for me to ride home to my boarding place, the Bannermans.

I think of the time it was almost 50 below zero and how I rode horseback through snow well over two feet deep, knowing I must go anyway, although there wouldn't be anyone there. I was wrong. There were five or six brave little souls awaiting my arrival and they had walked through all the snow.

I think too of how elated I used to feel as I was the highest paid teacher in the surrounding area. I received a salary of $840 per year.

There are many pleasant memories I could relate but will not bore you. To all of you good people of Square Butte, may I say it was good to know you. I hope I have contributed in some small way to your history book and thank you for the opportunity.

Rishaug, Fred and Avis F-F ⅃
written by Avis Rishaug

We came to Millarville to live after Fred was discharged from the army in 1945. We were familiar with the district as visitors to my parents, the Leftwich's, who lived at the Calmont Camp at the foot of the Home Hill. This camp consisted of about twelve families, all employed in the oil industry, who lived in skid houses that could be moved where ever their jobs took them.

Fred and I had been in the oilfields for a number of years before the war. I came with my family from the dried out area of Chinook, Alberta, where we had tried for years to make a living on a farm. Fred was born at Gleichen and had come to the Priddis district in 1933, driving the chuckwagon trailing cattle for Henry Samons, and he worked around that area until jobs opened up in the oilfields. He moved to Royalties in 1939 when the oil boom started and fifty cents an hour was high pay. Competition for a days work was keen, as there were lots of people looking for the small pay you received to live on.

While we lived at the Calmont Camp our daughter Linda was born. In 1946 we bought a house and rented a piece of land — later being able to buy it, part of SE section 3, township 21, range 3. Here we have made our home and raised our family. Our son Rick was born in 1951. Linda and Rick attended school at Millarville, belonged to all the various clubs and organizations, and were active in all community activities. Linda married George Bull, and has remained in the com-

Spring Cleaning. L. to R. Linda, Rick, and Fred Rishaug. A pet sheep given to Linda and Rick by Murdoch MacKay.

munity to raise her family of two girls, Bev and Shelley. She continues her active participation in the community.

Rick married Sandra Williams and lives in Turner Valley. He works for Imperial Oil at Quirk Creek, and has two children, Paul and Dawn. Rick and his dad work together raising some cattle and selling livestock handling equipment.

Fred worked on the steam drilling rigs until they drilled the last well, Home 39, which is the farthest north producer in the Turner Valley field. We farmed the Rawlinson flat for a few years, and rented land from Carlton-King for a while. We have always been interested in agriculture and livestock, usually had cattle, and at various times have had horses, sheep, pigs, chickens and all the other animals that children like. We both like to garden, so have always raised a big garden, planted many trees and enjoyed our yard and flower beds.

I can think back on all the wet years when the roads were nearly impassable, the rivers in flood, the early and very late snows, the changing landscape as our old neighbors were replaced.

Fred has worked for Home Oil since 1951 and is now looking forward to his retirement. Our plans include

Old Roanie, aged 34 years, a familiar sight in Rishaug's pasture at Millarville.

Feeding time — Winter 1977. Paul and Dawn Rishaug.

481

staying in Millarville, which has been our home for many years, and we still think it's the best.

Jack and Laura Robbins
by Carol Robbins

Laura A. Barraclough was born December, 1928 on the Cochrane Ranch, Millarville, to John and Emily Barraclough. She was the youngest of seven children. Being very musical, Laura learned to play the piano by ear, at the early age of four. She attended the Fordville School and, as many children of her age, she rode to school on horseback. She still enjoys horses and the sport of pleasure riding.

Andrew John Robbins was born February 23, 1927 to Edwin and Violet Robbins. His family moved from Carmangay to Priddis in 1936. They farmed ½ section S.W. 9-22-3W5 and S.E. 8-22-3W5. Jack took over the farm after his father's death in 1942.

Laura and Jack met in 1944 and were married in 1948. They operated a dairy farm from 1949 until 1965. During the first years of marriage they also cleared and broke most of the home quarter. They drove school bus for 23 years and can remember using a Jeep for a school bus, because the roads of the time called for such a vehicle. They progressed from the Jeep to a car, and then a large High School bus.

They had two sons, Edwin John, born August 2, 1948 and John Andrew, born March 11, 1950. Edwin married Valerie Carol McBean on August 5, 1967 and they have two daughters, Nicole Lee, born June 7, 1972 and Candace Lynne, born August 21, 1973. They live in Calgary.

John married Mary Jeanne Pearson on March 14, 1970. They have a son, John Andrew, born January 2, 1972 and a daughter, Laureen Jeanne, born May 15, 1973. They live in Port Alberni, British Columbia.

Roberts, Art and Rose (nee Jensen)

Art and Rose Roberts (nee Jensen) farmed in the Priddis district in the 1950's and are now farming in the Millarville area on the former Jensen family farm. Their son Ken and daughter Kathy attended Millarville public and later Oilfields High School. Ken is now employed locally and Kathy in Calgary.

Edward R. Roberts and Kathlyn M. Roberts (Luke)

Kaye — born in Winnipeg, educated in Calgary, worked with Trans-Canada Airlines prior to marriage in 1951.

Ed — born and educated in Calgary, flying instructor in World War II, discharged 1945, rank of Flying Officer.

Member of Institute of Chartered Accountants of Alberta.

President Kinsmen Club of Calgary in 1963.

Past member Board of Directors of Victorian Order of Nurses.

Presently member of K 40 Club of Calgary.

Presently member of Board of Directors of Calgary Exhibitions and Stampede.

Members of Glencoe Club.

Plan to build in 1978 on land formerly owned by Bill and Marj Winthrop.

Occupation — Business Manager of Jones, Black & Co., Barristers & Solicitors, Calgary.

Interested in gardening, community affairs, music.

Members of St. Martins Anglican Church.

Family: Brent, Son, University of Calgary student. Craig, Son, Mount Royal College student. Leslie, Daughter, attending Viscount Bennett High School.

Thomas and Mary Roberts

Thomas and Mary Roberts were transferred to Canada from Newton, North Wales, in 1911, when their employers, Pryce-Jones & Co. set up a store in Calgary. Later they joined the Hudson's Bay Co.

Thomas served in the first World War as London paymaster with the 113th Battalion Highlanders until illness overtook him. In 1920, with his allotment from the Soldiers Settlement Board, he and Mary bought part of the old Jonathan Cuffling place. They lived in a tent until Thomas had completed building their house. They farmed, raised livestock and milked cows until 1945, when they sold their land to Nevill Cannon. Moving to Okotoks, they resided with their only daughter and her husband, Gwendolyn and Charles Stagg, until Thomas had completed their new home next door to their daughter.

Gwen remembers his stubborn resistance to any help in erecting this structure — he was determined to drive every nail himself!

Thomas became very proficient with diamond willow and his granddaughters, Dorothy Hogge and Betty Sparrow, retain many of his lamp and plant stands and furniture today. We also recall his painstaking labour over constructing fly-fishing hooks. Thomas died in 1956 at the age of 85 and the house he built was sold to Allan King.

Mary was a wonderful, hardworking person. She often told stories of the Court of Queen Mary, where she apprenticed as a seamstress in her youth. Her handwork was beautiful and well-known through the area. Though she was stone deaf, she loved company and when television came, she watched the sports with avid interest. Mary resided with her daughter, Gwen, until her death in 1970. She was 96 years old.

Mr. and Mrs. John A. Robertson

Jack and Maude Robertson arrived in Millarville about April, 1941, with their adopted teenage daughters, Bonita and Margaret, also son Eugene and wife. The Robertsons Sr. lived near Calmont Camp, more specifically it was at Major 1 well head. Jack was employed as a separator man until his retirement to Calgary in 1953. Following the death of his wife in 1960, he returned to Millarville to live with Bob and

L. to R. Mrs. Robertson, Mrs. Donaldson, Margaret (Robertson) Lochhead.

Margaret Lochhead on the Ford Lochhead Kew Ranch. Three years later he passed away in the Turner Valley Hospital, aged 84 years.

In the 1940's both daughters attended High School at Millarville, walking the distance until finally a truck with a cab on the back picked up students from Home Oil Camp and former Plainview School students. Before the advent of this truck or the school bus which succeeded it, Margaret and Bonita walked a total of six miles when Sheep Creek (now Three Point Creek) was in flood, going around across the bridge and up to Millarville Store, then west to the school site, about 4 miles. Sometimes they took a short cut when the Creek allowed this, by leaving Herb Adams farm, walking through MacKay's land, crossing the creek on a pipe line, holding on to a cable.

Their brother Gene and his wife lived in a small camp near a temporary store on Elwyn Evan's land. Gene remained only a few years, then left to establish a private business (vacation resort) on Vancouver Island, having previously been in a managerial position in Lloydminster and later Dawson Creek. He and his second wife are now retired at Comax, B.C.

Jack and Maude had been active in community work and interested in the progress of the Social Credit Party. By radio, they enjoyed all sports. They attended church in Turner Valley and Black Diamond. Both of them enjoyed warm friendships in Millarville.

Their daughter Margaret married Bob Lochhead of Kew. They were united in marriage April 19, 1964. They now reside in Caroline.

Their daughter Bonita married locally, after a seventeen year absence from Millarville. Following a ten year period with Northern Canada Evangelical Mission in three provinces, she married a widower, Albert Iceton of Turner Valley. His two sons, now married, also live in Turner Valley. Bonita and Albert have a son, Edwin and a daughter Angela, born in 1962, and 1963. Both are attending school.

Robison Howard R̄3

by Rita Robison

Howard came from Gleichen in the spring of 1932 with his parents, Rulon and Gertrude Robison, his

Howard and Rita Robison

brother Lyle and twin sister, Hazel. His oldest brother, Harold, was teaching school at McLennan at the time.

They had purchased the south half of section 7-20-3-W5 from J. F. Dole, land previously owned by Mr. and Mrs. Jim McGregor.

They loaded their belongings on two wagons drawn by four horses. Since most of the roads weren't gravelled and being the spring of the year, it was sometimes necessary to put eight horses on a wagon to get through some of the mud holes. The trip took four days.

Bill and Julie Thomson with their children. Bill holding Sheila, Lori, left, and Vicki.

Howard rode horseback and drove the cattle. He recalls going through Okotoks on a Sunday morning when people were coming out of church. Okotoks had the longest main street he'd ever seen and seemed longer than ever with so many spectators.

Howard took over the ranch after his father's death in 1945. In 1946 he and I, Marguerite (Rita) Billo were married. I came to this area from Crossfield to teach at Plainview School (see Plainview School).

Howard and Rita had a daughter, Julie. She married Bill Thomson and they have three daughters. Lori, Vicki and Sheila. They live east of Black Diamond on the Roy Thomson ranch.

Plainview School Location 29-30-3-W5

by Marguerite (Rita) Robison

I came to teach at Plainview School January 3, 1945. The school had been closed for a time due to a teacher shortage during the war. I was one of quite a number of beginning teachers who were sent out to reopen one of the closed country schools. We had completed our training and practice teaching just before the Christmas holidays after which our duties began.

I was brought out to see my school the day before my job started and then taken to Sid Peel's, one-half mile south of the school, where I boarded the first six months.

We were on daylight saving time then so the first morning I set out for school carrying a lantern to light the way. One of the oldest boys, who lived near the school, had taken on the duties of janitor so he had started the fire when I arrived, but the room was still not very warm except near the stove and it was still dark even when the children began to arrive. The stove was a gas drum with legs on it located in the center of the room and the fuel for it was wood just about the length of the gas drum. I had attended two country schools myself as a child, but they were equipped with coal heaters so the fire could be kept over night and didn't require constant re-fueling.

I decided that first day to start school at ten o'clock until the days lengthened so we wouldn't have to go to school in the dark and wait for daylight to begin classes. Most of the children walked distances of one half mile to over three miles to school. Over the summer, those who lived the farthest acquired ponies so they could ride instead the next term.

I had 18 pupils, seven of which were in grade one. The others were divided up in the rest of the grades.

That winter was exceptionally mild and there was no snow until the Easter Holidays so we didn't have too hard a time keeping warm. We settled down to work and things went along quite smoothly. From Easter on there were a lot of storms and since the roads weren't gravelled we had many muddy walks to and from school.

By the next term the board had moved a teacherage near the school which was to be my home for that year. It was just two small rooms, but was easy to heat with the cook stove it contained and being so near the school was handy. My janitor had left and as the other older children lived too far from school to come early, I started the fire myself. When I first got up, I'd go over and start the fire and while the school was warming up I would go home to have breakfast. Unlike the first winter, this was a cold one. I was supplied with coal for the teacherage, but we still had to burn wood to heat the school. There was a bad storm the middle of November and it was very cold for several days. Only five children showed up so rather than try to heat the school I kept them in the teacherage.

My pupils were very cooperative and would do anything to help me. They brought in fire wood during recess and one of the boys kept me supplied with kindling to start the fire. He also looked after the fire through the day, enabling me to concentrate on my classes without interruption. I'm sure I couldn't have managed as efficiently without their assistance.

By the end of November we were very busy practicing for the Christmas concert which was quite an event for the children. Except for parties at Hallowe'en and Valentine's day it was the only other social function they had. To put on a program with so few to participate, meant that each child had many parts to learn and it was a lot of work for them. Having children of different ages, though, was an advantage as the program could be quite varied. All talents were uncovered and the concert turned out to be very successful.

June 29, 1946 I married Howard Robison and resigned from my position at Plainview. I was replaced by Jim Campbell, a young teacher from Calgary. He just stayed until Christmas so Plainview was again without a teacher. At the parents' request I returned after Christmas for the remainder of the term. There had been one major improvement during my absence. There was now a big coal heater. I have often thought since that if I had asked the school board for it they likely would have supplied it. However, it never occurred to me at the time to ask for anything that wasn't there.

During my time at Plainview I taught the following: Shirley and Merlin Hedley, Lavone and Bruce Adams, Richard, Lorna, Harold and Patsy Kary, Fred and Lucille Dudenhoeffer, Gordon Peel, Verna, Earl and Joy Orum, Frank, Melvin and Ken Adams, Arnold Danforth, Marlene and Donna Hanson, Garry Blanchard, Evelyn Smith, Milton, Jean and Don Sim, Maxine Way and Michael Rogers.

As the children were helpful, so were the parents and I couldn't have managed without their help in getting my mail and provisions as I had no means of transportation. Sid and Leah Peel were especially kind when I boarded with them, letting me use their saddle horse and after I lived in the teacherage, bringing my groceries or taking me to town with them.

Our daughter, Julie, was born in 1948 and in 1954 when she started school, I went back to teaching in

Turner Valley and taught there for 17 years until June 1971.

As they now bussed the children from surrounding areas, the enrollment was large enough that most of the time you taught one grade, or at most some of two grades. It wasn't much less work as I found that you could have just as many levels of learning ability in the one grade as you had grades in the one room school.

Heating or cleaning the school was no longer a problem to the teacher and with water, lights, washrooms in the school, not to mention all the teaching aids available, teaching school was quite different from my first experience.

Nevertheless, of all my years of teaching, the two years at Plainview are the most memorable.

Bob and Lori Rock

by Lori Rock

Bob and Lori Rock resided in the Millarville area for four years. Bob was born and raised in Bornholm, Ontario and came to Alberta in the fall of 1967 to see a prairie harvest. He decided to stay the winter to help his uncle, the late Bert Haney, build the R. Chalmers home. After making it through the winter, Bob decided to call Millarville his home. He worked on the drilling rigs for four years before joining the staff of Millarville Motors where he worked as a mechanic for six years. Bob is now employed by Esso Resources Canada Limited, at the Quirk Creek Gas Plant as a mechanic. Bob's parents, Harold and Florence Rock still reside in Mitchell, Ontario.

On March 10, 1973, Bob married Lori Hyland, eldest daughter of Keith and Monica Hyland, formerly of Turner Valley, now living in Arrowwood, Alberta. Keith, once an active participant in the rodeo circuit, has now retired into the administrative end of the rodeo business. Monica is the daughter of John and Ruby Nobert, long time residents of the Black Diamond area.

Lori was born and raised in Turner Valley and attended school in the Oilfields district. She is now working as the secretary for Esso Resources Canada Limited, Quirk Creek Gas Plant.

When they were first married, Bob and Lori lived on the Chalmers ranch, in the home of the late Mr. and Mrs. B. Chalmers, for about nine months. They then spent a short time in Arrowwood, where Bob discovered he was definitely not cut out to be a farmer. After six months, they returned to Millarville and spent three years in the home owned by R. Backs.

Bob and Lori are now living in Black Diamond, where they have purchased their first home.

James Rodgers

Born in 1893, the eldest son of Mr. and Mrs. James "Dublin" Rodgers of an old Irish family who came out to the Okotoks district in the early nineties. He spent his childhood days in the Okotoks area. He was a graduate of Ridleys College in Ontario.

When war broke out, Mr. Rodgers joined up as a private with the 31st Battalion and was later promoted a non-commissioned officer, following which he was made a Lieutenant. Transferring to the 50th Battalion, he was Commissioned a Captain.

On his return from the front, Mr. Rodgers joined the staff of the Bank of Montreal. He later resigned from the Bank to join the Alberta Provincial Police. He left the Police to take the appointment of Secretary-Treasurer of the Drumheller Municipal Hospital, a position he held until his death.

An outstanding sportsman, he helped to develop baseball, golf, cricket, hockey, tennis and football. He was particularly noted for his interest in hockey. After the war he acted as both Captain and Manager of the local team. Those were the great days of hockey in Okotoks when the local team under Jim's leadership won the Intermediate Championship three times.

He was later a member of the 1928 Drumheller Miners hockey team and later coached the Miners Club.

He was married to Agnes Cecilia Sandberg, a Rumsey school teacher. They had one son, James.

Mr. Rogers died in 1938 at the age of 45 years.

Rodgers, Michael ZR R.R. PR R.R. 7Z L.H. ⊠

I was born in 1939, only son of Pat and Nina Rodgers. I rode a horse to Plainview School until grade eight, a school bus to Sheep Creek School, then on to Mount Royal and S.A.I.T. in Calgary.

In 1962 I married Ellemae Anderson of Rose Valley, Saskatchewan, and lived on the N.W. ¼ of 22-20-4W5. In 1968 we built a home on the S.E. ¼ of 6-21-3W5 and moved in April. We are the third generation of my family to carry on ranching in these Foothills.

We have two children Nancy, born in 1963 and Shawn, born in 1965.

Shawn and Nancy Rodgers.

Rodgers, Robert Hugh Hull (Pat.)

by Michael Rodgers

Pat was born in Ireland in 1901, son of James and Maude Rodgers, who homesteaded west of Okotoks in

485

Pat Rodgers and Nina Rummel. 1925.

1886. He attended school at Panima and Okotoks before leaving home at an early age to work for various ranches in the foothills. One of his first jobs was freighting to the Burns Mine, also for Bob Carry and the South Sheep Stock Association, then on to the Cheadle Cattle Co.

In 1928, he married Nina von Rummel, youngest daughter of Gustav von Rummel-Waldau and Elsa Basilici. They lived on the Basilici home place, N.W.¼ of 25-20-4W5 and they were active in the ranching business until their passing in 1968 and 1969. They had one son, Michael, born in 1939.

Their entire married life was spent in the Foothill country they loved, and surrounded by the livestock which provided both their livelihood and their enjoyment. Theirs was an ideal partnership as they spent their married life living and working side by side, my mother being equally at home cooking Christmas dinner for thirty people or moving a herd of cattle all by herself in the Forest Reserve or by sweeping hay all day with a team of horses and having supper ready for the whole crew at six o'clock.

My dad, along with an appreciation for good livestock, loved sports, playing polo and hockey in his younger years and hunting all his life. He became an avid curler in later years.

Rodgers, William Jasper "Jappy"

William Jasper (Jappy) Rodgers was born in Calgary on March 4th, 1896. He grew up on the Hillside Ranch 8 miles west of Okotoks. Jappy attended the Panima School in the Okotoks area. At the age of 18, Jappy left the Hillside Ranch and started working for Douglas Hardwick on the Lazy H Ranch located in the Snake Valley, what is now the Lake McGregor district.

In the early spring of 1918, Jappy joined the Lord Strathcona Horse Regiment in Calgary and went to Vancouver with the remount department training horses that the Russians had bought. In the fall of 1918, Jappy married Lulu Hamilton, daughter of a pioneer

Pat and Nina Rodgers with Michael held by father. 1939.

Jappy Rodgers at Virginia Ranch about 1926.

family, the Hamiltons, of the Okotoks area. After the armistice day in November 1918 the horses in Vancouver were sold by public auction and in the early spring of 1919, Jappy returned to Calgary where he was hired by a Government Agency to handle horses for the Calgary Stockyards. While working there, he met Captain T. B. Jenkinson who owned a Polo Pony Ranch 20 miles north of Cochrane, called the Virginia Ranch. Jappy was hired by Mr. Jenkinson and partners, the Martin Brothers, to break young horses and train them for playing polo. Jappy and his wife Lulu, moved to the Virginia Ranch in the spring of 1920. Jappy spent several winters of the 9 years on the Virginia Ranch, playing polo at Coronado Beach in the San Diego area of Southern California.

The Rodgers children, Kathleen, Patricia and Douglas were all born on the Virginia Ranch. Jappy and family moved to a ranch of their own just 4 miles west of the Virginia Ranch in the spring of 1928, where they lived until Jappy retired and moved into the Big Hill Lodge in Cochrane of March 1977. He was predeceased by his wife, Lulu, in March of 1956. After a short illness, Jappy passed away on July 20, 1978.

Ross Brothers

The Rosses came from Stornaway, Isle of Lewis, Scotland, to Cape Breton, Nova Scotia in the good ship "Hector" in 1817. William Ross, our grandfather, the youngest of eleven children, was in Baddeck, N.S. in 1858 and moved with his family to Bruce County, Ontario. He took a farm and married Annie Christie Ferguson, and raised two boys, William Ferguson, our father, and Allan James Ferguson, who was killed in action with the R.A.F. in October 1918.

In 1902, they moved to a farm near Carman, Manitoba, where, after a couple of tough winters, Grandfather took the train to Calgary to check on those rumored Chinooks. When he saw people going about without the benifit of heavy coats, carpenters sawing and hammering bare-handed, and homes and buildings going up everywhere, in mid-January, he

knew he had found his Eldorado. He lost no time in selling the farm, and arrived in Calgary to stay in 1905.

He never changed his mind about Alberta, doing well in real estate, and serving as an Elder of Knox Church and a city alderman. He died suddenly in 1914. Grandmother Ross, who boasted two of her great-grandfathers were United Empire Loyalists, always claimed her family were in Canada two generations before Grandfather's folks left Scotland.

Dad had been a partner in the real estate business, and continued in that profession until his retirement. He married Judith Trotter in 1912. Her family, the Trotters, originally came from Thurlaston, Leistershire, England, to Ontario in 1870. Her father, J. O. Trotter, was a partner in Trotter Bros. in Woodstock, Ont. (1880s), ran his own shoe store in St. Catherines, where Mother was born in 1892, and, back in Woodstock, suffered a disastrous fire in 1904 which destroyed his third business. He was soon on his feet again and, encouraged by his brother Ralph, who was already in Calgary, he moved west in 1907. He operated the "Boy's Special Clothiers" at 236-8th Ave. W. where he employed his nephew, Tom Trotter as extra help on Saturdays.

Grandmother Trotter, (Minnie Scofield), whose grandfather was a United Empire Loyalist, was born, raised and married in Woodstock. She was a strict and proper Baptist, and a wonderful grandmother to a bunch of rowdy boys.

Mother attended "Sleepy Hollow" High School during its final year and Central High School during its first years. She worked as a legal secretary before she married.

We were a family of five boys, Bill, Don, Ken, Jack and Bruce, which Mother often complained of when she was out-voted 6 to 1, but when she put her foot down, she was in majority, and we toed the mark. We were all born and lived for some years at 707-5th Ave. W. where the Pacific Plaza now rises, and later at 628-7th Ave. W., the site of the J. J. Bowlen Building. It seems they do big things with the land when we move off.

Ross Family. L. to R. Jimmie, Don (in behind) Bill, Bruce, Carrie Ross. Picture taken at Tommy Trotter's.

Penny and Marnie Ross holding African lion cub.

Dad was a keen outdoorsman throughout his lifetime. We were all taught the joys of fishing, hunting and camping at the earliest possible age and, although we were probably spoiled by the superlative fishing and hunting available in the 20's, 30's and 40's, it has not all rubbed off yet.

Bill was an active skier for twenty-five years, serving the Calgary Ski Club in several capacities. During the first years that the club held races, he won a first, a second and a couple of thirds. After that he was listed among the "also rans". In the late forties he began working for game conservation with the Calgary Fish and Game Association, serving as president for two years. In late years he joined the Archaeological Society of Alberta.

Bill married Eileen Mae Moore, who was born on the homestead her folks had taken up on their arrival from Ireland in 1908. She later lived and attended school in Delburne and Calgary, and worked for Union Milk Co. before her marriage. She is active in the I.O.D.E. and has been awarded a life membership. They have two girls, Marjorie (Marnie) and Penny Lou. Both girls were keen on horses and riding, young animals, tame or wild, swimming in the creek, and attending brandings where they loved to wrestle the smaller calves, or administer the innoculations. All the spare time they could manage from school or job was spent at the ranch, checking on their pets and wild friends.

Marnie is married to Duane Kelly who was raised on a farming-ranching operation at Hussar. They met at computer courses at U. of Calgary and were very busy at graduation. Duane was recruited by I.B.M. before his graduation, and the happy couple were married shortly after. I.B.M. moved them to Vancouver, then to Toronto, to Regina, and then back to Vancouver. They have two children, Patrick Ross Kelly, 8, and Colleen Anne Kelly, 6.

Penny married Darrell Esligar in 1971 and Darrell was a welcome extra hand at the ranch. After six years they were divorced and Penny married Bob Birmingham in 1978. They both work in the oil industry.

In 1961 we decided we needed some land to pasture a few horses. When we saw "the old Jack Johnson Place" as it was called, our plans were drastically changed. It was much bigger and costlier than we had planned. On the advice of our good friends and generous neighbors, Frank and Maudie Sharp, and the Wildman family, we approached the owner "Pip" Graham, who offered a proposition we could not refuse. In what seemed no time, we became the proud owners of the N.½ of 1-21-4w5 and S.½ of 12-21-4w5, some of the most beautiful land in the country.

We were never able to stay on the place during the winter, so we were restricted to a summer operation. We pastured steers in the early years, then cows with calves, and later, bred yearling heifers. For a few years we rented extra pasture from Tom and Edith Trotter. Our wonderful friends and neighbors consistently gave more help than we can ever repay.

Our current hobbies are hunting, fishing, shooting and boating. Bill branched out into sailing in 1976 with the Chestermere Yacht Club. Since we both are now retired, these hobbies will receive renewed attention.

James and Gillian Ross

The Rosses are relative newcomers to the Millarville area having bought their acreage in January of 1970 and taking up residence on it in August of 1971. Neither are native Albertans. James was born in Winnipeg, Manitoba, to James and Mildred Ross. Gillian (Jill) was born in Wallington, Surrey, England, the daughter of a serviceman and an English mother, Joseph and Kathleen Katchenoski.

Following the war, the family returned to Canada to live in a small town seven miles east of Winnipeg, Transcona. There, Jill attended Central School, Westview School and the Transcona Collegiate Institute. It was at the latter that she met Jim, who had also been residing in Transcona, but on what Jill calls the wrong side of the tracks, in South Transcona. He had attended Springfield School up to Grade Ten, then had to continue his education at T.C.I.

Bill and Eileen Ross at the wedding of their daughter Penny.

James and Gillian Ross.

Following graduation, Jill went on to United College, now the University of Winnipeg. There she received her B.A. and later a certificate in Education from the University of Manitoba.

During this time Jim had been working as an apprentice electrician. After one winter of pulling wire in -30 degrees he opted for the warmth of a classroom at the University of North Dakota where he received a B. Sc. in Geology.

In 1966, Jim and Jill were married and took up residence on the University of North Dakota campus in one of hundreds of corrugated tin married students housing duplexes affectionately referred to as Silver City. Between battling voracious shrews, tenacious millipedes and snirt storms they completed their course work for Masters programs in Geology and English respectively.

In 1968, Jim was offered a position as petroleum geologist with Amerada Petroleum Corp. in Calgary, so they packed their worldly belongings into a fastback Mustang and headed west. Jim spent that summer doing extensive geological mapping in the Spray Lakes region west of Calgary. In September of that year, Jill took up the position of Senior English teacher at Cochrane High School and remained there until June of 1971.

In December of 1971, the Rosses first child, Alison Kathleen, was born. Their second daughter, Lesley Jean, arrived on October 30th, 1973.

During their time in Millarville, Jill has been an active member of the Christ Church Junior Guild and was founding librarian of the Millarville Public Library. Jim has been a director of the Meota Gas Coop.

At present, Jim is Exploration Supervisor for Amerada Minerals Corporation and Jill in Calgary manager for Pirjo-Liisa Fashions.

Roth Family
by Rudi Roth

I have very fond memories of the Ranch (E½ 22-21-4-W5th). I loved the solitude, the coyotes howl from the hills early in the morning, the moose and mule deer in the valley. The old log house and barn were in perfect harmony with the natural spirit and character of the Foothills. The neighbors were the most friendly people in the world.

We didn't live on the Ranch very long, end of 1958 and 1959. My Mother and three brothers, John, Peter, Willi and myself moved up from Lethbridge in order to be close to Calgary where John and Peter worked as Steelmen. However, the winter roads and driving conditions were of great concern to our Mother, she was always terribly worried from the time that John and Peter left in the morning until they came home in the evening, so we moved to Calgary. We tried to run the Ranch from the city but that proved to be a disaster.

Mother, John and Willi still live in Calgary.

John and his wife Elizabeth have two sons, John and Richard and a daughter named Elizabeth.

Willi and his wife Waltraud have two daughters, Diana and Anita.

Peter, with his wife Lorraine and two daughters Dorlaine and Lenay and son Kyle live in Surrey, B.C.

My wife Elsa and I and our two sons Robert and Ronald live in Edmonton.

Alexander Russell (Sandy) 1879-1946
by Billie Russell

Sandy Russell was born in Bathgate. In 1906 he took up a homestead at Pincher Creek, married Jean Jordon-Dick in 1914, a Scottish girl from Edinburgh, who never lost her Scottish burr. Their only child Lawrence (Laurie) was born in 1915 at Pincher Creek.

In 1917 Sandy moved his family north of Peace River. The winters were hard and in the summer there was no relief from the mosquitoes and flies for the cattle. They were miles from nowhere. They were so far north, the Indians had not seen a blonde child before and stroked Laurie's head as good luck omen, a child of the Sun.

Returning to Calgary in 1922, Sandy worked at his trade of Cabinet Maker for the C.P.R. repairing passenger cars. Later in 1924, in partnership with Bob Dick, he moved the family to Kew. Their buildings were on the N.W. ¼ 22-20-4W5, on Ware Creek. Sandy was a keen fly fisherman and in those years the streams abounded with fish.

In those years their neighbors were Eddie Behm, Mr. and Mrs. Bert Nichols, (later Tommy McMillan's place) Basilici family, Millions, Phillips (Walter and Georgie) and Seniors. The Russell home was a popular stopping place for the men hauling fire wood, posts and rails (fire killed) from the reserve. Jean always had out the welcome mat, she loved company, they stopped for a meal, or hot drink — all were welcome.

When the Richfield Company drilled a well on Billie Seniors place in 1929, Sandy built the cook house and sleeping quarters at the camp. He also worked at the well drilled on the Phillips lease, now Jim Silvester's in the 1930's.

In the late 1920's Paddy Rodgers, Ford Lochhead, Sandy and others organized to raise money, haul lumber by team and wagon and built the Kew Hall. Many share fond memories of good times had at the old hall. The hall was later moved from the original site and is the present Square Butte Hall.

When his wife Jean died in 1940, Sandy moved to his homestead on Quirk Creek, built a small log house and lived there till his death in 1946.

Lawrence Russell (Laurie)
by Billie Russell

Sandy's son Laurie, known as Scotty at school, attended Plainview, a ride of five miles from home.

After leaving school he ranched with his Father until Sandy retired.

Married Blodwen Evans (Billie) in 1940. After service in the army (the 25th Royal Engineers) he worked in the Oilfields of Turner Valley until his retirement in 1967.

In 1945, bought the original DePalezieux place at Millarville, travelled to work by Pony Express. The place was sold to Don Ricks and John Evans in 1971.

Our home is in Turner Valley, but we still enjoy the place at Quirk Creek in the summer. Laurie enjoys riding and working with horses.

We have three children, seven grandchildren. Larry is married to Myrna Howerton. They have four children, Shirley, David, Laurie Jay and Jean. They live at Cochrane.

Roy married Louise De Guarra. They have one child, Rene and live at Malta.

Sandy married Don Andersen. They have two children, Steven and Tracy and they live at Rocky Mountain House.

Bill and Peggy Sadler

During Bill and Peggy's stay at Ann Boon's place with their family, son Lawrence and daughters Dawn, Marjorie and Tootie, they enjoyed their four years in the community before moving to Calgary. One of the enjoyable activities they took part in were the cribbage parties. There was always time for a few games of crib at Sadlers, Harvey Goerlitz' and McNabs, with a big wind-up crib party New Year's Eve at one of the homes.

Mr. and Mrs. Bill Sadler, 1968. Their daughters Marj. and Toots.

George William (Curly) Sand
by Joan Kendall

Curly was born May 4th, 1909, at Chisholm, Minnesota. He came to the Kew area about 1946. He was hired by the North Fork Stockmen's Association to hunt grizzlies that were depredating the yearlings in

Curly Sand and wolf he shot, with dog Buck.

Paws of Grizzly bears shot by Curly Sand in Muskeg.

490

the Muskeg — a long open valley at the head of the North Fork of the Sheep River. In the two years time he hunted there he shot eleven grizzlies and numerous black bear. Having been mauled by a grizzly previously, he had no mercy on any bear unfortune enough to come within his sight.

Many were the tales Curly had to tell of hunting exploits and he could always be counted on to entertain young and old till well into the night. One always had the impression that there was a nebulous area where fact stopped and fiction began.

He was a fine horseman-had been a rodeo rider in his younger days and always had several good horses which he looked after with meticulous care. He was fond of dogs and was never without one or two. In later years he kept coon hounds which could be depended on to tree any cougar which left a track in the neighborhood.

He was living in the Cochrane area when he was stricken with a heart attack in 1971.

Margaret (King, Kayler) Saucier

by Margaret Saucier

Margaret is the daughter of William and Lucy King, born in the original Calgary General Hospital Nov. 8th, 1904.

After completing schooling to grade eleven, inclusive, at Duncan, B.C. she took grade twelve and Normal School (now S.A.I.T.) in Calgary. Her first teaching position was in May and June 1923, teaching grade three at Redcliff, Alberta. Her second teaching position was Sept. to Dec. 1923, grades one to eight in Willow Creek S.D. just north of MacLeod. It was closed Dec. 1923 due to lack of funds.

Her third teaching position was at Plainview School, in the Kew district, in January 1924 for 2½

1976. At Brugelette, Belgium. L. to R. Jim Beacham, Mary Beacham, Margaret Saucier. Front: Will Beacham, John Beacham.

years, teaching all grades one to nine. Transportation from Millarville was by saddle horse, except at Christmas 1924 as a raging blizzard had drifted in the roads. In 1925, the weather being solubrious the family Ford was called into action to transport the Christmas parcels etc. for the school Christmas party and concert.

Mrs. King died in the summer of 1926, thus Plainview had another teacher, Miss Dorothy Thomas of Okotoks, starting Sept. 1926.

In January 1927, Fordville School needed a teacher, this position Margaret filled until moving to Calgary Sept. 1928 where she taught until Dec. 1937. On January 1938, Margaret King and Carlton H. Kayler were married; the result of this union — four children, Mary Margaret, a graduate of the Vancouver General Hospital Nursing School, now the wife of Lieut. Col. James C. Beachman (Jim) R.C.E. and the mother of William, John and Richard Beacham.

The second child, William Edward Kaylor, is a graduate of Trinity College School (T.C.S.) and has a Bsc. in Agriculture from MacDonald College of McGill University. Edward is now married to Margaret Ades of Montreal and living in Grand Falls, Nfld. working with the provincial government. They have two children, Tana and Glen.

The third child of "Kay" and "Marg" — Frederick King, a graduate of Trinity College School with honors, had completed two and a half years of University when he died.

Richard John, number four, also a graduate of T.C.S. worked with seismic crews in Saskatchewan, Melville Island, Hinton and MacKenzie Delta, also various other jobs — completed his Bsc. in Agriculture at the U. of Alberta, 1978.

Carlton (Kay) Kayler with Mr. W. H. Colley, owned Terrils' Flowers Ltd., with greenhouses in east Calgary and a retail shop at 809, First St. S.W. In 1948, Kay Kayler bought out Harry Colley, thus becoming sole owner of the company. C. H. Kayler died in 1956. Margaret then assumed control of the business, becoming president of the company, with the help of

New Year's Day. 1966. Edward Kayler, King Kyler, Richard Kayler. William Beacham (3 weeks old).

two very good friends as directors: Mr. Robert Dinning (Pres. of P. Burns Co.) and Eric Connelly. A very good friend, Mr. Frank Burnet, Q.C. was company lawyer and general advisor. For the first few years Harry Colley returned annually to give his able assistance and experienced advice. Sixteen years later, in the spring of 1972, Terrils' Flowers Ltd. was sold. The business had expanded considerably with two new glass houses, a wholesale florist supply business at the east end plant and a second retail outlet uptown at the Calgary Inn.

Margaret continued to live at 2725-Carleton St. S.W. In 1974 she married John J. Saucier Q.C., then about to retire from his Calgary firm as a partner but to continue on as a consultant with his office in the firms' premises. In 1918, Jack Saucier and Billie King were on the same survey party into Burns Mine. Students were filling men's jobs as the majority of able bodied men, in 1918, were in the armed services. Jack, a native of Calgary, has been a friend of the King family for over 50 years.

Scatterty, James A. and Cathie (Sinclair-Smith)

written by James Scatterty

I was born in Calgary on September 20, 1939, the second son of Alex and Effie Scatterty. I have one brother, Ron, who moved to Edmonton; two sisters, Anne, living in Black Diamond and Joan, who is living in Okotoks.

My father passed away in 1959 and my mother is now remarried to Oswald Madsen.

We lived on my father's farm, NW¼-14-21-4-W5, till I was seven, then moved to the Spooner Ranch which is now owned by Bar Pipe Farms. I started school at Fordville and attended there until it closed, at which time we were bussed to Sheep Creek. When my parents moved to Calgary in 1955 I struck out to meet the world and went to work for Shaw Construction. It was during the next couple of years on my frequent visits to Millarville that I became re-acquainted with a girl I went to school with, namely Cathie Sinclair-Smith.

Cathie was born in Calgary, sometime in the 1940's, only daughter of Francis and Helen Sinclair-Smith. She has one brother, Stuart, who is married, has two boys, and is still on the farm. After completing her schooling in Fordville, Sheep Creek, Okotoks and Calgary, she went to work in Calgary for the Bank of Commerce. Cathie was involved with 4-H, is a charter member of the Millarville Ladies Junior Guild and a Director of the Priddis and Millarville Agriculture Society. Her hobbies are too numerous to mention. For the past six years she has been the secretary at the Millarville School.

During our courting days it was usually the custom to have Sunday dinner at her house, which invariably produced a roast of very rare mutton. As I didn't like

Jim and Cathie Scatterty, daughter Barbara, son Gerald.

sheep very much, especially raw, I thought maybe if I married her I could teach her the finer arts of cooking.

On October 17, 1959 we were married by Rev. W. Gant in Christ Church, Millarville.

Our first home was on the Spooner Ranch, then owned by E. V. Keith, where I went to work, while Cathie commuted to Calgary. We remained there until the ranch was sold to Lester Boulton, then moved to Rocky Mountain Ranch near Priddis. It was there that our first child, a son, Gerald, was born. We survived there for a couple of years, then moved to Falconer Farms where our daughter, Barbara, was born on July 16, 1962.

We stayed at Falconer Farms for twelve years during which time we learned a little about the race horse business; how to raise them and how not to bet on them. We also raised a few Charolais cattle.

In May, 1974, we moved onto our own land, SW¼-11-21-2-W5 and lived in a trailer while our house was being built. The first week in October saw us move into our not-quite finished home. During this time I was working for Bert Haney and did so until his death in 1977.

The construction business still seemed to be calling me and since then my brother and I have formed Scatterty Brothers Construction Company. Road-building and sub-divisions have been our main business so far but we have done seismic jobs as well.

Ronald Henry Scatterty

by Joan Goyette

Ronald was born in October, 1931, the first child of

Lois and Ronald Scatterty and family.

Alex and Effie Scatterty. He spent his childhood in Millarville and attended Fordville School. In 1949, he left and went to work for Shaw Construction for the next eight years. On October 26, 1957 he married Lois Velma Lowry, a girl from Sawyerville, Quebec and a cousin of his sister's husband, Don. In September, 1958 their first child, Rory Allen was born, followed in May, 1961 by Judy Anne. They lived in Calgary for about six years before moving to Edmonton in 1968. Ron worked for Consolidated Concrete for eleven years and then formed his own company, Alanco Construction in 1974. He has just recently formed another company with his brother Jim, called Scatterty Brothers Construction. Ron and his family still reside in Edmonton.

John and Sophie Schaal

by Sophie Schaal

We moved to the S.E.¼, Sec.33, T.21, R.3, W.5, in the month of November, 1949, and bought this quarter from Ed Hehr.

My mother, Mary Heth, and I came by car with my brother-in-law doing the driving. John came in the truck, bringing a load of furniture, the cat and dog, and last but not least on top of the load, crates of chickens. They blessed us with eggs along the way. Our machinery and livestock came by rail. My mother was an invalid from age thirty, or there about. She lived with us a year and eight months. We took her back to my sister's at Maple Creek then, and we alternated taking care of her at yearly intervals until she died here, and was buried in Queens Cemetery in Calgary, October, 1954.

It was not easy to pull up roots and leave the district where we were born, southeast of Maple Creek in

John and Sophie Schaal with nephew, 1955.

the district of Kealey Springs. Oddly enough, we never stopped pulling up roots for quite a few years.

There was not much cleared land on this quarter, so we had trees cut and cleared, then plowed, and then the everlasting root picking began. We didn't live here very long when we realized we could not make a living on one quarter, so bought the west half of 27-21-3-W5; this also did not have much cleared land, but we eventually cleared most of one quarter for hay and grain. The owner, when we bought was Moette. We sold this half section to J. C. Meeker in 1971, when John realized he wasn't able to carry on full time. Since then we have sold all the livestock. Our brand was J̃∩ L.H. (quarter circle J lazy S left hip). We still keep it registered. John's father had the original brand J∩, without the quarter circle. Electricity came into our area in 1951. But it was not until 1958 that we could afford to have bathroom facilities. Telephones came about 1960, and last but not least, natural gas. Up until then, we burned wood and coal. No more cold feet after the furnace was installed. One of my evening rituals was to put my feet in the oven before going to bed.

We are semi-retired now, but still want to keep the home quarter as long as we are able to do our own work.

Schaal Farm, taken 1976.

Farmstead of Walter Schaal, 1970.

Walter Schaal U4

Cattle brand

In October 1949 my wife, Lillian, daughter Beverley and son Garry came here from Kealey Springs, Saskatchewan, where I was born. We bought ¾ of a section of land from Bill Mackintosh, and live on SW 3-22-2-W5.

The first few years were rough. We had to pick roots every spring, we had no power but we did have a good spring. Water was piped into the house from the hill top and there was plenty of water for cattle. From December 1949 to February 28, 1950 we had a very cold winter. I froze my face several times hauling feed for cattle — six miles with horses and sleigh.

We had a real crop the first year, 1950; wheat went fifty bushels per acre which really helped to pay off the land. In the fall of 1952 and of 1953 I worked for Mr. Roedler, ten miles west, sawing lumber, I managed then to get enough lumber to build my barn.

My wife and I then got five milk cows and we also had chickens; we sold cream and eggs, enough to buy our food and clothing, for a few years.

Beverley and Garry went to school at Ballyhamage for a time, then a large school was built at Red Deer Lake and Ballyhamage was closed. All children in the area went to Red Deer Lake School in 1956. Beverley

went to Millarville for a couple of years then on to Calgary where she took a business course, then to work for the Industrial Development Bank.

Playing crib at Ruby and Jimmie McNab's; Walter Schaal, Bill Sadler, Robert Field and Jimmie McNab.

494

Beverley and Jack Macklin were married in 1960. They lived at Ballyhamage for several years, then moved up west of Olds, where they now farm. In 1969 Garry and Linda Watkins were married and live on SW 2-22-W5. They farm and run Simmental cattle, also do custom work.

A lot of my time in May and June is spent castrating calves for my neighbors, have a few drinks afterwards, swap a few good jokes, plenty of good food served, then go home tired but happy.

I have sold one-quarter-section of land, so hope to gradually cut down on work. I will stay on the farm as long as I can work and help out in the neighborhood.

Schiele, Gunther and Martha

Born in Germany, Mr. Schiele came to Canada in 1952, and moved to Vancouver, where he married his wife, Martha. In 1965, they moved to Calgary, where they presently still live, with their daughter, Nicole.

In 1973, they purchased the N.E. quarter of section 20-20-3W5 from the Peel family, which they use mostly for pasture and hay. This quarter section of beautiful country-side was originally homesteaded by J. J. Morrison, in 1908.

Schiele Family. Gunther, Martha and Nicole.

Conrad and Elizabeth Scheuerman

Conrad and Elizabeth Scheuerman, one son George, together with Conrad's parents, one brother and two sisters, emigrated to Calgary from Russia in 1912. The family first settled in Calgary. The brother, Adam, and sisters Katherine and Elizabeth, later moved to the United States. One sister, Mrs. Katherine Diel, who is 89 years old, still resides in Tacoma, Washington. She renewed family ties by visiting in Calgary in October, 1978. Conrad and his family resided in Calgary for a few years and David and Katheryn were born in Calgary.

In 1917 Conrad moved his family to Leader, Saskatchewan, taking up farming a few years later. During the period the family lived in Saskatchewan, Victor, Robert, John, Henry, Emma and Sam were born.

In 1934, after years of crop failures from drought, the family moved to the Okotoks district, having

Family of Elizabeth and Conrad Scheuerman. L. to R., back row: Sam, Vic, Bob, John. Front row: Hank, Kay, Dave, Emma, and George.

purchased the Richard Powes Libby land. Elizabeth, Conrad's father and the youngest children travelled by truck, while Conrad and the older children including Kay drove horses and wagons and herded the family livestock.

Conrad and his father passed away in 1941 and Elizabeth moved to Calgary, where she resided until her passing in 1967.

During World War II five of the boys served in the Armed Forces, four of them having overseas service. The husbands of both Kay and Emma were also members of the services.

All the children are married and with the exception of David, who died in 1972, reside in Western Canada and are engaged in various occupations. In July, 1978, a two-day reunion was held in Calgary and was attended by 107 family members. There are 8 surviving children, 32 grandchildren, and 43 great-grandchildren. Together with surviving spouses the family has grown to 118 members.

The Scheuerman Family
written by Emma Faulkner
Nov. 27, 1978

Parents Elizabeth and Conrad, children in order of age: George, David, Katherine (Kay), Victor, Robert, John, Henry, Emma and Samuel — seven boys and two girls, came to Okotoks from Estuary, Saskatchewan. We attended Ballyhamage School; the teacher at that time was Miss MacDougal. Later Sheilagh Jameson was teacher, until I finished Grade 9.

Dave, Vic, John and Henry served in the Forces overseas, Kay was working in Calgary, and later Dad passed away at age 54, so Mother, Sam and I came to live in Calgary too.

I married Sid Faulkner in 1946 and we had three children: Linda, Neil and Colleen. Sid was, and is, in the construction industry, I was in homemaking. After the children all got to school age I took a hairdressing course and opened and ran a Beauty Salon for six

Sid and Emma Faulkner.

Victor and Esther Scheuerman.

years. I sold the business and rested for a couple of years, later opened a Ladies Clothing Store (Emi-Jo's). As time passed the children all grew up and all got married. I now have four and 8/9 grandchildren.

So now I am getting old and I closed my store and in October 1978 I retired, but Sid is still active and busy. We hope to take a nice, long vacation, after 8/9 arrives, and live happily ever after.

Victor Scheuerman

Written by Victor Scheuerman, Dec. 1, 1978

Sept. 3 (or thereabout) 1934, we were getting much closer at last, having come from 10 miles south-east of Empress arriving in Okotoks from south, we stopped at Don Eastcott's garage and asked directions to the Dick Libby place north and west of there. After fair directions received, we crossed the tracks and headed west on the north side.

Four wagons, twelve horses in harness, machinery and equipment left over and hauled in, near Gene Goettlers, a rider comin' down the road on west side of Gene's place, turned out to be brother Dave. He was part of the threshing crew of Phil Miller's outfit, threshing at George Lumsdens at the time. Turned out — Phil was our neighbor at our new place. Needed more teams for threshin'. "Well, seein' as how you know where "Home is", and how to get back here why don't you drive my rig (Four on a grain tank) home and come back with a team and rack an I'll ride that over there and pitch bouquets in your place." While puttin' the harness on the horse, a little chap came over to the scene, an' "Did you just get off a wagon down there?" "Yes I did." "Had lunch?" "Yes, young timer." "Today?" "Well, not really." "Well you just tie those ponies back at the rack and come with me, and no argument." That was That.

Well, George Lumsden, Mrs., and Margaret were the first new people I met here, and a fine set of people they were. They fed the threshing crew in their house. I had the privilege of working for them in Spring of '35 for couple of months, fine people. After them, went to work for Ed Goettler for a couple of months then home to threshing (custom threshing for other people).

Worked out wherever possible (and whenever), for farmers in the DeWinton and Okotoks areas till the fall of '40. Then Nov. 17 I joined the Army. Nov. 20 arrived at Vancouver, B.C. This Is The Army. Well, seems everybody were bosses (except some of us). An' how they talked and ordered us about you'd think it was "us" who started this darned foolishness called "War". Well, we mopped, and dishwashed, made cinder paths, roads, parade square, etc., by cartin' washtubs and buckets of cinders (We're fightin' a loosin' battle for sure) finally, wooden buildings were completed and we moved into them, What a mess, "Clean em up," "Yes Sir".

Well, about May or June, Niagara-on-the-Lake, What a mess, "Clean it up" — "Yes Sir". Niagara Falls, never saw so much water flow over one hill in my life, before or since, guard duty along the canals, etc. During time off met again Esther Schimpfof from near home in Sask. and Nov. 30 we got married (37 yrs. ago now) about Dec. 2 or 3 South Alta Regt. moved to Debert, N.S. There from an infantry regt., we became an Armoured Regt. 29th Cdn. Armrd. Regt. S.A.R.

August '42 — a day or two after the Dieppe raid, we were on the boat at Halifax. Sept. 3 docked at Glasgow, and down into England, various places, fun and Games — war games, etc., then in '44 July or so over to France, Belgium, Holland, Germany, etc., as far as Oldenberg in Germany and they decided "That was it." Victory in Europe. V.E. Day.

Sept. 3, '45, onto the boat again in Glasgow an' headed home, while heading West on the train (homeward bound) we were told, we would be doing a Victory parade on arrival in Calgary. An' to make sure we do, we don't get our passes till after. Well word spread fast about, if they've never seen a stampede before, they will then, passes or no passes.

There wasn't a Victory parade by us and we had our passes in hand and pay.

I go by the old place out here occasionally an' some of the neighborhood see some of the ol' timers and places. This fall I even did same in Sask. ol' Saskedge school has only the Foundation left.

Stayed in Calgary after the War, have near 32 years in at Calgary brewing now.

Kenneth and Margaret Anne (Lyall) Schmitke

I was born August 15, 1947, second child and first daughter of Dick and Helen Lyall. We lived on a ranch southwest of the present location of the Square Butte Hall. Dad's parents (George and Ann Lyall) homesteaded there (N.W.¼ of 9-21-4w5). What a beautiful place to grow up in. I guess I practically learned to ride before I could walk. Dad and Mom said I spent more time with the animals than with them. A lot of the time they thought I was with the animals I was following a very dear friend and neighbor, Joe Bell, from here to there and back again. Poor Joe, I wonder if he knew he had a shadow.

Those foothills were beautiful for long, quiet rides, and outdoor fun of all kinds. Skating and tobogganing parties, family picnics, and regular get-togethers with our family and friends were our entertainment. Weekends nearly always found a bunch together for one reason or another. I remember a lot of fun parties at the original Square Butte Hall. It had its beginning as the community school, and later became the meeting place for monthly dances, wedding, showers, picnics, church services and the like. Those good times are something I will always cherish.

Jay, Ken and Evan Schmitke.

We went to Turner Valley a lot, both for business and to the theatre there. Jake Reimer would pick up a whole bunch of people on his bus route, and off we'd go: the Reimers, Birneys, Lyalls, Nylunds, Wildmans and whoever else wanted to go along.

I rode Jake's bus as long as I went to school. From grades one through nine at Sheep Creek (now Millarville) then ten through twelve at Turner Valley (now Oilfields) High School. We went to Millarville with Jake then via Bob Lochhead's bus to Turner Valley. I discovered a lot of new and interesting differences between living a quiet country life and life in small towns. Even bigger were the differences between small town and big city, as I learned upon graduation in 1965. At that time I moved to Calgary to live with Eldon and Barbara and look for work. After a lot of hunting, and encouragement from Barbara, I found a job with C.I.S. and moved to northwest Calgary to board with Gordon and Ethel Tarvis. October 1965, found me living with Don and Noreen Schmitke and the following spring I moved to Nylunds (Peggy and Hjalmar). In July of 1966, I changed jobs, and worked for Universal Sales and Service until the fall of 1969.

On June 29, 1968 (Mother's birthday) Ken and I were married in Okotoks United Church. Ken was born and raised on a farm four miles east of Black Diamond. He and I met in High School. We resided in Calgary until October 1969, when we were transferred to Whitecourt with Alberta Gas Trunk Line. Ken was a compressor station operator there until March 1971.

February 1971 found us blessed with our first born, a son named Kenneth Jay. March of that year we were back in Calgary. Ken had become a Controls Technician Trainee and worked out of the city at several stations in the area. In 1973, we bought a house in the Haysboro area in southwest Calgary. September of 1975, Ken started as a construction Inspector and spent a great deal of that winter in Camrose. In 1977, our second son, Evan Lyall was born.

Ken is still employed by the Alberta Gas Trunk Line as a construction inspector, so sees a great deal of Alberta. At this writing, he is working on the

Margaret Anne, Jay and Evan Schmitke.

building of a station at Eureka River (in the Fairview area) Jay is presently enrolled in Grade 2 at Eugene Coste elementary school, and Evan, thirteen months, keeps Mother out of mischief.

Leonard and Isobel Schrader
by Isobel Schrader

Leonard was born at Wilson Creek, Washington in 1911. On April 10, 1934, Leonard and I were married. I was born at Delmer, Ontario in 1915.

We settled on a quarter section 13 miles west of Bowden, Alberta. Our daughter Darlene Marie was born in February, 1940, and Linda Pearl in January, 1947. We increased to ½ section, then to ¾ section all in the same section.

After farming for 33 years, we retired to Calgary, where Linda was in University, and Darlene was teaching.

In the spring of 1967 we went to work on the Graham Ranches. It was a wonderful experience to get to know the Millarville district and to live in such a beautiful country. Linda also worked on the ranch in the summer, returning to University in the fall.

Thanks for the opportunity to write a few lines in your history.

June Collins Schulmeister

Soon after I was born on a farm near Collingwood, Ontario, my parents moved West where they farmed for seven years north of Tompkins, Saskatchewan, five years near Bethune, Saskatchewan, and ten years near Airdrie, Alberta, where my sister, Sheila, was born. While at Airdrie I attended Crescent Heights High School in Calgary, followed by teacher training at the Calgary Normal School in 1935-36.

My teaching experience began with two years in my home school district, Dry Creek, and two years near Byemoor, Alberta. For the next year and a half, because my father was ill and passed away in 1939, I did not teach.

From January 1 to June 30, 1942, it was my privilege to be in charge of Square Butte School. The class of 8 pupils ranging from Grade 1 to 9 was a lively and interesting group. My boarding place was the home of Mr. and Mrs. Kosling. By choice I walked the two miles to and from the little log school where the warmth from the cheerful fire of the wood-burning stove often had to dry me up after walking through wet bushes on the roadside in order to avoid the very muddy roads of a particularly wet spring. Exactly 30 years later my husband and I had the happy experience of attending the fiftieth anniversary reunion of teachers and pupils of Square Butte School.

After Square Butte I taught in Sunshine School near Crossfield, in Dalemead near Calgary, Bowness, and finally 18 years at Balmoral School in Calgary. In 1964 I retired from teaching.

Former pupils of Square Butte School at the reunion, May 21, 1972. Back row, Charlie Silvester, Jimmie Silvester, John Kendall, Frank Kendall. Front row, Marie (Dibby Kendall) Stewart, Minnie (Silvester) Marshall, June Collins Schulmeister (teacher in 1942).

In 1953 I married Jake Schulmeister who passed away in 1973. Since then I have continued to live in our Calgary home.

Scott, Carol (Lyall)

Carol Lyall, daughter of Dick and Helen Lyall, born on October 21, 1956 in the Calgary General Hospital. Residing at Millarville, on my parents ranch for 18 years, I attended Millarville School for 8 years, and spent the last 4 years at Oilfields High School in Black Diamond. During my years at home, I enjoyed the outdoors, participating in many school functions and was active in 4-H food and beef clubs in our community.

Dan and Carrol Scott on their wedding day.

The summer of 1973, my first experience away from home, I spent 6 weeks cooking for a Church camp at Waterton Lakes with Jane Glaister. Upon my graduation I took the opportunity of spending the summer at Mount Assiniboine, B.C., where I met many people from all over the world.

October of 1974, I returned to Calgary where I began my career as a banker. After working in the city for about 1½ years I decided I would like to see some of Canada's north country. From Calgary I transferred to Whitehorse, Yukon Territories where I stayed for the summer, then back to Calgary the fall of 1976. Still working for the bank I resided at Calgary and was married in April of 1977. My husband, Dan Scott, and I lived in Calgary for about 6 months. We now live at Longview, and both work in High River.

George A. Scott

My father George Scott, came to Alberta from Scotland in 1889 and spent many years in the Okotoks, Millarville and High River areas, as a ranch hand, mostly breaking horses. In later years he was employed by the Alberta Government as a inspector of brands and grazing lease inspector. My mother Saraha (Nellie) came to Okotoks from Ontario in 1904 to visit her sister Elizabeth Pugh. Instead of returning to Ontario she accepted a teaching position in Okotoks and taught there for several years. I was born in Okotoks and when just a few years old my parents, in 1910 rented the Middleton place northeast of Black Diamond, where we lived for three years. We returned to Okotoks and I attended public and high school there.

In 1927 we moved to Calgary where I spent one year at Crescent Heights High School then the Calgary Normal School and obtained my teacher's certificate. My first and only teaching job was at New Valley S.D. about four miles north of Black Diamond from 1930 to 1936. I left New Valley and spent one term at the Olds School of Agriculture and had intended going on the University for a degree in agriculture. When the term ended I returned to Millarville and Turner Valley

New Valley School. L. to R. Bruce Stanhope, Lily Frayne, Joan Oliver, Frank Cougar, Bill Fisher. Sitting: Isamay de Palezieux, Margaret Deane-Freeman, Doreen Oliver, Betty Hart, Elliene Burns.

where I worked at odd jobs until I obtained employment with Royalite, then Valley Pipe Line Co. with whom I remained for four years, until enlisting in the R.C.A.F. I was in the airforce almost five years and after my discharge returned to Calgary and Valley Pipe Line, working in their accounting department for one year then transferred to Imperial Oil and spent three years, 1947-1949 at Norman Wells N.W.T as an accounting clerk. In December 1949 came back to Calgary and worked in Imperials productions accounting department and five years at their Production Research Laboratory.

I retired in October 1972 and still live in Calgary where I keep busy with my greenhouse and gardening and when you have your place there is always something to do. I have also enjoyed going back to Imperials' Lab. and working on a part-time basis, mostly holiday relief.

I have two sisters, Margaret Wilson (Peggy) living in Victoria, B.C. and Betty White living in Sydney, Australia.

Preben Sebbelov and Family
as told by Elisabeth Sebbelov

On May 4, 1954, my husband, Preben, (born January, 1927) our eighteen month old son, Michael Scheel, (born July, 1952) and myself, Elisabeth, (born March, 1932) left our homeland in Denmark, to come to Canada for a planned one year to work on a turkey and chicken farm. We travelled by plane from Copenhagen to Amsterdam, and from Amsterdam to Montreal, quite painless; not true though for the last part. The three of us spent four nights and three days on a train, reaching Calgary on May 9th. We were unloaded at the station hoping somebody would be there to take us to our job. After waiting for close to an hour, a kind gentleman from C.P.R. escorted our foreign family to our new home. The farm at that time was outside the city limits but today is part of Calgary.

Our new house was an old and dirty army barrack containing little furniture. My husband was to look after 5000 chickens, 5000 turkeys and milk a few cows. The past few days let us experience a number of drastic lifestyle changes as we had left a lovely, well furnished old farm house to come to this seemingly unfriendly place. We managed, however, and soon met other Danes who had experienced similar difficulties as us and who had overcome them just as we would in the weeks that followed.

The biggest disadvantage in this new country was the language barrier. I did not read or speak any English. Preben, on the other hand, spoke fluent English and of course Michael, being young, picked it up quickly. It was up to them to teach me.

One luxury we got in Canada which we had never before thought of having was a car, a beautiful 1929 Essex Coupe with a rumble seat. It carried our small family all over the countryside in fine style.

Our first Christmas was something none of us looked forward to as we never before had spent a Christmas without our family. But as Christmas always does, it came closer and closer only too quickly. We received the parcels from Denmark and managed to buy a few personal gifts. Of course Michael and I baked the traditional cookies that we were so accustomed to. Our holiday spirits were easily dampened, though, when on December 23rd our boss informed Preben that we were out of jobs as of January 1st, due to financial difficulties. What a Christmas present! As soon as the holidays were over, my husband went searching for a new job. It took only one interview with a Millarville farmer, Virgil Ohlson, and we had a job starting February 2nd, 1955.

Preben was to look after pigs, milk cows and help in the fields. I was to cook for from three to five men. That proved to be a bit of a snag because my spoken English was still very limited and my written English almost hopeless. When I got meat from the locker or vegetables from the store, Mrs. Ohlson or some other helpful, patient person would have to come to my rescue and tell me what it was.

Little by little I learned to cook the typically Canadian vegetables such as beans, corn and turnips. Preben and Michael eventually got to like what we used to think was food for the barnyard animals.

Michael soon became his own little farmer. He had several types of livestock including two kittens, a puppy, a pony and of all things, a starved lamb that our good friend and neighbor, Percy Bennet came with. It appeared to be half dead but nevertheless, we put him behind the stove, fed him well and soon he had joined the gang. From then on, the sight around the farm was a small black lamb following the little blond boy, wearing a red corduroy hat.

About that time we came to love Canada and decided to add to our family. On April 1st, 1957, Ann Joergi was born in the Turner Valley Hospital. Needless to say, we were very proud of our two children.

In August of that same year, Preben and I decided it was time to look for a Canadian home of our own. We bought a small place on the townsite just outside of Turner Valley. Preben then began working as a carpenter; a man of many trades.

How nice it felt to live in a house we could actually call our home. We were growing to love this part of the country more and more. Our roots were definitely in Canada now.

Because Michael started school, Ann needed something to keep herself occupied during the day. It was then that her father bought a little goat from Rev. Gant, in Black Diamond. Those two found more mischief than could be imagined, but they did have fun.

Preben and I gave Ann another playmate on July 21st, 1960; Patricia. Michael and Ann both loved their little sister but Ann always had something against Patricia. Ann would say "Pete", (as Patricia was later nicknamed) refused to get herself into trouble like she could; Pete was too good, according to Ann.

Because Preben and I always wished for a family of four, and by now Ann had started school, we had Mark Scheel on June 3rd, 1964; a perfect family as far as we were concerned.

In January of 1970, our family planned on one more move. My husband had taken a job as manager on Graham's horse ranch, only a few miles east of Millarville and things seemed better if we were living on the place.

The children all loved horses and soon after we were settled, Michael began to work beside his Dad. Ann became interested in riding and it was not long before she was an active participant in the equestrian sport. Ann's interest gave Patricia the inspiration she needed to compete alongside her sister. Mark always liked horses as well but only rode when his sisters talked him into exercising their horses.

On August 5th, 1971, Preben, Michael and I became Canadian citizens. Because Michael was not of legal age, he did not have to be sworn in like we did. It was only required that he accompany us to watch the ceremonies.

In our minds, that was a big day. The feeling of being a working part of a country, like a spring in a watch, was exciting yet challenging. As it happened, Ann was competing in the Calgary Horse Show on that same day. We promised to go and see her after the ceremonies. To our great surprise, when we reached the barn, we found some of our friends gathered around a paper covered tack box, complete with a bottle of wine and glasses. The celebration? To welcome us as fellow Canadians; a real western welcome.

As happens in all families, children outgrow the nest and fly away. Michael and Ann both finished their high school in Black Diamond. Michael is now working for Simpson's Ranching in Cochrane. Ann works as a Rental Representative for Hertz-Rent-A-Car at the Calgary International Airport and is living in an apartment in Calgary.

Patricia is just now finishing her grade 12 and hopes to continue her education at Mt. Royal College, taking their two year course in interior design.

Both girls had a very successful and enlightening experienc s riding horses. Mark, now in grade 8, has not yet decided on a career, but seems positive he will go on to some form of secondary education.

Selman, James R. and Helen M. *JI*
SW¼ Sec. 29, Twp. 20, Rge. 3 W5th

The Selmans were born in Calgary and received their education there. Mr. Selman served in the Royal Canadian Navy on a Corvette and Mine Sweeper during the Second War, and, in the Army in Korea during the Korean War. He is presently with the Calgary Fire Department. Mr. Selman's grandfather, James B. Moore, came to Canada from Ireland in 1883 and in 1885 joined the N.W.M.P. and was trumpeter of the guard the day Louis Reil was hanged in Regina. His grandparents wedding day was celebrated at a ceremony of the Sun-Dance, the making of a warrior brave, at Ft. Macleod.

Mrs. Selman worked for a General Insurance Company for thirty years and owned and operated a Children's Holiday Dude Ranch for five years, entertaining from forty to fifty children a week.

After selling their acreage north of Okotoks, they purchased the Sim's quarter section in Kew, now Millarville area, in December '72 and moved in January '73 during a heavy snowstorm, into the little house which was built in 1937 and moved from Royalties to its present site in 1946. The house was heated by a coal furnace until 1976.

The Selmans are presently raising percentage Simmentals.

Seven Springs Ranch

by Doreen Spence HD

In 1966, part of the N.E.¼ of 26-21-4w5 was acquired from John Gouy by the Spence family (Harvey, Doreen Harvie, Roc and Dwayne.)

Harvey was born in Toronto, son of Frank Altona Spence and Jean Melba (Bennett) Spence. Both were from the Toronto area. Jean was an R.N. and served overseas during World War I. She met Frank in England and they were married at St. Marleybone Church in London. They returned to Toronto, and Frank was principal of Eastern Commerce School until his death in 1937.

Doreen's father, John Henry Notley (Harry) Dutton, came from England in 1904 and settled in the Cypress Hills for several years before taking up a homestead at Veteran, Alta. Doreen's mother was Lexy Phyllis Dowler, whose parents were original homesteaders of that area. She taught at Rae School before her marriage. Doreen was born at Veteran. The family moved to Drumheller in 1922, where Mr. Dutton was a B.A. Bulk Oil and Oliver and Cockshutt dealer until his retirement. They then settled in Calgary.

Harvey and Doreen were married in Christ Church in 1949.

Major Spence was still serving as Officer Commanding, R.C.E. Works Co'y. at Currie Barracks, Calgary until his retirement in 1969. The family could not "Move In" with Harvey still in active service, so for a year Phyllis (Backs) and Lyle Dahl were residents and then when they left Ron Arkes and his family moved on to the place for a five year period.

In 1970, the home place was split into two titles. Harvie moved onto the 30 acres west of the road after attending Olds College. At this time, Harvey Sr. was an active resident and with Harvie's assistance kept the home place going and attended to our cattles' wants. The family came out weekends and Harvey commuted to his job at City Hall after his retirement from the Army.

Spence Family. Roc, Harvie, Doreen, Harvey. Dwayne in front.

The family were committed in town as Doreen was teaching in the figure skating world. Doreen was the first Albertan to win a Canadian Championship in figure skating and to pass the Gold Medal, which is the highest award in figure skating.

Roc followed in the figure skating world and competed in Canadian Championships and is now teaching figure skating as well as having formal training as a Diesel mechanic. He was married in 1977 to Lori Nimis.

Harvie ran sheep on his side of the road while Harvey Sr. ran cows with HD brand. The working arrangements went well but in due course Harvie married Katherine Bye in 1976 and with added responsibilities found it necessary to move to Claresholm in 1978.

Dwayne has been his Dad's right hand man. He is attending Crescent Heights High School.

The Seven Springs Ranch was sold to Oden Consultants (Peter Hofer) in 1977.

The Spence family will always be a part of the Square Butte Community. We all hold very special memories of our years in the Valley.

Leland Case (Jake) Sevrens

by Lorraine Norgaard

I was only one year old when we moved from James River to Millarville area. My Dad worked for Major

Gas Waterlines. I was five when we moved back to Sundre and James River. I remember a little about the time we were there, like playing on a large wheel-axle and in the dump grounds. Once in awhile I would go to work with my Dad at the old pump house. There were two pumps. As I remember it, the building burned down while we were there. There are a lot of memories come to me as I write this.

My sister Leone was born while we were at Millarville. She now lives on the family farm with Mom and Dad and her husband Ed. Smart and two children, Tammy, age 14, Brian age 12.

My husband Ray and I have our own business in Innisfail. We have four children, Ella Jean 17, Rose 15, Leland 13, and Edna Mae 11. For the past four years, Mom and Dad have spent their winters in Arizona.

Dorothy Scott (Campbell) Shackleton
by Dorothy Scott (Campbell) Shackleton

My name was Dorothy Scott Campbell, a Calgarian in the second year of teaching who came to the little log school at Square Butte in 1937. There were fifteen students at that time, in grades one to ten. Marie Edlund had preceded me as teacher and Harry Hamilton followed after my two year term. I boarded with Mr. and Mrs. Fred Kosling. In the snap shots you will recognize my students as: (right to left in the standing group) Marie Kendall, Minnie Silvester, Dolores Gouy, Florie Hulme, Nina Ingevald, Renee Gouy, Joan Kosling, Alice Silvester, — Miss Campbell — Bill Kendall, Gordon McLay, John Kendall, Charlie Silvester, Frank Kendall — Joe Bannerman having taken the picture for us.

Ernest Silvester had finished in 1937-1938 (we missed him) and Marie Kendall came as a beginner in 1938-1939.

Square Butte was a community of friendly hospitable people and the school pupils were alert and exciting to teach. We all shared in putting on many community entertainments in the little school and had happy times together.

Miss Campbell's class at Square Butte School. R. to L. Frank Kendall, John Kendall, Gordon McLay, Bill Kendall, Miss Campbell, Alice Silvester, Joan Kosling, Renee Gouy, Nina Ingeveld, Florrie Hulme, Dolores Gouy, Minnie Silvester, Marie Kendall.

It was a great pleasure to attend the Square Butte Reunion and catch up with the events in the lives of my former students.

If they are interested in my activities after Square Butte, I'll briefly mention having taught the following year at Red Deer Lake, marrying Ernest Shackleton, both teaching at Milo for the two following years, then moving into Calgary, where our first daughter was born. Later, when my three girls were all in school, I taught at Briar Hill school for four years, and at Mount Royal College. I then attended the University of Calgary to get the Bachelor of Education and the Bachelor of Fine Arts, and also studied Speech Arts with Toronto Conservatory. As an Associate Speech teacher with Mount Royal Conservatory of music, I was a private speech teacher examiner and adjudicator of music festivals in the western provinces.

Five grandchildren now complete the pictures.

Though many students pass through a teacher's life, these snap shots of my Square Butte students bring the personality of each boy and girl back so vividly and we seem once more to be choosing sides for baseball, or sitting huddled around the rusty old stove for warmth on a blizzardy day, with cold sandwiches and hot cocoa or filled with excitement over our Christmas concerts.

Our one sorrowful memory through the years has been the sad untimely death of my dear pupil Gordon McLay, as a young man in Saskatchewan.

Congratulations to Square Butte-ers for your initiative in recording your community's history — and "thanks for the memory" of my (and your) fine boys and girls.

Frank and Maud E. Sharpe

Born in Atwood, Kansas, January 26, 1900, I came to Alberta in 1903, when my father took a homestead north west of Ponoka, where our nearest post office was Usona. After the bad winter of 1906-07, the family moved back to the United States, to Missouri, where we lived for two and a half years. Coming back to Canada, we lived at North Battleford, Saskatchewan. When the first World War was on, I joined the Army. As I was just fifteen years of age, my mother objected, so I was discharged.

My next move was to Montoya, New Mexico, where my father was living at the time. In 1916, I drove a team of mules to Roswell, New Mexico to work in the fruit. The first day we drove thirty miles before we made camp. That night, a flash flood came up, flooding our camp as well as others, who were camped nearby. Here we were stranded for four days. Although some of the wagons, which were returning from the fruit picking had lots of fruit with them, meat was very scarce. I was the youngest among the campers, so I chased rabbits to shoot with my .22 rifle to get meat for the camp. Some of the rabbits took me on quite a chase, but I managed to get enough of the

502

Maude Sharp on Sir Willow.

fast running little critters to help with the food problem.

I worked in the harvest in Ochiltree, Texas, for a month then started out with a team of mules, driving through Oklahoma to Bucklin, Kansas. Here I sold my team of mules, along with my complete outfit, for $135. I bought a ticket to Humboldt, Sask., where my sister was living. I was only there a short time, then returned to Alberta, and worked for a Dutch farmer near Wetaskiwin. Here I really learned to milk cows. The farmer had a herd of thirty some dairy cows, and his wife and I milked them all, besides doing other chores.

About this time my cousin came from North Battleford to buy horses which were scarce back there. I quit the cow milking and went along with my cousin, buying horses from the Hobbema Reserve and anywhere we could get them. We trailed these horses all the way back to North Battleford, where we received a good price for them, a lot more than we paid.

The first rodeo I ever won anything at was at St. Margaret, in Northern Saskatchewan. For first prize I won a saddle, which I kept for many years. This was in 1918. Two other fellows, Montana Bill, Bobby Hill and I put on four different rodeos, at Alsask, Richard, Midnight Lake and at Battleford. At Richard, there were only three riders to entertain the fairly large crowd, so I rode sixteen head of stock that afternoon and played baseball for North Battleford that evening.

In the spring of 1919 I went to Peace River where my sister and brother-in-law were living, then returned to Calgary that summer to compete in the Stampede. I split third and fourth with Powder River Thompson. From there we went to Wetaskiwin, then on to Saskatoon where the Prince of Wales was attending his first rodeo. He had his picture taken on my pick-up horse.

Jackie Cooper, Joe Fisher and I went to several American rodeos, at Yakima, Condon and Everett Washington, where I got first, Joe got second and Jackie got third. From there we went to Vancouver, B.C. where Welch and Strawberry Walls were putting on shows. I got third in the saddle riding. We went to Winnipeg in 1926, where I won third in the saddle riding, first in bareback and steer riding and also won the all-around. That year there was a show at Strathmore, where I won first, Slim Watrin second, Leo Watrin third and George McIntosh fourth. From there we went to Toronto with the Peter Welsh shows. In Toronto, I won bareback, steer riding and third in the saddle riding. The next show was Buffalo, New York, where I got second in steer riding and second in bareback.

In 1927, we all went back to Toronto for the second time. Almost all the Alberta boys rode in these shows. We rode in Columbus, Ohio, where I won a cup for bull riding, split second and third in the saddle riding. Pete Knight got first in the saddle riding at this show.

I went to Turner Valley and worked on the boiler gang and rodeoed in between. In 1931, at a show in Ellensburg, Wash. I won second in the saddle riding. In Pendleton, I lost a stirrup and didn't win any money. We went on to Sedalia, Missouri, then Madison Square Garden in New York, where I placed in three events. From a rodeo in Boston, I drove back to Montana with Ma (Marie) Gibson, one of the best cowgirls in rodeo. Herman Linder and Marie's son were also along. As we were leaving Boston, with Marie driving, a policeman was letting some children cross safely at a

L. to R. Frank Sharp, Maude Sharp and Marshall Copithorne at Calgary Stampede at ceremony honoring old time cowboys.

503

crosswalk. Marie nearly hit the policeman, who asked if there was anyone else in the car who could drive, so I took over. We got to Chicago, where Herman stayed and we started out again. I was so sleepy by this time that Marie took over the driving. However, she got turned around and we landed back in Chicago. Three days and nights later (with no sleep and much trouble) we finally arrived in Havre, Montana, and I bought a train ticket to Calgary.

In 1933, I rode in the Worlds Fair in Chicago, but could only ride bulls as only the top ten in each event were allowed to compete. From there we went to St. Louis, back to New York and Boston, then I travelled back to Omaha, Nebraska with Pete and Babe Knight. I rode bulls but didn't win much so went back to Calgary.

In 1937, I married Maud Mino, who I had met several years before at a party she had given for my cousins in North Battleford. Maud was born in Walker, Minnesota, and came to Canada with her family in 1910. They were early settlers of the North Battleford district. Maud worked in Calgary for the Hudson's Bay Co. before our marriage. We built a home in the Royalite Townsite in Turner Valley. About this time I was injured in a gas explosion, and I still feel the effects of that today. During the second World War, when drivers were scarce, Maud drove the Royalite work bus for three years, taking the workers to and from work, late shift and the early ones, and over some pretty bad roads.

In 1941, I judged at the Calgary Stampede. The following years I judged with Pete La Grandeur for four years, three years with Earl Thode, and also judged with Joe Fisher and Jack Wade. I judged the chuck wagon races for several years.

In 1945, we bought three quarters of land on Ware Creek in the Kew district. This was the S.W.¼ of 27-20-4-W5, N.W.¼ of 22-20-4-W5 and the S.E.¼ of 21-20-4-W5 and some lease. We started a ranch and a herd of cows. After tens years on Ware Creek we sold the place to Al and Alice Belanger, and bought land further east. When I was away judging at rodeos Maud would stay home and keep an eye on the animals. However, when our cow herd got too big, I spent all of my time on the ranch.

We have now sold our cows and most of our land, keeping the home place near Fisher Creek, the S.E.¼ of 7-21-3-W5, where we had built a new home and just enjoy life now that we have retired from active ranching.

Isabella Shaw

Isabella was the fifth child of Ernest and Alice Silvester of Kew, Alberta. She attended school in her growing years in the Square Butte area.

Later she did housework and cooking for the Larratt sawmill and cooking for the Joe Standish cook car serving the threshing crews.

In September of 1942 she joined the Canadian Women's Army Corp, serving at Vermillion, Currie and Suffield, Alberta. In February of 1944 she travelled overseas to serve in London, England. She returned to Canada in March, 1946 to receive her discharge.

After her discharge she took a sewing course in Calgary. In February of 1949, she married Alex Shaw. She returned with him to Carstairs, Alberta, and has lived on their farm there since.

They have three children. Ed, his wife and two children, of Athens, Greece, working for the J. & I. Case Co. over the middle east.

Barry works for Pan Arctic in the North. Donna the the only daughter, is married to Andy Morton of Didsbury, Alberta, and she works for the Senior Citizen's Home in Crossfield.

Isabella's interests are the legion (being president of the Ladies' Auxiliary for four years) and the Women of Unifarm. She was Assistant Cub Leader for three years.

Ron and Jo Shelley
by Ron and Jo Shelley
Brand right hip   ᔓ   left hip ᶜᣰ

Ronald Arthur Shelley was born in Calgary, Alberta, October 1940. He received his early education at Ramsay school and graduated from junior high at Colonel Walker. After graduating from high school at Western Canada Ron continued his education in accounting until his convocation from the University of Calgary where he received his Bachelor of Commerce degree in November of 1976, after previously attaining his Registered Industrial and Cost Accountant degree in September 1968. Ron, as a professional accountant, finds ample opportunity to practice his skills in the Millarville area.

Ron's father, Henry Alfred Shelley was born in Calgary and married Helen Winnifred Larter, also born in Calgary. Ron's grandparents on his father's side are John Thomas Shelley born in Hamilton, Ontario and married Ellen Hobestad who was born in North Dakota. John Thomas Shelley was Calgary's Fire Chief from 1945 to 1950. Ron's grandparents on his mother's side are Peter Larter born in Manchester, England and married Lottie Geneva Williams who was born in Chester, Nova Scotia. Ron has three brothers and one sister: Hank (deceased); Ellen (Marshall) Calgary; Ken, Edmonton and John, Calgary.

Ron married Marilyn Jo Whitlock in 1959 at St. Anne's Church in Calgary. Jo was born in Calgary, July 1941 and received her first nine years of education at St. Anne's school then received her grade twelve diploma from St. Mary's Girls High school in 1959.

Jo's father, Archie Whitlock was born in Idaho Falls, Idaho and married Margaret Devlin Gourlay who was born in Calgary. Jo's grandparents on her father's side are Gust A. Carlson born in Sweden and married Emily Anderson who was born in Nebraska of Swedish parents. They came to Idaho where Emily Carlson was remarried to Albert E. Whitlock who adopted her three sons, Archie, Frank and Earl. Jo's grandparents on her mother's side are Arthur P. Gourlay born in Scotland of Irish parents and married Mary Sutherland who was born in Scotland too. Jo has three sisters Peggy (Thomson), Betty (Anderson), both of Calgary and Gail (McCulloch) Vancouver.

We moved to Millarville from Calgary (Acadia District) with our four children in March 1973 having purchased our 40 acres from Dr. Black for $375.00 per acre. Our land location is (part of the Ingeveld homestead) Ptn. SW¼, Sec. 23, Twn. 21, Rge. 4, W5 Mer. The kids, two girls and two boys (Deborah Anne born May 1960; Daniel Dean born August 1961; Darrell Allen born August 1962 and Traci Lynn born April 1964) were at first mistaken for four girls because at that time long hair styles for boys was becoming quite popular in Calgary but not so in Millarville, consequently many children went home from school that first day our kids started saying that, "Four new girls have just started school." It didn't take long for our kids to adjust to the school bus, lunch kits, a small school, etc. and if asked shortly after if they wanted to move back to Calgary it was always "No Way." But the difference in the schooling was only a small part of the exciting changes.

The biggest thrill in moving to Millarville was that of the livestock. By the following year we owned cows, pigs, chickens, horses, dogs and even those very necessary cats. We tried a couple of times to do without cats but we definitely prefer cats to mice and now all our cats are our pets too. Ron and Jo were both born and raised in the Shamrock Hotel district near the Stockyards so we knew the difference between a cow and a pig but that's about all we knew when we moved out here. No one told us that all on one day we would be removing porcupine quills from pigs, horses and dogs; but that's exactly what we did.

Alex and Norma Lyall, our neighbours to the south, were always so patient teaching us or helping us to do all those crazy country tricks that city folks don't know how to do. Little things like turning cows properly (cows don't really respond to shoo — shoo); how to give a calf bolus; loading or unloading horses or just keeping the horses where they belonged. We had all kinds of help from our neighbours during our first couple of years. Like the time we flagged down Vern Blanchard to see if he could tell us how to milk a cow whose calf couldn't take all her milk. Vern parked his truck and came right over to show us what to do not just tell us. He made it look real easy but at least we aren't afraid to do it ourselves now. And how many times did we call on Ron Arkes for his know how, especially after we got Blossom, our milk cow. We were so nervous the first time we dried her up that poor Ron must have been over here every day reassuring us all that Blossom was not going to explode. A person could write a whole book just about our experiences with that damn cow. What a character she is. Of course she has to put up with two of us milking her at the same

time. Yes, Jo and one of the kids sit side by side and milk her. Blossom came from a Dairy Farm in B.C. and was used to a milking machine — that's why two of us milk her at the same time. Doc Roenisch dropped her off at the house one night and said, "Here's your milk cow". Thanks Doc! We had no milk pail, no stool, no nothin' but Doc was confident that we would manage and we did. We don't have to ask for as much help from our neighbours anymore but the help was greatly appreciated when we did need it.

Having four active children always keeps you involved in school matters as well as community affairs and we all really enjoy that. The baseball games and the hockey games too. Jo tried to get the girls in organized fastball so she was the Millarville representative when the Foothills Girls Fastball Association was formed in 1978 at which time there was junior and senior girls teams from Red Deer Lake — Priddis; Longview; Black Diamond and Millarville. Okotoks joined the league in 1979 too. Ron was president of the Valley Minor Hockey Association from 1976 to 1978. Like many parents in rural areas we spent countless hours transporting our children to various sports engagements anywhere from Midnapore to Stavely and from Bragg Creek to Blackie; a nuisance but much appreciated by the kids.

Debbie graduated from Oilfields High School in June 1978 and Danny is to do the same in June 1979. Darry did not adjust to High School as well as we would like so after a few months at Lord Beaverbrook in Calgary decided to try working for a while. Traci will graduate from grade nine at Millarville with plans to complete her high school at Oilfields.

The Shelley Family feel much a part of the life in and around our foothill community. Our hope is that we can continue sharing with all the good neighbours and friends we have found here good health and fortune all our remaining years.

Judith Lawna Shermerhorn (nee Latter)
Written by Judi Shermerhorn

I am Judi, born August 19, 1950, second daughter of the Latters, Roy and Grace.

Looking back over the years it seems to me that I was usually the one who 'did'. Not that the others didn't, it's just that the effects of what I did would last a long time. For example, one day Dad and Uncle Freddie (Barkley) had just finished putting up the last of our haystack and were ready to call it a day when they noticed I was missing. Where was I? On the very top at the edge of the stack, having a ball!! They just couldn't imagine how a four-year-old could have made it to the top without killing herself. Another time, Peg and I were trying to catch 'Stampede' to go for a ride. It was hard telling who was out to catch who, because it was I who ended up getting caught — square in the mouth by Stampede's back hoof and suddenly I was missing my front teeth. No, we did not pursue the idea of riding that day.

Judy and Roy Latter, 1952.

If my boot came off in the middle of a mucky barnyard I would carry on to my destination with one sock and one boot. (The sock usually started out the day as white). While Peg would run into the house to have her hands washed after each mud pie she made, I would carry on to the bitter end or until Mom made me come in for a washup. The idea that I could sleep anywhere and through anything probably began when Dad and Mom would take us with them to the dances at Millarville. When we got tired we would just fall asleep on a bench until everyone went home. They would always find me curled up directly under the band.

Peg and I spent hours one summer trying to catch pet magpies and once we had them we expected them to talk. I had heard that they required their tongues split, which I was ready to do until Dad and Mom convinced us it was not a very humane task for young ladies to undertake. I decided that I'd build a bird cage but my construction efforts did not hold up to the bird's thrashing about and we eventually let them go.

If we were good kids Dad would sometimes let us ride on the stoneboat behind Pete and Maggie, our plow horses. When we weren't bothering Dad to let us help him, we'd be out driving hundreds of miles in Uncle Cliff's old abandoned car that had been left on the hill behind the house for so long that a tree had grown up through the fender.

I remember the picnics the family would go on at Millarville Race Track. Mom always had her hands full trying to keep track of all of us and make sure we'd all end up in one place in time for dinner. She'd locate half of us and while she'd be off tracking down the rest, the first half would be off in the other direction. On the days of the Millarville Fair we'd begin packing the car early with all our entries. Cakes, pies, cookies, sewing and flowers — we must have had entries in half of the categories. There was always plenty of tears and frustration in the preparations for that day. With our oil stove, one slam of the back door, a jump in the next room, or someone running down the stairs would surely flop the would-be masterpieces in the oven. There were usually half-a-dozen cakes that would not pass inspection and these were left at home to be eaten before they spoiled.

I am the one credited with the breakage of two collarbones while clowning around with the family. During a small quarrel with Peg one evening I miscalculated in my attempt to 'kick her in the shins' and came in direct contact with the fridge, breaking my big toe. So as you see I was occasionally on the receiving line. We all had our share of chores in our family and one Saturday with Dad and Mom in town shopping, I had Peg so mad at me for walking across her freshly washed floor she chased me clear through the house with a dirty, wet floor mop.

I attended Red Deer Lake Elementary/Junior High School from 1956 to 1964, and Henry Wise Wood Senior High School, Calgary, from 1964 to 1967. Even attending a city school, where we were never allowed to wear slacks, didn't erase the tomboy from me. The vice-principal, Mr. John Semkuley, unexpectedly walked into the gym one morning before classes and caught Peg and me wrestling around on the floor.

Besides going to school we had other activities to keep us busy. I took Highland dancing, Tap Dancing, and singing lessons, played fastball with Midnapore and later coached the Kingsland Bantam Girls fastball team. I belonged to the Millarville 4-H Beef Club and the Red Deer Lake Hi-C. I became a member of the Red Deer Lake United Church, taught Sunday School, and sang in the church choir. In 1968 I enrolled at the University of Calgary. I have worked as a secretary for nine years and for the last two years as an accounting specialist.

I was married in 1971 and have two children: Shelley Lawna, born in 1971 and Daniel Earl Frederick, born in 1973. Our home is in the Kingsland Mobile Home Park, Calgary, where we have lived since 1972. Shelley is now in school and is a member of the local Brownie organization. Danny is attending Kindergarten and spends every free minute practising for the hockey team he joined this year.

Albert Silvester
by Ernie Silvester

Albert was the eldest son of Mr. and Mrs. Ernest Silvester. He was born in a tent at Cochrane, July 31, 1912. Albert attended Square Butte School when it was first built, but did not get much schooling as he had to help his dad a lot. He cut brush and thistles on the roads for many years. In 1939, he bought the N.E. quarter of 23-21-4w5 from Frank Ross. Albert milked cows and shipped cream up until 1948, when he became sick and had to quit work. In 1949, he sold the place to his brother Ernie. Albert worked for his Uncle George

Albert Silvester.

Arthur Silvester.

in the winter. In the summer he helped his dad, haying with horses for a good many years. In 1951, he bought the N.E. quarter of 24-20-4w5, and went back into milk cows. In 1964, he married Elsie Lynn. He became sick again and the doctors advised him to sell out. He loaded his cows, went into the house and passed away. He was buried in the cemetery at Christ Church, Millarville.

Arthur Silvester
AS RR

I was born the fourth child to Ernest and Alice Silvester Sr. on March 11th, 1916, at Kew, Alberta.

After receiving my basic education at Square Butte School I went to work for various lengths of time for some of the local ranchers some of which included: E. L. Kendall, G. Silvester, W. Patterson, and the Ballards and Beattys in the Okotoks area. In 1937 I purchased the NW ¼ of sec 8, Twp 20, R 3, W 5 from the Hudson's Bay Company which at that time was being leased by Russ Broomfield. Following the purchase of this quarter I began my own small ranching operation as well as worked for the neighbouring Broomfields. On March 11th, 1943 I enlisted in the army and served on the Front Line in Belgium, Holland and Germany. On March 11th, 1946 I was discharged and returned home to Canada.

Arthur Silvester's Family, Muriel and Phillip.

507

I exchanged marital vows with Grace Herridge, a girl I met while I was in the army, on February 6th, 1948 at Okotoks, Alberta. We made our home on my quarter section of land and continued to work for the Broomfields until I sold out to my brother Charlie in 1952. At that time I went to work for Alex Hartell for about one year and then obtained employment with Madison Natural Gas in Turner Valley where I purchased a home and continued to work until 1958. In that year I went to work as manager for Norman Gustavson, owner of High Noon Ranch, a position I have continued to hold until the present time.

Grace and I had two children, Muriel born in 1948 and Philip born in 1951. Both Muriel and Philip reside in Grande Prairie, Alberta and Muriel is married and has two sons.

Charles Silvester
-SC RR

I was born at Kew, Alberta August 13th, 1927, the 10th child of Ernest and Alice Silvester Sr. My basic formal education was received at Square Butte School and after school hours and weekends were spent helping with the many chores at home.

At the age of sixteen I went to work for Tom Merriam feeding cattle in the winter and operating cat for Howard Hampton during the spring, summer and fall. In 1950 I worked for Alex Shaw at Carstairs and in 1951 I worked for J. Schrader at Olds. I purchased the NW¼ of Sec. 8, Twp. 20, R 3, W 5 from my brother Arthur in 1952 and since that time have been managing my own small ranching operation as well as feeding

Jim Kilmeister and Charlie Silvester, with bear shot by Charlie in the Muskeg.

cattle during the winter months for Russ and Jack Broomfield. I also helped Herb McEathron with the fall threshing until a few years ago when Herb decided combining was easier. For summer pasture I have a forest reserve permit allowing me to run 50 head of cattle in the Muskeg area. I obtained this permit in 1954 which at that time was for only 25 head of cattle. When I first ran my cattle in the Muskeg, bears were a serious and constant threat however this problem has changed to wolves in recent years.

I have remained a bachelor all of my life.

Ernest and Marjorie Silvester and Family
by Ernest Silvester — E S L·R·

I was the 4th son of Ernest and Alice Silvester, born on June 5th, 1923. I was one of a family of thirteen. I received my schooling at Square Butte School. I had to walk two miles to and from school, and for quite a few years I was janitor, having to go early and light the wood fire to get the school warm before the teacher and children got there. The big wage was four dollars a month.

Ernie and Marjorie (Posgate) Silvester on their wedding day 1957.

Ernie Silvester Family. Back row, L. to R.: Tommy, Randy, Rick. Front: Cora and Gary.

508

Ernie Silvester's new cedar log house that was blown down by a big Chinook wind. January 15th, 1972.

Jim and Kathleen Silvester on their wedding day, July 24, 1967. L. to R. Virginia Cowan, Kathy, Jim and Charlie Silvester.

I worked on my dad's ranch for a number of years. In 1949, I bought the N.E.¼ of 23-21-4w5 from my brother, who was in ill health at the time. I never was interested in anything but ranching. In 1951 I went into ranching on my own. I bought another 80 acres adjacent to my first quarter, and I got a grazing permit in the Muskeg area, North Sheep district, about eight years later. I was moved down on the Fisher Creek range, which was much handier, as I had acquired section 31-21-4w5.

In 1957 I married Marjorie Rose Posgate, who grew up in the Millarville area and attended Millarville School. We have five children, four boys, Thomas B., Richard E., Randolph A., Gary D., and one girl, Cora Rose. My boys love hunting and fishing and all the children love horseback riding, so did Marjorie until she became ill. Marjorie passed away July 23, 1977.

One incident I would like to relate: on January 15, 1972, we had a new cedar log house, and we have a picture of what was left after the big wind that night. We moved in with a very good neighbor, Ivor and Elaine Lyster, for three weeks while the new house was being built. After this, every time the wind would start blowing, Gary was so scared he would run down into the basement.

I run approximately a 100 cow herd, brand —E S, left rib. Tom has finished high school and is now working for Husky Oil on Savanna Creek. Rick has finished school. He tried his hand at everything this past summer. He worked for the fire suppression crew in the Bow Crow Forest until they closed for the season. Now he is field clerk for the Northern Geophysical in Northern Alberta. The three younger children are in school. Gary and Cora go to Millarville School and Randy attends Bishop Grandin in Calgary.

The Jim Silvester Family

by Kathy Silvester   —E∃ R.R. E̅S̅ L.H. M-J

Jim was born to Mr. Ernest and Mrs. Alice Silvester June 20th, 1932, being the second youngest of a family of thirteen. Jim still lives on the ranch which his parents homesteaded in 1910, being the NW¼ of Sec 34-Twp. 20-R4-W 5. He attended school at Square

Butte which was a one-room one-teacher school. There were as many as eighteen pupils and sometimes as few as seven going to school at one time.

Sister Minnie and brothers Charlie, Jim and Tom all attended school together for a few years. They also did the janitor work which consisted of sweeping the floor and lighting the fire in the mornings before the rest of the children arrived.

After finishing grade nine, Jim came home to work for his Father on the ranch. The only time he worked away from home was in the Fall of 1949 through to 1957 during which time he helped Mr. G. A. Wonacott (Bert) and Mrs. J. Wylie with the threshing. Both of these families owned land south of the Red Deer Lake store.

In 1957 Jim purchased the SE¼ of Sec 3-Twp. 20-R 4-W 5 (formerly the Stagg place) from his Dad and in 1959 he purchased the NE¼ of Sec 3-Twp. 20-R 4-W 5. When his Dad passed away in 1964 Jim was left the home ½ section giving him one section of deeded land and 1¼ sections of leased land. Along with the land, he was also left his Father's cow brand -E∃ on the right ribs and the horse brand E̅S̅ on the left hip. Jim also has his own brand M-J on the left rib. In July 1967 Jim married Kathleen Jean Mathers.

I was born a farmer's daughter to Mr. William (Bill) and Mrs. Catherine (Cathy) Mathers on January 21st, 1945 in Aberdeenshire Scotland. My younger sister Dorothy passed away in 1947 and my younger brother William (Bill) is now married and lives in Southern England.

I attended school in Hatten until Dad passed away in 1955. At that time Mum sold the farm and we moved into Aberdeen. Upon completing my elementary education at Mile-End School, I attended Rosemount to obtain my secondary education. After leaving school I attended Craibstone Agricultural College for one year and then obtained employment on a farm in Kincardineshire.

I then took my nurses training and received my degree in 1965. It was while I was studying for my finals that I answered an advertisement in the local newspaper for a nanny on a ranch in Alberta, Canada. The job was to look after seven boys. I was accepted for the position and flew from Prestwick to Calgary March 7th, 1966 where Mr. J. A. Campbell, owner of Tullochewan Ranch at Black Diamond, met me. After a stormy drive home to the ranch, Mrs. Campbell was waiting to greet us. Next day I met the boys — John, Tony, William, Andrew, Neil, Matthew and Gordon. They ranged in age from 14 to 2 years. One nice day that summer the boys and myself took Mr. Campbell's canoe down to the slough and managed without effort to tip the canoe and ourselves upside down.

The following year, 1967, proved to be quite a memorable year for the Silvester family as far as weddings went, with two almost catastrophies.

Bill Eden and Maureen O'Hagen had their wedding date set for June 2nd. A few days before however, it began raining very heavily and as a consequence several roads and bridges were washed out. Because of the poor road conditions, the groom and bestman were almost stranded at Square Butte and the bride and bridesmaid in Black Diamond. However after loosing sleep and a lot of sweat everything went as planned.

Next came July 24th and the creeks were still a little high. My Mother and Brother came out for our wedding and were taken to Christ Church Millarville by Howard and Alice Hampton. My bridesmaid, Virginia Cowan, and myself later followed with Bob and Janet MacKay. The quickest way to the church from Campbell's Ranch was across Three Point Creek. As already mentioned the creeks were still a little high from the earlier rains — well we just broke over the hill at the creek and there was the Hampton car stuck right in the middle. But Bob, being Bob, said "Oh don't worry we'll make it all right" so in we went. Well we were just neck and neck with Howard's car and down we went. As the saying goes a bride should be late for her wedding — I was late all right, one hour late. It

was through the kindness of Charlie King and Joe Preston with a tractor that we weren't any later. Janet had very kindly covered the car seat with a white sheet so that we didn't get our dresses dirty. When we finally reached the other side we had to get out of the car to wring the water out of the sheet. About this time Mum was having fits as she thought it was my wedding dress that we were wringing the water out of. However all this time back at the church Charlie Silvester, best-man, and Jim were looking for a bottle to settle their nerves — which Archdeacon Gant had assured them was in the vestry. Fortunately they did not find it or they may have left. Worse still, the Square Butte Ladies who were catering for the reception almost gave up on us and went home.

In March 1968 we were blessed with our only daughter Ailsa MacIntosh. May 1970 saw the arrival of our first son Scott James and July 1971 saw the arrival of our second son Neil Craig.

May Silvester

I was born on the 16th of October 1921 at Kew, Alberta, the seventh child in a family of thirteen to Alice and Ernest Silvester Sr. I received my schooling at Square Butte School and my out-of-school hours were spent helping with the many chores at home.

At the age of sixteen I went to work for Mrs. Joe Standish and stayed there for a year and a half. I then went to work for Mrs. Garstin and in 1939 I commenced employment with the E. Wonacott family in the Red Deer Lake area where I have been to the present day. After Mrs. Wonacott passed away I stayed and kept house for her son Bert. In April of 1944 Bert moved to the NW¼ of sec 5-twp 22-R1-W5 which has been my place of residence since. Bert passed away on the 10th of September 1978 at the age of eighty-four.

Ernest Silvester Family. Back, L. to R.: Min, Ernie, Bella, Charlie, Albert. Centre: Daisy, May, Alice. Front: Arthur, Tom, Jim on Mrs. Silvester's lap.

Thomas Silvester
by Ernie Silvester

Tom was the youngest of thirteen children born to Mr. and Mrs. Ernest Silvester Sr., early Kew

The Jim Silvester family. Scott, Ailsa, Jim, Kathy and Neil.

Tommy Silvester

ranchers. He was born on the ranch June 8th, 1934. How well I remember that night: it was the only time Mother had to have a doctor's assistance. The doctor had to be brought the last three miles by saddle horse or wagon.

Tom attended Square Butte School and after finishing, stayed at the ranch, helping his dad and brother.

After a lengthy illness, he passed away at the Turner Valley hospital in 1958 at the age of twenty-three. He was laid to rest at Christ Church cemetery at Millarville. He is still survived by five brothers and six sisters.

Donald K. Sim

by Margaret Sim

Donald was born July 6th, 1936 in High River. He lived at Royalties until moving to Kew in 1946. He went to school at Royalties, Plainview and Sheep Creek. He worked with his brother on the pipe lines. June 1954, he went to work on the drilling rigs.

On August 6th, 1954, Donald married Margaret Nylund. Margaret was born in Calgary October 21, 1934 and was raised at Square Butte. She attended school there until grade nine, then attended the school at Sheep Creek. Before she married she worked in Calgary and at the Turner Valley Hospital.

Don and Margaret lived in Leslieville, Innisfail, Rimbey, Breton and Blue Ridge, while Don was working on the rigs. They moved to Turner Valley, January 1956, where they lived for five years, then moved to Carstairs in January, 1961. Don worked there for the Home Oil Co. until 1976, when he was transferred to Lethbridge. He has been with Home Oil for twenty-one years.

Donald Sim family. Back row, Lorna, Kathleen, Darrel, Diana. Front row, Margaret and Donald Sim.

Don Sim Family. Left to Right: Darrel and Heather Sim, Don and Margaret Sim, Kathy and Tom Bennett and Dixie Bennett on mother's knee. Front: Lorna and Diana Sim.

Their son Darrel was born November 13, 1955, at Turner Valley. He married Heather Yellowlees of Carstairs on September 4th, 1976. They are now living in their new home in Calgary.

Kathleen was born January 7th, 1957, at Turner Valley. She married Thomas Bennet of Carstairs on November 20th, 1976. They have one daughter, Dixie Lee. They live on a farm east of Carstairs.

Diana was born on June 22nd, 1960, at Turner Valley. Lorna was born May 30th, 1963, at Didsbury. They are both living at home and going to school, Diana in Grade 12, and Lorna in Grade nine.

Roy Sim and Family

Roy Sim and family. I came from Woodstock, Ontario to High River in 1926. My parents were Andrew and Jessie Sim of Innerkip, Ontario. That fall harvest was late so I worked in High River digging sewer ditches near the hospital. It was all dug by hand in those days. Sometimes we dug as deep as 10 to 11 feet. I worked there about 3 weeks, then went out stooking

Roy and Elsie Sim's family. L. to R. Jean, Donald, Glen, Milton.

with my brother Joe. The first field we started in was a half section all cut down, it sure made me feel homesick for a while as I was only 17 years old and never had been away from home before, but we were working for Mormon folk east of High River, and I think their motto was pleasure before work, and they took us all over to dances and shows which did not leave us in very good shape for stooking the next day, but helped ease the loneliness. Then came threshing; we did not get a very good run as it snowed quite early in the fall, so we lived in High River until February, then went threshing again, and finished when they were putting in the crop.

I went to work for a water well driller by the name of C. B. Larsen. We drilled wells west of High River to Longview and south. I really enjoyed working for him. Eventually, I went to work for my Uncle Fred Sim at East Longview where I met my wife Elsie Wells from Antelope, Saskatchewan near Swift Current. Her dad came from Ireland as a small boy. He grew up and worked near Stratford, Ontario. Her mother came from Milverton, Ontario.

Elsie and I were married in 1932. We worked for several farmers, then moved to Royalities in 1937 which was Little Chicago then. We lived there for 9 years. I worked for several Oil Companies, then for Imperial Oil which later became Royalite. I roughnecked on many of their wells, mostly in the south end of the field — Hartel, Little Chicago, Little New York and some around Turner Valley.

I was badly hurt on Royalite 73; very nearly lost my arm; was in the Turner Valley hospital and later sent to the Compensation Hospital in Banff for two months, then went back to work on the same rig, which I did not like very much. I never did care for the rigs after that, so was glad when they put me doing something else.

I learned later that the boys nailed my finger (which had been pulled off) above the Cathead. When the next Cathead man came on and saw it, he fainted.

I sure missed my finger for several winters as it used to get so cold.

I always wanted a piece of land so I could get the

Roy and Elsie Sim. Christmas Day, 1978.

family out of town. I heard of a quarter section up west of Turner Valley which was owned by Bill Calderwood in the Kew district. S.W.¼, 29-20-3W5. We bought it in 1945 and moved the following year in July 26th, 1946. We moved our house from Royalities which we built in 1937 for $300.00.

I worked for Imperial till 1948 when I went to work for Home Oil. I was there until I retired in 1969. Many times it was 7 days a week and nearly always Christmas and New Years. I could always use that extra money as I was getting the land cleared and getting a few cattle. My first brand was $\overline{RS}$. Later I bought Harry Orum's Brand $\overline{HA}$ and used it till I quit farming in 1972.

We had four children, Milton, Jean, Donald and Glen. Milton, who married Darlene Hendricks of Hardisty, Alberta, makes his home in Hardisty. He is assistant superintendent for Price Pipeline Co. Ltd. of Canada. Our daughter, Jean, married Douglas Godkin of Turner Valley, Alberta. They lived in Calgary till her death at the age of 29 in 1962. Donald married Margaret Nylund of the Square Butte district. They now live in Lethbridge. Don has worked for Home Oil for years and is now manager of the Retlaw Gas Plant north of Lethbridge.

Glen married Ivy Mitchel of Black Diamond, Alberta. They are now living at Carrot Creek east of Edmonton. He worked for Ottis Elevator Company for 15 years as foreman.

We sold our farm in 1972 to Mr. and Mrs. Jim Selman. We moved to Black Diamond January 31, 1973 where we still reside.

Simpson, Kenneth Wayne

Kenneth Wayne, born and raised in Nokomis, Saskatchewan. Lived in Regina, Saskatchewan a number of years where he met his wife Adeline Rose (nee Buczulak) of Jasmin, Saskatchewan. In May, 1965 they moved to Calgary, Alberta and shortly thereafter they made numerous friends in the city and country and purchased from Jake and Barbara Reimer an acreage, namely a portion of SW-4-22-4, W5M.

On May 10, 1971 a son Greg Owen was born and the only child of the couple.

Mr. Simpson a well known car and truck salesman has served many of the Millarville district folks. Fishing, hunting and the love of flying his Cessna 180 aircraft were his interests.

Unfortunate events occurred for the family in 1976 and once again on May 18, 1977 a tragedy, whereby Kenneth was killed in his private aircraft while on a business trip.

Adeline and Greg reside in Calgary where she works as an executive secretary for a downtown oil company. She and son can be seen at Square Butte district most any time either working or looking up friends.

Adeline Simpson and son Greg. Calgary Stampede July 1977.

Francis Stuart Sinclair-Smith

written by Stuart Sinclair-Smith
Cattle brand Ƨ left rib.

My father, Francis, came to the Millarville district in 1911. He served in the Great War of 1914-18, then returned and purchased Viewfield Ranch in 1919 — S 2-21-2-W5 and SW¼ 11-21-2-W5. He married Helen May Cannon in 1938; she was born and raised on S10-21-2-W5, only a mile from Viewfield. Cathie Helen, a daughter, was born in 1940. I arrived on the scene in 1942, destined to be a mobile punching bag for my sister.

Stuart and Ruby Sinclair-Smith, sons Jeffrey and Steven.

I took my schooling at the old Sheep Creek School about three miles west of Millarville. The school was moved to Millarville in 1951, where two more rooms were added. The one and only time I played hooky was at the old school. A bunch of the boys, big and small, decided to play hooky one day. The first thing that went wrong was the weather. It was in February and it must have been 20 degrees below zero. We tramped around in the kneedeep snow until about 1:30 in the afternoon, when we decided this hooky stuff was for people who lived in warmer parts. We sheepishly went back to the school where our irate teacher, Mrs. Clarke, made us all stand in the school porch — which by the way had no door we could close and no window to shut. We huddled there in a 20 mph. cross-wind until bus time.

In 1954 I joined the Royal Canadian Army Cadets in Turner Valley, headed by Lieut. W. Dube of Millarville. The Cadet Corps met every Monday night in what is now the Turner Valley Fire Hall. We were taught parade square drill, firearms, different types of radio drill, signals, and mechanics. I remember many winter evenings riding in the back of an army truck between Millarville and Turner Valley, and wondering what we had done to deserve the coldest truck in the entire Canadian Army. I was in the Cadet Corps for six years, during which time I attended a number of training camps in Vernon, B.C. I left the Cadet Corps in 1959, with the rank of Cadet Captain.

In the fall of 1959 I attended the School of Agriculture at Olds. I enrolled in the two-year course, and in 1961 graduated from the course in Practical Agriculture. The highlight of the course had to be the Sadie Hawkins dance. Some of the boys raided the hog barn and showed up at the dance in the gym with three liberally greased pigs. The staff was not amused as the pigs sought refuge amongst the chairs where they were seated. For some unknown reason the inhabitants of the boys' dormitory were confined to their rooms for the rest of the weekend.

I returned to Viewfield, and in 1963 met Ruby Lowe of Priddis. As with most families, the kids helped with the chores; Ruby and her sister were responsible for milking cows after school. When I would go and visit, invariably I would be early and the girls wouldn't be finished the milking. Being an up and coming hero, I would boldly grab a pail, a milking stool, and sit down under the cow which Ruby had pointed out. Nine times out of ten, the cow took an immediate dislike for my milking ability and a sloppy foot would be planted in the centre of my sparkling white shirt, and I would end up in the gutter. Nine out of ten times I would crawl out of the gutter and find Ruby and Jean barely able to breathe from laughing. Boy, you talk about love being blind, you should have seen me. Another favorite trick was to talk me into a wrist-twisting match; in full view of her parents, brothers and sister. I couldn't refuse for fear of being called chicken, and then she would rap my knuckles on the table. I never could figure out why her father looked at me out of the corner of his eye like that.

Love conquers all, and in July 1963 we were married in Christ Church, Millarville. We moved a small house from Hartell onto the farm and our first son, Jeffrey Stuart, was born in 1964.

Dad passed away suddenly in February 1966, just two weeks before our second son, Steven James, was born.

In June of 1967 I was asked to be head guide for an outfitting company in the Northwest Territories. The company was owned by Chuck Hayward of Red Deer Lake, and guided hunters in the McKenzie Mountains. This was my life's ambition, so it was off to the fabled North Country. I thought it would be great to see what the north was like for a summer, but the North tends to grow on you, and I guided for Chuck for six years. We were the first ever to take horses from the Yukon Territory overland to the McKenzie River, and later, were the first ever to trail horses completely around the Ragged Range, one of the highest and most formidable of the McKenzie Mountains. I have a veritable mountain of memories of horses, hunters and experiences. Ruby and the boys first came up in 1968, and loved it. They flew into the base camp at Little Dall Lake, a distance of 250 air miles, by float plane. They left home after school ended in June, and returned for school in September.

Chuck with his crew of guides would truck thirty-

Jeffrey and Steven Sinclair-Smith feeding orphaned lambs.

five head of horses from Millarville to the Canada Tungsten Mine, a distance of 1390 miles. From there, we would pack up and trail them into camp. It usually took twelve to fourteen days, depending on river conditions — flooding in the Nahanni and Broken Skull — to cover the 240 miles. There are many hair-raising tales that could be told about crossing those two rivers.

Ruby, and Chuck's wife, Laura, did the cooking and housekeeping at base camp. They are famous for their roast hind quarter of caribou and home-made bread and fresh blueberry pies. They are also renowned for their ability to provide a meal for fourteen hungry people on a moment's notice. We guided the hunters after Dall Sheep, Grizzly, Caribou, Wolf, Moose and Goat. Many lasting friendships were kindled on the thirteen-day hunting expeditions. In 1973, after three hazardous experiences in rivers, I decided to return to agriculture full time.

Mom was remarried on July 11, 1968. She married Joe Preston, who farms on N½ 31-20-2-W5.

Charles E. Sine 1913-
SW¼ 7-21-3-W5

My Mother and Father were born of American extraction, Minneapolis, Minnesota, from where they moved to Revelstoke, British Columbia in 1903. My Dad managed sawmills in those days, and later, when they were sold, opened retail lumber yards on the prairies, establishing their headquarters in Calgary in 1911. It was in Calgary where I was born.

After graduating from Dartmouth College in Hanover, New Hampshire in 1937 I started my business career with Revelstoke Sawmill Company and Atlas Lumber Company, and as a matter of fact just about the first job I had with the Company was at "Little Chicago" south of Black Diamond. That would have been in the late fall and winter of 1937/38. I worked with the Companies for 35 years, retiring in February 1972.

Sine Family. L. to R. Betty, Dixie and Charles (Chuck) Sine.

My wife Mary E. (Betty) was born in Lethbridge. Her Mother (Dixie Seatle) was born in Pincher Creek in 1889, and her Grandmother arrived in Southern Alberta via Milwaukee, Wisconsin and the Missouri River and presumably overland to Fort Macleod area from Fort Benton, Montana. Betty's Grandfather was with the Northwest Mounted Police and was stationed at various times in Fort Macleod, Pincher Creek, Lethbridge, Calgary, and Edmonton. He retired from the force, which by then was the Royal Canadian Mounted Police, as Ass't. Comm. J. O. Wilson in about 1915 and moved to Victoria, British Columbia. Betty's Father died when she was very young in Lethbridge, and her mother moved to Victoria with her family taking her two children.

Betty and I met in Victoria in 1946, right after the war, and were married the same year. We have three children, Brett is the eldest, married, and living in Victoria; Michael, single and living in Calgary; and daughter Dixie is married and living in Calgary.

We bought our quarter section from Maude and Frank Sharp in December 1968, and until the spring of 1971 we used it for picnicing and camping. We started building our home during the spring of 1971 after Maude Sharp found our well with her witching ability. We did not complete the house until the fall of 1972. It was not until July of 1973 that we took up permanent residence.

Fred Singer

Fred Singer worked for Malcolm Millar in the 30's and used to introduce himself as "Millar's foreman". He had an accent you could cut with a knife and claimed to be a Dutchman. Mr. Roedler Sr. said that from his accent he came from the south of Germany, and Singer didn't deny it. Sometime in the late 1930's or early 40's, he developed some disturbing symptoms and was told by the doctor that he had six months to live. He resolved to make the last six months worthwhile, and after liquidating what assets he had,

he proceeded to blow the works on wine, women and song — mainly the first two. At the end of six months he was still alive and in reasonably good shape, so he went back to the doctor who decided he must have been mistaken. Fred said it had been a lot of fun anyway.

Evelyn and Clell Sloan

Evelyn, the fifth of seven Field girls, married Clell Sloan, a business man from Calgary. They have lived in Calgary ever since and have a family of five sons and one daughter.

Clell and Evelyn (Field) Sloan, on their wedding day.

Front row: Clell and Evelyn Sloan with son Jamie, and daughter Shannon. Back row: four sons, Clark, Kent, Cameron and Craig.

515

Lynn and Garry Smith.

Garry Smith

by Doug Lawrence

Garry was born in Turner Valley in 1954, the youngest of four children born to Dorothy and Wilbur Smith. They resided on the farm in the Kew district, the south half of section 13-20-4w5. He was still very young when his father passed away. The family continued living on the farm until his mother married Doug Lawrence and they moved to his farm in the Red Deer Lake district, where Garry attended School. They were there four years when the farm was sold and they moved back to the farm at Kew. Garry then attended school at Millarville, later finishing at Turner Valley, where he excelled in gymnastics and basketball, and also played hockey.

Garry helped with the farm work and when the farm was sold and the family moved to Turner Valley, he was able to get a job locally, and then later in Calgary.

He was married to Lynn Kosak of Turner Valley, and they make their home in Turner Valley. Garry is very active helping the young hockey players in the winter.

Hilda Bernice Smith

by H. Smith

Born — February 4, 1921 on the farm near where the Calgary airport now stands; fourth daughter of Johnny and Emily Barraclough.

We moved into the Millarville area in 1928, travelling by team and wagon. I recall vividly, riding in the wagon with some new born calves and Dad had them tied down with a canvas over them. One of them kept getting its head out and hanging it on the wheel, so I had to keep putting its head in. We arrived at our new home which is where the Charles Bull Place is now.

I attended Ballyhamage and later Fordville schools; lived and worked at home on the farm until June of 1941 when I married George H. Smith (Ted), lived in and around Calgary until moving to Nanaimo, British Columbia in 1960.

We have two children, Margaret M. and Ronald D., and four grandchildren, all residing in Nanaimo, British Columbia.

Jamie Smith (Chalmers)

Jamie Smith (Chalmers) was born November 16, 1954 in Turner Valley, the third daughter of Jim and Wilma Chalmers of the Millarville area. She attended Sheep Creek School until the finish of grade eight, took grade nine at Turner Valley Elementary School and grade ten at Oilfields High School at Black Diamond. She was active in basketball, gymnastics, track and field, badminton, and volleyball during the school years. While in grade nine she helped instruct gymnastics (after school) to the lower grades at Millarville. Jamie was a member of the Busy Beavers 4-H Food Club for five years and the Busy Beavers 4-H Horse Club for one year. She attended Sunday School at Sheep Creek School and then joined the choir at Christ Church, Millarville.

In 1971, in Christ Church, Millarville, Jamie married Wade V. Smith of Hanna, Alta. Their daughter, Pamela Jean, was born in Turner Valley, and their son, Marty James, was born in the Holy Cross Hospital in Calgary. They resided in Turner Valley where Jamie was actively involved in "Time Out", and helped judge the gymnastics competitions in Turner Valley Elementary School for three years.

In March of 1979 Jamie, Pamela and Marty moved to High River. Jamie presently works as seamstress at the High River Dry Cleaners and as cook, waitress and cashier at the Dairy Inn.

Raymond L. Smith

by Doug Lawrence

Ray was born in High River in 1941, eldest son of Wilbur and Dorothy Smith. They lived on a farm in the Kew district, and also for a time in the oilfields, where Ray started school. Later the family moved back to the farm and Ray attended Plainview School until bussed to Millarville when Plainview School was closed. His father passed away during this time and his mother struggled on for some time, until she married Doug Lawrence and the family moved to Doug's farm in the Red Deer Lake area. Ray finished his schooling there. He worked for the M.D. in road construction for some time.

He married Iris Taylor of Okotoks, and they lived in High River for a while, then he gave up road work and did trucking, then spent some winters with an oil exploration outfit in the far north. He returned to trucking and they lived in various places and finally returned to Okotoks. By this time they had a family of

Ray Smith Family. Back: Ray, Iris, Darcy. Centre: Kim, Danny. Front: Shawn.

three, Darcy, Kim and Danny. Shawn joined the family later.

Ray went to work for the local sulpher plant, then returned to trucking. Its in his blood. He leads a busy life and is active in the Lion's club, and is a member of the Okotoks Volunteer Fire Brigade. Iris has also been busy, with her family, has assumed office and retail work at times. She is also keen on ceramics, etc.

Richard Milton (Dick) Smith

by Joan Kendall

Dick was born December 23, 1909, near Swan River, Manitoba. His life was spent in the lumber and sawmill business. In 1935, he came to Alberta to work with his brother Rexford in his sawmill business three miles south-west of Priddis. There they sawed mine timbers for the coal mine at Priddis and other lumber for sale.

In 1937 they moved to a timber tract on Roedler's land, now owned by Sedco. A planer and resaw were set up at Midnapore in 1946 to remanufacture the lumber sawn at the mill. The mill was moved to Dick Lyall's land at Square Butte about 1950 and in 1954 Dick moved his planer and resaw to Kendall's Lumber yard to process the lumber from this mill.

In the twenty-four years that Dick planed and resawed lumber at Kendall's Mill he pursued many other interests. He was always a collector — of antique machinery and a collector of guns. He had a varied assortment of the latter and never a hunting season passed that he did not make a few forays into the woods, usually returning with something for dinner.

He was always interested in teaching the young people about guns and conducted turkey shoots for them at Square Butte Hall, where his main concern was safety before fun.

In his last few years his main interest was the young people, those of the Square Butte Community and his many nephews and nieces — in fact it would be said that he was an uncle to every child he knew.

Dick Smith passed away March 28, 1978.

Mr. and Mrs. Rixford Smith

by Rix Smith

I was born in Midland, Ontario on May 26, 1899. My parents moved when I was a little scamper to Minnitonas, Manitoba, where they homesteaded in the wilderness. I was one of a family of ten.

In 1928 I came west to Calgary. I was a building contractor until 1934. I then moved to Priddis with my brother Dick, to N.W., Sec.5, T.22, W.5 and started manufacturing lath and lumber and mine timbers. In 1935 I married Katharine McLeod. In 1936 we moved to S.E. ¼, Sec.31, T.21, R.3, W.5. We then did logging and lumbering with Katharine doing the cooking for the men.

The lath was bought by the National Timber and Fence delivered to Red Deer, also the Calgary Lumber yards bought lath and lumber and some was sold locally. We also ran a planing mill.

It was here our son Hugh was born. Katharine later moved to Calgary to send the children to school. Gwen, our daughter, is Mrs. Riese — was born in Calgary, as well as our son Don. Dick and I continued with the lumbering business and later moved the planing mill to Midnapore. In 1953 we moved the mill to Parson, B.C. where I did logging and lumbering for several years.

We make our home in Midnapore and still sell building supplies.

Robin and Evelyn Smith

by Evelyn Smith

Being the ninth in a family of eleven children was a learning experience, as well as a lot of fun for me — especially with seven brothers! I was born in June, 1949 to Ernest and Mary Loewen, who lived and farmed in the Swalwell and Linden areas in Alberta.

Robin was born in Edmonton in June, 1948, the second in a family of four. His parents still reside there, but his mother grew up in the Nanton area as Jean McMasters.

We met at the University of Alberta, Edmonton, became good friends, and used to coffee more than study. Eventually, after I received my Bachelor of Arts degree and he received his Bachelor of Science, we got around to our first date. This led to our marriage at Mayfair Park in Edmonton in June, 1973. In August of that year, we moved to Guelph, Ontario where, three years later, Robin received his Bachelor of Landscape Architecture, and I received my "P.H.T.", that is, "Putting Hubby Through", by teaching Staff Education Courses at a local psychiatric hospital. After studies were completed, we toured Europe for a month, and returned to Alberta in October, 1976, where Robin is a landscape architect.

While in Ontario, we had a taste of country living and decided that we would like that situation again, if possible. We feel fortunate to be in the Millarville area, and are presently living on the N.W.¼, Sec. 30, T. 21, R. 2, W. 5. So far, we have one child, daughter Amanda, born in June, 1977. We thoroughly enjoy this friendly, active community nestled in the foothills of Alberta.

The Poplar Place

Ron Smith

In October of 1978, the Smiths moved onto the Westergaard place, a home originally built by the Warrens in 1973.

Ronald Smith was born in 1939 in Manchester, England, and lived there till he immigrated to Canada in 1965. His job as a sprinkler fitter took him all over Western Canada before he finally settled in Calgary, Alberta.

Mary Anne Smith was born in 1944 in New Westminster, B.C. She went to school in Delta and then onto the University of British Columbia where she obtained a Bachelor of Education Degree. She taught for two years in Abbotsford, B.C. and for two years in Whitehorse, Y.T.

Ron and Mary Anne met under the midnight sun and were married in Vancouver. They moved to Calgary where, on December 29, 1969, Alec Neil Smith was born. He was raised in Calgary till the age of 8 and is now being raised as a "country slicker".

Sharon Smith (Chalmers)

Sharon Smith (Chalmers) was born June 6, 1956 in Turner Valley, fourth daughter of Jim and Wilma Chalmers, ranchers of the Millarville area. She went to Sheep Creek School until grade 8 then took her high schooling at Oilfields High in Black Diamond. Being interested in sports, Sharon took an active part in Track and Field, basketball, and gymnastics while go-

Sharon and Cliff Smith with Shawn and Kelli.

ing to Sheep Creek School. She was a member of the Busy Beavers 4-H Food Club for 3 years.

In 1974 Sharon was married in Christ Church, Millarville to Clifford E. Smith from Hanna, Alta. In 1976, Kelli Marie, their daughter was born, and in 1978 their son, Shawn Clifford. Sharon has now been a First Aider with the St. John's of Calgary for 4 years. Cliff and Sharon, Kelli, and Shawn reside in Black Diamond.

Mary and James South

by Mary South

I was born in 1948 in Turner Valley, the second daughter of Ronald and Maud Birkenes (nee Glaister). My family lived in Turner Valley where my father was employed by Gulf Oil, so my sister and I attended the Turner Valley Elementary and Junior High and then the Oilfields High School.

In 1958 while still living in Turner Valley, my father bought a ¼ section in Millarville from Alex and Effie Scatterty (N.W.¼, Sec. 14, T. 21, R.3, W.5). We moved an old cabin on the place and bought four horses and became "weekend farmers". My sister, Margaret and myself spent many pleasant hours riding the surrounding district, building a tree house, skating on the dam, and riding or walking over for "tea" with our maternal grandparents, Mr. and Mrs. D. O. Glaister Sr., who resided on the next quarter.

In 1969 my father built a new house on the farm, retired from Gulf Oil and took up permanent residence in Millarville. By this time I was in my third year of Education at the University of Calgary and living with a girlfriend in Calgary. In 1970 I started teaching (Grades 4, 5 and 6) at Canyon Meadows Elementary School and commuted from my parents home in Millarville to Calgary daily. I taught school there for four years.

In July, 1972 I married James Thomas South (born 1943, Prince Albert, Saskatchewan). Jim spent his younger years in the Vulcan, Blackie, and Nanton districts, the second of three children born to Alexander and Catherine South. Alex was a welder and blacksmith by trade, but when Jim was ten his family loaded up all their belongings and went to the Manning district (Hotchkiss) to homestead a section of land. To supplement their income, both Jim and his brother along with their father worked in various lumber mills throughout the district, and worked on their education at the Manning High School, and from there worked on various jobs with the Alberta Forestry and Department of Highways.

He returned to the Vulcan district in 1964 where he worked for the county, and then finally in 1966 moved to Calgary where he became a heavy equipment operator for Canadian Western Natural Gas Co. In 1972, he bought his own backhoe and started his own company (Southco Excavating Ltd.) with a contract with Canadian Western and has been under contract there ever since.

After our marriage, we lived for a short time in Calgary where we both worked, but in March, 1973 because of my grandmother's death and my grandfather's ill health, we were asked by my family to move on to the farm in Millarville (N.E.¼, Sec.14, T.21, R.3, W.5) to care for it. We lived there for 3½ years renewing old friendships in the district and developing new ones. In 1974, I returned to the U of C to finish off my university education, and in 1975 our daughter Kimberly was born. In December, 1978 Jamie Dianne was born.

After my grandfather's death, the quarter was sold and Jim and I bought our own home and moved to Okotoks where we still reside.

Harvie Spence Family

by Kathy Spence

Harvie Spence was born to Harvey B. Spence and Doreen Lexy Dutton on August 4, 1950 in Chilliwack, B.C. The eldest of three sons, he came to Calgary with his parents in 1960.

Upon completion of high school he attended two years of Olds Agricultural College and moved to the Square Butte district in 1967. Harvie worked at Kendall's Sawmill while building up a herd of sheep. The next years saw Harvie phase out of his four hundred head of sheep into the cattle business. During this time he also drove a school bus.

On March 30, 1976 Harvie married Katherine Philomena Schmaltz. Kathy was raised on a mixed farm, in the Beiseker district, with her twelve brothers and sisters. She was educated through high school in Beiseker, Alberta before moving to the Calgary area where she met Harvie.

The Spences have four children, Duane, Deborah, Derrick and Dean. The three oldest children started their education at the Millarville School and took an active part in sports and community activities. Kathy also became involved in the community and drove a school bus.

Many winter nights found the Spences on moonlight snowmobile rides over the beautiful Square Butte

Debbie, Duane, Derrick and Dean Spence.

hills, with friends and neighbors. Summers were occupied at the Circle 8 Speedway in Calgary where Harvie and Kathy won several trophies in demolition derbies as well as stock car racing. Since obtaining his private pilots license in 1977 most of the family's leisure time is spent in the air. Harvie is presently working at his night endorsement and instrument ratings.

The fall of 1978 saw the Spences relocate in Claresholm, Alberta, where Harvie has taken the position of Automotive Equipment Operator for the Government of Alberta. Kathy has continued to drive school bus. The two oldest boys, Duane and Derrick, participate in minor hockey, which they began at Millarville, while Debbie continues her tap dancing and acrobat lessons. Baby Dean joins mom and dad as an avid sports spectator.

Evelyn and Walter Spink

Both were born and raised in Leeds, Yorkshire, England. They were childhood sweethearts. Walter worked in the coal mine and when work began to slacken off and times started to get tough, Eve and Walt decided to emigrate to Canada. So the year of '29 saw them set sail in the ship "Montrose" from Liverpool to St. John. From there they went by train to Calgary. After spending a few days there they continued their journey to Beaton, at the top of the Arrow Lakes in British Columbia. They were fortunate in getting work right away. Eve helped out in the hotel

Harvie and Kathy Spence.

Walter Spink.

owned by Mr. and Mrs. Lindsay, who became great friends, and Walter got a job in a gold mine; I believe the name was The Silver Dollar.

The year 1930 saw them back in Calgary — they had decided to try their hand at farming. So out they went to the Ballyhamage district, which was then about twenty miles from Calgary. The place they lived on is now owned by Cecelia and Bill Taylor. They then moved to a quarter-section kitty-corner to that one, and finally bought a quarter-section of NW13-21-2-5 which they owned until their decease.

They had a mixed farm, horses, cattle, pigs and poultry. Their cattle brand was $\widehat{EW}$ (rafter EW). Although they still owned the farm, Evelyn and Walter went to live in Calgary for a while. Walter got a job at P. Burns & Co. Ltd. as a retort operator. You could say they were week-end farmers until they moved back to the farm.

They had no children of their own so decided to adopt one. Catherine, or Cathy as she was known to her friends, started her education at Red Deer Lake School. She graduated from Henry Wisewood in Calgary and from there went into the Nursing School at Calgary General Hospital. She has since married and has two children, a boy and a girl.

Evelyn's sister, Pamela Scruton, came out from England in 1947, to live with them. She also worked for

Pam and Harry Styler at their wedding.

P. Burns & Co. until she went to join Eve and Walt on the farm. Eve was under the doctor's care for angina pectoris, so was unable to do any heavy work or help with the farm chores.

At the demise of Evelyn and Walter the farm was sold. Pam went to work at the Father Lacombe Nursing Home, which she enjoyed, until she married. She now lives in Calgary.

Albert James Stagg

by Jean Blakley

Albert was born in Milton, Ontario, January 7th, 1890. His parents Robert C. and Catherine Isabel (Fraser) Stagg had come to Canada from Inverness, Scotland, in 1885, settling at Milton, not far from Toronto. Albert and his twin sister, Elma (Stagg) Beatt, were the youngest in the large family.

In 1899, the elder Staggs decided to come to Calgary to make their home. Their eldest daughter, Elizabeth, had come west the previous year, accompanied by her brother Will and had been married to Joseph Fisher, a

Evelyn Spink.

Seated, Albert Stagg, Gwen Stagg, on chair arm. Front, L. to R. Wayne and Keith Stagg.

Millarville rancher. Two other brothers, George and Jack, had arrived later the same year.

The younger children attended an East Calgary school. At that time, during the warm weather, many of the students went bare legged, and some times bare footed. On one occasion, Albert had incurred the teacher's ire, and was switched on his bare legs. His twin sister jumped out of her seat and without asking permission, hurried home to tell her mother. On returning to the school room, she told her brother "Mother says for you to come home, and as for you, Miss — —, Mother will see you at prayer meeting tonight."

Albert spent much time on his brother-in-law's ranch at Millarville, and became a very good horseman. About 1908, he, with his father Robert Sr. and brother Robert Jr., each filed on a homestead in the Kew district. Albert's was the N.E.¼ of 3-21-4w5. Robert Sr. the N.W.¼ of 3-21-4w5, and brother Robert took the S.E.¼ of the same section. They acquired some horses, using the brand 

Albert joined the Armed Services during the first World War. After the war he had a truck and was one of the first to do trucking from the Millarville and Kew districts, hauling cream, etc. The roads left much to be desired during these years, just the usual dirt trails, and many mud holes during the wet years.

On June 11th, 1928, he was married to Gwendoline Godkin of Kindersley, Saskatchewan, at Everett, Wash. For nearly fifteen years, he worked for the Hudson's Bay Co. as a carpet and linoleum layer, later going in to business for himself. He kept the land at Kew, renting at times, later having it hayed on shares. In 1949 the land was bought by Ernest Silvester, and is now owned by Jim Silvester.

Albert and Gwen have two sons, The eldest, Albert Wayne, married Grace Webster of Chestermere Lake. Wayne has worked for the Hudson's Bay Co. for 30 years. They have one son, Robert Wayne, who is married to Marlee Dayman of Calgary.

The younger son, Roger Keith, is married to Patsy Walters of Le Duc. They have three sons, Randy, Terry and Darryl. Keith is a mechanical engineer with Angus Butler of Edmonton, where they make their home.

Albert passed away November 25th, 1961. Gwen makes her home in Calgary.

John C. (Jack) Stagg

by J. Blakley

Born in Inverness, Scotland, October 31, 1880, Jack came to Canada with his parents, Robert C. and Catherine (Fraser) Stagg, in 1885. With their seven children, they settled in Milton, Ontario, and Jack lived there until 1898. Times were hard in Ontario so Jack and his brother George decided to go west to what at that time was the Northwest Territories, later Alberta. Their older brother, Will, had accompanied

John C. Stagg.

their sister Elizabeth to Calgary, where she was married to Joseph Fisher of Millarville and their ranch was the boy's destination.

After a long train trip, during which their luggage had been stolen, they finally arrived in Calgary. At that time, the little city had a population of between 2000 and 4000. They had very little money, so they took off as soon as possible for Millarville, walking along the McLeod Trail, then cutting through the hills and eventually arriving at Sam Kieran's ranch. Here they were fed, given a small job haying. Mrs. Kieran was amazed that anyone would walk through the unfenced country, with all the half wild cattle and the bulls roaming around ready to chase anything that took their attention. They were given a bed for the night, and taken the next day to the Fisher ranch by team and wagon.

Jack's first years in the west were spent as a cowboy working for his brother-in-law, Joseph Fisher, and other neighboring ranchers. He met and knew John Ware, who was ranching in the Kew district at that time. Some of his fondest memories were of his early cowboy days, and of riding to Christ Church at Millarville, where the Rev. Webb-Peploe made all the young people feel welcome, later serving tea in their home after the church services.

As Jack got older, he worked in and around Calgary, where his parents had made their home, coming from the east the year following their son's arrival. Jack and his brother George started a small business, digging basements with horses at 40 cents a cubic yard, and any other work they could get in that line, but didn't make much, so gave it up after a year. He worked at the Burn's plant as a fireman, then later as night engineer, from 6:P.M. to 7:A.M. for $55 per month, a big wage in those days.

He married Laura Tuckett, and they had six children, three daughters and three sons. For some time, around 1915, they lived on the Stagg ranch at Kew, and later farmed in the Blackie district. He bought a farm near Michichi, in the Hand Hills country. This was during the dried out years of the 1920s, when the clouds would roll in and roll right out again, leaving not a trace of moisture. A few years of this and Jack brought his family to Calgary, where he once again worked as a fireman. The oilfields were just starting to require experienced steam engineers, so in 1928, Jack came to Black Diamond, his family remaining in Calgary until the following year, so once more Jack was back in the foothill country he liked so well, and he made his home in Black Diamond for many years.

In 1939, his wife Laura passed away, and by this time most of the family were on their own. In 1943, he married Martha Leeman, and the following year, 1944, they moved to the Kew district and took over the store and post office until 1946, then moved to Whiskey Row, a small settlement north of the town of Turner Valley, then on to Peace River, keeping house for his oldest son Grant, who was manager for a hardware store in that town. They returned to Black Diamond and bought a home, living there until his final illness. He was a man who had to keep busy, and this he did in many capacities. He was on the town council, and served as mayor of the town of Black Diamond, and served on the board of the Turner Valley Hospital, and later as chairman of that board. Even all this did not stop him from taking on carpenter work and one of the buildings he enjoyed working was the new Parish House for the Millarville Church he attended nearly seventy years before. After a long and busy life, Jack passed away in Calgary in 1969.

His oldest son, Grant, now makes his home in Victoria, B.C. Hazel married John Fisher and she lives in Fort St. John, B.C. They had four children, Carolyn, Gary, Brett and Bob. John passed away in 1966. Don makes his home in Edmonton, married Vona Riley. Jock married Louise Johnson, was killed in a car accident at Rainbow Lake in 1970.

Edith married Jack Pettinger, and they have two sons, Bob and Jim, make Calgary their home. The youngest daughter, Helen, married Alex Tait, lives in Edmonton.

Mrs. Jean Standish

by Audrey Tarry

Since her retirement from farming, and the sale of her farm in 1975, Mrs. Jean Standish moved to Victoria, B.C. where she has ownership in a delicatessen, and enjoys her garden, and the scent of the ocean air.

Audrey Standish Tarry, married in 1973, is now living at the Calgary Zoo, where husband, Greg, is a currator at the Zoo. They have two children, Sarah, born in Feb. 1976, and Bryce, born in Jan. 1978. Audrey nursed at the Calgary General Hospital until the birth of her children.

James Standish graduated from Western College of Veterinary Medicine in 1978, and plans to practice in Alberta.

Jane Standish is presently living in Red Deer and has recently completed a course in Real Estate, and is working there.

Eva Standish is still employed in northern B.C., where she has been since her graduation from high school in 1974.

David Standish lives with his mother, Jean, where he is presently completing high school.

Luella Standish-Nee Sleight

Luella Standish (nee Sleight) was born in Manitoba. She took her teacher training in Winnipeg. While in the process of taking this training, she met a native Albertan, Irving Standish. Irving was stationed in Manitoba while serving in the Royal Canadian Air Force. The two were married and moved to Irving's dairy farm in the Millarville district of Alberta.

In the fall of 1947, the Fordville School Board could not locate a teacher for their school. It looked as if the school would not open that fall. John and Ida Jackson offered to take Luella and baby son into their home, babysit Gordon, and provide transportation to school. This would be a temporary arrangement until a permanent teacher could be located. Everyone agreed to this situation, so the school was kept open. The teacher and students had a happy time together. Luella enjoyed those students — Pat and Roger Jones, who were relatives, Walter and Billy Jackson, who have remained life long friends, Blanchards, and Lila Croston, whose daughter Luella taught in Eugene Costo School in Calgary in the mid 1970's.

Later in the year, a permanent teacher was found. Luella had time to stay home and prepare for the birth of her daughter, Judy, in February, 1948. She had been carried to school every day. No wonder Judy also became a teacher!

Recollections of Fordville School

by R. Standish

My brother John and I went to Fordville School. beginning I believe, in about 1918, as Priddis School where we first went, was not operated for the full year. If memory serves me right, our first teacher there was Mr. Sturgeon — a teacher to remember. He always provided us with his jack knife to cut our own green willow to get punished for our wrongdoings (eg. blowing on a tight elastic band). Miss Edith Potter, my last teacher in Fordville (1923) was a person I will never forget. My brother and I left Fordville that year, after completing grade 10. From Fordville, I went to Calgary to complete Grades 11 and 12, and after one year of road building, went to Normal School in 1927-1928, graduating with a First Class Teaching Certificate.

Westoe School, about 1 mile east of the Priddis turn-off on Highway 22 west, was my first school — 1928-1929. The year 1929-1930 I taught at Panima, west of Okotoks. 1931-1932 I was at Glen Rock, east of Airdrie.

Back row, L.-R.: Nelson Standish, Lester Letts, Bill Lee, Edith King, John Jackson, Leonard Nelson, Bob Standish. Middle row: Eunice Shaw, Frances Jackson, Dick King, Edna Standish, Marjorie Lee. Front Row: Ellen Standish, Gordon Douglass, May Standish. Class of 1922 at Fordville School.

In 1932 I came to Fordville (No. 1908) and was there until June 30, 1941. When I was accepted as teacher of Fordville in 1932, I built a small home adjacent to the school grounds (on land owned by R. G. Spooner), and during the nine years of teaching, built our home "Rainbow's End" into a well known landmark on Highway 22.

When I returned to Fordville in 1932, it was like returning home, for many of the pupils had familiar names as follows (my apologies to those whose names do not at this moment come to mind): Cawthorne, Barraclough, Wilderman, Winthrop, Petersen, Standish, Holt, Shaw, and Blackie.

The nine years spent at Fordville have given me many memories: the hard times at term end, wondering if my contract would be renewed — but mostly the good times, being with good friends and neighbours — the skating parties, dances, social evenings, and Christmas Concerts, all of which now unfortunately seem to have disappeared from our social activities.

On June 30, 1941, I closed the door on my teaching career; beginning July 1, 1941, I began my 30 year career in the Oil Industry, retiring in 1971.

Bruce Fisher Stanhope

Bruce is the second son of Mary Isabel (Fisher) and Stanley Clarke Stanhope. Born in Calgary February 13th, 1922, he was brought to Millarville by his parents when he was three months of age.

When New Valley School started in 1928, he and his brother Jim were among the first students, Bruce taking from grade one to nine there, then on to Turner Valley High School for two years.

In 1942, he joined the Army, serving with the Signal Corps, in France, Belguim and Germany, returning to Canada in 1946. He was with Imperial Oil then joined the C.P.R. as a brakeman. He lost his right hand in an employment accident in August, 1947. From 1948 to 1952, he worked for the Alberta Liquor Board.

Shelley and Michael Stanhope.

In 1950, he was married to Evelyn Baldwin, then in 1952, he went with Alberta Govt. Telephones, where he is presently employed as Directory Production Manager.

Bruce and Evelyn have a family of two, Michael, born on the 6th of April, 1954, and Shelley, born the 21st of November, 1958. Both attended public and high school in Calgary. Michael is studying Environmental Biology, at Bamfield on Vancouver Island, has attended marine laboratories in Frobisher Bay and other areas in the far north and also in the Virgin Islands in the Caribbean Sea.

Shelley has just completed a course in Health Records at S.A.I.T. in Calgary.

David A. Stanhope

Born on August 21, 1932 the son of Stanley C. Stanhope and Mary Isabelle Stanhope (nee Fisher).

As a child lived with his parents and two older brothers Jim and Bruce on the farm located three-quarters of a mile south of New Valley School. Attended the school with his cousins Lila and Olive Piper and Louie, Jim, Anne and Lillybette Koehler, David Glaister and Ronnie Scatterty.

Moved to Calgary when his parents sold the farm to Bruce McLean in 1945.

Joined the Royal Canadian Navy in 1950 and served with the United Nations Forces in the Korean War during 1952 and 1953.

Married the former Miss Frances Charbonneau of Regina and Calgary in 1954 and has three sons and one daughter, John 23, Scott 19, Gerald 16, and Lisa 13.

After attending the Calgary Institute of Technology in 1956 and 1957, entered the employment of Gulf Oil Company in Edmonton and is presently employed as a Land Representative with Westcoast Transmission Company Limited in Vancouver.

Stanhope, James Fisher

Born in Calgary, Alberta, June 28th, 1919, to Stanley Clarke and Maybelle (Fisher) Stanhope. We lived in Calgary until 1921, when we moved to Millarville, where my parents had rented The Meadow, owned by the Fisher family. In 1923, we moved to land which my Grandfather Stanhope and my father had bought from Mr. Williams, the S.E. ¼ of 31-20-2w5 and the N.E. ¼ of 30-20-2w5.

When New Valley School was built, I started to attend school there in 1928, and stayed there until grade nine. Many times I sit and laugh to myself, remembering the day my brother Bruce knocked out my front tooth with his milk bottle. Of course I cannot say I wasn't deserving of the consequences since I was threatening to reveal to our mother that Bruce had got a licking in school that day. Still my only false front tooth. I still remember the good times and the one room school house and some teachers, George Scott being one.

While helping on the farm I lost three of my fingers from my right hand, getting them caught in a seeder.

My father got me a job at the Royalite Oil Machine Shop where I put in my welding apprenticeship. I then moved to Black Diamond to live with my Grandmother Stanhope so I would be closer to my job. In 1939 when war broke out I was given a deferment from the Army so I left for Vancouver to work in the shipyards as it was considered key work. I married Evelyn Webb from Black Diamond in 1941 in Vancouver, B.C. January 1946 our daughter Cheryl was born. Shipyards were winding down so I had an opportunity to go to Sacramento, California, which I did, in 1947 and we still live here in the Sacramento Valley. I have worked in machine shops and manufacturing plants since arriving here. In 1951 our son Darryl was born and in 1960 our second son, Barry, was born. I have worked in a shop for A. Teichert & Son, which is a large construction company and I am looking forward to retirement in 1981.

We are fortunate to have all three of our children and their families, including our two grandsons, living

Jim Stanhope having a ride on the family milk cow. L. to R. Netta Stanhope, Mrs. Stanhope sr., Mr. Stanhope sr., Stan Stanhope, Maybelle Stanhope, Jim on cow.

Jim and Evelyn Stanhope and sons Barry (front) and Darryl.

in Sacramento near us. Our daughter Cheryl married Joe Marvelli and gave us two grandsons. Cheryl has a credential in Early Childhood Education and Joe a Business Administration Degree. Cheryl is a Pre-School teacher and likes her job and 32 little ones. Darryl married Kimber McKnight from Sacramento, Darryl getting his degree in Civil Engineering in 1977 and Kimber received hers in Nutrition in 1978. Barry graduated from High School and is now enrolled in a Junior College nearby.

We have travelled to Canada many times since we left in 1947. Since my wife's and my folks are gone we visit our brothers and sisters. I still have many wonderful memories of our life in Canada and the beautiful places, which we will be visiting more when I retire.

Mary (Maybelle Fisher) and Stanley Stanhope
by Jean Blakley

Stanley Clarke Stanhope was born in Melford, Suffolk, England, in 1899, the eldest son of Arthur and Kate Stanhope. He came to Canada with his father in 1913 and a year later his mother came with his two sisters, Evelyn and Netta and a brother Bob. Stan worked with his father, who was a carpenter, later working at the Ogden C.P.R. shops, where he received his training to become a welder and boiler maker. The family settled in South Calgary and every working morning at six o'clock a special street car came and picked up the workers for Ogden.

In 1919, Stan married Mary Isabel (Maybelle) Fisher, eldest child of Joseph and Elizabeth Fisher of Millarville. Maybelle was born in Calgary and was one of the first children to be baptized in Christ Church, Millarville, which had been built in 1896. Maybelle was raised on the Fisher ranch and when only two years of age, her father bought an Indian pony for her to learn to ride. The pony was named Laggan and as Maybelle was of a very venturesome nature, the two of them

Mary Isabel (Maybelle Fisher) Stanhope and son Jim.

shared some exciting times. By the time Maybelle was eight years of age, she rode Laggan all over the hills.

One time when her father and the men working for him were at the Meadow, the lower ranch, and her mother and the younger children were at the Fisher Creek ranch, Maybelle and Laggan had taken off on one of their usual jaunts. Heavy rains started and before long the creeks were in flood stage and no girl or pony had put in appearance. Her mother became very worried and after two days knew she had to have help in locating her missing daughter. She saddled her horse with a side saddle and with great misgivings about leaving the younger children alone, swam her horse across Fisher Creek, then on six miles to Millar's crossing on Sheep Creek, also in flood and much higher than the first creek. Luckily she was able to swim her horse across safely, then on to the ranch buildings and here she found her daughter safe and sound, helping her father bake bread. The men were amazed, declaring none of them had dared cross the flooding creek. However, it had to be crossed once more to get back to the children at home.

There was no school in the district close enough for the children to attend school, so in 1912 the Fishers moved in to Calgary, living first in the Riverside district, then later moving to South Calgary, where a new

house had been built. It was here that Maybelle met and later married Stan.

By 1922, there were two small boys in the Stanhope family, Jim, three years old and Bruce, just a few months. Stan and Maybelle, with her brother, Bob Fisher, rented the Meadow, moved out to the old log house, in which for years only cowboys had lived. With lots of soap and water, and a bit of paint they soon had the place quite comfortable. They invested in a flock of sheep and as the flats of the Meadow were renowned for the hay they produced, the three of them were kept busy. At a time when not much baling was done, they baled the hay and hauled it in to Calgary, where it was stacked and sold. No trucks, the hauling was done as the haying had been, by horse power.

In 1923, that year is well remembered by old timers as the year of the big floods. The sheep were kept in a paddock below the stables, and the low lying Meadow was flooded. Stan was working in Calgary at the time and when the water came up to the sheep paddock, Maybelle and Bob had to swim in the swirling water to rescue the sheep. Stan's sister, Netta (now Mrs. Dick Knight) remembers when she was visiting having to sit on ewes that had lost their young, while Maybelle milked the swollen udders.

The same year, Stan and his father, Arthur Stanhope, bought the Williams place, the S.E. ¼ of 31-20-2w5 and the N.E. ¼ of 30-20-2w5. A house was built on each quarter and Mr. and Mrs. Stanhope sr. moved out from Calgary. The 1920's were the years of the freak hail storms, with stones not only the size of golf balls but chunks of ice frozen together. The storms were usually accompanied by fierce winds and several times the Stanhope farm was severely hit, crops ruined and even pigs killed.

Maybelle had a "green thumb" and over the years worked very hard, planting trees, shrubs and flowers. She planted 100 small trees on the east side of the farm, causing one neighbor to laughingly call them "Mrs. Stanhope's 100 little twigs." However, in a few years the little twigs grew to be fine big trees. Stanley hired Bert Hodgkins, an old timer of the Kew district, to help Maybelle, who raised a large flock of chickens and turkeys.

Stan worked in Turner Valley at the Royalite machine shop as well as doing a lot of farm work. Water was a problem and a good well was badly needed. After having about a dozen wells drilled, he took the advice of two local water witches, Tim Blakley and Fred Hodgkins, who each pin pointed an area close together. A well was drilled in between and a fair water well was found.

As a small boy in England, Stan had studied the piano and was an excellent pianist. During the 1920's and the 1930's he had a small orchestra, with Tommy Black on the drums and Johnnie Henderson on the violin, also Campbell Aird. They were a very lively band and played for many dances at the old Rancher's Hall and Turner Valley. These dances usually lasted

Stanley and Maybelle (Fisher) Stanhope. 1929.

until the wee small hours. At home, for his own and his family's pleasure, he would play the more classical kind of music.

In 1927, with Jim and Bruce ready for school, Stan and two of his neighbors, Jack King and Frank Mortimer, applied to have a school built and these three were the first trustees of New Valley School, which opened in January, 1928. It was named for a nearby oil well.

Stan was Government Land Assessor, a job which took him to other districts, but he continued to farm. Another son, David, was born in 1932, and he also attended New Valley School.

Mr. and Mrs. Stanhope sr. had moved to the town of Black Diamond and built a home there. About 1943, Stan and Maybelle sold their farm to Bruce McLean and bought a home in Calgary. Stan worked for Interprovincial Pipe Lines, eventually working out of Edmonton. He held this job until ill health forced him to retire. He passed away March 17th, 1967 and Maybelle passed away on November 29th, 1968.

Jack Steen — 1943
Horse Brand

Jack Steen was born in Montreal, Quebec on January 12, 1943, and moved with his family to Calgary, Alberta in 1954 where he completed his education. Jack met Patsy Allan who was born in Vancouver, British Columbia on April 18, 1946. They were married in Calgary on July 27, 1968. They have two children, Laurie Diane Steen born June 12, 1970 and James Tyler Steen born July 26, 1972.

They lived in Calgary for six years before buying 24 acres SW ¼, S31, T21, R3, W5 in February 1974. The property was heavily wooded with only limited living quarters on a small clearing. The last four and a half years have been spent adding onto the house, clearing portions of the property for pasture, fencing and building corrals. In this four and a half years the four Steen's have accumulated four riding horses, two large dogs and three cats.

Although Jack works hard for a large Stock Brokerage firm, Pitfield MacKay Ross Limited, they have participated actively in all community and school projects.

Jack and Patsy Steen with daughter Laurie and son James.

In 1967 Patsy was chosen Stampede Queen and since has been very active with the Calgary Exhibition & Stampede on the Creative Living Committee, and the Stampede Queen Alumni. Jack has been very active since 1970 with the Rodeo Committee. These volunteer committees help to contribute to make the Calgary Exhibition Stampede the Greatest Outdoor Show on Earth.

The four Steens' enjoy country living and the rural community life and have no desire to return to city living.

Stewart, David James (Dave) 1879-1962
by Lillian Stewart Anschetz

Dave and his wife Sarah, both of Irish Scotch ancestry, with their four children, moved to the Kew district in the spring of 1917. They settled on Section 19-20-3W5, known as the Scott place.

Dave had been a wheat farmer at Chinook, Alberta, and bred heavy horses, of which he brought many Percherons and Clydesdales to the ranch at Kew. The herd of Shorthorns acquired in Ontario in November, 1916, were moved as well. Later that summer a large flock of sheep was purchased and a page-wire fence around the farm became a necessity.

Needing more pasture land, Dave purchased a ¼ section from Billy Senior, N.W. 17-20-2W5 and a ¼ section from Fred Senior, the S.W. 17-20-3W5, also a ¼ section from Carl Ohlson. For several years Dave exhibited and won many ribbons at the Stock Show and Bull Sale in Calgary.

As the Stewart home was the closest to the Plainview School, one half mile, all of the children had a turn at doing the janitor work. Many were the cold mornings that the fire delighted in "going out". After Public School years all attended Crescent Heights High School, and Mrs. Stewart moved to Calgary to be with the family. Dave continued to spend a few more summers on the Chinook farm and winters with the family in Calgary.

The ranch was rented to the Robison family, and later the Boggs family. A land deal in 1932 put Dan

Maberly car about 1921. Mrs. Maberly and baby Walter inside car. Seated on running board, L. to R. Cameron Stewart, Bessie and Lillian Stewart, Mrs. Kosling, standing. Rements of old Scott corral in background.

Dudenhoeffer and his family on the Stewart ranch and Dave and his son on the Dudenhoeffer farm at Herronton.

In January 1943 Dave retired from active farming and went to Toronto, where he joined the "Home Guard." He spent six months Guard Duty at the large Anaconda Plant in New Toronto. Late in July he returned home on the sudden death of Mrs. Stewart, in her 70th year.

Spending winters in Vancouver and California and summers on the farm, Dave enjoyed an active life. A stroke in 1958 put him in a nursing home until his death in January, 1962, four weeks before his 83rd. birthday. His twin sister Mary died of a stroke ten months later.

Evelyn, the eldest child, had an over-abundance of energy, a tease, and could and did stir up many scraps with the younger members. Fred Senior had an explanation for it. "Must be the full of the moon, Evie is at it again."

High school in Calgary, Business College and Stenography followed for Evelyn. She worked for a number of years in the offices of the Alberta Wheat Pool and later in the offices of City Hall. After an illness of more than two years, she passed away at home. Besides her family, she was survived by her fiance in Toronto, Ontario. She was 26 years of age.

High School and Business College had little appeal for Bessie, the second daughter. At the age of 19 years, she married Henry (Hank) Treend of Hussar, youngest son of a well known former rancher, W. R. Treend, of Husser and later Calgary, until he moved to California. Bessie and Hank resided on the farm for many years, spending several winters in California visiting Mr. Treend Sr.

One night in early April, their son Ronald, less than three years old at the time, left the supper table early to play in the yard. By bed time, he and the two dogs were nowhere to be found. Darkness was settling down, all the hired men and the family were searching the surrounding fields and pastures. Carloads of neighbors as far as 25 miles distance came to join in the search. At 11:30 P.M. a neighbor found the boy deep in a hollow, two miles from the house. Only the Fox-terrier was at his side, barking when the neighbor came up close as he called out in the darkness. Ronald had tired and gone to sleep for a time. The man said later "He cried when he saw me and I cried too."

A "little boy lost" was not enough scare for the parents, there was another to come in a few weeks time. During the war, many country areas had "Home Guard Defence Units", made up of men from the farms and small town business men. They drilled usually on Sundays. The Army conducted the units and supplied the Army uniforms they wore. Hank Treend was an active member. Arriving home after the "drill" one Sunday evening, Ronald turned blue and nearly choked to death. Hank did not wait to remove all his army clothes, added some civilian clothes and rushed the boy to the Holy Cross Hospital in Calgary. There they were told it was a very expensive operation, $500 to $600 because of the needed instruments and what you had to know to do the operation. The midnight operation saved his life when ten pieces of peanuts were removed from the entrance to his lungs. He had to remain in hospital for two days in case of pneumonia. The doctor told them "Nuts never dissolve and would have been fatal."

Henry went to pay the doctor next day, prepared to pay $600 or more, the doctor looked at his strange attire, and said, "$50 will do just fine. Hank said later "I wrote the cheque, thanked him for the boy's life and left, shaking my head."

When the older son Ronald started to school, the family moved to the town of Husser. Small towns suffered from housing shortage as did all the cities after the war and the only accomodations available was an old butcher shop with full living accomodations built on the back of the store. They lived there for a few years and in June, 1949, their home was burned to the ground. Dry weather and high winds, and the old building was in the basement in less than ten minutes. Dave, visiting at the time, roused the family and all escaped the burning building, and most of their possessions were lost in the fire. A general store on one side and the town garage, 10 feet away, were lost to the fire as well.

The family then moved to Banff and purchased a number of houses and engaged in the tourist rental business. The boys attended school and both were active in sports. Ronald, an exceptionally fine skier, took part in school and community skiing activities, also inter-school district ski meets.

Neil, the younger boy, aged twelve years, had a nerve wracking session in hospital in February, under constant care with convulsions, twenty-six in a two week period. A brain operation in September of the same year, 1957, was necessary, and on February 2nd., 1958, while on a ski meet with his brother Ronald and the Banff Ski Team, he passed away in his sleep at Revelstoke, B.C. The doctor said "a blood clot to the brain."

The death was unexpected and a great shock to all the family. In September of that year, Bessie and Henry moved to Calgary. Ronald finished High School at Mount Royal College, then attended Technical School for a few months. He then joined the R.C.A.F. and was stationed at many places in Ontario, Alberta, B.C. and several years at the Norad Station at North Bay, Ontario. In early September 1960, he married Gladys Bond of London, Ontario.

One year later, August 8th, 1961, Ronald's parents, Bessie and Henry, met with a tragic death in their own home. The murderer, Norman Campbell, served a seven year and three months prison, and late November, 1976, ran head-on into a snow plow on the highway and was killed.

On leaving the R.C.A.F., Ronald worked for a time with the I.B.M. Co., Toronto, selling business machines and later for two other Companies of the same line. The Mohawk Computer Machines Co. transferred him to Vancouver, where he still resides. He and Gladys have two sons, Ronnie jr. and Danny and a daughter Karen. The two boys, Ronnie, 16 and Danny 15, at the time of this writing, are very accomplished swimmers and have won many ribbons in school and district swim meets. Karen, also a good swimmer, is more interested in a neighbors trotting horse, that she cares for in her spare time. She is now training to drive them in the sulkies.

After all the years of growing pains, schooling and the "hard Times" Lillian, the third daughter, a stenographer and comptometer operator, spent several years in the employ of the Hudson's Bay Co. offices. After her marriage in Winnipeg to Flt. Sgt. Jack Anschetz of the R.C.A.F. in June of 1942, Lillian left the Hudson's Bay in October of that year. Joining her husband, they spent six months in Victoria while Jack was stationed at R.C.A.F. Station, "Pat Bay" outside of Victoria. After a short leave, Flt. Sgt. Anschetz was sent overseas in April 1943. Lillian went to work in the offices of Burns and Co. until Jack returned from England after V.E. Day, May 1945.

Jack was one of six children, four sons and two daughters born to Conrad and Christina Anschetz, who lived and farmed in the Hanna district of Alberta. On leaving the Service with the rank of Flying Officer, Jack went back to his trade of projectionist. He worked in various theatres, among them the Grand, Uptown, and at.the present time the Palliser Square Theatres. He was the first man in Canada to operate a Twin House, the Westbrook Theatres in Calgary.

One daughter, Carole, was born to Lillian and Jack, in June, 1948. Carole went through the usual children's diseases and problems of growing up, while she attended King George Public and Junior High School and gained a High School diploma at Crescents Heights High School. She received her diploma at the Comptometer School with a 98%, the highest mark in the history of all the branches of the school across Canada. She worked in the offices of the A.P. Grain

L. to R. Jack Anschetz, Dave Stewart, Camille Stewart, Millicent Stewart, Lillian Anschetz, Bessie Treend, Cameron Stewart, Ronald Treend. Seated in front — David Stewart, Carole Anschetz.

Co. until the offices were moved to Winnipeg. Not wishing to move to Winnipeg, she went to work in the Hudson's Bay Audit Offices, where she worked for a number of years.

While at the Bay, Carole married Ted Nielsen, son of Kay and the late Brett Nielsen of Calgary. She left the Bay to attend Mount Royal College, taking a two year course in Design and Interior Decorating. At the present time she is in partnership with Miss Barbara Jackson, and they are engaged in the business of Design and decorating. Along with offices, restaurants etc. they have done many show homes.

Carole and Ted, a city transit driver, have no children so — Lillian and Jack are not grandparents.

Marie Anne (Dibby) Kendall Stewart

I was the fourth child born to Eugene Lamont and Katherine B. Kendall, on November 21, 1931. My schooling began in Square Butte School, which was two and a half miles from the ranch. Many experiences too numerous to recall on paper, but one comes to mind. One crisp winter's morning, John, Frank and I were hurrying down the icy trail, and I, of course, was in the rear on a two year old colt whose mother was a good distance ahead, ridden by John. The young colt didn't like being left and began to buck, but I was able to stay on and reach school before the bell rang. John told my parents that "She did a good job of riding, too."

My last year at Square Butte School there were five pupils, Margaret, George and Johnnie Nylund, Jimmy and Tommy Silvester, and myself. In the fall of 1944, there was no teacher assigned to the school. My father decided to send me to Portland, Oregon, to stay with my Grandmother and Aunt Alice.

That was indubitably the most traumatic event in my life. From boy's blue-jeans, horseback riding and ranch life, to dresses, street cars and city life. From a one-roomed school house to a two story eight room school, and 42 pupils in my grade. I was very home-

Floyd Stromstedt and wife Karen and son Cam.

Bill Stewart Family. Back, L. to R.: Cheryl, Scott, Marie. Front: Dean, Bill, and Marian.

sick and letters from home brought many tears. By June of 1945 I had grown five inches and coming home was wonderful. I travelled back and forth to Portland for the next four years, attending Ainsworth School and Catlin High School.

In 1949 I entered Mount Royal College for three years. Then I worked in the main branch of the Royal Bank in Calgary until I married William W. Stewart jr. of Priddis and we made our home on Bill's father's farm, the S.E. ¼ of 35-22-3W5. I was involved in the St. James Sewing Guild, Priddis Women's Institute and the Priddis Community Association.

My four children are: Marian Rosamond, born 1954. Cheryl Anne, born 1957. Scott Kendall, born 1958. Dean William, born 1968. Marian married Daryl F. Barkley and they have one son, Micheal Daryl, born in 1977.

In 1974, we sold our Priddis farm to Judy and Dick Armitage of Calgary. For seven months we rented a house on A. E. Cross's property, the S.W. 6-22-2W5, formerly owned by Lloyd Standish. While living there we purchased a farm from Gordon and Walter Befus on Gull Lake, west of the town of Lacombe, Alta., the N.W. 22-41-28-4. We moved to Lacombe in January 1975.

Floyd Stromstead

Floyd Stromstead was born and raised on a small farm in the Peace River district of Northern Alberta.

Upon graduating from high school in 1957, he went to Calgary to study voice production. Becoming a family man, he worked in the Calgary area at various endeavors. The call of the land was always in his blood, so when the opportunity came in 1972 to acquire a small piece of property near his friends Ron Mitchell and Ernie Geiger west of Millarville he jumped at the chance.

Floyd, his wife Karen and son Cam bought a small house from the Home Oil Co. Kew site and moved it to their little bit of heaven near the north end of John Ware Ridge. Continuing to work in Calgary to pay the bills, they enjoyed living in the Square Butte community.

However, the land values in the area escalated beyond any hope of expansion. In 1976, a quarter section near the home farm in the Peace country became available. So — Floyd, Karen, Cam and baby Carla took advantage of the price difference and trekked north to the land of good gardens, leaving behind a beautiful spot and a lot of good friends.

Greg and Susan (Lyall) Strother
by Susan Strother

I started my life out in Millarville where I lived for five years and then moved with my parents Tommy and Betty Lyall and sister Elizabeth to Calgary, Olds, Carstairs and Calgary again. I attended high school at Lord Beaverbrook and after I graduated I worked for the Toronto Dominion Bank and then the office for the drug department at Woodwards.

I met my husband Greg Storther in the summer of 1971 and we were married on May 6, 1972. Greg was born in Council Bluffs, Iowa, and lived much of his youth in Westboro, Missouri. He came with his family to Medicine Hat and then later to Calgary. His parents are Dr. Charles and Betty Strother, who now reside at Red Deer Lake. Greg is one of six children. He is employed by the Government of Canada as a Primary Products Inspector 3.

We bought our first home in Okotoks and resided in the town for five years. We moved to Lake Midnapore

Gregg and Susan Strothers with their children Leah Jo (held by father) and Laura Lee, on Mom's lap.

in November of 1978. We have two daughters: Leah Jo — 3½ years and Laura Lee — 18 months, both who were born in Calgary.

Stroud — James (Bud) and Alberta
by Gail Vickery

In the year of 1882, James Albert Stroud came west from Bruce County, Ontario, to homestead a section of land in the District of Deloraine, Manitoba. He married Sarah Mildred Western of Portage La Prairie, Manitoba, in 1894, and of the nine children of that marriage, Jim was the youngest. Jim was born in Youngstown, Alberta, in July, 1918, but at the tender age of one or two months, Jim and his mother returned to the family farm northwest of Deloraine, Manitoba, in the Thirlstane School District. Jim was educated and grew up in that district. In the late 1920's Jim's two oldest brothers invented and patented what was known as "Stroud's Wild Oat Blanket Mill" which was once displayed and sold at the Calgary Stampede.

Earl Henry Galloway came west from Guelph, Ontario, with his mother in 1909 to live at Waskada, Manitoba. Earl saw overseas action in World War I and in 1920 he married Hannah Holden of Dand, Manitoba. They had three children, the oldest being Alberta.

The Galloway family moved to Alida, Saskatchewan when Alberta was six years old. Alberta's father was postmaster there until 1938, when they moved back to Dand, Manitoba and made it possible for Alberta to meet Jim. In 1940, Alberta's father joined the Veteran Guards in World War II, so she, her mother and brother moved to Winnipeg, Manitoba. Alberta and Jim were married in December, 1941. Jim joined the Armoured Corp in January of 1942 and was sent overseas in September of that year. On arriving in England, he was assigned to the Calgary Tank Regiment, but was later transferred to the Three Rivers Regiment. Also in September of that year, their first child, Gail, was born in Winnipeg. Gail and Alberta lived in Winnipeg until Jim returned from overseas in October of 1945, having seen action in Africa, Italy and Holland. Upon his discharge in January, 1946, Jim and his family returned to Deloraine to take over and operate the family farm.

Their second child, Carol, was born in March, 1947, followed by their only son, Ronald, in July of 1952, and their youngest daughter, Joyce, in December of 1954.

Jim and his family moved to Brandon, Manitoba in 1958, having sold the farm and bought a house in the City. Jim took up employment with the Federal Civil Service, while Alberta joined the staff of the Assiniboie Extended Treatment Care Hospital, where she worked for fifteen years as a nurses' aid. In July, 1978, Jim retired from the Civil Service, having purchase 40 acres of Section 13-21-4-W5 North of Millarville. They were able to take possession of their new home on the acreage in March, 1979, and are enjoying their retirement to the fullest. Their youngest daughter, Joyce, married to musician Paul Jackson, formerly of Winnipeg, has two sons and lives in Brandon, Manitoba. Ron, their only son, married to Marlyn Martin of Lac Du Bonnet, Manitoba, since June, 1972, is living and working in Red Deer with their two sons. Their daughter Carol married Brian MacQuarrie, formerly of Ontario, in July, 1964. Brian is an air traffic controller at the International Airport in Calgary, and Carol and he live in Carstairs with their two sons. Their oldest daughter, Gail, who was married to Keith Vickery in Germany in 1962, is practising law in Calgary, and spends as much time as possible at the Millarville Property, which she owns with Jim and Alberta.

Jack and Blanche Stuart
by Blanche Stuart

Jack went to work for the Home Oil Co. the spring of 1951. He and two of our boys, Ross and Roy, moved to the half section south of the Home Camp, where Evert Danforth had lived.

Ross and Roy went to the Plainview School. That winter, Joyce and Ross stayed with their Dad and went to the school at Millarville. The next spring, 1952, I moved to the farm with the rest of the children from

Ross and Roy Stuart saddling goat for Bud and Bill.

Black Diamond, Roy, Bud, Bill, Harry, Allan and Lorne. Dale was born that winter.

The children went to the Sheep Creek School at Millarville; they walked a mile to the Home Camp and got the school bus. In 1953-54, Ross and Joyce got a ride with Mrs. Bowie to Turner Valley High School.

While we lived in the Millarville area, Bob joined the Airforce and Ruth worked in the Bassano Hospital and married Bernard Steinbeck.

Getting the older children to High School was quite a chore as there wasn't a bus yet, so we moved to Turner Valley in 1956, to the late Sam Virtue's house where we still live.

Bob and his wife, Joyce, have a farm at Eckville where they live with their four children.

Ruth and her husband, Bernard Steinbeck, live near Bassano, have five children and two grandchildren.

Joyce and her husband, Grant Berreth, have five children and live in Calgary.

Ross and wife Carol have three children, live in Winnipeg.

Roy and Cherie have three boys, live in Calgary.

Bud and Linda have two children, live in Medicine Hat.

Bill and Dolores have three children, live in Sparwood.

Harry and Linda have two children, live in Rimbey.

Allan and Gwen have one girl and live in Duchess.

Lorne and Margaret have one girl, live in Brooks.

Dale and Candy have two children, live in Red Deer.

Our family were all home on November 22, for our 45th wedding anniversary.

Jack Surtees
by Dorothy Surtees

Jack Surtees first came to America when he was fifteen years old, to a ranch in Cheyenne, Wyoming. His father recalled him to England two years later, but the call of the wide open spaces soon took him across the sea again, this time to Canada, where he joined the R.C.M.P. in Regina. He served his three years, then joined the Canadian Armed Forces and saw heavy fighting in France. After postwar occupation duties in Germany, he returned to Canada for his discharge. He took up a homestead in the Peace River Country, in the remote area of Donnelly.

Jack Surtees (left) and friend.

Stuart family. Top, Bob, Roy, Ross, Dale, (held by Bob) Joyce, Bill and Bud. Front, Harry, Lorne and Allan.

L. to R. Gerald Dixon, Jack Lee (centre) and Jack Surtees. Taken at the old Quirk ranch, later the Kendall Ranch.

With little money and years of back breaking toil clearing the land, and long distances for marketing his grain and livestock, he decided to sell and came south to his sister, Mrs. Mortimer, living at Cochrane. It was there he met me (Dorothy Lee). We were eventually married and took up farming in the Bluffton area at the beginning of the "Hungry Thirties". We were hailed out the first year, frozen out the second year so we were forced to return south to the Lee Ranch at Kew, where we remained until 1939, when Jack enlisted in the Calgary Highlanders and went overseas as an instructor until the end of the war.

Back to Canada and the land, this time in British Columbia, with a young son born in England. Several subsequent moves finally brought us to Victoria. Jack then retired until his death on October 8th, 1976.

Gordon M. and Ethel V. (Suttle) Tarves

by Ethel Tarves

Gordon was born at Birch Hill, Saskatchewan, and Ethel, Calgary, Alberta. We were married at Calgary in 1949.

We have two children, Donna Lynn born in 1950 and Dale Robert in 1954. Donna is married to Bob Nyren, who is an Engineer with Syncrude (Canada Ltd.), and they live in Edmonton. Dale works with Western Airlines in Calgary.

In 1964 we purchased 23 acres (ptn. of NW¼ 9-21-4-W5M) which was originally owned by Dick Lyall. We lived in the trailer on weekends and built our house in 1977.

We plan to make "Hidden Acres" our permanent residence.

Barbara Bernice Tate

by Bernice Tate

Born in 1938 (enroute to the hospital) to Jake and Barbara Reimer, I was the second child and first daughter. From the time I remember my early days were spent on the ranch where my mother lives today.

The first school I attended, was in the home of the Purdy's (now owned by Jim Davis). Mrs. Purdy taught all grades. After two years, my father bussed all of us, as well as the other children of the district to Square Butte School. When Square Butte was closed, we then went to Sheep Creek School. The next school for me was Millarville, where I finished my schooling.

While I was growing up, I devoted as much time as I could to riding with my sister Edie and the Birney girls, Bev and Audrey. On occasion, when the Indians happened to be passing through, we would pester them and kick up a little dust, much to our parents dislike.

I left the farm, in June of 1957, to work in Calgary. I married Frank Adams, of Pibrock, Alta., about four months later. My first child, Marilyn, was born October 24th, 1958. We moved to Okotoks in 1960, where Dana was born on the 20th of March, 1961, and Lacey came along on May 6th, 1962.

Tate Family. Marilyn, Bernice, John Dana. Front, Lacey.

My children and I moved to Calgary in 1968. The following year I was divorced. I worked for four years supporting my family, until John Tate requested that responsibility. We were married in Christ Church, Millarville, on September 29th, 1972.

My husband is a member of the R.C.A.F. and at that time we were based in Cold Lake Alberta. Our next home, for nine months, was Dartmouth, N.S. The next move took us to Victoria, B.C. which is where we live now. After my husband's career in the R.C.A.F. has run its course, we would like to retire on the ranch.

Taylor, Robert (Bill) and Cecilia

by Elaine Taylor

Cecilia Emily Fendall was born near Okotoks on March 6, 1911, only daughter of Emily and Arthur Fendall. In 1920, she moved with her family to the NW¼-23-21-2-W5, where she attended Ballyhamage School. Her family moved back to Okotoks in 1924 where her father died. She moved back into the same community when her mother kept house for David Wylie, whom Mrs. Fendall later married.

In 1929-30, Cecilia took dressmaking and millinery at the Institute of Technology and Art in Calgary (now called SAIT). Both a son, Robert, and a daughter, Elaine, took post-secondary education at SAIT.

Cecilia married Robert William Taylor in 1936. He was an upholsterer by trade and they met at Tynan Furniture, a well-known Calgary firm, where they were both employed. Robert Taylor was born in Nottingham, England, on April 29, 1911. He moved with his parents and brother to Calgary in 1912, and later settled on a farm in Lincoln Park, half a mile from the present site of the Glenmore Reservoir Bridge in southwest Calgary.

Robert and Cecilia Taylor, 1936.

They purchased the farm where Cecilia had lived as a girl and have run a mixed farm for over forty years. Land in the area was selling at $12.50 an acre and taxes in those days were about $12. Reasonable compared to prices these days! Cream, the chief cash crop, however, was worth $1.90 a five gallon can (special grade). They still use Arthur Fendall's cattle brand  .

There are four children in the Taylor family. The three eldest attended Ballyhamage School as did their mother.

1) Shirley, a teacher, has her Bachelor of Education degree and is married to Harvey Goerlitz. They live on a farm in the Alexandra School District.

2) Robert (Bob) farms the SW¼-22-21-2-W5 and does a lot of custom farming in the district. He and his wife Judy, have two children: 1) Robert John, born September 9, 1975, and 2) Billi-Jo Louise, born May 7, 1978.

3) Arthur farms east of Innisfail, Alberta. He and his wife Linda, have three children: 1) Sandra, born October 2, 1973, 2) Shannon, born July 13, 1975, and 3) Richard, born March 19, 1977.

4) Elaine, a SAIT graduate in journalism, is associate editor of the Canadian Petroleum Magazine in Calgary.

Robert (Bill) and Cecilia Taylor, 1936.

Robert L. and Lillian M. Tedrick
by Bob Tedrick

My parents Russell C. Tedrick and Mable C. Miracle were both born in Ohio, U.S.A. At a young age they settled in Vanguard, Saskatchewan. I was born in Waldeck, Sask. Dad died in 1973 and Mother resides in Swift Current.

Lillian's parents, Cornelius A. Wiebe and Mary Wiens were born in Russia. They immigrated to Canada after marriage and settled in Herbert, Saskatchewan where Lillian was born. They also reside in Swift Current.

We were married in Swift Current in 1956, and moved to Calgary in 1963. We have two children, a daughter Tracy Cyd and a son Trevor Nelson. Tracy would like to travel after graduation in June. Trevor is

Elaine Taylor.

Looking south across acreage toward "John Ware Ridge". Tracy on Beauty.

very busy with sports and attends John Ware Junior High School in Calgary.

My wife and I are in partnership in our own Geological Consulting firm. In October, 1970 we purchased 40 acres — approximately one-half mile West of the John Ware Memorial — from Mr. Ed. Mattheis. Most weekends are spent at the farm enjoying our horses and working with the honey bees.

David W. Tesky
by Joyce Teskey

David and Joyce moved to Millarville in 1965, building a home on the S.E.¼ of 1-21-3W5. David was born in Black Diamond in 1940. In his early teens he left for a years schooling in art and music in Toronto. Returning to Calgary he attended Queen Elizabeth High School and S.A.I.T.; upon graduation he gained employment with the Betty Shop, a chain of ladies' ready-to-wear clothing, in the area of display. In 1963 he married Joyce I. Jensen, a graduate nurse from the Holy Cross Hospital School of Nursing in Calgary. Joyce was from a farming community south of Drumheller, Alta.

Karen Tesky with Mark and Paul. Nov. 1978.

Karen M. was born in 1967. Three years later a change in life style began when David entered the University of Calgary, obtaining a degree in Education. Joyce worked at the Foothills Hospital during that four year period. Teaching jobs were scarce so the Teskey family took the opportunity to move to a tropical area of Australia, where David taught high school art for two years. It was during that period that Mark D. B. was born in 1975.

Following a six year absence from the Millarville area the family moved back to their home in July 1976. David was employed as an art teacher with the Calgary School Board, as well as maintaining a keen interest in ceramics in his Millarville studio built in 1977-78. To complete the family a son, Paul Jason, was born August 28, 1978.

Andy Thom

Andy Thom was a bachelor and seemed to have a base in Okotoks. He worked in the Millarville area and ended his days at the MacMillan place at Kew. He worked for Joe Standish one summer, and when Joe paid him off in the fall, he pleaded with Andy to put his summer's wages into a few head of cows or horses.

Jean (Chalmers) Thomson
by Ruth Maberley

Being the oldest of five in the Chalmers family and from an early age very considerate of others, resulted in Jean becoming a fine person, in settling childhood disputes and later in considering the fairest course of action for all concerned. Her many early companions became life-long friends. She enjoyed the outdoors but was equally happy indoors doing careful art work or household chores.

Following High School in Turner Valley, Jean took a secretarial course and worked for the Royal Bank at Consort, Okotoks and Turner Valley. She enjoyed riding, dancing, skating, playing baseball and all games and was never idle. In September, 1944, she married Roy Thomson and we are all thankful for the happy years they spent together on the Thomson ranch east of Black Diamond. First in a small house by Roy's parents and later on their own homesite just east of there.

While raising four sons, Bill, Bert, John and Gary, Jean was an active farm wife and mother, combining house chores, of meal preparations, sewing and preserving their large garden produce supply, with helping in the fields, riding, and with Community activities. She greatly enjoyed the Uniform Women's group, and the Rockettes, a group of women from the Big Rock area.

Sadly, Jean developed multiple sclerosis at an early age. Neither she, Roy, nor their family allowed this to embitter them, and made the most of life for themselves and for all who came in contact with them. All who called at Jean and Roy's were welcomed and made to feel at home. Many a person after visiting with her in her wheel chair went away feeling uplifted by her good common sense and thoughtfulness.

Three of Jean and Roy's sons are married. Bill married Julie Robison from west of Turner Valley. They live on Roy's home place and have three lovely daughters, Lori, Vicki and Sheila. Bill runs a caterpillar and truck business.

Bert received his Bachelor of Commerce degree from U.A.C. in 1972 and now lives in Black Diamond and works in Okotoks.

John worked on oil wells and on the home farm. He married Heather Parks of Black Diamond and they live there.

Gary is a journeyman electrician and works in Calgary. He married Joan Shortt of High River. They and their young son Jesse also live on Roy's home farm, so Roy has all his family close by, which helps, since we lost Jean in August 1976. All of us close to Jean have learned a little more of how to make the most of life. Her acceptance of her fate, her tremendous spirit and her concern for others will long remain with all of us who knew and loved her.

Gladys and Bill Threlfall
by Edith McNab

Gladys Threlfall (Field) the youngest daughter of Bud and Lola Field. Attended Ballyhamage School. After finishing school she helped a couple of the neighbors before going to work in Calgary at the Holy Cross Hospital. Coming from a very musical family Gladys bought herself an accordian and learned to play it. She married Bill Threlfall in 1952 who was in the Airforce at the time. He was stationed in Ontario, so Gladys went East with him. Staying in the East for several years. Having family of three boys Wayne, Lyle, Elwood. Elwood graduated from high school making the football team. He won a scholarship to Utah to train four years in football. He plans to make football his career. They also have two daughters Wendy and Lola, coincidentally were born on the same day November the first five years apart. Gladys and family reside in Calgary. Gladys' Mother, who plays a very

Gladys (Field) Threlfall, playing the accordion.

major part in their lives, is coming 83 this year spends the winter in Gladys' home. She is still active and very spry. Gladys donates a lot of her time keeping her smiling and happy. Mrs. Fields daughters are very thankful they have her with them to enjoy their children plus the great-grandchildren.

Mr. and Mrs. A. N. Thorssen
Albert E. and Joyce Thorssen
by A. E. Thorssen

Page 195 in the book "Our Foothills" displays a photograph of the Polkinghorne Ranch as it was known seventy years ago. This home, in its beautiful setting, was purchased in 1925 by A. Mulder and was home to R. Mulder for 23 years. It was subsequently purchased by A.N. and A. E. Thorssen in 1948.

A. N. Thorssen first came to Canada in the spring of 1907. At this time he was working at his Stone-mason trade in the area of Spokane and had a homestead near Dalkena, Washington. The Calgary Colonization Co. painted a vivid picture of the land in Alberta and thereby coaxed workers from Spokane into investigating farming possibilities around Calgary. Thus he purchased his first Alberta land in 1907; had it plowed and then sold it for a small profit. However meager the profit was it brought him back in 1908 when he acquired land north-east of Namaka, Alberta. It was in 1910 that he decided to try farming again, so after seeding the entire quarter to grain, he and his wife left for a visit to their native land, Sweden. Upon returning in August, he found the crop entirely dried up. The 1911 crop was lost to hail. That October, a

Gladys and Bill Threlfall on their wedding day.

Mr. and Mrs. A. N. Thorssen, Golden Wedding, 1958. 88 and 80 years respectively.

Albert and Joyce Thorssen at their home at Millarville.

daughter, Ethel Marjorie, was born; after all, they needed something to liven up the atmosphere. The third year after many tedious days behind the horses, another crop was finally on the way. This time, an old-timer by the name of "Jack-Frost" visited with such severity that all was lost again.

It was in this year of November that a son Albert E. was born; an added incentive to keep the home fires burning. He was also tempted to go back to his Stone-mason trade but realized that bricks and concrete were forcing that sort of work to the wayside. Although there were several partial crops lost on many occasions, for various reasons, still he proved that farming was worthwhile and yielded a good livelihood.

In 1917 he purchased a section and a half in the Mossleigh area. As there was no railroad at this time, all trading was done in Gleichen, 20 miles away. A steel bridge across the "Bow" made quick trips with the Model "T" possible. Some grain was hauled to Carseland, 13 miles distant, but this was not too satisfactory as two teams and a wagon load of grain, quite often caused the ferry to touch bottom. There just couldn't be anything more provoking to a farmer, than to be stranded with four horses and load of grain, half-way across the Bow River.

1925 saw the railroad through Arrowwood and in 1930 to Mossleigh. In 1932, A. E. Thorssen started his

farming career and formed a partnership with his dad in 1941. The "30's" were poor years. The war years were good for production but poor from a selling stand-point. This forced many farmers to go into cattle and hogs. We kept 200 head of cattle and between 4 to 500 head of hogs for many years. As we were short of summer pasture, we looked around and finally bought the N½ 21-21-3-W5, the Mulder place at Millarville, and before this deal was completed we had also purchased S.E.28-21-3W5 from Mr. Hambling, Mrs. Mulder's father. Then in 1949 S.W.28-21-3-W5 and S.E.29-21-3 was purchased from Herb Adams. This gave us ample pasture and for twenty years the cattle were trucked to summer pasture here and home to Mossleigh for winter feeding. We tried raising hay at Millarville, but a good portion of it used to disappear very mysteriously. We couldn't with a clear con-science, blame this entirely on the wild animals.

Mr. and Mrs. Thorssen enjoyed the Millarville country, often driving out from the prairies to spend several days in the former Mulder home. It brought back pleasant memories of their homeland, Sweden, as the country-side was very similar. Mrs. Thorssen passed away suddenly in 1962 and Mr. Thorssen followed in June 1963. This left A. E. Thorssen to farm alone. In 1967 he chose to marry a childhood friend, Joyce Clasen. The farm at Mossleigh was sold and a new house was built on section S.E.28-21-3-W5, a few miles north-west of Millarville.

We have carried on the cattle operation with the help of Cliff Clemis, who came with us from the farm at Mossleigh. Cliff does the farming necessary for raising winter feed and also looks after the cattle. The Polkinghorne or Mulder house was modernized in 1969, giving Cliff, a bachelor, ample living conditions. Except for this, the house has not been altered to any great extent.

We, Joyce and Al have lived here for nine years and enjoy it so that we have never as much as considered any other place to live.

Tosh, William Allan and Joan Elaine $\frac{T}{3}$ L.R

Allan's parents, Kathleen E. (Fisher) and William S. Tosh, (see pages 120 and 217 of Our Foothills), lived in the Millarville area when Allan was born in 1946. They lived on their ranch at SW 7-21-2-W5 until 1948, when due to his father's job with Bear Oil they moved to Edmonton and remained there until 1954.

On their return to the ranch Allan attended the Sheep Creek School and later the Oilfields High School in Black Diamond. During these years, Allan was a member of the Millarville 4H Beef Club and the Oilfields Cadet Corp under the leadership of Mr. Bill Dube (see page 60 of Our Foothills). Allan attended the Olds Agricultural College in 1964 and later the Mount Royal College. His stay at Mount Royal was cut short due to his father's ill health and Allan was required to return home and look after the ranch.

In 1969 Allan and Lance Winthrop attended an Auctioneers School in Billings, Montana. They graduated and again returned home.

Allan married Joan Monkman in 1971.

Joan is the daughter of Bruce and Mildred (Peppard) Monkman (see Chaps and Chinooks page 551 and Big Hill Country page 658). The Monkmans lived in the Rosscarrock Community in Calgary. Joan attended

Allan and Joan Tosh with L. Darren, R. held by mom, Trevor.

Allan Tosh presenting the W. S. Tosh Memorial Trophy to Bruce McMillan at Millarville Races, 1973. Horse is owned by Allan McMillan, named King of Bells.

the Rosscarrock, Melville Scott, Vincent Massey and Western Canada Schools. After graduation in 1964 and until marrying Allan, Joan worked for British American Oil, which later became Gulf Oil Co. Joan has one sister, Hazel Baxter, who lives in Calgary.

Allan has three sisters, Phyllis (Piper) Norris, of Turner Valley, Leila (Piper) Redford and Olive (Piper) Schwarz, both of Calgary.

In 1971, Allan's Dad passed away and since then Allan has been running the ranch. He has a herd of registered polled herefords and has been able to take bulls to the Calgary Bull Sales and other local sales. Allan's father was a horse racing enthusiast, therefore Allan presents a trophy at the Annual Millarville Races in his memory. Allan has served on the Central Board of the Race Track and Joan is a director for the Priddis, Millarville Fair.

Allan and Joan have two sons, Darren, born in 1976 and Trevor, born in 1978.

Brands $\frac{T}{3}$ Left Ribs and WST Left Ribs.

Kathleen Elizabeth Tosh

I was born in Calgary in the old General Hospital on 12th Ave., on the 31st of March, 1907, the fifth child of Joseph and Elizabeth Fisher of Millarville. Easter was also on the 31st of March that year and what started out to be a lovely sunny day turned into a blizzard by afternoon. The nurses from the hospital went out to the Easter parade decked out in all their finery and came back a very bedraggled looking bunch, the flowers and feathers blown off their pretty hats. My name, Kathleen, was given to me by Jack Dempsey, an old time cattleman, who thought it was such a nice Irish name, but my nickname came from my father, who always asked when he came in the house "Where's the cub?" This has stayed with me all my life and Oh! how I have tried to get rid of it. Good thing I didn't turn out to be tall and beautiful.

My early years were spent on the ranch on Fisher Creek, but the need for schooling caused my parents to

Kathleen (Cubbie Fisher) Tosh with her daughters. L. to R. Olive, Phyllis, Cubbie and Leila.

have a home in Calgary, where I attended King Edward School, then for a few years in Victoria for more schooling. We usually came back to Millarville for the summer holidays, staying at either the Meadow, the lower ranch, or the Upper Place, on Fisher Creek. I spent a lot of time riding with Jean and Harry and our favorite playhouse was the rock lined dug out that had been my father's first home when he came to the country. One summer, when we were staying at the Meadow, our eldest sister, Maybelle, took Jean and me to pick a pail of saskatoons which grew in great profusion there. At that time the irrigation ditches at the Meadow were running full of water. We were to return to Calgary that day as our holiday was over. When a call came from the buildings that everyone was ready to go and we must hurry, Maybelle decided the quickest way to go was to cross the water filled ditch. She picked up Jean and threw her across and she landed all right, but when she threw me her aim wasn't so good and I landed in the water. I was wearing a pongee silk dress, which ballooned around me and kept me floating to shallow water, I was unhurt, except for my dignity. I might add here that those trips to and from Calgary were made by team and wagon.

In 1923, the family came back to the ranch to live as by now my brothers were old enough to do the ranch work. The old Rancher's Hall was on our place and most of the social life of the community took place there. One event that was very popular was the 17th of March annual dance, and suddenly there were a lot of Irishmen in the country, at least for one night.

I married John Piper of Red Deer and had three daughters, Phyllis, Leila and Olive. We lived on a bush farm a few miles east of Red Deer during the early thirties and times were really hard. The prices for grain and stock was very low and a case of eggs wouldn't buy a pound of tea. We were there five years. After the sudden death of my husband in 1933, I came back to Millarville. Mother and my brother Bob were living at the Meadow at the time and the girls and I stayed with them while I applied for a Mothers

Allowance from the Gov't. I had left everything in Red Deer so had to start from scratch. When the allowance came through, $35 per month, I got $250 from the Fisher Estate and bought a house in Black Diamond for $500. Out of my $35 I made payments of $10 a month on the house and fed and clothed three girls and myself. That's when I learned to sew and make do with anything.

Eight years later I married Bill (Scotty) Tosh and we bought part of the Fisher place at Millarville. I milked cows and raised chickens. When we bought our first milk cow, Blossom, we didn't know if we had enough money in the bank to pay for her but we managed. Bill worked in the oil fields on the afternoon shift (4 to 12). I sold my house in Black Diamond and bought two good Hereford cows, which gave us a start in the cattle business. Our son Alan was born in August, 1946.

When the Turner Valley oil fields slowed down, Bill went to Trinidad to work in the oil drilling there. We had Christmas dinner with Tim and Jean Blakley, and Bill was to leave the next morning. I had volunteered to stay on the farm for the winter, although Alan was only four months old. After Christmas dinner was over, a young Indian, Webster Lefthand, stopped at Blakley's on his way home to Morley. I asked him how the rest of the winter would be and he replied "Winter hasn't even started yet." How right he was. On Ground Hog's Day, it started to snow and it snowed for weeks,

Cowboy Allan Tosh, son of Bill and Kathleen Tosh. About six years of age.

538

drifts getting higher all the time. The snow plow would clear the roads then it would blow right in again. Getting to the store for groceries was a real headache, but we managed to get through the winter. At times it got to 40 degrees below F. I will never forget the winter of 1947.

When Bill returned from Trinidad we moved to Edmonton and had a caretaker on the farm. We lived in Edmonton for six years, but came back to Millarville as often as possible. Alan started school in Edmonton.

We had a new house built on the Millarville land and when Bill was transferred back to Calgary, we lived on the farm and he drove into Calgary to his job.

By this time the girls were married and we only had Alan at home, so with time on my hands I got involved in community affairs. I was secretary for the Sheep Creek P.T.A. for a few years. I have been a member of the Millarville W.I. since 1955. When I was president, I called the first meeting to discuss compiling a book of the history of the district as a centennial project for the W.I. At that first meeting we had two ladies who had worked on the Gladys and Dinton history book attend to give us some ideas on how to go about starting. However, it was a larger project than we had anticipated, so a history association was formed, with most of the W.I. members joining, and as a result, the book "Our Foothills" was published. I represented Millarville for the new swimming pool in Turner Valley. We held an auction and gave the Pool Committee $3400. I was a leader in the 4-H Sewing Club with Betty Akins, later with Ruth Hoy.

When the World Conference for the A.C.W.W. was held in Ireland, a few members of our local W.I. group attended, and here we met women from all over the world. The Irish people were very kind to us and wearing the Maple Leaf opened many doors to us. The second conference we attended was in Lansing, Michigan, and while there made a trip to New York City. Esther Jackson and I were going up in the hotel elevator, and she was wearing her western costume, including a white hat. Someone in the elevator said "Hello Calgary," recognizing the white hat.

Bill passed away very suddenly on New Year's Eve day, in 1971. Since then I have kept very busy doing handicrafts, bowling etc. I was asked to take over the duties of treasurer for the Historical Society, when the first book "Our Foothills" was being produced. This took a lot of my time, and I was very busy but got to know many of my neighbors better and made new friends.

Alan and his wife, Joan, took over the ranch, and I was able to take another trip, this time to Scotland to visit my daughter Leila and her husband, who were living in Dundee, and also to visit our Fisher cousins in Carlisle, in Northern England. A cousin, Tom Fisher had visited his Canadian relatives the year before and we all enjoyed meeting him and his friend, Tom Mann, a well-known cattle judge in England. They had attended the Calgary Stampede, also the Angus Ban-

Kathleen (Cubbie) Tosh.

quet held during that week. When Tom knew I was coming, he told his wife, Margaret, "Now, Cubby takes a wee drink, smokes a cigarette and wears troosers. "Wearing "troosers" isn't as usual there as it is here. While there I had the pleasure of meeting two other cousins, sons of my father's brother, Harry Fisher, who had come west with my father in the 1880s, and homesteaded where Chubb and Nita Foster now live.

Alan and Joan live near me here on the ranch with their two young sons, Darren and Trevor, so I am enjoying my life and my hobbies. One I have recently taken up is weaving, using wool from the sheep Joan and Alan are raising.

Besides my son and three daughters, I have nine grandchildren, and three great-grandchildren.

Robert Treit

Born at Edmonton in October 1925, one of three children, an older brother now in Vancouver and a younger sister in White Rock, B.C.

I was educated in Edmonton and in the fall of 1943 joined the R.C.N.V.R. Most of my navy days were spent at the East Coast, the more memorable, at an Amunition Base at Renous, New Brunswick on the Banks of the Miramichi River. Time spent there was like a vacation, only to end two years from date of enlistment. After my discharge, I moved to Vancouver where I attempted to continue my life of leisure going from job to unemployment.

Treilane Acres

Tom and Edith Trotter.

The 1947 news of an Oil Strike at Leduc lured me back to Edmonton Alberta, and a job with Oilwell Division of U.S. Steel, of which I am now Manager of Production Equipment Sales for Canada.

In May of 1949 I married Marjorie Quigley of Three Hills, then nursing at the Royal Alexander Hospital in Edmonton. We have three children, Cheryl, residing in Vancouver, Susan in Calgary and Jamie (Mrs. Barton Pillidge) of Bragg Creek.

In 1962 my company transferred me to Calgary, and in 1967 purchased PLAN 6186 PARCEL "A" on the N.E. ¼-SEC 7 TWP 21-R 2-W5M, known as Camp Oliver, from the Diocese of Calgary. This property was originally donated to the Church by Wm. J. Oliver in the late 1930's to be used as a Church Camp for children. In the late 1940's it was abandoned for a larger camp.

When I first purchased the property we used it as a summer home and outings on weekends, it wasn't until 1974, when I built a new home making it my permanent residence.

The beautiful surroundings and solitude setting contributes to the relaxed living I enjoy away from the turmoil of 8th avenue, downtown. While continuing at my work everyday, I have ample time pursuing my hobbies, Curling and Cross Country Skiing in the Winter, and Golfing, Bird Watching and just smelling the flowers in the Summer at TREILANE ACRES, containing 1.212 Hectares.

Edith Lucy (King) Trotter

by Donna Trotter

Daughter of W.H. and Lucy (Wilkin) King, Edith was born at the ranch in 1908.

A party of four travelled slowly along the trail up to the Highwood Pass. This was the fall of 1932, following the marriage of Edith Lucy King to Thomas Wentworth Trotter of Turner Valley. There were no roads as today, only a game trail used by Indians and hunters. Bob Carry, guide and packer, accompanied

them as well as Zoe Trotter, Tom's sister, then a free lance writer for the Edmonton Journal. Thus started a life together, patterned by the wilderness south and west of Millarville.

Twenty years previously, W. H. King, Edith's father, had come up the other side of the Highwood Pass in search of coal. (Our Foothills, page 151.)

I remember most of my childhood sleeping in tents, endless picnics and weekend trips to remote areas. The sound of the night hawk is one of the most nostalgic of my childhood. Always the elusive Lost Lemon Mine played with our fantasies. There were many trips into Burns Lake, Carnarvon Lake and Pickle Jar Lakes, many over swollen spring streams.

While Edith spent many of her falls alone, Tom hunted in any spare time he had. He has now over fifty years experience of the area and knows it well. There are hot springs he discovered up Mist Creek that are recorded in his name.

Edith, a graduate of the Vancouver General Hospital, mother of three children, believed that family groups was the manner in which to raise your children. Along with our cousins, the R. H. King family of Millarville, we went on winter picnics, camped at

Edith Trotter with children. L. to R. Roddy, Donna, Diana, Edith. Hester Stevens — Guille, extreme left with dog.

540

Millarville and rode from Turner Valley to Millarville, slept overnight and then on to the Fair next day. The first Fair I attended was held at the Fordville School site. George Scott was the judge. He gave me second prize for my riding. The ring was a circle of people and there were two in the class. I rode bareback and was about five years of age. Later on the Fair was held at the Millarville Race Track.

The story I like the most involves my three uncles, Bill King, Dick King, Don Trotter and my father, Tom Trotter. They were robust roughnecks working in the Turner Valley Oilfields. As I recall, they were driving between Turner Valley and Millarville when they became stuck in the mud with a flat tire. Bill King lifted the car while the others changed the tire. Then all together, they lifted the car to another track so they could carry on. They were so proud of themselves we were to hear the story told for thirty years.

Tom and Edith Trotter had three children. Diana, born 1933, married Ike Lanier, a farmer from the Lethbridge area. They have four sons, William, Addison, Rodrick and David.

Donna, born 1935, has four children, Gordon, Deborah, Alix and Laura MacNiel, is now married to John Dodds and lives sixteen miles west of Olds.

Rodrick, who married Evelyn Fleay, has two sons Thomas and Daniel Trotter. They live in Sydney, Australia.

Len and Iris Turner

Len and Iris Turner and children moved to Millarville in the spring of 1975. Previously, we had lived our married life in Calgary, the birthplace of all the children.

Len was born in Camrose, Alberta, but spent his growing years in Carstairs, Alberta, where we are presently living. His parents, Ada and Ellis Turner farmed in this area and later moved into the town of Carstairs. His mother taught school there until her retirement 5 years ago. During this time his father, while living in town, carpentered and was on the

school board. He later was Mayor of Carstairs until they moved to their present residence in Ferintosh, Alberta.

Iris was born in Edmonton but between the ages of 2 and 19 she lived on the West Coast. Her parents, Asa and Dolly Douglas are fishermen and residing on Salt Spring Island. Asa had been a carpenter until moving to the coast, where he worked at fishing as well as boat building for many years. He built his own fishing boat large enough to take his whole family with him. In the summertime the whole family would live on the boat. Her mother worked alongside her dad and though he is now in his seventies, they are still going strong.

When Iris was 18 she moved to Victoria where she did office work at the Gov't. building. Through friends she met Len at a party. At this time he was a sailor based at Naden in Esquimalt and after a short period of going together, they decided to get married.

In April, Len's discharge from the Navy came through and they were married in Crossfield, Alberta, in October 1960. Len worked at various jobs until he started as a salesman for Silver Automotive in 1964 and for the next six years learned the automotive trade. 1970 was the opening of his own shop, Action Parts. Iris went to work as his secretary and the company has gone steadily forward from that time.

Shelley, our oldest, is graduating this June and plans a commercial arts course following a year working with other young people in a Gov't sponsored wilderness program. Lana and Julie are in grades 10 and 9 respectively and are both involved in Air Cadets. Barry is in grade four and a cub. They are happy here but miss the acreage at Millarville.

In 1975, we sold our home in Mapleridge in Calgary and moved into a newly constructed house on top of Whiskey Mountain. This acreage sub-division had the most breathtakenly beautiful scenery and peacefulness and together with the friendliness of the neighbors and others in the general area made our time in Millarville "The best years of our life."

Rob and Mariette Vanderham
Joe and Betty Mercier

by Mariette Vanderham   DL

The two quarters that make up the Driftline Ranch (SE 30-21-4-W5M — the home quarter, and SW 29-21-4-W5M) are on the eastern slopes of the Rocky Mountains. A crystal stream, named after an earlier settler Joseph Fisher, cuts through the land, adding to its charm. Three to four hundred foot high foothills surround it, and west lies the Rocky Mountain Forest Reserve. The land passed through the hands of James H. Adams, Dan Bannerman, R. G. MacKay, and the McBees of Longview before it became the property of J. Wallace Andrew. He sold the two quarters to James William Lucas, who used the land for summer grazing. In April 1967 Lucas sold the land to its present owners, Rob and Mariette Vanderham, and Joe and Betty Mercier.

Turner Family. Back: Julie, Lana. Front: Barry, Iris, Shelley, Len.

The Driftline Crowd. Vanderhams and Merciers. Summer, 1967.

Rob Vanderham finished his teen years in Holland under the German occupation. After the war he decided two brothers in the family lumber business took up all the room, so he came to Canada where wide open spaces beckoned. He worked on a farm near Airdrie for two years and saved money to go to Agricultural College where he majored in animal husbandry. Then by a twist of fate he ended up in the oil business. Love of cattle and the land stayed in his heart and the Driftline satisfies an old yearning. I am a 'dyed-in-the-wool' westerner. I grew up in Saskatoon, Sask. and was educated there. After teaching high school for a few years I met the irresistible Dutchman and we started our French-Irish-Dutch family. The family grew to seven children: Karen, Paul, Margot, Kristine, Mark, Maria and Gina. One day Robin and I hope to be able to enjoy country living full time.

Both Joe and Betty Mercier were born and raised in the drylands of Saskatchewan. To Joe the Driftline was the beginning of a lifelong dream to start a cattle ranch. His father had ranched in southwestern Saskatchewan until the growing demands of his family forced him to turn to farming. His heart remained with ranching, and when he died at 42 he left Joe, then nine years old, with the same love of the open range. A year after buying the Driftline they bought Hugh Macklin's land near Red Deer Lake, built a home, and moved there with their eight children: Peter, Daniel, Margaret, Joe, Jeanne, Tom, Robert and Barbara. For the past 11 years this has been the nucleus of their cattle operation with the Driftline their summer range.

We bought the land with the Mercier family in the spring of 1967. There were four adults and fifteen children on the place that summer, and there was never a dull moment. The first work party tackled garbage clean up which was a monumental job since past owners somewhere down the line had tossed tons (or so it seemed!) of bottles and cans down by the creek. Then came yard clean up, housework, fence repair, and drama of dramas, the moving of the outhouse, a

job somewhat overdue! The young boys dug until they were nearly out of sight, ropes were wound around the little building; some expert manoeuvering with the tractor and it was happily settled. The diggers weren't so happy. Was this all there was to it? After all that shovelling in the hot sun? No more excitement? So we decided to have an opening ceremony. As luck would have it there was a big roll of pink ribbon (??) in the outhouse. We wound it around the hut and across the door, took pictures of the diggers proudly waiting to cut it to formally open the outhouse, and drew lots to see who would use the new location first. Paul Vanderham entered to the roar of eighteen cheering voices.

And now for the bull. The story of the big bull called Blanco. Joe and Rob had the choice of two part Charolais. The semen test showed one was blank, so they bought the good one, called it Blanco because of its color and drove off satisfied, with the big brute in the truck. They talked and chuckled and bumped their way to the Driftline gate, jumped out and . . . no bull! They found him grazing peacefully a few miles back. Once in the field he really came alive, leaping on and off cows at a mad clip. Oh, how the thought of all those little calves warmed the new ranchers' hearts. The many months passed, and then what?? One lone calf! Had they made an honest mistake at the stockyards? At any rate Blanco lived up to his name in more ways than one.

And now to the dry 'Summer of the Bees' and our friendly rancher neighbor Ernie Silvester, who came to help with fencing. It was another hot day and the men and boys worked their way along the fence line checking, repairing and sweating. Ernie was ahead, and decided to mix fun with work. He stirred up a wasps' nest with a fence post and trudged on. All unsuspecting the group moved ahead, smack into a swarm of angry eager wasps. While they swatted and roared in pain, Ernie was swatting his knee and roaring with laughter. I just can't remember whether he was invited for cold beer that day!

I could go on. Like about the day a horse aptly called Rising Wolf gave a free, unscheduled demonstration on reproduction when we were all lunching at the picnic table. The eyes of the little city kids nearly popped out of their heads. Or about the time we bought an animal at the horse sale when we were sitting high in the bleachers and found when we came to get her she was 17½ hands high. Or about the late fall day Fred Ball was by and said one of our mares sure looked in foal. "Ah no, she's just fat" said Rob. "Well, I don't know", insisted Fred, "that sure looks like more than fat to me". Late February when we drove to the ranch to toss out a little extra feed the mare came trotting to the barn with a brand new colt by her side, it's little eartips frozen off. The reserve Stallion strikes again! We had three 'surprise' colts that way.

The Merciers and our family think its the most

beautiful place in the world, this Alberta Foothill land of ours. I think all the ranchers around here feel the same — its just God's country!

Venus Family
by Laura Venus

We bought the farm from Mr. and Mrs. Bartlam in 1941. Mr. Venus was still employed by the Union Oil Co. Mr. Bartlam had been unable to keep up the work necessary on the farm due to ill health, consequently the farm was in great need of cleaning, barns, pens, etc. As a result, we could not, or rather, were not able to employ a man to go out to the farm to operate it. This meant that the boys, Bob and Marvin, and myself took on the task of going to live on the farm and manage it. Should say we tried, at least. First came several years of cleaning everything, from barns to yard. Having accomplished this, it was a lovely place to live.

The neighbors, Prestons, Kohlers, McLeans and Ericsons, made life very pleasant for me. One could not wish to live in a community as friendly and helpful, could name many more, no one could be omitted.

The children remember the teacher, Miss Korpeki, especially Marvin and Audrey. They both remember that on Fridays she would have the preschool children come to school in the afternoons. Mothers could then go to town for shopping. The older children would entertain them, help them to write, draw, crayon, anything to entertain them. They were all very well behaved, and the teacher did not seem to have any discipline problems. On one such occasion, little Billy Jackson (then) shared Marvin's desk, and he stood up in the seat, put his arms around Marvin's neck and said "Marvin, I sure loves you." Marvin came home beaming.

Bob was in College, Audrey was in Calgary and Marvin and I were alone on the farm. It was winter, forty-five below zero, and we had four sows due to farrow. Thinking the pigs might freeze, we put up a heater in the pig pens, but we could not find a damper to put in the pipes. There was such a blizzard blowing, we thought the sparks from the chimney could easily put the pig pens on fire. We were so afraid of the little pigs freezing as they arrived, we decided to get four boxes and put each sow's little ones in each box and take them to the house where it was warm. People had told us that a sow would not take another sows piglets, that they would likely kill them, so by putting them in separate boxes it would be safe to take them back to their mothers when they were over farrowing. This was about four in the morning. We went to the house to take the pigs back to the pen, but the house being warm and the little pigs being very much alive, were all out of the boxes and were running helter-skelter all over everywhere. What to do now? There was no way of telling what little pig belonged to what sow. So we

just gathered them up, took them back to the pens, dumped them in the centre and let them fend for themselves. Out of forty-two we only lost three runts. That disproved the story that no sow will take anothers little ones.

We had a thirty pound turkey gobbler on the farm. He was gentle and quiet with us but did he hate Mr. Venus (Jack) with a vengeance. Jack came out on week ends and what a noise that turkey would make. He would wait for every chance to fly at Jack and take a peck at him. Needless to say the turkey was asking for a quick demise when Jack came out to the farm to stay.

We milked ten cows and would take the milk up to the milk house to separate it. From the barn to the closed in yard was about a hundred yards. We had a young horse that loved milk, we would look to see where he was, nowhere in sight, so we would make a dash to get to the gate and inside the yard, but that horse would appear from somewhere. Before we could get through the gate his head would be in one of the pails and the milk would be gone.

We had a black Aberdeen Angus cow, it must have been bred from a deer, that is the father must have been. No fence would keep her in. She would walk back from a fence twenty feet, then run and clear the fence without any difficulty. Mr. Ericson had put up a high new fence around his property to the south of us, and this cow could go over it with ease. In the spring she jumped in there for the last time; she got poisoned from a weed that is deadly poison and if I remember right it was wild larkspur. In the spring the roots are poisonous.

There was a short time when the coyotes were hazarding the surrounding district. A number of the farmers had lost the little pigs, especially if the sows got out and roamed. One day we missed ten little pigs; we looked for them all day and into the night. It was a beautiful moonlight night when we heard very quiet oink oink's and there, single file were ten little pigs coming down the dry creek bed, very quietly oinking all the way. When they got into their pen, were still being quiet, except for the oinks. One of them looked up at me and oink oinked, as much as to say "Yes we have been naughty, now we are going to sleep." It is a picture I will never forget.

We remember the Millarville Sports day, and especially the horse races. This was an event no one missed. I am quite sure you will have many comments about this social community gathering, everyone entered into the spirit of the day, from age one to ninety.

The Women's Institute was a very active group. There was only one regret I had when I lived there and belonged to the Institute. Many might remember we had a conference in the Valley, and the main issue of discussion was the cost of food. They voted to send a delegation to Ottawa to get Ottawa to take some action on it. I had asked the members to wait and take time to prepare the actual cost of producing each food item, butter, beef, pork, poultry. The cost of transportation from the farm, to wholesaler, to store and the final cost to the consumer. To prepare such a report would take six months, but having these figures, would have a good foundation to achieve what they were concerned about. The delegation was sent to Ottawa without taking time to have facts and figures regarding costs. As a result, Ottawa told them to go home. There was nothing gained as a result of haste. Had they taken time to prepare costs, perhaps we would not have had the inflation we have had since. At the best our government would have had to listen, with a force of women who knew what they were talking about.

Mr. Robaloyd (Indian) living in Black Diamond, was doing some trapping and walked along the line parallel to our property, and would always call in to see how we were. He was a very fine person, and on several occasions when there was illness, his thoughtfulness was appreciated. He will always be remembered.

We left Millarville in the fall of 1948 to reside in North Bend, B.C. Jack passed away in 1955. I remained there until 1975, when I sold the business and came to live in Chase, B.C.

Bob is with an oil company in Iran. Audrey is on a farm in Grindrod, B.C. Marvin is with the B.C.R. in Prince George. We all remember the farm and some of our most enjoyable times, and the many friends we made.

Many of the problems with our young people could be solved if the Government would have a large farm, where these young people could go. They would learn so much, as to be a farmer there is so much to learn. He must be carpenter, plumber, gardener, knowledge of all animals, and horticulturist. We will need young men and women to take up farming. This would be a good start, to have them become interested. In spite of the many handicaps there is to farming, there is no better life.

Ernie M. and Greta Verhulst

Ernie M. and Greta Verhulst came to Canada from Holland in 1958 with their daughter Yolanda. They arrived in Edmonton and stayed in the Immigration Hall for 14 days, while Ernie did some work as a laborer, such as roofing etc. Fourteen days later they moved to Calgary to stay with friends there, and Ernie did labor work most of that summer until he found work in his own field as an Electronic Technician.

In 1968 they bought 20 acres on Highway 22 near Millarville Section 35-20-3-W5 from Norm Gordon and started building their own home. In 1975 they sold their place to Mark Banjavich and bought 40 acres and house from Albert Kieboom. Section 28-20-3-5th being part of the former Dick Cooper place where they do

some farming raising some cattle and chinchilla's. The Verhurst now have six children.

Yolanda born in 1955 and is married to David Marston of Calgary. They live at Acme and have one daughter, Shannon. Larry born 1960; Steve born 1962; Shawna born 1970; Christine 1962; Alex born 1962 and all are living at home.

Anne Vincent

Born in Calgary, I am the youngest daughter of Esther and Bill Jackson. Received my education at Sheep Creek School. As kids we had many good times while attending Sheep Creek. I often think back to the Christmas Concerts at Ranchers' Hall, exchanging gifts and the candy bags. One other funny incident which comes to mind is the time when a certain Hugh used to tease the daylights out of me and one day he was making faces at me through the school window and I reached the boiling point and punched my fist at him through the glass; I didn't even cut my hand. A short while later though, I ran around the outside of the school after him and fell on the glass and cut my knees.

I worked at Millarville Store for Jappy and Martha Douglas a year before moving to Calgary in 1949. Attended Calgary Business College and upon graduating was employed by the Calgary City Police as a stenographer in the Court Reporters' Office. What a quick education for a green gal off the farm. A few days after I was there I typed a judgement re a bawdy house case. I spelled bawdy house, "body" house. Shortly after the judge received it he phoned me up and asked me to spell bawdy, and I said, "b-o-d-y", he sort of grunted a laugh and said, "You have the right idea, but the wrong spelling." I spent three years there and then decided to make a change and went with Burgess Building and Plumbing, I remained there for four years.

Warren, Anne, Suzy and Neil Vincent. 1973.

544

Warren and I were married in 1955. Our son Neil arrived in 1957, and Mary Anne in 1961. I returned to the working world in 1963 with the Supreme Court of Alberta. Since 1966, have been employed with the Calgary Board of Education as a school secretary.

Am a member of The Southern Alberta Pioneer and Descendants; The Calgary Foothills Wanderers Jeep Club. Participate in volunteer work at Heritage Park. Enjoy camping, cross country skiing and handicrafts when time permits.

Warren was born in Fort St. John, B.C. His grandfather Vincent was among the early pioneers who came to the Peace River country from the United States over the Edson Trail in covered wagons around 1912. His father ran the Clayhurst Ferry on the Peace River for many years.

Warren received his education at Dawson Creek and Rolla, B.C. He then joined the Lord Strathcona Horse Regiment of the armed forces in Calgary in 1949. He trained in Edmonton, Wainwright, Calgary, and Camp Borden, Ontario. He served in the tank corp in Korea for over a year.

Upon his discharge from the services he became employed with Burgess Building and Plumbing for a few years and then went with Bruce Robinson Electric. When that company dissolved, Warren and three other fellow employees opened up Guardian Appliance Sales and Service in 1969. Due to health reasons he sold his interest in Guardian in 1976 and has since been with the Calgary Co-op.

Warren is a member of the Royal Canadian Legion, Calgary Foothills Wanderers Jeep Club. He enjoys camping, fishing and wood working.

Our son Neil received all of his education in Calgary, graduating in 1976. During his school years he was involved in Cubs, Boy Scouts and Venturers. He participated in the Ice Stampede quite a few seasons. He delivered the early morning Albertan for several years. Then he went on to delivering drugs for Penley's Drug Store. He is presently taking Architectural drafting and working for Calgary Co-op. Neil enjoys most sports and is an enthusiastic skier.

Mary Anne (Suzy), our daughter, is in her last year of High School and expects to graduate June 1979. She has been active in C.G.I.T. Has worked part time for the past two years, at Laura Secord Candy Shops and is presently with the Hudson Bay Co. She is a avid lover of music, especially, "Rock", which she plays on piano. Mary Anne has not decided on a career as yet, but that will come in time.

Phill and Keri Vincent

Phill was born in Hamilton, Ontario, and came west to Calgary with his parents in 1953; his father being transferred with the army.

Keri was born in Calgary and lived there all her life until moving to Millarville.

Phill and Keri were married in May, 1976 and lived in Calgary for two and a half years before finding

Phill and Keri Vincent.

acreage in the Millarville area. They bought thirty acres and a house from Dr. and Mrs. Chopra, who owned the acreage for seven years prior to that. This was in the fall of 1978.

Phill is in the carpet business, and has been for the past fourteen years. He works in both the Calgary and Okotoks areas.

At the present time, they have no children, but both have lots of relatives in Calgary who enjoy coming out to the country for a visit.

Phill and Keri have found their new community and neighbours very friendly and lots of fun; and are looking forward to many enjoyable years in Millarville.

Virtue, S. L. (Jim.)

Having left the Millarville-Kew district in the winter of 1927-1928, as mentioned in the first book "Our Foothills", and living in the oil fields of Black Diamond and Turner Valley, I finished my schooling in Black Diamond and at the Turner Valley High School, which is now the Golf Club House. My teachers were Rev. D. J. C. Elson, Ian (Mack) McLaren, James Shearer, Clive Ballard, Mrs. Beisterfield, and Cecil Hart.

I started working for the Royalite Oil Co. in the fall of 1936 and served my apprenticeship under the late Art Cobb, Stan Stanhope and Alf Wilkes.

In 1938 I met Ida Archibald of Turner Valley, formerly of Nanton, Alberta, and we were married February 10th, 1939. I enlisted in the Canadian Army, Royal Canadian Engineers in June 1940 and served five and a half years in Canada and overseas.

Upon my discharge, I returned to work for the Royalite Oil Co. I continued to work for Royalite and then transferred to Imperial Oil where I worked on different drilling locations as a welder for rigs and transportation departments. I worked in Northern British Columbia and Alberta. The last thirteen years I was in the Arctic.

In 1975, I retired from Imperial Oil after 39 years service, due to illness. My wife and I make our home in Devon, Alberta. We enjoy working in our yard and garden, and helping our neighbors, and belonging to the Canadian Legion.

Our only child passed away in 1958 at age 15 years after a lengthy illness.

Elizabeth von Rummel

by Jean Blakley

Born in Munich, Germany, February 1897, Elizabeth (Lizzie) came to Alberta in 1911, when her mother, Mrs. Elsa Basilici, bought the Gate Ranch at Kew from Louis Taylor. While her mother and step-father went on to the ranch to arrange to have the place put in order, Lizzie and her two sisters, Jane and Nina, stayed at Gillespie's boarding house at Priddis. Here, they were first introduced to the western way of life, riding horses and Lizzie baked her first bread, under the capable instruction of Mrs. Gillespie.

After a few weeks spent at Priddis, the three girls were driven to the ranch by team and democrat, a distance of about twenty miles south west of Priddis. The girls immediately fell in love with the ranch, the grand view of the mountains, and the North Fork of Sheep River, which ran through the property, close to the buildings. They spent an ideal summer, but their first stay was short lived and they all returned to Germany. However, they came back the following year, 1912. Mrs. Basilici gave in to her daughters' pleading and they returned to Alberta, in time to attend the first Calgary Stampede.

The first World War in 1914 curtailed any more trips to Germany for a few years. Lizzie and her sisters were quite happy. They had made friends with the daughters of two neighboring ranchers, Tuck (Constance) Phillips and Molly and Isabel Fulton, a friendship which has lasted many years. These girls shared the same interests as Lizzie and her sisters, riding horses and camping, and they had a favorite spot on a small creek near Ware Creek where they had many happy camping trips, without the supervision of their elders.

As the girls grew older it wasn't all fun and games. A good Clydesdale stallion was bought and also some good mares and in a few years there was a good herd of horses on the ranch. Some of these horses had to be broken to drive, for haying and the other needs on a ranch, so Lizzie and her sisters did the job as well as any man could have done it. They also broke saddle horses for their own use. One annual event was the Priddis and Millarville Fair, and some of their horses were shown there. Lizzie was a director of this fair, and one time was a trustee of the Square Butte School board.

By 1936, with both sisters married and ranching on their own, Lizzie embarked on a new career in the mountain resorts. Her first job was at Mt. Assiniboine Lodge, and she was there 1936-37-38-39. From 1940 to 1949, she operated Skoki Lodge, north of Lake Louise, then in 1950 she bought Pat Brewster's concession at Sunburst Lake, in Mt. Assiniboine Provincial Park in

Elizabeth Rummel at Sunburst Lake Camp in Mt. Assiniboine Park, British Columbia, which Elizabeth owned for 20 years.

Camp near Ware Creek where Lizzie and her sisters, Jane and Nina and friends spent many happy times. L. to R. Isabel Fulton, Nina Rummel, Jane Rummel, Lizzie Rummel, Constance (Tuck) Phillips, and Connel Williams, who drove the girls and their gear to the camp with team and wagon. About 1919.

British Columbia. She was there for the next twenty years. There was no road in to Sunburst Lake so her supplies were brought in by pack horse, mostly by Ray McBride. Most of her guests were hikers and fishermen, and they also came in by walking. During her long stay at Sunburst Lake, many of her relatives walked in from the road's end at Spray Lakes. Her sister Jane made several trips in alone, and a couple of times came almost face to face with a bear, but she was unafraid and the bear went about his business. One time a large bear looked in on Lizzie and made off with a precious roast of beef.

She had one memorable trip out of Mt. Assiniboine after a fall in which her leg was broken. A helicopter was sent for and she was flown to a Calgary hospital, but was back at Sunburst Lake the following summer.

In 1970 Lizzie retired and bought a home in Canmore, but not one to sit idle, she worked for the Banff Archives. She has made several trips in to Assiniboine by helicopter with her friend, Jim Davies. On one of these trips she was accompanied by Tensing Norgay, co-climber with Sir Edmund Hilary of Mt. Everest, who wished to see Mt. Assiniboine.

In the more than thirty years that Lizzie has been in the mountain country, she has made many friends from all over the world, but probably the longest continued friendship has been with the Bearspaw family from Morley. David Bearspaw and his family first came to the Kew ranch in 1912, and were constant visitors for many years. In 1968, Lizzie attended the funeral at Morley of Mrs. David Bearspaw who passed away at age 106. Johnnie Bearspaw passed away a short time ago.

Lizzie still makes trips to Kew to visit the sons of her sisters, and their families. Michael Rodgers, Nina's son, is using the Z̄R brand used by the family for many years.

Irene (Adams) Waite   K

I made my appearance into the world April 21st, 1926, on the farm of my parents, Hazel and Herb Adams, the N.W.¼ of 33-20-3w5. There were already three brothers and three sisters. Three more sisters were born later.

I went to Plainview School for most of my schooling, riding horseback winter and summer. In the spring I used to help my brothers collect magpie and crow eggs on the way home from school. The winters were sometimes very miserable. The last year and a half of school was at Sheep Creek.

When I finished school I worked on the farm. In September of 1944 I joined the C.W.A.C. in Calgary. I took basic training and also a cook's course at Kitchener, Ontario. I spent that Christmas in Montreal, Quebec. I was stationed at Suffield, Alberta for thirteen months, then at Currie Barracks, Calgary, until my discharge in July, 1946.

I went to Yellowknife and worked there as a

Irene (Adams) Waite.

waitress and then cooked for the Consolidated Mining and Smelting Company for twenty-eight months.

I married Joseph C. Waite in June 1949 and lived by the Halfway Service Station on the S.E. corner of Sec. 25-22-3w5. Brian was born April 28th, 1950. Sandra was born April 12th, 1952. Janice was born October 23rd, 1956. Karen was born September 18th, 1958. We moved to the service station in 1960 and remained until we sold it in 1963 and moved to Chedderville District, near Rocky Mountain House. We purchased our farm, the north ½ of sec. 13-37-r7-w5, in March of 1964. Joe registered his brand ⅃ but in recent years when Brian became involved in the farm, he registered Grandfather Joseph Waite's brand Ɖ but due to changes in brand regulations he had to add a half diamond Ɖ .

The pioneering spirit needed to take over when we moved to the farm. There were old and poorly built buildings, no barn and a small house. When the wind would blow, it would come in one side of the house, run around and then go out the other side. We wrapped the house in plastic to keep a little heat in for the winter. We finally purchased a house in Rocky Mountain House to move to the farm but at the time there were only narrow steel covered bridges so we had to wait until the Clearwater River froze hard enough to bring the house across.

All the children graduated from high school and now: Brian is working on rigs and helping on the farm. Sandra is married to a R.C.M.P. constable, Jack

Doyle. They married in April 1975 in New Brunswick and they live in North Sidney, Nova Scotia, with son Tim and daughter Kathy. Janice is working on the farm looking after the cattle. Karen is living in Rocky Mountain House with her son Lesley. Joe is farming and I'm working in Rocky at the Mountview Hotel.

Wallace, Ruth

by R. Wallace

I was born at Mossleigh, Alberta, May 24, 1914. In 1918, my parents, Ada and Warren Bucher, bought the John Fulton ranch, the S.E.¼ of 36-20-R4-W5, at Kew and we moved there.

I attended the Plainview School for three years, riding horseback the two miles. I still remember how kind and helpful the older pupils were to the younger ones. On the way home we used to have horse races which were a lot of fun for everyone except for my sister, Janet MacKay, riding behind the saddle with me. No wonder my parents put a stop to this sport.

I saw my first hockey game at Kew. There was a rink near Walton's store. I don't recall how many players had proper hockey sticks but I do remember some of them were pieces of small trees or bushes with a crook at the bottom.

In 1923, we moved to Okotoks where I continued my schooling. Glen Wallace and I were married in 1932 and lived in Okotoks. We have four children, Harry of Calgary, Margaret Steinke of Edmonton, Jim of Medicine Hat and Douglas of Edmonton. We also have five granddaughters and four grandsons.

Glen worked for Shell Oil. In 1953, we were transferred to Weyburn, Sask. and in 1959 to Valleyview, Alta. He retired in 1968 and we moved to our farm at Worsley, in the Peace River district, where we still reside.

Ruth (Bucher) Wallace and her husband, Glen Wallace. 1954.

Eileen (Macturk) Wallin

by Eileen Wallin

In 1914 I arrived at Pine Lake from England. In 1917 I spent three months with Mr. and Mrs. Clem Gardiner, Pirmez Creek, and then stayed with Hastie and Helen Cochrane, whose ranch boarded Christ Church.

Mrs. Eileen (MacTurk) Wallin at Ballyhamage 1919. Sheilagh Jameson on her back.

I have fond memories of the Cochrane family, their neighbors, and good times at Ranchers Hall. Towards the end of the war I accompanied the family to Duncan, B.C. In 1921 I married Ernest Wallin at Pine Lake. Little did I know then I would make many trips back to the Millarville area to visit my daughter Una, son-in-law Fred Ball and my grandchildren.

I am presently living in Victoria and keep in touch with my friends Mrs. Cochrane, Elspeth and Ken.

Mary and Phillip Wallis

Mary and Phillip, with two very young children, Jane and Susan, came to George Smale's ranch in April, 1949. We shared life at the ranch with Johnny Grant — that very big hearted "master of all trades" who was so fond of an occasional bender. George and Clem Smale were living in Calgary at the time and left John to look after their affairs.

Very shortly after arriving we attended a dance in the old hall across the road — (Ranchers Hall) — our ranch supplied the electric power for lighting. The dance was put on by Don MacKay, Liberal candidate for Parliament (Don later became mayor of Calgary.)

From our ranch we used to be able to look across at Joe and Jane Fisher's place and see Dusty, that beautiful Palomino exercising in his corral. For years Dusty was ridden by Dick Cosgrove, infield manager at the Stampede.

My life throughout the next winter consisted mainly of hauling feed with the black and white team. I used to go past Joe Fisher's gate and further west was Tim Blakleys place, then over the creek, turn left, and go up the steep hill which became quite slippery for the team.

Due to a much poorer Bull Sale in March of 1950 than had been hoped for it was not possible to go on employing full time help at the ranch so after only one year we sadly left the area and went to Colpitts Ranches in Symons Valley north of Calgary.

Mr. and Mrs. J. T. Ward

The early years living on our place at Millarville were happy years, throwing the harness on Jean and

Nan, (our team of part Percherons) and visiting neighbors, with cups of tea always remembered.

So many former neighbors and dear friends have passed on, but we will never forget their kindly help, when times were hard, money scarce and we were very poor and inexperienced.

Jimmy never attended any of the schools mentioned but he always attended all the do's at Square Butte with Jim and me.

Mrs. Jones and her daughter Hilda boarded with us and the late Harry Fisher, our chore boy, drove them to Square Butte School. Mr. Vanderburg (another teacher) and his son were frequent guests for a home cooked meal.

While we have put our roots down in Calgary, a bit of our heart remains in Millarville. Our grandson has a home on our Millarville place.

John and Mildred Ware Family
by Nettie Ware

There were four boys and two girls in the Ware family, Robert, William, Arthur and Daniel. The girls were Janet and Mildred, who was named for her mother. Janet was the eldest of the family, born in Calgary the 9th of March, 1893, born in the same house that her father and mother were married in. Then there was Robert, the next oldest, born September 20th, 1894 at Millarville. Mildred and William, the twins, were born September, 1898, at Millarville.

Arthur was born at Millarville 4th of July 1900. Daniel was born in 1902, at Bantry, Alberta, the same year the family left the hills. He died when he was two years old at Blairmore and is buried in a pretty graveyard on the mountain side at Blairmore.

After we lost our father and mother within six months of each other, Grandma and Grandpa Lewis took us to look after and reared us. I, Janet, stayed at home with the Lewis' and helped as much as I could. The first school days were at Blairmore, in the Crow's Nest Pass. Robert went to school in Blairmore also, the others were too young.

The Lewis' left Blairmore and moved to Calgary where the rest of us went to the old West Calgary School. In 1914, when the First World war was on, Willie and Arthur joined up and went overseas. Arthur was not 16 years old in 1918. They both returned, but Willie had contracted tuberculosis, he died and was buried in the Field of Honor in Calgary.

Arthur and Robert went to work for the C.P.R. They stayed there until they retired. Arthur went to Vancouver to make his home. Robert lives in Calgary, has lived there most of his life. He was married but his wife died suddenly, had no children. The rest of us were not married, making no descendants on the Ware side of the family.

I was the only one born with a doctor in attendance. The others born at Millarville and no doctor. A friend, Mrs. Standish Sr. was with my mother. None of the boys took after their father, a cattleman. I, Janet

John Ware family with friends. L. to R. Arthur Ware, Mildred Ware, Grant MacEwan, Bob Ware, Front, Nettie Ware. Ellamae Rodgers and D. Johnson in wagon. Photo courtesy, Micheal Burn.

(Nettie) the eldest, is the one with a bit of everything and have enjoyed life in all my different vocations. It was at Millarville that Father brought in the anvil for the frost to get out and I licked it and was stuck there and have had a long tongue ever since. I can remember when Father dipped Robert in the irrigation that ran under the milk house. I ran. I remember going with Father to the Rineharts at Red Deer Lake. They had a piano, the first I had ever seen, a great curiosity. I have a very home like feeling towards Millarville and love our old friends there.

In 1972, I was appointed Alberta Pioneer Daughter. I have also had the honor of opening the John Ware School in Calgary, named for my father.

Wilfred and Winifred Waters

by Winifred Waters

My father, Harry Taylor, homesteaded in the Hand Hills district and Wilf's father, Bill Waters, homesteaded near Rocky Mountain House. We both moved to Calgary, Wilf when he was two and I when I was 12.

We were married in 1950, and have four children: Barbara, Mrs. Allen Traxel, a former Phs. Ed. teacher now has two boys and lives in Calgary. Kerry, a stenographer with the Provincial Gov't. lives in Calgary. Norman works with a wholesale distributing company and lives in Calgary. Neil is married to the former Pamela Arndt, is a salesman in Calgary.

Wilfred Waters and family. L. to R. Neil, Kerry, Norman, Wilf and Barbara. Front: Win.

In 1959, we bought 20 acres in the Midnapore district and built a house there. Here we spent many happy years. The children went to school in Midnapore and were then bused to Calgary. We belonged to the Midnapore and Red Deer Lake districts. We curled at Red Deer Lake, worshiped at the United Church there and enjoyed many dances and parties in the old hall.

I guess you judge a community by the people who live there and we had some of the finest friends and neighbors to be found anywhere in the world.

In 1978, we sold our land but kept the house. We bought 80 acres in the Millarville area from the Johnsons who lived in Priddis. This acreage just west of Ernie Silvester's slopes west and is just lovely for a home nestled in the hills. Here we had York Shaw move our house. Kinnard and Bill Shaw did a fantastic job of moving the large house and setting it on a foundation. The people in this area are just as friendly and helpful as we could wish for and we enjoyed our time spent in Millarville.

Donald James Wathen

by Don Wathen

Born July 30, 1928 in High River. Lived on a farm near Okotoks for thirty years to the day. Moved to Midnapore, DeWinton area July 30, 1958. In 1963 at Banff, Alberta, he married Dorothy Ellen Bowie. His life-long friend, Joe Foss was best man. Ever since. has shared the same good times together with many a Sunday (after the branding of cattle and work being done) getting together with friends for a good old singsong party. Been in the ranching, cattle buying and trucking business for 30 years. Bought cattle from Fort McLeod to Grand Prairie, through B.C. to Kamloops. Still very much in the cattle buying and selling business.

Thinking of retiring and selling out and moving to a warmer climate come fall.

Wedding of Dorothy Bowie and Don Wathen, Banff, 1963.

Don Wathen, winter 1978-79.

Earl George Watson

by Mary Ann Highmoor

Earl was born in Strathmore March 8, 1939 the second son of four of George and Irene. They lived on his Grandfather's (Angus Watson) farm seven miles south of Strathmore until Earl was the age of six when the family moved to East Calgary. George (Shorty) was well known at the Calgary Stockyards where he worked for Burns then Parslow and Denoon until he was badly injured by a Holstein bull in 1963.

Earl has many happy memories of growing up. For about four summers around 1948 George and family packed up the old Model A car, one horse trailer, mule, goat, coyote, geese and ducks and followed the northern rodeo circuit where he was hired as rodeo clown.

Earl attended Colonel Walker school for nine years and was a pupil of Harry Hamilton who was well

Watson Family. L. to R. George, Ronny, Vivian, Vernon, Randy and Earl Watson.

known as a stern disciplinarian. As a boy of fifteen the trading of horses became his life and school went by the wayside. Earl's family at this time had moved to a ten acre acreage three miles south of Forest Lawn from 1950-58. For four years he traded horses and was well known at auction sales in the area. The only problem with trading in horses was that all the horses came home and caused lots of headaches for his mother.

On December 12, 1959, Earl married Vivian Thompson of Calgary. In the same year he went to work for H.T.R. Gregg of Old Town Stock Farm which was to last for ten years.

While at Millarville much of their free time was spent hunting, fishing and holidaying in the mountains. One of the many times they were out riding with Glaisters, Lucille all of a sudden leaped off her horse, ripped off her slacks, of course they thought a whole swarm of bees had got her. They were wrong, it was only the matches in her pocket which had set fire.

On May 6, 1961 a son Randy was born to be followed by a second son Ronny on April 13, 1962.

In 1969 he worked for Jim Wright at De Winton and helped him establish a herd of Red Angus cattle.

Snap Lawson purchased Wright's farm and Earl worked for Snap for two years building an elaborate race horse facility. With waning interest in race horses, they moved to Windermere, B.C. to the Elkhorn Ranch owned by Sam Hanen, as ranch manager.

In 1970 they moved to the Halfway Corner where Earl did hoof trimming for a living.

In the summer of 1971 the opportunity came to guide for Chuck Hayward at Little Dahl Lake, N.W.T.

551

Vivian and the boys joined him later in the summer up there and they had one of the greatest times and experiences of their lives.

The fall of 1971 to spring of 1974 they lived at Millarville and Earl was ranch manager for Valley Cattle Co. (Seaman Bros.) and interested them in Red Angus cattle.

In May of 1974, after many years of dreaming of a place of his own Earl purchased a half section of land at Sangudo. At this time Vivian didn't care to venture north so she and the boys stayed at Millarville and are presently living at Okotoks.

In December 1974 Mary Ann and Holly Highmoor joined Earl at Sangudo.

The last five years have been spent building up ranch facilities and a commercial and purebred herd of Red Angus cattle.

The Wes Ways

by Lois Way

I was born in Nanton, Alta. longer ago than I care to remember, and attended school there from grades 1 to 12. In November 1936, I married Wes Way, who was born in Killarney, Manitoba, moved to Moose Jaw at age two and lived there until moving to Nanton, via the boxcar express in 1930.

In the spring of 1937 we moved to Black Diamond and started job and house hunting. There were lots of jobs but also lots of men looking for work, so it wasn't easy to find a job. Finding a house wasn't easy either, so for a while we stayed with my sister and brother-in-law, Ruby and Ed Sprague. They lived in Black Diamond for 8 years, during which time Ed had been employed as mechanic in the Royalite Garage in Turner Valley. A few weeks after, we managed to get an upstairs apartment in Scott's Apartment House; three bare rooms which we furnished with odds and ends of borrowed furniture, cupboards of packing boxes, fortunately plentiful in those days, sheets for curtains and a $12 gas stove. It wasn't much but it was home.

About the middle of March, 1937, Wes went to work for Cliff Shaw, rig building. One of their first rigs was a wooden derrick on the banks of the Highwood River and it was hardly finished when we had a bad wind storm, which completely demolished it. I don't remember whether it was rebuilt, but not by Cliff's crew. In April or May, Wes quit rig building and went to work on the pipe line for Tim Redford. In October we got lucky and when Fergy and Emily Ferguson moved out of Dave McRae's little house back of the store, we moved in. We managed to get a better stove, a new bed and dresser, chesterfield and chair. Things were beginning to look up.

In Jan. 1938, Wes went to work on the rigs, pipe-racking for Earl Bennet and continued with this work until 1946.

In April 1938, our first baby, Maxine, was born at home, with Dr. Harry Lander in attendance. Since most of the rigs Wes worked on were in the South end, we moved onto the Lish farm in Hartell in the spring of 1939 and lived there for two years. While there I grew some of the best gardens I ever had, and we started our cow herd with a cow and calf my brother had given me. While there our second daughter, Sharon, was born in December 1940, in the new Turner Valley Hospital and again Dr. Harry was our doctor. Wes went to the north end to work early in 1941, so back we moved, this time to the Brown farm across the road from Wilf Middleton's, and joining John Broomfields place. While there we farmed the place, bought a few more cows, a couple of horses and began to dream of being ranchers some day. In November, 1941, our son Wayne was born on one of the most hectic nights of the hospital's experience. I'll never forget it. There had been an explosion in the basement of the Black Diamond Hardware Store and three men had been severely burned. The wife of one of them was already in the delivery room when I was admitted around 11 P.M. I don't remember her last name but her first name was Bunny. They rolled me into the room on a stretcher and put a curtain between us, but before her baby was born, Buck George brought Millie in and they were waiting in the hall. As soon as Bunny had her baby, a girl, I was moved onto the table and Millie was put on the stretcher and shortly after, Helen Wallace from Whiskey Row was brought into the same room and put on a cot. I don't remember which of them had their baby first. I know Wayne was born at 12:10, and between 11:30 P.M. and 1 A.M. there were four babies, two boys and two girls. There were no rooms to put us in so Bunny was put in the room with her husband, I was rolled into the hall and Helen and Millie spent the night in the delivery room. When "Aunt" Mable McLeod came on duty the next morning and found me in the hall, eating steak for breakfast, she nearly had a fit. Probably somewhere in the hospital a hungry man was having poached eggs and tea.

Lois and Wes Way.

After living four years on the Brown place we bought the George Wambeke quarter west of the Duncan Smith place, and since there were no buildings, we lived in the old Bird house. It was pretty delapidated, but we managed. There were no school busses in those days, so in order to get Maxine started to school, I went to Nanton and lived in a four room apartment in my mother's house. For the next three years, Wes sprayed cattle for warbles, headquartering at the Bird place and the kids and I spent the school term in Nanton and Holidays in Turner Valley. Then we bought the Dunc Smith farm and built up a small ranch, living there until 1948.

Our nearest neighbors and very good friends were Wilbur (Smitty) and Dot Smith and their family. Our kids and the Smith kids rode to the Plainview School where Mrs. Howard Robison was the teacher.

I think it was in 1944 that Wes started contracting haying for Burn's Ranches. He would hay from July 1st to October 1st, then go back on the rigs for the winter. He did this for four years, then we moved back to Nanton to take over the R L Ranch for Mrs. Robertson, whose husband had been the first doctor in the Nanton area.

In August, 1948, I again headed for the Turner Valley Hospital and Dr. Harry Lander and there our son Danny was born.

In 1952, the R L was sold and we moved back to the old place west of Turner Valley. We were only there a short time when Wes and the Morrisons got the Peace River fever and in July of 1953 we headed north, kids, dogs, cats and all our worldly goods. For a couple of years we lived at East Pine, B.C. where Wes worked in sawmills and drove lumber trucks, but it wasn't the kind of work he really liked and once more he turned to his first love, cattle. We bought and settled on a place in the Groundbirch area, which is some 36 miles west of Dawson Creek. We are still raising cattle and once again we are alone.

Maxine married John Gripich, heavy duty mechanic and welder and they live in Cranbrook, B.C. John works for Interior Diesel and Maxine has her own Seamstress Centre and does drapes, alterations, etc. They have three boys, Dean, 21, employed at Kapps Transport Ltd. in Ft. St. John. Ken, 19, is buyer for a sporting goods store in Sparwood, B.C. Jamie, 14, is still going to school and is quite strong on sports.

Sharon married Gerald Sandul of Rycroft, Alta., where they live. Gerald farms and is also town foreman. They have one little girl, Tarla, aged 6.

Wayne married Sheila Moore from Chetwynd, B.C. and they also live in Cranbrook where Wayne is manager of the X-Pert Auto and Sheila works part time there as book-keeper and part time at Super A. They have two children, Shelley, 15, and Shawn, 11, both in school.

Danny married Loreen Torio of South Dawson and as yet have no family. They have a place at South Dawson, and have a nice herd of cattle. He is presently working for Slumberger of Canada and Loreen is employed as secretary in the Agriculture Office in Dawson Creek.

Patty (Hoy) and Robert Webb

I was born in Turner Valley, the only child of Nels and Ruth Hoy, who at the time were renting a farm west of Turner Valley. When I was three, Dad bought land at Millarville (2 miles east of the Millarville Race Track). There wasn't much for buildings on the place, just an old log house and a so-called barn; but with a lot of hard work, Dad and Mom built up a fine dairy farm. I enjoyed helping out with the farm work when I could. Taking a few days off school in the fall to help Dad bale straw was a real treat, as this appealed far more to me than going to school.

Wes and Lois Way with their family, Maxine, Sharon, Wayne and Danny.

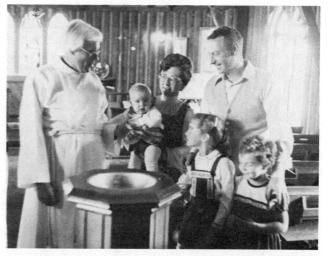

Ian Webb's Christening Oct. 29th, 1978; Archdeacon Gant, Patty holding Ian, Robert with Marney and Adele.

As Dad built up his Holstein herd into purebred show stock, I was exposed to the excitement and challenge of exhibiting and showing at various fairs. Being an only child, I had the opportunity to work with and learn from both my Mom and Dad. I thoroughly enjoyed the experience of working with the cattle and I also appreciate the basic skills I was taught in the home.

I attended Sheep Creek School and Oilfields High School. I was involved with the first Millarville 4-H Club, in which I spent six years, also two years in the Foothills Dairy Club. I was fortunate enough to win several awards in these Clubs but the one that gave me the greatest satisfaction was winning the Champion Showmanship award at the 4-H Show in Calgary.

After finishing school in 1964, I went to Calgary and worked for Campbell Floral, where I learned the basic techniques of flower arranging. During the summers of 1965 and 1966 I spent at the Banff Springs Hotel managing the Flower Shop. Later I managed Park Florist in the Britannia Shopping Center. After this shop was sold I worked for Whitburns Florist until I was married.

In September of 1968 I married Robert Webb, only son of John and Harriet Webb of Calgary. Robert was born raised and educated in Calgary. He attended Henry Wise Wood High School at the same time the Red Deer Lake students were going there. It was here that Robert met Bruce Bamford and Robin Arthurs and spent many week-ends and holidays at their farms, getting a good taste of country living. After finishing High School, Robert graduated from a Forestry program at N.A.I.T. and Hinton respectively. He was then positioned at Peace River Ranger Station and then the Three Creeks Ranger Station (about 30 miles east of Peace River). This is where we lived the first four months of our married life. We were then transferred to Sheep Creek Ranger Station (west of Turner Valley) where he worked and lived for the next year. At the end of that time, Robert decided to train for a plumber, so we left the Forestry and moved again to Calgary; living there for the next four years. During this time our daughters Marney and Adele were born. Even though we lived in Calgary, we were very much involved with Millarville activities.

In 1973 we were able to start building our new home on NW¼-8-21-2-w-5th at Millarville. We recently had an addition to our family when our son Ian was born. It has been a rewarding experience for us to live in this community. For me, I am able to be back home again among old friends and family; while Robert has been able to experience country living and the involvement in the community, which he had never encountered before. He now says, "he hopes we never have to move to the city because this is the only place to really live."

Alice (Webster) Landon and Paul Webster
by Alice Landon

We are the off-spring of Lena (Borup) Webster and

Back, L. to R.: Fred Porter, Jerry Porter. Front: Geraldine Porter Marsh, Alice Webster Porter Landen.

Gerald Webster. Both are deceased, Mother in 1958, and Dad in 1975.

I'm Alice, the oldest of the clan. I was born in Lethbridge, Alta. I have worked driving a Dry Cleaning truck, Taxi, and school bus, all in Calgary. I have one daughter, Gerry Marsh, who lives in Calgary. She has two daughters and two sons. Sherry lives at home, and Debbie is Mrs. Bruce Garbutt, and lives in Calgary with her husband. Patrick Jr. and Michael also live at home with Mum and Father, Pat Sr.

Number one son Fred, is in the Air Force, presently stationed at the base at Beaverlodge, Alberta. He is a Sgt. for the office personnel. He has two sons, David and Derek.

Number two son is a Civil Engineer and lives in Coquitlam, B.C. with his wife Penny and their children, Lisa, Wes and Jason.

After being widowed for a number of years and in a weak moment I said "Yes" again to Edmund Landon and we live in Calgary.

Our parents moved to Millarville where Paul, my brother was born. He has lived in Calgary, Victoria, B.C. and Chilliwack, B.C. and is back in Calgary again with his wife, Joan. He has two sons. Gerald is a Controller for a firm in Calgary. Gerald has a wife, Dorothy and two sons at home. Son number two, Wayne, is a salesman with a firm in Calgary. He and his wife, Bobby, have two sons at home.

Paul is a Steam Engineer and Maintenance man for the Lord Nelson Inn. After our parents left Millarville we all came to Calgary, where John was born. He lived in Calgary, Coronation and back to Calgary again, then moved to Nanaimo, B.C. where he lives with his wife, Doreen. He has two sons, one in Calgary, and the younger one lives in Victoria, B.C. John is a post man in Nanaimo and loves it.

John and Dorothy Weir
by John and Dorothy Weir
Brand: SS ‿ L·S

On the fifteenth of April, 1923, the Weir Family of

Lisdonwilly County Armaugh, Northern Ireland, began their journey to the Land of Milk & Honey; Gold Paved Streets and according to the pictures, large boats faring up and down the Bow River lined with beautiful houses with green grass. Father John, my mother Sara Jane, myself John Jr., my brothers Bob, William and Herb sailed on the S.S. Marvelle, suffering thru a long, bumpy journey and bouts of seasickness. Lifeboat drill every morning before breakfast allowed the crew to practise in case of an emergency. The Marvelle sank on it's return voyage but no souls were lost. Our arrival in Canada was highlighted by waiting three days for icebreakers to free us from the frozen mouth of the St. Lawrence. Our cross country journey brought us to Calgary on May 10, 1923. We were met by Dad's brother, my Uncle James and our cousins, James, George, Wilfred, Dorothy, Jean, Gwen, Florence and Lorna. Uncle James owned Weir's grocery on 4th Street N.E. We also met Dad's sister Sara and her husband Wm. Donaldson along with my cousin Albert. My brother Herb's first comment on arrival in -30 degrees F. temperature was "Mom, look at all the flour on the ground."

We moved close to Stanley Jones school and later moved to 31 Avenue in Tuxedo Park. I attended Tuxedo North Mount Pleasant and Balmoral schools.

Dad found work at Burns Meats but Mom suffered from homesickness for the first year. We managed to survive the hungry thirties when having a job was the exception and the unemployed were the majority. I worked for Revelstoke Saw Mills when we owed on our account. We would charge materials to be allowed to work and made a little extra by selling what we put on account.

I also worked at the Russel Hotel in Cochrane and in 1935 worked in the Dividend Gold Mine at Osoyoos, B.C.

I played softball back in Calgary for teams sponsored by the Independent Biscuit Company, The Avenue Grill and Dollar Cleaners.

The Weir Family. Back: John, Sharon, Dorothy Front: Darryl Weir.

I served in several capacities for the Tuxedo Park Community Assoc. and was president of the Ulster Assoc. in Calgary.

On July 3, 1942 I married Dorothy Larter, daughter of Peter and Lottie Larter of Capital Hill.

In 1943, I started work as carpenters assistant at the Imperial Refinery in Ogden. I worked my way up to General Works Foreman and after 32 years retired. On August 10, 1974 we moved to the home I had built on 40 acres near Millarville. The parcel (ptn. SW ¼, Sec. 23, Twn. 21, Rge. 4 Mer. W5) was one I had purchased from Dr. Black, but was originally owned by George Ingeveld. I stocked my homestead with three purebred red angus cows purchased from Dave Glaister. The next spring I had my first three calves. My herd has grown to eight cows, three yearling heifers, six crossbred calves and a Hereford bull. My fondness for my animals, including our two dogs and two cats, has amused my neighbors ever since our arrival.

On occasion we are visited by our daughter Sharon Rose of Calgary and our son Daryll Wayne, his wife Marg-Ann and our two grandsons, Chad and Kyle of Fairmont, B.C.

I have had the privilege of serving as president of the Square Butte Community Assoc. and in my two years of service the help of volunteers and willing workers made it a rewarding and gratifying experience.

Dorothy and I enjoy living here very much with the trees, mountain views and good neighbors.

By Kathleen Ruth Welch (Knights)

My family came from England in 1909 where all the children were born. I came slap-dab in the middle of the family of nine — so was always the "odd one". After starting my education in England I attended Fordville School up to Grade 8 and afterwards took a business course at Garbutt's Business College, subsequently working for the C.P.R., Department of Natural Resources until I married J. W. (Duckie) Welch in 1926. Duckie was born in Port Hope, Ontario, and moved to Okotoks with his family at an early age. He received his education in Okotoks and was one of the true pioneers of the Turner Valley oilfields. He began his career digging ditches and driving a four-horse team over dirt roads hauling pipe from Okotoks.

Duckie was a tool-dresser on a cable-tool rig at Jumping Pound at the time of our marriage. Our first home was a lean-to attached to an abandoned two-story farm house. It was in good shape and we were quite comfortable. However, the rig was about a half mile from the house on the opposite side of the creek, which was quite low in summer and easily waded or crossed by car. It was a different matter in the spring run-off though so Duckie built a raft to get to work. He was not very conversant in the principles of water travel and it turned out to be too heavy and frequently sank to at least shoe-top level! Fortunately, the spring run-off was short lived that year.

The next year we moved to Turner Valley and lived in "Poverty Flats" where we built a small house. However, along came the "Dirty Thirties" and no work in the oil fields. We sold out and moved to Calgary where my husband ran a service station for about a year. Then things picked up in the oil fields so back to Turner Valley, or more correctly the top of the Home Hill. Things gradually improved so we were able to get a home established again.

Duckie worked on various wells and then was made toolpush by W. S. Herron for Okalta Co., being the first Canadian boy to be promoted to that position. He had the distinction of supervising the drilling of Okalta No.6 to a depth of over 10,000 feet, which was the deepest hole drilled in the British Empire up to that time. He was also Field Superintendent for Commonwealth Drilling and at the time of his death held that position with Lion Oils.

Duckie passed away in November of 1943.

After my husband's death I worked in the office at Gas and Oil Products for five years and when the oil boom got going at Leduc, I obtained a position with Imperial Oil in their Devon office. One incident that sticks in my mind of the early days in Devon, which literally sprang up out of a wheat field, was getting stuck in the mud on my own two feet crossing the main street from the bank to the grocery store. I was finally rescued by a gallant gentleman — leaving my shoes behind. He almost left his too!

I worked for Imperial Oil for 10 years in Devon and Edmonton. When I reached their retirement age I went to work for the United Church Bissell Centre as Secretary-Receptionist where I stayed for over 12 years. I finally retired for good and moved to Calgary where I make my home.

We had two sons and a daughter. Larry, the oldest, has been in the oil business all of his working years and is at present Vice President of Sales for Interprovincial Steel and Pipe (IPSCo). He has a small ranch at Bragg Creek where he and his wife Barbara reside. He has two children.

Antonia (Toni) my daughter, has worked for Imperial Oil most of her working life, in Devon, Edmonton, five years at Quirk Creek (Millarville) and presently in Calgary.

Gordon, the youngest, went to School in Devon and attended U of A and U of C where he obtained a B.Sc. degree. He has lived in Edson ever since that time, being Principal of the High School and presently Superintendent with the Yellowhead School Division. He has also had a two year term as Mayor and several years on the Town Council. He and wife Paula reside in the town. He has three children.

This is truly the story of the ups and downs of life in the oil industry and holds many memories, some sad and some happy which of course is the lot of all those living on this planet, Earth.

Agnes and Al Wells

In 1973 we bought an acreage from the Cornforth family. The land is on the NW¼ 26-21-4-W5M. In August 1974 we started building our house there and we moved into it in February 1975. We previously sold our home on Elbow Drive in Calgary to Mrs. K. Kendall who was at that time a resident of Square Butte.

My husband, Al, is from Moosomin Sask. and my home is Stratford, Ont. My maiden name is Agnes Carnerie. Al is employed as an instructor in steam fitting and plumbing at S.A.I.T. in Calgary.

I had six children from a previous marriage. The children are; Beverly Ann (now Mrs. P. Coenjarts) and she lives with her husband and three children, Johnny, Jamie and Jody, in Sarnia, Ont., Peter Charles McManus and wife, Leslie; live in Calgary where Peter is a printer with the Albertan Newspaper and Leslie a registered nurse at the Holy Cross Hospital. Jean Margaret (now Mrs. K. Denton) resides with her husband, Keith, a cat operator with Whissell Enterprizes, and their son Trevor, in Calgary. Marian Eileen McManus the youngest, lives at home and is employed by the Energy Conservation Board in Calgary. Kenneth Andrew McManus, the eldest, deceased in 1974 at age twenty-eight; and Cameron Bruce McManus deceased in 1973 at the age of twenty-one. We have two grandsons, Robbie and Steve McManus, living in Lethbridge Alta., they are the sons of Kenneth McManus.

Wells residence.

George White, 1889-1960
by Alberta McIlveen

Born — 1889 at Ryton, England.

Dad emigrated to Calgary, Alberta in 1906 with his parents. He worked in Calgary until 1909. He then left Calgary with his older brother, Tom, and their father — also Johnny Barraclough, to homestead in what is now the Youngstown district. There was no town when they first arrived by covered wagon. They cut sod and built sod houses and barns, and broke some land. Dad

Edwin and Fred White, 1930's.

George White, Marjorie McIlveen, Elsie White, Alberta McIlveen. 3 generations. Sacks of leafmould on trailer and old trunk.

returned to Calgary for the winter, and in the spring of 1910 he married Elsie Barraclough (born 1888 at Triangle Yorkshire, England). Mother had emigrated to Calgary with her family in 1907 and had met dad two years later. Dad returned to the homestead to put in a crop, and spent most of the summer on the trail hauling supplies. I was born in Calgary, December, 1910, and three months later mother and I moved out to the homestead. We lived in the sod house (two rooms) for six years. It was cool in the summers and warm in the winter. I can remember the prairie fires, and mother locking me in where I'd be safe, while she went to help fight the fire with wet gunny sacks. By 1917 we were living in a frame house, where my sister and two brothers were born. Mother and Dad now had four children:

— Alberta — Born 1910; married John McIlveen. Widow — living in Calgary.
— Estelle — Born 1917; married Robert Bateman. Died — 1971.
— Edwin — Born 1920 — Lost at sea (St. Croix) — 1943.
— Fred — Born 1925, married Mona Hutt; widower — 1951; re-married in 1973 to Dorothy Blanchette; living in Calgary.

We returned to Calgary in 1926, and in 1929 Dad bought the S.E.¼, Sec. 33, T21-R3-W5. Mr. and Mrs. Roy Bemus were living on the place at the time. After

Dad took possession, he supplied Calgary greenhouses with leaf mould for several years, that he took off the place. He rented the pasture out for grazing cattle. Mother spent the summers out there with my sister and brothers. They would screen leaf mould, a chore the boys did not appreciate. Dad went out every weekend after work from spring till fall. In 1940, he started building a new house. This was a week-end project, and everybody was put to work. There had always been a lot of friends driving down on the weekends over the years. We'd often have 15 to 20 extra on a Sunday, making quite a crowd with 8 of us. Funny how they stop coming when there is work to be done. When the new house was closed in well enough for us to move in, Dad rented the log cabin to Ed Hehr. Then, about 1947, he sold the quarter section to Ed. I understand John Schaal has it now.

Dad passed away in 1960, and Mother in 1965.

I often think of the good times we had out there. Estelle and I attended a good many dances at the Priddis Hall and the Fordville School.

I still enjoy a drive down past the old place, especially in September when the fall colours are at their best.

Mary Kathleen (Blakley) White

I was born in Turner Valley June, 1937, youngest daughter of Tim and Jean Blakley. My early years were lived in a log house on the homestead of my grandfather, Joseph Fisher Sr. This land is now owned by my cousin, Peter Fisher.

Some of my fondest memories were riding horses and raising various animals with my older brother and sister. At one time we had a pen of rabbits, and one morning discovered one of these pets was missing, with the wire torn from the top of the pen. Next evening, brother Dennis, on hearing a noise and expecting his cousin Jody, ran out to meet him only to discover a bear about to help himself to another rabbit. I don't know who was the most frightened, Dennis or the bear.

We lived on the south side of Fisher Creek, which

caused many hazards and moments of anxiety for my mother, when we went to school or town. When the creek was low we would walk across on a log or Dad would drive us in his car. When the creek was in flood, horses were needed or we would have a holiday if it was too high.

When I was six years old it was time for me to start school. After a few months I decided that was enough schooling. I would play sick, and when that didn't work anymore, I would walk as far as the old Rancher's Hall with my sister and brother. There was an Indian family camped there so I would stay and play with their children for the day. When my sister and brother came back from school, I would go back home with them. That worked quite well until my parents found out what was going on. That's when I had to further my education.

In 1946 we moved to the north side of the creek where my parents reside today. Life was a little different then as I had four boys to grow up with, my brother Dennis, cousins Peter and Jody Fisher, and Michael Rodgers, a cousin of the Fisher boys. Michael lived about three miles from us but was over often. We did a lot of skating, skiing and riding horses. When we were skiing the boys would make jumps on the hill and send me over first to see if it was safe enough for them. There was one compensation with having the boys around; I had four escorts and chaperones, which didn't do much for their love life.

We lived three miles west of Sheep Creek School when it was at its old location, before it was moved to Millarville. My sister Charis, brother Dennis and I rode most times on Charis' pony. He would often buck us off and just stand and wait until we got back on, and continue on our way to school. In 1950, when Jake Reimer started to bus the Square Butte pupils to Sheep Creek School, I finally got to ride on a bus.

The old Rancher's Hall was on our place and much of the entertainment of the district was held there, dances and our annual Christmas concerts, which were the highlights of the school year.

In the summer of 1953, I worked in the Millarville Store, at that time owned by Jappy Douglass. My

Mary Kathleen Blakley. 1940.

L. to R. Alan, Dale, Mary and Gary White. 1979.

duties were store clerk and gas jockey. In 1954, I started to work in the Turner Valley telephone exchange, and was there for two and a half years. From there I went to Calgary and worked in the telephone exchange until my marriage to Dale White in 1957. He was from Turner Valley, had graduated from the high school there. We first lived in Edmonton, where Dale was employed by Chemical and Geological Labs. He was later transferred to Calgary. In 1961, he was employed by Petrofina Canada at their plant west of Cochrane, where we lived for a short time, then moved back to Calgary. Dale commutes daily to the Cochrane plant.

We have two sons. Alan Dale was born in Edmonton in 1958, graduated from Sir Winston Churchill High School, Calgary, in 1976 and is now attending Mount Royal College.

Gary Winston was born in Edmonton in 1959. He graduated from Sir Winston Churchill High School in 1978, is presently working but plans on further education.

Whitman, Orman B. (1905-1971)

by Paul Whitman

In the spring of 1956, a Calgary dentist, Dr. Orman Whitman, known to many as "the Doc", established a thoroughbred breeding and training ranch on the north fork of Sheep Creek, some eight miles west of the settlement of Millarville. (S.W.¼ 33-2-4-W5M — 90 acres). With the help of sons Peter, Paul, and daughter Adele, plus the able assistance of neighbors and friends, land was cleared and a log cabin and out-buildings were constructed.

Through the early years of kerosene lamps and woodstoves, washed out bridges and late spring snows, "the Doc", furthered by a considerable knowledge of pedigree patterns and breeding characteristics, weathered the annual foal production problems. As a result of his efforts and direction over the next seventeen years, thoroughbred horses from the Running W. Ranch raced on the Western Canadian circuit and tracks in Eastern Canada.

Subsequently, the eldest son Peter has moved his family to the Sexsmith district, and the breeding and training of quarter horses has followed at the ranch under the direction of Paul, his wife LaVerne (Gowing) and daughters Shannon and Alison. Adele and husband Tom Stanton of Calgary have continued in the thoroughbred breeding, and share in the management of the operation.

Neel de Wit-Wibaut

Rein de Wit, Geologist, and I, Neel de Wit-Wibaut, bought the N.E.¼ of section 27-21-4-W5 in 1963 from the Seamen Brothers. The first piece of land we looked at was at Kew and it was $30 an acre, which we thought was too much. Six years later we got this quarter section, scraping together all the money we had and paying three times the price of the Kew land.

We came to Canada in 1948 from our homeland, Holland. Rein was sent out by Shell Oil on a temporary basis. After a while we made the choice between staying with Shell and leaving Canada or leaving Shell and staying here. Rein took a job with the Geological Survey in 1950 and from that moment Canada became home. We lived six years in Ottawa, two years in Regina and twenty-four years in Calgary.

I was born in Amsterdam February 1915. My parents were both scientists (Father taught chemistry at the U. of Amsterdam and Mother worked as a microbiologist at the health department of the city of Amsterdam.) My parents never owned a house or a car, but we always had a maid and when the twins were born, also a nanny. We were four girls and I was the second. After high school we were to choose a profession and get a degree. I did not care too much for studying, all the same I got a degree in social work and did not mind giving it up when I married Rein in 1943, the blackest of war years. We produced three children, Sonja, Floris and Harriet. Sonja was born in 1944 during the battle of Groningen in the last weeks of the Hitler regime. Canadians were shooting (and hitting) the centre of the city of Groningen where the German Headquarters were located. A mortar hit our apartment and killed the nurse who was going to deliver Sonja — April 12, 1944. We survived.

After immigrating to Ottawa we lived without a car or washing machine, with outdoor facilities etc. the

Neel de Wit-Wibaut.

pioneering life. I had three toddlers and every summer Rein took off to the N.W. Territories. However, gradually life became a little easier. Like everybody else, we got a house, a car and indoor plumbing. As the children grew older I had time to do the thing I wanted, I joined the Calgary Philharmonic as a viola player, and I stayed with them eighteen years, a great experience.

In the meantime we had acquired the land and Rein took to the land as a born farmer. After work he went there, chopped, dug, seeded, built fences, from dawn to dusk, rain or shine. In 1973 Rein and I split up and divided our assets. I became the owner of the land. In 1975 I obtained a degree in the art of painting (B.F.A. University of Calgary.) The land has been an inspiration for me and my friends and children. Two other artists, Roy Hamill and Greg Frederick, built the place to what it is today. Although it is called Neel's Cabin, many people know the way to get there, feel at home and occupy themselves with things one cannot do in city surroundings — hike, ski, garden, sketch, do ceramics etc.

The valley is also utilized for grazing by Fred Ball's cattle and Lepp's horses. I am surrounded by very friendly people and also by a great variety of wild life, ranging from minute ants to huge moose. All of it I love. I think I owe that to my parents who taught us respect for living things and pointed out the miracles of the Universe. I, in turn, have adult children who now enjoy the Alberta foothills whenever they can. Sonja is an interpreter with the Government in Ottawa. Harriet is a psychologist at George Williams in Montreal and Floris is foreman with Western Geophysical, working around Drayton Valley.

In 1978, I obtained a beautiful source of water, fifty feet deep. It appeared to be an artesian well, so now I have running water, winter and summer. With all the water the beavers are preserving, it is certain that I belong with the sign of Aquarius in more than one respect.

Wilder, Jane (nee Glaister)

I was born on August 16, 1955 at the Turner Valley Hospital. In September, 1961 I started school at Millarville. Just before my thirteenth birthday I started working for Joan Kendall at Kendall's Sawmill. I cooked and cleaned house a few days a week until school started again. In 1969 I went to Ottawa on a sort of exchange trip, where I stayed for about a month. During the summer of 1970 I again worked on weekends for the Kendalls. In August of 1971 I went to Mount Assiniboine for three weeks to work. During the year 1971/72 my work was again with the Kendalls. On July 1st, 1972 I travelled to High Horizons Mountaineering Camp for Teenagers where I was head cook for the summer. I returned in the fall to attend Grade XII at the Turner Valley Oilfields High School in Black Diamond. At the end of June, 1973 I went to Canyon Church Camp as head cook, staying there until September when I moved back home to Mesa Creek Ranch On December 26, 1973 I moved to Radium Hot Springs, B.C. In January, 1974 I started cooking at the Radium Hot Springs Lodge and worked there until November, 1975. I moved back to Calgary and cooked at Sylvia's Kitchen until May, 1976. In June I moved to Whitehorse, Yukon Territories where I worked at the Shefield House, Airport Chalet, and Woolworth's. I did some travelling around and took a few flying lessons. I moved back home in October, 1976. I stayed a bit in Calgary, skied — when I could, generally bd around. Went back to Sylvia's Kitchen and worked a bit; helped Myrna Fisher between December '76 and March '77. Still no major changes to report . . . moved back to Radium, worked at the Hot Springs Lodge. Then, in November of '77 Kathy (younger sister) and I went to Switzerland. Kathy is married to David Flundra of Cochrane. We stayed a month, skiing.

On December 25th, 1977 I became engaged to Lloyd Wilder of Invermere, B.C. We were married on June 3, 1978 at Christ Church, Millarville. In November I became Manageress of Magilla's Fashion Boutique in Invermere where I am presently employed.

David V. Wildman   YE l.r. E l.h.
by David and Gail Wildman

I was born July 10th, 1941, in Rimbey, Alberta, the first child of Tom and Norma Wildman. With my parents, we moved from the farm, east of Rimbey, to the Square Butte district in May, 1947.

L. to R. George Nylund, John Nylund, David and Mary Ann Wildman. 1948.

I attended Square Butte School for two years, until it closed, then attended Sheep Creek School for the balance of my education, and took one year of Farm Mechanics at S.A.I.T. in Calgary.

Early childhood recollections include many hours spent on horses riding in the area with the Nylund boys and their cousin, Eldon Lyall; cold rides to school, hot days in the hayfield to come home to an even hotter barn to milk cows; skating on Fisher Creek with friends and cold wet rides trailing cows to the Forest Reserve in the spring and out again in the fall. These

Back: David and Gail Wildman. Front: Kirk, Brett, Jay.

early experiences with horses, cattle and the mountains, led me to jobs closely related in my later teens and early twenties.

I worked in the bush, logging, for Kendall Sawmills, for several winters. During the summer and fall of those years, I worked as a packer and guide in the Lake Louise area for Bert and June Mickle.

After my father's accidental death in 1960, more of my time was spent on the home ranch, putting up hay and feeding it out. I guided hunters in the fall, and had some good times catching wildies (wild horses) during the winter in the Forest Reserve.

In 1965, I married Gail Ross R.N., eldest daughter of Bob and Florence Ross of Winnipeg. We have three boys; David Jay, born in 1966; Brett Gregory, born in 1967; Kirk Michael, born in 1972.

In 1970, I purchased the S.E.¼ of 2-21-4w5 from my late uncle, Fred W. Wildman. I resold this quarter in 1974 to William Lucas of Vulcan.

From 1960 to 1970, our efforts were concentrated on building a commercial Hereford cow herd. In 1972, the nucleus of our present purebred Red Angus herd was established.

In 1974, my family and I purchased a larger holding in the Sangudo area, north of Edmonton, and moved in July. The present operation is grain farming and a 100 cow herd of Registered Red Angus cattle.

My family and I will always remember the experiences and the people in the Square Butte district 1947-1974. The silver tray presented to us when we left the district is proudly displayed in our new home.

Thomas Noble Wildman *GC L.R.*
Fredrick William Wildman *GC R.A.*
by Norma (Wildman) Lyall

Tom was born in 1902 at Innisfail, N.W.T., the second child of Marmaduke (Duke) and Dinah Wildman, followed in 1904 by the birth of Fred.

The Wildman children went to the Little Red Deer School, west of Innisfail, near where they lived, until Duke was called to war in 1916. Dinah and the seven children then moved to Chilliwack, B.C.

Fred and Tom, as the only boys in the family, cut cord wood and worked on farms to help their mother out. While in their teens, each fall they would go to Saskatchewan to harvest.

Not caring too much for Chilliwack, Tom came back to Innisfail area in 1922 and Fred in 1928. Then they bought a farm. They also worked for William Edgar and his son Wilford, to help make ends meet. In 1931, they sold their farm at Innisfail and bought two quarters of land, seven miles north of Gull Lake.

In 1940, Tom married Norma Edith Stewart of Rimbey. On July 10th 1941 our first child, David Vernon, was born, followed by Mary Ann on Feb. 27th, 1944.

In May 1947 we moved to Square Butte and Tom bought the N.E. ¼ of 2-21-4w5 and Fred purchased the S.E. ¼ of 2-21-4w5, from Percy and Gladys Keeping, originally the homesteads of Jimmie Spooner and Digby Dennett, then the home of the Dan Bannerman family. There were three quarters of lease land north of the home quarter.

At the Wildman Ranch. On horse, Allan Coxworth. L. to R. Tom, David, and Norma Wildman, Bernice Coxworth (sister of Tom and Fred), Fred Wildman. Front: Kay Coxworth, Mary Ann Wildman, Pat Coxworth.

Wildman Ranch buildings looking north west.

Fred Wildman and team hauling logs, winter 1947-48.

In July the horses were shipped from Rimbey to Calgary by rail and when they passed through the stockyards they contacted distemper. What a sorry sight it was that summer, trying to hay with sick horses.

In the winter of 1947-48 Fred and Tom logged on the home quarter. Buster Adams trucked his saw mill from Rimbey and they sawed in June and July, 1948.

Through the years we built a cow herd which summer grazed on the Muskeg in the north Fork Forest Reserve. Tom and Fred had a very closely knit life and lived under the same roof until Tom's death and then Fred lived on with Tom's family. Both men were small but very wiry. They were noted for being exceptionally good at stooking grain in their younger days. They were ambitious and cleared many acres of land and made improvements to their property where ever they lived. Tom was handy around the ranch, building and fixing things up and conducted all the business for the family.

When Bill Kendall started logging in the Forest Reserve, Fred and Tom worked for Bill, limbing and

Enjoying a cribbage game, Dec. 1962. L. to R. Fred and David Wildman, Jack Friesen and John Shick.

choking one winter. Fred worked for Bill several years after that in the winters.

In later years Tom's health was failing but in the spring of 1960 he was feeling better. On June 12th we moved the cattle to the Muskeg. We had a good crew with John and Margaret Kendall, Vern Blanchard, David, Mary Ann and myself. Bud and Marthe Pallister, Allen Gouy and Tom brought our lunch to the canyon, where we met them. On the way home Bud's Jeep went out of control on a hill and struck a tree, throwing Tom and Marthe to their death.

Fred never did learn to drive a tractor or truck, but what a lot of hair raising stories can be told about his runaways with horses. He must have had nine lives, for many times it was a wonder he wasn't killed in some of his wrecks.

One time he rode the Appaloosa over to Ivor Lyster's but on the way there he met up with Ivor's horses and one ass (Donkey) which brayed and set them off for quite a run, through two wire gates leading to Ivor's. Elaine saw them coming and called for Ivor to go catch his ass and save Fred. The horse and Fred were both trembling by this time.

Fred never had an enemy in his life, being a kindly man, never liking to have trouble between family or neighbors.

In 1969 Fred sold his quarter section to David, then in 1971, he retired to Chilliwack to live with his youngest sister, Bernice Coxworth. When returning on the ferry from visiting friends in Victoria, he quietly passed away Feb. 12th, 1975.

Ralph and Beatrice Willcock and Family

In January 1942, myself, my wife Beatrice and son Dick moved our house from Royalties, Alta. to the N.W.¼ of section 19, Twp. 21, about 7½ miles N.W. of Millarville.

I worked on a rig for Drilling Contractors. It was located on the 40 acres that joined our quarter on the

Willcock Family. Top: L. to R. Geraldine, and George. Centre: Beatrice and Dick. Bottom: Ralph.

north. I worked as back-up man for John Norman and then for Tim Blakley when he was set up drilling. I also cut logs and operated a sawmill for awhile.

In 1943 our daughter Geraldine was born and George was born in 1947.

We lived on a bench with a south slope, up out of the valley. We could grow cucumbers, pumpkin, squash, corn etc. We called it the banana belt.

Dick went to school at the old Sheep Creek School, situated about 2½ miles from the Millarville store, on the north side of the road. He sometimes walked or rode a horse the five miles from our place. One day, after he had left for school, he came running back, saying there was a black bear in the trees, so I picked up my rifle and went down the road with him, to find it was Gordon Larratt's black cow.

Another time, when I had come home about dark from working in the bush, Dick still wasn't home from school and it was 20 degrees below F. I ran down the road on foot and met him about ½ mile from home, strolling along, his jacket wide open, as happy as a lark. Didn't seem to think it was cold or anything to be concerned about. He was then about seven years old.

One incident that took place in 1942, was when Beatrice saw something moving through the bush up by the barn, so she went up to see what it was. By the time she got there it had its head in the garbage hole, so she went a little closer to be sure of what it was. It looked like a bear, but there was a lot of razzing about people who thought they saw bears. About then, the bear sensed her being there, and reared up and whoofed and as Bea said "I whoofed it back to the house."

Soon after the bear came down the pathway to the house and Bea took a picture through the window, her proof of her story. The bear stood on the banking of the house and left his imprint, which was 9 and three quarters inch long.

It had been raining almost continually and I was working at Bona Ventures, so she left Dick with her brother Melvin, who was staying with us, and walked in her bare feet (because her boots got too heavy and wide with mud) up to the rig to tell me. I came home and got my rifle and hunted for the bear the rest of that day and part of the next. About two days later Jim Colley shot it. It was a cross between a grizzly and a cinnamon and was a good sized bear.

Vern Cooper was watchman on the rig on the north side of our quarter, and used to walk through our place to get there. He always packed a 22 rifle with him but after seeing the track on the banking of our house, he packed a 30-06 instead.

It seemed that it was never going to quit raining that summer and sometimes we couldn't get our car within a couple of miles of our house, for weeks at a time. However, we hated to leave the place as everyone in the area was real friendly and we had some good times in the old Rancher's Hall that used to be to the west of Bill Jackson's place.

Picture of a very large bear, taken by Beatrice Willcock through window.

When we were contemplating moving on account of the school being so far away and no school bus, most people said we couldn't move our stockade log buildings, so Bea and I went out one day and put a jack under one corner of one of the buildings and raised it the full length of the building. The one building is a garage at Millarville Store and the other one is in Turner Valley, still with us. Not many logs are showing anymore, though, as it has been built on to a couple of times.

Stephen Bell bought our land after we moved to Turner Valley in 1948. I have retired from woodworking and cabinet shop I operated until August 30, 1976. I am spending most of my time now with my hobby of fifteen years, hunting agates, jaspers, precious opals etc. and cutting them to make rock clocks, rock lamps, rock tables and all types of jewelry.

Dick operates his own business "Snoopy's Oil Field Service." With his wife Sharon and four children they live on an acreage about 5½ miles N.W. of Lloydminster, Alta.

Geraldine and her husband Ron Hansen farm in the Standard area. They have two children.

George and his wife Donna own a General Store at Throne, Alta. They have two children.

Edgar (Dude) and May Willford

Ed was born in Redding, Nebraska, in 1898, and came to Canada with his parents when just a baby. The family lived in Okotoks for about six years then moved to the Black Diamond district. He grew up in the area, working on many farms and ranches. He also worked as a carpenter and various other jobs. For a few years he took fishing and hunting parties into the Kananaskis Lakes country, at a time when it was all done by pack horse. Dude acted as both guide and packer.

He married May Mitchell, daughter of Mr. and Mrs. Ben Mitchell, old-timers of the Turner Valley area. For a while, they lived a short distance north of the town of Turner Valley, later moving to an acreage near John Broomfields ranch. He worked as road foreman for the M.D. when the road was built from Turner Valley west to the Forest Reserve and on to the Big Horn Ranger Station. He also worked on the road which was built from George Silvester's ranch to the North Fork Ranger Station.

In 1933, John Broomfield exchanged his land in the Millarville district, the S.E.¼ of 20-21-3w5, for the acreage that Willfords owned, so in 1933, the family moved to the new home in Millarville in August, by team and wagon, helped by Mr. Bradshaw.

The Willford's children attended Sheep Creek School, when it was at its old location, riding horseback, no busses in those days.

In 1946, the land was sold to Mr. and Mrs. John Bowman, and the family moved to Turner Valley, where Ed worked for Western Propane. In 1953, Ed and May moved near Edmonton, where they lived until moving to Grand Centre, near Cold Lake, Alberta, in 1959. Ed passed away there in 1961, and May moved back to Turner Valley, passing away there in 1970.

Their son Hugh married Lillian Kohler and they make their home in Turner Valley.

Irene married Bob Massom, and they make their home in Claresholm.

Mamie is married to Doug Beatty, they live in Fort McLeod.

Florence married Jim Massom and they make their home in Brooks.

Ed (Dude) and May Willford with granddaughter, Yvonne. 1956.

John and Rilla Wills
by Rilla Wills

My Mother came from England and Dad from Scotland. They were married in London, Feb. 4, 1905 and sailed soon after to come to Canada. They arrived in Lethbridge and settled in Raymond where Dad worked on the irrigation. My sister, Ena and I were both born in Raymond. We moved to Lethbridge and attended public school there, then to Vulcan where we finished school. I worked in the bakery for a number of years before going to Calgary where I met John. We were married in 1940. We have one son Kenneth who married Verda Neilsen. They have three daughters, Verla, Mylene and Shauna.

John's Mother and Dad were born and raised in the north of England, Wigton, Cumbria, where they lived and farmed for many years before they came to Canada. They settled in the Sylvan Lake district raising Clydesdale horses, Shorthorn cattle, Suffolk sheep and Yorkshire pigs.

John and I have had quite a varied life working on ranches until we settled in East Calgary. We

On the farm at Millarville about 1938. Ed (Dude) Willford, (with violin) Hugh (reading) and sisters, Mamie, Florence and Irene.

John and Rilla Wills at Square Butte, with Tamie.

John and Rilla Wills with their family. Back: Kenneth, Verda, three daughters, Verla, Mylene, and Shauna. John and Rilla in front.

purchased Harvey Jr. a Thoroughbred stallion, bought and sold horses and ponies. I worked at Marilyn Masquerade for Acme Novelty.

Mr. Ransom was looking for someone to look after his home and family at Square Butte so we went out there taking Harvey Jr. and a few mares. We had six and a half years there the most enjoyable of our life. We made many good friends whom we'll never forget. We are now retired and live at Spruce View where we are always pleased to see old friends drop in.

Mr. and Mrs. Robert A. Willson
W5

Mr. and Mrs. Robert A. Willson (Margaret and Bob) of Calgary, bought the S.W.¼ of 14-21-4w5 in May 1974, from the estate of Lily Hulme- Hargreaves-Robinson, pioneers of the area.

Bob's people, on his father's side, were United Empire Loyalists in Ontario and Inverness Scottish through his mother. Margaret's grandparents came to Canada from England and Northern Ireland.

Both Margaret and Bob were born in Toronto and only recently lost the 1817 homestead farm by expropriation of the Ontario Government. They came west to Banff in 1965 to direct the Banff School of Advanced Management, and to Calgary in 1970, after residence in Ancaster and Toronto, Ontario, and Minneapolis, Minnesota. Eldest son Laird is in business, married to Janet Jacobson of Austin, Minnesota, and living in Vancouver. Daughter Martha Ann also works and lives there. Son Gary, an environmental planner, lives in Calgary. All are frequent visitors to the farm.

Bob Willson Family. L. to R. Gary David Willson, Margaret (mother) R. Laird, Martha Ann, seated Janet, Robert A. Willson (father).

Bob works in Calgary in management consulting and banking. Margaret is active in community service. Both are active church members and share interest in cross-country skiing, golf and reading. Margaret's personal hobbies are weaving and needlework. Bob's are history and photography.

The whole family moved into their new home, built from locally cut logs, on Christmas Eve, 1975, relying on a Franklin stove, sleeping bags and Christmas carols. The site is a few yards distant from the original Hulme log cabin, which was unfortunately beyond repair.

They are gradually expanding their small cow-calf herd and hay and feed crops. Their brand is W5.

Robert and Fae Winthrop
by Fae Winthrop

Bob was born in 1918 and grew up on his father's homestead — N.E.¼, Sec.30, T.21, R.2, W.5. He attended Fordville School.

I was born at Bassano in 1923, the second daughter of the Royal Burrows family. I have 4 sisters and one brother. Our family farmed at Countess until 1938, when we moved to the Millarville district. We lived 2 years on the S.½, Sec. 33, T. 21, R. 2, W. 5, and then rented the Charley Wilkinson place.

Bob and I were married in 1942. We started building a home on the S.½, Sec. 26, T.21, R.3, W.5. The Winthrops had bought this land from the Hudsons Bay several years earlier. It had only 10 acres cleared and no buildings on it. We bought a small house and garage, and moved them on.

The first year, we milked a few cows and used a granary to tie them in. Our first milk cows were mostly range cows we broke to milk. The first few years we shipped cream and raised pigs. In 1943 we built a barn. We used it for 2 or 3 years before we put a roof on it. Every time it rained outside, it also rained inside.

In 1943 Sharon was born, and in 1948, the twins Diane and Delaine were born. With this sudden in-

Bob and Fae Winthrop with grandson, Chad.

crease in our family, we needed more house room, so we built onto our house. I also rebelled at washing clothes on the scrub board, so we bought a washing machine with a gas motor — what luxury!

About 1949, we started shipping milk and continued until we sold our cows in 1967 and bought beef cattle.

We sold part of our land in 1971 and built a riding arena, mostly for team roping. We have practice sessions twice a week, and sometimes on Sundays we have jackpot team roping through the winter months.

Sharon lives in Calgary with her 3 children, Dale — 17 years, Ross — 16 years, and Marci — 13 years.

Diane lives at Okotoks and works in Calgary.

Delaine and her husband, Rudy Evenson live in their own home in our yard.

Wolf, Harry Otto Albert, Jr. and Phyllis Elaine Wolf (Nelson)

Harry and I were both born and raised in small suburban towns southeast of Chicago in the State of Illinois. We met one Sunday afternoon in the Veterans Club of Harry's home town, introduced by my older sister. She had known and worked with him for a short time, and decided to try her talents as matchmaker. I was only eighteen at the time, but Harry had been led to believe I was twenty-three. Although I was only in my first year of nurses training, Harry had been told by my sister that I was a full fledged R.N. He is several years my senior, and she felt he would not be interested, at the time, in meeting an eighteen year old student nurse. At his age now, however, he would probably relish the idea.

And so our relationship began, with the afternoon spent learning to play pool, and Harry as my able instructor. We parted that evening with an invitation from him to meet the next day when he would take me on an exciting sight-seeing tour of Marengo — a very small town about the size of our Okotoks, with its one industry being a mouse trap factory. Even today we still laugh about our first date, and my eager enthusiasm to view the mouse trap factory, so taken was I with this older sophisticated man.

It was many months later before he came to realize my true age. But by that time, age was inconsequential. We enjoyed being together, and that's all that mattered. We made the most of the few snatched hours a week we managed to spend with each other. Many hurried picnics were had while sitting in the weeds of some deserted area. I can still recall the startled looks of people walking down a path in the forest preserve when they would stumble upon Harry and me sitting in the weeds, dining on broasted chicken and champagne.

My free hours were few while I was a student. Dates were short due to rigid dorm curfews. Many an evening was spent at the harness races in Chicago, where I would bring my books and try to cram as much information into my reluctant brain as was possible during the short pauses between races. My grades would have suffered severely had not Harry accepted a job offer in Minneapolis, Minnesota during my second year of training. We became engaged to be married before he left and continued our romance through numerous letters, phone calls, and occasional visits once he had taken up residence in Minnesota.

Three weeks after my graduation, on September 10, 1966, during a formal traditional wedding ceremony, we became husband and wife. After a two week honeymoon, Harry brought me to our new home in Excelsior, Minnesota. There I got my registration papers, and began my nursing career at Fairview Southdale Hospital.

One year later, we bought our first house. Only a month after we moved in, on October 17, 1967, our first daughter was born. We named her Cara Michelle Wolf. Once again, Harry was offered a job in a different location, but this time in another country — Canada. Being young and eager for adventure, plus the benefits offered for this particular job, it didn't take us long to pick up the challenge and move our small family to Calgary, in the fall of 1969. It was here that our second child was born. On Harry's birthday, January 12, of 1970, we welcomed our son Hal, into the world. His legal name is Harry Otto Albert Wolf, III, but finding this just a bit lengthy for a tiny infant, we shortened it some, and call him "Hal".

We bought a home in Chinook Park, and resided there for five years. On April 21, 1975, Aaron Phillip was born, almost an exact duplicate in appearance and temperament as his older brother.

Shortly after Aaron's birth, Harry began looking for a home in the country. But after several disappointing months of viewing various prospects, and not finding the type of house we had in mind, we decided to purchase a parcel of land and construct our own. We bought twenty acres of land about a half mile from Plummer's Corner in the fall of 1975. (N.E.¼, Sec. 35,

T.21, R.3, W.5, Block 4) We took our ideas of what we wanted in our home to Wolfgang Wenzel, who designed the plans, and construction on the house began that following July. All was ready when we moved in on December 9, 1976.

Being a city girl all my life, I had serious reservations about our move to the country. After a few short months, however, I began to realize what a special privilege it was to be out here. Terrific neighbors, and friendly people in the community helped us to feel welcome. The constant beauty that surrounds us in all seasons brought added pleasure to each day. The children adjusted well to their new school, and all of us will cherish our days spent in Millarville.

We are the original and present owners of the Haus of Sausage in Okotoks. Our shop was opened on December 9, 1977, and Harry has just recently started H & H Sausage of Calgary, the manufacturing end of our business.

Lila Womack (Croston)

I was born in Calgary during the thirty's; the youngest of eight, four brothers, Murrey, Irvin, Bert, Melvin; and three sisters, Neva, Hazel, and Noreen. When I was seven, Dad decided to buy a sawmill and go into the lumber business, so our home was sold to cover the cost of the mill, and we packed our meager belongings, left the city and all its conveniences behind, and headed for the timber which was in the Midnapore district. It was all very exciting to me as a child, not thinking of how hard Dad and my brothers had to work in the bush falling the trees, limbing them, then skidding them by teams of horses to the mill, where they cut them into boards ready for sale. Dad was a good carpenter by trade, and it was his dream to get enough timber ahead to build a motel unit just outside the city as soon as he could get enough money ahead to start.

Just as the family logging operations were starting to run smoothly, in the midst of winter, Dad was bedridden with a stroke. Those were hard years for all of us; war called two brothers and Neva's husband, Irvin was married and living in Calgary, Melvin went to work at a farm near Red Deer Lake, while us younger ones continued school at Fordville School, via Mr. Barraclough's car. When weather didn't permit travel by car, he came by horse and democrat and we took short cuts through farmers' fields to arrive at school as usual.

Neva and her first daughter, Sharon, spent a lot of time with us, for they lived close by. They were a lot of company for Mom while the rest of us were gone all day. I was in my early teens by this time, and Sharon was like a living doll to me. Neva let me hold her, change her, and I just adored doing it. She was so tiny, some of the dolly clothes fit her. She was the brightest part of our lives in those dark years.

Mom had a cyst removed from her throat and short-ly after, Dad passed away in his sleep. By this time the war had ended and fortunately all three came home safely. Murrey and Melvin decided to go farming, so with the help of the VLA were able to get land in the Caroline district, which is forty miles west of Innisfail, Alberta, and wanted us to come too. So, once more we packed our belongings and headed out for parts unknown to any of us except Murrey, who had gone ahead to seed the fields and reap the harvest already.

The country was beautiful, and here we could start life anew. The change helped Mom to forget the sorrows of losing a husband, also she got stronger and started to enjoy life once more. We had no well yet, so learned to appreciate the good neighbour to the south who supplied us with water, which we hauled by wagon.

How well I remember those rough bumpy trips as the Rumley with its huge steel wheels pulled the wagon along the trail over to the next quarter to haul water. Oh, what an ornery critter to drive. I often wonder how the boys managed to get the crops in with the beast.

It was late fall when we arrived at our new home. We were all exhausted from the packing and long trip, so quickly unloaded the necessities, drained the truck radiator (didn't have anti-freeze, of course), and fell into bed. All would have been perfect next morn; we awoke to the thrill of looking out over our very own fields, finishing unloading, and set about figuring a way to get water for breakfast, since the last drop was drained out of the radiator, onto the ground the night before. Finally, one of the boys walked over to the nearest neighbour to carry back a pailfull, only to find, our new neighbours wouldn't hear of such a thing, and drove him, water and all, home.

That was my first meeting with the wonderful man who has been my husband for the past 27 years. Our first of many happy years we spent around the Caroline area, spent one winter at Nordegg, then to Vulcan before settling down in Calgary. Ray and I have found a lot of happiness together. The two children have made our happiness complete. We waited a long time for their arrival, but are thankful to have been blessed with a son, Larry Raymond, and a daughter, Marlene Lorraine. Both have brought us much joy. I only hope the good Lord sees fit to give us plenty more years to enjoy being together.

Thanks to the children, I overcame a lifetime of fear, and learned to swim. This summer, while visiting relatives abroad, we all had the pleasure of swimming in the beautiful Mediterranean Sea. While there, we cruised aboard the Enrico, from Genoa, Italy to Spain, Africa, Sicily, and Malta, where we spent 3 glorious weeks with Melvin, his wife and their family in their lovely villa. It was a thrill of a lifetime for all of us. We have never flown before, nor been off the continent, so we enjoyed it all. We saw lots of places; however, there is no place like home, it's nice to be back.

Index